Contemporary
Management

Fifth Edition

Gareth R. Jones
Texas A&M University

Jennifer M. George
Rice University

McGraw-Hill Irwin

Boston   Burr Ridge, IL   Dubuque, IA   Madison, WI   New York   San Francisco   St. Louis
Bangkok   Bogotá   Caracas   Kuala Lumpur   Lisbon   London   Madrid   Mexico City
Milan   Montreal   New Delhi   Santiago   ...   ...ipei   Toronto

The *McGraw-Hill* Companies

McGraw-Hill
Irwin

CONTEMPORARY MANAGEMENT

Published by McGraw-Hill/Irwin, a business unit of The McGraw-Hill Companies, Inc., 1221 Avenue of the Americas, New York, NY, 10020. Copyright © 2008 by The McGraw-Hill Companies, Inc. All rights reserved. No part of this publication may be reproduced or distributed in any form or by any means, or stored in a database or retrieval system, without the prior written consent of The McGraw-Hill Companies, Inc., including, but not limited to, in any network or other electronic storage or transmission, or broadcast for distance learning.

Some ancillaries, including electronic and print components, may not be available to customers outside the United States.

This book is printed on acid-free paper.

3 4 5 6 7 8 9 0 WCK/WCK 0 9 8

ISBN   978-0-07-128561-2
MHID   0-07-128561-X

www.mhhe.com

Brief Contents

Contents

Examples

Management in Action

Examples

Management in Action

Contents

Part Two The Environment of Management

Examples

Management in Action

Examples

Management in Action

Contents

Examples

Management in Action

Examples

Management in Action

Contents

Examples

Management in Action

Examples

Management in Action

Contents

Part Four Organizing and Controlling

Contents

Chapter Eleven — Organizational Control and Change 428

Chapter Twelve — Human Resource Management 476

Management in Action

Examples

Management in Action

Contents

Contents

Contents

Examples

Management in Action

Examples

Management in Action

Preface

The number and complexity of the strategic, organizational, and human resource challenges facing managers and all employees has continued to increase throughout the 2000s. In most companies, managers at all levels are playing "catch-up" as they work toward meeting these challenges by implementing new and improved management techniques and practices. The challenges facing managers continue to mount as changes in the environment such as global outsourcing impact organizations, large and small. Moreover, the revolution in digital information technology has transformed managerial decision making across all levels of a company's hierarchy and across all its functions.

Today, relatively small differences in performance between companies, for example, in the speed at which they can bring new products or services to market or in the ways they motivate their employees to find ways to reduce costs or improve performance, can combine to give one company a significant competitive advantage over another. Managers and companies that utilize proven management techniques and practices in their decision making and actions increase their effectiveness over time. Companies and managers that are slower to implement new management techniques and practices find themselves at a growing competitive disadvantage that makes it even more difficult to catch up. Thus, in many industries there is a widening gap between the most successful companies whose performance reaches new heights, and their weaker competitors because their managers have made better decisions about how to use a company's resources in the most efficient and effective ways.

In the fifth edition of our book, *Contemporary Management*, we keep to our theme of providing students with the most contemporary and up-to-date account of the changing environment of management and management practices. We mirror the changes taking place by incorporating recent developments in management theory into our text and by providing vivid, current examples of the way managers of well-known companies large and small have responded to the changes taking place.

In this edition, for example, we extend our treatment of global outsourcing and examine the many managerial issues that must be addressed when millions of functional jobs in information technology, customer service, and manufacturing are being sent to countries overseas. For example, increasing globalization means that managers must respond to the effects of major differences in the legal rules and regulations and ethical values and norms that prevail in countries around the globe. Many companies and their managers, for example, have been accused of ignoring "sweatshop" working conditions under which the products they sell are manufactured abroad. More generally, many people have begun to look closely at the way large global companies are managed and to scrutinize the behavior of their managers.

The ethics of top managers and the multitude of ethical issues managers and organizations face have remained at the forefront of public concern and also receive expanded treatment in our revision. New developments include the revelation that many companies have been rigging the time at which stock options are granted to managers to maximize the profits they can make when they sell them. And, following Hurricane Katrina and the poor performance of many nonprofits, the disclosure that many of their top executives earn more than a million dollars a year is very troubling. Thus, the ethics of managers of nonprofits are also being investigated and are discussed in our revision.

Other major challenges we continue to expand on in the new edition include the impact of the steadily increasing diversity of the workforce on companies, and how this increasing diversity makes it imperative for managers to understand how and why people differ so that they can effectively manage and reap the performance benefits of diversity. Similarly, across all functions and levels, managers and employees must continuously search out ways to "work smarter" and increase performance. Using new information technology to improve all aspects of an organization's operations to improve efficiency and customer responsiveness is a vital part of this process. So too is the continuing need to innovate and improve the quality of goods and services, and the ways they are produced, to allow an organization to compete effectively. We have significantly revised the fifth edition of *Contemporary Management* to address these challenges to managers and their organizations.

Major Content Changes and Chapter Reorganization

Encouraged by the increase in the number of instructors and students who are using our book with each new edition, and based on the reactions and suggestions of both users and reviewers, we have substantially revised and updated our book. First, we have altered the content of the book's chapters in many ways, adding new material that has become pertinent today and eliminating outdated management concepts. As usual, our goal has been to streamline our presentation and keep the focus on the many changes that have been taking place that have the most impact on managers and organizations.

One noticeable change in this edition is that we have eliminated Chapter 19 from the 4th edition on entrepreneurship and innovation and integrated the material that used to be in this chapter into three other chapters where it enriches and makes a good complement to the material covered. For example, the material on entrepreneurship has been incorporated into Chapter 7, now entitled "Decision Making, Learning, Creativity, and Entrepreneurship" because it complements the discussion of creativity and allows us to discuss the many different aspects involved in effective decision-making over time. The material on innovation has been woven into the discussion of functional–level strategy in Chapter 8 which allows us to deepen our discussion of how the creation of new goods and services is a key to competitive advantage.

Although we have reduced the number of chapters to eighteen, we have broadened the scope of many of the chapters (while keeping our streamlined student-oriented approach). Chapter 1, for example, now includes a discussion of crisis decision making and we discuss the managerial implications of crises that are the result of natural causes, man-made causes, or geopolitical conflicts. Chapter 1 also has an increased focus on ethics and diversity to prime students to consider the importance of understanding the implications of these complex, personal, and value-laden issues in later chapters. Chapter 2 has new coverage of the historical ethics of business, and how fortunes were made and lost by making management decisions that increased business performance but which eventually led to the passing of antitrust legislation to preserve fair competition and protect the public. Chapter 3 has updated coverage of the manager as a person and how personal characteristics of managers influence how they view and treat others and organizational culture and effectiveness.

Increasing public concern over ethical issues has led us to expand our coverage of the many issues involved in acting and managing ethically. We provide more conceptual tools to help students understand better how to make ethical decisions. Not only does our discussion in Chapter 4 include more approaches to understanding ethical issues, on the Web site that accompanies our book you will find a series of exercises that describe various ethical dilemma scenarios. These scenarios can be used to frame a "hands-on" class discussion that reflects how the various principles behind ethical decision making and action can work together to help people make the "right" ethical choices. Also, we have new coverage of the ethics of nonprofits whose managers must also be scrutinized to ensure that they do not spend organizational resources on their own personal goals rather than those of the people and causes they are meant to help. The new ethical exercise at the end of every chapter has also proved to be popular and we have refined and improved these as well.

Chapter 5, "Managing Diverse Employees in a Multicultural Environment," focuses on the effective management of the many faces of diversity in organizations for the benefit of all. Among the new issues we discuss are the effects of the population growth of Asians and Hispanics in the workplace, employee wage and position disparities and the advantages of ensuring fair treatment and representation, and the implications of disabilities and sexual orientation in the workplace. To address current issues, in an era when many companies are facing discrimination lawsuits involving hundreds of millions of dollars, we include new material on effectively managing diversity and eliminating discrimination and sexual harassment.

Chapter 6, which contains an integrated account of forces in both the domestic and global environments has also been expanded and refined to reflect the changes that have been occurring in the last few years, such as the increase in global outsourcing. The chapter also now contains expanded coverage of free trade and the many global regional free trade associations that have sprung up to break down barriers to the flow of goods and services and promote global value creation.

Another major change in chapter organization from the last edition, the two sequential chapters on strategy, has also proved popular. Reacting to reviewer comments, we have continued to refine our approach. Chapter 8 has been rewritten and focuses on corporate, global, and business level strategy. In Chapter 9, we have expanded our coverage of functional strategies for managing value-chain activities, incorporating the material on innovation from Chapter 19. These changes have allowed us to increase the links between the different levels of strategy making while still maintaining a strong focus on managing operations and processes.

We have updated and expanded our treatment of the many ways in which managers can effectively organize, manage, and lead employees in their companies. For example, Chapter 12 includes an updated discussion of outsourcing and its implications, Chapter 13 includes a discussion of protecting the natural environment as a source of intrinsic motivation and the critical role of self-management of behavior in developing new goods and services, Chapter 14 highlights the critical importance of effective leadership in organizations and factors that contribute to managers being effective leaders, and expanded coverage of the effective management of teams is provided in Chapter 15. As another example, Chapter 16 provides updated coverage of effective communication and how, given the multitude of advances in information technology, managers and organizations can use these advances in ways that help, rather than inadvertently detract from, organizational effectiveness and innovation. As a final example, Chapter 17 focuses on the critical task of effectively managing conflict and politics in organizations and how to negotiate effectively.

In reorganizing our chapters, we begin our treatment of the nature and significance of organizational culture in Chapter 3 ("Values, Attitudes, Emotions, and Culture: The Manager as a Person"). We have moved our discussion of organizational change to Chapter 11 ("Organizational Control and Change"), where we also discuss the ways in which culture powerfully shapes behavior in organizations. The new focus of Chapter 11 allows us to emphasize the important links between an organization's ability to control its activities, adapt to a rapidly changing environment, and innovate.

We feel confident that the major changes we have made to the fifth edition of *Contemporary Management* reflect the changes that are occurring in management and the workplace; we also feel they offer an account of management that will stimulate and challenge students to think about the their future in the world of organizations.

Unique Emphasis on Contemporary, Applied Management

In revising our book, we have kept at the forefront the fact that our users and reviewers are very supportive of our attempts to integrate contemporary management theories and issues into the analysis of management and organizations. As in previous editions, our goal has been to distill new and classic theorizing and research into a contemporary framework that is compatible with the traditional focus on management as planning, leading, organizing, and controlling but that transcends this traditional approach.

Users and reviewers report that students appreciate and enjoy our presentation of management, a presentation that makes its relevance obvious even to those who lack exposure to a real-life management context. Students like the book's content and the way we relate management theory to real-life examples to drive home the message that management matters both because it determines how well organizations perform and because managers and organizations affect the lives of people inside and outside the organization, such as customers and shareholders.

Our contemporary approach has led us to discuss many concepts and issues that are not addressed in other management textbooks and is also illustrated by the way we have chosen to organize and discuss these management issues. We have gone to great lengths to bring the manager back into the subject matter of management. That is, we have written our chapters from the perspective of current or future managers to illustrate, in a hands-on way, the problems and opportunities they face and how they can effectively meet them. For example, in Chapter 3 we provide an integrated treatment of personality, attitudes, emotions, and culture; in Chapter 4, a focus on ethics from a student's and a manager's perspective; and in Chapter 5, an in-depth treatment of effectively managing diversity and eradicating sexual harassment. In Chapters 8 and 9, our integrated treatment of strategy highlights the multitude of decisions managers must make as they go about performing their most important role—increasing organizational efficiency, effectiveness, and performance.

Our applied approach can also be clearly seen in the last three chapters of the book, which cover the topics of promoting effective communication, managing organizational conflict, politics, and negotiation, and using information technology in ways that increase organizational performance.

These chapters provide a student-friendly, behavioral approach to understanding the management issues entailed in persuasive communication, negotiation, and implementation of advanced information systems to build competitive advantage.

Flexible Organization

Another factor of interest to instructors concerns the way we have designed the grouping of chapters to allow instructors to teach the chapter material in the order that best suits their needs. For example, the more micro-oriented instructor can follow Chapters 1 through 5 with Chapters 12 through 16 and then do the more macro chapters. The more macro-oriented professor can follow Chapters 1 and 2 with Chapters 6 through 11, jump to 16 through 18, and then do the micro chapters, 3 through 5 and 12 through 15. Our sequencing of parts and chapters gives instructors considerable freedom to design the course that best suits their needs. Instructors are not tied to the planning, organizing, leading, and controlling framework, even though our presentation remains consistent with this approach.

Acknowledgments

Finding a way to integrate and present the rapidly growing literature on contemporary management and make it interesting and meaningful for students is not an easy task. In writing and revising the various drafts of *Contemporary Management*, we have been fortunate to have the assistance of several people who have contributed greatly to the book's final form. First, we are grateful to Kelly Lowry, our sponsoring editor, for her ongoing support and commitment to our project and for always finding ways to provide the resources that we needed to continually improve and refine our book. Second, we are grateful to Laura Spell, our developmental editor, for so ably coordinating the book's progress and to her and Anke Braun, our marketing manager, for providing us with concise and timely feedback and information from professors and reviewers that have allowed us to shape the book to the needs of its intended market. We also thank Artemio Ortiz for executing an awe-inspiring design; Mary Conzachi for coordinating the production process; and Elaine Morris (Rice University) and Patsy Hartmangruber (Texas A&M University) for providing excellent word-processing and graphic support. We are also grateful to the many colleagues and reviewers who provided us with useful and detailed feedback and perceptive comments and valuable suggestions for improving the manuscript.

Producing any competitive work is a challenge. Producing a truly market-driven textbook requires tremendous effort beyond simply obtaining reviews of a draft manuscript. Our goal was simple with the development of *Contemporary Management*: to be the most customer-driven principles-of-management text and supplement package ever published! With the goal of exceeding the expectations of both faculty and students, we executed one of the most aggressive product development plans ever undertaken in textbook publishing. Hundreds of faculty have taken part in developmental activities ranging from regional focus groups to manuscript and supplement reviews and surveys. Consequently, we're confident in assuring you and your students, our customers, that every aspect of our text and support package reflects your advice and needs. As you review it, we're confident that your reaction will be, "They listened!"

We extend our special thanks to the faculty who gave us detailed chapter-by-chapter feedback during the development of the Fifth Edition:

M. Ruhul Amin, Bloomsburg University of PA
James D. Bell, Texas State University
Danielle R. Blesi, Hudson Valley Community College
Marian Cox Crawford, University of Arkansas-Little Rock
Thomas W. Deckelman, Owens Community College
Richard S. DeFrank, University of Houston
Fred J. Dorn, University of Mississippi
Anne Kelly Hoel, University of Wisconsin-Stout
Daniel W. McAllister, University of Nevada-Las Vegas
Gary Renz, Webster University
Karen Overton, Houston Community College
L. Jeff Seaton, University of Tennessee–Martin

M. James Smas, Kent State University
Fred Slack, Indiana University of Pennsylvania

We also appreciate the advice we received from these faculty who assisted in various ways in the Fifth Edition development process:

Barry Ashmen, Bucks County Community College
James J. Barkocy, St. Joseph's College
Dan Baugher, Pace University
Melanie Jackson Bookout, Greenville Technical College
Stan Emanuel, University of South Carolina-Lancaster
Elizabeth Evans, Concordia University Wisconsin
Jeff Fahrenwald, Rockford College
John Finley, Columbus State University
Larry A. Flick, Three Rivers Community College
David A. Foote, Middle Tennessee State University
Shawnta S. Friday-Stroud, Florida A&M University
Claudia G. Green, Pace University
Brian Gregory, The University of Southern Mississippi
David A. Grossman, Florida Southern College
Kathleen K. Jones, University of North Dakota
Rusty Juban, Southeastern Louisiana University
Jordan Kaplan, Long Island University
Jerry Kinard, Western Carolina University
John Kohl, Texas A&M International University
Beverly Little, Western Carolina University
Susan Looney, Delaware Tech & Community College
Thomas R. Miller, The University of Memphis
Don C. Mosley, Jr., University of South Alabama
Satyanarayana Parayitam, McNeese State University
Linda Beats Putchinski, University of Central Florida
Cynthia L. Ruszkowski, Illinois State University
Robert Schwartz, The University of Toledo
Amy Sevier, The University of Southern Mississippi
Robin Sronce, University of Wisconsin–Green Bay
Kenneth R. Thompson, DePaul University
Dmitry Yarushkin, Grand View College

And, finally, our thanks go to our Fourth Edition reviewers:

Gerald Baumgardner, Pennsylvania College of Technology
Barry Bunn, Valencia Community College
Gerald Calvasina, Southern Utah University
Bruce H. Charnov, Hofstra University
Jay Christensen-Szalanski, University of Iowa
Teresa A. Daniel, Marshall University
Sandra Edwards, Northeastern State University
Kim Hester, Arkansas State University
Gwendolyn Jones, University of Akron
Kathleen Jones, University of North Dakota
Joanne E. Kapp, Siena College
Nicholas Mathys, DePaul University

Douglas L. Micklich, Illinois State University
Clive Muir, Stetson University

Finally, we are grateful to two incredibly wonderful children, Nicholas and Julia, for being all that they are and the joy they bring to all who know them.

Gareth R. Jones
Mays Business School
Texas A&M University

Jennifer M. George
Jesse H. Jones Graduate School of Management
Rice University

RICH AND RELEVANT EXAMPLES

An important feature of our book is the way we use real-world examples and stories about managers and companies to drive home the applied lessons to students. Our reviewers were unanimous in their praise of the sheer range and depth of the rich, interesting examples we use to illustrate the chapter material and make it come alive. Moreover, unlike boxed material in other books, our boxes are seamlessly integrated into the text; they are an integral part of the learning experience, and not tacked on or isolated from the text itself. This is central to our pedagogical approach.

Each chapter opens with "A Manager's Challenge," which poses a chapter-related challenge and then discusses how managers in one or more organizations responded to that challenge. "A Manager's Challenge" helps demonstrate the uncertainty and excitement surrounding the management process.

A Manager's Challenge
Steve Jobs Has to Change His Approach to Management

What is high-performance management?

In 1976, Steven P. Jobs sold his Volkswagen van, and his partner Steven Wozniak sold his two programmable calculators, and they used the proceeds of $1,350 to build a circuit board in Jobs's garage. So popular was the circuit board, which developed into the Apple II personal computer (PC), that in 1977 Jobs and Wozniak founded Apple Computer to make and sell it. By 1985 Apple's sales had exploded to almost $2 billion, but in the same year Jobs was forced out of the company he founded. Jobs's approach to management was a big part of the reason he lost control of Apple.[1]

Jobs saw his main task as leading the planning process to develop new and improved PCs. Although this was a good strategy, his management style was often arbitrary and overbearing. For example, Jobs often played favorites among the many project teams he created. His approach caused many conflicts and led to fierce competition, many misunderstandings, and growing distrust among members of the different teams.[2]

Steve Jobs addresses an audience in front of an image of him in the early days (on the right) with partner Steven Wozniak.

Jobs's abrasive management style also brought him into conflict with John Sculley, Apple's CEO. Employees became unsure whether Jobs (the chairman) or Sculley was leading the company. Both managers were so busy competing for control of Apple that the

Additional in-depth examples appear in boxes throughout each chapter. "Management Insight" boxes illustrate the topics of the chapter, while the "Ethics in Action," "Managing Globally," "Focus on Diversity," and "Information Technology Byte" boxes examine the chapter topics from each of these perspectives.

Ethics in Action

The Hidden Side of Valentine's Day

Every year on Valentine's Day tens of millions of roses are delivered to sweethearts and loved ones in the United States, and anyone who has bought roses knows that their price has been dropping. One of the main reasons for this is that rose growing is now concentrated in poorer countries in Central and South America. Rose growing has been a boon to poor countries, where the extra income women earn can mean the difference between starving or eating for their families. Ecuador, for example, is the fourth-biggest rose-growing nation in the world, and the industry employs over 50,000 women who tend, pick, and package roses for wages

Workers on some rose-growing farms in poorer countries are often subjected to unsafe working conditions that may harm their health, although they grow beautiful roses.

above the nation's national minimum. Most of these women are employed by Rosas del Ecuador, the company that controls the rose business in that country.

The hidden side of the global rose-growing business is that poorer countries tend to have lax or unenforced health and safety laws—a major reason why they have lower rose-growing costs. And, industry-watchers argue, many rose-growing companies and countries are *not* considering the well-being of their workers. For example, the CEO of Rosas del Ecuador, Erwin Pazmino, denies that workers are subjected to unsafe working conditions. Almost 60% of his workers have reported blurred vision, nausea, headaches, asthma, and other symptoms of pesticide poisoning, however.[58] Workers labor in hot, poorly ventilated greenhouses in which roses have been sprayed

Manager as a Person

Xerox's Anne Mulcahy Is a Manager to Copy

In 2001, Xerox, the well-known copier company, was near bankruptcy. The combination of aggressive Japanese competitors, which were selling low-price copiers, and a shift toward digital copying, which made Xerox's pioneering light-lens copying process obsolete, was resulting in plummeting sales. Losing billions of dollars, Xerox's board desperately searched for a new CEO who could revitalize the company's product line and change the way it operated.[19] The person they chose to plan the company's transformation was Anne Mulcahy, a 26-year Xerox veteran. Mulcahy began her career as a Xerox copier salesperson, transferred into

Anne Mulcahy worked her way up from Xerox copier salesperson to company president. The management skills she developed have made her a person who helps create value for people.

"Manager as a Person" boxes focus on how real managers brought about change to their organizations. These examples allow to reflect on how individual managers dealt with real-life on-the-job challenges related to various chapter concepts.

These are not boxes in the traditional sense; that is, they're not disembodied from the chapter narrative. These thematic applications are fully integrated into the reading. Students will no longer be forced to decide whether to read boxed material. These features are interesting and engaging for students while bringing the chapter content to life.

EXPERIENTIAL LEARNING FEATURES

We have given considerable time and attention to developing state-of-the-art experiential end-of-chapter learning exercises that drive home the meaning of management to students. These exercises are grouped together at the end of each chapter in the section called Management in Action.

TOPICS FOR DISCUSSION AND ACTION

A set of chapter-related questions and points for reflection, some of which ask students to research actual management issues and learn firsthand from practicing managers.

BUILDING MANAGEMENT SKILLS

A self-development exercise that asks students to apply what they have learned to their own experience of organizations and managers or to the experiences of others.

MANAGING ETHICALLY

An exercise that presents students with an ethical scenario or dilemma and asks them, either individually or in a group, to think about the issue from an ethical perspective to understand the issues facing practicing managers.

SMALL GROUP BREAKOUT EXERCISE

This unique exercise is designed to allow instructors in large classes to utilize interactive experiential exercises in groups of three to four students. The instructor calls on students to form into small groups simply by turning to people around them. All students participate in the exercise in class, and a mechanism is provided for the different groups to share what they have learned with one another.

 # Management in Action

Topics for Discussion and Action

Discussion

1. Describe the difference between efficiency and effectiveness, and identify real organizations that you think are, or are not, efficient and effective.
2. In what ways can managers at each of the three levels of management contribute to organizational efficiency and effectiveness?
3. Identify an organization that you believe is high-performing and one that you believe is low-performing. Give five reasons why you think the performance levels of the two organizations differ so much.
4. What are the building blocks of competitive advantage? Why is obtaining a competitive advantage important to managers?
5. In what ways do you think managers' jobs have changed the most over the last 10 years? Why have these changes occurred?

Action

6. Choose an organization such as a school or a bank; visit it; then list the different organizational resources it uses.
7. Visit an organization, and talk to first-line, middle, and top managers about their respective management roles in the organization and what they do to help the organization be efficient and effective.
8. Ask a middle or top manager, perhaps someone you already know, to give examples of how he or she performs the managerial tasks of planning, organizing, leading, and controlling. How much time does he or she spend in performing each task?
9. Like Mintzberg, try to find a cooperative manager who will allow you to follow him or her around for a day. List the roles the manager plays, and indicate how much time he or she spends performing them.

Building Management Skills
Thinking About Managers and Management

Think of an organization that has provided you with work experience and of the manager to whom you reported (or talk to someone who has had extensive work experience); then answer these questions.

1. Think of your direct supervisor. Of what department is he or she a member, and at what level of management is this person?
2. How do you characterize your supervisor's approach to management? For example, which particular management tasks and roles does this person perform most often?
3. What kinds of management skills does this manager have?
4. Do you think the tasks, roles, and skills of your supervisor are appropriate for the particular job he or she performs? How could this manager improve his or her task performance? How can IT affect this?
5. How did your supervisor's approach to management affect your attitudes and behavior? For example, how well did you perform as a subordinate, and how motivated were you?
6. Think of the organization and its resources. Do its managers utilize organizational resources effectively? Which resources contribute most to the organization's performance?

Managing Ethically

Think about an example of unethical behavior that you observed in the past. The incident could be something you experienced as an employee or a customer or something you observed informally.

1. Either by yourself or in a group, give three reasons why you think the behavior was unethical. For example, what rules or norms were broken? Who benefited or was harmed by what took place? What was the outcome for the people involved?
2. What steps might you take to prevent such unethical behavior and encourage people to behave in an ethical way?

Small Group Breakout Exercise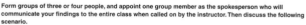
Opening a New Restaurant

Form groups of three or four people, and appoint one group member as the spokesperson who will communicate your findings to the entire class when called on by the instructor. Then discuss the following scenario.

You and your partners have decided to open a large, full-service restaurant in your local community; it will be open from 7 a.m. to 10 p.m. to serve breakfast, lunch, and dinner. Each of you is investing $50,000 in the venture, and together you have secured a bank loan for $300,000 more to begin operations. You and your partners have little experience in managing a restaurant beyond serving meals or eating in restaurants, and you now face the task of deciding how you will manage the restaurant and what your respective roles will be.

1. Decide what each partner's managerial role in the restaurant will be. For example, who will be responsible for the necessary departments and specific activities? Describe your managerial hierarchy.
2. Which building blocks of competitive advantage do you need to establish to help your restaurant succeed? What criteria will you use to evaluate how successfully you are managing the restaurant?
3. Discuss the most important decisions that must be made about (a) planning, (b) organizing, (c) leading, and (d) controlling, to allow you and your partners to utilize organizational resources effectively and build a competitive advantage.
4. For each managerial task, list the issues to solve, and decide which roles will contribute the most to your restaurant's success.

Exploring the World Wide Web

Go to the General Electric (GE) Web site at www.ge.com, click on "Our Company," then "company information," and then "Jeffrey Immelt," GE's CEO. You will see a list of recent articles that discuss his management style; click on arti-cles such as "The Immelt Revolution, 2005" in *BusinessWeek* and the *Financial Times* article titled "Man of the Year 2003."

Search these articles or others for information that describes Immelt's approach to planning, orga-nizing, leading, and controlling GE. What is his approach to managing? What effects has this approach had on GE's performance?

Be the Manager

Problems at Achieva

You have just been called in to help managers at Achieva, a fast-growing Internet software company that specializes in B2B network soft-ware. Your job is to help Achieva solve some management problems that have arisen because of its rapid growth.

Customer demand to license Achieva's software has boomed so much in just two years that more than 50 new software programmers have been added to help develop a new range of software products. Achieva's growth has been so swift that the company still operates informally, its organizational struc-ture is loose and flexible, and pro-grammers are encouraged to find solutions to problems as they go along. Although this structure worked well in the past, you have been told that problems are arising.

There have been increasing complaints from employees that good performance is not being rec-ognized in the organization and that they do not feel equitably treated. Moreover, there have been complaints about getting managers to listen to their new ideas and to act on them. A bad atmosphere is developing in the company, and recently several talented employ-ees left. Your job is to help Achieva's managers solve these problems quickly and keep the company on the fast track.

Questions

1. What kinds of organizing and controlling problems is Achieva suffering from?
2. What kinds of management changes need to be made to solve them?

Case in the News

BusinessWeek

HP's Ultimate Team Player

One July evening in Silicon Valley, Hewlett-Packard executive Ann Liv-ermore got the phone call she had waited months to receive. She rushed to the hospital, having learned that a kidney had been donated, and underwent an organ transplant, necessary due to com-plications from a childhood dis-ease. For most executives, it would have been an opportune time to call it quits after a 24-year career. But three days after the surgery, she was phoning HP Chief Execu-tive Mark V. Hurd and peppering lieutenants with questions. "I finally asked if someone would please go in there and take her laptop away," laughs Hurd.

Why didn't Livermore step down? Opportunity. While the $33 billion corporate-computing busi-ness she runs has long been one of the most glaring underachievers in tech, she's convinced the busi-ness is finally ready to show what it can do. Livermore and HP have spent 18 months overhauling the unit, and the benefits are only now becoming visible. "From the moment I left, I never thought of not coming back," says Livermore, who was out for 5 1/2 weeks. "We have a very special opportunity right now."

It's a dramatic reversal. A year ago her Technology Solutions Group, which sells servers, stor-age, and consulting services to corporations, was valued at next to nothing by Wall Street analysts. Mercilessly squeezed by IBM and Dell Inc., the unit struggled to show profits or promise. Yet Livermore's unit is now a key reason HP's stock

39

EXPLORING THE WORLD WIDE WEB

This is an Internet exercise designed to draw students into relevant material on the Web and give them the experience of judging its potential value while applying what they have learned.

BE THE MANAGER
This exercise presents a realistic scenario in which a man-ager/organization faces some kind of challenge, problem, or opportunity and the student plays the role of the focal manager figuring out how to address the challenge based on the chapter content. These exercise provide students with a real, hands-on way to take an action-oriented approach to solving "real" problems by applying what they've just learned in the chapter.

BUSINESSWEEK CASE IN THE NEWS
Each chapter has two cases for analysis that are actual or shortened versions of *BusinessWeek* articles. The accompanying discussion questions encour-age students to think about and analyze how real managers deal with real problems in the business world. These cases give instructors the opportunity to explore issues in more depth if they choose.

CHOOSING EXERCISES
Our idea in offering instructors such a wide array of exer-cises to promote the learning experience is that instructors can *choose and select* from these exercises and vary them over the semester so that students can learn the mean-ing of management through many different avenues. These exercises complement the chapter material and have been class tested to add to the overall learning experience. Students report that they enjoy and learn from them.

FOR INSTRUCTORS

INTEGRATED LEARNING SYSTEM

Great care was used in the creation of the supplemental materials to accompany *Contemporary Management*. Whether you are a seasoned faculty member or a newly minted instructor, you'll find our support materials to be the most thorough and thoughtful ever created!

INSTRUCTOR'S RESOURCE CD

This CD allows instructors to easily create their own custom presentations using resources that include the Instructor's Manual, PowerPoint, Test Bank, and Computerized Test Bank.

INSTRUCTOR'S MANUAL

Prepared by Stephanie Bibb of Chicago State University, the IM contains a chapter overview; learning objectives; key terms; list of resources available; notes for opening case; lecture outline; notes for end-of-chapter materials; lecture enhancers; and video case teaching notes. In addition, a new section and labels have been added that provide guidance on how to use the materials in the book and teaching package to help meet AACSB standards.

POWERPOINT® PRESENTATION

Approximately 400 slides feature reproductions of key tables and figures from the text as well as original content—prepared by Brad Cox of Midlands Tech. A new feature in the PowerPoint Presentation, "Movie Example" slides, will help you incorporate popular movies, such as *You've Got Mail* and *Apollo 13* into your management course. These slides appear at the end of each chapter presentation and include notes on how the movies can be used to generate discussion and to illustrate management concepts.

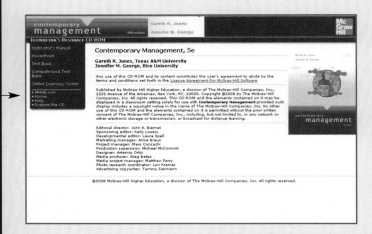

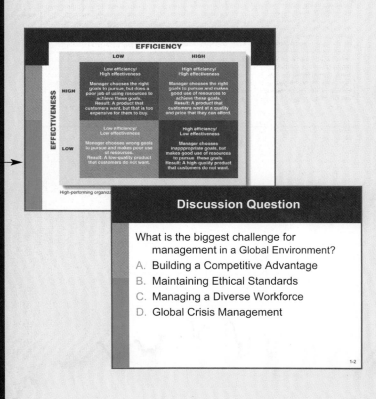

Video Case

Chapter 1 Video Case: Southwest CEO: Get to Know Gary Kelly

The major airline companies have faced turbulent times in recent years, and now the low-price carriers are facing a similar situation. The rising price of fuel has had an adverse effect on the discount carriers whose business model is based on low fares. Jet Blue, Air Tran, Spirit, and Southwest have all increased fares, in some cases making them higher than the major airlines' fares for some routes.

As chief executive officer (CEO) of Southwest Airlines, the most profitable airline in the United States, Gary Kelly has no easy job. When he took over as Southwest's CEO in 2004, he had huge shoes to fill. Former CEO Herb Kelleher, by all accounts, was an icon. Books were written about him, and his approach to running a business was studied in colleges and replicated in industry. Kelleher revolutionized the airline industry through his vision of bringing cheaper travel to the masses and developing a culture where employees thrived.[1] History has shown that a company with a coherent culture can survive the loss of a charismatic leader. Southwest has continued to prosper under Kelly, in large part because he grew up in the Southwest culture of "employees first, customer focus, and cost containment."

Kelly lives the culture daily. A flight to his ranch in Austin from headquarters at Love Field, Dallas, with his wife, Carol, is a good example. Kelly greets many employees by name. He sits in the very back of the plane, where it is the noisiest and most cramped, leaving the best seats for paying customers. He also enjoys mingling with passengers, telling them, "I'm just a guy who works in the office." The former high school star quarterback was an accountant before he became chief financial officer at Southwest, a position he held for 15 years. He had no aspirations to be CEO, nor did he seek the job. He perceived that the stress would be too much to deal with, but hasn't found that to be true.

In an era when most airlines are struggling, Southwest has continued to enjoy a competitive advantage over rivals because of its fuel-hedging contracts.[2] Kelly gets credit for locking up these contracts, which had Southwest paying less than competitors for its fuel. But tough tasks lie ahead. As these hedging contracts begin to expire, Southwest's fuel expenses are rising faster than those of rivals. Along with other airlines, Southwest has already had to raise fares. Additionally, Kelly faces a potentially contentious negotiation with Southwest pilots. Nonetheless, employees express total confidence in Kelly's ability.

The Southwest model is simple: Keep costs down, fly one type of plane—the 737—to keep parts and maintenance costs low, treat customers like kings, and treat employees even better. As well-known discounters like Home Depot and Dell struggle to maintain customer service while increasing operational efficiency, Southwest continues to have it both ways.[3] The management seems to understand

better than most that well-tr
workers mean fewer compl
which translates into lower
and greater sales. Many peo
competing airlines have take
cuts to work at Southwest.

Gary Kelly never said S
west employees—there are 3
of them—would not have to
hard and make sacrifices
instance, some gate agents
been asked to work multiple
at once to cut costs. What
sacrifices might lie ahead, no
is saying. For now, the com
prefers to remain profitab
expanding. What city will S
west serve next? A place
the airline can be financially
cessful, be it New York–La G
or Charlotte, North Caro
According to Kelly, any airlin
expand, but so far others ha
been able to match the grea
ple of Southwest. Heading
Austin with his wife, Gary
looks like just another one of
people, and it is this ever
quality that may help him na
the rough waters ahead.

Questions

1. What skills does Gary Ke possess that make him a cessful manager?

2. Why is responsiveness to tomers and employees a to success at Southwest lines?

3. What challenges lie ahea Gary Kelly, and what do y think will be needed to successfully meet them?

TEST BANK AND COMPUTERIZED TEST BANK The test bank has been thoroughly reviewed, revised, and improved, in response to customer feedback, by Eileen Hogan of Kutztown University. There are approximately 100 questions per chapter, including true-false, multiple-choice, and essay, each tagged with level of difficulty (corresponding to Bloom's taxonomy of educational objectives), AACSB standards, correct answer, and page references to the text. The new AACSB tags allow instructors to sort questions by the various standards and create reports to help give assurance that they are including the recommended learning experiences in their curricula.

CASE VIDEOS One video is provided on a Video DVD for each of the 18 chapters, and each has a corresponding written Video Case included on the book's Online Learning Center at www.mhhe.com/jonesgeorge5e. These videos illustrate application of the relevant chapter concepts and feature profiles of successful businesses and managers—such as Southwest CEO Gary Kelly or Andre Thornton, the former Cleveland Indian player who founded a company called Global Promotions and Incentives—as well as thought-provoking management topics and issues—such as the outcome of the Enron trial and recent immigrant rallies. Each case provides a written overview of the video content as well as additional background information and discussion questions that encourage students to critically examine and apply chapter concepts to analyzing the case.

NEW! MANAGEMENT IN THE MOVIES DVD Students will have fun will learning about management principles when they watch these short film clips from popular movies such as You've Got Mail, Apollo 13, and The Firm. Discussion questions and teaching notes for each clip are included on the Instructor's Resource CD and on the book Web site.

FOR STUDENTS

Student Study Guide

Prepared by Thomas J. Quirk of Webster University, the Study Guide has been completely updated with the goal of helping students master course content. Each chapter includes learning objectives; a chapter outline; and matching, true-false, multiple-choice, and essay questions, with answer keys including page references to the text.

The Contemporary Management Online Learning Center

www.mhhe.com/jonesgeorge5e

The Online Learning Center (OLC) is a Web site that follows the text chapter by chapter. OLC content is designed to reinforce and build on the text content. As students read the book, they can go online to take self-grading quizzes, review material, or work through interactive exercises. In the popular Build Your Management Skills section, students can find out more about their personal management styles and preferences by completing the Self-Assessments.

OLCs can be delivered multiple ways—professors and students can access them directly through the textbook Web site, through PageOut, or within a course management system (i.e., WebCT, Blackboard, or eCollege). In addition, a new series of chapter-by-chapter modules that include video overviews of key concepts along with animations and/or interactive exercises are available with Enhanced Cartridges for use in an online course management system or for individual purchase from the OLC.

Manager's Hot Seat

www.mhhe.com/mhs

In today's workplace, managers are confronted daily with issues like ethics, diversity, working in teams, and the virtual workplace. The Manager's Hot Seat interactive software allows students to watch as 15 real managers apply their years of experience to confront these issues.

BusinessWeek Edition and *The Wall Street Journal* Edition

Students can subscribe to *BusinessWeek* for a specially priced rate of $8.25 in addition to the price of this text or to *The Wall Street Journal* for 15 weeks at a specially priced rate of $20 in addition to the price of the text. With their WSJ subscription students will also receive the *How to Use the WSJ* handbook and access to www.wsj.com.

Authors

Gareth Jones is a Professor of Management in the Lowry Mays College and Graduate School of Business at Texas A&M University. He received his B.A. in Economics/Psychology and his Ph.D. in Management from the University of Lancaster, U.K. He previously held teaching and research appointments at the University of Warwick, Michigan State University, and the University of Illinois at Urbana-Champaign. He is a frequent visitor and speaker at universities in both the United Kingdom and the United States.

He specializes in strategic management and organizational theory and is well known for his research that applies transaction cost analysis to explain many forms of strategic and organizational behavior. He is currently interested in strategy process, competitive advantage, and information technology issues. He is also investigating the relationships between ethics, trust, and organizational culture and studying the role of affect in the strategic decision-making process.

He has published many articles in leading journals of the field, and his recent work has appeared in the *Academy of Management Review,* the *Journal of International Business Studies,* and *Human Relations.* An article on the role of information technology in many aspects of organizational functioning was published in the *Journal of Management.* One of his articles won the *Academy of Management Journal*'s Best Paper Award, and he is one of the most prolific authors in the *Academy of Management Review.* He is or has served on the editorial boards of the *Academy of Management Review,* the *Journal of Management,* and *Management Inquiry.*

Gareth Jones has taken his academic knowledge and used it to craft leading textbooks in management and three other major areas in the management discipline: organizational behavior, organizational theory, and strategic management. His books are widely recognized for their innovative, contemporary content and for the clarity with which they communicate complex, real-world issues to students.

Jennifer George is the Mary Gibbs Jones Professor of Management and Professor of Psychology in the Jesse H. Jones Graduate School of Management at Rice University. She received her B.A. in Psychology/Sociology from Wesleyan University, her M.B.A. in Finance from New York University, and her Ph.D. in Management and Organizational Behavior from New York University. Prior to joining the faculty at Rice University, she was a Professor in the Department of Management at Texas A&M University.

Professor George specializes in organizational behavior and is well known for her research on mood and emotion in the workplace, their determinants, and their effects on various individual and group-level work outcomes. She is the author of many articles in leading peer-reviewed journals such as the *Academy of Management Journal, the Academy of Management Review,* the *Journal of Applied Psychology, Organizational Behavior and Human Decision Processes, Journal of Personality and Social Psychology,* and *Psychological Bulletin.* One of her papers won the Academy of Management's Organizational Behavior Division Outstanding Competitive Paper Award and another paper won the *Human Relations* Best Paper Award. She is, or has been, on the editorial review boards of the *Journal of Applied Psychology, Academy of Management Journal, Academy of Management Review, Administrative Science Quarterly, Journal of Management, Organizational Behavior and Human Decision Processes, International Journal of Selection and Assessment,* and *Journal of Managerial Issues,* was a consulting editor for the *Journal of Organizational Behavior,* and was a member of the SIOP *Organizational Frontiers Series* editorial board. She is a Fellow in the American Psychological Association, the American Psychological Society, and the Society for Industrial and Organizational Psychology and a member of the Society for Organizational Behavior. Professor George is currently an Associate Editor for the *Journal of Applied Psychology.* She also has co-authored a widely used textbook titled *Understanding and Managing Organizational Behavior.*

CHAPTER 1

Managers and Managing

Learning Objectives

After studying this chapter, you should be able to:

- Describe what management is, why management is important, what managers do, and how managers utilize organizational resources efficiently and effectively to achieve organizational goals.

- Distinguish among planning, organizing, leading, and controlling (the four principal managerial tasks), and explain how managers' ability to handle each one affects organizational performance.

- Differentiate among three levels of management, and understand the tasks and responsibilities of managers at different levels in the organizational hierarchy.

- Distinguish between three kinds of managerial skill, and explain why managers are divided into different departments to perform their tasks more efficiently and effectively.

- Discuss some major changes in management practices today that have occurred as a result of globalization and the use of advanced information technology (IT).

- Discuss the principal challenges managers face in today's increasingly competitive global environment.

A Manager's Challenge

Steve Jobs Has to Change His Approach to Management

What is high-performance management?

In 1976, Steven P. Jobs sold his Volkswagen van, and his partner Steven Wozniak sold his two programmable calculators, and they used the proceeds of $1,350 to build a circuit board in Jobs's garage. So popular was the circuit board, which developed into the Apple II personal computer (PC), that in 1977 Jobs and Wozniak founded Apple Computer to make and sell it. By 1985 Apple's sales had exploded to almost $2 billion, but in the same year Jobs was forced out of the company he founded. Jobs's approach to management was a big part of the reason he lost control of Apple.[1]

Jobs saw his main task as leading the planning process to develop new and improved PCs. Although this was a good strategy, his management style was often arbitrary and overbearing. For example, Jobs often played favorites among the many project teams he created. His approach caused many conflicts and led to fierce competition, many misunderstandings, and growing distrust among members of the different teams.[2]

April 1, 2006

Steve Jobs addresses an audience in front of an image of him in the early days (on the right) with partner Steven Wozniak.

Jobs's abrasive management style also brought him into conflict with John Sculley, Apple's CEO. Employees became unsure whether Jobs (the chairman) or Sculley was leading the company. Both managers were so busy competing for control of Apple that the task of ensuring its resources were being used efficiently was neglected. Apple's costs soared, and its performance and profits fell.

Apple's directors became convinced Jobs's management style was the heart of the problem and asked him to resign. After he left Apple, Jobs started new ventures. First, he founded PC maker NEXT to develop a powerful new PC that would outperform Apple's PCs. Then he founded Pixar, a computer animation company, which become a huge success after it made blockbuster movies such as *Toy Story* and *Finding Nemo,* both distributed by Walt Disney.

In both these companies Jobs developed a clear vision for managers to follow, and he built strong management teams to lead the project teams developing the new PCs and movies. Jobs saw his main task as planning the companies' future product development strategies. However, he left the actual tasks of leading and organizing to managers below him. He gave them the autonomy to put his vision into practice. In both companies he encouraged a culture of collaboration and innovation to champion creative thinking.

In the meantime, Apple was struggling to compete against Michael Dell's new, low-cost PCs loaded with Microsoft's Windows software. Its performance was plummeting, and to help his old company survive, in 1996 Jobs convinced Apple to buy NEXT for $400 million and use its powerful operating system in new Apple PCs. Jobs began working inside Apple to lead its turnaround and was so successful that in 1997 he was asked to become its CEO.[3] Jobs agreed and continued to put the new management skills he had developed over time to good use.

The first thing he did was create a clear vision and goals to energize and motivate Apple employees. Jobs decided that to survive, Apple had to introduce state-of-the art, stylish PCs and related digital equipment. He instituted an across-the-board planning process and created a team structure that allowed programmers and engineers to pool their skills to develop new PCs. He delegated considerable authority to the teams, but he also established strict timetables and challenging "stretch" goals, such as bringing new products to market as quickly as possible, for these groups. One result of these efforts was Apple's sleek new line of iMac PCs, which were quickly followed by a wide range of futuristic PC-related products.

In 2003 Jobs announced that Apple was starting a new service called iTunes, an online music store from which people could download songs for 99 cents. At the same time, Apple introduced its iPod music player, which can store thousands of downloaded songs, and it quickly became a runaway success. By 2006 Apple had introduced many new generations of the iPod, each more compact, powerful, and versatile than previous models. By 2006 Apple had control of 70% of the digital music player market and 80% of the online music download business, and its stock price soared to new record levels![4]

The next milestone in Jobs's managerial history came in 2006 when it was announced that Walt Disney would buy its longtime partner Pixar for $7.4 billion in stock and so take full control of Pixar's movie-making skills. The deal put Steve Jobs in a powerful new position at Disney because his 7% stake in Pixar made him the largest individual Disney shareholder. Jobs also became a member of Disney's board of directors, so he now has a major responsibility to oversee the planning of Disney's new CEO, Robert Iger.[5]

Overview

The history of Steve Jobs's ups and downs as founder, manager, and now director of these companies illustrates many of the challenges facing people who become managers: Managing a company is a complex activity, and effective managers must possess many kinds of skills, knowledge, and abilities. Management is an unpredictable process. Making the right decision is difficult; even effective managers often make mistakes, but the most effective managers are the ones, like Jobs, who learn from their mistakes and continually strive to find ways to increase their companies' performance. Indeed, business analysts are joking that Iger had better do a good job at Disney or else Jobs might soon get his job. Then, he might merge Apple and Disney, and Mickey Mouse might find himself selling Apples and iPods!

In this chapter, we look at what managers do and what skills and abilities they must develop if they are to manage their organizations successfully over time. We also identify the different kinds of managers that organizations need and the skills and abilities they must develop if they are to be successful. Finally, we identify some of the challenges that managers must address if their organizations are to grow and prosper.

What Is Management?

When you think of a manager, what kind of person comes to mind? Do you see someone who, like Steve Jobs, can determine the future prosperity of a large for-profit company? Or do you see the administrator of a not-for-profit organization, such as a school, library, or charity, or the person in charge of your local Wal-Mart store or McDonald's restaurant, or the person you answer to if you have a part-time job? What do all these managers have in common? First, they all work in organizations. **Organizations** are collections of people who work together and coordinate their actions to achieve a wide variety of goals, or desired future outcomes.[6] Second, as managers, they are the people responsible for supervising and making the most of an organization's human and other resources to achieve its goals.

organizations Collections of people who work together and coordinate their actions to achieve a wide variety of goals, or desired future outcomes.

management The planning, organizing, leading, and controlling of human and other resources to achieve organizational goals efficiently and effectively.

Management, then, is the planning, organizing, leading, and controlling of human and other resources to achieve organizational goals efficiently and effectively. An organization's *resources* include assets such as people and their skills, know-how, and experience; machinery; raw materials; computers and information technology; and patents, financial capital, and loyal customers and employees.

From managers of large corporations like Steve Jobs to those who manage on a smaller scale like this McDonald's restaurant manager, all work in organizations and are responsible for making the most of resources to help achieve organizational goals.

Achieving High Performance: A Manager's Goal

One of the most important goals that organizations and their members try to achieve is to provide some kind of good or service that customers desire. The principal goal of CEO Steve Jobs is to manage Apple so that it creates a new stream of goods and services—such as more powerful PCs, improved PC customer support, more versatile Internet music players, and the ability to easily download diverse kinds of digital content from the Internet—that customers are willing to buy. In 2006 Apple led the field in many of these areas; indeed, it had taken over from Dell the leadership position in good PC customer support.[7]

Similarly, the principal goal of doctors, nurses, and hospital administrators is to increase their hospital's ability to make sick people well—and to do so cost-effectively. Likewise, the principal goal of each McDonald's restaurant manager is to produce burgers, salads, fries, and shakes that people want to pay for and eat so that they become loyal, return customers.

Organizational performance is a measure of how efficiently and effectively managers use available resources to satisfy customers and achieve organizational goals. Organizational performance increases in direct proportion to increases in efficiency and effectiveness (see Figure 1.1, page 7).

Efficiency is a measure of how well or how productively resources are used to achieve a goal.[8] Organizations are efficient when managers minimize the amount of input resources (such as labor, raw materials, and component parts) or the amount of time needed to produce a given output of goods or services. For example, McDonald's developed a more efficient fat fryer that not only reduces the amount of oil used in cooking by 30% but also speeds up the cooking of french fries. Steve Jobs instructed Apple's engineers not only to develop ever more compact, powerful, and multipurpose models of its iPod player but also to find cost-effective ways to do so, such as by outsourcing manufacturing to China.[9] A manager's responsibility is to ensure that an organization and its members perform as efficiently as possible all the activities needed to provide goods and services to customers.

Effectiveness is a measure of the appropriateness of the goals that managers have selected for the organization to pursue and of the degree to which the organization achieves those goals. Organizations are effective when managers choose appropriate goals and then achieve them. Some years ago, for example, managers at McDonald's decided on the goal of providing breakfast service to attract more customers. The choice of this goal has proved very smart, for sales of breakfast food now account for more than 30% of McDonald's revenues. Jobs's goal is to create a constant flow of innovative PC and digital entertainment products. High-performing organizations, such as Apple, McDonald's, Wal-Mart, Intel, Home Depot, Accenture, and Habitat for Humanity are simultaneously efficient and effective (see Figure 1.1). Effective managers are those who choose the right organizational goals to pursue and have the skills to utilize resources efficiently.

organizational performance A measure of how efficiently and effectively a manager uses resources to satisfy customers and achieve organizational goals.

efficiency A measure of how well or how productively resources are used to achieve a goal.

effectiveness A measure of the appropriateness of the goals an organization is pursuing and of the degree to which the organization achieves those goals.

Figure 1.1

Efficiency, Effectiveness, and Performance in an Organization

High-performing organizations are efficient *and* effective.

The study of management is becoming increasingly popular. Many aspiring managers are attracted to the responsibility and rewards that can accompany a management position.

Why Study Management?

Today, more students are competing for places in business courses than ever before; the number of people wishing to pursue Master of Business Administration (MBA) degrees—today's passport to an advanced management position—either on campus or from online universities and colleges is at an all-time high. Why is the study of management currently so popular?[10]

First, in any society or culture resources are valuable and scarce, so the more efficient and effective use that organizations can make of those resources, the greater the relative well-being and prosperity of people in that society. Because managers are the people who decide how to use many of a society's most valuable resources—its skilled employees, raw materials like oil and land, computers and information systems, and financial assets—they directly impact the well-being of a society and the people in it. Understanding what managers do and how they do it is of central importance to understanding how a society creates wealth and affluence for its citizens.

Second, although most people are not managers, and many may never intend to become managers, almost all of us encounter managers because most people have jobs and bosses. Moreover, many people today are working in groups and teams and have to deal with coworkers. Studying management helps people to deal with their bosses and their coworkers. It reveals how to understand other people at work and make decisions and take actions that win the attention and support of the boss. Management also teaches people not yet in positions of authority how to lead coworkers, solve conflicts between them, achieve team goals, and so increase performance.

Third, in any society, people are in competition for a very important resource—a job that pays well and provides an interesting and satisfying career—and understanding management is one important path toward obtaining this objective. In general, jobs become more interesting the more complex or responsible they are. Any person who desires a motivating job that changes over time might therefore do well to develop management skills and become promotable. A person who has been working for several years and then returns to school for an MBA can usually, after earning the degree, find a more interesting, satisfying job and one that pays significantly more than the previous job. Moreover, salaries increase rapidly as people move up the organizational hierarchy, whether it is a school system, a large for-profit business organization, or a not-for-profit charitable or medical institution.

Indeed, the salaries paid to top managers are enormous. For example, the CEOs and other top executives or managers of companies such as Apple, Dell, Walt Disney, GE, and McDonald's receive millions in actual salary each year. However, even more staggering is the fact that many top executives also receive stock or shares in the company they manage, as well as stock options that give them the right to sell these shares at a certain time in the future.[11] If the value of the stock goes up, then the managers keep the difference between the price they obtained the stock option for (say, $10) and what it is worth later (say, $33). By the time Michael Eisner resigned as CEO of Disney in 2005 he had received over $1 billion from selling his stock options. When Steve Jobs again became CEO of Apple, he decided he would accept a salary of only $1 a year. However, Jobs was also awarded stock options that, with the fast rise in Apple's stock price, were worth over $600 million by 2006 and will be worth double or treble this amount if Apple continues to perform well (he was also given the free use of a $90 million jet).[12] These incredible amounts of money provide some indication of both the responsibilities and the rewards that accompany the achievement of high management positions in major companies. What is it that managers actually do to receive such rewards?[13]

Essential Managerial Tasks

The job of management is to help an organization make the best use of its resources to achieve its goals. How do managers accomplish this objective? They do so by performing four essential managerial tasks: *planning, organizing, leading,* and *controlling* (see Figure 1.2). The arrows linking these tasks in Figure 1.2 suggest the sequence in which managers typically perform them. French manager Henri Fayol first outlined the nature of these managerial activities around the turn of the 20th century in *General and Industrial Management*, a book that remains the classic statement of what managers must do to create a high-performing organization.[14] Managers at all levels and in all departments—whether in small or large companies, for-profit or not-for-profit organizations, or organizations that operate in one country or throughout the world—are responsible for performing these four tasks, which we look at next. How well managers perform these tasks determines how efficient and effective their organizations are.

Planning

planning Identifying and selecting appropriate goals; one of the four principal tasks of management.

To perform the **planning** task, managers identify and select appropriate organizational goals and courses of action. The three steps involved in planning are (1) deciding which goals the organization will pursue, (2) deciding

Figure 1.2
Four Tasks of Management

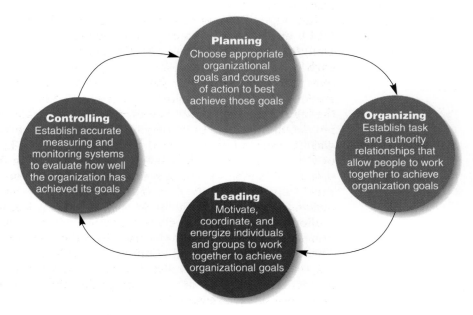

what courses of action to adopt to attain those goals, and (3) deciding how to allocate organizational resources to attain those goals. How well managers plan determines how effective and efficient the organization is—its performance level.[15]

As an example of planning in action, consider the situation confronting Michael Dell, founder and chairman of Dell Computer, the most profitable PC maker and Apple's main competitor.[16] In 1984, the 19-year-old Dell saw an opportunity to enter the PC market by assembling PCs and then selling them directly to customers. Dell began to plan how to put his idea into practice. First, he decided that his goal was to sell an inexpensive PC, to undercut the prices of companies like Compaq and Apple. Second, he had to decide on a course of action to achieve this goal. He decided to sell directly to customers by telephone and to bypass expensive computer stores that sold Compaq and Apple PCs. He also had to decide how to obtain low-cost components and how to tell potential customers about his products. Third, he had to decide how to allocate his limited funds (he had only $5,000) to buy labor and other resources. He chose to hire three people and work with them around a table to assemble his PCs.

Michael Dell sits in the dorm room at the University of Texas, Austin, where he launched his personal computer company as a college freshman. When he visited, the room was occupied by freshmen Russell Smith (left) and Jacob Frith, both from Plano, Texas.

Thus, to achieve his goal of making and selling low-price PCs, Dell had to plan, and as his organization grew, his plans changed and became progressively more complex. Dell and his managers are continually planning how to help the company maintain its position as the highest-performing PC maker. In 2003, Dell announced it would begin to sell printers and Internet music players, which brought it into direct competition with Hewlett-Packard (HP), the leading printer maker, and Apple, with its new PCs and iPod. It has since expanded the range of products it sells to include LCD screens of all sizes, digital cameras, TVs, and all kinds of broadband and other digital information services.

Dell's new plan has not worked very successfully, however. Apple remains the clear leader in the Internet music download and player business, and Dell's printers are not popular. Also, Dell's share of the PC market fell by 6% in 2006, and it was forced to lower prices to compete with HP, which is catching up with Dell in PC sales.[17] In addition, in 2006 Apple announced it would begin using Intel chips, which allows Microsoft's Windows to work on Apple PCs, so now Apple becomes a direct competitor with Dell.

strategy A cluster of decisions about what goals to pursue, what actions to take, and how to use resources to achieve goals.

As the battle between Dell, HP, and Apple suggests, the outcome of planning is a **strategy,** a cluster of decisions concerning what organizational goals to pursue, what actions to take, and how to use resources to achieve goals. The decisions that were the outcome of Michael Dell's planning formed a *low-cost strategy*. A low-cost strategy is a way of obtaining customers by making decisions that allow an organization to produce goods or services more cheaply than its competitors so that it can charge lower prices than they do. Throughout its history Dell has been constantly refining this strategy and exploring new strategies to reduce costs; Dell became the most profitable PC maker as a result of its low-cost strategy. By contrast, since its founding Apple's strategy has been to deliver new, exciting, and unique computer and digital products, such as its new futuristic PCs and iPods, to its customers—a strategy known as *differentiation*.[18] However, as the opening case notes, this strategy almost ruined Apple when customers bought cheaper Dell PCs rather than Apple's higher-priced PCs.

Planning is a complex, difficult activity because what goals an organization should pursue and how best to pursue them—which strategies to adopt—are almost always not immediately clear; planning is done under uncertainty. Managers take major risks when they commit organizational resources to pursue a particular strategy. Either success or failure is a possible outcome of the planning process. Dell succeeded spectacularly in the past with its low-cost strategy; but presently Apple is succeeding spectacularly with its differentiation strategy, and HP, after many problems, seems to be enjoying a turnaround. So Dell is under pressure and now its managers have to decide how to respond. In May 2006, Dell announced it would begin to package Google's popular software on its PCs; it also announced new initiatives to make its PCs more attractive to customers. So the managers of all these companies are continually planning how to outperform the others! In Chapter 8 we focus on the planning process and on the strategies organizations can select to respond to opportunities or threats in an industry. The story of Anne Mulcahy's rise to power at Xerox illustrates well how important planning and strategy making are to a manager's career success.

Manager as
a Person

Xerox's Anne Mulcahy Is a Manager to Copy

In 2001, Xerox, the well-known copier company, was near bankruptcy. The combination of aggressive Japanese competitors, which were selling low-price copiers, and a shift toward digital copying, which made Xerox's pioneering light-lens copying process obsolete, was resulting in plummeting sales. Losing billions of dollars, Xerox's board desperately searched for a new CEO who could revitalize the company's product line and change the way it operated.[19] The person they chose to plan the company's transformation was Anne Mulcahy, a 26-year Xerox veteran. Mulcahy began her career as a Xerox copier salesperson, transferred into

Anne Mulcahy worked her way up from Xerox copier salesperson to company president. The management skills she developed have made her a person who helps create value for people.

individuals, departments, and the organization as a whole to see whether they are meeting desired performance standards. Michael Dell learned early in his career how important this is; it took Steve Jobs longer. If standards are not being met, managers seek ways to improve performance.

The outcome of the control process is the ability to measure performance accurately and regulate organizational efficiency and effectiveness. To exercise control, managers must decide which goals to measure—perhaps goals pertaining to productivity, quality, or responsiveness to customers—and then they must design control systems that will provide the information necessary to assess performance, that is, to determine to what degree the goals have been met. The controlling task also allows managers to evaluate how well they themselves are performing the other three tasks of management—planning, organizing, and leading—and to take corrective action.

Michael Dell had difficulty establishing effective control systems because his company was growing so rapidly and he lacked experienced managers. In the 1990s Dell's costs soared because no controls were in place to monitor inventory, which had built up rapidly, and in 1994 Dell's new line of laptop computers crashed because poor quality control resulted in defective products, some of which caught fire. To solve these and other control problems, Michael Dell hired hundreds of experienced managers from other companies to put the right control systems in place. As a result, by 1998 Dell was able to make computers for about 10% less than its competitors, which created a major source of competitive advantage it has enjoyed ever since. By 2001 Dell became so efficient it drove its competitors out of the market because it had a 20% cost advantage over them.[23] Controlling, like the other managerial tasks, is an ongoing, fluid, always-changing process that demands constant attention and action. We cover the most important aspects of the control task in Chapters 9, 11, 17, 18, and 19.

The four managerial tasks—planning, organizing, leading, and controlling—are essential parts of a manager's job. At all levels in the managerial hierarchy, and across all jobs and departments in an organization, effective management means performing these four activities successfully—in ways that increase efficiency and effectiveness.

Performing Managerial Tasks: Mintzberg's Typology

Our discussion of managerial tasks may seem to suggest that a manager's job is highly orchestrated and that management is a logical, orderly process in which managers rationally calculate the best way to use resources to achieve organizational goals. In reality, being a manager often involves acting emotionally and relying on gut feelings. Quick, immediate reactions to situations, rather than deliberate thought and reflection, are an important aspect of managerial action.[24] Often, managers are overloaded with responsibilities, do not have time to spend on analyzing every nuance of a situation, and therefore make decisions in uncertain conditions without being sure which outcomes will be best.[25] Moreover, for top managers in particular, the current situation is constantly changing, and a decision that seems right today may prove to be wrong tomorrow. The range of problems that managers face is enormous *(high variety)*. Managers frequently must deal with many problems simultaneously *(fragmentation),* often must make snap decisions *(brevity),* and many times must rely on intuition and experience gained throughout their careers to do their jobs to the best of their abilities.[26]

Henry Mintzberg, by following managers around and observing what they actually *do*–hour by hour and day by day–identified 10 kinds of specific roles, or sets of job responsibilities, that capture the dynamic nature of managerial work.[27] He grouped these roles according to whether the responsibility was primarily decisional, interpersonal, or informational in nature; they are described in Table 1.1.

Table 1.1
Managerial Roles Identified by Mintzberg

Type of Role	Specific Role	Examples of Role Activities
DECISIONAL	**Entrepreneur**	Commit organizational resources to develop innovative goods and services; decide to expand internationally to obtain new customers for the organization's products.
	Disturbance Handler	Move quickly to take corrective action to deal with unexpected problems facing the organization from the external environment, such as a crisis like an oil spill, or from the internal environment, such as producing faulty goods or services.
	Resource Allocator	Allocate organizational resources among different tasks and departments of the organization; set budgets and salaries of middle and first-level managers.
	Negotiator	Work with suppliers, distributors, and labor unions to reach agreements about the quality and price of input, technical, and human resources; work with other organizations to establish agreements to pool resources to work on joint projects.
INTERPERSONAL	**Figurehead**	Outline future organizational goals to employees at company meetings; open a new corporate headquarters building; state the organization's ethical guidelines and the principles of behavior employees are to follow in their dealings with customers and suppliers.

(continued)

Table 1.1

Continued

Type of Role	Specific Role	Examples of Role Activities
	Leader	Provide an example for employees to follow; give direct commands and orders to subordinates; make decisions concerning the use of human and technical resources; mobilize employee support for specific organizational goals.
	Liaison	Coordinate the work of managers in different departments; establish alliances between different organizations to share resources to produce new goods and services.
INFORMATIONAL	**Monitor**	Evaluate the performance of managers in different tasks and take corrective action to improve their performance; watch for changes occurring in the external and internal environments that may affect the organization in the future.
	Disseminator	Inform employees about changes taking place in the external and internal environments that will affect them and the organization; communicate to employees the organization's vision and purpose.
	Spokesperson	Launch a national advertising campaign to promote new goods and services; give a speech to inform the local community about the organization's future intentions.

Given the many complex, difficult job responsibilities they have, it is no small wonder that many managers claim that they are performing their jobs well if they are right just half of the time.[28] And it is understandable that many experienced managers accept failure by their subordinates as a normal part of the learning experience and a rite of passage to becoming an effective manager. Managers and their subordinates learn both from their successes and from their failures.

Levels and Skills of Managers

To perform the four managerial tasks efficiently and effectively, organizations group or differentiate their managers in two main ways—by level in hierarchy and by type of skill. First, they differentiate managers according to their level or rank in the organization's hierarchy of authority.

The three levels of managers are first-line managers, middle managers, and top managers—arranged in a hierarchy. Typically, first-line managers report to middle managers, and middle managers report to top managers.

Second, organizations group managers into different departments (or functions) according to their specific set of job-related skills, expertise, and experiences, such as a manager's engineering skills, marketing expertise, or sales experience. A **department,** such as the manufacturing, accounting, engineering, or sales department, is a group of managers and employees who work together because they possess similar skills and experience or use the same kind of knowledge, tools, or techniques to perform their jobs. Within each department are all three levels of management. Next, we examine the reasons why organizations use a hierarchy of managers and group them, by the jobs they perform, into departments.

department A group of people who work together and possess similar skills or use the same knowledge, tools, or techniques to perform their jobs.

Levels of Management

As just discussed, organizations normally have three levels of management: first-line managers, middle managers, and top managers. (See Figure 1.3.) Managers at each level have different but related responsibilities for utilizing organizational resources to increase efficiency and effectiveness.

first-line manager A manager who is responsible for the daily supervision of nonmanagerial employees.

FIRST-LINE MANAGERS At the base of the managerial hierarchy are **first-line managers,** often called *supervisors*. They are responsible for the daily supervision of the nonmanagerial employees who perform many of the specific

Figure 1.3
Levels of Managers

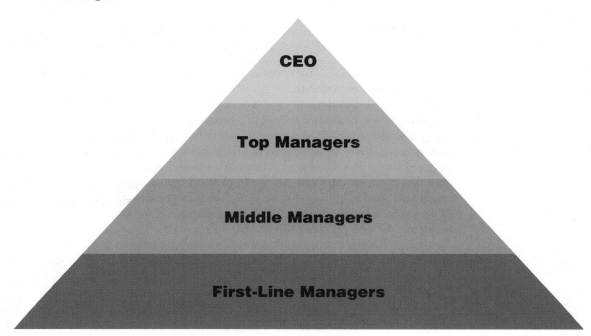

activities necessary to produce goods and services. First-line managers work in all departments or functions of an organization.

Examples of first-line managers include the supervisor of a work team in the manufacturing department of a car plant, the head nurse in the obstetrics department of a hospital, and the chief mechanic overseeing a crew of mechanics in the service function of a new-car dealership. At Dell, first-line managers include the supervisors responsible for controlling the quality of its computers or the level of customer service provided by telephone salespeople. When Michael Dell started his company, he personally controlled the computer assembly process and thus performed as a first-line manager or supervisor.

middle manager
A manager who supervises first-line managers and is responsible for finding the best way to use resources to achieve organizational goals.

MIDDLE MANAGERS Supervising the first-line managers are **middle managers,** responsible for finding the best way to organize human and other resources to achieve organizational goals. To increase efficiency, middle managers find ways to help first-line managers and nonmanagerial employees better utilize resources to reduce manufacturing costs or improve customer service. To increase effectiveness, middle managers evaluate whether the goals that the organization is pursuing are appropriate and suggest to top managers ways in which goals should be changed. Very often, the suggestions that middle managers make to top managers can dramatically increase organizational performance. A major part of the middle manager's job is developing and fine-tuning skills and know-how, such as manufacturing or marketing expertise, that allow the organization to be efficient and effective. Middle managers make thousands of specific decisions about the production of goods and services: Which first-line supervisors should be chosen for this particular project? Where can we find the highest-quality resources? How should employees be organized to allow them to make the best use of resources?

Behind a first-class sales force look for the middle managers responsible for training, motivating, and rewarding the salespeople. Behind a committed staff of high school teachers look for the principal who energizes them to find ways to obtain the resources they need to do outstanding and innovative jobs in the classroom.

top manager
A manager who establishes organizational goals, decides how departments should interact, and monitors the performance of middle managers.

TOP MANAGERS In contrast to middle managers, **top managers** are responsible for the performance of *all* departments.[29] They have *cross-departmental responsibility*. Top managers establish organizational goals, such as which goods and services the company should produce; they decide how the different departments should interact; and they monitor how well middle managers in each department utilize resources to achieve goals.[30] Top managers are ultimately responsible for the success or failure of an organization, and their performance (like that of Steve Jobs and Anne Mulcahy) is continually scrutinized by people inside and outside the organization, such as other employees and investors.[31]

The *chief executive officer (CEO)* is a company's most senior and important manager, the one all other top managers report to. Today, the term *chief operating officer (COO)* is often used to refer to the top manager who is being groomed to take over as CEO when the current CEO retires or leaves the company. Together, the CEO and COO are responsible for developing good working relationships among the top managers of various departments (manufacturing and marketing, for example); usually top managers have the title "vice president." A central concern of the CEO is the creation of a smoothly functioning

Figure 1.4

Relative Amount of Time That Managers Spend on the Four Managerial Tasks

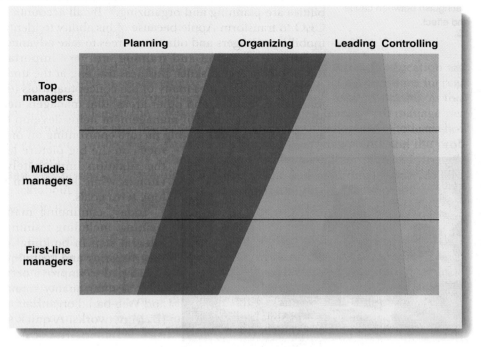

top-management team, a group composed of the CEO, the COO, and the department heads most responsible for helping achieve organizational goals.[32]

The relative importance of planning, organizing, leading, and controlling—the four principal managerial tasks—to any particular manager depends on the manager's position in the managerial hierarchy.[33] The amount of time that managers spend planning and organizing resources to maintain and improve organizational performance increases as they ascend the hierarchy (see Figure 1.4).[34] Top managers devote most of their time to planning and organizing, the tasks so crucial to determining an organization's long-term performance. The lower that managers' positions are in the hierarchy, the more time the managers spend leading and controlling first-line managers or nonmanagerial employees.

Managerial Skills

Both education and experience enable managers to recognize and develop the personal skills they need to put organizational resources to their best use. Michael Dell realized from the start that he lacked sufficient experience and technical expertise in marketing, finance, and planning to guide his company alone. Thus, he recruited experienced managers from other IT companies, such as IBM and HP, to help him build his company. Research has shown that education and experience help managers acquire and develop three types of skills: *conceptual, human,* and *technical* or job-specific.[35]

rate than its competitors.

conceptual skills

The ability to analyze and

CONCEPTUAL SKILLS   Conceptual skills are demonstrated in the ability
to analyze and diagnose a situation and to distinguish between cause and effect.

Figure 1.5
Types and Levels of Managers

Effective managers need all three kinds of skills—conceptual, human, and
technical—to help their organizations perform more efficiently and effectively. The absence of even one type of managerial skill can lead to failure.
One of the biggest problems that people who start small businesses confront,
for example, is their lack of appropriate conceptual and human skills. Someone who has the technical skills to start a new business does not necessarily
know how to manage the venture successfully. Similarly, one of the biggest
problems that scientists or engineers who switch careers from research to
management confront is their lack of effective human skills. Ambitious managers or prospective managers are constantly in search of the latest educational contributions to help them develop the conceptual, human, and
technical skills they need to perform at a high level in today's changing and
increasingly competitive global environment.

Developing new and improved skills through education and training has
become a major priority for both aspiring managers and the organizations
they work for. As we discussed earlier, many people are enrolling in
advanced management courses, but many companies, such as Motorola, GE,

and IBM, have established their own colleges to train and develop their employees and managers at all levels. Every year these companies put thousands of their employees through management programs designed to identify the employees who the company believes have superior competencies and whom it can develop to become its future top managers. In many organizations promotion is closely tied to a manager's ability to acquire the competencies that a particular company believes are important.[40] At 3M, for example, the ability to successfully lead a new product development team is viewed as a vital requirement for promotion; at IBM, the ability to attract and retain clients is viewed as a skill its consultants must possess. We discuss the various kinds of skills managers need to develop in most of the chapters of this book.

Recent Changes in Management Practices

The tasks and responsibilities of managers have been changing dramatically in recent years. Two major factors that have led to these changes are global competition and advances in new information technology (IT). Stiff competition for resources from organizations both at home and abroad has put increased pressure on all managers to improve efficiency and effectiveness. Increasingly, top managers are encouraging lower-level managers to look beyond the goals of their own departments and take a cross-departmental view to find new opportunities to improve organizational performance, as Michael Dell and Steve Jobs have done. Modern IT gives managers at all levels and in all areas access to more and better information and improves their ability to plan, organize, lead, and control. IT also provides employees with more job-related information and allows them to become more skilled, specialized, and productive.[41]

Restructuring and Outsourcing

To utilize IT to increase efficiency and effectiveness, CEOs and top-management teams have been restructuring organizations and outsourcing specific organizational activities to reduce the number of employees on the payroll and make more productive use of the remaining workforce.

restructuring
Downsizing an organization by eliminating the jobs of large numbers of top, middle, and first-line managers and nonmanagerial employees.

Restructuring involves simplifying, shrinking, or downsizing an organization's operations to lower operating costs, as Xerox did. Restructuring can be done by eliminating departments and reducing levels in the hierarchy, both of which result in the loss of large numbers of jobs of top, middle, or first-line managers and nonmanagerial employees. Modern IT's ability to increase efficiency has increased the amount of downsizing in recent years. For example, IT makes it possible for fewer employees to perform a given task because it increases each person's ability to process information and make decisions more quickly and accurately. U.S. companies are spending over $50 billion a year on advanced IT that improves efficiency and effectiveness. We discuss IT's many dramatic effects on management in Chapter 18 and throughout this book.

Restructuring, however, can produce some powerful negative outcomes. It can reduce the morale of the remaining employees, who are worried about their own job security, something Anne Mulcahey had to deal with at Xerox. And

New IBM managers participate in IBM's Basic Blue program at their Learning Center next door to headquarters. These meetings, of which more than 18,000 IBM managers have attended worldwide since launch in 1999, cover issues of people management, HR policies and programs and leadership development issues. The attendees in the class are new first-line managers recently promoted to management. The groups represent phase 2 of a nine-month program. Attendees have already completed six months of on-line e-learning.

particular client's specific needs. By using teams, IBM is now able to offer high-quality personalized service at a low price and compete effectively in the global marketplace.

Most of IBM's employees are concentrated in competency centers located in the countries in which IBM has the most clients and does the most business. These employees have a wide variety of skills, developed from their previous work experience, and the challenge facing IBM is to use these experts efficiently. To accomplish this, IBM used its own IT expertise to develop sophisticated software that allows it to create self-managed teams composed of IBM experts who have the optimum mix of skills to solve a client's particular problems.

Initially, IBM programmers analyzed the skills and experience of its 70,000 global employees and inputted the results into the software program. Now they analyze and code the nature of a client's specific problem and input that information. The IBM program then matches the specific problem to the skills of IBM's experts and identifies a list of "best fit" employees. One of IBM's senior managers then narrows down this list and decides on the actual composition of the self-managed team. Once selected, team members, from wherever they happen to be in the world, assemble as quickly as possible and go to work analyzing the client's problem. Together, team members then use their authority to develop the software and service package necessary to solve and manage the client's problem.

This new IT allows IBM to create an ever-changing set of global self-managed teams that form to solve the problems of IBM's global clients. At the same time, IBM's IT also optimizes the use of its whole talented workforce because each employee is being placed in his or her "most highly valued use," that is, in the team where the employee's skills can best increase efficiency and effectiveness. In addition, because each team inputs knowledge about its activities into IBM's internal information system, teams can watch and learn from one another—so their skills increase over time.

Challenges for Management in a Global Environment

Because the world has been changing more rapidly than ever before, managers and other employees throughout an organization must perform at higher and higher levels.[47] In the last 20 years, rivalry between organizations competing domestically (in the same country) and globally (in countries abroad) has increased dramatically. The rise of **global organizations,** organizations that operate and compete in more than one country, has put severe pressure on many organizations to identify better ways to use their resources and improve their performance. The successes of the German chemical companies Schering and Hoechst, Italian furniture manufacturer Natuzzi, Korean electronics

global organizations
Organizations that operate and compete in more than one country.

companies Samsung and LG, Brazilian plane maker Embraer, and Europe's Airbus Industries are putting pressure on companies in other countries to raise their level of performance to compete successfully against these global organizations.

Even in the not-for-profit sector, global competition is spurring change. Schools, universities, police forces, and government agencies are reexamining their operations because looking at the way activities are performed in other countries often reveals better ways to do them. For example, many curriculum and teaching changes in the United States have resulted from the study of methods that Japanese and European school systems use. Similarly, European and Asian hospital systems have learned much from the U.S. system—which may be the most effective, though not the most efficient, in the world.

Today, managers who make no attempt to learn from and adapt to changes in the global environment find themselves reacting rather than innovating, and their organizations often become uncompetitive and fail.[48] Five major challenges stand out for managers in today's world: building a competitive advantage, maintaining ethical standards, managing a diverse workforce, utilizing new information systems and technologies, and practicing global crisis management.

Building Competitive Advantage

competitive advantage The ability of one organization to outperform other organizations because it produces desired goods or services more efficiently and effectively than they do.

What are the most important lessons for managers and organizations to learn if they are to reach and remain at the top of the competitive environment of business? The answer relates to the use of organizational resources to build a competitive advantage. **Competitive advantage** is the ability of one organization to outperform other organizations because it produces desired goods or services more efficiently and effectively than its competitors. The four building blocks of competitive advantage are superior *efficiency; quality; speed, flexibility,* and *innovation;* and *responsiveness to customers* (see Figure 1.6).

Figure 1.6
Building Blocks of Competitive Advantage

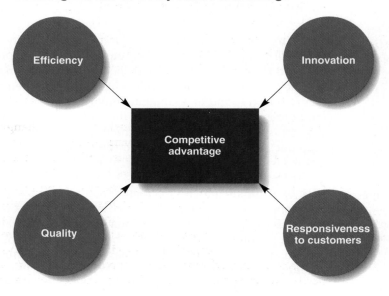

INCREASING EFFICIENCY   Organizations increase their efficiency when they reduce the quantity of resources (such as people and raw materials) they use to produce goods or services. In today's competitive environment, organizations continually search for new ways to use their resources to improve efficiency. Many organizations are training their workforces in the new skills and techniques needed to operate heavily computerized assembly plants. Similarly, cross-training gives employees the range of skills they need to perform many different tasks, and organizing employees in new ways, such as in self-managed teams, allows them to make good use of their skills. These are important steps in the effort to improve productivity. Japanese and German companies invest far more in training employees than do American or Italian companies.

Managers must improve efficiency if their organizations are to compete successfully with companies operating in Mexico, China, Malaysia, and other countries where employees are paid comparatively low wages. New methods must be devised either to increase efficiency or to gain some other competitive advantage—higher-quality goods, for example—if outsourcing and the loss of jobs to low-cost countries are to be prevented.

INCREASING QUALITY   The challenge from global organizations such as Korean electronics manufacturers, Mexican agricultural producers, and European marketing and financial firms also has increased pressure on companies to improve the skills and abilities of their workforces in order to improve the quality of their goods and services. One major thrust to improving quality has been to introduce the quality-enhancing techniques known as *total quality management (TQM)*. Employees involved in TQM are often organized into quality control teams and are responsible for finding new and better ways to perform their jobs; they also must monitor and evaluate the quality of the goods they produce. We discuss ways of managing TQM successfully in Chapter 9.

INCREASING SPEED, FLEXIBILITY, AND INNOVATION   Today, companies can win or lose the competitive race depending on their *speed*—how fast they can bring new products to market—or their *flexibility*—how easily they can change or alter the way they perform their activities to respond to the actions of their competitors. Companies that have speed and flexibility are agile competitors: Their managers have superior planning and organizing abilities; they can think ahead, decide what to do, and then speedily mobilize their resources to respond to a changing environment. We examine how managers can build speed and flexibility in their organizations in later chapters. Steve Jobs and Anne Mulcahy achieved their goal of making Apple and Xerox agile companies that can react to the continuous changes taking place in a digital world—now their problem is how to maintain their competitive advantage against Dell and Canon!

innovation The process of creating new or improved goods and services or developing better ways to produce or provide them.

Innovation, the process of creating new or improved goods and services that customers want or developing better ways to produce or provide goods and services, poses a special challenge. Managers must create an organizational setting in which people are encouraged to be innovative. Typically, innovation takes place in small groups or teams; management decentralizes control of work activities to team members and creates an organizational culture that rewards risk taking. For example, in 2006 a team composed of Apple and Nike employees came up with the idea for a new model of iPod that would be able to record and measure the distance its owner had run, among other things, and the companies formed an alliance to make it.[49] Managing innovation and creating a work setting that encourages risk taking are among the most difficult managerial tasks. Innovation is discussed in depth in Chapter 9.

INCREASING RESPONSIVENESS TO CUSTOMERS   Organizations compete for customers with their products and services, so training employees to be responsive to customers' needs is vital for all organizations, but particularly for service organizations. Retail stores, banks, and hospitals, for example, depend entirely on their employees to perform behaviors that result in high-quality service at a reasonable cost.[50] As many countries (the United States, Canada, and Switzerland are just a few) move toward a more service-based economy (in part because of the loss of manufacturing jobs to China, Malaysia, and other countries with low labor costs), managing behavior in service organizations is becoming increasingly important. Many organizations are empowering their customer service employees and giving them the authority to take the lead in providing high-quality customer service. As noted previously, the empowering of nonmanagerial employees changes the role of first-line managers and often leads to the more efficient use of organizational resources.

TURNAROUND MANAGEMENT   Because of intense global competition, companies like Kodak, Xerox, Apple, GM, Ford, Levi Strauss, Heinz, and a host of others lost their competitive advantage. For example, technological change and the move towards digital imaging led demand for Kodak's film and light-based Xerox copiers to plunge. Others like GM and Levi Strauss have suffered because low-cost competitors undercut their prices. The managers of these companies faced the challenge of turning around the performance of their companies by finding ways to restore competitive advantage—as Steve Jobs has done for Apple and Anne Mulcahey for Xerox.

Turnaround management is a particularly difficult and complex management task because it is done under conditions of great uncertainty. Customers, employees, and investors are unsure about the future; for example, will customer service be available, will employees retain their jobs, will investors get their money back? The risk of failure is greater for a troubled company, and usually a more radical restructuring and company reorganization are necessary to turn around its performance. Even Dell, for example, which has performed so spectacularly in the past, lost market share to competitors like HP and Apple in 2006. Its new CEO, Kevin Rollins—whom Michael Dell appointed because he perceived Rollins has great management skills—is working hard to find ways to help the company regain its commanding position. Few companies stay on top all the time—and the only place left is "down"—and this is why it is so important that managers continually monitor how well their company is performing compared to its rivals, as we discuss in Chapters 8 and 9.

Achieving a competitive advantage requires that managers use all their skills and expertise, as well as their companies' other resources, to improve efficiency, quality, innovation, and responsiveness to customers. We revisit this theme often as we examine the ways managers plan strategies, organize resources and activities, and lead and control people and groups to increase efficiency and effectiveness.

Maintaining Ethical and Socially Responsible Standards

Managers at all levels are under considerable pressure to make the best use of resources to increase the level at which their organizations perform.[51] For example, top managers feel pressure from shareholders to increase the performance of the entire organization to boost its stock price, improve profits, or raise dividends. In turn, top managers may then pressure middle managers to find new ways to use organizational resources to increase efficiency or quality and thus attract new customers and earn more revenues—and then middle managers hit on their department's supervisors.

Pressure to increase performance can be healthy for an organization because it leads managers to question the way the organization is working and it encourages them to find new and better ways to plan, organize, lead, and control. However, too much pressure to perform can be harmful.[52] It may induce managers to behave unethically, and even illegally, when dealing with people and groups inside and outside the organization.[53] For example, a purchasing manager for a nationwide retail chain might buy inferior clothing as a cost-cutting measure; or to secure a large foreign contract, a sales manager in a large defense company might offer bribes to foreign officials. In 2004, the four top executives of Lucent's Korean division were fired after it was revealed they used bribery to obtain lucrative contracts for Lucent in that country.[54]

The issue of social responsibility, discussed in Chapter 5, centers on deciding what, if any, obligations a company has toward the people and groups affected by its activities—such as employees, customers, or the communities in which it operates. Some companies have strong views about social responsibility; their managers believe they should protect the interests of others. But some managers may decide to act in an unethical way and put their own interests, or their company's, first, hurting others in the process. For example, Metabolife and NVE Pharmaceuticals used to make ephedra, a widely used dietary supplement. To protect their business, they did not reveal serious complaints about ephedra until forced to do so by lawsuits brought by people harmed by the drug. In 2003 Metabolife finally released over 16,000 customer reports about its ephedra products that listed nearly 2,000 adverse reactions, including 3 deaths.[55]

In 2004 the Food and Drug Administration (FDA) obtained the legal power to demand information from all the makers of ephedra pills. This revealed over 16,000 adverse-report events experienced by users, including at least 36 deaths. In 2004, it became illegal to make or sell ephedra in the United States.[56]

However, in their attempt to protect the $18 billion-a-year dietary supplement business, some pill makers continue to behave unethically. In particular, they have begun to use other chemical compounds that have ephedralike effects in new varieties of pills. The FDA has issued warnings about these pills and has received new powers to police dietary supplement makers; however, the old saying *Caveat emptor* remains true: "Buyer beware."[57] Another example showing why companies, managers, and customers need to think about the issues involved in acting in a socially responsible way is profiled in the following "Ethics in Action."

Ethics in Action

The Hidden Side of Valentine's Day

Every year on Valentine's Day tens of millions of roses are delivered to sweethearts and loved ones in the United States, and anyone who has bought roses knows that their price has been dropping. One of the main reasons for this is that rose growing is now concentrated in poorer countries in Central and South America. Rose growing has been a boon to poor countries, where the extra income women earn can mean the difference between starving or eating for their families. Ecuador, for example, is the fourth-biggest rose-growing nation in the world, and the industry employs over 50,000 women who tend, pick, and package roses for wages

Workers on some rose-growing farms in poorer countries are often subjected to unsafe working conditions that may harm their health, although they grow beautiful roses.

above the nation's national minimum. Most of these women are employed by Rosas del Ecuador, the company that controls the rose business in that country.

The hidden side of the global rose-growing business is that poorer countries tend to have lax or unenforced health and safety laws—a major reason why they have lower rose-growing costs. And, industry-watchers argue, many rose-growing companies and countries are *not* considering the well-being of their workers. For example, the CEO of Rosas del Ecuador, Erwin Pazmino, denies that workers are subjected to unsafe working conditions. Almost 60% of his workers have reported blurred vision, nausea, headaches, asthma, and other symptoms of pesticide poisoning, however.[58] Workers labor in hot, poorly ventilated greenhouses in which roses have been sprayed with pesticides and herbicides. Safety equipment such as masks and ventilators is scarce, and the long hours women work adds to chemical overexposure. If workers complain, they may be fired and blacklisted, which makes it very hard for them to find other jobs. So, to protect their families, well-being, workers rarely complain and thus their health remains at risk.

Clearly, rose buyers the world over need to be aware of the conditions under which roses are grown when deciding what brand of roses to buy—the company and country they are grown in, for example. A similar issue faced buyers of inexpensive footwear and clothing in the 1990s who became concerned when they learned about the sweatshop conditions in which garment and shoe workers around the world labored. Companies like Nike and Wal-Mart have made major efforts to stop sweatshop practices. They now employ hundreds of inspectors who police the factories overseas that make the products they sell. In a similar way, the main buyers and distributors of flowers for the U.S. market need to also consider the conditions under which roses are grown and the well-being of the workers who grow them.

Managing a Diverse Workforce

A major challenge for managers everywhere is to recognize the ethical need and legal requirement to treat human resources in a fair and equitable manner. Today, the age, gender, race, ethnicity, religion, sexual preference, and socio-economic makeup of the workforce present new challenges for managers. To create a highly trained and motivated workforce, as well as to avoid major class-action lawsuits, managers must establish human resource management (HRM) procedures and practices that are legal, are fair, and do not discriminate against any organizational members.[59]

In the past, white male employees dominated the ranks of management. Today increasing numbers of organizations are realizing that to motivate effectively and take advantage of the talents of a diverse workforce, they must make promotion opportunities available to all employees, including women and minorities.[60] Managers must recognize the performance-enhancing possibilities of a diverse workforce, such as the ability to take advantage of the skills and experiences of different kinds of people.[61] Union Bank of California, one of the 30 largest banks in the United States, is a good example of a company that has utilized the potential of its diverse employees.[62]

Based in San Francisco, Union Bank operates in one of the most diverse states in the nation, California, where more than half the population is Asian, black, Hispanic, or gay. Recognizing this fact, the bank always had a policy of hiring diverse employees. However, the bank did not realize the potential of its diverse employees to create a competitive advantage until 1996 when George Ramirez, a vice president at Union Bank, proposed that the bank create a marketing group to attract Hispanic customers. His idea was so successful that a group of African-American employees, and later Asian-American and gay and lesbian employees, proposed similar marketing campaigns.

After these groups' considerable success in recruiting new customers, it was clear to Union Bank's managers that they could use employee diversity to improve not only customer service (e.g., by staffing banks in Latino neighborhoods with Latino employees)[63] but also the quality of decision making inside the organization.[64] Furthermore, the bank's reputation of being a good place for minorities to work has attracted highly skilled and motivated minority job candidates.

As its former CEO Takahiro Moriguchi said when accepting a national diversity award for the company, "By searching for talent from among the disabled, both genders, veterans, gay, all ethnic groups and all nationalities, we gain access to a pool of ideas, energy, and creativity as wide and varied as the human race itself. I expect diversity will become even more important as the world gradually becomes a truly global marketplace."[65] Union Bank's diversity practices have become a model for many other companies seeking to emulate its success.[66]

Union Bank's customer service representatives, such as the employee pictured here, are well known for building relationships with their diverse customer groups to improve the level of customer service. The diverse nature of Union Bank's employees reflects the diverse customer groups the bank serves.

Managers who value their diverse employees not only invest in developing these employees' skills and capabilities but also succeed best in promoting performance over the long run.[67] The Gap, profiled in the following "Focus on Diversity" feature, offers a good example of how companies can take advantage of diversity to enhance their ability to satisfy customers and employees.

Focus on Diversity

People Are the Source of Competitive Advantage

Gap, the well-known clothing company, has always been responsive to the changing needs of its diverse customers; it is careful to employ clothes designers and salespeople who reflect the demographics of its customers. It ran into major problems in the 1990s, however, when suddenly its designers lost contact with its customers' needs and chose to make lines of unusual or garish clothing that appealed to no one. Gap's profits plunged as sales fell in its Gap, Banana Republic, and Old Navy stores, and investors felt it was in big trouble.

Gap hired a new CEO, Mickey Pressler, an ex-Disney executive, to somehow "revolutionize" its decision-making process. Pressler had learned at Disney how important it was to study customers' quickly changing needs. He restructured the design department by forming teams of diverse employees to investigate the demographics and changing needs of Gap's customers—to discover which customer needs were being met and, more importantly, which were not. These teams quickly figured out how to meet the needs of Gap's traditional, diverse customers, and its sales rose again.

The teams also made another important discovery: Gap had not recognized, and so was not adequately serving, the needs of a very lucrative market segment—specifically, the 46 million baby-boom-generation women, born between 1946 and 1964. These women have enormous spending power; indeed, they are the women who give their children and grandchildren the money to shop at Gap's stores!

Pressler realized his diverse employee teams had discovered a potentially profitable sales opportunity. He formed a team charged with the task of making all the thousands of decisions involved in opening a new chain of Gap stores that would stock clothing targeted at the needs of older, female, professional or casual customers who wanted to look good in clothes that fitted their lifestyle. So Gap opened Forth & Towne, its new chain aimed at female boomers age 35 and up. Five stores opened in 2005, and five additional stores were scheduled to open in 2006. Twenty more are planned in 2007 if Gap finds that its decision making has worked and its new chain proves popular—but finding a winning strategy is a complex task.

Today, more and more organizations are realizing that people are their most important resource and that developing and protecting human resources is an important challenge for management in a competitive global environment. We discuss the many issues surrounding the management of a diverse workforce in Chapter 5.

Utilizing IT and E-Commerce

As we discussed above, another important challenge for managers is the efficient utilization of new information technology.[68] New technologies such as computer-controlled manufacturing and Web-based IT that link and enable employees in new ways are continually being developed. Increasingly, new kinds of IT enable self-managed teams, providing them with more and more important information and allowing for virtual interactions over the Internet. This global coordination helps to improve quality and increase the pace of innovation. Microsoft, Hitachi, IBM, and most companies now search for new IT that can help them to build a competitive advantage. The importance of IT is discussed in detail in Chapters 16 and 18, and throughout the text you will find icons that alert you to examples of how IT is changing the way companies operate, such as happened at Empire and IBM, discussed earlier.

Practicing Global Crisis Management

Today, another challenge facing managers and organizations is global crisis management. The causes of global crises or disasters fall into three main categories: natural causes, man-made causes, and international terrorism and geopolitical conflicts. Crises that arise because of natural causes include the hurricanes, tsunamis, earthquakes, famines, and diseases that have devastated so many countries in the 2000s; hardly any country has been left untouched by their effects. Java, for example, which was inundated by the huge Pacific tsunami of 2004, experienced a devastating earthquake in 2006 that also killed thousands of people and left tens of thousands more homeless.

The Superdome is surrounded by floodwaters after Hurricane Katrina in New Orleans, September, 2005. Management has an important role to play in helping people, organizations, and indeed countries, respond to global crises such as this.

Man-made crises are the result of factors such as global warming, pollution, and the destruction of the natural habitat or environment. Pollution, for example, has become an increasingly significant problem for companies and countries to deal with. Companies in heavy industries such as coal and steel have polluted millions of acres of land around major cities in eastern Europe and Asia; billion-dollar cleanups are necessary. Disasters such as the 1986 Chernobyl nuclear power plant meltdown released over 1,540 times as much radiation into the air as occurred at Hiroshima; over 50,000 people died as a result, while hundreds of thousands more have been affected.

Man-made crises, such as global warming due to emissions of carbon dioxide and other gases, may have made the effects of natural disasters more serious. For example, increasing global temperatures and acid rain may have increased the intensity of hurricanes, led to unusually strong rains, and contributed to lengthy droughts. Scientists are convinced that global warming is responsible for the destruction of coral reefs (which are disappearing at a fast rate), forests, animal species, and the natural habitat in many parts of the world. The shrinking polar ice caps are expected to raise the sea level by a few, but vital, inches.

Finally, increasing geopolitical tensions, which are partly the result of the speed of globalization process itself, have upset the balance of world power as different countries and geographic regions attempt to protect their own economic and political interests. Rising oil prices, for example, have strengthened the bargaining power of major oil-supplying countries. This has led the United States to adopt global political strategies, including its war on terrorism, to secure the supply of oil vital to protect the national interest. In a similar way, countries in Europe have been forming contracts and allying with Russia to obtain its supply of natural gas, and Japan and China have been negotiating with Iran and Saudi Arabia. The rise of global terrorism and terrorist groups is to a large degree the result of changing political, social, and economic conditions that have made it easier for extremists to influence whole countries and cultures.

Management has an important role to play in helping people, organizations, and countries respond to global crises because it provides lessons on how to plan, organize, lead, and control the resources needed to both forestall and respond effectively to a crisis. Crisis management involves making important choices about how to (1) create teams to facilitate rapid decision making and communication, (2) establish the organizational chain of command and reporting relationships necessary to mobilize a fast response, (3) recruit and select the right people to lead and work in such teams, and (4) develop bargaining and negotiating strategies to manage the conflicts that arise whenever people and groups have different interests and objectives. How well managers make such decisions determines how quickly an effective response to a crisis can be implemented, and it sometimes can prevent or reduce the severity of the crisis itself.

Summary and Review

WHAT IS MANAGEMENT? A manager is a person responsible for supervising the use of an organization's resources to meet its goals. An organization is a collection of people who work together and coordinate their actions to achieve a wide variety of goals. Management is the process of using organizational resources to achieve organizational goals effectively and efficiently through planning, organizing, leading, and controlling. An efficient organization makes the most productive use of its resources. An effective organization pursues appropriate goals and achieves these goals by using its resources to create the goods or services that customers want.

MANAGERIAL TASKS The four principal managerial tasks are planning, organizing, leading, and controlling. Managers at all levels of the organization and in all departments perform these tasks. Effective management means managing these activities successfully.

LEVELS AND SKILLS OF MANAGERS Organizations typically have three levels of management. First-line managers are responsible for the day-to-day supervision of nonmanagerial employees. Middle managers are responsible for developing and utilizing organizational resources efficiently and effectively. Top managers have cross-departmental responsibility. Three main kinds of managerial skills are conceptual, human, and technical. The need to develop

6. Describe the way the organization treats its human resources. How does this treatment affect the attitudes and behaviors of the workforce?

7. If you could give your manager one piece of advice or change one management practice in the organization, what would it be?

8. How attuned are the managers in the organization to the need to increase efficiency, quality, innovation, or responsiveness to customers? How well do you think the organization performs its prime goals of providing the goods or services that customers want or need the most?

Managing Ethically

Think about an example of unethical behavior that you observed in the past. The incident could be something you experienced as an employee or a customer or something you observed informally.

1. Either by yourself or in a group, give three reasons why you think the behavior was unethical. For example, what rules or norms were broken? Who benefited or was harmed by what took place? What was the outcome for the people involved?

2. What steps might you take to prevent such unethical behavior and encourage people to behave in an ethical way?

Small Group Breakout Exercise

Opening a New Restaurant

Form groups of three or four people, and appoint one group member as the spokesperson who will communicate your findings to the entire class when called on by the instructor. Then discuss the following scenario.

You and your partners have decided to open a large, full-service restaurant in your local community; it will be open from 7 a.m. to 10 p.m. to serve breakfast, lunch, and dinner. Each of you is investing $50,000 in the venture, and together you have secured a bank loan for $300,000 more to begin operations. You and your partners have little experience in managing a restaurant beyond serving meals or eating in restaurants, and you now face the task of deciding how you will manage the restaurant and what your respective roles will be.

1. Decide what each partner's managerial role in the restaurant will be. For example, who will be responsible for the necessary departments and specific activities? Describe your managerial hierarchy.

2. Which building blocks of competitive advantage do you need to establish to help your restaurant succeed? What criteria will you use to evaluate how successfully you are managing the restaurant?

3. Discuss the most important decisions that must be made about (a) planning, (b) organizing, (c) leading, and (d) controlling, to allow you and your partners to utilize organizational resources effectively and build a competitive advantage.

4. For each managerial task, list the issues to solve, and decide which roles will contribute the most to your restaurant's success.

Exploring the World Wide Web

Go to the General Electric (GE) Web site at www.ge.com, click on "Our Company," then "company information," and then "Jeffrey Immelt," GE's CEO. You will see a list of recent articles that discuss his management style; click on articles such as "The Immelt Revolution, 2005" in *BusinessWeek* and the *Financial Times* article titled "Man of the Year 2003."

Search these articles or others for information that describes Immelt's approach to planning, organizing, leading, and controlling GE. What is his approach to managing? What effects has this approach had on GE's performance?

Be the Manager

Problems at Achieva

You have just been called in to help managers at Achieva, a fast-growing Internet software company that specializes in B2B network software. Your job is to help Achieva solve some management problems that have arisen because of its rapid growth.

Customer demand to license Achieva's software has boomed so much in just two years that more than 50 new software programmers have been added to help develop a new range of software products. Achieva's growth has been so swift that the company still operates informally, its organizational structure is loose and flexible, and programmers are encouraged to find solutions to problems as they go along. Although this structure worked well in the past, you have been told that problems are arising.

There have been increasing complaints from employees that good performance is not being recognized in the organization and that they do not feel equitably treated. Moreover, there have been complaints about getting managers to listen to their new ideas and to act on them. A bad atmosphere is developing in the company, and recently several talented employees left. Your job is to help Achieva's managers solve these problems quickly and keep the company on the fast track.

Questions

1. What kinds of organizing and controlling problems is Achieva suffering from?
2. What kinds of management changes need to be made to solve them?

BusinessWeek Case in the News

HP's Ultimate Team Player

One July evening in Silicon Valley, Hewlett-Packard executive Ann Livermore got the phone call she had waited months to receive. She rushed to the hospital, having learned that a kidney had been donated, and underwent an organ transplant, necessary due to complications from a childhood disease. For most executives, it would have been an opportune time to call it quits after a 24-year career. But three days after the surgery, she was phoning HP Chief Executive Mark V. Hurd and peppering lieutenants with questions. "I finally asked if someone would please go in there and take her laptop away," laughs Hurd.

Why didn't Livermore step down? Opportunity. While the $33 billion corporate-computing business she runs has long been one of the most glaring underachievers in tech, she's convinced the business is finally ready to show what it can do. Livermore and HP have spent 18 months overhauling the unit, and the benefits are only now becoming visible. "From the moment I left, I never thought of not coming back," says Livermore, who was out for 5 1/2 weeks. "We have a very special opportunity right now."

It's a dramatic reversal. A year ago her Technology Solutions Group, which sells servers, storage, and consulting services to corporations, was valued at next to nothing by Wall Street analysts. Mercilessly squeezed by IBM and Dell Inc., the unit struggled to show profits or promise. Yet Livermore's unit is now a key reason HP's stock is on a tear and the newly arrived Hurd is being hailed as a turn-around maestro. Thanks mostly to cost-cutting and operational improvements, the businesses turned in a 50% increase in operating earnings in fiscal 2005.

In many ways, Livermore is a perfect metaphor for HP. The 46-year-old is competent, respected, but not really feared by rivals. A standout tennis player and valedictorian of her high school in Greensboro, N.C., she earned a coveted Morehead Scholarship to the University of North Carolina at Chapel Hill. She went straight to business school at Stanford University. There, she won the annual competition for best business plan for running the doughnut concession.

Her secret? She solicited companies that were coming to interview students to buy her sweets by the dozen. When she joined HP, straight out of Stanford, she never expected to make a career of it. She had watched her father stay at the same insurance company for years and vowed not to get bogged down. But she fell in love with HP's unique culture. Especially appealing was HP's willingness to accommodate working mothers, through flexible working hours and other arrangements. Livermore could dote on her daughter, even as she roared through the ranks. By 1996 she was running the services arm. In 1999, she made a very public run at the CEO job—even hiring an internal press relations person to raise her profile. She lost out to Fiorina and then became a staunch ally.

Inauspicious Start

For all her success, Livermore still has something to prove. Wall Streeters are wary of her ability to deliver consistent financial results. Even some HP insiders ascribe her rise to a selfless willingness to follow orders. They're quick to point out that she's a solid general manager and universally well-liked, but question whether she can rally the troops to challenge a fierce foe like IBM. "She's extremely competent," says one insider, "but I don't see her as a key leader for the long-term." Completing the turnaround in the corporate business could help Livermore win over the naysayers.

Livermore had an inauspicious start in her current job. She took over the corporate computing business in early 2004. Just three months later, in August, it reported a disastrous quarter pushing the company's stock down 15%. Out of that crisis, Livermore has helped forge a comeback. Within days, she instructed HP veteran Scott Stallard to set up a war room to begin addressing the unit's many operational problems. Over the months that followed, she worked closely with a seven-person team to identify and improve 15 key weaknesses—everything from how HP worked with distributors to how it pulled together bids for customers.

Livermore recognizes that both she and HP have their doubters. But she believes time is on their side. "The fact is, there's no one better in the world at helping customers design, build, and manage data centers," she says. "We have not proudly or loudly enough put that stake in the ground. But we will." The company's future—and her own—may depend on it.

Questions for Discussion

1. What is Ann Livermore's approach to managing?

2. What kinds of skills do you think she needs the most to perform her job effectively?

Source: Peter Burrows, "HP's Ultimate Team Player." Reprinted from the January 30, 2006, issue of *BusinessWeek* by special permission. Copyright © 2006 by the McGraw-Hill Companies, Inc.

BusinessWeek

Case in the News

The Hardest Job in Silicon Valley

As Oracle Corp.'s senior vice president in charge of applications, John Wookey has one of the toughest jobs in software. Over the past two years, Chief Executive Lawrence J. Ellison has spent $19 billion buying 14 rivals in the corporate software market. His buying binge included paying $10 billion for PeopleSoft Inc. and $5.8 billion for Siebel Systems Inc. That was the easy part. Putting it all together is Wookey's job. "My head is the one on the chopping block if this doesn't work," deadpans Wookey. He's mostly joking, but in the past Ellison has been quick to fire executives who don't perform.

The plan is to meld the best of what Oracle has bought into a new suite of software code-named "Project Fusion." The integrated package will help corporations run everything from accounting and sales to customer relations and supply-chain management. Ellison's hope is that Fusion—together with all the new customers he landed with his acquisitions—will finally give him the edge he needs to overtake the top corporate applications company, Germany's SAP.

Stiff Competition

To get Oracle's market share growing, Wookey must build a new suite of software applications — using the latest technology and drawing the best from each of the acquired companies. He has to persuade customers to wait for him to finish his task and then gradually switch more of their computing jobs to run on Oracle software. And he has to fend off SAP, which is attempting to take advantage of customers' uncertainty and pick them off.

The grand vision to take on SAP by fusing the best of the rest is all Ellison's. But while he's the mastermind, Wookey is the foreman. Wookey has worked at Oracle for a decade, earning his stripes as an executive in the customer relations and accounting groups. His career took off after he ran a pet project of Ellison's: building applications for the health-care industry. He was promoted a year ago to run the entire applications business.

The two men stand in stark contrast to each other. Wookey once quipped during an Oracle event as he was taking the stage after Ellison that the Armani part of the program was ending and the Men's Wearhouse part was starting. While Ellison enjoys fast cars, fast boats, and fancy suits, Wookey is a devoted family man. He gets up at 4:15 a.m. every day for a jog and dog walk, works for several hours, then takes the kids to school. At work, while Ellison is brash and contentious, Wookey is a soft-spoken diplomat. He's known for his straight talk and dry wit.

That disarming style has made him the perfect goodwill ambassador to the customers Oracle has swallowed up through acquisitions during the past year. Since he took command of the Fusion project, he has crisscrossed the world making personal appeals to customers. To make sure he's on the right track with Fusion, he vets his plans with an advisory council of customers. Within Oracle, Wookey's greatest strength is as a consensus builder. Every Monday at midday, he presents progress reports to Ellison and Co-Presidents Charles E. Phillips Jr. and Safra A. Catz. After that, he meets with his 14 senior staff members to hash out nitty-gritty product details. There's vigorous debate over how the applications should be built and what features are most important. The Oracle of old might have been paralyzed, but Wookey keeps things moving.

Mr. Nice Guy

Typical of Wookey's style was a recent four-hour meeting with his top staff. Looking around the conference room, it was hard to tell who was in charge. Wookey didn't sit at the head of the table, and he let others do most of the talking. As developers argued over arcane technical matters, Wookey weighed in to resolve debates—often by reminding them what customers had asked for.

One of Wookey's most notable victories was holding on to the software writers who came to Oracle from acquired rivals. So far, nearly all of the developers to whom Oracle offered jobs are still with the company. "I had an image that everyone [at Oracle] had been growing horns," says John Schiff, a former People-Soft manager. "But John expressed the importance of family values, and you see it in his own behavior. It's just very comfortable."

If Wookey can meet his deadlines and take full advantage of Oracle software franchises, he'll have a fighting chance as the battle between the tech titans heats up. If not, he might find himself on another vacation. Only the next one could be permanent.

Questions for Discussion

1. What do you think are John Wookey's greatest skills as a manager?

2. In what way will these skills help him to perform his task at Oracle?

3. Why do he and Larry Ellison complement each other as managers?

Source: Sarah Lacy, "The Hardest Job in Silicon Valley." Reprinted from the January 23, 2006, issue of *BusinessWeek* by special permission. Copyright © 2006 by the McGraw-Hill Companies, Inc.

CHAPTER 2

The Evolution of Management Thought

Learning Objectives

After studying this chapter, you should be able to:

- Describe how the need to increase organizational efficiency and effectiveness has guided the evolution of management theory.

- Explain the principle of job specialization and division of labor, and tell why the study of person-task relationships is central to the pursuit of increased efficiency.

- Identify the principles of administration and organization that underlie effective organizations.

- Trace the changes in theories about how managers should behave to motivate and control employees.

- Explain the contributions of management science to the efficient use of organizational resources.

- Explain why the study of the external environment and its impact on an organization has become a central issue in management thought.

A Manager's Challenge

Finding Better Ways to Make Cars

What is the best way to manage the work process?

Car production has changed dramatically over the years as managers have applied different principles of management to organize and control work activities. Prior to 1900, small groups of skilled workers cooperated to hand-build cars with parts that often had to be altered and modified to fit together. This system, a type of *small-batch production,* was very expensive; assembling just one car took considerable time and effort; and skilled workers could produce only a few cars in a day. Although these cars were of high quality, they were too expensive. Managers of early car companies needed better techniques to increase efficiency, reduce costs, and sell more cars.

Henry Ford revolutionized the car industry. In 1913, Ford opened the Highland Park car plant in Detroit to produce the Model T Ford, and his team of manufacturing managers pioneered the development of *mass-production manufacturing,* a system that made the small-batch system almost obsolete overnight. In mass production, moving conveyor belts bring the cars to the workers. Each worker performs a single assigned task along a production line, and the speed of the conveyor

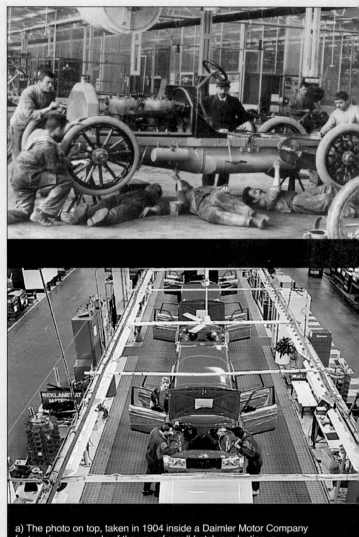

a) The photo on top, taken in 1904 inside a Daimler Motor Company factory, is an example of the use of small-batch production, a production system in which small groups of people work together and perform all the tasks needed to assemble a product. (b) In 1913, Henry Ford revolutionized the production process of a car by pioneering mass-production manufacturing, a production system in which a conveyor belt brings each car to the workers and each individual worker performs a single task along the production line. Even today cars are still built using this system, as evidenced in the photo of workers along a modern-day computerized automobile assembly line.

belt is the primary means of controlling workers' activities. Ford experimented to discover the most efficient way for each worker to perform an assigned task. The result was that each worker performed one narrow, specialized task, such as bolting on the door or attaching the door handle, and jobs in the Ford car plant became very repetitive. They required little use of a worker's skills.[1] Ford's management approach increased efficiency and reduced costs by so much that by 1920 he was able to reduce the price of a car by two-thirds and to sell more than 2 million cars a year.[2] Ford became the leading car company in the world, and competitors rushed to adopt the new mass-production techniques.

The next change in management thinking about car assembly occurred in Japan when Ohno Taiichi, a Toyota production engineer, pioneered the development of *lean manufacturing* in the 1960s after touring the U.S. plants of the Big Three car companies. The management philosophy behind lean manufacturing is to continuously find methods to improve the efficiency of the production process in order to reduce costs, increase quality, and reduce car assembly time. Lean production is based on the idea that if workers have input and can participate continually in the decision-making process, their skills and knowledge can be used to increase efficiency.

In lean manufacturing, workers work on a moving production line, but they are organized into small teams, each of which is responsible for a particular phase of car assembly, such as installing the car's transmission or electrical wiring system. Each team member is expected to learn the tasks of all members of that team, and each work group is responsible not only for assembling cars but also for continuously finding ways to increase quality and reduce costs. By 1970, Japanese managers had applied the new lean-production system so efficiently that they were producing higher-quality cars at lower prices than their U.S. counterparts. By 1980 Japanese companies dominated the global car market.

To compete with the Japanese, managers of U.S. carmakers visited Japan to learn the new management principles of lean production. As a result, companies such as General Motors (GM) established the Saturn plant to experiment with this new way of involving workers; GM also established a joint venture with Toyota called New United Motor Manufacturing Inc. (NUMMI) to learn how to achieve the benefits of lean production. Meanwhile, Ford and Chrysler began to change their work processes to take advantage of employees' skills and knowledge.

In the 1990s global car companies increased the number of robots used on the production line and began to use advanced IT to build and track the quality of cars being produced. Indeed, for a time it seemed that robots rather than employees would be building cars in the future. However, Toyota discovered something interesting at its first fully roboticized car plant. When only robots build cars, efficiency does not continually increase because, unlike people, robots cannot provide input to improve the work process. The crucial thing is to find the right balance between using people, machinery, computers, and IT.

In the 2000s, global car companies are continuing to compete fiercely to improve and perfect better ways of making cars. Toyota is constantly pioneering new ways to manage its assembly lines to increase efficiency, and other Japanese carmakers such as Honda and Nissan are catching up fast. Ford, Chrysler, and GM have also made great strides in the last decade, and they are closing the quality gap with Toyota and Nissan. In the 2000s, however, U.S. carmakers have been saddled with high overhead costs because of such factors as employee pensions and health benefits that add over $1,000 to the cost of every car they make. In addition, Japanese carmakers are introducing popular new car models at a faster pace and establishing U.S. plants to make them efficiently. Ford and GM are finding it hard to compete. In 2006 Ford announced plans to reduce its car-making capacity by 20% as it continues to lose market share; its managers are racing to develop the cars customers want to buy today (be effective) and to make them reliably and cost-effectively (be efficient).

Overview

As this sketch of the evolution of management thinking in global car manufacturing suggests, changes in management practices occur as managers, theorists, researchers, and consultants seek new ways to increase organizational efficiency and effectiveness. The driving force behind the evolution of management theory is the search for better ways to utilize organizational resources. Advances in management thought typically occur as managers and researchers find better ways to perform the principal management tasks: planning, organizing, leading, and controlling human and other organizational resources.

In this chapter, we examine how management thought has evolved in modern times and the central concerns that have guided ongoing advances in management theory. First, we examine the so-called classical management theories that emerged around the turn of the 20th century. These include scientific management, which focuses on matching people and tasks to maximize efficiency, and administrative management, which focuses on identifying the principles that will lead to the creation of the most efficient system of organization and management. Next, we consider behavioral management theories developed both before and after World War II; these focus on how managers should lead and control their workforces to increase performance. Then we discuss management science theory, which developed during World War II and has become increasingly important as researchers have developed rigorous analytical and quantitative techniques to help managers measure and control organizational performance. Finally, we discuss business in the 1960s and 1970s and focus on the theories developed to help explain how the external environment affects the way organizations and managers operate.

By the end of this chapter you will understand the ways in which management thought and theory have evolved over time. You will also understand how economic, political, and cultural forces have affected the development of these theories and the ways in which managers and their organizations behave. In Figure 2.1 we summarize the chronology of the management theories discussed in this chapter.

Figure 2.1
The Evolution of Management Theory

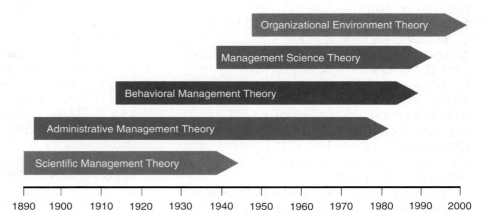

Scientific Management Theory

The evolution of modern management began in the closing decades of the 19th century, after the industrial revolution had swept through Europe and America. In the new economic climate, managers of all types of organizations—political, educational, and economic—were increasingly trying to find better ways to satisfy customers' needs. Many major economic, technical, and cultural changes were taking place at this time. The introduction of steam power and the development of sophisticated machinery and equipment changed the way goods were produced, particularly in the weaving and clothing industries. Small workshops run by skilled workers who produced hand-manufactured products (a system called *crafts production*) were being replaced by large factories in which sophisticated machines controlled by hundreds or even thousands of unskilled or semiskilled workers made products. For example, raw cotton and wool, which in the past had been spun into yarn by families or whole villages working together, were now shipped to factories where workers operated machines that spun and wove large quantities of yarn into cloth.

Owners and managers of the new factories found themselves unprepared for the challenges accompanying the change from small-scale crafts production to large-scale mechanized manufacturing. Moreover, many of the managers and supervisors in these workshops and factories were engineers who had only a technical orientation. They were unprepared for the social problems that occur when people work together in large groups in a factory or shop system. Managers began to search for new techniques to manage their organizations' resources, and soon they began to focus on ways to increase the efficiency of the worker-task mix.

Job Specialization and the Division of Labor

Initially, management theorists were interested in the subject of why the new machine shops and factory system were more efficient and produced greater quantities of goods and services than older, crafts-style production operations. Nearly 200 years before, Adam Smith had been one of the first writers to investigate the advantages associated with producing goods and services in factories. A famous economist, Smith journeyed around England in the 1700s studying the effects of the industrial revolution.[3] In a study of factories that produced various pins or nails, Smith identified two different manufacturing methods. The first was similar to crafts-style production, in which each worker was responsible for all of the 18 tasks involved in producing a pin. The other had each worker performing only 1 or a few of the 18 tasks that go into making a complete pin.

In a comparison of the relative performance of these different ways of organizing production, Smith found that the performance of the factories in which workers specialized in only one or a few tasks was much greater than the performance of the factory in which each worker performed all 18 pin-making tasks. In fact, Smith found that 10 workers specializing in a particular task could make 48,000 pins a day, whereas those workers who performed all the tasks could make only a few thousand at most.[4] Smith reasoned that this difference in performance was due to the fact that the workers who specialized became much more skilled at their specific tasks and as a group were thus able to produce a product faster than the group of workers who each performed many tasks. Smith concluded that increasing the level of job specialization—the process by which a division of labor occurs as different workers specialize in specific tasks over time—increases efficiency and leads to higher organizational performance.[5]

job specialization
The process by which a division of labor occurs as different workers specialize in different tasks over time.

Armed with the insights gained from Adam Smith's observations, other managers and researchers began to investigate how to improve job specialization to increase performance. Management practitioners and theorists focused on how managers should organize and control the work process to maximize the advantages of job specialization and the division of labor.

F. W. Taylor and Scientific Management

Frederick W. Taylor (1856–1915) is best known for defining the techniques of scientific management, the systematic study of relationships between people and tasks for the purpose of redesigning the work process to increase efficiency. Taylor was a manufacturing manager who eventually became a consultant and taught other managers how to apply his scientific management techniques. Taylor believed that if the amount of time and effort that each worker expends to produce a unit of output (a finished good or service) can be reduced by increasing specialization and the division of labor, the production process will become more efficient. According to Taylor, the way to create the most efficient division of labor could best be determined by scientific management techniques, rather than intuitive or informal rule-of-thumb knowledge. Based on his experiments and observations as a manufacturing manager in a variety of settings, he developed four principles to increase efficiency in the workplace:

scientific management The systematic study of relationships between people and tasks for the purpose of redesigning the work process to increase efficiency.

- Principle 1: *Study the way workers perform their tasks, gather all the informal job knowledge that workers possess, and experiment with ways of improving how tasks are performed.*

  To discover the most efficient method of performing specific tasks, Taylor studied in great detail and measured the ways different workers went about performing their tasks. One of the main tools he used was a *time-and-motion study,* which involves the careful timing and recording of the actions taken to perform a particular task. Once Taylor understood the existing method of performing a task, he then experimented to increase specialization. He tried different methods of dividing and coordinating the various tasks necessary to produce a finished product. Usually this meant simplifying jobs and having each worker perform fewer, more routine tasks, as at the pin factory or on Ford's car assembly line. Taylor also sought to find ways to improve each worker's ability to perform a particular task—for example, by reducing the number of motions workers made to complete the task, by changing the layout of the work area or the type of tools workers used, or by experimenting with tools of different sizes.

- Principle 2: *Codify the new methods of performing tasks into written rules and standard operating procedures.*

  Once the best method of performing a particular task was determined, Taylor specified that it should be recorded so that this procedure could be taught to all workers performing the same task. These new methods further

captured—at times quite humorously—in the movie *Cheaper by the Dozen,* a new version of which appeared in 2004, which depicts how the Gilbreths (with their 12 children) tried to live their own lives according to these efficiency principles and apply them to daily actions such as shaving, cooking, and even raising a family.[16]

Eventually, the Gilbreths became increasingly interested in the study of fatigue. They studied how the physical characteristics of the workplace contribute to job stress that often leads to fatigue and thus poor performance. They isolated factors that result in worker fatigue, such as lighting, heating, the color of walls, and the design of tools and machines. Their pioneering studies paved the way for new advances in management theory.

Fordism in Practice

From 1908 to 1914, through trial and error, Henry Ford's talented team of production managers pioneered the

perform *all* the steelmaking operations necessary to convert iron ore into finished products. For example, he constructed rolling mills to make steel rails *next* to his blast furnace so that iron ore could be converted into finished steel products in one continuous process. Carnegie's innovations led to a dramatic fall in steelmaking costs and revolutionized the U.S. steel industry. His new production methods reduced the price of U.S. steel from $135 a ton to $12 a ton! Despite the cheaper price, his company was still enormously profitable, and he ploughed back all his profits into building his steel business and constructed many new low-cost steel plants. By 1900, most of his competitors had been driven out of business because of his low prices; his company was the leading U.S. steelmaker, and he was one of the richest men in the world.

Although the story of Carnegie's new approach to management might seem like "business as usual," there is another side to Carnegie's management style. Critics say he increased profitability "on the backs" of his workers. Despite the enormous increase in productivity he had achieved by using the new mass-production steelmaking technology, he was continually driven by the need to find every way possible to reduce operating costs. To increase productivity, Carnegie gradually increased the normal workday from an already long 10 hours to 12 hours, six days a week. He also paid his workers the lowest wage rate possible even though their increasing skills in mastering the new technology were contributing to the huge increase in productivity. He also paid no attention to improving the safety of his mills, where workers toiled in dangerous conditions and thousands of workers were injured each year because of spills of molten steel. Any attempts by workers to improve their work conditions were uniformly rejected, and Carnegie routinely crushed any of the workers' attempts to unionize. Carnegie, in implementing new management techniques and creating the modern industrial company, also created the need for new administrative management theory—theory that could help managers find better ways of organizing and controlling resources to increase performance, as well as find new strategies for negotiating with and managing the increasingly unionized workforce that modern methods of production had brought into being.

Administrative Management Theory

administrative management The study of how to create an organizational structure and control system that leads to high efficiency and effectiveness.

Side by side with scientific managers like Carnegie studying the person-technology mix to increase efficiency, other managers and researchers were focusing on **administrative management,** the study of how to create an organizational structure and control system that leads to high efficiency and effectiveness. *Organizational structure* is the system of task and authority relationships that control how employees use resources to achieve the organization's goals. Two of the most influential early views regarding the creation of efficient systems of organizational administration were developed in Europe: Max Weber, a German professor of sociology, developed one theory; Henri Fayol, the French manager who developed the model of management introduced in Chapter 1, developed the other.

The Theory of Bureaucracy

Max Weber (1864–1920), wrote at the turn of the 20th century, when Germany was undergoing its industrial revolution.[18] To help Germany manage its growing industrial enterprises at a time when it was striving to become a world power, Weber developed the principles of **bureaucracy**—a formal system of organization and administration designed to ensure efficiency and effectiveness. A bureaucratic system of administration is based on the five principles summarized in Figure 2.2

bureaucracy A formal system of organization and administration designed to ensure efficiency and effectiveness.

- Principle 1: *In a bureaucracy, a manager's formal authority derives from the position he or she holds in the organization.*

  Authority is the power to hold people accountable for their actions and to make decisions concerning the use of organizational resources. Authority gives managers the right to direct and control their subordinates' behavior to achieve organizational goals. In a bureaucratic system of administration, obedience is owed to a manager, not because of any personal qualities—such as personality, wealth, or social status—but because the manager occupies a position that is associated with a certain level of authority and responsibility.[19]

authority The power to hold people accountable for their actions and to make decisions concerning the use of organizational resources.

- Principle 2: *In a bureaucracy, people should occupy positions because of their performance, not because of their social standing or personal contacts.*

  This principle was not always followed in Weber's time and is often ignored today. Some organizations and industries are still affected by social networks in which personal contacts and relations, not job-related skills, influence hiring and promotional decisions.

Figure 2.2

Weber's Principles of Bureaucracy

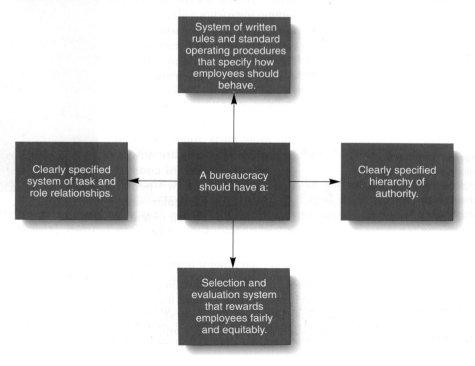

what the organization does best, and the emphasis is on continuously improving the goods and services the organization provides to its customers. Managers of top-performing companies resist the temptation to get sidetracked into pursuing ventures outside their area of expertise just because they seem to promise a quick return. These managers also focus on customers and establish close relationships with them to learn their needs, for responsiveness to customers increases competitive advantage.

The third set of management principles pertains to organizing and controlling the organization. Excellent companies establish a *division of work* and a *division of authority and responsibility* that will motivate employees to *subordinate their individual interests to the common interest*. Inherent in this approach is the belief that high performance derives from individual skills and abilities and that *equity, order, initiative,* and other indications of respect for the individual create the *esprit de corps* that fosters productive behavior. An emphasis on entrepreneurship and respect for every employee leads the best managers to create a structure that gives employees room to exercise *initiative* and motivates them to succeed. Because a simple, streamlined managerial hierarchy is best suited to achieve this outcome, top managers keep the *line of authority* as short as possible. They also decentralize authority to permit employee participation, but they keep enough control to maintain *unity of direction*.

As this insight into contemporary management suggests, the basic concerns that motivated Fayol continue to motivate management theorists.[25] The principles that Fayol and Weber set forth still provide a clear and appropriate set of guidelines that managers can use to create a work setting that makes efficient and effective use of organizational resources. These principles remain the bedrock of modern management theory; recent researchers have refined or developed them to suit modern conditions. For example, Weber's and Fayol's concerns for equity and for establishing appropriate links between performance and reward are central themes in contemporary theories of motivation and leadership.

Behavioral Management Theory

Because the writings of Weber and Fayol were not translated into English and published in the United States until the late 1940s, American management theorists in the first half of the 20th century were unaware of the contributions of these European pioneers. American management theorists began where Taylor and his followers left off. Although their writings were all very different, these theorists all espoused a theme that focused on **behavioral management,** the study of how managers should personally behave to motivate employees and encourage them to perform at high levels and be committed to achieving organizational goals.

behavioral management The study of how managers should behave to motivate employees and encourage them to perform at high levels and be committed to the achievement of organizational goals.

The Work of Mary Parker Follett

If F. W. Taylor is considered the father of management thought, Mary Parker Follett (1868–1933) serves as its mother.[26] Much of her writing about management and about the way managers should behave toward workers was a response to her concern that Taylor was ignoring the human side of the organization. She pointed out that management often overlooks the multitude of ways in which employees can contribute to the organization when managers allow them to participate and exercise initiative in their everyday work lives.[27] Taylor, for example, never proposed that managers should involve workers in analyzing their jobs to identify better ways to perform tasks or should even ask workers how they felt about their jobs. Instead, he used time-and-motion experts to analyze workers' jobs for them. Follett, in contrast, argued that because workers know the most about their jobs, they should be involved in job analysis and managers should allow them to participate in the work development process.

Mary Parker Follett, an early management thinker who advocated that "Authority should go with knowledge . . . whether it is up the line or down."

Follett proposed that "authority should go with knowledge . . . whether it is up the line or down." In other words, if workers have the relevant knowledge, then workers, rather than managers, should be in control of the work process itself, and managers should behave as coaches and facilitators—not as monitors and supervisors. In making this statement, Follett anticipated the current interest in self-managed teams and empowerment. She also recognized the importance of having managers in different departments communicate directly with each other to speed decision making. She advocated what she called "cross-functioning": members of different departments working together in cross-departmental teams to accomplish projects—an approach that is increasingly utilized today.[28]

Fayol also mentioned expertise and knowledge as important sources of managers' authority, but Follett went further. She proposed that knowledge and expertise, and not managers' formal authority deriving from their position in the hierarchy, should decide who will lead at any particular moment. She believed, as do many management theorists today, that power is fluid and should flow to the person who can best help the organization achieve its goals. Follett took a horizontal view of power and authority, in contrast to Fayol, who saw the formal line of authority and vertical chain of command as being most essential to effective management. Follett's behavioral approach to management was very radical for its time.

The Hawthorne Studies and Human Relations

Probably because of its radical nature, Follett's work was unappreciated by managers and researchers until quite recently. Most continued to follow in the footsteps of Taylor and the Gilbreths. To increase efficiency, they studied ways to improve various characteristics of the work setting, such as job specialization or the kinds of tools workers used. One series of studies was conducted from 1924 to 1932 at the Hawthorne Works of the Western Electric Company.[29] This research, now known as the *Hawthorne studies,* began as an attempt to investigate how characteristics of the work setting—specifically the level of lighting or

2. Which management approach (for example, Theory X or Y) do you propose to use to run your organization? In 50 words or less write a statement describing the management approach you believe will motivate and coordinate your subordinates, and tell why you think this style will be best.

Managing Ethically

Mr. Edens Profits from Watching His Workers' Every Move

Read the case below, "Mr. Edens Profits from Watching His Workers' Every Move," and think about the following issues.

Control is one of Ron Edens's favorite words. "This is a controlled environment," he says of the blank brick building that houses his company, Electronic Banking System Inc.

Inside, long lines of women sit at spartan desks, slitting envelopes, sorting contents and filling out "control cards" that record how many letters they have opened and how long it has taken them. Workers here, in "the cage," must process three envelopes a minute. Nearby, other women tap keyboards, keeping pace with a quota that demands 8,500 strokes an hour.

The room is silent. Talking is forbidden. The windows are covered. Coffee mugs, religious pictures and other adornments are barred from workers' desks.

In his office upstairs, Mr. Edens sits before a TV monitor that flashes images from eight cameras posted throughout the plant. "There's a little bit of Sneaky Pete to it," he says, using a remote control to zoom in on a document atop a worker's desk. "I can basically read that and figure out how someone's day is going."

This day, like most others, is going smoothly, and Mr. Edens's business has boomed as a result. "We maintain a lot of control," he says. "Order and control are everything in this business."

Mr. Edens's business belongs to a small but expanding financial service known as "lockbox processing." Many companies and charities that once did their paperwork in-house now "out-source" clerical tasks to firms like EBS, which processes donations to groups such as Mothers Against Drunk Driving, the Doris Day Animal League, Greenpeace and the National Organization for Women.

More broadly, EBS reflects the explosive growth of jobs in which workers perform low-wage and limited tasks in white-collar settings. This has transformed towns like Hagerstown—a blue-collar community hit hard by industrial layoffs in the 1970s—into sites for thousands of jobs in factory-sized offices.

Many of these jobs, though, are part time and most pay far less than the manufacturing occupations they replaced. Some workers at EBS start at the minimum wage of $4.25 an hour and most earn about $6 an hour. The growth of such jobs—which often cluster outside major cities—also completes a curious historic circle. During the Industrial Revolution, farmers' daughters went to work in textile towns like Lowell, Mass. In post-industrial America, many women of modest means and skills are entering clerical mills where they process paper instead of cloth (coincidentally, EBS occupies a former garment factory).

"The office of the future can look a lot like the factory of the past," says Barbara Garson, author of *The Electronic Sweatshop* and other books on the modern workplace. "Modern tools are being used to bring 19th-century working conditions into the white-collar world."

The time-motion philosophies of Frederick Taylor, for instance, have found a 1990s correlate in the phone, computer and camera, which can be used to monitor workers more closely than a foreman with a stopwatch ever could. Also, the nature of the work often justifies a vigilant eye. In EBS workers handle thousands of dollars in checks and cash, and Mr. Edens says cameras help deter would-be thieves. Tight security also reassures visiting clients. "If you're disorderly, they'll think we're out of control and that things could get lost," says Mr. Edens, who worked as a financial controller for the National Rifle Association before founding EBS in 1983.

But tight observation also helps EBS monitor productivity and weed out workers who don't keep up. "There's multiple uses," Mr. Edens says of surveillance. His desk is covered with computer printouts recording the precise toll of keystrokes tapped by each data-entry worker. He also keeps a day-to-day tally of errors. The work floor itself resembles an enormous classroom in the throes of exam period. Desks point toward the front, where a manager keeps watch from a raised platform that workers call "the pedestal" or "the birdhouse." Other supervisors are positioned toward the back of the room. "If you want to watch someone," Mr. Edens explains, "it's easier from behind because they don't know you're watching." There also is a black globe hanging from the ceiling, in which cameras are positioned.

Mr. Edens sees nothing Orwellian about this omniscience. "It's not a Big Brother attitude," he says. "It's more of a calming attitude."

But studies of workplace monitoring suggest otherwise. Experts say that surveillance can create a hostile environment in which workers feel pressured, paranoid and prone to stress-related illness. Surveillance also can be used punitively, to intimidate workers or to justify their firing.

Following a failed union drive at EBS, the National Labor Relations Board filed a series of complaints against the company, including charges that EBS threatened, interrogated, and spied on workers. As part of an out-of-court settlement, EBS reinstated a fired worker and posted a notice that it would refrain from illegal practices during a second union vote, which also failed.

"It's all noise," Mr. Edens says of the unfair labor charges. As to the pressure that surveillance creates, Mr. Edens sees that simply as "the nature of the beast." He adds: "It's got to add stress when everyone knows their production is being monitored. I don't apologize for that."

Mr. Edens also is unapologetic about the Draconian work rules he maintains, including one that forbids all talk unrelated to the completion of each task. "I'm not paying people to chat. I'm paying them to open envelopes," he says. Of the blocked windows. Mr. Edens adds: "I don't want them looking out—it's distracting. They'll make mistakes."

This total focus boosts productivity but it makes many workers feel lonely and trapped. Some try to circumvent the silence rule, like kids in a school library. "If you don't turn your head and sort of mumble out of the side of your mouth, supervisors won't hear you most of the time," Cindy Kesselring explains during her lunch break. Even so, she feels isolated and often longs for her former job as a waitress. "Work is your social life, particularly if you've got kids," says the 27-year-old mother. "Here it's hard to get to know people because you can't talk."

During lunch, workers crowd in the parking lot outside, chatting nonstop. "Some of us don't eat much because the more you chew the less you can talk," Ms. Kesselring says. There aren't other breaks and workers aren't allowed to sip coffee or eat at their desks during the long stretches before and after lunch. Hard candy is the only permitted desk snack.

New technology, and the breaking down of labor into discrete, repetitive tasks, also have effectively stripped jobs such as those at EBS of whatever variety and skills clerical work once possessed.

Workers in the cage (an antiquated banking term for a money-handling area) only open envelopes and sort contents; those in the audit department compute figures; and data-entry clerks punch in the information that the others have collected. If they make a mistake, the computer buzzes and a message such as "check digit error" flashes on the screen.

"We don't ask these people to think—the machines think for them," Mr. Edens says. "They don't have to make any decisions." This makes the work simpler but also deepens its monotony. In the cage, Carol Smith says she looks forward to envelopes that contain anything out of the ordinary, such as letters reporting that the donor is deceased. Or she plays mental games. "I think to myself, A goes in this pile, B goes here and C goes there—sort of like Bingo." She says she sometimes feels "like a machine," particularly when she fills out the "control card" on which she lists "time in" and "time out" for each tray of envelopes. In a slot marked "cage operator" Ms. Smith writes her code number, 3173. "That's me," she says.

Barbara Ann Wiles, a keyboard operator, also plays mind games to break up the boredom. Tapping in the names and addresses of new donors, she tries to imagine the faces behind the names, particularly the odd ones. "Like this one, Mrs. Fittizzi," she chuckles. "I can picture her as a very stout lady with a strong accent, hollering on a street corner." She picks out another: "Doris Angelroth—she's very sophisticated, a monocle maybe, drinking tea on an overstuffed mohair couch."

It is a world remote from the one Ms. Wiles inhabits. Like most EBS employees, she must juggle her low-paying job with child care. On this Friday, for instance, Ms. Wiles will finish her eight-hour shift at about 4 P.M., go home for a few hours, then return for a second shift from midnight to 8 A.M. Otherwise, she would have to come in on Saturday to finish the week's work.

This way I can be home on the weekend to look after my kids," she says.

Others find the work harder to leave behind at the end of the day. In the cage, Ms. Smith says her husband used to complain because she often woke him in the middle of the night. "I'd be shuffling my hands in my sleep," she says, mimicking the motion of opening envelopes.

Her cage colleague, Ms. Kesselring, says her fiancé has a different gripe. "He dodges me for a couple of hours after work because I don't shut up—I need to talk, talk, talk," she says. And there is one household task she can no longer abide.

"I won't pay bills because I can't stand to open another envelope," she says. "I'll leave letters sitting in the mailbox for days."

Questions

1. Which of the management theories described in the chapter does Ron Edens make most use of?

2. What do you think are the effects of this approach on (a) workers and (b) supervisors?

3. Do you regard Ron Eden's approach to management as ethical and acceptable or unethical and unacceptable in the 2000s? Why?

Source: Tony Horwitz, "Mr. Edens Profits from Watching His Workers' Every Move," *The Wall Street Journal,* December 1, 1994.

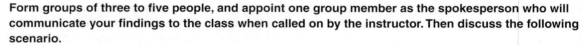

Small Group Breakout Exercise
Modeling an Open System

Form groups of three to five people, and appoint one group member as the spokesperson who will communicate your findings to the class when called on by the instructor. Then discuss the following scenario.

Think of an organization with which you are all familiar, such as a local restaurant, store, or bank. After choosing an organization, model it from an open-systems perspective. Identify its input, conversion, and output processes; and identify forces in the external environment that help or hurt the organization's ability to obtain resources and dispose of its goods or services.

Exploring the World Wide Web

Research Ford's Web site (www.ford.com), and locate and read the material on Ford's history and evolution over time. What have been the significant stages in the company's development? What problems and issues confronted managers at these stages? What are the challenges facing Ford's managers now?

Be the Manager

How to Manage a Hotel

You have been called in to advise the owners of an exclusive new luxury hotel. For the venture to succeed, hotel employees must focus on providing customers with the highest-quality customer service possible. The challenge is to devise a way of organizing and controlling employees that will promote high-quality service, that will encourage employees to be committed to the hotel, and that will reduce the level of employee turnover and absenteeism—which are typically high in the hotel business.

Questions

1. How do the various theories of management discussed in this chapter offer clues for organizing and controlling hotel employees?

2. Which parts would be the most important for an effective system to organize and control employees?

BusinessWeek Case in the News

What You Don't Know About Dell

Dell is the master at selling direct, bypassing middlemen to deliver PCs cheaper than any of its rivals. And few would quarrel that it's the model of efficiency, with a far-flung supply chain knitted together so tightly that it's like one electrical wire, humming 24/7. Yet all this has been true for more than a decade. And although the entire computer industry has tried to replicate Dell's tactics, none can hold a candle to the company's results.

As it turns out, it's how Michael Dell manages the company that has elevated it far above its sell-direct business model. What's Dell's secret? At its heart is his belief that the status quo is never good enough, even if it means painful changes for the man with his name on the door. When success is achieved, it's greeted with five seconds of praise followed by five hours of postmortem on what could have been done better. Says Michael Dell: "Celebrate for a nanosecond. Then move on." After the outfit opened its first Asian factory, in Malaysia, the CEO sent the manager who was heading the job one of his old running shoes to congratulate him. The message: This is only the first step in a marathon.

Just as crucial is Michael Dell's belief that once a problem is uncovered, it should be dealt with quickly and directly, without excuses. "There's no 'The dog ate my homework' here," says Dell. No, indeedy. After Randall D. Groves, then head of the server business, delivered 16 percent higher sales last year, he was demoted. Never mind that none of its rivals came close to that. It could have been better, say two former Dell executives. Groves referred calls to a Dell spokesman, who says Groves's job change was part of a broader reorganization.

Above all, Michael Dell expects everyone to watch each dime—and turn it into at least a quarter. Unlike most tech bosses, Dell believes every product should be profitable from Day One. To ensure that, he expects his managers to be walking databases, able to cough up information on everything from top-line growth to the average number of times a part has to be replaced in the first 30 days after a computer is sold.

But there's one number he cares about most: operating margin. To Dell, it's not enough to rack up profits or grow fast. Execs must do both to maximize long-term profitability. That means products need to be priced low enough to induce shoppers to buy, but not so low that they cut unnecessarily into profits. When Dell's top managers in Europe lost out on profits in 1999 because they hadn't cut costs far enough, they were replaced. "There are some organizations where people think they're a hero if they invent a new thing," says Rollins. "Being a hero at Dell means saving money."

It's this combination—reaching for the heights of perfection while burrowing down into every last data point—that no rival has been able to imitate. "It's like watching Michael Jordan stuff the basketball," says Merrill Lynch & Co. technology strategist Steven Milunovich. "I see it. I understand it. But I can't do it."

How did this Mike come by his management philosophy? It started 19 years ago, when he was ditching classes to sell homemade PCs out of his University of Texas dorm room. Dell was the scrappy underdog, fighting for his company's life against the likes of IBM and Compaq Computer Corp. with a direct-sales model that people thought was plain nuts. Now, Michael Dell is worth $17 billion, while his 40,000-employee company is about to top $40 billion in sales. Yet he continues to manage Dell with the urgency and determination of a college kid with his back to the wall. "I still think of us as a challenger," he says. "I still think of us attacking."

All this has kept Dell on track as rivals have gone off the rails. Since 2000, the company has been adding market share at a faster pace than at any time in its history—nearly three percentage points in 2002. A renewed effort to control costs sliced overhead expenses to just 9.6 percent of revenue in the most recent quarter and boosted productivity to nearly $1 million in revenue per employee. That's three times the revenue per employee at IBM and almost twice Hewlett-Packard Co.'s rate.

Still, for the restless Michael Dell, that's not nearly enough. He wants to make sure the company he has spent half his life building can endure after he's gone. So he and Rollins sketched out an ambitious financial target: $60 billion in revenues by 2006. That's twice what the company did in 2001 and enough to put it in league with the largest, most powerful companies in the world. Getting there will require the same kind of success that the company achieved in PCs—but in altogether new markets. Already, Michael Dell is moving the company into printers, networking, handheld computers, and tech services. His latest foray: Dell is entering the cutthroat $95 billion consumer-electronics market with a portable digital-music player, an online music store, and a flat-panel television set.

Dell also faces an innovation dilemma. Its penny-pinching ways leave little room for investments in product development and future technologies, especially compared with rivals. Even in the midst of the recession, IBM spent $4.75 billion or 5.9 percent of its revenues, on research and development in 2002, while HP ponied up $3.3 billion, or 4.8 percent of revenues. And Dell? Just a paltry $455 million, or 1.3 percent. Rivals say that handicaps Dell's ability to move much beyond PCs, particularly in such promising markets as digital imaging and utility computing. "Dell is a great company, but they are a one-trick pony," says HP CEO Carleton S. Fiorina. What's more, Dell has shown little patience for the costs of entering new markets, killing off products—like its high-end server—when they didn't produce quick profits, rather than staying committed to a long-term investment. "They're the best in the world at what they do," says IBM server chief William M. Zeitler. "The question is, will they be best at the Next Big Thing?"

Dell's track record suggests the CEO will meet his $60 billion revenue goal by 2006. Already, Dell has grabbed large chunks of the markets for inexpensive servers and data-storage gear. After just two quarters, its first handheld computer has captured 37 percent of the U.S. market for such devices. And Rollins says initial sales of Dell printers are double its internal targets. With the potential growth in PCs and new markets, few analysts doubt that Dell can generate the 15 percent annual growth needed to reach the mark.

Questions

1. What are the main principles behind Michael Dell's approach to managing?

2. List these principles then compare them to those developed by Henry Fayol. In what ways are they similar or different?

Source: Andrew Park and Peter Burrows, "What You Don't Know About Dell." Reprinted from the November 3, 2003, issue of *BusinessWeek* Online by special permission. © 2003 McGraw-Hill Companies, Inc.

Charm Offensive: Why America's CEOs are suddenly so eager to be loved

It's hard to avoid Lee Scott's tender side these days. In April the Wal-Mart chief executive told a convention of journalists that he plans to build stores in high-crime neighborhoods, in run-down malls, even on contaminated land. Why? Not because these are the best places to put a store. The idea, said Scott, is to "engage the community," reaching out to poor folks and minorities, the kind of "people and neighborhoods that need Wal-Mart most."

While Scott tries to recast the often vilified retailer as a force for good, ExxonMobil's new CEO, Rex W. Tillerson, is putting a friendlier face on the world's largest energy company, drawing loud applause at the company's May annual meeting after an investor thanked him for his "friendliness, humor, and candor." Then there's Anne M. Mulcahy, boosting morale by telling Xerox employees to take their birthdays off. Or General Electric's Jeffrey R. Immelt, refusing his last cash bonus in favor of performance-linked shares to show that he's aligned with shareholders.

Feel a sudden urge to hug a CEO? If so, it's likely because of all the thoughtful gestures and warm words coming out of America's corporate suites. In the pageant of business, senior executives seem to be battling for the congeniality prize. Humility, authenticity, and responsive leadership are new buzzwords at the top. Many chief executives talk about being "servant leaders" and team players.

They care openly about everything from employees to Mother Earth. In short, they're more likable.

Years of white-collar-crime headlines, as well as grumbling over executive pay, have created an environment that's less tolerant of boorish behavior. "Every CEO has a code of conduct and is eating in the cafeteria," says Leslie Gaines-Ross, chief reputation strategist at public relations firm Weber Shandwick.

Now, CEOs have to talk to everyone. With greater transparency in business, there's no place to hide. It's not enough to be popular with employees, board members, or the regulators perched outside your door. In today's wired world, how you treat workers and the planet can quickly come back to haunt you in a blog or an I-Hate-Your-Company Web site. Anyone can find out what it's like to work for you, says Libby Sartain, senior vice-president for human resources at Yahoo! , and that "dictates what kind of talent you get"—especially among younger workers.

Positive is More Potent

That's not to say all CEOs are experiencing a sudden surge of love for their fellow man. As with any management trend, there's an element of faddishness to the recent emphasis on humble, engaging leadership. Yet current thinking has shifted to emphasizing the benefits of model behavior.

A recent study in the *Harvard Business Review* found that people tend to choose work partners based on likability. Professor Kim S. Cameron at the University of Michigan's three-year-old Center for Positive Organizational Scholarship also cites studies showing

that likable people—those at the hub of what he calls "positive energy networks"—are four times more potent on the job than those who have influential jobs but are less popular. Rarely has there been more attention paid to personality in getting ahead. Mountains of leadership books and hours of coaching greet most high-potential executives. The recurring themes? Trust, inspiration, teamwork, authenticity. Jerks who deliver results are usually shoved into somebody's hands to learn a little tenderness before rising to the top job. "People are proud to have a coach now," says Judith Glaser, who coaches executive teams. "It shows they're being emotionally cultivated for a better job."

In contrast, those who don't make an effort to win friends stand out. Robert L. Nardelli of Home Depot was widely regarded as an operational genius during his time at GE. But insiders say Jeff Immelt performed equally well—and also had an exceptional ability with people. Since coming to the top job five years ago, Immelt has helped establish GE as a leader in eco-friendly products, innovation, and even diversity. Over at Home Depot, Nardelli has been accused of focusing on costs over customers, chipping away at morale, and ignoring shareholders. At the May annual meeting, he stayed 30 minutes and refused to take questions. "How could anyone not know that doesn't play in today's world?" asks one peer.

A Nod to Outrageous Pay

This is hardly the first time corporate leaders have put a benevolent face before the public. In the 1960s and '70s, as industry struggled to adapt to tumultuous times and the end of a booming postwar economy, business leaders adopted more statesmanlike roles. Their message to politicians and the public: We're all in this together. Earlier in the century, industrialists such as Andrew Carnegie and John D. Rockefeller made a show of spreading their largesse after amassing huge fortunes under controversial circumstances. More than a few critics accused them of trying to buy back their reputations.

With the fortunes being accumulated by the executive class today, it's not surprising that leaders feel a need to reach out. Median CEO compensation at 200 of the largest U.S. companies last year hovered around $8.4 million. That's a 10% jump over 2004. Outrageous pay is hardly the hallmark of a servant leader. The speech on "sacrifice" doesn't resonate when it comes from someone whose bonus is in the millions. No wonder a small but growing number of execs, from former Circuit City CEO W. Alan McCollough to Susan Lyne of Martha Stewart Living Omnimedia, are giving back cash. Says Lyne, who gave a third of her $625,500 bonus to employees.

Playing to a wide audience and cultivating positive publicity often does help the company. John Browne, group chief executive at

BP (BP), has spent millions trying to make his company the nicest, greenest oil giant on the block. While ExxonMobil is pulling in bigger profits, BP has posted stronger growth and better stock performance since 2001. In that time, BP has delivered a total shareholder return of 62%, compared with ExxonMobil's 49%. "We have to be responsible as a company and attract the best people of every background," says Browne, who won BP the prestigious Catalyst Award this year for advancing women in the organization. Such good vibes helped the company emerge with its reputation largely intact after a devastating refinery explosion in Texas last year that killed 15 people and led to a $21.3 million fine.

ExxonMobil's Raymond, in contrast, made money for investors but never did much to warm the public's heart. Greenpeace research director Kert Davies says "shareholders—really nice people like priests and nuns—tell me they have never dealt with anyone as stubborn, self-important, and rude." An ExxonMobil spokesman said Raymond doesn't comment on such observations. But it's notable that his successor makes a point of cracking jokes with journalists and listening politely to investors. To executive leadership consultant

Granville Toogood, Tillerson comes "across as a humble, concerned citizen of the world." The business strategy hasn't changed. The CEO is just nicer.

Treating people well makes you feel good. It makes others feel good. It can even cast a glow around your company. But the biggest incentive to woo the masses is a growing belief that it benefits the bottom line. As consultant Tim Sanders, author of The Likeability Factor, puts it: "If the average employee has a pit in his stomach instead of a song in his heart, your profits will go down."

Questions for Discussion

1. What new kinds of managerial skills are top managers having to learn?

2. In what ways can these skills help managers improve organizational performance?

3. How do these new skills relate to the skills talked about in the chapter such as those suggested by Fayol and Follerr?

Source: Diane Brady, "Charm Offensive: Why America's CEOs are suddenly so eager to be loved." June 26, 2006, BusinessWeek. Copyright © 2006 by the McGraw-Hill Companies, Inc.

CHAPTER 3

Values, Attitudes, Emotions, and Culture: The Manager as a Person

Learning Objectives

After studying this chapter, you should be able to:

- Describe the various personality traits that affect how managers think, feel, and behave.

- Explain what values and attitudes are and describe their impact on managerial action.

- Appreciate how moods and emotions influence all members of an organization.

- Describe the nature of emotional intelligence and its role in management.

- Define *organizational culture* and explain how managers both create and are influenced by organizational culture.

A Manager's Challenge

PAETEC's Culture of Care

How can managers promote organizational growth and effectiveness while sustaining a caring culture?

PAETEC Communications is a privately owned broadband telecommunications company that provides local, long distance, and Internet services in 29 markets across the United States.[1] When PAETEC was founded in 1998, it had less than 20 employees and revenues of only $150,000; today, it has approximately 1,200 employees and over $500 million in revenues.[2] Moreover, this phenomenal rate of growth occurred during a period when the telecommunications industry lost over 500,000 jobs.[3] PAETEC's amazing growth trajectory has not gone without notice; the company recently was ranked second in Deloitte Technology's Fast 500 list, which ranks the technology industry's top 500 fastest-growing companies in North America. Firms like Yahoo and eBay debuted on this list in their early days.[4]

PAETEC's growth and ongoing success are a tribute to the values of its five founders and

the culture they created. In particular, Arunas Chesonis, one of the founders and its current CEO, ensures that PAETEC's values are upheld by using them to guide the way he manages on a day-to-day basis. The four core values of PAETEC are "a caring culture, open communication, personalized solutions, and unmatched service and support."[5] The ways in which these values are enacted on a daily

PAETEC founder and current CEO Arunas Chesonis believes that when a company takes good care of its employees, they will take good care of their customers.

basis result in a satisfied, motivated, and loyal workforce whose members have developed a unique and distinct approach to the way they perform their jobs.[6]

An overarching principle at PAETEC is "Employees come first."[7] This does not mean that PAETEC doesn't care about customers;

Figure 3.1

The Big Five Personality Traits

Manager's personalities can be described by determining which point on each of the following dimensions best characterizes the manager in question:

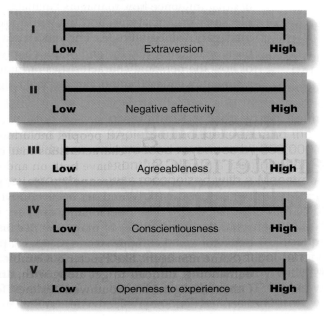

EXTRAVERSION   **Extraversion** is the tendency to experience positive emotions and moods and feel good about oneself and the rest of the world.

extraversion The tendency to experience positive emotions and moods and to feel good about oneself and the rest of the world.

Managers who are high on extraversion (often called *extraverts*) tend to be sociable, affectionate, outgoing, and friendly. Managers who are low on extraversion (often called *introverts*) tend to be less inclined toward social interactions and to have a less positive outlook. Being high on extraversion may be an asset for managers whose jobs entail especially high levels of social interaction. Managers who are low on extraversion may nevertheless be highly effective and efficient, especially when their jobs do not require excessive social interaction. Their more "quiet" approach may enable them to accomplish quite a bit of work in limited time. See Figure 3.2 for an example of a scale that can be used to measure a person's level of extraversion.

High levels of extraversion may be an asset for managers whose jobs entail a great deal of social interaction.

Figure 3.2

Measures of Extraversion, Agreeableness, Conscientiousness, and Openness to Experience

Listed below are phrases describing people's behaviors. Please use the rating scale below to describe how accurately each statement describes *you*. Describe yourself as you generally are now, not as you wish to be in the future. Describe yourself as you honestly see yourself, in relation to other people you know of the same sex as you are and roughly your same age.

1	2	3	4	5
Very inaccurate	Moderately inaccurate	Neither inaccurate nor accurate	Moderately accurate	Very accurate

_____ **1.** Am interested in people.

_____ **2.** Have a rich vocabulary.

_____ **3.** Am always prepared.

_____ **4.** Am not really interested in others.*

_____ **5.** Leave my belongings around.*

_____ **6.** Am the life of the party.

_____ **7.** Have difficulty understanding abstract ideas.*

_____ **8.** Sympathize with others' feelings.

_____ **9.** Don't talk a lot.*

_____ **10.** Pay attention to details.

_____ **11.** Have a vivid imagination.

_____ **12.** Insult people.*

_____ **13.** Make a mess of things.*

_____ **14.** Feel comfortable around people.

_____ **15.** Am not interested in abstract ideas.*

_____ **16.** Have a soft heart.

_____ **17.** Get chores done right away.

_____ **18.** Keep in the background.*

_____ **19.** Have excellent ideas.

_____ **20.** Start conversations.

_____ **21.** Am not interested in other people's problems.*

_____ **22.** Often forget to put things back in their proper place.*

_____ **23.** Have little to say.*

_____ **24.** Do not have a good imagination.*

_____ **25.** Take time out for others.

_____ **26.** Like order.

_____ **27.** Talk to a lot of different people at parties.

_____ **28.** Am quick to understand things.

_____ **29.** Feel little concern for others.*

_____ **30.** Shirk my duties.*

_____ **31.** Don't like to draw attention to myself.*

_____ **32.** Use difficult words.

_____ **33.** Feel others' emotions.

_____ **34.** Follow a schedule.

_____ **35.** Spend time reflecting on things.

_____ **36.** Don't mind being the center of attention.

_____ **37.** Make people feel at ease.

_____ **38.** Am exacting in my work.

_____ **39.** Am quiet around strangers.*

_____ **40.** Am full of ideas.

* Item is reverse-scored: 1 = 5, 2 = 4, 4 = 2, 5 = 1
Scoring: Sum responses to items for an overall scale.
     Extraversion = sum of items 6, 9, 14, 18, 20, 23, 27, 31, 36, 39
     Agreeableness = sum of items 1, 4, 8, 12, 16, 21, 25, 29, 33, 37
     Conscientiousness = sum of items 3, 5, 10, 13, 17, 22, 26, 30, 34, 38
     Openness to experience = sum of items 2, 7, 11, 15, 19, 24, 28, 32, 35, 40

Source: Lewis R. Goldberg, Oregon Research Institute, http://ipip.ori.org/ipip/.

negative affectivity
The tendency to experience negative emotions and moods, to feel distressed, and to be critical of oneself and others.

NEGATIVE AFFECTIVITY Negative affectivity is the tendency to experience negative emotions and moods, feel distressed, and be critical of oneself and others. Managers high on this trait may often feel angry and dissatisfied and complain about their own and others' lack of progress. Managers who are low on negative affectivity do not tend to experience many negative emotions and moods and are less pessimistic and critical of themselves and others. On the plus side, the critical approach of a manager high on negative affectivity may sometimes be effective if it spurs both the manager and others to improve their performance. Nevertheless, it is probably more pleasant to work with a manager who is low on negative affectivity; the better working relationships that such a manager is likely to cultivate also can be an important asset. Figure 3.3 is an example of a scale developed to measure a person's level of negative affectivity.

agreeableness The tendency to get along well with other people.

AGREEABLENESS   Agreeableness is the tendency to get along well with others. Managers who are high on the agreeableness continuum are likable, tend to be affectionate, and care about other people. Managers who are low on agreeableness may be somewhat distrustful of others, unsympathetic, uncooperative, and even at times antagonistic. Being high on agreeableness may be especially important for managers whose responsibilities require that they develop good,

Figure 3.3
A Measure of Negative Affectivity

Instructions: Listed below are a series of statements a person might use to describe her/his attitudes, opinions, interests, and other characteristics. If a statement is true or largely true, put a "T" in the space next to the item. Or if the statement is false or largely false, mark an "F" in the space.

Please answer every statement, even if you are not completely sure of the answer. Read each statement carefully, but don't spend too much time deciding on the answer.

_____ **1.** I often find myself worrying about something.

_____ **2.** My feelings are hurt rather easily.

_____ **3.** Often I get irritated at little annoyances.

_____ **4.** I suffer from nervousness.

_____ **5.** My mood often goes up and down.

_____ **6.** I sometimes feel "just miserable" for no good reason.

_____ **7.** Often I experience strong emotions—anxiety, anger—without really knowing what causes them.

_____ **8.** I am easily startled by things that happen unexpectedly.

_____ **9.** I sometimes get myself into a state of tension and turmoil as I think of the day's events.

_____ **10.** Minor setbacks sometimes irritate me too much.

_____ **11.** I often lose sleep over my worries.

_____ **12.** There are days when I'm "on edge" all of the time.

_____ **13.** I am too sensitive for my own good.

_____ **14.** I sometimes change from happy to sad, or vice versa, without good reason.

Scoring: Level of negative affectivity is equal to the number of items answered "True."

Source: Auke Tellegen, *Brief Manual for the Differential Personality Questionnaire*, Copyright © 1982. Reproduced by permission.

close relationships with others. Nevertheless, a low level of agreeableness may be an asset in managerial jobs that actually require that managers be antagonistic, such as drill sergeants, and some other kinds of military managers. See Figure 3.2 for an example of a scale that measures a person's level of agreeableness.

conscientiousness
The tendency to be careful, scrupulous, and persevering

CONSCIENTIOUSNESS   Conscientiousness is the tendency to be careful, scrupulous, and persevering.[22] Managers who are high on the conscientiousness continuum are organized and self-disciplined; those who are low on this trait might sometimes appear to lack direction and self-discipline. Conscientiousness has been found to be a good predictor of performance in many kinds of jobs, including managerial jobs in a variety of organizations.[23] CEOs of major companies, such as Meg Whitman of eBay and Bill Greehey of Valero Energy, often show signs of being high on conscientiousness—the long hours they work, their attention to detail, and their ability to handle their multiple responsibilities in an organized manner. Figure 3.2 provides an example of a scale that measures conscientiousness.

openness to experience   The tendency to be original, have broad interests, be open to a wide range of stimuli, be daring, and take risks.

OPENNESS TO EXPERIENCE   Openness to experience is the tendency to be original, have broad interests, be open to a wide range of stimuli, be daring, and take risks.[24] Managers who are high on this trait continuum may be especially likely to take risks and be innovative in their planning and decision making. Entrepreneurs who start their own businesses—like Bill Gates of Microsoft, Jeff Bezos of Amazon.com, and Anita Roddick of The Body Shop— are, in all likelihood, high on openness to experience, which has contributed to their success as entrepreneurs and managers. Arunas Chesonis, discussed in this chapter's "A Manager's Challenge," founded his own company and continues to explore new ways for it to grow—a testament to his high level of openness to experience. Managers who are low on openness to experience may be less prone to take risks and more conservative in their planning and decision making. In certain organizations and positions, this tendency might be an asset. The manager of the fiscal office in a public university, for example, must ensure that all university departments and units follow the university's rules and regulations pertaining to budgets, spending accounts, and reimbursements of expenses. Figure 3.2 provides an example of a measure of openness to experience.

Managers who initiate major changes in their organizations often are high on openness to experience, as is true of Gary Heiman, CEO of Standard Textile Co., who is profiled in the following "Managing Globally."

Managing Globally

Expanding into China

Gary Heiman is CEO of Standard Textile, a privately held company that manufactures and sells a wide variety of textile products, ranging from scrubs, surgical gowns, and industrial-strength insulated coveralls to decorator bedspreads and pillows, sheets, and towels.[25] Throughout Standard's history and to this very day, Heiman's openness to experience has led him to expand Standard's global presence. Standard was founded by Heiman's grandfather, and around 30 years ago, when Standard was selling sheets out of an apartment in Chicago, Heiman convinced his father to expand Standard's wholesale operations by opening a factory in Israel near the Negrev desert.[26] Today, Standard Textile manufactures and distributes products to hotels, hospitals, and factories, operates in 49 countries, has over 3,000 employees, and over $500 million in annual revenues.[27]

Around five years ago, Heiman's openness to experience led him to spend a year traveling around China, Pakistan, India, and the Philippines to find a location for a new manufacturing facility that would enable Standard to benefit from Asia's booming economic growth and relatively low labor costs. He decided to locate the $23 million facility in Linyi, China, a somewhat remote noncoastal city of 4 million people between Beijing and Shanghai.[28]

Chinese workers sew up garments on a production line. Heiman's openness to experience has led him to expand his garment business operations into 49 countries, including China.

Heiman's combination of high openness to experience and high conscientiousness helped him to overcome many hurdles in getting the Linyi facility up and running. At times, it seemed like nothing was going right, with problems ranging from polluted water to a heating system that didn't work, Chinese custom-made machine parts that didn't fit imported U.S. machines, and increased utility charges to run the plant.[29]

Heiman approached these challenges with adventurousness and determination, and bedsheets produced in Linyi are currently being shipped to the United States and will soon be sold in China. Labor costs in Linyi are around 80% less than the costs in the United States and around 40% less than those in Shanghai, and Heiman has found that Standard's Chinese employees are highly motivated and fast learners.[30] While expansions into China like Standard's are not without their critics, who fear that ultimately jobs will be lost in the United States, Standard has not laid off any U.S. employees and does not plan to do so.[31] Standard's investment in the Linyi manufacturing facility was both its largest investment to date and its most troublesome one in terms of overcoming problems to get the plant up and running, but true to his openness to experience, Heiman indicates that "the potential is simply awesome."[32]

Successful managers occupy a variety of positions on the Big Five personality-trait continua. One highly effective manager may be high on extraversion and negative affectivity, another equally effective manager may be low on both these traits, and still another may be somewhere in between. Members of an organization must understand these differences among managers because they can shed light on how managers behave and on their approach to planning, leading, organizing, or controlling. If subordinates realize, for example, that their manager is low on extraversion, they will not feel slighted when their manager seems to be aloof because they will realize that by nature he or she is simply not outgoing.

Managers themselves also need to be aware of their own personality traits and the traits of others, including their subordinates and fellow managers. A manager who knows that he has a tendency to be highly critical of other people might try to tone down his negative approach. Similarly, a manager who realizes that her chronically complaining subordinate tends to be so negative because of his personality may take all his complaints with a grain of salt and realize that things probably are not as bad as this subordinate says they are.

In order for all members of an organization to work well together and with people outside the organization, such as customers and suppliers, they must understand each other. Such understanding comes, in part, from an appreciation of some of the fundamental ways in which people differ from one another—that is, an appreciation of personality traits.

Other Personality Traits That Affect Managerial Behavior

Many other specific traits in addition to the Big Five describe people's personalities. Here we look at traits that are particularly important for understanding managerial effectiveness: locus of control, self-esteem, and the needs for achievement, affiliation, and power.

internal locus of control The tendency to locate responsibility for one's fate within oneself.

LOCUS OF CONTROL   People differ in their views about how much control they have over what happens to and around them. The locus-of-control trait captures these beliefs.[33] People with an **internal locus of control** believe that they themselves are responsible for their own fate; they see their own actions and behaviors as being major and decisive determinants of important outcomes such as attaining levels of job performance, being promoted, or being turned down for a choice job assignment. Some managers with an internal locus of control see the success of a whole organization resting on their shoulders. One example is Arunas Chesonis in "A Manager's Challenge." An internal locus of control also helps to ensure ethical behavior and decision making in an organization because people feel accountable and responsible for their own actions.

external locus of control The tendency to locate responsibility for one's fate in outside forces and to believe that one's own behavior has little impact on outcomes.

People with an **external locus of control** believe that outside forces are responsible for what happens to and around them; they do not think that their own actions make much of a difference. As such, they tend not to intervene to try to change a situation or solve a problem, leaving it to someone else.

Managers need to have an internal locus of control because they *are* responsible for what happens in organizations; they need to believe that they can and do make a difference, as does Arunas Chesonis at PAETEC Communications. Moreover, managers are responsible for ensuring that organizations and their members behave in an ethical fashion, and for this as well they need to have an internal locus of control—they need to know and feel they can make a difference.

self-esteem The degree to which individuals feel good about themselves and their capabilities.

SELF-ESTEEM   Self-esteem is the degree to which individuals feel good about themselves and their capabilities. People with high self-esteem believe that they are competent, deserving, and capable of handling most situations, as does Arunas Chesonis. People with low self-esteem have poor opinions of themselves, are unsure about their capabilities, and question their ability to succeed at different endeavors.[34] Research suggests that people tend to choose activities and goals consistent with their levels of self-esteem. High self-esteem is desirable for managers because it facilitates their setting and keeping high standards for themselves, pushes them ahead on difficult projects, and gives them the confidence they need to make and carry out important decisions.

need for achievement The extent to which an individual has a strong desire to perform challenging tasks well and to meet personal standards for excellence.

NEEDS FOR ACHIEVEMENT, AFFILIATION, AND POWER   Psychologist David McClelland has extensively researched the needs for achievement, affiliation, and power.[35] The **need for achievement** is the extent to which an individual has a strong desire to perform challenging tasks well and to meet personal standards for excellence. People with a high need for achievement often set clear goals for themselves and like to receive performance feedback.

need for affiliation
The extent to which an individual is concerned about establishing and maintaining good interpersonal relations, being liked, and having other people get along.

need for power The extent to which an individual desires to control or influence others.

The **need for affiliation** is the extent to which an individual is concerned about establishing and maintaining good interpersonal relations, being liked, and having the people around him or her get along with one another. The **need for power** is the extent to which an individual desires to control or influence others.[36]

Research suggests that high needs for achievement and for power are assets for first-line and middle managers and that a high need for power is especially important for upper-level managers.[37] One study found that U.S. presidents with a relatively high need for power tended to be especially effective during their terms of office.[38] A high need for affiliation may not always be desirable in managers because it might lead them to try too hard to be liked by others (including subordinates) rather than doing all they can to ensure that performance is as high as it can and should be. Although most research on these needs has been done in the United States, some studies suggest that these findings may also be applicable to people in other countries such as India and New Zealand.[39]

Research suggests that the needs for achievement and power are desirable personality traits in first-line and middle managers, while the need for power is especially important for upper-level managers.

Taken together, these desirable personality traits for managers—an internal locus of control, high self-esteem, and high needs for achievement and power—suggest that managers need to be take-charge people who not only believe that their own actions are decisive in determining their own and their organizations' fates but also believe in their own capabilities. Such managers have a personal desire for accomplishment and influence over others.

Values, Attitudes, and Moods and Emotions

What are managers striving to achieve? How do they think they should behave? What do they think about their jobs and organizations? And how do they actually feel at work? Some answers to these questions can be found by exploring managers' values, attitudes, and moods.

Values, attitudes, and moods and emotions capture how managers experience their jobs as individuals. *Values* describe what managers are trying to achieve through work and how they think they should behave. *Attitudes* capture their thoughts and feelings about their specific jobs and organizations. *Moods and emotions* encompass how managers actually feel when they are managing. Although these three aspects of managers' work experience are highly personal, they also have important implications for understanding how managers behave, how they treat and respond to others, and how, through their efforts, they help contribute to organizational effectiveness through planning, leading, organizing, and controlling.

Values: Terminal and Instrumental

terminal value A lifelong goal or objective that an individual seeks to achieve.

The two kinds of personal values are *terminal* and *instrumental*. A **terminal value** is a personal conviction about lifelong goals or objectives; an **instrumental value** is a personal conviction about desired modes of conduct or ways of behaving.[40] Terminal values often lead to the formation of **norms,** or informal rules of conduct, for behaviors considered important by most members of a group or organization, such as behaving honestly or courteously.

instrumental value A mode of conduct that an individual seeks to follow.

Milton Rokeach, one of the leading researchers in the area of human values, identified 18 terminal values and 18 instrumental values that describe each person's value system (see Figure 3.4).[41] By rank ordering the terminal values from 1 (most important as a guiding principle in one's life) to 18 (least important as a

norms Informal rules of conduct for behaviors considered important by most members of a group or organization.

Figure 3.4
Terminal and Instrumental Values

Terminal Values	Instrumental Values
A comfortable life (a prosperous life)	Ambitious (hardworking, aspiring)
An exciting life (a stimulating, active life)	Broad-minded (open-minded)
A sense of accomplishment (lasting contribution)	Capable (competent, effective)
A world at peace (free of war and conflict)	Cheerful (lighthearted, joyful)
A world of beauty (beauty of nature and the arts)	Clean (neat, tidy)
Equality (brotherhood, equal opportunity for all)	Courageous (standing up for your beliefs)
Family security (taking care of loved ones)	Forgiving (willing to pardon others)
Freedom (independence, free choice)	Helpful (working for the welfare of others)
Happiness (contentedness)	Honest (sincere, truthful)
Inner harmony (freedom from inner conflict)	Imaginative (daring, creative)
Mature love (sexual and spiritual intimacy)	Independent (self-reliant, self-sufficient)
National security (protection from attack)	Intellectual (intelligent, reflective)
Pleasure (an enjoyable, leisurely life)	Logical (consistent, rational)
Salvation (saved, eternal life)	Loving (affectionate, tender)
Self-respect (self-esteem)	Obedient (dutiful, respectful)
Social recognition (respect, admiration)	Polite (courteous, well-mannered)
True friendship (close companionship)	Responsible (dependable, reliable)
Wisdom (a mature understanding of life)	Self-controlled (restrained, self-disciplined)

Source: Milton Rokeach, *The Nature of Human Values.* Copyright © 1973 The Free Press. All rights Reserved. Reprinted with persmission of the Free Press, a Division of Simon & Schuster Adult Publishing Group.

value system The terminal and instrumental values that are guiding principles in an individual's life.

guiding principle in one's life) and then rank ordering the instrumental values from 1 to 18, people can give good pictures of their **value systems**—what they are striving to achieve in life and how they want to behave.[42] (You can gain a good understanding of your own values by rank ordering first the terminal values and then the instrumental values listed in Figure 3.4.)

Several of the terminal values listed in Figure 3.4 seem to be especially important for managers—such as *a sense of accomplishment (a lasting contribution)*, *equality (brotherhood, equal opportunity for all)*, and *self-respect (self-esteem)*. A manager who thinks a sense of accomplishment is of paramount importance might focus on making a lasting contribution to an organization by developing a new product that can save or prolong lives, as is true of managers at Medtronic (a company that makes medical devices such as cardiac pacemakers), or by opening a new foreign subsidiary. A manager who places equality at the top of his or her list of terminal values may be at the forefront of an organization's efforts to support, provide equal opportunities to, and capitalize on the many talents of an increasingly diverse workforce.

Other values are likely to be considered important by many managers, such as *a comfortable life (a prosperous life)*, *an exciting life (a stimulating, active life)*, *freedom (independence, free choice)*, and *social recognition (respect, admiration)*. The relative importance that managers place on each terminal value helps explain what they are striving to achieve in their organizations and what they will focus their efforts on.

Several of the instrumental values listed in Figure 3.4 seem to be important modes of conduct for managers, such as being *ambitious (hardworking, aspiring)*, *broad-minded (open-minded)*, *capable (competent, effective)*, *responsible (dependable, reliable)*, and *self-controlled (restrained, self-disciplined)*. Moreover, the relative importance a manager places on these and other instrumental values may be a significant determinant of actual behaviors on the job. A manager who considers being *imaginative (daring, creative)* to be highly important, for example, is more likely to be innovative and take risks than is a manager who considers this to be less important (all else being equal). A manager who considers being *honest (sincere, truthful)* to be of paramount importance may be a driving force for taking steps to ensure that all members of a unit or organization behave ethically. As indicated in the following "Ethics in Action," taking ethical action sometimes requires that managers be responsible in addition to being honest.

Ethics in Action

Taking Responsibility for Exposing Wrongdoing

Noreen Harrington, a former fund manager at the Hartz Group investment firm based in Secaucus, New Jersey, became aware of illegal activity in the firm by overhearing traders discussing after-hours trades. These traders managed hedge funds—investment funds that hold a variety of types of financial assets to offset risks and provide a consistent return to shareholders.[43] Harrington was not involved in these hedge funds herself but could not help overhearing the traders. From their conversation, she learned that some mutual fund managers were allowing the traders to buy and sell their shares in the fund after the market had closed.[44] This is illegal and unethical and gave the traders an unfair advantage over other investors in the mutual funds, who were able to trade only when the market was open.

Harrington told Edward J. Stern, a member of the Stern family that owns the Hartz Group, what she had overheard, but this changed nothing—the illegal trading carried on. Harrington resigned but kept an eye on the news, hoping that security regulators would uncover what she had witnessed.[45]

After a year of waiting, Harrington felt a responsibility to report the illegal trading, as it was most likely still going on and hurting ordinary investors. She relayed what she had observed as a Hartz manager to Eliot Spitzer, the New York State attorney general. Spitzer's investigation of her claim led the Stern family to settle the case for $40 million, although they admitted no wrongdoing. In taking responsibility for exposing what she knew was wrong, Harrington set events in motion that ultimately had a major impact on the mutual fund industry as a whole: Other funds were scrutinized and additional instances of after-hours trading were uncovered.[46] Harrington is currently Co-Chief Investment Officer for Alternative Institutional Partners and a founding member of organizations seeking to promote diversity in financial services and related industries such as 85Broads, Goldman Sachs Alumni Women's Network, and 100 Women in Hedge Funds.[47]

All in all, managers' value systems signify what managers as individuals are trying to accomplish and become in their personal lives and at work. Thus, managers' value systems are fundamental guides to their behavior and efforts at planning, leading, organizing, and controlling.

Attitudes

attitude A collection of feelings and beliefs.

An **attitude** is a collection of feelings and beliefs. Like everyone else, managers have attitudes about their jobs and organizations, and these attitudes affect how they approach their jobs. Two of the most important attitudes in this context are job satisfaction and organizational commitment.

job satisfaction The collection of feelings and beliefs that managers have about their current jobs.

JOB SATISFACTION   Job satisfaction is the collection of feelings and beliefs that managers have about their current jobs.[48] Managers who have high levels of job satisfaction generally like their jobs, feel that they are being fairly treated, and believe that their jobs have many desirable features or characteristics (such as interesting work, good pay and job security, autonomy, or nice coworkers). Figure 3.5 shows sample items from two scales that managers can use to measure job satisfaction. Levels of job satisfaction tend to increase as one moves up the hierarchy in an organization. Upper managers, in general, tend to be more satisfied with their jobs than entry-level employees. Managers' levels of job satisfaction can range from very low to very high and anywhere in between.

Figure 3.5
Sample Items from Two Measures of Job Satisfaction

Sample items from the Minnesota Satisfaction Questionnaire:
People respond to each of the items in the scale by checking whether they are:

[ ] Very dissatisfied   [ ] Satisfied
[ ] Dissatisfied   [ ] Very satisfied
[ ] Can't decide whether satisfied or not

On my present job, this is how I feel about . . .

___ **1.** Being able to do things that don't go against my conscience.

___ **2.** The way my job provides for steady employment.

___ **3.** The chance to do things for other people.

___ **4.** The chance to do something that makes use of my abilities.

___ **5.** The way company policies are put into practice.

___ **6.** My pay and the amount of work I do.

___ **7.** The chances for advancement on this job.

___ **8.** The freedom to use my own judgment.

___ **9.** The working conditions.

___ **10.** The way my coworkers get along with each other.

___ **11.** The praise I get for doing a good job.

___ **12.** The feeling of accomplishment I get from the job.

The Faces Scale
Workers select the face which best expresses how they feel about their job in general.

11   10   9   8   7   6   5   4   3   2   1

Source: Copyright © 1975 by the American Pyschological Association. Adapted by permission of Randall B. Dunham and J.B. Brett.

Focus on
Diversity

Changing Attitudes

An interesting trend in job attitudes has been observed among some managers in their 20s and 30s. For example, after Sandi Garcia graduated from the University of Wyoming with a degree in marketing, she landed a good job in Florida and was soon promoted into the managerial ranks. By all counts, Garcia should have been satisfied with her job—she was advancing in the company, making good money, and doing the kind of work she had hoped for. Ironically, Garcia found herself becoming increasingly dissatisfied with her job. Putting in 12-hour workdays was not unusual for Garcia, nor was it unusual for her to work during the weekends. Living a hectic, fast-paced life revolving around work soon made Garcia dream of a simpler life where she would have time to do things she enjoyed such as skiing, being

After living through changes in the corporate landscape, some younger workers are questioning what work should be and mean to them and making career changes.

with family and friends, and doing volunteer work. Garcia acted on her dream: She moved back to Wyoming, and is now more satisfied with a less demanding job at the Wyoming Business Council.[49]

Gregg Steiner was a high-tech manager on the West Coast who seemed to have everything, including a Malibu beach house. However, he was dissatisfied with a job that left him no free time to enjoy the beach or much else. Steiner quit the high-tech world and works at his now more modest home, handling customer service for his family's diaper rash ointment business (Pinxav).[50]

Young managers like Garcia and Steiner are not lazy, nor do they lack ambition. Rather, they have lived through changes in the corporate landscape that cause them to question what work should be and should mean to them. Some of these young managers have seen their parents slaving away at their jobs in corporate America year after year, only to be laid off in tough times. While their parents might never have questioned their commitment to their organizations, the need to work long hours, and the lack of time for much else other than work and raising a family, Garcia and Steiner desire the flexibility and time to live lives that are simpler but also richer in terms of meaningful activities. And they want to be in charge of their own lives rather than having their lives dictated by persons higher up the corporate hierarchy.[51]

Of course, for every young manager like Garcia and Steiner who voluntarily leaves the fast track for a more balanced life, there are other young prospective managers eager to take their place in the corporate world. And a job that is dissatisfying for one manager might be satisfying for another. In any case, in an era when trust in corporations has come under question (e.g., due to ethical lapses and fraud at companies like Enron), some young managers are seeking to invest themselves in things they can really trust.[52]

organizational citizenship behaviors (OCBs) Behaviors that are not required of organizational members but that contribute to and are necessary for organizational efficiency, effectiveness, and competitive advantage.

In general, it is desirable for managers to be satisfied with their jobs, for at least two reasons. First, satisfied managers may be more likely to go the extra mile for their organization or perform organizational citizenship behaviors (OCBs), behaviors that are not required of organizational members but that contribute to and are necessary for organizational efficiency, effectiveness, and competitive advantage.[53] Managers who are satisfied with their jobs are more likely to perform these "above and beyond the call of duty" behaviors, which can range from putting in extra-long hours when needed to coming up with truly creative ideas and overcoming obstacles to implement them (even when doing so is not part of the manager's job), or to going out of one's way to help a coworker, subordinate, or superior (even when doing so entails considerable personal sacrifice).[54]

A second reason why it is desirable for managers to be satisfied with their jobs is that satisfied managers may be less likely to quit.[55] A manager who is highly satisfied may never even think about looking for another position; a dissatisfied manager may always be on the lookout for new opportunities. Turnover can hurt an organization because it results in the loss of the experience and knowledge that managers have gained about the company, industry, and business environment.

A growing source of dissatisfaction for many lower- and middle-level managers, as well as for nonmanagerial employees, is the threat of unemployment and increased workloads from organizational downsizings. A recent study of 4,300 workers conducted by Wyatt Co. found that 76% of the employees of expanding companies are satisfied with their jobs but only 57% of the employees of companies that have downsized are satisfied.[56] Organizations that try to improve their efficiency through restructuring often eliminate a sizable number of first-line and middle management positions. This decision obviously hurts the managers who are laid off, and it also can reduce the job satisfaction levels of managers who remain. They might fear that they may be the next to be let go. In addition, the workloads of remaining managers often are dramatically increased as a result of restructuring, and this can contribute to dissatisfaction.

organizational commitment The collection of feelings and beliefs that managers have about their organization as a whole.

ORGANIZATIONAL COMMITMENT Organizational commitment is the collection of feelings and beliefs that managers have about their organization as a whole. Managers who are committed to their organizations believe in what their organizations are doing, are proud of what these organizations stand for, and feel a high degree of loyalty toward their organizations. Committed managers are more likely to go above and beyond the call of duty to help their company and are less likely to quit.[57] Organizational commitment can be especially strong when employees and managers truly believe in organizational values; it also leads to a strong organizational culture, as found in PAETEC.

Organizational commitment is likely to help managers perform some of their figurehead and spokesperson roles (see Chapter 1). It is much easier for a manager to persuade others both inside and outside the organization of the merits of what the organization has done and is seeking to accomplish if the manager truly believes in and is committed to the organization. Figure 3.6 is an example of a scale that managers can use to measure a person's level of organizational commitment.

Do managers in different countries have similar or different attitudes? Differences in the levels of job satisfaction and organizational commitment among managers in different countries are likely because these managers have different kinds of opportunities and rewards and because they face different economic, political, or sociocultural forces in their organizations' general environments. In countries with relatively high unemployment rates, such as France, levels of job satisfaction may be higher among employed managers because they may be happy simply to have a job.

Levels of organizational commitment from one country to another may depend on the extent to which countries have legislation affecting firings and layoffs and the extent to which citizens of a country are geographically mobile. In both France and Germany legislation protects workers (including managers) from being fired or laid off. U.S. workers, in contrast, have very little protection. In addition, managers in the United States are more willing to relocate than managers in France and Germany. In France citizens have relatively strong family and community ties; and in Germany housing is expensive and difficult to find. For those reasons citizens in both countries tend to be less geographically mobile than Americans.[58] Managers who know that their jobs are secure and who are reluctant to relocate (such as those in Germany and France) may be more committed to their organizations than managers who know that their organizations could lay them off any day and who would not mind geographic relocations.

Figure 3.6
A Measure of Organizational Commitment

People respond to each of the items in the scale by checking whether they:

[ ] Strongly disagree   [ ] Slightly agree
[ ] Moderately disagree   [ ] Moderately agree
[ ] Slightly disagree   [ ] Strongly agree
[ ] Neither disagree nor agree

_____ **1.** I am willing to put in a great deal of effort beyond that normally expected in order to help this organization be successful.

_____ **2.** I talk up this organization to my friends as a great organization to work for.

_____ **3.** I feel very little loyalty to this organization.*

_____ **4.** I would accept almost any type of job assignment in order to keep working for this organization.

_____ **5.** I find that my values and the organization's values are very similar.

_____ **6.** I am proud to tell others that I am part of this organization.

_____ **7.** I could just as well be working for a different organization as long as the type of work was similar.*

_____ **8.** This organization really inspires the very best in me in the way of job performance.

_____ **9.** It would take very little change in my present circumstances to cause me to leave this organization.*

_____ **10.** I am extremely glad that I chose this organization to work for over others I was considering at the time I joined.

_____ **11.** There's not too much to be gained by sticking with this organization indefinitely.*

_____ **12.** Often, I find it difficult to agree with this organization's policies on important matters relating to its employees.*

_____ **13.** I really care about the fate of this organization.

_____ **14.** For me this is the best of all possible organizations for which to work.

_____ **15.** Deciding to work for this organization was a definite mistake on my part.*

Scoring: Responses to items 1, 2, 4, 5, 6, 8, 10, 13, and 14 are scored such that 1 = strongly disagree; 2 = moderately disagree; 3 = slightly disagree; 4 = neither disagree nor agree; 5 = slightly agree; 6 = moderately agree; and 7 = strongly agree. Responses to "*" items 3, 7, 9, 11, 12, and 15 are scored 7 = strongly disagree; 6 = moderately disagree; 5 = slightly disagree; 4 = neither disagree nor agree; 3 = slightly agree; 2 = moderately agree; and 1 = strongly agree. Responses to the 15 items are averaged for an overall score from 1 to 7; the higher the score, the higher the level of organizational commitment.

Source: L.W. Porter and F.J. Smith, "Organizational Commitment Questionnaire," in J.D. Cook, S.J. Hepworth, T.D. Wall, and P.B. Warr, eds., *The Experience of Work: A Compendium and Review of 249 Measures and Their Use.* Academic Press, New York, 1981, pp. 84-86.

Moods and Emotions

Just as you sometimes are in a bad mood and at other times are in a good mood, so too are managers. A **mood** is a feeling or state of mind. When people are in a positive mood, they feel excited, enthusiastic, active, or elated.[59] When people

mood A feeling or state of mind.

are in a negative mood, they feel distressed, fearful, scornful, hostile, jittery, or nervous.[60] People who are high on extraversion are especially likely to experience positive moods; people who are high on negative affectivity are especially likely to experience negative moods. People's situations or circumstances also determine their moods; however, receiving a raise is likely to put most people in a good mood regardless of their personality traits. People who are high on negative affectivity are not always in a bad mood, and people who are low on extraversion still experience positive moods.[61]

emotions Intense, relatively short-lived feelings.

Emotions are more intense feelings than moods, are often directly linked to whatever caused the emotion, and are more short-lived. However, once whatever has triggered the emotion has been dealt with, the feelings may linger in the form of a less intense mood.[62]

For example, a manager who gets very angry when one of his subordinates has engaged in an unethical behavior may find his anger decreasing in intensity once he has decided how to address the problem. Yet he continues to be in a bad mood the rest of the day, even though he is not directly thinking about the unfortunate incident.[63]

Research has found that moods and emotions affect the behavior of managers and all members of an organization. For example,

As might be expected, research has shown that a manager's positive moods may contribute to improving employees' job performance and job satisfaction.

research suggests that the subordinates of managers who experience positive moods at work may perform at somewhat higher levels and be less likely to resign and leave the organization than the subordinates of managers who do not tend to be in a positive mood at work.[64] Other research suggests that under certain conditions creativity might be enhanced by positive moods, whereas under other conditions negative moods might push people to work harder to come up with truly creative ideas.[65]

Other research suggests that moods and emotions may play an important role in ethical decision making. For example, researchers at Princeton University found that when people are trying to solve difficult personal moral dilemmas, the parts of their brains that are responsible for emotions and moods are especially active.[66]

Recognizing the benefits of positive moods, the Northbrook, Illinois, accounting firm of Lipschultz, Levin, & Gray has gone to great lengths to promote positive feelings among its employees. Chief executive Steven Siegel claims that positive feelings promote relaxation and alleviate stress, increase revenues and attract clients, and reduce turnover. Positive moods are promoted in a variety of ways at Lipschultz, Levin, & Gray. Siegel has been known to put on a gorilla mask at especially busy times; clerks sometimes don chicken costumes; a foghorn announces the signing of a new client; employees can take a break and play miniature golf in the office, play darts, or exercise with a hula-hoop (even during tax time). A casual dress code also lightens things up at the firm. By all counts, positive moods seem to be paying off for this group of accountants, whose good feelings seem to be attracting new clients.

Patrick Corboy, president and chief executive of Austin Chemical, switched his account from a bigger firm to Lipschultz, Levin, & Gray because he found the people at the bigger firm to be "too stuffy and dour for us." Of the accountant William Finestone, who now manages the Austin Chemical account, Corboy says the following: "[He] is a barrel of laughs . . . Bill not only solves our problems more quickly but he puts us at ease, too."[67]

Nevertheless, sometimes negative moods can have their advantages. Some studies suggest that critical thinking and devil's advocacy may be promoted by a negative mood, and sometimes especially accurate judgments may be made by managers in negative moods.[68]

Managers and other members of an organization need to realize that how they feel affects how they treat others and how others respond to them, including their subordinates. For example, a subordinate may be more likely to approach a manager with a somewhat far-out but potentially useful idea if the subordinate thinks the manager is in a good mood. Likewise, when managers are in very bad moods, their subordinates might try to avoid them at all costs. Figure 3.7 is an example of a scale that managers can use to measure the extent to which a person experiences positive and negative moods at work.

Figure 3.7

A Measure of Positive and Negative Mood at Work

People respond to each item by indicating the extent to which the item descibes how they felt at work during the past week on the following scale:

1 = Very slightly or not at all	4 = Quite a bit
2 = A little	5 = Very much
3 = Moderately	

____	**1.** Active	____	**7.** Enthusiastic
____	**2.** Distressed	____	**8.** Fearful
____	**3.** Strong	____	**9.** Peppy
____	**4.** Excited	____	**10.** Nervous
____	**5.** Scornful	____	**11.** Elated
____	**6.** Hostile	____	**12.** Jittery

Scoring: Responses to items 1, 3, 4, 7, 9, and 11 are summed for a positive mood score; the higher the score, the more positive mood is experienced at work. Responses to items 2, 5, 6, 8, 10, and 12 are summed for a negative mood score; the higher the score, the more negative mood is experienced at work.

Source: A. P. Brief, M. J. Burke, J. M. George, B. Robinson, and J. Webster, "Should Negative Affectivity Remain an Unmeasured Variable in the Study of Job Stress?" *Journal of Applied Psychology* 73 (1988), 193–98; M. J. Burke, A. P. Brief, J. M. George, L. Robinson, and J. Webster, "Measuring Affect at Work: Confirmatory Analyses of Competing Mood Structures with Conceptual Linkage in Cortical Regulatory Systems," *Journal of Personality and Social Psychology* 57 (1989), 1901–1102.

Emotional Intelligence

In understanding the effects of managers' and all employees' moods and emotions, it is important to take into account their levels of emotional intelligence. **Emotional intelligence** is the ability to understand and manage one's own moods and emotions and the moods and emotions of other people.[69] Managers with a high level of emotional intelligence are more likely to understand how they are feeling and why, and they are more able to effectively manage their feelings. When managers are experiencing stressful feelings and emotions such as fear or anxiety, emotional intelligence enables them to understand why and manage these feelings so that they do not get in the way of effective decision making.[70]

Emotional intelligence also can help managers perform their important roles such as their interpersonal roles (figurehead, leader, and liaison).[71] Understanding how your subordinates feel, why they feel that way, and how to manage these feelings is central to developing strong interpersonal bonds with them.[72] Moreover, emotional intelligence has the potential to contribute to effective leadership in multiple ways[73] and can help managers make lasting contributions to society, as shown in the following "Manager as a Person."

emotional intelligence The ability to understand and manage one's own moods and emotions and the moods and emotions of other people.

Manager as
a Person

Bernie Goldhirsh's Legacy

Bernard (Bernie) Goldhirsh founded *INC.* magazine back in 1979, when entrepreneurs received more notoriety than respect, if they were paid attention to at all.[74] Goldhirsh was an entrepreneur himself at the time, with his own publishing company. He recognized the vast contributions entrepreneurs could make to society, creating something out of nothing, and also realized firsthand what a tough task entrepreneurs faced.[75] His emotional intelligence helped him to understand the challenges and frustrations entrepreneurs like himself faced and their need for support.

When Goldhirsh founded *INC.*, entrepreneurs had little they could turn to for advice, guidance, and solutions to management problems. *INC.* was born to fill this gap and provide entrepreneurs with information and support by profiling successful and unsuccessful entrepreneurial ventures, highlighting management techniques that work, and providing readers with firsthand accounts of how successful entrepreneurs developed and managed their businesses.[76]

Goldhirsh had an inquisitive mind and liked to go where his thoughts and conversations took him. Although he founded *INC.* magazine and inspired his staff, he let his writers and editors have free reign with the magazine's content. They were the experts he chose to write and edit the magazine, and he realized it was not his place to interfere with editorial matters. What he did do, and do very well, was inspire his staff to be enthusiastic about the mission of *INC.* and the role of the entrepreneur as a self-reliant explorer, going off into the unknown. As Goldhirsh put it, entrepreneurs create new businesses "from nothing, just blank canvas. . . . It's amazing.

Somebody goes into a garage, has nothing but an idea, and out of the garage comes a company, a living company. It's so special what they do. They are a treasure."[77]

Goldhirsh's emotional intelligence helped him recognize the many barriers entrepreneurs face and the emotional roller coaster of staking all one has on an idea that may or may not work. Goldhirsh believed that helping society understand the entrepreneurial process through *INC.* magazine not only helped entrepreneurs but also enlightened bankers, lawmakers, and the public at large about the role these visionaries play, the challenges they face, and the support their ventures depend on.[78]

When Goldhirsh was diagnosed with brain cancer at age 60, he sold *INC.* magazine at the urging of his doctors. From the proceeds of the sale, he distributed $20 million to *INC.*'s employees, and he dedicated $50 million to a foundation supporting brain cancer research. Goldhirsh inspired *INC.*'s employees to recognize that the magazine had only gotten started and had an important and growing future ahead, and this has certainly been the case.[79] It was a sad day at INC. when Goldhirsh passed away but also an opportunity to reflect on the ongoing contributions of a man who saw the ultimate good in entrepreneurship and whose efforts to support it live on today through the magazine he founded.[80]

Emotional intelligence helps managers understand and relate well to other people.[81] It also helps managers maintain their enthusiasm and confidence and energize subordinates to help the organization attain its goals.[82] Recent theorizing and research suggest that emotional intelligence may be especially important in awakening employee creativity.[83] Managers themselves are increasingly recognizing the importance of emotional intelligence. As Andrea Jung, CEO of Avon Products, indicates, "Emotional intelligence is in our DNA here at Avon because relationships are critical at every stage of our business."[84] An example of a scale that measures emotional intelligence is provided in Figure 3.8.

Organizational Culture

organizational culture
The shared set of beliefs, expectations, values, norms, and work routines that influence the ways in which individuals, groups, and teams interact with one another and cooperate to achieve organizational goals.

Personality is a way of understanding why all managers and employees, as individuals, characteristically think and behave in different ways. However, when people belong to the same organization, they often tend to share certain beliefs and values that lead them to act in similar ways.[85] Organizational culture comprises the shared set of beliefs, expectations, values, norms, and work routines that influence how members of an organization relate to one another and work together to achieve organizational goals. In essence, organizational culture reflects the distinctive ways organizational members go about performing their jobs and relating to others inside and outside the organization. It may, for example, be a distinctive way in which customers in a particular hotel chain are treated from the time they are greeted at check-in until their stay is completed; or it may be the shared work routines that research teams use to guide new product development. When organizational members share an intense commitment to cultural values, beliefs, and routines and use them to achieve their goals, a *strong* organizational culture exists.[86]

Figure 3.8
A Measure of Emotional Intelligence

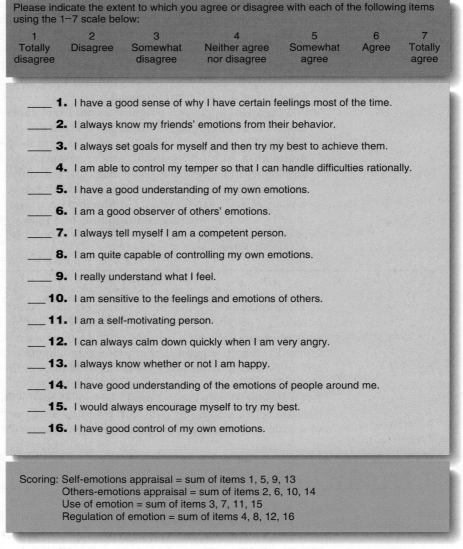

Please indicate the extent to which you agree or disagree with each of the following items using the 1–7 scale below:

1	2	3	4	5	6	7
Totally disagree	Disagree	Somewhat disagree	Neither agree nor disagree	Somewhat agree	Agree	Totally agree

____ **1.** I have a good sense of why I have certain feelings most of the time.

____ **2.** I always know my friends' emotions from their behavior.

____ **3.** I always set goals for myself and then try my best to achieve them.

____ **4.** I am able to control my temper so that I can handle difficulties rationally.

____ **5.** I have a good understanding of my own emotions.

____ **6.** I am a good observer of others' emotions.

____ **7.** I always tell myself I am a competent person.

____ **8.** I am quite capable of controlling my own emotions.

____ **9.** I really understand what I feel.

___ **10.** I am sensitive to the feelings and emotions of others.

___ **11.** I am a self-motivating person.

___ **12.** I can always calm down quickly when I am very angry.

___ **13.** I always know whether or not I am happy.

___ **14.** I have good understanding of the emotions of people around me.

___ **15.** I would always encourage myself to try my best.

___ **16.** I have good control of my own emotions.

Scoring: Self-emotions appraisal = sum of items 1, 5, 9, 13
Others-emotions appraisal = sum of items 2, 6, 10, 14
Use of emotion = sum of items 3, 7, 11, 15
Regulation of emotion = sum of items 4, 8, 12, 16

Source: K. Law, C. Wong, and L. Song. "The Construct and Criterion Validity of Emotional Intelligence and its Potential Utility for Management Studies." *Journal of Applied Psychology*, 89, no. 3, (2004), 496, C. S. Wong and K. S. Law. "The Effects of Leader and Follower Emotional Intelligence on Performance and Attitude: An Exploratory Study." *Leadership Quarterly* 13 (2002), 243–74.

When organizational members are not strongly committed to a shared system of values, beliefs, and routines, organizational culture is weak.

The stronger the culture of an organization, the more one can think about it as being the "personality" of an organization because it influences the way its members behave.[87] Organizations that possess strong cultures may differ on a wide variety of dimensions that determine how their members behave toward one another and perform their jobs. For example, organizations differ in terms of how members relate to each other (e.g., formally or informally), how important decisions are made (e.g., top-down or bottom-up), willingness to change (e.g., flexible or unyielding), innovation (e.g., creative or predictable), and playfulness (e.g., serious or serendipitous). In an innovative design firm like IDEO Product Development in Silicon Valley, employees are encouraged to adopt a playful attitude to their work, look outside the organization to find inspiration, and adopt a flexible approach toward product design that uses multiple perspectives.[88] IDEO's culture is vastly different from that of companies such as Citibank and ExxonMobil, in which employees treat each other in a more formal or deferential way, employees are expected to adopt a serious approach to their work, and decision making is constrained by the hierarchy of authority.

Managers and Organizational Culture

While all members of an organization can contribute to the development and maintenance of organizational culture, managers play a particularly important part in influencing organizational culture,[89] given their multiple and important roles (see Chapter 1). How managers create culture is most vividly evident in start-ups of new companies. Entrepreneurs who start their own companies are typically also the start-ups' top managers until the companies grow and/or become profitable. Often referred to as the firms' founders, these managers literally create their organizations' cultures.

Often, the founders' personal characteristics play an important role in the creation of organizational culture. Benjamin Schneider, a well-known management researcher, developed a model that helps to explain the role that founders' personal characteristics play in determining organizational culture.[90] His model, called the **attraction-selection-attrition (ASA) framework,** posits that when founders hire employees for their new ventures, they tend to be attracted to and choose employees whose personalities are similar to their own.[91] These similar employees are more likely to stay with the organization. While employees who are dissimilar in personality might be hired, they are more likely to leave the organization over time.[92] As a result of these attraction, selection, and attrition processes, people in the organization tend to have similar personalities, and the typical or dominant personality profile of organizational members determines and shapes organizational culture.[93]

attraction-selection-attrition (ASA) framework A model that explains how personality may influence organizational culture.

For example, when David Kelley became interested in engineering and product design challenges in the late 1970s, he realized that who he was as a person meant that he would not be happy working in the typical corporate environment. Kelley is high on openness to experience, driven to go where his interests take him, and not content to follow others' directives. Kelley recognized that he needed to start his own business and, with the help of other Stanford-schooled engineers and design experts, IDEO was born.[94]

From the start, IDEO's culture has embodied Kelley's spirited, freewheeling approach to work and design—from colorful and informal work spaces to an emphasis on networking and communicating with as many people as possible to understand a design problem. No project or problem is too big or too small for IDEO: The company designed the Apple Lisa computer and mouse (the precursor of the Mac) and the Palm as well as the Crest Neat Squeeze toothpaste dispenser and the Racer's Edge water bottle. Kelley hates rules, job titles, big

David Kelley, pictured here, started his own business because he knew he would not be content in the typical corporate environment. And today, his freewheeling spirit lives on in the culture at IDEO, the company he founded.

corner offices, and all the other trappings of large traditional organizations that stifle creativity. Employees who are attracted to, selected by, and remain with IDEO value creativity and innovation and embrace one of IDEO's mottos: "Fail often to succeed sooner."[95]

While ASA processes are most evident in small firms such as IDEO, they also can operate in large companies.[96] According to the ASA model, this is a naturally occurring phenomenon to the extent that managers and new hires are free to make the kinds of choices the model specifies. While people tend to get along well with others who are similar to themselves, too much similarity in an organization can actually impair organizational effectiveness. That is, similar people tend to view conditions and events in similar ways and thus can be resistant to change. Moreover, organizations benefit from a diversity of perspectives rather than similarity in perspectives (see Chapter 5). At IDEO, Kelley recognized early on how important it is to take advantage of the diverse talents and perspectives that people with different personalities, backgrounds, experiences, and education can bring to a design team. Hence, IDEO's design teams include not only engineers but others who might have a unique insight into a problem, such as anthropologists, communications experts, doctors, and users of a product. When new employees are hired at IDEO, they meet with many employees who have different backgrounds and characteristics—the focus is not on hiring someone who will "fit in" but, rather, on hiring someone who has something to offer and can "wow" different kinds of people with his or her insights.[97]

In addition to personality, other personal characteristics of managers shape organizational culture; these include managers' values, attitudes, moods and emotions, and emotional intelligence.[98] For example, both terminal and instrumental values of managers play a role in determining organizational culture. Managers who highly value freedom and equality, for example, might be more likely to stress the importance of autonomy and empowerment in their organizations, as well as fair treatment for all. As another example, managers who highly value being helpful and forgiving may not only be tolerant of mistakes but also be prone to emphasize the importance of organizational members' being kind and helpful to one another.

Managers who are satisfied with their jobs, are committed to their organizations, and experience positive moods and emotions might also encourage these attitudes and feelings in others. The result would be an organizational culture emphasizing positive attitudes and feelings. Research suggests that attitudes like job satisfaction and organizational commitment can be affected by the influence of others. Managers are in a particularly strong position to engage in social influence given their multiple roles. Moreover, research suggests that moods and emotions can be "contagious" and that spending time with people who are excited and enthusiastic can increase one's own levels of excitement and enthusiasm.

The Role of Values and Norms in Organizational Culture

Shared terminal and instrumental values play a particularly important role in organizational culture. *Terminal values* signify what an organization and its employees are trying to accomplish, and *instrumental values* guide the ways in which the organization and its members achieve organizational goals. In addition to values, shared norms also are a key aspect of organizational culture. Recall that norms are unwritten, informal rules or guidelines that prescribe appropriate behavior in particular situations. For example, norms at IDEO include not being critical of others' ideas, coming up with multiple ideas before settling on one, and developing prototypes of new products.[99]

Managers determine and shape organizational culture through the kinds of values and norms they promote in an organization. Some managers, like David Kelley of IDEO, cultivate values and norms that encourage risk taking, creative responses to problems and opportunities, experimentation, tolerance of failure in order to succeed, and autonomy.[100] Top managers at organizations such as Intel, Microsoft, and Sun Microsystems encourage employees to adopt such values to support their commitment to innovation as a source of competitive advantage.

Other managers, however, might cultivate values and norms that indicate to employees that they should always be conservative and cautious in their dealings with others and should try to consult with their superiors before making important decisions or any changes to the status quo. Accountability for actions and decisions is stressed, and detailed records are kept to ensure that policies and procedures are followed. In settings where caution is needed—nuclear power stations, large oil refineries, chemical plants, financial institutions, insurance companies—a conservative, cautious approach to making decisions might be highly appropriate.[101] In a nuclear power plant, for example, the catastrophic consequences of a mistake make a high level of supervision vital. Similarly, in a bank or mutual fund company, the risk of losing investors' money makes a cautious approach to investing highly appropriate.

Managers of different kinds of organizations deliberately cultivate and develop the organizational values and norms that are best suited to their task and general environments, strategy, or technology. Organizational culture is maintained and transmitted to organizational members through the values of the founder, the process of socialization, ceremonies and rites, and stories and language (see Figure 3.9).

VALUES OF THE FOUNDER   From the ASA model discussed above, it is clear that founders of an organization can have profound and long-lasting effects on organizational culture. Founders' values inspire the founders to start their own companies and, in turn, drive the nature of these new companies and their defining characteristics. Thus, an organization's founder and his or her terminal and instrumental values have a substantial influence on the values, norms, and standards of behavior that develop over time within the organization.[102] Founders set the scene for the way cultural values and norms develop because their own values guide the building of the company and they hire other managers and employees who they believe will share these values and help the

Figure 3.9

Factors that Maintain and Transmit Organizational Culture

organization to attain them. Moreover, new managers quickly learn from the founder what values and norms are appropriate in the organization and thus what is desired of them. Subordinates imitate the style of the founder and, in turn, transmit their values and norms to their subordinates. Gradually, over time, the founder's values and norms permeate the organization.[103]

A founder who requires a great display of respect from subordinates and insists on proprieties such as formal job titles and formal modes of dress encourages subordinates to act in this way toward their subordinates. Often, a founder's personal values affect an organization's competitive advantage. For example, McDonald's founder Ray Kroc insisted from the beginning on high standards of customer service and cleanliness at McDonald's restaurants; these became core sources of McDonald's competitive advantage. Similarly, Bill Gates, the founder of Microsoft, pioneered certain cultural values in Microsoft. Employees are expected to be creative and to work hard, but they are encouraged to dress informally and to personalize their offices. Gates also established a host of company events such as cookouts, picnics, and sports events to emphasize to employees the importance of being both an individual and a team player.

SOCIALIZATION   Over time, organizational members learn from each other which values are important in an organization and the norms that specify appropriate and inappropriate behaviors. Eventually, organizational members behave in accordance with the organization's values and norms—often without realizing they are doing so. **Organizational socialization** is the process by which newcomers learn an organization's values and norms and acquire the work behaviors necessary to perform jobs effectively.[104] As a result of their socialization experiences, organizational members internalize an organization's values and norms and behave in accordance with them not only because they think they have to but because they think that these values and norms describe the right and proper way to behave.[105]

At Texas A&M University, for example, all new students are encouraged to go to "Fish Camp" to learn how to be an "Aggie" (the traditional nickname of students at the university). They learn about the ceremonies that have developed over time to commemorate significant events or people in A&M's history. In addition, they learn how to behave at football games and in class and what it means to be an Aggie. As a result of this highly organized socialization program,

organizational socialization The process by which newcomers learn an organization's values and norms and acquire the work behaviors necessary to perform jobs effectively.

Texas A&M's Fish Camp is an annual orientation program designed to help freshmen (or Fish) make the transition from high school to college life. Texas A&M's Fish Camp runs for four days and is attended by over 4,500 freshmen each year.

by the time new students arrive on campus and start their first semester, they have been socialized into what a Texas A&M student is supposed to do, and they have relatively few problems adjusting to the college environment.

Most organizations have some kind of socialization program to help new employees learn the ropes—the values, norms, and culture of the organization. The military, for example, is well known for the rigorous socialization process it uses to turn raw recruits into trained soldiers. Organizations such as the Walt Disney Company also put new recruits through a rigorous training program to provide them with the knowledge they need not only to perform well in their jobs but also to ensure that each employee plays his or her part in helping visitors to Disneyland have fun in a wholesome theme park. New recruits at Disney are called "cast members" and attend Disney University to learn the Disney culture and their part in it. Disney's culture emphasizes the values of safety, courtesy, entertainment, and efficiency, and these values are brought to life for newcomers at Disney University. Newcomers also learn about the attraction area they will be joining (e.g., Adventureland or Fantasyland) at Disney University and then receive on-the-job socialization in the area itself from experienced cast members.[106] Through organizational socialization, founders and managers of an organization transmit to employees the cultural values and norms that shape the behavior of organizational members. Thus, the values and norms of founder Walt Disney live on today at Disneyland as newcomers are socialized into the Disney way.

CEREMONIES AND RITES Another way in which managers can create or influence organizational culture is by developing organizational ceremonies and rites—formal events that recognize incidents of importance to the organization as a whole and to specific employees.[107] The most common rites that organizations use to transmit cultural norms and values to their members are rites of passage, of integration, and of enhancement (see Table 3.1).[108]

Rites of passage determine how individuals enter, advance within, or leave the organization. The socialization programs developed by military organizations (such as the U.S. Army) or by large accountancy and law firms are rites of passage. Likewise, the ways in which an organization prepares people for promotion or retirement are rites of passage.

Table 3.1
Organizational Rites

Type of Rite	Example of Rite	Purpose of Rite
Rite of passage	Induction and basic training	Learn and internalize norms and values
Rite of integration	Office Christmas party	Build common norms and values
Rite of enhancement	Presentation of annual award	Motivate commitment to norms and values

Rites of integration, such as shared announcements of organizational successes, office parties, and company cookouts, build and reinforce common bonds among organizational members. IDEO uses many rites of integration to make its employees feel connected to one another and special. In addition to having wild "end-of-year" celebratory bashes, groups of IDEO employees periodically take time off to go to a sporting event, movie, or meal, or sometimes on a long bike ride or for a sail. These kinds of shared activities not only reinforce IDEO's culture but also can be a source of inspiration on the job (e.g., IDEO has been involved in the making of movies such as *The Abyss* and *Free Willy*). One 35-member design studio at IDEO led by Dennis Boyle has bimonthly lunch fests with no set agenda—anything goes. While enjoying great food, jokes, and camaraderie, studio members often end up sharing ideas for their latest great products, and the freely flowing conversation that results often leads to creative insights.[109]

A company's annual meeting also may be used as a ritual of integration, offering an opportunity to communicate organizational values to managers, other employees, and shareholders. Wal-Mart, for example, makes its annual stockholders' meeting an extravagant ceremony that celebrates the company's success. The company often flies thousands of its highest-performing employees to its annual meeting at its Bentonville, Arkansas, headquarters for a huge weekend entertainment festival complete with performances by country and western stars. Wal-Mart believes that rewarding its supporters with entertainment reinforces the company's high-performance values and culture. The proceedings are shown live over closed-circuit television in all Wal-Mart stores so that all employees can join in the rites celebrating the company's achievements.[110]

Rites of enhancement, such as awards dinners, newspaper releases, and employee promotions, let organizations publicly recognize and reward employees' contributions and thus strengthen their commitment to organizational values. By bonding members within the organization, rites of enhancement reinforce an organization's values and norms.

A Motorola sales representative wears her award ribbon while attending an employee recognition party. These events, or "rites of enhancement," reinforce an organization's values and norms.

STORIES AND LANGUAGE also communicate organizational culture. Stories (whether fact or fiction) about organizational heroes and villains and their actions provide important clues about values and norms. Such stories can reveal the kinds of behaviors that are valued by the organization and the kinds of practices that are frowned on.[111] At the heart of McDonald's rich culture are hundreds of stories that organizational members tell about founder Ray Kroc. Most of these stories focus on how Kroc established the strict operating values and norms that are at the heart of

McDonald's culture. Kroc was dedicated to achieving perfection in McDonald's quality, service, cleanliness, and value for money (QSC&V), and these four central values permeate McDonald's culture. For example, an often retold story describes what happened when Kroc and a group of managers from the Houston region were touring various restaurants. One of the restaurants was having a bad day operationally. Kroc was incensed about the long lines of customers, and he was furious when he realized that the product customers were receiving that day was not up to his high standards. To address the problem, he jumped up and stood on the front counter and got the attention of all customers and operating crew personnel. He introduced himself, apologized for the long wait and cold food, and told the customers that they could have freshly cooked food or their money back—whichever they wanted. As a result, the customers left happy, and when Kroc checked on the restaurant later, he found that his message had gotten through to its managers and crew—performance had improved. Other stories describe Kroc scrubbing dirty toilets and picking up litter inside or outside a restaurant. These and similar stories are spread around the organization by McDonald's employees. They are the stories that have helped establish Kroc as McDonald's "hero."

Because spoken language is a principal medium of communication in organizations, the characteristic slang or jargon—that is, organization-specific words or phrases—that people use to frame and describe events provides important clues about norms and values. "McLanguage," for example, is prevalent at all levels of McDonald's. A McDonald's employee described as having "ketchup in his (or her) blood" is someone who is truly dedicated to the McDonald's way—someone who has been completely socialized to its culture. McDonald's has an extensive training program that teaches new employees "McDonald's speak," and new employees are welcomed into the family with a formal orientation that illustrates Kroc's dedication to QSC&V.

The concept of organizational language encompasses not only spoken language but how people dress, the offices they occupy, the cars they drive, and the degree of formality they use when they address one another. Casual dress reflects and reinforces Microsoft's entrepreneurial culture and values. Formal business attire supports the conservative culture found in many banks, which emphasize the importance of conforming to organizational norms such as respect for authority and staying within one's prescribed role. Traders in the Chicago futures and options trading pits frequently wear garish and flamboyant ties and jackets to make their presence known in a sea of faces. The demand for magenta, lime green, and silver lamé jackets featuring bold images such as the Power Rangers—anything that helps the traders stand out and attract customers—is enormous.[112] When employees speak and understand the language of their organization's culture, they know how to behave in the organization and what is expected of them.

At IDEO, language, dress, the physical work environment, and extreme informality all underscore a culture that is adventuresome, playful, risk taking, egalitarian, and innovative. For example, at IDEO, employees refer to taking the consumers' perspective when designing products as "being left-handed." Employees dress in T-shirts and jeans, the physical work environment is continually evolving and changing depending upon how employees wish to personalize their workspace, no one "owns" a fancy office with a window, and rules are nonexistent.[113]

Culture and Managerial Action

While founders and managers play a critical role in the development, mainte-nance, and communication of organizational culture, this same culture shapes and controls the behavior of all employees, including managers themselves. For example, culture influences the way managers perform their four main func-tions: planning, organizing, leading, and controlling. As we consider these func-tions, we continue to distinguish between top managers who create organizational values and norms that encourage creative, innovative behavior and top managers who encourage a conservative, cautious approach by their subordinates. We noted earlier that both kinds of values and norms can be appropriate depending upon the situation and type of organization.

PLANNING   Top managers in an organization with an innovative culture are likely to encourage lower-level managers to participate in the planning process and develop a flexible approach to planning. They are likely to be willing to lis-ten to new ideas and to take risks involving the development of new products. In contrast, top managers in an organization with conservative values are likely to emphasize formal top-down planning. Suggestions from lower-level man-agers are likely to be subjected to a formal review process, which can signifi-cantly slow decision making. Although this deliberate approach may improve the quality of decision making in a nuclear power plant, it can have unintended consequences. In the past, at conservative IBM, the planning process became so formalized that managers spent most of their time assembling complex slide shows and overheads to defend their current positions rather than thinking about what they should be doing to keep IBM abreast of the changes taking place in the computer industry. When former CEO Lou Gerstner took over, he used every means at his disposal to abolish this culture, even building a brand-new campus-style headquarters to change managers' mind-sets. IBM's culture is undergoing further changes initiated by its current CEO, Samuel Palmisano.

ORGANIZING   What kinds of organizing will managers in innovative and in conservative cultures encourage? Valuing creativity, managers in innovative cul-tures are likely to try to create an organic structure, one that is flat, with few levels in the hierarchy, and one in which authority is decentralized so that employees are encouraged to work together to find solutions to ongoing problems. A prod-uct team structure may be very suitable for an organization with an innovative culture. In contrast, managers in a conservative culture are likely to create a well-defined hierarchy of authority and establish clear reporting relationships so that employees know exactly whom to report to and how to react to any problems that arise.

LEADING   In an innovative culture, managers are likely to lead by exam-ple, encouraging employees to take risks and experiment. They are support-ive regardless of whether employees succeed or fail. In contrast, managers in a conservative culture are likely to use management by objectives and to con-stantly monitor subordinates' progress toward goals, overseeing their every move. We examine leadership in detail in Chapter 13 when we consider the leadership styles that managers can adopt to influence and shape employee behavior.

CONTROLLING   The ways in which managers evaluate, and take actions to improve, performance differ depending upon whether the organizational culture emphasizes formality and caution or innovation and change. Managers who want to encourage risk taking, creativity, and innovation recognize that there are multiple potential paths to success and that failure must be accepted in order for creativity to thrive. Thus, they are less concerned about employees' performing their jobs in a specific, predetermined manner and in strict adherence to preset goals and more concerned about employees' being flexible and taking the initiative to come up with ideas for improving performance. Managers in innovative cultures are also more concerned about long-run performance than short-term targets because they recognize that real innovation entails much uncertainty that necessitates flexibility. In contrast, managers in cultures that emphasize caution and maintenance of the status quo often set specific, difficult goals for employees, frequently monitor progress toward these goals, and develop a clear set of rules that employees are expected to adhere to.

The values and norms of an organization's culture strongly affect the way managers perform their management functions. The extent to which managers buy into the values and norms of their organization shapes their view of the world and their actions and decisions in particular circumstances.[114] In turn, the actions that managers take can have an impact on the performance of the organization. Thus, organizational culture, managerial action, and organizational performance are all linked together.

This linkage is apparent at Hewlett-Packard (HP), a leader in the electronic instrumentation and computer industries. Established in the 1940s, HP developed a culture that is an outgrowth of the strong personal beliefs of the company's founders, William Hewlett and David Packard. As discussed in Chapter 2, Bill and Dave, as they are known within the company, formalized HP's culture in 1957 in a statement of corporate objectives known as the "HP Way." The basic values informing the HP Way stress serving everyone who has a stake in the company with integrity and fairness, including customers, suppliers, employees, stockholders, and society in general. Bill and Dave helped build this culture within HP by hiring like-minded people and by letting the HP Way guide their own actions as managers.

Although the Hewlett-Packard example and our earlier example of IDEO illustrate how organizational culture can give rise to managerial actions that ultimately benefit the organization, this is not always the case. The cultures of some organizations become dysfunctional, encouraging managerial actions that harm the organization and discouraging actions that might lead to an improvement in performance.[115] Recent corporate scandals at large companies like Enron, Tyco, and WorldCom show how damaging a dysfunctional culture can be to an organization and its members. For example, Enron's arrogant, "success-at-all costs" culture led to fraudulent behavior on the part of its top managers.[116] Unfortunately, hundreds of Enron employees have paid a heavy price for the unethical behavior of these top managers and the dysfunctional organizational culture. Not only have these employees lost their jobs, but many also have lost their life savings in Enron stock and pension funds, which became worth just a fraction of their former value before the wrongdoing at Enron came to light. We discuss ethics and ethical cultures in depth in the next chapter.

Summary and Review

ENDURING CHARACTERISTICS: PERSONALITY TRAITS Personality traits are enduring tendencies to feel, think, and act in certain ways. The Big Five general traits are extraversion, negative affectivity, agreeableness, conscientiousness, and openness to experience. Other personality traits that affect managerial behavior are locus of control, self-esteem, and the needs for achievement, affiliation, and power.

VALUES, ATTITUDES, AND MOODS AND EMOTIONS A terminal value is a personal conviction about lifelong goals or objectives; an instrumental value is a personal conviction about modes of conduct. Terminal and instrumental values have an impact on what managers try to achieve in their organizations and the kinds of behaviors they engage in. An attitude is a collection of feelings and beliefs. Two attitudes important for understanding managerial behaviors include job satisfaction (the collection of feelings and beliefs that managers have about their jobs) and organizational commitment (the collection of feelings and beliefs that managers have about their organizations). A mood is a feeling or state of mind; emotions are intense feelings that are short-lived and directly linked to their causes. Managers' moods and emotions, or how they feel at work on a day-to-day basis, have the potential to impact not only their own behavior and effectiveness but also those of their subordinates. Emotional intelligence is the ability to understand and manage one's own and other people's moods and emotions.

ORGANIZATIONAL CULTURE Organizational culture is the shared set of beliefs, expectations, values, norms, and work routines that influence how members of an organization relate to one another and work together to achieve organizational goals. Founders of new organizations and managers play an important role in creating and maintaining organizational culture. Organizational socialization is the process by which newcomers learn an organization's values and norms and acquire the work behaviors necessary to perform jobs effectively.

Management in Action

Topics for Discussion and Action

Discussion

1. Discuss why managers who have different types of personalities can be equally effective and successful.

2. Can managers be too satisfied with their jobs? Can they be too committed to their organizations? Why or why not?

3. Assume that you are a manager of a restaurant. Describe what it is like to work for you when you are in a negative mood.

4. Why might managers be disadvantaged by low levels of emotional intelligence?

Action

5. Interview a manager in a local organization. Ask the manager to describe situations in which he or she is especially likely to act in accordance with his or her values. Ask the manager to describe situations in which he or she is less likely to act in accordance with his or her values.

6. Watch a popular television show, and as you watch it, try to determine the emotional intelligence levels of the characters the actors in the show portray. Rank the characters from highest to lowest in terms of emotional intelligence. As you watched the show, what factors influenced your assessments of emotional intelligence levels.

7. Go to an upscale clothing store in your neighborhood, and go to a clothing store that is definitely not upscale. Observe the behavior of employees in each store as well as the store's environment. In what ways are the organizational cultures in each store similar? In what ways are they different?

Building Management Skills

Diagnosing Culture

Think about the culture of the last organization you worked for, your current university, or another organization or club to which you belong. Then, answer the following questions:

1. What values are emphasized in this culture?

2. What norms do members of this organization follow?

3. Who seems to have played an important role in creating the culture?

4. In what ways is the organizational culture communicated to organizational members.

Managing Ethically

Some organizations rely on personality and interest inventories to screen potential employees. Other organizations attempt to screen employees by using paper-and-pencil honesty tests.

Questions

1. Either individually or in a group, think about the ethical implications of using personality and interest inventories to screen potential employees. How might this practice be unfair to potential applicants? How might organizational members who are in charge of hiring misuse it?

2. Because of measurement error and validity problems, some relatively trustworthy people may "fail" an honesty test given by an employer. What are the ethical implications of trustworthy people "failing" honesty tests, and what obligations do you think employers should have when relying on honesty tests for screening purposes?

Small Group Breakout Exercise

Making Difficult Decisions in Hard Times

Form groups of three or four people, and appoint one member as the spokesperson who will communicate your findings to the whole class when called on by the instructor. Then discuss the following scenario.

You are on the top-management team of a medium-size company that manufactures cardboard boxes, containers, and other cardboard packaging materials. Your company is facing increasing levels of competition for major corporate customer accounts, and profits have declined significantly. You have tried everything you can to cut costs and remain competitive, with the exception of laying off employees. Your company has had a no-layoff policy for the past 20 years, and you believe it is an important part of the organization's culture. However, you are experiencing mounting pressure to increase your firm's performance, and your no-layoff policy has been questioned by shareholders. Even though you haven't decided whether to lay off employees and thus break with a 20-year tradition for your company, rumors are rampant in your organization that something is afoot, and employees are worried. You are meeting today to address this problem.

1. Develop a list of options and potential courses of action to address the heightened competition and decline in profitability that your company has been experiencing.

2. Choose your preferred course of action, and justify why you will take this route.

3. Describe how you will communicate your decision to employees.

4. If your preferred option involves a layoff, justify why. If it doesn't involve a layoff, explain why.

Exploring the World Wide Web

Go to IDEO's Web site (www.ideo.com) and read about this company. Try to find indicators of IDEO's culture that are provided on the Web site. How does the design of the Web site itself, and the pictures and words it contains, communicate the nature of IDEO's organizational culture? What kinds of people do you think would be attracted to IDEO? What kinds of people do you think would be likely to be dissatisfied with a job at IDEO?

Be the Manager

You have recently been hired as the vice president for human resources in an advertising agency. One of the problems that has been brought to your attention is the fact that in the creative departments at the agency, there are dysfunctionally high levels of conflict. You have spoken with members of each of these departments, and in each one it seems that there are a few members of the department who are creating all the problems. All of these individuals are valued contributors who have many creative ad campaigns to their credit. The very high levels of conflict are creating problems in the departments, and negative moods and emotions are much more prevalent than positive feelings. What are you going to do to both retain valued employees and alleviate the excessive conflict and negative feelings in these departments?

BusinessWeek Case in the News

An Open-Source Lightning Rod

One weekend back in December, Marc Fleury was hunched over his computer, absorbed in writing a fervent, almost preachy and completely self-serving blog about why IBM and BEA Systems Inc. will never be able to best his tiny but growing open-source company, JBoss Inc. His 6-year-old daughter walked up to him and asked: "Daddy, why are you still working on a Sunday? Is IBM still after you?" He laughed and replied: "Yes, darling . . . but now a whole industry is ganging up on us."

That's life in the Fleury household. The entrepreneur's favorite movie is *The Matrix* because, like its protagonist, Neo, he has long fancied himself working a boring day job and then saving the world at night. Fleury's company, JBoss, is a key player in the booming open-source movement that's shaking up every software company from Microsoft to Oracle to IBM, forcing them all to change their strategies or to collaborate with younger, faster-moving competitors that develop "open" software, distribute it freely on the Net, and make money by providing support and training for it. When JBoss took in venture capital in 2004, it was valued at $200 million, and those close to the company say Fleury and his family own nearly 50%.

Profit Motive

But while fleury, like Neo, is something of a cult figure, few people in the old or new software world want to think of him as their savior. Brash, outspoken, and frequently insulting, Fleury has clawed his way to the top of the open-source pile over the past six years. Part of the dislike arises because he's a threat. Even though JBoss brings in only $50 million a year in revenues, at most, from providing training, support, and maintenance services to its users, it has siphoned off some hundreds of millions in market value from the likes of BEA Systems and IBM by giving away free software.

Meanwhile, some open-source companies are put off by what they say is Fleury's money-grubbing, controlling style. It's out of keeping, they say, with the cooperative, do-it-for-the-greater-good ethos of the open-source movement. Stuart F. Cohen, head of Open Source Development Labs Inc. (OSDL), a nonprofit group that advocates for the development of Linux, the open-source operating system, remembers the first time he met Fleury. He had been invited to Atlanta to be on a panel at a JBoss customer event, and Fleury kept asking when he was going to take OSDL public. "To him, everyone is out to make money," he says. "That's not what this idea is really all about." Even competitors from the traditional software world criticize Fleury for having what they say is a cynical profit motive. "Marc Fleury has really exploited the open-source hype for his own personal financial gain," says one. Fleury's reply: "That's like someone telling the rapper 50 Cent he's not street enough."

If Fleury is focused on making money, perhaps that's because he spent a few frustrating years in Silicon Valley making none. His ambitions were nearly crushed in 2001 when he and his wife, Nathalie, and their young daughter left Silicon Valley penniless after he had spent years trying to build a software hosting company called Telkel. He was disillusioned and sick of playing the Silicon Valley game: putting together a business plan and shopping it around to "snooty" venture capitalists.

So he moved into his in-laws' house in Atlanta and focused on contributing to an open-source project that he and others had started in 1999, JBoss. All he wanted to do, he told his wife, was write code for free all day long. "She told me I was stupid," he says, and gave him a year to make $70,000 or else get a job. Then companies downloading JBoss software started asking him for training and support—and offering to pay. A year later, Fleury had made more than $100,000.

Demanding Personality

He's worth a lot more now, to the dismay of his critics. Some investors have even refused to invest in JBoss because of Fleury's style. "It's a strength and a weakness," says David R. Skok, a partner at Matrix and the company's biggest outside investor. "Because he's so disliked, it creates incredible controversy and incredible press. I think he knows that, and kind of plays that up." His personality may have played a part in what insiders say was an offer from Oracle Corp. earlier this year that fell apart. Oracle is said to have valued the small company at nearly $500 million—a big endorsement of open source that had entrepreneurs and venture capitalists licking their chops along with JBoss employees, who own a large chunk of its stock.

Neither Fleury nor Oracle will comment on what happened, but insiders say the deal died because of Fleury's demands about what his role would be at the combined company. With Oracle paying such a premium, the deal was going to be integrated its way, not his. Fleury will say only this: "One of the conditions of me selling to anyone is we remain whole and I remain the boss."

Fleury owns up to the reputation that he has developed. Sitting in an unkempt office in a flashy Atlanta building, he downs a giant cup of coffee before dribbling Visine into red-rimmed eyes. He spits sunflower seeds in a cup as he talks about why people hate him. The old software world? They're jealous. Open-source zealots? "They probably hate me at night because they didn't have the *cojones* to go out and do [what I've done]."

Of course, no one says you have to be a nice guy to make it in software—just ask people who have worked for Microsoft's Bill Gates or Oracle's Lawrence J. Ellison, whom Fleury names as personal heroes. And although Fleury didn't write the most salient parts of JBoss code and wasn't the one to fine-tune the business model, JBoss probably wouldn't be where it is without him. As much as he is despised outside the company, its executives and developers describe him as the visionary who holds JBoss together. "The public face of Marc is very abrasive, but inside the company, he really cares a lot about what you have to say," says Sacha Labourey, JBoss's chief technology officer and one of its first employees.

Fleury has hired some of the best contributors to the open-source project, who work for him remotely from around the world. He fancies himself a sort of record label managing "rock stars." He has always wanted to be a hotshot programmer himself. During his first tech job at Sun Microsystems Inc. in France, the company kept trying to push him into sales or middle management, and he insisted on software development. When he came to Silicon Valley with Sun in 1997, he continued to be frustrated when he couldn't break into its elite programming teams.

Now, as an employer of elite programmers, he gives them the freedom to take months on projects of their choosing. He rewards them with "genius grants" when they do something particularly innovative. "Managing superstars is one of the things I can do," he says. As Fleury talked to *BusinessWeek*, he was planning a surprise birthday bash for one of his "geniuses." The details: "We are going to get this horrible stretch limo and go out to dinner and [the clubs]."

A few weeks ago, Fleury's daughter had another question for him: "Daddy, is JBoss still going to be around when I'm big?" She's not the only one wondering about that. Red Hat, Novell, and Oracle are all said to be interested in the company. But quietly, several industry watchers say the cocksure Fleury blew his chance. Aside from Red Hat, there are few businesses that have proved they can scale up using the free-software model. Red Hat's steep earnings multiple, which tops 80, along with the $500 million that venture capitalists pumped into startups last year have some worried about an open-source bubble that may be nearing its limit.

If Fleury is kicking himself, he's certainly not doing it publicly. He and his investors say they're focused on getting ready for an initial public offering, which will come "sooner rather than later," according to Chief Operating Officer Rob Bearden. "They'll be rich," Fleury boldly says of investors and employees. "I'll create a generation of open-source millionaires, and I'm damn proud of that."

Source: S. Lacy "An Open-Source Lightning Rod." Reprinted from the April 10, 2006, issue of *BusinessWeek* by special permission. Copyright © by the McGraw-Hill Companies, Inc.

Questions

1. What personality traits does Marc Fleury appear to be high on?
2. What personality traits is he probably low on?
3. How would you describe his values and attitudes?
4. Do you think he is high or low on emotional intelligence? Why?

BusinessWeek

Case in the News

Bucking the Odds at Amylin

At least once a day, Ginger L. Graham follows a routine that many people with diabetes know all too well: She pricks her finger and tests her blood sugar. Graham, chief executive of Amylin Pharmaceuticals Inc., does not have diabetes. But her company just launched two new drugs to treat the disease, and Graham believes that to truly understand her customers, she must live the diabetic lifestyle. "I just think we don't appreciate how hard their lives are," she says. So she watches her diet, taking notice of foods that can cause dangerous glucose swings. But it's the finger sticks that are the toughest to get used to. "I dread it," confesses Graham, 50. "It's so unpleasant."

Those daily jabs are pretty much the only pain Graham is experiencing these days. In the spring, after 18 years of regulatory setbacks and near-death experiences, San Diego-based Amylin pulled off a rare feat in biotech, scoring Food & Drug Administration approval for both its first and second products. The back-to-back wins—which Graham celebrated by jumping into the fountain outside Amylin's headquarters—instantly transformed the company from a pure research outfit to a player in the pharma business. And Graham, who has been CEO since 2003, found herself facing brand new challenges, from cobbling together a salesforce to gearing up for commercial manufacturing. "We needed to hire 300 people all at once," she says.

For the most part, Amylin's transition is going swimmingly. In March the company introduced Symlin, an engineered form of a human hormone that insulin-dependent diabetics can take along with insulin to smooth out dangerous fluctuations in blood sugar. Two months later, Amylin launched Byetta, a drug derived from a hormone found in the saliva of desert-dwelling Gila monsters. The injected hormone, aimed at diabetics who are not yet dependent on insulin, helps them control their blood sugar. That, in turn, could keep patients from sliding toward insulin dependency. The company is on track to report 2005 sales of $122 million, analysts estimate. Because of its frantic expansion, Amylin's loss is expected to jump 38% over 2004, to about $216 million. But analysts believe the company could turn profitable by 2008 and surpass $1 billion in annual sales the following year.

Graham already has her scientists working on an improved version of Byetta, which may have to be injected only once a week, as opposed to twice a day. And the drug may offer an additional benefit: In August the company announced that in an early clinical trial, patients taking the longer-acting drug lost an average of nine pounds.

Considering that most diabetes treatments cause patients to gain weight—which in turn aggravates their condition—investors were stunned. "I don't think anyone has seen such compelling data," says Kris H. Jenner, a biotech analyst for T. Rowe Price Group Inc., which holds shares of Amylin. Hopes for the next generation of Byetta, which could be introduced by 2008, helped push Amylin's stock up 58% in 2005, to $39.70.

Dire Straits

There was a time when Amylin's fate seemed as precarious as that of the threatened Gila monster. In 1998, Graham was an executive at device maker Guidant Corp. and serving on Amylin's board when the company suffered some setbacks. Johnson & Johnson pulled out of a key research partnership, Amylin's share price fell to 31¢, and it was nearly delisted from the NASDAQ. Six weeks from running out of cash, the biotech stripped down from 300 employees to 37.

Amylin was in such dire straits that some board members invested their own money to keep it afloat. Graham contributed $200,000 to the cause. "I thought: 'This is somebody who puts her money where her mouth is,'" says Chief Operating Officer Daniel M. Bradbury. The company raised $33.5 million altogether, allowing it to continue studying its flagship drug Symlin, as well as Byetta, which Amylin acquired from its inventor in 1996.

Sleeping Beauty

In 2003, Graham was mulling early retirement when Amylin's board asked her to take over as CEO. She quickly abandoned the idea of spending her days riding horses and learning to play the harp her husband bought her as a retirement gift. But shortly into her tenure, Graham realized the job might be harder than she anticipated. Unexpectedly, the FDA said it wouldn't approve Symlin without more clinical trial data.

It was the second such request—and a chilling warning that the drug might never see the light of day. On the other hand, early studies of Byetta indicated that it might be a billion-dollar drug. Graham deliberated briefly before shifting all but 20 of the 350 employees then working at Amylin over to the Byetta team.

For the many employees who had staked their careers on Symlin, the move was painful. The mood at Amylin was grim, especially for Graham, who was simultaneously mourning the death of her mother. In a pep talk to the staff, Graham explained that Symlin was like Sleeping Beauty: "She was still beautiful, but she had to go to sleep." After Symlin was approved, Graham came to work dressed as the newly awakened Sleeping Beauty and handed out hardbound copies of the fairy tale.

Graham has always had a penchant for the theatrical. As a child growing up on a chicken farm in Arkansas, she competed in local rodeos, earning the title of Arkansas High School Rodeo Queen. "I could rope a calf or tie a goat or run barrels and poles," she says. As an undergraduate at the University of Arkansas she won the 1976 state title and then competed at the national Miss Rodeo America Pageant. Her speech about Arkansas garnered her the top prize in the public-speaking portion of the contest.

Competing in the male-dominated world of rodeo prepared Graham well for her first corporate gig, selling agricultural chemicals for a division of Eli Lilly & Co. As a woman working in agriculture at that time, Graham was such an oddity that her very presence offended some customers. One of Lilly's largest buyers refused to work with Graham and called her manager to demand that the previous sales rep—a man—return to the account. Her manager refused, and an undaunted Graham kept calling on the customer. "I hung out there, I got to know all the staff," she says. Her stubbornness paid off: He became a loyal customer.

The normally soft-spoken and approachable Graham can turn crusty if she's not getting her way. After returning to Lilly in 1986, Graham worked in a variety of divisions, ranging from finance to pharmaceuticals to medical devices. In 1987 she managed the sale of Elizabeth Arden to Fabergé for $735 million—then the largest cosmetics deal ever. When one of the Morgan Stanley bankers dragged his feet, "she had him backed into a corner and she was screaming at him," says Michael Hunt, who worked with her on the deal. "She was holding him accountable." In the middle of the negotiations, the Black Monday market crash forced the parties to restructure the financing. Still, Graham and Hunt managed to close it at the originally agreed-upon price.

Today, Graham is facing a delicate balancing act. She has to transform Amylin into a sales-driven company without letting go of the scrappy culture that inspired those original 37 survivors to stick by two promising drugs. "How do you infuse that into all these new people who didn't go through the Valley of Death?" asks Joseph C. Cook Jr., Amylin's former CEO and now chairman of the board. "Ginger worries about that." Graham vows to continue to spend heavily on research, nurturing Amylin's experimental drugs to treat obesity and heart failure. And she spends much of her time on the road, speaking to all of the newly hired salespeople.

The rodeo-queen-turned-CEO revels in telling new recruits about Amylin's two-decade fight for survival. One of her favorite stories describes an early Amylin investor who was so determined to nurture new treatments for his diabetic daughter that he FedExed a $6.2 million personal check to the company. Graham refers to these specimens of corporate lore as "cave paintings," and at her San Diego office she surrounds herself with symbols of Amylin's history, including figurines of Gila monsters and her personal copy of *Sleeping Beauty*. Every day they remind her of the challenge she has taken on. "I need to transfer what was," she says, "to what we're about to become."

Source: A. Weintraub, "Bucking the Odds at Amylin." Reprinted from the January 9, 2006, issue of *BusinessWeek* by special permission. Copyright © by the McGraw-Hill Companies.

Questions

1. How would you describe Ginger Graham's personality, values, and attitudes?

2. Do you think she is high or low on emotional intelligence? Why?

3. How would you describe Amylin's culture?

4. How did its culture come into being, and how and why is Graham trying to sustain this culture while Amylin undergoes major changes?

CHAPTER 4

Ethics and Social Responsibility

Learning Objectives

After studying this chapter, you should be able to:

- Explain the relationship between ethics and the law.

- Discuss why it is important to behave ethically.

- Differentiate between the claims of the different stakeholder groups that are affected by managers and their companies' actions.

- Describe four rules that can be used to help companies and their managers act in ethical ways.

- Identify the four main sources of managerial ethics.

- Distinguish between the four main approaches toward social responsibility that a company can take.

The Whole Foods Market supermarket chain was founded by two hippies in Austin, Texas, in 1978 as a natural counterculture food store. Today, it is the world's leading retailer of natural and organic foods, with 184 stores in North America and the United Kingdom. Whole Foods specializes in the sale of chemical- and drug-free meat, poultry, and produce; its products are the "purest" possible, meaning it selects the ones least adulterated by artificial additives, sweeteners, colorings, and preservatives. Despite the fact that it charges high prices for its pure produce, sales per store are growing fast and the company plans to double both the number of its stores and its $4 billion revenue by 2010. Why has Whole Foods been so successful? Because, says founder and CEO John Mackey, of the principles he established to manage his company since its beginning—principles founded on the need to behave in an ethical and socially responsible way toward everybody affected by its business.

Mackey says he started his business for three reasons—to have fun, to make money, and to contribute to the well-being of other people.[1] The company's mission is based on its members' collective responsibility to the well-being of the people and groups its

A customer makes her selections at the seafood section of a new Whole Foods market in Austin, Texas.

affects, its *stakeholders;* in order of priority, at Whole Foods these are customers, team members, investors, suppliers, community, and natural environment. Mackey measures his company's success on how well it satisfies the needs of these stakeholders. His ethical stance toward customers is that they are guaranteed that Whole Foods products are 100% organic, hormone-free, or as represented. To help achieve this promise, Whole Foods insists that its suppliers also behave in an ethical way so that it knows, for example, that the beef it sells comes from cows pastured on grass, not corn-fed in feed lots, and the chicken it sells is from free-range hens and not from hens that have been confined in tiny cages that prevent even movement.

His management approach toward "team members," as Whole Foods employees are called, is also based on a well-defined ethical position. Mackey says, "We put great emphasis at Whole Foods on the 'Whole People' part of the company mission. We believe in helping support our team members to grow as individuals—to become 'Whole People.' We consciously use Maslow's hierarchy of needs model [see Chapter 13] to help our team members to move up Maslow's hierarchy. As much as we are able, we attempt to manage through love instead of fear or greed. We allow tremendous individual initiative at Whole Foods and that's why our company is so innovative and creative."[2] Mackey claims that each supermarket in the chain is unique because in each one team members are constantly experimenting with new

and better ways to serve customers and improve their well-being. As team members learn, they become "self-actualized" or self-fulfilled, and this increase in their well-being translates into a desire to increase the well-being of other stakeholders. Mackey contrasts this supportive management approach with a "command and control" reward-based directive management approach, which he claims encourages the pursuit of self-interested rather than team- or company-based objectives.

Finally, Mackey's strong views on ethics and social responsibility also serve shareholders. Mackey does not believe the object of being in business is to primarily maximize profits for shareholders; he puts customers first. He believes, however, that companies that behave ethically, and strive to satisfy the needs of customers and employees, simultaneously satisfy the needs of investors because high profits are the result of loyal customers and committed employees. Indeed, since Whole Foods issued shares to the public in 1992, the value of those shares has increased 25 times—something that has certainly increased the well-being of the company's owners![3] Clearly, taking a strong position on ethics and social responsibility has worked so far at Whole Foods.

Overview

As the story of Whole Foods suggests, an ethical dimension is present in most kinds of management decision making but companies and managers can differ enormously in their commitment to stakeholders. Some companies, such as Whole Foods, make the need to behave ethically toward stakeholders the main priority. Others, such as Enron, pursue their own self-interest at the expense of their stakeholders. As a result, Enron collapsed and went bankrupt; its former top managers Ken Lay and Jeffrey Skilling were found guilty in 2006 of defrauding investors, and they face the prospect of spending the rest of their lives in jail.

In this chapter, we examine the nature of the obligations and responsibilities of managers and the companies they work for toward the people and society that are affected by their actions. First, we examine the nature of ethics and the sources of ethical problems. Second, we discuss the major groups of people, called *stakeholders,* who are affected by the way companies operate. Third, we look at four rules or guidelines that managers can use to decide whether a specific business decision is ethical or unethical. Finally, we consider the sources of managerial ethics and the reasons why it is important for a company to behave in a socially responsible manner. By the end of this chapter you will understand the central role that ethics plays in shaping the practice of management and the life of a people, society, and nation.

The Nature of Ethics

Suppose you see a person being mugged in the street. How will you behave? Will you act in some way to help, even though you risk being hurt? Will you walk away? Perhaps you might adopt a "middle way" and not intervene but call the police? Does the way you act depend on whether the person being mugged is a fit male, an elderly person, or even a street person? Does it depend on whether there are other people around, so you can tell yourself, "Oh well, someone else will help or call the police. I don't need to"?

Ethical Dilemmas

ethical dilemma The quandary people find themselves in when they have to decide if they should act in a way that might help another person or group even though doing so might go against their own self-interest.

The situation described above is an example of an **ethical dilemma,** the quandary people find themselves in when they have to decide if they should act in a way that might help another person or group, and is the "right" thing to do, even though doing so might go against their own self-interest.[4] A dilemma may also arise when a person has to decide between two different courses of action, knowing that whichever course he or she chooses will result in harm to one person or group even while it may benefit another. The ethical dilemma here is to decide which course of action is the "lesser of two evils."

People often know they are confronting an ethical dilemma when their moral scruples come into play and cause them to hesitate, debate, and reflect upon the "rightness" or "goodness" of a course of action. Moral scruples are thoughts and feelings that tell a person what is right or wrong; they are a part of a person's ethics. Ethics are the inner-guiding moral principles, values, and beliefs that people use to analyze or interpret a situation and then decide what is the "right" or appropriate way to behave. At the same time, ethics also indicate what is inappropriate behavior and how a person should behave to avoid doing harm to another person.

ethics The inner-guiding moral principles, values, and beliefs that people use to analyze or interpret a situation and then decide what is the "right" or appropriate way to behave.

The essential problem in dealing with ethical issues, and thus solving moral dilemmas, is that there are no absolute or indisputable rules or principles that can be developed to decide if an action is ethical or unethical. Put simply, different people or groups may dispute which actions are ethical or unethical depending on their own personal self-interest and specific attitudes, beliefs, and values—concepts we discussed in Chapter 3. How, therefore, are we and companies and their managers and employees to decide what is ethical and so act appropriately toward other people and groups?

Ethics and the Law

The first answer to this question is that society as a whole, using the political and legal process, can lobby for and pass laws that specify what people can and cannot do. Many different kinds of laws exist to govern business, for example, laws against fraud and deception and laws governing how companies can treat their employees and customers. Laws also specify what sanctions or punishments will follow if those laws are broken. Different groups in society lobby for which laws should be passed based on their own personal interests and beliefs with regard to what is right or wrong. The group that can summon most support is able to pass the laws that most closely align with its interests and beliefs. Once a law is passed, a decision about what the appropriate behavior is with regard to a person or situation is taken from the personally determined ethical realm to the societally determined legal realm. If you do not conform to the law, you can be prosecuted; and if you are found guilty of breaking the law, you can be punished. You have little say in the matter; your fate is in the hands of the court and its lawyers.

In studying the relationship between ethics and law, it is important to understand that *neither laws nor ethics are fixed principles,* cast in stone, which do not change over time. Ethical beliefs alter and change as time passes, and as they do so, laws change to reflect the changing ethical beliefs of a society. It was seen as ethical, and it was legal, for example, to acquire and possess slaves in ancient Rome and Greece and in the United States until the 19th century. Ethical views regarding whether slavery was morally right or appropriate changed, however. Slavery was made illegal in the United States when those in power decided that slavery degraded the very meaning of being human. Slavery is a statement about the value or worth of human beings and about their right to life, liberty, and the pursuit of happiness. And if I deny these rights to other people, how then can I claim to have any natural or "god-given" rights to these things myself?

Moreover, what is to stop any person or group that becomes powerful enough to take control of the political and legal process from enslaving me and denying me the right to be free and to own property? In denying freedom to others, one risks losing it oneself, just as stealing from others opens the door for them to steal from me in return. "Do unto others as you would have them do unto you" is a commonly used ethical or moral rule that people apply in such situations to decide what is the right thing to do. This moral rule is discussed in detail below.

Changes in Ethics over Time

There are many types of behavior—such as murder, theft, slavery, rape, driving while intoxicated—that most, if not all, people currently believe are totally unacceptable and unethical and should therefore be illegal. There are also, however, many other kinds of actions and behaviors whose ethical nature is open to dispute. Some people might believe that a particular behavior—for example, smoking tobacco or possessing guns—is unethical and so should be made illegal. Others might argue that it is up to the individual or a group to decide if such behaviors are ethical or not and thus whether a particular behavior should remain legal.

As ethical beliefs change over time, some people may begin to question whether existing laws that make specific behaviors illegal are still appropriate today. They might argue that although a specific behavior is deemed illegal, this does not make it unethical and thus the law should be changed. In the United States, for example, it is illegal to possess or use marijuana (cannabis). To justify this law, it is commonly argued that smoking marijuana leads people to try more dangerous drugs. Once the habit of taking drugs has been acquired, people can get hooked on them. More powerful drugs such as the murderous heroin are fearfully addictive, and most people cannot stop using them without help from others. Thus, the use of marijuana, because it might lead to further harm, is an unethical practice.

It has been documented medically, however, that the use of marijuana has many medical benefits for people with certain illnesses. For example, for cancer sufferers who are undergoing chemotherapy and for those with AIDS who are on potent medications, marijuana offers relief from many of the treatment's side effects, such as nausea and lack of appetite. Yet, in the United States, it is illegal in many states for doctors to prescribe marijuana for these patients, so their suffering goes on. Since 1996, however, 35 states have made it legal to prescribe marijuana for medical purposes; nevertheless, the federal government has sought to stop such state legislation. The U.S. Supreme Court ruled in 2005 that only Congress or the states could decide whether the medical use of the drug should be made legal, and people in many states are currently lobbying for a relaxation of state laws against its use for medical purposes.[5] In Canada there has been a widespread movement to decriminalize marijuana. While not making the drug legal, decriminalization removes the threat of prosecution even for uses that are not medically related. A major ethical debate is currently raging over this issue in many countries.

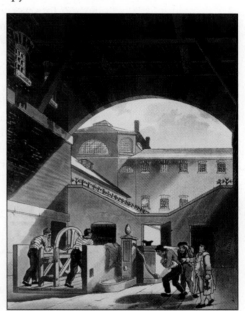

Coldbath Fields Prison, London, circa 1810. The British criminal justice system around this time was quite severe: There were over 350 different crimes for which a person could be executed, including sheep stealing. Thankfully in this case, as ethical beliefs change over time, so do laws.

The important point to note is that while ethical beliefs lead to the development of laws and regulations to prevent certain behaviors or encourage others, laws themselves can and do change or even disappear as ethical beliefs change. In Britain in 1830 there were over 350 different crimes for which a person could be executed, including sheep stealing. Today there are none; capital punishment and the death penalty are no longer legal. Thus, both ethical and legal rules are relative: No absolute or unvarying standards exist to determine how we should behave, and people are caught up in moral dilemmas all the time. Because of this we have to make ethical choices.

The previous discussion highlights an important issue in understanding the relationship between ethics, law, and business. Throughout the 2000s many scandals have plagued major companies such as Enron, Arthur Andersen, WorldCom, Tyco, Adelphia, and others. Managers in some of these companies clearly broke the law and used illegal means to defraud investors. At Enron, former chief financial officer Andrew Fastow, and his wife, pleaded guilty to falsifying the company's books so that they could siphon off tens of millions of dollars of Enron's money for their own use.

In other cases, some managers took advantage of loopholes in the law to divert hundreds of millions of dollars of company capital into their own personal fortunes. At WorldCom, for example, former CEO Bernie Ebbers used his position to place six personal, long-time friends on its 13-member board of directors. While this is not illegal, obviously these people would vote in his favor at board meetings. As a result of their support Ebbers received huge stock options and a personal loan of over $150 million from WorldCom. In return, his supporters were well rewarded for being directors; for example, Ebbers allowed them to use WorldCom's corporate jets for a minimal cost—something that saved them hundreds of thousands of dollars a year.[6]

In the light of these events some people said, "Well, what these people did was not illegal," implying that because such behavior was not illegal it was also not unethical. However, not being illegal does *not* make it ethical; such behavior is clearly unethical.[7] In many cases laws are passed *later* to close the loopholes and prevent unethical people, such as Fastow and Ebbers, from taking advantage of them to pursue their own self-interest at the expense of others. Like ordinary people, managers must confront the need to decide what is appropriate and inappropriate as they use a company's resources to produce goods and services for customers.[8]

Stakeholders and Ethics

Just as people have to work out the right and wrong ways to act, so do companies. When the law does not specify how companies should behave, their managers must decide what is the right or ethical way to behave toward the people and groups affected by their actions. Who are the people or groups that are affected by a company's business decisions? If a company behaves in an ethical way how does this benefit people and society? Conversely, how are people harmed by a company's unethical actions?

The people and groups affected by the way a company and its managers behave are called its stakeholders. **Stakeholders** supply a company with its productive resources; as a result, they have a claim on and stake in the company.[9] Since stakeholders can directly benefit or be harmed by its actions, the ethics of a company and its managers are important to them. Who are a company's major stakeholders? What do they contribute to a company, and what do they claim in return? Below we examine the claims of these stakeholders—stockholders, managers, employees, suppliers and distributors, customers, and community, society, and nation-state (Figure 4.1).

stakeholders The people and groups that supply a company with its productive resources and so have a claim on and stake in the company.

Stockholders

Stockholders have a claim on a company because when they buy its stock or shares they become its owners. Whenever the founder of a company decides to

Figure 4.1

Types of Company Stakeholders

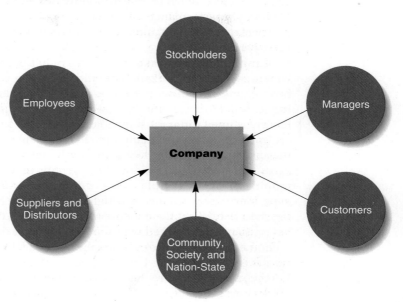

publicly incorporate the business to raise capital, shares of the stock of that company are issued. This stock grants its buyers ownership of a certain percentage of the company and the right to receive any future stock dividends. For example, in December 2004 Microsoft decided to pay the owners of its 5 billion shares a record dividend payout of $32 billion! Bill Gates received $3.3 billion in dividends based on his stockholding, and he donated this money to the Bill and Melinda Gates Foundation, to which he has reportedly donated over $25 billion to date, with the promise of much more to come.

Stockholders are interested in the way a company operates because they want to maximize the return on their investment. Thus, they watch the company and its managers closely to ensure that management is working diligently to increase the company's profitability.[10] Stockholders also want to ensure that managers are behaving ethically and not risking investors' capital by engaging in actions that could hurt the company's reputation. The fall of Enron from being one of the biggest and most profitable companies in the United States to declaring bankruptcy took less than one year after the illegal and unethical actions of its top managers came to light. The Enron tragedy was brought about by a handful of greedy top managers who abused their positions of trust. It has been estimated that Enron's collapse, by precipitating the crash of the stock market, caused the average U.S. household to lose over $66,000 of its hard-earned savings as trillions of dollars were wiped off the value of the stock of publicly traded U.S. companies.

Managers

Managers are a vital stakeholder group because they are responsible for using a company's financial capital and human resources to increase its performance and thus its stock price.[11] Managers have a claim on an organization because they bring to it their skills, expertise, and experience. They have the right to expect a good return or reward by investing their human capital to improve a company's performance. Such rewards include good salaries and benefits, the prospect of promotion and a career, and stock options and bonuses tied to company performance.

Managers are the stakeholder group that bears the responsibility to decide which goals an organization should pursue to most benefit stakeholders and how to make the most efficient use of resources to achieve those goals. In making such decisions, managers are frequently in the position of having to juggle the interests of different stakeholders, including themselves.[12] These decisions are sometimes very difficult and challenge managers to uphold ethical values because in some cases decisions that benefit some stakeholder groups (managers and stockholders) harm other groups (individual workers and local communities). For example, in economic downturns or when a company experiences performance shortfalls, layoffs may help to cut costs (thus benefiting shareholders) at the expense of the employees laid off. Many U.S. managers have recently been faced with this very difficult decision. On average about 1.6 million employees out of a total labor force of 140 million are affected by mass layoffs each year in the United States;[13] a million jobs from the United States, Europe, and Japan were outsourced to Asia in the year ending May 2006.[14] Layoff decisions are always difficult, as they not only take a heavy toll on workers, their families, and local communities but also mean the loss of the contributions of valued employees to an organization. Whenever decisions such as these are made—benefiting some groups at the expense of others—ethics come into play.

As we discussed in Chapter 1, managers must be motivated and given incentives to work hard in the interests of stockholders. Their behavior must also be scrutinized to ensure they do not behave illegally or unethically, pursuing goals that threaten stockholders and the company's interests.[15] Unfortunately, we have seen in the 2000s how easy it is for top managers to find ways to ruthlessly pursue their self-interest at the expense of stockholders and employees because laws and regulations were not strong enough to force them to behave ethically.

In a nutshell, the problem has been that in many companies corrupt managers focus not on building the company's capital and stockholders' wealth but on maximizing their own *personal capital and wealth*. In an effort to prevent future scandals the Securities and Exchange Commission (SEC), the government's top business watchdog, began to rework the rules governing a company's relationship with its auditor, as well as regulations concerning stock options, and to increase the power of outside directors to scrutinize a CEO. The SEC's goal is to turn many actions that were previously classified as only unethical into illegal behavior in the near future. For example, companies are now forced to reveal to stockholders the value of the stock options they give their top executives and directors, and when they give them these options, and this shows how much such payments reduce company profits. Managers and directors can now be prosecuted if they disguise or try to hide these payments. In 2006, SEC chairman Christopher Cox proposed new rules that would require that companies disclose myriad details of executive compensation packages.

Indeed, many experts are arguing that the rewards given to top managers, particularly the CEO and COO, have grown out of control in the 2000s. Top managers are today's "aristocrats," and through their ability to influence the board of directors and raise their own pay, they have amassed personal fortunes worth hundreds of millions of dollars. For example, according to a study by the Federal Reserve, U.S. CEO salaries have ballooned to more than 170 times the average worker's pay, up from 40 times in the 1970s—a staggering amount. Michael Eisner, CEO of Disney, received over $1 billion in Disney stock options. Jack Welch, the former CEO of General Electric and one of the most admired managers in the United States, received more than $500 million in GE stock options as a reward for his services. On his retirement he was also awarded $2.5 million in annual perks ranging from round-the-clock access to a corporate jet to free dry cleaning. When this information was revealed to the press, Welch quickly agreed to pay GE $2 million for these services.

Is it ethical for top managers to receive such vast amounts of money from their companies? Do they really earn it? Remember, this money could have gone to shareholders in the form of dividends. It could also have gone to reduce the huge salary gap between those at the top and those at the bottom of the hierarchy. Many people argue that the growing disparity between the rewards given to CEOs and to other employees is unethical and should be regulated. CEO pay has become too high because CEOs are the people who set and control one another's salaries and bonuses! They can do this because they sit on the boards of other companies, as outside directors, and thus can control the salaries and stock options paid to other CEOs. As the example of Bernie Ebbers at World-Com, discussed earlier, suggests, when a CEO can control and select many of the outside directors, the CEO can abuse his or her power. Others argue that because top managers play an important role in building a company's capital and wealth, they deserve a significant share of its profits. Jack Welch, for example, deserved his $500 million because he created hundreds of billions of dollars in stockholder wealth. On the other hand, since Bob Nardelli became CEO of Home Depot in 2002, he has recevied over $200 million in salary, bonus, stock, stock options, and other perks while Home Depot's total return to shareholders, a key benchmark of corporate performance, has fallen by 13% although its stock price has recovered. The debate over how much money CEOs and other top managers should be paid is currently raging. The issue of compensation is but one of the many issues facing nonprofits as well, as discussed in the following "Ethics in Action."

Ethics in Action

The Ethics of Some Nonprofits Are Not So Good

The many ethics scandals that have plagued companies in the 2000s might suggest that the issue of ethics is important only for profit-seeking companies, but this would be untrue. There are 1.8 million private nonprofit charitable and philanthropic organizations in the United States, and charges that their managers have acted in unethical and even illegal ways have grown in the 2000s. For example, many states and the federal government are investigating the huge salaries that the top executives of charitable institutions earn. One impetus for this was the revelation that the NYSE, which is classified as a charitable organization, paid its disgraced top executive Richard A. Grasso over $187 million in pension benefits. It turns out that over 200 nonprofits pay their top executives more than $1 million a year in salary and that the boards of trustees or directors of many of these organizations also enjoy lavish perks and compensation for attendance at board meetings. And, unlike for-profit companies, which are required by law to provide detailed reports of their operations to their shareholders, nonprofits do not have shareholders, so the laws governing disclosure are far weaker. As a result, the board and its top managers have considerable latitude to decide how they will spend a nonprofit's resources, and little oversight exists. To remedy this situation, many states and the federal government are considering new laws that would subject nonprofits to strict Sarbanes-Oxley-type regulations that force the disclosure of issues related to managerial compensation and financial integrity. There are also efforts in progress to strengthen the legal power of the IRS to oversee nonprofits' expenditures so that it has more scope to examine the way these organizations spend their resources on managerial and director compensation and perks.

Experts hope that the introduction of new rules and regulations to monitor and oversee how nonprofits spend their funds will result in much more value being created from the funds given by donors. After all, every cent that is spent just administering a nonprofit is a cent not being used to help the people (or cause) for whom the money was intended. Major ethical issues are involved because some badly run charities spend 70 cents of every dollar on administration costs! And recently charges have been leveled against charities such as the Red Cross for mishandling the hundreds of millions of dollars they received in donations after Hurricane Katrina struck. To compound this problem, there have also been charges that major insurance companies have been tardy in paying the claims of customers who lost their homes in the hurricane. By June 2006, although $38 billion in claims had been submitted, only $22 billion had been paid to claimants.

American Red Cross Disaster Relief workers distribute food to Hurricane Katrina refugees in Miami. Recently, charges have been leveled against charities such as the Red Cross for mishandling the hundreds of millions of dollars in donations after Hurricane Katrina.

Thousands of families are fighting insurance companies that argue that they are not liable because the damage and destruction was brought about by flooding, not by the storm, and flooding is not covered in a regular homeowner's policy. Clearly, the directors and managers of all organizations need to carefully consider the ethical issues involved in their decision making.

Employees

A company's employees are the hundreds of thousands of people who work in its various departments and functions, such as research, sales, and manufacturing. Employees expect that they will receive rewards consistent with their performance. One principle way that a company can act ethically toward employees and meet their expectations is by creating an occupational structure that fairly and equitably rewards employees for their contributions. Companies, for example, need to develop recruitment, training, performance appraisal, and reward systems that do not discriminate between employees and that employees believe are fair.

Suppliers and Distributors

No company operates alone. Every company is in a network of relationships with other companies that supply it with the inputs (e.g., raw materials, components, contract labor, and clients) that it needs to operate. It also depends on intermediaries such as wholesalers and retailers to distribute its products to the final customer. Suppliers expect to be paid fairly and promptly for their inputs; distributors expect to receive quality products at agreed-upon prices.

Once again, many ethical issues arise in the way companies contract and interact with their suppliers and distributors. Important issues concerning how and when payments are to be made or product quality specifications are governed by the terms of the legal contracts a company signs with its suppliers and distributors. Many other issues are dependent on business ethics. For example, numerous products sold in U.S. stores have been outsourced to countries that do not have U.S.-style regulations and laws to protect the workers who make these products. All companies must take an ethical position on the way they obtain and make the products they sell. Commonly this stance is published on the company's Web site. Table 4.1 presents part of the Gap's statement on its approach to global ethics (www.gapinc.com).

Customers

Customers are often regarded as the most critical stakeholder group since if a company cannot attract them to buy its products, it cannot stay in business. Thus, managers and employees must work to increase efficiency and effectiveness in order to create loyal customers and attract new ones. They do so by selling customers quality products at a fair price and providing good after-sales service. They can also strive to improve their products over time and provide guarantees to customers about the integrity of their products, as Whole Foods does. The way in which Whole Food views its responsbilities to stakeholders and its approach to ethical business is depticed in Figure 4.2.

Many laws exist that protect customers from companies that attempt to provide dangerous or shoddy products. Laws exist that allow customers to sue a company whose product causes them injury or harm, such as a defective tire or vehicle. Other laws force companies to clearly disclose the interest rates they charge on purchases—an important hidden cost that customers frequently do not factor into their purchase decisions. Every year thousands of companies are

Table 4.1
Some Principles from the Gap's Code of Vendor Conduct

As a condition of doing business with Gap Inc., each and every factory must comply with this Code of Vendor Conduct. Gap Inc. will continue to develop monitoring systems to assess and ensure compliance. If Gap Inc. determines that any factory has violated this Code, Gap Inc. may either terminate its business relationship or require the factory to implement a corrective action plan. If corrective action is advised but not taken, Gap Inc. will suspend placement of future orders and may terminate current production.

I. General Principles
Factories that produce goods for Gap Inc. shall operate in full compliance with the laws of their respective countries and with all other applicable laws, rules and regulations.

II. Environment
Factories must comply with all applicable environmental laws and regulations. Where such requirements are less stringent than Gap Inc.'s own, factories are encouraged to meet the standards outlined in Gap Inc.'s statement of environmental principles.

III. Discrimination
Factories shall employ workers on the basis of their ability to do the job, without regard to race, color, gender, nationality, religion, age, maternity or marital status.

IV. Forced Labor
Factories shall not use any prison, indentured or forced labor.

V. Child Labor
Factories shall employ only workers who meet the applicable minimum legal age requirement or are at least 14 years of age, whichever is greater. Factories must also comply with all other applicable child labor laws. Factories are encouraged to develop lawful workplace apprenticeship programs for the educational benefit of their workers, provided that all participants meet both Gap Inc.'s minimum age standard of 14 and the minimum legal age requirement.

VI. Wages & Hours
Factories shall set working hours, wages and overtime pay in compliance with all applicable laws. Workers shall be paid at least the minimum legal wage or a wage that meets local industry standards, whichever is greater. While it is understood that overtime is often required in garment production, factories shall carry out operations in ways that limit overtime to a level that ensures humane and productive working conditions.

prosecuted for breaking these laws, so "buyer beware" is an important rule customers must follow when buying goods and services.

Community, Society, and Nation

The effects of the decisions made by companies and their managers permeate all aspects of the communities, societies, and nations in which they operate. *Community* refers to physical locations like towns or cities or to social milieus like ethnic neighborhoods in which companies are located. A community provides a company with the physical and social infrastructure that allows it to operate; its

Figure 4.2
Whole Food Market's Stakeholder Approach to Ethical Business

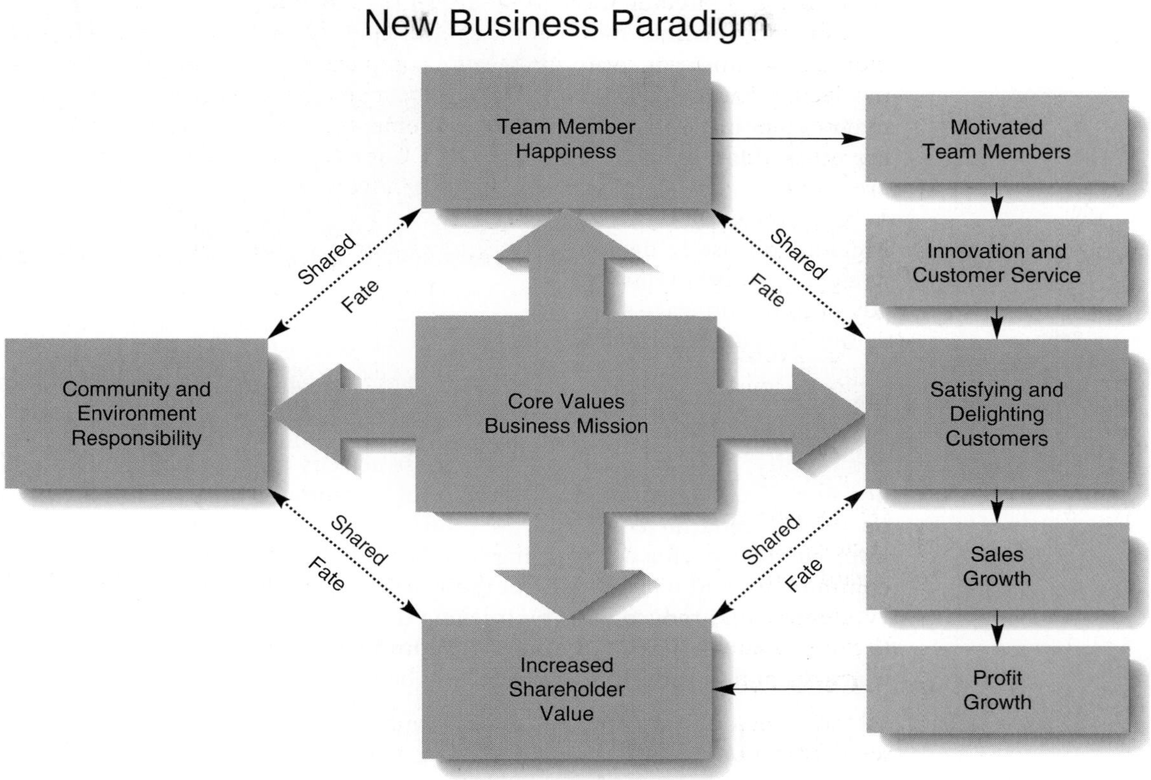

New Business Paradigm

Source: www.wholefoodsmarket.com.

utilities and labor force; the homes in which its managers and employees live; the schools, colleges, and hospitals that service their needs; and so on.

Through the salaries, wages, and taxes it pays, a company contributes to the economy of the town or region and often determines whether the community prospers or declines. Similarly, a company affects the prosperity of a society and a nation and, to the degree that a company is involved in global trade, all the countries it operates in and thus the prosperity of the global economy. We have already discussed the many issues surrounding global outsourcing and the loss of jobs in the United States, for example.

Although the individual effects of the way each McDonald's restaurant operates might be small, for instance, the combined effects of the way all McDonald's and other fast-food companies do business are enormous. In the United States alone, over 500,000 people work in the fast-food industry, and many thousands of suppliers like farmers, paper cup manufacturers, builders, and so on, depend on it for their livelihood. Small wonder then that the ethics of the fast-food business are scrutinized closely. The industry is the major lobbyer against attempts to raise the national minimum wage, which in 2006 was $5.15 an hour (a figure that has not changed since 1998), for example, because a higher minimum wage would substantially increase its operating costs. However, responding to protests about chickens raised in cages where they cannot move their wings, McDonald's—the largest egg buyer in the United States—issued new ethical guidelines concerning cage size and related matters that its egg suppliers must abide by if they are to retain its business. What ethical rules does McDonald's use to decide its stance toward minimum pay or minimum cage size?

In 2001 McDonald's announced new standards that would require egg suppliers to improve the conditions under which chickens are housed and treated. Since McDonald's is an important customer, suppliers are

Business ethics are also important because the failure of companies can have catastrophic effects on a community; a general decline in business activity affects a whole nation. The decision of a large company to pull out of a community, for example, can seriously threaten the community's future. Some companies may attempt to improve their profits by engaging in actions that, although not illegal, can hurt communities and nations. One of these actions is pollution. For example, many U.S. companies reduce costs by trucking their waste to Mexico, where it is legal to dump waste in the Rio Grande. The dumping pollutes the river from the Mexican side, and the effects are increasingly being felt on the U.S. side too.

Rules for Ethical Decision Making

When a stakeholder perspective is taken, questions on company ethics abound.[16] What is the appropriate way to manage the claims of all stakeholders? Company decisions that favor one group of stakeholders, for example, are likely to harm the interests of others.[17] High prices to customers may lead to high returns to shareholders and high salaries for managers in the short run. If in the long run customers turn to companies that offer lower-cost products, however, the result may be declining sales, laid-off employees, and the decline of the communities that support the high-price company's business activity.

When companies act ethically, their stakeholders support them. For example, banks are willing to supply them with new capital, they attract highly qualified job applicants, and new customers are drawn to their products. Thus ethical companies grow and expand over time, and all their stakeholders benefit. The result of unethical behavior is the loss of reputation and resources, shareholders who sell their shares, skilled managers and employees who leave the company, and customers who turn to the products of more reputable companies.

When making business decisions, managers must take the claims of all stakeholders into consideration.[18] To help themselves and employees make ethical decisions and behave in ways that benefit their stakeholders, managers can use four ethical rules or principles to analyze the effects of their business decisions on stakeholders: the *utilitarian, moral rights, justice,* and *practical* rules (Figure 4.3).[19] These rules are useful guidelines that help managers decide on the appropriate way to behave in situations where it is necessary to balance a company's self-interest against the interests of its stakeholders. Remember, the right choices will lead resources to be used where they can create the most value. If all companies make the right choices, all stakeholders will benefit in the long run.[20]

utilitarian rule An ethical decision is a decision that produces the greatest good for the greatest number of people.

UTILITARIAN RULE The **utilitarian rule** is that an ethical decision is a decision that produces the greatest good for the greatest number of people. To decide which is the most ethical course of business action, managers should first consider how different possible courses of business action would benefit or harm different stakeholders. They should then choose the course of action that provides the most benefits, or conversely the one that does the least harm, to stakeholders.[21]

The ethical dilemma for managers is, How do you measure the benefits and harms that will be done to each stakeholder group? Moreover, how do you evaluate the rights of different stakeholder groups, and the relative importance of each group, in coming to a decision? Since stockholders are the owners of the company, shouldn't their claims be held above those of employees? For example, managers might be faced with a choice of using global outsourcing to reduce costs and lower prices to customers or continuing with high-cost production at home. A decision to use global outsourcing benefits shareholders and customers but will result in major layoffs that will harm employees and the communities in which they live. Typically, in a capitalist society, like the United States, the interests of shareholders are put above those of employees, so production will move abroad. This is commonly regarded as being an ethical

Figure   4.3
Four Ethical Rules

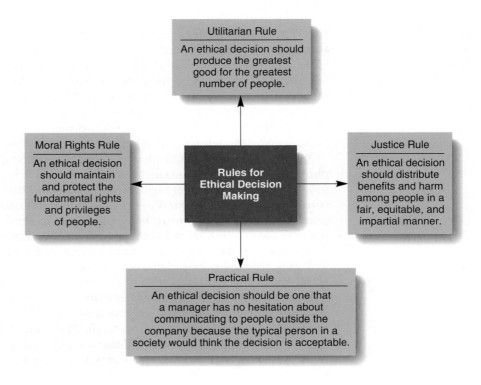

choice because in the long run the alternative, home production, might cause the business to collapse and go bankrupt, in which case greater harm will be done to all stakeholders.

moral rights rule An ethical decision is one that best maintains and protects the fundamental or inalienable rights and privileges of the people affected by it.

MORAL RIGHTS RULE   Under the moral rights rule, an ethical decision is a decision that best maintains and protects the fundamental or inalienable rights and privileges of the people affected by it. For example, ethical decisions protect people's rights to freedom, life and safety, property, privacy, free speech, and freedom of conscience. The adage "Do unto others as you would have them do unto you" is a moral rights principle that managers should use to decide which rights to uphold. Customers must also consider the rights of the companies and people who create the products they wish to consume (see Ethics in Actions box "Digital Piracy, Ethics, and Napster").

From a moral rights perspective, managers should compare and contrast different courses of business action on the basis of how each course will affect the rights of the company's different stakeholders. Managers should then choose the course of action that best protects and upholds the rights of *all* the stakeholders. For example, decisions that might result in significant harm to the safety or health of employees or customers would clearly be unethical choices.

The ethical dilemma for managers is that decisions that will protect the rights of some stakeholders often will hurt the rights of others. How should they choose which group to protect? For example, in deciding whether it is ethical to snoop on employees, or search them when they leave work to prevent theft, does an employee's right to privacy outweigh an organization's right to protect its property? Suppose a coworker is having personal problems and is coming in late and leaving early, placing you in the position of being forced to pick up the person's workload. Do you tell your boss even though you know this will probably get that person fired?

justice rule An ethical decision is a decision that distributes benefits and harms among people and groups in a fair, equitable, or impartial way.

JUSTICE RULE   The justice rule is that an ethical decision is a decision that distributes benefits and harms among people and groups in a fair, equitable, or impartial way. Managers should compare and contrast alternative courses of action based on the degree to which they will result in a fair or equitable distribution of outcomes for stakeholders. For example, employees who are similar in their level of skill, performance, or responsibility should receive the same kind of pay. The allocation of outcomes should not be based on differences such as gender, race, or religion.

The ethical dilemma for managers is to determine the fair rules and procedures for distributing outcomes to stakeholders. Managers must not give people they like bigger raises than they give to people they do not like, for example, or bend the rules to help their favorites. On the other hand, if employees want managers to act fairly toward them, then employees need to act fairly toward their companies and work hard and be loyal. Similarly, customers need to act fairly toward a company if they expect it to be fair to them—something people who illegally copy digital media should consider.

PRACTICAL RULE   Each of the above rules offers a different and complementary way of determining whether a decision or behavior is ethical, and all three rules should be used to sort out the ethics of a particular course of action. Ethical issues, as we just discussed, are seldom clear-cut, however, because the rights, interests, goals, and incentives of different stakeholders often conflict. For

practical rule An ethical decision is one that a manager has no reluctance about communicating to people outside the company because the typical person in a society would think it is acceptable.

this reason many experts on ethics add a fourth rule to determine whether a business decision is ethical: The **practical rule** is that an ethical decision is one that a manager has no hesitation or reluctance about communicating to people outside the company because the typical person in a society would think it is acceptable. A business decision is probably acceptable on ethical grounds if a manager can answer yes to each of these questions:

1.   Does my decision fall within the accepted *values* or *standards* that typically apply in business activity today?

2.   Am I willing to see the decision *communicated* to all people and groups *affected* by it—for example, by having it reported in newspapers or on television?

3.   Would the people with whom I have a *significant* personal relationship, such as family members, friends, or even managers in other organizations, *approve* of the decision?

Applying the practical rule to analyze a business decision ensures that managers are taking into account the interests of all stakeholders.[22] After applying this rule managers can judge if they have chosen to act in an ethical or unethical way and they must abide by the consequences. The following ethical insight, which describes the issues surrounding individuals copying digital content from the Internet, provides a good example to test these different ethical issues—what is the right or ethical thing to do in this situation?

Ethics in Action

Digital Piracy, Ethics, and Napster

Today, almost all written text, music, movies, and software are recorded in digital form and can be easily copied electronically and sent between personal computers through the Internet. Many sites on the Internet contain illegal copies of music, movies, and so on, that can be easily accessed and downloaded. Millions of people and companies have taken advantage of this to make illegal copies of music CDs, software programs, and DVDs. As a result, it has been estimated that over one-third of all CDs and cassettes recorded around the world were illegally produced and sold in the 2000s, and the music industry has lost tens of billions in sales revenues.[23]

As you can imagine, the managers of music and movie companies have been doing all they can to reduce illegal recording because it decreases their sales and profits. One enterprise that music company CEOs went after with a vengeance was Napster.[24] Shawn Fanning created Napster while he was an undergraduate student at Northeastern University. His roommate downloaded music from Internet sites using the MP3 format, which compresses digital files, making them faster to transmit and easier to store. As Fanning watched his roommate search the Internet for new material, he realized that it would be easy to create a software platform to help people easily locate and download digital music files stored in any PC that was logged into this platform. Fanning created the necessary software, and word of mouth did the rest; soon Napster was a phenomenon, and millions of people were swapping and downloading music.[25]

Managers in the music industry became desperate to stop this practice. The value of their companies' copyrights to songs and contracts with artists was being destroyed by this new technology that allowed pirating of their products. They sought legal injunctions against Napster to shut the company down, and since it was clearly violating copyright laws, the courts stopped Napster's operations. However, many other Internet sites then sprung up from which people can still download music and other digital media.

Illegal copying of digital files has taken a big bite out of CD and DVD sales, raising a number of legal and ethical questions.

The copying of digital material is illegal because it infringes on copyright laws that protect the rights of artists, authors, composers, and the companies that produce and distribute their work. Is this copying unethical? Is it an unacceptable or acceptable way to behave? Why are so many people doing it if it is illegal? The obvious answer is that people are doing it to pursue their own self-interest. Paying nothing for valuable digital media is attractive, and who, goes the argument, suffers anyway? Music companies have been making billions of dollars of profit out of music sales for decades. Songs may be the property of music stars like the Rolling Stones and Eminem, but these people are fabulously wealthy. Why shouldn't the average person benefit from digital technology? After all, the pleasure gained by hundreds of millions of people is more important than the harm done to only a few thousand musicians and a handful of music companies, so copying is not "really" unethical. It may be illegal, but it's not actually such a bad thing to do, is it?

Arguments like these may make people feel that their copying is doing no real harm to others. But what about the rights of artists and companies to profit from their property—the songs, books, and movies that result from their creative endeavors? The average person would not like it if a "poorer" person came along and said, "You don't need all those appliances, cars, and jewelry? I'll just help myself; you'll never miss it." Those who steal digital media not only are weakening the rights of musicians and writers to own property but also are weakening *their* rights to own property. Digital piracy is not a fair or equitable practice. And, although each person may argue that engaging in it doesn't have much of an effect since he or she is "only one person," if many people do it a major problem emerges.

To illustrate the problem, suppose that by 2010 about 80% of all music and movies are illegally copied rather than bought. What will musicians and music companies and movie stars and movie studios do? If these people and companies cannot protect their property and profit from it, then they are not going to make or sell digital products. Over time, music and movie companies will cease to operate. Creative people will find new ways to make money, or musicians will make music only for their own pleasure or in live concerts (where recording devices are not permitted!). The result will be a loss to everyone because no new music or movies will be made, and the world will become a less interesting place to live in.

It is no easy matter to determine what is a fair or equitable division of the value and profit in a particular business activity. Music companies have no desire to see their revenues fall because potential customers are "profiting" from their ability to make illegal copies of CDs. Music companies have a responsibility to make profits so that they can reward their stockholders, pay the musicians who receive royalties on their record sales, and pay their employees salaries. Of course, they also have a responsibility toward customers—they should charge only a fair price for their CDs. In fact, since Apple opened its iTunes store in 2001 and other online music stores followed suit, tens of millions of songs have been legally downloaded and paid for, something that indicates that millions of customers do accept their obligation to pay a fair price for the products they receive. At the same time, artists and companies also recognize they have to provide first-class content if customers are going to continue to purchase, rather than copy, digital content.

Why Should Managers Behave Ethically?

Why is it so important that managers, and people in general, should act ethically and temper their pursuit of self-interest by considering the effects of their actions on others? The answer is that the relentless pursuit of self-interest can lead to a collective disaster when one or more people start to profit from being unethical because this encourages other people to act in the same way.[26] Quickly, more and more people jump onto the bandwagon, and soon everybody is trying to manipulate the situation in the way that best serves their personal ends with no regard for the effects of their action on others. The situation brought about by Napster is an example of how what is called the "tragedy of the commons" works.

Suppose that in an agricultural community there is common land that everybody has an equal right to use. Pursuing self-interest, each farmer acts to make the maximum use of the free resource by grazing his or her own cattle and sheep. Collectively, all the farmers overgraze the land, which quickly becomes worn out. Then a strong wind blows away the exposed topsoil so tragically, the common land is destroyed. The pursuit of individual self-interest with no consideration for societal interests leads to disaster for each individual and for the whole society because scarce resources are destroyed.[27] In the Napster case the tragedy that would result if all people were to steal digital media would be the disappearance of music, movie, and book companies as creative people decided there was no point in their working hard to produce original songs, stories, and so on.

We can look at the effects of unethical behavior on business activity in another way. Suppose companies and their managers operate in an unethical society, meaning one in which stakeholders routinely try to cheat and defraud one another. If stakeholders expect each other to cheat, how long will it take them to negotiate the purchase and shipment of products? When they do not trust each other, stakeholders will probably spend hours bargaining over fair prices, and this is a largely unproductive activity that reduces efficiency and effectiveness.[28] All the time and effort that could be spent improving product quality or customer service is being lost because it is spent on negotiating and bargaining. Thus, unethical behavior ruins business commerce, and society has a lower standard of living because fewer goods and services are produced, as Figure 4.4 illustrates.

On the other hand, suppose companies and their managers operate in an ethical society, meaning that stakeholders believe they are dealing with others who are basically moral and honest. In this society stakeholders have a greater reason to trust others. Trust is the willingness of one person or group to have faith or confidence in the goodwill of another person, even though this puts them at risk (because the other might act in a deceitful way). When trust exists, stakeholders are more likely to signal their good intentions by cooperating and providing information that makes it easier to exchange and price goods and services. When one person acts in a trustworthy way, this encourages others to act in the same way. Over time. as greater trust between stakeholders develops,

trust The willingness of one person or group to have faith or confidence in the goodwill of another person, even though this puts them at risk

Figure 4.4
Some Effects of Ethical and Unethical Behavior

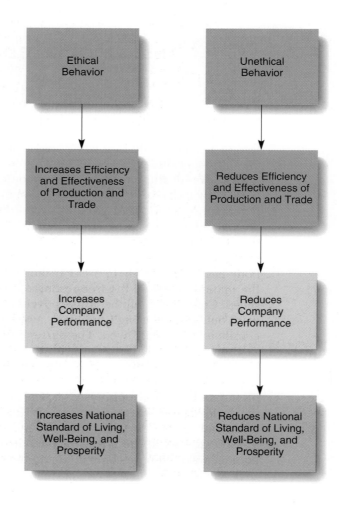

they can work together more efficiently and effectively and this raises company performance (see Figure 4.4). As people see the positive results of acting in an honest way, ethical behavior becomes a valued social norm and society in general becomes increasingly ethical.

As noted in Chapter 1, a major responsibility of managers is to protect and nurture the resources under their control. Any organizational stakeholders—managers, workers, stockholders, suppliers—who advance their own interests by behaving unethically toward other stakeholders, either by taking resources or by denying resources to others, waste collective resources. If other individuals or groups copy the behavior of the unethical stakeholder ("If he can do it, we can do it, too"), the rate at which collective resources are misused increases, and eventually there are few resources available to produce goods and services. Unethical behavior that goes unpunished creates incentives for people to put their unbridled self-interests above the rights of others.[29] When this happens, the benefits that people reap from joining together in organizations disappear very quickly.

An important safeguard against unethical behavior is the potential for loss of reputation.[30] **Reputation,** the esteem or high repute that people or organizations gain when they behave ethically, is an important asset. Stakeholders have valuable reputations that they must protect because their ability to earn a living and obtain resources in the long run depends on the way they behave on a day-to-day, week-to-week, and month-to-month basis.

If a manager misuses resources and other parties regard that behavior as being at odds with acceptable standards, the manager's reputation will suffer. Behaving unethically in the short run can have serious long-term consequences. A manager who has a poor reputation will have difficulty finding employment with other companies. Stockholders who see managers behaving unethically may refuse to invest in their companies, and this will decrease the stock price, undermine the companies' reputations, and ultimately put the managers' jobs at risk.[31]

All stakeholders have reputations to lose. Suppliers who provide shoddy inputs find that organizations learn over time not to deal with them, and eventually they go out of business. Powerful customers who demand ridiculously low prices find that their suppliers become less willing to deal with them, and resources ultimately become harder for them to obtain. Workers who shirk responsibilities on the job find it hard to get new jobs when they are fired. In general, if a manager or company is known for being unethical, other stakeholders are likely to view that individual or organization with suspicion and hostility, and the reputation of each will be poor. But if a manager or company is known for ethical business practices, each will develop a good reputation.[32]

In summary, in a complex, diverse society, stakeholders, and people in general, need to recognize they are all part of a larger social group. The way in which they make decisions and act not only affects them personally but also affects the lives of many other people. The problem is that for some people their daily struggle to survive and succeed or their total disregard for the rights of others can lead them to lose that "bigger" connection to other people. We can see our relationships to our families and friends, to our school, church, and so on. But we always need to go further and keep in mind the effects of our actions on other people—people who will be judging our actions and whom we might harm by acting unethically. Our moral scruples are like that "other person" but are inside our heads.

reputation The esteem or high repute that individuals or organizations gain when they behave ethically.

Ethics and Social Responsibility

Some companies, like Glaxo Smith Klein, Bristol Myers Squib, Prudential Insurance, Whole Foods, and Blue Cross–Blue Shield, are well-known for their ethical business practices.[33] Other companies, such as Arthur Andersen and Enron, which are now out of business, or WorldCom, Tyco, Qwest, and Adelphia, which have been totally restructured, repeatedly engaged in unethical and illegal business activities. What explains such differences between the ethics of these companies and their managers?

There are four main determinants of differences in ethics between people, employees, companies, and countries: *societal* ethics, *occupational* ethics, *individual* ethics, and *organizational* ethics, especially the ethics of a company's top managers.[34] (See Figure 4.5.)

Societal Ethics

societal ethics
Standards that govern how members of a society should deal with one another in matters involving issues such as fairness, justice, poverty, and the rights of the individual.

Societal ethics are standards that govern how members of a society should deal with one another in matters involving issues such as fairness, justice, poverty, and the rights of the individual. Societal ethics emanate from a society's laws, customs and practices and from the unwritten values and norms that influence how people interact with each other. People in a particular country may automatically behave ethically because they have *internalized* (i.e., made a part of their morals) certain values, beliefs, and norms that specify how they should behave when confronted with an ethical dilemma.

Figure 4.5
Sources of Ethics

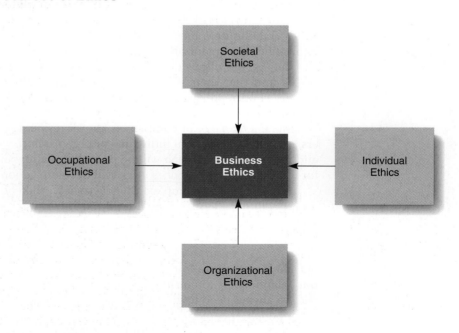

Societal ethics vary among societies. Countries like Germany, Japan, Sweden, and Switzerland are well known as being some of the most ethical countries in the world, with strong values about social order and the need to create a society that protects the welfare of all groups of their citizens. In other countries the situation is very different. In many economically poor countries bribery is standard practice to get things done—such as getting a telephone installed or a contract awarded. In the United States and other economically advanced countries, bribery is considered unethical and has been made illegal.

IBM experienced the problem of differences in ethical standards in its Argentinean division. Managers there became involved in an unethical scheme to secure a $250 million contract for IBM to provide and service the computers of one of Argentina's largest state-owned banks. After $6 million was paid to bribe the bank executives who agreed to give IBM the contract, IBM announced that it had fired the three top managers of its Argentine division. According to IBM, transactions like this, though unethical by IBM's standards, are not necessarily illegal under Argentine law. The Argentine managers were fired, however, for failing to follow IBM's organizational rules, which preclude the payment of bribes to obtain contracts in foreign countries. Moreover, the payment of bribes violates the U.S. *Foreign Corrupt Practices Act,* which forbids payment of bribes by U.S. companies to secure contracts abroad, makes companies liable for the actions of their foreign managers, and allows companies found in violation to be prosecuted in the United States. By firing the managers, IBM signaled that it would not tolerate unethical behavior by any of its employees, and it continues today to take a rigorous stance toward ethical issues.

Countries also differ widely in their beliefs about appropriate treatment for their employees. In general, the poorer a country is, the more likely employees are to be treated with little regard. One issue of particular concern on a global level is whether it is ethical to use child labor, as discussed in the following "Ethics in Action."

Ethics in Action

Is It Right to Use Child Labor?

In recent years, the number of U.S. companies that buy their products from low-cost foreign suppliers has been growing, and concern about the ethics associated with employing young children in factories has been increasing. In Pakistan, children as young as age six work long hours in deplorable conditions to make rugs and carpets for export to Western countries. Children in poor countries throughout Africa, Asia, and South America work in similar conditions. Is it ethical to employ children in factories, and should U.S. companies buy and sell products made by these children?

Opinions about the ethics of child labor vary widely. Robert Reich, an economist and secretary of labor in the first Clinton administration, believes that the practice is totally reprehensible and should be outlawed on a global level. Another view, championed by *The Economist* magazine, is that, while nobody wants to see children employed in factories, citizens of rich countries need to recognize that in poor countries children are often a family's only breadwinners. Thus, denying children employment would cause whole families to suffer, and one wrong (child labor) might produce a greater wrong (poverty). Instead, *The Economist* favors regulating the conditions under which children are employed and hopes that over time, as poor countries become richer, the need for child employment will disappear.

Many U.S. retailers typically buy their clo-

Afghan boys weave a rug while their father stands nearby inside their home in Kabul, Afghanistan. Afghan rug makers contract children to make rugs, paying their families roughly 8 U.S. dollars a yard. To make one 18-foot rug takes approximately one month, and the children often work in shifts around their schooling or other household duties.

thing from low-cost foreign suppliers, and managers in these companies have had to take their own ethical stance on child labor. Managers in Wal-Mart, Target, JCPenney, and Gap Inc. (see Table 4.1) have followed U.S. standards and rules and have policies dictating that their foreign suppliers not employ child labor. They also vow to sever ties with any foreign supplier found to be in violation of this standard.

Apparently, however, retailers differ widely in the way they choose to enforce such policies. It has been estimated that more than 300,000 children under age 14 are being employed in garment factories in Guatemala, a popular low-cost location for clothing manufacturers that supply the U.S. market. These children frequently work more than 60 hours a week and often are paid less than $3 a day, close to the minimum wage in Guatemala. Many U.S. retailers do not check up on their foreign suppliers. Clearly, if U.S. retailers are to be true to their ethical stance on this troubling issue, they cannot ignore the fact that they are buying clothing made by children and they must do more to regulate the conditions under which these children work.

Occupational Ethics

occupational ethics
Standards that govern how members of a profession, trade, or craft should conduct themselves when performing work-related activities.

Occupational ethics are standards that govern how members of a profession, trade, or craft should conduct themselves when performing work-related activities.[35] For example, medical ethics govern the way doctors and nurses should treat their patients. Doctors are expected to perform only necessary medical procedures and to act in the patient's interest and not in their own. The ethics of scientific research require that scientists conduct their experiments and present their findings in ways that ensure the validity of their conclusions. Like society at large, most professional groups can impose punishments for violations of ethical standards.[36] Doctors and lawyers can be prevented from practicing their professions if they disregard professional ethics and put their own interests first.

Within an organization, occupational rules and norms often govern how employees such as lawyers, researchers, and accountants should make decisions to further stakeholder interests. Employees internalize the rules and norms of their occupational group (just as they do those of society) and often follow them automatically when deciding how to behave. Because most people tend to follow established rules of behavior, people often take ethics for granted. However, when occupational ethics are violated, such as when scientists fabricate data to disguise the harmful effects of products, ethical issues come to the forefront of attention. In 2005, for example, researchers in Korea were found to have fabricated data that showed they had successfully cloned a dog. On the other hand, top researchers in pharmaceutical companies have been accused of deliberately hiding research evidence that revealed the harmful effects of products such as Merck's Vioxx heart drug and Guidant's heart pacemaker, so doctors and patients could not make informed medical treatment decisions. Table 4.2 lists some failures or lapses in professional ethics according to type of functional manager.

Table 4.2
Some Failures in Professional Ethics

For manufacturing and materials management managers:
- Releasing products that are not of a consistent quality because of defective inputs.
- Producing batches of the product that may be dangerous or defective and harm customers.
- Compromising workplace health and safety to reduce costs (e.g., to maximize output, employees are not given adequate training to maintain and service machinery and equipment).

For sales and marketing managers:
- Knowingly making unsubstantiated product claims.
- Engaging in sales campaigns that use covert persuasive or subliminal advertising to create customer need for the product.
- Marketing to target groups such as the elderly, minorities, or children to build demand for a product.
- Having ongoing campaigns of unsolicited junk mail, spam, door-to-door, or telephone selling.

For accounting and finance managers:
- Engaging in misleading financial analysis involving creative accounting or "cooking the books" to hide salient facts.
- Authorizing excessive expenses and perks to managers, customers, and suppliers.
- Hiding the level and amount of top-management and director compensation.

For human resource managers:
- Failing to act fairly, objectively, and in a uniform way toward different employees or kinds of employees because of personal factors such as personality and beliefs.
- Excessively encroaching on employee privacy through non-job-related surveillance or personality, ability, and drug testing.
- Failing to respond to employee observations and concerns surrounding health and safety violations, hostile workplace issues, or inappropriate or even illegal behavior by managers or employees.

Individual Ethics

individual ethics
Personal standards and values that determine how people view their responsibilities to others and how they should act in situations when their own self-interests are at stake.

Individual ethics are personal standards and values that determine how people view their responsibilities to other people and groups and thus how they should act in situations when their own self-interests are at stake.[37] Sources of individual ethics include the influence of one's family, peers, and upbringing in general. The experiences gained over a lifetime—through membership in social institutions such as schools and religions, for example—also contribute to the development of the personal standards and values that a person uses to evaluate a situation and decide what is the morally right or wrong way to behave. However, suppose you are the son or daughter of a mobster and your upbringing and education take place in an organized-crime context; this affects the way you evaluate a situation. You may come to believe that it is ethical to do anything and perform any act, up to and including murder, if it benefits your family or friends. These are your ethics. They are obviously not the ethics of the wider society and so are subject to sanction. In a similar way, managers and employees in an organization may come to believe that actions they take to promote or protect their organization are more important than any harm these actions may cause to other stakeholders. So they behave unethically or illegally, and when this is discovered, they also are sanctioned.

In general, many decisions or behaviors that one person finds unethical, such as using animals for cosmetics testing, may be acceptable to another person. If decisions or behaviors are not illegal, individuals may agree to disagree about their ethical beliefs, or they may try to impose their own beliefs on other people and make those ethical beliefs the law. In all cases, however, people should develop and follow the ethical criteria described earlier to balance their self-interests against those of others when determining how they should behave in a particular situation.

Organizational Ethics

organizational ethics
The guiding practices and beliefs through which a particular company and its managers view their responsibility toward their stakeholders.

Organizational ethics are the guiding practices and beliefs through which a particular company and its managers view their responsibility toward their stakeholders. The individual ethics of a company's founders and top managers are especially important in shaping the organization's code of ethics. Organizations whose founders had a vital role in creating a highly ethical code of organizational behavior include UPS, Procter & Gamble, Johnson & Johnson, and

Former Enron Corp Chief Financial Officer Andrew Fastow (center) is escorted by U.S. marshals as Fastow leaves court in Houston March 7, 2006, after his first day of testimony against former bosses Ken Lay and Jeff Skilling.

the Prudential Insurance Company. Johnson & Johnson's code of ethics—its credo—reflects a well-developed concern for its stakeholders (see Figure 4.7

on page 158). Company credos, such as that of Johnson & Johnson, are meant to deter self-interested, unethical behavior; to demonstrate to managers and employees that a company will not tolerate people who, because of their own poor ethics, put their personal interests above the interests of other organizational stakeholders and ignore the harm that they are inflicting on others; and to demonstrate that those who act unethically will be punished.

Managers or workers may behave unethically if they feel pressured to do so by the situation they are in and by unethical top managers. People typically confront ethical issues when weighing their personal interests against the effects of their actions on others. Suppose a manager knows that promotion to vice president is likely if she can secure a $100 million contract but getting the contract requires bribing the contract giver with $1 million. The manager reasons that performing this act will ensure her career and future, and what harm would it do anyway? Bribery is common, and she knows that even if she decides not to pay the million, somebody else surely will. So what to do? Research seems to suggest that people who realize they have most at stake in a career sense or a monetary sense are the ones most likely to act unethically. And it is exactly in this situation that a strong code of organizational ethics can help people behave in the right or appropriate way. *The Wall Street Journal*'s detailed code of ethics (see http://nytco.com/business-ethics.html), for example, was crafted by its editors to ensure the integrity and honesty of its journalists as they report sensitive information.

If a company's top managers consistently endorse the ethical principles in its corporate credo, they can prevent employees from going astray. Employees are much more likely to act unethically when a credo does not exist or is disregarded. Arthur Andersen, for example, did not follow its credo at all; its unscrupulous partners ordered middle managers to shred records that showed evidence of their wrongdoing. Although the middle managers knew this was wrong, they followed the orders because they responded to the personal power and status of the partners and not the company's code of ethics. They were afraid they would lose their jobs if they did not behave unethically, but their actions still cost them their jobs.

Top managers play a crucial role in determining a company's ethics. It is clearly important, then, that when making appointment decisions, the board of directors should scrutinize the reputations and ethical records of top managers. It is the responsibility of the board to decide whether a prospective CEO has the maturity, experience, and integrity needed to head a company and be entrusted with the capital and wealth of the organization, on which the fate of all its stakeholders depends. In the 2000s it was disclosed that the top managers of several major companies did not have the kinds of degrees or experience they had claimed on their résumés and that they had acted unethically to get their current jobs. For example, the former CEO of RadioShack claimed degrees he had not received.

Clearly, a track record of success is not enough to decide whether a top manager is capable of moral decision making, for a manager might have achieved this success through unethical or illegal means. It is important to investigate prospective top managers and examine their credentials. While the best predictor of future behavior is often past behavior, the board of directors needs to be on guard against unprincipled executives who use unethical means to rise to the top of the organizational hierarchy. For this reason it is necessary that a company's directors continuously monitor the behavior of top executives. In the 2000s this increased scrutiny has led to the dismissal of many top executives for breaking ethical rules concerning issues such as excessive personal loans, stock options, inflated expense accounts, and even sexual misconduct as the following "Ethics in Action" discusses.

Ethics in Action

Habitat for Humanity Has to Rebuild Goodwill

Habitat for Humanity is the 20th-largest U.S. charity, and its mission is to build cost-effective, modest new homes for needy families, who repay the charity by helping to build new homes for other families and by repaying low-interest-rate mortgages. Founded decades ago by Millard and Linda Fuller, it receives over $1 billion in donations a year. In 2004, a scandal struck the charity when Millard Fuller

Habitat's board of directors brought in former Walt Disney and Best Buy executive Jonathan Reckford, pictured here, as its new CEO to "clean house."

was accused of sexually harassing a female employee. So much bad press and organizational turmoil was caused by this event, which was denied by Fuller, that Habitat's board of directors decided to oust Fuller as CEO, even though the board's investigation failed to substantiate the charges. One main reason for the ousting was that a charity's reputation is a major factor that determines how much donors contribute to it, and the board was convinced that only a new leader could help Habitat reestablish its good name. A second, reason, however, was that in the 2000s the efficiency and effectiveness of nonprofits have been questioned, and many analysts believe that nonprofits need to introduce new management techniques in order to improve their level of performance. Indeed, one study estimated that nonprofits could save $100 billion by using such techniques as total quality management and benchmarking, which involve an organization's imitating a company that excels in performing some functional activity.[38]

So Habitat's board of directors searched for a new CEO who could simultaneously help the organization rebuild its reputation and improve its performance, The person they chose was Johnathan Reckford, an ex-Walt Disney and Best Buy executive who, having made his personal fortune, had retired from business and was devoting himself to good works. Reckford relished the challenge of using his management skills to find better ways to use Habitat's $1 billion in donations and to attract more donors, including companies such as Whirlpool, which donates home appliances, and Owens Corning, which donates home insulation, free of charge for all the houses Habitat builds.

Quickly Reckford began to introduce best-practice techniques. For example, modeling companies like Dell and Wal-Mart that use their huge buying power to lower the costs of their inputs, he emphasized the need for "scale" or volume purchasing of building products to lower costs. He introduced new kinds of output controls to provide detailed feedback on vital aspects of Habitat's performance, such as the number of new houses it built in different regions and countries and the time and cost of construction involved per house. He also introduced better human resource management practices, including creating a promotion ladder in Habitat and raising salaries to competitive levels found in other nonprofits. He decided to move Habitat's headquarters from the small city in which it had been founded to Atlanta, Georgia, to make it easier to hire skilled functional managers. Finally, he established a new set of goals and priorities for the company, and given that Reckford took over only a month after Hurricane Katrina struck, one obvious priority was to rebuild homes along the Gulf Coast. Habitat's goal is to complete 1,000 permanent homes by 2007.

Approaches to Social Responsibility

social responsibility
The way a company's managers and employees view their duty or obligation to make decisions that protect, enhance, and promote the welfare and well-being of stakeholders and society as a whole.

A company's ethics are the result of differences in societal, organizational, occupational, and individual ethics. In turn, a company's ethics determine its stance or position on social responsibility. A company's stance on **social responsibility** is the way its managers and employees view their duty or obligation to make decisions that protect, enhance, and promote the welfare and well-being of stakeholders and society as a whole.[39] As we noted earlier, when no laws exist that specify how a company should act toward stakeholders, managers must decide what the right, ethical, and socially responsible thing to do is. Differences in business ethics can lead companies to take very different positions or views on what their responsibility is toward their stakeholders.

Many kinds of decisions signal a company's beliefs about its obligations to make socially responsible business decisions. (See Table 4.3.) The decision to spend money on training and educating employees—investing in them—is one such decision; so is the decision to minimize or avoid layoffs whenever possible. The decision to act promptly and warn customers when a batch of defective merchandise has been accidentally sold is another one. Companies that try to hide such problems show little regard for social responsibility. In the 1990s, both GM and Ford tried to hide the fact that several of their vehicles had defects that rendered them dangerous to drive; the companies were penalized with hundreds of millions of dollars in damages for their unethical behavior. On the other hand, in 2006, when HP discovered one of its most popular cameras could catch fire if users attempted to recharge ordinary batteries, it quickly announced a software fix for the problem; informing the public was the right thing to do.[40] The way a company announces business problems or admits its mistakes provides strong clues about its stance on social responsibility.

Table 4.3
Forms of Socially Responsible Behavior

Managers are being socially responsible and showing their support for their stakeholders when they:
- Provide severance payments to help laid-off workers make ends meet until they can find another job.
- Provide workers with opportunities to enhance their skills and acquire additional education so that they can remain productive and do not become obsolete because of changes in technology.
- Allow employees to take time off when they need to and provide health care and pension benefits for employees.
- Contribute to charities or support various civic-minded activities in the cities or towns in which they are located. (Target and Levi Strauss both contribute 5% of their profits to support schools, charities, the arts, and other good works.)
- Decide to keep open a factory whose closure would devastate the local community.
- Decide to keep a company's operations in the United States to protect the jobs of American workers rather than move abroad.
- Decide to spend money to improve a new factory so that it will not pollute the environment.
- Decline to invest in countries that have poor human rights records.
- Choose to help poor countries develop an economic base to improve living standards.

Four Different Approaches

obstructionist approach Companies and their managers choose *not* to behave in a socially responsible way and instead behave unethically and illegally.

The strength of companies' commitment to social responsibility can range from low to high (see Figure 4.6). At the low end of the range is an **obstructionist approach,** in which companies and their managers choose *not* to behave in a socially responsible way. Instead, they behave unethically and illegally and do all they can to prevent knowledge of their behavior from reaching other organizational stakeholders and society at large. Managers at the Mansville Corporation adopted this approach when they sought to hide evidence that asbestos causes lung damage; so too did tobacco companies when they sought to hide evidence that cigarette smoking causes lung cancer.

Top managers at Enron also acted in an obstructionist way when they prevented employees from selling Enron shares in their pension funds even before employees knew the company was in trouble. At the same time, top managers sold hundreds of millions of dollars' worth of their own Enron stock. Senior partners at Arthur Andersen who instructed their subordinates to shred files chose, like the managers of all these organizations, an obstructionist approach. The result was not only a loss of reputation but devastation for the organization and for all stakeholders involved. All these companies are no longer in business. The unethical behavior characteristic of the obstructionist approach is exemplified in the way Beech-Nut's management team in the 1980s put personal interests before customers' health and above the law.

Figure 4.6

Four Approaches to Social Responsibility

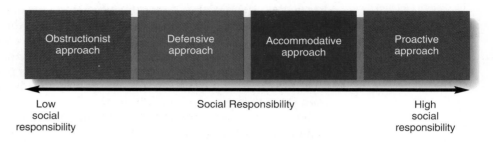

Ethics in Action

Apple Juice or Sugar Water?

In the early 1980s Beech-Nut, a maker of baby foods, was in grave financial trouble as it strove to compete with Gerber Products, the market leader. Threatened with the bankruptcy of the company if it could not lower its operating costs, Beech-Nut entered into an agreement with a low-cost supplier of apple juice concentrate. The agreement would save the company over $250,000 annually at a time when every dollar counted. Soon, one of Beech-Nut's food scientists became concerned about the quality of the concentrate. He believed that it was not made from apples alone but contained large quantities of corn syrup and cane sugar. He brought this information to the attention of top managers at Beech-Nut, but they were obsessed with the need to keep costs down and chose to ignore his concerns. The company continued to produce and sell its product as pure apple juice.[41]

Eventually investigators from the U.S. Food and Drug Administration (FDA) confronted Beech-Nut with evidence that the concentrate was adulterated. The top managers issued denials and quickly shipped the remaining stock of apple juice to the market before their inventory could be seized. The scientist who had questioned the purity of the apple juice had resigned from Beech-Nut, but he decided to blow the whistle on the company. He told the FDA that Beech-Nut's top management had known of the problem with the concentrate and had acted to maximize company profits rather than to inform customers about the additives in the apple juice. In 1987, the company pleaded guilty to charges that it had deliberately sold adulterated juice and was fined over $2 million. Its top managers were also found guilty and were sentenced to prison terms.

Consumer trust in Beech-Nut products plummeted, as did the value of Beech-Nut stock. The company's reputation was ruined, and it was eventually sold to Ralston Purina, now owned by Nestlé, which installed a new management team and a new ethical code of values to guide future business decisions.

defensive approach
Companies and their managers behave ethically to the degree that they stay within the law and abide strictly with legal requirements.

A **defensive approach** indicates at least a commitment to ethical behavior.[42] Defensive companies and managers stay within the law and abide strictly with legal requirements but make no attempt to exercise social responsibility beyond what the law dictates–thus they can and often do act unethically. These are the kinds of companies, like Computer Associates and WorldCom, that give their managers large stock options and bonuses even when company performance is declining. The managers are the kind who sell their stock in advance of other stockholders because they know that their company's performance is about to fall. Although acting on inside information is illegal, it is often very hard to prove since top managers have the right to sell their shares whenever they choose. The founders of most dot-com companies took advantage of this legal loophole to sell hundreds of millions of dollars of their dot-com shares before their stock prices collapsed. When making ethical decisions, such managers put their own interests first and commonly harm other stakeholders.

accommodative approach Companies and their managers behave legally and ethically and try to balance the interests of different stakeholders as the need arises.

An **accommodative approach** is an acknowledgment of the need to support social responsibility. Accommodative companies and managers agree that organizational members ought to behave legally and ethically, and they try to balance the interests of different stakeholders against one another so that the claims of stockholders are seen in relation to the claims of other stakeholders. Managers adopting this approach want to make choices that are reasonable in the eyes of society and want to do the right thing when called on to do so.

This approach is the one taken by the typical large U.S. company, which has the most to lose from unethical or illegal behavior. Generally, the older and more reputable a company, the more likely are its managers to curb attempts by their subordinates to act unethically. Large companies like GM, Intel, Du Pont, and Dell seek every way to build their companies' competitive advantages. Nevertheless, they reign in attempts by their managers to behave unethically or illegally, knowing the grave consequences such behavior can have on future profitability.

proactive approach
Companies and their managers actively embrace socially responsible behavior, going out of their way to learn about the needs of different stakeholder groups and utilizing organizational resources to promote the interests of all stakeholders.

Companies and managers taking a **proactive approach** actively embrace the need to behave in socially responsible ways. They go out of their way to learn about the needs of different stakeholder groups and are willing to utilize organizational resources to promote the interests not only of stockholders but also of the other stakeholders. Such companies are at the forefront of campaigns for causes such as a pollution-free environment, recycling and conservation of resources, the minimization or elimination of the use of animals in drug and cosmetics testing, and the reduction of crime, illiteracy, and poverty. For example, companies like McDonald's, Green Mountain Coffee, Ben and Jerry's, Whole Foods, and Target all have a reputation for being proactive in the support of stakeholders such as their suppliers or the community in which they operate.

Why Be Socially Responsible?

Several advantages result when companies and their managers behave in a socially responsible manner. First, demonstrating its social responsibility helps a company build a good reputation. Reputation is the trust, goodwill, and confidence others have in a company that leads them to want to do business with it. The reward for a good company reputation is increased business and improved ability to obtain resources from stakeholders. Reputation thus can enhance profitability and build stockholder wealth. Therefore, behaving socially responsibly is the economically right thing to do because companies that do so benefit from increasing business and rising profits.

A second major reason for companies to act socially responsibly toward employees, customers, and society is that in a capitalist system companies, as well as the government, have to bear the costs of protecting their stakeholders, providing health care and income, paying taxes, and so on. So if all companies in a society act socially responsibly, the quality of life as a whole increases.

Moreover, the way companies behave toward their employees determines many of a society's values and norms and the ethics of its citizens, as noted above. It has been suggested that if all organizations adopted a caring approach and agreed that their responsibility is to promote the interests of their employees, a climate of caring would pervade the wider society. Experts point to Japan, Sweden, Germany, the Netherlands, and Switzerland as countries where organizations are highly socially responsible and where, as a result, crime, poverty, and unemployment rates are relatively low, literacy rates are relatively high, and sociocultural values promote harmony between different groups of people. Business activity affects all aspects of people's lives, so the way business behaves toward stakeholders affects how stakeholders will behave toward business. You "reap what you sow," as the adage goes.

The Role of Organizational Culture

While an organization's code of ethics guides decision making when ethical questions arise, managers can go one step further by ensuring that important ethical values and norms are key features of an organization's culture. For example, Herb Kelleher and Coleen Barrett created Southwest Airlines' culture in which promoting employee well-being is a main company priority; this translates into organizational values and norms dictating that layoffs should be avoided and employees should share in the profits the company makes.[43] Google, UPS, and Toyota, are among the many companies who espouse similar values. When ethical values and norms such as these are part of an organization's culture, they help organizational members resist self-interested action because they recognize that they are part of something bigger than themselves.[44]

Managers' roles in developing ethical values and standards in other employees are very important. Employees naturally look to those in authority to provide leadership, just as a country's citizens look to its political leaders, and managers become ethical role models whose behavior is scrutinized by subordinates. If top managers are perceived as being self-interested, and not ethical, their subordinates are not likely to behave in an ethical manner. Employees may think that if it's all right for a top manager to

Google employees Yadi Arewal, right, and Harpreet Arewal, left, dance during the annual Google Dance at Google headquarters in Mountain View, California. Google is one of many companies known for having a culture that promotes employee well-being.

engage in dubious behavior, it's all right for them too, and for employees this might mean slacking off, reducing customer support, and not taking supportive kinds of actions to help their company. The actions of top managers such as CEOs and the president of the United States are scrutinized so closely for ethical improprieties because their actions represent the values of their organizations and, in the case of the president, the values of the nation.

Figure 4.7

Johnson & Johnson's Credo

Our Credo

We believe our first responsibility is to the doctors, nurses and patients,
to mothers and fathers and all others who use our products and services.
In meeting their needs everything we do must be of high quality.
We must constantly strive to reduce our costs
in order to maintain reasonable prices.
Customers' orders must be serviced promptly and accurately.
Our suppliers and distributors must have an opportunity
to make a fair profit.

We are responsible to our employees,
the men and women who work with us throughout the world.
Everyone must be considered as an individual.
We must respect their dignity and recognize their merit.
They must have a sense of security in their jobs.
Compensation must be fair and adequate,
and working conditions clean, orderly and safe.
We must be mindful of ways to help our employees fulfill
their family responsibilities.
Employees must feel free to make suggestions and complaints.
There must be equal opportunity for employment, development
and advancement for those qualified.
We must provide competent management,
and their actions must be just and ethical.

We are responsible to the communities in which we live and work
and to the world community as well.
We must be good citizens—support good works and charities
and bear our fair share of taxes.
We must encourage civic improvements and better health and education.
We must maintain in good order
the property we are privileged to use,
protecting the environment and natural resources.

Our final responsibility is to our stockholders.
Business must make a sound profit.
We must experiment wlth new ideas.
Research must be carried on, innovative programs developed
and mistakes paid for.
New equipment must be purchased, new facilities provided
and new products launched.
Reserves must be created to provide for adverse times.
When we operate according to these principles,
the stockholders should realize a fair return.

Johnson & Johnson

Source: © Johnson & Johnson. Used with permission.

ethics ombudsman A manager responsible for communicating and teaching ethical standards to all employees and monitoring their conformity to those standards.

Managers can also provide a visible means of support to develop an ethical culture. Increasingly, organizations are creating the role of ethics officer, or **ethics ombudsman,** to monitor their ethical practices and procedures. The ethics ombudsman is responsible for communicating ethical standards to all employees, for designing systems to monitor employees' conformity to those standards, and for teaching managers and employees at all levels of the organization how to respond to ethical dilemmas appropriately.[45] Because the ethics ombudsman has organizationwide authority, organizational members in any department can communicate instances of unethical behavior by their managers or coworkers without fear of retribution. This arrangement makes it easier for everyone to behave ethically. In addition, ethics ombudsmen can provide guidance when organizational members are uncertain about whether an action is ethical. Some organizations have an organizationwide ethics committee to provide guidance on ethical issues and help write and update the company code of ethics.

Ethical organizational cultures encourage organizational members to behave in a socially responsible manner. In fact, managers at Johnson & Johnson take social responsibility so seriously that their organization is often held up as an example of a socially responsible firm. The Johnson & Johnson Credo (see Figure 4.7) is one of the many ways in which social responsibility is emphasized at the company. As discussed in the "Ethics in Action" below, Johnson & Johnson's ethical organizational culture provides the company and its various stakeholder groups with numerous benefits.

Ethics in Action

Johnson & Johnson's Ethical Culture

Johnson & Johnson is so well known for its ethical culture that it has been judged as having the best corporate reputation for two years in a row based on a survey of over 26,000 consumers conducted by Harris Interactive and the Reputation Institute at New York University.[46] Johnson & Johnson grew from a family business led by General Robert Wood Johnson in the 1930s to a major maker of pharmaceutical and medical products. Attesting to the role of managers in creating ethical organizational cultures, Johnson emphasized the importance of ethics and responsibility to stakeholders and wrote the first Johnson & Johnson Credo in 1943.[47]

The credo continues to guide employees at Johnson & Johnson today and outlines the company's commitments to its different stakeholder groups. It emphasizes that the organization's first responsibility is to doctors, nurses, patients, and consumers. Following this group are suppliers and distributors, employees, communities, and, lastly, stockholders.[48] This credo has served managers and employees at Johnson & Johnson well and guided some difficult decision making, such as the decision to recall all Tylenol capsules in the U.S. market after cyanide-laced capsules were responsible for seven deaths in Chicago.

True to its ethical culture and outstanding reputation, consumer well-being always comes before profit considerations at Johnson & Johnson. For example, around 20 years ago, Johnson & Johnson's baby oil was used as a tanning product at a time when the harmful effects of sun exposure were not well known by the public.[49] The product manager for baby oil at the time, Carl Spalding, was making a presentation to top management about marketing plans when the company's president, David Clare, mentioned that tanning might not be healthy.[50] Before launching his planned marketing campaign, Spalding looked into the health-related concerns connected with tanning and discovered some evidence suggesting that health problems could arise from too much exposure to the sun. Even though the evidence was not definitive, Spalding recommended that baby oil no longer be marketed as a tanning aid, a decision that resulted in a 50% decrease in sales of baby oil, to the tune of $5 million.[51]

The ethical values and norms in Johnson & Johnson's culture, along with its credo, guide managers such as Spalding to make the right decision in difficult situations. Hence, it is understandable why Johnson & Johnson is renowned for its corporate reputation. An ethical culture and outstanding reputation have other benefits in addition to helping employees make the right decisions in questionable situations. Jeanne Hamway, vice president for recruiting, finds that Johnson & Johnson's reputation helps the company recruit and attract a diverse workforce.[52] Moreover, when organizations develop an outstanding reputation, their employees often are less tempted to act in a self-interested or unethical manner. For example, managers at Johnson & Johnson suggest that since employees in the company never accept bribes, the company is known as one in which bribes should not be offered in the first place.[53] All in all, ethical cultures such as Johnson & Johnson's benefit various stakeholder groups in multiple ways.

Summary and Review

THE NATURE OF ETHICS Ethical issues are central to the way companies and their managers make decisions, and they affect not only the efficiency and effectiveness of the way companies operate but also the prosperity of a nation. The result of ethical behavior is a general increase in company performance and in a nation's standard of living, well being, and wealth.

An ethical dilemma is the quandary people find themselves in when they have to decide if they should act in a way that might help another person or group, and is the "right" thing to do, even though it might go against their own self-interest. Ethics are the inner-guiding moral principles, values, and beliefs that people use to analyze or interpret a situation and then decide what is the "right" or appropriate way to behave.

Ethical beliefs alter and change as time passes, and as they do so laws change to reflect the changing ethical beliefs of a society.

STAKEHOLDERS AND ETHICS Stakeholders are people and groups who have a claim on and a stake in a company. The main stakeholder groups are stockholders, managers, employees, suppliers and distributors, customers, and a community, society, and nation. Companies and their managers need to make ethical business decisions that promote the well being of their stakeholders and avoid doing them harm.

To determine if a business decision is ethical, managers can use four ethical rules to analyze it: the utilitarian, moral rights, justice, and practical rules.

Managers should behave ethically because this avoids the tragedy of the commons and results in a general increase in efficiency, effectiveness, and company performance. The main determinants of differences in a manager's, company's, and country's business ethics are societal, occupational, individual, and organizational.

ETHICS AND SOCIAL RESPONSIBILITY   A company's stance on social responsibility is the way its managers and employees view their duty or obligation to make decisions that protect, enhance, and promote the welfare and well-being of stakeholders and society as a whole.

APPROACHES TO SOCIAL RESPONSIBILITY   There are four main approaches to social responsibility: obstructionist, defensive, accommodative, and proactive. The rewards from behaving in a socially responsible way are a good reputation, the support of all organizational stakeholders, and thus superior company performance.

Management in Action

Topics for Discussion and Action

Discussion

1. What is the relationship between ethics and the law?

2. Why do the claims and interests of stakeholders sometimes conflict?

3. Why should managers use ethical criteria to guide their decision making?

4. As an employee of a company, what are some of the most unethical business practices that you have encountered in its dealings with stakeholders?

5. What are the main determinants of business ethics?

Action

1. Find a manager and ask about the most important ethical rules that he or she uses to make the right decisions.

2. Find an example of (a) a company that has an obstructionist approach to social responsibility and (b) one that has an accommodative approach.

Building Management Skills
Dealing with Ethical Dilemmas

Use the chapter material to decide how you, as a manager, should respond to each of the following ethical dilemmas.

1. You are planning to leave your job to go work for a competitor; your boss invites you to an important meeting where you will learn about new products your company will be bringing out next year. Do you go to the meeting?

2. You're the manager of sales in an expensive sports-car dealership. A young executive who has just received a promotion comes in and wants to buy a car that you know is out of her price range. Do you encourage the executive to buy it so that you can receive a big commission on the sale?

3. You sign a contract to manage a young rock band, and that group agrees to let you produce their next seven records, for which they will receive royalties of 5%. Their first record is a smash hit and sells millions. Do you increase their royalty rate on their future records?

Managing Ethically

As the chapter discussed, Arthur Andersen's culture had become so strong that some of the company's partners and their subordinates acted unethically and pursued their own interests at the expense of other stakeholders. Many employees knew they were doing wrong but were afraid to refuse to follow orders. At Beech-Nut, the company's ethical values completely broke down; some managers joked about the harm being done to stakeholders.

Questions

1. Why is it that an organization's values and norms can become too strong and lead to unethical behavior?

2. What steps can a company take to prevent this problem—to stop its values and norms from becoming so inwardly focused that managers and employees lose sight of their responsibility to their stakeholders?

Small Group Breakout Exercise

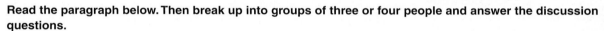

Is Chewing Gum the "Right" Thing to Do?

Read the paragraph below. Then break up into groups of three or four people and answer the discussion questions.

In the United States the right to chew gum is taken for granted. Although it is often against the rules to chew gum in a high school classroom, church, and so on, it is legal to do so on the street. If you possess or chew gum on a street in Singapore, you can be arrested. Chewing gum has been made illegal in Singapore because those in power believe that it creates a disgusting mess on pavements and feel that people cannot be trusted to dispose of their gum properly and thus should have no right to use it.

1. What makes chewing gum acceptable in the United States and unacceptable in Singapore?

2. Why can you chew gum on the street but not in a church?

3. How can you use ethical principles to decide when gum chewing is ethical or unethical and if and when it should be made illegal?

Exploring the World Wide Web

Go to Wal-Mart's Web site (www.walmart.com) and read the information there about the company's stance on the ethics of global outsourcing and the treatment of workers in countries abroad. Then search the Web for some recent stories about Wal-Mart's global purchasing practices and reports on the enforcement of its code of conduct.

1. What ethical principles guide Wal-Mart's approach to global purchasing?

2. Does Wal-Mart appear to be doing a good job of enforcing its global code of conduct?

Be the Manager

Creating an Ethical Code

You are an entrepreneur who has decided to go into business and open a steak and chicken restaurant. Your business plan requires that you hire at least 20 people as chefs, waiters, and so on. As the owner, you are drawing up a list of ethical principles that each of these people will receive and must agree to when he or she accepts a job offer. These principles outline your view of what is right or acceptable behavior and what will be expected both from you and from your employees.

Create a list of the five main ethical rules or principles you will use to govern the way your business operates. Be sure to spell out how these principles relate to your stakeholders; for example, state the rules you intend to follow in dealing with your employees and customers.

BusinessWeek

Case in the News

Cleaning Up Boeing

When W. James McNerney Jr. decided that Boeing Co.'s top managers needed a loud wake-up call, the new chief executive chose the obvious place to sound the alarm: the company's annual executive retreat. A year earlier, the event had been held at the posh Mission Hills Country Club in Palm Springs, CA, and nobody apparently had a better time than McNerney's predecessor, Harry Stonecipher. After a day devoted largely to socializing and playing golf, the former CEO, surrounded by Boeing's elite, closed down the bar and then fired up a cigar. It was at the same event that the married Stonecipher began a relationship with a female vice-president at Boeing—a misjudgment that ultimately paved the way for his humiliating ouster, and for McNerney's appointment as CEO.

The "Palm Springs fling," as it became known at Boeing, marked an all-time low for the company. It followed a three-year binge of widely publicized corporate misbehavior highlighted by the jailing of Boeing's former chief financial officer for holding illegal job negotiations with a senior Pentagon official, the indictment of a manager for allegedly stealing some 25,000 pages of proprietary documents from his former employer, Lockheed Martin Corp., and the judicial finding that Boeing had abused attorney-client privilege to help cover up internal studies showing that female employees were paid less than men. Scandals involving multiple forms of misconduct in geographically scattered locations enveloped nearly every division at Boeing, leaving little doubt that the legendary company, even as it began to enjoy a cyclical boom, was plagued by a poisonous culture.

Given that backdrop, nobody was particularly shocked when the 2006 annual retreat was moved to the more quotidian Hyatt Regency in Orlando and pared from three days to one and a half. The real surprises began during a breakfast speech when the normally upbeat McNerney launched into the sharpest critique of the company he had ever aired before such a large audience. Speaking without notes, McNerney said that "management had gotten carried away with itself," that too many executives had become used to "hiding in the bureaucracy," that the company had failed to "develop the best leadership." The next day, McNerney introduced General Counsel Douglas G. Bain, who really lowered the boom, railing against Boeing's pervasive "culture of silence." To grab the group's attention, Bain rattled off the federal prison numbers of two jailed former employees. "These are not ZIP Codes," Bain snapped. With McNerney looking on in clear support, Bain warned the audience that many prosecutors "believe that Boeing is rotten to the core."

The challenge of cleaning out the rot at the heart of Boeing is one for which McNerney, 56, has spent his entire professional life preparing. Since earning his master's degree from Harvard Business School in 1975, he has uprooted his family every two or three years in search of the next professional test. He started in brand marketing at Procter & Gamble Co., jumped to

McKinsey & Co., and then climbed the ranks through General Electric Co. for 18 years, where he topped out as CEO of GE's aircraft engine business, one of Boeing's most important business partners. After losing in a three-way race to replace Jack Welch as CEO of GE, McNerney was snapped up by 3M Co. in 2001 to turn around the struggling manufacturer. A short time later, he joined Boeing's board.

Straight Arrow

McNerney is a leader who both understands and cares about the aerospace giant. The series of ethical violations that surfaced at Boeing grated on the arrow-straight McNerney when he was a director, as did the fact that in 2003 the iconic company lost its status as the world's No. 1 commercial aircraft company to Airbus. Now McNerney has what he has always wanted: a chance to seal his legacy at one of America's most important companies. But to do so, he'll have to reinvent the 153,000-employee, $55 billion colossus, which, besides losing its moral compass, has not yet reached its profit-making potential. "I think the culture had morphed in dysfunctional ways in some places," the polished, soft-spoken McNerney said in a recent conversation with *BusinessWeek*, his first extensive interview since taking the job. "There are elements of our culture that I think we all would like to change."

Specifically, McNerney wants to unite a balkanized management team that has been at war ever since Boeing merged with McDonnell Douglas Corp. in 1997. The distinct cultures of the two companies never meshed, and the differences calcified into bitter rivalries. Having spent his first six months on the job in a "deep dive" learning about the company, McNerney believes that internal rivalry not only is at the root of the company's ethical scandals but also has prevented managers from cutting costs and sharing good ideas effectively. His prescription includes some predictable elements, including exerting more effective central leadership over Boeing's three divisions, changing the way executives are paid, and encouraging managers to exploit the giant manufacturer's cost-cutting leverage. But it also includes some unusual ones, such as encouraging managers to talk more openly about Boeing's severe ethical lapses. "I want to try to make it OK to have that dialogue," says McNerney. The scandals at Boeing aren't "something that happened in a separate part of the company that half of us aren't responsible for."

Relentless ethical scandals and bitter infighting, he believes, have dampened the aerospace giant's performance. "If we can get the values lined up with performance, then this is an absolutely unbeatable company," says McNerney. Rather than simply giving speeches about management virtue, insiders say that McNerney is trying to lead by example. He wins praise from co-workers for paying attention to the small things like remembering people's names, listening closely to their presentations, and not embarrassing underlings in public. That marks a sharp distinction from the blunt Stonecipher and the remote Philip M. Condit, who stepped down as CEO in 2003 in the wake of the Pentagon scandals.

More important, McNerney asks different types of questions than Stonecipher and Condit. "Phil or Harry would get into the weeds on the technical stuff," says this executive. "But Jim is more interested in the human side. He is interested in how to . . . create a culture where people speak up and take the risk and stop a production line because something is wrong."

Revamping pay is another powerful tool McNerney is using to reform Boeing's culture. In the old days, no points were awarded for collaborating with other units or following ethics rules. Now pay and bonuses are directly linked to how well executives embrace a set of six leadership attributes such as "Living Boeing Values." That includes new criteria such as promoting integrity and avoiding abusive behavior. McNerney is also giving managers financial incentives that better reflect the cyclical nature of the aerospace industry. Boeing's past long-term incentive system, called Performance Shares, paid out based on a higher stock price. But that system failed to consider management's performance during the down cycles inherent in the industry, thus offering managers few incentives to find a way to improve performance during a downturn.

Questions for Discussion

1. What kinds of factors resulted in Boeing's unethical culture?

2. What steps is its new CEO taking to change Boeing's culture and make ethical behavior the center of attention?

Source: Stanley Holmes, "Cleaning Up Boeing." Reprinted from the March 13, 2006, issue of *BusinessWeek* by special permission. Copyright © 2006 by the McGraw-Hill Companies, Inc.

Case in the News

Fixing Apple's "Sweatshop" Woes

As workers in the United States and elsewhere commanded ever higher wages, manufacturers shifted operations elsewhere, including such places as Mexico and Japan, and later Taiwan and China. Many companies, Apple among them, get outside companies to handle the manufacturing entirely, often in places where labor costs are low and workplace regulations differ from those in the United States and Europe.

On June 25, it was reported that Apple Computer's iPod portable media players are made in what was portrayed as sweatshop conditions. The plant specified in the report is operated in Longhua, China by an outfit called Foxconn, the trade name given to Hon Hai Precision Industry. Known as a contract electronics manufacturer—a company whose sole purpose is to manufacture products for other companies it is said to employ some 200,000 people who live in dormitories crammed with up to 100 people at a time, for wages that appear to Western eyes shockingly low—about $50 a month.

Last year, Hon Hai eclipsed Flextronics, the Singapore-based electronics giant, as the world's biggest contract manufacturer. Hon Hai's other clients include Hewlett-Packard, Nokia, and Sony. Hon Hai executives initially took issue with the report, pointing out what they said were inconsistencies: Its entire corporate workforce is only 160,000 people, and so how could a single plant employ 200,000? A later report appeared on ChinaCSR.com, a Web site devoted to promoting corporate responsibility in China. In that account, Hon Hai admitted to breaking some local laws regarding overtime. It also said its salary structure had been misinterpreted in media reports and that it complies with minimum-wage laws.

Walking the Walk?

Apple, clearly wanting to avoid unpleasant appearances, had sent a team to investigate. Some reports have suggested the investigation was complete, but at the time of printing, it was not. "We are still investigating the working conditions at Foxconn's manufacturing plant in Longhua'" says Apple spokesman Steve Dowling. "This is a thorough audit, which includes employee working and living conditions, interviews of employees and managers, compliance with overtime and wage regulations, and other areas as necessary to insure adherence to Apple's supplier code of conduct. Apple's supplier code of conduct sets the bar higher than accepted industry standards and we take allegations of noncompliance very seriously."

Clearly, much about this situation is not yet known, and Apple is to be commended for springing into action when the allegations surfaced. Steve Jobs is a socially conscious person, and he associates with people of the same ilk. Former Vice President Al Gore is on the Apple board of directors. Apple makes a special U2-branded version of the iPod whose front man is global activist Bono, the band's lead singer. Such high-profile folks linked with Apple—and more importantly for Apple, a lot of its customers—will eagerly await the investigation's outcome.

What are the possible scenarios, starting with the worst-case? For the sake of argument, let's assume that the allegations are true, and that working conditions at the plant are horrible. In this case, it would be incumbent on Apple to either demand rapid and sweeping changes at Hon Hai's plant, or to take its business elsewhere. Certainly, other companies could build iPods, but such a change wouldn't happen without major disruption to Apple's business. Products could be delayed or go in short supply. This would anger shareholders, and could cause serious damage to Apple's reputation.

No Hiding

But Apple would clearly want to avoid the kind of public-relations problems that for so long plagued Nike about sweatshops in Vietnam. Stigmas like the one in that case don't go away fast. Decisive, corrective action would be the order of the day, even if it hurts business.

Consider the opposite scenario. Let's say that Apple's investigation finds nothing amiss or improper with the way iPods are made by Hon Hai and the conditions under which its employees work. Apple and Hon Hai jointly brand the story as fiction and go their merry way, making iPods and money.

Both scenarios call for transparency. If the findings are bad, people will wonder if the whole story has been told. If the findings are good, questions may linger, nevertheless, and doubt will fester. Some will wonder if it's really humane to buy an iPod. Regardless of the findings, Apple should make every effort to disclose whatever it finds—good or bad—immediately.

And it should ask for help from an independent authority to verify whatever the company finds and to help oversee whatever corrective action is taken—if any is ultimately needed.

Be a Model

I'd suggest the U.K.-based Catholic Agency for Overseas Development. In 2003, the agency reported on working conditions in the PC industry—again at contract manufacturers—and spurred changes from companies such as Dell, HP, and IBM, which were targeted in the first report. They've since updated their supplier codes of conduct to address issues the agency raised.

Apple has a Supplier Code of Conduct as well, which can be read at this site. Among the actions it forbids are corporal punishment of workers. Working hours are to be no more than 60 hours in a single week, including overtime. Plus, workers must be allowed one day off each week. Dowling says Apple's code of conduct is intended to exceed standards established by the International Labor Organization. "We set the bar high," he says.

But is it enough to demand that another company do things in a manner you prefer? High-profile companies like Apple are often held to higher standards because they lead in what they do. The industry follows Apple in how computers are made and personal electronics are designed. Apple should also set an example for how their products are made.

Controlling its Destiny

One way to do that: build a factory in China. Rather than hire a Chinese company to build iPods, why couldn't Apple build them in China in its own factory? It has $8.2 billion in cash and would be in good corporate company. I can think of at least two electronics companies, Motorola and Plantronics, that both build products at wholly owned facilities in China. Plantronics spent $23 million to build a 270,000 square-foot plant for wireless-phone headsets. It employs 425 now, and expects the headcount there to grow to 2,000.

An Apple factory built to accommodate good working standards in China would give the company total control over conditions, environmental practices, and all the other things that manufacturers like to brag about these days. It would erase any concerns—warranted or not—about worker exploitation there.

It would be no small undertaking: Expensive, complicated, fraught with bureaucracy. But it could be done. No one said running the world's most influential technology company would be easy.

Questions for Discussion

1. What kinds of ethical criteria could Apple use to decide if it should continue to buy from Foxcomm, or establish its own factory in China?

2. If it decides to continue to buy its components what kinds of safeguard could it put in place?

Source: Arik Hesseldahl, "Fixing Apple's 'Sweatshop' Woes." Reprinted from the June 29, 2006, issue of *BusinessWeek* by special permission. Copyright © 2006 by the McGraw-Hill Companies, Inc.

CHAPTER 5

Managing Diverse Employees in a Multicultural Environment

Learning Objectives

After studying this chapter, you should be able to:

- Discuss the increasing diversity of the workforce and of the organizational environment.

- Explain the central role that managers play in the effective management of diversity.

- Explain why the effective management of diversity is both an ethical and a business imperative.

- Discuss how perception and the use of schemas can result in unfair treatment.

- List the steps managers can take to effectively manage diversity.

- Identify the two major forms of sexual harassment and how they can be eliminated.

A Manager's Challenge

Diversity in the Boardroom and on the Police Force

How can managers diversify nontraditional work groups and organizations?
For any demographic group such as women, Hispanics, and African–Americans, nontraditional work groups and organizations are work settings in which the demographic group in question is very underrepresented. For example, given that women make up about half of the population, a nontraditional organization for women is one in which less than 25% of its employees are women.[1] Recognizing that diversity on multiple dimensions makes good business sense, managers are increasingly seeking to diversify jobs and work groups that traditionally have comprised very few women or minorities.

In the United States and other countries such as Norway and Sweden, efforts to diversify nontraditional work settings are occurring at every organizational level.[2]

The need for diversification at the very top of organizations is reflected in the composition of boards of directors.[3] According to a recent study of the boards of directors of Fortune 100 companies, of 1,195 total board

Boston Mayor Menino says he chose Kathleen O'Toole, pictured here, to be the city's Chief of Police because she was the best person for the job.

seats, only 202 seats are occupied by women, 120 by African–Americans, 46 by Hispanics, and 12 by Asian–Americans.[4] Additionally, some minorities and women serve on multiple boards, which means that the numbers of women and minority directors are actually lower than the number of seats they occupy. For example, Bonnie G. Hill, an African–American woman, sits on six boards of directors, including Albertson's.[5] According to Ilene H. Lange, president of Catalyst, a nonprofit organization focused on women's advancement in business and a member of the Alliance for Board Diversity, which conducted the study, "The business case for diversity on boards is very strong and compelling. . . . We document that in the highest levels of corporations, there is under-representation as compared to lower levels in organizations."[6]

Leonard Schaeffer, former chairman of the board of directors of Wellpoint Health Networks in Thousand Oaks, California, and currently a member of Amgen Inc.'s board, suggests that managers can diversify boards of directors if they try.[7] Moreover, Schaeffer believes that boards should reflect the diversity in the population for business reasons. Having different experiences, backgrounds, and perspectives represented on a board can help ensure that the organization appeals to diverse markets for its goods and services and makes well-informed decisions that take into account all relevant information. As Schaeffer puts it, "Women make most health-care decisions in American families, so if we are going to reach out to our customers, we need gender diversity."[8] Consistent with Wellpoint's experience, when Jill Kerr Conway was on Nike's board of directors in the early 1990s, her valuable input led Nike to launch its successful women's sports apparel division.[9]

At lower levels in organizations, more managers and employees alike are beginning to question why certain jobs, such as those in construction, tend to be dominated by men. Linda Simpson created her own handywoman-referral service in Denver, Colorado, to help customers and handywomen connect for their mutual benefit.[10] Often, in certain nontraditional jobs, people think that women are underrepresented because of size and strength issues. However, petite women such as Jeannette Patane of Fairbanks, Alaska, have successful careers as handywomen. And for many positions such as painter and electrician, physical differences between men and women really don't enter the picture even though many people assume they do.[11]

In the health care arena, Dr. Harry R. Gibbs, a cardiologist and vice president of Institutional Diversity at the M. D. Anderson Cancer Center in Houston, Texas, believes that the effective management of diversity is important in all aspects of health care research and delivery and that a proactive approach to managing diversity is a necessity.[12] Whether it is scientific research, disease detection, participation in drug trials, laboratory testing, or marketing to patients, diversity enters into the equation. And in all of these venues, good communication is a necessity, as are mutual understanding and the ability to converse in the same language, whether it be English, Spanish, or Chinese.[13]

What about law enforcement? Women currently make up less than 15% of the 880,000 members of the police forces in the United States;[14] in urban areas with populations of 50,000 or more, less than 13% of police officers are women.[15] Traditionally, even if a woman became a law enforcement officer, it was very unlikely that she would ever rise to the top and assume a leadership position. Often, the reasoning revolved around issues of physical strength. However, this situation is changing as women are currently assuming high-level leadership positions in law enforcement. For example, Kathleen O'Toole is chief of police for the Boston Police Department, and both the San Francisco and Detroit police departments have female chiefs of police.[16] Boston Mayor Menino, who chose O'Toole for the top spot, indicates that he did so because she was the best person for the job and that gender was not a factor in the decision.[17] As decision makers like Menino increasingly recognize that leaders in law enforcement need many of the same leadership qualities that are important in other kinds of organizations—intelligence, interpersonal skills, education, experience, and the ability and desire to make difficult decisions—excluding women from serious consideration for such positions for irrelevant reasons will hopefully decline.

Overview

The effective management of diversity means much more than hiring diverse employees. It means learning to appreciate and respond appropriately to the needs, attitudes, beliefs, and values that diverse people bring to an organization. It also means correcting misconceptions about why and how different kinds of employee groups are different from one another and finding the most effective way to utilize the skills and talents of diverse employees.

In this chapter, we focus on the effective management of diversity in an environment that is becoming increasingly diverse in all respects. Not only is the diversity of the global workforce increasing, but suppliers and customers are also becoming increasingly diverse. Managers need to proactively manage diversity to be able to attract and retain the best employees and effectively compete in a diverse global environment. For example, managers at the audit and consulting firm Deloitte & Touche have instituted a program to encourage minority suppliers to compete for its business, and the firm sponsors schools and colleges that supply a stream of well-trained recruits.[18]

Sometimes well-intentioned managers inadvertently treat one group of employees differently from another group, even though there are no performance-based differences between the two groups. As illustrated in the opening case, women were traditionally excluded from top-management positions in law enforcement for reasons that were irrelevant to performance in leadership roles. This chapter explores why differential treatment occurs and the steps managers and organizations can take to ensure that diversity, in all respects, is effectively managed for the good of all organizational stakeholders.

The Increasing Diversity of the Workforce and the Environment

diversity Differences among people in age, gender, race, ethnicity, religion, sexual orientation, socioeconomic background, and capabilities/disabilities.

One of the most important management issues to emerge over the last 30 years has been the increasing diversity of the workforce. **Diversity** is dissimilarities—differences—among people due to age, gender, race, ethnicity, religion, sexual orientation, socioeconomic background, education, experience, physical appearance, capabilities/disabilities, and any other characteristic that is used to distinguish between people (see Figure 5.1).

Diversity raises important ethical issues and social responsibility issues (see Chapter 4). It is also a critical issue for organizations, one that if not handled well can bring an organization to its knees, especially in our increasingly global environment. There are several reasons why diversity is such a pressing concern and issue both in the popular press and for managers and organizations:

- There is a strong ethical imperative in many societies that diverse people receive equal opportunities and be treated fairly and justly. Unfair treatment is also illegal.

- Effectively managing diversity can improve organizational effectiveness.[19] When managers effectively manage diversity, they not only encourage other managers to treat diverse members of an organization fairly and justly but also realize that diversity is an important organizational resource that can help an organization gain a competitive advantage.

Figure 5.1

Sources of Diversity in the Workplace

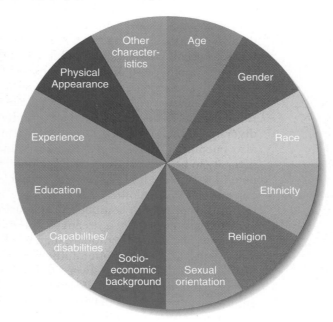

- There is substantial evidence that diverse individuals continue to experience unfair treatment in the workplace as a result of biases, stereotypes, and overt discrimination.[20] In one study, résumés of equally qualified men and women were sent to high-priced Philadelphia restaurants (where potential earnings are high). Though equally qualified, men were more than twice as likely as women to be called for a job interview and more than five times as likely to receive a job offer.[21] Findings from another study suggest that both women and men tend to believe that women will accept lower pay than men; this is a possible explanation for the continuing gap in pay between men and women.[22]

Other kinds of diverse employees may face even greater barriers. For example, the federal Glass Ceiling Commission Report indicated that African–Americans have the hardest time being promoted and climbing the corporate ladder, that Asians are often stereotyped into technical jobs, and that Hispanics are assumed to be less well educated than other minority groups.[23] (The term **glass ceiling** alludes to the invisible barriers that prevent minorities and women from being promoted to top corporate positions.)[24]

Before we can discuss the multitude of issues surrounding the effective management of diversity, we must document just how diverse the U.S. workforce is becoming.

glass ceiling A metaphor alluding to the invisible barriers that prevent minorities and women from being promoted to top corporate positions.

Age

According to the latest data from the U.S. Census Bureau, the median age of a person in the United States is the highest it has ever been, 36.2 years.[25] Moreover, by 2030, it is projected that 20% of the population will be over 65.[26] Title

Table 5.1

Major Equal Employment Opportunity Laws Affecting Human Resources Management

Year	Law	Description
1963	Equal Pay Act	Requires that men and women be paid equally if they are performing equal work.
1964	Title VII of the Civil Rights Act	Prohibits discrimination in employment decisions on the basis of race, religion, sex, color, or national origin; covers a wide range of employment decisions, including hiring, firing, pay, promotion, and working conditions.
1967	Age Discrimination in Employment Act	Prohibits discrimination against workers over the age of 40 and restricts mandatory retirement.
1978	Pregnancy Discrimination Act	Prohibits discrimination against women in employment decisions on the basis of pregnancy, childbirth, and related medical decisions.
1990	Americans with Disabilities Act	Prohibits discrimination against disabled individuals in employment decisions and requires that employers make accommodations for disabled workers to enable them to perform their jobs.
1991	Civil Rights Act	Prohibits discrimination (as does Title VII) and allows for the awarding of punitive and compensatory damages, in addition to back pay, in cases of intentional discrimination.
1993	Family and Medical Leave Act	Requires that employers provide 12 weeks of unpaid leave for medical and family reasons, including paternity and illness of a family member.

VII of the Civil Rights Act of 1964 and the Age Discrimination in Employment Act of 1967 are the major federal laws prohibiting age discrimination.[27] While we discuss federal employment legislation in more depth in Chapter 12, major equal employment opportunity legislation that prohibits discrimination among diverse groups is summarized in Table 5.1.

The aging of the population suggests managers need to be vigilant that employees are not discriminated against because of age. Moreover, managers need to ensure that the policies and procedures they have in place treat all workers fairly, regardless of their ages.

Gender

Women and men are almost equally represented in the U.S. workforce (approximately 53.5% of the U.S. workforce is male and 46.5% female),[28] yet women's median weekly earnings are estimated to be $572 compared to $714 for men.[29] Thus, the gender pay gap appears to be as alive and well as the glass ceiling. According to the nonprofit organization Catalyst, which studies women in business, while women comprise about 50.5% of the employees in managerial and professional positions, only around 15.7% of corporate officers in the 500 largest U.S. companies (i.e., Fortune 500) are women, only 5.2% of the top earners are women, only 7.9% of those with the highest-ranking titles in corporate America are women (e.g., CEO or executive vice president), and only eight Fortune 500 companies have women as CEOs.[30] These women, such as Andrea Jung, CEO of Avon Products, and Meg Whitman, CEO of eBay, stand out among their male peers and often receive a disparate amount of attention in the media. (We address this issue later, when we discuss the effects of being salient.) Women are also very underrepresented on boards of directors–they currently hold 13.6% of the board seats of Fortune 500 companies.[31] However, as Sheila Wellington, president of Catalyst, indicates, "Women either control or influence nearly all consumer purchases, so it's important to have their perspective represented on boards."[32]

Additionally, research conducted by consulting firms suggests that female executives outperform their male colleagues on skills such as motivating others, promoting good communication, turning out high-quality work, and being a good listener.[33] For example, the Hagberg Group performed in-depth evaluations of 425 top executives in a variety of industries, with each executive rated by approximately 25 people. Of the 52 skills assessed, women received higher ratings than men on 42 skills, although at times the differences were small.[34] Results of a recent study conducted by Catalyst found that organizations with higher proportions of women in top-management positions had significantly better financial performance than organizations with lower proportions of female top managers.[35] All in all, studies such as these make one wonder why the glass ceiling continues to hamper the progress of women in business (a topic we address later in the chapter).

Race and Ethnicity

The U.S. Census Bureau typically distinguishes between the following races: American Indian or Alaska Native (native Americans of origins in North, Central, or South America), Asian (origins in the Far East, Southeast Asia, or India), African–American (origins in Africa), Native Hawaiian or Pacific Islander (origins in the Pacific Islands such as Hawaii, Guam, and Somoa), and white (origins in Europe, the Middle East, or North Africa). While ethnicity refers to a grouping of people based on some shared characteristic such as national origin, language, or culture, the U.S. Census Bureau treats ethnicity in terms of whether a person is Hispanic or not Hispanic. Hispanics, also referred to as Latinos, are people whose origins are in Spanish cultures such as those of Cuba, Mexico, Puerto Rico, and South and Central America. Hispanics can be of different races.[36] According to a recent poll, most Hispanics prefer to be identified by their country of origin (e.g., Mexican, Cuban, or Salvadoran) rather than by the overarching term *Hispanic.*[37]

The racial and ethnic diversity of the U.S. population is increasing at an exponential rate, as is the composition of the workforce.[38] According to the U.S. Census Bureau, approximately one of every three U.S. residents belongs to a minority group (i.e., is not a non-Hispanic white); approximately 67% of the population is white, 13.4% is African–American, 14.4% is Hispanic, and 4.8% is Asian.[39] As indicated in the following "Managing Globally," the diversity of the U.S. population based on race and ethnicity will increase dramatically over the next few decades.

Managing Globally

Asians and Hispanics Projected to Be Fastest-Growing Group

According to projections released by the U.S. Census Bureau, the composition of the U.S. population in 2050 will be quite different from its composition in 2000. It is estimated that the Hispanic and Asian populations will triple during this 50-year period.[40] While the overall population in the United States is projected to grow from 282.1 million in 2000 to 419.9 million in 2050 (a 49% increase), estimated percentage growth rates for different ethnic and racial groups show that racial and ethnic diversity will definitely be on the rise.[41] Interestingly, while the U.S. population will increase by almost 50% in this next half-century, populations in many European countries are actually expected to decline.[42]

Percentage growth rates for African–Americans, Asians, Hispanics (of any race), and other races are well above the overall population growth estimate, while the percentage growth rate for non-Hispanic whites is far below this figure.[43] More specifically, from 2000 to 2050, African–Americans, Asians, Hispanics (of any race), other races, and non-Hispanic whites have estimated growth rates of 71.3%, 212.9%, 187.9%, 217.1%, and 7.4%, respectively.[44]

In addition to experiencing increased racial and ethnic diversity, the U.S. population is also projected to get older. While the overall population growth rate is an estimated 48.8%, the segments of the population in the age groups of 45–64, 65–84, and 85 and over are expected to grow by 49.1%, 113.8%, and 388.9%, respectively.[45] The U.S. Census Bureau made these projections based on Census 2000 data and assumptions regarding immigration patterns, mortality rates, and birth rates during the 2000-2050 period. For example, assumptions regarding immigration from China and India to the United States in the next several decades contribute to the projected high rate of growth in the Asian segment of the population.[46] All in all, these projections underscore the fact that the effective management of diversity in the workplace will only increase in importance in the years ahead.[47]

Puerto Rican Day Parade in New York City. It is estimated that the U.S. Hispanic and Asian populations will triple by 2050.

The increasing racial and ethnic diversity of the workforce and the population as a whole underscores the importance of effectively managing diversity. Statistics compiled by the National Urban League suggest that much needs to be done in terms of ensuring that diverse employees are provided with equal opportunities. For example, African–Americans' earnings are approximately 73% of the earnings of whites,[48] and of 10,092 corporate officers in Fortune 500 companies, only 106 are African–American women.[49] In the remainder of this chapter, we focus on the fair treatment of diverse employees and explore why this is such an important challenge and what managers can do to meet it. We begin by taking a broader perspective and considering how increasing racial and ethnic diversity in an organization's environment (e.g., customers and suppliers) affects decision making and organizational effectiveness.

At a general level, managers and organizations are increasingly being reminded that stakeholders in the environment are diverse and expect organizational decisions and actions to reflect this diversity. For example, the NAACP (National Association for the Advancement of Colored People) and Children Now (an advocacy group) have lobbied the entertainment industry to increase the diversity in television programming, writing, and producing.[50] The need for such increased diversity is more than apparent. For example, while Hispanics make up 12.5% of the U.S. population (or 35 million potential TV viewers), only about 2% of the characters in prime-time TV shows are Hispanics (i.e., of the 2,251 characters in prime-time shows, only 47 are Hispanic), according to a study conducted by Children Now.[51] Moreover, only about 1.3% of the evening network TV news stories are reported by Hispanic correspondents, according to the Center for Media and Public Affairs.[52]

Pressure is mounting on networks to increase diversity for a variety of reasons revolving around the diversity of the population as a whole, TV viewers, and consumers. For example, home and automobile buyers are increasingly diverse, reflecting the increasing diversity of the population as a whole.[53] Moreover, managers have to be especially sensitive to avoid stereotyping different groups when they communicate with potential customers. For example, Toyota Motor Sales USA made a public apology to the Reverend Jesse Jackson and his Rainbow Coalition for using a print advertisement depicting an African–American man with a Toyota RAV4 sport utility image embossed on his gold front tooth.[54]

Religion

Title VII of the Civil Rights Act prohibits discrimination based on religion (as well as based on race/ethnicity, country of origin, and sex; see Table 5.1 and Chapter 12). In addition to enacting Title VII, in 1997 the federal government issued "The White House Guidelines on Religious Exercise and Expression in the Federal Workplace."[55] These guidelines, while technically applicable only in federal offices, also are frequently relied on by large corporations. The guidelines require that employers make reasonable accommodations for religious practices such as observances of holidays as long as doing so does not entail major costs or hardships.[56]

A key issue for managers when it comes to religious diversity is recognizing and being aware of different religions and their beliefs, with particular attention being paid to when religious holidays fall. For example, critical meetings should not be scheduled during a holy day for members of a certain faith, and managers should be flexible in allowing people to have time off for religious observances. According to Lobna Ismail, director of a diversity training company in Silver Spring, Maryland, when managers acknowledge, respect, and make even small accommodations for religious diversity, employee loyalty is often enhanced. For example, allowing employees to leave work early on certain days instead of taking a lunch break or posting holidays for different religions on the company calendar can go a long way toward making individuals of diverse religions feel respected and valued as well as enable them to practice their faith.[57]

Capabilities/Disabilities

The Americans with Disabilities Act (ADA) of 1990 prohibits discrimination against persons with disabilities and also requires that employers make reasonable accommodations to enable these people to effectively perform their jobs. In force for more than a decade, the ADA is not uncontroversial. On the surface, few would argue with the intent of this legislation. However, as managers attempt to implement policies and procedures to comply with the ADA, they face a number of interpretation and fairness challenges.

On the one hand, some people with real disabilities warranting workplace accommodations are hesitant to reveal their disabilities to their employers and claim the accommodations they deserve.[58] On the other hand, some employees abuse the ADA by seeking unnecessary accommodations for disabilities that may or may not exist.[59] Thus, it is perhaps not surprising that the passage of the ADA does not appear to have increased employment rates significantly for those with disabilities.[60] A key challenge for managers is to promote an environment in which employees needing accommodations feel comfortable disclosing their need and, at the same time, to ensure that the accommodations not only enable those with disabilities to effectively perform their jobs but also are perceived to be fair by those not disabled.[61]

In addressing this challenge, often managers must educate both themselves and their employees about the disabilities, as well as the very real capabilities, of those who are disabled. For example, during Disability Awareness Week, administrators at Notre Dame University sought to increase the public's knowledge of disabilities while also heightening awareness of the abilities of persons who are disabled.[62] The University of Houston conducted a similar program called "Think Ability."[63] According to Cheryl Amoruso, director of the University of Houston's Center for Students with Disabilities, many people are unaware of the prevalence of disabilities as well as misinformed about their consequences. She suggests, for example, that although students may not be able to see, they can still excel in their coursework and have very successful careers.[64] Accommodations enabling such students to perform up to their capabilities are covered under the ADA.

The ADA also protects employees with acquired immune deficiency syndrome (AIDS) from being discriminated against in the workplace. AIDS is caused by the human immunodeficiency virus (HIV) and is transmitted through sexual contact, infected needles, and contaminated blood products. HIV is not spread through casual, nonsexual contact. Yet, out of ignorance, fear, or prejudice, some people wish to avoid all contact with anyone infected with HIV. Infected individuals may not

One way managers can educate employees about HIV and AIDS is by hanging AIDS awareness posters in the workplace, such as the one shown here.

necessarily develop AIDS, and some individuals with HIV are able to remain effective performers of their jobs, while not putting others at risk.[65]

AIDS awareness training can help people overcome their fears and also provide managers with a tool to prevent illegal discrimination against HIV-infected employees. Such training focuses on educating employees about HIV and AIDS, dispelling myths, communicating relevant organizational policies, and emphasizing the rights of HIV-positive employees to privacy and an environment that allows them to be productive.[66] The need for AIDS awareness training is underscored by some of the problems HIV-positive employees experience once others in their workplace become aware of their condition.[67] Moreover, organizations are required to make reasonable accommodations to enable people with AIDS to effectively perform their jobs.

Thus, managers have an obligation to educate employees about HIV and AIDS, dispel myths and the stigma of AIDS, and ensure that HIV-related discrimination is not occurring in the workplace. For example, Home Depot has provided HIV training and education to its store managers; such training was sorely needed given that over half of the managers indicated it was the first time they had the opportunity to talk about AIDS.[68] Moreover, advances in medication and treatment mean that more infected individuals are able to continue working or are able to return to work after their condition improves.[69] Thus, managers need to ensure that these employees are fairly treated by all members of their organizations. And managers and organizations that do not treat HIV-positive employees in a fair manner, as well as provide reasonable accommodations (e.g., allowing time off for doctor visits or to take medicine), risk costly lawsuits.

Socioeconomic Background

The term *socioeconomic background* typically refers to a combination of social class and income-related factors. From a management perspective, socioeconomic diversity (and, in particular, diversity in income levels) requires that managers be sensitive and responsive to the needs and concerns of individuals who might not be as well off as others. U.S. welfare reform in the mid- to late 1990s emphasized the need for single mothers and others receiving public assistance to join or return to the workforce. In conjunction with a strong economy, this led to record declines in the number of families, households, and children living below the poverty level, according to the 2000 U.S. census.[70] However, the economic downturn in the early 2000s, along with increased terrorism and the tragic collapse of the World Trade Center in New York City, resulted in domestic and international repercussions. These suggest that some past gains, which lifted families out of poverty, have been reversed. In a very strong economy, it is much easier for poor people with few skills to find jobs; in a weak economy, when companies lay off employees in hard times, people who need their incomes the most are unfortunately often the first to lose their jobs.[71]

Even with all the gains from the 1990s, the U.S. Census Bureau estimates that 6,825,399 families had incomes below the poverty level in 2000, with 3,581,475 of these families being headed by single women.[72] The Census Bureau relies on predetermined threshold income figures, based on family size and composition, adjusted annually for inflation, to determine the poverty level. Families whose income falls below the threshold level are considered poor.[73] For example, in

2000 a family of four with two children under 18 was considered poor if their annual income fell below $17,463.[74] When workers earn less than $10 or $15 per hour, it is often difficult, if not impossible, for them to meet their families' needs.[75] Moreover, increasing numbers of families are facing the challenge of finding suitable child care arrangements that enable the adults to work long hours and/or through the night to maintain an adequate income level. New information technology has led to more and more businesses operating 24 hours a day, creating real challenges for workers on the night shift, especially those with children.[76]

Hundreds of thousands of parents across the country are scrambling to find someone to care for their children while they are working the night shift, commuting several hours a day, working weekends and holidays, or putting in long hours on one or more jobs. This has led to the opening of day care facilities that operate around the clock as well as to managers seeking ways to provide such care for children of their employees. For example, the Children's Choice Learning Center in Las Vegas, Nevada, operates around the clock to accommodate employees working nights in neighboring casinos, hospitals, and call centers. Randy Donahue, a security guard who works until midnight, picks his children up from the center when he gets off work; his wife is a nurse on the night shift. There currently are five Children's Choice Learning Centers in the United States operating 24 hours a day, and plans are under way to add seven more.[77]

Judy Harden, who focuses on families and child care issues for the United Workers Union, indicates that the demands families are facing necessitate around-the-clock and odd-hour child care options. Many parents simply do not have the choice of working at hours that allow them to take care of their children at night and/or on weekends, never mind when the children are sick.[78] In 1993, Ford Motor Company built an around-the-clock child care facility for 175 children of employees in Livonia, Michigan. However, a recent survey of child care needs indicates that many employees in other locations require such a facility. Some parents and psychologists feel uneasy having children separated from their families for so much time and particularly at night. Most agree that unfortunately for many families this is not a choice but a necessity.[79]

A father drops his children off at a daycare facility before going to work. Managers need to be aware that many employees deal with challenging socioeconomic factors such as long commutes and finding suitable child care arrangements.

Socioeconomic diversity suggests that managers need to be sensitive and responsive to the needs and concerns of workers who may be less fortunate than themselves in terms of income and financial resources, child care and elder care options, housing opportunities, and existence of sources of social and family support. Moreover—and equally important—managers should try to provide such individuals with opportunities to learn, advance, and make meaningful contributions to their organizations while improving their economic well-being.

Sexual Orientation

Approximately 2% to 10% of the U.S. population is gay or lesbian.[80] While no federal law prohibits discrimination based on sexual orientation, 14 states have such laws, and a 1998 executive order prohibits sexual orientation discrimination in civilian federal offices. Moreover, an increasing number of organizations recognize the minority status of gay and lesbian employees, affirm their rights to fair and equal treatment, and provide benefits to same-sex partners of gay and lesbian employees. For example, 95% of Fortune 500 companies prohibit discrimination based on sexual orientation, and 70% of the Fortune 500 provide domestic-partner benefits.[81] As indicated in the following "Focus on Diversity," there are many steps that managers can take to ensure that sexual orientation is not used to unfairly discriminate among employees.

Focus on Diversity

Gays and Lesbians in the Workplace

While gays and lesbians have made great strides in terms of attaining fair treatment in the workplace, much more needs to be done. In a recent study conducted by Harris Interactive Inc. (a research firm) and Witeck Communications Inc. (a marketing firm), over 40% of gay and lesbian employees indicated that they had been unfairly treated, denied a promotion, or pushed to quit their jobs because of their sexual orientation.[82] Given continued harassment and discrimination despite the progress that has been made,[83] many gay and lesbian employees fear disclosing their sexual orientation in the workplace and thus live a life of secrecy. While there are a few openly gay top managers, such as David Geffen, cofounder of DreamWorks SKG, and Allan Gilmour, former vice chairman and CFO of Ford and currently a member of the board of directors of Whirlpool and DTE Energy Company, many others choose not to disclose or discuss their personal lives, including long-term partners.[84]

Thus, it is not surprising that many managers are taking active steps to educate and train their employees in regard to issues of sexual orientation. S. C. Johnson & Sons, Inc., maker of Raid insecticide and Glade air fresheners in Racine, Wisconsin, provides mandatory training to its plant managers to overturn stereotypes, as does Eastman Kodak. Other organizations such as Lucent Technologies, Microsoft, and Southern California Edison send employees to seminars conducted at prominent business schools. Companies like Raytheon, IBM, Eastman Kodak, and Lockheed Martin provide assistance to their gay and lesbian employees through gay and lesbian support groups.[85]

More generally, the presence of a gay, lesbian, bisexual, and transgender (GLBT) rights movement in the workplace is steadily increasing. From an individual employee perspective, sometimes these rights boil down to receiving the same kind of treatment as one's heterosexual coworkers. For example, when Daniel Kline applied to use United Parcel Service's Management Initiated Transfer to follow his partner of 27 years to another state, he was initially denied. This program allows employees to transfer to UPS offices in other states and retain their seniority when the employee's spouse accepts a job in another state. Kline's partner was transferred from United Airlines' office in San Francisco to its office in Chicago, and Kline was hoping to remain with UPS when he, too, moved to Chicago. After Kline took his case to the Lambda Legal Defense and Education Fund, a GLBT advocacy organization, and threatened legal action based on California's antidiscrimination laws, UPS reversed its position and allowed the transfer.[86]

Clearly, many highly qualified potential and current employees might happen to be gay or lesbian. An organization that does not welcome and support such employees not only is unfairly discriminating against this group but also is losing the contributions of valued potential employees. Additionally, an organization that discriminates against this group risks alienating customers. Fifteen million consumers are in the GLBT group in the United States, and according to research conducted by MarketResearch.com, their purchasing power is around $485 billion.[87]

Other Kinds of Diversity

There are other kinds of diversity that are important in organizations, critical for managers to deal with effectively, and also potential sources of unfair treatment. For example, organizations and teams need members with diverse backgrounds and experiences. This is clearly illustrated by the prevalence of cross-functional teams in organizations whose members might come from various departments such as marketing, production, finance, and sales (teams are covered in depth in Chapter 15). A team responsible for developing and introducing a new product, for example, often will need the expertise of employees not only from R&D and engineering but also from marketing, sales, production, and finance.

Other types of diversity can also affect how employees are treated in the workplace. For example, employees differ from each other in how attractive they are [based on the standards of the culture(s) in which an organization operates] and in terms of body weight. Whether individuals are attractive or thin or unattractive or overweight, in most cases, has no bearing on their job performance unless they have jobs in which physical appearance plays a role, such as modeling. Yet sometimes these physical sources of diversity end up influencing advancement rates and salaries. For example, a recent study published in the *American Journal of Public Health* found that highly educated obese women earned approximately 30% less per year than women who were not obese and men (regardless of whether or not the men were obese).[88] Clearly, managers need to ensure that all employees are treated fairly, regardless of their physical appearance.

Managers and the Effective Management of Diversity

The increasing diversity of the environment—which, in turn, increases the diversity of an organization's workforce—increases the challenges managers face in effectively managing diversity. Each of the kinds of diversity discussed above presents managers with a particular set of issues they need to appreciate before they can respond to them effectively. Understanding these issues is not always a simple matter, as many informed managers have discovered. Research on how different groups are currently treated and the unconscious biases that might adversely affect them is critical because it helps managers become aware of the many subtle and unobtrusive ways in which diverse employee groups can come to be treated unfairly over time. There are many more steps managers can take to become sensitive to the ongoing effects of diversity in their organizations, take advantage of all the contributions diverse employees can make, and prevent diverse employees from being unfairly treated.

Critical Managerial Roles

In each of their managerial roles (see Chapter 1), managers can either promote the effective management of diversity or derail such efforts; thus, they are critical to this process. For example, in their interpersonal roles, managers can convey that the effective management of diversity is a valued goal and objective (figurehead role), can serve as a role model and institute policies and procedures to ensure that diverse organizational members are treated fairly (leader role), and can enable diverse individuals and groups to coordinate their efforts and cooperate with each other both inside the organization and at the organization's boundaries (liaison role). In Table 5.2 we summarize some of the ways in which managers can ensure that diversity is effectively managed as they perform their different roles.

Given the formal authority that managers have in organizations, they typically have more influence than rank-and-file employees. When managers commit to supporting diversity, as was true of Leonard Schaeffer and Mayor Menino in "A Manager's Challenge," their authority and positions of power and status influence other members of an organization to make a similar commitment.[89] Research on social influence supports such a link, as people are more likely to be influenced and persuaded by others who have high status.[90]

Moreover, when managers commit to diversity, their commitment legitimizes the diversity management efforts of others.[91] In addition, resources are devoted to such efforts, and all members of an organization believe that their diversity-related efforts are supported and valued. Consistent with this reasoning, top-management commitment and rewards for the support of diversity are

Table 5.2

Managerial Roles and the Effective Management of Diversity

Type of Role	Specific Role	Example
Interpersonal	Figurehead	Convey that the effective management of diversity is a valued goal and objective.
	Leader	Serve as a role model and institute policies and procedures to ensure that diverse members are treated fairly.
	Liaison	Enable diverse individuals to coordinate their efforts and cooperate with one another.
Informational	Monitor	Evaluate the extent to which diverse employees are being treated fairly.
	Disseminator	Inform employees about diversity policies and initiatives and the intolerance of discrimination.
	Spokesperson	Support diversity initiatives in the wider community and speak to diverse groups to interest them in career opportunities.
Decisional	Entrepreneur	Commit resources to develop new ways to effectively manage diversity and eliminate biases and discrimination.
	Disturbance handler	Take quick action to correct inequalities and curtail discriminatory behavior.
	Resource allocator	Allocate resources to support and encourage the effective management of diversity.
	Negotiator	Work with organizations (e.g., suppliers) and groups (e.g., labor unions) to support and encourage the effective management of diversity.

often cited as critical ingredients for the success of diversity management initiatives.[92] Additionally, seeing managers express confidence in the abilities and talents of diverse employees causes other organizational members to be similarly confident and helps to reduce any misconceived misgivings they may have as a result of ignorance or stereotypes.[93]

Two other important factors emphasize why managers are so central to the effective management of diversity. The first factor is that women, African–Americans, Hispanics, and other minorities often start out at a slight disadvantage due to the ways in which they are perceived by others in organizations, particularly in work settings where they are a numerical minority. As Virginia Valian, a psychologist at Hunter College who studies gender, indicates, "In most organizations women begin at a slight disadvantage. A woman does not walk into the room with the same status as an equivalent man, because she is less likely than a man to be viewed as a serious professional."[94]

The second factor is that research suggests that slight differences in treatment can cumulate and result in major disparities over time. Even small differences–such as a very slight favorable bias toward men for promotions–can lead to major differences in the number of male and female managers over time.[95] Thus, while women and other minorities are sometimes advised not to make "a mountain out of a molehill" when they perceive they have been unfairly treated, research conducted by Valian and others suggests that molehills (i.e., slight differences in treatment based on irrelevant distinctions such as race, gender, or ethnicity) can turn into mountains over time (i.e., major disparities in important outcomes such as promotions) if they are ignored.[96] Once again, managers have the obligation, from both an ethical and business perspective, to ensure that neither large nor small disparities in treatment and outcomes due to irrelevant distinctions such as race or ethnicity occur in organizations.

The Ethical Imperative to Manage Diversity Effectively

Effectively managing diversity not only makes good business sense (which is discussed in the next section) but also is an ethical imperative in U.S. society. Two moral principles provide managers with guidance in their efforts to meet this imperative: distributive justice and procedural justice.

distributive justice A moral principle calling for the distribution of pay raises, promotions, and other organizational resources to be based on meaningful contributions that individuals have made and not on personal characteristics over which they have no control.

DISTRIBUTIVE JUSTICE The principle of distributive justice dictates that the distribution of pay raises, promotions, job titles, interesting job assignments, office space, and other organizational resources among members of an organization should be fair. The distribution of these outcomes should be based on the meaningful contributions that individuals have made to the organization (such as time, effort, education, skills, abilities, and performance levels) and not on irrelevant personal characteristics over which individuals have no control (such as gender, race, or age).[97] Managers have an obligation to ensure that distributive justice exists in their organizations. This does not mean that all members of an organization receive identical or similar outcomes; rather, it means that members who receive more outcomes than others have made substantially higher or more significant contributions to the organization.

Is distributive justice common in organizations in corporate America? Probably the best way to answer this question is by saying that things are getting better. Fifty years ago, overt discrimination against women and minorities was not uncommon; today, organizations are inching closer toward the ideal of distributive justice. Statistics comparing the treatment of women and minorities with the treatment of other employees suggest that most managers would need to take a proactive approach to achieve distributive justice in their organizations.[98] For example, across occupations, women consistently earn less than men (see Table 5.3) according to data collected by the U.S. Bureau of Labor Statistics.[99] Even in occupations dominated by women, such as teacher assistants and elementary and secondary school teachers, men tend to earn more than women.[100]

In many countries, managers have not only an ethical obligation to strive to achieve distributive justice in their organizations but also a legal obligation to treat all employees fairly. They risk being sued by employees who believe that they are not being fairly treated. That is precisely what six African–American employees at Texaco did when they experienced racial bias and discrimination.[101]

procedural justice A moral principle calling for the use of fair procedures to determine how to distribute outcomes to organizational members.

PROCEDURAL JUSTICE   The principle of procedural justice requires that managers use fair procedures to determine how to distribute outcomes to organizational members.[102] This principle applies to typical procedures such as appraising subordinates' performance, deciding who should receive a raise or a promotion, and deciding whom to lay off when an organization is forced to downsize. Procedural justice exists, for example, when managers (1) carefully appraise a subordinate's performance, (2) take into account any environmental obstacles to high performance beyond the subordinate's control, such as lack of

Table 5.3
Weekly Salaries by Sex and Occupation

Occupation	Men	Women	Women's Salaries as a Percentage of Men's
Management	$1,172	$849	72
Business and finance	1,014	744	73
Computer and mathematics	1,130	906	80
Architecture and engineering	1,094	827	76
Life, physical, and social science	970	773	80
Community and social service	746	655	88
Law	1,480	796	54
Education, training, library	904	708	78
Art, entertainment, sports, media	837	648	77
Health care	1,002	770	77
Service	463	366	79
Sales and office work	658	502	76
Resources and construction	613	449	73
Production and transportation	570	407	71

Median Weekly Salaries

Source: "Median Weekly Earnings of Full-Time Wage and Salary Workers by Selected Characteristics," www.bls.gov, May 1, 2004.

supplies, machine breakdowns, or dwindling customer demand for a product, and (3) ignore irrelevant personal characteristics such as the subordinate's age or ethnicity. Like distributive justice, procedural justice is necessary not only to ensure ethical conduct but also to avoid costly lawsuits.

Effectively Managing Diversity Makes Good Business Sense

The diversity of organizational members can be a source of competitive advantage, helping an organization provide customers with better goods and services.[103] The variety of points of view and approaches to problems and opportunities that diverse employees provide can improve managerial decision making. Suppose the Budget Gourmet frozen-food company is trying to come up with some creative ideas for new frozen meals that will appeal to health-conscious, time-conscious customers tired of the same old frozen-food fare. Which group do you think is likely to come up with the most creative ideas: a group of white women with master's degrees in marketing from Yale University who grew up in upper-middle-class families in the Northeast or a racially mixed group of men and women who grew up in families with varying income levels in different parts of the country and attended a mix of business schools (New York University, Oklahoma State, University of Michigan, UCLA, Cornell University, Texas A&M University, and Iowa State)? Most people would agree that the diverse group is likely to come up with a wider range of creative ideas. Although this example is simplistic, it underscores one way in which diversity can lead to a competitive advantage.

Just as the workforce is becoming increasingly diverse, so too are the customers who buy an organization's goods or services. In an attempt to suit local customers' needs and tastes, managers of Target's chain of 623 discount stores vary the selection of products available in stores in different cities and regions. For example, the Target store in Phoenix, Arizona, stocks religious candles and Spanish-language diskettes and Disney videos to appeal to local Hispanic Catholics; the Target store in Scottsdale, Arizona, stocks in-line skates and bicycle baby trailers that appeal to well-to-do yuppies.[104]

Diverse members of an organization are likely to be attuned to what goods and services diverse segments of the market want and do not want. Major car companies, for example, are increasingly assigning women to their design teams to ensure that the needs and desires of female customers (a growing segment of the market) are taken into account in new car design.

For Darden Restaurants, the business case for diversity rests on market share and growth. Darden seeks to satisfy the needs and tastes of diverse customers by providing menus in Spanish in communities with large Hispanic populations.[105] Similarly, market share and growth and the identification of niche markets led Tracey Campbell to cater to travelers with disabilities.[106] She heads InnSeekers, a telephone and online listing resource for bed and breakfasts. Nikki Daruwala works for the Calvert Group in Bethesda, Maryland, a mutual fund that emphasizes social responsibility and diversity. She indicates that profit alone is more than enough of an incentive to effectively manage diversity. As she puts it, "You can look at an automaker. There are more women making decisions about car buying or home buying . . . $3.72 trillion per year are spent by women."[107]

Ethics in Action

Habitat International's Valuable Employees

Habitat International was founded by current CEO David Morris, and his father Saul, over 20 years ago and has an enviable track record of success.[124] Habitat is a manufacturer and contractor of indoor–outdoor carpet and artificial grass and a supplier to home improvement companies like Lowe's and Home Depot. Habitat's profits have steadily increased over the years and the factory's defect rate is less than 0.5%; only around 10 carpets have been incorrectly cut in the entire history of the firm, which, during its busy season from January to June, produces 15,000 rugs daily.[125]

Morris attributes Habitat's success to its employees, 75% of whom have either a physical or a mental disability or both.[126] Habitat has consistently provided employment opportunities to people with disabilities such as Down syndrome, schizophrenia, or cerebral palsy.[127] The company has also hired the homeless, recovering alcoholics, and non-English-speaking refugees from other countries. And these

The first clue that Habitat isn't your run-of-the mill factory may be the gigantic animal sculptures at the plant entrance in Chattanooga, Tennessee. The Habitat team produces the sculptures, which can also be seen at restaurants, parks, garden centers, medical centers, museums and other sites.

very same employees were relied on by plant manager Connie Presnell when she needed to fill a rush order by assigning it to a team of her fastest workers.[128] Habitat pays its employees regionally competitive wages and has very low absence and turnover rates. Employees who need accommodations to perform their jobs are provided them, and Habitat has a highly motivated, satisfied, and committed workforce.[129]

While Habitat has actually gained some business from clients who applaud its commitment to diversity, Habitat's ethical values and social responsibility have also led the company to forgo a major account when stereotypes reared their ugly head. A few years ago, CEO Morris dropped the account of a distribution company because its representatives had made derogatory comments about his employees. Although it took Habitat two years to regain the lost revenues from this major account, Morris had absolutely no regrets.[130] Habitat's commitment to diversity and fair treatment is a win–win situation; the company is thriving, and so too are its employees.[131]

bias The systematic tendency to use information about others in ways that result in inaccurate perceptions.

Inaccurate perceptions leading to unfair treatment of diverse members of an organization also can be due to biases. Biases are systematic tendencies to use information about others in ways that result in inaccurate perceptions. Because of the way biases operate, people often are unaware that their perceptions of others are inaccurate. There are several types of biases.

The *similar-to-me effect* is the tendency to perceive others who are similar to ourselves more positively than we perceive people who are different.[132] The similar-to-me effect is summed up by the saying, "Birds of a feather flock together." It can lead to unfair treatment of diverse employees simply because they are different from the managers who are perceiving them, evaluating them, and making decisions that affect their future in the organization.

Managers (particularly top managers) are likely to be white men. Although these managers may endorse the principles of distributive and procedural justice, they may unintentionally fall into the trap of perceiving other white men more positively than they perceive women and minorities. This is the similar-to-me effect. Being aware of this bias as well as using objective information about employees' capabilities and performance as much as possible in decision making about job assignments, pay raises, promotions, and other outcomes can help managers avoid the similar-to-me effect.

Social status, a person's real or perceived position in a society or an organization, can be the source of another bias. The *social status effect* is the tendency to perceive individuals with high social status more positively than we perceive those with low social status. A high-status person may be perceived as smarter and more believable, capable, knowledgeable, and responsible than a low-status person, even in the absence of objective information about either person.

Imagine being introduced to two people at a company Christmas party. Both are white men in their late 30s, and you learn that one is a member of the company's top-management team and the other is a supervisor in the mailroom. From this information alone, you might assume that the top manager is smarter, more capable, more responsible, and even more interesting than the mailroom supervisor. Because women and minorities have traditionally had lower social status than white men, the social status effect may lead some people to perceive women and minorities less positively than they perceive white men.

Have you ever stood out in a crowd? Maybe you were the only man in a group of women; or maybe you were dressed formally for a social gathering, and everyone else was in jeans. Salience (i.e., conspicuousness) is another source of bias. The *salience effect* is the tendency to focus attention on individuals who are conspicuously different from us. When people are salient, they often feel as though all eyes are watching them, and this perception is not too far off the mark. Salient individuals are more often the object of attention than are other members of a work group, for example. A manager who has six white subordinates and one Hispanic subordinate reporting to her may inadvertently pay more attention to the Hispanic in group meetings because of the salience effect.

Individuals who are salient are often perceived to be primarily responsible for outcomes and operations and are evaluated more extremely, in either a positive or a negative direction.[133] Thus, when the Hispanic subordinate does a good job on a project, she receives excessive praise, and when she misses a deadline, she is excessively chastised.

Management in Action

Topics for Discussion and Action

Discussion

1. Discuss why violations of the principles of distributive and procedural justice continue to occur in modern organizations. What can managers do to uphold these principles in their organizations?

2. Why do workers who test positive for HIV sometimes get discriminated against?

3. Why would some employees resent accommodations made for employees with disabilities that are dictated by the Americans with Disabilities Act?

4. Discuss the ways in which schemas can be functional and dysfunctional.

5. Discuss an occasion when you may have been treated unfairly because of stereotypical thinking. What stereotypes were applied to you? How did they result in your being treated unfairly?

6. How does the similar-to-me effect influence your own behavior and decisions?

7. Why is mentoring particularly important for minorities?

8. Why is it important to consider the numbers of different groups of employees at various levels in an organization's hierarchy?

9. Think about a situation in which you would have benefited from mentoring but a mentor was not available. What could you have done to try to get the help of a mentor in this situation?

Action

10. Choose a Fortune 500 company not mentioned in the chapter. Conduct research to determine what steps this organization has taken to effectively manage diversity and eliminate sexual harassment.

Building Management Skills
Solving Diversity-Related Problems

Think about the last time that you (1) were treated unfairly because you differed from a decision maker on a particular dimension of diversity or (2) observed someone else being treated unfairly because that person differed from a decision maker on a particular dimension of diversity. Then answer these questions:

1. Why do you think the decision maker acted unfairly in this situation?

2. In what ways, if any, were biases, stereotypes, or overt discrimination involved in this situation?

3. Was the decision maker aware that he or she was acting unfairly?

4. What could you or the person who was treated unfairly have done to improve matters and rectify the injustice on the spot?

5. Was any sexual harassment involved in this situation? If so, what kind was it?

6. If you had authority over the decision maker (e.g., if you were his or her manager or supervisor), what steps would you take to ensure that the decision maker no longer treated diverse individuals unfairly?

Managing Ethically

Some companies require that their employees work very long hours and travel extensively. Employees with young children, employees taking care of elderly relatives, and employees who have interests outside the workplace sometimes find that their careers are jeopardized if they try to work more reasonable hours or limit their work-related travel. Some of these employees feel that it is unethical for their manager to expect so much of them in the workplace and not understand their needs as parents and caregivers.

Questions

1. Either individually or in a group, think about the ethical implications of requiring long hours and extensive amounts of travel for some jobs.

2. What obligations do you think managers and companies have to enable employees to have a balanced life and meet nonwork needs and demands?

Small Group Breakout Exercise

Determining If a Problem Exists

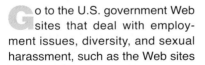

Form groups of three or four people, and appoint one member as the spokesperson who will communicate your findings to the whole class when called on by the instructor. Then discuss the following scenario.

You and your partners own and manage a local chain of restaurants, with moderate to expensive prices, that are open for lunch and dinner during the week and for dinner on weekends. Your staff is diverse, and you believe that you are effectively managing diversity. Yet on visits to the different restaurants you have noticed that your African–American employees tend to congregate together and communicate mainly with each other. The same is true for your Hispanic employees and your white employees. You are meeting with your partners today to discuss this observation.

1. Discuss why the patterns of communication that you observed might be occurring in your restaurants.

2. Discuss whether your observation reflects an underlying problem. If so, why? If not, why not?

3. Discuss whether you should address this issue with your staff and in your restaurants. If so, how and why? If not, why not?

Exploring the World Wide Web

Go to the U.S. government Web sites that deal with employment issues, diversity, and sexual harassment, such as the Web sites of the Equal Employment Opportunity Commission (EEOC) and the Bureau of Labor Statistics. After reviewing these Web sites, develop a list of tips to help managers effectively manage diversity and avoid costly lawsuits.

Be the Manager

You are Maria Herrera and have been recently promoted to the position of director of financial analysis for a medium-size consumer goods firm. During your first few weeks on the job, you took the time to have lunch with each of your subordinates to try to get to know them better. You have 12 direct reports who are junior and senior financial analysts who support different product lines. Susan Epstein, one of the female financial analysts you had lunch with, made the following statement, "I'm so glad we finally have a woman in charge. Now, hopefully things will get better around here." You pressed Epstein to elaborate, but she clammed up. She indicated that she didn't want to

entrepreneur who teaches at the Kellogg School of Management, became a director at SC Johnson & Son Inc. in the late '90s. Then-CEO William Perez took a risk, since Rogers was 41 and lacked major board experience. But Perez was soon taking Rogers' advice—for example, investing in venture capital firms that back black businesses. "It's not like I fell off the watermelon truck," says Rogers, who is also a director at SuperValu and Amcor Financial. "Boards sometimes have to go outside their normal blueprint to find people."

When Arbitron Inc., the radio-industry researcher, was looking for a black perspective, it made Shellye L. Archambeau a director. The CEO of San Francisco business software maker MetricStream Inc. isn't a big name. But she has operating experience and technology expertise, both skills Arbitron needed. Plus, she adds a fresh point of view about the data Arbitron produces for its minority-owned media customers. "It's important to have someone on the board [who] understands that," says Philip Guarascio, chair of the board's nominating committee. "It adds to the richness of the discussion."

Questions

1. Why are boards of directors seeking to increase the diversity of their members?

2. How might diversity increase the effectiveness of boards of directors?

3. Why, as Steven Rogers suggests, might "boards . . . have to go outside their normal blueprint to find people"?

4. What are some of the benefits for top managers of being a member of one or more boards of directors?

Source:R. O. Crockett, "The Rising Stock of Black Directors." Reprinted from the February 27, 2006, issue of *BusinessWeek* by special permission. Copyright © 2004 by the McGraw-Hill Companies.Chapter 5U.S.

CHAPTER 6

Managing in the Global Environment

Learning Objectives

After studying this chapter, you should be able to:

- Explain why the ability to perceive, interpret, and respond appropriately to the global environment is crucial for managerial success.

- Differentiate between the global task and global general environments.

- Identify the main forces in both the global task and general environments and describe the challenges that each force presents to managers.

- Explain why the global environment is becoming more open and competitive and identify the forces behind the process of globalization that increase the opportunities, complexities, challenges, and threats that managers face.

- Discuss why national cultures differ and why it is important that managers be sensitive to the effects of falling trade barriers and regional trade associations on the political and social systems of nations around the world.

Why is managing the global environment so complex today?

IKEA is the largest furniture chain in the world, and in 2006 the Swedish company operated over 231 stores in 33 countries. In 2005 IKEA sales were almost $15 billion, or over 20% of the global furniture market, but to its managers and employees this is just the tip of the iceberg. They believe IKEA is poised for massive growth throughout the world in the coming decade because it can provide what the average customer wants: well-designed and well-made contemporary furniture at an affordable price. IKEA's ability to provide customers with affordable furniture is very much the result of its approach to globalization, to the way it treats its global employees and operates its global store empire. In a nutshell, IKEA's global approach revolves around simplicity, attention to detail, cost-consciousness, and responsiveness in every aspect of its operations and behavior.

IKEA's global approach derives from the personal values and beliefs of its founder,

Employees at each IKEA store, including this one in Montpellier, France, are expected to cooperate to solve problems and get the job one.

Ingvar Kamprad, about how companies should treat their employees and customers. Kamprad, who is in his late 70s, was born in Smaland, a poor Swedish province whose citizens are well known for being entrepreneurial, frugal, and hardworking. Kamprad definitely absorbed these values, for when he entered the furniture business, he made them the core of his management approach. He teaches store managers and employees his values; his beliefs about the need to operate in a no-frills, cost-conscious way; and his view that they are all in business "together," by which he means that every person who works in his global empire plays an essential role and has an obligation to everyone else.

What does Kamprad's approach mean in practice? It means that all IKEA's members fly coach class on business trips, stay in inexpensive hotels, and keep traveling expenses to a minimum. It also means that IKEA stores operate on the simplest set of rules and procedures possible and that employees are expected to cooperate to solve problems and get the job done. Many famous stories exist about the frugal Kamprad, such as that even he always flies coach class and that when he takes a coke can from the mini-bar in a hotel room, he replaces it with one bought in a store—despite the fact that he is a multibillionaire ranked in the top 20 on the *Forbes* list of the world's richest people!

IKEA's employees see what his global approach means as soon as they are recruited to work in a store in one of the many countries in which the company operates. They start learning about IKEA's global corporate culture by performing jobs at the bottom of the ladder, and they are quickly trained to perform all the various jobs involved in store operations. During this process they internalize IKEA's global values and norms, which center on the importance the company attaches to their taking the initiative and responsibility for solving problems and for focusing on the customer. Employees are rotated between departments and sometimes stores, and rapid promotion is possible for those who demonstrate the enthusiasm and togetherness that signifies they have bought into IKEA's global culture.

Most of IKEA's top managers rose from its ranks, and the company holds "breaking the bureaucracy weeks" in which they are required to work in stores and warehouses for a week each year to make sure they and all employees stay committed to IKEA's global values. No matter which country they operate in, all employees wear informal clothes to work at IKEA—Kamprad has always worn an open-neck shirt—and there are no marks of status such as executive dining rooms or private parking places. Employees believe that if they buy into IKEA's work values, behave in ways that keep its growing global operations streamlined and efficient, and focus on being one step ahead of potential problems, they will share in its success. Promotion, training, above-average pay, a generous store bonus system, and the personal well-being that comes from working in a company where people feel valued are some of the rewards that Kamprad pioneered to build and strengthen IKEA's global approach.

Whenever IKEA enters a new country, it sends its most experienced store managers to establish its global approach in its new stores. When IKEA first entered the United States, the attitude of U.S. employees puzzled its managers. Despite their obvious drive to succeed and good education, employees seemed reluctant to take the initiative and assume responsibility. IKEA's managers discovered that their U.S. employees were afraid mistakes would result in the loss of their jobs, so the managers strove to teach employees the "IKEA way." The approach paid off: The United States has become the company's second-best country market, and IKEA plans to open many more U.S. stores, as well as stores around the world, over the next decade.

Overview

Top managers of a global company like IKEA are always operating in an environment where they are competing with other companies for scarce and valuable resources. Managers of companies large and small have concluded that to survive and prosper in the 21st century, most organizations must become **global organizations,** organizations that operate and compete not only domestically, at home, but also globally, in countries around the world. Operating in the global environment is uncertain and unpredictable because it is complex and constantly changing.

global organization
An organization that operates and competes in more than one country.

If organizations are to adapt to this changing environment, their managers must learn to understand the forces that operate in it and how these forces give rise to opportunities and threats. In this chapter, we examine why the environment, both domestically and globally, has become more open, vibrant, and competitive. We examine how forces in the task and general environments affect global organizations and their managers. By the end of this chapter, you will appreciate the changes that have been taking place in the environment and understand why it is important for managers to develop a global perspective as they strive to increase organizational efficiency and effectiveness.

What Is the Global Environment?

The **global environment** is a set of forces and conditions in the world outside an organization's boundary that affect the way it operates and shape its behavior.[1] These forces change over time and thus present managers with *opportunities* and *threats*. Changes in the global environment, such as the development of efficient new production technology, the availability of lower-cost components, or the opening of new global markets, create opportunities for managers to make and sell more products, obtain more resources and capital, and thereby strengthen their organization. In contrast, the rise of new global competitors, a global economic recession, or an oil shortage poses threats that can devastate an organization if managers are unable to sell its products and revenues and profits plunge. The quality of managers' understanding of forces in the global environment and their ability to respond appropriately to those forces, such as IKEA's managers ability to make and sell furniture customers around the world want to buy, are critical factors affecting organizational performance.

global environment
The set of global forces and conditions that operate beyond an organization's boundaries but affect a manager's ability to acquire and utilize resources.

In this chapter we explore the nature of these forces and consider how managers can respond to them. To identify opportunities and threats caused by forces in the environment, it is helpful for managers to distinguish between the *task environment* and the more encompassing *general environment* (see Figure 6.1, page 212).

The **task environment** is the set of forces and conditions that originate with global suppliers, distributors, customers, and competitors; these forces and conditions affect an organization's ability to obtain inputs and dispose of its outputs. The task environment contains the forces that have the most *immediate* and *direct* effect on managers because they pressure and influence managers on a daily basis. When managers turn on the radio or television, arrive at their offices in the morning, open their mail, or look at their computer screens, they are likely to learn about problems facing them because of changing conditions in their organization's task environment.

task environment The set of forces and conditions that originate with suppliers, distributors, customers, and competitors and affect an organization's ability to obtain inputs and dispose of its outputs because they influence managers on a daily basis.

general environment
The wide-ranging global, economic, technological, sociocultural, demographic, political, and legal forces that affect an organization and its task environment.

The **general environment** includes the wide-ranging global, economic, technological, sociocultural, demographic, political, and legal forces that affect the organization and its task environment. For the individual manager, opportunities and threats resulting from changes in the general environment are often more difficult to identify and respond to than are events in the task environment. However, changes in these forces can have major impacts on managers and their organizations.

The Task Environment

Forces in the task environment result from the actions of suppliers, distributors, customers, and competitors both at home and abroad (see Figure 6.1). These four groups affect a manager's ability to obtain resources and dispose of outputs on a daily, weekly, and monthly basis and thus have a significant impact on short-term decision making.

Figure 6.1
Forces in the Global Environment

Suppliers

suppliers Individuals and organizations that provide an organization with the input resources that it needs to produce goods and services.

Suppliers are the individuals and companies that provide an organization with the input resources (such as raw materials, component parts, or employees) that it needs to produce goods and services. In return, the supplier receives payment for those goods and services. An important aspect of a manager's job is to ensure a reliable supply of input resources.

Take Dell Computer, for example, the company we focused on in Chapter 1. Dell has many suppliers of component parts such as microprocessors (Intel and AMD) and disk drives (Quantum and Seagate Technologies). It also has suppliers of preinstalled software, including the operating system (Microsoft) and specific applications software (IBM, Oracle, and America Online). Dell's providers of capital, such as banks and financial institutions, are also important suppliers. Cisco Systems and Oracle are important providers of Internet hardware and software for dot-coms.

Dell has several suppliers of labor. One source is the educational institutions that train future Dell employees and therefore provide the company with skilled workers. Another is trade unions, organizations that represent employee interests and can control the supply of labor by exercising the right of unionized workers to strike. Unions also can influence the terms and conditions under which labor is employed. Dell's workers are not unionized; when layoffs became necessary due to an economic slowdown in the early 2000s, Dell had few problems in laying off workers to reduce costs. In organizations and industries where unions are very strong, however, an important part of a manager's job is negotiating and administering agreements with unions and their representatives.

Changes in the nature, number, or type of suppliers results in forces that produce opportunities and threats to which managers must respond if their organizations are to prosper. For example, a major supplier-related threat that confronts managers arises when suppliers' bargaining position is so strong that they can raise the prices of the inputs they supply to the organization. A supplier's bargaining position is especially strong when (1) the supplier is the sole source of an input and (2) the input is vital to the organization.[2] For example, for 17 years G. D. Searle was the sole supplier of NutraSweet, the artificial sweetener used in most diet soft drinks. Not only was NutraSweet an important ingredient in diet soft drinks, but it also was one for which there was no acceptable substitute (saccharin and other artificial sweeteners raised health concerns). Searle earned its privileged position because it invented and held the patent for NutraSweet. Patents prohibit other organizations from introducing competing products for 17 years. In 1992, Searle's patent expired, and many companies began to produce products similar to NutraSweet. Prior to 1992, Searle was able to demand a high price for NutraSweet, charging twice as much as the price of an equivalent amount of sugar. Paying that price raised the costs of soft-drink manufacturers, including Coca-Cola and PepsiCo, which had no alternative but to buy the product.[3] In the 2000s Splenda, made by McNeil Nutritionals owned by Tate & Lyle, a British company, has replaced NutraSweet as the artificial sweetener of choice, and NutraSweet's price has fallen while Splenda now commands a high price from soft-drink companies.[4]

In contrast, when an organization has many suppliers for a particular input, it is in a relatively strong bargaining position with those suppliers and can demand low-cost, high-quality inputs from them. Often, an organization can use its power with suppliers to force them to reduce their prices, as Dell frequently does. Dell, for example, is constantly searching for low-cost suppliers abroad to keep its PC prices competitive. At a global level, organizations have the opportunity to buy products from suppliers overseas or to become their own suppliers and manufacture their own products abroad.

It is important that managers recognize the opportunities and threats associated with managing the global supply chain. On the one hand, gaining access to low-cost products made abroad represents an opportunity for U.S companies to lower their input costs. On the other hand, managers who fail to utilize low-cost overseas suppliers create a threat and put their organizations at a competitive disadvantage.[5] Levi Strauss, for example, was slow to realize that it could not compete with the low-priced jeans sold by Wal-Mart and other retailers, and it was eventually forced to close almost all of its U.S. jean factories and utilize low-cost overseas suppliers to keep the price of its jeans competitive. Now it sells its low-priced jeans in Wal-Mart! The downside to global outsourcing is, of course, the loss of millions of U.S. jobs, an issue we have discussed in previous chapters.

A common problem facing managers of large global companies such as Ford, Procter & Gamble, and IBM is managing the development of a global network of suppliers that will allow their companies to keep costs down and quality high. For example, Boeing's popular 777 jet airline requires 132,500 engineered parts produced around the world by 545 suppliers.[6] While Boeing makes the majority of these parts, eight Japanese suppliers make parts for the 777's fuselage, doors, and wings; a Singapore supplier makes the doors for the plane's forward landing gear; and three Italian suppliers manufacture wing flaps. Boeing's rationale for buying so many inputs from overseas suppliers is that these suppliers are the best in the world at performing their particular activity and doing business with them helps Boeing to produce a

The purchasing activities of global companies have become increasingly complicated in recent years. More than 500 suppliers around the world produce parts for Boeing's popular 777 and even more will be needed for the new Dreamliner.

high-quality final product, a vital requirement given the need for aircraft safety and reliability.[7] Its new plane, the Dreamliner, uses even more parts made by overseas suppliers, and Boeing has outsourced some of the plane's assembly to companies' abroad—something that has led to the charge that is giving away the source of its competitive advantage!

The purchasing activities of global companies have become increasingly complicated as a result of the development of a whole range of skills and competences in different countries around the world. It is clearly in their interests to search out the lowest-cost, best-quality suppliers no matter where they may be. Also, the Internet makes it possible for companies to coordinate complicated, arm's-length exchanges involving the purchasing of inputs and the disposal of outputs.

global outsourcing
The purchase of inputs from overseas suppliers or the production of inputs abroad to lower production costs and improve product quality or design.

Global outsourcing is the process by which organizations purchase inputs from other companies or produce inputs themselves throughout the world to lower their production costs and improve the quality or design of their products.[8] To take advantage of national differences in the cost and quality of resources such as labor or raw materials, GM might build its own engines in one country, transmissions in another, and brakes in a third and buy other components from hundreds of global suppliers. Trade expert Robert Reich once calculated that of the $20,000 that customers pay GM for a Pontiac Le Mans, about $6,000 goes to South Korea, where the Le Mans is assembled; $3,500, to Japan for advanced components such as engines, transaxles, and electronics; $1,500, to Germany, where the Le Mans was designed; $800, to Taiwan, Singapore, and Japan for small components; $500, to Britain for advertising and marketing services; and about $100, to Ireland for data-processing services. The remaining $7,000 goes to GM—and to the lawyers, bankers, and insurance agents that GM retains in the United States.[9]

Is the Le Mans a U.S. product? Yes, but it is also a Korean product, a Japanese product, and a German product. Today, such global exchanges are becoming so complex that specialized organizations are emerging to help manage global organizations' supply chains, that is, the flow of inputs necessary to produce a product. One example is Li & Fung, profiled below in "Managing Globally."

Managing Globally

Global Supply Chain Management

Finding the overseas suppliers that offer the lowest-priced and highest-quality products is an important task facing the managers of global organizations. Since these suppliers are located in thousands of cities in many countries around the world, finding them is a difficult business. Often, global companies use the services of overseas intermediaries or brokers, located near these suppliers, to find the one that best meets their input requirements. Li & Fung, now run by brothers Victor and William Fung, is one of the brokers that has helped hundreds of global companies to locate suitable overseas suppliers, especially suppliers in mainland China.[10]

In the 2000s, however, managing global companies' supply chains became a more complicated task. To reduce costs, overseas suppliers were increasingly *specializing* in just one part of the task of producing a product. For example, in the past, a company such as Target might have negotiated with an overseas supplier to manufacture 1 million units of some particular shirt at a certain cost per unit. But with specialization, Target might find it can reduce the costs of producing the shirt even further by splitting apart the operations involved in its production and having *different* overseas suppliers, often in *different* countries, perform each operation. For example, to get the lowest cost per unit, rather than negotiating with a single overseas supplier over the price of making a particular shirt, Target might first negotiate with a yarn manufacturer in Vietnam to make the yarn; then ship the yarn to a Chinese supplier to weave it into cloth; and then ship the cloth to several different factories in Malaysia and the Philippines to cut the fabric and sew the shirts. Then, another overseas company might take responsibility for packaging and shipping the shirts to wherever in the world they are required. Because a company such as Target has thousands of different clothing products under production, and they change all the time, the problems of managing such a supply chain to get the full cost savings from global expansion are clearly difficult and costly.

Li & Fung capitalized on this opportunity. Realizing that many global companies do not have the time or expertise to find such specialized low-price suppliers, its founders moved quickly to provide such a service. Li & Fung employs 3,600 agents who travel across 37 countries to locate new suppliers and inspect existing suppliers to find new ways to help its global clients get lower prices or higher-quality products. Global companies are happy to outsource their supply chain management to Li & Fung because they realize significant cost savings. Even though they pay a hefty fee to Li & Fung, they avoid the costs of employing their own agents. As the complexity of supply chain management continues to increase, more and more companies like Li & Fung are appearing.

Distributors

distributors

Organizations that help other organizations sell their goods or services to customers.

Distributors are organizations that help other organizations sell their goods or services to customers. The decisions that managers make about how to distribute products to customers can have important effects on organizational performance. For example, package delivery companies such as Federal Express, UPS, and the U.S. Postal Service became vital distributors for the millions of items bought online and shipped to customers by dot-com companies.

The changing nature of distributors and distribution methods can bring opportunities and threats for managers. If distributors become so large and powerful that they can control customers' access to a particular organization's goods and services, they can threaten the organization by demanding that it reduce the prices of its goods and services.[11] For example, the huge retail distributor Wal-Mart controls its suppliers' access to a great number of customers and thus often demands that its suppliers reduce their prices. If an organization such as Procter & Gamble refuses to reduce its prices, Wal-Mart might respond by buying products only from Procter & Gamble's competitors—companies such as Unilever and Dial. In 2004, Wal-Mart announced that by 2006 all its suppliers must adopt a new wireless scanning technology that will reduce its cost of distributing products to its stores or it will stop doing business with them.[12]

In contrast, the power of a distributor may be weakened if there are many options. This has been the experience of the three broadcast television networks—ABC, NBC, and CBS, which "distribute" TV programs. Their ability to demand lower prices from the producers of television programs has been weakened because today hundreds of new cable television channels exist that have reduced the three networks' share of the viewing audience to less than 40%, down from more than 90% a decade ago. Similarly, because there are at least four major package delivery companies—USPS, FedEx, UPS, and DHL—dot-coms and other companies would not really be threatened if one delivery firm tried to increase its prices; they could simply switch delivery companies.

It is illegal for distributors to collaborate or collude to keep prices high and thus maintain their power over buyers; however, this frequently happens. In the early 2000s, several European drug companies conspired to keep the price of vitamins artificially high. In 2005 the three largest global makers of flash memory, including Samsung, were found guilty of price fixing. All these companies paid hundreds of millions of dollars in fines, and many of their top executives were sentenced to jail terms.

Customers

customers Individuals and groups that buy the goods and services that an organization produces.

Customers are the individuals and groups that buy the goods and services that an organization produces. For example, Dell's customers can be segmented into several distinct groups: (1) individuals who purchase PCs for home use, (2) small companies, (3) large companies, (4) government agencies, and (5) educational institutions. Changes in the number and types of customers or in customers' tastes and needs result in opportunities and threats. An organization's success depends on its response to customers. In the PC industry, customers are demanding lower prices and increased multimedia capability, and PC companies must respond to the changing types and needs of customers.[13] A school, too, must adapt to the changing needs of its customers. For example, if more Spanish-speaking students enroll, additional classes in English as a second language may need to be scheduled. A manager's ability to identify an organization's main customers and produce the goods and services they want is a crucial factor affecting organizational and managerial success.

The most obvious opportunity associated with expanding into the global environment is the prospect of selling goods and services to new customers, as Amazon.com's CEO Jeff Bezos discovered when he began to start operating in many countries abroad. Similarly, Accenture and Cap Gemini, two large consulting companies, have established operations throughout the world and recruit and train thousands of overseas consultants to serve the needs of customers in a wide variety of countries.

Today, many products are becoming global products and have gained wide acceptance from customers in countries around the globe. This consolidation is occurring both for consumer goods and for business products and has created enormous opportunities for managers. The global acceptance of Coca-Cola, Apple iPods, McDonald's hamburgers, Doc Martin boots, and Nokia cell phones is a sign that the tastes and preferences of consumers in different countries may not be so different after all.[14] Likewise, large global markets currently exist for business products such as telecommunications equipment, electronic components,

An iPod advertisement adorns a Metro Train in Shanghai. Today, many products such as the iPod have become popular with customers around the world.

computer services, and financial services. Thus, Motorola sells its telecommunications equipment, Intel its microprocessors, and SAP its business systems management software to customers throughout the world.

Competitors

competitors
Organizations that produce goods and services that are similar to a particular organization's goods and services.

One of the most important forces that an organization confronts in its task environment is competitors. **Competitors** are organizations that produce goods and services similar to a particular organization's goods and services. In other words, competitors are organizations vying for the same customers. Dell's competitors include other domestic manufacturers of PCs (such as Apple, HP, and Gateway) as well as overseas competitors (such as Sony and Toshiba in Japan and Lenovo, the Chinese company that bought IBM's PC division in 2005). Dot-com stockbroker E*Trade has other dot-com competitors, like Ameritrade and Scottrade, as well as bricks-and-clicks competitors, such as Merrill Lynch and Charles Schwab.

Rivalry between competitors is potentially the most threatening force that managers must deal with. A high level of rivalry often results in price competition, and falling prices reduce access to resources and lower profits. In the 2000s, competition in the PC industry became intense not only because of an economic slowdown but also because Dell was aggressively cutting costs and prices to increase its global market share.[15] IBM exited the PC business because it was losing millions in its battle against low-cost rivals, and Gateway and HP also suffered, while Dell's profits soared. By 2006, however, HP's fortunes had recovered as it lowered its costs and offered new PCs with AMD's popular chips, while Dell's profit margins had shrunk.

Because fierce competition drives down prices and profits, unethical companies often try to find ways to collude with competitors to keep prices high. Boeing adopted a different, very unsavory, method to gain market share and beat its rivals. In 2006 Boeing agreed to pay $615 million in fines to end a three-year Justice Department investigation into contracting scandals involving Boeing, thereby avoiding criminal charges or admission of wrongdoing. Boeing had been under investigation for improperly acquiring proprietary competitive information about Lockheed Martin's bidding intentions for government rocket-launching contracts. Once it knew how much Lockheed was willing to bid, it could then simply undercut its price by a few million to win the billion dollar auction! The government stripped Boeing of $1 billion worth of the contracts it had won through its improper use of the

Former Boeing CFO Michael Sears, left, walks with his attorney from the U.S. District Court in Alexandria, Virginia, in February 2005. Sears was sentenced to four months for his role in aiding and abetting illegal contract negotiations.

Lockheed documents. Additionally, Boeing illegally recruited senior U.S. Air Force procurement officer Darleen Druyun while she still had authority over billions of dollars in other Boeing contracts. Druyun served nine months in prison for violating federal conflict-of-interest laws. Michael Sears, formerly chief financial officer at Boeing, was fired in 2003 and spent four months in federal prison for illegally recruiting her. The scandals also led to the resignation of Boeing Chairman Phil Condit. Clearly, Boeing went to "enormous" lengths to beat its rivals, and supposedly it had a strong code of ethics that should have prevented such illegal actions!

Although extensive rivalry between existing competitors is a major threat to profitability, so is the potential for new competitors to enter the task environment. **Potential competitors** are organizations that are not presently in a task environment but could enter if they so choose. Amazon.com, for example, is not currently in the retail furniture or appliance business, but it could enter these businesses if its managers decided it could profitably sell such products online. When new competitors enter an industry, competition increases and prices and profits decrease.

potential competitors
Organizations that presently are not in a task environment but could enter if they so choose.

BARRIERS TO ENTRY　In general, the potential for new competitors to enter a task environment (and thus increase competition) is a function of barriers to entry.[16] **Barriers to entry** are factors that make it difficult and costly for a company to enter a particular task environment or industry.[17] In other words, the more difficult and costly it is to enter the task environment, the higher are the barriers to entry. The higher the barriers to entry, the fewer the competitors in an organization's task environment and thus the lower the threat of competition. With fewer competitors, it is easier to obtain customers and keep prices high.

Barriers to entry result from three main sources: economies of scale, brand loyalty, and government regulations that impede entry (see Figure 6.2). **Economies of scale** are the cost advantages associated with large operations. Economies of scale result from factors such as manufacturing products in very large quantities, buying inputs in bulk, or making more effective use of organizational resources than do competitors by fully utilizing employees' skills and knowledge. If organizations already in the task environment are large and enjoy significant economies of scale, then their costs are lower than the costs that potential entrants will be, and newcomers will find it very expensive to enter the

barriers to entry
Factors that make it difficult and costly for an organization to enter a particular task environment or industry.

economies of scale
Cost advantages associated with large operations.

Figure 6.2
Barriers to Entry and Competition

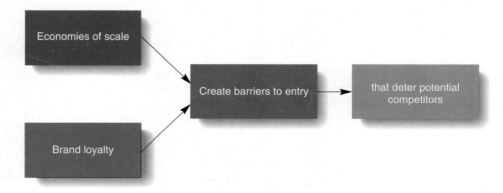

industry. Amazon.com, for example, enjoys significant economies of scale relative to most other dot-com companies.[18]

brand loyalty
Customers' preference for the products of organizations currently existing in the task environment.

Brand loyalty is customers' preference for the products of organizations currently existing in the task environment. If established organizations enjoy significant brand loyalty, then a new entrant will find it extremely difficult and costly to obtain a share of the market. Newcomers must bear huge advertising costs to build customer awareness of the goods or services they intend to provide.[19] Both Amazon.com and Yahoo, for example, two of the first dot-coms to go online, enjoy a high level of brand loyalty and have some of the highest Web site hit rates of all dot-coms (the latter also allows them to increase their advertising revenues).

In some cases, *government regulations* function as a barrier to entry at both the industry and the country levels. Many industries that were deregulated, such as air transport, trucking, utilities, and telecommunications, experienced a high level of new entry after deregulation; this forced existing companies in those industries to operate more efficiently or risk being put out of business.

At the national and global level, administrative barriers are government policies that create a barrier to entry and limit imports of goods by overseas companies. Japan is well known for the many ways in which it attempts to restrict the entry of overseas competitors or lessen their impact on Japanese firms. For example, why do Dutch companies export tulip bulbs to almost every country in the world except Japan? Japanese customs inspectors insist on checking every tulip bulb by cutting the stems vertically down the middle, and even Japanese ingenuity cannot put them back together.[20] Japan has come under intense pressure to relax and abolish such regulations, as the following suggests.

American Rice Invades Japan

Managing Globally

The Japanese rice market, similar to many other Japanese markets, was closed to overseas competitors until 1993 to protect Japan's thousands of high-cost, low-output rice farmers. Rice cultivation is expensive in Japan because of the country's mountainous terrain, so Japanese consumers have always paid high prices for rice. Under overseas pressure, the Japanese government opened the market, and overseas competitors are now allowed to export to Japan 8 percent of its

A Japanese businessman receives a lunch box at a Nippon restaurant shop at the Tokyo Railway Station. Nippon began selling lunch boxes prepared from U.S. rice, frozen and imported from the United States, in 2001, drawing harsh protests from Japanese rice farmers.

annual rice consumption. Despite the still-present hefty overseas tariff on rice–$2.33 per 2.2 pounds–U.S. rice sells for $14 dollars per pound bag, while Japanese rice sells for about $19. With the recession affecting Japan, price-conscious consumers are turning to overseas rice, which has hurt domestic farmers.

In the 2000s, however, an alliance between organic rice grower Lundberg Family Farms of California and the Nippon Restaurant Enterprise Co. found a new way to break into the Japanese rice market. Because there is no tariff on rice used in processed foods, Nippon takes the U.S. organic rice and converts it into "O-bento," an organic hot boxed lunch packed with rice, vegetables, chicken, beef, and salmon, all imported from the United States. The new lunches, which cost about $4 compared to a Japanese rice bento that costs about $9, are sold at railway stations and other outlets throughout Japan.[21] They are proving to be very popular and are creating a storm of protest from Japanese rice farmers, who already have been forced to leave 37 percent of their rice fields idle and grow less profitable crops because of the entry of U.S. rice growers. Japanese and overseas companies are increasingly forming alliances to find new ways to break into the high-price Japanese market, and, little by little, Japan's restrictive trade practices are being whittled away.

In summary, intense rivalry among competitors creates a task environment that is highly threatening and causes difficulty for managers trying to gain access to the resources an organization needs. Conversely, low rivalry results in a task environment where competitive pressures are more moderate and managers have greater opportunities to acquire the resources they need for their organizations to be effective.

The General Environment

Economic, technological, sociocultural, demographic, political, and legal forces in the general environment can have profound effects on forces in the task environment, effects that may not be evident to managers. For example, the sudden, dramatic upheavals in the Internet and dot-com industry environment in the early 2000s were brought about by a combination of changing Internet and digital technology, the softening U.S. stock market and economy, and increasing fears about global recession. These changes triggered intense competition between dot-com companies that further worsened the industry situation.

The implication is clear: Managers must constantly analyze forces in the general environment because these forces affect ongoing decision making and planning. Next, we discuss the major forces in the general environment, and examine their impact on an organization's task environment.

Economic Forces

economic forces
Interest rates, inflation, unemployment, economic growth, and other factors that affect the general health and well-being of a nation or the regional economy of an organization.

Economic forces affect the general health and well-being of a country or world region. They include interest rates, inflation, unemployment, and economic growth. Economic forces produce many opportunities and threats for managers. Low levels of unemployment and falling interest rates give more people more money to spend, and as a result organizations have an opportunity to sell more goods and services. Good economic times affect supplies: Resources become easier to acquire, and organizations have an opportunity to flourish, as high-tech companies did throughout the 1990s. The high-techs made record profits as the economy boomed in large part because of advances in information technology and growing global trade.

In contrast, worsening macroeconomic conditions, as in the 2000s, pose a major threat because they limit managers' ability to gain access to the resources their organizations need. Profit-seeking organizations such as retail stores and hotels have fewer customers for their goods and services during economic downturns. Nonprofits such as charities and colleges receive fewer donations during economic downturns. Even a moderate deterioration in national or regional economic conditions can seriously reduce performance. A relatively mild recession was a major factor in the staggering collapse of dot-com companies in the early 2000s.

Poor economic conditions make the environment more complex and managers' jobs more difficult and demanding. Managers may need to reduce the number of individuals in their departments and increase the motivation of remaining employees, and managers and workers alike may need to identify ways to acquire and utilize resources more efficiently. Successful managers realize the important effects that economic forces have on their organizations, and they pay close attention to what is occurring in the national and regional economies to respond appropriately.

Technological Forces

technology The combination of skills and equipment that managers use in the design, production, and distribution of goods and services.

Technology is the combination of tools, machines, computers, skills, information, and knowledge that managers use in the design, production, and distribution of goods and services. **Technological forces** are outcomes of changes in the technology that managers use to design, produce, or distribute goods and services. The overall pace of technological change has accelerated greatly in the last decade because of advances in microprocessors and computer hardware and software, and technological forces have increased in magnitude.[22]

technological forces Outcomes of changes in the technology that managers use to design, produce, or distribute goods and services.

Technological forces can have profound implications for managers and organizations. Technological change can make established products obsolete—for example, typewriters, black-and-white televisions, bound sets of encyclopedias—forcing managers to find new ways to satisfy customer needs. Although technological change can threaten an organization, it also can create a host of new opportunities for designing, making, or distributing new and better kinds of goods and services. More powerful microprocessors developed by Intel caused a revolution in IT that spurred demand for PCs, contributed to the success of companies such as Dell and HP, but led to the decline of mainframe computer makers such as IBM.[23] However, IBM responded in the last decade by changing its emphasis from providing computer hardware to providing advanced computer services and consulting, and it has regained its strong global position. Managers must move quickly to respond to such changes if their organizations are to survive and prosper. Today Intel is being pressured by chip maker AMD, which was first to develop a powerful 64-bit PC chip, the Athlon, and has moved quickly to develop its own 64-bit chips.[24]

Changes in IT are altering the very nature of work itself within organizations, including that of the manager's job. Telecommuting along the information superhighway, videoconferencing, and text messaging are now everyday activities that provide opportunities for managers to supervise and coordinate geographically dispersed employees. Salespeople in many companies work from home offices and commute electronically to work. They communicate with other employees through companywide electronic mail networks and use video cameras attached to PCs for "face-to-face" meetings with coworkers who may be across the country.

Sociocultural Forces

sociocultural forces
Pressures emanating from the social structure of a country or society or from the national culture.

social structure The arrangement of relationships between individuals and groups in a society.

Sociocultural forces are pressures emanating from the social structure of a country or society or from the national culture, pressures that were discussed at length in the previous chapter. Pressures from both sources can either constrain or facilitate the way organizations operate and managers behave. **Social structure** is the arrangement of relationships between individuals and groups in a society. Societies differ substantially in social structure. In societies that have a high degree of social stratification, there are many distinctions among individuals and groups. Caste systems in India and Tibet and the recognition of numerous social classes in Great Britain and France produce a multilayered social structure in each of those countries. In contrast, social stratification is lower in relatively egalitarian New Zealand and in the United States, where the social structure reveals few distinctions among people. Most top managers in France come from the upper classes of French society, but top managers in the United States come from all strata of American society.

Societies also differ in the extent to which they emphasize the individual over the group. For example, the United States emphasizes the primacy of the individual, and Japan emphasizes the primacy of the group. This difference may dictate the methods managers need to use to motivate and lead employees. **National culture** is the set of values that a society considers important and the norms of behavior that are approved or sanctioned in that society. Societies differ substantially in the values and norms that they emphasize. For example, in the United States individualism is highly valued, and in Korea and Japan individuals are expected to conform to group expectations.[25] National culture, discussed at length later in this chapter, also affects the way managers motivate and coordinate employees and the way organizations do business. Ethics, an important aspect of national culture, was discussed in detail in Chapter 4.

national culture The set of values that a society considers important and the norms of behavior that are approved or sanctioned in that society.

Social structure and national culture not only differ across societies but also change within societies over time. In the United States, attitudes toward the roles of women, love, sex, and marriage changed in each past decade. Many people in Asian countries such as Hong Kong, Singapore, Korea, and Japan think that the younger generation is far more individualistic and "American-like" than previous generations. Currently, throughout much of eastern Europe, new values that emphasize individualism and entrepreneurship are replacing communist values based on collectivism and obedience to the state. The pace of change is accelerating.

Individual managers and organizations must be responsive to changes in, and differences among, the social structures and national cultures of all the countries in which they operate. In today's increasingly integrated global economy, managers are likely to interact with people from several countries, and many managers live and work abroad. Effective managers are sensitive to differences between societies and adjust their behaviors accordingly.

Managers and organizations must respond to social changes within a society. One example is the rage for "low-carb" foods, which affected not only large businesses like Krispy Kreme but also smaller ones such as this local diner.

Managers and organizations also must respond to social changes within a society. In the last few decades, for example, Americans have become increasingly interested in their personal health and fitness. Managers who recognized this trend early and exploited the opportunities that resulted from it were able to reap significant gains for their organizations. PepsiCo used the opportunity presented by the fitness trend and took market share from archrival Coca-Cola by being the first to introduce diet colas and fruit-based soft drinks. Quaker Oats made Gatorade the most popular sports drink and brought out a whole host of low-fat food products. The health trend, however, did not offer opportunities to all companies; to some it posed a threat. Tobacco companies came under intense pressure due to consumers' greater awareness of negative health impacts from smoking. Hershey Foods and other manufacturers of candy bars have been threatened by customers' desires for low-fat, healthy foods. The rage for "low-carb" foods in the 2000s led to a huge increase in demand for meat and hurt bread and doughnut companies such as Kraft and Krispy Kreme.

Demographic Forces

demographic forces
Outcomes of changes in, or changing attitudes toward, the characteristics of a population, such as age, gender, ethnic origin, race, sexual orientation, and social class.

Demographic forces are outcomes of changes in, or changing attitudes toward, the characteristics of a population, such as age, gender, ethnic origin, race, sexual orientation, and social class. Like the other forces in the general environment, demographic forces present managers with opportunities and threats and can have major implications for organizations. We examined the nature of these challenges in depth in our discussion of diversity in Chapter 5, so we will not discuss these forces again here.

We will just note one important change occurring today: Most industrialized nations are experiencing the aging of their populations as a consequence of falling birth and death rates and the aging of the baby-boom generation. In Germany, for example, the percentage of the population over age 65 is expected to rise to 20.7% by 2010 from 15.4% in 1990. Comparable figures for Canada are 14.4% and 11.4%; for Japan, 19.5% and 11.7%; and for the United States, 13.5% and 12.6%.[26] In the United States the percentage increase is far smaller because of the huge wave of immigration during the 1990s and the large families that new immigrants typically have. However, the absolute number of older people has increased substantially and is increasing opportunities for organizations that cater to older people; the home health care and recreation industries, for example, are seeing an upswing in demand for their services.

The aging of the population also has several implications for the workplace. Most significant are a relative decline in the young people joining the workforce and an increase in the number of active employees willing to postpone retirement past the traditional retirement age of 65. These changes suggest that organizations need to find ways to motivate and utilize the skills and knowledge of older employees, an issue that many Western societies have yet to tackle.

Political and Legal Forces

political and legal forces Outcomes of changes in laws and regulations, such as the deregulation of industries, the privatization of organizations, and the increased emphasis on environmental protection.

Political and legal forces are outcomes of changes in laws and regulations. They result from political and legal developments that take place within a nation, within a world region, or across the world and significantly affect managers and organizations everywhere. Political processes shape a nation's laws and the international laws that govern the relationships between nations. Laws constrain the operations of organizations and managers, and thus create both opportunities and threats.[27] For example, throughout much of the industrialized world there has been a strong trend toward deregulation of industries previously controlled by the state and privatization of organizations once owned by the state.

In the United States, deregulation of the airline industry in 1978 ushered into the task environment of commercial airlines major changes that are still working themselves out. Deregulation allowed 29 new airlines to enter the industry between 1978 and 1993. The increase in airline-passenger carrying capacity after deregulation led to excess capacity on many routes, intense competition, and fare wars. To respond to this more competitive task environment, in the 1980s airlines looked for ways to reduce operating costs. The development of hub-and-spoke systems, the rise of nonunion airlines, and the introduction of no-frills discount service are all responses to increased competition in the airlines' task environment. By the 1990s, once again in control of their environments, airlines were making record profits. However, soaring oil prices in the 2000s wiped out these profits, and airlines found themselves once again under pressure. In 2004, for example, both United Airlines and Delta announced that they were close to bankruptcy, and their futures were uncertain.[28]

Another important political and legal force affecting managers and organizations is the political integration of countries that has been taking place during the past decades.[29] Increasingly nations are joining together into political unions that allow for the free exchange of resources and capital. The growth of the European Union (EU) is one example: Common laws govern trade and commerce between EU member countries, and the European Court has the right to examine the business of global organizations and to approve any proposed mergers between overseas companies that operate inside the EU. For example, Microsoft's anticompetitive business practices have come under scrutiny, and the court refused to approve a proposed merger between GE and Honeywell that had been approved by U.S. regulators. The North American Free Trade Agreement (NAFTA), discussed later in the chapter, has more modest political goals, but as with the EU, it has changed the laws that affect international commerce by lowering the barriers to the free flow of goods and services between member nations.[30]

Indeed, international agreements to abolish laws and regulations that restrict and reduce trade between countries have been having profound effects on global organizations. The fall in legal trade barriers creates enormous opportunities for companies in one country to sell goods and services in other countries. But, by allowing nondomestic companies to compete in a nation's domestic market for customers, falling trade barriers also pose a serious threat because they increase competition in the task environment. Between 1973 and 2006, for example, Japanese competitors increase their share of the U.S. car market from 3% to 30%.[31] This growth would not have been possible without relatively low trade barriers, which allowed producers in Japan to export cars to the United States. However, competition from Toyota, Honda, and other Japanese companies has forced U.S. car companies to improve their operations. Finding new ways to design and make cars is an ongoing process as they fight to protect their market share, which was continuing to fall in 2006–Japanese carmakers' market share had grown to over 33%. In essence, the removal of legal restrictions to global trade has the same effect as deregulating industries and removing restrictions against competition: It increases the intensity of competition in the task environment and forces conservative, slow-moving companies to become more efficient, improve product quality, and learn new values and norms to compete in the global environment.

Deregulation, privatization, and the removal of legal barriers to trade are just a few of the many ways in which changing political and legal forces can challenge organizations and managers. Others include increased emphasis on environmental protection and the preservation of endangered species, increased emphasis on safety in the workplace, and legal constraints against discrimination on the basis of race, gender, or age. Managers face major challenges when they seek to take advantage of the opportunities created by changing political, legal, and economic forces, as the example of Nestlé in the next section suggests.

The Changing Global Environment

In the 21st century, any idea that the world is composed of a set of distinct national countries and markets that are separated physically, economically, and culturally from one another has vanished. Managers now recognize that companies exist and compete in a truly global market. Today, managers regard the global environment as a source of important opportunities and threats that they must respond to. Managers constantly confront the challenges of global competition–establishing operations in a country abroad or obtaining inputs from suppliers abroad–or the challenges of managing in a different national culture.[32] (See Figure 6.3.)

In essence, as a result of falling trade barriers, managers view the global environment as open, that is, as an environment in which companies are free to buy goods and services from, and sell goods and services to, whichever companies and countries they choose. They also are free to compete against each other to attract customers around the world. They must establish an international network of operations and subsidiaries to build global competitive advantage. Coca-Cola and PepsiCo, for example, have competed aggressively for 20 years to develop the strongest global soft-drink empire, just as Toyota and Honda have built hundreds of car plants around the world to provide the vehicles that global customers like.

In this section, we first explain how this open global environment is the result of globalization and the flow of capital around the world. Next, we examine how specific economic, political, and legal changes, such as the lowering of barriers to trade and investment, have increased globalization and led to greater interaction and exchanges between organizations and countries. Then we discuss how declining barriers of distance and culture have also increased the pace of globalization, and we consider the specific implications of these changes for managers

Figure 6.3
The Global Environment

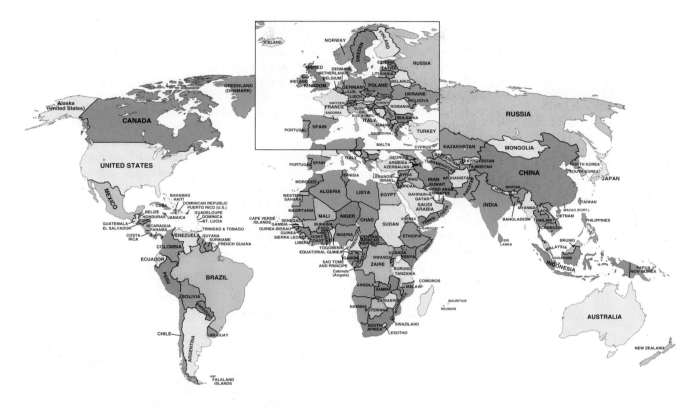

and organizations. Finally, we note that nations still differ widely from each other because they have distinct cultural values and norms and that managers must appreciate these differences if they are to compete successfully across countries.

The Process of Globalization

globalization The set of specific and general forces that work together to integrate and connect economic, political, and social systems *across* countries, cultures, or geographical regions so that nations become increasingly interdependent aned similar.

Perhaps the most important reason why the global environment has become more open and competitive is the increase in globalization. **Globalization** is the set of specific and general forces that work together to integrate and connect economic, political, and social systems *across* countries, cultures, or geographic regions. The result of globalization is that nations and peoples become increasingly *interdependent* because the same forces affect them in similar ways. The fates of peoples in different countries become interlinked as the world's markets and businesses become increasingly interconnected. And, as nations become more interdependent, they become more similar to one another in the sense that people develop a similar liking for products as diverse as cell phones, iPods, blue jeans, coke, Manchester United, curry, green tea, Japanese cars, and Columbian coffee. One outcome of globalization is that the world is becoming a "global village": Products, service, or people can become well known throughout the world—something Nestlé, with its products like Kit-Kat bars, is taking advantage of, as the following "Managing Globally" describes.

Managing Globally

Nestlé's Food Empire

Nestlé is the world's largest food company, with over $50 billion in annual sales, 224,000 employees, and 500 factories in 80 countries. In 2006, it made and sold over 8,000 food products, including such popular brands as Kit-Kat chocolate bars, Taster's Choice coffee, Carnation Instant milk, and Stouffer's Foods. At its corporate headquarters in Vevey, Switzerland, CEO Peter Brabeck-Latmathe, who has been in charge since 1997, is responsible for boosting Nestlé's global performance. He has faced many challenges.[33]

Brabeck has been working to increase Nestlé's revenues and profits by entering attractive markets in both developed and emerging nations as trade barriers fall. He is continuing the global expansion that Nestlé began in the 1990s, when, for example, it bought the U.S. food companies Carnation and Buitoni Pasta, the British chocolate maker Rowntree, the French bottled-water company Perrier, and the Mexican food maker Ortega. Under Brabeck, Nestlé spent $18 billion to acquire U.S. companies Ralston Purina, Dreyer's Ice-cream, and Chef America. Brabeck intends not only to develop these food brands in the United States but also to modify their products to suit the tastes of customers in countries around the world. He is particularly anxious to enter emerging markets such as those in eastern Europe and Asia to take advantage of the enormous numbers of potential new customers in these regions. In this way Nestlé can leverage its well-known products and brand image around the world to drive up its performance.

South Korean promoters make coffee with the new Latte Creamer in a huge cup during a Nestlé Korea sales event in Seoul.

Increasing global revenues from increased product sales is only the first leg of Brabeck's global business model, however. He is also anxious to increase Nestlé's operating efficiency and reduce the cost of managing its global operations. As you can imagine, with 224,000 employees and 500 factories the costs of organizing Nestlé's global activities are enormous. Brabeck benchmarked its operating costs to those of competitors such as Kraft Foods and Unilever and found Nestlé's costs were significantly higher than theirs. Brabeck cut the workforce by 20% percent, closed 150 factories, and reduced operating costs by over 12%, with more cuts to come. Nestlé is also using advanced IT both to reduce the number of its global suppliers and to negotiate more favorable supply contracts with them—moves that should result in a significant drop in purchasing costs. To improve the efficiency of its purchasing and retailing functions, Nestlé has developed e-business Web sites where it lists the detailed specifications of the inputs it requires from suppliers.

Brabeck hopes Nestlé's new streamlined operating structure will result in an increased flow of information that will allow it to capitalize on what has always been its main source of competitive advantage: superior innovation. In 1886 Henri Nestlé, a pharmacist living in Vevey, invented an infant formula made from cow's milk and wheat flour that could be used as a substitute for mother's milk. Since then the company he founded has been a pioneer in food product innovation. One of his company's later innovations was Nescafe instant coffee, introduced in 1938 and still the best-selling brand in the world today. Brabeck's global vision for Nestlé is therefore driven by three main goals: (1) Expand Nestlé's range of products, and offer them to new and existing customers in countries throughout the world; (2) find lower-cost ways to make and sell these products; and (3) speed up Nestlé's product innovation by leveraging its expertise across its food businesses to create more attractive food products that will increase its global market share. If his plan works, then Brabeck will be well on the way to making Nestlé not only the largest but also the most profitable global food company.

But what drives or spurs globalization? What makes people and companies like Nestlé, Toyota, or Microsoft want to venture into an uncertain global environment that puts into motion the complex set of forces that result in globalization? The answer is that the path of globalization is shaped by the ebb and flow of *capital*, that is, valuable wealth-generating assets, as it moves through companies, countries, and world regions seeking its most highly valued use, that is, the investment through which capital can earn the greatest returns (wealth). Managers, employees, and companies like Nestlé are motivated to try to profit or benefit by using their skills to make products customers around the world want to buy. The four principal forms of capital that flow between countries are:

- *Human capital:* the flow of people around the world through immigration, migration, and emigration.
- *Financial capital:* the flow of money capital across world markets through overseas investment, credit, lending, and aid.
- *Resource capital:* the flow of natural resources and semifinished products between companies and countries such as metals, minerals, lumber, energy, food products, microprocessors, and auto parts.
- *Political capital:* the flow of power and influence around the world using diplomacy, persuasion, aggression, and force of arms to protect a country's or world region or political bloc's access to the other forms of capital.

Most of the changes associated with globalization are the result of these four capital flows and the interactions between them, as nations compete on the world stage to protect and increase their standards of living and to further the political goals and social causes that are espoused by their societies' cultures. The next sections look at the factors that have increased the rate at which capital flows between companies and countries. In a positive sense the faster the flow, the more capital is being utilized where it can create the most value, in the sense of people moving to where their skills earn them more money, or investors switching to the stocks or bonds that give them higher dividends or interest, or companies finding lower-cost sources of inputs. In a negative sense, however, a fast flow of capital also means that individual countries or world regions can find themselves in trouble when companies and investors move their capital to invest it in more productive ways in other countries or world regions, often those with lower labor costs or rapidly expanding markets. When capital leaves a country, the result is higher unemployment, recession, and lower a standard of living for its people.

Declining Barriers to Trade and Investment

One of the main factors that has speeded globalization by freeing the movement of capital has been the decline in barriers to trade and investment, discussed earlier. During the 1920s and 1930s, many countries erected formidable barriers to international trade and investment in the belief that this was the best way to promote their economic well-being. Many of these barriers were high tariffs on imports of manufactured goods. A **tariff** is a tax that a government imposes on imported or, occasionally, on exported goods. The aim of import tariffs is to protect domestic industries and jobs, such as those in the auto or steel industry, from overseas competition by raising the price of goods from abroad. In 2001, for example, the U.S. government increased the tariffs on the import of overseas steel to protect U.S. steelmakers; however, under pressure from the European Union, these tariffs were significantly reduced in 2003.

The reason for removing tariffs is that, very often, when one country imposes an import tariff, others follow suit and the result is a series of retaliatory moves as countries progressively raise tariff barriers against each other. In the 1920s this behavior depressed world demand and helped usher in the Great Depression of the 1930s and massive unemployment. It was to avoid tariffs on U.S. goods entering Europe that the steel tariffs were reduced. In short, rather than protecting jobs and promoting economic well-being, governments of countries that resort to raising high tariff barriers ultimately reduce employment and undermine economic growth.[34]

GATT AND THE RISE OF FREE TRADE After World War II, advanced Western industrial countries, having learned from the Great Depression, committed themselves to the goal of removing barriers to the free flow of resources and capital between countries. This commitment was reinforced by acceptance of the principle that free trade, rather than tariff barriers, was the best way to foster a healthy domestic economy and low unemployment.[35]

The **free-trade doctrine** predicts that if each country agrees to specialize in the production of the goods and services that it can produce most efficiently, this will make the best use of global capital resources and will result in lower prices.[36] For example, if Indian companies are highly efficient in the

tariff A tax that a government imposes on imported or, occasionally, exported goods.

free-trade doctrine The idea that if each country specializes in the production of the goods and services that it can produce most efficiently, this will make the best use of global resources.

production of textiles and U.S. companies are highly efficient in the production of computer software, then under a free-trade agreement capital would move to India and be invested there to produce textiles, while capital from around the world would flow to the United States and be invested in its innovative computer software companies. Consequently, prices of both textiles and software should fall because each good is being produced in the location where it can be made at the lowest cost, benefiting consumers and making the best use of scarce capital. This doctrine is, of course, responsible for the increase in global outsourcing and the loss of millions of U.S. jobs in textiles and manufacturing as capital is invested in factories in China and Malaysia. However, millions of jobs have also been created because of new capital investments in high-tech, IT, and the service sector that in theory should offset manufacturing job losses in the long run.

Historically, countries that accepted this free-trade doctrine set as their goal the removal of barriers to the free flow of goods, services, and capital between countries. They attempted to achieve this through an international treaty known as the General Agreement on Tariffs and Trade (GATT). In the half-century since World War II, there have been eight rounds of GATT negotiations aimed at lowering tariff barriers. The last round, the Uruguay Round, involved 117 countries and was completed in December 1993. This round succeeded in lowering tariffs by over 30 percent from the previous level. It also led to the dissolving of GATT and its replacement by the World Trade Organization (WTO), which today, in 2006, continues the struggle to reduce tariffs and has more power to sanction countries that break global agreements.[37] On average, the tariff barriers among the governments of developed countries declined from over 40% in 1948 to about 3% in 2000, causing a dramatic increase in world trade.[38]

Declining Barriers of Distance and Culture

Historically, barriers of distance and culture also closed the global environment and kept managers focused on their domestic market. The management problems Unilever, the huge British-based, global soap and detergent maker, experienced at the turn of the 20th century illustrate the effect of these barriers.

Founded in London during the 1880s by William Lever, a Quaker, Unilever had a worldwide reach by the early 1900s and operated subsidiaries in most major countries of the British Empire, including India, Canada, and Australia. Lever had a very hands-on, autocratic management style and found his far-flung business empire difficult to control. The reason for Lever's control problems was that communication over great distances was difficult. It took six weeks to reach India by ship from England, and international telephone and telegraph services were very unreliable.

Another problem that Unilever encountered was the difficulty of doing business in societies that were separated from Britain by barriers of language and culture. Different countries have different sets of national beliefs, values, and norms, and Lever found that a management approach that worked in Britain did not necessarily work in India or Persia (now Iran). As a result, management practices had to be tailored to suit each unique national culture. After Lever's death in 1925, top management at Unilever lowered or *decentralized* (see Chapter 10) decision-making authority to the managers of the various national subsidiaries so that they could develop a management approach that suited the country in which they were operating. One result of this strategy was that the subsidiaries grew distant and remote from one another—something that reduced Unilever's performance.[39]

Since the end of World War II, a continuing stream of advances in communications and transportation technology have worked to reduce the barriers of distance and culture that affected Unilever and all global organizations. Over the last 30 years, global communication has been revolutionized by developments in satellites, digital technology, the Internet and global computer networks, and video teleconferencing that allow for the transmission of vast amounts of information and make reliable, secure, and instantaneous communication possible between people and companies anywhere in the world.[40] This revolution has made it possible for a global organization—a tiny garment factory in Li & Fung's network or a huge company such as Nestlé or Unilever—to do business anywhere, anytime, and to search for customers and suppliers around the world.

One of the most important innovations in transportation technology that has made the global environment more open has been the growth of commercial jet travel, which reduced the time it takes to get from one location to another. Because of jet travel, New York is now closer to Tokyo than it was to Philadelphia in the days of the 13 colonies—a fact that makes control of far-flung international businesses much easier today than in William Lever's era. In addition to making travel faster, modern communications and transportation technologies have also helped reduce the cultural distance between countries. The Internet and its millions of Web sites facilitate the development of global communications networks and media that are helping to create a worldwide culture above and beyond unique national cultures. Moreover, television networks such as CNN, MTV, ESPN, BBC, and HBO can now be received in many countries, and Hollywood films are shown throughout the world.

Effects of Free Trade on Managers

The lowering of barriers to trade and investment and the decline of distance and culture barriers has created enormous opportunities for companies to expand the market for their goods and services through exports and investments in overseas countries. Although managers at some organizations, like Barnes & Noble, have shied away from trying to sell their goods and services overseas, the situation of Wal-Mart and Lands' End, which have developed profitable global operations, is more typical. The shift toward a more open global economy has created not only more opportunities to sell goods and services in markets abroad but also the opportunity to buy more from other countries. Indeed, the success in the United States of Lands' End has been based in part on its managers' willingness to import low-cost clothes and bedding from overseas manufacturers. Lands' End purchases clothing from manufacturers in Hong Kong, Malaysia, Taiwan, and China because U.S. textile makers often do not offer the same quality, styling, flexibility, or price.[41] Indeed, most clothing companies, such as Levi Strauss, Wal-Mart, and Target, are major players in the global environment by virtue of their purchasing activities, even if like Target or Dillard's they sell only in the United States.

The manager's job is more challenging in a dynamic global environment because of the increased intensity of competition that goes hand in hand with the lowering of barriers to trade and investment. Thus, as discussed above, the job of the average manager in a U.S. car company became a lot harder from the mid-1970s on as a result of the penetration of the U.S. market by efficient Japanese competitors. Recall that Levi Strauss closed its last U.S. clothing factory in 2001 because it could not match the prices of low-cost overseas jeans manufacturers that compete with Levi's to sell to clothing chains such as Wal-Mart, Dillard's, and Target.

REGIONAL TRADE AGREEMENTS The growth of regional trade agreements such as the North American Free Trade Agreement (NAFTA), and most recently the Central American Free Trade Agreement (CAFTA), also presents opportunities and threats for managers and their organizations. Table 6.1 outlines some of the most active regional trade associations; they have been formed between countries in most continents or world regions.

In North America, NAFTA, which became effective on January 1, 1994, had the aim of abolishing the tariffs on 99% of the goods traded between Mexico, Canada, and the United States by 2004. Although it has not achieved this lofty goal, NAFTA has removed most barriers on the cross-border flow of resources, giving, for example, financial institutions and retail businesses in Canada and the United States unrestricted access to the Mexican marketplace. After NAFTA was signed, there was a flood of investment into Mexico from the United States, as well as many other countries such as Japan. Wal-Mart, Costco, Radio Shack, and other major U.S. retail chains have expanded their operations in Mexico; Wal-Mart, for example, is stocking many more products from Mexico in its U.S. stores, and its Mexican store chain is also expanding rapidly.

The establishment of free-trade areas creates an opportunity for manufacturing organizations because it allows them to reduce their costs. They can do this either by shifting production to the lowest-cost location within the free-trade area (for example, U.S. auto and textile companies shifting production to Mexico) or by serving the whole region from one location, rather than establishing separate operations in each country. Some managers, however, view regional free-trade agreements

Mexican workers at CyOptics in Matamoros, Mexico, a high-tech manufacturing facility just across the U.S. border from Brownsville, TX. CyOptics, a U.S-owned company, designs, develops and markets a range of optical chips and components for communications systems. The more competitive environment brought about by NAFTA poses both opportunities and threats for managers.

Table 6.1

Most Active Regional Global Free-Trade Associations

Regional Associations	Area (km²)	Population	GDP ($US) in Millions	Per Capita	Member states
European Union (EU)	3,977,487	460,124,266	11,723,816	25,480	25
Caribbean Community and Common Market (CARICOM)	462,344	14,565,083	64,219	4,409	15
Economic Community of West African States (ECOWAS)	5,112,903	251,646,263	342,519	1,361	15
Economic and Monetary Community of Central Africa (CEMAC)	3,020,142	34,970,529	85,136	2,435	6
East African Community (EAC)	1,763,777	97,865,428	104,239	1,065	3
South American Community of Nations (CSN)	17,339,153	370,158,470	2,868,430	7,749	10
Cooperation Council of the Arab States of the Gulf (GCC)	2,285,844	35,869,438	536,223	14,949	6
Southern African Customs Union (SACU)	2,693,418	51,055,878	541,433	10,605	5
Common Market for Eastern and Southern Africa (COMESA)	3,779,427	118,950,321	141,962	1,193	5
North American Free Trade Agreement (NAFTA)	21,588,638	430,495,039	12,889,900	29,942	3
Association of Southeast Asian Nations (ASEAN)	4,400,000	553,900,000	2,172,000	4,044	10
South Asian Association for Regional Cooperation (SAARC)	5,136,740	1,467,255,669	4,074,031	2,777	8
Euro-Mediterranean Free Trade Area (Agadir)	1,703,910	126,066,286	513,674	4,075	4
Eurasian Economic Community (EurAsEC)	20,789,100	208,067,618	1,689,137	8,118	6
Central American Common Market (CACM)	422,614	37,816,598	159,536	4,219	5
Pacific Islands Forum (PARTA)	528,151	7,810,905	23,074	2,954	14

Source: *CIA World Factbook 2005,* IMF WEO database.

as a threat because they expose a company based in one member country to increased competition from companies based in the other member countries. NAFTA has had this effect; today Mexican managers find themselves facing the threat of head-to-head competition in some industries against efficient U.S. and Canadian companies. But the opposite is true as well: U.S. and Canadian managers are experiencing threats in labor-intensive industries, such as the flooring tile and textile industries, where Mexican businesses have a cost advantage.

In July 2005 the U.S. House of Representatives approved the formation of CAFTA, a regional trade agreement designed to eliminate tariffs on products between the United States and all countries in Central America. By 2006, the Dominican Republic, El Salvador, Guatemala, Nicaragua, and Honduras had also approved and implemented the agreement, but Costa Rica has not. CAFTA is seen as a stepping stone toward establishing the Free Trade Area of the Americas (FTAA), an ambitious attempt to establish a free-trade agreement that would increase economic prosperity throughout the Americas. FTAA would include all South American and Caribbean nations, except Cuba, as well as those of North and Central America. However, the economic problems many countries have been experiencing, together with major political and ideological differences—such as the political resistance within the United States because of jobs lost to Mexico and Canada—have slowed down the process of integration and globalization. The more competitive environment NAFTA has brought about has increased both the opportunities that managers can take advantage of and the threats they must respond to in performing their jobs effectively.

The Role of National Culture

Despite evidence that countries are becoming more similar to one another because of globalization, and that the world is on the verge of becoming a global village, the cultures of different countries still vary widely because of critical differences in their values, norms, and attitudes. As noted earlier, national culture includes the values, norms, knowledge, beliefs, moral principles, laws, customs, and other practices that unite the citizens of a country.[42] National culture shapes individual behavior by specifying appropriate and inappropriate behavior and interaction with others. People learn national culture in their everyday lives by interacting with those around them. This learning starts at an early age and continues throughout their lives.

Cultural Values and Norms

values Ideas about what a society believes to be good, right, desirable, or beautiful.

The basic building blocks of national culture are values and norms. **Values** are ideas about what a society believes to be good, right, desirable, or beautiful. They provide the basic underpinnings for notions of individual freedom, democracy, truth, justice, honesty, loyalty, social obligation, collective responsibility, the appropriate roles for men and women, love, sex, marriage, and so on. Values are more than merely abstract concepts; they are invested with considerable emotional significance. People argue, fight, and even die over values such as freedom.

Although deeply embedded in society, values are not static; however, change in a country's values is likely to be slow and painful. For example, the value systems of many formerly communist states, such as Russia, are undergoing significant changes as those countries move away from a value system that emphasizes the state and toward one that emphasizes individual freedom. Social turmoil often results when countries undergo major changes in their values.

norms Unwritten rules and codes of conduct that prescribe how people should act in particular situations.

Norms are unwritten rules and codes of conduct that prescribe appropriate behavior in particular situations and shape the behavior of people toward one another. Two types of norms play a major role in national culture: folkways and

folkways The routine social conventions of everyday life.

mores. Folkways are the routine social conventions of everyday life. They concern customs and practices such as dressing appropriately for particular situations, good social manners, eating with the correct utensils, and neighborly behavior. Although folkways define the way people are expected to behave, violation of folkways is not a serious or moral matter. People who violate folkways are often thought to be eccentric or ill-mannered, but they are not usually considered to be evil or bad. In many countries, initially foreigners may be excused for violating folkways because they are unaccustomed to local behavior, but repeated violations are not excused because foreigners are expected to learn appropriate behavior.

mores Norms that are considered to be central to the functioning of society and to social life.

Mores are norms that are considered to be central to the functioning of society and to social life. They have much greater significance than folkways. Accordingly, the violation of mores can be expected to bring serious retribution. Mores include proscriptions against theft, adultery, and incest. In many societies mores have been enacted into law. Thus, all advanced societies have laws against theft and incest. However, there are many differences in mores from one society to another.[43] In the United States, for example, drinking alcohol is widely accepted; but in Saudi Arabia, the consumption of alcohol is viewed as a violation of social norms and is punishable by imprisonment (as many U.S. citizens working in Saudi Arabia have discovered).

Hofstede's Model of National Culture

Researchers have spent considerable time and effort identifying similarities and differences in the values and norms of different countries. One model of national culture was developed by Geert Hofstede.[44] As a psychologist for IBM, Hofstede collected data on employee values and norms from more than 100,000 IBM employees in 64 countries. Based on his research, Hofstede developed five dimensions along which national cultures can be placed (see Figure 6.4).[45]

Figure 6.4

Hofstede's Model of National Culture

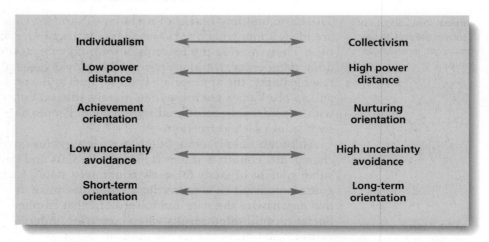

Source: Geert Hofstede, Bram Nevijen, Denise Daval Ohayv, and Geert Sanders, "Measuring Organizational Cultures: A Qualitative and Quantitative Study Across Twenty Cases," *Administrative Science Quarterly,* volume 35, Number 2 (June 1990), pp. 286–316. Approval of request for permission to reprint. © Johnson Graduate School of Management, Cornell University.

individualism A worldview that values individual freedom and self-expression and adherence to the principle that people should be judged by their individual achievements rather than by their social background.

collectivism A worldview that values subordination of the individual to the goals of the group and adherence to the principle that people should be judged by their contribution to the group.

INDIVIDUALISM VERSUS COLLECTIVISM   The first dimension, which Hofstede labeled "individualism versus collectivism," has a long history in human thought. **Individualism** is a worldview that values individual freedom and self-expression and adherence to the principle that people should be judged by their individual achievements rather than by their social background. In Western countries, individualism usually includes admiration for personal success, a strong belief in individual rights, and high regard for individual entrepreneurs.[46]

In contrast, **collectivism** is a worldview that values subordination of the individual to the goals of the group and adherence to the principle that people should be judged by their contribution to the group. Collectivism was widespread in communist countries but has become less prevalent since the collapse of communism in most of those countries. Japan is a noncommunist country where collectivism is highly valued.

Collectivism in Japan traces its roots to the fusion of Confucian, Buddhist, and Shinto thought that occurred during the Tokugawa period in Japanese history (1600–1870s).[47] One of the central values that emerged during this period was strong attachment to the group—whether a village, a work group, or a company. Strong identification with the group is said to create pressures for collective action in Japan, as well as strong pressure for conformity to group norms and a relative lack of individualism.[48]

Managers must realize that organizations and organizational members reflect their national culture's emphasis on individualism or collectivism. Indeed, one of the major reasons why Japanese and American management practices differ is that Japanese culture values collectivism and U.S. culture values individualism, as the following "Managing Globally" suggests.[49]

Managing Globally

A *Gaijin* Works to Turn Around Sony

Sony, the Japanese electronics maker, used to be renowned for using its innovation and engineering prowess to turn out blockbuster new products such as the Walkman and Trinitron TV. In the 1990s product engineers at Sony turned out an average of four new product ideas every day. Why? A large part of the answer was Sony's culture, called the "Sony Way," which emphasized communication, cooperation, and harmony between groups of engineers across the company to foster innovation and change. Engineers were given considerable freedom to pursue their own ideas, and the managers of different product

New Sony CEO Howard Stringer shakes hands with new Sony President and COO Ryoji Chubachi at a news conference in Tokyo. In his effort to revamp the company, Stringer will need to confront difficult, challenging cultural differences.

groups championed their own innovations, but problems arose with Sony's approach in the 2000s.

Companies in Korea, Taiwan, and China, began to innovate new technologies like digital LCD screens and flash memory that made Sony's technologies obsolete. Companies like Apple and Nokia came out with the iPod, smart phones, and tablet computers that better fitted customer needs than Sony's "old-generation" products such as the Walkman. One reason that Sony experienced major problems responding to these changes was that its culture had changed with its success. The top managers of its many divisions had become used to acting as if they had control of a fiefdom, and, protected by the Japanese tradition of lifetime employment, they worked to promote their own division's interests, not their company's. This competition had increased Sony's bureaucracy and slowed its decision making, making it much harder for Sony to take advantage of its pipeline of new product innovations! At the same time, its research was becoming enormously expensive, as divisions demanded more and more funds to create innovative new products.

Sensing this was a crucial turning point in their company's history, Sony's Japanese top managers turned to a *gaijin,* or non-Japanese, executive to lead their company. Their choice was Sir Howard Stringer, a Welshman, who headed Sony's North American operations and had been instrumental in cutting costs and increasing the profits of Sony's U.S. division. Stringer cannot speak Japanese, but luckily for him many of Sony's top executives speak English.

Now that he is in command, he faces the problem of reducing costs in Japan, where many Japanese companies have a policy of lifetime employment. He has made it clear that layoffs will be forthcoming, as Sony must reduce its high operating costs. He has also made it clear that the politicking going on between Sony's different product groups must stop and that managers must prioritize new products, investing only in those that have the highest chance of success, for Sony must reduce its huge R&D budget. Indeed, he wants to make engineering, not management, the focus once again at Sony and eliminate the tall, bloated hierarchy that has developed over time—by, for example, downsizing corporate headquarters. In Stringer's own words, the culture or "business of Sony has been management, not making products." However, he has to accomplish this in Japan, which has a national culture known for its collectivist, long-term orientation and for its distrust of *gaijin* or overseas values. And, these same values operate inside Sony, so Stringer will have to be hard-headed and push Sony to make the best use of its resources.

power distance The degree to which societies accept the idea that inequalities in the power and well-being of their citizens are due to differences in individuals' physical and intellectual capabilities and heritage.

POWER DISTANCE By **power distance** Hofstede meant the degree to which societies accept the idea that inequalities in the power and well-being of their citizens are due to differences in individuals' physical and intellectual capabilities and heritage. This concept also encompasses the degree to which societies accept the economic and social differences in wealth, status, and well-being that result from differences in individual capabilities.

Societies in which inequalities are allowed to persist or grow over time have *high power distance*. In high-power-distance societies, workers who are professionally successful amass wealth and pass it on to their children, and, as a result, inequalities may grow over time. In such societies, the gap between rich and poor, with all the attendant political and social consequences, grows very large. In contrast, in societies with *low power distance,* large inequalities between citizens are not allowed to develop. In low-power-distance countries, the government uses taxation and social welfare programs to reduce inequality and improve the welfare of the least fortunate. These societies are more attuned to preventing a large gap between rich and poor and minimizing discord between different classes of citizens.

Advanced Western countries such as the United States, Germany, the Netherlands, and the United Kingdom have relatively low power distance and high individualism. Economically poor Latin American countries such as Guatemala and Panama, and Asian countries such as Malaysia and the Philippines, have high power distance and low individualism.[50] These findings suggest that the cultural values of richer countries emphasize protecting the rights of individuals and, at the same time, provide a fair chance of success to every member of society.

ACHIEVEMENT VERSUS NURTURING ORIENTATION Societies that have an **achievement orientation** value assertiveness, performance, success, competition, and results. Societies that have a **nurturing orientation** value the quality of life, warm personal relationships, and services and care for the weak. Japan and the United States tend to be achievement-oriented; the Netherlands, Sweden, and Denmark are more nurturing-oriented.

UNCERTAINTY AVOIDANCE Societies as well as individuals differ in their tolerance for uncertainty and risk. Societies low on **uncertainty avoidance** (such as the United States and Hong Kong) are easygoing, value diversity, and tolerate differences in personal beliefs and actions. Societies high on uncertainty avoidance (such as Japan and France) are more rigid and skeptical about people whose behaviors or beliefs differ from the norm. In these societies, conformity to the values of the social and work groups to which a person belongs is the norm, and structured situations are preferred because they provide a sense of security.

LONG-TERM VERSUS SHORT-TERM ORIENTATION The last dimension that Hofstede described is orientation toward life and work.[51] A national culture with a **long-term orientation** rests on values such as thrift (saving) and persistence in achieving goals. A national culture with a **short-term orientation** is concerned with maintaining personal stability or happiness and living for the present. Societies with a long-term orientation include Taiwan and Hong Kong, well known for their high rate of per capita savings. The United States and France have a short-term orientation, and their citizens tend to spend more and save less.

National Culture and Global Management

Differences among national cultures have important implications for managers. First, because of cultural differences, management practices that are effective in one country might be troublesome in another. General Electric's managers learned this while trying to manage Tungsram, a Hungarian lighting products

achievement orientation A worldview that values assertiveness, performance, success, and competition.

nurturing orientation A worldview that values the quality of life, warm personal friendships, and services and care for the weak.

uncertainty avoidance The degree to which societies are willing to tolerate uncertainty and risk.

long-term orientation A worldview that values thrift and persistence in achieving goals.

short-term orientation A worldview that values personal stability or happiness and living for the present.

company GE acquired for $150 million. GE was attracted to Tungsram, widely regarded as one of Hungary's best companies, because of Hungary's low wage rates and the possibility of using the company as a base from which to export lighting products to western Europe. GE transferred some of its best managers to Tungsram and hoped it would soon become a leader in Europe. Unfortunately, many problems arose.

One of the problems resulted from major misunderstandings between the American managers and the Hungarian workers. The Americans complained that the Hungarians were lazy; the Hungarians thought the Americans were pushy. The Americans wanted strong sales and marketing functions that would pamper customers. In the prior command economy, sales and marketing activities were unnecessary. In addition, Hungarians expected GE to deliver Western-style wages, but GE came to Hungary to take advantage of the country's low-wage structure.[52] As Tungsram's losses mounted, GE managers had to admit that, because of differences in basic attitudes between countries, they had underestimated the difficulties they would face in turning Tungsram around. Nevertheless, by 2001, these problems had been solved, and the increased efficiency of GE's Hungarian operations made General Electric a major player in the European lighting market, causing it to invest another $1 billion.[53]

Often, management practices must be tailored to suit the cultural contexts within which an organization operates. An approach effective in the United States might not work in Japan, Hungary, or Mexico because of differences in national culture. For example, U.S.-style pay-for-performance systems that emphasize the performance of individuals alone might not work well in Japan, where individual performance in pursuit of group goals is the value that receives emphasis.

Managers doing business with individuals from another country must be sensitive to the value systems and norms of that country and behave accordingly. For example, Friday is the Islamic Sabbath. Thus, it would be impolite and inappropriate for a U.S. manager to schedule a busy day of activities for Saudi Arabian managers on a Friday.

A culturally diverse management team can be a source of strength for an organization participating in the global marketplace. Compared to organizations with culturally homogeneous management teams, organizations that employ managers from a variety of cultures have a better appreciation of how national cultures differ, and they tailor their management systems and behaviors to the differences. Indeed, one of the advantages that many Western companies have over their Japanese competitors is greater willingness to build an international team of senior managers.[54]

Summary and Review

WHAT IS THE GLOBAL ENVIRONMENT? The global environment is the set of forces and conditions that operate beyond an organization's boundaries but affect a manager's ability to acquire and utilize resources. The global environment has two components, the task environment and the general environment.

THE TASK ENVIRONMENT The task environment is the set of forces and conditions that originate with global suppliers, distributors, customers, and competitors that influence managers on a daily basis. The opportunities and threats associated with forces in the task environment become more and more complex as a company expands globally.

THE GENERAL ENVIRONMENT   The general environment comprises wider-ranging global economic, technological, sociocultural, demographic, political, and legal forces that affect an organization and its task environment.

THE CHANGING GLOBAL ENVIRONMENT   In recent years there has been a marked shift toward a more open global environment in which capital flows more freely as people and companies search for new opportunities to create profit and wealth. This has hastened the process of globalization. Globalization is the set of specific and general forces that work together to integrate and connect economic, political, and social systems across countries, cultures, or geographic regions so that nations become increasingly interdependent aned similar. The process of globalization has been furthered by declining barriers to international trade and investment and declining barriers of distance and culture.

Management in Action

Topics for Discussion and Action

Discussion

1. Why is it important for managers to understand the nature of the forces in the global environmental that are acting on them and their organizations?

2. Which organization is likely to face the most complex task environment, a biotechnology company trying to develop a new cure for cancer or a large retailer like The Gap or Macy's? Why?

3. The population is aging because of declining birth rates, declining death rates, and the aging of the baby-boom generation. What might some of the implications of this demographic trend be for (a) a pharmaceutical company and (b) the home construction industry?

4. How do political, legal, and economic forces shape national culture? What characteristics of national culture do you think have the most important effect on how successful a country is in doing business abroad?

5. After the passage of NAFTA, many U.S. companies shifted production operations to Mexico to take advantage of lower labor costs and lower standards for environmental and worker protection. As a result, they cut their costs and were better able to survive in an increasingly competitive global environment. Was their behavior ethical—that is, did the ends justify the means?

Action

6. Choose an organization, and ask a manager in that organization to list the number and strengths of forces in the organization's task environment. Ask the manager to pay particular attention to identifying opportunities and threats that result from pressures and changes in customers, competitors, and suppliers.

Building Management Skills

Analyzing an Organization's Environment

Pick an organization with which you are familiar. It can be an organization in which you have worked or currently work or one that you interact with regularly as a customer (such as the college that you are currently attending). For this organization do the following:

1. Describe the main forces in the global task environment that are affecting the organization.

2. Describe the main forces in the global general environment that are affecting the organization.

3. Explain how environmental forces affect the job of an individual manager within this organization. How do they determine the opportunities and threats that its managers must confront?

Managing Ethically

In recent years, the number of U.S. companies that buy their inputs from low-cost overseas suppliers has been growing, and concern about the ethics associated with employing young children in factories has been increasing. In Pakistan and India, children as young as six years old work long hours to make rugs and carpets for export to Western countries or clay bricks for local use. In countries like Malaysia and in Central America, children and teenagers routinely work long hours in factories and sweatshops to produce the clothing that is found in most U.S. discount and department stores.

Questions

1. Either by yourself or in a group, discuss whether it is ethical to employ children in factories and whether U.S. companies should buy and sell products made by these children? What are some arguments for and against child labor?

2. If child labor is an economic necessity, what ways could be employed to make it as ethical a practice as possible? Or is it simply unethical?

Small Group Breakout Exercise

How to Enter the Copying Business

Form groups of three to five people, and appoint one group member as the spokesperson who will communicate your findings to the whole class when called on by the instructor. Then discuss the following scenario.

You and your partners have decided to open a small printing and copying business in a college town of 100,000 people. Your business will compete with companies like FedEx Kinko's. You know that over 50% of small businesses fail in their first year, so to increase your chances of success, you have decided to do a detailed analysis of the task environment of the copying business to discover what opportunities and threats you will encounter. As a group:

1. Decide what you must know about (a) your future customers, (b) your future competitors, and (c) other critical forces in the task environment if you are to be successful.

2. Evaluate the main barriers to entry into the copying business.

3. Based on this analysis, list some of the steps you would take to help your new copying business succeed.

Exploring the World Wide Web

Go to Fuji Films' Web site (http://home.fujifilm.com), and then click on "corporate," "profile," and "global operations" and read about Fuji's global activities.

1. How would you characterize the way Fuji manages the global environment? For example, how has Fuji responded to the needs of customers in different countries?

2. How have increasing global competition and declining barriers of distance and culture been affecting Fuji's operations?

Be the Manager

The Changing Environment of Retailing

You are the new manager of a major clothing store that is facing a crisis. This clothing store has been the leader in its market for the last 15 years. In the last three years, however, two other major clothing store chains have opened up, and they have steadily been attracting customers away from your store—your sales are down 30%. To find out why, your store surveyed former customers and learned that they perceive the store as not keeping up with changing fashion trends and new forms of customer service. In examining the way the store operates, you found out that the 10 purchasing managers who buy the clothing and accessories for the store have been buying increasingly from the same clothing suppliers and have become reluctant to try new ones. Moreover, salespeople rarely, if ever, make suggestions for changing the way the store operates, they don't respond to customer requests, and the culture of the store has become conservative and risk-averse.

Questions

1. Analyze the major forces in the task environment of a retail clothing store.

2. Devise a program that will help other managers and employees to better understand and respond to their store's task environment.

BusinessWeek

Case in the News

Do You Need to Be Green?

Karin de Gier hasn't always been green. In 2001 she founded San Francisco-based Zwanette Design to produce cabinets, tables, and other custom-made furniture. As she learned more about woodworking, de Gier also learned more about toxic glues, sustainable forestry, and green building principles. De Gier, now 45, soon realized green building was in line with her own values. Out went the toxic glues. In came bamboo, fiberboard, and woods certified by the Forestry Stewardship Council as harvested from sustainably managed forests. And although de Gier had to jack up prices 30% to cover her higher materials costs, orders for her two-employee, $100,000 shop doubled last year, to 15. "There are some very motivated and committed customers out there," says de Gier.

Those committed customers are encouraging companies of all stripes to go green. And for good reason: The Organic Trade Assn. says sales of organic foods, now about $14 billion and 2.5% of the market for food, are expected to expand by 20% annually over the next few years. Green building is forecast to grow from a $7.4 billion market last year to $38 billion in 2010, according to the National Association of Home Builders. While each industry is affected in its own unique way and at a different rate, it's clear that for many, green business is a huge opportunity. But is it one your company should tackle?

That's a timely question, and answering it has probably never been trickier. Historically, sporting the green label has helped some small companies gain traction in a crowded market. It has allowed them to charge a premium for their products, often one as high as 20% to 30%. Those hefty markups are one reason many green companies have been profitable: A 2003 report by McKinsey & Co. found a portfolio of green and socially responsible companies returned between 5% and 14% annually in a 10-year period.

That's likely to change as more big players enter the market, bringing competitors to sectors that haven't encountered them. The enviable markups that have allowed small companies to become both green and profitable may become as endangered as the spotted owl. The onslaught has already started. France's Group Danone took majority control of organic yogurt pioneer Stonyfield Farms in 2003, and Colgate-Palmolive purchased

Tom's of Maine in March of this year. Also in March, mega-retailer Wal-Mart Stores said it plans to double the number of organic foods it carries, to 400, and to "democratize" organic food by selling it at lower prices than are now readily available. "Larger producers will aim for volume, pushing organic to the mainstream. That means pricing pressure and prices coming down," says John Stayton, co-founder and director of the Green MBA program at San Francisco's New College of California. "There will be winners and losers, the losers being those smaller companies that can't compete with larger producers."

Of course, the reach of the green movement may well be determined by just how far prices fall, something that is still uncertain. "Consumers are driven by time and money," says Harry Balzer, vice president of the NPD Group, a consumer research firm based in Port Washington, N.Y. "The wheels of permanent change are ease and convenience, which organic doesn't seem to offer over nonorganic products, and low cost. If the prices don't come down, it will remain a niche."

All of which makes the decision of whether to go green more difficult than ever. First, you've got to figure out what being green actually means in your industry. Since the movement began in the 1970s with a handful of farmers eschewing chemical pesticides, green has been commonly understood as products made with organic ingredients. But the term refers to processes, too: using fewer natural resources and less energy. Increasingly, green companies have a socially responsible agenda as well, paying living wages, supporting minority groups or workers in less

developed countries, and becoming active in their own communities.

Then decide what green means to your business. If you have a services company, being green will most likely mean reexamining the way you do business rather than changing the service you provide. If you decide to make a green product, you'll need to address not only costs—they'll likely go up— and marketing, but also credibility.

Baby Steps

Going green doesn't have to involve an all-out change in philosophy. There's a lot to be said for taking baby steps and observing how they affect your business, your customers, and your employees. Carol Cone, chairman of Boston-based Cone Inc., which links companies with appropriate causes, recommends that entrepreneurs look at greening their operations before they think about changing any product, especially those that are successful. "Try lessening the impact of your packaging," she says. Are you shipping your product in a box within a box, as Wal-Mart recently asked its suppliers to stop doing? That's easy enough to fix. "Lessen your energy use," she suggests. Maybe you could switch at least partly to wind or solar power or a greener manufacturing process. A volunteer program that meshes with your company's goals might be another tack, says Jacquelyn Ottman, founder of J. Ottman Consulting in New York, which specializes in green product marketing. And make sure to promote your achievements on your Web site and to your staff. "Your employees, especially if they're young, want to know about it," says Cone. That goes double for potential recruits.

Another way to green your operations is to reconsider your wage structure and benefits. Joshua Scott Onysko, founder of Pangea Organics, a Boulder (Colo.) company that manufactured and sold $3 million of "ecocentric body care" products in 2005, pays each of his 15 workers at least $12.75 an hour. That's more than $6 above the minimum wage, but it's what Onysko considers to be a living wage in his area. Mark Inman's $3.5 million, Sebastopol (Calif.) organic coffee company, Taylor Maid Farms, works with coffee farmers to help them maintain organic methods, and also invests in schools and clinics for the workers, all of which adds about 10 cents to each pound of coffee it sells. Health insurance for Inman's 15 employees is fully paid by the company—workers don't shell out for co-payments or contribute to premiums. "If you claim to be a green company, you have to act like one," says Inman.

Next is the tougher part: figuring out if you need a green product. Here, the circumstances of your individual business and industry loom even larger. Beyond food, industries that are seeing a lot of green players include body care, building, clothing, home furnishings, and, of course, energy. Start with a market analysis, suggests Ottman. "Are your customers interested in buying green? Are your competitors already offering green products, and if so, what can you offer that is distinct from theirs?" It's also worth asking if a greener product will make your customers more loyal.

Clever Marketing

As green products proliferate, such innovative marketing will be key to attracting consumers' attention. One hurdle is overcoming the long-held perception that green means shoddy. Early organic products were often considered of lesser quality, says Ottman, and among a wide swath of consumers "that stigma still exists." Further, consumers have had enough gloom-and-doom messages. "Consumers want upbeat messages," says Ottman. "They don't want to hear about how the planet is going to hell in a handbasket."

The challenge is to create a brand consumers will buy whether or not it is good for the environment. "If you have an idea for an alternative to cotton shirts, make sure it is fashionable first and the green aspect is second or third down the list," says Sonora Beam, co-founder and creative director of Digital Hive Ecological Design, a green consulting firm in San Francisco. Many people are buying green products not because it's the right thing to do, says Beam, "but because they look or taste good."

Getting an organic product into stores isn't necessarily any easier than getting placement for a traditional product. As with any new item, finding slots in mass-market grocery chains can be difficult as well as costly, and many supermarket chains are producing their own green labels. Whole Foods Market, the nation's largest organic retailer, is, not surprisingly, a tough sell. But hotels, restaurants, and cafes are a more direct, fresher channel to expose consumers to green brands.

Questions for Discussion

1. In what ways do the growing popularity of green products change the opportunities and threats facing companies in an industry?

2. What are some ways small companies could compete with large established companies by selling green products?

BusinessWeek Case in the News

The Future of Outsourcing

Globalization has been brutal to midwestern manufacturers like the Paper Converting Machine Co. For decades, PCMC's Green Bay (Wis.) factory thrived by making ever-more-complex equipment to weave, fold, and print packaging for everything from potato chips to baby wipes.

But PCMC has fallen on hard times. First came the 2001 recession. Then, two years ago, one of the company's biggest customers told it to slash its machinery prices by 40% and urged it to move production to China. Last year, a St. Louis holding company, Barry-Wehmiller Cos., acquired the manufacturer and promptly cut workers and nonunion pay. In five years sales have plunged by 40%, to $170 million, and the workforce has shrunk from 2,000 to 1,100. Employees have been traumatized, says operations manager Craig Compton, a muscular former hockey player." All you hear about is China and all these companies closing or taking their operations overseas."

But now, Compton says, he is "probably the most optimistic I've been in five years." Hope is coming from an unusual source. As part of its turnaround strategy, Barry-Wehmiller plans to shift some design work to its 160-engineer center in Chennai, India. By having U.S. and Indian designers collaborate 24/7, explains Vasant Bennett, president of Barry-Wehmiller's engineering services unit, PCMC hopes to slash development costs and time, win orders it often missed due to engineering constraints—and keep production in Green Bay. Barry-Wehmiller says the strategy already has boosted profits at some of the 32 other midsize U.S. machinery makers it has bought. "We can compete and create great American jobs," vows CEO Robert Chapman. "But not without offshoring."

Come again? Ever since the offshore shift of skilled work sparked widespread debate and a political firestorm three years ago, it has been portrayed as the killer of good-paying American jobs. "Benedict Arnold CEOs" hire software engineers, computer help staff, and credit-card bill collectors to exploit the low wages of poor nations. U.S. workers suddenly face a grave new threat, with even highly educated tech and service professionals having to compete against legions of hungry college grads in India, China, and the Philippines willing to work twice as hard for one-fifth the pay.

Workers' fears have some grounding in fact. The prime motive of most corporate bean counters jumping on the offshoring bandwagon has been to take advantage of such "labor arbitrage"—the huge wage gap between industrialized and developing nations. And without doubt, big layoffs often accompany big outsourcing deals.

The changes can be harsh and deep. But a more enlightened, strategic view of global sourcing is starting to emerge as managers get a better fix on its potential. The new buzzword is "transformational outsourcing." Many executives are discovering offshoring is really about corporate growth, making better use of skilled U.S. staff, and even job creation in the U.S., not just cheap wages abroad. True, the labor savings from global sourcing can still be substantial. But it's peanuts compared to the enormous gains in efficiency, productivity, quality, and revenues that can be achieved by fully leveraging offshore talent.

Thus entrepreneurs such as Chapman see a chance to turn around dying businesses, speed up their pace of innovation, or fund development projects that otherwise would have been unaffordable. More aggressive outsourcers are aiming to create radical business models that can give them an edge and change the game in their industries. Old-line multinationals see offshoring as a catalyst for a broader plan to overhaul outdated office operations and prepare for new competitive battles. And while some want to downsize, others are keen to liberate expensive analysts, engineers, and salesmen from routine tasks so they can spend more time innovating and dealing with customers. "This isn't about labor cost," says Daniel Marovitz, technology managing director for Deutsche Bank's global businesses. "The issue is that if you don't do it, you won't survive."

The new attitude is emerging in corporations across the U.S. and Europe in virtually every industry. Ask executives at Penske Truck Leasing why the company outsources dozens of business processes to Mexico and India, and they cite greater efficiency and customer service. Ask managers at U.S.-Dutch professional publishing giant Wolters Kluwer why they're racing to shift software development and editorial work to India and the Philippines, and they will say it's about being able to pump out a greater variety of books, journals, and Web-based content more rapidly.

Here's what such transformations typically entail: Genpact, Accenture, IBM Services, or another big outsourcing specialist dispatches teams to meticulously dissect the workflow of an entire human resources, finance, or info tech department. The team then helps build a new IT platform, redesigns all processes, and administers programs, acting as a virtual subsidiary. The contractor then disperses work among global networks of staff ranging from the U.S. to Asia to Eastern Europe.In recent years, Procter & Gamble, DuPont, Cisco Systems, Unilever, and Marriott were among those that signed such megadeals worth billions.

Some observers even believe Big Business is on the cusp of a new burst of productivity growth, ignited in part by offshore outsourcing as a catalyst. "Once this transformation is done," predicts Arthur H. Harper, former CEO of General Electric Co.'s equipment management businesses, "I think we will end up with companies that deliver products faster at lower costs, and are better able to compete against anyone in the world." As executives shed more operations, they also are spurring new debate about how the future corporation will look. Some management pundits theorize about the "totally disaggregated corporation," wherein every function not regarded as crucial is stripped away.

Of course, corporations have been outsourcing management of IT systems to the likes of Electronic Data Systems, IBM, and Accenture for more than a decade, while Detroit has long given engineering jobs to outside design firms. Futurists have envisioned "hollow" and "virtual" corporations since the 1980s.

It hasn't happened yet. Reengineering a company may make sense on paper, but it's extremely expensive and entails big risks if executed poorly. Corporations can't simply be snapped apart and reconfigured like LEGO sets, after all. They are complex, living organisms that can be thrown into convulsions if a transplant operation is botched. Valued employees send out their résumés, customers are outraged at deteriorating service, a brand name can be damaged. In consultant surveys, what's more, many U.S. managers complain about the quality of offshored work and unexpected costs.

But as companies work out such kinks, the rise of the offshore option is dramatically changing the economics of reengineering. With millions of low-cost engineers, financial analysts, consumer marketers, and architects now readily available via the Web, CEOs can see a quicker payoff. "It used to be that companies struggled for a few years to show a 5% or 10% increase in productivity from outsourcing," says Pramod Bhasin, CEO of Genpact, the 19,000-employee back-office-processing unit spun off by GE last year. "But by offshoring work, they can see savings of 30% to 40% in the first year" in labor costs. Then the efficiency gains kick in. A $10 billion company might initially only shave a few million dollars in wages after transferring back-office procurement or bill collection overseas. But better management of these processes could free up hundreds of millions in cash flow annually.

Those savings, in turn, help underwrite far broader corporate restructuring that can be truly transformational. DuPont has long wanted to fix its unwieldy system for administering records, payroll, and benefits for its 60,000 employees in 70 nations, with data scattered among different software platforms and global business units. By awarding a long-term contract to Cincinnati-based Convergys Corp., the world's biggest call-center operator, to redesign and administer its human resources programs, it expects to cut costs 20% in the first year and 30% a year afterward.

The management challenges will grow more urgent as rising global salaries dissipate the easy cost gains from offshore outsourcing. The winning companies of the future will be those most adept at leveraging global talent to transform themselves and their industries, creating better jobs for everyone.

Questions for Discussion

1. In what ways can outsourcing contribute to a company's competitive advantage?

2. How can outsourcing help create jobs at home? Will it create more jobs than it takes abroad?

Source: Pete Engardio, Michael Arndt, and Dean Foust, "The Future of Outsourcing: How it's transforming whole industries and changing the way we work." Reprinted from the January 30, 2006, issue of *BusinessWeek* by special permission. Copyright © 2006 by the McGraw-Hill Companies, Inc.

BusinessWeek

Nokia Connects

It wasn't hard for Wang Ninie to decide on a mobile phone. In early March the twentysomething Beijing entrepreneur saw a golden Nokia handset with a flower pattern etched into the trim, one of the company's "L'Amour" line of high-end designer phones. "I fell in love with it," she says. At $470, the phone wasn't cheap. No matter."I didn't even look at other phones," says Wang. Jeevanlal Pitodia is equally smitten with Nokia. The 27-year-old Bombay fruit vendor used to spend his days pounding the pavement in the city's alleys, hawking oranges, apples, and bananas. Last September, Pitodia ponied up $56 for his first handset, a simple but sturdy Nokia 1100. Now he sits

Case in the News

under a colorful beach umbrella, earning as much as $10 a day taking orders by phone for both himself and nearby vendors. "I tried many phones, but Nokia is the most user-friendly," says Pitodia.

More than any other handset maker, Nokia Corp. has connected with the likes of Wang and Pitodia and their billions of countrymen. In both China and India, the Finnish company is the top brand. In China last year, it had nearly 31% of a crowded market, well ahead of the 10% controlled by No. 2 Motorola Inc. In India, Nokia has a 60% share, with sales last year of about $1 billion.

Nokia isn't letting up: On March 11 it opened its first Indian factory, a $150 million facility near the southern city of Madras that will

turn out as many as 20 million inexpensive phones annually both for the local market and for export. And the company is doubling the size of its plant in the Chinese city of Dongguan, near Hong Kong.The two Asian giants are of fundamental importance for Nokia. The Finnish company has played catch-up in the U.S., where Motorola has beaten it with hot-selling models such as the ultra-thin RAZR. But the U.S. market is nearly saturated. The company that can control Asia's Big Two will have a lead in the global handset wars.

Caught Off Guard

Just a few years ago, Nokia faced big troubles in both countries. In India, growth was sluggish. In China, Nokia not only trailed

Motorola but was threatened by domestic players such as TCL and Ningbo Bird, newcomers to the business that had quickly gobbled up almost half of the market with their inexpensive but well-designed handsets. The local upstarts flooded stores nationwide with armies of sales assistants flogging their brands. "Our people would put up posters, and within 30 minutes they would be torn down," recalls Colin Giles, manager of Nokia's China handset business.

To fight back, Giles pushed through big changes. Nokia decentralized, going from three Chinese sales offices in 2003 to 70 today. Instead of eight national distributors, Nokia now has 50 provincial ones. And since rivals were having great success with handsets designed for local users, Nokia introduced its own China-specific models with software that lets them write Chinese characters with a stylus. The result: Nokia sold 27.5 million handsets in China last year, triple what it sold in 2003. Since 2002, when India's cellular market took off, Nokia has drawn on its China experience to consolidate its lead. In 2004 the company launched two India-specific models, which included a flashlight, dust cover, and slip-free grip (handy during India's scorching, sweaty summers). Nokia introduced software in seven Indian regional languages and the company's marketers pitched the phones through ads tailored to India, with one early campaign showing burly truck drivers calling home on Nokia handsets.

Fierce Rivals

Nokia has also reaped the fruits of rivals' missteps. Motorola was slower in reacting to the threat from the Chinese locals and has had a tougher time bouncing back because it didn't change its strategy for a long time. The Chinese upstarts, meanwhile, suffered from sharp reversals due to disappointing quality.

Rivals say the time is right to eat into Nokia's lead. Samsung in the past focused solely on the middle to high end of the market in India but began selling lower-cost phones last year Aad opened a new factory in Gurgaon, near Delhi. Motorola revamped its structure in China, expanding its salesforce and strengthening its distribution network to cover 300 cities. By February, Motorola had boosted its market share by several percentage points. And in India, Motorola is planning to market phones costing as little as $35. Motorola Vice President Allen Burnes calls India "pivotal" and says the company will open its first factory there in 18 months.

Questions for Discussion

1. What are the opportunities associated with being first into a major new country market?

2. What are the threats associated with being late in entering a major new country market?

3. How can a company help its products compete effectively in a growing market?

Source: Bruce Einhorn, Nandini Lakshman, Manjeet Kripalani, and Jack Ewing, "Nokia Connects." Reprinted from the March 27, 2006, issue of *BusinessWeek* by special permission. Copyright © 2006 by the McGraw-Hill Companies, Inc.

CHAPTER 7

Decision Making, Learning, Creativity, and Entrepreneurship

Learning Objectives

After studying this chapter, you should be able to:

- Differentiate between programmed and nonprogrammed decisions, and explain why nonprogrammed decision making is a complex, uncertain process.

- Describe the six steps that managers should take to make the best decisions, and explain how cognitive biases can lead managers to make poor decisions.

- Identify the advantages and disadvantages of group decision making, and describe techniques that can improve it.

- Explain the role that organizational learning and creativity play in helping managers to improve their decisions.

- Describe how managers can encourage and promote entrepreneurship to create a learning organization, and differentiate between entrepreneurs and intrapreneurs.

A Manager's Challenge

Decision Making and Learning Are the Key to Entrepreneurial Success

Why is decision making and learning an ongoing challenge for managers of businesses large and small?

All managers must make decisions day in and day out under considerable uncertainty. And sometimes those decisions come back to haunt them if they turn out poorly. Sometimes, even highly effective managers make bad decisions; other times, factors beyond a manager's control, such as unforeseen changes in the environment, cause a good decision to result in unexpected negative consequences. Effective managers recognize the critical importance of making decisions on an ongoing basis as well as learning from prior decisions.

Decision making has been an ongoing challenge for Marc Shuman, founder and president of GarageTek, headquartered in Syosset, New York.[1] Since founding his company less than 10 years ago, he has met this challenge time and time again, recognizing when decisions need to be made and learning from feedback about prior decisions.

Shuman was working with his father in a small business, designing and building

interiors of department stores, when he created and installed a series of wall panels with flexible shelving for a store to display its

GarageTek founder and President Marc Shuman.

merchandise. When he realized that some of his employees were using the same concept in their own homes to organize the clutter in their basements and garages, he recognized that he had a potential opportunity to start a new business, GarageTek, designing and installing custom garage systems to organize and maximize storage capacities and uses for home garage space. A booming housing market, the popularity of closet organizing systems, and the recognition that many people's lives were getting busier and more complicated led him to believe that homeowners would be glad to pay someone to design and install a system that would help them gain control over some of the clutter in their lives.[2]

Schuman decided to franchise his idea, as he feared that other entrepreneurs were probably having similar thoughts and competition could be around the corner. His franchising arrangement was as follows: Franchisees would pay a $25,000 franchise fee and remit 8% of their annual revenues back to GarageTek. GarageTek, in turn, would provide three days of training and a detailed manual as well as promote the business through national advertising. As long as would-be franchisees had some background in business, marketing, and selling and around $200,000 to invest in supplies and local advertising for their franchise, they were granted a franchise. Shuman projected that within 18 months of opening, new franchises would start earning a profit.[3]

Within three years, GarageTek had 57 franchises in 33 states contributing revenues to the home office of around $12 million. While this would seem to be an enviable track record of success, Shuman recognized that although many of the franchises were succeeding, some were having very serious problems. With the help of a consulting company, Shuman and home office managers set about trying to figure out why some of the franchises were failing. They gathered detailed information about each franchise, ranging from the market served, pricing strategies, costs, managerial talent, and franchisee investment. From this information, Shuman learned that the struggling franchises tended either to have lower levels of capital investment behind them or to be managed by nonowners.[4]

Shuman faced a tough decision. While his franchise agreement gave him the right to close franchises that were not generating sufficient revenues, doing so could create a lot of ill will, bad publicity, and potential lawsuits. Also, he was the one who had granted these franchises in the first place, and perhaps he had not provided franchisees with the training and support they needed.[5]

Shuman decided to give the failing franchises around six months to get back on their feet, during which time he would monitor their performance and try to help them improve. While a few franchisees did manage to turn their businesses around, others were not so fortunate and some of them were sold. As Shuman puts it, "Some guys were left with some pretty hard feelings."[6]

Shuman learned from this experience. He now has new decision criteria for accepting new franchisees to help ensure that their investments of time and money lead to a successful franchise. Interested franchisees need to have a minimum of $250,000 in assets that are readily convertible into cash if need be; they must have a net worth of at least $1 million; their locations need to serve an area of at least 250,000 single-family homes with resident owners; and the franchisees must commit to manage and operate the franchise themselves. They also need to fly to the home office, meet with Shuman and other top managers, and take a screening test to see if they have some of the qualities that top franchisees share, such as being independent and inventive. Shuman also decided to track franchises' performance closely so that potential problems can be quickly identified and hopefully solved.[7]

Shuman also decided to give new franchisees much more training and support than he had in the past. Now, new franchises receive two weeks of training at the home office, on-site assistance in sales, marketing, and operations, a multivolume training manual, a sales and marketing kit, and access to databases and GarageTek's intranet. Franchisees learn from each other through monthly conference calls and regional and national meetings.

In 2005, GarageTek's sales increased by over 30%, to around $20 million, and plans are under way for opening additional franchises. For Shuman, however, making good decisions and learning from prior ones are still an ongoing challenge; in his words, "We're not, by any stretch, done."[8]

Overview

"A Manager's Challenge" indicates how decision making and learning from prior decisions are an ongoing challenge for managers that can have a profound influence on organizational effectiveness. Shuman's decision to seize an opportunity and start GarageTek and his subsequent decisions along the way have had a profound effect on his business. Likewise, the decisions that managers make at all levels in large corporations have a profound impact on the effectiveness of the corporations.[9] The decisions managers make—managers like GarageTek's Shuman, Valero Energy's Bill Greehey, and eBay's Meg Whitman[10]—and the effects that these decisions have on the decision-making process throughout an organization, profoundly influence organizational effectiveness. Yet such decisions can be very difficult to make because they are fraught with uncertainty.

In this chapter, we examine how managers make decisions, and we explore how individual, group, and organizational factors affect the quality of the decisions they make and ultimately determine organizational performance. We discuss the nature of managerial decision making and examine some models of the decision-making process that help reveal the complexities of successful decision making. Then we outline the main steps of the decision-making process; in addition, we explore the biases that may cause capable managers to make poor decisions both as individuals and as members of a group. Next, we examine how managers can promote organizational learning and creativity and improve the quality of decision making throughout an organization. Finally, we discuss the important role of entrepreneurship in promoting organizational creativity, and we differentiate between entrepreneurs and intrapreneurs. By the end of this chapter, you will appreciate the critical role of management decision making in creating a high-performing organization.

The Nature of Managerial Decision Making

Every time managers act to plan, organize, direct, or control organizational activities, they make a stream of decisions. In opening a new restaurant, for example, managers have to decide where to locate it, what kinds of food to provide to customers, which people to employ, and so on. Decision making is a basic part of every task managers perform. In this chapter we study how these decisions are made.

As we discussed in the last three chapters, one of the main tasks facing a manager is to manage the organizational environment. Forces in the external environment give rise to many opportunities and threats for managers and their organizations. In addition, inside an organization managers must address many opportunities and threats that may arise during the course of utilizing organizational resources. To deal with these opportunities and threats, managers must make decisions—that is, they must select one solution from a set of alternatives. **Decision making** is the process by which managers respond to the opportunities and threats that confront them by analyzing the options and making determinations, or *decisions*, about specific organizational goals and courses of action. Good decisions result in the selection of appropriate goals and courses of action that increase organizational performance; bad decisions result in lower performance.

Decision making in response to opportunities occurs when managers search for ways to improve organizational performance to benefit customers, employees, and other stakeholder groups. In "A Manager's Challenge," Marc Shuman saw

decision making The process by which managers respond to opportunities and threats by analyzing options and making determinations about specific organizational goals and courses of action.

an opportunity to start a new business designing and installing custom garage solutions. *Decision making in response to threats* occurs when events inside or outside the organization are adversely affecting organizational performance and managers are searching for ways to increase performance.[11] At GarageTek, the poor performance of some franchises was a threat that prompted Shuman to make a number of decisions to improve the performance and viability of his company.[12] Decision making is central to being a manager, and whenever managers engage in planning, organizing, leading, and controlling–their four principal tasks–they are constantly making decisions.

Managers are always searching for ways to make better decisions to improve organizational performance. At the same time, they do their best to avoid costly mistakes that will hurt organizational performance. Examples of spectacularly good decisions include Liz Claiborne's decision in the 1980s to focus on producing clothes for the growing number of women entering the workforce–a decision that contributed to making her company one of the largest clothing manufacturers. Also, Bill Gates's decision to buy a computer operating system for $50,000 from a small company in Seattle and sell it to IBM for the new IBM personal computer turned Gates and Microsoft, respectively, into the richest man and richest software company in the United States. Examples of spectacularly bad decisions include the decision by managers at NASA and Morton Thiokol to launch the *Challenger* space shuttle–a decision that resulted in the deaths of six astronauts in 1986. Also, the decision of Ken Olsen, founder of Digital Equipment Corporation, to stay with mainframe computers in the 1980s and not allow his engineers to spend the company's resources on creating new kinds of personal computers because of his belief that "personal computers are just toys" was a decision that cost Olsen his job as CEO and almost ruined his company.

Programmed and Nonprogrammed Decision Making

Regardless of the specific decisions that a manager makes, the decision-making process is either programmed or nonprogrammed.[13]

programmed decision making Routine, virtually automatic decision making that follows established rules or guidelines.

PROGRAMMED DECISION MAKING Programmed decision making is a *routine*, virtually automatic process. Programmed decisions are decisions that have been made so many times in the past that managers have developed rules or guidelines to be applied when certain situations inevitably occur. Programmed decision making takes place when a school principal asks the school board to hire a new teacher whenever student enrollment

An employee takes inventory of office supplies. The decision making process involved in such a routine, repetitive task is an example of programmed decision making.

increases by 40 students; when a manufacturing supervisor hires new workers whenever existing workers' overtime increases by more than 10%; and when an office manager orders basic office supplies, such as paper and pens, whenever the inventory of supplies on hand drops below a certain level. Furthermore, in the last example, the office manager probably orders the same amount of supplies each time.

This decision making is called *programmed* because office managers, for example, do not need to repeatedly make new judgments about what should be done. They can rely on long-established decision rules such as these:

- *Rule 1:* When the storage shelves are three-quarters empty, order more copy paper.
- *Rule 2:* When ordering paper, order enough to fill the shelves.

Managers can develop rules and guidelines to regulate all routine organizational activities. For example, rules can specify how a worker should perform a certain task, and rules can specify the quality standards that raw materials must meet to be acceptable. Most decision making that relates to the day-to-day running of an organization is programmed decision making. Examples include decision making about how much inventory to hold, when to pay bills, when to bill customers, and when to order materials and supplies. Programmed decision making occurs when managers have the information they need to create rules that will guide decision making. There is little ambiguity involved in assessing when the stockroom is empty or counting the number of new students in class.

NONPROGRAMMED DECISION MAKING   Suppose, however, managers are not at all certain that a course of action will lead to a desired outcome. Or, in even more ambiguous terms, suppose managers are not even clear about what they are really trying to achieve. Obviously, rules cannot be developed to predict uncertain events. Nonprogrammed decision making is required for these *nonroutine* decisions. Nonprogrammed decisions are made in response to unusual or novel opportunities and threats. Nonprogrammed decision making occurs when there are no ready-made decision rules that managers can apply to a situation. Rules do not exist because the situation is unexpected or uncertain and managers lack the information they would need to develop rules to cover it. Examples of nonprogrammed decision making include decisions to invest in a new kind of technology, develop a new kind of product, launch a new promotional campaign, enter a new market, expand internationally, or start a new business, as did Shuman in "A Manager's Challenge."

How do managers make decisions in the absence of decision rules? They may rely on their intuition—feelings, beliefs, and hunches that come readily to mind, require little effort and information gathering, and result in on-the-spot decisions.[14] Or they may make reasoned judgments—decisions that take time and effort to make and result from careful information gathering, generation of alternatives, and evaluation of alternatives. "Exercising" one's judgment is a more rational process than "going with" one's intuition. For reasons that we examine later in this chapter, both intuition and judgment often are flawed and can result in poor decision making. Thus, the likelihood of error is much greater in nonprogrammed decision making than in programmed decision making.[15] In the remainder of this chapter, when we talk about decision making, we are referring to *nonprogrammed* decision making because it causes the most problems for managers and is inherently challenging.

nonprogrammed decision making Nonroutine decision making that occurs in response to unusual, unpredictable opportunities and threats.

intuition Feelings, beliefs, and hunches that come readily to mind, require little effort and information gathering, and result in on-the-spot decisions.

reasoned judgment A decision that takes time and effort to make and results from careful information gathering, generation of alternatives, and evaluation of alternatives.

Sometimes managers have to make rapid decisions and don't have the time for careful consideration of the issues involved. They must rely on their intuition to quickly respond to a pressing concern. For example, when fire chiefs, captains, and lieutenants manage firefighters battling dangerous, out-of-control fires, they often need to rely on their expert intuition to make on-the-spot decisions that will protect the lives of the firefighters and save the lives of others, contain the fires, and preserve property—decisions made in emergency situations entailing high uncertainty, high risk, and rapidly changing conditions.[16] Other times, managers do have the time available to make reasoned judgments but there are no established rules to guide their decisions, such as when deciding whether or not to proceed with a proposed merger.

Regardless of the circumstances, making nonprogrammed decisions can result in effective or ineffective decision making. As indicated in the following "Manager as a Person," managers have to be on their guard to avoid being overconfident in decisions that result from their intuition and reasoned judgment.

Fire chiefs and firefighters gather to plan strategy at the scene of a brush fire in Los Angeles' Griffith Park. In a crisis like this, managers don't have much time for decision making and, therefore, must rely on their expert intuition.

Manager as a Person

Curbing Overconfidence

Should managers be confident in their intuition and reasoned judgments?[17] Decades of research by Nobel Prize winner Daniel Kahneman, his long-time collaborator the late Amos Tversy, and other researchers suggests that managers (like all people) tend to be overconfident in the decisions they make (whether based on intuition or reasoned judgment). And with overconfidence comes the failure to evaluate and rethink the wisdom of the decisions one makes and to learn from mistakes.[18]

Kahneman distinguishes between the intuitions of managers who are truly expert in the content domain of a decision and the intuition of managers who have some knowledge and experience but are not true experts.[19] While the intuition of both types can be faulty, that of experts is less likely to be flawed. This is why fire captains can make good decisions and why expert chess players can make good moves, in both cases without spending much time or deliberating carefully on what, for nonexperts, is a very complicated set of circumstances. What distinguishes expert managers from those with "some" expertise is that the experts have extensive experience under conditions in which they receive quick and clear feedback about the outcomes of their decisions.[20]

Unfortunately, managers who have some experience in a content area but are not true experts tend to be overly confident in their intuition and their judgments.[21] As Kahneman puts it, "People jump to statistical conclusions on the basis of very weak evidence. We form powerful intuitions about trends and about the replicability of results on the basis of information that is truly inadequate."[22] Not only do managers, and all people, tend to be overconfident about their intuitions and judgments, but they also tend not to learn from mistakes. Compounding this undue optimism is a very human tendency to be overconfident in one's own abilities and influence over unpredictable events. Surveys have found that the majority of people think they are above average, make better decisions, and are less prone to making bad decisions than others (of course, it is impossible for most people to be above average on any dimension).[23]

A recent example of managerial overconfidence is particularly telling. Research has consistently found that mergers tend to turn out poorly—post-merger profitability declines, stock prices decline, and so forth. (For example, Chrysler had the biggest profits of the three largest automobile makers in the United States when it merged with Daimler; the merger has not worked out well, and Chrysler would have been better off if it never had happened.)[24] So one would imagine that top executives and boards of directors would learn from this research and from articles in the business press about the woes of merged companies (e.g., the AOL–Time Warner merger).[25] Evidently not. According to a recent study by Hewitt Associates, top executives and board members are, if anything, planning on increasing their involvement in mergers over the next few years. These top managers evidently overconfidently believe that they can succeed where others have failed.[26]

Jeffrey Pfeffer, a professor at Stanford University's Graduate School of Business, suggests that managers can avoid the perils of overconfidence by critically evaluating the decisions they have made and the outcomes of those decisions. They should admit to themselves when they have made a mistake and really learn from their mistakes (rather than dismissing them as flukes or situations out of their control). In addition, managers should be leery of too much agreement at the top. As Pfeffer puts it, "If two people agree all the time, one of them is redundant".[27]

The classical and the administrative decision-making models reveal many of the assumptions, complexities, and pitfalls that affect decision making. These models help reveal the factors that managers and other decision makers must be aware of to improve the quality of their decision making. Keep in mind, however, that the classical and administrative models are just guides that can help managers understand the decision-making process. In real life, the process is typically not cut-and-dried, but these models can help guide a manager through it.

The Classical Model

classical decision-making model A prescriptive approach to decision making based on the assumption that the decision maker can identify and evaluate all possible alternatives and their consequences and rationally choose the most appropriate course of action.

One of the earliest models of decision making, the **classical model,** is *prescriptive*, which means that it specifies how decisions *should* be made. Managers using the classical model make a series of simplifying assumptions about the nature of the decision-making process (see Figure 7.1). The premise of the classical model is

Figure 7.1
The Classical Model of Decision Making

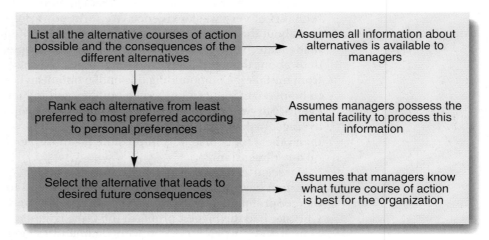

that once managers recognize the need to make a decision, they should be able to generate a complete list of *all* alternatives and consequences and make the best choice. In other words, the classical model assumes that managers have access to *all* the information they need to make the **optimum decision,** which is the most appropriate decision possible in light of what they believe to be the most desirable future consequences for the organization. Furthermore, the classical model assumes that managers can easily list their own preferences for each alternative and rank them from least to most preferred to make the optimum decision.

The Administrative Model

James March and Herbert Simon disagreed with the underlying assumptions of the classical model of decision making. In contrast, they proposed that managers in the real world do *not* have access to all the information they need to make a decision. Moreover, they pointed out that even if all information were readily available, many managers would lack the mental or psychological ability to absorb and evaluate it correctly. As a result, March and Simon developed the **administrative model** of decision making to explain why decision making is always an inherently uncertain and risky process—and why managers can rarely make decisions in the manner prescribed by the classical model. The administrative model is based on three important concepts: *bounded rationality, incomplete information,* and *satisficing.*

BOUNDED RATIONALITY March and Simon pointed out that human decision-making capabilities are bounded by people's cognitive limitations—that is, limitations in their ability to interpret, process, and act on information.[28] They argued that the limitations of human intelligence constrain the ability of decision makers to determine the optimum decision. March and Simon coined the term **bounded rationality** to describe the situation in which the number of alternatives a manager must identify is so great and the amount of information so vast that it is difficult for the manager to even come close to evaluating it all before making a decision.[29]

optimum decision
The most appropriate decision in light of what managers believe to be the most desirable future consequences for the organization.

administrative model
An approach to decision making that explains why decision making is inherently uncertain and risky and why managers usually make satisfactory rather than optimum decisions.

bounded rationality
Cognitive limitations that constrain one's ability to interpret, process, and act on information.

Figure 7.2
Why Information Is Incomplete

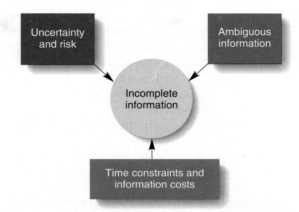

INCOMPLETE INFORMATION   Even if managers did have an unlimited ability to evaluate information, they still would not be able to arrive at the optimum decision because they would have incomplete information. Information is incomplete because the full range of decision-making alternatives is unknowable in most situations and the consequences associated with known alternatives are uncertain.[30] In other words, information is incomplete because of risk and uncertainty, ambiguity, and time constraints (see Figure 7.2).

RISK AND UNCERTAINTY   As we saw in Chapter 6, forces in the organizational environment are constantly changing. Risk is present when managers know the possible outcomes of a particular course of action and can assign probabilities to them. For example, managers in the biotechnology industry know that new drugs have a 10% probability of successfully passing advanced clinical trials and a 90% probability of failing. These probabilities reflect the experiences of thousands of drugs that have gone through advanced clinical trials. Thus, when managers in the biotechnology industry decide to submit a drug for testing, they know that there is only a 10% chance that the drug will succeed, but at least they have some information on which to base their decision.

When **uncertainty** exists, the probabilities of alternative outcomes *cannot* be determined and future outcomes are *unknown*. Managers are working blind. Since the probability of a given outcome occurring is *not* known, managers have little information to use in making a

risk The degree of probability that the possible outcomes of a particular course of action will occur.

uncertainty Unpredictability.

When Apple introduced the Newton, shown here, managers were working under conditions of extreme uncertainty. Because Apple was the first to market this type of product, there was no body of well-known data that managers could draw on to calculate the probability of a successful product launch.

decision. For example, in 1993, when Apple Computer introduced the Newton, its personal digital assistant (PDA), managers had no idea what the probability of a successful product launch for a PDA might be. Because Apple was the first to market this totally new product, there was no body of well-known data that Apple's managers could draw on to calculate the probability of a successful launch. Uncertainty plagues most managerial decision making.[31] Although Apple's initial launch of its PDA was a disaster due to technical problems, an improved version was more successful. In fact, Apple created the PDA market that has boomed during the 2000s as new and different wireless products have been introduced.

As indicated in the following "Information Technology Byte," a major source of uncertainty for top managers revolves around being unable to accurately predict future demand for products and services.

Information Technology Byte

Revising Plans Never Ends for Craig Knouf

Having a good business plan is essential for entrepreneurs to obtain funding from banks, venture capitalists, and other sources of funds. Once entrepreneurs have secured funding and their businesses are up and running, their business plans are typically reviewed only once a year as part of an annual planning process, unless, of course, the entrepreneurs are seeking to obtain additional funds. These business plans are inherently fraught with uncertainty, as is starting a new business and having it actually succeed. However, viewing a business plan as a work in progress that should be evolving on an almost continuous basis has turned out to be a blessing for Craig Knouf, founder, CEO, and majority owner of Associated Business Systems (ABS), a Portland, Oregon, supplier of office equipment.[32]

Knouf estimates that he has revised his business plan over 120 times since founding ABS in 1997; he makes a point of reviewing and, if necessary, revising ABS's business plan on a monthly basis after consulting with the firm's seven vice presidents. As Knouf puts it, "If you only looked at the plan every quarter, by the time you realize the mistake, you're five months off. . . . You're done. You're not going to get back on track."[33] Of course, the reason why managers like Knouf have to continually rethink their decisions is the inherent uncertainty in all that they do. As a case in point, in the early years Knouf never anticipated that scanners would be a significant part of his business. But during his monthly reviews of the business, he noticed that sales of office equipment with scanning capabilities were steadily increasing. Acting on what his sales data were telling him, Knouf quickly added products with scanning capabilities to his company's offerings.[34]

Knouf's ability to appreciate the inherent uncertainty of the best-made plans and decisions, and the benefit of frequently changing courses of action in response to feedback from customers and the market, has certainly paid off handsomely for his company. Since its founding in 1997, ABS's revenues have grown from $880,000 to over $32.5 million.[35] ABS appeared on *INC.* magazine's list of fastest-growing private companies and was on the *Portland Business Journal*'s list of fastest-growing companies in Oregon.[36] Even suppliers have taken notice of ABS's ability to stay in touch with the market, provide excellent, timely service to customers, and actively respond to changing market conditions.[37] For example, ABS was one of only eight distributors across the United States selected by Hewlett-Packard to launch a new line of high-speed copiers with multiple functions such as printing and scanning.[38] Management experts agree that Knouf's approach to planning makes good business sense. As Eric Siegel, Wharton Business School lecturer and president of Siegel Management Consultants, puts it, "The world turns; things change. . . . What you commit to a document on Dec. 19 is not necessarily appropriate on Jan. 19."[39]

ambiguous information Information that can be interpreted in multiple and often conflicting ways.

AMBIGUOUS INFORMATION   A second reason why information is incomplete is that much of the information managers have at their disposal is **ambiguous information.** Its meaning is not clear—it can be interpreted in multiple and often conflicting ways.[40] Take a look at Figure 7.3. Do you see a young woman or an old woman? In a similar fashion, managers often interpret the same piece of information differently and make decisions based on their own interpretations.

TIME CONSTRAINTS AND INFORMATION COSTS   The third reason why information is incomplete is that managers have neither the time nor the money to search for all possible alternative solutions and evaluate all the potential consequences of those alternatives. Consider the situation confronting a Ford Motor Company purchasing manager who has one month to choose a supplier for a small engine part. Of the thousands of potential suppliers for this part, there are 20,000 in the United States alone. Given the time available, the purchasing manager cannot contact all potential suppliers and ask each for its terms (price, delivery schedules, and so on). Moreover, even if the time were available, the costs of obtaining the information, including the manager's own time, would be prohibitive.

Figure 7.3
Ambiguous Information: Young Woman or Old Woman?

satisficing Searching for and choosing an acceptable, or satisfactory, response to problems and opportunities, rather than trying to make the best decision.

SATISFICING   March and Simon argue that managers do not attempt to discover every alternative when faced with bounded rationality, an uncertain future, unquantifiable risks, considerable ambiguity, time constraints, and high information costs. Rather, they use a strategy known as **satisficing,** exploring a limited sample of all potential alternatives.[41] When managers satisfice, they search for and choose acceptable, or satisfactory, ways to respond to problems and opportunities rather than trying to make the optimal decision.[42] In the case of the Ford purchasing manager's search, for example, satisficing may involve asking a limited number of suppliers for their terms, trusting that they are representative of suppliers in general, and making a choice from that set. Although this course of action is reasonable from the perspective of the purchasing manager, it may mean that a potentially superior supplier is overlooked.

March and Simon pointed out that managerial decision making is often more art than science. In the real world, managers must rely on their intuition and judgment to make what seems to them to be the best decision in the face of uncertainty and ambiguity.[43] Moreover, managerial decision making is often fast-paced, as managers use their experience and judgment to make crucial decisions under conditions of incomplete information. Although there is nothing wrong with this approach, decision makers should be aware that human judgment is often flawed. As a result, even the best managers sometimes end up making very poor decisions.[44]

Steps in the Decision–Making Process

Using the work of March and Simon as a basis, researchers have developed a step-by-step model of the decision-making process and the issues and problems that managers confront at each step. Perhaps the best way to introduce this model is to examine the real-world nonprogrammed decision making that Scott McNealy had to engage in at a crucial point in Sun Microsystems' history.

In early August 1985, Scott McNealy, CEO of Sun Microsystems[45] (a hardware and software computer workstation manufacturer focused on network solutions), had to decide whether to go ahead with the launch of the new Carrera workstation computer, scheduled for September 10. Sun's managers had chosen the date nine months earlier when the development plan for the Carrera was first proposed. McNealy knew that it would take at least a month to prepare for the September 10 launch and that the decision could not be put off.

Customers were waiting for the new machine, and McNealy wanted to be the first to provide a workstation that took advantage of Motorola's powerful 16-megahertz 68020 microprocessor. Capitalizing on this opportunity would give Sun a significant edge over Apollo, its main competitor in the workstation market. McNealy knew, however, that committing to the September 10 launch date was risky. Motorola was having production problems with the 16-megahertz 68020 microprocessor and could not guarantee Sun a steady supply of these chips. Moreover, the operating system software was not completely free of bugs.

If Sun launched the Carrera on September 10, the company might have to ship some machines with software that was not fully operational, was prone to crash the system, and utilized Motorola's less-powerful 12 megahertz 68020 microprocessor instead of the 16-megahertz version.[46] Of course, Sun could later upgrade the microprocessor and operating system software in any machines purchased by early customers, but the company's reputation would

Figure 7.4
Six Steps in Decision Making

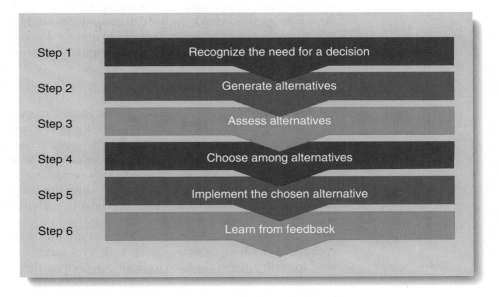

suffer as a result. If Sun did not go ahead with the September launch, the company would miss an important opportunity.[47] Rumors were circulating in the industry that Apollo would be launching a new machine of its own in December.

Scott McNealy clearly had a difficult decision to make. He had to decide quickly whether to launch the Carrera, but he was not in possession of all the facts. He did not know, for example, whether the microprocessor or operating system problems could be resolved by September 10; nor did he know whether Apollo was going to launch a competing machine in December. But he could not wait to find these things out—he had to make a decision. We'll see what he decided later in the chapter.

Many managers who must make important decisions with incomplete information face dilemmas similar to McNealy's. There are six steps that managers should consciously follow to make a good decision (see Figure 7.4).[48] We review them in the remainder of this section.

Recognize the Need for a Decision

The first step in the decision-making process is to recognize the need for a decision. Scott McNealy recognized this need, and he realized that a decision had to be made quickly.

Some stimuli usually spark the realization that there is a need to make a decision. These stimuli often become apparent because changes in the organizational environment result in new kinds of opportunities and threats. This happened at Sun Microsystems. The September 10 launch date had been set when it seemed that Motorola chips would be readily available. Later, with the supply of chips in doubt and bugs remaining in the system software, Sun was in danger of failing to meet its launch date.

The stimuli that spark decision making are as likely to result from the actions of managers inside an organization as they are from changes in the external environment.[49] An organization possesses a set of skills, competencies, and resources in its employees and in departments such as marketing, manufacturing, and research and development. Managers who actively pursue opportunities to use these competencies create the need to make decisions. Managers thus can be proactive or reactive in recognizing the need to make a decision, but the important issue is that they must recognize this need and respond in a timely and appropriate way.[50]

Generate Alternatives

Having recognized the need to make a decision, a manager must generate a set of feasible alternative courses of action to take in response to the opportunity or threat. Management experts cite failure to properly generate and consider different alternatives as one reason why managers sometimes make bad decisions.[51] In the Sun Microsystems decision, the alternatives seem clear: to go ahead with the September 10 launch or to delay the launch until the Carrera was 100% ready for market introduction. Often, however, the alternatives are not so obvious or so clearly specified.

One major problem is that managers may find it difficult to come up with creative alternative solutions to specific problems. Perhaps some of them are used to seeing the world from a single perspective—they have a certain "managerial mind-set." In a manner similar to that of Digital's Olsen, many managers find it difficult to view problems from a fresh perspective. According to best-selling management author Peter Senge, we all are trapped within our personal mental models of the world—our ideas about what is important and how the world works.[52] Generating creative alternatives to solve problems and take advantage of opportunities may require that we abandon our existing mind-sets and develop new ones—something that usually is difficult to do.

The importance of getting managers to set aside their mental models of the world and generate creative alternatives is reflected in the growth of interest in the work of authors such as Peter Senge and Edward de Bono, who have popularized techniques for stimulating problem solving and creative thinking among managers.[53] Later in this chapter, we discuss the important issues of organizational learning and creativity in detail.

Evaluate Alternatives

Once managers have generated a set of alternatives, they must evaluate the advantages and disadvantages of each one.[54] The key to a good assessment of the alternatives is to define the opportunity or threat exactly and then specify the criteria that *should* influence the selection of alternatives for responding to the problem or opportunity. One reason for bad decisions is that managers often fail to specify the criteria that are important in reaching a decision.[55] In general, successful managers use four criteria to evaluate the pros and cons of alternative courses of action (see Figure 7.5):

1. *Legality:* Managers must ensure that a possible course of action is legal and will not violate any domestic and international laws or government regulations.

2. *Ethicalness:* Managers must ensure that a possible course of action is ethical and will not unnecessarily harm any stakeholder group. Many of the decisions that managers make may help some organizational stakeholders and harm others (see Chapter 3). When examining alternative courses of action, managers need to be very clear about the potential effects of their decisions.

Figure 7.5
General Criteria for Evaluating Possible Courses of Action

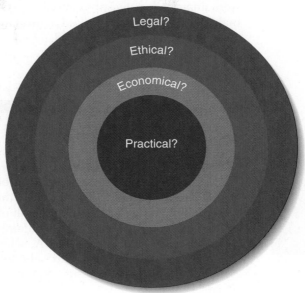

Is the possible course of action:

Legal?

Ethical?

Economical?

Practical?

3. *Economic feasibility:* Managers must decide whether the alternatives are economically feasible—that is, whether they can be accomplished given the organization's performance goals. Typically, managers perform a cost-benefit analysis of the various alternatives to determine which one will have the best net financial payoff.

4. *Practicality:* Managers must decide whether they have the capabilities and resources required to implement the alternative, and they must be sure that the alternative will not threaten the attainment of other organizational goals. At first glance, an alternative might seem to be economically superior to other alternatives, but if managers realize that it is likely to threaten other important projects, they might decide that it is not practical after all.

Very often, a manager must consider these four criteria simultaneously. Scott McNealy framed the problem at hand at Sun Microsystems quite well. The key question was whether to go ahead with the September 10 launch date. Two main criteria were influencing McNealy's choice: the need to ship a machine that was as "complete" as possible (the *practicality* criterion) and the need to beat Apollo to market with a new workstation (the *economic feasibility* criterion). These two criteria conflicted. The first suggested that the launch should be delayed; the second, that the launch should go ahead. McNealy's actual choice was based on the relative importance that he assigned to these two criteria. In fact, Sun Microsystems went ahead with the September 10 launch, which suggests that McNealy thought the need to beat Apollo to market was the more important criterion.

Some of the worst managerial decisions can be traced to poor assessment of the alternatives, such as the decision to launch the *Challenger* space shuttle, mentioned earlier. In that case, the desire of NASA and Morton Thiokol managers to demonstrate to the public the success of the U.S. space program in order to ensure future funding *(economic feasibility)* conflicted with the need to ensure the safety of the astronauts *(ethicalness)*. Managers deemed the economic criterion more important and decided to launch the space shuttle even though there were unanswered questions about safety. Tragically, some of the same decision-making problems that resulted in the *Challenger* tragedy led to the demise of the *Columbia* space shuttle in 2003, 17 years later, killing all seven astronauts on board.[56]

NASA Focused on Changing Culture

Ethics in Action

Seventeen years after the *Challenger* disaster, history repeated itself on February 1, 2003, when *Columbia* broke up over Texas on the final day of its mission, killing all seven astronauts on board.[57] While different specific causes resulted in each of these tragedies, they were both at least partially the result of a deeper, more widespread problem: a flawed safety culture at NASA, where concerns with budgets and schedules were emphasized at the expense of safety.[58]

Both the Columbia Accident Investigation Board (CAIB) and a NASA team headed by Al Diaz, director of the Goddard Space Flight Center, concluded—after intensive investigations involving employees at all ranks, outside contractors, and engineering and scientific data—that NASA's flawed, can-do culture, emphasizing budgets and schedules over safety, was partially to blame for the *Columbia* tragedy.[59] Commenting on the CAIB report and their own investigations, the Diaz team stated:

Had the fate of STS-107 been the result of a small number of well-defined problems in a single program, finding solutions would be a relatively straightforward matter. But the CAIB determined that such is not the case. . . . It was their conclusion that the mistakes made on STS-107 were not isolated failures but rather were indicative of systemic flaws that existed prior to the accident. The Diaz Team believes that some of these systemic flaws exist beyond the shuttle program.[60]

The Columbia crew waved to onlookers on their way to the launch pad for liftoff. Leading the way were Pilot William "Willie" McCool (left) and Commander Rick Husband. Following in the second row were Mission Specialists Kalpana Chawla (left) and Laurel Clark; in the rear were Payload Specialist Ilan Ramon (left), Payload Commander Michael Anderson, and Mission Specialist David Brown. Ramon was the first astronaut from Israel to fly on a shuttle.

In both the *Challenger* and the *Columbia* disasters, safety questions were raised before the shuttles were launched; safety concerns took second place to budgets, economic feasibility, and schedules; top decision makers seemed to ignore or downplay the inputs of those with relevant technical expertise; and speaking up was discouraged.[61] Rather than making safety a top priority, decision makers seemed overly concerned with keeping on schedule and within budget.[62] The day before *Columbia* lifted off, mission managers were presented with data indicating that a ring that linked the rocket boosters to the external tank failed to meet strength requirements. Rather than postponing the launch to address this problem, a shuttle manager temporarily waived the requirements based on what later turned out to be faulty data.[63] After foam had broken loose the next day during liftoff (a recurring problem) and struck the left wing, NASA engineers repeatedly and doggedly requested images of the affected area to assess the extent of the damage and perhaps plan a rescue mission. Mission managers actively opposed their requests and no images were obtained.[64]

Bill Parsons, who now heads the troubled shuttle program, is committed to changing the organization's culture.[65] Among other things, he is trying to improve communication, encourage all employees to speak up without fear of retribution, make sure that all employees' inputs are heard, ensure that technical expertise is taken into account when making decisions, and, above all, emphasize safety.[66] Currently, NASA engineers are trying to develop fillers and wrappings that astronauts can use to repair unexpected cracks, gashes, and holes on shuttles during space flights.[67] And efforts are under way to prevent foam insulation from breaking off fuel tanks when shuttles are launched.[68] New launch restrictions have been put in place; for example, launches must take place during daylight so any potential foam shedding can be documented.[69] Above all else, Parsons is trying to change the culture so that safety is a top priority, technical expertise is respected, and shuttles are not launched until all known problems are addressed.[70]

Choose Among Alternatives

Once the set of alternative solutions has been carefully evaluated, the next task is to rank the various alternatives (using the criteria discussed in the previous section) and make a decision. When ranking alternatives, managers must be sure *all* the information available is brought to bear on the problem or issue at hand. As the Sun Microsystems case indicates, however, identifying all *relevant* information for a decision does not mean that the manager has *complete* information; in most instances, information is incomplete.

Perhaps more serious than the existence of incomplete information is the often-documented tendency of managers to ignore critical information, even when it is available. We discuss this tendency in detail below when we examine the operation of cognitive biases and groupthink.

Implement the Chosen Alternative

Once a decision has been made and an alternative has been selected, it must be implemented, and many subsequent and related decisions must be made. After a course of action has been decided—say, to develop a new line of women's clothing—thousands of subsequent decisions are necessary to implement it. These decisions would involve recruiting dress designers, obtaining fabrics, finding high-quality manufacturers, and signing contracts with clothing stores to sell the new line.

Although the need to make subsequent decisions to implement the chosen course of action may seem obvious, many managers make a decision and then fail to act on it. This is the same as not making a decision at all. To ensure that a decision is implemented, top managers must assign to middle managers the responsibility for making the follow-up decisions necessary to achieve the goal. They must give middle managers sufficient resources to achieve the goal, and they must hold the middle managers accountable for their performance. If the middle managers are successful at implementing the decision, they should be rewarded; if they fail, they should be subject to sanctions.

Learn from Feedback

The final step in the decision-making process is learning from feedback. Effective managers like Marc Shuman in "A Manager's Challenge" always conduct a retrospective analysis to see what they can learn from past successes or failures.[71] Managers who do not evaluate the results of their decisions do not learn from experience; instead, they stagnate and are likely to make the same mistakes again and again.[72] To avoid this problem, managers must establish a formal procedure with which they can learn from the results of past decisions. The procedure should include these steps:

1. Compare what actually happened to what was expected to happen as a result of the decision.
2. Explore why any expectations for the decision were not met.
3. Derive guidelines that will help in future decision making.

Managers who always strive to learn from past mistakes and successes are likely to continuously improve the decisions they make. A significant amount of learning can take place when the outcomes of decisions are evaluated, and this assessment can produce enormous benefits.

Cognitive Biases and Decision Making

heuristics Rules of thumb that simplify decision making.

systematic errors Errors that people make over and over and that result in poor decision making.

In the 1970s psychologists Daniel Kahneman and Amos Tversky suggested that because all decision makers are subject to bounded rationality, they tend to use **heuristics,** rules of thumb that simplify the process of making decisions.[73] Kahneman and Tversky argued that rules of thumb are often useful because they help decision makers make sense of complex, uncertain, and ambiguous information. Sometimes, however, the use of heuristics can lead to systematic errors in the way decision makers process information about alternatives and make decisions. **Systematic errors** are errors that people make over and over and that result in poor decision making. Because of cognitive biases, which are caused by systematic errors, otherwise-capable managers may end up making bad decisions.[74] Four sources of bias that can adversely affect the way managers make decisions are prior hypotheses, representativeness, the illusion of control, and escalating commitment (see Figure 7.6).

Figure 7.6
Sources of Cognitive Bias at the Individual and Group Levels

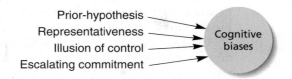

Prior-Hypothesis Bias

Decision makers who have strong prior beliefs about the relationship between two variables tend to make decisions based on those beliefs *even when presented with evidence that their beliefs are wrong.* In doing so, they are falling victim to **prior-hypothesis bias.** Moreover, decision makers tend to seek and use information that is consistent with their prior beliefs and to ignore information that contradicts those beliefs.

Representativeness Bias

Many decision makers inappropriately generalize from a small sample or even from a single vivid case or episode. An interesting example of the **representativeness bias** occurred after World War II, when Seawell Avery, the CEO of Montgomery Ward, shelved plans for national expansion to meet competition from Sears because he believed there would be a depression after the war. The basis for Avery's belief was the occurrence of the Great Depression after World War I. However, there was no second Great Depression, and Avery's poor decision allowed Sears to establish itself as the number-one nationwide retailer. Avery's mistake was generalizing from the post-World War I experience and assuming that "depressions always follow wars."

Illusion of Control

Other errors in decision making result from the **illusion of control,** the tendency of decision makers to overestimate their ability to control activities and events. Top-level managers seem to be particularly prone to this bias. Having worked their way to the top of an organization, they tend to have an exaggerated sense of their own worth and are overconfident about their ability to succeed and to control events.[75] The illusion of control causes managers to overestimate the odds of a favorable outcome and, consequently, to make inappropriate decisions. For example, Nissan used to be controlled by Katsuji Kawamata, an autocratic CEO who thought he had the ability to run the car company single-handedly. He made all the decisions, some of which resulted in a series of spectacular mistakes, including changing the company's name from Datsun to Nissan.

Escalating Commitment

Having already committed significant resources to a course of action, some managers commit more resources to the project *even if they receive feedback that the project is failing.*[76] Feelings of personal responsibility for a project apparently bias

escalating commitment A source of cognitive bias resulting from the tendency to commit additional resources to a project even if evidence shows that the project is failing.

the analysis of decision makers and lead to this **escalating commitment**. The managers decide to increase their investment of time and money in a course of action and ignore evidence that it is illegal, unethical, uneconomical, or impractical (see Figure 7.5). Often, the more appropriate decision would be to cut their losses and run.

A tragic example of where escalating commitment can lead is the *Challenger* disaster. Apparently, managers at both NASA and Morton Thiokol were so anxious to keep the shuttle program on schedule that they ignored or discounted any evidence that would slow the program down. Thus, the information offered by two Thiokol engineers, who warned about O-ring failure in cold weather, was discounted, and the shuttle was launched on a chilly day in January 1986.

Another example of escalating commitment occurred during the 1960s and 1970s when large U.S. steelmakers responded to low-cost competition from minimills and foreign steelmakers by increasing their investments in the technologically obsolete steelmaking facilities they already possessed, rather than investing in new, cutting-edge technology.[77] This decision was irrational because investment in obsolete technology would never enable them to lower their costs and compete successfully. Similarly, overly optimistic top managers at Lucent Technologies escalated their commitment to growth, engaging in practices like discounting and vendor loans that ultimately may have hurt organizational performance.[78]

Be Aware of Your Biases

How can managers avoid the negative effects of cognitive biases and improve their decision-making and problem-solving abilities? Managers must become aware of biases and their effects, and they must identify their own personal style of making decisions.[79] One useful way for managers to analyze their decision-making style is to review two decisions that they made recently—one decision that turned out well and one that turned out poorly. Problem-solving experts recommend that managers start by determining how much time to spend on each of the decision-making steps, such as gathering information to identify the pros and cons of alternatives or ranking the alternatives, to make sure that they spend sufficient time on each step.[80]

Another recommended technique for examining decision-making style is for managers to list the criteria they typically use to assess and evaluate alternatives—the heuristics (rules of thumb) they typically employ, their personal biases, and so on—and then critically evaluate the appropriateness of these different factors.

Many individual managers are likely to have difficulty identifying their own biases, so it is often advisable for managers to scrutinize their own assumptions by working with other managers to help expose weaknesses in their decision-making style. In this context, the issue of group decision making becomes important.

Group Decision Making

Many, perhaps most, important organizational decisions are made by groups or teams of managers rather than by individuals. Group decision making is superior to individual decision making in several respects. When managers work as a team to make decisions and solve problems, their choices of alternatives are less likely to fall victim to the biases and errors discussed previously.

They are able to draw on the combined skills, competencies, and accumulated knowledge of group members and thereby improve their ability to generate feasible alternatives and make good decisions. Group decision making also allows managers to process more information and to correct one another's errors. And in the implementation phase, all managers affected by the decisions agree to cooperate. When a group of managers makes a decision (as opposed to one top manager making a decision and imposing it on subordinate managers), the probability that the decision will be implemented successfully increases. (We discuss how to encourage employee participation in decision making in Chapter 13.)

There are some potential disadvantages associated with group decision making. Groups often take much longer than individuals to make decisions. Getting two or more managers to agree to the same solution can be difficult because managers' interests and preferences are often different. In addition, just like decision making by individual managers, group decision making can be undermined by biases. A major source of group bias is *groupthink*.

The Perils of Groupthink

groupthink A pattern of faulty and biased decision making that occurs in groups whose members strive for agreement among themselves at the expense of accurately assessing information relevant to a decision.

Groupthink is a pattern of faulty and biased decision making that occurs in groups whose members strive for agreement among themselves at the expense of accurately assessing information relevant to a decision.[81] When managers are subject to groupthink, they collectively embark on a course of action without developing appropriate criteria to evaluate alternatives. Typically, a group rallies around one central manager, such as the CEO, and the course of action that manager supports. Group members become blindly committed to that course of action without evaluating its merits. Commitment is often based on an emotional, rather than an objective, assessment of the optimal course of action.

The decision President Kennedy and his advisers made to launch the unfortunate Bay of Pigs invasion in Cuba in 1962, the decisions made by President Johnson and his advisers from 1964 to 1967 to escalate the war in Vietnam, the decision made by President Nixon and his advisers in 1972 to cover up the Watergate break-in, and the decision made by NASA and Morton Thiokol in 1986 to launch the ill-fated *Challenger* shuttle—all were likely influenced by groupthink. After the fact, decision makers such as these who may fall victim to groupthink are often surprised that their decision-making process and outcomes were so flawed.

When groupthink occurs, pressures for agreement and harmony within a group have the unintended effect of discouraging individuals from raising issues that run counter to majority opinion. For example, when managers at NASA and Morton Thiokol fell victim to groupthink, they convinced each other that all was well and that there was no need to delay the launch of the *Challenger* space shuttle.

Devil's Advocacy and Dialectical Inquiry

The existence of cognitive biases and groupthink raises the question of how to improve the quality of group and individual decision making so that managers make decisions that are realistic and are based on a thorough evaluation of

Figure 7.7
Devil's Advocacy and Dialectical Inquiry

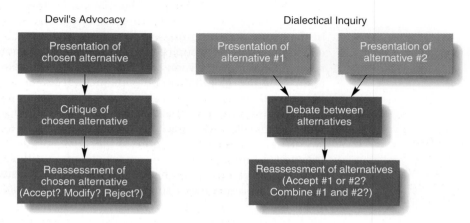

Devil's Advocacy

Presentation of chosen alternative

↓

Critique of chosen alternative

↓

Reassessment of chosen alternative (Accept? Modify? Reject?)

Dialectical Inquiry

Presentation of alternative #1   Presentation of alternative #2

↓

Debate between alternatives

↓

Reassessment of alternatives (Accept #1 or #2? Combine #1 and #2?)

devil's advocacy
Critical analysis of a preferred alternative, made in response to challenges raised by a group member who, playing the role of devil's advocate, defends unpopular or opposing alternatives for the sake of argument.

alternatives. Two techniques known to counteract groupthink and cognitive biases are devil's advocacy and dialectic inquiry (see Figure 7.7).[82]

Devil's advocacy is a critical analysis of a preferred alternative to ascertain its strengths and weaknesses before it is implemented.[83] Typically, one member of the decision-making group plays the role of devil's advocate. The devil's advocate critiques and challenges the way the group evaluated alternatives and chose one over the others. The purpose of devil's advocacy is to identify all the reasons that might make the preferred alternative unacceptable after all. In this way, decision makers can be made aware of the possible perils of recommended courses of action.

dialectical inquiry
Critical analysis of two preferred alternatives in order to find an even better alternative for the organization to adopt.

Dialectical inquiry goes one step further. Two groups of managers are assigned to a problem, and each group is responsible for evaluating alternatives and selecting one of them.[84] Top managers hear each group present its preferred alternative, and then each group critiques the other's position. During this debate, top managers challenge both groups' positions to uncover potential problems and perils associated with their solutions. The goal is to find an even better alternative course of action for the organization to adopt.

Both devil's advocacy and dialectical inquiry can help counter the effects of cognitive biases and groupthink.[85] In practice, devil's advocacy is probably the easier method to implement because it involves less commitment in managerial time and effort than does dialectical inquiry.

Diversity Among Decision Makers

Another way to improve group decision making is to promote diversity in decision-making groups (see Chapter 4).[86] Bringing together managers of both genders from various ethnic, national, and functional backgrounds broadens the range of life experiences and opinions that group members can draw on as they generate, assess, and choose among alternatives. Moreover, diverse groups are sometimes less prone to groupthink because group members already differ from each other and thus are less subject to pressures for uniformity.

Organizational Learning and Creativity

organizational learning The process through which managers seek to improve employees' desire and ability to understand and manage the organization and its task environment.

learning organization An organization in which managers try to maximize the ability of individuals and groups to think and behave creatively and thus maximize the potential for organizational learning to take place.

creativity A decision maker's ability to discover original and novel ideas that lead to feasible alternative courses of action.

The quality of managerial decision making ultimately depends on innovative responses to opportunities and threats. How can managers increase their ability to make nonprogrammed decisions, decisions that will allow them to adapt to, modify, and even drastically alter their task environments so that they can continually increase organizational performance? The answer is by encouraging organizational learning.[87]

Organizational learning is the process through which managers seek to improve employees' desire and ability to understand and manage the organization and its task environment so that employees can make decisions that continuously raise organizational effectiveness.[88] A **learning organization** is one in which managers do everything possible to maximize the ability of individuals and groups to think and behave creatively and thus maximize the potential for organizational learning to take place. At the heart of organizational learning is **creativity,** the ability of a decision maker to discover original and novel ideas that lead to feasible alternative courses of action. Encouraging creativity among managers is such a pressing organizational concern that many organizations hire outside experts to help them develop programs to train their managers in the art of creative thinking and problem solving.

Creating a Learning Organization

How do managers go about creating a learning organization? Learning theorist Peter Senge identified five principles for creating a learning organization (see Figure 7.8):[89]

1. For organizational learning to occur, top managers must allow every person in the organization to develop a sense of *personal mastery.* Managers must empower employees and allow them to experiment and create and explore what they want.

2. As part of attaining personal mastery, organizations need to encourage employees to develop and use *complex mental models*-sophisticated ways of thinking that challenge them to find new or better ways of performing a task—to

Figure 7.8
Senge's Principles for Creating a Learning Organization

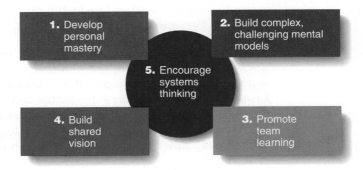

deepen their understanding of what is involved in a particular activity. Here Senge is arguing that managers must encourage employees to develop a taste for experimenting and risk taking.[90]

3.   Managers must do everything they can to promote group creativity. Senge thinks that *team learning* (learning that takes place in a group or team) is more important than individual learning in increasing organizational learning. He points out that most important decisions are made in subunits such as groups, functions, and divisions.

4.   Managers must emphasize the importance of *building a shared vision*—a common mental model that all organizational members use to frame problems or opportunities.

5.   Managers must encourage *systems thinking* (a concept drawn from systems theory, discussed in Chapter 2). Senge emphasizes that to create a learning organization, managers must recognize the effects of one level of learning on another. Thus, for example, there is little point in creating teams to facilitate team learning if managers do not also take steps to give employees the freedom to develop a sense of personal mastery.

Building a learning organization requires that managers change their management assumptions radically. Developing a learning organization is neither a quick nor an easy process. Senge has been working with Ford Motor Company to help managers make Ford a learning organization. Why does Ford want this? Top management believes that to compete successfully, Ford must improve its members' ability to be creative and make the right decisions.

Increasingly, managers are being called on to promote global organizational learning. For example, managers at Wal-Mart use the lessons derived from its failures and successes in one country to promote global organizational learning across the many countries in which it now operates. For instance, when Wal-Mart entered Malaysia, it was convinced customers there would respond to its one-stop shopping format. It found, however,

Smiling workers and happy customers at the many tills of the Monks Cross ASDA. ASDA was formed by a group of farmers and now has 265 stores and 19 depots across the United Kingdom. It was bought by Wal-Mart in 1999, and in 2004 was the UK's second largest grocery chain, employing over 100,000 workers whose friendliness and cheer are hallmarks of the 'colleague culture' aimed for by senior management. Known as a value supermarket, its merger with Wal-Mart allows it to pursue its mission of low prices.

that Malaysians enjoy the social experience of shopping in a lively market or bazaar and thus did not like the impersonal efficiency of the typical Wal-Mart store. As a result, Wal-Mart has learned the importance of designing store layouts to appeal specifically to the customers of each country in which it operates.

When purchasing and operating a chain of stores in another country, such as the British ASDA chain, Wal-Mart now strives to retain what customers value in the local market while taking advantage of all of its own accumulated organizational learning. For example, Wal-Mart improved ASDA's information technology used for inventory and sales tracking in stores and enrolled ASDA in Wal-Mart's global purchasing operations, which has enabled the chain to pay less for certain products, sell them for less, and, overall, significantly increase sales. At the same time, Wal-Mart empowered local ASDA managers to run the stores; as the president of ASDA indicates, "This is still essentially a British business in the way it's run day to day."[91] Clearly, global organizational learning is essential for companies such as Wal-Mart that have significant operations in multiple countries.

For organizations whose life blood rests on research and development, such as those in the pharmaceutical industry, facilitating learning and creativity is of utmost importance, as indicated in the following "Ethics in Action."

Ethics in Action

Learning, Creativity, and Social Responsibility at GlaxoSmithKline

When entrenched pharmaceutical companies SmithKline Beecham and Glaxo Wellcome merged to become GlaxoSmithKline (Glaxo), the future of Glaxo was on shaky grounds with few promising new drugs in the pipeline and patents expiring on other top drugs.[92,93] Tadataka (Tachi) Yamada, currently Glaxo's director of research and development (R&D), reinvented the 15,000-people-strong R&D function of the merged company to develop many promising new drugs and, virtually, save the company.[94]

What did Yamada decide that changed the fate of Glaxo? Taking a bold step, he decided *not* to do what typically is done after such a mega-merger—consolidate R&D across the newly merged companies, lay off employees, and focus on cutting costs. Rather, Yamada went back to his research roots (he has an MD degree and was formerly the chairman of the Internal Medicine Department at the University of Michigan Medical School).[95] He decided that to develop new drugs, R&D employees need to think and act like entrepreneurs—making decisions that they believe in and being highly motivated to follow through to make them a success.[96]

Tachi Yamada faced some tough decisions in taking on the task of reinventing the 15,000-people-strong R&D function at the newly merged company, GlaxoSmithKline.

Yamada restructured R&D at Glaxo by forming autonomous, entrepreneurial start-up labs to develop new drugs. Rather than consolidating decision making at the top, which usually happens after a merger, he empowered researchers in the labs to make the decisions that would either revive Glaxo or seal its fate. Yamada's bold experiment was a testament to his belief that the research scientists responsible for discovering and developing new drugs should be making the key decisions—not top executives, who are a step removed from the research process on a day-to-day basis. Given the huge investments and lengthy time horizons involved—developing a new drug and getting it approved by the U.S. Food and Drug Administration (FDA) typically takes about 10 years and costs about $800 million—giving research scientists the final say on what new drugs to pursue was a dramatic departure from the tradition of having top managers make such decisions.[97]

Yamada divided R&D at Glaxo into small, semiautonomous labs, each with a primary research focus, such as cardiovascular disease or cancer. Rather than operating as R&D typically does in a large company, these labs resemble biotech start-ups: Each has its own top managers, budget, and staff (kept deliberately small, at no more than 400 employees). Not only do the labs decide what drugs to pursue, but they also follow through with their decisions into the clinical testing phase. Previously, as is typical in large pharmaceutical companies, once R&D discovered new drugs, it passed them on to other units responsible for getting the drugs into clinical testing. Yamada wanted the researchers who were closest to the new discoveries to take ownership of them, make key decisions on how to proceed, and be responsible for their success (or failure). Importantly, researchers are rewarded for their expanded role in drug development; those who succeed at discovering a new drug and moving it into clinical testing are rewarded with bonuses and royalties.[98]

Today, Glaxo spends $14 million per day on R&D, has scores of new drugs and vaccines at various levels of testing, and has one of the largest pharmaceutical product pipelines in the industry. A socially responsible company, Glaxo is committed to developing drugs and vaccines to combat three priority diseases in the poorest countries: HIV/AIDS, malaria, and tuberculosis.[99] Glaxo provides poor countries with drugs at discounted, nonprofit prices and makes substantial donations to treat diseases afflicting the world's poor. For example, as a member of the Global Alliance to Eliminate Lymphatic Filariasis, Glaxo has committed to donate up to 6 billion albendazole tablets (a $1 billion commitment) to help eliminate that disease in poor countries.[100] All in all, learning, creativity, and social responsibility appear to be alive and well at Glaxo.

Promoting Individual Creativity

Research suggests that when certain conditions are met, managers are more likely to be creative. As just discussed, people must be given the opportunity and freedom to generate new ideas. Creativity declines when managers look over the shoulders of talented employees and try to "hurry up" a creative solution. How would you feel if your boss said you had one week to come up with a new product idea to beat the competition? Creativity results when employees have an opportunity to experiment, to take risks, and to make mistakes and learn from them. And employees must not fear that they will be looked down on or penalized for ideas that might at first seem outlandish, as it is sometimes those ideas that yield truly innovative products and services, as indicated in the following "Focus on Diversity."

Focus on Diversity

Asking Different Questions and Providing Different Answers

Ideas for truly creative goods, products, and services sometimes come from asking different kinds of questions and seeking different kinds of answers. When George Ohr discovered the wonders of making clay pots at a potter's wheel in the late 1800s, he learned as much as he could about pots. Then he questioned everything that people at the time thought pots should look like, and he provided answers in his own unique form of pottery art.[101]

Disdained at the time, Ohr's pottery is now so revered for its creativity and beauty that his pots command five-digit prices. Famed architect Frank Gehry designed the Ohr-O'Keefe museum in Ohr's hometown of Biloxi, Mississippi, to display Ohr's work (completion and opening of the museum were delayed by damages sustained from Hurricane Katrina in 2005).[102] Ohr turned pot making on its head. Each of his pots was unique: He would form perfect shapes and then crumple them like newspaper; he would make delicate, paper-thin pots; he carved writings into his pots; and he used bright, bold colors—all unheard of at the time and hailed as innovations decades later. It was only after Ohr's death that the art world recognized the genius and beauty in his work, which came from Ohr's unique answers to the question of pottery as an art form.[103]

Asking the right questions and providing different kinds of answers can lead to creativity in other arenas as well.[104] Dr. William Hunter has followed this approach ever since.[105] Now, as CEO of Angiotech Pharmaceuticals in Vancouver, California, he encourages his employees to do the same.[106] As a physician, he wondered whether drugs that were administered in massive doses to combat diseases like cancer could be used to cure or prevent other ailments when used in more moderate doses. And he also asked why medical implants like catheters and stents rarely

Creativity can sometimes seem initially outlandish. George Ohr turned pot making on its head in the early 1800s by questioning every pot-making norm of the time. Now his techniques are hailed as innovations.

included administrations of drugs. After extensive research, the answers to these questions led to the development of paclitaxel-coated coronary stents, a successful public offering of stock in Angiotech, and more questions for future research.[107]

Hunter learned that stents were not coated with drugs because of the questions stent manufacturers asked physicians. Typically, they would ask surgeons for advice on how to make better stents. Hunter, on the other hand, asked surgeons why stents sometimes fail and cause problems for about 20% of patients receiving them. The answer to this question is that stents used to open arteries can cause scar tissue to form around the stent, ultimately clogging the artery once again for certain patients. So why aren't stents coated with drugs that might help prevent the problem? Well, pharmaceutical companies have very long time horizons and spend large amounts of money on developing and testing new drugs. Medical equipment makers that develop and manufacture stents typically have much shorter time horizons. Hunter reasoned that paclitaxel, used in large dosages to stop the growth of cancer tumors, might prevent the growth of scar tissue when coated on stents in much smaller dosages.

After years of testing, Angiotech has a successful new product in paclitaxel-coated stents with only a 3% failure rate.[108] However, Hunter is the first to acknowledge that creative success and failure go hand in hand. For example, Angiotech unsuccessfully tried to develop a form of paclitaxel to treat multiple sclerosis. As Hunter puts it, "You have to celebrate the failures. . . . If you send the message that the only road to career success is experiments that work, people won't ask risky questions, or get any dramatically new answers."[109] If he were alive today, George Ohr would likely concur.

Highly innovative companies like 3M are well known for the wide degree of freedom they give their managers and employees to ask different questions and seek their answers. For example, at 3M employees are expected to spend a certain percentage of their time on projects of their own choosing, a policy that fosters creativity.

Once managers have generated alternatives, creativity can be fostered by providing them with constructive feedback so that they know how well they are doing. Ideas that seem to be going nowhere can be eliminated and creative energies refocused in other directions. Ideas that seem promising can be promoted, and help from other managers can be obtained as well.[110]

Top managers must stress the importance of looking for alternative solutions and should visibly reward employees who come up with creative ideas. Being creative can be demanding and stressful. Employees who believe that they are working on important, vital issues are motivated to put forth the high levels of effort that creativity demands. Creative people like to receive the acclaim of others, and innovative organizations have many kinds of ceremonies and rewards to recognize creative employees. For example, 3M established the Carlton Hall of Fame to recognize successful innovators. These employees not only become members of the hall of fame but also receive financial rewards through the Golden Step program.

These ad agency employees are conducting a brainstorming session. Brainstorming can be used to generate multiple ideas and solutions for solving problems.

Promoting Group Creativity

To encourage creativity at the group level, organizations can make use of group problem-solving techniques that promote creative ideas and innovative solutions. These techniques can also be used to prevent groupthink and to help managers uncover biases. Here, we look at three group decision-making techniques: *brainstorming*, the *nominal group technique*, and the *Delphi technique.*

BRAINSTORMING   *Brainstorming* is a group problem-solving technique in which managers meet face-to-face to generate and debate a wide variety of alternatives from which to make a decision.[111] Generally, from 5 to 15 managers meet in a closed-door session and proceed like this:

- One manager describes in broad outline the problem the group is to address.

- Group members then share their ideas and generate alternative courses of action.

- As each alternative is described, group members are not allowed to criticize it; everyone withholds judgment until all alternatives have been heard. One member of the group records the alternatives on a flip chart.

- Group members are encouraged to be as innovative and radical as possible. Anything goes; and the greater the number of ideas put forth, the better. Moreover, group members are encouraged to "piggyback" or build on each other's suggestions.

- When all alternatives have been generated, group members debate the pros and cons of each and develop a short list of the best alternatives.

    Brainstorming is very useful in some problem-solving situations—for example, when managers are trying to find a new name for a perfume or for a model of car. But sometimes individuals working alone can generate more alternatives. The main reason for the loss of productivity in brainstorming appears to be **production blocking,** which occurs because group members cannot always simultaneously make sense of all the alternatives being generated, think up additional alternatives, and remember what they were thinking.[112]

NOMINAL GROUP TECHNIQUE   To avoid production blocking, the **nominal group technique** is often used. It provides a more structured way of generating alternatives in writing and gives each manager more time and opportunity to come up with potential solutions. The nominal group technique is

production blocking A loss of productivity in brainstorming sessions due to the unstructured nature of brainstorming.

nominal group technique A decision-making technique in which group members write down ideas and solutions, read their suggestions to the whole group, and discuss and then rank the alternatives.

especially useful when an issue is controversial and when different managers might be expected to champion different courses of action. Generally, a small group of managers meet in a closed-door session and adopt the following procedures:

- One manager outlines the problem to be addressed, and 30 or 40 minutes are allocated for group members, working individually, to write down their ideas and solutions. Group members are encouraged to be innovative.

- Managers take turns reading their suggestions to the group. One manager writes all the alternatives on a flip chart. No criticism or evaluation of alternatives is allowed until all alternatives have been read.

- The alternatives are then discussed, one by one, in the sequence in which they were first proposed. Group members can ask for clarifying information and critique each alternative to identify its pros and cons.

- When all alternatives have been discussed, each group member ranks all the alternatives from most preferred to least preferred, and the alternative that receives the highest ranking is chosen.[113]

DELPHI TECHNIQUE   Both the nominal group technique and brainstorming require that managers meet together to generate creative ideas and engage in joint problem solving. What happens if managers are in different cities or in different parts of the world and cannot meet face-to-face? Videoconferencing is one way to bring distant managers together to brainstorm. Another way is to use the **Delphi technique,** a written approach to creative problem solving.[114] The Delphi technique works like this:

delphi technique
A decision-making technique in which group members do not meet face-to-face but respond in writing to questions posed by the group leader.

- The group leader writes a statement of the problem and a series of questions to which participating managers are to respond.

- The questionnaire is sent to the managers and departmental experts who are most knowledgeable about the problem. They are asked to generate solutions and mail the questionnaire back to the group leader.

- A team of top managers records and summarizes the responses. The results are then sent back to the participants, with additional questions to be answered before a decision can be made.

- The process is repeated until a consensus is reached and the most suitable course of action is apparent.

Entrepreneurship and Creativity

entrepreneur
An individual who notices opportunities and decides how to mobilize the resources necessary to produce new and improved goods and services.

Entrepreneurs are individuals who notice opportunities and decide how to mobilize the resources necessary to produce new and improved goods and services. Entrepreneurs make all of the planning, organizing, leading, and controlling decisions necessary to start new business ventures. Thus entrepreneurs are an important source of creativity in the organizational world. These people are the Bill Gateses or Liz Claibornes of the world, who make vast fortunes when their businesses succeed. Or they are among the millions of people who start new business ventures only to lose their money when they fail. Despite the fact that an estimated 80% of small businesses fail in the first three to five years, by some estimates 38% of men and 50% of women in today's workforce want to start their own companies.[115]

Many managers, scientists, and researchers employed by companies also engage in entrepreneurial activity, and they are an important source of organizational creativity. They are involved in innovation, developing new and improved products and ways to make them, which we describe in detail in Chapter 9. Such employees notice opportunities for either quantum or incremental product improvements and are responsible for managing the product development process. These individuals are known as **intrapreneurs,** to distinguish them from entrepreneurs who start their own businesses. But, in general, entrepreneurship involves creative decision making that provides customers with new or improved goods and services.

There is an interesting relationship between entrepreneurs and intrapreneurs. Many managers with intrapreneurial talents become dissatisfied if their superiors decide neither to support nor to fund new product ideas and development efforts that the managers think will succeed. What do intrapreneurial managers who feel that they are getting nowhere do? Very often they decide to leave their current organizations and start their own companies to take advantage of their new product ideas! In other words, intrapreneurs become entrepreneurs and found companies that often compete with the companies they left. To avoid losing these individuals, top managers must find ways to facilitate the entrepreneurial spirit of their most creative employees. In the remainder of this section we consider issues involved in promoting successful entrepreneurship in both new and existing organizations.

intrapreneur
A manager, scientist, or researcher who works inside an organization and notices opportunities to develop new or improved products and better ways to make them.

Entrepreneurship and New Ventures

The fact that a significant number of entrepreneurs were frustrated intrapreneurs provides a clue about the personal characteristics of people who are likely to start a new venture and bear all the uncertainty and risk associated with being an entrepreneur.

CHARACTERISTICS OF ENTREPRENEURS   Entrepreneurs are likely to possess a particular set of the personality characteristics we discussed in Chapter 4. First, they are likely to be high on the personality trait of *openness to experience*, meaning that they are predisposed to be original, to be open to a wide range of stimuli, to be daring, and to take risks. Entrepreneurs also are likely to have an *internal locus of control,* believing that they are responsible for what happens to them and that their own actions determine important outcomes such as the success or failure of a new business. People with an external locus of control, in contrast, would be very unlikely to leave a secure job in an organization and assume the risk associated with a new venture.

Entrepreneurs are likely to have a high level of *self-esteem* and feel competent and capable of handling most situations—including the stress and uncertainty surrounding a plunge into a risky new venture. Entrepreneurs are also likely to have a high *need for achievement* and have a strong desire to perform challenging tasks and meet high personal standards of excellence. A good example of an entrepreneur with these qualities who founded a new company and has led it successfully since then is Omar Maden, profiled in the following "Manager as a Person."

Manager as a Person

Omar Maden Creates a New Company

In 1962, 15-year old Omar Maden fled Cuba alone and penniless and was resettled with foster parents in Portland, Oregon. Five years later he was drafted into the U.S. Army during the Vietnam war, and the former Afro-Cuban found himself working on command and control communication technology for artillery and missiles. At the end of the war, Maden's superior officers encouraged him to remain in the Army because of his considerable technical skills. Maden became an Army information technology expert, and rose through the ranks to become a major. He was transferred to the Pentagon, where he was responsible for implementing some key logistics communication technologies.[116]

Omar Maden has successfully guided his company through the transition from fulfilling government contracts to selling its high-tech expertise to the private sector.

After retiring from the Army in the mid-1980s, Maden decided he could use his IT skills to become an independent consultant. Using a home equity loan and his personal savings, he started Maden Technologies. Soon his previous employer, the Army, began to call on his services. Maden's big break came when he was hired to oversee deployment of the Army's logistics center for the Desert Storm campaign during the first war with Iraq. He and his team of highly trained IT analysts fashioned a field communication system that offered Desert Storm's commanders instantaneous performance feedback, which put them in total control of all mobile military resources. Maden's systems excelled, and his success in managing this venture led to more contracts. Within 10 years Maden Technologies had become one of the Pentagon's largest research and development contractors.

Since 1995, Maden has organized his IT analysts into teams to develop the different communication products that the Army needed. For example, one team converted the military's internal e-mail system into a battlefield tool that allows everyone to communicate with everyone else. Another team developed a smart card that has embedded in it a soldier's complete personal, medical, and military record. The cards were issued to 4 million Army personnel.

Moreover, using his military experience, Maden has been careful to assign authority for each project to the members of the team responsible for developing each product to encourage innovation and entrepreneurial behavior. Team members are given wide authority to make decisions, and each team works closely with its customers—Army officers—so that the team can be sure it is designing a product that matches the Army's needs.[117]

Realizing that his company's technological innovations and skills could be used more widely, in the 2000s Maden has been trying to reposition his company as a technology service provider to industry. His employees have been pushing him to do this because they have received large stock options for their major contributions and are anxious to see their company succeed on a national level. Clearly, entrepreneurship and innovation go hand in hand at Maden Technologies.

ENTREPRENEURSHIP AND MANAGEMENT Given that entrepreneurs are predisposed to activities that are somewhat adventurous and risky, in what ways can people become involved in entrepreneurial ventures? One way is to start a business from scratch. Taking advantage of modern IT, many people are starting solo ventures. The total number of small-office and home-office workers is more than 40 million, and each year more than a million new solo entrepreneurs join the ranks of the more than 29 million self-employed.

When people who go it alone succeed, they frequently need to hire other people to help them run the business. Michael Dell, for example, began his computer business as a college student and within weeks had hired several people to help him to assemble computers from the component parts he bought from suppliers. From his solo venture grew Dell Computer, the largest PC maker in the world today.

entrepreneurship The mobilization of resources to take advantage of an opportunity to provide customers with new or improved goods and services.

Some entrepreneurs who found a new business often have difficulty deciding how to manage the organization as it grows; entrepreneurship is *not* the same as management. Management encompasses all the decisions involved in planning, organizing, leading, and controlling resources. Entrepreneurship is noticing an opportunity to satisfy a customer need and then deciding how to find and use resources to make a product that satisfies that need. When an entrepreneur has produced something that customers want, entrepreneurship gives way to management, as the pressing need becomes providing the product both efficiently and effectively. Frequently, a founding entrepreneur lacks the skills, patience, and experience to engage in the difficult and challenging work of management. Some entrepreneurs find it very hard to delegate authority because they are afraid to risk their company by letting others manage it. As a result, they become overloaded, and the quality of their decision making declines. Other entrepreneurs lack the detailed knowledge necessary to establish state-of-the-art information systems and technology or to create the operations management procedures that are vital to increase the efficiency of their organizations' production systems. Thus, to succeed, it is necessary to do more than create a new product; an entrepreneur must hire managers who can create an operating system that will let a new venture survive and prosper.

Intrapreneurship and Organizational Learning

The intensity of competition today, particularly from agile, small companies, has made it increasingly important for large, established organizations to promote and encourage intrapreneurship to raise the level of innovation and organizational

Management in Action

Topics for Discussion and Action

Discussion

1. What are the main differences between programmed decision making and nonprogrammed decision making?

2. In what ways do the classical and administrative models of decision making help managers appreciate the complexities of real-world decision making?

3. Why do capable managers sometimes make bad decisions? What can individual managers do to improve their decision-making skills?

4. In what kinds of groups is groupthink most likely to be a problem? When is it least likely to be a problem? What steps can group members take to ward off groupthink?

5. What is organizational learning, and how can managers promote it?

6. What is the difference between entrepreneurship and intrapreneurship?

Action

7. Ask a manager to recall the best and the worst decisions he or she ever made. Try to determine why these decisions were so good or so bad.

8. Think about an organization in your local community, your university, or an organization that you are familiar with that is doing poorly. Now think of questions managers in the organization should ask stakeholders to elicit creative ideas for turning around the organization's fortunes.

Building Management Skills

How Do You Make Decisions?

Pick a decision that you made recently and that has had important consequences for you. It may be your decision about which college to attend, which major to select, whether to take a part-time job, or which part-time job to take. Using the material in this chapter, analyze the way in which you made the decision. In particular:

1. Identify the criteria you used, either consciously or unconsciously, to guide your decision making.

2. List the alternatives you considered. Were they all possible alternatives? Did you unconsciously (or consciously) ignore some important alternatives?

3. How much information did you have about each alternative? Were you making the decision on the basis of complete or incomplete information?

4. Try to remember how you reached the decision. Did you sit down and consciously think through the implications of each alternative, or did you make the decision on the basis of intuition? Did you use

any rules of thumb to help you make the decision?

5. In retrospect, do you think that your choice of alternative was shaped by any of the cognitive biases discussed in this chapter?

6. Having answered the previous five questions, do you think in retrospect that you made a reasonable decision? What, if anything, might you do to improve your ability to make good decisions in the future?

Managing Ethically

Sometimes groups make extreme decisions—decisions that are either more risky or more conservative than they would have been if individuals acting alone had made them. One explanation for the tendency of groups to make extreme decisions is diffusion of responsibility. In a group, responsibility for the outcomes of a decision is spread among group members, so each person feels less than fully accountable. The group's decision is extreme because no individual has taken full responsibility for it.

Questions

1. Either alone or in a group, think about the ethical implications of extreme decision making by groups.

2. When group decision making takes place, should members of a group each feel fully accountable for outcomes of the decision? Why or why not?

Small Group Breakout Exercise

Brainstorming

Form groups of three or four people, and appoint one member as the spokesperson who will communicate your findings to the class when called on by the instructor. Then discuss the following scenario.

You and your partners are trying to decide which kind of restaurant to open in a centrally located shopping center that has just been built in your city. The problem confronting you is that the city already has many restaurants that provide different kinds of food at all price ranges. You have the resources to open any type of restaurant. Your challenge is to decide which type is most likely to succeed.

Use the brainstorming technique to decide which type of restaurant to open. Follow these steps:

1. As a group, spend 5 or 10 minutes generating ideas about the alternative restaurants that the members think will be most likely to succeed. Each group member should be as innovative and creative as possible, and no suggestions should be criticized.

2. Appoint one group member to write down the alternatives as they are identified.

3. Spend the next 10 or 15 minutes debating the pros and cons of the alternatives. As a group, try to reach a consensus on which alternative is most likely to succeed.

After making your decision, discuss the pros and cons of the brainstorming method, and decide whether any production blocking occurred.

When called on by the instructor, the spokesperson should be prepared to share your group's decision with the class, as well as the reasons the group made its decision.

Exploring the World Wide Web

Go to www.brainstorming. co.uk. This Web site contains "Training on Creativity Techniques" and "Creativity Puzzles." Spend at least 30 minutes on the training and/or puzzles. Think about what you have learned. Come up with specific ways in which you can be more creative in your thinking and decision making based on what you have learned.

Be the Manager

You are a top manager who was recently hired by an oil field services company in Oklahoma to help it respond more quickly and proactively to potential opportunities in its market. You report to the chief operating officer (COO), who reports to the CEO, and you have been on the job for eight months. Thus far, you have come up with three initiatives you carefully studied, thought were noteworthy, and proposed and justified to the COO. The COO seemed cautiously interested when you presented the proposals, and each time he indicated he would think about them and discuss them with the CEO as considerable resources were involved. Each time, you never heard back from the COO, and after a few weeks elapsed, you casually asked the COO if there was any news on the proposal in question. For the first proposal, the COO said, "We think it's a good idea but the timing is off. Let's shelve it for the time being and reconsider it next year." For the second proposal, the COO said, "Mike [the CEO] reminded me that we tried that two years ago and it wasn't well received in the market. I am surprised I didn't remember it myself when you first described the proposal but it came right back to me once Mike mentioned it." For the third proposal, the COO simply said, "We're not convinced it will work."

You believe that your three proposed initiatives are viable ways to seize opportunities in the marketplace, yet you cannot proceed with any of them. Moreover, for each proposal, you invested considerable amounts of time and have even worked to bring others on board to support the proposal, only to have it shot down by the CEO. When you interviewed for the position, both the COO and the CEO claimed they wanted "an outsider to help them step out of the box and innovate." Yet your experience to date has been just the opposite.

BusinessWeek

Case in the News

Five Offshore Practices that Pay Off

From Dell Inc. to Reuters Group PLC, corporations have run into trouble as they've shifted jobs offshore. But they've persisted since the process is so critical to corporate success. Take Bank of America Corp., for example, which attracted media attention when it laid off hundreds of information technology workers after forcing some of them to train their Indian replacements. But BofA learned from its mistake. "It caused us to make a greater commitment to [retraining] our associates and to explaining the context of changes in the marketplace," says Barbara J. Desoer, BofA's global technology, service, and fulfillment executive. Now BofA gives its workers six to eight months' notice before an offshore move, enough time to train for new assignments or to hunt for jobs.

What are the pitfalls to avoid when outsourcing? What are the best practices to follow? These questions are more pressing than ever as outsourcing turns companies inside out. "The era of lift, shift, and labor arbitrage is coming to an end," says Sanjeev Aggarwal, chief executive of IBM Daksh Business Services, Big Blue's New Delhi call center operation. "It's all about business transformation today." This playbook offers guidelines companies must keep in mind as they consider such a profound change.

1. Go offshore for the right reasons

Despite the lure of lower costs and the promise of big gains in efficiency and innovation, it may make sense not to go offshore at all. Can you boost efficiency and competitiveness by shaking up operations or improving technology at home? What's the risk of a damaging backlash from your customers or community? "Offshoring is a powerful lever, but just one [of many]" for companies aiming to stay competitive, says Ramesh Venkataraman, McKinsey & Co.'s tech partner for Asia.

Don't decide to send work offshore simply because your competitors are doing it. And don't outsource a mess! "If you have a broken process, shifting it overseas won't fix it," notes Ananda Mukerji, CEO of Bombay call center operator and researcher ICICI OneSource Ltd.

2. Choose your model carefully

As you develop your strategy, weigh whether you should set up your own subsidiary offshore—known as a "captive" operation—or contract with outside specialists. The appeal of opening your own outfit is that you keep firm control of proprietary technology and processes. For that reason, Boeing Co. opened its own center in Moscow, where it employs 1,100 skilled but relatively low-cost aerospace engineers on a range of projects, including the design of titanium parts for the new 787 Dreamliner jet. Likewise, Chicago-based law firm Baker & McKenzie has its own English-speaking team in Manila that drafts documents and does market research.

One downside of captive units, warns Gartner Inc., is that they can wind up costing the head office more than it would to hire large outside outsourcers that spread overhead among numerous customers. For that reason, many companies are shooting for the best of both worlds. BofA established its own India subsidiary, yet also teamed up with Infosys Technologies and Tata Consultancy Services Ltd. to shift 30% of its IT resources offshore. Since 2001, says the bank, offshoring has helped save it $100 million and, more important, improved product quality.

3. Get your people on board

Keep in mind that employees and middle managers can make your bold move happen—or stop you in your tracks. Dutch bank ABN Amro was aware of this risk when it decided in 2004 to boost efficiency and product quality by uniting retail, investment, private banking, and asset management businesses under one technology platform, to be developed offshore. Senior executives feared resistance. "When you first approach outsourcing, it's a religious issue," says Lars Gustavsson, ABN Amro's London-based group chief information officer. "People either believe in it or they don't."

To counter potential opposition, the bank set up a full-time communications department dedicated to explaining the move to middle managers and staff. Senior executives held town hall meetings with employees and involved the unions in managing the shift. And the bank gathered together its 12 chief technology officers into a committee that made decisions by consensus about redeploying the workforce and selecting outsourcing partners. Although some 1,500 jobs will be lost, ABN Amro is helping

with severance and retraining—and still expects to save more than $300 million annually starting in 2007.

4. Be prepared to invest time and effort

As Gartner points out, 80% of companies cite cost-cutting as the main reason for outsourcing. But you won't save as much after the initial year unless you're prepared to invest serious management time and effort. "It took a heck of a lot more involvement on the part of myself and my team than I expected," acknowledges Frank Cocuzza, chief financial officer of Penske Truck Leasing, which has shifted work on more than 30 business operations to India, Mexico, China, and Brazil since 2000.

To keep its leasing and logistics businesses humming, Penske invests heavily in teaching its contractors English language skills—not just so that call-center workers sound fluent to U.S. customers but also so that Penske's own managers can better understand them. Offshore workers also receive intensive training in Penske's business practices. And Cocuzza sends operational managers to meet with their offshore counterparts at least twice a year.

Quality control is also important once the offshore project is up and running, particularly for more complicated tasks. What's often lacking in offshore partners "is a lot of deep process knowledge, whether it's mortgage processing, insurance, or other areas," says Gartner Research Director Frances Karamouzis.

5. Treat your partners as equals

While working with offshore partners can be scary at first, outsourcing veterans agree that the gains are greater if you regard them as equals. "If you try to treat these suppliers as a body shop—telling them exactly what to do and how to do it—it does not go well," says Christopher Cartwright, CEO of the corporate and financial services division of Dutch-American publisher Wolters Kluwer.

Cartwright headed the company's pilot offshore project in 2003, when it contracted with Tata Consultancy and HCL Technologies Ltd. to develop new technology for delivering the publisher's compliance products online. "We tried to map out everything so there would be no doubt what we wanted," he recalls. "We didn't invite the partner to help us determine the best way" to make the project work, he adds. Cartwright felt his company did not get the maximum payoff from its initial project as a result. Now he ensures that his company's project managers and software architects work closely with their counterparts from India onshore for a period to organize their work efficiently.

In a very different industry, HT Capital Management Ltd., a $300 million hedge fund in Hong Kong, has teamed up with New Delhi-based Evalueserve Inc. Four financial analysts from the Indian company write research and market analysis for HT, working closely with four analysts from HT. "We make them feel part of our team," says Ophelia Tong, HT's investment director.

Outsourcing is still more of an art than a science. But it's now part of the corporate toolkit, and it's important to use this tool right.

Source: M. Kripalani, "Five Offshore Practices That Pay Off." Reprinted from the January 30, 2006, issue of *BusinessWeek* by special permission. Copyright © 2006 by the McGraw-Hill Companies.

Questions

1. Is the decision to offshore a programmed or nonprogrammed decision?

2. To what extent are risk and uncertainty involved in this decision?

3. What criteria do managers need to consider when making decisions about offshoring?

4. Why is it important for managers to learn from the feedback they receive in the context of offshoring?

BusinessWeek

Case in the News

Steering Patients through the System

For Kara J. Troti, becoming an entrepreneur meant leaving her corporate law career. It meant resigning from a nonprofit board she no longer has time for and giving up her vacations. And in the early days it meant taking out a home-equity loan and moving to a smaller house.

But the new Kara Trott—the superbusy one in the more modest home—has never been happier. The company she started in 1999, Quantum Health in Columbus, Ohio, helps patients navigate the complexities of the health-care system. "When someone is diagnosed with cancer or diabetes, it is the most difficult time in their lives," says Trott, 44. "It gives me the greatest satisfaction that I help people make the right decisions during those critical moments."

In her prior life many of Trott's legal clients had been hospitals or doctors. She witnessed the insurance industry's attempts to shift health-care costs by cutting reimbursements to physicians and hospitals and by increasing employees' deductibles and co-payments. Trott also had worked as a consumer products consultant, and she thought some of the techniques used in that industry, such as providing incentives to get people to buy, could be applied to health care to encourage patients to reduce spending. That would help everyone in the system, from patients on up. "I wanted to create something and make a change in people's lives," says Trott. "Of course, everybody was skeptical."

Undeterred, she tracked health-care decisions from 2,800 patients, 260 physicians, and 140 employers, using data supplied largely by her law firm's clients. She found that half of the patients left their physicians' offices not knowing what to do. Only 15% got answers to their questions, and 61% of the time patients chose the wrong type of specialist. That misstep generated an average of $3,500 in extra costs. And Trott found that most patients wanted more guidance in choosing health care.

Data in hand, Trott quit her job. She told employers that her company would call their employees when they made doctors' appointments. Quantum would arm the employees with pertinent questions, help them choose the right specialists, give them advice about which tests to take, and ensure that tests weren't duplicated. Quantum would get a percentage of any savings the employers reaped. It would also offer workers incentives to stay well, such as by slashing co-pays for preventive care visits.

Her pitch worked. Trott's first customers, mostly small, self-insured companies, averaged 6% increases in their health-care expenditures in 2001, compared with a national average of about 11% at the time. In 2004, according to a study of 600 patients by Appleton (Wis.) benefits consultant Associated Health Group, Quantum made 970 telephone calls to patients, compared with 27 by a disease management company assigned to assist employees with chronic ailments. "Quantum takes disease management to the nth degree," says Associated's vice-president, Jeff Prickette.

Still, the first few years were slow going. "In the health-care business it takes an average of three years before people believe that results you're generating aren't an anomaly," says Trott. She invested $400,000 of her own money and raised $300,000 from family and friends before taking out a Small Business Administration-backed loan in 2004 for $730,000. In 2002 she hired a professional management team, including her husband, strategy consultant Randy Gebhardt, as COO.

Now, Quantum is on a tear. Last year the number of patients Quantum oversees doubled, to 52,000. Trott doubled her own employee base, to 55, and 2005 revenues shot up 40%, to $7 million. "If we had gone to employers in 1999 talking about the importance of wellness and disease management, they would have laughed me out," says Trott. Now they're begging her to come in.

Source: P. Gogoi, "Steering Patients Through the System." Reprinted from the February

Questions

1. What factors contributed to Kara Trott's decision to become an entrepreneur?

2. Was this a programmed or a nonprogrammed decision?

3. Compared with the classical model, why does the administrative model of decision making better describe Trott's process in making this decision?

4. How has Trott learned from feedback?

CHAPTER 8

The Manager as a Planner and Strategist

After studying this chapter, you should be able to:

- Identify the three main steps of the planning process and explain the relationship between planning and strategy.

- Describe some techniques managers can use to improve the planning process so that they can better predict the future and mobilize organizational resources to meet future contingencies.

- Differentiate between the main types of business-level strategies and explain how they give an organization a competitive advantage that may lead to superior performance.

- Differentiate between the main types of corporate-level strategies and explain how they are used to strengthen a company's business-level strategy and competitive advantage.

- Describe the vital role managers play in implementing strategies to achieve an organization's mission and goals.

A Manager's Challenge

Can Mattel's Planners Help Barbie Compete with Bratz?

Why is it hard to compete in an industry?

The rapid pace at which forces in the global environment are changing is causing managers of all kinds of companies to reexamine the way their products create value for customers and to find ways to increase that value. Otherwise, these companies will get left behind by competitors that do respond faster to changing conditions, such as changing technology or customer tastes and fads and fashions. Nowhere is this truer than in the global toy industry, where a vicious combat is raging in the doll business, with annual sales of $10 billion.

Mattel, the largest global toy company, has earned tens of billions of dollars from its world's best-selling doll, Barbie, since she was introduced 50 years ago. Mothers who played with the original dolls bought them for their daughters, and then granddaughters, and Barbie became an American and then a global icon. Barbie and Barbie accessories account for almost 50% of Mattel's toy sales, so protecting its star product is crucial. Barbie's status as the world's best-selling doll

led Mattel's managers to make major errors in their planning and strategy making in the last decade, however.

Look out, Barbie! Here come the Bratz dolls.

The Barbie doll was created in the 1960s when most women were homemakers; her voluptuous shape was a response to a dated view of what the "ideal" woman should look like. In the last decades, changing cultural views about the role of girls, women, and women working after marriage altered the tastes of doll buyers in fundamental ways. Barbie's continuing success as measured by sales, however, led a series of

Mattel CEOs, including Mattel's current CEO Bob Eckert and his top managers, to underestimate how quickly the needs of doll buyers has been changing. Mattel's managers collectively bought into an "If it's not broken, don't fix it" approach. Indeed, given that Barbie is still the best-seller, managers decided it might be very dangerous to make major changes to her appearance because customers might not like them—and might stop buying the doll. Mattel's top managers continued to bet on Barbie's ongoing success, and no major changes were planned for the Barbie brand.[1]

So Mattel was unprepared when a challenge came along in the form of a new kind of doll, the Bratz doll, introduced by MGA Entertainment. Over the years many competitors to Barbie had emerged—selling dolls is very profitable—but no other doll had matched Barbie's appeal to young girls (or their mothers). The marketers and designers behind the Bratz line of dolls, however, spent a lot of time and money to discover what the new generation of girls, especially those aged 7 to 11, wanted from a doll so that they could design a doll to better satisfy their needs. Their research suggested that what was needed was a brash, individualized doll that would appeal to girls brought up in a fast-changing fashion, music, and television market and age. Bratz dolls have larger heads and oversized eyes, wear lots of makeup and short dresses, and are multicultural to give each doll "personality and attitude."[2] This careful planning paid off: The Bratz dolls did meet the needs of "tween," relationship-oriented girls, and the new line took off. MGA quickly licensed the rights to make and sell the doll to toy companies overseas, and Bratz soon became a serious competitor to Barbie.

Now Mattel's planners were in trouble. Bratz's success showed them they needed to redefine the doll and Barbie business; they had to reexamine who their customers were, what needs dolls were satisfying in the 2000s, and, most importantly, how to change Barbie to bring her up to date. And they had to do this quickly under intense pressure because of the prospect of losing billions in Barbie sales. Mattel's top managers and doll designers went to work. They changed Barbie's "extreme" vital statistics; they killed off her old-time boyfriend and replaced him with Blaine, an Aussie surfer; they created new models of hip Barbie dolls; and so on. Mattel's managers also recognized they had waited much too long to introduce new lines of dolls to meet the changed needs of tweens and other girls in the 2000s. So they quickly designed and introduced the new "My Scene" line of dolls in 2002, obvious imitations of Bratz dolls that have not competed successfully against Bratz. Mattel also introduced a line called Flava in 2003 to appeal to even younger girls, but this line flopped completely. To make things worse, the changes they made to the Barbie brand, such as her looks, clothing, and boyfriend, came too late to revive the brand, and sales continued to fall.

All this poor planning and strategy is serious stuff for Mattel because its profits and stock price hinge on Barbie's continuing success. Indeed, its stock price, which reached a high of $40 in 1999, was only $16 in 2005, so stockholders lost billions of dollars on their investment in the company.[3] Analysts argue that Mattel's planning has consistently failed; managers have not developed the strategies needed to stay up to with date with changing customer needs in the toy business and to introduce new and improved products fast enough. Time will tell if Mattel's managers can find new strategies to reverse the decline in its doll sales. But strategy making at Mattel has changed forever; managers recognize they must find a better way to plan in a fast-changing global environment.

Overview

As the opening case suggests, in an uncertain, fast-changing competitive environment managers must continually evaluate how well products are meeting customer needs, and they must engage in thorough, systematic planning to find new strategies to better meet those needs. This chapter explores the manager's role both as planner and as strategist. First, we discuss the nature and importance of planning, the kinds of plans managers develop, and the levels at which planning takes place. Second, we discuss the three major steps in the planning process: (1) determining an organization's mission and major goals, (2) choosing or formulating strategies to realize the mission and goals, and (3) selecting the most effective ways to implement and put these strategies into action. We also examine several techniques, such as scenario planning and SWOT analysis, that can help managers improve the quality of their planning; and we discuss a range of strategies that managers can use to give their companies a competitive advantage over their rivals. By the end of this chapter, you will understand the vital role managers carry out when they plan, develop, and implement strategies to create a high-performing organization.

Planning and Strategy

planning Identifying and selecting appropriate goals and courses of action; one of the four principal functions of management.

strategy A cluster of decisions about what goals to pursue, what actions to take, and how to use resources to achieve goals.

mission statement A broad declaration of an organization's purpose that identifies the organization's products and customers and distinguishes the organization from its competitors.

Planning, as we note in Chapter 1, is a process that managers use to identify and select appropriate goals and courses of action for an organization.[4] The organizational plan that results from the planning process details the goals of the organization and the specific set of strategies that managers will implement to attain those goals. Recall, from Chapter 1, that a **strategy** is a cluster of related managerial decisions and actions to help an organization attain one of its goals. Thus, planning is both a goal-making and a strategy-making process.

In most organizations, planning is a three-step activity (see Figure 8.1). The first step is determining the organization's mission and goals. A **mission statement** is a broad declaration of an organization's overriding purpose, what it is

Figure 8.1
Three Steps in Planning

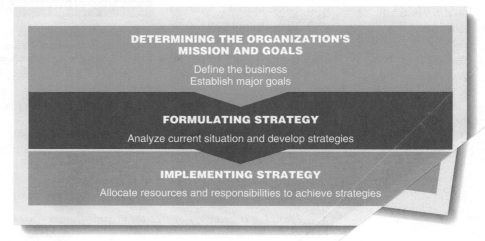

DETERMINING THE ORGANIZATION'S MISSION AND GOALS
Define the business
Establish major goals

FORMULATING STRATEGY
Analyze current situation and develop strategies

IMPLEMENTING STRATEGY
Allocate resources and responsibilities to achieve strategies

seeking to achieve from its activities; this statement is also intended to identify what is *unique or important* about its products to its employees and customers as well as to *distinguish or differentiate* the organization in some ways from its competitors. (Three examples of mission statements, those created by Cisco Systems, Wal-Mart, and AT&T, are illustrated later, in Figure 8.4.)

The second step is formulating strategy. Managers analyze the organization's current situation and then conceive and develop the strategies necessary to attain the organization's mission and goals. The third step is implementing strategy. Managers decide how to allocate the resources and responsibilities required to implement the strategies among people and groups within the organization.[5] In subsequent sections of this chapter we look in detail at the specifics of each of these steps. But first we examine the general nature and purpose of planning.

The Nature of the Planning Process

Essentially, to perform the planning task, managers (1) establish and discover where an organization is at the *present time*, (2) determine where it should be in the future, its *desired future state;* and (3) decide how to *move it forward* to reach that future state. When managers plan, they must forecast what may happen in the future in order to decide what to do in the present. The better their predictions, the more effective will be the strategies they formulate to take advantage of future opportunities and counter emerging competitive threats in the environment. As previous chapters noted, however, the external environment is uncertain and complex, and managers typically must deal with incomplete information and bounded rationality. This is why planning and strategy making is such a difficult and risky activity, and as at Mattel, if managers' predictions are wrong and strategies fail, organizational performance falls.

A group of managers plots their future course of action. Their ability to predict the future will have a significant impact on the organization's success.

Why Planning Is Important

Almost all managers participate in some kind of planning because they must try to predict future opportunities and threats and develop a plan and strategies that will result in a high-performing organization. Moreover, the absence of a plan often results in hesitations, false steps, and mistaken changes of direction that can hurt an organization or even lead to disaster. Planning is important for four main reasons:

1. *Planning is necessary to give the organization a sense of direction and purpose.*[6] A plan states what goals an organization is trying to achieve and what strategies it

intends to use to achieve them. Without the sense of direction and purpose that a formal plan provides, managers may interpret their own specific tasks and jobs in ways that best suit themselves. The result will be an organization that is pursuing multiple and often conflicting goals and a set of managers who do not cooperate and work well together. By stating which organizational goals and strategies are important, a plan keeps managers on track so that they use the resources under their control efficiently and effectively.

2. *Planning is a useful way of getting managers to participate in decision making about the appropriate goals and strategies for an organization.* Effective planning gives all managers the opportunity to participate in decision making. At Intel, for example, top managers, as part of their annual planning process, regularly request input from lower-level managers to determine what the organization's goals and strategies should be.

3. *A plan helps coordinate managers of the different functions and divisions of an organization to ensure that they all pull in the same direction and work to achieve its desired future state.* Without a well-thought-out plan, for example, it is possible that the members of the manufacturing function will produce more products than the members of the sales function can sell, resulting in a mass of unsold inventory. This happened to high-flying Internet router supplier Cisco Systems in the early 2000s when manufacturing, which previously had been able to sell all the routers it produced, found it had over $2 billion of inventory that the sales force could not sell; customers now wanted new kinds of optical routers that Cisco had not planned to develop—even though sales had told manufacturing that customer needs were changing.

4. *A plan can be used as a device for controlling managers within an organization.* A good plan specifies not only which goals and strategies the organization is committed to but also *who* bears the responsibility for putting the strategies into action to attain the goals. When managers know that they will be held accountable for attaining a goal, they are motivated to do their best to make sure the goal is achieved.

Henri Fayol, the originator of the model of management we discussed in Chapter 1, said that effective plans should have four qualities: unity, continuity, accuracy, and flexibility.[7] *Unity* means that at any one time only one central, guiding plan is put into operation to achieve an organizational goal; more than one plan to achieve a goal would cause confusion and disorder. *Continuity* means that planning is an ongoing process in which managers build and refine previous plans and continually modify plans at all levels—corporate, business, and functional—so that they fit together into one broad framework. *Accuracy* means that managers need to make every attempt to collect and utilize all available information at their disposal in the planning process. Of course, managers must recognize the fact that uncertainty exists and that information is almost always incomplete (for reasons we discussed in Chapter 7). Despite the need for continuity and accuracy, however, Fayol emphasized that the planning process should be *flexible* enough so that plans can be altered and changed if the situation changes; managers must not be bound to a static plan.

Levels of Planning

In large organizations planning usually takes place at three levels of management: corporate, business or division, and department or functional. Consider

Figure 8.2
Levels of Planning at General Electric

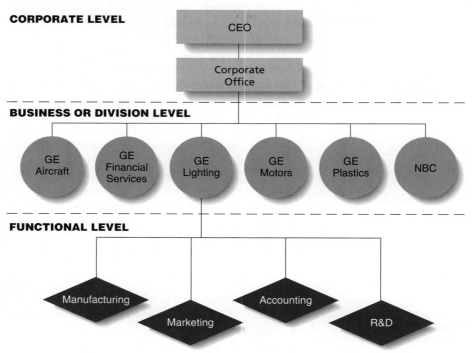

how General Electric (GE) operates. One of the world's largest global organizations, GE competes in over 150 different businesses or industries,.[8] GE has three main levels of management: corporate level, business or divisional level, and functional level (see Figure 8.2). At the corporate level are CEO and chairman Jeffrey Immelt, his top management team, and their corporate support staff. Together, they are responsible for planning and strategy making for the organization as a whole.

Below the corporate level is the business level. At the business level are the different *divisions* or *business units* of the company that compete in distinct industries; GE has over 150 divisions, including GE Aircraft Engines, GE Financial Services, GE Lighting, GE Motors, GE Plastics, and NBC. Each division or business unit has its own set of *divisional managers* who control planning and strategy for their particular division or unit. So, for example, GE Lighting's divisional managers plan how to operate globally to reduce costs while meeting the needs of customers in different countries.

Going down one more level, each division has its own set of *functions* or *departments,* such as manufacturing, marketing, human resource management (HRM), and research and development (R&D). For example, GE Aircraft has its own marketing function, as do GE Lighting, GE Motors, and NBC. Each division's *functional managers* are responsible for the planning and strategy making necessary to increase the efficiency and effectiveness of their particular function. So, for example, GE Lighting's marketing managers are responsible for increasing the effectiveness of its advertising and sales campaigns in different countries to improve lightbulb sales.

Figure 8.3
Levels and Types of Planning

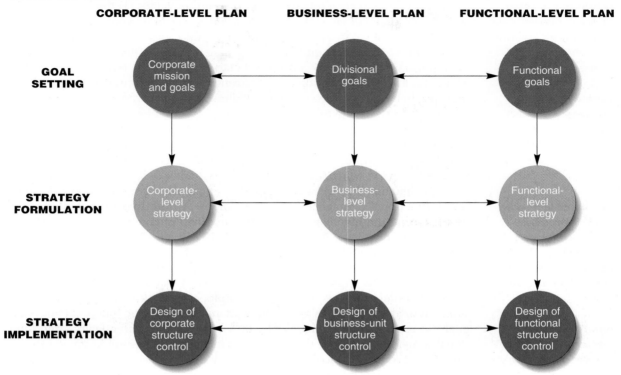

Levels and Types of Planning

As just discussed, planning at GE, as at all other large organizations, takes place at each level. Figure 8.3 shows the link between these three levels and the three steps in the planning and strategy-making process illustrated in Figure 8.1.

The **corporate-level plan** contains top management's decisions concerning the organization's mission and goals, overall (corporate-level) strategy, and structure (see Figure 8.3). **Corporate-level strategy** specifies in which industries and national markets an organization intends to compete and why. One of the goals stated in GE's corporate-level plan is that GE should be first or second in market share in every industry in which it competes. A division that cannot attain this goal may be sold to another company. GE Medical Systems was sold to Thompson of France for this reason. Another GE goal is to acquire other companies that can help a division build its market share to reach its corporate goal of being first or second in an industry. Over the last decade, GE acquired several large financial services companies to meet this goal and has transformed the GE Financial Services Division into one of the largest financial services operations in the world.

In general, corporate-level planning and strategy is the primary responsibility of top or corporate managers.[9] The corporate-level goal that GE should be first or second in every industry in which it competes was first articulated by former CEO Jack Welch. Now, Welch's hand-picked successor, Jeffrey Immelt, and his top-management team decide which industries GE should compete in.

corporate-level plan Top management's decisions pertaining to the organization's mission, overall strategy, and structure.

corporate-level strategy A plan that indicates in which industries and national markets an organization intends to compete.

The corporate-level plan provides the framework within which divisional managers create their business-level plans. At the business level, the managers of each division create a **business-level plan** that details (1) the long-term divisional goals that will allow the division to meet corporate goals and (2) the division's business-level strategy and structure necessary to achieve divisional goals. **Business-level strategy** outlines the specific methods a division, business unit, or organization will use to compete effectively against its rivals in an industry. Managers at GE's lighting division (currently number two in the global lighting industry, behind the Dutch company Philips NV) develop strategies designed to help their division take over the number-one spot and better contribute to GE's corporate goals. The lighting division's specific strategies might focus on ways to reduce costs in all departments to lower prices and so gain market share from Philips. For example, GE is currently expanding its European lighting operations in Hungary, which, as we discussed in Chapter 5, is a low-cost location.[10]

At the functional level, the business-level plan provides the framework within which functional managers devise their plans. A **functional-level plan** states the goals that the managers of each function will pursue to help their division attain its business-level goals, which, in turn, will allow the entire company to achieve its corporate goals. **Functional-level strategy** is a plan of action that managers of individual functions (such as manufacturing or marketing) can take to add value to an organization's goods and services and thereby increase the value customers receive. Thus, for example, consistent with the lighting division's strategy of driving down costs, its manufacturing function might adopt the goal "To reduce production costs by 20% over the next three years," and functional strategies to achieve this goal might include (1) investing in state-of-the-art European production facilities and (2) developing an electronic global business-to-business network to reduce the costs of inputs and inventory holding. The many ways in which managers can use functional-level strategy to strengthen business-level strategy are discussed in detail in Chapter 9.

In the planning process, it is important to ensure that planning across the three different levels is *consistent*–functional goals and strategies should be consistent with divisional goals and strategies, which, in turn, should be consistent with corporate goals and strategies, and vice versa. When consistency is achieved, the whole company operates in harmony; activities at one level reinforce and strengthen those at the other levels, increasing efficiency and effectiveness. To help accomplish this, each function's plan is linked to its division's business-level plan, which, in turn, is linked to the corporate plan. Although few organizations are as large and complex as GE, most plan in the same way as GE and have written plans, which are frequently updated, to guide managerial decision making.

Time Horizons of Plans

Plans differ in their **time horizon,** the period of time over which they are intended to apply or endure. Managers usually distinguish among *long-term plans,* with a time horizon of five years or more; *intermediate-term plans,* with a horizon between one and five years; and *short-term plans*, with a horizon of one year or less.[11] Typically, corporate- and business-level goals and strategies require long- and intermediate-term plans, and functional-level goals and strategies require intermediate- and short-term plans.

Although most companies operate with planning horizons of five years or more, this does not mean that managers undertake major planning exercises only once every five years and then "lock in" a specific set of goals and strategies

business-level plan Divisional managers' decisions pertaining to divisions' long-term goals, overall strategy, and structure.

business-level strategy A plan that indicates how a division intends to compete against its rivals in an industry.

functional-level plan Functional managers' decisions pertaining to the goals that they propose to pursue to help the division attain its business-level goals.

functional-level strategy A plan that indicates how functional managers intend to increase the value of the organization's goods and services.

time horizon The intended duration of a plan.

for that time period. Most organizations have an annual planning cycle that is usually linked to the annual financial budget (although a major planning effort may be undertaken only every few years). So, a corporate- or business-level plan that extends over several years is typically treated as a *rolling plan*, a plan that is updated and amended every year to take account of changing conditions in the external environment. Thus, the time horizon for an organization's 2007 corporate-level plan might be 2012; for the 2008 plan it might be 2013; and so on. The use of rolling plans is essential because of the high rate of change in the environment and the difficulty of predicting competitive conditions five years in the future. Rolling plans enable managers to make midcourse corrections if environmental changes warrant or to change the thrust of the plan altogether if it no longer seems appropriate. The use of rolling plans allows managers to plan flexibly, without losing sight of the need to plan for the long term.

Standing Plans and Single-Use Plans

Another distinction often made between plans is whether they are standing plans or single-use plans. Managers create standing and single-use plans to help achieve an organization's specific goals. *Standing plans* are used in situations in which programmed decision making is appropriate. When the same situations occur repeatedly, managers develop policies, rules, and standard operating procedures (SOPs) to control the way employees perform their tasks. A policy is a general guide to action; a rule is a formal, written guide to action; and a standing operating procedure is a written instruction describing the exact series of actions that should be followed in a specific situation. For example, an organization may have a standing plan about ethical behavior by employees. This plan includes a policy that all employees are expected to behave ethically in their dealings with suppliers and customers; a rule that requires any employee who receives from a supplier or customer a gift worth more than $10 to report the gift; and an SOP that obliges the recipient of the gift to make the disclosure in writing within 30 days.

In contrast, *single-use plans* are developed to handle nonprogrammed decision making in unusual or one-of-a-kind situations. Examples of single-use plans include *programs*, which are integrated sets of plans for achieving certain goals, and *projects*, which are

Astronaut John W. Young, commander of the Apollo 16 lunar landing mission, jumps up from the lunar surface as he salutes the U.S. Flag at the Descartes landing site during the first Apollo 16 extravehicular activity (EVA-1) on April 20, 1972. The construction of a lunar module capable of reaching the moon and returning to earth provides a dramatic example of a single-use plan.

specific action plans created to complete various aspects of a program. One of NASA's major programs was to reach the moon, and one project in this program was to develop a lunar module capable of landing on the moon and returning to the earth.

Scenario Planning

Earlier, we noted that effective plans have four qualities: unity, continuity, accuracy, and flexibility. One of the most widely used planning methods or techniques that can help managers create plans that have these qualities is scenario planning. Scenario planning (also known as *contingency planning*) is the generation of multiple forecasts of future conditions followed by an analysis of how to respond effectively to each of those conditions.

As noted previously, planning is about trying to forecast and predict the future in order to be able to anticipate future opportunities and threats. The future, however, is inherently unpredictable. How can managers best deal with this unpredictability? This question preoccupied managers at Royal Dutch Shell, the third-largest global oil company, in the 1980s. In 1984, oil was $30 a barrel and most analysts and managers, including Shell's, believed that it would hit $50 per barrel by 1990. Although these high prices guaranteed high profits, Shell's top managers decided to conduct a scenario-planning exercise. Shell's corporate and divisional managers were told to use scenario planning to generate different future scenarios of conditions in the oil market and then to develop a set of plans that detailed how they would respond to these opportunities and threats if any such scenario occurred.

One scenario used the assumption that oil prices would fall to $15 per barrel, and managers had to decide what they should do in such a case. Managers went to work with the goal of creating a plan consisting of a series of recommendations. The final plan included proposals to cut oil exploration costs by investing in new technologies, to accelerate invest-

As we know all too well, oil and gas prices are unpredictable. Oil industry managers, therefore, sometimes use scenario planning to deal with this chaotic market.

ments in cost-efficient oil-refining facilities, and to weed out unprofitable gas stations.[12] In reviewing these proposals, top management came to the conclusion that even if oil prices continued to rise, all of these actions would benefit Shell and increase its profit margin. So they decided to put the cost-cutting plan into action. As it happened, in the mid-1980s oil prices did not rise; they collapsed to $15 a barrel, but Shell, unlike its competitors, had already taken steps to be profitable in a low-oil-price world. Consequently, by 1990 the company was twice as profitable as its major competitors.

As this example suggests, because the future is unpredictable—the $30-a-barrel oil level was not reached again until the 2000s, for example—the best way to improve planning is first to generate "multiple futures," or scenarios of the future, based on different assumptions about conditions that *might prevail* in the future and then to develop different plans that detail what a company *should do* in the event that one of these scenarios actually occurs. Scenario planning is a learning tool that raises the quality of the planning process and can bring real benefits to an organization.[13] Shell's success with scenario planning influenced many other companies to adopt similar systems. By 1990, more than 50% of Fortune 500 companies were using some version of scenario planning, and the number has increased since then.[14]

The great strength of scenario planning is its ability not only to anticipate the challenges of an uncertain future but also to educate managers to think about the future—*to think strategically.*[15] Unfortunately, as we described in the opening case, Mattel's managers had not engaged in a formal-scenario planning exercise to forecast how changing societal and cultural factors might change customer needs for its dolls and how the company should respond by bringing out new lines of dolls to meet those changing needs. As a result, Mattel's managers made major decision-making errors that allowed the planners behind the Bratz dolls to gain a time advantage that has enabled them to establish the brand as a leading player in the doll market, and now Mattel has to play catch-up.

Determining the Organization's Mission and Goals

As we discussed earlier, determining the organization's mission and goals is the first step of the planning process. Once the mission and goals are agreed upon and formally stated in the corporate plan, they guide the next steps by defining which strategies are appropriate and which are inappropriate.[16] Figure 8.4 presents managers' vision of the mission and goals of three companies, Cisco, Wal-Mart, and AT&T.

Figure 8.4
Three Mission Statements

COMPANY	MISSION STATEMENT
Cisco	Cisco solutions provide competitive advantage to our customers through more efficient and timely exchange of information, which in turn leads to cost savings, process efficiencies, and closer relationships with our customers, prospects, business partners, suppliers, and employees.
Wal-Mart	We work for you. We think of ourselves as buyers for our customers, and we apply our considerable strengths to get the best value for you. We've built Wal-Mart by acting on behalf of our customers, and that concept continues to propel us. We're working hard to make our customers' shopping easy.
AT&T	We are dedicated to being the world's best at bringing people together—giving them easy access to each other and to the information and services they want and need—anytime, anywhere.

Defining the Business

To determine an organization's *mission*—the overriding reason it exists to provide customers with goods or services they value—managers must first *define its business* so that they can identify what kind of value customers are receiving. To define the business, managers must ask three related questions about a company's products: (1) *Who* are our customers? (2) *What* customer needs are being satisfied? (3) *How* are we satisfying customer needs?[17] Managers ask these questions to identify the customer needs that the organization satisfies and the way the organization satisfies those needs. Answering these questions helps managers to identify not only the customer needs they are satisfying now but the needs they should try to satisfy in the future and who their true competitors are. All of this information helps managers plan and establish appropriate goals.

The opening case on Mattel shows the important role the process of defining the business, in this case the doll business, has on the outcome of the planning process. Mattel failed to identify adequately who its customers were—that girls themselves were having much more input into the buying process; that their needs had changed—that girls wanted personalized, hip dolls they could relate too; and that Mattel was offering girls "cookie-cutter" Barbies that did *not* meet these needs. Had Mattel's managers defined the doll business of the 2000s appropriately, perhaps by using scenario planning, they would have recognized which kinds of dolls needed to be developed to satisfy the changing needs of its customers.

In the 1990s, while Mattel believed Barbie was safe, its managers did recognize that customer preferences were changing rapidly because of the growing popularity of electronic toys and computer games. Sales of computer games had increased dramatically as more and more parents saw the educational opportunities offered by games that children would enjoy playing. Moreover, many kinds of computer games could be played with other people over the Internet, so it seemed that in the future the magic of electronics and information technology would turn the toy world upside down. Fearing they would lose their customers to the new computer-game companies, Mattel's managers decided that the quickest and easiest way to redefine its business and become a major player in the computer-game market would be to acquire one of these companies. So in 1998 Mattel paid $3.5 billion for The Learning Company, the maker of such popular games as "Thinking Things." Its goal was to use this company's expertise and knowledge to build an array of new computer games, especially games linked to the company's core products. In this way Mattel hoped to better meet the needs of its existing customers and cater to the needs of the new computer-game customers.[18]

While Mattel's managers correctly sensed that customers' needs were changing, the way in which it decided to satisfy customers' new needs—namely, by buying The Learning Company—was not the right decision.[19] The skills required to rapidly develop new games linked to Mattel's products were not present in The Learning Company, and few popular games were forthcoming. Moreover, the $3.5 billion Mattel spent to acquire the company would have been better spent on updating its core toys, such as Barbie, and developing new lines of dolls and toys. In 2001, Mattel finally sold The Learning Company and focused on its core toys, but sales of Barbie products faltered; and in 2004, international Barbie sales dipped by 11% and domestic sales by 15%. CEO Eckert announced, "Our biggest challenge ahead is reinvigorating the fashion [doll] business. We're directing tremendous time, energy and resources to regain our momentum in the fashion doll category."[20] However, as we discussed earlier, so far Mattel has not been successful. The message is clear: Companies and their managers have to listen closely to their customers to decide how best to meet their changing needs and preferences.

Establishing Major Goals

Once the business is defined, managers must establish a set of primary goals to which the organization is committed. Developing these goals gives the organization a sense of direction or purpose. In most organizations, articulating major goals is the job of the CEO, although other managers have input into the process. Thus, at Mattel, CEO Eckert's primary goal is still to be the leader in every segment of the toy market in which the company competes, even though this is very challenging at present. However, the best statements of organizational goals are ambitious—that is, they stretch the organization and require that all its members work to improve its performance.[21] The role of **strategic leadership,** the ability of the CEO and top managers to convey a compelling vision of what they want to achieve to their subordinates, is important here. If subordinates buy into the vision, and model their behaviors on the leader, they develop a willingness to undertake the hard, stressful work that is necessary for creative, risk-taking strategy making.[22] Many popular books such as *Built to Last* provide lucid accounts of strategic leaders establishing "big, hairy, audacious goals (BHAGs)" that serve as rallying points for their subordinates.[23]

Although goals should be challenging, they should also be realistic. Challenging goals give managers at all levels an incentive to look for ways to improve organizational performance, but a goal that is clearly unrealistic and impossible to attain may prompt managers to give up.[24] Bob Eckert must be careful not to discourage Mattel's doll designers by setting unrealistic sales targets, for example.

Finally, the time period in which a goal is expected to be achieved should be stated. Time constraints are important because they emphasize that a goal must be attained within a reasonable period; they inject a sense of urgency into goal attainment and act as a motivator. Mattel's managers committed themselves to reviving the Barbie line and significantly increasing sales by 2006, but they have been unable to achieve this and their new plan has the goal of doing this by 2009.[25]

strategic leadership
The ability of the CEO and top managers to convey a compelling vision of what they want the organization to achieve to their subordinates.

Formulating Strategy

strategy formulation
The development of a set of corporate-, business-, and functional strategies that allow an organization to accomplish its mission and achieve its goals.

In **strategy formulation** managers work to develop the set of strategies (corporate, divisional, and functional) that will allow an organization to accomplish its mission and achieve its goals.[26] Strategy formulation begins with managers' systematically analyzing the factors or forces inside an organization, and outside in the global environment, that affect the organization's ability to meet its goals now and in the future. SWOT analysis and the five forces model are two useful techniques managers can use to analyze these factors.

Figure 8.5
Planning and Strategy Formulation

SWOT Analysis

SWOT analysis A plan-
ning exercise in which
managers identify organi-
zational strengths (S) and
weaknesses (W) and envi-
ronmental opportunities
(O) and threats (T).

SWOT analysis is a planning exercise in which managers identify *internal* organizational strengths (S) and weaknesses (W) and *external* environmental opportunities (O) and threats (T). Based on a SWOT analysis, managers at the
different levels of the organization select the corporate-, business-, and
functional-level strategies to best position the organization to achieve its
mission and goals (see Figure 8.5). In Chapter 5 we discussed forces in the
task and general environments that have the potential to affect an organization.
We noted that changes in these forces can produce opportunities that an organization might take advantage of and threats that may harm its current situation.

The first step in SWOT analysis is to identify an organization's strengths and
weaknesses. Table 8.1 (page 309) lists many important strengths (such as high-
quality skills in marketing and in research and development) and weaknesses
(such as rising manufacturing costs and outdated technology). The task facing
managers is to identify the strengths and weaknesses that characterize the present state of their organization.

The second step in SWOT analysis begins when managers embark on a full-
scale SWOT planning exercise to identify potential opportunities and threats in
the environment that affect the organization at the present or may affect it in the
future. Examples of possible opportunities and threats that must be anticipated
(many of which were discussed in Chapter 6) are listed in Table 8.1. Scenario
planning is often used to strengthen this analysis.

With the SWOT analysis completed, and strengths, weaknesses, opportunities, and threats identified, managers can continue the planning process and
determine specific strategies for achieving the organization's mission and goals.
The resulting strategies should enable the organization to attain its goals by taking advantage of opportunities, countering threats, building strengths, and correcting organizational weaknesses. To appreciate how managers use SWOT
analysis to formulate strategy, consider how Douglas Conant, CEO of Campbell Soup, has used it to find strategies to turn around the performance of the
troubled food products maker in the 2000s.

Table 8.1
Questions for SWOT Analysis

Potential Strengths	Potential Opportunities	Potential Weaknesses	Potential Threats
Well-developed strategy?	Expand core business(es)?	Poorly developed strategy?	Attacks on core business(es)?
Strong product lines?	Exploit new market segments?	Obsolete, narrow product lines?	Increase in domestic competition?
Broad market coverage?	Widen product range?	Rising manufacturing costs?	Increase in foreign competition?
Manufacturing competence?	Extend cost or differentiation advantage?	Decline in R&D innovations?	Change in consumer tastes?
Good marketing skills?	Diversify into new growth businesses?	Poor marketing plan?	Fall in barriers to entry?
Good materials management systems?	Expand into foreign markets?	Poor materials management systems?	Rise in new or substitute products?
R&D skills and leadership?	Apply R&D skills in new areas?	Loss of customer goodwill?	Increase in industry rivalry?
Human resource competencies?	Enter new related? businesses	Inadequate human resources?	New forms of industry competition?
Brand-name reputation?	Vertically integrate forward?	Loss of brand name?	Potential for takeover?
Cost of differentiation advantage?	Vertically integrate backward?	Growth without direction?	Changes in demographic factors?
Appropriate management style?	Overcome barriers to entry?	Loss of corporate direction?	Changes in economic factors?
Appropriate organizational structure?	Reduce rivalry among competitors?	Infighting among divisions?	Downturn in economy?
Appropriate control systems?	Apply brand-name capital in new areas?	Loss of corporate control?	Rising labor costs?
Ability to manage strategic change?	Seek fast market growth?	Inappropriate organizational structure and control systems?	Slower market growth?
Others?	Others?	High conflict and politics?	Others?
		Others?	

Manager as
a Person

Douglas Conant Reheats Campbell Soup

Campbell Soup Co., one of the oldest and best-known global food companies, saw demand for its major product, condensed soup, plummet by 30% between 1998 and 2004 as customers switched from high-salt, processed soups to healthier low-fat, low-salt varieties. Campbell's profits and stock price plunged as its condensed soup business collapsed, and in 2001 its directors brought in a new CEO, Douglas Conant, to help the troubled company. Conant decided it was necessary to develop a three-year turnaround plan to help the company strengthen its market position against aggressive competitors such as General Mills, whose Progresso Soup division had attracted away many of Campbell's customers with its innovative new lines of healthier soup.

One of Conant's first actions was to initiate a thorough SWOT planning exercise. *External analysis* of the environment identified the growth of the organic- and health-food segment of the food market and the increasing number of other kinds of convenience foods as a threat to Campbell's core soup business. It also revealed three growth opportunities: (1) the growing market for health and sports drinks, in which Campbell already was a competitor with its V8 juice, (2) the growing market for quality bread and cookies, in which Campbell competed with its Pepperidge

Campbell Soup Co. Chief Executive Douglas Conant answers a question in his office, as he holds a carton of one of the company's newer products, a ready to serve, restaurant quality soup, Campbell Select Gold Label, in February, 2006 at the company headquarters in Camden, N.J.

Farms brand, and (3) chocolate products, where Campbell's Godiva brand had enjoyed increasing sales throughout the 1990s.

With the analysis of the environment complete, Conant turned his attention to his organization's resources and capabilities. His *internal analysis* of Campbell identified a number of major weaknesses. These included staffing levels that were too high relative to its competitors and high costs associated with manufacturing its soups because of the use of outdated machinery.

Also, Conant noted that Campbell had a very conservative culture in which people seemed to be afraid to take risks—something that was a real problem in an industry where customer tastes are always changing and new products must be developed constantly. At the same time, the SWOT analysis identified an enormous strength: Campbell enjoyed huge economies of scale because of the enormous quantity of food products that it makes, and it also had a first-rate R&D division capable of developing exciting new food products.

Using the information gained from this SWOT analysis, Conant and his managers decided that Campbell needed to use its product development skills to revitalize its core products and modify or reinvent them in ways that would appeal to increasingly health-conscious and busy consumers. Moreover, it needed to expand its franchise in the health- and sports-, snack-, and luxury-food segments of the market. Also, to increase sales, Campbell's needed to tap into new food outlets, such as corporate cafeterias, college dining halls, and other mass eateries, to expand consumers' access to its foods. Finally, Conant decided to decentralize authority to managers at lower levels in the organization and make them responsible for developing new soup, bread, and chocolate products that met customers changing needs. In this way he hoped to revitalize Campbell's slow-moving culture and speed the flow of improved and new products to the market.

Conant put his new plan into action, sales of new soup products increased, and he began to put more emphasis on sales of soup at outlets such as 7-11 and Subway and less on supermarket sales.[27] By 2004, analysts felt that he had made a significant difference in Campbell's performance but that there was still a lot to do, as Campbell's operating margins were still shrinking. Carrying on the SWOT analysis, Conant decided Campbell should produce more products to meet the needs of the "low-carb diet," such as new kinds of low-carb bread and cookies. He also decided to shrink the company's operations to lower costs. His goal was to raise profit margins to the level of his major competitors Kraft and General Mills by 2007 using a new three-year plan based on this SWOT analysis.[28]

By 2006 Conant had substantially achieved his goals: Sales of soup had recovered, the Pepperidge Farm and Godiva divisions were earning record sales and profits, and Campbell was in the process of developing a new kind of low-salt soup that it claimed would have no loss in flavor.[29] Campbell's stock price soared, and Conant and employees at all levels received bonuses that rewarded their intense efforts to turn around the company. With a new culture of innovation permeating the organization, Campbell's future looks bright indeed.[30]

The Five Forces Model

A well-known model that helps managers focus on the five most important competitive forces, or potential threats, in the external environment is Michael Porter's five forces model. We discussed the first four forces in the list below in Chapter 6. Porter identified these five factors as major threats because they affect how much profit organizations competing within the same industry can expect to make:

- *The level of rivalry among organizations in an industry:* The more that companies compete against one another for customers—for example, by lowering the prices of their products or by increasing advertising—the lower is the level of industry profits (low prices mean less profit).

- *The potential for entry into an industry:* The easier it is for companies to enter an industry—because, for example, barriers to entry, such as brand loyalty, are low—the more likely it is for industry prices and therefore industry profits to be low.

- *The power of large suppliers:* If there are only a few large suppliers of an important input, then suppliers can drive up the price of that input, and expensive inputs result in lower profits for companies in an industry.

- *The power of large customers:* If only a few large customers are available to buy an industry's output, they can bargain to drive down the price of that output. As a result, industry producers make lower profits.

- *The threat of substitute products:* Often, the output of one industry is a substitute for the output of another industry (plastic may be a substitute for steel in some applications, for example; similarly, bottled water is a substitute for cola). When a substitute for their product exists, companies cannot demand very high prices for it or customers will switch to the substitute, and this constraint keeps their profits low.

Porter argued that when managers analyze opportunities and threats, they should pay particular attention to these five forces because they are the major threats that an organization will encounter. It is the job of managers at the corporate, business, and functional levels to formulate strategies to counter these threats so that an organization can manage its task and general

perform at a high level, and generate high profits. At Campbell, Conant performs such an analysis to identify the opportunities and threats stemming from the actions of food industry rivals. For example, as noted earlier, General Mill's Progresso Soups division developed healthier kinds of soups, and this resulted in increased rivalry that lowered Campbell's sales and profits until Campbell succeeded at making new lines of healthy soups itself. Today, both companies are competing to be the first to develop and market a new line of tasty but low-salt soups; in 2006, analysts believed Campbell's would be the first to do so and thus gain a competitive advantage over General Mills.

hypercompetition
Permanent, ongoing, intense competition brought about in an industry by advancing technology or changing customer tastes.

Today, competition is tough in most industries, whether companies make cars, soup, computers, or dolls. The term **hypercompetition** applies to industries that are characterized by permanent, ongoing, intense competition brought about by advancing technology or changing customer tastes and fads and fashions.[31] Clearly, planning and strategy formulation is much more difficult and risky when hypercompetition prevails in an industry.

Formulating Business-Level Strategies

Michael Porter, the researcher who developed the five forces model, also developed a theory of how managers can select a business-level strategy, a plan to gain a competitive advantage in a particular market or industry.[32] Indeed, Porter argued that business-level strategy creates a competitive advantage because it allows an organization (or a division of a company) to *counter and reduce* the threat of the five industry forces. That is, successful business-level strategy reduces rivalry, prevents new competitors from entering the industry, reduces the power of suppliers or buyers, and lowers the threat of substitutes—and this raises prices and profits.

According to Porter, to obtain these higher profits managers must choose between two basic ways of increasing the value of an organization's products: *differentiating the product* to increase its value to customers or *lowering the costs* of making the product. Porter also argues that managers must choose between serving the whole market or serving just one segment or part of a market. Based on those choices, managers choose to pursue one of four business-level strategies: low cost, differentiation, focused low cost, or focused differentiation (see Table 8.2).

Table 8.2
Porter's Business-Level Strategies

	Number of Market Segments Served	
Strategy	Many	Few
Low cost	✓	
Focused low cost		✓
Differentiation	✓	
Focused differentiation		✓

Low-Cost Strategy

low-cost strategy
Driving the organization's costs down below the costs of its rivals.

With a **low-cost strategy,** managers try to gain a competitive advantage by focusing the energy of all the organization's departments or functions on driving the company's costs down below the costs of its industry rivals. This strategy, for example, would require that manufacturing managers search for new ways to reduce production costs, R&D managers focus on developing new products that can be manufactured more cheaply, and marketing managers find ways to lower the costs of attracting customers. According to Porter, companies pursuing a low-cost strategy can sell a product for less than their rivals sell it and yet still make a good profit because of their lower costs. Thus, such organizations enjoy a competitive advantage based on their low prices. For example, BIC pursues a low-cost strategy; it offers customers razor blades priced lower than Gillette's and ball-point pens less expensive than those offered by Cross or Waterman. Also, when existing companies have low costs and can charge low prices, it is difficult for new companies to enter the industry because entering is always an expensive process.

BIC is an example of a company that pursues a low-cost strategy, offering razors and pens at a lower cost than its competitors.

Differentiation Strategy

differentiation strategy Distinguishing an organization's products from the products of competitors on dimensions such as product design, quality, or after-sales service.

With a **differentiation strategy,** managers try to gain a competitive advantage by focusing all the energies of the organization's departments or functions on *distinguishing* the organization's products from those of competitors on one or more important dimensions, such as product design, quality, or after-sales service and support. Often, the process of making products unique and different is expensive. This strategy, for example, often requires that managers increase spending on product design or R&D to differentiate the product, and costs rise as a result. Organizations that successfully pursue a differentiation strategy may be able to charge a *premium price* for their products, a price usually much higher than the price charged by a low-cost organization. The premium price allows organizations pursuing a differentiation strategy to recoup their higher costs. Coca-Cola, PepsiCo, and Procter & Gamble are some of the many well-known companies that pursue a strategy of differentiation. They spend enormous amounts of money on advertising to differentiate, and create a unique image for, their products. Also, differentiation makes industry entry difficult because new companies have no brand name to help them compete and customers don't perceive other products to be close substitutes, so this also allows for premium pricing and results in high profits.

"Stuck in the Middle"

According to Porter's theory, managers cannot simultaneously pursue both a low-cost strategy and a differentiation strategy. Porter identified a simple correlation: Differentiation raises costs and thus necessitates premium pricing to recoup those high costs. For example, if BIC suddenly began to advertise heavily to try to build a strong global brand image for its products, BIC's costs would rise. BIC then could no longer make a profit simply by pricing its blades or pens lower than Gillette or Cross. According to Porter, managers must choose between a low-cost strategy and a differentiation strategy. He refers to managers and organizations that have not made this choice as being "stuck in the middle."

Organizations stuck in the middle tend to have lower levels of performance than do those that pursue a low-cost or a differentiation strategy. To avoid being stuck in the middle, top managers must instruct departmental managers to take actions that will result in either low cost or differentiation.

However, exceptions to this rule can be found. In many organizations managers have been able to drive costs below those of rivals and simultaneously differentiate their products from those offered by rivals.[33] For example, Toyota's production system is the most efficient in the world, as we discuss in the next chapter. This efficiency gives Toyota a low-cost strategy vis-á-vis its rivals in the global car industry. At the same time, Toyota has differentiated its cars from those of rivals on the basis of superior design and quality. This superiority allows the company to charge a premium price for many of its popular models.[34] Thus, Toyota seems to be simultaneously pursuing both a low-cost and a differentiated business-level strategy. This example suggests that although Porter's ideas may be valid in most cases, very well managed companies such as Toyota, McDonald's, and Dell Computer may have both low costs and differentiated products—and so make the highest profits of any company in an industry.

Focused Low-Cost and Focused Differentiation Strategies

focused low-cost strategy Serving only one segment of the overall market and trying to be the lowest-cost organization serving that segment.

focused differentiation strategy Serving only one segment of the overall market and trying to be the most differentiated organization serving that segment.

Both the differentiation strategy and the low-cost strategy are aimed at serving many or most segments of a particular market, such as for cars or computers. Porter identified two other business-level strategies that aim to serve the needs of customers in only one or a few market segments.[35] Managers pursuing a focused low-cost strategy serve one or a few segments of the overall market and aim to make their organization the lowest-cost company serving that segment. By contrast, managers pursuing a focused differentiation strategy serve just one or a few segments of the market and aim to make their organization the most differentiated company serving that segment.

Companies pursuing either of these strategies have chosen to *specialize* in some way by directing their efforts at a particular kind of customer (such as serving the needs of babies or affluent customers) or even the needs of customers in a specific geographic region (customers on the East or West Coast). BMW, for example, pursues a focused differentiation strategy, producing cars exclusively for higher-income customers. By contrast, Toyota pursues a differentiation strategy and produces cars that appeal to consumers in almost *all* segments of the car market, from basic transportation (Toyota Tercel), through the middle of the market (Toyota Camry), to the high-income end of the market (Lexus). An interesting example of how a company pursuing a focused low-cost strategy, by specializing on one market segment, can compete with powerful differentiators is profiled in the following "Management Insight."

Management Insight

Different Ways to Compete in the Soft-Drink Business

"Coke" and "Pepsi" are household names worldwide. Together, Coca-Cola and PepsiCo control over 70% of the global soft-drink market and over 75% of the U.S. soft-drink market. Their success can be attributed to the differentiation strategies they developed to produce and promote their products—strategies that have made them two of the most profitable global organizations. There are several parts to their differentiation strategies. First, both companies built global brands by manufacturing the soft-drink concentrate that gives cola its flavor but then selling the concentrate in a syrup form to bottlers throughout the world. The bottlers are responsible for producing and distributing the actual cola. They add carbonated water to the syrup, package the resulting drink, and distribute it to vending machines, supermarkets,

SEIZING THE FUTURE: DRIVING RETAILER BRAND POWER

www.cott.com

Cott advertises the fact that any retailer can put its own company name, for example, "Sam's Cola" on its generic Cola.

restaurants, and other retail outlets. The bottlers must also sign an exclusive agreement that prohibits them from bottling or distributing the products of competing soft-drink companies. This creates a barrier to entry that helps prevent new companies from entering the industry.

Second, Coca-Cola and PepsiCo charge the bottlers a *premium price* for the syrup; they then invest a large part of the profits in advertising to build and maintain brand awareness. The money they spend on advertising (in 2005 each company spent over $500 million) to develop a global brand name helps Coca-Cola and PepsiCo differentiate their products so that consumers are more likely to buy a Coke or a Pepsi than a lesser-known cola. Moreover, brand loyalty allows both companies to charge a premium or comparatively high price for what is, after all, merely colored water and flavoring.

In the last decade the global soft-drink environment has undergone a major change, however, because of Gerald Pencer, a Canadian entrepreneur who came up with a new strategy for competing against these powerful differentiators. Pencer's strategy was to produce a high-quality, low-priced cola, manufactured and bottled by the Cott Corporation, of which he was CEO at the time, but to sell it as the private-label house brand of major retail stores such as Wal-Mart (Sam's Cola brand) and supermarket chains such as Kroger's (Big K brand), thus bypassing the bottlers. Pencer could implement his *focused low-cost* strategy and charge a low price for his soft drinks because he did not need to spend any money on advertising (the retail stores did that) and because Cott's soft drinks are distributed by the store chains and retailers using their efficient national distribution systems, such as the nationwide trucking system developed by giant retailer Wal-Mart. Retailers are willing to do this because Cott's low-cost soft drinks allow them to make much more profit than they receive from selling Coke or Pepsi. At the same time, the products build their store-brand image.

Pencer implemented this plan first in Canada and then quickly expanded into the United States as retailers' demand for his products grew. He then went on to supply the international market by offering to sell soft-drink concentrate to global retailers at prices lower than Coca-Cola and PepsiCo. By 2004 Cott was the world's largest supplier of retailer-branded carbonated soft drinks.[36] It has manufacturing facilities in Canada, the United States, and the United Kingdom and a syrup concentrate production plant in Columbus, Georgia, which supply most of the private-label grocery store, drugstore, mass-merchandising, and convenience store chains in these countries. However, note that while Cott is the leading supplier of retailer-branded sodas, it is still focusing on its low-cost strategy. It makes no attempt to compete with Coke and Pepsi, which pursue differentiation strategies and whose brand-name sodas dominate the global soda market.

Increasingly, smaller companies are finding it easier to pursue a focused strategy and compete successfully against large, powerful, low-cost and differentiated companies because of advances in IT that lower costs and enable them to reach and attract customers. By establishing a storefront on the Web, thousands of small, specialized companies have been able to carve out a profitable niche against large bricks-and-mortar competitors. Zara, a Spanish manufacturer of fashionable clothing whose sales have soared in recent years, provides an excellent example of the way even a small bricks-and-mortar company can use IT to pursue a focused strategy and compete globally.[37] Zara has managed to position itself as the low-price, low-cost leader in the fashion segment of the clothing market, against differentiators like Gucci, Dior, and Armani, because it has applied IT to its specific needs. Zara has created IT that allows it to manage its design and manufacturing process in a way that minimizes the inventory it has to carry—the major cost borne by a clothing retailer. However, its IT also gives its designers instantaneous feedback on which clothes are selling well and in which countries, and this gives Zara a competitive advantage from differentiation. Specifically, Zara can manufacture more of a particular kind of dress or suit to meet high customer demand, decide which clothing should be sold in its rapidly expanding network of global stores, and constantly change the mix of clothes it offers customers to keep up with fashion—at low cost.

Zara's IT also allows it to manage the interface between its design and manufacturing operations more efficiently. Zara takes only five weeks to design a new collection and then a week to make it. Fashion houses like Channel and Armani, by contrast, can take six or more months to design the collection and then three more before it is available in stores.[38] This short time to market gives Zara great flexibility and allows the company to respond quickly to the rapidly changing fashion market, in which fashions can change several times a year. Because of the quick manufacturing-to-sales cycle and just-in-time fashion, Zara offers its clothes collections at relatively low prices and still makes profits that are the envy of the fashion clothing industry.[39]

Zara has been able to pursue a focused strategy that is simultaneously low cost and differentiated because it has developed many kinds of strengths in functions such as clothing design, marketing, and IT that have given it a competitive advantage. Developing functional-level strategies that strengthen business-level strategy and increase competitive advantage is a vital managerial task. Discussion of this important issue is left until the next chapter. First, we need to go up one planning level and examine how corporate strategy helps an organization achieve its mission and goals.

Zara's use of IT allows it to pursue a focused strategy of being the low-price/cost leader in the clothing market fashion segment.

Formulating Corporate-Level Strategies

Once managers have formulated the business-level strategies that will best position a company, or a division of a company, to compete in an industry and outperform its rivals, they must look to the future. If their planning has been successful the company will be generating high profits, and their task now is to plan how to invest these profits to increase performance over time.

Recall that *corporate-level strategy* is a plan of action that involves choosing in which industries and countries a company should invest its resources to achieve its mission and goals. In choosing a corporate-level strategy, managers ask: How should the growth and development of our company be managed to increase its ability to create value for customers (and thus increase its performance) over the long run? Managers of effective organizations actively seek out new opportunities to use a company's resources to create new and improved goods and services for customers. Examples of organizations whose product lines are growing rapidly are Google, chipmaker AMD, Apple, and Toyota, whose managers pursue any feasible opportunity to use their companies' skills to provide customers with new products.

In addition, some managers must help their organizations respond to threats due to changing forces in the task or general environment that have made their business-level strategies less effective and reduced profits. For example, customers may no longer be buying the kinds of goods and services a company is producing (high-salt soup, bulky computer monitors or televisions), or other organizations may have entered the market and attracted away customers (this happened to Intel in the 2000s after AMD began to produce more powerful chips). Top managers aim to find corporate strategies that can help the organization strengthen its business-level strategies and thus respond to these changes and improve performance.

The principal corporate-level strategies that managers use to help a company grow and keep it at the top of its industry, or to help it retrench and reorganize to stop its decline, are (1) concentration on a single industry, (2) vertical integration, (3) diversification, and (4) international expansion. An organization will benefit from pursuing any one or more of these strategies only when the strategy helps further increase the value of the organization's goods and services so that more customers buy them. Specifically, to increase the value of goods and services, a corporate-level strategy must help a company, or one of its divisions, either (1) lower the costs of developing and making products or (2) increase product differentiation so that more customers want to buy the products even at high or premium prices. Both of these outcomes strengthen a company's competitive advantage and increase its performance.

Concentration on a Single Industry

concentration on a single industry
Reinvesting a company's profits to strengthen its competitive position in its current industry.

Most growing companies reinvest their profits to strengthen their competitive position in the industry in which they are currently operating; in doing so, they pursue the corporate-level strategy of **concentration on a single industry**. Most commonly an organization uses its functional skills to develop new kinds of products or it expands the number of locations in which it uses those skills. For example, Apple is expanding the range of its iPods and mobile wireless computers, while McDonald's, which began as one restaurant in California, focused all its efforts on using its resources to quickly expand across the United States to become the biggest and most profitable U.S. fast-food company.

On the other hand, concentration on a single industry becomes an appropriate corporate-level strategy when managers see the need to *reduce* the size of their organizations to increase performance. Managers may decide to get out of certain industries when, for example, the business-level strategy pursued by a particular division no longer works and the division has lost its competitive advantage. To improve performance, managers now sell off low-performing divisions, concentrate remaining organizational resources in one industry, and try to develop new products customers want to buy. This happened to electronics maker Hitachi when customers were increasingly switching from bulky CRT monitors to newer, flat LCD monitors. Hitachi announced it was closing its three CRT factories in Japan, Singapore, and Malaysia and would use its resources to invest in the new LCD technology.[40]

By contrast, when organizations are performing effectively, they often decide to enter new industries in which they can use their resources to create more valuable products. Thus they begin to pursue vertical integration or diversification.

Vertical Integration

vertical integration
Expanding a company's operations either backward into an industry that produces inputs for its products or forward into an industry that uses, distributes, or sells its products.

When an organization is performing well in its industry, managers often see new opportunities to create value by either producing the inputs it uses to make its products or distributing and selling its products to customers. Managers at E. & J. Gallo Winery, for example, realized that they could lower Gallo's costs if the company produced its own wine bottles rather than buying bottles from a glass company that was earning good profits from its bottle sales to Gallo. So Gallo established a new division to produce glass bottles more cheaply than buying them; it quickly found that it could also produce new-shaped bottles to help differentiate its wines. **Vertical integration** is a corporate-level strategy in which a company expands its business operations either

Figure 8.6

Stages in a Vertical Value Chain

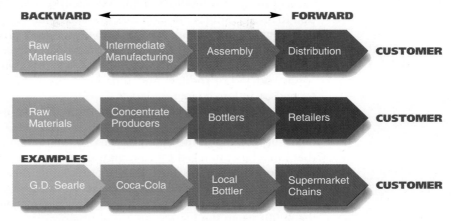

backward into a new industry that produces inputs for the company's products *(backward vertical integration)* or forward into a new industry that uses, distributes, or sells the company's products *(forward vertical integration)*.[41] A steel company that buys iron ore mines and enters the raw materials industry to supply the ore needed to make steel is engaging in backward vertical integration. A PC maker that decides to enter the retail industry and open a chain of company-owned retail outlets to sell its PCs is engaging in forward integration. For example, in 2001 Apple Computer entered the retail industry when it decided to set up a chain of Apple Stores to sell its computers; Dell announced it would open its own stores in 2006.

Figure 8.6 illustrates the four main stages in a typical raw material–to-customer value chain; value is added to the product at each stage by the activities involved in each industry. For a company based in the assembly stage, backward integration would involve establishing a new division in the intermediate manufacturing or raw material production industries; and forward integration would involve establishing a new division to distribute its products to wholesalers or a retail division to sell directly to customers. A division at one stage or one industry receives the product produced by the division in the previous stage or industry, transforms it in some way—adding value—and then transfers the output at a higher price to the division at the next stage in the chain.

As an example of how this industry value chain works, consider the cola segment of the soft-drink industry. In the raw material industry, suppliers include sugar companies and manufacturers of artificial sweeteners such as NutraSweet and Splenda, which are used in diet colas. These companies sell their products to companies in the soft-drink industry that make concentrate—such as Coca-Cola and PepsiCo, which mix these inputs with others to produce the cola concentrate. In the process, they add value to these inputs. The concentrate producers then sell the concentrate to companies in the bottling and distribution industry, which add carbonated water to the concentrate and package the resulting drink—again adding value to the concentrate. Next, the bottlers distribute and sell the soft drinks to retailers, including stores such as Costco and Wal-Mart and fast-food chains such as McDonald's. Companies in the retail industry add value by making the product accessible to customers, and they profit from direct sales to customers. Thus, value is added by companies at each stage in the raw material-to-consumer chain.

The reason managers pursue vertical integration is that it allows them either to add value to their products by making them special or unique or to lower the costs of making and selling them. An example of using forward vertical integration to increase differentiation is Apple's decision to open its own stores to make its unique products more accessible to customers who could try them out before they bought them. An example of using forward vertical integration to lower costs is Matsushita's decision to open company-owned stores to sell its Panasonic and JVC products and thus keep the profit that otherwise would be earned by independent retailers.[42]

Although vertical integration can strengthen an organization's competitive advantage and increase its performance, it can also reduce an organization's flexibility to respond to changing environmental conditions and create threats that must be countered by changing the organization's strategy. For example, IBM used to produce most of the components it used to make its own mainframe computers. While this made sense in the 1970s when IBM enjoyed a major competitive advantage, it became a major handicap for the company in the 1990s when the increasing use of organizationwide networks of PCs meant slumping demand for mainframes. IBM had lost its competitive advantage and found itself with an excess-capacity problem in its component operations. Closing down this capacity, and exiting the computer components industry, cost IBM over $5 billion.[43]

Thus, when considering vertical integration as a strategy to add value, managers must be careful because sometimes it may reduce a company's ability to create value when the environment changes. This is why so many companies now outsource the production of component parts to other companies and, like IBM, have exited the components industry—by vertically *disintegrating* backward. IBM, however, found a profitable new opportunity for forward vertical integration in the 1990s: It entered the IT consulting services industry to provide advice to large companies about how to install and manage their computer hardware and software.[44] Providing IT services has been a major source of IBM's profitability in the 2000s.

Diversification

diversification
Expanding a company's business operations into a new industry in order to produce new kinds of valuable goods or services.

Diversification is the corporate-level strategy of expanding a company's business operations into a new industry in order to produce new kinds of valuable goods or services.[45] Examples include PepsiCo's diversification into the snack-food business with the purchase of Frito Lay, tobacco giant Philip Morris's diversification into the brewing industry with the acquisition of Miller Beer, and GE's move into broadcasting with its acquisition of NBC. There are two main kinds of diversification: related and unrelated.

related diversification
Entering a new business or industry to create a competitive advantage in one or more of an organization's existing divisions or businesses.

RELATED DIVERSIFICATION Related diversification is the strategy of entering a new business or industry to create a competitive advantage in one or more of an organization's existing divisions or businesses. Related diversification can add value to an organization's products if managers can find ways for its various divisions or business units to share their valuable skills or resources so that synergy is created.[46] **Synergy** is obtained when the value created by two divisions cooperating is greater than the value that would be created if the two divisions operated separately and independently. For example, suppose two or more of the divisions of a diversified company can utilize the same manufacturing facilities, distribution channels, or advertising campaigns—that is, share functional activities.

synergy Performance gains that result when individuals and departments coordinate their actions.

Each division has to invest fewer resources in a shared functional activity than it would have to invest if it performed the functional activity by itself. Related diversification can be a major source of cost savings when divisions share the costs of performing a functional activity.[47] Similarly, if one division's R&D skills can be used to improve another division's products and increase their differentiated appeal, this synergy can give the second division an important competitive advantage over its industry rivals—so the company as a whole benefits from diversification.

The way Procter & Gamble's disposable diaper and paper towel divisions cooperate is a good example of the successful production of synergies. These divisions share the costs of procuring inputs such as paper and packaging, a joint sales force sells both products to retail outlets, and both products are shipped using the same distribution system. This resource sharing has enabled both divisions to reduce their costs, and as a result, they can charge lower prices than their competitors and so attract more customers.[48] In addition, the divisions can share the research costs involved in developing new and improved products, such as finding more absorbent material, that increase both products' differentiated appeal. This is something that is also at the heart of 3M's corporate strategy, which is discussed in the following "Management Insight."

Management Insight

How to Make Related Diversification Work

3M is a 100-year-old industrial giant that in 2005 generated over $16 billion in revenues and $1.4 billion in profits from its more than 50,000 individual products, ranging from sandpaper and sticky tape to medical devices, office supplies, and electronic components. From the beginning, 3M has pursued related diversification and created new businesses by leveraging its skills in research and development. Today, the company is composed of more than 40 separate divisions positioned in six major business groups: transportation, health care, industrial, consumer and office, electronics and communications, and specialty materials. The company currently operates with the goal of producing 40% of sales revenues from products introduced within the previous four years.[49]

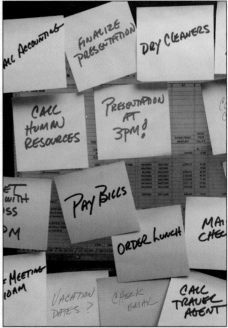

How did we survive without Post-It Notes? 3M's focus on helping customers solve problems has been one key to its success in using a related diversification strategy.

How does 3M do it? First, the company is a science-based enterprise with a strong tradition of innovation and risk taking. Risk taking is encouraged, and failure is not punished but seen as a natural part of the process of creating new products and business. Second, 3M's management is relentlessly focused on the company's customers and the problems they face. Many of 3M's products have come from helping customers to solve difficult problems. Third, managers set stretch goals that require the company to create new products and businesses at a rapid rate. Fourth, employees are given considerable autonomy to pursue their own ideas; indeed, 15% of employees' time can be spent working on projects of their own choosing without management approval. Many products have resulted from this autonomy, including the ubiquitous Post-it notes. Fifth, while products belong to business units and it is business units that are responsible for generating profits, the technologies belong to every unit within the company. Anyone at 3M is free to try to develop new applications for a technology developed by its business units. Finally, 3M organizes many companywide meetings where researchers from its different divisions are brought together to share the results of their work. It also implemented an IT system that promotes the sharing of technological knowledge between researchers so that new opportunities can be identified.

In sum, to pursue related diversification successfully, managers search for new businesses where they can use the existing skills and resources in their departments and divisions to create synergies, add value to new products and businesses, and improve their competitive position and that of the entire company. In addition, managers may try to acquire a company in a new industry because they believe it possesses skills and resources that will improve the performance of one or more of their existing divisions. If successful, such skill transfers can help an organization to lower its costs or better differentiate its products because they create synergies between divisions.

unrelated diversification Entering a new industry or buying a company in a new industry that is not related in any way to an organization's current businesses or industries.

UNRELATED DIVERSIFICATION Managers pursue unrelated diversification when they establish divisions or buy companies in new industries that are *not* linked in any way to their current businesses or industries. One main reason for pursuing unrelated diversification is that, sometimes, managers can buy a poorly performing company, transfer their management skills to that company, turn around its business, and increase its performance—all of which creates value.

Another reason for pursuing unrelated diversification is that purchasing businesses in different industries lets managers engage in *portfolio strategy,* which is apportioning financial resources among divisions to increase financial returns or spread risks among different businesses, much as individual investors do with their own portfolios. For example, managers may transfer funds from a rich division (a "cash cow") to a new and promising division (a "star") and, by appropriately allocating money between divisions, create value. Though used as a popular explanation in the 1980s for unrelated diversification, portfolio strategy ran into increasing criticism in the 1990s because it simply does not work.[50] Why? As managers expand the scope of their organization's operations and enter more and more industries, it becomes increasingly difficult for top managers to be knowledgeable about all of the organization's diverse businesses. Managers do not have the time to process all of the information required to adequately assess the strategy and performance of each division, and so the performance of the entire company often falls.

This problem arose at General Electric in the 1970s, as its former CEO Reg Jones commented: "I tried to review each business unit plan in great detail. This effort took untold hours and placed a tremendous burden on the corporate executive office. After a while I began to realize that no matter how hard we would work, we could not achieve the necessary in-depth understanding of the 40-odd business unit plans."[51] Unable to handle so much information, top managers are overwhelmed and eventually make important resource allocation decisions on the basis of only a superficial analysis of the competitive position of each division. This usually results in value being lost rather than created.[52]

Thus, although unrelated diversification can potentially create value for a company, research evidence suggests that *too much* diversification can cause managers to lose control of their organization's core business. As a result, diversification can reduce value rather than create it.[53] Because of this, during the last decade there has been an increasing trend for diversified companies to divest many of their unrelated, and sometimes related, divisions. Managers in companies like Tyco, Dial, and Textron sold off many or most of their divisions and focused on increasing the performance of the core division that remained—in other words, they went back to a strategy of concentrating on a single industry.[54]

International Expansion

As if planning whether or not to vertically integrate, diversify, or concentrate on the core business was not a difficult enough task, corporate-level managers also must decide on the appropriate way to compete internationally. A basic question confronts the managers of any organization that needs to sell its products abroad and compete in more than one national market: To what extent should the organization customize features of its products and marketing campaign to different national conditions?[55]

global strategy Selling the same standardized product and using the same basic marketing approach in each national market.

multidomestic strategy Customizing products and marketing strategies to specific national conditions.

If managers decide that their organization should sell the same standardized product in each national market in which it competes, and use the same basic marketing approach, they adopt a **global strategy**.[56] Such companies undertake very little, if any, customization to suit the specific needs of customers in different countries. But if managers decide to customize products and marketing strategies to specific national conditions, they adopt a **multidomestic strategy.** Matsushita, with its Panasonic brand, has traditionally pursued a global strategy, selling the same basic TVs, video cameras, and DVD and MP3 players in every country in which it does business and often using the same basic marketing approach. Unilever, the European food and household products company, has pursued a multidomestic strategy. Thus, to appeal to German customers, Unilever's German division sells a different range of food products and uses a different marketing approach than its North American division.

Both global and multidomestic strategies have advantages and disadvantages. The major advantage of a global strategy is the significant cost savings associated with not having to customize products and marketing approaches to different national conditions. For example, Rolex watches, Ralph Lauren or Tommy Hilfiger clothing, Channel or Armani clothing or accessories or perfume, Dell computers, Chinese-made plastic toys and buckets, and U.S.-grown rice and wheat are all products that can be sold using the same marketing across many countries by simply changing the language. Thus, companies can save a significant amount of money. The major disadvantage of pursuing a global strategy is that, by ignoring national differences, managers may leave themselves vulnerable to local competitors that do differentiate their products to suit local tastes. This occurred in the British consumer electronics industry. Amstrad, a British computer and electronics company, got its start by recognizing and responding to local consumer needs. Amstrad captured a major share of the British audio market by ignoring the standardized inexpensive music centers marketed by companies pursuing a global strategy, such as Sony and Matsushita. Instead, Amstrad's product was encased in teak rather than metal and featured a control panel tailor-made to appeal to British consumers' preferences. To remain competitive in this market, Matsushita had to place more emphasis on local customization of its Panasonic and JVC brands.

The advantages and disadvantages of a multidomestic strategy are the opposite of those of a global strategy. The major advantage of a multidomestic strategy is that by customizing product offerings and marketing approaches to

A study in contrasts. Matsushita, with its Panasonic brand (shown on the top), has largely pursued a global strategy, selling the same basic TVs and VCRs in every market and using a similar marketing message. Unilever, on the other hand, has pursued a multidomestic strategy, tailoring its product line and marketing approach to specific locations. On the bottom, the CEO of Hindustan Lever, Ltd., Keki Dadiseth, holds a box of Surf detergent.

local conditions, managers may be able to gain market share or charge higher prices for their products. The major disadvantage is that customization raises production costs and puts the multidomestic company at a price disadvantage because it often has to charge prices higher than the prices charged by competitors pursuing a global strategy. Obviously, the choice between these two strategies calls for trade-offs.

Managers at Gillette, the well-known razor blade maker acquired by Procter & Gamble in 2005, created a strategy that combined the best features of both international strategies. Like Procter & Gamble, Gillette has always been a global organization because its managers quickly saw the advantages of selling its core product, razor blades, in as many countries as possible. Gillette's strategy over the years has been pretty constant: Find a new country with a growing market for razor blades, form a strategic alliance with a local razor blade company and take a majority stake in it, invest in a large marketing campaign, and then build a modern factory to make razor blades and other products for the local market. For example, when Gillette entered Russia after the breakup of the Soviet Union, it saw a huge opportunity to increase sales. It formed a joint venture with a local company called Leninets Concern, which made a razor known as the Sputnik, and then with this base began to import its own brands into Russia.

When sales growth rose sharply, Gillette decided to offer more products in the market and built a new plant in St. Petersburg.[57]

In establishing factories in countries where labor and other costs are low and then distributing and marketing its products to countries in that region of the world, Gillette pursued a global strategy. However, all of Gillette's research and development and design activities are located in the United States. As it develops new kinds of razors, it equips its foreign factories to manufacture them when it decides that local customers are ready to trade up to the new product. So, for example, Gillette's latest razor may be introduced in a country abroad years later than in the United States. Thus, Gillette is customizing its product offering to the needs of different countries and so also pursues a multidomestic strategy.

By pursuing this kind of international strategy, Gillette achieves low costs and still differentiates and customizes its product range to suit the needs of each country or world region.[58] Procter & Gamble pursues a similar international strategy, and the merger between them to create the world's largest consumer products company came about because of the value that could be realized by pursuing related diversification at a global level. For example, Procter & Gamble's corporate managers realized that substantial global synergies could be obtained by combining their global manufacturing, distribution, and sales operations across countries and world regions. These synergies have resulted in billions of dollars in cost savings.[59] At the same time, by pooling their knowledge of the needs of customers in different countries, the combined company can better differentiate and position its products throughout the world. P&G's strategy is working; its principal competitors Colgate and Unilever have not performed well in the 2000s, and P&G is developing a commanding global position.

CHOOSING A WAY TO EXPAND INTERNATIONALLY As we have discussed, a more competitive global environment has proved to be both an opportunity and a threat for organizations and managers. The opportunity is that organizations that expand globally are able to open new markets, reach more customers, and gain access to new sources of raw materials and to low-cost suppliers of inputs. The threat is that organizations that expand globally are likely to encounter new competitors in the foreign countries they enter and must respond to new political, economic, and cultural conditions.

Before setting up foreign operations, managers of companies such as Amazon.com, Lands' End, GE, P&G, Dell, and Boeing needed to analyze the forces in the environment of a particular country (such as Korea or Brazil) in order to choose the right method to expand and respond to those forces in the most appropriate way. In general, four basic ways to operate in the global environment are importing and exporting, licensing and franchising, strategic alliances, and wholly owned foreign subsidiaries, Gillette's preferred approach. We briefly discuss each one, moving from the lowest level of foreign involvement and investment required of a global organization and its managers, and the least amount of risk, to the high end of the spectrum (see Figure 8.7).[60]

exporting Making products at home and selling them abroad.

IMPORTING AND EXPORTING The least complex global operations are exporting and importing. A company engaged in **exporting** makes products at home and sells them abroad. An organization might sell its own products abroad or allow a local organization in the foreign country to distribute its products. Few risks are associated with exporting because a company does not have to invest in developing manufacturing facilities abroad. It can further reduce its investment abroad if it allows a local company to distribute its products.

Figure 8.7

Four Ways to Expand Internationally

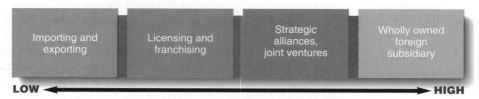

Level of foreign involvement and investment
and degree of risk

importing Selling at home products that are made abroad.

A company engaged in **importing** sells at home products that are made abroad (products it makes itself or buys from other companies). For example, most of the products that Pier 1 Imports, The Bombay Company, and The Limited sell to their customers are made abroad. In many cases the appeal of a product—Irish glass, French wine, Italian furniture, or Indian silk—is that it is made abroad. The Internet has made it much easier for companies to inform potential foreign buyers about their products; detailed product specifications and features are available online, and informed buyers can communicate easily with prospective sellers.

licensing Allowing a foreign organization to take charge of manufacturing and distributing a product in its country or world region in return for a negotiated fee.

LICENSING AND FRANCHISING   In **licensing,** a company (the licenser) allows a foreign organization (the licensee) to take charge of both manufacturing and distributing one or more of its products in the licensee's country or world region in return for a negotiated fee. Chemical maker Du Pont might license a local factory in India to produce nylon or Teflon. The advantage of licensing is that the licenser does not have to bear the development costs associated with opening up in a foreign country; the licensee bears the costs. The risks associated with this strategy are that the company granting the license has to give its foreign partner access to its technological know-how and so risks losing control over its secrets.

franchising Selling to a foreign organization the rights to use a brand name and operating know-how in return for a lump-sum payment and a share of the profits.

Whereas licensing is pursued primarily by manufacturing companies, franchising is pursued primarily by service organizations. In **franchising,** a company (the franchiser) sells to a foreign organization (the franchisee) the rights to use its brand name and operating know-how in return for a lump-sum payment and share of the franchiser's profits. Hilton Hotels might sell a franchise to a local company in Chile to operate hotels under the Hilton name in return for a franchise payment. The advantage of franchising is that the franchiser does not have to bear the development costs of overseas expansion and avoids the many problems associated with setting up foreign operations. The downside is that the organization that grants the franchise may lose control over the way in which the franchisee operates and product quality may fall. In this way, franchisers, such as Hilton, Avis, and McDonald's, risk losing their good names. American customers who buy McDonald's hamburgers in Korea may reasonably expect those burgers to be as good as the ones they get at home. If they are not, McDonald's reputation will suffer over time. Once again, the Internet facilitates communication between partners and allows them to better meet each other's expectations.

strategic alliance An agreement in which managers pool or share their organization's resources and know-how with a foreign company, and the two organizations share the rewards and risks of starting a new venture.

STRATEGIC ALLIANCES   One way to overcome the loss-of-control problems associated with exporting, licensing, and franchising is to expand globally by means of a strategic alliance. In a **strategic alliance,** managers pool or share their organization's resources and know-how with those of a foreign company, and the two organizations share the rewards or risks of starting a new venture in a foreign country. Sharing resources allows a U.S. company, for example, to take advantage of the high-quality skills of foreign manufacturers and the specialized knowledge of foreign managers about the needs of local customers and to reduce the risks involved in a venture. At the same time, the terms of the alliance give the U.S. company more control over how the good or service is produced or sold in the foreign country than it would have as a franchiser or licenser.

joint venture A strategic alliance among two or more companies that agree to jointly establish and share the ownership of a new business.

A strategic alliance can take the form of a written contract between two or more companies to exchange resources, or it can result in the creation of a new organization. A **joint venture** is a strategic alliance among two or more companies that agree to jointly establish and share the ownership of a new business.[61] An organization's level of involvement abroad increases in a joint venture because the alliance normally involves a capital investment in production facilities abroad in order to produce goods or services outside the home country. Risk, however, is reduced. The Internet and global teleconferencing provide the increased communication and coordination necessary for partners to work together on a global basis. For example, Coca-Cola and Nestlé formed a joint venture to market their teas, coffees, and health-oriented beverages in more than 50 countries.[62] Similarly, BP Amoco and Italy's ENI formed a joint venture to build a $2.5 billion gas-liquefaction plant in Egypt.[63]

wholly owned foreign subsidiary Production operations established in a foreign country independent of any local direct involvement.

WHOLLY OWNED FOREIGN SUBSIDIARIES When managers decide to establish a **wholly owned foreign subsidiary,** they invest in establishing production operations in a foreign country independent of any local direct involvement. Many Japanese car component companies, for example, have established their own operations in the United States to supply U.S.-based Japanese carmakers such as Toyota and Honda with high-quality car components.

Operating alone, without any direct involvement from foreign companies, an organization receives all of the rewards and bears all of the risks associated with operating abroad.[64] This method of international expansion is much more expensive than the others because it requires a higher level of foreign investment and presents managers with many more threats. However, investment in a foreign subsidiary or division offers significant advantages: It gives an organization high potential returns because the organization does not have to share its profits with a foreign organization, and it reduces the level of risk because the organization's managers have full control over all aspects of their foreign subsidiary's operations. Moreover, this type of investment allows managers to protect their technology and know-how from foreign organizations. Large, well-known companies like Du Pont, General Motors, and P&G, which have plenty of resources, make extensive use of wholly owned subsidiaries.

Obviously, global companies can use many of these different corporate strategies simultaneously to create the most value and strengthen their competitive position. We discussed above how P&G pursues related diversification at the global level, while it also pursues an international strategy that is a mixture of global and multidomestic. P&G also pursues vertical integration: It operates factories that make many of the specialized chemicals used in its products; it operates in the container industry and makes the thousands of different glass and plastic bottles and jars that contain its products; it prints its own product labels; and it distributes its products using its own fleet of trucks. Although P&G is highly diversified, it still puts the focus on its core individual product lines because it is famous for pursuing brand management—it concentrates resources around each brand, which is in effect managed as a "separate company." So P&G is trying to add value in every way it can from its corporate- and business-level strategies. At the business-level, for example, P&G aggressively pursues differentiation and it charges premium prices for its products. However, it also strives to lower its costs and pursues the corporate-level strategies just discussed to achieve this. The way in which the largest global package delivery company chose to expand globally also illustrates the complex issues surrounding global expansion.

Managing Globally

How DHL Entered the U.S. Package Delivery Business

In 1971, Federal Express (FedEx) turned the package delivery world upside down when it began to offer overnight package delivery by air. Its founder, Fred Smith, had seen the opportunity for next-day delivery because both the U.S. Postal Service and United Parcel Service (UPS) were, at that time, taking several days to deliver packages. Smith was convinced there was pent-up demand for overnight delivery, and he was also convinced that customers would be willing to pay a high premium price to get such a unique new service, at least $15 a package at that time.[65] Smith was right; customers were willing to pay high prices for fast reliable delivery. By discovering and tapping into an unmet customer need, he redefined the package delivery industry.

When DHL entered the package delivery market with its purchase of Airborne Express, it gained a differentiation advantage over FedEx and UPS at the global level.

Several companies imitated FedEx's new strategy and introduced their own air overnight service. None, however, could match FedEx's state-of-the-art information system that allowed continuous tracking of all packages in transit. Several of its competitors went out of business. A few, like Airborne Express, managed to survive by focusing or specializing on serving the needs of one particular group of customers—corporate customers—and by offering lower prices than FedEx.

The well-known road delivery package company UPS initiated an overnight air delivery service of its own in 1998.[66] UPS managers realized that the future of package delivery lay both on the road and in the air because different customer groups, with different needs, were emerging. It began to aggressively imitate FedEx's state-of-the-art operating and information systems, especially its tracking system. Slowly and surely UPS increased the number of overnight packages that it was delivering. In 1999, UPS announced two major innovations. First, it introduced a new tracking and shipping information system that matched, and even exceeded, the sophistication of the FedEx tracking system because it could work with any IT system used by corporate customers. (By contrast, customers had to install and use FedEx's proprietary IT, an approach that caused more work and cost for them.) Second, UPS integrated its overnight air service into its nationwide delivery service and created a seamless interface between these two different aspects of its business. This gave it a differentiation advantage over FedEx because UPS can deliver short-range and mid-distance packages, those being shipped within about 500 miles, more quickly than FedEx, as well as match the speed and reliability of FedEx's long-range operations.

In the early 2000s competition between FedEx and UPS further increased, but in 2003 both companies received a major shock when the largest global package delivery company, DHL, announced that it was purchasing Airborne Express in order to enter the U.S. package delivery market.[67] Thus DHL bought the wholly owned subsidiary it needed to become a direct competitor of FedEx and UPS, and these companies went to court to try to block the purchase. They did not want DHL to enter the market because it is the world's largest package delivery company, and its entry would give it a differentiation advantage over them at the global level. They were unable to prevent DHL's entering the market, as U.S. regulators believed its entry would spur healthy competition in the industry.

Since 2003 all three companies have worked hard to find new ways to differentiate themselves. FedEx purchased Kinko's Copies and has made each of its new FedExKinko's stores a base for its global delivery operations. DHL began to promote and advertise its global delivery system as the most efficient in the world. Both UPS and FedEx formed strategic alliances with delivery companies in countries around the world to develop their own efficient global delivery systems. The fight is ongoing as each company strives to become the global leader in each world region in which it operates.

Planning and Implementing Strategy

After identifying appropriate business and corporate strategies to attain an organization's mission and goals, managers confront the challenge of putting those strategies into action. Strategy implementation is a five-step process:

1. Allocating responsibility for implementation to the appropriate individuals or groups.
2. Drafting detailed action plans that specify how a strategy is to be implemented.
3. Establishing a timetable for implementation that includes precise, measurable goals linked to the attainment of the action plan.
4. Allocating appropriate resources to the responsible individuals or groups.
5. Holding specific individuals or groups responsible for the attainment of corporate, divisional, and functional goals.

The planning process goes beyond just identifying effective strategies; it also includes plans to ensure that these strategies are put into action. Normally, the plan for implementing a new strategy requires the development of new functional strategies, the redesign of an organization's structure, and the development of new control systems; it might also require a new program to change an organization's culture. These are issues we address in the next three chapters.

Summary and Review

PLANNING   Planning is a three-step process: (1) determining an organization's mission and goals; (2) formulating strategy; (3) implementing strategy. Managers use planning to identify and select appropriate goals and courses of action for an organization and to decide how to allocate the resources they need to attain those goals and carry out those actions. A good plan builds commitment for the organization's goals, gives the organization a sense of direction and purpose, coordinates the different functions and divisions of the organization, and controls managers by making them accountable for specific goals. In large organizations planning takes place at three levels: corporate, business or divisional, and functional or departmental. Long-term plans have a time horizon of five years or more; intermediate-term plans, between one and five years; and short-term plans, one year or less.

DETERMINING MISSION AND GOALS AND FORMULATING STRATEGY   Determining the organization's mission requires that managers define the business of the organization and establish major goals. Strategy formulation requires that managers perform a SWOT analysis and then choose appropriate strategies at the corporate, business, and functional levels. At the business level, managers are responsible for developing a successful low-cost and/or differentiation strategy, either for the whole market or a particular segment of it. At the functional level, departmental managers develop strategies to help the organization either to add value to its products by differentiating them or to lower the costs of value creation. At the corporate level, organizations use strategies such as concentration on a single industry, vertical integration, related and unrelated diversification, and international expansion to strengthen their competitive advantage by increasing the value of the goods and services provided to customers.

IMPLEMENTING STRATEGY   Strategy implementation requires that managers allocate responsibilities to appropriate individuals or groups, draft detailed action plans that specify how a strategy is to be implemented, establish a timetable for implementation that includes precise, measurable goals linked to the attainment of the action plan, allocate appropriate resources to the responsible individuals or groups, and hold individuals or groups accountable for the attainment of goals.

Management in Action

Topics for Discussion and Action

Discussion

1. Describe the three steps of planning. Explain how they are related.

2. How can scenario planning help managers predict the future?

3. What is the relationship among corporate-, business-, and functional-level strategies, and how do they create value for an organization?

4. Pick an industry and identify four companies in the industry that pursue one of the four main business-level strategies (low-cost, focused low-cost, etc.)

5. What is the difference between vertical integration and related diversification?

Action

6. Ask a manager about the kinds of planning exercises he or she regularly uses. What are the purposes of these exercises, and what are their advantages or disadvantages?

7. Ask a manager to identify the corporate- and business-level strategies used by his or her organization.

Building Management Skills
How to Analyze a Company's Strategy

Pick a well-known business organization that has received recent press coverage and that provides its annual reports at its Web site. From the information in the articles and annual reports:

1. What is (are) the main industry(ies) in which the company competes?

2. What business-level strategy does the company seem to be pursuing in this industry? Why?

3. What corporate-level strategies is the company pursuing? Why?

4. Have there been any major changes in its strategy recently? Why?

Managing Ethically

A few years ago, IBM announced that it had fired the three top managers of its Argentine division because of their involvement in a scheme to secure a $250 million contract for IBM to provide and service the computers of one of Argentina's largest state-owned banks. The three executives paid $14 million of the contract money to a third company, CCR, which paid nearly $6 million to phantom companies. This $6 million was then used to bribe the bank executives who agreed to give IBM the contract.

These bribes are not necessarily illegal under Argentine law. Moreover, the three managers argued that all companies have to pay bribes to get new business contracts and they were not doing anything that managers in other companies were not.

Questions

1. Either by yourself or in a group decide if the business practice of paying bribes is ethical or unethical.

2. Should IBM allow its foreign divisions to pay bribes if all other companies are doing so?

3. If bribery is common in a particular country, what effect would this likely have on the nation's economy and culture?

Small Group Breakout Exercise
Low Cost or Differentiation?

Form groups of three or four people, and appoint one member as spokesperson who will communicate your findings to the class when called on by the instructor. Then discuss the following scenario.

You are a team of managers of a major national clothing chain, and you have been charged with finding a way to restore your organization's competitive advantage. Recently, your organization has been experiencing increasing competition from two sources. First, discount stores such as Wal-Mart and Target have been undercutting your prices because they buy their clothes from low-cost foreign manufacturers while you buy most of yours from high-quality domestic suppliers. Discount stores have been attracting your customers who buy at the low end of the price range. Second, small boutiques opening in malls provide high-price designer clothing and are attracting your customers at the high end of the market. Your company has become stuck in the middle, and you have to decide what to do: Should you start to buy abroad so that you can lower your prices and begin to pursue a low-cost strategy? Should you focus on the high end of the market and become more of a differentiator? Or should you try to pursue both a low-cost strategy and a differentiation strategy?

1. Using scenario planning, analyze the pros and cons of each alternative.

2. Think about the various clothing retailers in your local malls and city, and analyze the choices they have made about how to compete with one another along the low-cost and differentiation dimensions.

Exploring the World Wide Web

Go to the corporate Web site of Google (www.google.com/corporate/execs.html), click on "corporate info," and explore this site; in particular, click on "Google's history" and "The 10 Things" that guide Google's corporate philosophy.

1. How would you describe Google's mission and goals?

2. What is Google's business-level strategy?

3. What is Google's corporate-level strategy?

Be the Manager

A group of investors in your city is considering opening a new upscale supermarket to compete with the major supermarket chains that are currently dominating the city's marketplace. They have called you in to help them determine what kind of upscale supermarket they should open. In other words, how can they best develop a competitive advantage against existing supermarket chains?

Questions

1. List the supermarket chains in your city, and identify their strengths and weaknesses.

2. What business-level strategies are these supermarkets currently pursuing?

3. What kind of supermarket would do best against the competition? What kind of business-level strategy should it pursue?

BusinessWeek

Case in the News

Lilly's Labs Go Global

Across the nation, so-called teaching hospitals have teamed up with Eli Lilly to find out, in experiments on volunteer patients, whether its newest drugs are safe and effective. Increasingly, Lilly is moving its research and development, including clinical trials, to China, India, and the former Soviet bloc. The reason: It's much, much cheaper to do this work in these nations, and Lilly considers the work itself to be as good as in the U.S. or Western Europe.

Lilly isn't the only member of Big Pharma relocating R&D operations to the developing world. Industry titan Pfizer is testing drugs in Russia, while AstraZeneca has been conducting clinical trials in China. But Lilly seems to be ahead of many of its peers.

Costly Development.

In general, Lilly also seems to get more from its labs. The Indianapolis-based drugmaker is renowned for its product pipeline. In the last five years, it has introduced eight drugs in the U.S.—more than even some of its larger rivals—and its execs say Lilly should be able to keep up that pace at least for the next several years.

Like other drugmakers, Lilly is getting squeezed by the rising cost of developing drugs. Company executives now put that cost at $1.1 billion per drug, including expenses on all the products that don't make it to the market. And they say this price tag looks likely to hit $1.5 billion in 2010. Lilly execs have set a goal of lowering that tab to $800 million instead. This is where India and China come in.

CEO Sidney Taurel says Lilly today is doing 20% of its chemistry work in China where costs are one-quarter that in the U.S. or Western Europe. Lilly helped start a lab in Shanghai in 2003, a year after industry pioneer Novo Nordisk opened a small research facility in Beijing. The startup, Chem-Explorer, works exclusively for Lilly and has a staff of 230 chemists today. Now, Lilly is expanding its R&D efforts to include clinical trials. These are the late-stage experiments to prove a drug can be used on humans. Typically, in the last phase of testing, a large sample of prescreened people with a disease or condition is given a drug over 12 months and carefully monitored by physicians and researchers to see how the drug performs against either a placebo or an existing product.

The tests are enormously expensive. Lilly estimates that each Phase III test costs at least $50 million a year. In fact, Lilly is spending more than $300 million right now to test an anticlotting pill, prasugrel, for heart patients. And one way to reduce costs is doing some of these studies where the quality of the data generated is very high—China, India, and Eastern Europe, the old Soviet bloc nations—and the costs are low.

What about concerns that Lilly's experimental drugs will be ripped off during these trials in India or China, where intellectual property isn't often respected and counterfeit drugs are common? John Lechleiter, Lilly's president and chief operating officer, says Lilly has not had this problem in clinical trials. The more these two countries develop, he adds, the less concerned management is.

Lilly execs say outsourcing is picking up momentum. "The research is less expensive per patient outside of the U.S., but at the same high quality," Lechleiter says. "It also helps speed up the development process. In our business, time is money." He explains that a patent is effective from the date of a drug's discovery, not when the drug hits the market. So the faster Lilly can move the product out of the lab, the longer it can secure patent protection—and high profit margins—in the marketplace. Lilly's drug Arzoxifene, for example, is benefiting from offshore testing. Aimed at treating both osteoporosis and breast cancer, Arzoxifene is in the final stage of tests on 9,000 people, and most of this research is being done in India and Brazil. Lilly hopes to seek market approval for the drug from the FDA in 2009.

Questions for Discussion

1. Why is Lilly moving some of its value-creation operations overseas?

2. How is this changing its business-level strategy?

Case in the NEWS

Toyota: Way, Way Off-Road

Looking for the biggest Toyota on the market? You'd do well to skip the Tundra pickups and Sequoia SUVs down at your local dealer. Instead, take a trip to the Toyota factory in Kasugai, a city of 300,000 about three hours west of Tokyo. There, the models on the assembly line don't amount to much in terms of acceleration or horsepower, but boy, are they ever roomy—as in multiple bedrooms, a living room, kitchen, bath, and patio.

The Kasugai plant is one of three Toyota factories in Japan that make prefabricated houses. Just like Toyota's cars, these come with fancy, foreign-sounding names and plenty of options, such as solar roof panels and keyless entry. For those with a Corolla-size budget, the top-selling, 1,300-sq.-ft. Smart Stage runs about $175,000, excluding land. For the Camry set, there's the 1,800-square-foot Espacio Mezzo, with three bedrooms and a garage, selling for about $225,000, though add-ons can take buyers into Lexus territory: At least one big spender laid out $860,000 for a super-size version.

Even as Detroit's carmakers have shed virtually all of their non-core assets, the world's most successful car company is heading in the opposite direction. Toyota controls dozens of businesses that have virtually nothing to do with automaking, ranging in size from resort developer Nagasaki Sunset Marina (77% owned by Toyota), with just five employees, to Toyota Financial Services Corp., a wholly owned subsidiary with 8,000 workers and $1.7 billion in operating profits in fiscal 2005. All told,

revenues for Toyota's nonauto businesses jumped 15.5%, to $10.3 billion, in the year through March, and are up 50% since 2003. While last year's total still represented less than 6% of Toyota's overall sales of $180 billion, if broken out the company's sideline businesses would rank No. 192 among companies in the Standard & Poor's 500-stock index.

Odorless Manure

Houses are just the beginning. The automaker owns 100% of Delphys Inc., an advertiser with revenues of $660 million. There's Toyota Amenity, a wholly owned subsidiary with 69 employees that provides consulting services for hotels, wedding halls, and restaurants. To profit from the graying of Japan, there's Good Life Design, a 51%-owned company that offers support services to medical institutions. And should its employees go hungry, Toyota could turn to Toyota Bio Indonesia, a grower and processor of sweet potatoes. Established in 2001, the subsidiary is 90% owned by Toyota and aimed for sales of $860,000 in 2005.

Then there's Tokyo-based Toyota Roof Garden. As its name suggests, the subsidiary—70% owned by Toyota—designs and sells greenery for rooftops, using peat from China to create lush spaces high above the streets. Toyota expects the business to grow as governments across Japan promote planting on roofs to combat rising temperatures in cities. And on July 1 the unit began selling a new composting ingredient developed with contact lens maker Menicon Co. that, among other things, removes offensive odors from manure.

What's the point? One clue can be found in Toyota's history. The company started out making power looms for Japan's textile industry. But Toyota founder Kiichiro Toyoda, after dismantling and rebuilding engines on Chevrolets imported to Japan, quickly recognized the potential for autos. In 1935 he built his first car, the A1. Two years later, Toyota Motor Corp. (TM) was spun off. Following that tradition of corporate exploration, since 1986 Toyota has had a New Business Project Committee to look into concepts in five areas, including factory automation, electronics, and biotechnology.

Image is another factor. Just as Toyota has used its Prius hybrid to build an eco-friendly profile—while churning out ever more big trucks and SUVs—investing relatively small sums in new technologies can go a long way in the PR stakes. While few of its nonauto businesses are huge profit drivers, Toyota says the aim of such sidelines is to use its technology and intellectual assets to "enrich society."

Not all the investments are totally unrelated to autos. Some of those Indonesian sweet potatoes, for example, are used to make biodegradable plastics that have found their way into Toyota cars. Panasonic EV Energy, 60% Toyota-owned, develops batteries for hybrids. And like many other automakers, Toyota rakes in big bucks from financing its vehicles.

Still, Toyota says it can find synergies in many activities that have nothing to do with cars. At Kasugai, Toyota's houses are 85% completed at the plant before being transported by road and built in just six hours. To improve efficiency, the company borrows knowhow from its fabled Toyota Production System with its principles of just-in-time delivery and kaizen, or continuous improvement. Anticorrosive paint is applied evenly to houses' steel frames using methods adopted from car production. And just as in all Toyota's Japan auto factories, a banner proclaiming "good thinking, good products" hangs from the roof. "We follow the Toyota way in housing," says Senta Morioka, a managing officer at Toyota.

Where possible, Toyota also uses components developed for cars in its houses. One example is the keyless entry system which uses a radio sensor to lock or unlock the doors automatically. And to help keep out burglars, the windows are made of the shatter-resistant glass that Toyota uses in its windshields.

Yet for all that, many wonder what a car company like Toyota is doing in housing, roof gardens, and advertising. For the most part, analysts and investors turn a blind eye. One reason, of course, is that it's difficult to quibble with a company that posted earnings of $12.5 billion last year, enjoys operating margins near the top of the auto industry, and is poised to sweep past General Motors Corp. (GM) as the world's biggest carmaker in the next year or so. "There's a certain amount of complaining about this kind of stuff [from investors], but it's a rounding error when compared with their total spending," says Christopher Richter, an analyst at brokerage CLSA Asia-Pacific Markets in Tokyo.

Questions for Discussion

1. In owning these different businesses Toyota is pursuing the three kinds of coprorate-level strategies discussed in the chapter. What are the strategies? Why is it pursuing each of them?

2. In what ways could Toyota use its skills to enter new businesses and industries to create a significant amount of value for the company?

Source: Ian Rowley and Hiroko Tashiro, "Toyota: Way, Way Off-Road." Reprinted from the July 17, 2006, issue of *BusinessWeek* by special permission. Copyright © 2006 by the McGraw-Hill Companies.

Appendix
How to Develop a Business Plan

A **business plan** is a detailed, written statement that explains the purpose of creating a new venture—either a new company or a new project in an existing company—to provide new or improved products to customers. The purpose of a business plan is to guide the development, production, and marketing of a new and improved product and to accomplish this it must contain several important kinds of information: (1) It explains the purpose of the new venture, it outlines its mission and goals, and describes what kinds of product it will make and sell and why they will appeal to customers; (2) it explains why and how the new venture will be able to compete successfully against established competitors; and (3) it explains how the entrepreneur, business owner, or manager intends to obtain, use, and organize the resources the company will need to make and sell these products. The steps in the development of a business plan are listed in Table 8A.1.

If the assumptions in the business plan work out as intended, a company will have succeeded in creating a profitable new product. If the business plan does not work out because entrepreneurs and managers have made mistaken assumptions about customers' needs, or underestimated how much it will cost to make and sell the product, the new venture will be unprofitable and will probably be ended. To increase the chances of success it is therefore vital that the entrepreneur or managers do an accurate and thorough job of analyzing current industry conditions and formulating the right set of strategies.

Table 8A.1
Developing a Business Plan

1. Notice a Product Opportunity, and Develop a Basic Business Idea
   - Goods/services
   - Customers/markets
2. Conduct a Strategic (SWOT) Analysis
   - Identify opportunities
   - Identify threats
   - Identify strengths
   - Identify weaknesses
3. Decide Whether the Business Opportunity Is Feasible
4. Prepare a Detailed Business Plan
   - Executive summary: Statement of mission, goals, and financial objectives
   - Company Background Information
   - List of necessary Functional and Organizational Strategies and resources
   - Organizational time line of events

Developing a Business Plan

Planning for a new business venture begins when an entrepreneur notices an opportunity to develop a new or improved good or service. Similarly, planning for a new business venture or project *inside of* an established company begins when a manager notices an opportunity. On the one hand, an entrepreneur might notice an opportunity in the fast-food market to provide customers with healthy fast food such as rotisserie chicken served with fresh vegetables. This is what the founders of the Boston Market restaurant chain did. On the other hand, a manager at McDonald's might notice an opportunity to create a new kind of hamburger or fast-food product to attract more customers. And, in fact, the idea for the Big Mac and Egg McMuffin came from two of McDonald's franchisees who independently developed and tested these new products and then shared them with the whole McDonald's Company.

There is no formalized way in which a person can "come up" with a new idea for an attractive new product. Many successful new products result from continuous hard thinking and from intuition and luck. They can also result from a formal, in-house strategic planning process as product development and marketing managers brainstorm ideas for new products or new ways to package and deliver them to customers. Once a new product idea has been generated, the crucial next step in creating a business plan is to test the feasibility of the new idea and the strategies behind it.

To accomplish this, an entrepreneur or functional experts perform a detailed SWOT analysis, the strategic planning exercise discussed in Chapter 8 (see Table 8.1). For example, in the fast food industry, to assess the viability of selling rotisserie chicken served with fresh vegetables, an entrepreneur needs to analyze opportunities and threats. One potential threat might be that if the new idea succeeds, McDonald's or KFC might decide to imitate the idea and rush to do so. If this happens, whatever competitive advantage the entrepreneur may have had will be short-lived. (KFC actually did this after Boston Market was successfully launched.) As the entrepreneur conducts a thorough analysis of the competitive environment, he or she must be willing to abandon an idea if it seems likely that industry threats will be difficult to counter so that the risks involved are too great to bear.

Entrepreneurs and managers must not become so committed to their ideas that they discount potential threats and forge ahead—only to lose all of the money they invested in their venture. Unfortunately, people make this mistake all the time in the restaurant business and the failure rate of new restaurants is very high.

If the environmental analysis suggests that the product idea is feasible, however, the next step is to examine the strengths and weaknesses of the idea. For a new company venture the main strength is likely to be the resources possessed by the entrepreneur. Does the entrepreneur have access to an adequate source of funds? Does the entrepreneur have any experience in the fast-food industry such as having been a chef or managed a restaurant? To identify weaknesses, the entrepreneur needs to assess what kinds of functional resources will be necessary to establish a viable new venture—such as a chain of chicken restaurants—and how much money will be required to fund it.

Thus the first three steps in creating a business plan for a new venture are listed next. First, notice a product opportunity and develop a mission statement and goals that focuses on the product, customer needs, and potential markets. Second, conduct a SWOT analysis to identify opportunities, threats, strengths, and weaknesses. Third, make an initial assessment of whether the new venture is feasible and if it is, then write the detailed business plan.

Writing a Detailed Business Plan

Once these steps are completed, the hard work of writing up the detailed business plan begins. The business plan will be used to (1) continue the process of testing, assessing, and fine-tuning the proposed set of strategies, and (2) to attract the banks or investors who will provide the capital needed to launch the venture (or, in the case of an exiting company, get the buy-in of top managers). Business plans are formatted in many ways, but a typical format is as follows:

THE EXECUTIVE SUMMARY   The executive summary is an opening, two-page statement of the organization's mission, goals, and financial objectives. The summary also contains a statement of the organization's strategic objectives, including an in-depth analysis of a new product's market potential based on the SWOT analysis that has already been conducted. Finally, it outlines the

CHAPTER 9

Value-Chain Management: Functional Strategies for Competitive Advantage

Learning Objectives

After studying this chapter, you should be able to:

- Explain the role of functional strategy and value-chain management in achieving superior quality, efficiency, innovation, and responsiveness to customers.

- Describe what customers want, and explain why it is so important for managers to be responsive to their needs.

- Explain why achieving superior quality is so important, and understand the challenges facing managers and organizations that seek to implement total quality management.

- Explain why achieving superior efficiency is so important, and understand the different kinds of techniques that need to be employed to increase efficiency.

- Differentiate between two forms of innovation, and explain why innovation and product development is a crucial component of the search for competitive advantage.

A Manager's Challenge

Toyota's Approach to Building Competitive Advantage

How can managers increase operating performance?

Toyota has long been known as a company that constantly strives to improve its car design and production systems to enhance efficiency, quality, innovation, and customer responsiveness. It pioneered the system of "lean production," a functional strategy that changes the way cars are assembled and results in dramatic improvements in vehicle reliability. And Toyota has always pursued total quality management, or *kaizen,* a functional strategy that makes production-line employees responsible for finding ways to continuously make incremental improvements to work procedures that drive down costs and drive up quality. Over time, the thousands of suggestions employees' make, individually and in quality groups or circles, result in innovations to the car assembly process that lead to major improvements in the final product. Employees receive cash bonuses and rewards for their contributions, which enable Toyota to continuously increase car quality and reduce manufacturing costs.

In the 2000s, however, under the leadership of Toyota's chairman, Jujio Cho, and president, Katsuaki Watanabe, the company

Assembly line workers for Japanese auto giant Toyota put tires onto Toyota's vehicle "Wish" at the company's Tsutsumi plant in Toyota, central Japan.

sought new strategies to further improve efficiency and quality and strengthen its competitive advantage over rivals such as Volkswagen, Ford, and DaimlerChrysler.[1] It began to implement a series of new strategies, each directed at improving the way its various functions operate. One new manufacturing strategy to strengthen its kaizen program is "pokayoke," or mistake-proofing. This initiative concentrates on the stages of the assembly process that have led to most previous quality problems; employees are required to double- and triple-check a particular stage to discover defective parts or to fix improper assembly operations that would have led to subsequent customer complaints. Another strategy is "CCC21," which involves working with the company's suppliers to find ways to reduce the costs of Toyota's car components by 30%—a goal that will result in billions of dollars in savings. Toyota also implemented a new manufacturing process called GBL that uses a sophisticated new assembly process to hold a car body firmly in place during production. This allows welding and assembly operations to be performed more accurately, resulting in better-quality cars. GBL has also enabled Toyota to build factories that can assemble several different car models on the same production line with no loss in efficiency or quality. This is a major competitive advantage. The company's global network of plants can now quickly switch among the kinds of cars they are making depending upon buyers' demands for various models at different points in time.

Other new functional strategies focus on revamping Toyota's development and design process to keep up with changing customer needs and demographics; for example, the age of the average Toyota car buyer has been steadily increasing, which is a major competitive problem. Despite Toyota's climbing global sales (which exceeded $160 billion in 2006), the company has often been criticized for failing to understand the needs of different kinds of customers. Analysts blamed the problem on centralized decision making at the company and a culture that had long been dominated by Toyota's cautious and frugal Japanese designers. Rather than designing innovative, flexible vehicles that customers were increasingly demanding, Toyota continued to focus on cutting costs and increasing quality. When the company's U.S. designers, for example, argued with designers in Tokyo that U.S. customers wanted an eight-cylinder pickup truck, and that Toyota needed to make such a vehicle to compete with GM and Ford, they were ignored. Headquarters also turned a deaf ear to the call to make innovative vehicles that would appeal to younger customers. Slow sales of its small pickups and compact cars soon showed that the company was not being responsive to customers and that design changes were necessary.

To speed innovation and the new product development process, Cho championed two new functional strategies that radically alter the way vehicles are designed: PDCA and Obeya. Obeya is based on frequent brainstorming sessions between product engineers, designers, production managers, and marketers and is designed to speed new-model cars to the market. PDCA, or "plan-do-check-action," is a strategy designed to empower the company's designers outside Japan to intervene in the product development process and champion vehicle designs that meet the needs of local customers. The results of promoting a flexible, decentralized car design process were the speedy introduction of the rugged eight-cylinder Tundra pickup truck and the angular ScionxB compact in the United States, as well as the Yaris, Toyota's best-selling European car. The Yaris was designed in Europe, and its success there led to its subsequent introduction in Japan, where it also sold well.

Toyota's mastery of value-chain management through implementing groundbreaking functional strategies has made it by far the most profitable of the major carmakers. Its functional strategies strengthen its ability to pursue both low cost and differentiation business-level strategies and have given it a widening competitive advantage over its rivals. Toyota replaced Ford as the world's second-largest carmaker in 2004, and it seems likely it will replace GM as the world's biggest carmaker before too long.

Overview

Toyota has developed many kinds of strategies to encourage managers in value-creating functions like manufacturing, materials management, and product development to improve the way functional activities are performed to promote the organization's competitive advantage. In this chapter we focus on the functional-level strategies managers can use to achieve superior efficiency, quality, innovation, and responsiveness to customers and so build competitive advantage. We also examine the nature of an organization's value chain and discuss how the combined or cooperative efforts of managers across the value chain are required if an organization is to achieve its mission and goal of maximizing the amount of value its products provide customers. By the end of this chapter, you will understand the vital role value-chain management plays in building competitive advantage and creating a high-performing organization.

Functional Strategies, the Value Chain, and Competitive Advantage

As we noted in Chapter 8, there are two basic business-level strategies managers can use to add value to an organization's products and achieve a competitive advantage over industry rivals. First, managers can pursue a *low-cost strategy* and lower the costs of creating value in order to attract customers by keeping product prices as low as or lower than competitors' prices. Second, managers can pursue a *differentiation strategy* and add value to a product by finding ways to make it superior in some way to the products of other companies. If they are successful, and customers see greater value in the product, then like Toyota they are able to charge a premium or higher price for the product. The four specific ways in which managers can lower costs and/or increase differentiation to obtain a competitive advantage were mentioned in Chapter 1 and are reviewed below; how organizations seek to achieve them is the topic of this chapter. (See Figure 9.1.)

Figure 9.1

Four Ways to Create a Competitive Advantage

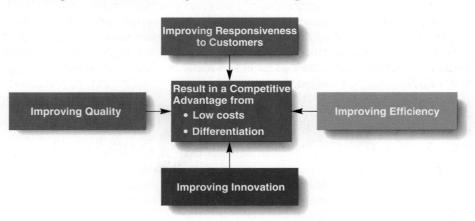

1. *Achieve superior efficiency.* Efficiency is a measure of the amount of inputs required to produce a given amount of outputs. The fewer the inputs required to produce a given output, the higher is efficiency and the lower the cost of outputs. For example, in 1990 it took the average Japanese auto company 16.8 employee-hours to build a car, while the average American car company took 25.1 employee-hours. Japanese companies at that time were more efficient and had lower costs than their American rivals.[2] By 2004, U.S. companies had adopted more efficient manufacturing methods and narrowed the cost gap significantly; however, as the opening case suggests, Toyota continually works to reduce costs to maintain its position as the most efficient carmaker in the world.

2. *Achieve superior quality.* Quality means producing goods and services that have attributes—such as design, styling, performance, and reliability—that customers perceive as being superior to those found in competing products.[3] Providing high-quality products creates a brand-name reputation for an organization's products, and this enhanced reputation allows it to charge higher prices. In the car industry, for example, besides Toyota's efficiency-based cost advantage, the higher quality of Toyota's products also enables the company to outperform its rivals because customers are willing to pay a premium price for its cars.

3. *Achieve superior innovation, speed, and flexibility.* Anything new or better about the way an organization operates or the goods and services it produces is the result of innovation. Successful innovation gives an organization something *unique* or different about its products that rivals lack—more sophisticated products, production processes, or strategies and structures that strengthen its competitive advantage. Innovation adds value to products, and allows the organization to further differentiate itself from rivals and attract customers willing to pay a premium price for unique products. Toyota is widely credited with pioneering innovations in the way cars are built that have made them more reliable, quiet, and comfortable and allowed it to charge a premium price for them. For example, a Toyota Corolla or Camry is always priced a thousand or more dollars above its equivalent U.S. competitor such as the Ford Focus or Five Hundred or the Chevy Cobalt, Grand Prix, or Pontiac G6, and many customers are willing to pay the higher price.

4. *Attain superior responsiveness to customers.* An organization that is responsive to customers tries to satisfy their needs and give them *exactly* what they want. An organization that treats customers better than its rivals do also provides a valuable service some customers may be willing to pay a higher price for. Managers can increase responsiveness by providing excellent after-sales service and support and by working with customers to provide improved products or services in the future. Today, Toyota, like other carmakers, is always on the lookout for changing customer needs, and as "A Manager's Challenge described, managers across its functions apply innovative strategies to design new cars to better meet those needs.

One way to measure how much managers are concerned with customer responsiveness is to look at the range of products a company makes and how fast it changes and improves them to better meet their needs. Figure 9.2 shows the range of vehicles that Toyota currently makes and the kinds of customers it is targeting according to the price they are willing or able to pay. As the figure illustrates, there are few major gaps in Toyota's product range; the company makes a variety of vehicles that are designed to be responsive to the needs of the largest possible range of customers.

Figure 9.2

Toyota's Product Lineup

Price	Sports Utility Vehicles	Passenger/ Sports Sedans	Passenger Vans	Personal Luxury Vehicles	Sports Cars	Pickup Trucks
11–20K	RAV4 Scion xB FJ Cruiser	Echo, Matrix, Corolla, Yaris Scion xA			Celica GT	Tacoma
21–30K	4-Runner, Highlander	Prius, Camry, Avalon	Sienna	Avalon	MR2, Spyder	Tundra
31–45K	Sequoia, RX350	GS 350, IS 350		ES 350	Camry Solara	Tundra Double Cab
46–75K	Land Cruiser, GX, LX	GS 450		LS 460	SC 430	

☐ No vehicle in category

Functional Strategies and Value-Chain Management

functional-level strategy A plan of action to improve the ability of each of an organization's functions to perform its task-specific activities in ways that add value to an organization's goods and services.

value chain The coordinated series or sequence of functional activities necessary to transform inputs such as new product concepts, raw materials, component parts, or professional skills into the finished goods or services customers value and want to buy.

value-chain management The development of a set of functional-level strategies that support a company's business-level strategy and strengthen its competitive advantage.

Functional-level strategy is a plan of action to improve the ability of each of an organization's functions or departments (such as manufacturing or marketing) to perform its task-specific activities in ways that add value to an organization's goods and services. A company's **value chain** is the coordinated series or sequence of functional activities necessary to transform inputs such as new product concepts, raw materials, component parts, or professional skills into the finished goods or services customers value and want to buy (see Figure 9.3). Each functional activity along the chain *adds value* to the product when it lowers costs or gives the product differentiated qualities that increase the price a company can charge for it.

Value-chain management is the development of a set of functional-level strategies that support a company's business-level strategy and strengthen its competitive advantage. Functional managers develop the strategies that result in increased efficiency, quality, innovation, and/or responsiveness to customers and thus strengthen an organization's competitive advantage. So the better the fit between functional- and business-level strategies, the greater will be the organization's competitive advantage, and the better able the organization is to achieve its mission and goal of maximizing the amount of value it gives customers—something Toyota excels at. Each function along the value chain has an important role to play in the value-creation process.

As Figure 9.3 suggests, the starting point of the value chain is often the search for new and improved products that will better appeal to customers, so the activities of the product development and marketing functions become

Figure 9.3

Functional Activities and the Value Chain

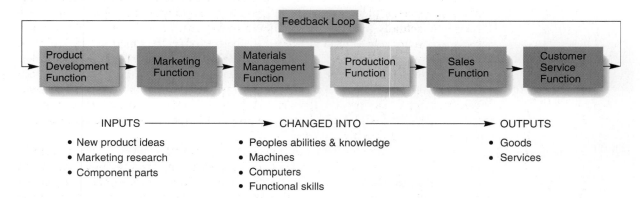

important. *Product development* is the engineering and scientific research activities involved in innovating new or improved products that add value to a product. For example, Toyota's engineers developed a hybrid gas-saving technology that has proved popular among car buyers. Once a new product has been developed, then the *marketing function's* task is to persuade customers that the product meets their needs and convince them to buy it. Marketing can help create value through brand positioning and advertising that increases customer perceptions about the utility of a company's product. For example, in the 1980s the French company Perrier persuaded U.S. customers that carbonated bottled water was worth $1.50 per liter bottle rather than the 25 cents it cost to purchase a gallon of spring water. Perrier's marketing function had developed strategies that made customers want to buy the product, and major U.S. companies such as Coca-Cola and PepsiCo rushed to bring out their own bottled-water labels to capitalize on customers' growing appetite for bottled water.

Even the best-designed product can fail if the marketing function hasn't devised a careful plan to persuade people to buy it and try it out—or to make sure customers really want it. For this reason, marketing often conducts consumer research to discover unmet customer product needs and to find better ways to tailor existing products to satisfy customer needs. Marketing then presents its suggestions to product development, which performs its own research to discover how best to design and make the new or improved products.

At the next stage of the value chain, the *materials management function* controls the movement of physical materials from the procurement of inputs through production and to distribution and delivery to the customer. The efficiency with which this is carried out can significantly lower costs and create more value. Wal-Mart, the U.S. retailing giant, has the most efficient materials management function in the retail industry. By tightly controlling the flow of goods from its suppliers through its stores and into the hands of customers, Wal-Mart has eliminated the need to hold large inventories of goods. Lower inventories mean lower costs, and hence greater value creation. Similarly, Toyota insists that its suppliers establish car component plants close to its factories so that it does not have to bear the cost of holding a large inventory of car components—a significant cost savings.

The *production function* is responsible for the creation, assembly or provision of a good or service, for transforming inputs into outputs. For physical products, when we talk about production, we generally mean manufacturing and assembly. For services such as banking or retailing, production takes place when the service is actually provided or delivered to the customer (for example, when a bank originates a loan for a customer, it is engaged in "production" of the loan). By performing its activities efficiently, the production function helps to lower costs. For example, the efficient production operations of Honda and Toyota have made them more profitable than competitors such as Renault, Volkswagen, and Ford. The production function can also perform its activities in a way that is consistent with high product quality, which leads to differentiation (and higher value) and to lower costs.

At the next stage in the value chain, the *sales function* plays a crucial role in locating customers and then informing and persuading them to buy company's products. Personal selling, that is, direct face-to-face communication by salespeople with existing and potential customers to promote a company's products is a crucial value-chain activity. Which products retailers choose to stock, for example, or which drugs doctors choose to prescribe often depend upon the salesperson's ability to inform and persuade customers that *his or her* company's product is superior and thus a the best choice.

Finally, the role of the *customer service function* is to provide after-sales service and support. This function can create a perception of superior value in the minds of customers by solving customer problems and supporting customers after they have purchased the product. For example, FedEx can get its customers' parcels to any point in the world within 24 hours, thereby lowering the cost of its own value-creation activities. Finally, customer service controls the electronic systems for tracking sales and inventory, pricing products, selling products, dealing with customer inquires, and so on, all of which can greatly increase responsiveness to customers. Indeed, an important activity of sales and customer service is to inform product development and marketing about why a product is meeting or not meeting customers needs so that the product can be redesigned or improved. Hence, the feedback loop links the end of the value chain to its beginning (see Figure 9.3).

In the rest of this chapter we examine the functional strategies used to manage the value chain to improve quality, efficiency, innovation, and responsiveness to customers. Notice, however, that achieving superior quality, efficiency, and innovation is *part* of attaining superior responsiveness to customers. Customers want value for their money, and managers who develop functional strategies that result in a value chain capable of creating innovative, high-quality, low-cost products best deliver this value to customers. For this reason, we begin by discussing how functional managers can increase responsiveness to customers.

Improving Responsiveness to Customers

All organizations produce outputs—goods or services—that are consumed by customers, who, in buying these products, provide the monetary resources most organizations need to survive. Since customers are vital to organizational survival, managers must correctly identify who their customers are and pursue strategies that result in products that best meet their needs. This is why the marketing function plays such an important part in the value chain, and good value-chain management requires that marketing managers focus on defining their company's business in terms of the customer *needs* it is satisfying and not by the *type of products* it makes—or the result can be disaster.[4] For example, Kodak's managers said "no thanks" when the company was offered the rights to "instant photography," which was later marketed by Polaroid. Why did they make this mistake? Because the managers adopted a product-oriented approach to their business which didn't put the needs of customers first. Kodak's managers believed their job was to sell high-quality, glossy photographs to people; why would they want to become involved in instant photography, which results in inferior-quality photographs? In reality, Kodak was not satisfying people's needs for high-quality photographs; it was satisfying the need customers had to *capture and record the images of their lives*—their birthday parties, weddings, graduations, and so on. And people wanted those images quickly so that they could share them right away with other people—which is why today digital photography has taken off. In the 2000s, Kodak is in serious trouble because its film-based photographic business has declined sharply, and it is losing billions as it tries to position itself in the digital market to give customers what they want.

Kodak has fallen behind in the digital camera market by focusing more on products than on customers.

What Do Customers Want?

Given that satisfying customer demands is central to the survival of an organization, an important question is, "What do customers want?" Although specifying *exactly* what customers want is not possible because their needs vary from product to product, it is possible to identify some general product attributes or qualities that most customers desire:

1. A lower price to a higher price.
2. High-quality products to low-quality products.
3. Quick service and good after-sales service to slow service and poor after-sales support.
4. Products with many useful or valuable features to products with few features.
5. Products that are, as far as possible, customized or tailored to their unique needs.

Managers know that the more desired product attributes a company's value chain builds into its products, the higher the price that must be charged to cover the costs of developing and making the product. So what do managers of a customer-responsive organization try to do? They try to develop functional strategies that allow the organization's value chain to deliver to customers either *more* desired product attributes for the *same price* or the *same* product attributes for a *lower price*.[5] For example, by increasing the efficiency of its manufacturing process, and by finding new ways to design cars that are less expensive, Toyota has been able to increase the number of luxury features in its cars at very little or no extra cost, compared to its competitors. Similarly, Wal-Mart's "price roll-backs" or reductions are possible because it constantly searches for lower-cost suppliers or more efficient ways to manage its product inventory and deliver it to stores. It told its suppliers, for example, that if they did not put new radio frequency tags (that allow inventory to be monitored electronically as it moves around) on their products by 2006, it would cease to buy from them.[6] In general, new IT has allowed many organizations to offer new models of products with more attributes at a price similar to or even lower than that of earlier models, and so in the last decade customers have been able to choose from a wider variety of higher-quality products and receive quicker customer service.

Managing the Value Chain to Increase Responsiveness to Customers

Because satisfying customers is so important, managers try to design and improve the way their value chains operate so that they can supply products that have the desired attributes—quality, cost, and features. For example, the need to respond to customer demands for competitively priced, quality cars drove U.S. carmakers like Ford and GM to imitate Japanese companies and copy the way Toyota and Honda perform their value-chain activities. Today, the imperative of satisfying customer needs shapes the activities of GM's materials management and manufacturing functions. As an example of the link between responsiveness to customers and an organization's value chain, consider how Southwest Airlines, the most profitable U.S. airline, operates.[7]

A Southwest ticket agent assists a customer. Southwest's operating system is geared toward satisfying customer demands for low-priced, reliable, and convenient air travel, making it one of the most consistently successful airlines in recent years. To help keep flights on schedule, Southwest's workforce has been cross-trained to perform multiple tasks. For example, the person who checks tickets might also help with baggage loading.

The major reason for Southwest's success is that it has striven to pursue functional strategies that improve the way its value chain operates to give customers what they want. Southwest commands high customer loyalty precisely because it can deliver products, such as flights from Houston to Dallas, which have all the desired attributes: reliability, convenience, and low price. In each one of its functions, Southwest's strategies revolve around finding ways to lower costs. For example, Southwest offers a no-frills approach to in-flight customer service; no meals are served onboard, and there are no first-class seats. Southwest does not subscribe to the big reservation computers used by travel agents because the booking fees are too costly. Also, the airline flies only one aircraft, the fuel-efficient Boeing 737, which keeps training and maintenance costs down. All this translates into low prices for customers.

Southwest's reliability derives from the fact that it has the quickest aircraft turnaround time in the industry. A Southwest ground crew needs only 15 minutes to turn around an incoming aircraft and prepare it for departure. This speedy operation helps to keep flights on time. Southwest has such a quick turnaround because it has a flexible workforce that has been cross-trained to perform multiple tasks. Thus, the person who checks tickets might also help with baggage loading if time is short.

Southwest's convenience comes from its scheduling multiple flights every day between its popular locations, such as Dallas and Houston, and its use of airports that are close to downtown areas (Hobby at Houston and Love Field at Dallas) instead of using more distant, major airports.[8] In sum, Southwest's excellent value-chain management has given it a competitive advantage in the airline industry.

Although managers must seek to improve their responsiveness to customers by improving the way the value chain operates, they should not offer a level of responsiveness to customers that results in costs becoming *too high*—something that threatens an organization's future performance and survival. For example, a company that customizes every product to the unique demands of individual customers is likely to find that its costs will get out of control. This happened to Toyota in the 1990s when its managers' push to offer customers many different choices of specifications for a particular model of car increased costs faster than it generated additional sales. At one point, Toyota factories were producing literally thousands of variations of Toyota's basic models, such as the Camry and Corolla! Toyota's managers decided that the costs of extreme customer responsiveness exceeded the benefits, and they reduced the number of models and specifications of its cars.[9] This is why today most models of Toyota vehicles listed in Figure 9.2 are assembled to three main levels of specifications—basic, sports, or luxury packages. Customers have less choice, but they also pay a lower price and still get more of the attributes they desire.

Customer Relationship Management

customer relationship management (CRM)
A technique that uses IT to develop an ongoing relationship with customers to maximize the value an organization can deliver to them over time.

One functional strategy managers can use to get close to customers and understand their needs is **customer relationship management (CRM)**. CRM is a technique that uses IT to develop an ongoing relationship with customers to maximize the value an organization can deliver to them over time. In the 2000s, most large companies have installed sophisticated CRM IT to track customers' changing demands for a company's products; it has become a vital tool used to maximize responsiveness to customers. CRM IT monitors, controls, and links each of the functional activities involved in marketing, selling, and delivering products to customers, such as monitoring the delivery of products through the distribution channel, monitoring salespeople's selling activities, setting product pricing, and coordinating after-sales service. CRM systems have three interconnected components, sales and selling, after-sales service and support, and marketing.

Suppose that a sales manager has access only to sales data that show the total sales revenue each salesperson had generated in the last 30 days. This information does not break down how much revenue came from sales to existing customers versus sales to new customers. What important knowledge is being lost? First, if most revenues are earned from sales to existing customers, this suggests that the money being spent by a company to advertise and promote its products is not attracting new customers and so is being wasted. Second, important dimensions involved in sales are pricing, financing, and order processing. In many companies, to close a deal, a salesperson has to send the paperwork to a central sales office that handles matters such as approving the customer for special financing and determining specific shipping and delivery dates. In some companies, different departments handle these activities, and it can take a long time to get a response from them; this keeps customers waiting—something that often leads to lost sales. Until CRM systems were introduced, these kinds of problems were widespread and resulted in missed sales and higher operating costs. Today the sales and selling CRM software contains *best sales practices* that analyze this information and then recommend ways to improve the way the sales process operates. One company that has improved its sales, and after-sales, practices by implementing CRM is discussed in the following "Information Technology Byte."

Information Technology Byte

How CRM Helped Empire HealthChoice

Empire HealthChoice Inc., the largest health insurance provider in New York, sells its policies through 1,800 sales agents. For years, these agents were responsible for collecting all of the customer-specific information needed to determine the price of each policy. Once they had collected the necessary information, the agents called Empire to get their price quotes. After waiting days to get these quotes, the agents relayed them back to customers, who often then modified their requests to reduce the cost of their policies. When this occurred, the agent had to telephone Empire again to get a revised price quote. Because this frequently happened several times with each transaction, it often took more than 20 days to close a sale and another 10 days for customers to get their insurance cards.[10]

Recognizing these delays were resulting in lost sales, Empire decided to examine how a CRM system could help improve the sales process. Its managers chose a Web-based system so that agents themselves could calculate the insurance quotes online. Once an agent has entered a customer's data, a quote is generated in just a few seconds. The agent can continually modify a policy while sitting face-to-face with the customer until the policy and price are agreed upon. As a result, the sales process can now be completed in a few hours, and customers receive their insurance cards in 2 to 3 days rather than 10.[11]

When a company implements after-sales service and support CRM software, salespeople are required to input detailed information about their follow-up visits to customers. Because the system is now tracking and documenting every customer's case history, salespeople have instant access to a record of everything that occurred during previous phone calls or visits. They are now in a much better position to be responsive to customers' needs and build customer loyalty, so a company's after-sales service improves. Telephone providers like Sprint and MCI, for example, require that telephone sales reps collect information about all customers' inquiries, complaints, and requests, and this is recorded electronically in customer logs. The CRM module can analyze the information in these logs to evaluate whether the customer service reps are meeting or exceeding the company's required service standards.

The CRM system also identifies the top 10 reasons why customer complaints are arising. Sales managers can then work to eliminate the sources of these problems and improve after-sales support procedures. The CRM system also identifies the top 10 best service and support practices, which can then be taught to all sales reps.

Finally, as a CRM system processes information about changing customer needs, this improves the way marketing operates in many ways. Marketing managers, for example, now have access to detailed customer profiles, including data on purchases and the reasons why individuals were or were not attracted to a company's products. Armed with this knowledge, marketing can better identify customers and the specific product attributes they desire. It may become clear, for example, that a customer group that marketing had targeted has a specific need that is not being satisfied by a product—such as a need for a cell phone containing a 5-megapixel digital camera and an MP3 player. With real-time information, marketing can work with product development to redesign the product to better meet customer needs. In sum, a CRM system is a comprehensive method of gathering crucial information about the way customers respond to a company's products. It is a powerful functional strategy used to better align a company's products with customer needs.

Improving Quality

As noted earlier, high-quality products possess attributes such as superior design, features, reliability, and after-sales support; these products are designed to better meet customer requirements.[12] Quality is a concept that can be applied to the products of both manufacturing and service organizations—goods such as a Toyota car or services such as Southwest Airlines flight service or customer service in a Citibank branch. Why do managers seek to control and improve the quality of their organizations' products?[13] There are two reasons (see Figure 9.4).

First, customers usually prefer a higher-quality product to a lower-quality product. So an organization able to provide, *for the same price*, a product of higher quality than a competitor's product is serving its customers better—it is being more responsive to its customers. Often, providing high-quality products creates a brand-name reputation for an organization's products. In turn, this enhanced reputation may allow the organization to charge more for its products than its competitors are able to charge, and thus it makes even greater profits. In 2005 Lexus was ranked number one, as it has been for the last decade, on the J. D. Power list of the 10 most reliable carmakers, and Toyota was close behind.[14]

Figure 9.4

The Impact of Increased Quality on Organizational Performance

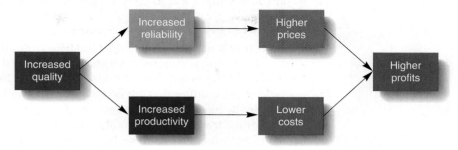

The high quality of Toyota/Lexus vehicles enables the company to charge higher prices for its cars than the prices charged by rival carmakers.

The second reason for trying to boost product quality is that higher product quality can increase efficiency and thereby lower operating costs and boost profits. Achieving high product quality lowers operating costs because of the effect of quality on employee productivity: Higher product quality means less employee time is wasted in making defective products that must be discarded or in providing substandard services, and thus less time has to be spent fixing mistakes. This translates into higher employee productivity, which means lower costs.

Total Quality Management

total quality management (TQM)
A management technique that focuses on improving the quality of an organization's products and services.

At the forefront of the drive to improve product quality is a functional strategy known as total quality management.[15] **Total quality management (TQM)** focuses on improving the quality of an organization's products and stresses that *all* of an organization's value-chain activities should be directed toward this goal. TQM requires the cooperation of managers in every function of an organization, and across functions, if it is to succeed.[16] The following 10 steps are necessary for managers to implement a successful TQM program:

1. *Build organizational commitment to quality.* TQM will do little to improve the performance of an organization unless all employees embrace it, and this often requires a change in an organization's culture.[17] At Citibank, discussed in detail in the next "Management Insight," the process of changing culture began at the top. First, a group of top managers, including the CEO, received training in TQM from consultants from Motorola. Each member of the top-management group was then given the responsibility of training a group at the next level in the hierarchy, and so on down through the organization until all 100,000 employees had received basic TQM training.

2. *Focus on the customer.* TQM practitioners see a focus on the customer as the starting point.[18] According to TQM philosophy, the customer, not managers in quality control or engineering, defines what quality is. The challenge is fourfold: (1) to identify what customers want from the good or service that the company provides; (2) to identify what the company actually provides to customers; (3) to identify the gap that exists between what customers want and what they actually get (the quality gap); and (4) to formulate a plan for closing the quality gap. The efforts of Citibank managers to increase responsiveness to customers illustrate this aspect of TQM well.

Management
Insight

Citibank Uses TQM to Increase Customer Loyalty

Citibank is one of the leading global financial institutions and has established a goal of becoming the premier institution in the 21st century. To achieve this lofty goal, Citibank has started to use TQM to increase its responsiveness to customers, recognizing that, ultimately, its customer base and customer loyalty determine the bank's future success.

As the first step in its TQM effort, Citibank identified the factors that dissatisfy its customers. When analyzing the complaints, it found that most concerned the time it took to complete a customer's request, such as responding to an account problem or getting a loan. So Citibank's managers began to examine how they handled each kind of customer request. For each distinct request, they formed a cross-functional team that broke down the request into the steps required, between people and departments, to complete the response. In analyzing the steps, teams found that many of them were often unnecessary and could be replaced by using the right information systems. They also found that very often delays occurred because employees simply did not know how to handle a request. They were not being given the right kind of training, and when they couldn't handle a request, they simply put it aside until a supervisor could deal with it.

By spending time training employees on how to handle specific requests, Citibank managers significantly improved their customer service record.

Citibank's second step to increase its responsiveness was to implement an organizationwide TQM program. Managers and supervisors were charged with reducing the complexity of the work process and finding the most effective way to process each particular request, such as a request for a loan. Managers were also charged with training employees to answer each specific request. The results were remarkable. For example, in the loan department the TQM program reduced the number of handoffs necessary to process a request by 75%. The department's average response time dropped from several hours to 30 minutes. By 2000, more than 92,000 employees worldwide had been trained in the new TQM processes, and Citibank could easily measure TQM's effectiveness by the increased speed with which it was handling an increased volume of customer requests.

3. *Find ways to measure quality.* Another crucial element of TQM is the development of a measuring system that managers can use to evaluate quality. Devising appropriate measures is relatively easy in manufacturing companies, where quality can be measured by criteria such as defects per million parts. It is more difficult in service companies, where outputs are less tangible. However, with a little creativity, suitable quality measures can be devised as they were by managers at Citibank. Similarly, at L.L.Bean, the mail-order retailer, managers use the percentage of orders that are correctly filled as one of their quality measures.

4. *Set goals and create incentives.* Once a measure has been devised, managers' next step is to set a challenging quality goal and to create incentives for reaching that goal. At Citibank, the CEO set an initial goal of reducing customer complaints by 50%. One way of creating incentives to attain a goal is to link rewards, such as bonus pay and promotional opportunities, to the goal.

5. *Solicit input from employees.* Employees are a major source of information about the causes of poor quality, so it is important that managers establish a system for soliciting employee suggestions about improvements that can be made. Quality circles—groups of employees who meet regularly to discuss ways to increase quality—are often created to achieve this goal. Companies also create self-managed teams to further quality improvement efforts.

6. *Identify defects and trace them to their source.* A major source of product defects is the production system; a major source of service defects is poor customer service procedures. TQM preaches the need for managers to identify defects in the work process, trace those defects back to their source, find out why they occurred, and make corrections so that they do not occur again. Today, IT makes the measurement of quality much easier.

7. *Introduce just-in-time inventory systems.* Inventory is the stock of raw materials, inputs, and component parts that an organization has on hand at a particular time. When the materials management function designs a just-in-time (JIT) inventory system, parts or supplies arrive at the organization when they are needed, not before. Also, under a JIT inventory system, defective parts enter an organization's operating system immediately; they are not warehoused for months before use. This means that defective inputs can be quickly spotted. JIT is discussed more later in the chapter.

8. *Work closely with suppliers.* A major cause of poor-quality finished goods is poor-quality component parts. To decrease product defects, materials managers must work closely with suppliers to improve the quality of the parts they supply. Managers at Xerox worked closely with suppliers to get them to adopt TQM programs, and the result was a huge reduction in the defect rate of component parts. Managers also need to work closely with suppliers to get them to adopt a JIT inventory system, also required for high quality.

9. *Design for ease of production.* The more steps required to assemble a product or provide a service, the more opportunities there are for making a mistake. It follows that designing products that have fewer parts or finding ways to simplify providing a service should be linked to fewer defects or customer complaints. For example, Dell continually redesigns the way it assembles its computers to reduce the number of assembly steps required and it constantly searches for new ways to reduce the number of components that have to be linked together. The consequence of these redesign efforts has been a fall in assembly costs and marked improvement in product quality that has led to Dell's becoming the number-one global PC maker.

quality circles Groups of employees who meet regularly to discuss ways to increase quality.

inventory The stock of raw materials, inputs, and component parts that an organization has on hand at a particular time.

just-in-time (JIT) inventory system A system in which parts or supplies arrive at an organization when they are needed, not before.

10. *Break down barriers between functions.* Successful implementation of TQM requires substantial cooperation between the different value-chain functions. Materials managers have to cooperate with manufacturing managers to find high-quality inputs that reduce manufacturing costs; marketing managers have to cooperate with manufacturing so that customer problems identified by marketing can be acted on; information systems have to cooperate with all of the other functions of the company to devise suitable IT training programs; and so on.

In essence, to increase quality, all functional managers need to cooperate to develop goals and spell out exactly how they will be achieved. Managers should embrace the philosophy that mistakes, defects, and poor-quality materials are not acceptable and should be eliminated. Functional managers should spend more time working with employees and providing them with the tools they need to do the job. Managers should create an environment in which employees will not be afraid to report problems or recommend improvements. Output goals and targets need to include not only numbers or quotas but also some indicators of quality to promote the production of defect-free output. Functional managers also need to train employees in new skills to keep pace with changes in the workplace. Finally, achieving better quality requires that managers develop organizational values and norms centered on improving quality.

Improving Efficiency

The third goal of value-chain management is to increase the efficiency of the various functional activities. The fewer the input resources required to produce a given volume of output, the higher will be the efficiency of the operating system. So efficiency is a useful measure of how well an organization utilizes all of its resources—such as labor, capital, materials, or energy—to produce its outputs, or goods and services. Developing functional strategies to improve efficiency is an extremely important issue for managers because increased efficiency lowers production costs, which allows an organization to make a greater profit or to attract more customers by lowering its price. Several important functional strategies are discussed below.

Facilities Layout, Flexible Manufacturing, and Efficiency

The strategies managers use to lay out or design an organization's physical work facilities also determine its efficiency. First, the way in which machines and workers are organized or grouped together into workstations affects the efficiency of the operating system. Second, a major determinant of efficiency is the cost associated with setting up the equipment needed to make a particular product. **Facilities layout** is the strategy of designing the machine-worker interface to increase operating system efficiency. **Flexible manufacturing** is a strategy based on the use of IT to reduce the costs associated with the product assembly

facilities layout The strategy of designing the machine-worker interface to increase operating system efficiency.

flexible manufacturing The set of techniques that attempt to reduce the costs associated with the product assembly process or the way services are delivered to customers.

process or the way services are delivered to customers. For example, this might be the way computers are made on a production line or the way patients are routed through a hospital.

FACILITIES LAYOUT   The way in which machines, robots, and people are grouped together affects how productive they can be. Figure 9.5 shows three basic ways of arranging workstations: product layout, process layout, and fixed-position layout.

In a *product layout,* machines are organized so that each operation needed to manufacture a product or process a patient is performed at workstations arranged in a fixed sequence. In manufacturing, workers are stationary in this arrangement, and a moving conveyor belt takes the product being worked on to the next workstation so that it is progressively assembled. Mass production is the familiar name for this layout; car assembly lines are probably the best-known example. It used to be that product layout was efficient only when products were created in large quantities; however, the introduction of modular assembly lines controlled by computers is making it efficient to make products in small batches.

In a *process layout,* workstations are not organized in a fixed sequence. Rather, each workstation is relatively self-contained, and a product goes to whichever workstation is needed to perform the next operation to complete the product. Process layout is often suited to manufacturing settings that produce a variety of custom-made products, each tailored to the needs of a different kind of customer. For example, a custom furniture manufacturer might use a process layout so that different teams of workers can produce different styles of chairs or tables made from different kinds of woods and finishes. Such a layout also describes

Figure 9.5
Three Facilities Layouts

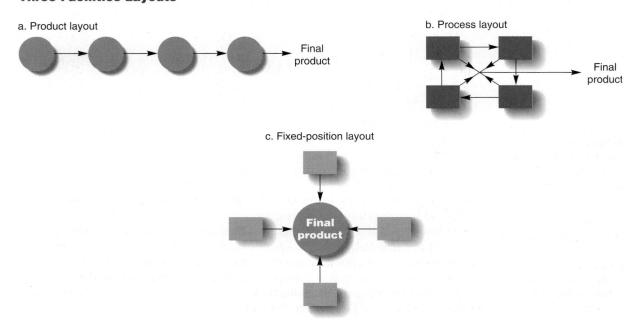

a. Product layout

Final product

b. Process layout

Final product

c. Fixed-position layout

Final product

how a patient might go through a hospital from emergency room, to X-ray room, to operating theater, and so on. A process layout provides the flexibility needed to change a product, whether it is a PC or a patient. Such flexibility, however, often reduces efficiency because it is expensive.

In a *fixed-position layout,* the product stays in a fixed position. Its component parts are produced in remote workstations and brought to the production area for final assembly. Increasingly, self-managed teams are using fixed-position layouts. Different teams assemble each component part and then send the parts to the final assembly team, which makes the final product. A fixed-position layout is commonly used for products such as jet airlines, mainframe computers, and gas turbines—products that are complex and difficult to assemble or so large that moving them from one workstation to another would be difficult. The effects of moving from one facilities layout to another can be dramatic, as the following "Manager as a Person" suggests.

Manager as a Person

Paddy Hopkirk Improves Facilities Layout

Paddy Hopkirk established his car accessories business in Bedfordshire, England, shortly after he had shot to car-racing fame by winning the Monte Carlo Rally. Sales of Hopkirk's accessories, such as bicycle racks and axle stands, were always brisk, but Hopkirk was the first to admit that his operating system left a lot to be desired, so he invited consultants to help reorganize the system.

After analyzing his factory's operating system, the consultants realized that the source of the problem was the facilities layout Hopkirk had established. Over time, as sales grew, Hopkirk simply added new workstations to the operating system as they were needed. The result was a process layout in which the product being assembled moved in the irregular sequences shown in the "Before Change" half of Figure 9.6. The consultants suggested that to save time and effort, the workstations should be reorganized into the sequential product layout shown in the "After Change" illustration.

Once this change was made, the results were dramatic. One morning the factory was an untidy sprawl of workstations surrounded by piles of crates holding semifinished components. Two days later, when the 170-person workforce came back to work, the machines had been brought together into tightly grouped workstations arranged in the fixed sequence shown in the illustration. The piles of components had disappeared, and the newly cleared floor space was neatly marked with color-coded lines mapping out the new flow of materials between workstations.

In the first full day of production, efficiency increased by as much as 30%. The space needed for some operations had been cut in half, and work in progress had been cut considerably. Moreover, the improved layout allowed some jobs to be combined, freeing operators for deployment elsewhere in the factory. An amazed Hopkirk exclaimed, "I was expecting a change but nothing as dramatic as this . . . it is fantastic."[19]

Figure 9.6

Changing a Facilities Layout

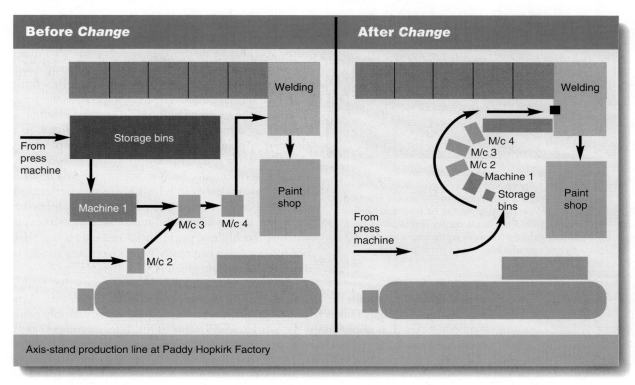

Axis-stand production line at Paddy Hopkirk Factory

Source: "The Application of Kaizen to Facilities Layout," *Financial Times* of January 4, 1994, p. 12. Reprinted by permission of Financial Times Syndication, London.

FLEXIBLE MANUFACTURING In a manufacturing company, a major source of costs is the costs associated with setting up the equipment needed to make a particular product. One of these is the cost of production that is forgone because nothing is produced while the equipment is being set up. For example, components manufacturers often need as much as half a day to set up automated production equipment when switching from production of one component part (such as a washer ring for the steering column of a car) to another (such as a washer ring for the steering column of a truck). During this half-day, a manufacturing plant is not producing anything, but employees are paid for this "nonproductive" time.

It follows that if setup times for complex production equipment can be reduced, so can setup costs, and efficiency will rise, that is, the time that plant and employees spend in actually producing something will increase. This simple insight has been the driving force behind the development of flexible manufacturing techniques.

Flexible manufacturing aims to reduce the time required to set up production equipment.[20] By redesigning the manufacturing process so that production equipment geared for manufacturing one product can be quickly replaced with equipment geared to make another product, setup times and costs can be reduced dramatically. Another favorable outcome from flexible manufacturing is that a company is able to produce many more varieties of a product than before in the

Housing units move on the production line as employees of Toyota Motor Corporation work during the installation process at the company's Kasugai Housing Works, one of the plants of Toyota home-brand houses on Kasugai, Aichi Prefecture, Japan. Toyota entered the housing industry 30 years ago where it applies the plant technology and experience it gained through producing cars.

same amount of time. Thus flexible manufacturing increases a company's ability to be responsive to its customers.

Increasingly, organizations are experimenting with new designs for operating systems that not only allow workers to be more productive but also make the work process more flexible, thus reducing setup costs. Some Japanese companies are experimenting with facilities layouts arranged as a spiral, as the letter *Y,* and as the number 6, to see how these configurations affect setup costs and worker productivity. At a camcorder plant in Kohda, Japan, for example, Sony changed from a fixed-position layout in which 50 workers sequentially built a camcorder to a flexible spiral process design in which 4 workers perform all the operations necessary to produce the camcorder. This new layout allows the most efficient workers to work at the highest pace, and it reduces setup costs because workers can easily switch from one model to another, increasing efficiency by 10%.[21]

An interesting example of a company that built a new factory to obtain the benefits from flexible manufacturing is German company Igus Inc. Igus makes over 28,000 polymer bearings and energy supply cable products used in applications the world over. In the 1990s, Igus's managers realized they needed to build a new factory that could handle the company's rapidly growing product line. The product line was changing constantly as new products were innovated and old ones became obsolete. At Igus new products are often introduced on a daily basis, so this need for flexibility is the company's prime requirement. Moreover, because many of its products are highly customized, the specific and changing needs of its customers drive new product development.

Igus's new factory was designed with the need for flexibility in mind. As big as three football fields, nothing in the factory is tied down or bolted to the floor. All the machines, computers, and equipment can be moved and repositioned to suit changing product requirements. Moreover, all Igus employees are trained to be flexible and can perform many of the production tasks necessary. For example, when one new product line proved popular with customers, its employees and production operations were relocated four times as it grew into larger spaces. Igus can change its operating system at a moment's notice and with minimal disruption, and since the company operates seven days a week, 24 hours a day, these changes are occurring constantly.

To facilitate these changes, workers are equipped with power scooters to move around the plant quickly and reconfigure operations. This also allows them to move quickly to wherever in the factory their skills are most needed. Employees are also equipped with mobile phones so that they are always on call. Igus's decision to create a flexible factory of the future has paid off. In the last decade its global sales have tripled.

Just-in-Time Inventory and Efficiency

As noted earlier, a just-in-time inventory system gets components to the assembly line just as they are needed and thus drives down costs. Using a JIT inventory system, component parts travel from suppliers to the assembly line in a small-wheeled container known as a *kanban*. Assembly-line workers empty the kanbans and then the empty container is sent back to the supplier as the signal to produce another small batch of component parts, and so the process repeats itself. This system can be contrasted with a just-in-case view of inventory, which leads an organization to stockpile excess inputs in a warehouse just in case it needs them to meet sudden upturns in demand.

JIT inventory systems have major implications for efficiency. Major cost savings can result from increasing inventory turnover and reducing inventory holding costs, such as warehousing and storage costs and the cost of capital tied up in inventory. Although companies that manufacture and assemble products can obviously use JIT to great advantage, so can service organizations.[22] Wal-Mart, the biggest retailer in the United States, uses JIT systems to replenish the stock in its stores at least twice a week. Many Wal-Mart stores receive daily deliveries. Wal-Mart's main competitors, Kmart and Sears, typically replenish their stock every two weeks. Wal-Mart can maintain the same service levels as these competitors but at one-fourth the inventory holding cost, a major source of cost saving. Faster inventory turnover has helped Wal-Mart achieve an efficiency-based competitive advantage in the retailing industry.[23] Even a small company can benefit from a kanban, as the experience of United Electric suggests in the following "Management Insight."

Management
Insight

United Electric's Kanban System

United Electric Controls, headquartered in Watertown, Massachusetts, is the market leader in the application of threshold detection and switching technology. At one time, the company simply warehoused its inputs and dispensed them as needed. Then it decided to reduce costs by storing these inputs at their point of use in the production system. However, this also caused problems because inventories of some inputs actually started to increase while other inputs were used up without anyone knowing which input caused a stoppage in production.

So managers decided to experiment with a supplier kanban system even though United Electric had fewer than 40 suppliers and they were totally up to date with its input requirements. Managers decided to store a three-week supply of parts in a central storeroom, a supply large enough to avoid unexpected shortages.[24] They began by asking their casting supplier to deliver inputs in kanbans and bins. Once a week, this supplier checks up on the bins to determine how much stock needs to be delivered the following week. Other suppliers were then asked to participate in this system, and now more than 35 of its major suppliers operate some form of the kanban system.

By all measures of performance, the results of using the kanban system have been successful. Inventory holding costs have fallen sharply. Products are delivered to all customers on time. And even new products' design-to-production cycles have dropped by 50% because suppliers are now involved much earlier in the design process so that they can supply new inputs as needed.

Self-Managed Work Teams and Efficiency

Another functional strategy to increase efficiency is the use of self-managed work teams.[25] The typical team consists of 5 to 15 employees who produce an entire product instead of just parts of it.[26] Team members learn all team tasks and move from job to job. The result is a flexible workforce, because team members can fill in for absent coworkers. The members of each team also assume responsibility for scheduling work and vacations, ordering materials, and hiring new members–previously all responsibilities of first-line managers. Because people often respond well to being given greater autonomy and responsibility, the use of empowered self-managed teams can increase productivity and efficiency. Moreover, cost savings arise from eliminating supervisors and creating a flatter organizational hierarchy, which further increases efficiency.

The effect of introducing self-managed teams is often an increase in efficiency of 30% or more, sometimes much more. After the introduction of flexible manufacturing technology and self-managed teams, a GE plant in Salisbury, North Carolina, increased efficiency by 250% compared with other GE plants producing the same products.[27]

Process Reengineering and Efficiency

process reengineering The fundamental rethinking and radical redesign of business processes to achieve dramatic improvement in critical measures of performance such as cost, quality, service, and speed.

The value chain is a collection of functional activities or business processes that take one or more kinds of inputs and transform them to create an output that is of value to the customer.[28] **Process reengineering** involves the fundamental rethinking and radical redesign of business processes (and thus the *value chain*) to achieve dramatic improvements in critical measures of performance such as cost, quality, service, and speed.[29] Order fulfillment, for example, can be thought of as a business process: When a customer's order is received (the input), many different functional tasks must be performed as necessary to process the order, and then the ordered goods are delivered to the customer (the output). Process reengineering boosts efficiency when it reduces the number of order-fulfillment tasks that must be performed, or reduces the time they take, and so reduces operating costs.

For an example of process reengineering in practice, consider how Ford used it. One day a manager from Ford was working at its Japanese partner Mazda and discovered quite by accident that Mazda had only five people in its accounts payable department. The Ford manager was shocked, since Ford's U.S. operation had 500 employees in accounts payable. He reported his discovery to Ford's U.S. managers, who decided to form a task force to figure out why the difference existed.

Ford managers discovered that procurement began when the purchasing department sent a purchase order to a supplier and sent a copy of the purchase order to Ford's accounts payable department. When the supplier shipped the goods and they arrived at Ford, a clerk at the receiving dock completed a form describing the goods and sent the form to accounts payable. The supplier, meanwhile, sent accounts payable an invoice. Thus, accounts payable received three documents relating to these goods: a copy of the original purchase order, the receiving document, and the invoice. If the information in all three was in agreement (most of the time it was), a clerk in accounts payable issued payment. Occasionally, however, all three documents did not agree. And Ford discovered that accounts payable clerks spent most of their time straightening out the 1% of instances in which the purchase order, receiving document, and invoice contained conflicting information.[30]

Ford managers decided to reengineer the procurement process to simplify it. Now when a buyer in the purchasing department issues a purchase order to a supplier, that buyer also enters the order into an online database. As before, suppliers send goods to the receiving dock. When the goods arrive, the clerk at the receiving dock checks a computer terminal to see whether the received shipment matches the description on the purchase order. If it does, the clerk accepts the goods and pushes a button on the terminal keyboard that tells the database the goods have arrived. Receipt of the goods is recorded in the database, and a computer automatically issues and sends a check to the supplier. If the goods do not correspond to the description on the purchase order in the database, the clerk at the dock refuses the shipment and sends it back to the supplier.

Payment authorization, which used to be performed by accounts payable, is now accomplished at the receiving dock. The new process has come close to eliminating the need for an accounts payable department. In some parts of Ford, the size of the accounts payable department has been cut by 95%. By reducing the head count in accounts payable, the reengineering effort reduced the amount of time wasted on unproductive activities, thereby increasing the efficiency of the total organization.

Information Systems, the Internet, and Efficiency

With the rapid spread of computers, the explosive growth of the Internet and corporate intranets, and high-speed digital Internet technology, the information systems function is moving to center stage in the quest for operating efficiencies and a lower cost structure. The impact of information systems on productivity is wide-ranging and potentially affects all other activities of a company. For example, Cisco Systems has been able to realize significant cost savings by moving its ordering and customer service functions online. The company has just 300 service agents handling all of its customer accounts, compared to the 900 it would need if sales were not handled online. The difference represents an annual saving of $20 million a year. Moreover, without automated customer service functions, Cisco calculates that it would need at least 1,000 additional service engineers, which would cost around $75 million.

Dell Computer also makes extensive use of the Internet to lower its costs; by 2004 more than 90% of Dell's PCs were sold online.[31] Dell's Web site allows customers to customize their orders to get the system that best suits their particular requirements. In this way, Dell increases its customer responsiveness. Dell has also put much of its customer service function online, reducing the need for telephone calls to customer service representatives and saving costs in the process. Each week, some 200,000 people access Dell's online troubleshooting tips. Each of these visits to Dell's Web site saves the company a potential $15, which is the average cost of a technical support call.[32] If just 10% of these online visitors were to call Dell by telephone instead, it would cost the company $15.6 million per year.

Dell, like most other large companies today, uses the Internet to manage its value chain, feeding real-time information about order flow to its suppliers, which use this information to schedule their own production, providing components to Dell on a just-in-time basis. This approach reduces the costs of coordination both between the company and its customers and between the company and its suppliers. By using Web-based programs to automate customer and supplier interactions, the number of people required to manage these interfaces can be substantially reduced, thereby reducing costs. This trend extends beyond high-tech companies. Banks and financial service companies are finding that they can substantially reduce costs by moving customer accounts and support functions online. Such a move reduces the need for customer service representatives, bank tellers, stockbrokers, insurance agents, and others. For example, it costs about $1 to execute a transaction at a bank, such as shifting money from one account to another; over the Internet the same transaction costs about $0.01.

Improving Innovation

As discussed in Chapter 6, *technology* comprises the skills, know-how, experience, body of scientific knowledge, tools, machines, computers, and equipment used in the design, production, and distribution of goods and services. Technology is involved in all functional activities, and the rapid advance of technology today is a significant factor in managers' attempts to improve the way their value chains innovate new kinds of goods and services or ways to provide them.

Two Kinds of Innovation

Two principal kinds of innovation can be identified based on the nature of the technological change that brings them about. **Quantum product innovation** results in the development of new, often radically different, kinds of goods and services because of fundamental shifts in technology brought about by pioneering discoveries. Examples are the creation of the Internet and the World Wide Web, which have revolutionized the computer industry, and biotechnology, which has transformed the treatment of illness by creating new, genetically engineered medicines. McDonald's development t of the principles behind the provision of fast food also qualifies as a quantum product innovation.

Incremental product innovation results in gradual improvements and refinements to existing products over time as existing technologies are perfected and functional managers, like those at Toyota, learn how to perform value-chain activities in better ways—ways that add more value to products. For example, Google's staffers have made thousands of incremental improvements to the company's search engine itself since its debut, changes that have enhanced the engine's search capabilities, given the engine the ability to work on all kinds of mobile devices, and made it available to users who search in their native tongues.

quantum product innovation The development of new, often radically different, kinds of goods and services because of fundamental shifts in technology brought about by pioneering discoveries.

incremental product innovation The gradual improvement and refinement to existing products that occurs over time as existing technologies are perfected.

Quantum product innovations are relatively rare; most managers' activities are focused on incremental product innovations that result from ongoing technological advances. For example, every time Dell or HP puts a new, faster Intel or AMD chip into a PC, or Google improves its search engine's capability, the company is making incremental product innovations. Similarly, every time auto engineers redesign a car model, and every time McDonald's managers work to improve the flavor and texture of burgers, fries, and salads, their product development efforts are intended to lead to incremental product innovations. Incremental innovation is frequently as important as or more important than quantum innovation. Indeed, as discussed below, it is often managers' ability to successfully manage incremental product development that results in success or failure in an industry.

In the 1950s, McDonald's revolutionized the restaurant business with its fast food principles.

The need to speed innovation and quickly develop new and improved products becomes especially important when the technology behind the product is advancing rapidly. This is because the first companies in an industry to adopt the new technology will be able to develop products that better meet customer needs and gain a "first-mover" advantage over their rivals. Indeed, managers who do not quickly adopt and apply new technologies to innovate products may soon find they have no customers for their products—and destroy their organizations.

Increasingly, to become more responsive to existing customers and attract new customers, managers are trying to outdo each other by being the first to market with a product that incorporates a new technology or that plays to a new fashion trend. In the car industry, for example, a particular car model used to be kept in production for five years, but today this has dropped to three years as car companies compete to attract new and existing customers to buy their newest models. In sum, the greater the rate of technological change in an industry, the more important it is for managers to innovate.

Strategies to Promote Innovation and Speed Product Development

product development
The management of the value-chain activities involved in bringing new or improved goods and services to the market.

There are several ways in which managers can promote innovation and encourage the development of new products. **Product development** is the management of the value-chain activities involved in bringing new or improved goods and services to the market. The steps that Monte Peterson, former CEO of Thermos, took to develop a new barbecue grill show how good product development should proceed. Peterson had no doubt about how to increase Thermos's sales of barbecue grills: motivate Thermos's functional managers to create new and improved models. So Peterson assembled a cross-functional product development team of six functional managers (from marketing, engineering, manufacturing, sales, and finance) and told them to develop a new barbecue grill within 18 months. To ensure that they were not spread too thin, he assigned them to this team only. Peterson also arranged for leadership of the team to rotate. Initially, to focus on what customers wanted, the marketing manager would take the lead; then, when technical developments became the main consideration, leadership would switch to engineering; and so on.

Team members christened the group the "Lifestyle team." To find out what people really wanted in a grill, the marketing manager and nine subordinates spent a month on the road visiting customers. What they found surprised them. The stereotype of Dad slaving over a smoky barbecue grill was wrong: more women were barbecuing. Many cooks were tired of messy charcoal, and many homeowners did not like rusty grills that spoiled the appearance of their decks. Moreover, environmental and safety issues were increasing in importance. In California charcoal starter fluid is considered a pollutant and is banned; in New Jersey the use of charcoal and gas grills on the balconies of condos and apartments has been prohibited to avoid fires. Based on these findings, the team decided that Thermos had to produce a barbecue grill that not only made the food taste good but also looked attractive, used no pollutants, and was safe for balcony use (which meant it had to be electric).

Within one year the basic attributes of the product were defined, and leadership of the team moved to engineering. The critical task for engineering was to design a grill that gave food the cookout taste that conventional electric grills could not provide because they did not get hot enough. To raise the cooking temperature, Thermos's engineers designed a domed vacuum top that trapped heat inside the grill, and they built electric heat rods directly into the surface of the grill. These features made the grill hot enough to sear meat and give it brown barbecue lines and a barbecue taste.

Manufacturing had been active from the early days of the development process, making sure that any proposed design could be produced economically. Because manufacturing was involved from the beginning, the team avoided some costly mistakes. At one critical team meeting the engineers said they wanted tapered legs on the grill. Manufacturing explained that tapered legs would have to be custom-made—and would raise manufacturing costs—and persuaded the team to go with straight legs.

When the new grill was introduced on schedule, it was an immediate success. The study of many product development successes, such as that of Thermos's Lifestyle team, suggests three strategies managers can implement to increase the likelihood that their product development efforts will result in innovative, and successful, new products.

INVOLVE BOTH CUSTOMERS AND SUPPLIERS Many new products fail when they reach the marketplace because they were designed with scant attention to customer needs. Successful product development requires inputs from more than just an organization's members; also needed are inputs from customers and suppliers. At Thermos, team members spent a month on the road visiting customers to identify their needs. The revolutionary electric barbecue grill was a direct result of this process. In other cases, companies have found it worthwhile to include customer representatives as peripheral members of their product development team. Boeing, for example, has included customers, the major airlines, in the design of its most recent commercial jet aircraft, the 777 and the new Dreamliner. Boeing builds a mockup of the aircraft's cabin and then, over a period of months, allows each airline's representatives to experiment with repositioning the galleys, seating, aisles, and bathrooms to best meet the needs of their particular airline. Boeing has learned a great deal from this process.

ESTABLISH A STAGE-GATE DEVELOPMENT FUNNEL

One of the most common mistakes that managers make in product development is trying to fund too many new projects at any one time. This approach spreads the activities of the different value-chain functions too thinly over too many different projects. As a consequence, no single project is given the functional resources and attention that are required to make it succeed.

One strategy for solving this problem is for managers to develop a structured process for evaluating product development proposals and deciding which to support and which to reject. A common solution is to establish a **stage-gate development funnel,** a technique that forces managers to make choices among competing projects so that functional resources are not spread thinly over too many projects. The funnel gives functional managers control over product development and allows them to intervene and take corrective action quickly and appropriately (see Figure 9.7).

At stage 1, the development funnel has a wide mouth, so top managers initially can encourage employees to come up with as many new product ideas as possible. Managers can create incentives for employees to come up with ideas. Many organizations run "bright-idea programs" that reward employees whose ideas eventually make it through the development process. Other organizations allow research scientists to devote a certain amount of work time to their own projects. Top managers at 3M, for example, have a 15% rule: They expect a research scientist to spend 15% of the workweek working on a project of his or her own choosing. Ideas may be submitted by individuals or by groups. Brainstorming (see Chapter 7) is a technique that managers frequently use to encourage new ideas.

stage-gate development funnel
A planning model that forces managers to make choices among competing projects so that organizational resources are not spread thinly over too many projects.

Figure 9.7
A Stage-Gate Development Funnel

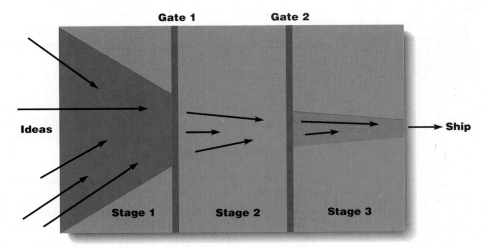

New product ideas are written up as brief proposals. The proposals are submitted to a cross-functional team of managers, who evaluate each proposal at gate 1. The cross-functional team considers a proposal's fit with the organization's strategy and its technical feasibility. Proposals that are consistent with the strategy of the organization and are judged technically feasible pass through gate 1 and into stage 2. Other proposals are turned down (although the door is often left open for reconsidering a proposal at a later date).

product development plan A plan that specifies all of the relevant information that managers need in order to decide whether to proceed with a full-blown product development effort.

The primary goal in stage 2 is to draft a detailed product development plan. The **product development plan** specifies all of the relevant information that managers need to make a decision about whether to go ahead with a full-blown product development effort. The product development plan should include strategic and financial objectives, an analysis of the product's market potential, a list of desired product features, a list of technological requirements, a list of financial and human resource requirements, a detailed development budget, and a time line that contains specific milestones (for example, dates for prototype completion and final launch).

A cross-functional team of managers normally drafts this plan. Good planning requires a good strategic analysis (see Chapter 8), and team members must be prepared to spend considerable time in the field with customers, trying to understand their needs. Drafting a product development plan generally takes about three months. Once completed, the plan is reviewed by a senior management committee at gate 2 (see Figure 9.7). These managers focus on the details of the plan to see whether the proposal is attractive (given its market potential) and viable (given the technological, financial, and human resources that would be needed to develop the product). Senior managers making this review keep in mind all other product development efforts currently being undertaken by the organization. One goal at this point is to ensure that limited organizational resources are used to their maximum effect.

contract book A written agreement that details product development factors such as responsibilities, resource commitments, budgets, time lines, and development milestones.

At gate 2 projects are rejected, sent back for revision, or allowed to pass through to stage 3, the development phase. Product development starts with the formation of a cross-functional team that is given primary responsibility for developing the product. In some companies, at the beginning of stage 3 top managers and cross-functional team members sign a **contract book,** a written agreement that details factors such as responsibilities, resource commitments, budgets, time lines, and development milestones. Signing the contract book is viewed as the symbolic launch of a product development effort. The contract book is also a document against which actual development progress can be measured. At Motorola, for example, team members and top management negotiate a contract and sign a contract book at the launch of a development effort, thereby signaling their commitment to the objectives contained in the contract.

The stage 3 development effort can last anywhere from 6 months to 10 years, depending on the industry and type of product. Some electronics products have development cycles of 6 months, but it takes from 3 to 5 years to develop a new car, about 5 years to develop a new jet aircraft, and as long as 10 years to develop a new medical drug.

ESTABLISH CROSS-FUNCTIONAL TEAMS   A smooth-running cross-functional team also seems to be a critical component of successful product development, as the experience of Thermos suggests. Marketing, engineering,

Figure 9.8
Members of a Cross-Functional Product Development Team

Team
leader

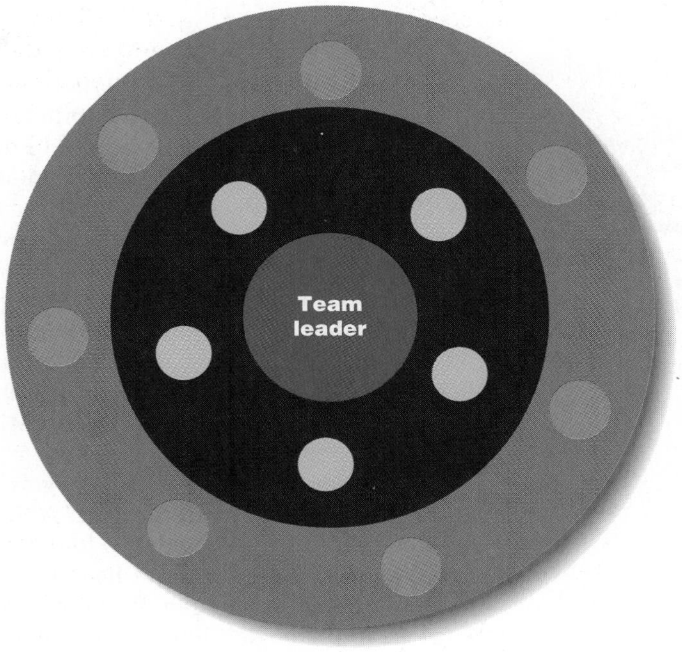

core members The
members of a team who
bear primary responsibility
for the success of a project
and who stay with a
project from inception to
completion.

and manufacturing personnel are **core members** of a successful product development team—the people who have primary responsibility for the product development effort. Other people besides core members work on the project as and when the need arises, but the core members (generally from three to six individuals) stay with the project from inception to completion of the development effort (see Figure 9.8).

The reason for using a cross-functional team is to ensure a high level of coordination and communication among managers in different functions. Input from both marketing and manufacturing members of Thermos's Lifestyle team determined the characteristics of the barbecue that the engineers on the team ended up designing.

If a cross-functional team is to succeed, it must have the right kind of leadership and it must be managed in an effective manner. To be successful, a product development team needs a team leader who can rise above a functional background and take a cross-functional view. In addition to having effective leadership, successful cross-functional product development teams have several other key characteristics. Often, core members of successful teams are located close to one another, in the same office space, to foster a sense of shared mission and commitment to a development program. Successful teams develop a clear sense of their objectives and how they will be achieved, the purpose again being to create a sense of shared mission. The way in which Google uses many of these strategies to promote innovation is discussed in the following "Management Insight."

Management
Insight

How Google Encourages Innovation and Product Development

The history of Google, the Internet search engine company, began in 1995 when two Stanford graduate computer science students, Sergey Brin and Larry Page, decided to collaborate to develop a new kind of search engine technology. They understood the limitations of existing search engines, and by 1998 they had developed a superior engine that they felt was ready to go online. They raised $1 million from family, friends, and risk-taking "angel" investors to buy the hardware necessary to connect Google to the Internet.

At first, Google answered 10,000 inquiries a day, but in a few months it was answering 500,000. By fall 1999, it was handling 3 million; by fall 2000, 60 million; and in spring 2001, 100 million per day. In the 2000s Google has become the leading search engine; it is one of the top-five most used Internet companies, and rivals like Yahoo and Microsoft are working hard to catch up and beat Google at its own game.

Google's explosive growth is largely due to the culture of innovation its founders cultivated from the start. Although by 2004 Google had grown to 1,900 employees worldwide, its founders claim that Google still maintains a small-company feel because its culture empowers its employees, who are called staffers or "Googlers," to create the best software possible. Brin and Page created Google's innovative culture in several ways.

From the beginning, lacking space and seeking to keep operating costs low, Google staffers worked in "high-density clusters." Three or four employees, each equipped with a high-powered Linux workstation, shared a desk, couch, and chairs that were large rubber balls, working together to improve the company's technology. Even when Google moved into more spacious surroundings at its "Googleplex" head-quarters building, staffers continued to work in shared spaces. Google designed the building so that staffers are constantly meeting one another in its funky lobby; in its Google Café, where everyone eats together; in its state-of-the-art recreational facilities; and in its "snack rooms," equipped with bins packed with cereals, gummi bears, yogurt, carrots, and

From the beginning, Google employees have worked in "high-density" clusters.

make-your-own cappuccino. Google also created many social gatherings of employees, such as a TGIF open meeting and a twice-weekly outdoor roller hockey game where staffers are encouraged to bring down the founders.[33]

All this attention to creating what might be the "grooviest" company headquarters in the world did not come about by chance. Brin and Page knew that Google's most important strength would be its ability to attract the best software engineers in the world and then motivate them to perform well. Common offices, lobbies, cafés, and so on, bring staffers into close contact with one another, develop collegiality, and encourage them to share their new ideas with their colleagues and to constantly improve Google's search engine technology and find new ways to expand the company. The freedom Google gives its staffers to pursue new ideas is a clear indication of its founders' desire to empower them to be innovative and to look off the beaten path for new ideas. Finally, recognizing that staffers who innovate important new software applications should be rewarded for their achievements, Google's founders give them stock in the company, effectively making staffers its owners as well.

Their focus on innovation did not blind Brin and Page to the need to build a viable competitive strategy so that Google could compete effectively in the cutthroat search engine market. They recognized, however, that they lacked business experience; they had never had to craft strategies to compete with giants like Microsoft and Yahoo. Moreover, they also had never been responsible for building a strong set of value-chain functions. So they recruited a team of talented and experienced functional managers to help them manage their company. They also decided to give responsibility for the company's value-chain management to a new CEO, Eric Schmidt, who came from Novell, where he had been in charge of strategic planning and technology development.

Brin and Page's understanding that successful product development requires building a strong organizational architecture has paid off. In August 2004, Google went public, and its shares, which were sold at $85 a share, were worth over $100 each by the end of the first day of trading and $500 by 2006. This has made Brin and Page's stake in the company worth billions – clearly it can pay to focus on improving innovation.

Google prospers because of its founders' ability to create a culture that encourages staffers to be innovative and because of their willingness to delegate authority for product development to managers and staffers. Managing innovation is an increasingly important aspect of a manager's job in an era of dramatic changes in advanced IT. Promoting successful new product development is difficult and challenging, and some product development efforts are much more successful than others. Google is performing at a high level, while thousands of other dot-coms, including many search engine companies such as Magellan and Openfind, have gone out of business.

In sum, managers need to recognize that successful innovation and product development cuts across roles and functions and requires a high level of cooperation. They should recognize the importance of common values and norms in promoting the high levels of cooperation and cohesiveness necessary to build a culture for innovation. They also should reward successful innovators and make heroes of the employees and teams that develop successful new products. Finally, managers should fully utilize the product development techniques just discussed to guide the process.

Managing the Value Chain: Some Remaining Issues

Achieving improved quality, efficiency, and responsiveness to customers often requires a profound change in the way managers plan, lead, control, and organize a company's value-chain activities. For example, planning often involves managers at all levels, and customers are brought into the planning process. The use of self-managed teams and empowered workers changes the way managers lead and organize employees, and employees become responsible for controlling many more dimensions of their work activities.

Obtaining the information necessary to improve the value chain becomes an important and never-ending task for functional managers. It is their job to collect relevant information about the competitive environment, such as (1) the future intentions of competitors, (2) the identity of new customers for the organization's products, and (3) the identity of new suppliers of crucial or low-cost inputs. They also need to seek out new ways to use resources more efficiently to hold down costs or to get close to customers and learn what they want.

Two issues that arise from the constant need to improve a company's value chain are, first, the need to use boundary-spanning roles to obtain valuable functional information and, second, the need to consider the ethical implications of adopting advanced value-chain management techniques.

Boundary-Spanning Roles

The ability of functional managers to gain access to the information they need to improve value-chain management is critical. The history of business is littered with numerous once-great companies whose managers did not recognize, and adapt their value chains to respond to, significant changes taking place in the competitive environment. Examples include Digital Equipment, a former leading computer maker now defunct because its CEO believed that "personal computers are just toys," and Eastern Airlines and Pan-Am, which were unable to survive because of their high operating costs in a competitive airline industry. History is also marked by companies whose managers made the wrong value-chain choices because they misinterpreted the competitive environment. Examples include Motorola managers who invested more than $3 billion in the Iridium satellite project that was abandoned in 2000 and the managers of thousands of dot-coms who underestimated the costs involved with delivering online products and services reliably to customers.

boundary spanning
Interacting with individuals and groups outside the organization to obtain valuable information from the environment.

Managers can learn to perceive, interpret, and appreciate better the competitive environments by practicing **boundary spanning**—interacting with individuals and groups outside the organization to obtain valuable information from the environment.[34] Managers who engage in boundary-spanning activities seek ways not only to respond to forces in the environment but also to directly influence and manage the perceptions of suppliers and customers in that environment to increase their organizations' access to resources.

To understand how boundary spanning works, see Figure 9.9. A functional manager in a boundary-spanning role in organization X establishes a personal or virtual link with a manager in a boundary-spanning role in organization Y. The two managers communicate and share information that helps both of

Figure 9.9
The Nature of Boundary-Spanning Roles

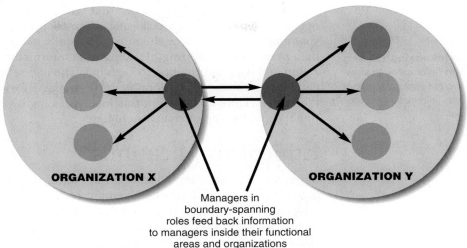

ORGANIZATION X   ORGANIZATION Y

Managers in
boundary-spanning
roles feed back information
to managers inside their functional
areas and organizations

them understand the changing forces and conditions in the environment. These managers then share this information with other functional managers in their respective organizations so that all managers become better informed about events outside their own organization's boundaries. As a result, the managers in both organizations can make value-chain decisions that lead to higher-performing operating systems.

For an example of a manager performing a boundary-spanning role, consider the situation of a purchasing manager for Taco Bell. The purchasing manager is charged with finding the lowest-cost supplier of low-fat cheese and sour cream. To perform this task, the manager could write to major food companies and ask for price quotes. Or the manager could phone food company managers personally, develop informal yet professional relationships with them, and, over time, learn from them which food companies are active in the low-fat-food area and what they envision for the future. By developing such relationships, the purchasing manager will be able to provide Taco Bell with valuable information that will allow its purchasing department to make well-informed choices. This flow of information from the environment may, in turn, allow marketing to develop more effective sales campaigns or allow product development to develop better-looking and better-tasting tacos. Note that personal communication is often necessary to supplement the information provided by IT.

What would happen if managers in all of an organization's functions performed boundary-spanning roles? The richness of the information available to managers throughout the organization probably would lead to an increase in the quality of managers' decision making and planning, enabling them to produce goods and services that customers prefer or to create advertising campaigns that attract new customers.

Searching for and collecting information to understand how changing trends and forces in the environment are affecting a company's operating system is an important boundary-spanning activity. Many organizations employ functional experts whose only job is to scan professional journals, trade association publications, and newspapers to identify changes in technology, government regulations, fashion trends, and so on, that will affect the way their organization operates. However, merely collecting information is not enough for the boundary-spanning manager. He or she must interpret what the information means and then practice **gatekeeping,** deciding what information to allow into the organization and what information to keep out. The nature of the information that the gatekeeper chooses to pass on to other managers will influence the decisions they make. Thus, accurate information processing is vital, and utilizing information technology can obviously help here.[35]

gatekeeping Deciding what information to allow into the organization and what information to keep out.

Ethical Implications

Managers also need to understand the ethical implications of the adoption of many of the value-chain management techniques discussed in this chapter. Although TQM, JIT, flexible manufacturing, and reengineering can all increase quality, efficiency, and responsiveness to customers, they may do so at great cost to employees. Employees may see the demands of their jobs increase as the result of TQM or, worse, may see themselves reengineered out of a job. For example, Toyota is the most efficient car manufacturer in the world, but some of its gains have been achieved at a significant cost to its employees, as discussed in the following "Ethics in Action."

Ethics
in Action

The Human Cost of Improving Productivity

Hisashi Tomiki is the leader of a four-man self-managed team in a Toyota production plant, 200 miles south of Tokyo, Japan. Tomiki and his team work at a grueling pace to build cowls (steel chambers onto which windshields and steering columns are attached). Consider this description of Tomiki at work:

> In two minutes Tomiki fits 24 metal pieces into designated slots on three welding machines; runs two large metal sheets through each of the machines, which weld on the parts; and fuses the two sheets together with two spot welds. There is little room for error. Once or twice an hour a mistake is made or a machine sticks, causing the next machine in line to stop. A yellow light flashes. Tomiki runs over. The squad must fix the part and work faster to catch up. A red button halts the production line if the problems are severe, but there is an unspoken rule against pushing it. Only once this day does Tomiki call in a special maintenance worker.[36]

The experience of workers like Tomiki has become increasingly common—especially in the 2000s when the threat of outsourcing has led workers to accept management demands for a faster work pace. Workers are heard to complain that constant attempts to increase quality and reduce costs really means continuous speedup and added job stress from the increase in the pressure put on employees to perform. Although some pressure is good, beyond a certain point it can seriously harm employees. Moreover, consider the following quote from Jerry Miller, a former employee of US West, whose team of billing clerks reengineered themselves out of a job:

> When we first formed our teams, the company came in talking teams and empowerment and promised that we wouldn't lose any jobs. It turns out all this was a big cover. The company had us all set up for reengineering. We showed them how to streamline the work, and now 9,000 people are gone. It was cut-your-own-throat. It makes you feel used.[37]

Is it ethical to continually increase the demands placed on employees, regardless of the human cost in terms of job stress? It is obvious that the answer is no. Employee support is vital if the organization is to function effectively. What kinds of work pressures are legitimate, and what pressures are excessive? There is no clear answer to this question. Ultimately the issue comes down to the judgment of responsible managers seeking to act ethically.

Summary and Review

VALUE-CHAIN MANAGEMENT AND COMPETITIVE ADVANTAGE To achieve high performance, managers try to improve their responsiveness to customers, the quality of their products, and the efficiency of their organization. To achieve these goals, managers can use a number of value-chain management techniques to improve the way an organization's operating system operates.

IMPROVING RESPONSIVENESS TO CUSTOMERS To achieve high performance in a competitive environment, it is imperative that the organization's value chain is managed to produce outputs that have the attributes customers desire. One of the central tasks of value-chain management is to develop new and improved operating systems that enhance the ability of the organization to economically deliver more of the product attributes that customers desire for the same price. Techniques such as CRM and TQM, JIT, flexible manufacturing, and process reengineering are popular because they promise to do this. As important as responsiveness to customers is, however, managers need to recognize that there are limits to how responsive an organization can be and still cover its costs.

IMPROVING QUALITY Managers seek to improve the quality of their organization's output because doing so enables them to better serve customers, to raise prices, and to lower production costs. Total quality management focuses on improving the quality of an organization's products and services and stresses that all of an organization's operations should be directed toward this goal. Putting TQM into practice requires having an organizationwide commitment to TQM, having a strong customer focus, finding ways to measure quality, setting quality improvement goals, soliciting input from employees about how to improve product quality, identifying defects and tracing them to their source, introducing just-in-time inventory systems, getting suppliers to adopt TQM practices, designing products for ease of manufacture, and breaking down barriers between functional departments.

IMPROVING EFFICIENCY   Improving efficiency requires one or more of the following: the introduction of a TQM program, the adoption of flexible manufacturing technologies, the introduction of just-in-time inventory systems, the establishment of self-managed work teams, and the application of process reengineering. Top management is responsible for setting the context within which efficiency improvements can take place by, for example, emphasizing the need for continuous improvement. Functional-level managers bear prime responsibility for identifying and implementing efficiency-enhancing improvements in operating systems.

IMPROVING PRODUCT INNOVATION   When technology is changing, managers must quickly innovate new and improved products to protect their competitive advantage. Some value-chain strategies managers can use to help them achieve this are (1) involve both customers and suppliers in the development process; (1) establish a stage-gate development funnel for evaluating and controlling different product development efforts; and (3) establish cross-functional teams composed of individuals from different functional departments, and give each team a leader who can rise above his or her functional background.

Management in Action

Topics for Discussion and Action

Discussion

1. What is CRM, and in what ways can it help improve responsiveness to customers?

2. What are the main challenges to be overcome in implementing a successful total quality management program?

3. What is efficiency, and what are some of the strategies that managers can use to increase it?

4. Why is it important for managers to pay close attention to value-chain management if they wish to be responsive to their customers?

5. What is innovation, and what are some of the strategies that managers can use to develop successful new products?

Action

6. Ask a manager how responsiveness to customers, quality, efficiency, and innovation are defined and measured in his or her organization.

7. Go to a local store, restaurant, or supermarket, observe how customers are treated, and list the ways in which you think the organization is being responsive or unresponsive to the needs of its customers. How could this business improve its responsiveness to customers?

Building Management Skills

Managing the Value Chain

Choose an organization with which you are familiar—one that you have worked in or patronized or one that has received extensive coverage in the popular press. The organization should be involved in only one industry or business. Answer these questions about the organization:

1. What is the output of the organization?

2. Describe the value-chain activities that the organization uses to produce this output.

3. What product attributes do customers of the organization desire?

4. Try to identify improvements that might be made to the organization's value chain to boost its responsiveness to customers, quality, efficiency, and innovation.

Managing Ethically

Go back and review the "Ethics in Action" on the human costs of Toyota's production system. After implementing efficiency-improving techniques, many companies commonly lay off employees who are no longer needed. And, frequently, remaining employees must perform more tasks more quickly, a situation that can generate employee stress and other work-related problems.

Questions

1. Either by yourself or in a group think through the ethical implications of using some new functional strategy to improve organizational performance.

2. What criteria would you use to decide which kind of strategy is ethical to adopt and/or how far to push employees to raise the level of their performance?

3. How big a layoff, if any, is acceptable? If layoffs are acceptable, what could be done to reduce their harm to employees?

Small Group Breakout Exercise

How to Compete in the Sandwich Business

Form groups of three or four people, and appoint one member as the spokesperson who will communicate your findings to the class when called on by the instructor. Then discuss the following scenario.

You and your partners are thinking about opening a new kind of sandwich shop that will compete head-to-head with Subway and Thundercloud Subs. Because these chains have good brand-name recognition, it is vital that you find some source of competitive advantage for your new sandwich shop, and you are meeting to brainstorm ways of obtaining one.

1. Identify the product attributes that a typical sandwich shop customer wants the most.

2. In what ways do you think you will be able to improve on the operations and processes of existing sandwich shops and increase responsiveness to customers through better (a) product quality, (b) efficiency, or (c) innovation?

Exploring the World Wide Web

Go to GM's Web site by typing the following address:
http://media.gm.com/servlet/GatewayServlet?target=http://image.emerald.gm.com/gmnews/viewmonthlyreleasedetail.do?domain=3&docid=19989

This address leads to a page that discusses TQM at GM's Livonia engine plant. (If the link has changed, search for the 2004 press release containing the keyword "Livonia.")

Read the press release; then go back to the principles of TQM discussed in this chapter. How has GM used TQM to attain superior quality and efficiency at its Livonia plant?

Be the Manager

How to Build Flat-Panel Displays

You are the top manager of a start-up company that will produce innovative new flat-screen displays for PC makers like Dell and HP. The flat-screen-display market is highly competitive, so there is also considerable pressure to reduce costs because prices fall rapidly. Also, PC makers are demanding ever-higher quality and better features to please customers. In addition, they demand that delivery of your product meets their production schedule needs. Functional managers want your advice on how to best meet these requirements, especially as they are in the process of recruiting new workers and building a production facility.

Questions

1. What kinds of techniques discussed in the chapter can help your functional managers to increase efficiency?

2. In what ways can these managers go about developing a program to increase (1) quality? (2) innovation?

3. What critical lessons do these managers need to learn about value-chain management?

BusinessWeek

Case in the News

No One Does Lean Like the Japanese

Two years ago, Matsushita Co.'s factory in Saga, on Japan's southern island of Kyushu, was looking mighty lean. The plant had doubled efficiency over the previous four years, and machinery stretching the length of the spotless facility could churn out cordless phones, fax machines, and security cameras in record time.

But Matsushita officials still saw fat that could be trimmed. So the plant's managers, Hitoshi Hirata and Hirofumi Tsuru, ripped out the conveyer belts and replaced them with clusters of robots. New software synchronizes production so each robot is ready to jump into action as soon as the previous step is completed. And if one robot breaks down, the work flow can be shifted to others that do the same job. "It used to be 2 1/2 days into a production run before we had our first finished product. But now the first is done in 40 minutes," Hirata says. "Next year we'll try to shorten the cycle even more."

Japan, of course, has long been a global leader in lean production. Japanese companies invented just-in-time manufacturing, where parts arrive at the loading dock right when they're needed. But now, as these companies face increasing competition from low-cost rivals in Korea, China, and elsewhere in Asia, they're working double-time to stay ahead. And to ensure that they produce what consumers are actually buying, they're rearranging factories so they can quickly shift gears to make gadgets that are hot, and ease up on those that are selling more slowly.

Network Hub

Matsushita's, Saga plant is at the forefront of that effort. Kunio Nakamura Matsushita's chairman, has often praised Saga as an example for the rest of the company as it seeks to cut plant inventories in half from 2004 levels by next March. "To get the most from our manufacturing strengths, we must lower inventories," Nakamura told employees last fall. In his speech, Nakamura cited Saga, which now makes a batch of 500 phones per eight-hour shift, vs. 1,500 phones in three days before the most recent changes. While that means Saga can make twice as many phones per week, the company is also trimming inventory costs because components such as chips, keypads, and circuit boards spend one-third as much time in the factory.

Those efficiency gains multiply when you look at the big picture. Saga is a "mother plant," or the hub of an overseas manufacturing network. Weeks after Hirata and Tsuru gave the green light to the new layout, six other Matsushita plants in China, Malaysia, Mexico, and Britain started copying the setup. Most have since been able to cut their inventories and have seen a similar boost in production, today churning out a total of 150,000 phones per shift.

That's just the kind of effort that has helped Matsushita bounce back from a $3.7 billion loss in 2002. The company on Apr. 29 announced its best earnings in more than a decade. And in the year ending next March, Matsushita expects net profit to increase by 23%, to $1.7 billion, on a 1% rise in sales, to $78 billion.

Matsushita has learned much from Hirata and Tsuru. They dress in factory-issued bamboo-green zip-up jackets and indoor-only shoes, and twice daily they join most of the 280 employees for calisthenics on the factory floor. But their real focus is on boosting efficiency. Their brainstorming began two years ago, when they discovered that a bottleneck on the assembly line meant that robots

sat idle for longer than they were working. So they broke the line into stations, or "cells," that allowed them to double up on slower robots to make things flow more smoothly.

In test runs, the new setup worked, but with so many machines going at once it was tough to choreograph the production process. In the past, a person was assigned to schedule everything from deliveries of supplies to work shifts to maintenance. But that wouldn't fly in a factory that had to be prepared to shift gears for a sudden spike or dip in demand. Instead the managers found software that would do the trick.

The next step was figuring out how to apply the changes globally. With 75 markets to cater to, the seven factories in Saga's group make 35 million phones, faxes, printers, and other products annually. It was a logistical nightmare: There were 1,500 shape and color variations for phones alone, and engineers needed to rearrange as

many as 77 circuit-board parts for each new model. Retooling the robots for every type of board was simply too time-consuming, so Matsushita engineers designed a circuit-board that would need only slight changes for each model. Despite the faster pace, Hirata says defects are at an all-time low: under 1% in every factory.

Questions for Discussion

1. What value–chain techniques has Matsushita been using to improve its performance lately?

2. Given its losses, Panasonic has been well behind Toyota in putting lean production into practice. Why is it difficult for all companies to do implement lean production?

Source: Kenji Hall, "No One Does Lean Like the Japanese." Reprinted from the July 10, 2006 , issue of *BusinessWeek* by special permission. Copyright © 2006 by the McGraw-Hill Companies.

CHAPTER 10

Managing Organizational Structure and Culture

Learning Objectives

After studying this chapter, you should be able to:

- Identify the factors that influence managers' choice of an organizational structure.

- Explain how managers group tasks into jobs that are motivating and satisfying for employees.

- Describe the types of organizational structures managers can design, and explain why they choose one structure over another.

- Explain why managers must coordinate jobs, functions, and divisions using the hierarchy of authority and integrating mechanisms.

- List the four sources of organizational culture, and differentiate between a strong, adaptive culture and a weak, inert culture.

- Explain why the culture of a company leads to competitive advantage.

A Manager's Challenge

A Centralized, Military-Style Structure and Culture Transform
Home Depot

How should managers organize to improve performance?

In the 2000s, Home Depot, the home improvement supply chain, has changed its organizational structure and culture in major ways to better motivate and coordinate employees and improve its performance. The company's founders, Bernie Marcus and Arthur Blank, opened their first store in Atlanta, Georgia, in 1979, and their mission was to create a home improvement "superstore" that could offer customers a range and variety of products at low prices that no other home improvement store could match. The huge success of their first store encouraged them to expand, and the founders set their stamp on the company by establishing organizational values and norms. They wanted to motivate their managers to act in an entrepreneurial way, so they created a culture based on values and norms that encouraged this. Individual store managers had considerable freedom to order and stock products that suited the needs of local and regional customers.[1]

With his military background, Bob Nardelli understood the advantages of having a centralized chain of command and uniform, standardized operating procedures.

The founders' decentralized approach to operating the store chain worked well until Home Depot's huge profits attracted new competitors, such as Lowe's, into the home improvement market. Lowe's managers had watched Home Depot's rapid growth and were convinced they could do better. In particular, they believed Home Depot's weakness was its poor-quality customer service and poor store layout, which was very similar to a warehouse. Lowe's managers designed stores that were responsive to customers so that ordinary, "unskilled" homeowners would feel happy shopping in them. They decided that Lowe's culture should be based on values and norms that emphasized providing good service and help to customers. They did not encourage store managers to be entrepreneurial; indeed, they decided to stock a standardized range of products in all their stores to reduce costs. The structure and culture they created worked: Lowe's quickly caught up with Home Depot in the 1990s, and Home Depot's stock collapsed when investors feared its strategy and structure were no longer working.

Home Depot's founders decided it was time for a change; they searched for a new CEO to turn around their company's performance. Bob Nardelli, a former GE top manager, was their choice. Nardelli had a reputation for finding ways to lower costs and overhead while giving customers what they want.[2] From his military background, he understood the advantages of a centralized chain of command and uniform, standardized operating procedures to get the job done quickly and efficiently. He also understood the importance of being responsive to customers—after all, the military has a culture based on making its individual members feel part of a "team."

Since 2002 Nardelli has worked to develop a military-style structure and culture for Home Depot.[3] He has recentralized authority over time and taken away store managers' ability to choose what products to stock for their individual stores. His goal is to streamline and centralize Home Depot's purchasing activities at its Atlanta headquarters and thus reduce costs. At the same time, to be responsive to customers, he has increased the number of new, innovative products Home Depot stocks. Nardelli created a sophisticated organization-wide IT system that provides store-by-store performance comparisons; top management has real-time, militarylike information on how its "forces" are succeeding in the field, and each store manager knows where he or she "ranks" in this hierarchy based on their store's performance. The military culture also emphasizes close attention to customer needs, however; employees are expected to watch customers, anticipate their need for help, lead them to the aisle where the products they need can be found, and help them select a product or refer them to the "expert soldier" who can provide this advice. To motivate managers and employees, Nardelli created a bonus system based on the performance of each store or "platoon": if employees achieve their goals, they can earn substantial amounts of money.

Within 18 months his new organizational structure and culture worked: Home Depot's costs fell, and its sales increased as customers responded to the new products its stores were now stocking and the new way employees responded to customer needs. This promising beginning has convinced Nardelli that his military style of organizing is the right approach for increasing efficiency in the future. In fact, he has been busily recruiting ex-military officers, who already have been socialized into values and norms that emphasize team performance and the need to look up the chain of command to get the "orders of the day"—in this case, the ones that most efficiently and effectively satisfy the needs of customers. By 2006 Home Depot had recruited more than 17,000 ex-military personnel to manage its 1,600 stores, and Nardelli's personal assistant is an ex-marine staff colonel.[4]

Overview

Home Depot's experience suggests that the way ~~zation~~ is designed has a major effect on the way emp~~loyees~~ behave and how well the organization operates. Moreover, with competiti~~on~~ heating up in the building supply industry, a major challenge facing Bob Nardelli was identifying the best way to organize people and resources efficiently and effectively. To meet that challenge, Nardelli decided to radically change the way Home Depot operated.

In Part 4 of this book, we examine how managers can organize and control human and other resources to create high-performing organizations. To organize and control (two of the four functions of management identified in Chapter 1), managers must design an organizational architecture that makes the best use of resources to produce the goods and services customers want. **Organizational architecture** is the combination of organizational structure, culture, control systems, and human resource management (HRM) systems that together determine how efficiently and effectively organizational resources are used.

By the end of this chapter, you will be familiar not only with various forms of organizational structures and cultures but also with various factors that determine the organizational design choices that managers make. Then, in Chapters 11 and 12, we examine issues surrounding the design of an organization's control systems and HRM systems.

organizational architecture The organizational structure, control systems, culture, and human resource management systems that together determine how efficiently and effectively organizational resources are used.

Designing Organizational Structure

organizational structure A formal system of task and reporting relationships that coordinates and motivates organizational members so that they work together to achieve organizational goals.

Organizing is the process by which managers establish the structure of working relationships among employees to allow them to achieve organizational goals efficiently and effectively. **Organizational structure** is the formal system of task and job reporting relationships that determines how employees use resources to achieve organizational goals.[5] *Organizational culture,* discussed in Chapter 3, is the shared set of beliefs, values, and norms that influence the way people and groups work together to achieve organizational goals. **Organizational design** is the process by which managers create a specific type of organizational structure and culture so that a company can operate in the most efficient and effective way.[6]

Once a company decides what kind of work attitudes and behaviors it wants from its employees, managers create a particular arrangement of task and authority relationships, and promote specific cultural values and norms, to obtain these desired attitudes and behaviors—just as Bob Nardelli did for Home Depot. The challenge facing all companies is to design a structure and culture that (1) *motivates* managers and employees to work hard and to develop supportive job behaviors and attitudes and (2) *coordinates* the actions of employees, groups, functions, and divisions to ensure they work together efficiently and effectively.

organizational design The process by which managers make specific organizing choices that result in a particular kind of organizational structure.

As noted in Chapter 2, according to contingency theory, managers design organizational structures to fit the factors or circumstances that are affecting the company the most and causing them the most uncertainty.[7] Thus, there is no one best way to design an organization: Design reflects each organization's specific situation, and researchers have argued that in some situations stable, mechanistic structures may be most appropriate while in others flexible, organic structures might be the most effective. Four factors are important determinants of the type of organizational structure or culture managers select: the nature of

rs Affecting Organizational Structure

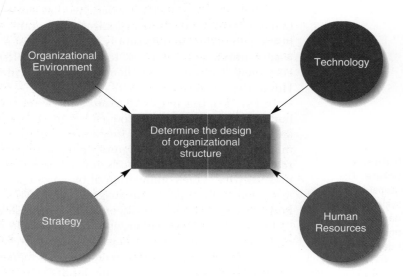

the organizational environment, the type of strategy the organization pursues, the technology (and particularly information technology) the organization uses, and the characteristics of the organization's human resources (see Figure 10.1).[8]

The Organizational Environment

In general, the more quickly the external environment is changing and the greater the uncertainty within it, the greater are the problems facing managers in trying to gain access to scarce resources. In this situation, to speed decision making and communication and make it easier to obtain resources, managers typically make organizing choices that result in more flexible structures and entrepreneurial cultures.[9] They are likely to decentralize authority, empower lower-level employees to make important operating decisions, and encourage values and norms that emphasize change and innovation—a more organic from of organizing.

In contrast, if the external environment is stable, resources are readily available, and uncertainty is low, then less coordination and communication among people and functions are needed to obtain resources. Managers can make organizing choices that bring more stability or formality to the organizational structure and can establish values and norms that emphasize obedience and being a team player. Managers in this situation prefer to make decisions within a clearly defined hierarchy of authority and to use detailed rules, standard operating procedures (SOPs), and restrictive norms to guide and govern employees' activities—a more mechanistic form of organizing.

As we discussed in Chapter 6, change is rapid in today's marketplace, and increasing competition both at home and abroad is putting greater pressure on managers to attract customers and increase efficiency and effectiveness. Consequently, interest in finding ways to structure organizations—such as through empowerment and self-managed teams—to allow people and departments to behave flexibly has been increasing.

Strategy

As discussed in Chapter 8, once managers decide on a strategy, they must choose the right means of implementing it. Different strategies often call for the use of different organizational structures and cultures. For example, a differentiation strategy aimed at increasing the value customers perceive in an organization's goods and services usually succeeds best in a flexible structure with a culture that values innovation; flexibility facilitates a differentiation strategy because managers can develop new or innovative products quickly—an activity that requires extensive cooperation among functions or departments. In contrast, a low-cost strategy that is aimed at driving down costs in all functions usually fares best in a more formal structure with more conservative norms, which gives managers greater control over the activities of an organization's various departments.[10]

In addition, at the corporate level, when managers decide to expand the scope of organizational activities by vertical integration or diversification, for example, they need to design a flexible structure to provide sufficient coordination among the different business divisions.[11] As discussed in Chapter 8, many companies have been divesting businesses because managers have been unable to create a competitive advantage to keep them up to speed in fast-changing industries. By moving to a more flexible structure, managers gain more control over their different businesses. Finally, expanding internationally and operating in many different countries challenges managers to create organizational structures that allow organizations to be flexible on a global level.[12] As we discuss later, managers can group their departments or divisions in several ways to allow them to effectively pursue an international strategy.

Technology

Recall that technology is the combination of skills, knowledge, machines, and computers that are used to design, make, and distribute goods and services. As a rule, the more complicated the technology that an organization uses, the more difficult it is to regulate or control it because more unexpected events can arise. Thus, the more complicated the technology, the greater is the need for a flexible structure and progressive culture to enhance managers' ability to respond to unexpected situations—and give them the freedom and desire to work out new solutions to the problems they encounter. In contrast, the more routine the technology, the more appropriate is a formal structure, because tasks are simple and the steps needed to produce goods and services have been worked out in advance.

What makes a technology routine or complicated? One researcher who investigated this issue, Charles Perrow, argued that two factors determine how complicated or nonroutine technology is: task variety and task analyzability.[13] *Task variety* is the number of new or unexpected problems or situations that a person or function encounters in performing tasks or jobs. *Task analyzability* is the degree to which programmed solutions are available to people or functions to solve the problems they encounter. Nonroutine or complicated technologies are characterized by high task variety and low task analyzability; this means that many varied problems occur and that solving these problems requires significant nonprogrammed decision making. In contrast, routine technologies are characterized by low task variety and high task analyzability; this means that the problems encountered do not vary much and are easily resolved through programmed decision making.

Examples of nonroutine technology are found in the work of scientists in an R&D laboratory who develop new products or discover new drugs, and they are seen in the planning exercises an organization's top-management team uses to chart the organization's future strategy. Examples of routine technology include typical mass-production or assembly operations, where workers perform the same task repeatedly and where managers have already identified the programmed solutions necessary to perform a task efficiently. Similarly, in service organizations such as fast-food restaurants, the tasks that crew members perform in making and serving fast food are very routine.

Human Resources

A final important factor affecting an organization's choice of structure and culture is the characteristics of the human resources it employs. In general, the more highly skilled its workforce, and the greater the number of employees who work together in groups or teams, the more likely an organization is to use a flexible, decentralized structure and a professional culture based on values and norms that foster employee autonomy and self-control. Highly skilled employees, or employees who have internalized strong professional values and norms of behavior as part of their training, usually desire greater freedom and autonomy and dislike close supervision.

Flexible structures, characterized by decentralized authority and empowered employees, are well suited to the needs of highly skilled people. Similarly, when people work in teams, they must be allowed to interact freely and develop norms to guide their own work interactions, which also is possible in a flexible organizational structure. Thus, when designing organizational structure and culture, managers must pay close attention to the needs of the workforce and to the complexity and kind of work employees perform.

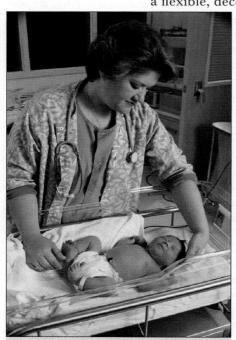

Highly skilled employees, such as this nurse, have internalized strong professional values and norms of behavior through their education and training. Such employees usually desire freedom and autonomy and dislike close supervision. Flexible structures, characterized by decentralized authority and empowered employees, are well suited to the needs of highly skilled people.

In summary, an organization's external environment, strategy, technology, and human resources are the factors to be considered by managers in seeking to design the best structure and culture for an organization. The greater the level of uncertainty in the organization's environment, the more complex its strategy and technologies, and the more highly qualified and skilled its workforce, the more likely managers are to design a structure and a culture that are flexible, can change quickly, and allow employees to be innovative in their responses to problems, customer needs, and so on. The more stable the organization's environment, the less complex and more well understood its strategy or technology, and the less skilled its workforce, the more likely managers are to design an organizational structure that is formal and controlling and a culture whose values and norms prescribe how employees should act in particular situations.

Later in the chapter we discuss how managers can create different kinds of organizational cultures. First, however, we discuss how managers can design flexible or formal organizational structures. The way an organization's structure works depends on the organizing choices managers make about three issues:

- How to group tasks into individual jobs.
- How to group jobs into functions and divisions.
- How to allocate authority and coordinate or integrate functions and divisions.

Grouping Tasks into Jobs: Job Design

job design The process by which managers decide how to divide tasks into specific jobs.

The first step in organizational design is **job design,** the process by which managers decide how to divide into specific jobs the tasks that have to be performed to provide customers with goods and services. Managers at McDonald's, for example, have decided how best to divide the tasks required to provide customers with fast, cheap food in each McDonald's restaurant. After experimenting with different job arrangements, McDonald's managers decided on a basic division of labor among chefs and food servers. Managers allocated all the tasks involved in actually cooking the food (putting oil in the fat fryers, opening packages of frozen french fries, putting beef patties on the grill, making salads, and so on) to the job of chef. They allocated all the tasks involved in giving the food to customers (such as greeting customers, taking orders, putting fries and burgers into bags, adding salt, pepper, and napkins, and taking money) to food servers. In addition, they created other jobs—the job of dealing with drive-through customers, the job of keeping the restaurant clean, and the job of overseeing employees and responding to unexpected events. The result of the job design process is a *division of labor* among employees, one that McDonald's managers have discovered through experience is most efficient.

Establishing an appropriate division of labor among employees is a critical part of the organizing process, one that is vital to increasing efficiency and effectiveness. At McDonald's, the tasks associated with chef and food server were split into different jobs because managers found that, for the kind of food McDonald's serves, this approach was most efficient. It is efficient because when each employee is given fewer tasks to perform (so that each job becomes more specialized), employees become more productive at performing the tasks that constitute each job.

At Subway sandwich shops, however, managers chose a different kind of job design. At Subway, there is no division of labor among the people who make the sandwiches, wrap the sandwiches, give them to customers, and take the money. The

At Subway, the role of chef and server is combined into one, making the job "larger" than the jobs of McDonald's more specialized food servers. The idea behind job enlargement is that increasing the range of tasks performed by the worker will reduce boredom and fatigue. Would you prefer a "larger" job?

roles of chef and food server are combined into one. This different division of tasks and jobs is efficient for Subway and not for McDonald's because Subway serves a limited menu of mostly submarine-style sandwiches that are prepared to order. Subway's production system is far simpler than McDonald's, because McDonald's menu is much more varied and its chefs must cook many different kinds of foods.

Managers of every organization must analyze the range of tasks to be performed and then create jobs that best allow the organization to give customers the goods and services they want. In deciding how to assign tasks to individual jobs, however, managers must be careful not to take **job simplification,** the process of reducing the number of tasks that each worker performs, too far.[14] Too much job simplification may reduce efficiency rather than increase it if workers find their simplified jobs boring and monotonous, become demotivated and unhappy, and, as a result, perform at a low level.

job simplification The process of reducing the number of tasks that each worker performs.

Job Enlargement and Job Enrichment

In an attempt to create a division of labor and design individual jobs to encourage workers to perform at a higher level and be more satisfied with their work, several researchers have proposed ways other than job simplification to group tasks into jobs: job enlargement and job enrichment.

Job enlargement is increasing the number of different tasks in a given job by changing the division of labor.[15] For example, because Subway food servers make the food as well as serve it, their jobs are "larger" than the jobs of McDonald's food servers. The idea behind job enlargement is that increasing the range of tasks performed by a worker will reduce boredom and fatigue and may increase motivation to perform at a high level—increasing both the quantity and the quality of goods and services provided.

job enlargement Increasing the number of different tasks in a given job by changing the division of labor.

Job enrichment is increasing the degree of responsibility a worker has over a job by, for example, (1) empowering workers to experiment to find new or better ways of doing the job, (2) encouraging workers to develop new skills, (3) allowing workers to decide how to do the work and giving them the responsibility for deciding how to respond to unexpected situations, and (4) allowing workers to monitor and measure their own performance.[16] The idea behind job enrichment is that increasing workers' responsibility increases their involvement in their jobs and thus increases their interest in the quality of the goods they make or the services they provide.

job enrichment Increasing the degree of responsibility a worker has over his or her job.

In general, managers who make design choices that increase job enrichment and job enlargement are likely to increase the degree to which people behave flexibly rather than rigidly or mechanically. Narrow, specialized jobs are likely to lead people to behave in predictable ways; workers who perform a variety of tasks and who are allowed and encouraged to discover new and better ways to perform their jobs are likely to act flexibly and creatively. Thus, managers who enlarge and enrich jobs create a flexible organizational structure, and those who simplify jobs create a more formal structure. If workers are grouped into self-managed work teams, the organization is likely to be flexible because team members provide support for each other and can learn from one another.

The Job Characteristics Model

J. R. Hackman and G. R. Oldham's job characteristics model is an influential model of job design that explains in detail how managers can make jobs more interesting and motivating.[17] Hackman and Oldham's model (see Figure 10.2) also describes the likely personal and organizational outcomes that will result from enriched and enlarged jobs.

According to Hackman and Oldham, every job has five characteristics that determine how motivating the job is. These characteristics determine how employees react to their work and lead to outcomes such as high performance and satisfaction and low absenteeism and turnover:

- *Skill variety:* The extent to which a job requires that an employee use a wide range of different skills, abilities, or knowledge. Example: The skill variety required by the job of a research scientist is higher than that called for by the job of a McDonald's food server.

- *Task identity:* The extent to which a job requires that a worker perform all the tasks necessary to complete the job, from the beginning to the end of the production process. Example: A craftsworker who takes a piece of wood and transforms it into a custom-made desk has higher task identity than does a worker who performs only one of the numerous operations required to assemble a television.

- *Task significance:* The degree to which a worker feels his or her job is meaningful because of its effect on people inside the organization, such as co-workers, or on people outside the organization, such as customers. Example: A teacher who sees the effect of his or her efforts in a well-educated and well-adjusted student enjoys high task significance compared to a dishwasher who monotonously washes dishes as they come to the kitchen.

- *Autonomy:* The degree to which a job gives an employee the freedom and discretion needed to schedule different tasks and decide how to carry them out. Example: Salespeople who have to plan their schedules and decide

Figure 10.2

The Job Characteristics Model

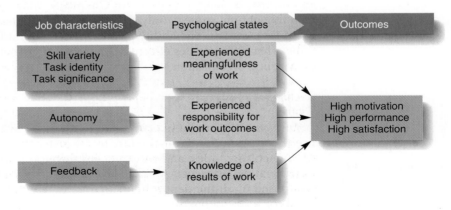

how to allocate their time among different customers have relatively high autonomy compared to assembly-line workers, whose actions are determined by the speed of the production line.

- *Feedback:* The extent to which actually doing a job provides a worker with clear and direct information about how well he or she has performed the job. Example: An air traffic controller whose mistakes may result in a midair collision receives immediate feedback on job performance; a person who compiles statistics for a business magazine often has little idea of when he or she makes a mistake or does a particularly good job.

Hackman and Oldham argue that these five job characteristics affect an employee's motivation because they affect three critical psychological states (see Figure 10.2). The more employees feel that their work is *meaningful* and that they are *responsible for work outcomes and responsible for knowing how those outcomes affect others*, the more motivating work becomes and the more likely employees are to be satisfied and to perform at a high level. Moreover, employees who have jobs that are highly motivating are called on to use their skills more and to perform more tasks, and they are given more responsibility for doing the job. All of the foregoing are characteristic of jobs and employees in flexible structures where authority is decentralized and where employees commonly work with others and must learn new skills to complete the range of tasks for which their group is responsible.

Grouping Jobs into Functions and Divisions

Once managers have decided which tasks to allocate to which jobs, they face the next organizing decision: how to group jobs together to best match the needs of the organization's environment, strategy, technology, and human resources. Most top-management teams decide to group jobs into departments and develop a functional structure to use organizational resources. As the organization grows, managers design a divisional structure or a more complex matrix or product team structure.

Choosing a structure and then designing it so that it works as intended is a significant challenge. As noted in Chapter 7, managers reap the rewards of a well-thought-out strategy only if they choose the right type of structure to implement the strategy. The ability to make the right kinds of organizing choices is often what differentiates effective from ineffective managers and creates a high-performing organization.

Functional Structure

A *function* is a group of people, working together, who possess similar skills or use the same kind of knowledge, tools, or techniques to perform their jobs. Manufacturing, sales, and research and development are often organized into functional departments. A **functional structure** is an organizational structure composed of all the departments that an organization requires to produce its goods or services. Figure 10.3 shows the functional structure that Pier 1 Imports, the home furnishings company, uses to supply its customers with a range of goods from around the world to satisfy their desires for new and innovative products.

functional structure
An organizational structure composed of all the departments that an organization requires to produce its goods or services.

Figure 10.3

The Functional Structure of Pier 1 Imports

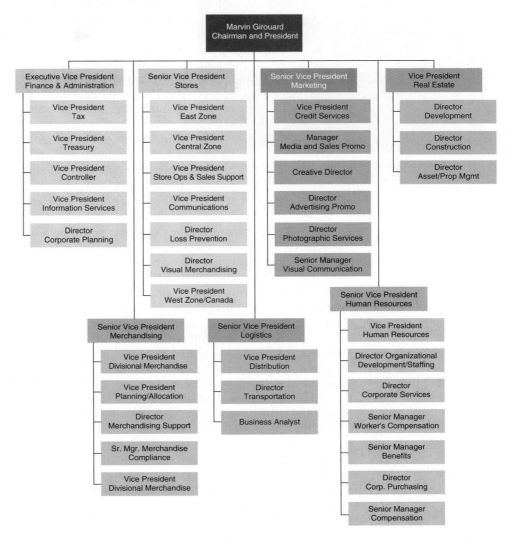

Pier 1's main functions are finance and administration, merchandising (purchasing the goods), stores (managing the retail outlets), logistics (managing product distribution), marketing, human resources, and real estate. Each job inside a function exists because it helps the function perform the activities necessary for high organizational performance. Thus, within the logistics department are all the jobs necessary to efficiently distribute and transport products to stores, and inside the marketing department are all the jobs (such as promotion, photography, and visual communication) that are necessary to increase the appeal of Pier 1's products to customers.

There are several advantages to grouping jobs according to function. First, when people who perform similar jobs are grouped together, they can learn from observing one another and thus become more specialized and can perform at a higher level. The tasks associated with one job often are related to the tasks associated with another job, which encourages cooperation within a function. In Pier 1's marketing

Pier 1 Imports Chairman and CEO Marvin J. Girouard heads the functional structure at the popular home décor store.

department, for example, the person designing the photography program for an ad campaign works closely with the person responsible for designing store layouts and with visual communication experts. As a result, Pier 1 is able to develop a strong, focused marketing campaign to differentiate its products.

Second, when people who perform similar jobs are grouped together, it is easier for managers to monitor and evaluate their performance.[18] Imagine if marketing experts, purchasing experts, and real-estate experts were grouped together in one function and supervised by a manager from merchandising. Obviously, the merchandising manager would not have the expertise to evaluate all these different people appropriately. However a functional structure allows workers to evaluate how well coworkers are performing their jobs, and if some workers are performing poorly, more experienced workers can help them develop new skills.

Finally, managers appreciate functional structure because it allows them to create the set of functions they need in order to scan and monitor the competitive environment and obtain information about the way it is changing.[19] With the right set of functions in place, managers are then in a good position to develop a strategy that allows the organization to respond to its changing situation. Employees in marketing can specialize in monitoring new marketing developments that will allow Pier 1 to better target its customers. Employees in merchandising can monitor all potential suppliers of home furnishings both at home and abroad to find the goods most likely to appeal to Pier 1's customers and manage Pier 1's global outsourcing supply chain.

As an organization grows, and particularly as its task environment and strategy change because it is beginning to produce a wider range of goods and services for different kinds of customers, several problems can make a functional structure less efficient and effective.[20] First, managers in different functions may find it more difficult to communicate and coordinate with one another when they are responsible for several different kinds of products, especially as the organization grows both domestically and internationally. Second, functional managers may become so preoccupied with supervising their own specific departments and achieving their departmental goals that they lose sight of organizational goals. If that happens, organizational effectiveness will suffer because managers will be viewing issues and problems facing the organization only from their own, relatively narrow, departmental perspectives.[21] Both of these problems can reduce efficiency and effectiveness.

Divisional Structures: Product, Market, and Geographic

divisional structure
An organizational structure composed of separate business units within which are the functions that work together to produce a specific product for a specific customer.

As the problems associated with growth and diversification increase over time, managers must search for new ways to organize their activities to overcome the problems associated with a functional structure. Most managers of large organizations choose a **divisional structure** and create a series of business units to produce a specific kind of product for a specific kind of customer. Each *division* is a collection of functions or departments that work together to produce the product. The goal behind the change to a divisional structure is to create smaller, more manageable units within the organization. There are three forms of divisional structure (see Figure 10.4).[22] When managers organize divisions according to the *type of good or service* they provide, they adopt a product structure. When managers organize divisions according to the *area of the country or world* they operate in, they adopt a geographic structure. When managers organize divisions according to *the type of customer* they focus on, they adopt a market structure.

PRODUCT STRUCTURE   Imagine the problems that managers at Pier 1 would encounter if they decided to diversify into producing and selling cars, fast food, and health insurance—in addition to home furnishings—and tried to use their existing set of functional managers to oversee the production of all four kinds of

Figure 10.4

Product, Market, and Geographic Structures

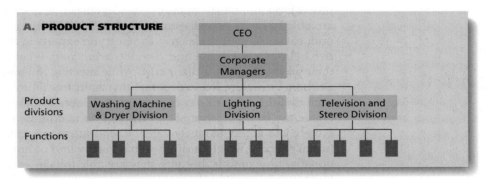

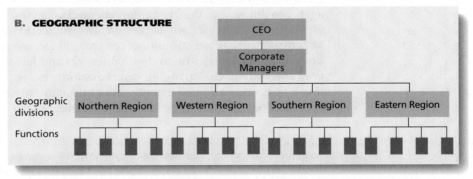

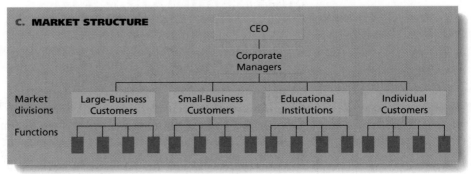

products. No manager would have the necessary skills or abilities to oversee those four products. No individual marketing manager, for example, could effectively market cars, fast food, health insurance, and home furnishings at the same time. To perform a functional activity successfully, managers must have experience in specific markets or industries. Consequently, if managers decide to diversify into new industries or to expand their range of products, they commonly design a product structure to organize their operations (see Figure 10.4a).

product structure An organizational structure in which each product line or business is handled by a self-contained division.

Using a **product structure,** managers place each distinct product line or business in its own self-contained division and give divisional managers the responsibility for devising an appropriate business-level strategy to allow the division to compete effectively in its industry or market.[23] Each division is self-contained because it has a complete set of all the functions—marketing, R&D, finance, and so on—that it needs to produce or provide goods or services efficiently and effectively. Functional managers report to divisional managers, and divisional managers report to top or corporate managers.

Grouping functions into divisions focused on particular products has several advantages for managers at all levels in the organization. First, a product structure allows functional managers to specialize in only one product area, so they are able to build expertise and fine-tune their skills in this particular area. Second, each division's managers can become experts in their industry; this expertise helps them choose and develop a business-level strategy to differentiate their products or lower their costs while meeting the needs of customers. Third, a product structure frees corporate managers from the need to supervise directly each division's day-to-day operations; this latitude allows corporate managers to create the best corporate-level strategy to maximize the organization's future growth and ability to create value. Corporate managers are likely to make fewer mistakes about which businesses to diversify into or how to best expand internationally, for example, because they are able to take an organizationwide view.[24] Corporate managers also are likely to evaluate better how well divisional managers are doing, and they can intervene and take corrective action as needed.

The extra layer of management, the divisional management layer, can improve the use of organizational resources. Moreover, a product structure puts divisional managers close to their customers and lets them respond quickly and appropriately to the changing task environment. A pharmaceutical company that has recently adopted a new product structure to better organize its activities is profiled in the following "Management Insight."

Management Insight

GlaxoSmithKline's New Product Structure

The need to innovate new kinds of prescription drugs in order to boost performance is a continual battle for pharmaceutical companies. In the 2000s, many of these companies have been merging to try to increase their research productivity, and one of them, GlaxoSmithKline, was created from the merger between Glaxo Wellcome and SmithKline Beecham.[25] Prior to the merger, both companies experienced a steep decline in the number of new prescription drugs their scientists were able to invent. The problem facing the new company's top managers was how to best use and combine the talents of

When Glaxo Wellcome and SmithKline Beechum merged, managers resolved the problem of how to coordinate the activities of thousands of research scientists by organizing them into product divisions focusing on clusters of diseases.

the scientists and researchers from both of the former companies to allow them to quickly innovate exciting new drugs.

Top managers realized that after the merger there would be enormous problems associated with coordinating the activities of the thousands of research scientists who were working on hundreds of different kinds of drug research programs. Understanding the problems associated with large size, the top managers decided to group the researchers into eight smaller product divisions to allow them to focus on particular clusters of diseases such as heart disease or viral infections. The members of each product division were told that they would be rewarded based on the number of new prescription drugs they were able to invent and the speed with which they could bring these new drugs to the market.

To date, GlaxoSmithKline's new product structure has worked well. The company claimed that by 2005 research productivity had more than doubled since the reorganization. The number of new drugs moving into clinical trials had doubled from 10 to 20, and the company had 148 new drugs that were being tested.[26] Moreover, the company claims that the morale of its researchers has increased and turnover has fallen because the members of each division enjoy working together and collaborating to innovate lifesaving new drugs. The company expects to have the best new drug pipeline in its industry in the next three to four years.

geographic structure
An organizational structure in which each region of a country or area of the world is served by a self-contained division.

GEOGRAPHIC STRUCTURE When organizations expand rapidly both at home and abroad, functional structures can create special problems because managers in one central location may find it increasingly difficult to deal with the different problems and issues that may arise in each region of a country or area of the world. In these cases, a geographic structure, in which divisions are broken down by geographic location, is often chosen (see Figure 10.4b). To achieve the corporate mission of providing next-day mail service, Fred Smith, CEO of FedEx, chose a geographic structure and divided up operations by creating a division in each region. Large retailers like Macy's, Neiman Marcus, and Brooks Brothers also use a geographic structure. Since the needs of retail customers differ by region—for example, surfboards in California and down parkas in the Midwest—a geographic structure gives retail regional managers the flexibility they need to choose the range of products that best meets the needs of regional customers.

In adopting a *global geographic structure*, such as shown in Figure 10.5a, managers locate different divisions in each of the world regions where the organization operates. Managers are most likely to do this when they pursue a multidomestic strategy, because customer needs vary widely by country or world region. For example, if products that appeal to U.S. customers do not sell in Europe, the Pacific Rim, or South America, then managers must customize the products to meet the needs of customers in those different world regions; a global geographic structure with global divisions will allow them to do this.

In contrast, to the degree that customers abroad are willing to buy the same kind of product, or slight variations thereof, managers are more likely

Figure 10.5

Global Geographic and Global Product Structures

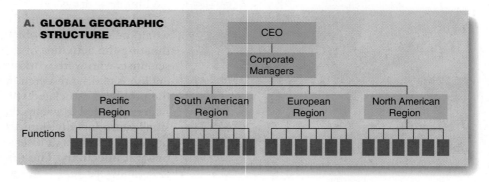

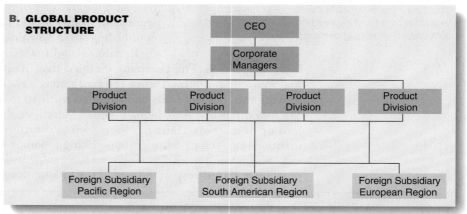

to pursue a global strategy. In this case they are more likely to use a global product structure. In a *global product structure*, each product division, not the country and regional managers, takes responsibility for deciding where to manufacture its products and how to market them in countries worldwide (see Figure 10.5b). Product division managers manage their own global value chains and decide where to establish foreign subsidiaries to distribute and sell their products to customers in foreign countries. As we noted at the beginning of this chapter, an organization's strategy is a major determinant of its structure both at home and abroad.

MARKET STRUCTURE   Sometimes the pressing issue facing managers is to group functions according to the type of customer buying the product, in order to tailor the products the organization offers to each customer's unique demands. A PC maker like Dell, for example, has several kinds of customers, including large businesses (which might demand networks of computers linked to a mainframe computer), small companies (which may need just a few PCs linked together), educational users in schools and universities (which might want thousands of independent PCs for their students), and individual users (who may want a high-quality multimedia PC so that they can play the latest video games).

market structure An organizational structure in which each kind of customer is served by a self-contained division; also called *customer structure.*

To satisfy the needs of diverse customers, a company might adopt a **market structure,** which groups divisions according to the particular kinds of customers they serve (see Figure 10.4c). A market structure allows managers to be responsive to the needs of their customers and allows them to act flexibly in making decisions in response to customers' changing needs. Dell, for example, moved from a functional to a market structure when it created four market divisions that are each focused on being responsive to a particular type of customer: corporate, small business, home computer users, and government and state agencies. Its new structure worked spectacularly well, as its sales soared through the 1990s.

Matrix and Product Team Designs

Moving to a product, market, or geographic divisional structure allows managers to respond more quickly and flexibly to the particular set of circumstances they confront. However, when customer needs or information technology is changing rapidly and the environment is very uncertain, even a divisional structure may not provide managers with enough flexibility to respond to the environment quickly. To operate effectively under these conditions, managers must design the most flexible kind of organizational structure available: a matrix structure or a product team structure (see Figure 10.5).

matrix structure An organizational structure that simultaneously groups people and resources by function and by product.

MATRIX STRUCTURE   In a **matrix structure,** managers group people and resources in two ways simultaneously: by function and by product.[27] Employees are grouped by *functions* to allow them to learn from one another and become more skilled and productive. In addition, employees are grouped into *product teams* in which members of different functions work together to develop a specific product. The result is a complex network of reporting relationships among product teams and functions that makes the matrix structure very flexible (see Figure 10.6a). Each person in a product team reports to two managers: (1) a functional boss, who assigns individuals to a team and evaluates their performance from a functional perspective, and (2) the boss of the product team, who evaluates their performance on the team. Thus, team members are known as *two-boss employees.* The functional employees assigned to product teams change over time as the specific skills that the team needs change. At the beginning of the product development process, for example, engineers and R&D specialists are assigned to a product team because their skills are needed to develop new products. When a provisional design has been established, marketing experts are assigned to the team to gauge how customers will respond to the new product. Manufacturing personnel join when it is time to find the most efficient way to produce the product. As their specific jobs are completed, team members leave and are reassigned to new teams. In this way the matrix structure makes the most use of human resources.

To keep the matrix structure flexible, product teams are empowered and team members are responsible for making most of the important decisions involved in product development.[28] The product team manager acts as a facilitator, controlling the financial resources and trying to keep the project on time and within budget. The functional managers try to ensure that the product is the best that it can be in order to maximize its differentiated appeal.

Figure 10.6

Matrix and Product Team Structures

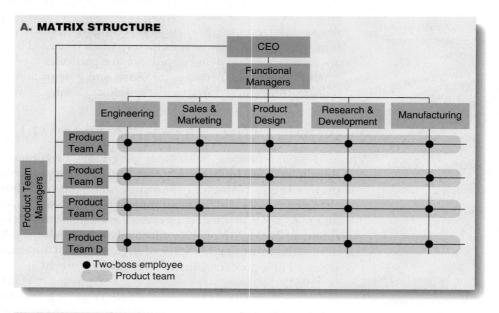

A. MATRIX STRUCTURE

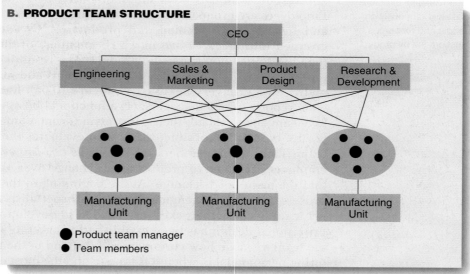

B. PRODUCT TEAM STRUCTURE

High-tech companies that operate in environments where new product development takes place monthly or yearly have used matrix structures successfully for many years, and the need to innovate quickly is vital to the organization's survival. The flexibility afforded by a matrix structure allows managers to keep pace with a changing and increasingly complex environment.[29]

PRODUCT TEAM STRUCTURE   The dual reporting relationships that are at the heart of a matrix structure have always been difficult for managers and employees to deal with. Often, the functional boss and the product boss make conflicting demands on team members, who do not know which boss to satisfy first. Also, functional and product team bosses may come into conflict over precisely who is in charge of which team members and for how long. To avoid these problems, managers have devised a way of organizing people and resources that still allows an organization to be flexible but makes its structure easier to operate: a product team structure.

product team structure An organizational structure in which employees are permanently assigned to a cross-functional team and report only to the product team manager or to one of his or her direct subordinates.

The product team structure differs from a matrix structure in two ways: (1) It does away with dual reporting relationships and two-boss managers, and (2) functional employees are permanently assigned to a cross-functional team that is empowered to bring a new or redesigned product to market. A cross-functional team is a group of managers brought together from different departments to perform organizational tasks. When managers are grouped into cross-functional teams, the artificial boundaries between departments disappear, and a narrow focus on departmental goals is replaced with a general interest in working together to achieve organizational goals. The results of such changes have been dramatic: DaimlerChrysler can introduce a new model of car in two years, down from five; Black & Decker can innovate new products in months, not years; and Hallmark Cards can respond to changing customer demands for types of cards in weeks, not months.

cross-functional team A group of managers brought together from different departments to perform organizational tasks.

Members of a cross-functional team report only to the product team manager or to one of his or her direct subordinates. The heads of the functions have only an informal, advisory relationship with members of the product teams—the role of functional managers is only to counsel and help team members, share knowledge among teams, and provide new technological developments that can help improve each team's performance (see Figure 10.6b).[30]

A committee looks over an artist's work during a meeting at Hallmark in Kansas City. At Hallmark, cross-functional teams like this one can respond quickly to changing customer demands.

Increasingly, organizations are making empowered cross-functional teams an essential part of their organizational architecture to help them gain a competitive advantage in fast-changing organizational environments. For example, Newell Rubbermaid, the well-known maker of more than 5,000 household products, moved to a product team structure because its managers wanted to speed up the rate of product innovation. Managers created 20 cross-functional teams composed of five to seven people from marketing, manufacturing, R&D, and other functions.[31] Each team focuses its energies on a particular product line, such as garden products, bathroom products, or kitchen products. These teams develop more than 365 new products a year.

hybrid structure The structure of a large organization that has many divisions and simultaneously uses many different organizational structures.

Hybrid Structure

A large organization that has many divisions and simultaneously uses many different structures has a hybrid structure. Most large organizations use product division structures and create self-contained divisions; then each division's managers select the structure that best meets the needs of the particular environment, strategy, and so on. Thus, one product division may choose to operate with a functional structure, a second may choose a geographic structure, and a third may choose a product team structure because of the nature of the division's products or the desire to be more responsive to customers' needs. Federated Department Stores, the largest U.S. department store company, uses a hybrid structure based on grouping by customer and by geography.

As shown in Figure 10.7, in 2005 Federated operated its four main store chains, Macy's, Bloomingdales, Marshall Field's, and Foley's, as independent divisions in a market division structure. Beneath this organizational layer is another layer of structure because both Macy's and Bloomingdale's operate with a geographic structure that groups stores by region. Macy's for example, has several different regional divisions that handle its over 700 stores. Each regional office is responsible for coordinating the market needs of the stores in its region and for responding to regional customer needs. The regional office feeds information back to divisional headquarters, where centralized merchandising functions make decisions for all stores. In 2006, to further reduce costs, Macy's decided to incorporate all its Marshall Field's and Foley's stores into its Macy's and Bloomingdales divisions, so now it operates two larger store chains that operate across all regions of the country.

Organizational structure may thus be likened to the layers of an onion. The outer layer provides the overarching organizational framework—most commonly a product or market division structure—and each inner layer is the structure that each division selects for itself in response to the contingencies it faces—such as a geographic or product team structure. The ability to break a large organization into smaller units or divisions makes it much easier for managers to change structure when the need arises—for example, when a change in technology or an increase in competition in the environment necessitates a change from a functional to a product team structure.

Figure 10.7
Federated's Hybrid Structure

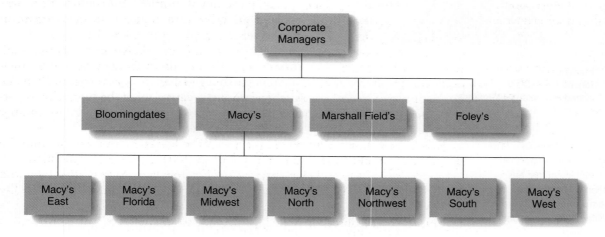

Coordinating Functions and Divisions

The more complex the structure a company uses to group its activities, the greater are the problems of *linking and coordinating* its different functions and divisions. Coordination becomes a problem because each function or division develops a different orientation toward the other groups that affects the way it interacts with them. Each function or division comes to view the problems facing the company from its own particular perspective; for example, they may develop different views about the major goals, problems, or issues facing a company.

At the functional level, the manufacturing function typically has a very short-term view; its major goal is to keep costs under control and get the product out the factory door on time. By contrast, the product development function has a long-term viewpoint because developing a new product is a relatively slow process and high product quality is seen as more important than low costs. Such differences in viewpoint may make manufacturing and product development managers reluctant to cooperate and coordinate their activities to meet company goals. At the divisional level, in a company with a product structure, employees may become concerned more with making *their* division's products a success than with the profitability of the entire company. They may refuse, or simply not see, the need to cooperate and share information or knowledge with other divisions.

The problem of linking and coordinating the activities of different functions and divisions becomes more and more acute as the number of functions and divisions increases. We look first at how managers design the hierarchy of authority to coordinate functions and divisions so that they work together effectively. Then we focus on integration and examine the different integrating mechanisms that managers can use to coordinate functions and divisions.

Allocating Authority

authority The power to hold people accountable for their actions and to make decisions concerning the use of organizational resources.

As organizations grow and produce a wider range of goods and services, the size and number of their functions and divisions increase. To coordinate the activities of people, functions, and divisions and to allow them to work together effectively, managers must develop a clear hierarchy of authority.[32] **Authority** is the power vested in a manager to make decisions and use resources to achieve organizational goals by virtue of his or her position in an organization. The **hierarchy of authority** is an organization's *chain of command*—the relative authority that each manager has—extending from the CEO at the top, down through the middle managers and first-line managers, to the nonmanagerial employees who actually make goods or provide services. Every manager, at every level of the hierarchy, supervises one or more subordinates. The term **span of control** refers to the number of subordinates who report directly to a manager.

hierarchy of authority An organization's chain of command, specifying the relative authority of each manager.

span of control The number of subordinates who report directly to a manager.

Figure 10.8 shows a simplified picture of the hierarchy of authority and the span of control of managers in McDonald's in 2004. At the top of the hierarchy is Jim Skinner, CEO and vice chairman of McDonald's board of directors, who took control in 2004.[33] Skinner is the manager who has ultimate responsibility for McDonald's performance, and he has the authority to decide how to use organizational resources to benefit McDonald's stakeholders.[34] Mike Roberts is

Figure 10.8

The Hierarchy of Authority and Span of Control at McDonald's Corporation

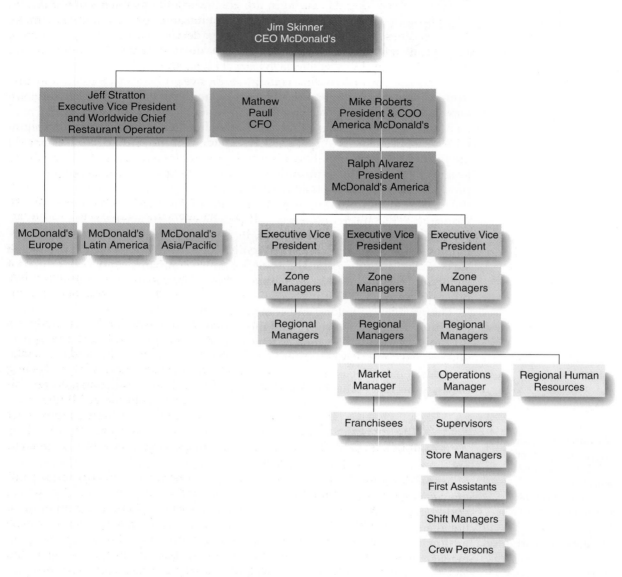

line manager
Someone in the direct line or chain of command who has formal authority over people and resources at lower levels.

staff manager
Someone responsible for managing a specialist function, such as finance or marketing.

next in line, he is president and COO and is responsible for overseeing all of McDonald's U.S. restaurant operations. Roberts reports directly to Skinner, as does chief financial officer Mathew Paull. Unlike the other managers, Paull is not a **line manager,** someone in the direct line or chain of command who has formal authority over people and resources. Rather, Paull is a **staff manager,** responsible for one of McDonald's specialist functions, finance. Worldwide chief operations officer Jeff Stratton is responsible for overseeing all functional aspects of McDonald's overseas operations, which are headed by the presidents of world regions: Europe, Latin America, and Asia/Pacific. Of special mention is Ralph Alvarez, who is president of McDonald's U.S. operations and reports to Roberts.

Managers at each level of the hierarchy confer on managers at the next level down the authority to make decisions about how to use organizational resources. Accepting this authority, those lower-level managers then become responsible for their decisions and are accountable for how well they make those decisions. Managers who make the right decisions are typically promoted, and organizations motivate managers with the prospects of promotion and increased responsibility within the chain of command.

Below Alvarez are the other main levels or layers in the McDonald's domestic chain of command—executive vice presidents of its West, Central, and East regions, zone managers, regional managers, and supervisors. A hierarchy is also evident in each company-owned McDonald's restaurant. At the top is the store manager; at lower levels are the first assistant, shift managers, and crew personnel. McDonald's managers have decided that this hierarchy of authority best allows the company to pursue its business-level strategy of providing fast food at reasonable prices.

TALL AND FLAT ORGANIZATIONS   As an organization grows in size (normally measured by the number of its managers and employees), its hierarchy of authority normally lengthens, making the organizational structure taller. A *tall* organization has many levels of authority relative to company size; a *flat* organization has fewer levels relative to company size (see Figure 10.9).[35] As a hierarchy becomes taller, problems that make the organization's structure less flexible and slow managers' response to changes in the organizational environment may result.

Communication problems may arise when an organization has many levels in the hierarchy. It can take a long time for the decisions and orders of upper-level managers to reach managers further down in the hierarchy, and it can take a long time for top managers to learn how well their decisions worked. Feeling out of touch, top managers may want to verify that lower-level managers are following orders and may require written confirmation from them. Middle managers, who know they will be held strictly accountable for their actions, start devoting too much time to the process of making decisions to improve their chances of being right. They might even try to avoid responsibility by making top managers decide what actions to take.

Another communication problem that can result is the distortion of commands and messages being transmitted up and down the hierarchy, which causes managers at different levels to interpret what is happening differently. Distortion of orders and messages can be accidental, occurring because different managers interpret messages from their own narrow, functional perspectives. Or distortion can be intentional, occurring because managers low in the hierarchy decide to interpret information in a way that increases their own personal advantage.

Another problem with tall hierarchies is that they usually indicate that an organization is employing many managers, and managers are expensive. Managerial salaries, benefits, offices, and secretaries are a huge expense for organizations. Large companies such as IBM and General Motors pay their managers billions of dollars a year. In the early 2000s, hundreds of thousands of middle managers were laid off as dot-coms collapsed and high-tech companies such as HP and Lucent attempted to reduce costs by restructuring and downsizing their workforces.

THE MINIMUM CHAIN OF COMMAND   To ward off the problems that result when an organization becomes too tall and employs too many managers,

Figure 10.9
Tall and Flat Organizations

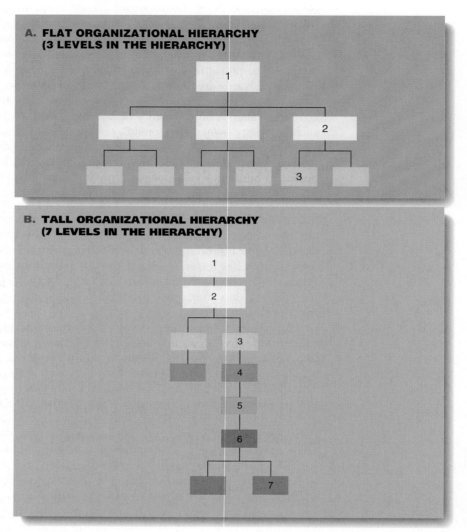

top managers need to ascertain whether they are employing the right number of middle and first-line managers and whether they can redesign their organizational architecture to reduce the number of managers. Top managers might well follow a basic organizing principle—the principle of the minimum chain of command—which states that top managers should always construct a hierarchy with the fewest levels of authority necessary to efficiently and effectively use organizational resources.

Effective managers constantly scrutinize their hierarchies to see whether the number of levels can be reduced—for example, by eliminating one level and giving the responsibilities of managers at that level to managers above and by empowering employees below. One manager who is constantly trying to empower employees and keep the hierarchy flat is Colleen C. Barrett, the number-two executive of Southwest Airlines.[36] Barrett is the highest-ranking woman in the airline industry. At Southwest, she is well known for continually reaffirming Southwest's message that employees should feel free to go above and beyond their prescribed roles to provide better customer service. Her central message is that Southwest values and trusts its employees, who are empowered to take responsibility. Southwest employees are encouraged not to look to their superiors for guidance but, rather, to find ways on their own to do the job better. As a result, Southwest keeps the number of its middle managers to a minimum. The need to empower workers is increasing as companies battle low-cost foreign competitors by searching for new ways to reduce costs, as the following "Managing Globally" suggests.

Managing Globally

How to Use Empowered Self-Managed Teams

In the United States, over 2.3 million manufacturing jobs were lost to factories in low-cost countries abroad in 2003. While many large U.S. manufacturing companies have given up the battle, some companies like electronics maker Plexus Corp., based in Neenah, Wisconsin, have been able to find ways of organizing that allow them to survive and prosper in a low-cost manufacturing world. How have they done this? By creating empowered work teams.

In the 1990s, Plexus saw the writing on the wall as more and more of its customers began to outsource the production of electronic components or even the whole product itself to manufacturers abroad. U.S. companies cannot match the efficiency of manufacturers abroad in producing high volumes of a single product, such as millions of a particular circuit board used in a laptop computer. So Plexus's managers decided to focus their efforts on developing a manufacturing technology called "low-high" that could efficiently produce low volumes of many different kinds of products.

Plexus's managers formed a team to design an organizational structure based on creating four "focused factories" in which control over production decisions is given to the workers, who perform all the operations involved in making a product. The managers cross-trained workers so that they can perform any particular operation in their "factory." With this approach, when work slows down at any point in the production of a particular product, a worker further along the production process can move back to help solve the problem that has arisen at the earlier stage.[37]

Furthermore, managers organized workers into self-managed teams that are empowered to make all the decisions necessary to make a particular

Like Plexus, assembly line workers in Amsterdam, NY, make radio antenna subassemblies in small, interrelated work groups for major U.S. auto manufacturers. Small work groups combined with clever investment in equipment enable the factory to remain competitive in factories that employ cheap overseas labor.

product in one of the four factories. Since each product is different, these teams have to make their decisions quickly if they are to assemble the product in a cost-effective way. The ability of the teams to make rapid decisions and respond to unexpected contingencies is vital on a production line, where time is money—every minute a production line is not moving adds hundreds or thousands of dollars to production costs. Also, a second reason for empowering teams is that when a changeover takes place from making one product to making another, nothing is being produced, so it is vital that changeover time be kept to a minimum. At Plexus, managers, by allowing teams to experiment and by providing guidance, have reduced changeover time from hours to as little as 30 minutes, so the line is making products over 80% of the time.[38] This incredible flexibility, brought about by the way employees are organized, is the reason why Plexus is so efficient and can compete against low-cost manufacturers abroad.

CENTRALIZATION AND DECENTRALIZATION OF AUTHORITY

decentralizing authority Giving lower-level managers and nonmanagerial employees the right to make important decisions about how to use organizational resources.

Another way in which managers can keep the organizational hierarchy flat is by **decentralizing authority**, that is, by giving lower-level managers and nonmanagerial employees the right to make important decisions about how to use organizational resources.[39] If managers at higher levels give lower-level employees the responsibility of making important decisions and only *manage by exception*, then the problems of slow and distorted communication noted previously are kept to a minimum. Moreover, fewer managers are needed because their role is not to make decisions but to act as coach and facilitator and to help other employees make the best decisions. In addition, when decision making is low in the organization and near the customer, employees are better able to recognize and respond to customer needs.

Decentralizing authority allows an organization and its employees to behave in a flexible way even as the organization grows and becomes taller. This is why managers are so interested in empowering employees, creating self-managed work teams, establishing cross-functional teams, and even moving to a product team structure. These design innovations help keep the organizational architecture flexible and responsive to complex task and general environments, complex technologies, and complex strategies.

Although more and more organizations are taking steps to decentralize authority, *too much* decentralization has certain disadvantages. If divisions, functions, or teams are given too much decision-making authority, they may begin to pursue their own goals at the expense of organizational goals. Managers in engineering design or R&D, for example, may become so focused on making the best possible product that they fail to realize that the best product may be so expensive that few people will be willing or able to buy it. Also, too much decentralization can result in a lack of communication among functions or divisions, and this prevents the synergies that result from cooperation ever materializing and organizational performance suffers.

Top managers must seek the balance between centralization and decentralization of authority that best meets the four major contingencies an organization faces (see Figure 10.1). If managers are in a stable environment, are using well-understood technology, and are producing staple kinds of products (such as cereal, canned soup, books, or televisions), then there is no pressing need to decentralize authority, and managers at the top can maintain control of much of organizational decision making.[40] However, in uncertain, changing environments where high-tech companies are producing state-of-the-art products, top managers must often empower employees and allow teams to make important strategic decisions so that the organization can keep up with the changes taking place. Even in high-tech situations, however, too much decentralization can result in problems, as the following "Management Insight" suggests.

Management Insight

Microsoft Centralizes to Meet Google's Challenge

Microsoft has been racing to compete against companies like Yahoo and, especially, Google, which are developing innovative Web-based software products to attract broadband users. In the 2000s, however, Microsoft has been hindered by its slow decision making, and its top managers decided that the source of the problem was its structure: As the company had grown and adopted a more complex divisional structure, too much authority had been decentralized.

In 2005 Microsoft consisted of seven major business units, each of which was headed by a top executive. In each business unit, the executive was in charge of the managers who led the hundreds of product teams working on related software applications. This structure allowed each business unit to make quick decisions internally, but many potential synergies *between* the business units—particularly in the area of developing integrated Web-based applications—were going unnoticed. So new products were not being developed, and the result was that Google, a much smaller company that operates with a product team structure, was forging ahead of Microsoft.

Bill Gates, Steve Ballmer, and a team of other top Microsoft executives decided that a radical overhaul of the company's structure was necessary to change the way companywide decisions were made and speed organizational learning. The top-management team has decided to consolidate the activities of the seven different units into three principal divisions, each of which will be headed by a top manager with a proven record of fast product innovation. The three divisions are the Microsoft Platform Products and Services Division, responsible for the Windows platform, servers, and tools; the Microsoft Business Division, responsible for its Office products and software for small and midsize businesses; and the Microsoft Entertainment and Devices Division, responsible for its Xbox console and games, mobile phones, and other hand-held products.[41]

The idea is that this reorganization will reduce the infighting and miscommunication that was slowing product development between the seven units. In the past, to solve such problems, Gates or Ballmer often had to intervene, and this slowed decision making. Now the head of each division can react faster, intervene, and solve problems as they arise because each division is more centralized. The result should be a faster flow of Web-based products inside each division.

In the new structure, however, the three executives in charge of the divisions will wield enormous power in the company. And although this reorganization has centralized control over product decision making, it has also added another layer in Microsoft's hierarchy. Thus the danger exists that the new structure might make the company even more bureaucratized, causing the potential gains to go unrealized.[42] In 2006 it was still unclear whether or not Microsoft's new structure was working. Has the reorganization just created three new fiefdoms and more bureaucracy? Or will the change allow Microsoft to come out with its own Windows Web-based offerings that will make Google's products such as e-mail storing, desktop searching, and rumored Web-based word processing less attractive to customers?[43]

Integrating and Coordinating Mechanisms

Much coordination takes place through the hierarchy of authority. However, several problems are associated with establishing contact among managers in different functions or divisions. As discussed earlier, managers from different functions and divisions may have different views about what must be done to achieve organizational goals. But if the managers have equal authority (as functional managers typically do), the only manager who can tell them what to do is the CEO, who has the ultimate authority to resolve conflicts. The need to solve everyday conflicts, however, wastes top-management time and slows strategic decision making; indeed, one sign of a poorly performing structure is the number of problems sent up the hierarchy for top managers to solve.

integrating mechanisms
Organizing tools that managers can use to increase communication and coordination among functions and divisions.

To increase communication and coordination among functions or between divisions and to prevent these problems from emerging, top managers incorporate various **integrating mechanisms** into their organizational architecture. The greater the complexity of an organization's structure, the greater is the need for coordination among people, functions, and divisions to make the organizational structure work efficiently and effectively.[44] Thus, when managers choose to adopt a divisional, matrix, or product team structure, they must use complex integrating mechanisms to achieve organizational goals. Several integrating mechanisms are available to managers to increase communication and coordination.[45] Figure 10.10 lists these mechanisms, as well as examples of the individuals or groups that might use them.

LIAISON ROLES   Managers can increase coordination among functions and divisions by establishing liaison roles. When the volume of contacts between two functions increases, one way to improve coordination is to give one manager in each function or division the responsibility for coordinating with the other. These managers may meet daily, weekly, monthly, or as needed. A liaison role is illustrated in Figure 10.10; the small dot represents the person within a function who has responsibility for coordinating with the other function. Coordinating is part of the liaison's full-time job, and usually

Figure 10.10

Types and Examples of Integrating Mechanisms

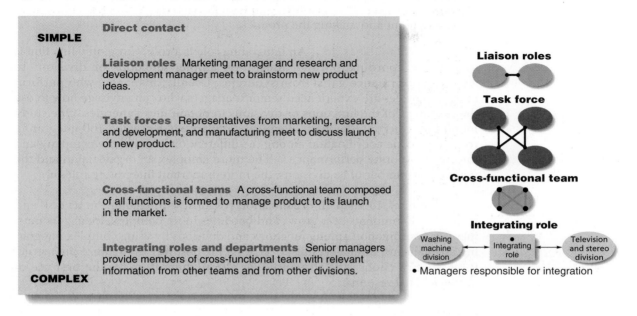

SIMPLE

Direct contact

Liaison roles Marketing manager and research and development manager meet to brainstorm new product ideas.

Task forces Representatives from marketing, research and development, and manufacturing meet to discuss launch of new product.

Cross-functional teams A cross-functional team composed of all functions is formed to manage product to its launch in the market.

Integrating roles and departments Senior managers provide members of cross-functional team with relevant information from other teams and from other divisions.

COMPLEX

Liaison roles

Task force

Cross-functional team

Integrating role

Washing machine division ← Integrating role → Television and stereo division

• Managers responsible for integration

an informal relationship develops between the people involved, greatly easing strains between functions. Furthermore, liaison roles provide a way of transmitting information across an organization, which is important in large organizations whose employees may know no one outside their immediate function or division.

TASK FORCES When more than two functions or divisions share many common problems, direct contact and liaison roles may not provide sufficient coordination. In these cases, a more complex integrating mechanism, a **task force,** may be appropriate (see Figure 10.10). One manager from each relevant function or division is assigned to a task force that meets to solve a specific, mutual problem; members are responsible for reporting to their departments on the issues addressed and the solutions recommended. Task forces are often called *ad hoc committees* because they are temporary; they may meet on a regular basis or only a few times. When the problem or issue is solved, the task force is no longer needed; members return to their normal roles in their departments or are assigned to other task forces. Typically, task force members also perform many of their normal duties while serving on the task force.

task force A committee of managers from various functions or divisions who meet to solve a specific, mutual problem; also called *ad hoc* committee.

CROSS-FUNCTIONAL TEAMS In many cases, the issues addressed by a task force are recurring problems, such as the need to develop new products or find new kinds of customers. To address recurring problems effectively, managers are increasingly using permanent integrating mechanisms such as cross-functional teams. An example of a cross-functional team is a new product development committee that is responsible for the choice, design, manufacturing, and marketing of a new product. Such an activity obviously requires a great deal of integration among functions if new products are to be successfully introduced, and using a complex integrating mechanism such as a cross-functional team accomplishes this. As discussed earlier, in a product team structure people and resources are grouped into permanent cross-functional teams to speed products to market. These teams assume long-term responsibility for all aspects of development and making the product.

INTEGRATING ROLES   An integrating role is a role whose only function is to increase coordination and integration among functions or divisions to achieve performance gains from synergies. Usually, managers who perform integrating roles are experienced senior managers who can envisage how to use the resources of the functions or divisions to obtain new synergies. One study found that Du Pont, the giant chemical company, had created 160 integrating roles to provide coordination among the different divisions of the company and improve corporate performance.[46] The more complex an organization and the greater the number of its divisions, the more important integrating roles are.

In summary, to keep an organization responsive to changes in its task and general environments as it grows and becomes more complex, managers must increase coordination among functions and divisions by using complex integrating mechanisms. Managers must decide on the best way to organize their structures, that is, choose the structure that allows them to make the best use of organizational resources.

Organizational Culture

The second principal issue in organizational design is to create, develop, and maintain an organization's culture. As we discussed in Chapter 3, **organizational culture** is the shared set of beliefs, expectations, values, and norms that influence how members of an organization relate to one another and cooperate to achieve organizational goals. Culture influences the work behaviors and attitudes of individuals and groups in an organization because its members adhere to shared values, norms, and expected standards of behavior. Employees *internalize* organizational values and norms and then let these values and norms guide their decisions and actions.[47]

A company's culture is a result of its pivotal or guiding values and norms. A company's *values* are the shared standards that its members use to evaluate whether or not they have helped the company achieve its vision and goals. The values a company might adopt include any or all of the following standards: excellence, stability, predictability, profitability, economy, creativeness, morality, and usefulness. A company's *norms* specify or prescribe the kinds of shared beliefs, attitudes, and behaviors that its members should observe and follow. Norms are informal, but powerful, rules about how employees should behave or conduct themselves in a company if they are to be accepted and help it to achieve its goals. Norms can be equally as constraining as the formal written rules contained in a company's handbook. Companies might encourage workers to adopt norms such as working hard, respecting traditions and authority, and being courteous to others; being conservative, cautious, and a "team player"; being creative and courageous and taking risks; being honest and frugal and maintaining high personal standards. Norms may also prescribe certain very specific behaviors such as keeping one's desk tidy, cleaning up at the end of the day, taking one's turn to bring doughnuts, and even wearing blue jeans and a t-shirt on Fridays.

Ideally, a company's norms help the company achieve its values. For example, a new computer company whose culture is based on values of excellence and innovation may try to attain this high standard by encouraging workers to adopt norms about being creative, taking risks, and working hard now and looking long-term for rewards (this combination of values and norms leads to an *entrepreneurial* culture in a company). On the other hand, a bank or insurance company that has values of stability and predictability may emphasize norms of cautiousness and obedience to authority (the result of adopting these values and norms would be a *stable, conservative* culture in a company).

Over time, members of a company learn from one another how to perceive and interpret various events that happen in the work setting and to respond to them in ways that reflect the company's guiding values and norms. This is why organizational culture is so important: When a strong and cohesive set of organizational values and norms is in place, employees focus on thinking about what is best for the organization in the long run—all their decisions and actions become oriented toward helping the organization perform well. For example, a teacher spends personal time after school coaching and counseling students; an R&D scientist works 80 hours a week, evenings, and weekends to help speed up a late project; a salesclerk at a department store runs after a customer who left a credit card at the cash register. An interesting example of a company founder who built a strong culture by focusing on values and norms is Sam Walton, profiled in the following "Manager as a Person."

Manager as a Person

Sam Walton and Wal-Mart's Culture

Wal-Mart, headquartered in Bentonville, Arkansas, is the largest retailer in the world. In 2005, it sold over $500 billion worth of products.[48] A large part of Wal-Mart's success is due to the nature of the culture that its founder, the late Sam Walton, established for the company. Walton wanted all his managers and workers to take a hands-on approach to their jobs and be totally committed to Wal-Mart's main goal, which he defined as total customer satisfaction. To motivate his employees, Walton created a culture that gave employees at all levels, who are called "associates," continuous feedback about their performance and the company's performance.

To involve his associates in the business and encourage them to develop work behaviors focused on pr established strong cultural values a norms associates are expected to fo encourages associates, in Walton come within 10 feet of a custome and ask him if you can help him." The "sundown rule" states that employees should strive to answer customer requests by sundown of the day they are made. The Wal-Mart cheer ("Give me a W, give me an A," and so on) is used in all its stores.[49]

The strong customer-oriented values that Walton created are exemplified in the stories Wal-Mart members tell one another about associates' concern for customers. They include stories like the one about Sheila, who risked her own safety when she jumped in front of a car to prevent a little boy from being struck; about Phyllis, who administered CPR to a customer who had suffered a heart attack in her store; and about Annette, who gave up the Power Ranger she had on layaway for her own son to fulfill the birthday wish of a customer's son.[50] The strong Wal-Mart culture helps to control and motivate employees to achieve the stringent output and financial targets the company has set for itself.[51]

A notable way Wal-Mart builds its culture is through its annual stockholders' meeting, an extravagant ceremony celebrating the company's success.[52] Every year Wal-Mart flies thousands of its highest performers to its annual meeting at corporate headquarters in Arkansas for a show featuring famous singers, rock bands, and comedians. Wal-Mart feels that expensive entertainment is a reward its employees deserve and that the event reinforces the company's high-performance values and culture. The proceedings are even broadcast live to all of Wal-Mart's stores so that employees can celebrate the company's achievements together.[53]

Since Sam Walton's death, however, Wal-Mart's increasing rise to prominence (it is the nation's largest private employer, with over 1 million employees) has brought attention to the "hidden side" of its culture. Critics have claimed that few ordinary Wal-Mart employees receive any reasonably priced health care or other benefits and that the company pays employees only the minimum wage or a little above it. They also contend that employees don't question these policies because managers have socialized them into believing that this has to be the case—that the only way Wal-Mart can keep its prices low is by keeping their pay and benefits low. In the 2000s, however, Wal-Mart's managers have responded to a barrage of criticism that it must do more to improve its human resource practices. While it still stresses the need to keep costs low, it has started to increase pay and health care benefits and has established new career ladders for its very loyal employees, who seem to be still following Sam Walton's 10-foot-attitude rule to the letter.

Where Does Organizational Culture Come From?

In managing organizational architecture, an important question that arises is, Where does organizational culture come from? Why do different companies have different cultures? Why might a culture that for many years helped an organization achieve its goals suddenly harm the organization?

Organizational culture is shaped by the interaction of four main factors: the personal and professional characteristics of people within the organization, organizational ethics, the nature of the employment relationship, and the design of its organizational structure (see Figure 10.11). These factors work together to produce different cultures in different organizations and cause changes in culture over time.

Figure 10.11
Sources of an Organization's Culture

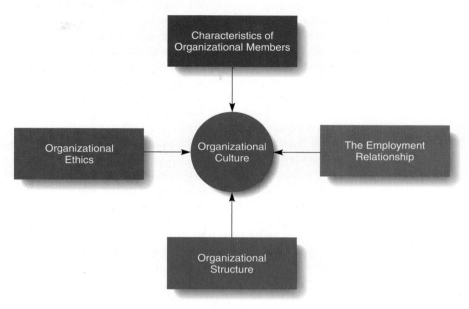

CHARACTERISTICS OF ORGANIZATIONAL MEMBERS The ultimate source of organizational culture is the people who make up the organization. If you want to know why organizational cultures differ, look at the way the characteristics of their members differ. Organizations A, B, and C develop distinctly different cultures because they attract, select, and retain people who have different values, personalities, and ethics.[54] Recall the attraction-selection-attrition model from Chapter 3. People may be attracted to an organization whose values match theirs; similarly, an organization selects people who share its values. Over time, people who do not fit in leave. The result is that people inside the organization become more and more similar, the values of the organization become more and more pronounced and clear-cut, and the culture becomes more and more distinct from that of similar organizations.[55]

The fact that an organization's members become similar over time and come to share the same values may actually hinder their ability to adapt and respond to changes in the environment.[56] This happens when the organization's values and norms become *so* strong and promote *so* much cohesiveness in members' attitudes that the members begin to misperceive the environment.[57] To prevent this situation at Microsoft, which has strong, cohesive values that bond its members, Bill Gates worked hard to make it clear that employees should express their own personal views, even though they might differ from his and other top managers' views. One example of how Gates's understanding of culture worked to Microsoft's advantage occurred when the company started its Internet service, MSN. Microsoft believed the popularity of its Windows platform would allow it to control the future development of the Internet, even though Netscape had introduced a popular browser. Two concerned Microsoft programmers working in its Internet division wrote a memo to top managers arguing that Microsoft would end up with *no* control over the Internet, given the rapid pace at which the Internet was developing. They also argued that Netscape's browser would become the dominant means by which people would access the Internet. The programmers argued that to compete with Netscape, Microsoft should rush to develop its own Web browser. After reading their memo, Gates convened a major organizationwide meeting. Top managers listened while all of the issues were aired, and then they admitted they were wrong. The company then diverted most of its human talent to developing its own browser as quickly as possible. Within one year, the first version of Internet Explorer was ready, and Microsoft gave it away free to users.

Companies like Microsoft need a strong set of values that emphasize innovation and hard work. However, they need to be careful that their success doesn't lead members to believe their company will always be the best in the business, or "invincible." Some companies have made this mistake. The old IBM of the 1980s believed its control of the mainframe market made it invincible; IBM employees laughed off the potential threat personal computers posed. The CEO of another dominant computer maker at that time, Digital Equipment, reportedly commented that "personal computers are just toys." Within a few years, Digital Equipment was experiencing huge losses. Today, Microsoft is facing the same problem in its battle with Google as the latter seeks to move PC operations, such as word processing and storage, online—a move that threatens Microsoft's power over the desktop PC world.

ORGANIZATIONAL ETHICS   An organization can purposefully develop some kinds of cultural values to control the way its members behave. One important class of values in this category stems from **organizational ethics,** the moral values, beliefs, and rules that establish the appropriate way for an organization and its members to deal with each other and with people outside the organization. Recall from Chapter 4 that ethical values rest on principles stressing the importance of treating organizational stakeholders fairly and equitably. Managers and employees are constantly making choices about the right, or ethical, thing to do, and to help them make ethical decisions, top managers purposefully implant ethical values into an organization's culture.[58] Consequently, ethical values, and the rules and norms that embody them, become an integral part of an organization's culture and determine how its members will manage situations and make decisions.

organizational ethics
The moral values, beliefs, and rules that establish the appropriate way for an organization and its members to deal with each other and with people outside the organization.

THE EMPLOYMENT RELATIONSHIP   A third factor shaping organizational culture is the nature of the employment relationship a company establishes with its employees via its human resource policies and practices. Recall from Chapter 1 our discussion of the changing relationship between organizations and their employees due to the growth of outsourcing and employment of contingent workers. Like a company's hiring, promotion, and layoff policies, human resource policies, along with pay and benefits, can influence how hard employees will work to achieve the organization's goals, how attached they will be to the organization, and whether or not they will buy into its values and norms.[59] As we discuss in Chapter 12, an organization's human resource policies are a good indicator of the values in its culture concerning its responsibilities to employees. Consider the effects of a company's promotion policy, for example: A company with a policy of promoting from within will fill higher-level positions with employees who already work for the organization. On the other hand, a company with a policy of promotion from without will fill its open positions with qualified outsiders. What does this say about each organization's culture?

Promoting from within will bolster strong values and norms that build loyalty, align employees' goals with the organization, and encourage employees to work hard to advance within the organization. If employees see no prospect of being promoted from within, they are likely to look for better opportunities elsewhere, cultural values and norms result in self-interested behavior, and cooperation and cohesiveness fall. The tech sector has gone through great turmoil in recent years, and an estimated 1 million U.S. tech employees lost their jobs following the burst of the dot-com bubble. Apple, HP, and IBM—long well known for their strong employee-oriented values that emphasized long-term employment and respect for employees—were among the many companies forced to lay off employees, and their cultures have been changed forever as a result. To rebuild their cultures, and make their remaining employees feel like "owners," many companies have HRM pay policies that reward superior performance with bonuses and stock options.[60] For example, Southwest Airlines and Google established companywide stock option systems that encourage their employees to be innovative and responsive to customers.

ORGANIZATIONAL STRUCTURE We have seen how the values and norms that shape employee work attitudes and behaviors derive from an organization's people, ethics, and HRM policies. A fourth source of cultural values comes from the organization's structure. *Different kinds of structure give rise to different kinds of culture,* so to create a certain culture, managers often need to design a particular type of structure. Tall and highly centralized structures give rise to totally different sets of norms, rules, and cultural values than do structures that are flat and decentralized. In a tall, centralized organization people have little personal autonomy, and norms that focus on being cautious, obeying authority, and respecting traditions emerge because predictability and stability are desired goals. In a flat, decentralized structure people have more freedom to choose and control their own activities, and norms that focus on being creative and courageous and taking risks appear, giving rise to a culture in which innovation and flexibility are desired goals.

Whether a company is centralized or decentralized also leads to the development of different kinds of cultural values. By decentralizing authority and empowering employees, an organization can establish values that encourage and reward creativity or innovation. In doing this, an organization signals employees that it's okay to be innovative and do things their own way—as long as their actions are consistent with the good of the organization. Conversely, in some organizations, it is important that employees do not make decisions on their own and that their actions be open to the scrutiny of superiors. In cases like this, centralization can be used to create cultural values that reinforce obedience and accountability. For example, in nuclear power plants, values that promote stability, predictability, and obedience to authority are deliberately fostered to prevent disasters.[61] Through norms and rules, employees are taught the importance of behaving consistently and honestly, and they learn that sharing information with supervisors, especially information about mistakes or errors, is the only acceptable form of behavior.[62]

An organization that seeks to manage and change its culture must take a hard look at all four factors that shape culture: the characteristics of its members, its ethical values, its human resource policies, and its organizational structure. However, changing a culture can be difficult because of the way these factors interact and affect one another.[63] Often, a major reorganization is necessary for a cultural change to occur, as we discuss in the next chapter.

Strong, Adaptive Cultures Versus Weak, Inert Cultures

Many researchers and managers believe that employees of some organizations go out of their way to help the organization because it has a strong and cohesive organizational culture—an adaptive culture that controls employee attitudes and behaviors. *Adaptive cultures* are those whose values and norms help an organization to build momentum and to grow and change as needed to achieve its goals and be effective. By contrast, *inert cultures* are those whose values and norms fail to motivate or inspire employees; they lead to stagnation and, often, failure over time. What leads to a strong adaptive culture or one that is inert and hard to change?

Researchers have found that organizations with strong adaptive cultures, like 3M, UPS, Microsoft, and IBM, invest in their employees. They demonstrate their commitment to their members by, for example, emphasizing the long-term nature of the employment relationship and trying to avoid layoffs. These companies develop long-term career paths for their employees and spend a lot of money on training and development to increase employees' value to the organization. In these ways, terminal and instrumental values pertaining to the worth of human resources encourage the development of supportive work attitudes and behaviors.

In adaptive cultures employees often receive rewards linked directly to their performance and to the performance of the company as a whole. Sometimes, employee stock ownership plans (ESOPs) are developed in which workers as a group are allowed to buy a significant percentage of their company's stock. Workers who are owners of the company have additional incentive to develop skills that allow them to perform highly and search actively for ways to improve quality, efficiency, and performance. At Dell, for example, employees are able to buy Dell stock at a steep 15% discount, and this allows them to build a sizable stake in the company over time.

Some organizations, however, develop cultures with values that do not include protecting and increasing the worth of their human resources as a major goal. Their employment practices are based on short-term employment according to the needs of the organization and on minimal investment in employees who perform simple, routine tasks. Moreover, employees are not often rewarded on the basis of their performance and thus have little incentive to improve their skills or otherwise invest in the organization to help it to achieve goals. If a company has an inert culture, poor working relationships frequently develop between the organization and its employees, and instrumental values of noncooperation, laziness, and loafing and work norms of output restriction are common.

Moreover, an adaptive culture develops an emphasis on entrepreneurship and respect for the employee and allows the use of organizational structures, such as the cross-functional team structure, that empower employees to make decisions and motivate them to succeed. By contrast, in an inert culture, employees are content to be told what to do and have little incentive or motivation to perform beyond minimum work requirements. As you might expect, the emphasis is on close supervision and hierarchical authority, which result in a culture that makes it difficult to adapt to a changing environment.

Nokia, the world's largest wireless phone maker, headquartered in Finland, is a good example of a company in which managers strive to create an adaptive culture.[64] Nokia's president, Matti Alahuhta, believes that Nokia's cultural values are based on the Finnish character: Finns are down-to-earth, rational, straightforward people. They are also very friendly and democratic people who do not believe in a rigid hierarchy based either on a person's authority or on social class. Nokia's culture reflects these values because innovation and decision making are pushed right down to the bottom line, to teams of employees who take up the challenge of developing the ever-smaller and more sophisticated phones for which the company is known. Bureaucracy is kept to a minimum at Nokia; its adaptive culture is based on informal and personal relationships and norms of cooperation and teamwork.

To help strengthen its culture, Nokia has built a futuristic open-plan steel and glass building just outside Helsinki. Here, in an open environment, its research and development people can work together to innovate new kinds of wireless phones. More than one out of every three of Nokia's 60,000 employees work in research; what keeps these people together and focused is Nokia's company mission to produce phones that are better, cheaper, smaller, and easier to use than competitor's phones.[65] This is the "Nokia Way," a system of cultural values and norms that can't be written down but is always present in the values that cement people together and in the language and stories that its members use to orient themselves to the company.

Another company with an adaptive culture is GlaxoSmithKlein, the prescription drug maker discussed earlier in the chapter. Much of GSK's success can be

An aerial view of the cafeteria at Nokia's headquarters in Espoo, Finland. The open architecture of the building reflects the company's culture, which is based on giving employees the space and freedom to pursue their dreams of improving Nokia's products.

attributed to its ability to attract the very best research scientists, who come because its adaptive culture nurtures scientists and emphasizes values and norms of innovation. Scientists are given great freedom to pursue intriguing ideas even if the commercial payoff is questionable. Moreover, researchers are inspired to think of their work as a quest to alleviate human disease and suffering worldwide, and GSK has a reputation as an ethical company whose values put people above profits.

Although the experience of Nokia and GSK suggests that organizational culture can give rise to managerial actions that ultimately benefit the organization, this is not always the case. The cultures of some organizations become dysfunctional, encouraging managerial actions that harm the organization and discouraging actions that might lead to an improvement in performance.[66] For example, Sunflower Electric Power, a electricity generation and transmission cooperative, almost went bankrupt in the early 2000s. A state committee of inquiry that was set up to find the source of the problem put the blame on Sunflower's CEO. The committee decided that he had created an abusive culture based on fear and blame that encouraged managers to fight over and protect their turf—an inert culture. Managers were afraid to rock the boat or make suggestions since they could not predict what would happen to them.

The CEO was fired, and a new CEO, Chris Hauck, was appointed to change the cooperative's culture. He found it very hard to do so, as his senior managers were so used to the old values and norms. One top manager, for example, engaged so frequently in the practice of berating one supervisor that the man became physically sick.[67] Hauck fired this and other managers as a signal that such behavior would no longer be tolerated. With the help of consultants, he went about the process of changing values and norms to emphasize cooperation, teamwork, and respect for others. Clearly, managers can influence the way their organizational culture develops over time.[68]

Summary and Review

DESIGNING ORGANIZATIONAL STRUCTURE The four main determinants of organizational structure are the external environment, strategy, technology, and human resources. In general, the higher the level of uncertainty associated with these factors, the more appropriate is a flexible, adaptable structure as opposed to a formal, rigid one.

GROUPING TASKS INTO JOBS Job design is the process by which managers group tasks into jobs. To create more interesting jobs, and to get workers to act flexibly, managers can enlarge and enrich jobs. The job characteristics model is a tool managers can use to measure how motivating or satisfying a particular job is.

GROUPING JOBS INTO FUNCTIONS AND DIVISIONS Managers can choose from many kinds of organizational structures to make the best use of organizational resources. Depending on the specific organizing problems they face, managers can choose from functional, product, geographic, market, matrix, product team, and hybrid structures.

COORDINATING FUNCTIONS AND DIVISIONS No matter which structure managers choose, they must decide how to distribute authority in the organization, how many levels to have in the hierarchy of authority, and what balance to strike between centralization and decentralization to keep the number of levels in the hierarchy to a minimum. As organizations grow, managers must increase integration and coordination among functions and divisions. Four integrating mechanisms that facilitate this are liaison roles, task forces, cross-functional teams, and integrating roles.

ORGANIZATIONAL CULTURE Organizational culture is the set of values, norms, and standards of behavior that control the ways individuals and groups in an organization interact with one another and work to achieve organizational goals. The four main sources of organizational culture are the characteristics of its members, organizational ethics, the nature of the employment relationship, and the design of organizational structure. The way in which managers work to influence these four factors determines whether an organization's culture is strong and adaptive or is inert and difficult to change.

Management in Action

Topics for Discussion and Action

Discussion

1. Would a flexible or a more formal structure be appropriate for these organizations: (a) a large department store, (b) a Big Five accountancy firm, (c) a biotechnology company? Explain your reasoning.

2. Using the job characteristics model as a guide, discuss how a manager can enrich or enlarge subordinates' jobs.

3. How might a salesperson's job or a secretary's job be enlarged or enriched to make it more motivating?

4. When and under what conditions might managers change from a functional to (a) a product, (b) a geographic, or (c) a market structure?

5. How do matrix structure and product team structure differ? Why is product team structure more widely used?

6. What is organizational culture, and how does it affect the way employees behave?

Action

7. Find and interview a manager and identify the kind of organizational structure that his or her organization uses to coordinate its people and resources. Why is the organization using that structure? Do you think a different structure would be more appropriate? Which one?

8. With the same or another manager, discuss the distribution of authority in the organization. Does the manager think that decentralizing authority and empowering employees is appropriate?

9. Interview some employees of an organization, and ask them about the organization's values and norms, the typical characteristics of employees, and the organization's ethical values and socialization practices. Using this information, try to describe the organization's culture and the way it affects the way people and groups behave.

Building Management Skills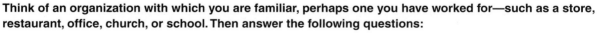
Understanding Organizing

Think of an organization with which you are familiar, perhaps one you have worked for—such as a store, restaurant, office, church, or school. Then answer the following questions:

1. Which contingencies are most important in explaining how the organization is organized? Do you think it is organized in the best way?

2. Using the job characteristics model, how motivating do you think the job of a typical employee in this organization is?

3. Can you think of any ways in which a typical job could be enlarged or enriched?

4. What kind of organizational structure does the organization use? If it is part of a chain, what kind of structure does the entire organization use? What other structures discussed in the chapter might allow the organization to operate more effectively? For example, would the move to a product

team structure lead to greater efficiency or effectiveness? Why or why not?

5. How many levels are there in the organization's hierarchy? Is authority centralized or decentralized? Describe the span of control of the top manager and of middle or first-line managers.

6. Is the distribution of authority appropriate for the organization and its activities? Would it be possible to flatten the hierarchy by decentralizing authority and empowering employees?

7. What are the principal integrating mechanisms used in the organization? Do they provide sufficient coordination among individuals and functions? How might they be improved?

8. Now that you have analyzed the way this organization is structured, what advice would you give its managers to help them improve the way it operates?

Managing Ethically

Suppose an organization is downsizing and laying off many of its middle managers. Some top managers charged with deciding who to terminate might decide to keep the subordinates they like, and who are obedient to them, rather than the ones who are difficult or the best performers. They might also decide to lay off the most highly paid subordinates even if they are high performers. Think of the ethical issues involved in designing a hierarchy, and discuss the following issues.

Questions

1. What ethical rules (see Chapter 5) should managers use to decide which employees to terminate when redesigning their hierarchy?

2. Some people argue that employees who have worked for an organization for many years have a claim on the organization at least as strong as that of its shareholders. What do you think of the ethics of this position—can employees claim to "own" their jobs if they have contributed significantly to the organization's past success? How does a socially responsible organization behave in this situation?

Small Group Breakout Exercise

Bob's Appliances

Form groups of three or four people, and appoint one member as the spokesperson who will communicate your findings to the class when called on by the instructor. Then discuss the following scenario.

Bob's Appliances sells and services household appliances such as washing machines, dishwashers, ranges, and refrigerators. Over the years, the company has developed a good reputation for the quality of its customer service, and many local builders patronize the store. Recently, some new appliance retailers, including Circuit City and REX, have opened stores that also provide numerous appliances. To attract more customers, however, these stores also carry a complete range of consumer electronics products—televisions, stereos, and computers. Bob Lange, the owner of Bob's Appliances, has decided that if he is to stay in business, he must widen his product range and compete directly with the chains.

In 2002, he decided to build a 20,000-square-foot store and service center, and he is now hiring new employees to sell and service the new line of consumer electronics. Because of his company's increased size, Lange is not sure of the best way to organize the employees. Currently, he uses a functional structure; employees are divided into sales, purchasing and accounting, and repair. Bob is wondering whether selling and servicing consumer electronics is so different from selling and servicing appliances that he should move to a product structure (see figure) and create separate sets of functions for each of his two lines of business.[69]

You are a team of local consultants whom Bob has called in to advise him as he makes this crucial choice. Which structure do you recommend? Why?

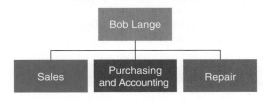

FUNCTIONAL STRUCTURE

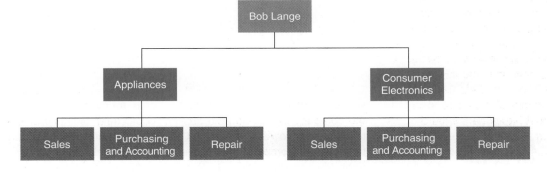

PRODUCT STRUCTURE

Exploring the World Wide Web

Go to the Web site of Kraft, the food services company www. kraft.com). Click on "brands" and then on "North America," and answer the following questions:

1. What kind of international structure do you think Kraft uses to manage its food operations?

2. Given the information on these pages, what kind of organizational structure do you think Kraft uses to manage its U.S. operations?

Why do you think it uses this structure?

3. What do you think are the main challenges Kraft faces in managing its food business to improve performance?

Be the Manager

Speeding Up Web Site Design

You have been hired by a Web site design, production, and hosting company whose new animated Web site designs are attracting a lot of attention and a lot of customers. Currently, employees are organized into different functions such as hardware, software design, graphic art, and Web site hosting, as well as functions such as marketing and human resources. Each function takes its turn to work on a new project from initial customer request to final online Web site hosting.

The problem the company is experiencing is that it typically takes one year from the initial idea stage to the time that the Web site is up and running; the company wants to shorten this time by half to protect and expand its market niche. In talking to other managers, you discover that they believe the company's current functional structure is the source of the problem—it is not allowing employees to develop Web sites fast enough to satisfy customers' demands. They want you to design a better one.

Questions

1. Discuss ways in which you can improve the way the current functional structure operates so that it speeds Web site development.

2. Discuss the pros and cons of moving to a (a) multidivisional, (b) matrix, and (c) product team structure to reduce Web site development time.

3. Which of these structures do you think is most appropriate and why?

4. What kind of culture would you help create to make the company's structure work more effectively?

BusinessWeek

Case in the News

Information Technology: Stopping the Sprawl at HP

When Randy Mott joined Wal-Mart fresh out of college in 1978, its in-house tech staff had only 30 members and company founder Sam Walton had not yet become a believer in the power of computing to revolutionize retailing. But Mott and his cohorts developed a network of computerized distribution centers that made it simple to open and run new stores with cookie-cutter efficiency.

Then in the early 1990s, Mott, by this time chief information officer, persuaded higher-ups to invest in a so-called data warehouse. That let the company collect and sift customer data to analyze buying trends as no company ever had—right down to which flavor of Pop-Tarts sells best at a given store.

By the time Mott took his latest job last summer, as CIO of HP, he had become a rock star of sorts among the corporate techie set—an executive who not only understood technology and how it could be used to improve a business but how to deliver those benefits. Besides his 22-year stint at Wal-Mart, Mott helped Dell hone its already huge IT advantage. By melding nearly 100 separate systems into a single data warehouse, Mott's team enabled Dell to quickly spot rising inventory for a particular chip, for instance, so the company could offer online promotions for devices containing that part before the price fell too steeply.

Now Mott, 49, is embarking on his boldest and most challenging project yet: a three-year, $1 billion-plus makeover of HP's internal tech systems that will replace 85 loosely connected data centers around the world with six cutting-edge facilities—two each in Austin, Atlanta, and Houston. Mott is pushing sweeping changes in the way HP operates, slashing thousands of smaller projects at the decentralized company to focus on a few corporatewide initiatives—including scrapping 784 isolated databases for one companywide data warehouse. Says Mott: "We want to make HP the envy of the technology world." If it works, Mott's makeover could have more impact than any new HP advertising campaign, printer, or PC—and could turbocharge the company's already impressive turnaround. HP posted profits of $1.5 billion in its second quarter, up 51% from the year before, on a 5% increase in sales. If Mott is successful, HP's annual spending on tech should be cut in half in the years ahead, from $3.5 billion in 2005, say insiders.

More important, a Wal-Mart-style data warehouse could help HP make headway on its most vexing problem in recent years: how to capitalize on its vast product breadth. While HP sells everything from $10 ink cartridges to multimillion-dollar supercomputers, the company has operated more like a conglomerate of separate companies than a one-stop tech superstore. "We shipped 55 million printers, 30 million PCs, and 2 million servers last year," says CEO Hurd. "If we can integrate all that information, it would enable us to know exactly how we're doing in Chicago on a given day, or whether the CIO of a big customer also happens to own any of our products at home."

Mott's initiatives may well stir up a hornet's nest within HP. They will likely require thousands of layoffs, while requiring the support of remaining staffers in a company that has long resisted centralized control. Mott is testing the limits of the HP culture, taking away the right of thousands of IT workers to purchase their own tech equipment.

But Mott has the absolute backing of Hurd, who began recruiting him shortly after arriving at HP in February 2005. The pair have known each other for years. At both Wal-Mart and Dell, Mott bought data warehousing gear from Hurd, who was a leading evangelist for the technology during his years at NCR Corp. Hurd eventually wooed Mott in July on the strength of a $15 million pay package and a promise to support him if he'd sign on for the aggressive three-year transformation.

Still, Mott's greatest strength may be that while a technologist, he has the management skills to actually make IT take root in a company's culture. Linda M. Dillman, a onetime Wal-Mart CIO and now its executive vice president for risk management and benefits administration, recalls how Mott championed the deployment of IT by showing how it achieved Wal-Mart's business goals. Underlings say Mott's low-key Southern charm belies an intensity that typically brings him into the office by 6:15 a.m. He has no patience for quick summaries during grueling two-day-long business reviews he convenes once a month. That certainly jibes with Hurd's view of the world—which is why he's centralizing HP's balkanized information systems, even while working to decentralize operational control The idea is to make sure all of HP's businesses are working off the same set of data, and to give them the tools to quickly make the best decisions for the entire company—say, a single customer management system, so executives can know the full breadth of what any account buys from HP.

Questions

1. In what ways is Randy Mott trying to change HP's structure and the way it works?

2. In what ways has he been trying to change HP's culture?

3. How will the changes he has made affect HP's competitive advantage and performance?

Source: Peter Burrows, "Information Technology: Stopping the Sprawl at HP." Reprinted from the May 29, 2006, issue of *BusinessWeek* by special permission. Copyright © 2006 by the McGraw-Hill Companies, Inc.

BusinessWeek

Case in the News

The Art of Motivation

It was about 2 p.m. on March 9 when three Nucor Corp. electricians got the call from their colleagues at the Hickman (Ark.) plant. It was bad news: Hickman's electrical grid had failed. For a minimill steelmaker like Nucor, which melts scrap steel from autos, dishwashers, mobile homes, and the like in an electric arc furnace to make new steel, there's little that could be worse. The trio immediately dropped what they were doing and headed out to the plant. Malcolm McDonald, an electrician from the Decatur (Ala.) mill, was in Indiana visiting another facility. He drove down, arriving at 9 o'clock that night. Les Hart and Bryson Trumble, from Nucor's facility in Hertford County, N.C., boarded a plane that landed in Memphis at 11 p.m. Then they drove two hours to the troubled plant.

No supervisor had asked them to make the trip, and no one had to. They went on their own. Camping out in the electrical substation with the Hickman staff, the team worked 20-hour shifts to get the plant up and running again in three days instead of the anticipated full week. There wasn't any direct financial incentive for them to blow their weekends, no extra money in their next paycheck, but for the company their contribution was huge. Hickman went on to post a first-quarter record for tons of steel shipped.

What's most amazing about this story is that at Nucor it's not considered particularly remarkable. Says Executive Vice President John J. Ferriola, who oversees the Hickman plant and seven others, "It happens daily." In an industry as Rust Belt as they come, Nucor has nurtured one of the most dynamic and engaged workforces around. The 11,300 nonunion employees at the Charlotte (N.C.) company don't see themselves as worker bees waiting for instructions from above. Nucor's flattened hierarchy and emphasis on pushing power to the front line lead its employees to adopt the mindset of owner-operators. It's a profitable formula as Nucor's 387% return to shareholders suggests. Nucor gained renown in the late 1980s for its radical pay practices, which base the vast majority of most workers' income on their performance. An upstart nipping at the heels of the integrated steel giants, Nucor had a close-knit culture that was the natural outgrowth of its underdog identity. Legendary leader F. Kenneth Iverson's radical insight: that employees, even hourly clock-punchers, will make an extraordinary effort if you reward them richly, treat them with respect, and give them real power.

Nucor is an upstart no more, and the untold story of how it has clung to that core philosophy even as it has grown into the largest steel company in the U.S. is in many ways as compelling as the celebrated tale of its brash youth. Iverson retired in 1999. Under CEO Daniel R. DiMicco, a 23-year veteran, Nucor has snapped up 13 plants over the past five years while managing to instill its unique culture in all of the facilities it has bought, an achievement that makes him a more than worthy successor to Iverson.

At Nucor the art of motivation is about an unblinking focus on the people on the front line of the business. It's about talking to them, listening to them, taking a risk on their ideas, and accepting the occasional failure. It's a culture built in part with symbolic gestures. Every year, for example, every single employee's name goes on the cover of the annual report. And, like Iverson before him, DiMicco flies commercial, manages without an executive parking space, and really does make the coffee in the office when he takes the last cup.

Although he has an Ivy League pedigree, including degrees from Brown University and the University of Pennsylvania, DiMicco retains the plain-talking style of a guy raised in a middle-class family in Mt. Kisco, N.Y. Only 65 people—yes, 65—work alongside him at headquarters.

Money is where the rubber meets the road. Nucor's unusual pay system is the single most daring element of the company's model and the hardest for outsiders and acquired companies to embrace. An experienced steelworker at another company can easily earn $16 to $21 an hour. At

Nucor the guarantee is closer to $10. A bonus tied to the production of defect-free steel by an employee's entire shift can triple the average steelworker's take-home pay.

With demand for steel scorching these days, payday has become a regular cause for celebration. Nucor gave out more than $220 million in profit sharing and bonuses to the rank and file in 2005. The average Nucor steelworker took home nearly $79,000 last year. Add to that a $2,000 one-time bonus to mark the company's record earnings and almost $18,000, on average, in profit sharing. Not only is good work rewarded, but bad work is penalized. Bonuses are calculated on every order and paid out every week. At the Berkeley mill in Huger, S.C., if workers make a bad batch of steel and catch it before it has moved on, they lose the bonus they otherwise would have made on that shipment. But if it gets to the customer, they lose three times that.

Managers don't just ask workers to put a big chunk of their pay at risk. Their own take-home depends heavily on results as well. Department managers typically get a base pay that's 75% to 90% of the market average. But in a great year that same manager might get a bonus of 75% or even 90%, based on the return on assets of the whole plant. "In average-to-bad years, we earn less than our peers in other companies. That's supposed to teach us that we don't want to be average or bad. We want to be good," says James M. Coblin, Nucor's vice president for human resources.

Compared with other U.S. companies, pay disparities are modest at Nucor. Today, the typical CEO makes more than 400 times what a factory worker takes home. Last year, Nucor's chief executive collected a salary and bonus precisely 23 times that of his average steelworker. DiMicco did well by any reasonable standard, making some $2.3 million in salary and bonus (plus long-term pay equaling $4.9 million), but that's because Nucor is doing well. When things are bad, DiMicco suffers, too.

Executive pay is geared toward team building. The bonus of a plant manager, a department manager's boss, depends on the entire corporation's return on equity.

So there's no glory in winning at your own plant if the others are failing. But to focus only on pay would be to miss something special about the culture Nucor has created. There's a healthy competition among facilities and even among shifts, balanced with a long history of cooperation and idea-sharing. Since there's always room for improvement, plant managers regularly set up contests for shifts to try to outdo one another on a set goal, generally related to safety, efficiency, or output. Ryan says Nucor's Utah plant is the benchmark these days. It is the most profitable, with the lowest costs per ton. "They've got everything down to a science," says Ryan admiringly. "It gives you something to shoot for."

Questions

1. What is Nucor's managers' approach to organizing and controlling?

2. In what ways has this approach affected its organizational structure and culture?

Source: Nanette Byrnes and Michael Arndt, "The Art of Motivation." Reprinted from the May 1, 2006, issue of *BusinessWeek* by special permission. Copyright © 2006 by the McGraw-Hill Companies, Inc.

CHAPTER 11

Organizational Control and Change

Learning Objectives

After studying this chapter, you should be able to:

- Define organizational control, and describe the four steps of the control process.

- Identify the main output controls, and discuss their advantages and disadvantages as means of coordinating and motivating employees.

- Explain why control affects employees' well-being and satisfaction.

- Identify the main behavior controls, and discuss their advantages and disadvantages as means of coordinating and motivating employees.

- Discuss the relationship between organizational control and change, and explain why managing change is a vital management task.

A Manager's Challenge

Microsoft Has Problems Controlling and Evaluating Its Employees

What is the best way to control people and resources?

From the beginning Microsoft organized its software engineers into small work groups and teams so that team members could cooperate, learning from and helping each other, and so speed the development of innovative software. Each team works on a subset of the thousands of programs that together make up its Windows operating system and applications software, which is loaded on over 90% of PCs today.[1] In the past, much of Microsoft's reward system was based on team performance; employees of successful teams that quickly developed innovative software received valuable stock options and other benefits. Microsoft's team-based reward system encouraged team members to work together intensively and cooperate to meet team goals. At the same time, the contributions of exceptional team members were recognized; these individuals received rewards such as promotion to become the managers or leaders of new teams as the company grew. This reward system resulted in a continuous series of improved Windows operating and applications software such as

When team members are only rewarded for their individual contributions, they may choose self-interest over team goals. Here, a team member is paying the price for selfish behavior.

Windows 95, 98, 2000, XP, and its Office, Money, and Internet Explorer suites.

In 2006, however, Microsoft ran into serious problems with the development of Vista, its newest operating system. Vista had been scheduled to come out in the summer of 2006, but unforeseen delays had put the project six months behind schedule, delaying the planned launch until spring 2007. Some analysts believed it might even be later than that, and they blamed the delays on Microsoft's current reward system, which, because it is now primarily based on individual performance contributions, is hurting team performance.

As Microsoft grew over time (it now employs over 60,000 people), it developed a more and more rigid performance evaluation system that became increasingly based on each engineer's individual performance. The manager of each team is expected to rate the performance of each team member on a scale of 2.5, 3.0, and so on to 5, the highest individual performance rating. Microsoft adopted this system to try to increase the perceived fairness of its evaluation system. However, employees still work principally in teams, and the emphasis on individual performance negatively affects the relationships among team members since the members are aware that they are in competition for the highest ratings. For example, when confronted with a situation in which they could help other team members but doing so might hurt their own personal performance evaluations, they behave self-interestedly and this hurts overall team performance. Moreover, Microsoft is highly secretive about employees' performance evaluations, current salaries, and raises. Indeed, employees are told *not* to share such information and can get fired if they do.[2]

To make matters worse, the way these evaluations are made by team managers is also highly secretive. And employees believe that when the managers of different teams meet together to discuss which teams (as a unit) have achieved the highest level of team performance, these evaluations are distorted by favoritism. Specifically, leaders of the teams who are liked by *their* managers (often because the leaders actively support their

managers) receive higher team evaluations than do leaders of teams who are not perceived as supportive by their managers. Because evaluations are biased by personal likes and dislikes, the performance evaluation system is now regarded as being highly political. Increasingly, engineers and teams perceive they are being evaluated not objectively—by the results achieved—but subjectively, by the ability of an engineer or team leader to "make the right pitch" and curry favor with his or her direct superior. As a result, team members are increasingly pursuing their own interests at the expense of others, and so team performance is declining across the organization.[3]

One team member, for example, commented that although she had received awards for good work, low performance evaluations from her current team leader had prevented her from moving to a new, more cohesive and less political team. As you can imagine, when team members feel that their personal performance contributions are not being adequately recognized, and that even the performance of different teams is not being judged fairly, many performance problems arise.[4] And one of these problems is that many of Microsoft's best software engineers have left to join rivals like Google and Yahoo as a result of their failure to achieve the recognition they think they deserved at Microsoft.[5]

Clearly, when people work in teams, both member's contribution to the team and each team's contribution to the goals of the organization must be fairly evaluated. This is no easy thing to do. It depends on managers' ability to create an organizational control system that measures performance accurately and fairly and links performance evaluations to rewards so that employees stay motivated and coordinate their activities to achieve the organization's mission and goals.

Overview

As we discussed in Chapter 10, the first task facing managers is to establish a structure of task and job reporting relationships that allows organizational members to use resources most efficiently and effectively. Structure alone, however, does not provide the incentive or motivation for people to behave in ways that help achieve organizational goals. When managers make choices about how to influence, shape, and regulate the activities of organizational divisions, functions, and employees to achieve the organization's mission and goals, they establish the second foundation of organizational architecture, organizational control. An organization's structure provides the organization with a skeleton, but its control systems give it the muscles, sinews, nerves, and sensations that allow managers to regulate and govern its activities. The control systems also provide managers with specific feedback on how well the organization and its members are performing.

The managerial functions of organizing and controlling are inseparable, and effective managers must learn to make them work together in a harmonious way. Microsoft's problem is that the changes that have occurred to its control system (new performance evaluation measures) as the company expanded are now hurting its ability to motivate its employees.

In this chapter, we look in detail at the nature of organizational control and describe the main steps in the control process. We also discuss the different types of control systems that are available to managers to shape and influence organizational activities—*output control, behavior control,* and *clan control.*[6] Finally, we discuss the important issue of organizational change, change that is possible only when managers have put in place a control system that allows them to alter the way people and groups behave and alter or transform the way the organization operates. Control is the essential ingredient that is needed to bring about and manage organizational change efficiently and effectively. By the end of this chapter, you will appreciate the rich variety of control systems available to managers and understand why developing an appropriate control system is vital to increasing the performance of an organization and its members.

What Is Organizational Control?

As noted in Chapter 1, *controlling* is the process whereby managers monitor and regulate how efficiently and effectively an organization and its members are performing the activities necessary to achieve organizational goals. As discussed in previous chapters, when planning and organizing, managers develop the organizational strategy and structure that they hope will allow the organization to use resources most effectively to create value for customers. In controlling, managers monitor and evaluate whether the organization's strategy and structure are working as intended, how they could be improved, and how they might be changed if they are not working.

Control, however, does not mean just reacting to events after they have occurred. It also means keeping an organization on track, anticipating events that might occur, and then changing the organization to respond to whatever opportunities or threats have been identified. Control is concerned with keeping employees motivated, focused on the important problems confronting the organization, and working together to make the changes that will help an organization improve its performance over time.

The Importance of Organizational Control

To understand the importance of organizational control, consider how it helps managers obtain superior efficiency, quality, responsiveness to customers, and innovation—the four building blocks of competitive advantage.

To determine how efficiently they are using their resources, managers must be able to accurately measure how many units of inputs (raw materials, human resources, and so on) are being used to produce a unit of output. Managers also must be able to measure how many units of outputs (goods and services) are being produced. A control system contains the measures or yardsticks that allow managers to assess how efficiently the organization is producing goods and services. Moreover, if managers experiment with changing the way the organization produces goods and services to find a more efficient way of producing them, these measures tell managers how successful they have been. For example, when managers at Ford decided to adopt a product team structure to design, engineer, and manufacture new car models, they used measures such as time taken to design a new car and cost savings per car produced to evaluate how well the new structure worked in comparison with the old structure. They found that the new one performed better. Without a control system in place, managers have no idea how well their organization is performing and how its performance can be improved—information that is becoming increasingly important in today's highly competitive environment.

Today, much of the competition among organizations revolves around increasing the quality of goods and services. In the car industry, for example, cars within each price range compete against one another in features, design, and reliability. Thus, whether a customer will buy a Ford Five Hundred, GM Grand Prix, Chrysler Sebring, Toyota Camry, or Honda Accord depends significantly on the quality of each product. Organizational control is important in determining the quality of goods and services because it gives managers feedback on product quality. If the managers of carmakers consistently measure the number of customer complaints and the number of new cars returned for repairs, or if school principals measure how many students drop out of school or how achievement scores on nationally based tests vary over time, they have a good indication of how much quality they have built into their product—be it an educated student or a car that does not break down. Effective managers create a control system that consistently monitors the quality of goods and services so that they can make continuous improvements to quality—an approach to change that gives them a competitive advantage.

Managers can help make their organizations more responsive to customers if they develop a control system, such as a CRM system, that allows them to evaluate how well customer-contact employees are performing their jobs. Monitoring employee behavior can help managers find ways to increase employees' performance levels, perhaps by revealing areas in which skill training can help employees or in which new procedures can allow employees to perform their jobs better. Also, when employees know that their behaviors are being monitored, they may have more incentive to be helpful and consistent in how they act toward customers. To improve customer service, for example, Ford regularly surveys customers about their experiences with particular Ford dealers. If a dealership receives too many customer complaints, Ford's managers investigate

A Ford salesperson talks with a prospective car buyer. In the car industry, managers not only need to control the quality of their products but also the quality of their customer service. To improve its customer service, Ford implemented a control system that consists of regularly surveying customers about their experience with particular dealers. If a dealership receives too many complaints, Ford's managers investigate and propose solutions.

the dealership to uncover the sources of the problems and suggest solutions; if necessary, they might even threaten to reduce the number of cars a dealership receives to force the dealer to improve the quality of its customer service.

Finally, controlling can raise the level of innovation in an organization. Successful innovation takes place when managers create an organizational setting in which employees feel empowered to be creative and in which authority is decentralized to employees so that they feel free to experiment and take risks. Deciding on the appropriate control systems to encourage risk taking is an important management challenge; organizational culture becomes important in this regard. To encourage product teams at Ford to perform highly, top managers monitored the performance of each team separately—by examining how each team reduced costs or increased quality, for example—and used a bonus system related to performance to pay each team. The product team manager then evaluated each team member's individual performance, and the most innovative employees received promotions and rewards based on their superior performance.

Control Systems and IT

control systems
Formal target-setting, monitoring, evaluation, and feedback systems that provide managers with information about how well the organization's strategy and structure are working.

Control systems are formal target-setting, monitoring, evaluation, and feedback systems that provide managers with information about whether the organization's strategy and structure are working efficiently and effectively.[7] Effective control systems alert managers when something is going wrong and give them time to respond to opportunities and threats. An effective control system has three characteristics: It is flexible enough to allow managers to respond as necessary to unexpected events; it provides accurate information and gives managers a true picture of organizational performance; and it provides managers with the information in a timely manner because making decisions on the basis of outdated information is a recipe for failure.

New forms of IT have revolutionized control systems because they facilitate the flow of accurate and timely information up and down the organizational hierarchy and between functions and divisions. Today, employees at all levels of the organization routinely feed information into a company's information system or network and start the chain of events that affect decision making at some other part of the organization. This could be the department store clerk whose scanning of purchased clothing tells merchandise managers what kinds of clothing need to be reordered or the salesperson in the field who feeds into a wireless laptop the CRM information necessary to inform marketing about customers' changing needs or problems.

feedforward control
Control that allows managers to anticipate problems before they arise.

Control and information systems are developed to measure performance at each stage in the process of transforming inputs into finished goods and services (see Figure 11.1). At the input stage, managers use **feedforward control** to anticipate problems before they arise so that problems do not occur later, during the conversion process.[8] For example, by giving stringent product

Scanning devices, such as the one shown here, are becoming common in all types of work processes, as more companies require real-time information about their products and customers.

concurrent control
Control that gives managers immediate feedback on how efficiently inputs are being transformed into outputs so that managers can correct problems as they arise.

specifications to suppliers in advance (a form of performance target), an organization can control the quality of the inputs it receives from its suppliers and thus avoid potential problems during the conversion process. Also, IT can be used to keep in contact with suppliers and to monitor their progress. Similarly, by screening job applicants, often by viewing their résumés electronically, and using several interviews to select the most highly skilled people, managers can lessen the chance that they will hire people who lack the necessary skills or experience to perform effectively. In general, the development of management information systems promotes feedforward control that provides managers with timely information about changes in the task and general environments that may impact their organization later on. Effective managers always monitor trends and changes in the external environment to try to anticipate problems. (We discuss management information systems in detail in Chapter 18.)

At the conversion stage, **concurrent control** gives managers immediate feedback on how efficiently inputs are being transformed into outputs so that managers can correct problems as they arise. Concurrent control through IT alerts managers to the need to react quickly to whatever is the source of the problem, be it a defective batch of inputs, a machine that is out of alignment, or a worker who lacks the skills necessary to perform a task efficiently. Concurrent control is at the heart of total quality management programs (discussed in Chapter 9), in which workers are expected to constantly monitor the quality of the goods or services they provide at every step of the production process and inform managers as soon as they discover problems. One of the strengths of Toyota's production system, for example, is that individual workers are given the authority to push a button to stop the assembly line whenever they discover a quality problem. When all problems have been corrected, the result is a finished product that is much more reliable.

Figure 11.1
Three Types of Control

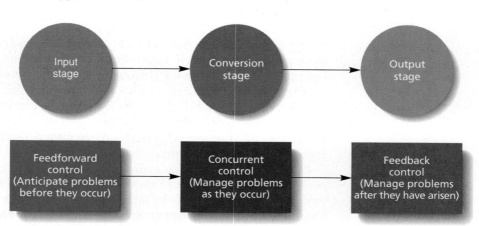

feedback control

Control that gives managers information about customers' reactions to goods and services so that corrective action can be taken if necessary.

At the output stage, managers use **feedback control** to provide information about customers' reactions to goods and services so that corrective action can be taken if necessary. For example, a feedback control system that monitors the number of customer returns alerts managers when defective products are being produced, and a management information system (MIS) that measures increases or decreases in relative sales of different products alerts managers to changes in customer tastes so that they can increase or reduce the production of specific products.

The Control Process

The control process, whether at the input, conversion, or output stage, can be broken down into four steps: establishing standards of performance, and then measuring, comparing, and evaluating actual performance (see Figure 11.2).[9]

● Step 1: *Establish the standards of performance, goals, or targets against which performance is to be evaluated.*

At step 1 in the control process managers decide on the standards of performance, goals, or targets that they will use in the future to evaluate the performance of the entire organization or part of it (such as a division, a function, or an individual). The standards of performance that managers select measure efficiency, quality, responsiveness to customers, and innovation.[10] If managers decide to pursue a low-cost strategy, for example, then they need to measure efficiency at all levels in the organization.

At the corporate level, a standard of performance that measures efficiency is operating costs, the actual costs associated with producing goods and services, including all employee-related costs. Top managers might set a corporate goal of "reducing operating costs by 10% for the next three years" to increase efficiency. Corporate managers might then evaluate divisional managers for their ability to reduce operating costs within their respective divisions, and divisional managers might set cost-saving targets for functional managers. Thus, performance standards selected at one level affect those at the other levels, and

Figure 11.2

Four Steps in Organizational Control

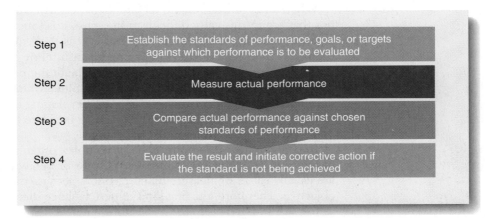

Step 1	Establish the standards of performance, goals, or targets against which performance is to be evaluated
Step 2	Measure actual performance
Step 3	Compare actual performance against chosen standards of performance
Step 4	Evaluate the result and initiate corrective action if the standard is not being achieved

ultimately the performance of individual managers is evaluated in terms of their ability to reduce costs. For example, in 2001 struggling Xerox Corp. named Anne Mulcahy as CEO and gave her the challenging task of turning around the company's fortunes. She was selected because of her 25-year reputation as a person who had been highly successful in reducing costs and increasing efficiency in Xerox's general markets division.[11] By 2004, Mulcahy had succeeded: Xerox began to make a profit again, as it now could make the products customers wanted, and Xerox's TQM program—a kind of control system—is helping to continuously improve its performance.

The number of standards or indicators of performance that an organization's managers use to evaluate efficiency, quality, and so on, can run into the thousands or hundreds of thousands. Managers at each level are responsible for selecting those standards that will best allow them to evaluate how well the part of the organization they are responsible for is performing.[12] Managers must be careful to choose the standards of performance that allow them to assess how well they are doing with all four of the building blocks of competitive advantage. If managers focus on just one (such as efficiency) and ignore others (such as determining what customers really want and innovating a new line of products to satisfy them), managers may end up hurting their organization's performance.

● Step 2: *Measure actual performance.*

Once managers have decided which standards or targets they will use to evaluate performance, the next step in the control process is to measure actual performance. In practice, managers can measure or evaluate two things: (1) the actual *outputs* that result from the behavior of their members and (2) the *behaviors* themselves (hence the terms *output control* and *behavior control* used below).[13]

Sometimes both outputs and behaviors can be easily measured. Measuring outputs and evaluating behavior is relatively easy in a fast-food restaurant, for example, because employees are performing routine tasks. Managers at Home Depot, discussed in the last chapter, are rigorous in using output control to measure the flow of inventory through its stores. Similarly, managers of a fast-food restaurant can quite easily measure outputs by counting how many customers their employees serve and how much money customers spend. Managers can easily observe each employee's behavior and quickly take action to solve any problems that may arise.

When an organization and its members perform complex, nonroutine activities that are intrinsically difficult to measure, it is much more difficult for managers to measure outputs or behavior.[14] It is very difficult, for example, for managers in charge of R&D departments at Intel or AMD, or at Microsoft or Google, to measure performance or to evaluate the performance of individual members because it can take several years to determine whether the new products that their engineers and scientists are developing are going to be profitable. Moreover, it is impossible for a manager to measure how creative an engineer or scientist is by watching his or her actions!

In general, the more nonroutine or complex organizational activities are, the harder it is for managers to measure outputs or behaviors.[15] Outputs, however, are usually easier to measure than behaviors because they are more tangible and objective. Therefore, the first kind of performance measures that managers tend to use are those that measure outputs. Then managers develop performance measures or standards that allow them to evaluate behaviors to determine whether employees at all levels are working toward organizational goals. Some simple behavior measures are (1) do employees come to work on time, and (2) do employees consistently follow the established rules for greeting and serving customers? Each type of output and behavior control and the way it is used at the different organizational levels—corporate, divisional, functional, and individual—is discussed in detail subsequently.

● Step 3: *Compare actual performance against chosen standards of performance.*

During step 3, managers evaluate whether—and to what extent—performance deviates from the standards of performance chosen in step 1. If performance is higher than expected, managers might decide that they set performance standards too low and may raise them for the next time period to challenge their subordinates.[16] Managers at Japanese companies are well known for the way they try to raise performance in manufacturing settings by constantly raising performance standards to motivate managers and workers to find new ways to reduce costs or increase quality—reread the Chapter 9 opening case on Toyota from an organizational control perspective.

However, if performance is too low and standards were not reached, or if standards were set so high that employees could not achieve them, managers must decide whether to take corrective action.[17] It is easy to take corrective action when the reasons for poor performance can be identified—for instance, high labor costs. To reduce costs, managers can search for low-cost foreign sources of supply, invest more in technology, or implement cross-functional teams. More often, however, the reasons for poor performance are hard to identify. Changes in the environment, such as the emergence of a new global competitor, a recession, or an increase in interest rates, might be the source of the problem. Within an organization, perhaps the R&D function underestimated the problems it would encounter in developing a new product or the extra costs of doing unforeseen research. If managers are to take any form of corrective action, step 4 is necessary.

● Step 4: *Evaluate the result and initiate corrective action (that is, make changes) if the standard is not being achieved.*

The final step in the control process is to evaluate the results and bring about change as appropriate. Whether performance standards have been met or not, managers can learn a great deal during this step. If managers decide that the level of performance is unacceptable, they must try to change the way work activities are performed to solve the problem. Sometimes, performance problems occur because the work standard was too high—for example, a sales target was too optimistic and impossible to achieve. In this case, adopting more realistic standards can reduce the gap between actual performance and desired performance.

However, if managers determine that something in the situation is causing the problem, then to raise performance they will need to change the way resources are being utilized.[18] Perhaps the latest technology is not being used; perhaps workers lack the advanced training needed to perform at a higher level; perhaps the organization needs to buy its inputs or assemble its products abroad to compete against low-cost rivals; perhaps it needs to restructure itself or reengineer its work processes to increase efficiency.

Figure 11.3
Three Organizational Control Systems

Type of control	Mechanisms of control
Output control	Financial measures of performance Organizational goals Operating budgets
Behavior control	Direct supervision Management by objectives Rules and standard operating procedures
Clan control	Values Norms Socialization

The simplest example of a control system is the thermostat in a home. By setting the thermostat, you establish the standard of performance with which actual temperature is to be compared. The thermostat contains a sensing or monitoring device, which measures the actual temperature against the desired temperature. Whenever there is a difference between them, the furnace or air-conditioning unit is activated to bring the temperature back to the standard. In other words, corrective action is initiated. This is a simple control system, for it is entirely self-contained and the target (temperature) is easy to measure.

Establishing targets and designing measurement systems are much more difficult for managers because the high level of uncertainty in the organizational environment causes managers to rarely know what might happen. Thus, it is vital for managers to design control systems to alert them to problems so that they can be dealt with before they become threatening. Another issue is that managers are not just concerned about bringing the organization's performance up to some predetermined standard; they want to push that standard forward, to encourage employees at all levels to find new ways to raise performance.

In the following sections, we consider three important types of control systems that managers use to coordinate and motivate employees to ensure they pursue superior efficiency, quality, innovation, and responsiveness to customers: output control, behavior control, and clan control (see Figure 11.3). Managers use all three to shape, regulate and govern organizational activities, no matter what specific organizational structure is in place. However, as Figure 11.3 suggests, an important element of control is embedded in organizational culture, which is discussed later.

Output Control

All managers develop a system of output control for their organizations. First, they choose the goals or output performance standards or targets that they think will best measure efficiency, quality, innovation, and responsiveness to customers. Then they measure to see whether the performance goals and standards are being achieved at the corporate, divisional, functional, and individual employee levels of the organization. The three main mechanisms that managers use to assess output or performance are financial measures, organizational goals, and operating budgets.

Financial Measures of Performance

Top managers are most concerned with overall organizational performance and use various financial measures to evaluate it. The most common are profit ratios, liquidity ratios, leverage ratios, and activity ratios. They are discussed below and summarized in Table 11.1.[19]

- *Profit ratios* measure how efficiently managers are using the organization's resources to generate profits. *Return on investment (ROI),* an organization's net income before taxes divided by its total assets, is the most commonly used financial performance measure because it allows managers of one organization to compare performance with that of other organizations. ROI allows managers to assess an organization's competitive advantage. *Operating margin* is calculated by dividing a company's operating profit

Table 11.1
Four Measures of Financial Performance

Profit Ratios

Return on investment	$=$	$\dfrac{\text{net profit before taxes}}{\text{total assets}}$	Measures how well managers are using the organization's resources to generate profits.
Operating margin	$=$	$\dfrac{\text{total operating profit}}{\text{sales revenues}}$	A measure of how much percentage profit a company is earning on sales; the higher the percentage, the better a company is utilizing its resources to make and sell the product.

Liquidity Ratios

Current ratio	$=$	$\dfrac{\text{current assets}}{\text{current liabilities}}$	Do managers have resources available to meet claims of short-term creditors?
Quick ratio	$=$	$\dfrac{\text{current assets} - \text{inventory}}{\text{current liabilities}}$	Can managers pay off claims of short-term creditors without selling inventory?

Leverage Ratios

Debt-to-assets ratio	$=$	$\dfrac{\text{total debt}}{\text{total assets}}$	To what extent have managers used borrowed funds to finance investments?
Times-covered ratio	$=$	$\dfrac{\text{profit before interest and taxes}}{\text{total interest charges}}$	Measures how far profits can decline before managers cannot meet interest changes. If ratio declines to less than 1, the organization is technically insolvent.

Activity Ratios

Inventory turnover	$=$	$\dfrac{\text{cost of goods sold}}{\text{inventory}}$	Measures how efficiently managers are turning inventory over so that excess inventory is not carried.
Days sales outstanding	$=$	$\dfrac{\text{current accounts receivable}}{\begin{array}{c}\text{sales for period}\\ \text{divided by days in period}\end{array}}$	Measures how efficiently managers are collecting revenues from customers to pay expenses.

(the amount it has left after all the costs of making the product and running the business have been deducted) by sales revenues. This measure provides managers with information about how efficiently an organization is utilizing its resources; every attempt to reduce costs will be reflected in increased operating profit, for example. Also, operating margin is a means of comparing one year's performance to another; for example, if managers discover operating margin has improved by 5% from one year to the next, they know that their organization is building a competitive advantage.

- *Liquidity ratios* measure how well managers have protected organizational resources to be able to meet short-term obligations. The *current ratio* (current assets divided by current liabilities) tells managers whether they have the resources available to meet the claims of short-term creditors. The *quick ratio* tells whether they can pay these claims without selling inventory.

- *Leverage ratios,* such as the *debt-to-assets ratio* and the *times-covered ratio,* measure the degree to which managers use debt (borrow money) or equity (issue new shares) to finance ongoing operations. An organization is highly leveraged if it uses more debt than equity. Debt can be very risky when net income or profit fail to cover the interest on the debt—as some people learn too late, when the size of their paychecks does not allow them to pay off their credit cards.

- *Activity ratios* provide measures of how well managers are creating value from organizational assets. *Inventory turnover* measures how efficiently managers are turning inventory over so that excess inventory is not carried. *Days sales outstanding* provides information on how efficiently managers are collecting revenue from customers to pay expenses.

The objectivity of financial measures of performance is the reason why so many managers use them to assess the efficiency and effectiveness of their organizations. When an organization fails to meet performance standards such as ROI, revenue, or stock price targets, managers know that they must take corrective action. Thus, financial controls tell managers when a corporate reorganization might be necessary, when they should sell off divisions and exit from businesses, or when they should rethink their corporate-level strategies.[20] Today, financial controls are being taught to all organizational employees, as the following "Management Insight" describes.

Management Insight

Making the Financial Figures Come Alive

You might think that financial control is the province of top managers and that employees lower in the organization don't need to worry about the numbers or about how their specific activities affect those numbers. However, some top managers make a point of showing employees exactly how their activities affect financial ratios, and they do so because employees' activities directly affect a company's costs and its sales revenues. One of those managers is Michael Dell.

Dell goes to enormous lengths to convince employees that they need to watch every dime spent in making the PCs that have made his company so prosperous, as well as in saying every word or making every phone call or service call that is needed to sell or repair them. Dell believes that all his managers need to have at their fingertips detailed information about Dell's cost structure, including assembly costs, selling costs, and after-sales costs, in order to squeeze out every cent of operating costs. And one good reason for this is that Dell puts a heavy emphasis on the operating-margin financial ratio in measuring his company's performance. Dell doesn't care about how much profits or sales are growing individually; he cares about how these two figures work together, because only if profits are growing faster than sales is the company increasing its long-run profitability by operating more efficiently and effectively.

So he insists that his managers search for every way possible to reduce costs or make customers happier and then help employees learn the new procedures to achieve these goals. At Dell's boot camp for new employees, in Austin, Texas, he has been known to bring financial charts that show employees how each minute spent on performing some job activity, or how each mistake made in assembling or packing a PC, affects bottom-line profitability. In the 2000s Dell's repeated efforts to slice costs while building customer loyalty have boosted efficiency and operating margins; it is much more efficient than HP or Gateway. However, these companies are applying Dell's principles and closing the performance gap, and in the 2000s all kinds of companies have begun training sessions in which employees at all levels are taught how their specific job activities, and the way their functions operate, affect the financial ratios used to judge how well an organization is performing.

Although financial information is an important output control, financial information by itself does not provide managers with all the information they need about the four building blocks of competitive advantage. Financial results inform managers about the results of decisions they have already made; they do not tell managers how to find new opportunities to build competitive advantage in the future. To encourage a future-oriented approach, top managers must establish organizational goals that encourage middle and first-line managers to achieve superior efficiency, quality, innovation, and responsiveness to customers.

Organizational Goals

Once top managers consult with lower-level managers and set the organization's overall goals, they establish performance standards for the divisions and functions. These standards specify for divisional and functional managers the level at which their units must perform if the organization is to achieve its overall goals.[21] Each division is given a set of specific goals to achieve (see Figure 11.4). We saw in Chapter 8, for example, that Jeffrey Immelt, CEO of GE, has established the goal of having each GE division be first or second in its industry in profit. Divisional managers then develop a business-level strategy (based on achieving superior efficiency or innovation) that they hope will allow them to achieve that goal.[22] In consultation with functional managers, they specify the functional goals that the managers of different functions need to achieve to allow the division to achieve its goals. For example, sales managers

Figure 11.4
Organizationwide Goal Setting

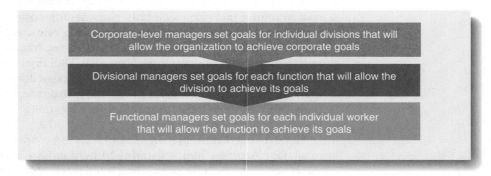

might be evaluated for their ability to increase sales; materials management managers, for their ability to increase the quality of inputs or lower their costs; R&D managers, for the number of products they innovate or the number of patents they receive. In turn, functional managers establish goals that first-line managers and nonmanagerial employees need to achieve to allow the function to achieve its goals.

Output control is used at every level of the organization, and it is vital that the goals set at each level harmonize with the goals set at other levels so that managers and other employees throughout the organization work together to attain the corporate goals that top managers have set.[23] It is also important that goals be set appropriately so that managers are motivated to accomplish them. If goals are set at an impossibly high level, managers might work only half-heartedly to achieve them because they are certain they will fail. In contrast, if goals are set so low that they are too easy to achieve, managers will not be motivated to use all their resources as efficiently and effectively as possible. Research suggests that the best goals are specific, difficult goals—goals that challenge and stretch managers' ability but are not out of reach and do not require an impossibly high expenditure of managerial time and energy. Such goals are often called *stretch goals*.

Deciding what is a specific, difficult goal and what is a goal that is too difficult or too easy is a skill that managers must develop. Based on their own judgment and work experience, managers at all levels must assess how difficult a certain task is, and they must assess the ability of a particular subordinate manager to achieve the goal. If they do so successfully, challenging, interrelated goals—goals that reinforce one another and focus on achieving overall corporate objectives—will energize the organization.

Operating Budgets

operating budget A budget that states how managers intend to use organizational resources to achieve organizational goals.

Once managers at each level have been given a goal or target to achieve, the next step in developing an output control system is to establish operating budgets that regulate how managers and workers attain their goals. An **operating budget** is a blueprint that states how managers intend to use organizational resources to achieve organizational goals efficiently. Typically, managers at one level allocate to subordinate managers a specific amount of resources to use to produce goods and services. Once they have been given a budget, these lower-level managers must decide how to allocate money for different organizational activities. They are then evaluated for their ability to stay within the budget and to make the best use of available resources. For example, managers at GE's washing machine division might have a budget of $50 million to spend on developing and selling a new line of washing machines. They must decide how much money to allocate to the various functions such as R&D, engineering, and sales so that the division generates the most customer revenue and makes the biggest profit.

Large organizations often treat each division as a singular or stand-alone responsibility center. Corporate managers then evaluate each division's contribution to corporate performance. Managers of a division may be given a fixed budget for resources and be evaluated on the amount of goods or services they can produce using those resources (this is a cost or expense budget approach). Or managers may be asked to maximize the revenues from the sales of goods and services produced (a revenue budget approach). Or managers may be evaluated on the difference between the revenues generated by the sales of goods and services and the budgeted cost of making those goods and services (a profit budget approach). Japanese companies' use of operating budgets and challenging goals to increase efficiency is instructive in this context.

In summary, three components—objective financial measures, challenging goals and performance standards, and appropriate operating budgets—are the essence of effective output control. Most organizations develop sophisticated output control systems to allow managers at all levels to keep accurate account of the organization so that they can move quickly to take corrective action as needed.[24] Output control is an essential part of management. The way in which Wal-Mart is using output control to expand internationally is discussed in the following "Managing Globally."

Wal-Mart Uses Output Control to Expand Internationally

Managing Globally

Retailing giant Wal-Mart has been aggressively expanding internationally in recent years to raise its performance. After moving into Mexico and Europe in the last decade, it began to contemplate entering the Japanese market. An opportunity arose in 2004 when Japan's third-largest supermarket chain, Daiei, which had been losing money for years and was heavily in debt, was put up for sale. Why was a supermarket chain in one of the world's most lucrative markets struggling?

Unlike efficient Japanese carmakers, which employ state-of-the-art IT-based output control systems to collect the detailed information needed to increase their efficiency, Japan's retailers had lagged behind in adopting the new systems. A major reason for this was historical. Until the 1990s, Japan's Large Scale Retail Store Law allowed small Japanese retailers to block the opening of large, efficient new stores in their neighborhoods for 10 years or more. Although the Japanese government weakened the law so that local storeowners could delay a store opening for only 18 months, there was no history of low-cost competition in the Japanese retail market. So retailers, such as supermarket chains, had never been forced to develop output controls to become more efficient.

A second reason for Daiei's problems revolved around Japan's system of distributing Japanese products. Traditionally, Japanese manufacturers sold their products only by means of wholesalers with which they had developed long-term business relationships. Because the wholesalers added their own price markup and controlled distribution, this made it much more difficult for supermarkets to compete on price and lowered competition. Less competition reduced the incentive for Japanese retailers to invest in materials management output control systems to increase their efficiency.

While Wal-Mart has successfully entered some Asian markets, so far attempts to open its doors in Japan have been blocked.

In contrast, Wal-Mart's focus on developing sophisticated output controls to monitor all aspects of its purchasing and sales activities made it the most efficient U.S. discount retailer in the 1990s. In fact, its skills in materials management allowed it to enter the U.S. supermarket industry and become a major competitor there. So, in the 2000s, to further its global expansion, Wal-Mart bought a significant stake in Seiyu Ltd., Japan's fourth-largest supermarket, Then, in 2004, it tried to buy the troubled Japanese supermarket chain, Daiei, in order to combine it with its Seiyu division. Its managers believed that if Wal-Mart transplanted its proprietary IT-based output control systems into its expanded Japanese store operations, it could increase Seiyu's and Daiei's efficiency by so much that its supermarket chain would become highly profitable and eventually dominate the Japanese supermarket industry. Wal-Mart also planned to purchase lower-priced goods from abroad to sell in its Japanese stores, using its sophisticated global supply chain, which allows it to identify and purchase products efficiently from manufacturers throughout the world.

To Wal-Mart's annoyance, Japan's Industrial Revitalization Corp., which had the power to select the buyer for Daiei's 260 locations across Japan, decided it did not want Wal-Mart to become one of the largest retailers in Japan and thus threaten domestic Japanese companies. It rejected Wal-Mart Stores' bid for Daiei, but the world's largest retailer is still keeping its eyes peeled for other opportunities in the lucrative Japanese market, whose citizens pay some of the highest prices in the world for their food and other consumer products.

Problems with Output Control

When designing an output control system, managers must be careful to avoid some pitfalls. For example, they must be sure that the output standards they create motivate managers at all levels and do not cause managers to behave in inappropriate ways to achieve organizational goals.

Suppose top managers give divisional managers the goal of doubling profits over a three-year period. This goal seems challenging and reachable when it is jointly agreed upon, and in the first two years profits go up by 70%. In the third year, however, an economic recession hits and sales plummet. Divisional managers think it is increasingly unlikely that they will meet their profit goal. Failure will mean losing the substantial monetary bonus tied to achieving the goal. How might managers behave to try to preserve their bonuses?

One course of action they might take is to find ways to reduce costs, since profit can be increased either by raising sales revenues or reducing costs. Thus, divisional managers might cut back on expensive research activities, delay maintenance on machinery, reduce marketing expenditures, and lay off middle managers and workers to reduce costs so that at the end of the year they will make their target of doubling profits and receive their bonuses. This tactic might help them achieve a short-run goal—doubling profits—but such actions could hurt long-term profitability or ROI (because a cutback in R&D can reduce the rate of product innovation, a cutback in marketing will lead to the loss of customers, and so on).

Problems of this sort occurred at Gillette in the early 2000s. Its new CEO, James Kilts, attributed a large part of the recent fall in its sales and profits to the overly ambitious sales and profit goals that his predecessor had set for managers of its divisions (razors and toiletries, Braun appliances, and Duracell batteries). To achieve these ambitious sales targets, divisional managers slashed advertising budgets and loaded up on inventory, hoping to sell it quickly and generate large revenues. However, this backfired when customer demand dropped and a recession occurred.

Kilts saw that Gillette's managers had not been focusing on the right way to reduce costs. Because managers' salaries and bonuses were based on their ability to meet the ambitious goals that had been set for them, they had acted with a short-term mind-set. Managers had not been thinking about the long-term goal of trying to find the best balance between keeping costs under control, keeping customers happy, and keeping the pipeline of new products full.

Kilts announced that henceforth Gillette would no longer provide specific and unrealistic sales and earning targets that created a "circle of doom" and led managers to behave in ways that would prevent them from achieving company goals—such as reducing advertising to reduce costs. Kilts decided that Gillette would set long-term goals based on carefully drawn marketing plans that targeted products customers wanted and that would lead to long-term sales growth.[25]

Kilt's strategy for Gillette worked, and his actions demonstrate that achieving long-run effectiveness is what managers of all organizations should be most concerned about. Thus, managers must consider carefully how flexible they should be when using output control. If conditions change (as they will because of uncertainty in the task and general environments), it is probably better for top managers to communicate to managers lower in the hierarchy that they are aware of the changes taking place and are willing to revise and lower goals and standards. Indeed, many organizations schedule yearly revisions of their five-year plan and goals and use scenario planning to avoid the problems Gillette experienced.

Changes to output controls happen at all levels in an organization and for all sorts of reasons. In 2006, for example, Wal-Mart announced that it would relax its "no-tolerance" policy and not prosecute shoplifters unless they were between the ages of 18 and 65 and took products valued at more than $25. Previously, Wal-Mart's strict no-tolerance output control regularly picked up teenagers or the very old taking some product worth a couple of dollars; then they would be hauled away by local police forces that sometimes had to add an extra officer just to meet Wal-Mart's needs. Henceforth, first-time shoplifters will receive only warnings, and Wal-Mart will now focus on professional shoplifters, and its own employees, who steal the bulk of the merchandise from its stores each year.

The message is clear: Although output control is a useful tool for keeping managers and employees at all levels motivated and the organization on track, it is only a guide to appropriate action. Managers must be sensitive to how they use output control and must constantly monitor its effects at all levels in the organization—and on customers and other stakeholders.

Behavior Control

Organizational structure by itself does not provide any mechanism that motivates managers and nonmanagerial employees to behave in ways that make the structure work or even improve the way it works—hence the need for control. Put another way, managers can develop an organizational structure that has the right grouping of divisions and functions, and an effective chain of command, but it will work as designed *only* if managers also establish control systems that motivate and shape employee behavior in ways that *match* this structure.[26] Output control is one method of motivating employees; behavior control is another method. This section examines three mechanisms of behavior control that managers can use to keep subordinates on track and make organizational structures work as they are designed to work: direct supervision, management by objectives, and rules and standard operating procedures (see Figure 11.3).

Direct Supervision

The most immediate and potent form of behavior control is direct supervision by managers who actively monitor and observe the behavior of their subordinates, teach subordinates the behaviors that are appropriate and inappropriate, and intervene to take corrective action as needed. Moreover, when managers personally supervise subordinates, they lead by example and in this way can help subordinates develop and increase their own skill levels. (Leadership is the subject of Chapter 14.) Thus, control through personal supervision can be a very effective way of motivating employees and promoting behaviors that increase efficiency and effectiveness, as the example of the senior manager profiled in the following "Manager as a Person" suggests.[27]

Manager as a Person

Tom LaSorda Is Close to Chrysler's Employees

In the past, Chrysler (part of DaimlerChrysler's global empire) was often criticized for its managers' failure to get close to employees and effectively communicate to them its current problems and future plans. Its top decision makers were often isolated from what was going on in its car plants; they looked to the measures of the output controls coming in. Also, employees often felt they were kept in the dark; they had little idea of how well their plants were performing or where their company was going—or how they could help Chrysler and themselves. Managers and employees were not sharing information about the company's performance and what might be needed to improve it, and this contributed to Chrysler's deteriorating performance during the 1990s.

In the 2000s, Chrysler has taken many steps to remedy this communication problem and bring managers and employees, at all levels of the company, closer together to deal with the major problems it faces. Chrysler's top executives recognized that only intense cooperation between employees and managers could produce the efforts needed to turn around its performance. A major step Chrysler took to encourage cooperation was to promote managers who understand the concerns and problems facing its employees—and how to talk to them. And, who better could speak to workers than managers whose parents had worked in Chrysler plants and who were raised in homes where events at the company were a major topic of conversation?

One of these managers is Tom LaSorda, Chrysler's current CEO, whose father was the United Auto Workers (UAW) president of one of Chrysler's Canadian auto plants and whose grandfather was also a union leader at that company. With his union roots, LaSorda has firsthand knowledge of what issues concern autoworkers at a time when thousands of them are losing their jobs because of intense global competition.[28] LaSorda remembers from his childhood the time that his father was laid off for six months when the economy collapsed; he also knows what it is like to live from paycheck to paycheck, as most American families do.

CEO Tom LaSorda's first-hand knowledge of auto workers' concerns helps him commnicate with employees.

Dieter Zetsche, the German-born former CEO of Chrysler who engineered its recent turnaround, recognized LaSorda's unqiue skills—the background and experience that enables him to effectively communicate with employees, as well as his proven management skills. Zetsche mentored LaSorda, and when his own success resulted in his being promoted to CEO of the whole of Daimler-Chrysler, he decided down-to-earth LaSorda, who is at his best when interacting with ordinary people, was the best choice as Chrysler's next CEO.[29] LaSorda spends a lot of time walking around Chrysler's plants, making direct contact with workers and UAW executives, and is the first Chrysler CEO to ever address union members at their annual meeting.

How have LaSorda's skills in talking and relating to union employees and officials paid off? Analysts say that Chrysler has enjoyed more conciliatory dealings with employees and the UAW than has GM or Ford. Not only has the UAW agreed to a painful 24,000 layoffs in the last five years; it also has agreed to change work practices that resulted in high operating costs, and it is working with the company to find ways to lower health care costs. These are all major factors that have been hurting the competitiveness of Chrysler and the Big Three U.S. carmakers. In return, LaSorda has worked to improve the future prospects of the laid-off workers. Chrysler has provided major funding to allow new companies to open up car-parts operations near Chrysler's plants to provide new jobs, and it provided new training, education, and severance benefits to laid-off employees. It has also behaved fairly to current employees. As he says, "When you're running a business, you do what's best for all," and he hopes that in the long run this will translate into thousands of new, well-paying auto jobs.[30]

As the work of Tom LaSorda suggests, direct supervision allows managers at all levels to become personally involved with their subordinates and allows them to mentor subordinates and develop their management skills. Nevertheless, certain problems are associated with direct supervision. First, it is very expensive because a manager can personally manage only a relatively small number of subordinates effectively. Therefore, if direct supervision is the main kind of control being used in an organization, a lot of managers will be needed and costs will increase. For this reason, output control is usually preferred to behavior control; indeed, output control tends to be the first type of control that managers at all levels use to evaluate performance.

Second, while employees react positively to LaSorda's personal style, direct supervision can *demotivate* subordinates. This occurs if employees feel that they are under such close scrutiny that they are not free to make their own decisions or if they feel that they are not being evaluated in an accurate and impartial way—as seems to be happening at Microsoft, as we discussed in "A Manager's Challenge." Team members and other employees may start to pass the buck, avoid responsibility, and cease to cooperate with other team members if they feel that their manager is not accurately evaluating their performance and is favoring some people over others.

Third, as noted previously, for many jobs personal control through direct supervision is simply not feasible. The more complex a job is, the more difficult it is for a manager to evaluate how well a subordinate is performing. The performance of divisional and functional managers, for example, can be evaluated only over relatively long time periods (which is why an output control system is developed) so it makes little sense for top managers to continually monitor their performance. However, managers can still work to communicate the organization's mission and goals to their subordinates and reinforce the values and norms in the organization's culture through their own personal style.

Management by Objectives

To provide a framework within which to evaluate subordinates' behavior and, in particular, to allow managers to monitor progress toward achieving goals, many organizations implement some version of management by objectives. **Management by objectives (MBO)** is a formal system of evaluating subordinates on their ability to achieve specific organizational goals or performance standards and to meet operating budgets.[31] Microsoft's performance evaluation system is an example of management by objectives, and most organizations use some form of MBO system because it is pointless to establish goals and then fail to evaluate whether or not they are being achieved. Management by objectives involves three specific steps:

management by objectives (MBO) A goal-setting process in which a manager and each of his or her subordinates negotiate specific goals and objectives for the subordinate to achieve and then periodically evaluate the extent to which the subordinate is achieving those goals.

● Step 1: *Specific goals and objectives are established at each level of the organization.*

MBO starts when top managers establish overall organizational objectives, such as specific financial performance goals or targets. Then objective setting cascades down throughout the organization as managers at the divisional and functional levels set their goals to achieve corporate objectives.[32] Finally, first-level managers and employees jointly set goals that will contribute to achieving functional objectives.

● Step 2: *Managers and their subordinates together determine the subordinates' goals.*

An important characteristic of management by objectives is its participatory nature. Managers at every level sit down with each of the subordinate managers who report directly to them, and together they determine appropriate and feasible goals for the subordinate and bargain over the budget that the subordinate will need to achieve his or her goals. The participation of subordinates in the objective-setting process is a way of strengthening their commitment to achieving their goals and meeting their budgets.[33] Another reason why it is so important for subordinates (both individuals and teams) to participate in goal setting is that doing so enables them to tell managers what they think they can realistically achieve.[34]

● Step 3: *Managers and their subordinates periodically review the subordinates' progress toward meeting goals.*

Once specific objectives have been agreed on for managers at each level, managers are accountable for meeting those objectives. Periodically, they sit down with their subordinates to evaluate their progress. Normally, salary raises and promotions are linked to the goal-setting process, and managers who achieve their goals receive greater rewards than those who fall short. (The issue of how to design reward systems to motivate managers and other organizational employees is discussed in Chapter 13.)

In the companies that have decentralized responsibility for the production of goods and services to empowered teams and cross-functional teams, management by objectives works somewhat differently. Managers ask each team to develop a set of goals and performance targets that the team hopes to achieve—goals that are consistent with organizational objectives. Managers then negotiate with each team to establish its final goals and the budget the team will need to achieve them. The reward system is linked to team performance, not to the performance of any one team member.

Cypress Semiconductor offers an interesting example of how IT can be used to manage the MBO process quickly and effectively. In the fast-moving semiconductor business a premium is placed on organizational adaptability. At Cypress, CEO T. J. Rodgers was facing a problem: How could he control his growing, 1,500-employee organization without developing a bureaucratic management hierarchy? Rodgers believed that a tall hierarchy hinders the ability of an organization to adapt to changing conditions. He was committed to maintaining a flat and decentralized organizational structure with a minimum of management layers. At the same time, he needed to control his employees to ensure that they perform in a manner consistent with the goals of the company.[35] How could he achieve this without resorting to direct supervision and the lengthy management hierarchy that it implies?

To solve this problem, Rodgers implemented an online information system through which he can monitor what every employee and team is doing in his fast-moving and decentralized organization. Each employee maintains a list of 10 to 15 goals, such as "Meet with marketing for new product launch" or "Make sure to check with customer X." Noted next to each goal are when it was agreed upon, when it is due to be finished, and whether it has been finished. All of this information is stored on a central computer. Rodgers claims that he can review the goals of all employees in about four hours and that he does so each week.[36] How is this possible? He *manages by exception* and looks only for employees who are falling behind. He then calls them, not to scold but to ask whether there is anything he can do to help them get the job done. It takes only about half an hour each week for employees to review and update their lists. This system allows Rodgers to exercise control over his organization without resorting to the expensive layers of a management hierarchy and direct supervision.

As Microsoft's experience suggests, however, MBO does not always work out so well. Managers and their subordinates at all levels must believe that performance evaluations are accurate and fair. Any suggestion that personal biases and political objectives play a part in the evaluation process can lower or even destroy MBO's effectiveness as a control system. This is why many organizations work so hard to protect the integrity of their systems. Jack Welsh, the former CEO of GE, was well known for his support of objective performance appraisal. Indeed, he systematically fired GE managers who worked the system to their own advantage and "smiled up but kicked down" to further their own goals at the expense of GE's. Currently, Microsoft is working hard to change the way its evaluation system is working and correct the biases and errors that can creep into any control system over time.

Bureaucratic Control

bureaucratic control
Control of behavior by means of a comprehensive system of rules and standard operating procedures.

When direct supervision is too expensive and management by objectives is inappropriate, managers might turn to another mechanism to shape and motivate employee behavior: bureaucratic control. **Bureaucratic control** is control by means of a comprehensive system of rules and standard operating procedures (SOPs) that shapes and regulates the behavior of divisions, functions, and individuals. In Chapter 2, we discussed Weber's theory of bureaucracy and noted that all organizations use bureaucratic rules and procedures but some use them more than others.[37] Recall that rules and SOPs are formal, written instructions that specify a series of actions to be taken to achieve a given end; for example, if *A* happens, then do *B*. A simple set of rules developed by the supervisor of some custodial workers (Crew G) at a Texas A&M University building clearly established task responsibilities and clarified expectations (see Table 11.2).

Rules and SOPs guide behavior and specify what employees are to do when they confront a problem that needs a solution. It is the responsibility of a manager to develop rules that allow employees to perform their activities efficiently and effectively. Rules and SOPs also clarify people's expectations about one another and prevent misunderstandings over responsibility or the use of power. Such guidelines can prevent a supervisor from arbitrarily increasing a subordinate's workload and prevent a subordinate from ignoring tasks that are a legitimate part of the job.

When employees follow the rules that managers have developed, their behavior is *standardized*–actions are performed the same way time and time again–and the outcomes of their work are predictable. And, to the degree that managers can make employees' behavior predictable, there is no need to monitor the outputs of behavior because *standardized behavior leads to standardized outputs,* such as goods and services of the same uniform quality. Suppose a

Table 11.2
Team Rules of Conduct

1. All employees must call their supervisor or leader before 5:55 a.m. to notify of absence or tardiness.
2. Disciplinary action will be issued to any employee who abuses sick leave policy.
3. Disciplinary action will be issued to any employee whose assigned area is not up to custodial standards.
4. If a door is locked when you go in to clean an office, it's your responsibility to lock it back up.
5. Name tags and uniforms must be worn daily.
6. Each employee is responsible for buffing hallways and offices. Hallways must be buffed weekly, offices periodically.
7. All equipment must be put in closets during 9:00 a.m. and 11 a.m. breaks.
8. Do not use the elevator to move trash or equipment from 8:50 to 9:05, 9:50 to 10:05, 11:50 to 12:05, or 1:50 to 2:05, to avoid breaks between classes.
9. Try to mop hallways when students are in classrooms, or mop floors as you go down to each office.
10. Closets must be kept clean, and all equipment must be clean and operative.
11. Each employee is expected to greet building occupants with "Good morning."
12. Always knock before entering offices and conference rooms.
13. Loud talking, profanity, and horseplay will not be tolerated inside buildings.
14. All custodial carts must be kept uniform and cleaned daily.
15. You must have excellent "public relations" with occupants at all times.

worker at Toyota comes up with a way to attach exhaust pipes that reduces the number of steps in the assembly process and increases efficiency. Always on the lookout for ways to standardize and improve procedures, managers make this idea the basis of a new rule that says, "From now on, the procedure for attaching the exhaust pipe to the car is as follows." If all workers follow the rule to the letter, every car will come off the assembly line with its exhaust pipe attached in the new way and there will be no need to check exhaust pipes at the end of the line.

In practice, mistakes and lapses of attention do happen, so output control is used at the end of the line, and each car's exhaust system is given a routine inspection. However, the number of quality problems with the exhaust system is minimized because the rule (bureaucratic control) is being followed. Service organizations such as retail stores, fast-food restaurants, and home-improvement stores also attempt to standardize employee behavior, for example, customer-service quality, by instructing employees on the correct way to greet customers or the appropriate way to serve and bag food. Employees are trained to follow the rules that have proved to be most effective in a particular situation, and the better trained the employees are, the more standardized is their behavior and the more trust managers can have that outputs (such as food quality) will be consistent. An interesting example of how creating the wrong rules can reduce performance is discussed in the following "Management Insight."

Management Insight

How to Kill Customer Satisfaction

In the early 2000s, Gateway, the PC maker, saw its customer satisfaction rating plummet from third to fifth in consumer satisfaction with PC makers. This drop caused Gateway's managers considerable anxiety because they used this measure of customer satisfaction as an important indicator of their company's ongoing performance. Such a drop is very serious to a computer maker because the volume of its online sales depends on how easy it is for customers to put their mail-order computer together when it reaches their homes and how easy it is for them to get advice and good service when they encounter a software or hardware problem. Customer satisfaction ratings also directly affect a company's profits, and as Gateway's computer shipments slipped, the company began to lose money.

Why did customer satisfaction plummet? Mike Ritter, director of Gateway consumer marketing, discovered that the source of customer dissatisfaction was a series of new rules and policies the company had instituted for its customer service reps to follow because of its desire to reduce the increasing costs of after-sales service. As Gateway's product line had broadened and many different software and hardware options were made available to customers, the complexity of its customer service procedures had increased. Employees had to have a great deal more information at their disposal to solve customer problems. These problems were often made more serious when customers installed additional software on their computers, which then caused problems with the software already installed on the Gateway machine. As everyone who has installed new software knows, it can take considerable time to iron out the problems and get the new installation to work. Gateway was spending millions of dollars in employee time to solve these problems and desired to reduce this cost.

Ritter discovered that of the 15 rules and procedures the company had instituted for its customer service reps to follow, two rules in particular were the source of customer dissatisfaction. The first rule concerned the issue of customer-installed software. Gateway had told its service reps to inform customers that if they installed any other software on their machines, this would invalidate Gateway's warranty. This infuriated customers, who asked, Why shouldn't they install other necessary software? The second rule was one that rewarded customer support reps on the basis of how quickly they handled customer calls, meaning that the more calls they handled in an hour or day, the higher their bonuses.

Success in the PC business is highly dependent on customer service.

The joint effect of these two rules was that customer reps were now motivated to minimize the length of a service call and, in particular, were unwilling to help solve customer problems that resulted from installation of "outlawed software" since doing so took a lot of time. Obviously customers resented this treatment; the result was the big decline in customer satisfaction.

Once Gateway's managers realized the source of the problem, they abolished the 15 rules immediately. Within one month customer satisfaction jumped by over 10%. As Gateway's managers discovered, to prevent unexpected problems, it is necessary to carefully choose and evaluate the rules and policies used to control employees' behavior.

In contrast to the situation at Gateway, Dave Lilly, an ex-nuclear submarine commander, chose the right rules for site-ROCK, whose business is hosting and managing other companies' Web sites to keep them up and running and error-free. A customer's site that goes down or runs haywire is the major enemy. To maximize the performance of his employees and to increase their ability to respond to unexpected online events, Lilly decided that they needed a comprehensive set of rules and SOPs to cover all the major known problems.[38] Lilly insisted that every problem-solving procedure should be written down and recorded. SiteROCK's employees developed over 30 thick binders that list all the processes and checklists they need to follow when an unexpected event happens to solve a specific problem.

Moreover, again drawing from his military experience, Lilly instituted a "two-man rule": Whenever the unexpected happens, each employee must immediately tell a coworker and the two together should attempt to solve the problem. The goal is simple: Use the rules to achieve a quick resolution of a complex issue. If the existing rules don't work, then employees must experiment; and when they find a solution, the solution is turned into a new rule to be included in the procedures book to aid the future decision making of all employees in the organization.

Problems with Bureaucratic Control

Like all organizations, siteROCK makes extensive use of bureaucratic control because rules and SOPs effectively control routine organizational activities. With a bureaucratic control system in place, managers can manage by exception and intervene and take corrective action only when necessary. However, managers need to be aware of a number of problems associated with bureaucratic control, because such problems can reduce organizational effectiveness.[39]

First, establishing rules is always easier than discarding them. Organizations tend to become overly bureaucratic over time as managers do everything according to the rule book. If the amount of red tape becomes too great, decision making slows and managers react slowly to changing conditions. This sluggishness can imperil an organization's survival if agile new competitors emerge. Once a siteROCK employee has found a better rule, the old one is discarded.

Second, because rules constrain and standardize behavior and lead people to behave in predictable ways, there is a danger that people become so used to automatically following rules that they stop thinking for themselves. Thus, too much standardization can actually *reduce* the level of learning taking place in an organization and get the organization off track if managers and workers focus on the wrong issues. An organization thrives when its members are constantly thinking of new ways to increase efficiency, quality, and customer responsiveness. By definition, new ideas do not come from blindly following standardized procedures. Similarly, the pursuit of innovation implies a commitment by managers to discover new ways of doing things; innovation, however, is incompatible with the use of extensive bureaucratic control.

Managers must therefore be sensitive about the way they use bureaucratic control. It is most useful when organizational activities are routine and well understood and when employees are making programmed decisions—for example, in mass-production settings such as Ford or in routine service settings such as stores like Target or Midas Muffler. Bureaucratic control is much less useful in situations where nonprogrammed decisions have to be made and managers have to react quickly to changes in the task environment.

To use output control and behavior control, managers must be able to identify the outcomes they want to achieve and the behaviors they want employees to perform to achieve those outcomes. For many of the most important and significant organizational activities, however, output control and behavior control are inappropriate for several reasons:

- A manager cannot evaluate the performance of workers such as doctors, research scientists, or engineers by observing their behavior on a day-to-day basis.

- Rules and SOPs are of little use in telling a doctor how to respond to an emergency situation or a scientist how to discover something new.

- Output controls such as the amount of time a surgeon takes for each operation or the costs of making a discovery are very crude measures of the quality of performance.

How can managers attempt to control and regulate the behavior of their subordinates when personal supervision is of little use, when rules cannot be developed to tell employees what to do, and when outputs and goals cannot be measured at all or can be measured usefully only over long periods?

Clan Control

clan control One source of control increasingly being used by organizations is **clan control,** which takes advantage of the power of internalized values and norms to guide and constrain employee attitudes and behavior in ways that increase organizational performance.[40] The first function of a control system is to shape the behavior of organizational members to ensure they are working toward organizational goals and to take corrective action if those goals are not being met. The second function of control, however, is to keep organizational members focused on thinking about what is best for their organization in the future and to keep them looking for new opportunities to use organizational resources to create value. Clan control serves this dual function of keeping organizational members goal-directed while open to new opportunities because it takes advantage of the power of organizational culture, discussed in the previous chapter.

Organizational culture functions as a kind of control system because managers can deliberately try to influence the kind of values and norms that develop in an organization—values and norms that specify appropriate and inappropriate behaviors and so determine the way its members behave.[41] We discussed the sources of organizational culture and the way managers can help create different kinds of cultures in Chapter 9, so there is no need to repeat this discussion here. Instead, the following "Management Insight" describes how one CEO created a very specific kind of company culture, one that survives until this day.

clan control The control exerted on individuals and groups in an organization by shared values, norms, standards of behavior, and expectations.

Management Insight

James Casey Creates a Culture for UPS

United Parcel Service (UPS) controls more than three-fourths of the U.S ground and air parcel service, delivering over 10 million packages a day in its fleet of 150,000 trucks.[42] It is also the most profitable company in its industry. UPS employs over 250,000 people, and since its founding as a bicycle messenger service in 1907 by James E. Casey, UPS has developed a culture that has been a model for competitors such as FedEx and the U.S. Postal Service.

From the beginning, Casey made efficiency and economy the company's driving values and loyalty, humility, discipline, dependability, and intense effort the key norms and standards UPS employees should adopt. UPS has always gone to extraordinary lengths to develop and maintain these values and norms in its workforce.

UPS drivers must follow strict guidelines regarding appearance, job performance, and customer interactions.

First, its operating systems from the top of the company down to its trucking operations are the subject of intense scrutiny by the company's 3,000 industrial engineers. These engineers are constantly on the lookout for ways to measure outputs and behaviors to improve efficiency. They time every part of an employee's job. Truck drivers, for example, are instructed in extraordinary detail on how to perform their tasks: They must step from their truck with their right foot first, fold their money face-up, carry packages under their left arm, walk at a pace of 3 feet per second, and slip the key ring holding their truck keys over their third finger.[43] Employees are not allowed to have beards, must be carefully groomed, and are instructed in how to deal with customers. Drivers who perform below average receive visits from training supervisors who accompany them on their delivery routes and instruct them on how to raise their performance level. Not surprisingly, as a result of this intensive training and close behavior control, UPS employees internalize the company's strong norms about the appropriate ways to behave to help the organization achieve its values of economy and efficiency.

Its search to find the best set of output controls leads UPS to constantly develop and introduce the latest in IT into the company's operations, particularly its materials management operations. In fact, today UPS offers a consulting service to other companies in the area of global supply chain management. Its goal is to teach other companies how to pursue its values of efficiency and economy, values that the company has been pursuing for the last hundred years as a result of the values of its founder.

Organizational Change

organizational change The movement of an organization away from its present state and toward some desired future state to increase its efficiency and effectiveness.

As we have discussed above, many problems can arise if an organization's control systems are not designed correctly. One of these problems is that an organization cannot change or adapt in response to a changing environment unless it has effective control over its activities. Companies can lose this control over time, as happened to Home Depot and Gateway, or they can change in ways that make them more effective, as happened to UPS and Wal-Mart. **Organizational change** is the movement of an organization away from its present state and toward some desired future state to increase its efficiency and effectiveness.

Interestingly enough, there is a fundamental tension or need to balance two opposing forces in the control process that influences the way organizations change. As just noted, organizations and their managers need to be able to control their activities and make their operations routine and predictable. At the same time, however, organizations have to be responsive to the need to change, and managers and employees have to "think on their feet" and realize when they need to depart from routines to be responsive to unpredictable events. In other words, even though adopting the right set of output and behavior controls is essential for improving efficiency, because the environment is dynamic and uncertain employees also need to feel that they have the autonomy to depart from routines as necessary to increase effectiveness. (See Figure 11.5.)

It is for this reason that many researchers believe that the highest-performing organizations are those that are constantly changing—and thus become experienced at doing so—in their search to become more efficient and effective. And

Figure 11.5
Organizational Control and Change

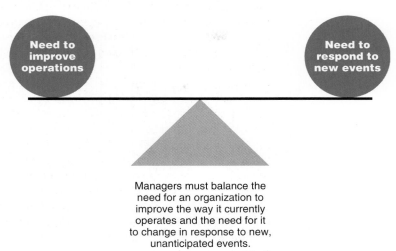

Managers must balance the
need for an organization to
improve the way it currently
operates and the need for it
to change in response to new,
unanticipated events.

companies like UPS, Dell, and Home Depot are constantly changing the mix
of their activities to move forward even as they are seeking to make their existing operations more efficient. For example, UPS entered the air express parcel
market, bought a chain of mailbox stores, and began offering a consulting service. At the same time, it has been increasing the efficiency of its ground transport network.

Lewin's Force-Field Theory of Change

Researcher Kurt Lewin developed a theory about organizational change.
According to his *force-field theory,* a wide variety of forces arise from the way an
organization operates, from its structure, culture, and control systems, that
make organizations resistant to change. At the same time, a wide variety of
forces arise from changing task and general environments that push organizations toward change. These two sets of forces are always in opposition in an
organization.[44] When the forces are evenly balanced, the organization is in a
state of inertia and does not change. To get an organization to change, managers must find a way to *increase* the forces for change, *reduce* resistance to
change, or do *both* simultaneously. Any of these strategies will overcome inertia
and cause an organization to change.

Figure 11.6 illustrates Lewin's theory. An organization at performance level
P1 is in balance: Forces for change and resistance to change are equal. Management, however, decides that the organization should strive to achieve performance level P2. To get to level P2, managers must *increase* the forces for
change (the increase is represented by the lengthening of the up-arrows), *reduce*
resistance to change (the reduction is represented by the shortening of the
down-arrows), or both. If managers pursue any of the three strategies successfully, the organization will change and reach performance level P2. Before we
look in more detail at the techniques that managers can use to overcome

Figure 11.6
Lewin's Force-Field Model of Change

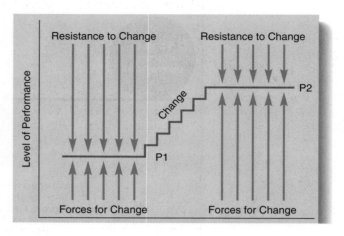

resistance and facilitate change, we need to look at the types of change they can implement to increase organizational effectiveness.

Evolutionary and Revolutionary Change

evolutionary change
Change that is gradual, incremental, and narrowly focused.

Managers continually face choices about how best to respond to the forces for change. There are several types of change that managers can adopt to help their organizations achieve desired future states.[45] In general, types of change fall into two broad categories: evolutionary change and revolutionary change.[46]

Evolutionary change is gradual, incremental, and narrowly focused. Evolutionary change is not drastic or sudden but, rather, is a constant attempt to improve, adapt, and adjust strategy and structure incrementally to accommodate to changes taking place in the environment.[47] Sociotechnical systems theory and total quality management, or kaizen, are two instruments of evolutionary change. Such improvements might entail utilizing technology in a better way or reorganizing the work process.

Technological change, such as this "robot" doctor at Hackensack University Medical Center in Hackensack, New Jersey, can bring about revolutionary change. Information technology has the potential to transform the health-care industry.

Some organizations, however, need to make major changes quickly. Faced with drastic, unexpected changes in the environment (for example, a new technological breakthrough) or with an impending disaster resulting from mismanagement, an organization might need to act quickly and decisively. In this case, revolutionary change is called for.

revolutionary change
Change that is rapid, dramatic, and broadly focused.

Revolutionary change is rapid, dramatic, and broadly focused. Revolutionary change involves a bold attempt to quickly find new ways to be effective. It is likely to result in a radical shift in ways of doing things, new goals, and a new structure for the organization. The process has repercussions at all levels in the organization—corporate, divisional, functional, group, and individual. Reengineering, restructuring, and innovation are three important instruments of revolutionary change.

Managing Change

The need to constantly search for ways to improve efficiency and effectiveness makes it vital that managers develop the skills necessary to manage change effectively. Several experts have proposed a model of change that managers can follow to implement change successfully, that is, to move an organization away from its present state and toward some desired future state to increase its efficiency and effectiveness.[48] Figure 11.7 outlines the steps in this process. In the rest of this section we examine each one.

ASSESSING THE NEED FOR CHANGE   Organizational change can affect practically all aspects of organizational functioning, including organizational structure, culture, strategies, control systems, and groups and teams, as well as the human resource management system and critical organizational processes such as communication, motivation, and leadership. Organizational change can bring alterations in the ways managers carry out the critical tasks of planning, organizing, leading, and controlling and the ways they perform their managerial roles.

Deciding how to change an organization is a complex matter because change disrupts the status quo and poses a threat, prompting employees to resist attempts to alter work relationships and procedures. Organizational learning, the process through which managers try to increase organizational members' abilities to understand and appropriately respond to changing conditions, can be an important impetus for change and can help all members of an organization, including managers, effectively make decisions about needed changes.

Assessing the need for change calls for two important activities: recognizing that there is a problem and identifying its source. Sometimes the need for change is obvious, such as when an organization's performance is suffering. Often, however, managers have trouble determining that something is going wrong because problems develop gradually; organizational performance may slip for a number of years before a problem becomes obvious. Thus, during the first step in the change process, managers need to recognize that there is a problem that requires change.

Figure 11.7
Four Steps in the Organizational Change Process

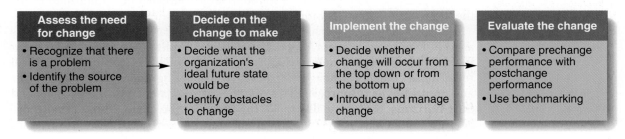

Often the problems that managers detect have produced a gap between desired performance and actual performance. To detect such a gap, managers need to look at performance measures—such as falling market share or profits, rising costs, or employees' failure to meet their established goals or stay within budgets—which indicate whether change is needed. These measures are provided by organizational control systems, discussed earlier in the chapter.

To discover the source of the problem, managers need to look both inside and outside the organization. Outside the organization, they must examine how changes in environmental forces may be creating opportunities and threats that are affecting internal work relationships. Perhaps the emergence of low-cost competitors abroad has led to conflict among different departments that are trying to find new ways to gain a competitive advantage. Managers also need to look within the organization to see whether its structure is causing problems between departments. Perhaps a company does not have integrating mechanisms in place to allow different departments to respond to low-cost competition.

DECIDING ON THE CHANGE TO MAKE   Once managers have identified the source of the problem, they must decide what they think the organization's ideal future state would be. In other words, they must decide where they would like their organization to be in the future—what kinds of goods and services it should be making, what its business-level strategy should be, how the organizational structure should be changed, and so on. During this step, managers also must engage in planning how they are going to attain the organization's ideal future state.

This step in the change process also includes identifying obstacles or sources of resistance to change. Managers must analyze the factors that may prevent the company from reaching its ideal future state. Obstacles to change are found at the corporate, divisional, departmental, and individual levels of the organization.

Corporate-level changes in an organization's strategy or structure, even seemingly trivial changes, may significantly affect how divisional and departmental managers behave. Suppose that to compete with low-cost foreign competitors, top managers decide to increase the resources spent on state-of-the-art machinery and reduce the resources spent on marketing or R&D. The power of manufacturing managers would increase, and the power of marketing and R&D managers would fall. This decision would alter the balance of power among departments and might lead to increased conflict as departments start fighting to retain their status in the organization. An organization's present strategy and structure are powerful obstacles to change.

Whether a company's culture is adaptive or inert facilitates or obstructs change. Organizations with entrepreneurial, flexible cultures, such as high-tech companies, are much easier to change than are organizations with more rigid cultures, such as those sometimes found in large, bureaucratic organizations like the military or General Motors.

The same obstacles to change exist at the divisional and departmental levels as well. Division managers may differ in their attitudes toward the changes that top managers propose and, if their interests and power seem threatened, will resist those changes. Managers at all levels usually fight to protect their power and control over resources. Given that departments have different goals and time horizons, they may also react differently to the changes that other managers propose. When top managers are trying to reduce costs, for example, sales managers may resist attempts to cut back on sales expenditures if they believe that problems stem from manufacturing managers' inefficiencies.

At the individual level, too, people are often resistant to change because change brings uncertainty and uncertainty brings stress. For example, individuals may resist the introduction of a new technology because they are uncertain about their abilities to learn it and effectively use it.

These obstacles make organizational change a slow process. Managers must recognize the potential obstacles to change and take them into consideration. Some obstacles can be overcome by improving communication so that all organizational members are aware of the need for change and of the nature of the changes being made. Empowering employees and inviting them to participate in the planning for change also can help overcome resistance and allay employees' fears. In addition, managers can sometimes overcome resistance by emphasizing group or shared goals such as increased organizational efficiency and effectiveness. In Home Depot's case, the company's declining performance made many of its managers who had previously resisted change realize that the change was ultimately in everyone's best interests because it would increase organizational performance. However, many of its store managers did leave the company because they didn't like its new culture and operating system. The larger and more complex an organization is, the more complex is the change process.

IMPLEMENTING THE CHANGE   Generally, managers implement—that is, introduce and manage—change from the top down or from the bottom up.[49] Top-down change is implemented quickly: Top managers identify the need for change, decide what to do, and then move quickly to implement the changes throughout the organization. For example, top managers may decide to restructure and downsize the organization and then give divisional and departmental managers specific goals to achieve. With top-down change, the emphasis is on making the changes quickly and dealing with problems as they arise; it is revolutionary in nature, such as the change that took place at Home Depot.

Bottom-up change is typically more gradual or evolutionary. Top managers consult with middle and first-line managers about the need for change. Then, over time, managers at all levels work to develop a detailed plan for change. A major advantage of bottom-up change is that it can co-opt resistance to change from employees. Because the emphasis in bottom-up change is on participation and on keeping people informed about what is going on, uncertainty and resistance are minimized. Home Depot's new CEO did not have the luxury of adopting an evolutionary approach; he had to take swift action to turn around the company.

EVALUATING THE CHANGE   The last step in the change process is to evaluate how successful the change effort has been in improving organizational performance.[50] Using measures such as changes in market share, in profits, or in the ability of managers to meet their goals, managers compare how well an organization is performing after the change with how well it was performing before. Managers also can use **benchmarking,** comparing their performance on specific dimensions with the performance of high-performing organizations to decide how successful a change effort has been. For example, when Xerox was doing poorly in the 1980s, it benchmarked the efficiency of its distribution operations against that of L.L.Bean, the efficiency of its central computer operations against that of John Deere, and the efficiency of its marketing abilities against that of Procter & Gamble. Those three companies are renowned for their skills in these different areas, and by studying how they performed, Xerox was able to

top-down change A fast, revolutionary approach to change in which top managers identify what needs to be changed and then move quickly to implement the changes throughout the organization.

bottom-up change A gradual or evolutionary approach to change in which managers at all levels work together to develop a detailed plan for change.

benchmarking The process of comparing one company's performance on specific dimensions with the performance of other, high-performing organizations.

dramatically increase its own performance. Benchmarking is a key tool in total quality management, an important change program discussed in Chapter 9.

In summary, organizational control and change are closely linked because organizations operate in environments that are constantly changing and so managers must be alert to the need to change their strategies and structures. High-performing organizations are those whose managers are attuned to the need to continually modify the way they operate and which adopt techniques like empowered work groups and teams, benchmarking, and global outsourcing to remain competitive in a global world.

Summary and Review

WHAT IS ORGANIZATIONAL CONTROL?   Controlling is the process whereby managers monitor and regulate how efficiently and effectively an organization and its members are performing the activities necessary to achieve organizational goals. Controlling is a four-step process: (1) establishing performance standards, (2) measuring actual performance, (3) comparing actual performance against performance standards, and (4) evaluating the results and initiating corrective action if needed.

OUTPUT CONTROL   To monitor output or performance, managers choose goals or performance standards that they think will best measure efficiency, quality, innovation, and responsiveness to customers at the corporate, divisional, departmental or functional, and individual levels. The main mechanisms that managers use to monitor output are financial measures of performance, organizational goals, and operating budgets.

BEHAVIOR CONTROL   In an attempt to shape behavior and induce employees to work toward achieving organizational goals, managers utilize direct supervision, management by objectives, and bureaucratic control by means of rules and standard operating procedures.

CLAN CONTROL   Clan control is the control exerted on individuals and groups by shared values, norms, and prescribed standards of behavior. An organization's culture is deliberately fashioned to put emphasis on the values and norms top managers believe will lead to high performance.

ORGANIZATIONAL CHANGE   There is a need to balance two opposing forces in the control process that influences the way organizations change. On the one hand, managers need to be able to control organizational activities and make their operations routine and predictable. On the other hand, organizations have to be responsive to the need to change, and managers must understand when they need to depart from routines to be responsive to unpredictable events. The four steps in managing change are (1) assessing the need for change, (2) deciding on the changes to make, (3) implementing change, and (4) evaluating the results of change.

Management in Action

Topics for Discussion and Action

Discussion

1. What is the relationship between organizing and controlling?

2. How do output control and behavior control differ?

3. Why is it important for managers to involve subordinates in the control process?

4. What kind of controls would you expect to find most used in (a) a hospital, (b) the Navy, (c) a city police force? Why?

5. What are the main obstacles to organizational change? What techniques can managers use to overcome these obstacles?

Action

6. Ask a manager to list the main performance measures that he or she uses to evaluate how well the organization is achieving its goals.

7. Ask the same or a different manager to list the main forms of output control and behavior control that he or she uses to monitor and evaluate employee behavior.

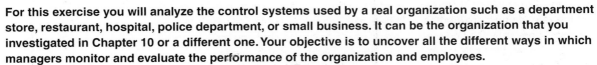

Building Management Skills
Understanding Controlling

For this exercise you will analyze the control systems used by a real organization such as a department store, restaurant, hospital, police department, or small business. It can be the organization that you investigated in Chapter 10 or a different one. Your objective is to uncover all the different ways in which managers monitor and evaluate the performance of the organization and employees.

1. At what levels does control take place in this organization?

2. Which output performance standards (such as financial measures and organizational goals) do managers use most often to evaluate performance at each level?

3. Does the organization have a management-by-objectives system in place? If it does, describe it. If it does not, speculate about why not.

4. How important is behavior control in this organization? For example, how much of managers' time is spent directly supervising employees? How formalized is the organization? Do employees receive a book of rules to instruct them about how to perform their jobs?

5. What kind of culture does the organization have? What are the values and norms? What effect does the organizational culture have on the way employees behave or treat customers?

6. Based on this analysis, do you think there is a fit between the organization's control systems and its culture? What is the nature of this fit? How could it be improved?

Managing Ethically

Some managers and organizations go to great lengths to monitor their employees' behavior, and they keep extensive records about employees' behavior and performance. Some organizations also seem to possess norms and values that cause their employees to behave in certain ways.

Questions

1. Either by yourself or in a group, think about the ethical implications of organizations' monitoring and collecting information about their employees. What kind of information is it ethical to collect or unethical to collect? Why? Should managers and organizations inform subordinates they are collecting such information?

2. Similarly, some organizations' cultures, like those of Arthur Andersen, the accounting firm, and of Enron, seemed to have developed norms and values that caused their members to behave in unethical ways. When and why does a strong norm that encourages high performance become one that can cause people to act unethically? How can organizations keep their values and norms from becoming "too strong"?

Small Group Breakout Exercise

How Best to Control the Sales Force?

Form groups of three or four people, and appoint one member as the spokesperson who will communicate your findings to the class when called on by the instructor. Then discuss the following scenario.

You are the regional sales managers of an organization that supplies high-quality windows and doors to building supply centers nationwide. Over the last three years, the rate of sales growth has slackened. There is increasing evidence that, to make their jobs easier, salespeople are primarily servicing large customer accounts and ignoring small accounts. In addition, the salespeople are not dealing promptly with customer questions and complaints, and this inattention has resulted in a drop in after-sales service. You have talked about these problems, and you are meeting to design a control system to increase both the amount of sales and the quality of customer service.

1. Design a control system that you think will best motivate salespeople to achieve these goals.

2. What relative importance do you put on (a) output control, (b) behavior control, and (c) organizational culture in this design?

Exploring the World Wide Web

Go to the Web site of UBS, an investment bank (www.ubs.com). Click on "careers" and then on "our culture," and read the statement about the bank's values and norms.

1. How would you expect UBS's values and norms to affect its employees' behavior?

2. How does UBS design its organizational structure to shape its culture?

Be the Manager

You have been asked by your company's CEO to find a way to improve the performance of its teams of Web design and Web hosting specialists and programmers. Each team works on a different aspect of Web site production, and while each is responsible for the quality of its own performance, its performance also depends on how well the other teams perform. Your task is to create a control system that will help to increase the performance of each team separately and facilitate cooperation among the teams. This is necessary because the various projects are interlinked and affect one another just as the different parts of a car must fit together. Since competition in the Web site production market is intense, it is imperative that each Web site be up and running as quickly as possible and incorporate all the latest advances in Web site software technology.

Questions

1. What kind of output controls will best facilitate positive interactions both within the teams and among the teams?

2. What kind of behavior controls will best facilitate positive interactions both within the teams and among the teams?

3. How would you go about helping managers develop a culture to promote high team performance?

BusinessWeek Case in the News

Cracking the Whip at Wyeth

When Robert R. Ruffolo Jr. signed on at Wyeth in 2000, his mandate was simple: shake up the drugmaker's mediocre research and development operation. He has certainly succeeded. One of Ruffolo's first moves as executive vice president for R&D was conducting a top-to-bottom review of Wyeth's pipeline.

Shredding It Up

Since jumping ship at SmithKline Beecham (GSK) in 2000, the 55-year-old Ruffolo has ripped apart and reassembled Wyeth's $2.7 billion research operation. Among his controversial changes: a series of quotas for how many compounds must be churned out by company scientists. For some of them, having to hit a hard-and-fast number seemed an athema to the complex and at times serendipitous drug-development process.

But Ruffolo held bonuses hostage to managers' meeting that goal. More recently he began studying industries from aerospace to computer hardware manufacturing in a bid to better manage innovation. But don't expect him to steal from the playbooks of industry rivals. "Until recently, this industry didn't have to focus too much on productivity," he says. "The solutions to our problems aren't going to come from our competitors."

Wyeth's efforts to energize its labs reflect a major challenge in the drug business. In recent years the output from big-pharma R&D has been almost universally disappointing. According to the Tufts Center for the Study of Drug Development, only 58 new drugs were approved by the Food & Drug Administration from 2002 to 2004, down 47% from the peak of 110 from 1996 to 1998. The reasons are myriad, including a wealth of good treatments that are already available for many diseases and increased vigilance from regulators and physicians on safety. But with financial pressures building as more drugs go off-patent and as payers push back against rising drug costs, pharma companies can't afford to battle that problem by simply throwing bigger bucks at research.

That's why Ruffolo, who took over all of Wyeth R&D in mid-2002, is looking for ways to bring greater efficiency to the innovation process. His goal may not be unusual, but his hard-nosed approach to getting there is.

After signing on at Wyeth, Ruffolo followed Wyeth CEO Robert A. Essner's charge to "rattle the cage." Ruffolo moved quickly to instill discipline. With the help of outside consultants, 70 scientists at the company took a hard look at recent projects that had succeeded and failed. They came to a stunning conclusion: Often, drugs with the lowest chance of paying off ended up with the most resources. Why? Scientists continued to plow money and staff into troubled projects in an attempt to rescue them.

So Ruffolo instituted the review process that sent everyone scrambling. Under that system, a value is determined for every project in the pipeline based on a host of factors, including the cost of developing it, the likelihood of success, and expected future sales. That culminates in an annual review that determines which projects move forward, which get put on the back burner, and which are killed. That new rigor made people more willing to terminate troubled projects. That's critical in the drug business since late-stage human trials are so expensive.

Smart Decisions

Brenda Reis, an assistant vice president in Wyeth R&D, had to make one of those tough calls. In 2004 her group was developing a new oral contraceptive. As part of Ruffolo's portfolio-review process they determined what sort of safety and effectiveness they would need from the drug in order to make it a hit.

In late summer of 2004, Reis recalls, the group of 12 people leading the project sat in stunned silence as they digested disappointing data from midstage human testing of the drug. The product was triggering a side effect that would seriously limit its potential. A few weeks later the group recommended the development of the compound be dropped. Her team was given an internal company award for stopping the project—a move that sent a clear signal that the company would reward good decision making.

Ruffolo has set firm targets for how many compounds need to move forward at each stage of the development process. Take discovery scientists, the group that identifies new ways to attack diseases and creates compounds to be passed on to another group for more extensive testing. When Ruffolo came in, that group was

moving just four drug candidates out of its labs every year. Ruffolo set the new target at 12—with no increase in resources or head count. The target has been met every year since its 2001 implementation. This year, the bar has been raised to 15.

Too Much Pressure?

Those targets forced big changes in the R&D operation. For one thing, scientists needed to standardize more of what they did in an effort to move compounds more quickly through their shop. Case in point: At the old Wyeth, researchers could design the early human safety studies—known as Phase I trials—in almost any way they wanted. Under the new regime, researchers pick from four or five standardized formats. That helped cut the time for a Phase I trial from 18 months to six.

The approach has critics. Some former executives say he seemed out of touch with the anxiety his new demands created among scientists. Dr. Philip Frost, chief scientific officer at biotech ImClone Systems (IMCL), describes Ruffolo as a "bully" at times. Ruffolo doesn't agree with that characterization, but he acknowledges that when it comes to the targets, "I forced it on them."

Critics also argue that Ruffolo went too far in trying to boost output. William J. Weiss, who left Wyeth in early 2004 and is now director of drug evaluation at biotech Cumbre in Dallas, says quotas like those set by Ruffolo can prompt scientists to "overlook problems with some compounds" in order to make their numbers. In fact, Wyeth has seen an increased failure rate for compounds in midstage testing recently. Ruffolo says that this has occurred throughout

the industry. Still, even supporters such as C. Richard Lyttle, CEO at pharmaceutical company Radius Health in Cambridge, Mass., point out that those sorts of productivity pressures can also force people to zero in on the projects that are the safest gambles. Ruffolo says he specifically put fewer controls in at the so-called exploratory phase, when scientists tend to have eureka moments of, say, spotting a new cellular target they want to hit with a drug. "I don't think you can manage creativity," he says. "But I think you can manage the outcome after you have that creative effort."

Has Ruffolo's prescription worked? UBS Investment Research analyst Carl Seiden says Wyeth's pipeline has shown major improvement, with a number of potentially hot-selling products likely to hit in the next few years. Among them: a new antidepressant based on its current blockbuster Effexor and a new schizophrenia treatment.

Questions

1. What kinds of control systems tend to be used to measure the performance of R&D scientists?

2. What kind of control system did Ruffolo institute? What are the various parts or measures of the control system he instituted?

3. What are the pros and cons of his system? Does it seem to be working?

Source: Amy Barrett, "Cracking the Whip at Wyeth." Reprinted from the February 6, 2006, issue of *BusinessWeek* by special permission. Copyright © 2006 by the McGraw-Hill Companies, Inc.

BusinessWeek

Case in the News

How Failure Breeds Success

Ever heard of Choglit? How about OK Soda or Surge? Long after "New Coke" became nearly synonymous with innovation failure, these products joined Coca-Cola Co.'s graveyard of beverage busts. Given that history, failure hardly seems like a subject CEO E. Neville Isdell would want to trot out in front of investors. But Isdell did just that, deliberately airing the topic at Coke's annual meeting in April. "You will see some failures," he told the crowd. "As we take more risks, this is something we must accept as part of the regeneration process."

Warning Coke investors that the company might experience some flops is a little like warning Atlantans they might experience afternoon thunderstorms in July. But Isdell thinks it's vital. He wants Coke to take bigger risks, and to do that, he knows he needs to convince employees and shareholders that he will tolerate the failures that will inevitably result. That's the only way to change Coke's traditionally risk-averse culture. And given the importance of this goal, there's no podium too big for sending the signal.

While few CEOs are as candid about the potential for failure as Isdell, many are wrestling with the same problem, trying to get their organizations to cozy up to the risk-taking that innovation requires. A warning: It's not going to be an easy shift. After years of cost-cutting initiatives and growing job insecurity, most employees don't exactly feel like putting themselves on the line. Add to that the heightened expectations by management on individual performance, and it's easy to see why so many opt to play it safe.

Indeed, for a generation of managers weaned on the rigors of Six Sigma error-elimination programs, embracing failure—gasp!—is close to blasphemy. Stefan H. Thomke, a professor at Harvard Business School and author of Experimentation Matters, says that when he talks to business groups, "I try to be provocative and say: 'Failure is not a bad thing.' I always have lots of people staring at me, [thinking] 'Have you lost your mind?' That's O.K. It gets their attention. [Failure] is so important to the experimental process."

That it is. Crucial, in fact. After all, that's why true, breakthrough innovation—an imperative in today's globally competitive world, in which product cycles are shorter than ever—is so extraordinarily hard. It requires well-honed organizations built for efficiency and speed to do what feels unnatural: Explore. Experiment. Foul up, sometimes. Then repeat.

Granted, not all failures are praiseworthy. Some flops are just that: bad ideas. The eVilla, Sony Corp.'s $500 "Internet appliance." The Pontiac Aztek, GM's ugly duckling "crossover" SUV. But intelligent failures—those that happen early and inexpensively and that contribute new insights about your customers—should be more than just tolerable. They should be encouraged. "Figuring out how to master this process of failing fast and failing cheap and fumbling toward success is probably the most important thing companies have to get good at," says Scott Anthony, the managing director at consulting firm Innosight.

Perhaps most important, it means designing ways to measure performance that balance accountability with the freedom to make mistakes. People may fear failure, but they fear the consequences of it even more. "The performance culture really is in deep conflict with the learning culture," says Paul J. H. Schoemaker, CEO of consulting firm Decision Strategies International Inc. "It's an unusual executive who can balance these."

Some organizations have tried to measure performance in a way that accounts for these opposing pressures. At IBM Research, engineers are evaluated on both one- and three-year time frames. The one-year term determines the bonus, while the three-year period decides rank and salary. The longer frame can help neutralize a year of setbacks. "A three-year evaluation cycle sends an important message to our researchers, demonstrating our commitment to investing in the early, risky stages of innovation," says Armando Garcia, vice president for technical strategy and worldwide operations at IBM Research.

In addition to making sure performance evaluations take a long-term view, managers should also think about celebrating smart failures. (Those who repeat their mistakes, of course, should hardly be rewarded.) Thomas D. Kuczmarski, a Chicago new-product development consultant, even proposes "failure parties" as a way of recognizing that it's part of the creative process. "What most companies do is put a wall around a failure as if it's radioactive," says Kuczmarski. Most companies don't spend enough time and resources looking backward. General Electric Co. (GE) is trying to do just that. The company, which is well-known for sharing best practices across its many units, has recently begun formally discussing failures, too. Last September the company set up a two-hour conference call for managers of eight "imagination breakthroughs" that didn't live up to expectations and were being shelved, or "retired," in GE's parlance. Such discussions can be nerve-racking, especially in companies where failure has traditionally been met with tough consequences. That was the case at GE, which is now three years into the effort spearheaded by Chairman and CEO Jeffrey R. Immelt to make innovation the new mantra at the $150 billion behemoth.

Some companies have gone even further, taking a comprehensive look at all their previous failures. That was the case at Corning Inc., which found itself teetering on the brink of bankruptcy after the once red-hot market for its optical fiber collapsed during the telecom bust. Following that debacle, then-Corning CEO James R. Houghton asked Joseph A. Miller Jr., executive vice president and chief technology officer, to produce an in-depth review of the company's 150-year history of innovation, documenting both failures and successes.

That's why W.L. Gore & Associates Inc. in Newark, Del., makers of the waterproof fabric Gore-Tex, recognizes outsiders—people within Gore but not on the product development team—who make the call on projects that need to be pulled. When Brad Jones led Gore's Industrial Products Div., which makes sealants and filtration systems, he handed out "Sharp Shooter" trophies to these outside managers when a project was effectively killed. These marksmen, so to speak, freed from the trappings of familiarity, can identify potential snags that the team may have overlooked. "We're effusive in our thanks for that contribution," says Jones. "We ask them to write up what they learned from it, and how we could have made the decision [to kill the project] faster."

A company's reaction in the face of intelligent failures can send tremors or thrills through a culture. If top executives are accepting, people will embrace risk. But if managers react harshly, people will retreat from it.

Questions

1. Why can studying failure help managers to better manage the control process and improve performance?

2. What kind of specific changes in control systems would studying failure lead to?

Source: Jena McGregor, William C. Symonds, Dean Foust, Diane Brady, and Moira Herbst , "How Failure Breeds Success." Reprinted from the July 10, 2006, issue of *BusinessWeek* by special permission. Copyright © 2006 by the McGraw-Hill Companies, Inc.

CHAPTER 12

Human Resource Management

After studying this chapter, you should be able to:

- Explain why strategic human resource management can help an organization gain a competitive advantage.

- Describe the steps managers take to recruit and select organizational members.

- Discuss the training and development options that ensure organizational members can effectively perform their jobs.

- Explain why performance appraisal and feedback is such a crucial activity, and list the choices managers must make in designing effective performance appraisal and feedback procedures.

- Explain the issues managers face in determining levels of pay and benefits.

A Manager's Challenge

Democracy in Action at Semco

How can managers provide employees with freedom and flexibility at work while ensuring their companies' survival and profitability?

Ricardo Semler was 21 years old (and one of the youngest graduates from the Harvard Business School MBA program) when he took his father's place as head of the family business, Semco, based in Sao Paolo, Brazil, in 1984.[1] His father, Antonio, had founded Semco in 1954 as a machine shop; the company went on to become a manufacturer of marine pumps for the shipbuilding industry, with $4 million a year in revenues when Ricardo Semler took over. Today, Semco's revenues are over $200 million a year from a diverse set of businesses ranging from industrial machinery, cooling towers, and facility management to environmental consulting and Web-based HRM outsourcing and inventory management services. Semco prides itself on being a premier provider of goods and services in its markets, provides goods and services only in markets that are complex and thus difficult for competitors to enter, and therefore has loyal customers who are willing to pay the higher prices it charges. In addition to growing over 30% a year and generating its own cash to support

this growth (Semco is a private company), Semco is very profitable.[2]

Semler is the first to admit that Semco's phenomenal success is due to its human

Ricardo Semler believes in treating employees like adults.

resources—its employees. In fact, Semler so firmly believes in Semco's employees that he and the other top managers are reluctant to tell employees what to do. Semco has no rules, regulations, or organizational charts; hierarchy is eschewed; and workplace democracy rules the day. Employees have levels of autonomy unheard of in other companies, and flexibility and trust are built into every aspect of human resource management at Semco.[3]

Semler believes in employees' willingness and desire to be productive and efficient, make significant contributions to Semco, and ensure its continued profitability (which also benefits the employees in terms of their own compensation). Thus, employees have maximum freedom and determine issues ranging from where and when they work to how they are paid.[4] This approach flies in the face of contemporary management thought, yet Semco's ongoing success has made it a living case study in the business community. Semler himself has become a best-selling author of business books, such as *Maverick* and *The Seven-Day Weekend*, frequently gives lectures to global audiences, and is the author of widely read *Harvard Business Review* articles.[5]

Human resource practices at Semco revolve around maximizing the contributions employees make to the company, and this begins by hiring individuals who want, can, and will contribute. Semco strives to ensure that all selection decisions are based on relevant and complete information. Job candidates are first interviewed as a group; the candidates meet many employees, receive a tour of the company, and interact with potential coworkers. This gives Semco a chance to size up candidates in ways more likely to reveal their true natures, and it gives the candidates a chance to learn about Semco. Once finalists are identified from the pool, multiple Semco employees interview each one five or six more times to choose the best person(s) to be hired. The result is that both Semco and new hires make very informed decisions and are mutually committed to making the relation a success.[6]

Once hired, entry-level employees participate in the Lost in Space program, in which they rotate through different positions and units of their own choosing for about a year.[7] In this way, the new hires learn about their options and can decide where their interests lie, and the units they work in learn about the new hires. At the end of the year, the new employees may be offered a job in one of the units in which they worked, or they may seek a position elsewhere in Semco. Seasoned Semco employees are also encouraged to rotate positions and work in different parts of the company to keep them fresh, energized, and motivated and to give them the opportunity to contribute in new ways as their interests change.[8]

Employees at Semco are free to choose when and where they work.[9] Semler realizes that employees have lives outside the workplace and gives them the freedom to manage their work and free time; he does not expect them to work excessive hours either. What is expected of all employees and all units at Semco is performance.[10]

Performance is appraised at Semco in terms of results. Every six months, all business units are required to demonstrate that their continued operation is producing value for Semco and its customers. If a unit cannot do so, the unit will be disbanded. Similarly, all employees and managers must demonstrate that they are making valuable contributions and deserve to be "rehired." For example, each manager's performance is anonymously appraised by all of the employees who report to him or her, and the appraisals are made publicly available in Semco. As Semler puts it,

> We treat our employees like adults. . . . If they screw up, they take the blame. And since they have to be rehired every six months, they know their jobs are always at risk. Ultimately, all we care about is performance. An employee who spends two days a week at the beach but still produces real value for customers and coworkers is a better employee than one who works ten-hour days but creates little value.[11]

Employees also can choose how they are paid from a combination of 11 different compensation options, ranging from fixed salaries, bonuses, and profit sharing to royalties on sales or profits and arrangements based on meeting annual self-set goals. Flexibility in compensation promotes risk taking and innovation, according to Semler, and maximizes returns to employees in terms of their pay and to the company in terms of revenues and profitability.[12]

Flexibility, autonomy, the ability to change jobs often, and control of working hours and even compensation are some of the ways by which Semler strives to ensure that employees are involved in their work because they *want* to be; turnover at Semco is less than 1% annually.[13] And with human resource practices geared toward maximizing contributions and performance, Semco is well poised to continue to provide value to its customers.

Overview

Managers are responsible for acquiring, developing, protecting, and utilizing the resources that an organization needs to be efficient and effective. One of the most important resources in all organizations is human resources–the people involved in the production and distribution of goods and services. Human resources include all members of an organization, ranging from top managers to entry-level employees. Effective managers like Ricardo Semler in "A Manager's Challenge" realize how valuable human resources are and take active steps to make sure that their organizations build and fully utilize their human resources to gain a competitive advantage.

This chapter examines how managers can tailor their human resource management system to their organization's strategy and structure. We discuss in particular the major components of human resource management: recruitment and selection, training and development, performance appraisal, pay and benefits, and labor relations. By the end of this chapter, you will understand the central role human resource management plays in creating a high-performing organization.

Strategic Human Resource Management

human resource management (HRM) Activities that managers engage in to attract and retain employees and to ensure that they perform at a high level and contribute to the accomplishment of organizational goals.

strategic human resource management The process by which managers design the components of an HRM system to be consistent with each other, with other elements of organizational architecture, and with the organization's strategy and goals.

Organizational architecture (see Part 4) is the combination of organizational structure, control systems, culture, and a human resource management system that managers develop to use resources efficiently and effectively. **Human resource management (HRM)** includes all the activities managers engage in to attract and retain employees and to ensure that they perform at a high level and contribute to the accomplishment of organizational goals. These activities make up an organization's human resource management system, which has five major components: recruitment and selection, training and development, performance appraisal and feedback, pay and benefits, and labor relations (see Figure 12.1).

Strategic human resource management is the process by which managers design the components of an HRM system to be consistent with each other, with other elements of organizational architecture, and with the organization's strategy and goals.[14] The objective of strategic HRM is the development of an HRM system that enhances an organization's efficiency, quality, innovation, and responsiveness to customers–the four building blocks of competitive advantage. At Semco in "A Manager's Challenge," HRM practices ensure that employees make meaningful contributions, are innovative, are efficient, and provide value to customers.

As part of strategic human resource management, some managers have adopted "Six Sigma" quality improvement plans. These plans ensure that an organization's products and services are as free of error or defects as possible through a variety of human resource–related initiatives. Jack Welch, former CEO of General Electric Company, has indicated that these initiatives have saved his company millions of dollars, and other companies, such as Whirlpool and Motorola, also have implemented Six Sigma initiatives. In order for such initiatives to be effective, however, top managers have to be committed to Six Sigma, employees must be motivated, and there must be demand for the products or services of the organization in the first place. David Fitzpatrick, head of Deloitte Consulting's Lean Enterprise Practice, estimates that most Six Sigma plans are not effective because the conditions for effective Six Sigma are not in

Figure 12.1

Components of a Human Resource Management System

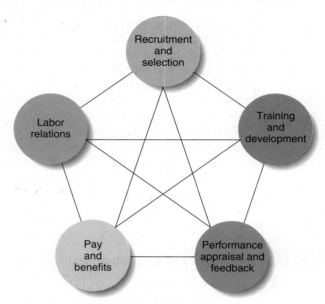

Each component of an HRM system influences
the others, and all five must fit together

place. For example, if top managers are not committed to the quality initiative, they may not devote the necessary time and resources to make it work and may lose interest in it prematurely.[15]

Effective strategic human resource management can not only help organizations be responsive to customers but also help corporate customers develop their own strategies and effectively utilize their own human resources, as indicated in the following "Information Technology Byte."

Information
Technology
Byte

IBM's Global Researchers Help Corporate Customers Achieve Their Goals

Information technology giant IBM is shifting its focus from making mainframe computers to providing customers with complex technological services.[16] As part of this strategic change in focus, IBM is putting its scientists, mathematicians, and researchers in close contact with major corporate customers so that these specialists can learn firsthand the major challenges customers face in their technology needs. Learning about customers' businesses and challenges enables the IBM specialists to develop solutions, based on their expertise, that customers might not be aware of or even think possible. Once customers realize that they will have IBM's best and brightest not only working on their current problems and challenges but also considering how

In order to beat the competition, IBM concluded that J.P. Morgan Chase should act like a single bank, so that in any customer interaction, an employee would be able to pull all relevant information about that customer instantly.

they can take advantage of future developments, it is easier to convince them to choose IBM for their technology needs.[17]

For example, IBM mathematician Howard Sacher spent over a year meeting with top managers in charge of technology at JPMorgan Chase, learning about the current state of banking and future challenges and exploring how IBM could develop technological solutions to put Chase ahead of its competition in terms of responsiveness to customers.[18] Sacher determined that Chase should act like a single bank with its customers so that any Chase employee interacting with a customer at any branch would be able to pull up all relevant information about that customer instantly. Developing the technology to make the "one-bank" mentality a reality is actually a complicated problem due to Chase's multitude of services, ways of interacting with customers, record-keeping procedures, and so forth.[19] Moreover, the technology needs to be in step with future developments and new technologies that banks will be unfolding to provide better service in the future. Sacher's efforts paid off when Chase awarded IBM a $5 billion contract to develop and manage its technological infrastructure.[20]

Moreover, in an effort to both reduce costs and increase the quality of service, IBM is globalizing its services workforce of around 200,000 employees (43,000 of whom work in India).[21] The focus of globalization is on skills rather than location. Thus, for any given project, IBM is striving to assemble the most highly skilled team of employees to serve customers' needs.[22] Using the latest developments in IT, IBM is able to serve clients from a distance over the Internet. Drawing on a database of employee skills and mathematical formulas, IBM can assemble a team of employees that will best meet customers' needs, even if those employees are physically spread around the globe.[23] Clearly, as IBM strategically manages its own human resources, the services it provides to corporate customers enables customers, in turn, to do the same—a win-win situation.

Overview of the Components of HRM

Managers use *recruitment and selection*, the first component of an HRM system, to attract and hire new employees who have the abilities, skills, and experiences that will help an organization achieve its goals. Microsoft Corporation, for example, has the goal of remaining the premier computer software company in the world. To achieve this goal, Bill Gates realizes the importance of hiring only the best software designers: hundreds of highly qualified candidates are interviewed and rigorously tested. This careful attention to selection has contributed to Microsoft's competitive advantage. Microsoft has little trouble recruiting top

Health Act of 1970, require that managers ensure that employees are protected from workplace hazards and safety standards are met.

In Chapter 4, we explained how effectively managing diversity is an ethical and business imperative, and we discussed the many issues surrounding diversity. EEO laws and their enforcement make the effective management of diversity a legal imperative as well. The Equal Employment Opportunity Commission (EEOC) is the division of the Department of Justice that enforces most of the EEO laws and handles discrimination complaints. In addition, the EEOC issues guidelines for managers to follow to ensure that they are abiding by EEO laws. For example, the Uniform Guidelines on Employee Selection Procedures issued by the EEOC (in conjunction with the Departments of Labor and Justice and the Civil Service Commission) provide managers with guidance on how to ensure that the recruitment and selection component of human resource management complies with Title VII of the Civil Rights Act (which prohibits discrimination based on gender, race, color, religion, and national origin).[29]

Contemporary challenges that managers face related to the legal environment include how to eliminate sexual harassment (see Chapter 5 for an in-depth discussion of sexual harassment), how to make accommodations for employees with disabilities, how to deal with employees who have substance abuse problems, and how to manage HIV-positive employees and employees with AIDS.[30] HIV-positive employees are infected with the virus that causes AIDS but may show no AIDS symptoms and may not develop AIDS in the near future. Often, such employees are able to perform their jobs effectively, and managers must take steps to ensure that they are allowed to do so and are not discriminated against in the workplace.[31] Employees with AIDS may or may not be able to perform their jobs effectively, and, once again, managers need to ensure that they are not unfairly discriminated against.[32] Many organizations have instituted AIDS awareness training programs to educate organizational members about HIV and AIDS, dispel unfounded myths about how HIV is spread, and ensure that individuals infected with the HIV virus are treated fairly and are able to be productive as long as they can be while not putting others at risk.[33]

While the Age Discrimination in Employment Act prohibits discrimination against workers over 40, increasing numbers of older workers are finding themselves unemployed with few promising job prospects,[34] as discussed in the following "Focus on Diversity."

Focus on
Diversity

Is It Age Discrimination?

There are approximately 77 million Americans classified as baby boomers, born in the post–World War II period of economic posterity between 1946 and 1964.[35] As baby boomers enter their 50s and 60s, some are finding their preretirement years to be fraught with anxiety and stress: After working hard to climb the corporate ladder for several decades, they are out of jobs and have few prospects.[36]

Take the case of Bob Miller, a top manager in the insurance and financial services industry, who lost his job at Zurich Financial a few years ago. Miller had a strong résumé, work history, and network of contacts in his field, as well as prior success at landing new jobs; he had been laid off

Milly Baltes works as a document clerk at the Orange County Clerk's office through an AARP senior jobs training program.

from five positions during his career and always ended up with a new job that was better than the previous one. Not so today. Miller, now in his mid-50s, is still looking for work. And he has company. A member of the Marketing Executives Networking Group (MENG), Miller has realized that many of his 1,300 co-members are in the same boat as he is—former top managers in corporate marketing who can't find a job.[37]

Increasing numbers of older workers are filing age discrimination lawsuits. However, these can be hard to win and sometimes are dismissed by the courts before they even go to trial because of a failure to demonstrate deliberate bias. Occasionally, such cases are settled out of court, such as the case of a 48-year-old business analyst at GE Capital who was laid off seven months after receiving a raise for outstanding performance.[38]

Some older workers who once were at the very top of the corporate hierarchy are now hiring themselves out as temporary workers. Tatum Partners, a white-collar temp agency based in Atlanta, specializes in finding work for former top managers as temporary chief financial officers or chief information officers; the agency has around 400 clients. Sam Horgan, one of Tatum's clients, had changed jobs only once before he was 47; between 47 and 56, he had six different employers; and now, at 57, he finds that full-time employment opportunities have dried up. As he puts it, "If I'm between jobs and I'm getting well into my 50s, I'm a leper with executive recruiters."[39] For Tatum, temporary assignments help pay the bills, provide him with meaningful work that makes use of his skills and experience, and mean that he no longer has to sit through demoralizing job interviews that often seem pointless due to his age.[40]

Ironically, just as age discrimination seems to be on the minds of many an out-of-work baby boomer, some organizations are realizing they will have a shortage of skilled and experienced workers if they don't hold on to valuable employees. There is a shortage of petroleum engineers in the United States (the average age of these employees is 50), and Georgia Pacific is trying to retain older researchers with PhD's by offering them a variety of incentives. Demographer Ken Bychtwald believes that organizations will need to roughly double their employment of older workers in the next 10 years. Bychtwald notes, "The managers trying to move everybody in their 50s out the door are taking their companies off a demographic cliff."[41] Clearly, some older workers who lost their jobs and can't find new ones might feel as if they are off a cliff. And their former employers might face age discrimination lawsuits.

Recruitment and Selection

Recruitment includes all the activities managers engage in to develop a pool of qualified candidates for open positions.[42] **Selection** is the process by which managers determine the relative qualifications of job applicants and their potential for performing well in a particular job. Prior to actually recruiting and selecting employees, managers need to engage in two important activities: human resource planning and job analysis (Figure 12.2).

recruitment Activities that managers engage in to develop a pool of qualified candidates for open positions.

selection The process that mangers use to determine the relative qualifications of job applicants and their potential for performing well in a particular job.

human resource planning Activities that managers engage in to forecast their current and future needs for human resources.

outsource To use outside suppliers and manufacturers to produce good and services.

Human Resource Planning

Human resource planning includes all the activities managers engage in to forecast their current and future human resource needs. Current human resources are the employees an organization needs today to provide high-quality goods and services to customers. Future human resource needs are the employees the organization will need at some later date to achieve its longer-term goals.

As part of human resource planning, managers must make both demand forecasts and supply forecasts. *Demand forecasts* estimate the qualifications and numbers of employees an organization will need given its goals and strategies. *Supply forecasts* estimate the availability and qualifications of current employees now and in the future, as well as the supply of qualified workers in the external labor market.

As a result of their human resource planning, managers sometimes decide to **outsource** to fill some of their human resource needs. Instead of recruiting and selecting employees to produce goods and services, managers contract with people who are not members of their organization to produce goods and services. Managers in publishing companies, for example, frequently contract with freelance editors to copyedit new books that they intend to publish. Kelly Services is an organization that provides temporary typing, clerical, and secretarial workers to managers who want to use outsourcing to fill some of their human resource requirements in these areas.

Two reasons why human resource planning sometimes leads managers to outsource are flexibility and cost. First, outsourcing can give managers increased flexibility, especially when accurately forecasting human resource needs is difficult, human resource needs fluctuate over time, or finding skilled workers in a particular area is difficult. Second, outsourcing can sometimes allow managers to make use of human resources at a lower *cost*. When work is outsourced, costs can be lower for a number of reasons: The organization does not have to provide benefits to workers; managers are able to contract for work only when the work is needed; and managers do not have to invest in training. Outsourcing can be used for functional activities such as after-sales service on appliances and equipment, legal work, and the management of information systems. Roy Richie, general counsel for the Chrysler Corporation, uses temporary

Figure 12.2
The Recruitment and Selection System

attorneys to write contracts and fill some of his department's human resource needs. As he says, "The math works. . . . Savings can be tremendous."[43]

Outsourcing does have its disadvantages, however.[44] When work is outsourced, managers may lose some control over the quality of goods and services. Also, individuals performing outsourced work may have less knowledge of organizational practices, procedures, and goals and less commitment to an organization than regular employees. In addition, unions resist outsourcing because it has the potential to eliminate some of their members. To gain some of the flexibility and cost savings of outsourcing and avoid some of its disadvantages, a number of organizations, such as Microsoft and IBM, rely on a pool of temporary employees to, for example, debug programs.

A major trend reflecting the increasing globalization of business is the outsourcing of office work, computer programming, and technical jobs from the United States and countries in western Europe, with high labor costs, to countries like India and China, with low labor costs.[45] For example, computer programmers in India and China earn a fraction of what their U.S. counterparts earn. According to estimates by Gartner Inc., outsourcing (or *offshoring*, as it is also called when work is outsourced to other countries) of information technology and business process work is valued at over $34 billion per year.

As companies gain experience in outsourcing software and technological services, managers are learning what kinds of work can be effectively outsourced and what work should probably not be outsourced. In India, for example, the workforce is highly trained and motivated, and cities like Bangalore are bustling with high-tech jobs and companies like Infosys Technologies, providing software services to companies abroad. Managers who have outsourcing experience have found that outsourcing works best for tasks that can be rule-based, do not require closeness/familiarity with customers and/or the customs and culture of the country in which the company is based, and do not require creativity.[46] When the work requires the recognition and solution of problems rather than the application of preexisting algorithms, creativity in developing solutions, and independent thinking and judgment without the guidance of standard operating procedures, performance might suffer from outsourcing. Essentially, the more complex and uncertain the work and the more it depends on being close to customers and the company itself, the less advantageous outsourcing tends to be.[47]

Nonetheless, there are many kinds of tasks that can be effectively outsourced, and the cost savings for these tasks can be considerable.[48] And some managers believe that many tasks can be effectively outsourced, even those requiring creativity.

General Electric (GE) and McKinsey & Co. are two companies at the forefront of offshoring, seeing it as a way not only to cut costs but to grow (while boosting efficiency).[49] GE Capital first started off with an office in Delhi, India, because the company was having a difficult time filling positions in its growing business of mortgage refinancing. Called GE Capital Investment Services, the office had around 300 employees in the late 1990s. Today, Genpact (a company owned by GE and two private equity firms) has over 20,000 employees, offices in Mexico, Romania, Hungary, India, China, and the United States, and over $490 million in revenues.[50]

Employment Web sites like www.monster.com are popular external recruitment tools. One advantage of such Web sites is that they can reach out to a broad applicant pool and can be used to fill global positions.

McKinsey and GE have such a legacy in offshoring that many current top managers of outsourcing companies were former McKinsey and GE employees. For example, the current president and CEO of Genpact, Pramod Bhasin, was a former GE employee.[51] As another example, Rizwan Koita, a former employee of McKinsey in London and New Delhi, has gone on to found two outsourcing companies, TransWork Information Services Ltd (recently purchased by AV Birla Group) and Citius Tech. Inc.[52] Additionally, other former employees of GE and McKinsey have used their knowledge and experience of outsourcing in subsequent positions in other organizations. For example, Robert Nardelli, CEO of Home Depot, was a former top manager at GE; Home Depot outsources its back-office functions in merchandising and management and call-center operations to Tata Consultancy Service Ltd. in India.[53]

Job Analysis

job analysis Identifying the tasks, duties, and responsibilities that make up a job and the knowledge, skills, and abilities needed to perform the job.

Job analysis is a second important activity that managers need to undertake prior to recruitment and selection.[54] **Job analysis** is the process of identifying (1) the tasks, duties, and responsibilities that make up a job (the *job description*) and (2) the knowledge, skills, and abilities needed to perform the job (the *job specifications*).[55] For each job in an organization, a job analysis needs to be done.

A job analysis can be done in a number of ways, including observing current employees as they perform the job or interviewing them. Often, managers rely on questionnaires compiled by jobholders and their managers. The questionnaires ask about the skills and abilities needed to perform the job, job tasks and the amount of time spent on them, responsibilities, supervisory activities, equipment used, reports prepared, and decisions made.[56] The Position Analysis Questionnaire (PAQ) is a comprehensive standardized questionnaire that many managers rely on to conduct job analyses.[57] It focuses on behaviors jobholders perform, working conditions, and job characteristics and can be used for a variety of jobs.[58] The PAQ contains 194 items organized into six divisions: (1) information input (where and how the jobholder acquires information to perform the job), (2) mental processes (reasoning, decision making, planning, and information processing activities that are part of the job), (3) work output (physical activities performed on the job and machines and devices used), (4) relationships with others (interactions with other people that are necessary to perform the job), (5) job context (the physical and social environment of the job), and (6) other job characteristics (such as work pace).[59] A trend, in some organizations, is toward more flexible jobs in which tasks and responsibilities change and cannot be clearly specified in advance. For these kinds of jobs, job analysis focuses more on determining the skills and knowledge workers need to be effective and less on specific duties.

After managers have completed human resource planning and job analyses for all jobs in an organization, they will know their human resource needs and the jobs they need to fill. They will also know the knowledge, skills, and abilities that potential employees need to perform those jobs. At this point, recruitment and selection can begin.

External and Internal Recruitment

As noted earlier, recruitment is what managers do to develop a pool of qualified candidates for open positions.[60] They traditionally have used two main types of recruiting: external and internal, which is now supplemented by recruiting over the Internet.

EXTERNAL RECRUITING   When managers recruit externally to fill open positions, they look outside the organization for people who have not worked for the organization previously. There are multiple means through which managers can recruit externally: advertisements in newspapers and magazines, open houses for students and career counselors at high schools and colleges or on-site at the organization, career fairs at colleges, and recruitment meetings with groups in the local community.

Many large organizations send teams of interviewers to college campuses to recruit new employees. External recruitment can also take place through informal networks, as occurs when current employees inform friends about open positions in their companies or recommend people they know to fill vacant spots. Some organizations use employment agencies for external recruitment, and some external recruitment takes place simply through walk-ins—job hunters coming to an organization and inquiring about employment possibilities.

With all the downsizings and corporate layoffs that have taken place in recent years, you might think that external recruiting would be a relatively easy task for managers. However, it often is not, because even though many people may be looking for jobs, many of the jobs that are opening up require skills and abilities that these job hunters do not have. Managers needing to fill vacant positions and job hunters seeking employment opportunities are increasingly relying on the Internet to make connections with each other through employment Web sites such as Monster.com[61] and Jobline International. Jobline is Europe's largest electronic recruiting site, with operations in 12 countries.[62] Major corporations such as Coca-Cola, Cisco, Ernst & Young, Canon, and Telia have relied on Jobline to fill global positions.[63]

External recruiting has both advantages and disadvantages for managers. Advantages include having access to a potentially large applicant pool, being able to attract people who have the skills, knowledge, and abilities that an organization needs to achieve its goals, and being able to bring in newcomers who may have a fresh approach to problems and be up to date on the latest technology. These advantages have to be weighed against the disadvantages, including the relatively high costs of external recruitment. Employees recruited externally also lack knowledge about the inner workings of the organization and may need to receive more training than those recruited internally. Finally, when employees are recruited externally, there is always uncertainty concerning whether they will actually be good performers.

INTERNAL RECRUITING   When recruiting is internal, managers turn to existing employees to fill open positions. Employees recruited internally are either seeking **lateral moves** (job changes that entail no major changes in responsibility or authority levels) or promotions. Internal recruiting has several advantages. First, internal applicants are already familiar with the organization (including its goals, structure, culture, rules, and norms). Second, managers already know the candidates; they have considerable information about their skills and abilities and actual behavior on the job. Third, internal recruiting can help boost levels of employee motivation and morale, both for the employee who gets the job and for other workers. Those who are not seeking a promotion or who may not be ready for one can see that promotion is a possibility in the future; or a lateral move can alleviate boredom once a job has been fully mastered and can also be a useful way to learn new skills. Finally, internal recruiting is normally less time-consuming and expensive than external recruiting.

Given the advantages of internal recruiting, why do managers rely on external recruiting as much as they do? The answer lies in the disadvantages of internal

lateral move A job change that entails no major changes in responsibility or authority levels.

recruiting–among them, a limited pool of candidates and a tendency among those candidates to be set in the organization's ways. Often, the organization simply does not have suitable internal candidates. Sometimes, even when suitable internal applicants are available, managers may rely on external recruiting to find the very best candidate or to help bring new ideas and approaches into their organization. When organizations are in trouble and performing poorly, external recruiting is often relied on to bring in managerial talent with a fresh approach. For example, when IBM's performance was suffering in the 1990s and the board of directors was looking for a new CEO, rather than consider any of IBM's existing top managers for this position, the board recruited Lou Gerstner, an outsider who had no previous experience in the computer industry.

HONESTY IN RECRUITING   At times, when trying to recruit the most qualified applicants, managers may be tempted to paint overly rosy pictures of both the open positions and the organization as a whole. They may worry that if they are totally honest about advantages and disadvantages, they either will not be able to fill positions or will have fewer or less qualified applicants. A manager trying to fill a secretarial position, for example, may emphasize the high level of pay and benefits the job offers and fail to mention the fact that the position is usually a dead-end job offering few opportunities for promotion.

Research suggests that painting an overly rosy picture of a job and the organization is not a wise recruiting strategy. Recruitment is more likely to be effective when managers provide potential applicants with an honest assessment of both the advantages and the disadvantages of the job and organization. Such an assessment is called a **realistic job preview** (RJP).[64] RJPs can reduce the number of new hires who quit when their jobs and organizations fail to meet their unrealistic expectations, and they help applicants decide for themselves whether the job is right for them.

Take the earlier example of the manager trying to recruit a secretary. The manager who paints a rosy picture of the job might have an easy time filling it but might end up with a secretary who expects to be promoted quickly to an administrative assistant position. After a few weeks on the job, the secretary may realize that a promotion is highly unlikely no matter how good his or her performance, become dissatisfied, and look for and accept another job. The manager then has to recruit, select, and train another new secretary. The manager could have avoided this waste of valuable organizational resources by using a realistic job preview. The RJP would have increased the likelihood of hiring a secretary who was comfortable with few promotional opportunities and subsequently would have been satisfied to remain on the job.

realistic job preview (RJP) An honest assessment of the advantages and disadvantages of a job and organization.

The Selection Process

Once managers develop a pool of applicants for open positions through the recruitment process, they need to find out whether each applicant is qualified for the position and likely to be a good performer. If more than one applicant meets these two conditions, managers must further determine which applicants are likely to be better performers than others. They have several selection tools to help them sort out the relative qualifications of job applicants and appraise their potential for being good performers in a particular job. These tools include background information, interviews, paper-and-pencil tests, physical ability tests, performance tests, and references (see Figure 12.3).[65]

Figure 12.3
Selection Tools

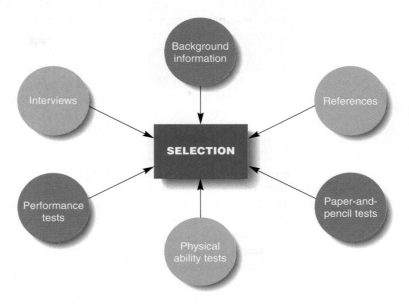

BACKGROUND INFORMATION   To aid in the selection process, managers obtain background information from job applications and from résumés. Such information might include the highest levels of education obtained, college majors and minors, type of college or university attended, years and type of work experience, and mastery of foreign languages. Background information can be helpful both to screen out applicants who are lacking key qualifications (such as a college degree) and to determine which qualified applicants are more promising than others. For example, applicants with a BS may be acceptable, but those who also have an MBA are preferable.

Increasing numbers of organizations are performing background checks to verify that the background information prospective employees provide is accurate (and also to uncover any negative information such as crime convictions),[66] as indicated in the following "Ethics in Action."

Background Checks on the Rise

Ethics
in Action

In February 2006, the CEO of RadioShack Corp., David Edmondson, resigned after admitting that he had misstated information regarding his education on his résumé. Edmondson had worked at RadioShack for over 10 years before assuming the top position in May 2005. In a public apology, Edmondson indicated, "The contents of my résumé and the company's Web site were clearly incorrect. I clearly misstated my academic record, and the responsibility for these misstatements is mine alone."[67]

According to ADP Employer Services, an outsourcing company that performs payroll and human resource functions for organizations, more and more companies are performing background checks on prospective employees and

The number of background checks is on the rise, as employees seek to avoid surprises after hiring decisions are made.

are uncovering inaccuracies, inconsistencies, and negative information such as prior convictions or driving violations.[68] According to a recent survey ADP conducted, about half of all background checks turn up an inconsistency between the education and credentials applicants list and the information other sources provide (e.g., universities or prior employers). And in some cases, background checks reveal convictions and driving violations.[69]

Fresh Direct, an online grocer that delivers groceries to customers living in apartments in New York City, faced a crisis when it found out that one of its delivery employees was stalking and harassing some of its female customers.[70] The screening firm that Fresh Direct employed at the time had failed to uncover the individual's felony and misdemeanor convictions. Fresh Direct has since switched to another background-check firm and also signed up with Verified Person, which supplies Fresh Direct with biweekly updates of any new convictions of current employees.[71]

In light of recent immigration legislation (see Chapter 6), some employers like Dunkin' Donuts are relying on a federal program called Basic Pilot to verify prospective employees' legal work status, mitigate against inadvertently hiring illegal immigrants, and verify the accuracy of Social Security numbers.[72] In the Basic Pilot program, employers submit the I-9 Employment Eligibility Verification Form, which they are required to complete and maintain for all employees, to the federal government to be checked against Social Security Administration (SSA) and Department of Homeland Security (DHS) databases.[73] According to the chief legal officer of Dunkin' Brands, Stephen Horn, "Dunkin' Brands is participating in [the] Basic Pilot program because we see it as a way to help our franchisees comply with the laws when the authenticity of their new hires' credentials are difficult to discern."[74]

While background checks can help deter unethical behavior in organizations, they also raise difficult ethical dilemmas in their own right. For example, sometimes learning of a minor conviction that has no bearing on a prospective employee's ability to perform a job might nonetheless bias an employer to not hire the person. Also, sometimes the information provided by backgrounds checks is inaccurate.[75] According to Scott Vinson, vice president of government relations for the National Council of Chain Restaurants, flaws in the SSA and DHS databases, as well as employer errors, result in the Basic Pilot program's having a high number of false negatives (meaning that individuals who are actually eligible for employment are not confirmed as eligible). Some of these flaws and errors are more prevalent for recent legal immigrants due to spelling errors in uncommon names.[76] Clearly, there are multiple ethical issues involved in the use of background checks.

INTERVIEWS   Virtually all organizations use interviews during the selection process. Interviews may be structured or unstructured. In *a structured interview*, managers ask each applicant the same standard questions (e.g., "What are your unique qualifications for this position?" and "What characteristics of a job are most important for you?"). Particularly informative questions may be those that prompt an interviewee to demonstrate skills and abilities needed for the job by answering the question. Sometimes called *situational interview questions,* these often present interviewees with a scenario that they would likely encounter on the job and ask them to indicate how they would handle it.[77] For example, applicants for a sales job may be asked to indicate how they would respond to a customer who complains about waiting too long for service, a customer who is indecisive, and a customer whose order is lost.

An *unstructured interview* proceeds more like an ordinary conversation. The interviewer feels free to ask probing questions to discover what the applicant is like and does not ask a fixed set of questions determined in advance. In general, structured interviews are superior to unstructured interviews because they are more likely to yield information that will help identify qualified candidates, are less subjective, and may be less influenced by the interviewer's biases.

Even when structured interviews are used, however, the potential exists for the interviewer's biases to influence his or her judgment. Recall from Chapter 5 how the similar-to-me effect can cause people to perceive others who are similar to themselves more positively than those who are different and how stereotypes can result in inaccurate perceptions. Interviewers must be trained to avoid these biases and sources of inaccurate perceptions as much as possible. Many of the approaches to increasing diversity awareness and diversity skills described in Chapter 5 are used to train interviewers to avoid the effects of biases and stereotypes. In addition, using multiple interviewers can be advantageous as their individual biases and idiosyncrasies may cancel one another out.[78]

When conducting interviews, managers cannot ask questions that are irrelevant to the job in question; otherwise, their organizations run the risk of costly lawsuits. It is inappropriate and illegal, for example, to inquire about an interviewee's spouse or to ask questions about whether an interviewee plans to have children. Because questions such as these are irrelevant to job performance, they are discriminatory and violate EEO laws (see Table 12.1). Thus, interviewers need to be instructed in EEO laws and informed about questions that may violate those laws.

Managers can use interviews at various stages in the selection process. Some use interviews as initial screening devices; others use them as a final hurdle that applicants must jump. Regardless of when they are used, managers typically use other selection tools in conjunction with interviews because of the potential for bias and for inaccurate assessments of interviewees. Even though training and structured interviews can eliminate the effects of some biases, interviewers can still come to erroneous conclusions about interviewees' qualifications. Interviewees, for example, who make a bad initial impression or are overly nervous in the first minute or two of an interview tend to be judged more harshly than other, less nervous candidates, even if the rest of the interview goes well.

PAPER-AND-PENCIL TESTS The two main kinds of paper-and-pencil tests used for selection purposes are ability tests and personality tests. *Ability tests* assess the extent to which applicants possess the skills necessary for job performance, such as verbal comprehension or numerical skills. Autoworkers hired by General Motors, Chrysler, and Ford, for example, are typically tested for their ability to read and to do mathematics.[79]

Personality tests measure personality traits and characteristics relevant to job performance. Some retail organizations, for example, give job applicants honesty tests to determine how trustworthy they are. The use of personality tests (including honesty tests) for hiring purposes is controversial. Some critics maintain that honesty tests do not really measure honesty (that is, they are not valid) and can be faked by job applicants. Before using any paper-and-pencil tests for selection purposes, managers must have sound evidence that the tests are actually good predictors of performance on the job in question. Managers who use tests without such evidence may be subject to costly discrimination lawsuits.

PHYSICAL ABILITY TESTS   For jobs requiring physical abilities, such as firefighting, garbage collecting, and package delivery, managers use physical ability tests that measure physical strength and stamina as selection tools. Autoworkers are typically tested for mechanical dexterity because this physical ability is an important skill for high job performance in many auto plants.[80]

PERFORMANCE TESTS   *Performance tests* measure job applicants' performance on actual job tasks. Applicants for secretarial positions, for example, typically are required to complete a keyboarding test that measures how quickly and accurately they type. Applicants for middle- and top-management positions are sometimes given short-term projects to complete—projects that mirror the kinds of situations that arise in the job being filled—to assess their knowledge and problem-solving capabilities.[81]

Assessment centers, first used by AT&T, take performance tests one step further. In a typical assessment center, about 10 to 15 candidates for managerial positions participate in a variety of activities over a few days. During this time they are assessed for the skills an effective manager needs—problem-solving, organizational, communication, and conflict resolution skills. Some of the activities are performed individually; others are performed in groups. Throughout the process, current managers observe the candidates' behavior and measure performance. Summary evaluations are then used as a selection tool.

An interviewee studies a question on a paper-and-pencil test. In addition to interviews, employers may use other employment tools to assess a job applicant's qualifications, such as ability tests that measure verbal comprehension or numerical skills.

REFERENCES   Applicants for many jobs are required to provide references from former employers or other knowledgeable sources (such as a college instructor or adviser) who know the applicants' skills, abilities, and other personal characteristics. These individuals are asked to provide candid information about the applicant. References are often used at the end of the selection process to confirm a decision to hire. Yet the fact that many former employers are reluctant to provide negative information in references sometimes makes it difficult to interpret what a reference is really saying about an applicant.

In fact, several recent lawsuits filed by applicants who felt that they were unfairly denigrated or had their privacy invaded by unfavorable references from former employers have caused managers to be increasingly wary of providing any negative information in a reference, even if it is accurate. For jobs in which the jobholder is responsible for the safety and lives of other people, however, failing to provide accurate negative information in a reference does not just mean that the wrong person might get hired; it may also mean that other people's lives will be at stake.

THE IMPORTANCE OF RELIABILITY AND VALIDITY   Whatever selection tools a manager uses, these tools need to be both reliable and valid. **Reliability** is the degree to which a tool or test measures the same thing each time it is administered. Scores on a selection test should be very similar if the same person is assessed with the same tool on two different days; if there is quite a bit of variability, the tool is unreliable. For interviews, determining reliability is more complex because the dynamic is personal interpretation. That is why the reliability of interviews can be increased if two or more different qualified interviewers interview the same candidate. If the interviews are reliable, the interviewers should come to similar conclusions about the interviewee's qualifications.

reliability The degree to which a tool or test measures the same thing each time it is used.

Validity is the degree to which a tool measures what it purports to measure—for selection tools, it is the degree to which the test predicts performance on the tasks or job in question. Does a physical ability test used to select firefighters, for example, actually predict on-the-job performance? Do assessment center ratings actually predict managerial performance? Do keyboarding tests predict secretarial performance? These are all questions of validity. Honesty tests, for example, are controversial because it is not clear that they validly predict honesty in such jobs as retailing and banking.

validity The degree to which a tool or test measures what it purports to measure.

Managers have an ethical and legal obligation to use reliable and valid selection tools. Yet reliability and validity are matters of degree rather than all-or-nothing characteristics. Thus, managers should strive to use selection tools in such a way that they can achieve the greatest degree of reliability and validity. For ability tests of a particular skill, managers should keep up to date on the latest advances in the development of valid paper-and-pencil tests and use the test with the highest reliability and validity ratings for their purposes. Regarding interviews, managers can improve reliability by having more than one person interview job candidates.

Training and Development

Training and development help to ensure that organizational members have the knowledge and skills needed to perform jobs effectively, take on new responsibilities, and adapt to changing conditions. **Training** primarily focuses on teaching organizational members how to perform their current jobs and helping them acquire the knowledge and skills they need to be effective performers. **Development** focuses on building the knowledge and skills of organizational members so that they are prepared to take on new responsibilities and challenges. Training tends to be used more frequently at lower levels of an organization; development tends to be used more frequently with professionals and managers.

training Teaching organizational members how to perform their current jobs and helping them acquire the knowledge and skills they need to be effective performers.

development Building the knowledge and skills of organizational members so that they are prepared to take on new responsibilities and challenges.

Before creating training and development programs, managers should perform a **needs assessment** to determine which employees need training or development and what type of skills or knowledge they need to acquire (see Figure 12.4).[82]

needs assessment An assessment of which employees need training or development and what type of skills or knowledge they need to acquire.

Types of Training

There are two types of training: classroom instruction and on-the-job training.

CLASSROOM INSTRUCTION   Through classroom instruction, employees acquire knowledge and skills in a classroom setting. This instruction may take place within the organization or outside it, such as courses at local colleges and universities. Many organizations actually establish their own formal instructional divisions—some are even called "colleges"—to provide needed classroom instruction.

Figure 12.4
Training and Development

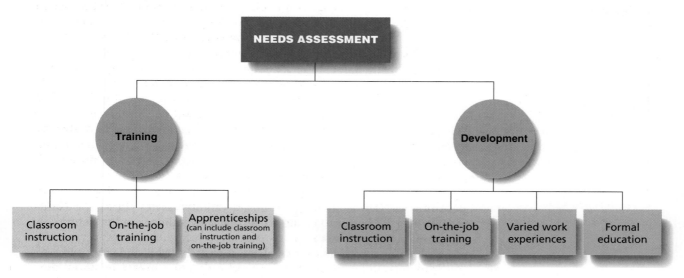

At Ethan Allen Interiors Inc., for example, employees from stores around the country attend Ethan Allen College at company headquarters in Danbury, Connecticut. During classes, employees acquire in-depth knowledge about the company's products and learn how to listen to customers and accurately assess their needs. In addition, the college provides instruction on such diverse topics as floor plans and window treatments. Training at Ethan Allen is an ongoing process. Veteran employees attend two- or three-day sessions at the college to brush up on their skills and keep abreast of the latest developments. M. Farooq Kathwari, chairman and CEO of Ethan Allen, believes that the classroom instruction that employees receive at Ethan Allen College has contributed significantly to his company's competitive advantage.[83]

Classroom instruction frequently includes the use of videos and role playing in addition to traditional written materials, lectures, and group discussions. *Videos* can be used to demonstrate appropriate and inappropriate job behaviors. For example, by watching an experienced salesperson effectively deal with a loud and angry customer in a video clip, inexperienced salespeople can develop skills in handling similar situations. During *role playing*, trainees either directly participate in or watch others perform actual job activities in a simulated setting. At McDonald's Hamburger University, for example, role playing helps franchisees acquire the knowledge and skills they need to manage their restaurants.

Simulations also can be part of classroom instruction, particularly for complicated jobs that require an extensive amount of learning and in which errors carry a high cost. In a simulation, key aspects of the work situation and job tasks are duplicated as closely as possible in an artificial setting. For example, air traffic controllers are trained by simulations because of the complicated nature of the work, the extensive amount of learning involved, and the very high costs of air traffic control errors.

on-the-job training
Training that takes place in the work setting as employees perform their job tasks.

ON-THE-JOB TRAINING   In **on-the-job training,** learning occurs in the work setting as employees perform their job tasks. On-the-job training can be

At many restaurants, new employees receive on-the-job training in which they shadow more experienced waiters and waitresses as they go about their work.

provided by coworkers or supervisors or can occur simply as jobholders gain experience and knowledge from doing the work, as is the case at Semco in "A Manager's Challenge." Newly hired waiters and waitresses in chains such as Red Lobster or The Olive Garden often receive on-the-job training from experienced employees. The supervisor of a new bus driver for a campus bus system may ride the bus for a week to ensure that the driver has learned the routes and follows safety procedures. Chefs learn to create new and innovative dishes by experimenting with different combinations of ingredients and cooking techniques. For all on-the-job training, employees learn by doing.

Managers often use on-the-job training on a continuing basis to ensure that their subordinates keep up to date with changes in goals, technology, products, or customer needs and desires. For example, sales representatives at Mary Kay Cosmetics Inc. receive ongoing training so that they are not only knowledgeable about new cosmetic products and currently popular colors but also reminded of Mary Kay's guiding principles. Mary Kay's expansion into Russia has been very successful, in part because of the ongoing training that Mary Kay's Russian salespeople receive.[84]

Types of Development

Although both classroom instruction and on-the-job training can be used for development purposes as well as training, development often includes additional activities such as varied work experiences and formal education.

VARIED WORK EXPERIENCES Top managers need to develop an understanding of, and expertise in, a variety of functions, products and services, and markets. To develop executives who will have this expertise, managers frequently make sure that employees with high potential have a wide variety of different job experiences, some in line positions and some in staff positions. Varied work experiences broaden employees' horizons and help them think more about the big picture. For example, one- to three-year stints overseas are being used increasingly to provide managers with international work experiences. With organizations becoming more global, managers need to develop an understanding of the different values, beliefs, cultures, regions, and ways of doing business in different countries.

Another development approach is mentoring. (Recall from Chapter 5 that a *mentor* is an experienced member of an organization who provides advice and guidance to a less experienced member, called a *protégé*.) Having a mentor can help managers seek out work experiences and assignments that will contribute to their development and can enable them to gain the most possible from varied work experiences.[85] While some mentors and protégés hook up informally, organizations have found that formal mentorship programs can be valuable ways to contribute to the development of managers and all employees, as indicated in the following "Focus on Diversity."

Focus on
Diversity

Development Through Mentoring

Lynn Tyson, vice president of investor relations and global corporate communications at Dell,[86] never had a mentor help her navigate her rise to the top, and she says, "Most of the time I was shaking in my shoes." Realizing the benefits of mentors for protégé development, and for the ability of organizations to retain valued members, Tyson worked to develop a formal mentoring program at Dell. Tyson currently mentors 40 protégés and derives tremendous satisfaction from knowing that she has "the ability to make a difference in somebody's career."[87]

Formal mentoring programs ensure that mentoring takes place in an organization, structure the process, and make sure that diverse organizational members have equal access to mentors. Participants receive training, efforts are focused on matching up mentors and protégés so that meaningful developmental relationships ensue, and organizations can track reactions and assess the potential benefits of mentoring. Formal mentoring programs can also ensure that diverse members of an organization receive the benefits of mentoring. A recent study conducted by David A. Thomas, a professor at the Harvard Business School, found that members of racial minority groups at three large corporations who were very successful in their careers had the benefit of mentors. Formal mentorship programs help organizations make this valuable development tool available to all employees.[88]

When diverse members of an organization lack mentors, their progress in the organization and advancement to high-level positions can be hampered. Ida Abott, a lawyer and consultant on work-related issues, recently presented a paper to the Minority Corporate Counsel Association in which she concluded, "The lack of adequate mentoring has held women and minority lawyers back from achieving professional success and has led to high rates of career dissatisfaction and attrition."[89]

Mentoring can benefit all kinds of employees in all kinds of work.[90] John Washko, a manager at the Four Seasons hotel chain, benefited from the mentoring he received from Stan Bromley on interpersonal relations and how to deal with employees; mentor Bromley, in turn, found that participating in the Four Seasons mentoring program helped him develop his own management style.[91] More generally, development is an ongoing process for all managers, and mentors often find that mentoring contributes to their own personal development.

FORMAL EDUCATION   Many large corporations reimburse employees for tuition expenses they incur while taking college courses and obtaining advanced degrees. This is not just benevolence on the part of the employer or even a simple reward given to the employee; it is an effective way to develop employees who are able to take on new responsibilities and more challenging positions. For similar reasons, corporations spend thousands of dollars sending managers to executive development programs such as executive MBA programs. In these programs, experts teach managers the latest in business and management techniques and practices.

To save time and travel costs, managers are increasingly relying on *long-distance learning* to formally educate and develop employees. Using videoconferencing technologies, business schools such as the Harvard Business School, the University of Michigan, and Babson College are teaching courses on video screens in corporate conference rooms. Business schools are also customizing courses and degrees to fit the development needs of employees in a particular company. The University of Michigan uses long-distance learning, for example, to provide instruction for customized MBA degrees for employees of the Daewoo Corporation in Korea and Cathay Pacific Airways Ltd. in Hong Kong. In conjunction with Westcott Communications Inc., eight business schools have formed a new venture, Executive Education Network, to create and operate satellite classrooms in major corporations; almost 100 companies have already signed on, including Eastman Kodak Company, Walt Disney Company, and Texas Instruments.[92]

Transfer of Training and Development

Whenever training and development take place off the job or in a classroom setting, it is vital for managers to promote the transfer of the knowledge and skills acquired *to the actual work situation.* Trainees should be encouraged and expected to use their newfound expertise on the job.

Performance Appraisal and Feedback

performance appraisal The evaluation of employees' job performance and contributions to their organization.

performance feedback The process through which mangers share performance appraisal information with subordinates, give subordinates an opportunity to reflect on their own performance, and develop, with subordinates, plans for the future.

The recruitment/selection and training/development components of a human resource management system ensure that employees have the knowledge and skills needed to be effective now and in the future. Performance appraisal and feedback complement recruitment, selection, training, and development. **Performance appraisal** is the evaluation of employees' job performance and contributions to the organization. **Performance feedback** is the process through which managers share performance appraisal information with their subordinates, give subordinates an opportunity to reflect on their own performance, and develop, with subordinates, plans for the future. Before performance feedback, performance appraisal must take place. Performance appraisal could take place without providing performance feedback, but wise managers are careful to provide feedback because it can contribute to employee motivation and performance.

Performance appraisal and feedback contribute to the effective management of human resources in several ways. Performance appraisal gives managers important information on which to base human resource decisions.[93] Decisions about pay raises, bonuses, promotions, and job moves all hinge on the accurate appraisal of performance. Performance appraisal can also help managers determine which workers are candidates for training and development and in what areas. Performance feedback encourages high levels of employee motivation and performance. It lets good performers know that their efforts are valued and appreciated. It also lets poor performers know that their lackluster performance needs improvement. Performance feedback can provide both good and poor performers with insight on their strengths and weaknesses and ways in which they can improve their performance in the future.

A manager shares performance appraisal information with an employee, and together, they make plans for the future.

Types of Performance Appraisal

Performance appraisal focuses on the evaluation of traits, behaviors, and results.[94]

TRAIT APPRAISALS   When trait appraisals are used, managers assess subordinates on personal characteristics that are relevant to job performance, such as skills, abilities, or personality. A factory worker, for example, may be evaluated based on her ability to use computerized equipment and perform numerical calculations. A social worker may be appraised based on his empathy and communication skills.

Three disadvantages of trait appraisals often lead managers to rely on other appraisal methods. First, possessing a certain personal characteristic does not ensure that the personal characteristic will actually be used on the job and result in high performance. For example, a factory worker may possess superior computer and numerical skills but be a poor performer due to low motivation. The second disadvantage of trait appraisals is linked to the first. Because traits do not always show a direct association with performance, workers and courts of law may view them as unfair and potentially discriminatory. The third disadvantage of trait appraisals is that they often do not enable managers to provide employees with feedback that they can use to improve performance. Because trait appraisals focus on relatively enduring human characteristics that change only over the long term, employees can do little to change their behavior in response to performance feedback from a trait appraisal. Telling a social worker that he lacks empathy provides him with little guidance about how to improve his interactions with clients, for example. These disadvantages suggest that managers should use trait appraisals only when they can demonstrate that the assessed traits are accurate and important indicators of job performance.

BEHAVIOR APPRAISALS   Through behavior appraisals, managers assess how workers perform their jobs—the actual actions and behaviors that workers exhibit on the job. Whereas trait appraisals assess what workers are *like*, behavior appraisals assess what workers *do*. For example, with a behavior appraisal, a manager might evaluate a social worker on the extent to which he looks clients in the eye when talking with them, expresses sympathy when they are upset, and refers them to community counseling and support groups geared toward the specific problem they are encountering. Behavior appraisals are especially useful when *how* workers perform their jobs is important. In educational organizations such as high schools, for example, the number of classes and students taught is important, but also important is how they are taught or the methods teachers use to ensure that learning takes place.

Behavior appraisals have the advantage of providing employees with clear information about what they are doing right and wrong and how they can improve their performance. And because behaviors are much easier for employees to change than traits, performance feedback from behavior appraisals is more likely to lead to performance improvements.

RESULT APPRAISALS For some jobs, *how* people perform the job is not as important as *what* they accomplish or the results they obtain. With result appraisals, managers appraise performance by the results or the actual outcomes of work behaviors, as is the case at Semco in "A Manager's Challenge." Take the case of two new-car salespersons. One salesperson strives to develop personal relationships with her customers. She spends hours talking to them and frequently calls them up to see how their decision-making process is going. The other salesperson has a much more hands-off approach. He is very knowledgeable, answers customers' questions, and then waits for them to come to him. Both salespersons sell, on average, the same number of cars, and the customers of both are satisfied with the service they receive, according to postcards that the dealership mails to customers asking for an assessment of their satisfaction. The manager of the dealership appropriately uses result appraisals (sales and customer satisfaction) to evaluate the salespeople's performance because it does not matter which behavior salespeople use to sell cars as long as they sell the desired number and satisfy customers. If one salesperson sells too few cars, however, the manager can give that person performance feedback about his or her low sales.

OBJECTIVE AND SUBJECTIVE APPRAISALS Whether managers appraise performance in terms of traits, behaviors, or results, the information they assess is either *objective* or *subjective*. Objective appraisals are based on facts and are likely to be numerical—the number of cars sold, the number of meals prepared, the number of times late, the number of audits completed. Managers often use objective appraisals when results are being appraised because results tend to be easier to quantify than traits or behaviors. When *how* workers perform their jobs is important, however, subjective behavior appraisals are more appropriate than result appraisals.

Subjective appraisals are based on managers' perceptions of traits, behaviors, or results. Because subjective appraisals rest on managers' perceptions, there is always the chance that they are inaccurate (we discuss managerial perception in more detail in the next chapter). This is why both researchers and managers have spent considerable time and effort on determining the best way to develop reliable and valid subjective measures of performance.

Some of the more popular subjective measures such as the graphic rating scale, the behaviorally anchored rating scale (BARS), and the behavior observation scale (BOS) are illustrated in Figure 12.5.[95] When graphic rating scales are used, performance is assessed along a continuum with specified intervals. With a BARS, performance is assessed along a scale with clearly defined scale points containing examples of specific behaviors. A BOS assesses performance by how often specific behaviors are performed. Many managers may use both objective and subjective appraisals. For example, a salesperson may be appraised both on the dollar value of sales (objective) and the quality of customer service (subjective).

In addition to subjective appraisals, some organizations employ *forced rankings* whereby supervisors must rank their subordinates and assign them to different categories according to their performance (which is subjectively appraised). For example, middle managers at Ford Motor Company are ranked by their supervisors in a forced distribution from A to C, with 10% of them receiving A's, 80% receiving B's, and 10% receiving C's.[96] The first year an employee receives a C, he or she does not receive a bonus, and after two years of C performance, a

objective appraisal
An appraisal that is based on facts and is likely to be numerical.

subjective appraisal
An appraisal that is based on perceptions of traits, behaviors, or results.

Figure 12.5

Subjective Measures of Performance

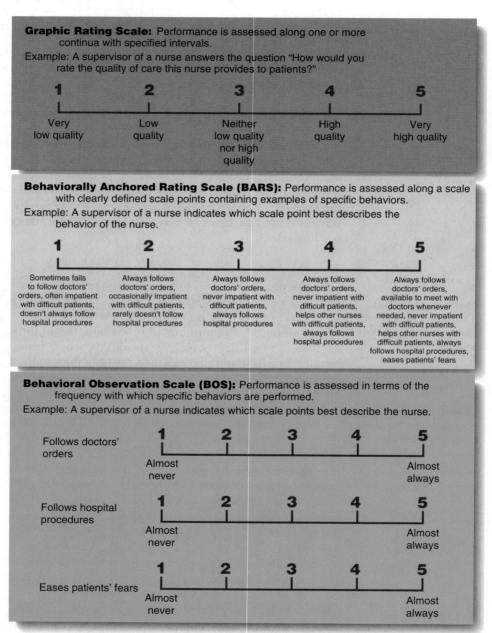

Graphic Rating Scale: Performance is assessed along one or more continua with specified intervals.

Example: A supervisor of a nurse answers the question "How would you rate the quality of care this nurse provides to patients?"

1	2	3	4	5
Very low quality	Low quality	Neither low quality nor high quality	High quality	Very high quality

Behaviorally Anchored Rating Scale (BARS): Performance is assessed along a scale with clearly defined scale points containing examples of specific behaviors.

Example: A supervisor of a nurse indicates which scale point best describes the behavior of the nurse.

1	2	3	4	5
Sometimes fails to follow doctors' orders, often impatient with difficult patients, doesn't always follow hospital procedures	Always follows doctors' orders, occasionally impatient with difficult patients, rarely doesn't follow hospital procedures	Always follows doctors' orders, never impatient with difficult patients, always follows hospital procedures	Always follows doctors' orders, never impatient with difficult patients, helps other nurses with difficult patients, always follows hospital procedures	Always follows doctors' orders, available to meet with doctors whenever needed, never impatient with difficult patients, helps other nurses with difficult patients, always follows hospital procedures, eases patients' fears

Behavioral Observation Scale (BOS): Performance is assessed in terms of the frequency with which specific behaviors are performed.

Example: A supervisor of a nurse indicates which scale points best describe the nurse.

Follows doctors' orders

1	2	3	4	5
Almost never				Almost always

Follows hospital procedures

1	2	3	4	5
Almost never				Almost always

Eases patients' fears

1	2	3	4	5
Almost never				Almost always

demotion or even firing is possible. Employees tend to not like these systems, as they believe they are unfair. For example, managers at Ford have filed a class-action lawsuit because they feel Ford's ranking system is unfair.[97] Relying on relative performance through ranking systems can force managers to rate some of their subordinates as unsatisfactory even if this might not be true and can also result in an employee's performance being downgraded not because of any change he or she has made but because coworkers have improved their performance. In other organizations that use ranking systems, employees tend to voice similar concerns. For example, forced-ranking systems can result in a zero-sum, competitive environment that can discourage cooperation and teamwork.[98]

Who Appraises Performance?

We have been assuming that managers or the supervisors of employees evaluate performance. This is a pretty reasonable assumption, for supervisors are the most common appraisers of performance; indeed, each year 70 million U.S. citizens have their job performance appraised by their managers or supervisors.[99] Performance appraisal is an important part of most managers' job duties. Managers are responsible for not only motivating their subordinates to perform at a high level but also making many decisions hinging on performance appraisals, such as pay raises or promotions. Appraisals by managers can be usefully augmented by appraisals from other sources (see Figure 12.6).

SELF, PEERS, SUBORDINATES, AND CLIENTS When self-appraisals are used, managers supplement their evaluations with an employee's assessment of his or her own performance. Peer appraisals are provided by an employee's coworkers. Especially when subordinates work in groups or teams, feedback from peer appraisals can motivate team members while providing managers with important information for decision making. A growing number of companies are having subordinates appraise their managers' performance and leadership as well. And sometimes customers or clients provide assessments of employee performance in terms of responsiveness to customers and quality of service. Although appraisals from each of these sources can be useful, managers need to be aware of potential issues that may arise when they

Figure 12.6
Who Appraises Performance?

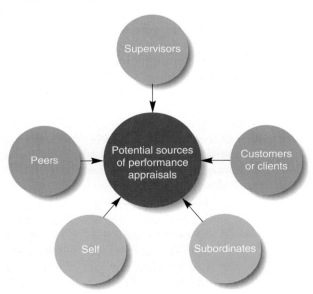

are used. Subordinates sometimes may be inclined to inflate self-appraisals, especially if organizations are downsizing and they are worried about their job security. Managers who are appraised by their subordinates may fail to take needed but unpopular actions out of fear that their subordinates will appraise them negatively.

Some of these potential issues can be mitigated to the extent that there are high levels of trust in an organization. At Dell, for example, all employees appraise their supervisors every six months, including founder and chairman Michael Dell and CEO Kevin Rollins. During one of these "Tell Dell" surveys, Dell and Rollins learned that some of their subordinates saw them as "cold technocrats."[100] Since learning of this, Dell, Rollins, and other top managers are taking steps to be warmer and more down to earth. Dell and Rollins expect other managers and supervisors to respond proactively to the feedback they receive from appraisals from subordinates. Given their approach, perhaps it is not surprising that Dell was named America's Most Admired Company by *Fortune* magazine in 2005.[101]

360-DEGREE PERFORMANCE APPRAISALS   To improve motivation and performance, some organizations include 360-degree appraisals and feedback in their performance appraisal systems, especially for managers. In a 360-degree appraisal, a variety of people, beginning with the manager and including peers or co-workers, subordinates, superiors, and sometimes even customers or clients, appraise a manager's performance. The manager receives feedback based on evaluations from these multiple sources.

The growing number of companies using 360-degree appraisals and feedback include AT&T Corp., Allied Signal Inc., Eastman Chemical Co., and Baxter International Inc.[102] For 360-degree appraisals and feedback to be effective, there has to be trust throughout an organization. More generally, trust is a critical ingredient in any performance appraisal and feedback procedure. In addition, research suggests that 360-degree appraisals should focus on behaviors rather than traits or results and that managers need to carefully select appropriate raters. Moreover, appraisals tend to be more honest when made anonymously, as is the case at Semco in "A Manager's Challenge," and when raters have been trained in how to use 360-degree appraisal forms.[103] Additionally, managers need to think carefully about the extent to which 360-degree appraisals are appropriate for certain jobs and be willing to modify any appraisal system they implement if they become aware of unintended problems it creates.[104]

Even when 360-degree appraisals are used, it is sometimes difficult to design an effective process by which subordinates' feedback can be communicated to their managers. Advances in information technology provide organizations with a potential solution to this problem. For example, ImproveNow.com has online questionnaires that subordinates fill out to evaluate the performance of their managers and provide the managers with feedback. Each subordinate of a particular manager completes the questionnaire independently, all responses are tabulated, and the manager is given specific feedback on behaviors in a variety of areas, such as rewarding good performance, looking out for subordinates' best interest and being supportive, and having a vision for the future.[105]

For example, Sonia Russomanno, a manager at Alliance Funding, a New Jersey mortgage lending organization, was evaluated online by her nine subordinates through ImproveNow. She received an overall grade of B and specific feedback on a variety of dimensions. This experience drove home to Russomanno the

360-degree appraisal
A performance appraisal by peers, subordinates, superiors, and sometimes clients who are in a position to evaluate a manager's performance.

importance of getting honest feedback from her subordinates and listening to it to improve her performance as a manager. As a result, she has changed how she rewards her subordinates, and she plans on using this service in the future to see how she is doing.[106]

Effective Performance Feedback

For the appraisal and feedback component of a human resource management system to encourage and motivate high performance, managers must provide their subordinates with feedback. To generate useful information to feed back to their subordinates, managers can use both formal and informal appraisals. Formal appraisals are conducted at set times during the year and are based on performance dimensions and measures that have been specified in advance. A salesperson, for example, may be evaluated by his or her manager twice a year on the performance dimensions of sales and customer service, sales being objectively measured from sales reports, and customer service being measured with a BARS (see Figure 12.5).

Managers in most large organizations use formal performance appraisals on a fixed schedule dictated by company policy, such as every six months or every year. An integral part of a formal appraisal is a meeting between the manager and the subordinate in which the subordinate is given feedback on performance. Performance feedback lets subordinates know which areas they are excelling in and which areas need improvement; it also should provide them with guidance for improving performance.

Realizing the value of formal appraisals, managers in many large corporations have committed substantial resources to updating their performance appraisal procedures and training low-level managers in how to use them and provide accurate feedback to employees. Top managers at the pharmaceutical company Hoffmann-La Roche Inc., for example, recently spent $1.5 million updating and improving their performance appraisal procedures. Alan Rubino, vice president of human resources for Hoffmann-La Roche, believes that this was money well spent because "people need to know exactly where they stand and what's required of them." Before Hoffmann-La Roche's new system was implemented, managers attended a three-day training and development session to improve their performance appraisal skills. The new procedures call for every manager and subordinate to develop a performance plan for subordinates for the coming year—a plan that is linked to the company's strategy and goals and approved by the manager's own superiors. Formal performance appraisals are conducted every six months, during which actual performance is compared to planned performance.[107]

Formal performance appraisals supply both managers and subordinates with valuable information; but subordinates often want feedback on a more frequent basis, and managers often want to motivate subordinates as the need arises. For these reasons many companies, including Hoffman-La Roche, supplement formal performance appraisal with frequent informal appraisals, for which managers and their subordinates meet as the need arises to discuss ongoing progress and areas for improvement. Moreover, when job duties, assignments, or goals change, informal appraisals can provide workers with timely feedback concerning how they are handling their new responsibilities.

Managers often dislike providing performance feedback, especially when the feedback is negative, but doing so is an important managerial activity.[108] Here are some guidelines for giving effective performance feedback that contributes to employee motivation and performance:

formal appraisal An appraisal conducted at a set time during the year and based on performance dimensions and measures that were specified in advance.

informal appraisal An unscheduled appraisal of ongoing progress and areas for improvement.

- *Be specific and focus on behaviors or outcomes that are correctable and within a worker's ability to improve.* Example: Telling a salesperson that he is too shy when interacting with customers is likely to do nothing more than lower his self-confidence and prompt the salesperson to become defensive. A more effective approach would be to give the salesperson feedback about specific behaviors to engage in—greeting customers as soon as they enter the department, asking customers whether they need help, and volunteering to help customers find items.

- *Approach performance appraisal as an exercise in problem solving and solution finding, not criticizing.* Example: Rather than criticizing a financial analyst for turning in reports late, the manager helps the analyst determine why the reports are late and identify ways to better manage her time.

- *Express confidence in a subordinate's ability to improve.* Example: Instead of being skeptical, a first-level manager tells a subordinate that he is confident that the subordinate can increase quality levels.

- *Provide performance feedback both formally and informally.* Example: The staff of a preschool receives feedback from formal performance appraisals twice a year. The director of the school also provides frequent informal feedback such as complimenting staff members on creative ideas for special projects, noticing when they do a particularly good job handling a difficult child, and pointing out when they provide inadequate supervision.

- *Praise instances of high performance and areas of a job in which a worker excels.* Example: Rather than focusing on just the negative, a manager discusses the areas her subordinate excels in as well as the areas in need of improvement.

- *Avoid personal criticisms and treat subordinates with respect.* Example: An engineering manager acknowledges her subordinates' expertise and treats them as professionals. Even when the manager points out performance problems to subordinates, she refrains from criticizing them personally.

- *Agree to a timetable for performance improvements.* Example: A first-level manager and his subordinate decide to meet again in one month to determine whether quality levels have improved.

In following these guidelines, managers need to remember *why* they are giving performance feedback: to encourage high levels of motivation and performance. Moreover, the information that managers gather through performance appraisal and feedback helps them determine how to distribute pay raises and bonuses.

Pay and Benefits

Pay includes employees' base salaries, pay raises, and bonuses and is determined by a number of factors such as characteristics of the organization and the job and levels of performance. Employee *benefits* are based on membership in an organization (and not necessarily on the particular job held) and include sick days, vacation days, and medical and life insurance. In Chapter 13, we discuss the ways in which pay can motivate organizational members to perform at a high level, as well as the different kinds of pay plans managers can use to help an organization achieve its goals and gain a competitive advantage. As you will learn, it is important for pay to be linked to behaviors or results that contribute to organizational effectiveness, as is true at Semco in "A Manager's Challenge." Next, we focus on establishing an organization's pay level and pay structure.

Pay Level

pay level The relative position of an organization's pay incentives in comparison with those of other organizations in the same industry employing similar kinds or workers.

Pay level is a broad comparative concept that refers to how an organization's pay incentives compare, in general, to those of other organizations in the same industry employing similar kinds of workers. Managers must decide if they want to offer relatively high wages, average wages, or relatively low wages. High wages help ensure that an organization is going to be able to recruit, select, and retain high performers, but high wages also raise costs. Low wages give an organization a cost advantage but may undermine the organization's ability to select and recruit high performers and to motivate current employees to perform at a high level. Either of these situations may lead to inferior quality or inadequate customer service.

In determining pay levels, managers should take into account their organization's strategy. A high pay level may prohibit managers from effectively pursuing a low-cost strategy. But a high pay level may be well worth the added costs in an organization whose competitive advantage lies in superior quality and excellent customer service. As one might expect, hotel and motel chains with a low-cost strategy, such as Days Inn and Hampton Inns, have lower pay levels than chains striving to provide high-quality rooms and services, such as Four Seasons and Hyatt Regency.

Pay Structure

pay structures The arrangement of jobs into categories reflecting their relative importance to the organization and its goals, levels of skill required, and other characteristics.

After deciding on a pay level, managers have to establish a pay structure for the different jobs in the organization. A **pay structure** clusters jobs into categories reflecting their relative importance to the organization and its goals, levels of skill required, and other characteristics managers consider to be important. Pay ranges are established for each job category. Individual jobholders' pay within job categories is then determined by factors such as performance, seniority, and skill levels.

There are some interesting global differences in pay structures. Large corporations based in the United States tend to pay their CEOs and top managers higher salaries than do their European or Japanese counterparts. Also, the pay differential between employees at the bottom of the corporate hierarchy and those higher up is much greater in U.S. companies than in European or Japanese companies.[109]

Concerns have been raised over whether it is equitable or fair for CEOs of large companies in the United States to be making hundreds of thousands or millions of dollars in years when their companies are restructuring and laying off a large portion of their workforces.[110] Robert Allen, for example, the CEO of AT&T, came under intense scrutiny in 1996 because he was earning $5 million a year when AT&T announced plans to lay off thousands of employees. As indicated in the following "Ethics in Action," hefty pay packages for current top managers, and those leaving top-management posts, are alive and well in corporate America.

Ethics in Action

Is CEO Pay Over the Top?

CEOs in the United States continue to earn phenomenal amounts of money despite public outcry and disgruntled shareholders.[111] Today, the average CEO earns over 430 times what the average hourly worker earns.[112] Is a pay structure with such a huge pay differential ethical? Shareholders and the public are increasingly asking this very question and asking large corporations to rethink their pay structures.[113] As a result of increasing scrutiny, pay levels of top managers are much more likely to be linked to the performance of their companies and their meeting of predetermined targets than they were before.[114]

Even more mind-boggling are the severance packages some CEOs and top managers receive when they leave their organizations. Steven Heyer was president and chief operating officer of Coca-Cola for three years; upon departing the company in June 2004, he received a $24 million severance package.[115] Departing Coca-Cola CEO Douglas Daft received over $30 million in a severance package in 2004 even though the company's performance was far less than stellar during his leadership. Douglas Ivestor, CEO of Coca-Cola prior to Daft, continues to receive $675,000 per year from a consulting contract with the company, even though he received over $100 million in his severance package.[116]

When it comes to CEO pay, how much is too much?

Coca-Cola is not alone in paying phenomenal severance pay to departing top managers. For example, when Richard H. Brown left Electronic Data Systems Corp. as CEO in 2003 amid poor financial performance, he received a severance package of over $45 million. Leo Mullins, who retired from his position as CEO of Delta Airlines, received over $15 million in severance compensation.[117] Carly Fiorina was given $42 million in cash, stock, and benefits when she departed the top post at Hewlett-Packard in 2005. (A group of four pension funds that are HP shareholders is suing Hewlett-Packard over Fiorina's generous severance pay; they allege that the package violates a board of directors' policy, adopted in 2003, limiting severance payouts to 2.99 times a top manager's salary and annual bonus.)[118]

Why do companies pay departing executives so excessively? Some say offering such "golden parachutes" is necessary to recruit top talent. For some companies, generous departing payouts help ensure that confidential company information stays confidential and that ex-CEOs do not damage the reputation of the company with negative statements to the press.[119] In any case, in an era in which many workers are struggling to find and keep jobs and make ends meet, more and more people are questioning whether it is ethical for some top managers to be making so much money. Granted, some very highly paid CEOs have done wonders for their companies and created real value.[120] But what about those poorly performing CEOs who are pushed from their jobs with millions in severance pay to break their fall?

Benefits

Organizations are legally required to provide certain benefits to their employees, including workers' compensation, Social Security, and unemployment insurance. Workers' compensation provides employees with financial assistance if they become unable to work due to a work-related injury or illness. Social Security provides financial assistance to retirees and disabled former employees. Unemployment insurance provides financial assistance to workers who lose their jobs due to no fault of their own. The legal system in the United States views these three benefits as ethical requirements for organizations and thus mandates that they be provided.

Other benefits such as health insurance, dental insurance, vacation time, pension plans, life insurance, flexible working hours, company-provided day care, and employee assistance and wellness programs are provided at the option of employers. Benefits enabling workers to simultaneously balance the demands of their jobs and of their lives away from the office or factory are of growing importance for many workers who have competing demands on their all-too-scarce time and energy, as is the case at Semco in "A Manager's Challenge."

In some organizations, top managers determine which benefits might best suit the employees and organization and offer the same benefit package to all employees. Other organizations, realizing that employees' needs and desires might differ, offer cafeteria-style benefit plans that let employees themselves choose the benefits they want. Cafeteria-style benefit plans sometimes assist managers in dealing with employees who feel unfairly treated because they are unable to take advantage of certain benefits available to other employees who, for example, have children. Some organizations have success with cafeteria-style benefit plans; others find them difficult to manage.

As health care costs are escalating and overstretched employees are finding it hard to take time out to exercise and take care of their health, more companies are providing benefits and incentives to promote employee wellness. AstraZeneca International offers its employees on-site counseling with a nutritionist and pays employees $125 for voluntarily taking a health risk assessment that covers wellness-related factors such as weight and nutrition.[121] Dole Food Company rewards employees with points toward gift certificates for participating in wellness activities provided on-site, such as yoga classes.[122]

For new parents, leaving an infant with a caregiver for 8 or 10 hours a day while they are at work can be traumatic. To ease the trauma and allow new parents to bond with their babies, Health Newsletter Direct, based in Evanston, Illinois, allows employees to bring their babies to work.[123] Since the program was instituted, 14 parents have taken advantage of it. Mark Tatara, the first father to bring his baby to work, says this of the program: "The closeness with my child means more to me than I ever could have imagined . . . and my coworkers were excited about him being here."[124]

Same-sex domestic-partner benefits are also being used to attract and retain valued employees. Gay and lesbian workers are more and more reluctant to work for companies that do not provide them with the same kinds of benefits for their partners as those provided for partners of the opposite sex.[125]

cafeteria-style benefit plan A plan from which employees can choose the benefits that they want.

Labor Relations

Labor relations are the activities that managers engage in to ensure that they have effective working relationships with the labor unions that represent their employees' interests. Although the U.S. government has responded to the potential for unethical and unfair treatment of workers by creating and enforcing laws regulating employment (including the EEO laws listed in Table 12.1), some workers believe that a union will ensure that their interests are fairly represented in their organizations.

labor relations The activities that managers engage in to ensure that they have effective working relationships with the labor unions that represent their employees' interests.

Before we describe unions in more detail, let's take a look at some examples of important employment legislation. In 1938 the government passed the Fair Labor Standards Act, which prohibited child labor and made provisions for minimum wages, overtime pay, and maximum working hours to protect workers' rights. In 1963 the Equal Pay Act mandated that men and women performing equal work (work requiring the same levels of skill, responsibility, and effort performed in the same kind of working conditions) receive equal pay (see Table 12.1). In 1970 the Occupational Safety and Health Act mandated procedures for managers to follow to ensure workplace safety. These are just a few of the U.S. government's efforts to protect workers' rights. State legislatures also have been active in promoting safe, ethical, and fair workplaces.

Unions

Unions exist to represent workers' interests in organizations. Given that managers have more power than rank-and-file workers and that organizations have multiple stakeholders, there is always the potential that managers might take steps that benefit one set of stakeholders such as shareholders while hurting another such as employees. For example, managers may decide to speed up a production line to lower costs and increase production in the hopes of increasing returns to shareholders. Speeding up the line, however, could hurt employees forced to work at a rapid pace and may increase the risk of injuries. Also, employees receive no additional pay for the extra work they are performing. Unions would represent workers' interests in a scenario such as this one.

Congress acknowledged the role that unions could play in ensuring safe and fair workplaces when it passed the National Labor Relations Act of 1935. This act made it legal for workers to organize into unions to protect their rights and interests and declared certain unfair or unethical organizational practices to be illegal. The act also established the National Labor Relations Board (NLRB) to oversee union activity. Currently, the NLRB conducts certification elections, which are held among the employees of an organization to determine whether they want a union to represent their interests. The NLRB also makes judgments concerning unfair labor practices and specifies practices that managers must refrain from.

Employees might vote to have a union represent them for any number of reasons.[126] They may think that their wages and working conditions are in need of improvement. They may believe that managers are not treating them with respect. They may think that their working hours are unfair or that they need more job security or a safer work environment. Or they may be dissatisfied with management and find it difficult to communicate their concerns to their bosses. Regardless of the specific reason, one overriding reason is power: A united group inevitably wields more power than an individual, and this type of power may be especially helpful to employees in some organizations.

Although these would seem to be potent forces for unionization, some workers are reluctant to join unions. Sometimes this reluctance is due to the perception that union leaders are corrupt. Some workers may simply believe that belonging to a union might not do them much good or may actually cause more harm than good while costing them money in membership dues. Employees also might not want to be forced into doing something they do not want to, such as striking because the union thinks it is in their best interest. Moreover, although unions can be a positive force in organizations, sometimes they also can be a negative force, impairing organizational effectiveness. For example, when union leaders resist needed changes in an organization or are corrupt, organizational performance can suffer.

The percentage of U.S. workers represented by unions today is smaller than it was in the 1950s, an era when unions were especially strong.[127] The American Federation of Labor–Congress of Industrial Organizations (AFL-CIO) includes 64 voluntary member unions representing 13 million workers.[128] Union influence in manufacturing and heavy industries has been on the decline, presumably because their workers no longer see the need to be represented by unions. Recently, however, unions have made inroads in other segments of the workforce, particularly the low-wage end. Garbage collectors in New Jersey, poultry plant workers in North Carolina, and janitors in Baltimore are among the growing numbers of low-paid workers who are currently finding union membership attractive. North Carolina poultry workers voted in a union in part because they thought it was unfair that they had to buy their own gloves and hairnets used on the job and had to ask their supervisors' permission to go to the restroom.[129]

Union membership and leadership, traditionally dominated by white men, are becoming increasingly diverse. For example, Linda Chavez-Thompson is the executive vice president of the AFL-CIO and the first woman and Hispanic to hold a top-management position in the federation.[130] Labor officials in Washington, DC, also are becoming increasingly diverse. Elaine L. Chao, the 24th U.S. secretary of labor, is the first Asian-American woman to hold an appointment in a U.S. president's cabinet. Chao, who has extensive management experience as a former CEO of the United Way of America and also as a former director of the Peace Corps, is committed to equal opportunity in the workplace, the well-being of workers and their families, and increased flexibility in the workplace.[131]

Collective Bargaining

collective bargaining
Negotiations between labor unions and managers to resolve conflicts and disputes about issues such as working hours, wages, benefits, working conditions, and job security.

Collective bargaining is negotiation between labor unions and managers to resolve conflicts and disputes about important issues such as working hours, wages, working conditions, and job security. Before sitting down with management to negotiate, union members sometimes go on strike to drive home their concerns to managers. Once an agreement that union members support has been reached (sometimes with the help of a neutral third party called a *mediator*), union leaders and managers sign a contract spelling out the terms of the collective bargaining agreement. We discuss conflict and negotiation in depth in Chapter 16, but some brief observations are in order here because collective bargaining is an ongoing consideration in labor relations.

The signing of a contract, for example, does not bring the collective bargaining process to a halt. Disagreement and conflicts can arise over the interpretation of the contract. In such cases, a neutral third party called an *arbitrator* is usually called in to resolve the conflict. An important component of a collective bargaining agreement is a *grievance procedure* through which workers who believe they are not being fairly treated are allowed to voice their concerns and have their interests represented by the union. Workers who think that they were unjustly fired in violation of a union contract, for example, may file a grievance, have the union represent them, and get their jobs back if an arbitrator agrees with them.

Union members sometimes go on strike when managers make decisions that the members think will hurt them and are not in their best interests. This is precisely what happened in 1996 when General Motors' North American assembly plants employing 177,000 workers were idled for 18 days. The strike originated in GM's Dayton, Ohio, brake assembly plants due to management's decision to buy some parts from other companies rather than make them in GM's own plants.[132] The United Auto Workers Union called a strike because outsourcing threatens union members' jobs. The agreement that the union and management, bargaining collectively, reached allowed the outsourcing to continue but contained provisions for the creation of hundreds of new jobs as well as for improvements in working conditions.[133]

Summary and Review

STRATEGIC HUMAN RESOURCE MANAGEMENT
Human resource management (HRM) includes all the activities that managers engage in to ensure that their organizations are able to attract, retain, and effectively utilize human resources. Strategic HRM is the process by which managers design the components of a human resource management system to be consistent with each other, with other elements of organizational architecture, and with the organization's strategies and goals.

RECRUITMENT AND SELECTION   Before recruiting and selecting employees, managers must engage in human resource planning and job analysis. Human resource planning includes all the activities managers engage in to forecast their current and future needs for human resources. Job analysis is the process of identifying (1) the tasks, duties, and responsibilities that make up a job and (2) the knowledge, skills, and abilities needed to perform the job. Recruitment includes all the activities that managers engage in to develop a pool of qualified applicants for open positions. Selection is the process by which managers determine the relative qualifications of job applicants and their potential for performing well in a particular job.

TRAINING AND DEVELOPMENT   Training focuses on teaching organizational members how to perform effectively in their current jobs. Development focuses on broadening organizational members' knowledge and skills so that they will be prepared to take on new responsibilities and challenges.

PERFORMANCE APPRAISAL AND FEEDBACK   Performance appraisal is the evaluation of employees' job performance and contributions to the organization.

Performance feedback is the process through which managers share performance appraisal information with their subordinates, give them an opportunity to reflect on their own performance, and develop with them plans for the future. Performance appraisal provides managers with useful information for decision-making purposes. Performance feedback can encourage high levels of motivation and performance.

PAY AND BENEFITS   Pay level is the relative position of an organization's pay incentives in comparison with those of other organizations in the same industry employing similar workers. A pay structure clusters jobs into categories according to their relative importance to the organization and its goals, the levels of skill required, and other characteristics. Pay ranges are then established for each job category. Organizations are legally required to provide certain benefits to their employees; other benefits are provided at the discretion of employers.

LABOR RELATIONS   Labor relations include all the activities managers engage in to ensure that they have effective working relationships with the labor unions that represent their employees' interests. The National Labor Relations Board oversees union activity. Collective bargaining is the process through which labor unions and managers resolve conflicts and disputes and negotiate agreements.

Management in Action

Topics for Discussion and Action

Discussion

1. Discuss why it is important for human resource management systems to be in sync with an organization's strategy and goals and with each other.

2. Discuss why training and development are ongoing activities for all organizations.

3. Describe the type of development activities you think middle managers are most in need of.

4. Evaluate the pros and cons of 360-degree performance appraisals and feedback. Would you like your performance to be appraised in this manner? Why or why not?

5. Discuss why two restaurants in the same community might have different pay levels.

6. Explain why union membership is becoming more diverse.

Action

7. Interview a manager in a local organization to determine how that organization recruits and selects employees.

Building Management Skills

Analyzing Human Resource Systems

Think about your current job or a job that you have had in the past. If you have never had a job, then interview a friend or family member who is currently working. Answer the following questions about the job you have chosen:

1. How are people recruited and selected for this job? Are the recruitment and selection procedures that the organization uses effective or ineffective? Why?

2. What training and development do people who hold this job receive? Is it appropriate? Why or why not?

3. How is performance of this job appraised? Does performance feedback contribute to motivation and high performance on this job?

4. What levels of pay and benefits are provided on this job? Are these levels appropriate? Why or why not?

Managing Ethically

Some managers do not want to become overly friendly with their subordinates because they are afraid that if they do so, their objectivity when conducting performance appraisals and making decisions about pay raises and promotions will be impaired. Some subordinates resent it when they see one or more of their coworkers being very friendly with the boss; they are concerned about the potential for favoritism. Their reasoning runs something like this: If two subordinates are equally qualified for a promotion and one is a good friend of the boss and the other is a mere acquaintance, who is more likely to receive the promotion?

Questions

1. Either individually or in a group, think about the ethical implications of managers' becoming friendly with their subordinates.

2. Do you think that managers should feel free to socialize and become good friends with their subordinates outside the workplace if they so desire? Why or why not?

Small Group Breakout Exercise
Building a Human Resource Management System

Form groups of three or four people, and appoint one group member as the spokesperson who will communicate your findings to the class when called on by the instructor. Then discuss the following scenario.

You and your two or three partners are engineers who minored in business at college and have decided to start a consulting business. Your goal is to provide manufacturing-process engineering and other engineering services to large and small organizations. You forecast that there will be an increased use of outsourcing for these activities. You discussed with managers in several large organizations the services you plan to offer, and they expressed considerable interest. You have secured funding to start your business and now are building the HRM system. Your human resource planning suggests that you need to hire between five and eight experienced engineers with good communication skills, two clerical/secretarial workers, and two MBAs who between them have financial, accounting, and human resource skills. You are striving to develop your human resources in a way that will enable your new business to prosper.

1. Describe the steps you will take to recruit and select (a) the engineers, (b) the clerical/secretarial workers, and (c) the MBAs.

2. Describe the training and development the engineers, the clerical/secretarial workers, and the MBAs will receive.

3. Describe how you will appraise the performance of each group of employees and how you will provide feedback.

4. Describe the pay level and pay structure of your consulting firm.

Exploring the World Wide Web

Go to www.net-temps.com, a Web site geared toward temporary employment. Imagine that you have to take a year off from college and are seeking a one-year position. Guided by your own interests, use this Web site to learn about your options and possible employment opportunities. What are the potential advantages of online job searching and recruiting? What are the potential disadvantages? Would you ever rely on a Web site like this to help you find a position? Why or why not?

Be the Manager

You are Walter Michaels and have just received some disturbing feedback. You are the director of human resources for Maxi Vision Inc., a medium-size window and glass-door manufacturer. You recently initiated a 360-degree performance appraisal system for all middle and upper managers at Maxi Vision, including yourself but excluding the most senior executives and the top-management team.

You were eagerly awaiting the feedback you would receive from the managers who report to you; you had recently implemented several important initiatives that affected them and their subordinates, including a complete overhaul of the organization's performance appraisal system. While the managers who report to you were evaluated based on 360-degree appraisals, their own subordinates were evaluated using a 20-question BARS scale you recently created that focuses on behaviors. Conducted annually, appraisals are an important input into pay raise and bonus decisions.

You were so convinced that the new performance appraisal procedures were highly effective that you hoped your own subordinates would mention them in their feedback to you. And boy did they! You were amazed to learn that the managers *and* their subordinates thought the new BARS scales were unfair, inappropriate, and a waste of time. In fact, the managers' feedback to you was that their own performance was suffering, based on the 360-degree appraisals they received, because their subordinates hated the new appraisal system and partially blamed their bosses, who were part of management. Some managers even admitted giving all their subordinates approximately the same scores on the scales so that their pay raises and bonuses would not be affected by their performance appraisals.

You couldn't believe your eyes when you read these comments. You had spent so much time developing what you thought was the ideal rating scale for this group of employees. Evidently, for some unknown reason, they were being very closed-minded and wouldn't give it a chance. Your own supervisor was aware of these complaints and said that it was a top priority for you to fix "this mess" (with the implication that you were responsible for creating it). What are you going to do?

BusinessWeek   Case in the News

You Are What You Post

One drizzly night in Seattle in 2001, Josh Santangelo was hanging out on his computer, clicking through an obscure Web site called Fray. After reading a post that asked if anyone had ever had a bad drug trip, the 22-year-old straightened up and began banging away. "Actually yes, about 36 hours ago . . . " he wrote. "Two Rolls Royces and four hits of liquid later, I was at a Playboy-themed birthday party with a head as dense as a brick. . . . It's hard to say no," he explained, "when a pretty girl is popping things into your mouth."

That was back when Santangelo was an up-all-night raver in giant pants and flame-red hair. Today he's a Web development guy with a shaved head who shows up at meetings on time and in khakis. Clients have included such family-friendly enterprises as Walt Disney and Nickelodeon, as well as Starbucks, AT&T, and Microsoft. You can read all about it if you Google him, right alongside the bold-faced entry: "Josh Santangelo on drugs and . . . "

Oh, the horror. Shortly after Santangelo's late-night overshare, famed blogger Jason Kottke linked to it on his site. That bagged so much traffic that five years later the "drug dump" still ranks No. 7 out of a total 92,600 Google hits that come up when you type in Santangelo's name. He says with a half-laugh that so far "it hasn't hurt me too bad," but he fears for the MySpacing, YouTubing, Facebooking masses—the bloggers and vloggers (video bloggers) who fail to realize that there is no such thing as an eraser on the Internet. "I see people do that sort of thing now, and I think: 'Oh man, that could come back and bite you.' "

Do you give good Google? It's the preoccupation du jour as Google hits become the new Q ratings for the creative class. Search engines provide endless opportunities for ego surfing, Google bombing (influencing traffic so it spikes a particular site), and Google juicing (enhancing one's "brand" in the era of microcelebrity). Follow someone too closely and you could be accused of being a Google stalker. Follow yourself too closely: Google narcissist.

But Googling people is also becoming a way for bosses and head-hunters to do continuous and stealthy background checks on employees, no disclosure required. Google is an end run around discrimination laws, inasmuch as employers can find out all manner of information—some of it for a nominal fee—that is legally off limits in interviews: your age, your martial status, the value of your house (along with an aerial photograph of it), the average net worth of your neighbors, fraternity pranks, stuff you wrote in college, liens, bankruptcies, political affiliations, and the names and ages of your children. Former Delta Air Lines flight attendant Ellen Simonetti lost her

job because she posted suggestive pictures of herself in uniform on her "Queen of Sky" blog—even though she didn't mention the airline by name. "We need Sarbanes and Oxley to come up with a Fair Google Reporting Act," says Brian Sullivan, CEO of recruitment firm Christian & Timbers. "I mean, what the hell do you do if there is stuff out there on Google that is unflattering or, God forbid, incorrect?"

Not a whole lot. That's because today there are two of you. There's the analog, warm-blooded version: the person who presses flesh at business conferences and interprets the corporate kabuki in meetings. Then there's the online you, your digital doppelgänger; that's the one that is growing larger and more impossible to control every day.

Because anyone, anywhere, at any time can say anything about you on the Web, reputations are scarily open-source. And because entire companies dedicate themselves to recording every inch of information on the Web, it's becoming difficult to unplug from the Google matrix, let alone make anything on the Internet go away. "This takes people's own agency out of how they want to present themselves," says Alice Marwick, a technology consultant and PhD candidate in New York University's Culture & Communications Department. The Internet started out with avatars and anonymity. Now online and offline are bleeding together. "It's consolidating personal information into the aggregate," says Marwick, even though "our social practices haven't figured out how to keep up with the technology."

Search engines make it possible for employers to scour all manner

of digital dirt to vet employees. Online profile company Ziggs.com CEO Tim DeMello fired an intern after he discovered that on the intern's Facebook profile he divulged that while at Ziggs he would "spend most of my days screwing around on IM and talking to my friends and getting paid for it."

There's also the risk of having no hits at all. (Translation: You are not a player.) Or the risk of having one too many. For lawyers, Google is paradise, often delivering more damning information than the discovery process does. Employment attorney Eric C. Bellafronto was recently on the phone with a client who had an employee with a history of being MIA. The slacker's excuse that day was that he was in Arizona taking care of a sick grandmother. While talking to the client, Bellafronto Googled the suspected faker and up came the fact that he was in Sacramento, being arraigned in federal court.

"People Can See Everything"

Schools are warning parents about Google's danger to the MySpace generation, for whom the Internet functions as a virtual diary-meets-barstool confessional. Adolescents try on identities and new behaviors like sweaters. Only now they are trying them on in front of the world. A Pew Research survey found that more than half of all online teenagers are ripping, mixing, and burning their own content, usually placing their creations right alongside their names and photos. The teenagers on the "companies and coworkers" section of MySpace who are talking smack about employers like Blockbuster, Target, and Gap are clearly unaware of the implications. "People need to realize that this is like putting stuff up on the 6 o'clock news," says employment lawyer Garry G. Mathiason, a partner at San Francisco's Littler Mendelson. "Once you've opened the drapes, people can see everything. They can see your past life."

That's why Dave Fonseca, a senior at the University of Massachusetts, pulled his Facebook profile down in December. "Employers are looking at these things," he says. (It's easy for people to get passwords and noodle around on the site.) Fonseca even knows the verb for people who get fired for what they put on their Web sites: "dooced." The name comes from Dooce.com, the blog of Heather B.

Armstrong, who got canned after writing about her job on her blog. Even Friendster, a social networking site that thrives on getting people to reveal everything about themselves, has been insistent on old-school discretion in-house. The company terminated esteemed engineer Joyce Park 18 months ago for mentioning Friendster on her blog, Troutgirl. The rumor on the Web was that the offending entry referred to Friendster's earlier sluggish performance. But the info was already widely known.

Oh, the irony.

Questions

1. Why are some managers and search firms googling prospective employees?

2. Why are some managers googling current employees?

3. What are the risks to employees of putting personal information on the Internet and writing blogs?

4. What are the ethical issues involved in using Google and the Internet to find information about prospective and current employees?

Source: M. Conlin, "You Are What You Post." Reprinted from the March 27, 2006, issue of *BusinessWeek* by special permission. Copyright © 2006 by the McGraw-Hill Companies.

BusinessWeek

Case in the News

The Struggle to Measure Performance

Holiday Shopping, year-end deadlines, and emotional family dramas aren't the only stresses in December. "Tis the season for companies to embark on that dreaded annual rite, the often bureaucratic and always time-consuming performance review. The process can be brutal: As many as one-third of U.S. corporations evaluate employees based on systems that pit them against their colleagues, and some even lead to the firing of low performers.

Fans say such "forced ranking" systems ensure that managers take a cold look at performance. But the practice increasingly is coming under fire. Following a string of discrimination lawsuits from employees who feel they were ranked and yanked based on age and not merely their performance, fewer companies are adopting the controversial management tool. Critics charge that it unfairly penalizes groups made up of stars and hinders collaboration and risk-taking, a growing concern for companies that are trying to innovate their way to growth. And a new study calls into question the long-term value of forced rankings. "It creates a zero-sum game, and so it tends to discourage cooperation," says Steve Kerr, a managing director at Goldman Sachs Group Inc., who heads the firm's leadership training program.

More Flexibility

Even General Electric Co., the most famous proponent of the practice, is trying to inject more flexibility into its system. Former Chief Executive Jack Welch required managers to divide talent into three groups—a top 20%, a middle 70%, and a bottom 10%, many of whom were shown the door. Eighteen months ago, GE launched a proactive campaign to remind managers to use more common sense in assigning rankings. "People in some locations take [distributions] so literally that judgment comes out of the practice," says Susan P. Peters, GE's vice-president for executive development.

Striking that balance between strict yardsticks and managerial judgment is something every company, from GE to Yahoo! to American Airlines, is grappling with today. But finding a substitute for a rigid grading system is not an easy task. It drives truth into a process frequently eroded by grade inflation and helps leaders identify managers who are good at finding top talent.

That's one reason GE isn't abandoning its system. But it has removed all references to the 20/70/10 split from its online performance management tool and now presents the curve as a set of guidelines. The company's 200,000 professional employees tend to fall into Welch's categories anyway, but individual groups are freer to have a somewhat higher number of "A" players or even, says Peters, no "bottom 10s." Even those low achievers are getting some kinder treatment, from a new appellation—the "less effectives"—to more specific coaching and intervention than in the past.

The changes are key for a company trying to evolve its culture from a Six Sigma powerhouse to one that also values innovation. Tempering such rigid performance metrics, says Peters, "enables individuals and organizations to be more comfortable with risk-taking and with failure." To drive that point home, the company's top 5,000 managers were evaluated for the first time this year on five traits, such as imagination and external focus, that represent the company's strategic goals.

Performance Art

Review season is here, with all the time-consuming bureaucracy and stress that comes with it. Here are five ideas to help put performance back into the process:

- **Meet More Often.** Time-strapped managers may sound a collective groan, but year-end reviews on their own are hardly enough. The best managers meet at least three times a year, if not four—once to set goals, once or twice for an update, and finally, to review—with many informal check-ins in between. In this quickly shifting economy, goals may change, and fewer surprises will surface at year-end.

- **Make Room for Risk.** As innovation trumps efficiency, some companies—including GE—are putting some wiggle room into their rankings and ratings. But more flexible guidelines have to have teeth, too: Low-performing units shouldn't get more than their share of top grades, for example. Exceptions should go to people who set aggressive goals and come close to achieving them.

- **Adjust Goals Along with Grades.** While many companies use "calibration" sessions to check that performance assessments level out among different managers, less than 10% fine-tune upfront goals across groups, according to Hewitt Associates.

- **Choose Words Wisely.** Whether or not you strip the labels off your performance reviews entirely, as Yahoo has, faint-praise terms such as "fully satisfies" make essential B-players feel like also-rans. Try "strong" or "successful" to drive home their value.

- **Build Trust.** With so much focus on the tools and tricks of performance management, it's easy to lose sight of what really matters: the conversation. The University of Michigan's Dave Ulrich suggests putting three simple words—"help me understand"—in front of difficult feedback.

New Data

Separating Stars from slackers remains a long-standing part of GE's performance-driven culture. But for most companies, especially those without such cultures, the benefits of adopting a forced ranking system are likely to dissipate over the long term.

A recent study lends hard data to that theory. Steve Scullen, an associate professor of management at Drake University in Des Moines, found that forced ranking, including the firing of the bottom 5% or 10%, results in an impressive 16% productivity improvement—but only over the first couple of years. After that, Scullen says, the gains drop off, from 6% climbs in the third and fourth years to basically zero by year 10. "It's a terrific idea for companies in trouble, done over one or two years, but to do it as a long-term solution is not going to work," says Dave Ulrich, a business professor at the University of Michigan at Ann Arbor. "Over time it gets people focused on competing with each other rather than collaborating."

One company that recently decided to dump forced rankings altogether is Chemtura, a $3 billion specialty chemicals company formed by the July merger of Crompton in Middlebury, Conn., and Great Lakes Chemical in Indianapolis. "The system forced me to turn people who were excellent performers into people who were getting mediocre ratings," says Eric Wisnefsky, Chemturs's vice-president for corporate finance. "That demotivates them, and they'd follow up with asking: 'What could I do differently next year?' That's a very difficult question to answer when you feel that people actually met all your expectations." Chemtura's new process still assigns grades. But to better motivate employees in the middle, labels such as "satisfactory" have been upgraded to phrases such as "successful performance."

Yahoo, too, was looking for better dialogue and less demoralizing labels when it made substantial changes this year to its rating system, which compared employees' performance to an absolute standard rather than to each other. Libby Sartain, Yahoo's senior vice-president for human resources, knew that review discussions at the Sunnyvale (Calif.) tech leader frequently included the wink-wink "I wanted to put you here, but I was forced by human resources to do something different" comment that discredits so many appraisals. This year, Yahoo stripped away its performance labels, partly in hopes that reviews would center more on substance and less on explaining away a grade.

But that doesn't mean Yahoo went all Pollyanna on its employees. To do a better job of finding and showering top performers with the rewards necessary to keep them from jumping ship in talent-tight Silicon Valley, the company also instituted a "stack-ranking" system this year to determine how compensation increases are distributed. It asks managers to rank employees within each unit—a group of 20 people would be ranked 1 through 20, for example—with raises and bonuses distributed accordingly. During reviews, employees are told how their increases generally compare to those of others.

Some Yahoo managers are livid about the new system. "It's going to kill morale," laments one senior engineering manager who says he's getting a stronger message to cull his bottom performers. Yahoo says its new program doesn't automatically weed out a bottom group and was designed specifically to reward its stars.

Indeed, what Yahoo has introduced in place of its old system shows how hard it is for companies to find ways to foster merit-driven cultures that coddle standouts while staying tough on low performers. Whether a company calls it stack ranking, forced ranking, or differentiation, "there's no magic process," says Sartain. "We just want to make sure we're making our bets and that we're investing in the people we most want to keep. That's what this is all about."

Questions

1. Why do some companies use forced ranking as part of their performance appraisal process?

2. What are some of the potential disadvantages of performance appraisals systems that use forced rankings?

3. Why might rigid performance metrics have the potential to stifle creativity and innovation?

4. Why did Yahoo change its performance appraisal system, and what are the pros and cons of its new system?

Source: J. McGregor, "The Struggle to Measure Performance." Reprinted from the January 9, 2006, issue of *BusinessWeek* by special permission. Copyright © 2006 by the McGraw-Hill Companies.

CHAPTER 13

Motivation and Performance

Learning Objectives

After studying this chapter, you should be able to:

- Explain what motivation is and why managers need to be concerned about it.

- Describe from the perspectives of expectancy theory and equity theory what managers should do to have a highly motivated workforce.

- Explain how goals and needs motivate people and what kinds of goals are especially likely to result in high performance.

- Identify the motivation lessons that managers can learn from operant conditioning theory and social learning theory.

- Explain why and how managers can use pay as a major motivation tool.

A Manager's Challenge

How can managers motivate employees in an industry known for high levels of turnover and low levels of motivation?

Kip Tindell and Garrett Boone founded the Container Store in Dallas, Texas, in 1978 and currently serve as CEO and chairman, respectively. When they opened their first store, they were out on the floor trying to sell customers their storage and organization products that would economize on space and time and make purchasers' lives a little less complicated. The Container Store has grown to include 37 stores in 17 U.S. markets from coast to coast; although the original store in Dallas had only 1,600 square feet, the stores today average around 25,000 square feet.[1] The phenomenal growth in the size of the stores has been matched by impressive growth rates in sales and profits.[2] Surprisingly enough, Tindell and Boone can still be found on the shop floor tidying shelves and helping customers carry out their purchases.[3] And that, perhaps, is an important clue to the secret of their success. The Container Store has been consistently ranked among *Fortune* magazine's "100 Best Companies to Work

A Container Store employee cheerfully assists a customer.

For" for seven years running.[4] In 2006, the Container Store was sixth on this list.[5]

Early on, Tindell and Boone recognized that people are the Container Store's most valuable asset and that after hiring great people, one of the most important managerial tasks is motivating them. One would think that

sense of accomplishment and achievement from helping the organization to achieve its goals and gain competitive advantages. Jobs that are interesting and challenging or high on the five characteristics described by the job characteristics model (see Chapter 9) are more likely to lead to intrinsic motivation than are jobs that are boring or do not make use of a person's skills and abilities. An elementary school teacher who really enjoys teaching children, a computer programmer who loves solving programming problems, and a commercial photographer who relishes taking creative photographs are all intrinsically motivated. For these individuals, motivation comes from performing their jobs whether it be teaching children, finding bugs in computer programs, or taking pictures.

For some people, intrinsic motivation comes from protecting the natural environment and encouraging others to do the same, as indicated in the following "Ethics in Action."

Ethics in Action

McDonough Protects the Planet

William McDonough's intrinsic motivation comes from saving the natural environment from pollution and waste and encouraging large corporations and their managers to do the same.[20] McDonough, an environmental designer, is the founder and principal of Williman McDonough & Partners, an architecture and community design firm, and a cofounder of MBDC, a process and product design firm. MBDC, cofounded with Dr. Michael Braungart, focuses on developing ways for organizations to produce goods and services without producing waste and polluting the natural environment. McDonough and Braungart helped the furniture manufacturer Herman Miller design a factory that, through its use of solar heating and cooling, has energy consumption savings of around 30%. They also helped create a new material for the soles of Nike athletic shoes that biodegrades without the customary release of toxic chemicals.[21]

The Herman Miller "GreenHouse" office in Holland, Michigan.

McDonough is so intrinsically motivated to protect our environment that for him, even recycling is not enough. Products made from recycled materials contain some of the toxic substances in the original products. Plastic bottles, for example, are often recycled, but the heavy metals and carcinogens in the bottles still find their ways into the new products made from them. And these new products eventually wind up in landfills, polluting the environment.[22]

McDonough and Braungart advocate that managers and organizations adopt "cradle-to-cradle design," which they introduced in their book *Cradle to Cradle: Remaking the Way We Make Things* (published by Northpoint Press; translated into Chinese, Korean, German, Spanish, and Italian).[23] Cradle-to-cradle design entails manufacturing products using biodegradable raw materials so that when a product is no longer useful, the materials it was made of either can be used over and over again in other products or will organically decompose. For example, McDonough recently designed a new carpet (called "A Walk in the Garden") for the Shaw industries unit of Berkshire Hathaway that is made of nylon pellets and polymers that can be reused again and again after the original carpet wears out.[24] This is in contrast to material from recyclable carpets being used to make other products which ultimately end up in landfills when they are discarded. Moreover, manufacturing costs for a Walk in the Garden are 10% lower than for some of Shaw's other carpet lines.[25]

Currently, McDonough is collaborating with the China Housing Industry Association to help it design sustainable housing in seven new Chinese cities using materials that contain no harmful chemicals and in ways that result in minimal energy costs for heating and cooling.[26] Clearly, McDonough's intrinsic motivation to protect and preserve the natural environment is enabling other managers and organizations to proactively address this ethical concern in a socially responsible manner.

extrinsically motivated behavior
Behavior that is performed to acquire material or social rewards or to avoid punishment.

Extrinsically motivated behavior is behavior that is performed to acquire material or social rewards or to avoid punishment; the source of motivation is the consequences of the behavior, not the behavior itself. A car salesperson who is motivated by receiving a commission on all cars sold, a lawyer who is motivated by the high salary and status that go along with the job, and a factory worker who is motivated by the opportunity to earn a secure income are all extrinsically motivated. Their motivation comes from the consequences they receive as a result of their work behaviors.

People can be intrinsically motivated, extrinsically motivated, or both intrinsically and extrinsically motivated.[27] A top manager who derives a sense of accomplishment and achievement from managing a large corporation and strives to reach year-end targets to obtain a hefty bonus is both intrinsically and extrinsically motivated. Similarly, a nurse who enjoys helping and taking care of patients and is motivated by having a secure job with good benefits is both intrinsically and extrinsically motivated. At the Container Store, employees are both extrinsically motivated, because they receive relatively high salaries and generous benefits, and intrinsically motivated, because they genuinely enjoy and get a sense of satisfaction out of doing their work and serving customers and look forward to coming to work each day. Whether workers are intrinsically motivated, extrinsically motivated, or both depends on a wide variety of factors: (1) workers' own personal characteristics (such as their personalities, abilities, values, attitudes, and needs), (2) the nature of their jobs (such as whether they have been enriched or where they are on the five core characteristics of the job characteristics model), and (3) the nature of the organization (such as its structure, its culture, its control systems, its human resource management system, and the ways in which rewards such as pay are distributed to employees).

Regardless of whether people are intrinsically or extrinsically motivated, they join and are motivated to work in organizations to obtain certain outcomes.

outcome Anything a person gets from a job or organization.

input Anything a person contributes to his or her job or organization.

An **outcome** is anything a person gets from a job or organization. Some outcomes, such as autonomy, responsibility, a feeling of accomplishment, and the pleasure of doing interesting or enjoyable work, result in intrinsically motivated behavior. Other outcomes, such as pay, job security, benefits, and vacation time, result in extrinsically motivated behavior.

Organizations hire people to obtain important inputs. An **input** is anything a person contributes to the job or organization, such as time, effort, education, experience, skills, knowledge, and actual work behaviors. Inputs such as these are necessary for an organization to achieve its goals. Managers strive to motivate members of an organization to contribute inputs—through their behavior, effort, and persistence—that help the organization achieve its goals. How do managers do this? They ensure that members of an organization obtain the outcomes they desire when they make valuable contributions to the organization. Managers use outcomes to motivate people to contribute their inputs to the organization. Giving people outcomes when they contribute inputs and perform well aligns the interests of employees with the goals of the organization as a whole because when employees do what is good for the organization, they personally benefit.

This alignment between employees and organizational goals as a whole can be described by the motivation equation depicted in Figure 13.1. Managers seek to ensure that people are motivated to contribute important inputs to the organization, that these inputs are put to good use or focused in the direction of high performance, and that high performance results in workers' obtaining the outcomes they desire.

Each of the theories of motivation discussed in this chapter focuses on one or more aspects of this equation. Each theory focuses on a different set of issues that managers need to address to have a highly motivated workforce. Together, the theories provide a comprehensive set of guidelines for managers to follow to promote high levels of employee motivation. Effective managers, such as Tindell and Boone in "A Manager's Challenge," tend to follow many of these guidelines, whereas ineffective managers often fail to follow them and seem to have trouble motivating organizational members.

Figure 13.1
The Motivation Equation

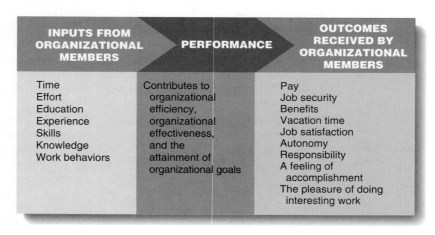

Expectancy Theory

expectancy theory
The theory that motivation will be high when workers believe that high levels of effort lead to high performance and high performance leads to the attainment of desired outcomes.

expectancy In expectancy theory, a perception about the extent to which effort results in a certain level of performance.

Expectancy theory, formulated by Victor H. Vroom in the 1960s, posits that motivation is high when workers believe that high levels of effort lead to high performance and high performance leads to the attainment of desired outcomes. Expectancy theory is one of the most popular theories of work motivation because it focuses on all three parts of the motivation equation: inputs, performance, and outcomes. Expectancy theory identifies three major factors that determine a person's motivation: *expectancy, instrumentality,* and *valence* (see Figure 13.2).[28]

Expectancy

Expectancy is a person's perception about the extent to which effort (an input) results in a certain level of performance. A person's level of expectancy determines whether he or she believes that a high level of effort results in a high level of performance. People are motivated to put forth a lot of effort on their jobs only if they think that their effort will pay off in high performance—that is, if they have high expectancy. Think about how motivated you would be to study for a test if you thought that no matter how hard you tried, you would get a D. Think about how motivated a marketing manager would be who thought that no matter how hard he or she worked, there was no way to increase sales of an unpopular product. In these cases, expectancy is low, so overall motivation is also low.

Members of an organization are motivated to put forth a high level of effort only if they think that doing so leads to high performance.[29] In other words, in order for people's motivation to be high, expectancy must be high. Thus, in attempting to influence motivation, managers need to make sure that their subordinates believe that if they do try hard, they can actually succeed. One way

Figure 13.2
Expectancy, Instrumentality, and Valence

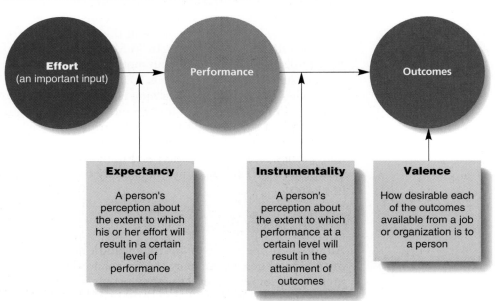

managers can boost expectancies is through expressing confidence in their subordinates' capabilities. Garrett Boone in "A Manager's Challenge" expressed confidence in his subordinates when he stated, "Everybody we hire, we hire as a leader. Anybody in our store can take an action that you might think of typically being a manager's action."[30]

In addition to expressing confidence in subordinates, another way for managers to boost subordinates' expectancy levels and motivation is by providing training so that people have all the expertise needed for high performance. For example, the Best Buy chain of over 629 stores selling electronics, computers, music and movies, and gadgets of all sorts boosts salespeople's expectancies by providing them with extensive training in on-site meetings and online. Electronic learning terminals in each department not only help salespeople learn how different systems work and can be sold as an integrated package but also enable them to keep up to date with the latest advances in technology and products. Salespeople also receive extensive training in how to determine customers' needs.[31]

Instrumentality

instrumentality In expectancy theory, a perception about the extent to which performance results in the attainment of outcomes.

Expectancy captures a person's perceptions about the relationship between effort and performance. **Instrumentality,** the second major concept in expectancy theory, is a person's perception about the extent to which performance at a certain level results in the attainment of outcomes (see Figure 13.2). According to expectancy theory, employees are motivated to perform at a high level only if they think that high performance will lead to (or is *instrumental* for attaining) outcomes such as pay, job security, interesting job assignments, bonuses, or a feeling of accomplishment. In other words, instrumentalities must be high for motivation to be high—people must perceive that because of their high performance they will receive outcomes.[32]

Managers promote high levels of instrumentality when they clearly link performance to desired outcomes. In addition, managers must clearly communicate this linkage to subordinates. By making sure that outcomes available in an organization are distributed to organizational members on the basis of their performance, managers promote high instrumentality and motivation. When outcomes are linked to performance in this way, high performers receive more outcomes than low performers. In "A Manager's Challenge," Boone and Tindell raise levels of instrumentality and motivation for Container Store employees by linking pay raises to performance.

Another example of high instrumentality contributing to high motivation can be found in the Cambodian immigrants who own, manage, and work in more than 80% of the doughnut shops in California.[33] These immigrants see high performance as leading to many important outcomes such as income, a comfortable existence, family security, and the autonomy provided by working in a small business. Their high instrumentality contributes to their high motivation to succeed.

Valence

Although all members of an organization must have high expectancies and instrumentalities, expectancy theory acknowledges that people differ in their preferences for outcomes. For many people, pay is the most important outcome of working. For others, a feeling of accomplishment or enjoying one's work is

Figure 13.3
Expectancy Theory

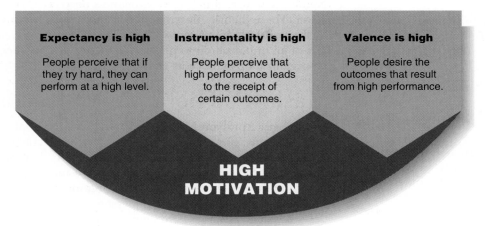

Expectancy is high	Instrumentality is high	Valence is high
People perceive that if they try hard, they can perform at a high level.	People perceive that high performance leads to the receipt of certain outcomes.	People desire the outcomes that result from high performance.

HIGH MOTIVATION

---

valence In expectancy theory, how desirable each of the outcomes available from a job or organization is to a person.

more important than pay. The term **valence** refers to how desirable each of the outcomes available from a job or organization is to a person. To motivate organizational members, managers need to determine which outcomes have high valence for them—are highly desired—and make sure that those outcomes are provided when members perform at a high level. From "A Manager's Challenge," it appears that not only pay but also autonomy, a stimulating work environment, enthusiastic coworkers, and generous benefits are highly valent outcomes for many employees at the Container Store.

Bringing It All Together

According to expectancy theory, high motivation results from high levels of expectancy, instrumentality, and valence (see Figure 13.3). If any one of these factors is low, motivation is likely to be low. No matter how tightly desired outcomes are linked to performance, if a person thinks it is practically impossible to perform at a high level, then motivation to perform at a high level is exceedingly low. Similarly, if a person does not think that outcomes are linked to high performance, or if a person does not desire the outcomes that are linked to high performance, then motivation to perform at a high level is low.

Need Theories

need A requirement or necessity for survival and well-being.

need theories Theories of motivation that focus on what needs people are trying to satisfy at work and what outcomes will satisfy those needs.

A **need** is a requirement or necessity for survival and well-being. The basic premise of **need theories** is that people are motivated to obtain outcomes at work that will satisfy their needs. Need theory complements expectancy theory by exploring in depth which outcomes motivate people to perform at a high level. Need theories suggest that to motivate a person to contribute valuable inputs to a job and perform at a high level, a manager must determine what needs the person is trying to satisfy at work and ensure that the person receives outcomes that help to satisfy those needs when the person performs at a high level and helps the organization achieve its goals.

There are several need theories. Here we discuss Abraham Maslow's hierarchy of needs, Clayton Alderfer's ERG theory, Frederick Herzberg's motivator-hygiene theory, and David McClelland's needs for achievement, affiliation, and power. These theories describe needs that people try to satisfy at work. In doing so, they provide managers with insights about what outcomes motivate members of an organization to perform at a high level and contribute inputs to help the organization achieve its goals.

Maslow's Hierarchy of Needs

Maslow's hierarchy of needs An arrangement of five basic needs that, according to Maslow, motivate behavior. Maslow proposed that the lowest level of unmet needs is the prime motivator and that only one level of needs is motivational at a time.

Psychologist Abraham Maslow proposed that all people seek to satisfy five basic kinds of needs: physiological needs, safety needs, belongingness needs, esteem needs, and self-actualization needs (see Table 13.1).[34] He suggested that these needs constitute a **hierarchy of needs,** with the most basic or compelling needs—physiological and safety needs—at the bottom. Maslow argued that these lowest-level needs must be met before a person strives to satisfy needs higher up in the hierarchy, such as self-esteem needs. Once a need is satisfied, Maslow proposed, it ceases to operate as a source of motivation. The lowest level of *unmet* needs in the hierarchy is the prime motivator of behavior; if and when this level is satisfied, needs at the next-highest level in the hierarchy motivate behavior.

Table 13.1
Maslow's Hierarchy of Needs

	Needs	Description	Examples of How Managers Can Help People Satisfy These Needs at Work
Highest-level needs	**Self-actualization needs**	The needs to realize one's full potential as a human being	By giving people the opportunity to use their skills and abilities to the fullest extent possible
	Esteem needs	The needs to feel good about oneself and one's capabilities, to be respected by others, and to receive recognition and appreciation	By granting promotions and recognizing accomplishments
	Belongingness needs	Needs for social interaction, friendship, affection, and love	By promoting good interpersonal relations and organizing social functions such as company picnics and holiday parties
	Safety needs	Needs for security, stability, and a safe environment	By providing job security, adequate medical benefits, and safe working conditions
Lowest-level needs (most basic or compelling)	**Physiological needs**	Basic needs for things such as food, water, and shelter that must be met in order for a person to survive	By providing a level of pay that enables a person to buy food and clothing and have adequate housing

The lowest level of unsatisfied needs motivates behavior; once this level of needs is satisfied, a person tries to satisfy the needs at the next level.

Jobs that involve artist expression, such as dancing, can help people fulfill higher-level needs.

Although this theory identifies needs that are likely to be important sources of motivation for many people, research does not support Maslow's contention that there is a need hierarchy or his notion that only one level of needs is motivational at a time.[35] Nevertheless, a key conclusion can be drawn from Maslow's theory: People try to satisfy different needs at work. To have a motivated workforce, managers must determine which needs employees are trying to satisfy in organizations and then make sure that individuals receive outcomes that satisfy their needs when they perform at a high level and contribute to organizational effectiveness. By doing this, managers align the interests of individual members with the interests of the organization as a whole. By doing what is good for the organization (that is, performing at a high level), employees receive outcomes that satisfy their needs.

In our increasingly global economy, managers must realize that citizens of different countries might differ in the needs they seek to satisfy through work.[36] Some research suggests, for example, that people in Greece and Japan are especially motivated by safety needs and that people in Sweden, Norway, and Denmark are motivated by belongingness needs.[37] In less developed countries with low standards of living, physiological and safety needs are likely to be the prime motivators of behavior. As countries become wealthier and have higher standards of living, needs related to personal growth and accomplishment (such as esteem and self-actualization) become important as motivators of behavior.

Alderfer's ERG Theory

Alderfer's ERG theory
The theory that three universal needs—for existence, relatedness, and growth—constitute a hierarchy of needs and motivate behavior. Alderfer proposed that needs at more than one level can be motivational at the same time.

Clayton **Alderfer's ERG theory** collapses the five categories of needs in Maslow's hierarchy into three universal categories—existence, relatedness, and growth—also arranged in a hierarchy (see Table 13.2). Alderfer agrees with Maslow that as lower-level needs become satisfied, a person seeks to satisfy higher-level needs. Unlike Maslow, however, Alderfer believes that a person can be motivated by needs at more than one level at the same time. A cashier in a supermarket, for example, may be motivated both by existence needs and by relatedness needs. The existence needs motivate the cashier to come to work regularly and not make mistakes so that his job will be secure and he will be able to pay his rent and buy food. The relatedness needs motivate the cashier to become friends with some of the other cashiers and have a good relationship with the store manager. Alderfer also suggests that when people experience *need frustration* or are unable to satisfy needs at a certain level, they will focus all the more on satisfying the needs at the next-lowest level in the hierarchy.[38]

As with Maslow's theory, research does not support some of the specific ideas outlined in ERG theory, such as the existence of the three-level need hierarchy that Alderfer proposed.[39] However, for managers, the important message from ERG theory is the same as that from Maslow's theory: Determine what needs your subordinates are trying to satisfy at work, and make sure that they receive outcomes that satisfy these needs when they perform at a high level to help the organization achieve its goals.

Table 13.2
Alderfer's ERG Theory

	Needs	Description	Examples of How Managers Can Help People Satisfy These Needs at Work
Highest-level needs	**Growth needs**	The needs for self-development and creative and productive work	By allowing people to continually improve their skills and abilities and engage in meaningful work
	Relatedness needs	The needs to have good interpersonal relations, to share thoughts and feelings, and to have open two-way communication	By promoting good interpersonal relations and by providing accurate feedback
Lowest-level needs	**Existence needs**	Basic needs for food, water, clothing, shelter, and a secure and safe environment	By promoting enough pay to provide for the basic necessities of life and safe working conditions

As lower-level needs are satisfied, a person is motivated to satisfy higher-level needs. When a person is unable to satisfy higher-level needs (or is frustrated), motivation to satisfy lower-level needs increases.

Herzberg's Motivator-Hygiene Theory

Herzberg's motivator-hygiene theory A need theory that distinguishes between motivator needs (related to the nature of the work itself) and hygiene needs (related to the physical and psychological context in which the work is performed) and proposes that motivator needs must be met for motivation and job satisfaction to be high.

Adopting an approach different from Maslow's and Alderfer's, Frederick Herzberg focuses on two factors: (1) outcomes that can lead to high levels of motivation and job satisfaction and (2) outcomes that can prevent people from being dissatisfied. According to Herzberg's motivator-hygiene theory, people have two sets of needs or requirements: motivator needs and hygiene needs.[40] *Motivator needs* are related to the nature of the work itself and how challenging it is. Outcomes, such as interesting work, autonomy, responsibility, being able to grow and develop on the job, and a sense of accomplishment and achievement, help to satisfy motivator needs. To have a highly motivated and satisfied workforce, Herzberg suggested, managers should take steps to ensure that employees' motivator needs are being met.

Hygiene needs are related to the physical and psychological context in which the work is performed. Hygiene needs are satisfied by outcomes such as pleasant and comfortable working conditions, pay, job security, good relationships with coworkers, and effective supervision. According to Herzberg, when hygiene needs are not met, workers are dissatisfied, and when hygiene needs are met, workers are not dissatisfied. Satisfying hygiene needs, however, does not result in high levels of motivation or even high levels of job satisfaction. For motivation and job satisfaction to be high, motivator needs must be met.

Many research studies have tested Herzberg's propositions, and, by and large, the theory fails to receive support.[41] Nevertheless, Herzberg's formulations have contributed to our understanding of motivation in at least two ways. First, Herzberg helped to focus researchers' and managers' attention on the important distinction between intrinsic motivation (related to motivator needs) and extrinsic motivation (related to hygiene needs), covered earlier in the chapter. Second, his theory prompted researchers and managers to study how jobs could be designed or redesigned so that they are intrinsically motivating.

McClelland's Needs for Achievement, Affiliation, and Power

need for achievement The extent to which an individual has a strong desire to perform challenging tasks well and to meet personal standards for excellence.

Psychologist David McClelland has extensively researched the needs for achievement, affiliation, and power.[42] The **need for achievement** is the extent to which an individual has a strong desire to perform challenging tasks well and to meet personal standards for excellence. People with a high need for achievement often set clear goals for themselves and like to receive performance feedback. The **need for affiliation** is the extent to which an individual is concerned about establishing and maintaining good interpersonal relations, being liked, and having the people around him or her get along with each other. The **need for power** is the extent to which an individual desires to control or influence others.[43]

need for affiliation The extent to which an individual is concerned about establishing and maintaining good interpersonal relations, being liked, and having the people around him or her get along with each other.

While each of these needs is present in each of us to some degree, their importance in the workplace depends upon the position one occupies. For example, research suggests that high needs for achievement and for power are assets for first-line and middle managers and that a high need for power is especially important for upper managers.[44] One study found that U.S. presidents with a relatively high need for power tended to be especially effective during their terms of office.[45] A high need for affiliation may not always be desirable in managers and other leaders because it might lead them to try too hard to be liked by others (including subordinates) rather than doing all they can to ensure that performance is as high as it can and should be. Although most research on these needs has been done in the United States, some studies suggest that the findings may be applicable to people in other countries as well, such as India and New Zealand.[46]

need for power The extent to which an individual desires to control or influence others.

Other Needs

Clearly more needs motivate workers than the needs described by the above four theories. For example, more and more workers are feeling the need for work-life balance and time to take care of their loved ones while simultaneously being highly motivated at work. Interestingly enough, recent research suggests that being exposed to nature (even just being able to see some trees from your office window) has many salutary effects and a lack of such exposure can actually impair well-being and performance.[47] Thus, having some time during the day when one can at least see nature may be another important need.

Managers of successful companies often strive to ensure that as many of their valued employees' needs as possible are satisfied in the workplace. This is illustrated by the following "Information Technology Byte" on the SAS Institute.

Information
Technology
Byte

High Motivation Rules at the SAS Institute

Keeping company with the Container Store in *Fortune* magazine's list of the 100 best companies to work for is the SAS Institute, which ranked 30th in 2006.[48] The SAS Institute is the world's largest privately owned software company, with over 10,000 employees worldwide and approximately $1.6 billion in sales.[49] Every indicator suggests that SAS employees are highly motivated and perform well while also working 35-hour weeks. How do managers at SAS do it? In large part, by ensuring that employees are highly motivated and the variety of needs they bring to the workplace are satisfied by doing a good job at SAS.[50]

Satisfying the need for intrinsically motivating work has also been a key priority at SAS. Managers strive to make sure that each employee is motivated by the work he or she performs, and employees are encouraged to change jobs to prevent becoming bored with their work (even if the job changes require that SAS provide additional training). Moreover, in contrast to the approach at some of the company's competitors, all new product development work at SAS is performed in-house, so employees have the opportunity to experience the excitement of developing a new product and seeing it succeed.[51]

An SAS Institute employee makes her way to the dining hall on the 200-acre SAS campus located in Cary, N.C. SAS Institute is known as one of the best companies to work for in the country, offering jogging paths, a gymnasium, and a Montessori preschool on the campus.

The SAS Institute satisfies employees' needs for economic security by paying them fairly and providing them with secure jobs. Employees have their own offices, and the work environment is rich in pleasant vistas, whether they be artwork on the walls or views of the rolling hills of Cary, North Carolina, at company headquarters. Managers at SAS realize that needs for work-life balance are a top priority for many of their employees and seek to satisfy these needs in a variety of ways, including 35-hour workweeks, on-site day care and medical care, unlimited sick days, and high chairs in the company cafeteria so that employees can dine with their kids. Moreover, employees and their families are encouraged to use the 200 acres that surround company headquarters for family walks and picnics.[52]

Since the company was founded, CEO James Goodnight has been committed to motivating employees to develop creative and high-quality products that meet customers' needs. Today, 96% of the top 100 companies in the Fortune 500 list use SAS products for a wide variety of purposes including risk management, monitoring and measuring performance, managing relations with suppliers and customers, and detecting fraud.[53] SAS also provides educational software for schools and teachers through SAS in School.[54] Clearly, motivating employees and helping to satisfy their needs is a win-win situation for SAS.

Equity Theory

equity theory A theory of motivation that focuses on people's perceptions of the fairness of their work outcomes relative to their work inputs.

Equity theory is a theory of motivation that concentrates on people's perceptions of the fairness of their work *outcomes* relative to, or in proportion to, their work *inputs*. Equity theory complements expectancy and need theories by focusing on how people perceive the relationship between the outcomes they receive from their jobs and organizations and the inputs they contribute. Equity theory was formulated in the 1960s by J. Stacy Adams, who stressed that what is important in determining motivation is the *relative* rather than the *absolute* levels of outcomes a person receives and inputs a person contributes. Specifically, motivation is influenced by the comparison of one's own outcome-input ratio with the outcome-input ratio of a referent.[55] The *referent* could be another person or a group of people who are perceived to be similar to oneself; the referent also could be oneself in a previous job or one's expectations about what outcome-input ratios should be. In a comparison of one's own outcome-input ratio to a referent's ratio, one's *perceptions* of outcomes and inputs (not any objective indicator of them) are key.

Equity

equity The justice, impartiality, and fairness to which all organizational members are entitled.

Equity exists when a person perceives his or her own outcome-input ratio to be equal to a referent's outcome-input ratio. Under conditions of equity (see Table 13.3), if a referent receives more outcomes than you receive, the referent contributes proportionally more inputs to the organization, so his or her outcome-input ratio still equals your ratio. Maria Sanchez and Claudia King, for example, both work in a shoe store in a large mall. Sanchez is paid more per hour than King but also contributes more inputs, including being responsible for some of the store's bookkeeping, closing the store, and periodically depositing cash in the bank. When King compares her outcome-input ratio to Sanchez's (her referent's), she perceives the ratios to be equitable because Sanchez's higher level of pay (an outcome) is proportional to her higher level of inputs (bookkeeping, closing the store, and going to the bank).

Similarly, under conditions of equity, if you receive more outcomes than a referent, then your inputs are perceived to be proportionally higher. Continuing

Table 13.3
Equity Theory

Condition	Person		Referent	Example
Equity	$\dfrac{\text{Outcomes}}{\text{Inputs}}$	$=$	$\dfrac{\text{Outcomes}}{\text{Inputs}}$	An engineer perceives that he contributes more inputs (time and effort) and receives proportionally more outcomes (a higher salary and choice job assignments) than his referent.
Underpayment inequity	$\dfrac{\text{Outcomes}}{\text{Inputs}}$	$<$ (less than)	$\dfrac{\text{Outcomes}}{\text{Inputs}}$	An engineer perceives that he contributes more inputs but receives the same outcomes as his referent.
Overpayment inequity	$\dfrac{\text{Outcomes}}{\text{Inputs}}$	$>$ (greater than)	$\dfrac{\text{Outcomes}}{\text{Inputs}}$	An engineer perceives that he contributes the same inputs but receives more outcomes than his referent.

with our example, when Sanchez compares her outcome-input ratio to King's (her referent's) ratio, she perceives them to be equitable because her higher level of pay is proportional to her higher level of inputs.

When equity exists, people are motivated to continue contributing their current levels of inputs to their organizations to receive their current levels of outcomes. If people wish to increase their outcomes under conditions of equity, they are motivated to increase their inputs.

Inequity

inequity Lack of fairness.

Inequity, lack of fairness, exists when a person's outcome-input ratio is not perceived to be equal to a referent's. Inequity creates pressure or tension inside people and motivates them to restore equity by bringing the two ratios back into balance.

There are two types of inequity: underpayment inequity and overpayment inequity (see Table 13.3). **Underpayment inequity** exists when a person's own outcome-input ratio is perceived to be *less* than that of a referent. In comparing yourself to a referent, you think that you are *not* receiving the outcomes you should be, given your inputs. **Overpayment inequity** exists when a person perceives that his or her own outcome-input ratio is *greater* than that of a referent. In comparing yourself to a referent, you think that you are receiving *more* outcomes than you should be, given your inputs.

underpayment inequity The inequity that exists when a person perceives that his or her own outcome-input ratio is less than the ratio of a referent.

overpayment inequity The inequity that exists when a person perceives that his or her own outcome-input ratio is greater than the ratio of a referent.

Ways to Restore Equity

According to equity theory, both underpayment inequity and overpayment inequity create tension that motivates most people to restore equity by bringing the ratios back into balance.[56] When people experience *underpayment* inequity, they may be motivated to lower their inputs by reducing their working hours, putting forth less effort on the job, or being absent or they may be motivated to increase their outcomes by asking for a raise or a promotion. Susan Richie, a financial analyst at a large corporation, noticed that she was working longer hours and getting more work accomplished than a coworker who had the same position, yet they both received the exact same pay and other outcomes. To restore equity, Richie decided to stop coming in early and staying late. Alternatively, she could have tried to restore equity by trying to increase her outcomes, say, by asking her boss for a raise.

When people experience *underpayment* inequity and other means of equity restoration fail, they can change their perceptions of their own or the referent's inputs or outcomes. For example, they may realize that their referent is really working on more difficult projects than they are or that they really take more time off from work than their referent does. Alternatively, if people who feel that they are underpaid have other employment options, they may leave the organization. As an example, John Steinberg, an assistant principal in a high school, experienced underpayment inequity when he realized that all of the other assistant principals of high schools in his school district had received promotions to the position of principal even though they had been in their jobs for a shorter time than he had been. Steinberg's performance had always been appraised as being high, so after his repeated requests for a promotion went unheeded, he found a job as a principal in a different school district.

When people experience *overpayment* inequity, they may try to restore equity by changing their perceptions of their own or their referent's inputs or outcomes. Equity can be restored when people realize that they are contributing more inputs than they originally thought. Equity also can be restored by perceiving the referent's inputs to be lower or the referent's outcomes to be higher than one originally thought. When equity is restored in this way, actual inputs and outcomes are unchanged and the person being overpaid takes no real action. What is changed is how people think about or view their or the referent's inputs and outcomes. For instance, Mary McMann experienced overpayment inequity when she realized that she was being paid $2 an hour more than a coworker who had the same job as she did in a record store and who contributed the same amount of inputs. McMann restored equity by changing her perceptions of her inputs. She realized that she worked harder than her coworker and solved more problems that came up in the store.

Experiencing either overpayment or underpayment inequity, you might decide that your referent is not appropriate because, for example, the referent is too different from yourself. Choosing a more appropriate referent may bring the ratios back into balance. Angela Martinez, a middle manager in the engineering department of a chemical company, experienced overpayment inequity when she realized that she was being paid quite a bit more than her friend, who was a middle manager in the marketing department of the same company. After thinking about the discrepancy for a while, Martinez decided that engineering and marketing were so different that she should not be comparing her job to her friend's job even though they were both middle managers. Martinez restored equity by changing her referent; she picked a middle manager in the engineering department as a new referent.

Motivation is highest when as many people as possible in an organization perceive that they are being equitably treated—their outcomes and inputs are in balance. Top contributors and performers are motivated to continue contributing a high level of inputs because they are receiving the outcomes they deserve. Mediocre contributors and performers realize that if they want to increase their outcomes, they have to increase their inputs. Managers of effective organizations, like Tindell and Boone at the Container Store, realize the importance of equity for motivation and performance and continually strive to ensure that employees believe they are being equitably treated.

The dot-com boom, its subsequent bust, and a recession, along with increased global competition, have resulted in some workers' putting in longer and longer working hours (i.e., increasing their inputs) without any kind of increase in their outcomes. For those whose referents are not experiencing a similar change, perceptions of inequity are likely. According to Jill Andresky Fraser, author of *White Collar Sweatshop*, over 25 million U.S. workers work more than 49 hours per week in the office, almost 11 million work more than 60 hours per week in the office, and many also put in additional work hours at home. Moreover, advances in information technology, such as e-mail and cell phones, have resulted in work intruding on home time, vacation time, and even special occasions.[57]

Goal-Setting Theory

Goal-setting theory focuses on motivating workers to contribute their inputs to their jobs and organizations; in this way it is similar to expectancy theory and equity theory. But goal-setting theory takes this focus a step further by considering as well how managers can ensure that organizational members focus their inputs in the direction of high performance and the achievement of organizational goals.

Ed Locke and Gary Latham, the leading researchers on goal-setting theory, suggest that the goals that organizational members strive to attain are prime determinants of their motivation and subsequent performance. A *goal* is what a person is trying to accomplish through his or her efforts and behaviors.[58] Just as you may have a goal to get a good grade in this course, so do members of an organization have goals that they strive to meet. For example, salespeople at Neiman Marcus strive to meet sales goals, while top managers pursue market share and profitability goals.

Goal-setting theory suggests that to stimulate high motivation and performance, goals must be *specific* and *difficult*.[59] Specific goals are often quantitative—a salesperson's goal to sell $200 worth of merchandise per day, a scientist's goal to finish a project in one year, a CEO's goal to reduce debt by 40% and increase revenues by 20%, a restaurant manager's goal to serve 150 customers per evening. In contrast to specific goals, vague goals such as "doing your best" or "selling as much as you can" do not have much motivational impact.

Difficult goals are hard but not impossible to attain. In contrast to difficult goals, easy goals are those that practically everyone can attain, and moderate goals are goals that about one-half of the people can attain. Both easy and moderate goals have less motivational power than difficult goals.

Regardless of whether specific, difficult goals are set by managers, workers, or teams of managers and workers, they lead to high levels of motivation and performance. When managers set goals for their subordinates, their subordinates must accept the goals or agree to work toward them; also, they should be committed to them or really want to attain them. Some managers find that having subordinates participate in the actual setting of goals boosts their acceptance of and commitment to the goals. In addition, organizational members need to receive *feedback* about how they are doing; feedback can often be provided by the performance appraisal and feedback component of an organization's human resource management system (see Chapter 12). More generally, goals and feedback are integral components of performance management systems such as management by objectives (see Chapter 11).

Specific, difficult goals affect motivation in two ways. First, they motivate people to contribute more inputs to their jobs. Specific, difficult goals cause people to put forth high levels of effort, for example. Just as you would study harder if you were trying to get an A in a course instead of a C, so too will a salesperson work harder to reach a $200 sales goal instead of a $100 sales goal. Specific, difficult goals also cause people to be more persistent than easy, moderate, or vague goals when they run into difficulties. Salespeople who are told to sell as much as possible might stop trying on a slow day, whereas having a specific, difficult goal to reach causes them to keep trying.

A second way in which specific, difficult goals affect motivation is by helping people focus their inputs in the right direction. These goals let people know what they should be focusing their attention on, be it increasing the quality of customer service or sales or lowering new product development times. The fact

Specific, difficult goals can encourage people to exert high levels of effort and to focus efforts in the right direction.

that the goals are specific and difficult also frequently causes people to develop *action plans* for reaching them.[60] Action plans can include the strategies to attain the goals and timetables or schedules for the completion of different activities crucial to goal attainment. Like the goals themselves, action plans also help ensure that efforts are focused in the right direction and that people do not get sidetracked along the way.

Although specific, difficult goals have been found to increase motivation and performance in a wide variety of jobs and organizations both in the United States and abroad, recent research suggests that they may detract from performance under certain conditions. When people are performing complicated and very challenging tasks that require them to focus on a considerable amount of learning, specific, difficult goals may actually impair performance.[61] Striving to reach such goals may direct some of a person's attention away from learning about the task and toward trying to figure out how to achieve the goal. Once a person has learned the task and it no longer seems complicated or difficult, then the assignment of specific, difficult goals is likely to have its usual effects. Additionally, for work that is very creative and uncertain, specific, difficult goals may be detrimental.

Learning Theories

The basic premise of **learning theories** as applied to organizations is that managers can increase employee motivation and performance by the ways they link the outcomes that employees receive to the performance of desired behaviors and the attainment of goals. Thus, learning theory focuses on the linkage between performance and outcomes in the motivation equation (see Figure 13.1).

learning theories
Theories that focus on increasing employee motivation and performance by linking the outcomes that employees receive to the performance of desired behaviors and the attainment of goals.

Learning can be defined as a relatively permanent change in a person's knowledge or behavior that results from practice or experience.[62] Learning takes place in organizations when people learn to perform certain behaviors to receive certain outcomes. For example, a person learns to perform at a higher level than in the past or to come to work earlier because he or she is motivated to obtain the outcomes that result from these behaviors, such as a pay raise or praise from a supervisor. In "A Manager's Challenge," the Container Store's emphasis on training ensures that new hires learn how to provide excellent customer service and all employees continue their learning throughout their careers with the Container Store.

learning A relatively permanent change in knowledge or behavior that results from practice or experience.

Of the different learning theories, operant conditioning theory and social learning theory provide the most guidance to managers in their efforts to have a highly motivated workforce.

operant conditioning theory The theory that people learn to perform behaviors that lead to desired consequences and learn not to perform behaviors that lead to undesired consequences.

Operant Conditioning Theory

According to **operant conditioning theory,** developed by psychologist B. F. Skinner, people learn to perform behaviors that lead to desired consequences and learn not to perform behaviors that lead to undesired consequences.[63] Translated into motivation terms, Skinner's theory means that people will be motivated to perform at a high level and attain their work goals to the extent that high performance and goal attainment allow them to obtain outcomes they desire. Similarly, people avoid performing behaviors that lead to outcomes they do not desire. By linking the performance of *specific behaviors* to the attainment of *specific outcomes*, managers can motivate organizational members to perform in ways that help an organization achieve its goals.

Operant conditioning theory provides four tools that managers can use to motivate high performance and prevent workers from engaging in absenteeism and other behaviors that detract from organizational effectiveness. These tools are positive reinforcement, negative reinforcement, extinction, and punishment.[64]

positive reinforcement Giving people outcomes they desire when they perform organizationally functional behaviors.

POSITIVE REINFORCEMENT   Positive reinforcement gives people outcomes they desire when they perform organizationally functional behaviors. These desired outcomes, called *positive reinforcers*, include any outcomes that a person desires, such as pay, praise, or a promotion. Organizationally functional behaviors are behaviors that contribute to organizational effectiveness; they can include producing high-quality goods and services, providing high-quality customer service, and meeting deadlines. By linking positive reinforcers to the performance of functional behaviors, managers motivate people to perform the desired behaviors.

negative reinforcement Eliminating or removing undesired outcomes when people perform organizationally functional behaviors.

NEGATIVE REINFORCEMENT   Negative reinforcement also can encourage members of an organization to perform desired or organizationally functional behaviors. Managers using negative reinforcement actually eliminate or remove undesired outcomes once the functional behavior is performed. These undesired outcomes, called *negative reinforcers*, can range from a manager's constant nagging or criticism to unpleasant assignments or the ever-present threat of losing one's job. When negative reinforcement is used, people are motivated to perform behaviors because they want to stop receiving or avoid undesired outcomes. Managers who try to encourage salespeople to sell more by threatening them with being fired are using negative reinforcement. In this case, the negative reinforcer is the threat of job loss, which is removed once the functional behavior is performed.

Whenever possible, managers should try to use positive reinforcement. Negative reinforcement can create a very unpleasant work environment and even a negative culture in an organization. No one likes to be nagged, threatened, or exposed to other kinds of negative outcomes. The use of negative reinforcement sometimes causes subordinates to resent managers and try to get back at them.

IDENTIFYING THE RIGHT BEHAVIORS FOR REINFORCEMENT   Even managers who use positive reinforcement (and refrain from using negative reinforcement) can get into trouble if they are not careful to identify the right behaviors to reinforce—behaviors that are truly functional for the organization. Doing this is not always as straightforward as it might seem. First, it is crucial for managers to choose behaviors over which subordinates have control; in other words, subordinates must have the freedom and opportunity to perform the behaviors that are being reinforced. Second, it is crucial that these behaviors contribute to organizational effectiveness.

EXTINCTION   Sometimes members of an organization are motivated to perform behaviors that actually detract from organizational effectiveness. According to operant conditioning theory, all behavior is controlled or determined by its consequences; one way for managers to curtail the performance of dysfunctional behaviors is to eliminate whatever is reinforcing the behaviors. This process is called **extinction.**

extinction Curtailing the performance of dysfunctional behaviors by eliminating whatever is reinforcing them.

Suppose a manager has a subordinate who frequently stops by his office to chat—sometimes about work-related matters but at other times about various topics ranging from politics to last night's football game. The manager and the subordinate share certain interests and views, so these conversations can get quite involved, and both seem to enjoy them. The manager, however, realizes that these frequent and sometimes lengthy conversations are actually causing him to stay at work later in the evenings to make up for the time he loses during the day. The manager also realizes that he is actually reinforcing his subordinate's behavior by acting interested in the topics the subordinate brings up and responding at length to them. To extinguish this behavior, the manager stops acting interested in these non-work-related conversations and keeps his responses polite and friendly but brief. No longer being reinforced with a pleasurable conversation, the subordinate eventually ceases to be motivated to interrupt the manager during working hours to discuss non-work-related issues.

PUNISHMENT Sometimes managers cannot rely on extinction to eliminate dysfunctional behaviors because they do not have control over whatever is reinforcing the behavior or because they cannot afford the time needed for extinction to work. When employees are performing dangerous behaviors or behaviors that are illegal or unethical, the behavior needs to be eliminated immediately. Sexual harassment, for example, is an organizationally dysfunctional behavior that cannot be tolerated. In such cases managers often rely on **punishment,** administering an undesired or negative consequence to subordinates when they perform the dysfunctional behavior. Punishments used by organizations range from verbal reprimands to pay cuts, temporary suspensions, demotions, and firings. Punishment, however, can have some unintended side effects—resentment, loss of self-respect, a desire for retaliation—and should be used only when necessary.

punishment Administering an undesired or negative consequence when dysfunctional behavior occurs.

To avoid the unintended side effects of punishment, managers should keep in mind these guidelines:

- Downplay the emotional element involved in punishment. Make it clear that you are punishing a person's performance of a dysfunctional behavior, not the person himself or herself.

- Try to punish dysfunctional behaviors as soon after they occur as possible, and make sure the negative consequence is a source of punishment for the individuals involved. Be certain that organizational members know exactly why they are being punished.

- Try to avoid punishing someone in front of others, for this can hurt a person's self-respect and lower esteem in the eyes of coworkers as well as make coworkers feel uncomfortable.[65] Even so, making organizational members aware that an individual who has committed a serious infraction has been punished can sometimes be effective in preventing future infractions and teaching all members of the organization that certain behaviors are unacceptable. For example, when organizational members are informed that a manager who has sexually harassed subordinates has been punished, they learn or are reminded of the fact that sexual harassment is not tolerated in the organization.

Managers and students alike often confuse negative reinforcement and punishment. To avoid such confusion, keep in mind the two major differences between them. First, negative reinforcement is used to promote the performance of functional behaviors in organizations; punishment is used to stop the performance of dysfunctional behaviors. Second, negative reinforcement entails the *removal* of a negative consequence when functional behaviors are performed; punishment entails the *administration* of negative consequences when dysfunctional behaviors are performed.

organizational behavior modification (OB MOD) The systematic application of operant conditioning techniques to promote the performance of organizationally functional behaviors and discourage the performance of dysfunctional behaviors.

ORGANIZATIONAL BEHAVIOR MODIFICATION   When managers systematically apply operant conditioning techniques to promote the performance of organizationally functional behaviors and discourage the performance of dysfunctional behaviors, they are engaging in **organizational behavior modification (OB MOD)**.[66] OB MOD has been successfully used to improve productivity, efficiency, attendance, punctuality, safe work practices, customer service, and other important behaviors in a wide variety of organizations such as banks, department stores, factories, hospitals, and construction sites.[67] The five basic steps in OB MOD are described in Figure 13.4.

Figure 13.4
Five Steps in OB MOD

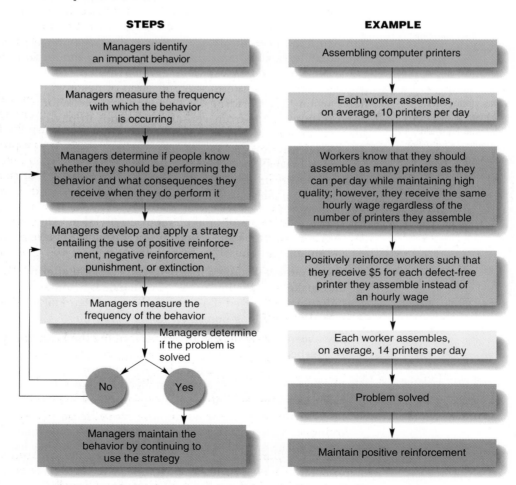

Source: Adapted from *Organizational Behavior Modification and Beyond* by F. Luthans and R. Kreitner (Scott, Foresman, 1985). With permission of the authors.

OB MOD works best for behaviors that are specific, objective, and countable, such as attendance and punctuality, making sales, or putting telephones together, all of which lend themselves to careful scrutiny and control. OB MOD may be questioned because of its lack of relevance to certain work behaviors (for example, the many work behaviors that are not specific, objective, and countable). Some people also have questioned it on ethical grounds. Critics of OB MOD suggest that it is overly controlling and robs workers of their dignity, individuality, freedom of choice, and even creativity. Supporters counter that OB MOD is a highly effective means of promoting organizational efficiency. There is some merit to both sides of this argument. What is clear, however, is that when used appropriately, OB MOD provides managers with a technique to motivate the performance of at least some organizationally functional behaviors.[68]

Social Learning Theory

social learning theory
A theory that takes into account how learning and motivation are influenced by people's thoughts and beliefs and their observations of other people's behavior.

Social learning theory proposes that motivation results not only from direct experience of rewards and punishments but also from a person's thoughts and beliefs. Social learning theory extends operant conditioning's contribution to managers' understanding of motivation by explaining (1) how people can be motivated by observing other people perform a behavior and be reinforced for doing so *(vicarious learning),* (2) how people can be motivated to control their behavior themselves *(self-reinforcement),* and (3) how people's beliefs about their ability to successfully perform a behavior affect motivation *(self-efficacy).*[69] We look briefly at each of these motivators.

vicarious learning
Learning that occurs when the learner becomes motivated to perform a behavior by watching another person perform it and be reinforced for doing so; also called *observational learning.*

VICARIOUS LEARNING Vicarious learning, often called *observational learning,* occurs when a person (the learner) becomes motivated to perform a behavior by watching another person (the model) perform the behavior and be positively reinforced for doing so. Vicarious learning is a powerful source of motivation on many jobs in which people learn to perform functional behaviors by watching others. Salespeople learn how to be helpful to customers, medical school students learn how to treat patients, law clerks learn how to practice law, and nonmanagers learn how to be managers, in part, by observing experienced members of an organization perform these behaviors properly and be reinforced for them. In general, people are more likely to be motivated to imitate the behavior of models who are highly competent, are (to some extent) experts in the behavior, have high status, receive attractive reinforcers, and are friendly or approachable.[70]

To promote vicarious learning, managers should strive to have the learner meet the following conditions:

- The learner observes the model performing the behavior.
- The learner accurately perceives the model's behavior.
- The learner remembers the behavior.
- The learner has the skills and abilities needed to perform the behavior.
- The learner sees or knows that the model is positively reinforced for the behavior.[71]

At the Ritz-Carlton hotel chain, vicarious learning is used around the globe to ensure that new employees learn how to provide outstanding service to guests, as profiled in the following "Managing Globally."

Managing Globally

Learning from Others at Ritz-Carlton

The Ritz-Carlton luxury hotel chain is a truly global organization with 28,000 employees working in 59 hotels in over 20 countries worldwide ranging from the United States, Italy, Japan, and China to Bahrain, Turkey, and the United Arab Emirates. Five new hotels in China alone are planned to open their doors soon.[72] To appeal to its global clientele, Ritz-Carlton partners with NewspapersDirect so that guests can have access to over 150 daily newspapers from 40 countries.[73]

Ritz-Carlton is known worldwide for its high-quality customer service, which is reflected in the first sentence of its credo: "The Ritz-Carlton Hotel is a place where the genuine care and comfort of our guests is our highest mission."[74] Making sure each new employee learns how to provide "the finest personal service" to guests—whether they be in Philadelphia, Pennsylvania, or Osaka, Japan—is of foremost importance for achieving this mission.[75] At Ritz-Carlton, new employees learn how to provide outstanding service to guests through vicarious learning.

Consider how a new room-service waiter at the Ritz-Carlton in Boston would learn how to perform his job.[76] After a two-day orientation program, he would be teamed up with and follow an experienced room-service waiter for several days, observing how the waiter interacts with guests and how guests respond. The newcomer would pick up tips along the way about providing outstanding service, such as trying to anticipate what guests might want even if they don't ask for it themselves. For instance, a guest ordering one dinner, an ice cream for dessert, and a bottle of wine might want two wine glasses, and the dinner should stay hot while the ice cream should stay cold. After the newcomer observes the experienced waiter model appropriate behavior for a while, he would begin to play a more active role interacting with and serving guests. However, the experienced waiter (the model) would never be out of sight until the newcomer has learned all he needs to pass a test administered by the in-room dining services manager.[77] New employees in other areas of the hotel also learn vicariously from observing their more experienced counterparts model appropriate behaviors.

Vicarious learning has paid off handsomely for Ritz-Carlton. The chain continues to receive accolades such as the prestigious Malcolm Baldrige National Quality Award, first place in the *Business Travel News'* Top U.S. Hotel Chain survey, and designation as "most prestigious brand" by the Luxury Institute's Brand Status Index Survey.[78]

self-reinforcer Any desired or attractive outcome or reward that a person gives to himself or herself for good performance.

SELF-REINFORCEMENT   Although managers are often the providers of reinforcement in organizations, sometimes people motivate themselves through self-reinforcement. People can control their own behavior by setting goals for themselves and then reinforcing themselves when they achieve the goals.[79] **Self-reinforcers** are any desired or attractive outcomes or rewards that people can give to themselves for good performance, such as a feeling of accomplishment, going to a movie, having dinner out, buying a new CD, or taking time out for a golf game. When members of an organization control their own behavior through self-reinforcement, managers do not need to spend as much time as they ordinarily would trying to motivate and control behavior through the administration of consequences because subordinates are controlling and motivating themselves. In fact, this self-control is often referred to as the *self-management of behavior.*

Chinese students at the prestigious Jiaotong University in Shanghai exemplify how strong motivation through self-control can be. These students, many of whom are aspiring engineers, live in spartan conditions (a barely lit small room is home for seven students) and take exceptionally heavy course loads. They spend their spare time reading up on subjects not covered in their classes, and many ultimately hope to obtain engineering jobs overseas with high-tech companies. Illustrating high self-control, 22-year-old Yan Kangrong spends his spare time reading computer textbooks and designing software for local companies. As Kangrong puts it, "We learn the basics from teachers. . . . But we need to expand on this knowledge by ourselves."[80]

When employees are highly skilled and are responsible for creating new goods and services, managers typically rely on self control and self management of behavior, as is the case at Google, profiled in the following "Information Technology Byte."

Information Technology Byte

Self-Management at Google

The largest search engine on the Internet today, Google is also the most popular search engine in Argentina, Australia, Belgium, Brazil, Canada, Denmark, France, Germany, India, Italy, Mexico, Spain, Sweden, Switzerland, the United Kingdom, and the United States.[81] Google employs over 5,600 people, many of whom are top-notch engineers focused on developing the most efficient search algorithms to give users exactly what they want at breakneck speed.[82]

Employees at Google are given the flexibility and autonomy to experiment, take risks, and sometimes fail as they work on new projects. They are encouraged to learn from their failures and apply what they learn to subsequent projects.[83] Self-control and self-management of behavior reign at Google. In fact, Google's engineers are given one day a week to work on their own projects that they are highly involved with, and new products such as Google News often emerge from these projects.[84]

Managers at Google, including founders Larry Page and Sergey Brin, believe that good ideas can come from anyone in the company, and thus all employees are encouraged to come up with the next big idea. Self-control and self-management of behavior have paid off handsomely for Google, which has experienced a phenomenal rate of growth in revenues and earnings since Page and Brin founded the company in 1998.[85]

self-efficacy A person's belief about his or her ability to perform a behavior successfully.

SELF-EFFICACY   Self-efficacy is a person's belief about his or her ability to perform a behavior successfully. Even with all the most attractive consequences or reinforcers hinging on high performance, people are not going to be motivated if they do not think that they can actually perform at a high level. Similarly, when people control their own behavior, they are likely to set for themselves difficult goals that will lead to outstanding accomplishments only if they think that they have the capability to reach those goals. Thus, self-efficacy influences motivation both when managers provide reinforcement and when workers themselves provide it.[86] The greater the self-efficacy, the greater is the motivation and performance. In "A Manager's Challenge," Tindell and Boone boost self-efficacy when they express confidence in their employees and view them all as leaders. Such verbal persuasion, as well as a person's own past performance and accomplishments and the accomplishments of other people, plays a role in determining a person's self-efficacy.

Pay and Motivation

In Chapter 12, we discussed how managers establish a pay level and structure for an organization as a whole. Here we focus on how, once a pay level and structure are in place, managers can use pay to motivate employees to perform at a high level and attain their work goals. Pay is used to motivate entry-level workers, first-line and middle managers, and even top managers such as CEOs. Pay can be used to motivate people to perform behaviors that help an organization achieve its goals, and it can be used to motivate people to join and remain with an organization.

Each of the theories described in this chapter alludes to the importance of pay and suggests that pay should be based on performance:

- *Expectancy theory:* Instrumentality, the association between performance and outcomes such as pay, must be high for motivation to be high. In addition, pay is an outcome that has high valence for many people.
- *Need theories:* People should be able to satisfy their needs by performing at a high level; pay can be used to satisfy several different kinds of needs.
- *Equity theory:* Outcomes such as pay should be distributed in proportion to inputs (including performance levels).
- *Goal-setting theory:* Outcomes such as pay should be linked to the attainment of goals.
- *Learning theories:* The distribution of outcomes such as pay should be contingent on the performance of organizationally functional behaviors.

merit pay plan A compensation plan that bases pay on performance.

As these theories suggest, to promote high motivation, managers should base the distribution of pay to organizational members on performance levels so that high performers receive more pay than low performers (other things being equal).[87] At General Mills, for example, the pay of all employees, ranging from mailroom clerks to senior managers, is based, at least in part, on performance.[88] A compensation plan basing pay on performance is often called a **merit pay plan.** Once managers have decided to use a merit pay plan, they face two important choices: whether to base pay on individual, group, or organizational performance or to use salary increases or bonuses.

Basing Merit Pay on Individual, Group, or Organizational Performance

Managers can base merit pay on individual, group, or organizational performance. When individual performance (such as the dollar value of merchandise a salesperson sells, the number of loudspeakers a factory worker assembles, and a lawyer's billable hours) can be accurately determined, individual motivation is likely to be highest when pay is based on individual performance.[89] When members of an organization work closely together and individual performance cannot be accurately determined (as in a team of computer programmers developing a single software package), pay cannot be based on individual performance, and a group- or organization-based plan must be used. When the attainment of organizational goals hinges on members' working closely together and cooperating with each other (as in a small construction company that builds custom homes), group- or organization-based plans may be more appropriate than individual-based plans.[90]

It is possible to combine elements of an individual-based plan with a group- or organization-based plan to motivate each individual to perform highly and, at the same time, motivate all individuals to work well together, cooperate with one another, and help one another as needed. Lincoln Electric, a very successful company and a leading manufacturer of welding machines, uses a combination individual- and organization-based plan.[91] Pay is based on individual performance. In addition, each year the size of a bonus fund depends on organizational performance. Money from the bonus fund is distributed to people on the basis of their contributions to the organization, attendance, levels of cooperation, and other indications of performance. Employees of Lincoln Electric are motivated to cooperate and help one another because when the firm as a whole performs well, everybody benefits by having a larger bonus fund. Employees also are motivated to contribute their inputs to the organization because their contributions determine their share of the bonus fund.

Salary Increase or Bonus?

Managers can distribute merit pay to people in the form of a salary increase or a bonus on top of regular salaries. Although the dollar amount of a salary increase or bonus might be identical, bonuses tend to have more motivational impact for at least three reasons. First, salary levels are typically based on performance levels, cost-of-living increases, and so forth, from the day people start working in an organization, which means that the absolute level of the salary is based largely on factors unrelated to *current* performance. A 5% merit increase in salary, for example, may seem relatively small in comparison to one's total salary. Second, a current salary increase may be affected by other factors in addition to performance, such as cost-of-living increases or across-the-board market adjustments. Third, because organizations rarely reduce salaries, salary levels tend to vary less than performance levels do. Related to this point is the fact that bonuses give managers more flexibility in distributing outcomes. If an organization is doing well, bonuses can be relatively high to reward employees for their contributions. However, unlike salary increases, bonus levels can be reduced when an organization's performance lags. All in all, bonus plans have

A steelworker at Nucor burns impurities from a tube used to pour molten steel in Decatur, Alabama. Nucor steelworkers can receive bonuses tied to performance and quality that are from 130 to 150 percent of their regular pay.

employee stock option A financial instrument that entitles the bearer to buy shares of an organization's stock at a certain price during a certain period of time or under certain conditions.

more motivational impact than salary increases because the amount of the bonus can be directly and exclusively based on performance.[92]

Consistent with the lessons from motivation theories, bonuses can be linked directly to performance and vary from year to year and employee to employee, as at Gradient Corporation, a Cambridge, Massachusetts, environmental consulting firm.[93] Another organization that successfully uses bonuses is Nucor Corporation. Steelworkers at Nucor tend to be much more productive than steelworkers in other companies—probably because they can receive bonuses tied to performance and quality that are from 130% to 150% of their regular or base pay.[94]

In addition to receiving pay raises and bonuses, high-level managers and executives are sometimes granted employee stock options. **Employee stock options** are financial instruments that entitle the bearer to buy shares of an organization's stock at a certain price during a certain period of time or under certain conditions.[95] For example, in addition to salaries, stock options are sometimes used to attract high-level managers. The exercise price is the stock price at which the bearer can buy the stock, and the vesting conditions specify when the bearer can actually buy the stock at the exercise price. The option's exercise price is generally set equal to the market price of the stock on the date it is granted, and the vesting conditions might specify that the manager has to have worked at the organization for 12 months or perhaps met some performance target (increase in profits) before being able to exercise the option. In high-technology firms and start-ups, options are sometimes used in a similar fashion for employees at various levels in the organization.[96]

From a motivation standpoint, stock options are used not so much to reward past individual performance but, rather, to motivate employees to work in the future for the good of the company as a whole. This is true because stock options issued at current stock prices have value in the future only if an organization does well and its stock price appreciates; thus, giving employees stock options should encourage them to help the organization improve its performance over time.[97] At high-technology start-ups and dot-coms, stock options have often motivated potential employees to leave promising jobs in larger companies and work for the start-ups. In the late 1990s and early 2000s, many dot-commers were devastated to learn not only that their stock options were worthless, because their companies went out of business or were doing poorly, but also that they were unemployed. Unfortunately, stock options have also lead to unethical behavior; for example, sometimes individuals seek to artificially inflate the value of a company's stock to increase the value of stock options.

Examples of Merit Pay Plans

Managers can choose among several merit pay plans, depending on the work that employees perform and other considerations. Using *piece-rate pay*, an individual-based merit plan, managers base employees' pay on the number of units each employee produces, whether televisions, computer components, or welded auto parts. Managers at Lincoln Electric use piece-rate pay to determine individual pay levels. Advances in information technology are currently simplifying the administration of piece-rate pay in a variety of industries. For example, farmers typically allocated piece-rate pay to farmworkers through a laborious, time-consuming process. Now, they can rely on metal buttons the size of a dime that farmworkers clip to their shirts or put in their pockets. Made by Dallas Semiconductor Corporation, these buttons are customized for use in farming by Agricultural Data Systems, based in Laguna Niguel, California.[98] Each button contains a semiconductor linked to payroll computers by a wandlike probe in the field.[99] The wand relays the number of boxes of fruit or vegetables that each worker picks as well as the type and quality of the produce picked, the location it was picked in, and the time and the date. The buttons are activated by touching them with the probe; hence, they are called Touch Memory Buttons. Managers generally find that the buttons save time, improve accuracy, and provide valuable information about their crops and yields.[100]

Using *commission pay*, another individual-based merit pay plan, managers base pay on a percentage of sales. Managers at the successful real-estate company Re/Max International Inc. use commission pay for their agents, who are paid a percentage of their sales. Some department stores, such as Neiman Marcus, use commission pay for their salespeople.

Examples of organizational-based merit pay plans include the Scanlon plan and profit sharing. The *Scanlon plan* (developed by Joseph Scanlon, a union leader in a steel and tin plant in the 1920s) focuses on reducing expenses or cutting costs; members of an organization are motivated to come up with and implement cost-cutting strategies because a percentage of the cost savings achieved during a specified time is distributed to the employees.[101] Under *profit sharing*, employees receive a share of an organization's profits. Approximately 16% of the employees in medium or large firms receive profit sharing, and about 25% of small firms give their employees a share of the profits.[102] Regardless of the specific kind of plan that is used, managers should always strive to link pay to the performance of behaviors that help an organization achieve its goals.

Japanese managers in large corporations have long shunned merit pay plans in favor of plans that reward seniority. However, more and more Japanese companies are adopting merit-based pay due to its motivational benefits; among such companies are SiteDesign,[103] Tokio Marine and Fire Insurance, and Hissho Iwai, a trading organization.[104]

Summary and Review

THE NATURE OF MOTIVATION Motivation encompasses the psychological forces within a person that determine the direction of the person's behavior in an organization, the person's level of effort, and the person's level of persistence in the face of obstacles. Managers strive to motivate people to contribute their inputs to an organization, to focus these inputs in the direction of high performance, and to ensure that people receive the outcomes they desire when they perform at a high level.

EXPECTANCY THEORY According to expectancy theory, managers can promote high levels of motivation in their organizations by taking steps to ensure that expectancy is high (people think that if they try, they can perform at a high level), instrumentality is high (people think that if they perform at a high level, they will receive certain outcomes), and valence is high (people desire these outcomes).

NEED THEORIES   Need theories suggest that to motivate their workforces, managers should determine what needs people are trying to satisfy in organizations and then ensure that people receive outcomes that satisfy these needs when they perform at a high level and contribute to organizational effectiveness.

EQUITY THEORY   According to equity theory, managers can promote high levels of motivation by ensuring that people perceive that there is equity in the organization or that outcomes are distributed in proportion to inputs. Equity exists when a person perceives that his or her own outcome-input ratio equals the outcome-input ratio of a referent. Inequity motivates people to try to restore equity.

GOAL-SETTING THEORY   Goal-setting theory suggests that managers can promote high motivation and performance by ensuring that people are striving to achieve specific, difficult goals. It is important for people to accept the goals, be committed to them, and receive feedback about how they are doing.

LEARNING THEORIES Operant conditioning theory suggests that managers can motivate people to perform highly by using positive reinforcement or negative reinforcement (positive reinforcement being the preferred strategy). Managers can motivate people to avoid performing dysfunctional behaviors by using extinction or punishment. Social learning theory suggests that people can also be motivated by observing how others perform behaviors and receive rewards, by engaging in self-reinforcement, and by having high levels of self-efficacy.

PAY AND MOTIVATION   Each of the motivation theories discussed in this chapter alludes to the importance of pay and suggests that pay should be based on performance. Merit pay plans can be individual-, group-, or organization-based and can entail the use of salary increases or bonuses.

Management in Action

Topics for Discussion and Action

Discussion

1. Discuss why two people with similar abilities may have very different expectancies for performing at a high level.

2. Describe why some people have low instrumentalities even when their managers distribute outcomes based on performance.

3. Analyze how professors try to promote equity to motivate students.

4. Describe three techniques or procedures that managers can use to determine whether a goal is difficult.

5. Discuss why managers should always try to use positive reinforcement instead of negative reinforcement.

Action

6. Interview three people who have the same kind of job (such as salesperson, waiter/waitress, or teacher), and determine what kinds of needs each is trying to satisfy at work.

7. Interview a manager in an organization in your community to determine the extent to which the manager takes advantage of vicarious learning to promote high motivation among subordinates.

Building Management Skills

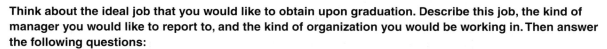

Diagnosing Motivation

Think about the ideal job that you would like to obtain upon graduation. Describe this job, the kind of manager you would like to report to, and the kind of organization you would be working in. Then answer the following questions:

1. What would be your levels of expectancy and instrumentality on this job? Which outcomes would have high valence for you on this job? What steps would your manager take to influence your levels of expectancy, instrumentality, and valence?

2. Whom would you choose as a referent on this job? What steps would your manager take to make you feel that you were being equitably treated? What would you do if, after a year on the job, you experienced underpayment inequity?

3. What goals would you strive to achieve on this job? Why? What role would your manager play in determining your goals?

4. What needs would you strive to satisfy on this job? Why? What role would your manager play in helping you satisfy these needs?

5. What behaviors would your manager positively reinforce on this job? Why? What positive reinforcers would your manager use?

6. Would there be any vicarious learning on this job? Why or why not?

7. To what extent would you be motivated by self-control on this job? Why?

8. What would be your level of self-efficacy on this job? Why would your self-efficacy be at this level? Should your manager take steps to boost your self-efficacy? If not, why not? If so, what would these steps be?

Managing Ethically

Sometimes pay is so contingent upon performance that it creates stress for employees. Imagine a salesperson who knows that if sales targets are not met, she or he will not be able to make a house mortgage payment or pay the rent.

Questions

1. Either individually or in a group, think about the ethical implications of closely linking pay to performance.

2. Under what conditions might contingent pay be most stressful, and what steps can managers take to try to help their subordinates perform effectively and not experience excessive amounts of stress?

Small Group Breakout Exercise

Increasing Motivation

Form groups of three or four people, and appoint one member as the spokesperson who will communicate your findings to the class when called on by the instructor. Then discuss the following scenario.

You and your partners own a chain of 15 dry-cleaning stores in a medium-size town. All of you are concerned about a problem in customer service that has surfaced recently. When any one of you spends the day, or even part of the day, in a particular store, clerks seem to provide excellent customer service, spotters are making sure all stains are removed from garments, and pressers are doing a good job of pressing difficult items such as silk blouses. Yet during those same visits customers complain to you about such things as stains not being removed and items being poorly pressed in some of their previous orders; indeed, several customers have brought garments in to be redone. Customers also sometimes comment on having waited too long for service on previous visits. You and your partners are meeting today to address this problem.

1. Discuss the extent to which you believe that you have a motivation problem in your stores.

2. Given what you have learned in this chapter, design a plan to increase the motivation of clerks to provide prompt service to customers even when they are not being watched by a partner.

3. Design a plan to increase the motivation of spotters to remove as many stains as possible even when they are not being watched by a partner.

4. Design a plan to increase the motivation of pressers to do a top-notch job on all clothes they press, no matter how difficult.

Exploring the World Wide Web

If you had the chance to choose which well-known corporation you would work for, which would it be? Now go to the Web site of that company and find out as much as you can about how it motivates employees. Also, using *Google* and other search engines, try to find articles in the news about this company. Based upon what you have learned, would this company still be your top choice? Why or why not?

Be the Manager

You supervise a team of marketing analysts who work on different snack products in a large food products company. The marketing analysts have recently received undergraduate degrees in business or liberal arts and have been on the job between one and three years. Their responsibilities include analyzing the market for their respective products, including competitors; tracking current marketing initiatives; and planning future marketing campaigns. They also need to prepare quarterly sales and expense reports for their products and estimated budgets for the next three quarters; to prepare these reports, they need to obtain data from financial and accounting analysts assigned to their products.

When they first started on the job, you took each marketing analyst through the reporting cycle, explaining what needs to be done and how to accomplish it and emphasizing the need for timely reports. While preparing the reports can be tedious, you think the task is pretty straightforward and easily accomplished if the analysts plan ahead and allocate sufficient time for it. When reporting time approaches, you remind the analysts through e-mails and emphasize the need for accurate and timely reports in team meetings.

You believe that this element of the analysts' jobs couldn't be more straightforward. However, at the end of each quarter, the majority of the analysts turn their reports in a day or two late, and, worse yet, your own supervisor (whom the reports are eventually turned in to) has indicated that information is often missing and sometimes the reports contain errors. Once you started getting flak from your supervisor about this problem, you decided you better fix things, and quick. You met with the marketing analysts, explained the problem, told them to turn the reports in to you a day or two early so that you could look them over, and more generally emphasized that they really needed to get their act together. Unfortunately, things have not improved much, and you are spending more and more of your own time doing the reports. What are you going to do?

BusinessWeek

Case in the News

A Real Stake in Your Customers

Nancy Kramer had a surprise up her sleeve. A few weeks before last January's annual meeting of Resource Interactive, the marketing agency she founded, Kramer sent an e-mail to her 140 employees. With mock seriousness, she said she needed some *"verrrrrryyyyyy"* important information before the meeting: their height in centimeters, favorite candy, shoe size, and favorite movie. Employees weren't thrown by the quirky message: Kramer, who co-produced the infamous Victoria's Secret online fashion show, once hired a pancake flipper to come to the office (employees caught their breakfast on a plate) and sometimes lies on the floor during meetings.

For the annual gathering, the only info she really needed was shoe size. Kramer and Kelly Mooney, with whom she runs the company, were about to introduce a new employee benefit called REEF, or Resource Employee Equity Fund, and were giving each staffer a pair of flip-flops by the surfwear brand REEF. The fund holds one share of stock per employee for each of Resource's publicly traded clients. Employees vest in the fund after a year.

Kramer's idea is an innovative approach to motivating employees and keeping them focused on their clients' businesses. "I wanted our employees to have the awareness of how clients are pressured," she says. "If [the stock price] does go down, what can we do to help?"

Ed Razek, Limited Brands' chief marketing officer, is impressed with Kramer's effort to turn her employees into shareholders. While other agencies might show their commitment by wearing clothes made by a client or driving its vehicles, he says, REEF is different. "It's ongoing, and it has value over time. Kelly and Nancy are telling their people very pointedly that what they do has to be measured."

Kramer's focus on results comes after 25 years of working with clients. She started out in media sales for an Ohio radio station, where she got to know a couple of manufacturer's sales reps. With them, Kramer launched Columbus-based Resource in 1981, at age 26. She eventually bought out her partners and built Resource into a full-service marketing firm with a growing Internet business.

Kramer got the idea for REEF in the late 1990s as she watched newly public bicoastal agencies toss stock options to their employees. But the boom went bust before Kramer could give REEF a try, and attracting talent was hardly her problem anymore. In early 2001, client bankruptcies erased half of her sales in 90 days.

But the idea stayed with her. As her company grew to $16 million in revenues and was ranked by *AdWeek* as one of the top 50 interactive agencies, Kramer decided to revisit it. She approached Merrill Lynch in 2004. "They said, 'It's too complicated,'" Mooney recalls. Merrill Lynch spokeswoman Jennifer Grigas says the adviser told Kramer

the plan would be difficult to implement and described some of its financial implications. Kramer's tax advisers at PricewaterhouseCoopers also initially questioned the idea. After 18 months of planning, Kramer and Moody laid out $1,337 per employee to buy one share of each of the firm's publicly traded clients (including Procter & Gamble and Hewlett-Packard). They also boosted associates' salaries the first year to offset any income tax hits.

Since its inception, the fund has done slightly better than the Standard & Poor's 500-stock index, which has returned just 0.3%. Still, there's more to the benefit than money, says John Kadlic, who joined Resource in May as executive director of business development. "Certainly, there was a financial interest," he says, noting that REEF, as well as Resource's reputation as a great place to work, was a factor in his

decision to join. "But it was more about what it said to me about their values." There are few better ways to win a talent war than that.

Questions

1. How does Resource Interactive motivate its employees?

2. How might the Resource Employment Equity Fund (REEF) contribute to employee motivation?

3. What behaviors might REEF motivate employees to perform?

4. How might REEF boost instrumentalities for employees at Resource Interactive?

Source: J. McGregor, "A Real Stake in Your Customers." Reprinted from the June 19, 2006, issue of *BusinessWeek* by special permission. Copyright © 2006 by the McGraw-Hill Companies.

BusinessWeek

Case in the News

Open Season on Open Source?

In 1999, Ethan Galstad was thinking about starting a business with a friend. Among other things on their to-do list was digging up software to monitor their network and flag any problems. They couldn't afford any of the programs on the market, however, so Galstad wrote his own. Almost on a whim, he posted it on an open-source Web site where geeks around the world browse code and download programs for free.

Galstad's original business idea never took off. But his software quickly became a hit. Some 50,000

companies downloaded the open-source project, called Nagios, and rely on it to monitor their networks. Galstad, now 31, works with other coders around the world to keep the software up to date and earns money by consulting. "It has really grown on its own, beyond anything I could have imagined," he says.

Galstad is one of the many true believers who have helped turn open-source software into a booming field. The highest-profile, open-source project is the free operating system Linux. Yet there are dozens of other projects to develop open-source versions of almost any software companies pay money for.

The projects, whether organized by a company or by a nonprofit, are typically supported by an army of volunteers. Altogether, tens of thousands of programmers work together on open-source software, typically sharing their code with one another over the Net.

Their success has had a far-reaching impact on the tech industry. Linux has spread to more than 25% of the world's servers and has become a legitimate rival to Microsoft Corp.'s Windows. The open-source approach is compelling enough that IBM and Sun Microsystems Inc. have become major supporters, utterly changing how they market software. There's even talk of taking the open-source method into semiconductors and tech hardware.

Yet in recent weeks the open-source community has been thrown into tumult. Software giant Oracle Corp. has acquired two small open-source companies and is in negotiations to buy at least one more. Many experts believe this is the beginning of a broader trend in which established tech companies scoop up promising open-source startups. While the validation is thrilling for Galstad and others in the community, it's also unsettling. Many young idealists who set out to create an alternative to the tech Establishment now find themselves becoming part of it. "When your main goal is to turn a profit, you start to lose some of the things that made open-source projects thrive," Galstad says.

The fear is that a round of buyouts could undermine the ethos of open source. Many coders volunteer their time, spending nights and weekends testing bugs and writing patches because they see themselves as part of an important, grassroots movement. Will that motivation remain if they're just helping to fill the coffers of Oracle or other tech giants?

Oracle, which has quickly become the most aggressive acquirer in the field, is undeterred. After striking deals for database companies Innobase Oy and Sleepycat Software, it's in talks to purchase JBoss, an open-source company that makes so-called middleware, for as much as $500 million. Sources close to Oracle say this is only the beginning of an open-source shopping spree. These companies, though they typically charge little or nothing up front for their software, bring in predictable and profitable subscription fees. "We are moving aggressively into open source," said Chief Executive Lawrence J. Ellison at a Feb. 8 investor conference. "We are not going to fight this trend."

Feeling the Tug

For decades, the only people who cared about open source were the geeks who stayed up for all hours swilling Jolt Cola and writing code. But the movement has gone mainstream in recent years. IBM has been one of its biggest champions, pushing Linux and hiring some of its best engineers. The company has more than 900 software engineers working on open-source projects. Venture capitalists have rushed into the field, too, pouring millions into scores of startups.

The outside money has led to the creation of two parallel open-source worlds. On one side are the traditionalists who have been around longer and typically don't have outside investors. They tap into the worldwide community of coders to polish their software. Then there are the newcomers who took venture money to set up shop in the booming field. They don't engage much with the network of open-source coders, doing most development themselves. For them, open-source is less about community and more about marketing. As traditionalists are offered venture money, many are being pulled into the second group.

Galstad is one of the people feeling the tug. He says he has received dozens of unsolicited calls from venture capitalists interested in taking a stake in Nagios. But he isn't tempted. He figures that if he takes venture money he'll have to start looking for a way to cash the investors out, probably through a sale. That could drive him into the hands of a big software company, where he may not be able to pursue the projects he wants. "Once you incorporate, you get shareholders who want to see their investment turn a profit, and all of a sudden the goals and ideals of the project are going to change," he says.

He's in good company. Many open-source projects, such as Linux and the popular Firefox Web browser, are supported by non-profit foundations that can't be sold. In addition, some of the most successful open-source companies are resisting outside capital, including Digium Inc., which makes low-cost telephone systems for small companies. Mark Spencer, Digium's 28-year-old CEO, has warned several peers about cashing out. "If you give up control of the company, either through percentage ownership or by giving up control on the board, you are effectively selling your company, not taking an investment," he says.

But others see outside cash as a huge help in getting their software into the hands of people who want to use it. Consider Teodor Danciu. Three years ago the Romanian coder wrote JasperReports, a business analytics program that several hundred thousand companies have downloaded. He was updating it on nights and weekends when its popularity became too much for him to handle. So he sold to a Silicon Valley startup, which renamed itself JasperSoft Corp. and hired him as part of the deal. He says it was the perfect opportunity for him to do what he loves: working on the code full-time while making money. Meanwhile, the business arm can invest more resources in support and training than he could on his own.

Day Jobs

Coders such as Danciu have a powerful role model in Linus Torvalds, the Finnish programmer who wrote Linux in 1991. Torvalds strikes a balance between community and cash. He focuses on managing the Linux code while leaving the business aspects to companies such as Red Hat and Novell and the nonprofit Open Source Development Labs (OSDL), which organizes advocacy groups around the operating system. He and his followers haven't resisted commercialization. Torvalds draws a salary from OSDL, and many of his Linux contributors have day jobs at companies such as IBM and Oracle. Andrew Morton, Torvalds' top lieutenant, says such efforts have helped make the code stronger.

A big reason people such as Morton and Torvalds are sanguine is their belief that while open-source companies may be for sale, open-source communities aren't. If contributors feel that Ellison & Co. are taking the software in the wrong direction, they can balk and start up a new project, taking along any of the open code they want. That would hurt Oracle's open-source credibility and leave it with little to show for the millions it has spent. "If Larry thinks he can have his way in the open-source community, he's going to find he can't get any developers to work [with him]," says Bruce Perens, a key figure in the open-source movement.

Questions

1. What are the sources of motivation for open-source programmers?

2. Why is Galstad reluctant to have venture capitalists invest in Nagios?

3. What are the sources of motivation for Teodur Danciu?

4. How has Linus Torvalds sustained his motivation since writing Linux in 1991?

Source: S. Lacy, "Open Season on Open Source?" Reprinted from the March 13, 2006, issue of *BusinessWeek* by special permission. Copyright © 2006 by the McGraw-Hill Companies.

CHAPTER 14

Leadership

Learning Objectives

After studying this chapter, you should be able to:

- Explain what leadership is, when leaders are effective and ineffective, and the sources of power that enable managers to be effective leaders.

- Identify the traits that show the strongest relationship to leadership, the behaviors leaders engage in, and the limitations of the trait and behavior models of leadership.

- Explain how contingency models of leadership enhance our understanding of effective leadership and management in organizations.

- Describe what transformational leadership is, and explain how managers can engage in it.

- Characterize the relationship between gender and leadership.

A Manager's Challenge

Judy McGrath and MTV Networks

How can a manager continuously transform a hip company in a rapidly changing environment?

As chairperson and CEO of MTV Networks, Judy McGrath has one of the most challenging and encompassing leadership positions in the media industry.[1] MTV Networks, a unit of Viacom, is home to the original MTV as well as Nickelodeon, VH1, Comedy Central, LOGO, MTV2, Nick at Nite, NOGGIN, TV Land, CMT, mtvU, the N, and Spike TV.[2] MTV Networks is accessed by more than 440 million households in over 165 viewing territories. Operating in an industry and markets whose rate of change is parallel to none, keeping MTV Networks hip and maintaining its appeal in an ever-changing digital landscape is a daunting task.[3]

McGrath certainly seems up to the challenge; in 2006, she received the Vanguard Award for Distinguished Leadership, and she was ranked 10th in *Fortune* magazine's list of the most powerful women in business in 2005.[4] Interestingly enough, McGrath, who

was born in Scranton, Pennsylvania, first came to New York City in the late 1970s with hopes of combining her love of rock music with her

MTV Chairman and CEO Judy McGrath

college degree in English literature to write for *Rolling Stone* magazine. Instead, McGrath started writing for *Mademoiselle* magazine and later for *Glamour*. In 1981, friends told her about the newly launched MTV, and she took a job there writing promotional pieces. And the rest has been history. With MTV from its earliest days, McGrath is now in the top post.[5]

McGrath is far from what comes to some people's minds when they think of a traditional CEO. Widely read, she is very attuned to pop culture, is nurturing of employees and talent alike, and is a creative leader who encourages the same in others; she has been credited with creating a very inclusive culture at MTV, where all employees are listened to and heard. She is down to earth, as comfortable planning strategies with top managers as she is interacting with hip-hoppers or seeing live indie music acts. McGrath's confidence and high energy are matched by her knowledge of the industry, creativity, and integrity.[6]

Her personal leadership style emphasizes empowering all members of the MTV organization as well as its viewers. According to McGrath, creativity and innovation stem from employees at all ranks, leaders and managers should listen to employees' ideas, and change must be the rule of the day in a dynamic environment.[7] She has also strived to empower the MTV viewing audience and raise viewers' awareness about important social concerns with award-winning programming such as the *Fight For Your Rights* series (e.g., "Take a Stand Against Violence," "Protect Yourself" (an AIDS awareness initiative), and "Take a Stand Against Discrimination").[8]

McGrath networks with wide-ranging contacts on a daily basis, keeping up with the latest developments in the industry and pop culture and always on the lookout for new ideas and opportunities. She is visionary and can see possibilities and opportunities where others might see just risks or potential downsides. She works hard, perseveres, and believes that anything is possible. Under her leadership, MTV has launched scores of successful new programs, all of which were risky and could have failed. As she puts it, "Falling flat on your face is a great motivator. The smartest thing we can do when confronted by something truly creative is to get out of the way."[9] That is what McGrath did when two producers came to her with the idea of filming people going through their day-to-day lives (with a soundtrack, of course, of new music);

so started reality TV and MTV's *The Real World* series, which is in its 17th season.

McGrath faces new challenges as she leads MTV forward. MTV's programming is now part of the media Establishment, and in an era of broadband, iPods, and online everything, she realizes that MTV cannot rest on its laurels: It must continually transform itself to maintain its hip and edgy focus and continue to appeal to its audience. Thus, McGrath is pushing MTV to deliver services from multiple digital platforms ranging from cell phones to new broadband channels to video games.[10]

In order to spearhead this digital transformation, McGrath is expanding from MTV's tradition of developing its own offerings to seeking partnerships and acquisitions. For example, MTV Networks has partnered with Microsoft Corp. to offer a new digital music download service called URGE.[11] MTV has recently purchased Web sites such as IFILM Corp., which is devoted to amateur short movies, and Neopets (popular with the younger set). McGrath is seeking synergies between digital acquisitions such as these and MTV's existing lineup. For example, IFILM debuted a show on VH1, and Nickelodeon is developing products for Neopets.[12]

To help transform MTV into a digital company, McGrath recently hired media consultant Michael Wolf to be MTV's president and chief operating officer and also created the position of chief digital officer. Wolf and McGrath are focusing on how to increase MTV's digital revenues over the next few years from around $150 million per year to over $500 million and how to use online platforms to deliver MTV's massive video offerings. They are also exploring all sorts of deals with advertisers, mobile phone companies, and consumer products companies.[13]

Clearly, challenging times lie ahead for McGrath as she seeks to transform MTV in the digital era. Her vision and decisiveness, combined with her style of empowering employees, encouraging risk taking and creativity, and making sure that all enjoy the ride suggest that MTV is in good hands.[14]

Overview

Judy McGrath exemplifies the many facets of effective leadership. In Chapter 1 we explained that one of the four primary tasks of managers is leading. Thus, it should come as no surprise that leadership is a key ingredient in effective management. When leaders are effective, their subordinates or followers are highly motivated, committed, and high-performing. When leaders are ineffective, chances are good that their subordinates do not perform up to their capabilities, are demotivated, and may be dissatisfied as well. CEO Judy McGrath is a leader at the very top of an organization, but leadership is an important ingredient for managerial success at all levels of organizations: top management, middle management, and first-line management. Moreover, leadership is a key ingredient for managerial success for organizations large and small.

In this chapter we describe what leadership is and examine the major leadership models that shed light on the factors that contribute to a manager's being an effective leader. We look at trait and behavior models, which focus on what leaders are like and what they do, and contingency models—Fiedler's contingency model, path-goal theory, and the leader substitutes model—each of which takes into account the complexity surrounding leadership and the role of the situation in leader effectiveness. We also describe how managers can use transformational leadership to dramatically affect their organizations. By the end of this chapter, you will have a good appreciation of the many factors and issues that managers face in their quest to be effective leaders.

The Nature of Leadership

leadership The process by which an individual exerts influence over other people and inspires, motivates, and directs their activities to help achieve group or organizational goals.

leader An individual who is able to exert influence over other people to help achieve group or organizational goals.

Leadership is the process by which a person exerts influence over other people and inspires, motivates, and directs their activities to help achieve group or organizational goals.[15] The person who exerts such influence is a **leader.** When leaders are effective, the influence they exert over others helps a group or organization achieve its performance goals. When leaders are ineffective, their influence does not contribute to, and often detracts from, goal attainment. As "A Manager's Challenge" makes clear, Judy McGrath is taking multiple steps to inspire and motivate MTV's employees so that they help MTV achieve its goals.

Beyond facilitating the attainment of performance goals, effective leadership increases an organization's ability to meet all the contemporary challenges discussed throughout this book, including the need to obtain a competitive advantage, the need to foster ethical behavior, and the need to manage a diverse workforce fairly and equitably. Leaders who exert influence over organizational members to help meet these goals increase their organizations' chances of success.

In considering the nature of leadership, we first look at leadership styles and how they affect managerial tasks and at the influence of culture on leadership styles. We then focus on the key to leadership, *power*, which can come from a variety of sources. Finally, we consider the contemporary dynamic of empowerment and how it relates to effective leadership.

Personal Leadership Style and Managerial Tasks

A manager's *personal leadership style*—that is, the specific ways in which a manager chooses to influence other people—shapes the way that manager approaches planning, organizing, and controlling (the other principal tasks of managing). Consider Judy McGrath's personal leadership style in "A Manager's

Keith Chong hangs up a freshly pressed shirt at his dry-cleaning business in Glendale, California. As owner and manager of a dry-cleaning business, Chong takes a hands-on approach to leadership.

Challenge": She is down to earth, nurturing of employees and talent, and at the same time decisive and visionary. She empowers employees, encourages them to be creative and take risks, and fosters an inclusive culture at MTV Networks.[16]

Managers at all levels and in all kinds of organizations have their own personal leadership styles that determine not only how they lead their subordinates but also how they perform the other management tasks. Michael Kraus, owner and manager of a dry-cleaning store in the northeastern United States, for example, takes a hands-on approach to leadership. He has the sole authority for determining work schedules and job assignments for the 15 employees in his store (an organizing task), makes all important decisions by himself (a planning task), and closely monitors his employees' performance and rewards top performers with pay increases (a control task). Kraus's personal leadership style is effective in his organization. His employees are generally motivated, perform highly, and are satisfied, and his store is highly profitable.

Developing an effective personal leadership style often is a challenge for managers at all levels in an organization. This challenge is often exacerbated when times are tough, due, for example, to an economic downturn or a decline in customer demand. The dot-com bust and the slowing economy in the early 2000s provided many leaders with just such a challenge.

While leading is one of the four principal tasks of managing, a distinction is often made between managers and leaders. When this distinction is made, managers are thought of as those organizational members who establish and implement procedures and processes to ensure smooth functioning and who are accountable for goal accomplishment.[17] Leaders look to the future, chart the course for the organization, and attract, retain, motivate, inspire, and develop relationships with employees based on trust and mutual respect.[18] Leaders provide meaning and purpose, seek innovation rather than stability, and impassion employees to work together to achieve the leaders' vision.[19]

The personal leadership style of founders often has an enduring effect on organizations, as indicated in the following "Ethics in Action."

Ethics in Action

John Mackey's Personal Leadership Style

John Mackey, cofounder and CEO of the Whole Foods Market, has grown Whole Foods from a single 10,000-square-foot store in Austin, Texas, into a thriving organization with over 180 stores and 39,000 employees (see "A Manager's Challenge" in Chapter 4). Whole Foods is ranked 479th on the *Fortune* 500 list of the biggest companies in America (by sales).[20] Whole Foods started out to promote healthy eating, and in its early days, the stores were dominated by nuts, grains, and fresh produce. The stores today stock all sorts of food products as long as they are healthy; Whole Food does not carry food containing trans fats, artificial colors or flavors, or chemical preservatives or made from animals that are not treated humanely.[21]

Mackey is casual and informal but also opinionated, blunt, and direct.[22] He combines good business sense and an eye for the bottom line with spirituality and ethical values. Whole Foods markets tend to have profit margins and prices that are higher than those of typical grocery stores; Mackey is a firm believer in the merits of capitalism and making money. On the spiritual side, he has indicated that "love is the only reality. Everything else is merely a dream or illusion."[23]

Mackey's opinionated and direct nature carries over into the ethical values he promotes at Whole Foods. While acknowledging that Whole Foods has multiple stakeholders, he maintains that the interests of customers and employees come before the interest of shareholders and that the local community and the natural environment are important stakeholders for Whole Foods. While Mackey is against labor unions, he is employee-focused and strives to treat employees well and make sure they are satisfied with their jobs (employees are called "team members").[24] Mackey does not believe in huge pay differentials between top managers and rank-and-file team members; at Whole Foods, no salary can be set higher than 14 times that of the average team member, and 94% of the stock options that Whole Foods gives to its team members are granted to nonexecutives. In 2006, Whole Foods was ranked 15th in *Fortune*'s "100 Best Companies to Work For".[25] Five percent of Whole Foods' profits each year are donated to charity, and Whole Foods pays its team members for performing community service.[26]

Whole Foods' mission, the company's Declaration of Interdependence, was formulated in 1985 by Mackey and around 60 team members during a series of weekend retreats and was revised once in the 1980s and twice in the 1990s.[27] The declaration emphasizes interdependence among multiple stakeholders—including customers, team members, shareholders, communities, the natural environment, and business partners—in helping Whole Foods live up to its motto, "Whole Foods, Whole People, Whole Planet."[28] Prominent themes in the declaration are high quality; customer satisfaction; frequent, open, and honest communication; team-member happiness and fulfillment; the embracing of diversity; community involvement; and active support of environmental sustainability. The Declaration of Interdependence, or parts of it, not only is espoused by team members but is visible in Whole Foods stores on posters and in free pamphlets. Even so, Whole Foods acknowledges that things might not always be just as they should be at the company and that working and living by the declaration's principles is a work in progress.[29] What is never in question is Mackey's passion to pursue what he believes in. In 2005, Whole Foods started two foundations, The Animal Compassion Foundation to help ranchers and meat producers treat animals humanely, and the Whole Planet Foundation, which provides microloans to women in poor, developing countries to start their own businesses.[30]

Leadership Styles Across Cultures

Some evidence suggests that leadership styles vary not only among individuals but also among countries or cultures. Some research indicates that European managers tend to be more humanistic or people-oriented than both Japanese and American managers. The collectivistic culture in Japan places prime emphasis on the group rather than the individual, so the importance of individuals' own personalities, needs, and desires is minimized. Organizations in the United States tend to be very profit-oriented and thus tend to downplay the importance of individual employees' needs and desires. Many countries in Europe have a more individualistic perspective than Japan and a more humanistic perspective than the United States, and this may result in some European managers' being more people-oriented than their Japanese or American counterparts. European managers, for example, tend to be reluctant to lay off employees, and when a layoff is absolutely necessary, they take careful steps to make it as painless as possible.[31]

Another cross-cultural difference occurs in time horizons. While managers in any one country often differ in their time horizons, there are also national differences. For example, U.S. organizations tend to have a short-run profit orientation, and thus U.S. managers' personal leadership styles emphasize short-run performance. Japanese organizations tend to have a long-run growth orientation, so Japanese managers' personal leadership styles emphasize long-run performance. Justus Mische, a personnel manager at the European organization Hoechst, suggests that "Europe, at least the big international firms in Europe, have a philosophy between the Japanese, long term, and the United States, short term."[32] Research on these and other global aspects of leadership is in its infancy; as it continues, more cultural differences in managers' personal leadership styles may be discovered.

Power: The Key to Leadership

No matter what one's leadership style, a key component of effective leadership is found in the *power* the leader has to affect other people's behavior and get them to act in certain ways.[33] There are several types of power: legitimate, reward, coercive, expert, and referent power (see Figure 14.1).[34] Effective leaders take steps to ensure that they have sufficient levels of each type and that they use the power they have in beneficial ways.

legitimate power The authority that a manager has by virtue of his or her position in an organization's hierarchy.

LEGITIMATE POWER Legitimate power is the authority a manager has by virtue of his or her position in an organization's hierarchy. Personal leadership style often influences how a manager exercises legitimate power. Take the case of Carol Loray, who is a first-line manager in a greeting card company and leads a group of 15 artists and designers. Loray has the legitimate power to hire new employees, assign projects to the artists and designers, monitor their work, and appraise their performance. She uses this power effectively. She always makes sure that her project assignments match the interests of her subordinates as much as possible so that they will enjoy their work. She monitors their work to make sure they are on track but does not engage in close supervision, which can hamper creativity. She makes sure her performance appraisals are developmental, providing concrete advice for areas where improvements could be made. Recently, Loray negotiated with her manager to increase her legitimate power so that now she can initiate and develop proposals for new card lines.

reward power The ability of a manager to give or withhold tangible and intangible rewards.

REWARD POWER Reward power is the ability of a manager to give or withhold tangible rewards (pay raises, bonuses, choice job assignments) and

Figure 14.1
Source of Managerial Power

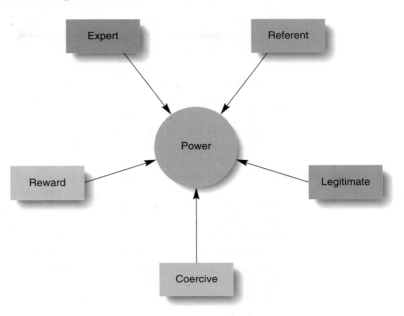

intangible rewards (verbal praise, a pat on the back, respect). As you learned in Chapter 12, members of an organization are motivated to perform at a high level by a variety of rewards. Being able to give or withhold rewards based on performance is a major source of power that allows managers to have a highly motivated workforce. Managers of salespeople in retail organizations like Neiman Marcus and Dillard's Department Stores, in car dealerships like Daimler-Chrysler and Ford, and in travel agencies like Liberty Travel and the Travel Company often use their reward power to motivate their subordinates. Subordinates in organizations such as these often receive commissions on whatever they sell and rewards for the quality of their customer service, which motivate them to do the best they can.

Effective managers use their reward power in such a way that subordinates feel that their rewards signal that they are doing a good job and their efforts are appreciated. Ineffective managers use rewards in a more controlling manner (wielding the "stick" instead of offering the "carrot") that signals to subordinates that the manager has the upper hand. Managers also can take steps to increase their reward power. Carol Loray had the legitimate power to appraise her subordinates' performance, but she lacked the reward power to distribute raises and end-of-year bonuses until she discussed with her own manager why this would be a valuable motivational tool for her to use. Loray now receives a pool of money each year for salary increases and bonuses and has the reward power to distribute them as she sees fit.

coercive power The ability of a manager to punish others.

COERCIVE POWER   Coercive power is the ability of a manager to punish others. Punishment can range from verbal reprimands to reductions in pay or working hours to actual dismissal. In the previous chapter, we discussed how punishment can have negative side effects such as resentment and retaliation and should be used only when necessary (for example, to curtail a dangerous behavior). Managers who rely heavily on coercive power tend to be ineffective as leaders and sometimes even get fired themselves. William J. Fife is one example; he was fired from his position as CEO of Giddings and Lewis Inc., a manufacturer of factory equipment, because of his overreliance on coercive power. In meetings, Fife often verbally criticized, attacked, and embarrassed top managers. Realizing how destructive Fife's use of punishment was for them and the company, these managers complained to the board of directors, who, after a careful consideration of the issues, asked Fife to resign.[35]

Excessive use of coercive power seldom produces high performance and is questionable ethically. Sometimes it amounts to a form of mental abuse, robbing workers of their dignity and causing excessive levels of stress. Overuse of coercive power can even result in dangerous working conditions. Better results and, importantly, an ethical workplace that respects employee dignity can be obtained by using reward power.

expert power Power that is based on the special knowledge, skills, and expertise that a leader possesses.

EXPERT POWER   Expert power is based on the special knowledge, skills, and expertise that a leader possesses. The nature of expert power varies, depending on the leader's level in the hierarchy. First-level and middle managers often have technical expertise relevant to the tasks that their subordinates perform. Their expert power gives them considerable influence over subordinates. Carol Loray has expert power: She is an artist herself and has drawn and designed some of her company's top-selling greeting cards. Judy McGrath, in "A Manager's Challenge," has expert power from over 25 years' experience in the media industry, as well as from her efforts to stay attuned to pop culture through extensive networking, reading, and ever-ready openness for the new and the quirky. As indicated in the following "Manager as a Person," the kinds of positions that leaders with expert power assume depends upon who they are as individuals and the kinds of challenges that appeal to them.

Manager as
a Person

Liane Pelletier Uses Her Expert Power in Alaska

Liane Pelletier was a senior vice president at Sprint when a recruiting firm called her to see if she was interested in becoming CEO of Alaska Communications Systems (ACS).[36] With over 15 years' experience in the telecommunications industry, she definitely had the skills, knowledge, and expertise to head ACS. Like many top managers, Connecticut-born Pelletier hesitated about making a move to Alaska—but she didn't hesitate for long.[37]

Pelletier loves adventure and new experiences; the opportunity to leverage her industry experience and take on the challenge of transforming ACS made her decision an easy one. For Pelletier, Alaska was not such a far-flung place to move to: She had traveled widely, on excursions ranging from hiking the Appalachian Trail to boating down the Amazon

Liane Pelletier loves adventure, whether it's snowshoeing in Alaska or transforming the state's telecommunication systems.

River. And now snowshoeing in Alaska is one of her new leisure activities.[38]

ACS is Alaska's largest local exchange carrier and the only in-state provider with its own local, long distance, wireless, and Internet infrastructure. As an experienced top manager in telecommunications, Pelletier sees her role at ACS as an exciting opportunity.[39] When she came to ACS, she realized that the company was focused on products rather than customers: Different divisions would provide different kinds of services to customers without taking into account that the same customers might be using other services provided by other parts of the company. Pelletier restructured ACS around customers and how to better meet their needs through the multiple products and services ACS offers. Now, sales and service at ACS are integrated across product lines, and employees receive training so that they are knowledgeable about all of ACS's products and services.[40] Pelletier's vision for ACS revolves around customer-focused growth and improved wireless services. Already her efforts have paid off for the company in terms of increases in ACS's earnings and stock price.[41] Clearly, ACS is fortunate that Pelletier assumed the top post and is applying her expertise to enable the company to better serve its customers and expand its range of products.[42]

Some top managers derive expert power from their technical expertise. Craig Barret, chairman of the board of directors of Intel, has a PhD in materials science from Stanford University and is very knowledgeable about the ins and outs of Intel's business—producing semiconductors and microprocessors.[43] Similarly, Bill Gates, chairman of Microsoft, and CEO Steve Ballmer have expertise in software design; and Tachi Yamada, executive director and chairman of research and development at GlaxoSmithKline (profiled in "Ethics in Action" in Chapter 7), has an MD and was an active researcher and chairman of the Internal Medicine Department of the University of Michigan Medical School. Many top-level managers, however, lack technical expertise and derive their expert power from their abilities as decision makers, planners, and strategists. Jack Welch, the former, well-known leader and CEO of General Electric, summed it up this way: "The basic thing that we at the top of the company know is that we don't know the business. What we have, I hope, is the ability to allocate resources, people, and dollars."[44]

Effective leaders take steps to ensure that they have an adequate amount of expert power to perform their leadership roles. They may obtain additional training or education in their fields, make sure they keep up to date with the latest developments and changes in technology, stay abreast of changes in their fields through involvement in professional associations, and read widely to be aware of momentous changes in the organization's task and general environments. Expert power tends to be best used in a guiding or coaching manner rather than in an arrogant, high-handed manner.

referent power Power that comes from subordinates' and coworkers' respect, admiration, and loyalty.

REFERENT POWER Referent power is more informal than the other kinds of power. Referent power is a function of the personal characteristics of a leader; it is the power that comes from subordinates' and co-workers' respect, admiration, and loyalty. Leaders who are likable and whom subordinates wish to use as a role model are especially likely to possess referent power, as is true of Judy McGrath in "A Manager's Challenge."

In addition to being a valuable asset for top managers like McGrath, referent power can help first-line and middle managers be effective leaders as well. Sally Carruthers, for example, is the first-level manager of a group of secretaries in the finance department of a large state university. Carruthers's secretaries are known to be among the best in the university. Much of their willingness to go above and beyond the call of duty has been attributed to Carruthers's warm and caring nature, which makes each of them feel important and valued. Managers can take steps to increase their referent power, such as taking time to get to know their subordinates and showing interest in and concern for them.

Empowerment: An Ingredient in Modern Management

empowerment Expanding employees' tasks and responsibilities.

More and more managers today are incorporating into their personal leadership styles an aspect that at first glance seems to be the opposite of being a leader. In Chapter 1, we described how empowerment—the process of giving employees at all levels the authority to make decisions, be responsible for their outcomes, improve quality, and cut costs—is becoming increasingly popular in organizations. When leaders empower their subordinates, the subordinates typically take over some of the responsibilities and authority that used to reside with the leader or manager, such as the right to reject parts that do not meet quality standards, the right to check one's own work, and the right to schedule work activities. Empowered subordinates are given the power to make some of the decisions that their leaders or supervisors used to make.

Empowerment might seem to be the opposite of effective leadership because managers are allowing subordinates to take a more active role in leading themselves. In actuality, however, empowerment can contribute to effective leadership for several reasons:

- Empowerment increases a manager's ability to get things done because the manager has the support and help of subordinates who may have special knowledge of work tasks.

- Empowerment often increases workers' involvement, motivation, and commitment, and this helps ensure that they are working toward organizational goals.

- Empowerment gives managers more time to concentrate on their pressing concerns because they spend less time on day-to-day supervisory activities.

Effective managers like Judy McGrath realize the benefits of empowerment. The personal leadership style of managers who empower subordinates often entails developing subordinates' ability to make good decisions as well as being their guide, coach, and source of inspiration. Empowerment is a popular trend in the United States at companies as diverse as United Parcel Service (a package delivery company) and Coram Healthcare Corporation (a provider of medical equipment and services). Empowerment is also taking off around the world.[45]

For instance, companies in South Korea (such as Samsung, Hyundai, and Daewoo), in which decision making typically was centralized with the founding families, are now empowering managers at lower levels to make decisions.[46]

Trait and Behavior Models of Leadership

Leading is such an important process in all organizations–nonprofit organizations, government agencies, and schools, as well as for-profit corporations–that it has been researched for decades. Early approaches to leadership, called the *trait model* and the *behavior model*, sought to determine what effective leaders are like as people and what they do that makes them so effective.

The Trait Model

The trait model of leadership focused on identifying the personal characteristics that cause effective leadership. Researchers thought effective leaders must have certain personal qualities that set them apart from ineffective leaders and from people who never become leaders. Decades of research (beginning in the 1930s) and hundreds of studies indicate that certain personal characteristics do appear to be associated with effective leadership. (See Table 14.1 for a list of these.)[47] Notice that although this model is called the "trait" model, some of the personal characteristics that it identifies are not personality traits per se but, rather, are concerned with a leader's skills, abilities, knowledge, and expertise. As "A Manager's Challenge" shows, Judy McGrath certainly appears to possess many of these characteristics (such as intelligence, knowledge and expertise, self-confidence, high energy, and integrity and honesty). Leaders who do not possess these traits may be ineffective.

Traits alone are not the key to understanding leader effectiveness, however. Some effective leaders do not possess all of these traits, and some leaders who do possess them are not effective in their leadership roles. This lack of a consistent relationship between leader traits and leader effectiveness led researchers to

Table 14.1
Traits and Personal Characteristics Related to Effective Leadership

Trait	Description
Intelligence	Helps managers understand complex issues and solve problems
Knowledge and expertise	Helps managers make good decisions and discover ways to increase efficiency and effectiveness
Dominance	Helps managers influence their subordinates to achieve organizational goals
Self-confidence	Contributes to managers' effectively influencing subordinates and persisting when faced with obstacles or difficulties
High energy	Helps managers deal with the many demands they face
Tolerance for stress	Helps managers deal with uncertainty and make difficult decisions
Integrity and honesty	Helps managers behave ethically and earn their subordinates' trust and confidence
Maturity	Helps managers avoid acting selfishly, control their feelings, and admit when they have made a mistake

shift their attention away from traits and to search for new explanations for effective leadership. Rather than focusing on what leaders are like (the traits they possess), researchers began looking at what effective leaders actually do—in other words, at the behaviors that allow effective leaders to influence their subordinates to achieve group and organizational goals.

The Behavior Model

After extensive study in the 1940s and 1950s, researchers at Ohio State University identified two basic kinds of leader behaviors that many leaders in the United States, Germany, and other countries engaged in to influence their subordinates: *consideration* and *initiating structure*.[48]

consideration

Behavior indicating that a manager trusts, respects, and cares about subordinates.

CONSIDERATION   Leaders engage in **consideration** when they show their subordinates that they trust, respect, and care about them. Managers who truly look out for the well-being of their subordinates and do what they can to help subordinates feel good and enjoy their work perform consideration behaviors. In "A Manager's Challenge," Judy McGrath engages in consideration when she listens to employees and fosters an inclusive, nurturing culture at MTV Networks.

At Costco Wholesale Corporation, CEO Jim Senegal believes that consideration not only is an ethical imperative but also makes good business sense,[49] as indicated in the following "Ethics in Action."

Consideration at Costco

Ethics in Action

Managers at Costco, including CEO Jim Senegal, believe that consideration is so important that one of the principles in Costco's Code of Ethics is "Take Care of Our Employees."[50] Costco Wholesale Corporation is the fifth-largest retailer, and the top warehouse retailer, in the United States.[51] Wages at Costco are an average of $17 per hour, over 40% higher than the average hourly wage at Wal-Mart, Costco's major competitor.[52] Costco pays the majority of health insurance costs for its employees (employees pay around 8% of health insurance costs compared to an industry average of around 25%), and part-time employees receive health insurance after they have been with the company six months. Overall, about 85% of Costco employees are covered by health insurance at any point in time, compared with less than 45% of employees at Target and Wal-Mart.[53]

Jim Senegal believes that caring about the well-being of his employees is a win-win proposition as Costco's employees are satisfied, committed, loyal, and motivated. Additionally, turnover and employee theft rates at Costco are much lower than industry averages.[54] In the retail industry, turnover tends to be very high and costly since for every employee who quits, a new hire needs to be recruited, tested, interviewed, and trained. Even though pay and benefits are higher at Costco than at rival Wal-Mart, Costco actually has lower labor costs as a percentage of sales and higher sales per square foot of store space than Wal-Mart.[55]

Additionally, treating employees well helps build customer loyalty at Costco. Surely, customers enjoy the bargains and low prices that come from

Loyal Costco customers like these know that their bargains don't come at the expense of employees' paychecks and benefits.

shopping in a warehouse store, the relatively high quality of the goods Costco stocks, and Costco's policy of not marking up prices by more than 14% or 15% (relatively low markups for retail) even if the goods would sell with higher markups. However, customers are also very loyal to Costco because they know that the company treats its employees so well and that their bargains are not coming at the expense of employees' paychecks and benefits.[56]

Costco started out as a single warehouse store in Seattle, Washington, in 1983. Now, the company has 457 stores (including stores in South Korea, Taiwan, Japan, Canada, and Britain) and over 44 million members who pay $45 per year to shop at Costco stores.[57] Costco's growth and financial performance are enviable. For example, for the first half of fiscal 2006, net sales were $26.45 billion (11% higher than in the same period in fiscal 2005) and earnings were $512 million. Clearly, consideration has paid off for Costco and for its employees.[58]

initiating structure

Behavior that managers engage in to ensure that work gets done, subordinates perform their jobs acceptably, and the organization is efficient and effective.

INITIATING STRUCTURE Leaders engage in **initiating structure** when they take steps to make sure that work gets done, subordinates perform their jobs acceptably, and the organization is efficient and effective. Assigning tasks to individuals or work groups, letting subordinates know what is expected of them, deciding how work should be done, making schedules, encouraging adherence to rules and regulations, and motivating subordinates to do a good job are all examples of initiating structure.[59] Michael Teckel, the manager of an upscale store selling imported men's and women's shoes in a midwestern city, engages in initiating structure when he establishes weekly work, lunch, and break schedules to ensure that the store has enough salespeople on the floor. Teckle also initiates structure when he discusses the latest shoe designs with his subordinates so that they are knowledgeable with customers, when he encourages adherence to the store's refund and exchange policies, and when he encourages his staff to provide high-quality customer service and to avoid a hard-sell approach. In "A Manager's Challenge," Judy McGrath engaged in initiating structure when she hired Michael Wolf to be MTV's president and chief operating officer and created the new position of chief digital officer.

Initiating structure and consideration are independent leader behaviors. Leaders can be high on both, low on both, or high on one and low on the other. Many effective leaders like Meg Whitman of eBay engage in both of these behaviors.

Leadership researchers have identified leader behaviors similar to consideration and initiating structure. Researchers at the University of Michigan, for example, identified two categories of leadership behaviors, *employee-centered behaviors* and *job-oriented behaviors*, that correspond roughly to consideration and initiating structure, respectively.[60] Models of leadership popular with consultants also tend to zero in on these two kinds of behaviors. For example, Robert

Blake and Jane Mouton's Managerial Grid focuses on *concern for people* (similar to consideration) and *concern for production* (similar to initiating structure). Blake and Mouton advise that effective leadership often requires both a high level of concern for people and a high level of concern for production.[61] As another example, Paul Hersey and Kenneth Blanchard's model focuses on *supportive behaviors* (similar to consideration) and *task-oriented behaviors* (similar to initiating structure). According to Hersey and Blanchard, leaders need to consider the nature of their subordinates when trying to determine the extent to which they should perform these two behaviors.[62]

You might expect that effective leaders and managers would perform both kinds of behaviors, but research has found that this is not necessarily the case. The relationship between performance of consideration and initiating-structure behaviors and leader effectiveness is not clear-cut. Some leaders are effective even when they do not perform consideration or initiating-structure behaviors, and some leaders are ineffective even when they do perform both kinds of behaviors. Like the trait model of leadership, the behavior model alone cannot explain leader effectiveness. Realizing this, researchers began building more complicated models of leadership, models focused not only on the leader and what he or she does but also on the situation or context in which leadership occurs.

Contingency Models of Leadership

Simply possessing certain traits or performing certain behaviors does not ensure that a manager will be an effective leader in all situations calling for leadership. Some managers who seem to possess the "right" traits and perform the "right" behaviors turn out to be ineffective leaders. Managers lead in a wide variety of situations and organizations and have various kinds of subordinates performing diverse tasks in a multiplicity of environmental contexts. Given the wide variety of situations in which leadership occurs, what makes a manager an effective leader in one situation (such as certain traits or behaviors) is not necessarily what that manager needs to be equally effective in a different situation. An effective army general might not be an effective university president; an effective manager of a restaurant might not be an effective manager of a clothing store; an effective coach of a football team might not be an effective manager of a fitness center; and an effective first-line manager in a manufacturing company might not be an effective middle manager. The traits or behaviors that may contribute to a manager's being an effective leader in one situation might actually result in the same manager being an ineffective leader in another situation.

Contingency models of leadership take into account the situation or context within which leadership occurs. According to contingency models, whether or not a manager is an effective leader is the result of the interplay between what the manager is like, what he or she does, and the situation in which leadership takes place. Contingency models propose that whether a leader who possesses certain traits or performs certain behaviors is effective depends on, or is contingent on, the situation or context. In this section, we discuss three prominent contingency models developed to shed light on what makes managers effective leaders: Fred Fiedler's contingency model, Robert House's path-goal theory, and the leader substitutes model. As you will see, these leadership models are complementary; each focuses on a somewhat different aspect of effective leadership in organizations.

Fiedler's Contingency Model

Fred E. Fiedler was among the first leadership researchers to acknowledge that effective leadership is contingent on, or depends on, the characteristics of the leader *and* of the situation. Fiedler's contingency model helps explain why a manager may be an effective leader in one situation and ineffective in another; it also suggests which kinds of managers are likely to be most effective in which situations.[63]

LEADER STYLE As with the trait approach, Fiedler hypothesized that personal characteristics can influence leader effectiveness. He used the term *leader style* to refer to a manager's characteristic approach to leadership and identified two basic leader styles: *relationship-oriented* and *task-oriented*. All managers can be described as having one style or the other.

relationship-oriented leaders Leaders whose primary concern is to develop good relationships with their subordinates and to be liked by them.

Relationship-oriented leaders are primarily concerned with developing good relationships with their subordinates and being liked by them. Relationship-oriented managers focus on having high-quality interpersonal relationships with subordinates. This does not mean, however, that the job does not get done when such leaders are at the helm. But it does mean that the quality of interpersonal relationships with subordinates is a prime concern for relationship-oriented leaders. Lawrence Fish, for example, is the chairman of Citizens Financial Group Inc. of Providence, Rhode Island, which has tripled its assets in the last three years. As the top manager who helped to engineer this rapid growth, Fish has never lost sight of the importance of good relationships and personally writes a thank-you note to at least one of his subordinates each day.[64]

task-oriented leaders Leaders whose primary concern is to ensure that subordinates perform at a high level.

Task-oriented leaders are primarily concerned with ensuring that subordinates perform at a high level and focus on task accomplishment. Some task-oriented leaders, like the top managers of the family-owned C. R. England Refrigerated Trucking Company based in Salt Lake City, Utah, go so far as to closely measure and evaluate performance on a weekly basis to ensure subordinates are performing as well as they can.[65]

In his research, Fiedler measured leader style by asking leaders to rate the co-worker with whom they have had the most difficulty working (called the *least-preferred coworker* or *LPC*) on a number of dimensions, such as whether the person is boring or interesting, gloomy or cheerful, enthusiastic or unenthusiastic, cooperative or uncooperative. Relationship-oriented leaders tend to describe the LPC in relatively positive terms; their concern for good relationships leads them to think well of others. Task-oriented leaders tend to describe the LPC in negative terms; their concern for task accomplishment causes them to think badly about others who make getting the job done difficult. Thus, relationship-oriented and task-oriented leaders are sometimes referred to as *high*-LPC and *low*-LPC leaders, respectively.

SITUATIONAL CHARACTERISTICS According to Fiedler, leadership style is an enduring characteristic; managers cannot change their style, nor can they adopt different styles in different kinds of situations. With this in mind,

Developing good relations with employees can make the "situation" more favorable for leading.

leader–member relations The extent to which followers like, trust, and are loyal to their leader; a determinant of how favorable a situation is for leading.

task structure The extent to which the work to be performed is clear-cut so that a leader's subordinates know what needs to be accomplished and how to go about doing it; a determinant of how favorable a situation is for leading.

position power The amount of legitimate, reward, and coercive power that a leader has by virtue of his or her position in an organization; a determinant of how favorable a situation is for leading.

Fiedler identified three situational characteristics that are important determinants of how favorable a situation is for leading: leader–member relations, task structure, and position power. When a situation is favorable for leading, it is relatively easy for a manager to influence subordinates so that they perform at a high level and contribute to organizational efficiency and effectiveness. In a situation unfavorable for leading, it is much more difficult for a manager to exert influence.

LEADER-MEMBER RELATIONS   The first situational characteristic that Fiedler described, leader–member relations, is the extent to which followers like, trust, and are loyal to their leader. Situations are more favorable for leading when leader–member relations are good.

TASK STRUCTURE   The second situational characteristic that Fiedler described, task structure, is the extent to which the work to be performed is clear-cut so that a leader's subordinates know what needs to be accomplished and how to go about doing it. When task structure is high, the situation is favorable for leading. When task structure is low, goals may be vague, subordinates may be unsure of what they should be doing or how they should do it, and the situation is unfavorable for leading.

Task structure was low for Geraldine Laybourne when she was a top manager at Nickelodeon, the children's television network. It was never precisely clear what would appeal to her young viewers, whose tastes can change dramatically, or how to motivate her subordinates to come up with creative and novel ideas.[66] In contrast, Herman Mashaba, founder and owner of Black Like Me, a hair care products company based in South Africa, seems to have relatively high task structure in his leadership situation. His company's goals are to produce and sell inexpensive hair care products to native Africans, and managers accomplish these goals by using simple yet appealing packaging and distributing the products through neighborhood beauty salons.[67]

POSITION POWER   The third situational characteristic that Fiedler described, position power, is the amount of legitimate, reward, and coercive power a leader has by virtue of his or her position in an organization. Leadership situations are more favorable for leading when position power is strong.

COMBINING LEADER STYLE AND THE SITUATION   By taking all possible combinations of good and poor leader–member relations, high and low task structure, and strong and weak position power, Fiedler identified eight leadership situations, which vary in their favorability for leading (see Figure 14.2). After extensive research, he determined that relationship-oriented leaders are most effective in moderately favorable situations (IV, V, VI, and VII in Figure 14.2) and task-oriented leaders are most effective in situations that are either very favorable (I, II, and III) or very unfavorable (VIII).

PUTTING THE CONTINGENCY MODEL INTO PRACTICE   Recall that, according to Fiedler, leader style is an enduring characteristic that managers cannot change. This suggests that to be effective, either managers need to be placed in leadership situations that fit their style or situations need to be

Figure 14.2
Fielder's Contingency Theory of Leadership

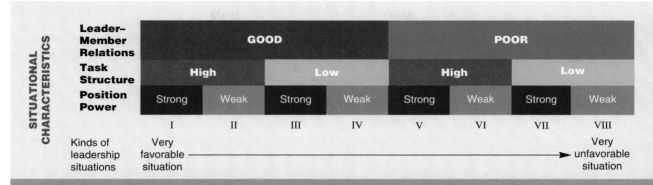

SITUATIONAL CHARACTERISTICS	Leader–Member Relations	GOOD				POOR			
	Task Structure	High		Low		High		Low	
	Position Power	Strong	Weak	Strong	Weak	Strong	Weak	Strong	Weak
		I	II	III	IV	V	VI	VII	VIII

Kinds of leadership situations   Very favorable situation ──────────────────────► Very unfavorable situation

Relationship-oriented leaders are most effective in moderately favorable situations for leading (IV, V, VI, VII).
Task-oriented leaders are most effective in very favorable situations (I, II, III) or very unfavorable situations (VIII) for leading.

changed to suit the managers. Situations can be changed, for example, by giving a manager more position power or taking steps to increase task structure, such as by clarifying goals.

Take the case of Mark Compton, a relationship-oriented leader employed by a small construction company, who was in a very unfavorable situation and having a rough time leading his construction crew. His subordinates did not trust him to look out for their well-being (poor leader–member relations); the construction jobs he supervised tended to be novel and complex (low task structure); and he had no control over the rewards and disciplinary actions his subordinates received (weak position power). Recognizing the need to improve matters, Compton's supervisor gave him the power to reward crew members with bonuses and overtime work as he saw fit and to discipline crew members for poor-quality work and unsafe on-the-job behavior. As his leadership situation improved to moderately favorable, so too did Compton's effectiveness as a leader and the performance of his crew.

Research studies tend to support some aspects of Fiedler's model but also suggest that, like most theories, it needs some modifications.[68] Some researchers have questioned what the LPC scale really measures. Others find fault with the model's premise that leaders cannot alter their styles. That is, it is likely that at least some leaders can diagnose the situation they are in and, when their style is inappropriate for the situation, modify their style so that it is more in line with what the leadership situation calls for.

House's Path-Goal Theory

path-goal theory A contingency model of leadership proposing that leaders can motivate subordinates by identifying their desired outcomes, rewarding them for high performance and the attainment of work goals with these desired outcomes, and clarifying for them the paths leading to the attainment of work goals.

In what he called **path-goal theory,** leadership researcher Robert House focused on what leaders can do to motivate their subordinates to achieve group and organizational goals.[69] The premise of path-goal theory is that effective leaders motivate subordinates to achieve goals by (1) clearly identifying the outcomes that subordinates are trying to obtain from the workplace, (2) rewarding subordinates with these outcomes for high performance and the attainment of work goals, and (3) clarifying for subordinates the *paths* leading to the attainment of work *goals*. Path-goal theory is a contingency model because it proposes that the steps managers should take to motivate subordinates depend on both the nature of the subordinates and the type of work they do.

Based on the expectancy theory of motivation (see Chapter 12), path-goal theory provides managers with three guidelines to follow to be effective leaders:

1. *Find out what outcomes your subordinates are trying to obtain from their jobs and the organization.* These outcomes can range from satisfactory pay and job security to reasonable working hours and interesting and challenging job assignments. After identifying these outcomes, the manager should have the *reward power* needed to distribute or withhold the outcomes. Mark Crane, for example, is the vice principal of a large elementary school. Crane determined that the teachers he leads are trying to obtain the following outcomes from their jobs: pay raises, autonomy in the classroom, and the choice of which grades they teach. Crane had reward power for the latter two outcomes, but the school's principal determined how the pool of money for raises was to be distributed each year. Because Crane was the first-line manager who led the teachers and was most familiar with their performance, he asked the principal (his boss) to give him some say in determining pay raises. Realizing that this made a lot of sense, his principal gave Crane full power to distribute raises and requested only that Crane review his decisions with him prior to informing the teachers about them.

2. *Reward subordinates for high performance and goal attainment with the outcomes they desire.* The teachers and administrators at Crane's school considered several dimensions of teacher performance to be critical to achieving their goal of providing high-quality education: excellent in-class instruction, special programs to enhance student interest and learning (such as science and computer projects), and availability for meetings with parents to discuss their children's progress and special needs. Crane distributed pay raises to the teachers based on the extent to which they performed highly on each of these dimensions. The top-performing teachers were given first choice of grade assignments and also had practically complete autonomy in their classrooms.

3. *Clarify the paths to goal attainment for subordinates, remove any obstacles to high performance, and express confidence in subordinates' capabilities.* This does not mean that a manager needs to tell subordinates what to do. Rather, it means that a manager needs to make sure that subordinates are clear about what they should be trying to accomplish and have the capabilities, resources, and confidence levels needed to be successful. Crane made sure that all the teachers understood the importance of the three targeted goals and asked them whether, to reach them, they needed any special resources or supplies for their classes. Crane also gave additional coaching and guidance to teachers who seemed to be struggling. For example, Patrick Conolly, in his first year of teaching after graduate school, was unsure about how to use special projects in a third-grade class and how to react to parents who were critical. Conolly's actual teaching was excellent, but he even felt insecure about how he was doing on this dimension. To help build Conolly's confidence, Crane told Conolly that he truly thought he could be one of the school's top teachers (which was true). He gave Conolly some ideas about special projects that worked particularly well with the third grade, such as a writing project. Crane also role-played teacher-parent interactions with Conolly.

Conolly played the role of a particularly dissatisfied or troubled parent, while Crane played the role of a teacher trying to solve the underlying problem while making the parent feel that his or her child's needs were being met. Crane's efforts to clarify the paths to goal attainment for Conolly paid off: Within two years the local PTS voted Conolly teacher of the year.

Path-goal theory identifies four kinds of leadership behaviors that motivate subordinates:

- *Directive behaviors* are similar to initiating structure and include setting goals, assigning tasks, showing subordinates how to complete tasks, and taking concrete steps to improve performance.

- *Supportive behaviors* are similar to consideration and include expressing concern for subordinates and looking out for their best interests.

- *Participative behaviors* give subordinates a say in matters and decisions that affect them.

- *Achievement-oriented behaviors* motivate subordinates to perform at the highest level possible by, for example, setting very challenging goals, expecting that they be met, and believing in subordinates' capabilities.

Which of these behaviors should managers use to lead effectively? The answer to this question depends, or is contingent on, the nature of the subordinates and the kind of work they do.

Directive behaviors may be beneficial when subordinates are having difficulty completing assigned tasks, but they might be detrimental when subordinates are independent thinkers who work best when left alone. *Supportive* behaviors are often advisable when subordinates are experiencing high levels of stress. *Participative* behaviors can be particularly effective when subordinates' support of a decision is required. *Achievement-oriented* behaviors may increase motivation levels of highly capable subordinates who are bored from having too few challenges, but they might backfire if used with subordinates who are already pushed to their limit.

Effective managers seem to have a knack for determining what kinds of leader behaviors are likely to work in different situations and result in increased effectiveness, as indicated in the following "Management Insight."

Management Insight

Supporting Creativity

What do playing in an orchestra and designing high-status automobiles have in common? Both activities require creativity from artistic individuals. Effectively leading workers who are engaged in creative activities can be a challenge. For example, too much initiating structure can inhibit their creativity. Roger Nierenberg, conductor of the Stamford, Connecticut, Symphony Orchestra, has long recognized this, and rather than being overly controlling with musicians, he emphasizes supportive behaviors. Nierenberg utilizes positive feedback to support his musicians, never blames them when things go wrong, and provides direction in an encouraging manner.[70]

Nierenberg's positive, encouraging style of leading and conducting also can be applied in more traditional work environments. For example, in his leadership classes for managers at major corporations, such as Lucent Technologies and Georgia-Pacific, he coaches the managers on how to commit to a course of action and direct their subordinates to attain it in a supportive, uncritical manner.[71]

This approach to leading creative workers is applied in other countries as well. For example, Chris Bangle, who heads BMW's global design efforts in Munich, Germany, takes great pains to shield creative designers of BMW interiors and exteriors from critical comments or negative feedback from others in the organization, such as market analysts and engineers. Rather than receiving critiques, designers need, above all else, support from leadership and the freedom to explore different designs, as well as encouraging direction to reach closure in a reasonably timely fashion.[72] Bangle sees this kind of encouraging and supportive leadership as key to BMW's competitive advantage in designing cars like "moving works of art that express the driver's love of quality."[73]

The Leader Substitutes Model

leadership substitute
A characteristic of a subordinate or of a situation or context that acts in place of the influence of a leader and makes leadership unnecessary.

The leader substitutes model suggests that leadership is sometimes unnecessary because substitutes for leadership are present. A **leadership substitute** is something that acts in place of the influence of a leader and makes leadership unnecessary. This model suggests that under certain conditions managers do not have to play a leadership role—that members of an organization sometimes can perform highly without a manager exerting influence over them.[74] The leader substitutes model is a contingency model because it suggests that in some situations leadership is unnecessary.

Take the case of David Cotsonas, who teaches English at a foreign-language school in Cyprus, an island in the Mediterranean Sea. Cotsonas is fluent in Greek, English, and French, is an excellent teacher, and is highly motivated. Many of his students are businesspeople who have some rudimentary English skills and wish to increase their fluency to be able to conduct more of their business in English. He enjoys not only teaching them English but also learning about the work they do, and he often keeps in touch with his students after they finish his classes. Cotsonas meets with the director of the school twice a year to discuss semiannual class schedules and enrollments.

With practically no influence from a leader, Cotsonas is a highly motivated top performer at the school. In his situation, leadership is unnecessary because substitutes for leadership are present. Cotsonas's teaching expertise, his motivation, and his enjoyment of his work all are substitutes for the influence of a leader—in this case, the school's director. If the school's director were to try to exert influence over the way Cotsonas goes about performing his job, Cotsonas would probably resent this infringement on his autonomy, and it is unlikely that his performance would improve because he is already one of the school's best teachers.

As in Cotsonas's case, *characteristics of subordinates*—such as their skills, abilities, experience, knowledge, and motivation—can be substitutes for leadership.[75] *Characteristics of the situation or context*—such as the extent to which the work is interesting and enjoyable—also can be substitutes. When work is interesting and enjoyable, as it is for Cotsonas, jobholders do not need to be coaxed into performing because performing is rewarding in its own right. Similarly, when managers *empower* their subordinates or use *self-managed work teams* (discussed in detail in Chapter 15), the need for leadership influence from a manager is decreased because team members manage themselves.

Substitutes for leadership can increase organizational efficiency and effectiveness because they free up some of managers' valuable time and allow managers to focus their efforts on discovering new ways to improve organizational effectiveness. The director of the language school, for example, was able to spend much of his time making arrangements to open a second school in Rhodes, an island in the Aegean Sea, because of the presence of leadership substitutes, not only in the case of Cotsonas but in that of most of the other teachers at the school as well.

Bringing It All Together

Effective leadership in organizations occurs when managers take steps to lead in a way that is appropriate for the situation or context in which leadership occurs and for the subordinates who are being led. The three contingency models of leadership discussed above help managers hone in on the necessary ingredients for effective leadership. They are complementary in that each one looks at the leadership question from a different angle. Fiedler's contingency model explores how a manager's leadership style needs to be matched to that person's leadership situation for maximum effectiveness. House's path-goal theory focuses on how managers should motivate subordinates and describes the specific kinds of behaviors that managers can engage in to have a highly motivated workforce. The leadership substitutes model alerts managers to the fact that sometimes they do not need to exert influence over subordinates and thus can free up their time for other important activities. Table 14.2 recaps these three contingency models of leadership.

Table 14.2
Contingency Models of Leadership

Model	Focus	Key Contingencies
Fiedler's Contingency Model	Describes two leader styles, relationship-oriented and task-oriented, and the kinds of situations in which each kind of leader will be most effective	Whether or not a relationship-oriented or a task-oriented leader is effective is contingent on the situation
House's Path-Goal Theory	Describes how effective leaders motivate their followers	The behaviors that managers should engage in to be effective leaders are contingent on the nature of the subordinates and the work they do
Leader Substitutes Model	Describes when leadership is unnecessary	Whether or not leadership is necessary for subordinates to perform highly is contingent on characteristics of the subordinates and the situation

Transformational Leadership

Time and time again, throughout business history, certain leaders seem to literally transform their organizations, making sweeping changes to revitalize and renew operations. For example, in the 1990s, the CEO and president of the German electronics company Siemens, Heinrich von Pierer, dramatically transformed his company. When von Pierer took over in 1992, Siemens had a rigid hierarchy in place, was suffering from increased global competition, and was saddled with a conservative, perfectionist culture that stifled creativity and innovation and slowed decision making. Von Pierer's changes at Siemens have been nothing short of revolutionary.[76] At the new Siemens, subordinates critique their managers, who receive training in how to be more democratic and participative and spur creativity. Employees are no longer afraid to speak their minds, and the quest for innovation is a driving force throughout the company.

transformational leadership Leadership that makes subordinates aware of the importance of their jobs and performance to the organization and aware of their own needs for personal growth and that motivates subordinates to work for the good of the organization.

Von Pierer literally transformed Siemens and its thousands of employees into being more innovative and taking the steps needed to gain a competitive advantage during his tenure as CEO from 1992 to 2005 (von Pierer is currently the chairman of Siemens' Supervisory Board).[77] When managers have such dramatic effects on their subordinates and on an organization as a whole, they are engaging in transformational leadership. **Transformational leadership** occurs when managers change (or transform) their subordinates in three important ways:[78]

1. *Transformational managers make subordinates aware of how important their jobs are for the organization and how necessary it is for them to perform those jobs as best they can so that the organization can attain its goals.* Von Pierer sent the message throughout Siemens not only that innovating, cost cutting, and increasing customer service and satisfaction were everyone's responsibilities but also that improvements could be and needed to be made in these areas. For example, when von Pierer realized that managers in charge of microprocessor sales were not aware of the importance of their jobs and of performing them in a top-notch fashion, he had managers from Siemens's top microprocessor customers give Siemens's microprocessor managers feedback about their poor service and unreliable delivery schedules. The microprocessor managers quickly realized how important it was for them to take steps to improve customer service.

2. *Transformational managers make their subordinates aware of the subordinates' own needs for personal growth, development, and accomplishment.* Von Pierer made Siemens's employees aware of their own needs in this regard through numerous workshops and training sessions, empowerment of employees throughout the company, the development of fast-track career programs, and increased reliance on self-managed work teams.[79]

3. *Transformational managers motivate their subordinates to work for the good of the organization as a whole, not just for their own personal gain or benefit.* Von Pierer's message to Siemens's employees was clear: Dramatic changes in the way they performed their jobs were crucial for the future viability and success of Siemens. As von Pierer put it, "We have to keep asking ourselves: Are we flexible enough? Are we changing enough?"[80] One way von Pierer tried to get all employees thinking in these terms was by inserting into the company magazine, distributed to all employees, self-addressed postcards urging employees to send their ideas for improvements directly to him.

Table 14.3
Transformational Leadership

Transformational Managers
- Are charismatic
- Intellectually stimulate subordinates
- Engage in developmental consideration

Subordinates of Transformational Managers
- Have increased awareness of the importance of their jobs and high performance
- Are aware of their own needs for growth, development, and accomplishment
- Work for the good of the organization and not just their own personal benefit

When managers transform their subordinates in these three ways, subordinates trust the managers, are highly motivated, and help the organization achieve its goals. As a result of von Pierer's transformational leadership, for example, a team of Siemens's engineers working in blue jeans in a rented house developed a tool control system in one-third the time and at one-third the cost of other similar systems developed at Siemens.[81] How do managers like von Pierer transform subordinates and produce dramatic effects in their organizations? There are at least three ways in which transformational leaders can influence their followers: by being a charismatic leader, by intellectually stimulating subordinates, and by engaging in developmental consideration (see Table 14.3).

Being a Charismatic Leader

charismatic leader
An enthusiastic, self-confident leader who is able to clearly communicate his or her vision of how good things could be.

Transformational managers are **charismatic leaders.** They have a vision of how good things could be in their work groups and organizations that is in contrast with the status quo. Their vision usually entails dramatic improvements in group and organizational performance as a result of changes in the organization's structure, culture, strategy, decision making, and other critical processes and factors. This vision paves the way for gaining a competitive advantage. From "A Manager's Challenge," it is clear that part of Judy McGrath's vision for MTV Networks is increasing its digital offerings and transforming MTV into a truly digital company.

Charismatic leaders are excited and enthusiastic about their vision and clearly communicate it to their subordinates, as does Judy McGrath. The excitement, enthusiasm, and self-confidence of a charismatic leader contribute to the leader's being able to inspire followers to enthusiastically support his or her vision.[82] People often think of charismatic leaders or managers as being "larger than life." The essence of charisma, however, is having a vision and enthusiastically communicating it to others. Thus, managers who appear to be quiet and earnest can also be charismatic.

Stimulating Subordinates Intellectually

Transformational managers openly share information with their subordinates so that they are aware of problems and the need for change. The manager causes subordinates to view problems in their groups and throughout the organization from a different perspective, consistent with the manager's vision. Whereas in the past subordinates might not have been aware of some problems, may have viewed problems as a "management issue" beyond their concern, or may have viewed problems as insurmountable, the transformational manager's **intellectual stimulation** leads subordinates to view problems as challenges that they can and will meet and conquer. The manager engages and empowers subordinates to take personal responsibility for helping solve problems.[83]

intellectual stimulation Behavior a leader engages in to make followers be aware of problems and view these problems in new ways, consistent with the leader's vision.

Engaging in Developmental Consideration

developmental consideration Behavior a leader engages in to support and encourage followers and help them develop and grow on the job.

When managers engage in **developmental consideration,** they not only perform the consideration behaviors described earlier, such as demonstrating true concern for the well-being of subordinates, but go one step further. The manager goes out of his or her way to support and encourage subordinates, giving them opportunities to enhance their skills and capabilities and to grow and excel on the job.[84] Heinrich von Pierer engaged in developmental consideration in numerous ways, such as providing counseling sessions with a psychologist for managers who were having a hard time adapting to the changes at Siemens and sponsoring hiking trips to stimulate employees to think and work in new ways.[85]

All organizations, no matter how large or small, successful or unsuccessful, can benefit when their managers engage in transformational leadership. Moreover, while the benefits of transformational leadership are often most apparent when an organization is in trouble, transformational leadership can be an enduring approach to leadership, leading to long-run organizational effectiveness.

The Distinction Between Transformational and Transactional Leadership

transactional leadership Leadership that motivates subordinates by rewarding them for high performance and reprimanding them for low performance.

Transformational leadership is often contrasted with transactional leadership. In **transactional leadership,** managers use their reward and coercive powers to encourage high performance. When managers reward high performers, reprimand or otherwise punish low performers, and motivate subordinates by reinforcing desired behaviors and extinguishing or punishing undesired ones, they are engaging in transactional leadership.[86] Managers who effectively influence their subordinates to achieve goals yet do not seem to be making the kind of dramatic changes that are part of transformational leadership are engaging in transactional leadership.

Many transformational leaders engage in transactional leadership. They reward subordinates for a job well done and notice and respond to substandard performance. But they also have their eyes on the bigger picture of how much better things could be in their organizations, how much more their subordinates are capable of achieving, and how important it is to treat their subordinates with respect and to help them reach their full potential.

Research has found that when leaders engage in transformational leadership, their subordinates tend to have higher levels of job satisfaction and performance.[87] Additionally, subordinates of transformational leaders may be more likely to trust their leaders and their organizations and feel that they are being fairly treated, and this, in turn, may positively influence their work motivation (see Chapter 13).[88]

Gender and Leadership

The increasing number of women entering the ranks of management, as well as the problems some women face in their efforts to be hired as managers or promoted into management positions, has prompted researchers to explore the relationship between gender and leadership. Although there are relatively more women in management positions today than there were 10 years ago, there are still relatively few women in top management and, in some organizations, even in middle management.

When women do advance to top-management positions, special attention often is focused on them and the fact that they are women. For example, women CEOs of large companies are still very rare; those who make it to the very top post, such as Meg Whitman of eBay, Judy McGrath of MTV Networks, and Andrea Jung of Avon, are very salient. As business writer Linda Tischler puts it, "In a workplace where women CEOs of major companies are so scarce . . . they can be identified, like rock stars, by first name only."[89] While women have certainly made inroads into leadership positions in organizations, they continue to be very underrepresented in top leadership posts (see Chapter 5). For example, it is estimated that the percentage of women in top leadership/partner positions in law firms is less than 16%. Less than 7% of the top-earning medical doctors are women, and of the corporate officers of the Fortune 500 largest U.S. companies, less than 16% are women.[90]

A widespread stereotype of women is that they are nurturing, supportive, and concerned with interpersonal relations. Men are stereotypically viewed as being directive and focused on task accomplishment. Such stereotypes suggest that women tend to be more relationship-oriented as managers and engage in more consideration behaviors, whereas men are more task-oriented and engage in more initiating-structure behaviors. Does the behavior of actual male and female managers bear out these stereotypes? Do women managers lead in different ways than men do? Are male or female managers more effective as leaders?

Research suggests that male and female managers who have leadership positions in organizations behave in similar ways.[91] Women do not engage in more consideration than men, and men do not engage in more initiating structure than women. Research does suggest, however, that leadership style may vary between women and men. Women tend to be somewhat more participative as leaders than are men, involving subordinates in decision making and seeking their input.[92] Male managers tend to be less participative than are female managers, making more decisions on their own and wanting to do things their own way. Moreover, research suggests that men tend to be harsher when they punish their subordinates than do women.[93]

There are at least two reasons why female managers may be more participative as leaders than are male managers.[94] First, subordinates may try to resist the influence of female managers more than they do the influence of male managers. Some subordinates may never have reported to a woman before; some may incorrectly see a management role as being more appropriate for a man than for a woman; and some may just resist being led by a woman. To overcome this resistance and encourage subordinates' trust and respect, women managers may adopt a participative approach.

A second reason why female managers may be more participative is that they sometimes have better interpersonal skills than male managers.[95] A participative approach to leadership requires high levels of interaction and involvement between a manager and his or her subordinates, sensitivity to subordinates' feelings, and the ability to make decisions that may be unpopular with subordinates but necessary for goal attainment. Good interpersonal skills may help female managers have the effective interactions with their subordinates that are crucial to a participative approach.[96] To the extent that male managers have more difficulty managing interpersonal relationships, they may shy away from the high levels of interaction with subordinates necessary for true participation.

The key finding from research on leader behaviors, however, is that male and female managers do *not* differ significantly in their propensities to perform different leader behaviors. Even though they may be more participative, female managers do not engage in more consideration or less initiating structure than male managers.

Perhaps a question even more important than whether male and female managers differ in the leadership behaviors they perform is whether they differ in effectiveness. Consistent with the findings for leader behaviors, research suggests that across different kinds of organizational settings, male and female managers tend to be *equally effective* as leaders.[97] Thus, there is no logical basis for stereotypes favoring male managers and leaders or for the existence of the "glass ceiling" (an invisible barrier that seems to prevent women from advancing as far as they should in some organizations). Because women and men are equally effective as leaders, the increasing number of women in the workforce should result in a larger pool of highly qualified candidates for management positions in organizations, ultimately enhancing organizational effectiveness.[98]

An important factor for women's advancement to top leadership positions is obtaining a variety of work experiences.[99] Varied work experiences have proved very beneficial for Kathleen Ligocki, CEO and president of Tower Automotive, Inc., as profiled in the following "Focus on Diversity."

Focus on Diversity

Kathleen Ligocki Leads Tower Automotive

Kathleen Ligocki occupies perhaps one of the highest leadership positions held by a woman in the automotive industry. As CEO and a director of Tower Automotive, Ligocki leads an automobile components and assemblies firm that supplies car parts to every major automaker, has approximately $2.8 billion in revenues, and operates in 13 countries in addition to the United States, ranging from Mexico, Germany, and Japan to Poland, Slovakia, Brazil, and India.[100]

With a BA in Chinese history and Renaissance art from Indiana University, Ligocki had no plans for a career in the automotive industry.[101] Upon receiving her undergraduate degree, she took a job as a foreman in a General Motors (GM) factory to earn money for graduate school. Much to her surprise, she realized she loved her work and went on to a number of different positions at GM and later at the Ford Motor Company; along the way, she also earned a master's degree from the Wharton Business School.[102] Ligocki's

Tower Automotive CEO Kathleen Ligocki draws on her prior experience in various positions at Ford to lead Tower.

positions at Ford included director of strategies, CEO of Ford Mexico, and, most recently, vice president of Ford's Customer Service Division.[103]

Bill Ford was so impressed with Ligocki's leadership capabilities that he remarked just weeks before she accepted the Tower top post that she might someday be the one to lead Ford. In fact, when she discussed potentially leaving Ford to become CEO of Tower with Ford top managers, they tried to convince her to stay but also appreciated the kind of opportunity she would have at Tower. As Ligocki put it, "They encouraged me to stay, but they also understood—maybe Bill better than anybody—that this was an opportunity to run a publicly traded company. Tower was a company I thought had great strategic strengths. But it needed operational work, which was a lot of what I had done at GM and Ford. So I felt I could offer something to the company."[104]

Varied work experiences in both line and administrative positions have paid off for Ligocki in terms of having a very motivating and rewarding career and being especially well suited for her current leadership position.[105]

Emotional Intelligence and Leadership

Do the moods and emotions leaders experience on the job influence their behavior and effectiveness as leaders? Research suggests that this is likely to be the case. For example, one study found that when store managers experienced positive moods at work, salespeople in their stores provided high-quality customer service and were less likely to quit.[106] Another study found that groups whose leaders experienced positive moods had better coordination while groups whose leaders experienced negative moods exerted more effort; members of groups with leaders in positive moods also tended to experience more positive moods themselves and members of groups with leaders in negative moods tended to experience more negative moods.[107]

Moreover, a leader's level of emotional intelligence (see Chapter 3) may play a particularly important role in leadership effectiveness.[108] For example, emotional intelligence may help leaders develop a vision for their organizations, motivate their subordinates to commit to this vision, and energize them to enthusiastically work to achieve this vision. Moreover, emotional intelligence may enable leaders to develop a significant identity for their organization and instill high levels of trust and cooperation throughout the organization while maintaining the flexibility needed to respond to changing conditions.[109]

Emotional intelligence also plays a crucial role in how leaders relate to and deal with their followers, particularly when it comes to encouraging followers to be creative.[110] Creativity in organizations is an emotion-laden process, as it often entails challenging the status quo, being willing to take risks and accept and learn from failures, and doing much hard work to bring creative ideas to fruition in terms of new products, services, or procedures and processes when uncertainty is bound to be high.[111] Leaders who are high on emotional intelligence are more likely to understand all the emotions surrounding creative endeavors, to be able to awaken and support the creative pursuits of their followers, and to provide the kind of support that enables creativity to flourish in organizations.[112]

Summary and Review

THE NATURE OF LEADERSHIP Leadership is the process by which a person exerts influence over other people and inspires, motivates, and directs their activities to help achieve group or organizational goals. Leaders are able to influence others because they possess power. The five types of power available to managers are legitimate power, reward power, coercive power, expert power, and referent power. Many managers are using empowerment as a tool to increase their effectiveness as leaders.

TRAIT AND BEHAVIOR MODELS OF LEADERSHIP The trait model of leadership describes personal characteristics or traits that contribute to effective leadership. However, some managers who possess these traits are not effective leaders, and some managers who do not possess all the traits are nevertheless effective leaders. The behavior model of leadership describes two kinds of behavior that most leaders engage in: consideration and initiating structure.

CONTINGENCY MODELS OF LEADERSHIP Contingency models take into account the complexity surrounding leadership and the role of the situation in determining whether a manager is an effective or ineffective leader. Fiedler's contingency model explains why managers may be effective leaders in one situation and ineffective in another. According to Fiedler's model, relationship-oriented leaders are most effective in situations that are moderately favorable for leading, and task-oriented leaders are most effective in situations that are very favorable or very unfavorable for leading. House's path-goal theory describes how effective managers motivate their subordinates by determining what outcomes their subordinates want, rewarding subordinates with these outcomes when they achieve their goals and perform at a high level, and clarifying the paths to goal attainment. Managers can engage in four different kinds of behaviors to motivate subordinates: directive behaviors, supportive behaviors, participative behaviors, or achievement-oriented behaviors. The leader substitutes model suggests that sometimes managers do not have to play a leadership role because their subordinates perform highly without the manager having to exert influence over them.

TRANSFORMATIONAL LEADERSHIP Transformational leadership occurs when managers have dramatic effects on their subordinates and on the organization as a whole and inspire and energize subordinates to solve problems and improve performance. These effects include making subordinates aware of the importance of their own jobs and high performance, making subordinates aware of their own needs for personal growth, development, and accomplishment, and motivating subordinates to work for the good of the organization and not just their own personal gain. Managers can engage in transformational leadership by being charismatic leaders, by intellectually stimulating subordinates, and by engaging in developmental consideration. Transformational managers also often engage in transactional leadership by using their reward and coercive powers to encourage high performance.

GENDER AND LEADERSHIP   Female and male managers do not differ in the leadership behaviors that they perform, contrary to stereotypes suggesting that women are more relationship-oriented and men more task-oriented. Female managers sometimes are more participative than male managers, however. Research has found that women and men are equally effective as managers and leaders.

EMOTIONAL INTELLIGENCE AND LEADERSHIP   The moods and emotions leaders experience on the job, and their ability to effectively manage these feelings, can influence their effectiveness as leaders. Moreover, emotional intelligence has the potential to contribute to leadership effectiveness in multiple ways, including encouraging and supporting creativity among followers.

Management in Action

Topics for Discussion and Action

Discussion

1. Describe the steps managers can take to increase their power and ability to be effective leaders.

2. Think of specific situations in which it might be especially important for a manager to engage in consideration and in initiating structure.

3. For your current job or for a future job you expect to hold, describe what your supervisor could do to strongly motivate you to be a top performer.

4. Discuss why managers might want to change the behaviors they engage in, given their situation, their subordinates, and the nature of the work being done. Do you think managers are able to readily change their leadership behaviors? Why or why not?

5. Discuss why substitutes for leadership can contribute to organizational effectiveness.

6. Describe what transformational leadership is, and explain how managers can engage in it.

7. Discuss why some people still think that men make better managers than women even though research indicates that men and women are equally effective as managers and leaders.

8. Imagine that you are working in an organization in an entry-level position after graduation and have come up with what you think is a great idea for improving a critical process in the organization that relates to your job. In what ways might your supervisor encourage you to actually implement your idea? How might your supervisor discourage you from even sharing your idea with others?

Action

9. Interview a manager to find out how the three situational characteristics that Fiedler identified are affecting his or her ability to provide leadership.

10. Find a company that has dramatically turned around its fortunes and improved its performance. Determine whether a transformational manager was behind the turnaround and, if one was, what this manager did.

Building Management Skills

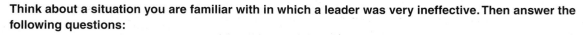

Analyzing Failures of Leadership

Think about a situation you are familiar with in which a leader was very ineffective. Then answer the following questions:

1. What sources of power did this leader have? Did the leader have enough power to influence his or her followers?

2. What kinds of behaviors did this leader engage in? Were they appropriate for the situation? Why or why not?

3. From what you know, do you think this leader was a task-oriented leader or a relationship-oriented leader? How favorable was this leader's situation for leading?

4. What steps did this leader take to motivate his or her followers? Were these steps appropriate or inappropriate? Why?

5. What signs, if any, did this leader show of being a transformational leader?

Managing Ethically

Managers who verbally criticize their subordinates, put them down in front of their coworkers, or use the threat of job loss to influence behavior are exercising coercive power. Some employees subject to coercive power believe that using it is unethical.

Questions

1. Either alone or in a group, think about the ethical implications of the use of coercive power.

2. To what extent do managers and organizations have an ethical obligation to put limits on the amount of coercive power that is exercised?

Small Group Breakout Exercise

Improving Leadership Effectiveness

Form groups of three to five people, and appoint one member as the spokesperson who will communicate your findings and conclusions to the class when called on by the instructor. Then discuss the following scenario.

You are a team of human resource consultants who have been hired by Carla Caruso, an entrepreneur who has started her own interior decorating business. A highly competent and creative interior decorator, Caruso established a working relationship with most of the major home builders in her community. At first, she worked on her own as an independent contractor. Then because of a dramatic increase in the number of new homes being built, she became swamped with requests for her services and decided to start her own company.

She hired a secretary-bookkeeper and four interior decorators, all of whom are highly competent. Caruso still does decorating jobs herself and has adopted a hands-off approach to leading the four decorators who report to her because she feels that interior design is a very personal, creative endeavor. Rather than pay the decorators on some kind of commission basis (such as a percentage of their customers' total billings),

she pays them a premium salary, higher than average, so that they are motivated to do what's best for a customer's needs and not what will result in higher billings and commissions.

Caruso thought everything was going smoothly until customer complaints started coming in. The complaints ranged from the decorators' being hard to get hold of, promising unrealistic delivery times, and being late for or failing to keep appointments to their being impatient and rude when customers had trouble making up their minds. Caruso knows that her decorators are very competent and is concerned that she is not effectively leading and managing them. She wonders, in particular, if her hands-off approach is to blame and if she should change the manner in which she rewards or pays her decorators. She has asked for your advice.

1. Analyze the sources of power that Caruso has available to her to influence the

decorators. What advice can you give her to either increase her power base or use her existing power more effectively?

2. Given what you have learned in this chapter (for example, from the behavior model and path-goal theory), does Caruso seem to be performing appropriate leader behaviors in this situation? What advice can you give her about the kinds of behaviors she should perform?

3. What steps would you advise Caruso to take to increase the decorators' motivation to deliver high-quality customer service?

4. Would you advise Caruso to try to engage in transformational leadership in this situation? If not, why not? If so, what steps would you advise her to take?

Exploring the World Wide Web

Go to the Web site of the Center for Creative Leadership (www.ccl.org). Spend some time browsing through the site to learn more about this organization, which specializes in leadership.

Then click on "Coaching" and read about the different coaching programs and options the center provides. How do you think leaders might benefit from coaching? What kinds of leaders/managers may find coaching especially beneficial? Do you think coaching services such as those provided by the Center for Creative Leadership can help leaders become more effective? Why or why not?

Be the Manager

You are the CEO of a medium-size company that makes window coverings such as Hunter Douglas blinds and Douettes. Your company has a real cost advantage in terms of being able to make custom window coverings at costs that are relatively low in the industry. However, the performance of your company has been lackluster. In order to make needed changes and improve performance, you met with the eight other top managers in your company and charged them with identifying problems and missed opportunities in each of their areas and coming up with an action plan to address the problems and take advantage of opportunities.

Once you gave the managers the okay, they were charged with implementing their action plans in a timely fashion and monitoring the effects of their initiatives on a monthly basis for the next 8 to 12 months.

You approved each of the manager's action plans, and a year later most of the manager's were reporting that their initiatives had been successful in addressing the problems and opportunities they had identified a year ago. However, overall company performance continues to be lackluster and shows no signs of improvement. You are confused and starting to question your leadership capabilities and approach to change. What are you going to do to improve the performance and effectiveness of your company?

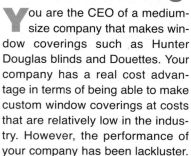

Case in the News

Making the Elephant Dance

You don't get to be a chief executive by waffling your way to the top. Most stick with the playbook and are steadfast and unflinching, or at least they want to be.

The company's share price was in free-fall: From 1992 to 1999, Campbell had watched the stock rise from 20 to 100, but in a little more than a year it had plunged half the way back down. Over two years, from 1999 to 2001 invested capital is expected to rise to 15.5% in 2006, up from 8.8% in 2003. But Campbell denies any interest in replacing GM and CEO G. Richard Wagoner Jr., who, in any event, has the support of his board. "It's a heck of an honor," Campbell says, "but you won't see me there."

"We were adrift," Campbell says. "We were doing all the things we used to do but were not getting results." "It was a very dramatic shift," says Jack J. Pelton, then an engineering executive at Textron's Cessna Aircraft unit and now its CEO. People were not even "sure what each of the peer group businesses did."

That soft correction is fare for a CEO, especially one who had ridden the old model to substantial professional success. "It's like doing a total 180," says Cowen & Co. analyst Cai von Rumohr. "It's like saying: 'Everything I've done in my career until now has been wrong.'"

Simplify, Simplify

To develop talent executives were transferred from posts in one unit to another. And to help coax along managers who didn't see much benefit in caring what happened outside of their unit, incentive compensation was linked to company-wide performance. As logical as those moves sound, they were still "hard for individual businesses to grasp," Campbell says. "They might have to spend money to get with it. I had to convince them the short term pain was worth it."

Finally, the business model improvements began to show their merit. Without the worry over earnings per share, Campbell felt able to invest in Cessna during some of its bleakest post-9/11 moments, when profits fell 47%. Cessna managers asked for hundreds of millions of dollars in investment, and "we didn't turn down one penny—not a one—even though it cost us earnings-per-share in the short term," claims Campbell. "The old me might not have said yes." As a result, Cessna emerged to meet the upturn with a bevy of new products.

Since the transformation began, Campbell has shed 45 pounds, as well as his old-fashioned, buttoned-up demeanor. "Lewis was a very formal guy," says Ed Orzetti, who was recruited by Campbell from General Electric Co. to help run cross-company initiatives and who has since left. "He let his hair down and became much more engaged."

Questions

1. How would you characterize Lewis Campbell's personal leadership style?

2. What traits does Campbell appear to be high on?

3. What leadership behaviors has Campbell engaged in?

4. In what ways has Lewis Campbell been a transformational leader at Textron?

Source: B. Hindo, "Making the Elephant Dance." Reprinted from the May 1, 2006, issue of *BusinessWeek,* by special permission. Copyright © 2006 by the McGraw-Hill Companies.

BusinessWeek

Case in the News

A Sister Act That's Wowing Them

When Rowland Schaefer, the founder and CEO of Claire's Stores Inc., was felled by a stroke in late 2002, the company was caught unprepared. Even at 86, the iron-willed Schaefer hadn't groomed a successor and had only promoted his two daughters, Bonnie and Marla, to vice-chair positions to appease the board. Left with few choices, the board tapped the two sisters as "acting co-CEOs"—but gave them orders to begin searching for a seasoned executive who could step in if their father wasn't able to return. "They had Claire's in their blood, but they were not proven quantities," says director Bruce G. Miller, a managing director at Ryan Beck & Co.

Privately, though, Bonnie and Marla chafed at the idea of bringing in an outsider to run the $1.3 billion retailer, which sells inexpensive baubles, bangles, and bows for teens and tweens. The pair had worked most of their adult lives at Claire's and figured any outsider would need at least a year to learn the business. "We said, 'We know all this stuff, let's just go do it,'" recalls Bonnie, 52, who handles real estate and store operations from the company's headquarters in Pembroke Pines, Fla. Marla, who is four years older and the more extroverted of the two, oversees merchandising and investor relations from New York. Together they form a unique executive partnership—a long-distance sister act built on their complementary strengths. "We like to say we share a brain," says Marla.

Back in 2002 the sisters simply ignored the directors' orders and threw themselves into the job. They did so well that after a year the board dropped the "acting" from their title. Smart move, because in the first two years of their tenure, profits nearly doubled, to $143 million, on a 28% rise in revenues—a performance that earned them a No. 56 ranking on *BusinessWeek*'s 2005 list of Hot Growth companies. For the fiscal year ended Jan. 31, analysts expect Claire's to record an additional 19% increase in profits. Investors clearly have bought in: Shares of Claire's have soared 157% since Bonnie and Marla took charge in November, 2002. "Wall Street was highly skeptical at first, but they've done a great job," says Eric Beder, analyst at

Brean Murray, Carret & Co., a New York securities firm.

The Schaefer sisters admit they benefited from shifting fashions. Grunge was dead, and teen girls were into accessories again. But analysts credit them with revitalizing a company that had been slowed by two troublesome acquisitions—a boys' apparel division called Mr. Rags (which was sold in May, 2002) and a second accessories chain called Afterthoughts.

Girl Magnets

Bonnie and Marla quickly reshaped the Afterthoughts unit, which had been renamed Icings, to appeal to the 17-to-27 crowd. Buying became more scientific: Instead of relying on the personal whims of the buyers, as their father had, they began using more market research to ensure they were on the cutting edge of teen trends. The sisters pushed more jewelry, which carries high margins. They also became more aggressive about licensing celebrity names they hope appeal to young teens: The company in February launched an exclusive line of Mary-Kate- and Ashley cosmetics, and later this spring it will unveil a line of costume jewelry hand-picked by pop singer Mariah Carey. "The stores have become a hangout for teen girls," says Eugene Fram, professor of marketing at the Rochester Institute of Technology.

Meanwhile, Bonnie and Marla reorganized the management structure to break down fiefdoms "and make sure everyone was rowing in the same direction," says Bonnie. To help them drill deeper into store data and, they hope, spot sales trends earlier, the two recently hired the company's first-ever chief information officer. And while it was Rowland Schaefer who pushed the company

into Europe and Japan in the 1990s, his daughters are taking the international expansion to the next level. To get a toehold in markets they don't know well, Bonnie and Marla have begun franchising the Claire's name to retailers in countries such as South Africa, Kuwait, and the United Arab Emirates.

That the sisters adapted to their new roles so well shouldn't be surprising, since they grew up in the business. Marla was a teenager when she took her first business trip to Europe with her father. She later gravitated toward merchandising, which required frequent travel to Asia to find suppliers to produce the 11,500 or so items that Claire's stocks. Bonnie, who says her father fired her from her first job as an assistant store manager because she "didn't have the right work ethic," returned a year later and found her niche on the real estate team, which contracts for space with mall landlords. Neither bothered with business school; their training was on the job.

Close as . . . Sisters

But it wasn't easy for them to be taken seriously as they came up the ranks; the Schaefer family (their father is still alive) controls roughly one-third of the outstanding shares of the company. "No one believes you're there for any reason other than that you're a member of the family," says Marla. And the two say it was difficult to get their father, even when he was in his 80s, to cede any power. "We would pry his fingers off and say, 'Let us do it, let us do it, Dad, we're adults now,'" recalls Bonnie. "It's not that he was giving over daily control. We were taking it."

As co-CEOs, they've found a way to make what could be an

uncomfortable arrangement work. They talk on the phone several times a day, and when they're together they often finish each other's sentences. Even as Bonnie, complains that Marla keeps interrupting her, she twice reaches over to pick lint from her sister's sweater. "Never in my wildest dreams did I think I'd be working things out with my sister," Bonnie jokes. Indeed, they vowed from the outset to smooth over any problems privately so that employees would never see a schism between them. "We have our differences of opinion," admits Marla. "But we also know that if we're not together on something, no one in the company is going to buy into it."

When it comes to thinking about their own successor(s), Bonnie and Marla aren't necessarily counting on the next generation of Schaefers. Bonnie doesn't have children, and Marla's daughters are just 15 and 13. If they ever show interest in Claire's, she says, she'll insist they first take a job elsewhere "to have an appreciation of working in a family business."

Questions

1. What are the sources of Marla and Bonnie Schaefer's power at Claire's?

2. What traits does each sister appear to be high on?

3. Why did the board originally appoint them as "acting co-CEOs"?

4. Are the Schaefer sisters transformational leaders? Why or why not?

Source: D. Foust, "A Sister Act That's Wowing Them." Reprinted from the March 13, 2006, issue of *BusinessWeek* by special permission. Copyright © 2006 by the McGraw-Hill Companies.

CHAPTER 15

Effective Groups and Teams

Learning Objectives:

After studying this chapter, you should be able to:

- Explain why groups and teams are key contributors to organizational effectiveness.

- Identify the different types of groups and teams that help managers and organizations achieve their goals.

- Explain how different elements of group dynamics influence the functioning and effectiveness of groups and teams.

- Explain why it is important for groups and teams to have a balance of conformity and deviance and a moderate level of cohesiveness.

- Describe how managers can motivate group members to achieve organizational goals and reduce social loafing in groups and teams.

A Manager's Challenge

Teams Work Wonders at Louis Vuitton and Nucor Corporation

How can managers use teams in different kinds of organizations and work environments to gain a competitive advantage?

Groups and teams are relied on in all kinds of organizations, from those specializing in heavy industrial manufacturing to those in high-tech fields ranging from computer software development to biotechnology. Relying on groups and teams to accomplish work tasks is one thing; managing groups and teams in ways that enable them to truly excel and help an organization gain and maintain a competitive advantage is another, much more challenging endeavor. Managers at Louis Vuitton, the most profitable luxury brand in the world, and managers at Nucor Corporation, the largest producer of steel and biggest recycler in the United States, have succeeded in effectively using teams to produce luxury accessories and steel, respectively. Teams at both companies not only are effective but truly excel and have helped to make the companies leaders in their respective industries.[1]

Louis Vuitton, with $4.8 billion in revenues in 2005 and over $1.4 billion in profits from recurring operations, is the largest and most

A team member assembles classic Louis Vuitton bags at the company's fine leather goods factory in the Normandy town of Ducey in France.

profitable producer of high-end luxury accessories.[2] Impeccable quality and high standards are a must for Louis Vuitton; when customers purchase a handbag such as the Boulogne Multicolor with a $1,500 price tag, they expect only the best. Teams at Louis Vuitton are so effective at making handbags and other accessories that not only are customers never disappointed but Vuitton's profit margins are much higher than those of its competitors such as Prada and Gucci.[3]

Teams with between 20 and 30 members make Vuitton handbags and accessories. The teams work on only one particular product at a time; a team with 24 members might produce about 120 handbags per day. Team members are empowered to take ownership for the goods they produce, are encouraged to suggest improvements, and are kept up to date on key facts such as products' selling prices and popularity. As Thierry Nogues, a team leader at a Vuitton factory in Ducey, France, puts it, "Our goal is to make everyone as multiskilled and autonomous as possible."[4]

In the case of the Boulogne Multicolor, a team found out that some of the studs on the handbag were interfering with the smooth operation of the zipper. The team's discovery led to a small design change that completely eliminated the problem.[5] By being involved in all aspects of the goods they produce, and having the skills and autonomy to ensure that all goods produced live up to the Vuitton brand name, employees take pride in their work and are highly motivated.

Nucor, headquartered in Charlotte, North Carolina, has operations in 17 states manufacturing all kinds of steel products ranging from steel joists, bars, and beams to steel decks and metal building systems.[6] Nucor has 11,300 employees and in 2005 had sales of $12.7 billion.[7]

Production workers at Nucor are organized into teams ranging in size from 8 to 40 members based on the kind of work the team is responsible for, such as rolling steel or operating a furnace. Team members have considerable autonomy to make decisions and creatively respond to problems and opportunities, and there are relatively few

layers in the corporate hierarchy, supporting the empowerment of teams.[8] Teams develop their own informal rules for behavior and make their own decisions. As long as team members follow organizational rules and policies (e.g., for safety) and meet quality standards, they are free to govern themselves. Managers act as coaches or advisers rather than supervisors, helping teams out when they need some additional outside assistance.[9]

To ensure that production teams are motivated to help Nucor achieve its goals, team members are eligible for weekly bonuses based on the team's performance. Essentially, these production workers receive base pay that does not vary and are eligible to receive weekly bonus pay that can average from 80% to 150% of their regular pay.[10] The bonus rate is predetermined by the work a team performs and the capabilities of the machinery they use. Given the immediacy of the bonus and its potential magnitude, team members are highly motivated to perform at a high level, develop informal rules that support high performance, and strive to help Nucor reach its goals. Moreover, because all members of a team receive the same amount of weekly bonus money, they are motivated to do their best for the team, cooperate, and help one another out.[11]

Crafting a luxury handbag and making steel joists couldn't be more different from each other in certain ways. Yet the highly effective teams at Louis Vuitton and Nucor share some fundamental qualities. These teams really do take ownership of their work and are highly motivated to perform effectively. Team members have the skills and knowledge they need to be effective, they are empowered to make decisions about their work, and they know that their teams are making vital contributions to their organizations.[12]

Overview

Louis Vuitton and Nucor are not alone in using groups and teams to produce goods and services that best meet customers' needs. Managers in large companies such as Du Pont, Microsoft, and Ford and in small companies such as Web Industries, Perdue Farms, and Risk International Services are all relying on teams to help them gain a competitive advantage.[13] In this chapter we look in detail at how groups and teams can contribute to organizational effectiveness and the types of groups and teams used in organizations. We discuss how different elements of group dynamics influence the functioning and effectiveness of groups, and we describe how managers can motivate group members to achieve organizational goals and reduce social loafing in groups and teams. By the end of this chapter, you will appreciate why the effective management of groups and teams is a key ingredient for organizational performance and a source of competitive advantage.

Groups, Teams, and Organizational Effectiveness

A **group** may be defined as two or more people who interact with each other to accomplish certain goals or meet certain needs.[14] A **team** is a group whose members work *intensely* with one another to achieve a specific common goal or objective. As these definitions imply, all teams are groups but not all groups are teams. The two characteristics that distinguish teams from groups are the *intensity* with which team members work together and the presence of a *specific, overriding team goal or objective.*

group Two or more people who interact with each other to accomplish certain goals or meet certain needs.

As described in "A Manager's Challenge," members of production teams in Louis Vuitton and in Nucor work intensely together to achieve their goals, whether they are crafting high-quality handbags or making steel beams. In contrast, the accountants who work in a small CPA firm are a group: They may interact with one another to achieve goals such as keeping up to date on the latest changes in accounting rules and regulations, maintaining a smoothly functioning office, satisfying clients, and attracting new clients. But they are not a team because they do not work intensely with one another. Each accountant concentrates on serving the needs of his or her own clients.

team A group whose members work intensely with one another to achieve a specific common goal or objective.

Because all teams are also groups, whenever we use the term *group* in this chapter, we are referring to both groups *and* teams. As you might imagine, because members of teams work intensely together, teams can sometimes be difficult to form and it may take time for members to learn how to effectively work together. Groups and teams can help an organization gain a competitive advantage because they can (1) enhance its performance, (2) increase its responsiveness to customers, (3) increase innovation, and (4) increase employees' motivation and satisfaction (see Figure 15.1). In this section, we look at each of these contributions in turn.

Groups and Teams as Performance Enhancers

synergy Performance gains that result when individuals and departments coordinate their actions.

One of the main advantages of using groups is the opportunity to obtain a type of **synergy:** People working in a group are able to produce more or higher-quality outputs than would have been produced if each person had worked

Figure 15.1

Groups' and Teams' Contributions to Organizational Effectiveness

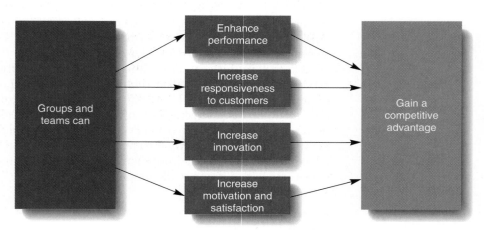

separately and all their individual efforts were later combined. The essence of synergy is captured in the saying "The whole is more than the sum of its parts." Factors that can contribute to synergy in groups include the ability of group members to bounce ideas off one another, to correct one another's mistakes, to solve problems immediately as they arise, to bring a diverse knowledge base to bear on a problem or goal, and to accomplish work that is too vast or all-encompassing for any one individual to achieve on his or her own. At Louis Vuitton and Nucor in "A Manager's Challenge," the kinds of work the production teams are responsible for could not be performed by an individual acting alone; it is only through the combined efforts of team members that luxury accessories and steel products can be produced efficiently and effectively.

Synergy in space. Astronaut Lisa M. Nowak (foreground) checks procedures as astronaut Stephanie D. Wilson (center) works with the Mobile Service System (MSS) and Canadarm2 controls in the Destiny laboratory of the International Space Station while Space Shuttle Discovery was docked to the station in July, 2006. Wilson used the station's arm to move the Italian-built Leonardo Multi-Purpose Logistics Module (MPLM) from the shuttle cargo bay to install on the station's Unity node. Astronaut Jeffrey N. Williams (background) assisted Wilson.

To take advantage of the potential for synergy in groups, managers need to make sure that groups are composed of members who have complementary skills and knowledge relevant to the group's work. For example, at Hallmark Cards, synergies are created by bringing together all the different functions needed to create and produce a greeting card in a cross-functional team (a team composed of members from different departments or functions; see Chapter 10). For instance, artists, writers, designers, and marketing experts work together as members of a team to develop new cards.[15]

At Hallmark, the skills and expertise of the artists complement the contributions of the writers and vice versa. Managers also need to give groups enough autonomy so that the groups, rather than the manager, are solving problems and determining how to achieve goals and objectives, as is true in the cross-functional teams at Hallmark and the production teams in Louis Vuitton and Nucor in

"A Manager's Challenge." To promote synergy, managers need to empower their subordinates and be coaches, guides, and resources for groups while refraining from playing a more directive or supervisory role, as is true at Louis Vuitton and Nucor. The potential for synergy in groups may be the reason why more and more managers are incorporating empowerment into their personal leadership styles (see Chapter 14).

When tasks are complex and involve highly sophisticated and rapidly changing technologies, achieving synergies in teams often hinges on having the appropriate mix of backgrounds and areas of expertise represented on the team. In large organizations with operations in many states and countries, it is often difficult for managers to determine which employees might have the expertise needed on a particular team or for a certain project. As indicated in the following "Information Technology Byte," new software applications can help managers identify employees with the expertise needed to achieve real synergies.

Information Technology Byte

Achieving Synergies By Identifying Expertise

Lockheed Martin Corporation has over 130,000 employees working in 939 different locations in over 450 cities in the United States and around the world.[16] These vast human resources provide Lockheed Martin with a tremendous amount of expertise to draw on to solve vexing problems and better meet customers' needs. However, it is a real challenge for managers to identify who in the company might actually have the expertise needed for a particular project or team.

Enter ActiveNet, a software application provided by Tacit Knowledge Systems Inc.[17] ActiveNet scans documents in a company's computer systems, ranging from e-mails and instant messages to Word and PowerPoint documents, to identify areas of expertise based on what people write and the content of documents they produce;[18] the software creates searchable employee profiles based on this content.[19] For example, a Lockheed team of researchers in California was concerned about the potential for condensation to accumulate in missile canisters. Given all the work Lockheed does with missiles, it was likely that someone in the company had worked on this problem before. Through ActiveNet, the team was able to identify a researcher working in another California facility who had expertise in this area.[20]

Northrop Grumman has over 125,000 employees and faces similar challenges in identifying expertise needed to achieve synergies.[21] For example, when Werner Hinz, a Grumman engineer, was preparing a bid for the Pentagon to develop a new, unmanned airplane that could travel faster than the speed of sound, he needed someone with expertise in hypersonics on his team. Hinz couldn't think of any employees he knew with this expertise, so he used ActiveNet by typing in key phrases. ActiveNet provided Hinz with the name of an employee he had actually met and who worked in the same building as Hinz but whom Hinz did not know much

At Amazon, teams adhere to the two-pizza rule; that is, no team should need more than two pizzas to feed its members.

While Bezos gives teams autonomy to develop and run with their ideas, he also believes in the careful analysis and testing of ideas. A great advocate of the power of facts, data, and analysis, Bezos feels that whenever an idea can be tested through analysis, analysis should rule the day. When an undertaking is just too large or too uncertain or when data are lacking and hard to come by, Bezos and other experienced top managers make the final call.[28] But in order to make such judgment calls about implementing new ideas (either by data analysis or expert judgment), what really is needed are truly creative ideas. To date, teams have played a very important role in generating ideas that have helped Amazon be responsive to its customers, have a widely known Internet brand name, ride out the dot-com bust, and be the highly successful and innovative company it is today.[29]

Groups and Teams as Motivators

Managers often decide to form groups and teams to accomplish organizational goals and then find that using groups and teams brings additional benefits. Members of groups, and especially members of teams (because of the higher intensity of interaction in teams), are likely to be more and satisfied than they would have been if they were working on their own. The experience of working alongside other highly charged and motivated people can be very stimulating. In addition, working on a team can be very motivating: Team members more readily see how their efforts and expertise directly contribute to the achievement of team and organizational goals, and they feel personally responsible for the outcomes or results of their work. This has been the case at Louis Vuitton, Nucor, and Hallmark Cards.

The increased motivation and satisfaction that can accompany the use of teams can also lead to other outcomes, such as lower turnover. This has been Frank B. Day's experience as founder and CEO of Rock Bottom Restaurants Inc. To provide high-quality customer service, Day has organized the restaurants' employees into wait staff teams, whose members work together to refill beers, take orders, bring hot chicken enchiladas to the tables, or clear off the tables. Team members share the burden of undesirable activities and unpopular shift times, and customers no longer have to wait until a particular waitress or waiter is available. Motivation and satisfaction levels in Rock Bottom restaurants seem to be higher than in other restaurants, and turnover is about one-half of that experienced in other U.S. restaurant chains.[30]

Working in a group or team can also satisfy organizational members' needs for engaging in social interaction and feeling connected to other people. For workers who perform highly stressful jobs, such as hospital emergency and operating room staff, group membership can be an important source of social support and motivation. Family members or friends may not be able to fully understand or appreciate some sources of work stress that these group members experience firsthand. Moreover, group members may cope better with work stressors when they are able to share them with other members of their group. In addition, groups often devise techniques to relieve stress, such as the telling of jokes among hospital operating room staff.

Why do managers in all kinds of organizations rely so heavily on groups and teams? Effectively managed groups and teams can help managers in their quest for high performance, responsiveness to customers, and employee motivation. Before explaining how managers can effectively manage groups, however, we will describe the types of groups that are formed in organizations.

Types of Groups and Teams

To achieve their goals of high performance, responsiveness to customers, innovation, and employee motivation, managers can form various types of groups and teams (see Figure 15.2). **Formal groups** are those managers establish to achieve organizational goals. The formal work groups are *cross-functional* teams composed of members from different departments, such as those at Hallmark Cards, and *cross-cultural* teams composed of members from different cultures or countries, such as the teams at global carmakers. As you will see, some of the groups discussed in this section also can be considered to be cross-functional (if they are composed of members from different departments) or cross-cultural (if they are composed of members from different countries or cultures).

Sometimes organizational members, managers or nonmanagers, form groups because they feel that groups will help them achieve their own goals or meet their own needs (for example, the need for social interaction). Groups formed in this way are **informal groups.** Four nurses who work in a hospital and have lunch together twice a week constitute an informal group.

formal group A group that managers establish to achieve organizational goals.

informal group A group that managers or nonmanagerial employees form to help achieve their own goals or meet their own needs.

top-management team A group composed of the CEO, the president, and the heads of the most important departments.

The Top-Management Team

A central concern of the CEO and president of a company is to form a **top-management team** to help the organization achieve its mission and goals. Top-management teams are responsible for developing the strategies that result in an organization's competitive advantage; most have between five and seven members. In forming their top-management teams, CEOs are well advised to stress

Figure 15.2
Types of Groups and Teams in Organizations

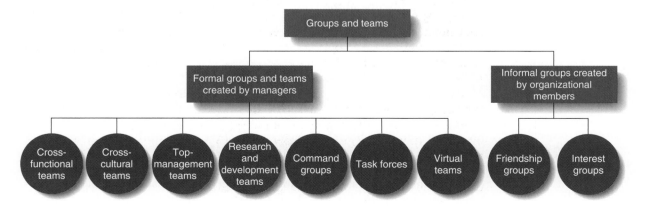

Top-management teams are responsible for developing the strategies that result in an organization's competitive advantage.

diversity—diversity in expertise, skills, knowledge, and experience. Thus, many top-management teams are also cross-functional teams: They are composed of members from different departments, such as finance, marketing, production, and engineering. Diversity helps ensure that the top-management team will have all the background and resources it needs to make good decisions. Diversity also helps guard against *groupthink*, faulty group decision making that results when group members strive for agreement at the expense of an accurate assessment of the situation (see Chapter 6).

Research and Development Teams

research and development team A team whose members have the expertise and experience needed to develop new products.

Managers in pharmaceuticals, computers, electronics, electronic imaging, and other high-tech industries often create **research and development teams** to develop new products. Managers select R&D team members on the basis of their expertise and experience in a certain area. Sometimes R&D teams are cross-functional teams with members from departments such as engineering, marketing, and production in addition to members from the research and development department.

Command Groups

command group A group composed of subordinates who report to the same supervisor; also called *department* or *unit*.

Subordinates who report to the same supervisor compose a **command group.** When top managers design an organization's structure and establish reporting relationships and a chain of command, they are essentially creating command groups. Command groups, often called *departments* or *units*, perform a significant amount of the work in many organizations. In order to have command groups that help an organization gain a competitive advantage, managers not only need to motivate group members to perform at a high level but also need to be effective leaders. Examples of command groups include the salespeople in a large department store in New York who report to the same supervisor, the employees of a small swimming pool sales and maintenance company in Florida who report to a general manager, the telephone operators at the MetLife insurance company who report to the same supervisor, and workers on an automobile assembly line in the Ford Motor Company who report to the same first-line manager.

Task Forces

task force A committee of managers or nonmanagerial employees from various departments or divisions who meet to solve a specific, mutual problem; also called *ad hoc committee*.

Managers form **task forces** to accomplish specific goals or solve problems in a certain time period; task forces are sometimes called *ad hoc committees*. For example, Michael Rider, owner and top manager of a chain of six gyms and fitness centers in the Midwest, created a task force composed of the general managers of each of the six gyms to determine whether the fitness centers should institute a separate fee schedule for customers who wanted to use the centers only for aerobics classes (and not use other facilities such as weights, steps, tracks, and swimming pools). The task force was given three months to prepare a report summarizing the pros and cons of the proposed change in fee schedules. Once the task force completed its report and reached the conclusion that the change in fee structure probably would reduce revenues rather than increase them and thus should not be implemented, it was disbanded. As in Rider's case, task forces can be a valuable tool for busy managers who do not have the time to personally explore an important issue in depth.

Sometimes managers need to form task forces whose work, so to speak, is never done. The task force may be addressing a long-term or enduring problem or issue facing an organization, such as how to most usefully contribute to the local community or how to make sure that the organization provides opportunities for potential employees with disabilities. Task forces that are relatively permanent are often referred to as *standing committees*. Membership in standing committees changes over time. Members may have, for example, a two- or three-year term on the committee, and memberships expire at varying times so that there are always some members with experience on the committee. Managers often form and maintain standing committees to make sure that important issues continue to be addressed.

Self-Managed Work Teams

self-managed work team A group of employees who supervise their own activities and monitor the quality of the goods and services they provide.

Self-managed work teams are teams in which team members are empowered and have the responsibility and autonomy to complete identifiable pieces of work. On a day-to-day basis, team members decide what the team will do, how it will do it, and which team members will perform which specific tasks.[31] Managers provide self-managed work teams with their overall goals (such as assembling defect-free computer keyboards) but let team members decide how to meet those goals. Managers usually form self-managed work teams to improve quality, increase motivation and satisfaction, and lower costs. Often, by creating self-managed work teams, they combine tasks that individuals working separately used to perform, so the team is responsible for the whole set of tasks that yields an identifiable output or end product.

In response to increasing competition, Johnson Wax, maker of well-known household products including Pledge furniture polish, Glade air freshener, and Windex window cleaner,[32] formed self-managed work teams to find ways to cut costs. Traditionally, Johnson Wax used assembly-line production, in which workers were not encouraged or required to do much real thinking on the job, let alone determine how to cut costs. Things could not be more different at Johnson Wax now. Consider, for example, the nine-member self-managed work team that is responsible for molding plastic containers. Team members choose their own leader, train new members, have their own budget to manage, and are responsible for figuring out how to cut costs of molding plastic containers. Kim Litrenta, a long-time employee of Johnson's Waxdale, Wisconsin, plant sums up the effects of the change from assembly-line production to self-managed work teams this way: "In the past you'd have no idea how much things cost because you weren't involved in decisions. Now it's amazing how many different ways people try to save money."[33]

Managers can take a number of steps to ensure that self-managed work teams are effective and help an organization gain a competitive advantage:[34]

- Give teams enough responsibility and autonomy to be truly self-managing. Refrain from telling team members what to do or solving problems for them even if you (as a manager) know what should be done.

- Make sure that a team's work is sufficiently complex so that it entails a number of different steps or procedures that must be performed and results in some kind of finished end product.

- Carefully select members of self-managed work teams. Team members should have the diversity of skills needed to complete the team's work, have the ability to work with others, and want to be part of a team.

- As a manager, realize that your role vis-á-vis self-managed work teams calls for guidance, coaching, and supporting, not supervising. You are a resource for teams to turn to when needed.

- Analyze what type of training team members need, and provide it. Working in a self-managed work team often requires that employees have more extensive technical and interpersonal skills.

Managers in a wide variety of organizations have found that self-managed work teams help the organization achieve its goals, as is true at Louis Vuitton and Nucor in "A Manager's Challenge."[35] However, self-managed work teams can run into trouble. Members are often reluctant to discipline one another by withholding bonuses from members who are not performing up to par or by firing members.[36] Buster Jarrell, a manager who oversees self-managed work teams in AES Corporation's Houston plant, has found that although self-managed work teams are highly effective, they have a very difficult time firing team members who are performing poorly.[37]

The Dallas office of the New York Life Insurance Co. recently experimented with having members of self-managed teams evaluate one another's performance and determine pay levels. Team members did not feel comfortable assuming this role, however, and managers ended up handling these tasks.[38] One reason for team members' discomfort may be the close personal relationships they sometimes develop with one another. In addition, members of self-managed work teams may actually take longer to accomplish tasks, such as when team members have difficulties coordinating their efforts.

Virtual Teams

virtual team A team whose members rarely or never meet face-to-face but, rather, interact by using various forms of information technology such as e-mail, computer networks, telephone, fax, and videoconferences.

Virtual teams are teams whose members rarely or never meet face-to-face but, rather, interact by using various forms of information technology such as e-mail, computer networks, telephone, fax, and videoconferences. As organizations become increasingly global, -and as the need for specialized knowledge increases due to advances in technology, managers can create virtual teams to solve problems or explore opportunities without being limited by the fact that team members need to be working in the same geographic location.[39]

Take the case of an organization that has manufacturing facilities in Australia, Canada, the United States, and Mexico and is encountering a quality problem in a complex manufacturing process. Each of its facilities has a quality control team headed by a quality control manager. The vice president for production does not try to solve the problem by forming and leading a team at one of the four manufacturing facilities; instead, she forms and leads a virtual team composed of the quality control managers of the four plants and the plants' general managers. When these team members communicate via e-mail and videoconferencing, a wide array of knowledge and experience is brought to bear to solve the problem.

The principal advantage of virtual teams is that they enable managers to disregard geographic distances and form teams whose members have the knowledge, expertise, and experience to tackle a particular problem or take advantage of a specific opportunity.[40] Virtual teams also can include members who are not actually employees of the organization itself; a virtual team might include members of a company that is used for outsourcing. More and more companies, including Hewlett-Packard, Price-waterhouseCoopers, Lotus Development, Kodak, Whirlpool, and VeriFone, are either using or exploring the use of virtual teams.[41]

There are two forms of information technologies that members of virtual teams rely on, synchronous technologies and asynchronous technologies.[42] *Synchronous technologies* enable virtual team members to communicate and interact with one another in real time simultaneously and include videoconferencing, teleconferencing, and electronic meetings. *Asynchronous technologies* delay communication and include e-mail, electronic bulletin boards, and Internet Web sites. Many virtual teams use both kinds of technology depending on what projects they are working on.

Increasing globalization is likely to result in more organizations relying on virtual teams to a greater extent.[43] One of the major challenges members of virtual teams face is building a sense of camaraderie and trust among team members who rarely, if ever, meet face-to-face. To address this challenge, some organizations schedule recreational activities, such as ski trips, so that virtual team members can get together. Other organizations make sure that virtual team members have a chance to meet in person soon after the team is formed and then schedule periodic face-to-face meetings to promote trust, understanding, and cooperation in the teams.[44] The need for such meetings is underscored by research that suggests that while some virtual teams can be as effective as teams that meet face-to-face, virtual team members might be less satisfied with teamwork efforts and have fewer feelings of camaraderie or cohesion. (Group cohesiveness is discussed in more detail later in the chapter.)[45]

Research also suggests that it is important for managers to keep track of virtual teams and intervene when necessary by, for example, encouraging members of teams who do not communicate often enough to monitor their team's progress and make sure that team members actually have the time, and are recognized for, their virtual teamwork.[46] Additionally, when virtual teams are experiencing downtime or rough spots, managers might try to schedule face-to-face team time to bring team members together and help them focus on their goals.[47]

friendship group An informal group composed of employees who enjoy one another's company and socialize with one another.

Friendship groups like this one can help satisfy employees' needs for interpersonal interaction, provide social support in times of stress, and can increase job satisfaction. Since group members often discuss work-related problems, they may even end up generating solutions that can be used on the job.

Friendship Groups

The groups described so far are formal groups created by managers. **Friendship groups** are informal groups composed of employees who enjoy one another's company and socialize with one another. Members of friendship groups may have lunch together, take breaks together, or meet after work for meals, sports, or other activities. Friendship groups help satisfy employees' needs for interpersonal interaction, can provide needed social support in times of stress, and can contribute to people's feeling good at work and being satisfied with their jobs. Managers themselves often form friendship groups. The informal relationships that managers build in friendship groups can often help them solve work-related problems because members of these groups typically discuss work-related matters and offer advice.

Interest Groups

interest group An informal group composed of employees seeking to achieve a common goal related to their membership in an organization.

Employees form informal **interest groups** when they seek to achieve a common goal related to their membership in an organization. Employees may form interest groups, for example, to encourage managers to consider instituting flexible working hours, providing on-site child care, improving working conditions, or more proactively supporting environmental protection. Interest groups can provide managers with valuable insights into the issues and concerns that are foremost in employees' minds. They also can signal the need for change.

Group Dynamics

The ways in which groups function and, ultimately, their effectiveness hinge on group characteristics and processes known collectively as *group dynamics*. In this section, we discuss five key elements of group dynamics: group size, tasks, and roles; group leadership; group development; group norms; and group cohesiveness.

Group Size, Tasks, and Roles

Managers need to take group size, group tasks, and group roles into account as they create and maintain high-performing groups and teams.

GROUP SIZE The number of members in a group can be an important determinant of members' motivation and commitment and group performance. There are several advantages to keeping a group relatively small—between two and nine members. Compared with members of large groups, members of small groups tend to (1) interact more with each other and find it easier to coordinate their efforts, (2) be more motivated, satisfied, and committed, (3) find it easier to share information, and (4) be better able to see the importance of their personal contributions for group success. A disadvantage of small rather than large groups is that members of small groups have fewer resources available to accomplish their goals.

Large groups—with 10 or more members—also offer some advantages. They have more resources at their disposal to achieve group goals than small groups do. These resources include the knowledge, experience, skills, and abilities of group members as well as their actual time and effort. Large groups also enable managers to obtain the advantages stemming from the **division of labor**—splitting the work to be performed into particular tasks and assigning tasks to individual workers. Workers who specialize in particular tasks are likely to become skilled at performing those tasks and contribute significantly to high group performance.

division of labor Splitting the work to be performed into particular tasks and assigning tasks to individual workers.

The disadvantages of large groups include the problems of communication and coordination and the lower levels of motivation, satisfaction, and commitment that members of large groups sometimes experience. It is clearly more difficult to share information with, and coordinate the activities of, 16 people rather than 8 people. Moreover, members of large groups might not think that their efforts are really needed and sometimes might not even feel a part of the group.

In deciding on the appropriate size for any group, managers attempt to gain the advantages of small-group size and, at the same time, form groups with sufficient resources to accomplish their goals and have a well-developed division of labor, as is true at Louis Vuitton and Nucor in "A Manager's Challenge." As a general rule of thumb, groups should have no more members than necessary to achieve a division of labor and provide the resources needed to achieve group goals. In R&D teams, for example, group size is too large when (1) members spend more time communicating what they know to others than applying what they know to solve problems and create new products, (2) individual productivity decreases, and (3) group performance suffers.[48]

GROUP TASKS   The appropriate size of a high-performing group is affected by the kind of tasks the group is to perform. An important characteristic of group tasks that affects performance is **task interdependence,** the degree to which the work performed by one member of a group influences the work performed by other members.[49] As task interdependence increases, group members need to interact more frequently and intensely with one another and their efforts have to be more closely coordinated if they are to perform at a high level. Management expert James D. Thompson identified three types of task interdependence: pooled, sequential, and reciprocal (see Figure 15.3).[50]

task interdependence
The degree to which the work performed by one member of a group influences the work performed by other members.

Figure 15.3
Types of Task Interdependence

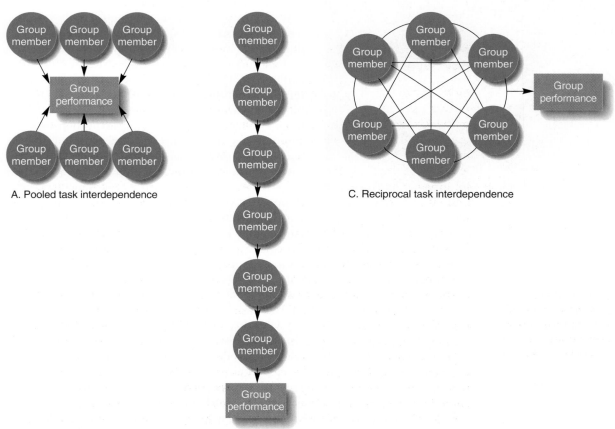

A. Pooled task interdependence

B. Sequential task interdependence

C. Reciprocal task interdependence

pooled task interdependence The task interdependence that exists when group members make separate and independent contributions to group performance.

POOLED TASK INTERDEPENDENCE Pooled task interdependence exists when group members make separate and independent contributions to group performance; overall group performance is the sum of the performance of the individual members (see Figure 15.3a). Examples of groups that have pooled task interdependence include a group of teachers in an elementary school, a group of salespeople in a department store, a group of secretaries in an office, and a group of custodians in an office building. In these examples, group performance, whether it be the number of children who are taught and the quality of their education, the dollar value of sales, the amount of secretarial work completed, or the number of offices cleaned, is determined by summing the individual contributions of group members.

For groups with pooled interdependence, managers should determine the appropriate group size primarily from the amount of work to be accomplished. Large groups can be effective because group members work independently and do not have to interact frequently with one another. Motivation in groups with pooled interdependence will be highest when managers reward group members based on individual performance.

sequential task interdependence The task interdependence that exists when group members must perform specific tasks in a predetermined order.

SEQUENTIAL TASK INTERDEPENDENCE Sequential task interdependence exists when group members must perform specific tasks in a predetermined order; certain tasks have to be performed before others, and what one worker does affects the work of others (see Figure 15.3b). Assembly lines and mass-production processes are characterized by sequential task interdependence.

With sequential interdependence, such as in this printing press operation, it is difficult to identify individual performance because one group member's performance depends on how well others perform their tasks.

When group members are sequentially interdependent, group size is usually dictated by the needs of the production process—for example, the number of steps needed in an assembly line to efficiently produce a CD player. With sequential interdependence, it is difficult to identify individual performance because one group member's performance depends on how well others perform their tasks. A slow worker at the start of an assembly line, for example, causes all workers further down to work slowly. Thus, managers are often advised to reward group members for group performance. Group members will be motivated to perform highly because if the group performs well, each member will benefit. In addition, group members may put pressure on poor performers to improve so that group performance and rewards do not suffer.

reciprocal task interdependence The task interdependence that exists when the work performed by each group member is fully dependent on the work performed by other group members.

RECIPROCAL TASK INTERDEPENDENCE Reciprocal task interdependence exists when the work performed by each group member is fully dependent on the work performed by other group members; group members have to share information, intensely interact with one another, and coordinate their efforts in order for the group to achieve its goals (see Figure 15.3c). In general, reciprocal task interdependence characterizes the operation of teams, rather than other kinds of groups. The task interdependence of R&D teams, top-management teams, and many self-managed work teams is reciprocal.

When group members are reciprocally interdependent, managers are advised to keep group size relatively small because of the necessity of coordinating team members' activities. Communication difficulties can arise in teams with reciprocally interdependent tasks because team members need to interact frequently with one another and be available when needed. As group size increases, communication difficulties increase and can impair team performance.

When a group's members are reciprocally interdependent, managers also are advised to reward group members on the basis of group performance. Individual levels of performance are often difficult for managers to identify, and group-based rewards help ensure that group members will be motivated to perform at a high level and make valuable contributions to the group. Of course, if a manager can identify instances of individual performance in such groups, they too can be rewarded to maintain high levels of motivation. Microsoft and many other companies reward group members for their individual performance as well as for the performance of their group.

group role A set of behaviors and tasks that a member of a group is expected to perform because of his or her position in the group.

GROUP ROLES A **group role** is a set of behaviors and tasks that a member of a group is expected to perform because of his or her position in the group. Members of cross-functional teams, for example, are expected to perform roles relevant to their special areas of expertise. In our earlier example of cross-functional teams at Hallmark Cards, it is the role of writers on the teams to create verses for new cards, the role of artists to draw illustrations, and the role of designers to put verse and artwork together in an attractive and appealing card design. The roles of members of top-management teams are shaped primarily by their areas of expertise—production, marketing, finance, research and development—but members of top-management teams also typically draw on their broad-based expertise as planners and strategists.

In forming groups and teams, managers need to clearly communicate to group members the expectations for their roles in the group, what is required of them, and how the different roles in the group fit together to accomplish group goals. Managers also need to realize that group roles often change and evolve as a group's tasks and goals change and as group members gain experience and knowledge. Thus, to get the performance gains that come from experience or "learning by doing," managers should encourage group members to take the initiative to assume additional responsibilities as they see fit and modify their assigned roles. This process, called **role making,** can enhance individual and group performance.

role making Taking the initiative to modify an assigned role by assuming additional responsibilities.

In self-managed work teams and some other groups, group members themselves are responsible for creating and assigning roles. Many self-managed work teams also pick their own team leaders. When group members create their own roles, managers should be available to group members in an advisory capacity, helping them effectively settle conflicts and disagreements. At Johnsonville Foods, for example, the position titles of first-line managers have been changed to "advisory coach" to reflect the managers' new role vis-á-vis the self-managed work teams they oversee.[51]

Group Leadership

All groups and teams need leadership. Indeed, as we discussed in detail in Chapter 14, effective leadership is a key ingredient for high-performing groups, teams, and organizations. Sometimes managers assume the leadership role in groups and teams, as is the case in many command groups and top-management teams. Or a manager may appoint a member of a group who is not a manager to be

CHAPTER 16

Promoting Effective Communication

Learning Objectives

After studying this chapter, you should be able to:

- Explain why effective communication helps an organization gain a competitive advantage.

- Describe the communication process, and explain the role of perception in communication.

- Define information richness, and describe the information richness of communication media available to managers.

- Describe the communication networks that exist in groups and teams.

- Explain how advances in technology have given managers new options for managing communication.

- Describe important communication skills that managers need as senders and as receivers of messages.

A Manager's Challenge

Jong-Yong Yun Reaps the Benefits of Face-to-Face Communication at Samsung Electronics

How can managers achieve a good balance between face-to-face and electronic communication?

Advances in information technology have changed the way managers and all organizational members communicate with one another. E-mail has become such a ubiquitous part of organizational life that some managers and employees are loathe to be out of touch even when on the road, on vacation, or after working hours when not near their PCs or laptops—hence, the popularity of the Blackberry, which allows users to send and receive e-mail anywhere on a device the size of a cell phone.

Of course, these technological advances are supposed to help organizational members work smarter and better and improve communication. Have they lived up to their promise? Some managers think not and fear that e-mail has taken on a life of its own, hindering rather than enhancing communication and productivity. Take the case of Vickie

Farrell, vice president of Teradata, a unit of NCR Corporation.[1] Farrell believes that the ever-present stream of e-mail messages, and

Communication devices such as the Blackberry give today's managers 24/7 access to e-mail.

the expectations on the part of senders that they will be responded to quickly, interferes with productivity, creativity, and innovation. It is hard to think, never mind engage in forward-looking thinking and develop truly creative ideas, when being bombarded with a constant stream of e-mail messages and responding to them. Managers and many employees could spend most of their days sending and receiving e-mails without getting any other work done—especially the kind of work that requires all of one's attention to deal with a vexing problem, think long term, and develop creative solutions. As Farrell puts it, "The messages keep coming and coming. . . . Now it has gotten to the point where you can spend your entire day doing nothing but answering e-mail. It's intrusive and disruptive."[2] Farrell deliberately sets time aside during the day when she will not look at or answer e-mails so that she can focus on her "real" work.[3]

Jong-Yong Yun, the celebrated CEO and vice chairman of Samsung Electronics, is one manager who seems to have a good handle on communication. Leading a company that is at the forefront of information technology,[4] Yun knows how powerful and efficient electronic communication can be. At the same time, as a leader, he knows that e-mail, videoconferences, and other forms of electronic communication cannot replace face-to-face contact when managers are dealing with important issues in today's dynamic workplace.[5] Since becoming CEO in 1996, Yun has literally transformed Samsung into the most profitable global consumer electronics company and biggest manufacturer of memory chips in the world.[6] Prior to Yun's leadership, Samsung was a complacent bureaucracy, pursuing growth and not too concerned about profits.[7]

Yun believes that the heart of any business is in the field and that no matter how convenient electronic communication can be (which he, of course, takes advantage of), it is no replacement for face-to-face communication. Thus, Yun devotes a lot of his time to communicating with employees on-site and face-to-face—both in Korea (where Samsung is based) and in other countries—so that he can personally witness ongoing operations and talk to employees at all levels about the challenges they face and opportunities for improvements. Yun explains,

> This gives me the opportunity to freely discuss matters with the person directly involved, from the top management to the junior staff of that work site. While many people believe that developments in digital technology have brought convenience . . . I still believe that no innovation can replace the valuable information that is gathered through direct discussions.[8]

Yun visits plants, sales offices, and even retailers to learn what is going on in the field, listens to employees regardless of their rank or position in the company, and frequently asks questions of those closest to operations to learn firsthand of problems and opportunities.[9] Of course, he also takes advantage of information technology (but not as a replacement for face-to-face contact). Thus, he instituted an electronic hotline whereby any employee can send him suggestions or complaints with confidentiality guaranteed. For example, employees in one R&D unit in a factory complained that they were having trouble getting an air conditioner that was needed to keep important equipment at the proper temperature; the air conditioner was in place the day after the complaint was received.[10]

Yun has propelled Samsung into being a global force with annual profits of over $9 billion on sales of over $71 billion.[11] Thus, it is not surprising that Yun has received numerous accolades in the business press, such as being ranked among the most powerful businesspeople in Asia by *Fortune* magazine and one of the best managers by *BusinessWeek* magazine.[12] And while Yun excels as a leader and manager in numerous ways, clearly, his commitment to good communication has contributed to his ongoing success at Samsung Electronics.[13]

Overview Even with all the advances in information technology that are available to managers, face-to-face communication continues to play a very important role in organizations, as Yun realizes in "A Manager's Challenge." While Yun certainly takes advantage of IT to receive and respond quickly to employee concerns, he also recognizes the importance of communicating with employees in person at their work sites. Ironically, the proliferation of e-mail has its downside as well; managers like Vickie Farrell are deliberately scheduling time-outs from e-mail to take control of their workdays and engage in strategic thinking.[14] The experiences of Farrell, Yun, and other managers and employees underscore the fact that IT is a tool to improve human communication, not a substitute for human communication. Hence, managers must never lose sight of the fact that people are at the center stage of effective communication. Ineffective communication is detrimental for managers, employees, and organizations; it can lead to poor performance, strained interpersonal relations, poor-quality service, and dissatisfied customers. For an organization to be effective and gain a competitive advantage, managers at all levels need to be good communicators.

In this chapter, we describe the nature of communication and the communication process and explain why all managers and their subordinates need to be effective communicators. We describe the communication media available to managers and the factors they need to consider in selecting a communication medium for each message they send. We consider the communication networks that organizational members rely on, and we explore how advances in information technology have expanded managers' range of communication options. We describe the communication skills that help managers be effective senders and receivers of messages. By the end of this chapter, you will have a good appreciation of the nature of communication and the steps that managers can take to ensure that they are effective communicators.

Communication and Management

communication The sharing of information between two or more individuals or groups to reach a common understanding.

Communication is the sharing of information between two or more individuals or groups to reach a common understanding.[15] "A Manager's Challenge" highlights some important aspects of this definition. First and foremost, no matter how electronically based, communication is a human endeavor and involves individuals and groups. Second, communication does not take place unless a common understanding is reached. Thus, when you call a business to speak to a person in customer service or billing and are bounced back and forth between endless automated messages and menu options and eventually hang up in frustration, communication has not taken place.

The Importance of Good Communication

In Chapter 1, we described how an organization can gain a competitive advantage when managers strive to increase efficiency, quality, responsiveness to customers, and innovation. Good communication is essential for attaining each of these four goals and thus is a necessity for gaining a competitive advantage.

Managers can *increase efficiency* by updating the production process to take advantage of new and more efficient technologies and by training workers to operate the new technologies and expand their skills. Good communication is necessary for managers to learn about new technologies, implement them in their organizations, and train workers in how to use them. Similarly, *improving quality* hinges on effective communication. Managers need to communicate to all members of an organization the meaning and importance of high quality and the routes to attaining it. Subordinates need to communicate quality problems and suggestions for increasing quality to their superiors, and members of self-managed work teams need to share their ideas on improving quality with one another.

Good communication can also help to increase *responsiveness to customers.* When the organizational members who are closest to customers, such as department store salespeople and bank tellers, are empowered to communicate customers' needs and desires to managers, managers are better able to respond to these needs. Managers, in turn, must communicate with other organizational members to determine how best to respond to changing customer preferences.

Innovation, which often takes place in cross-functional teams, also requires effective communication. Members of a cross-functional team developing a new electronic game, for example, must effectively communicate with one another to develop a game that customers will want to play, that will be engaging, interesting, and fun, and that can potentially lead to sequels. Members of the team also must communicate with managers to secure the resources they need for developing the game and to keep managers informed of progress on the project. Innovation in organizations is increasingly taking place on a global level, making effective communication all the more important, as illustrated in the following "Managing Globally."

Managing
Globally

Global Communication Enables Global Innovation

GE Healthcare Technologies, based in Waukesha, Wisconsin, is a unit of GE Healthcare (headquarted in the United Kingdom) that makes CT scanners and has approximately $12 billion in revenues.[16] In order to make the best scanners that meet the needs of doctors and patients around the world with next-generation technology, new product development and manufacture is truly a global endeavor at GE Healthcare Technologies. Take the case of the new LightSpeed VCT scanner series (*VCT* stands for "volume controlled tomography"), which costs in the millions and is among the quickest and highest-resolution scanners available in the world.[17] The LightSpeed can perform a full-body scan in under 10 seconds and yields a three-dimensional picture of patients' hearts within five heartbeats.[18]

The LightSpeed was developed through true global collaboration. GE managers not only spoke with doctors (including cardiologists and radiologists) around the world to find out what their needs were and what kinds of tests they would perform with the LightSpeed but also gathered information about differences among patients in various countries. Engineers in Hino (Japan), Buc

The team responsible for GE's LightSpeed VCT scanner, which can perform a full-body scan in less than 10 seconds, was made up of individuals from at least six different countries.

(France), and Waukesha developed the electronics for the LightSpeed. Other parts, such as the automated table that patients lie on, are made in Beijing (China) and Hino. Software for the LightSpeed was written in Haifa (Israel), Bangalore (India), Buc, and Waukesha.[19]

Effective global communication was a challenge and a necessity to successfully develop the Light-Speed series. As Brian Duchinsky, GE's general manager for global CT, puts it, "If we sat around in this cornfield west of Milwaukee, we wouldn't come up with the same breadth of good ideas. But yet, getting six countries on the phone to make a decision can be a pain."[20]

GE managers facilitated effective communication in a number of ways—participating daily in conference calls, making sure that teams in different countries depended on one another, developing an internal Web site devoted to the LightSpeed, encouraging teams to ask one another for help, and holding face-to-face meetings in different locations. While much communication took place electronically, such as through conference calls, face-to-face meetings were also important. As Bob Armstrong, GE's general manager for engineering, indicates, "You need to get your people together in one place if you want them to really appreciate how good everyone is, and how good you are as a team."[21]

sender The person or group wishing to share information.

message The information that a sender wants to share.

encoding Translating a message into understandable symbols or language.

noise Anything that hampers any stage of the communication process.

receiver The person or group for which a message is intended.

medium The pathway through which an encoded message is transmitted to a receiver.

Effective communication is necessary for managers and all members of an organization to increase efficiency, quality, responsiveness to customers, and innovation and thus gain a competitive advantage for the organization. Managers therefore must have a good understanding of the communication process if they are to perform effectively.

The Communication Process

The communication process consists of two phases. In the *transmission phase*, information is shared between two or more individuals or groups. In the *feedback phase*, a common understanding is ensured. In both phases, a number of distinct stages must occur for communication to take place (see Figure 16.1).[22]

Starting the transmission phase, the **sender,** the person or group wishing to share information with some other person or group, decides on the **message,** what information to communicate. Then the sender translates the message into symbols or language, a process called **encoding;** often messages are encoded into words. **Noise** is a general term that refers to anything that hampers any stage of the communication process.

Once encoded, a message is transmitted through a medium to the **receiver,** the person or group for which the message is intended. A **medium** is simply the pathway, such as a phone call, a letter, a memo, or face-to-face communication in a meeting, through which an encoded message is transmitted to a receiver. At

Figure 16.1
The Communication Process

Transmission phase

Message → Encoding → Medium → Decoding by receiver

Sender   **Noise**   Receiver (now sender)

Decoding by sender (now receiver) ← Medium ← Encoding ← Message

Feedback phase

decoding Interpreting and trying to make sense of a message.

verbal communication The encoding of messages into words, either written or spoken.

nonverbal communication The encoding of messages by means of facial expressions, body language, and styles of dress.

the next stage, the receiver interprets and tries to make sense of the message, a process called **decoding.** This is a critical point in communication.

The feedback phase is initiated by the receiver (who becomes a sender). The receiver decides what message to send to the original sender (who becomes a receiver), encodes it, and transmits it through a chosen medium (see Figure 16.1). The message might contain a confirmation that the original message was received and understood or a restatement of the original message to make sure that it has been correctly interpreted, or it might include a request for more information.

The original sender decodes the message and makes sure that a common understanding has been reached. If the original sender determines that a common understanding has not been reached, sender and receiver cycle through the whole process as many times as needed to reach a common understanding. Feedback eliminates misunderstandings, ensures that messages are correctly interpreted, and enables senders and receivers to reach a common understanding.

The encoding of messages into words, written or spoken, is **verbal communication.** We can also encode messages without using written or spoken language. **Nonverbal communication** shares information by means of facial expressions (smiling, raising an eyebrow, frowning, dropping one's jaw), body language (posture, gestures, nods, and shrugs), and even style of dress (casual, formal, conservative, trendy). For example, as they walk around GM plants, top managers in General Motors wear slacks and sports jackets rather than suits to communicate or signal that GM's old bureaucracy has been dismantled and that the company is decentralized and more informal than it used to be.[23] The trend toward increasing empowerment of the workforce has led some managers to dress informally to communicate that all employees of an organization are team members, working together to create value for customers.

Nonverbal communication can be used to back up or reinforce verbal communication. Just as a warm and genuine smile can back up words of appreciation for a job well done, a

Nonverbal communication shares information by means of facial expressions, body language, and even style of dress.

concerned facial expression can back up words of sympathy for a personal problem. In such cases, the congruence between the verbal and the nonverbal communication helps to ensure that a common understanding is reached.

Sometimes when members of an organization decide not to express a message verbally, they inadvertently do so nonverbally. People tend to have less control over nonverbal communication, and often a verbal message that is withheld gets expressed through body language or facial expressions. A manager who agrees to a proposal that she or he actually is not in favor of may unintentionally communicate her or his disfavor by grimacing.

Sometimes nonverbal communication is used to send messages that cannot be sent through verbal channels. Many lawyers are well aware of this communication tactic. Lawyers are often schooled in techniques of nonverbal communication, such as choosing where to stand in the courtroom for maximum effect and using eye contact during different stages of a trial. Lawyers sometimes get into trouble for using inappropriate nonverbal communication in an attempt to influence juries. In a Louisiana court, prosecuting attorney Thomas Pirtle was admonished and fined $2,500 by Judge Yada Magee for shaking his head in an expression of doubt, waving his arms indicating disfavor, and chuckling when the attorneys for the defense were stating their case.[24]

The Role of Perception in Communication

Perception plays a central role in communication and affects both transmission and feedback. In Chapter 5, we defined *perception* as the process through which people select, organize, and interpret sensory input to give meaning and order to the world around them. We mentioned that perception is inherently subjective and is influenced by people's personalities, values, attitudes, and moods as well as by their experience and knowledge. When senders and receivers communicate with each other, they are doing so based on their own subjective perceptions. The encoding and decoding of messages and even the choice of a medium hinge on the perceptions of senders and receivers.

In addition, perceptual biases can hamper effective communication. Recall from Chapter 5 that *biases* are systematic tendencies to use information about others in ways that result in inaccurate perceptions. In Chapter 5, we described a number of biases that can result in the unfair treatment of diverse members of an organization. The same biases also can lead to ineffective communication. For example, *stereotypes*—simplified and often inaccurate beliefs about the characteristics of particular groups of people—can interfere with the encoding and decoding of messages.

Suppose a manager stereotypes older workers as being fearful of change. When this manager encodes a message to an older worker about an upcoming change in the organization, she may downplay the extent of the change so as not to make the older worker feel stressed. The older worker, however, fears change no more than his younger colleagues fear it and thus decodes the message to mean that only a minor change is going to be made. The older worker fails to adequately prepare for the change, and his performance subsequently suffers because of his lack of preparation for the change. Clearly, the ineffective communication was due to the manager's inaccurate assumptions about older workers. Instead of relying on stereotypes, effective managers strive to perceive other people accurately by focusing on their actual behaviors, knowledge, skills, and abilities. Accurate perceptions, in turn, contribute to effective communication.

The Dangers of Ineffective Communication

Because managers must communicate with others to perform their various roles and tasks, managers spend most of their time communicating, whether in meetings, in telephone conversations, through e-mail, or in face-to-face interactions. Indeed, some experts estimate that managers spend approximately 85% of their time engaged in some form of communication.[25]

Effective communication is so important that managers cannot just be concerned that they themselves are effective communicators; they also have to help their subordinates be effective communicators. When all members of an organization are able to communicate effectively with one another and with people outside the organization, the organization is much more likely to perform highly and gain a competitive advantage.

When managers and other members of an organization are ineffective communicators, organizational performance suffers and any competitive advantage the organization might have is likely to be lost. Moreover, poor communication sometimes can be downright dangerous and even lead to tragic and unnecessary loss of human life. For example, researchers from Harvard University recently studied the causes of mistakes, such as a patient receiving the wrong medication, in two large hospitals in the Boston area. They discovered that some mistakes in hospitals occur because of communication problems—physicians' not having the information they need to correctly order medications for their patients or nurses' not having the information they need to correctly administer medications. The researchers concluded that some of the responsibility for these mistakes lies with hospital management, which has not taken active steps to improve communication.[26]

Communication problems in the cockpit of airplanes and between flying crews and air traffic controllers are unfortunately all too common, sometimes with deadly consequences. In the late 1970s, two jets collided in Tenerife (one of the Canary Islands) because of miscommunication between a pilot and the control tower, and 600 people were killed. The tower radioed to the pilot, "Clipper 1736 report clear of runway." The pilot mistakenly interpreted this message to mean that he was cleared for takeoff.[27] Unfortunately, errors like this one are not a thing of the past. A safety group at NASA tracked more than 6,000 unsafe flying incidents and found that communication difficulties caused approximately 529 of them.[28] And NASA has its own communication difficulties.[29] In 2004, NASA released a report detailing communication problems at the International Space Station jointly managed and staffed by NASA and the Russian space agency; the problems included inadequate record keeping, missing information, and failure to keep data current.[30]

Information Richness and Communication Media

To be effective communicators, managers (and other members of an organization) need to select an appropriate communication medium for *each* message they send. Should a change in procedures be communicated to subordinates in a memo sent through e-mail? Should a congratulatory message about a major accomplishment be communicated in a letter, in a phone call, or over lunch? Should a layoff announcement be made in a memo or at a plant meeting? Should the members of a purchasing team travel to Europe

Figure 16.2

The Information Richness of Communication Media

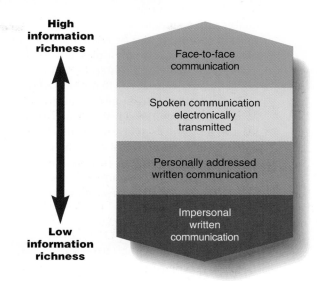

to cement a major agreement with a new supplier, or should they do so through faxes? Managers deal with these questions day in and day out.

There is no one best communication medium for managers to rely on. In choosing a communication medium for any message, managers need to consider three factors. The first and most important is the level of information richness that is needed. **Information richness** is the amount of information a communication medium can carry and the extent to which the medium enables the sender and receiver to reach a common understanding.[31] The communication media that managers use vary in their information richness (see Figure 16.2).[32] Media high in information richness are able to carry an extensive amount of information and generally enable receivers and senders to come to a common understanding.

The second factor that managers need to take into account in selecting a communication medium is the *time* needed for communication, because managers' and other organizational members' time is valuable. Managers at United Parcel Service, for example, dramatically reduced the amount of time they spent on communicating by using videoconferences instead of face-to-face communication, which required that managers travel overseas.[33]

The third factor that affects the choice of a communication medium is the *need for a paper or electronic trail* or some kind of written documentation that a message was sent and received. A manager may wish to document in writing, for example, that a subordinate was given a formal warning about excessive lateness.

In the remainder of this section we examine four types of communication media that vary along these three dimensions (information richness, time, and paper or electronic trail).[34]

information richness
The amount of information that a communication medium can carry and the extent to which the medium enables the sender and receiver to reach a common understanding.

Face-to-Face Communication

Face-to-face communication is the medium that is highest in information richness. When managers communicate face-to-face, they not only can take advantage of verbal communication but also can interpret each other's nonverbal signals such as facial expressions and body language. A look of concern or puzzlement can sometimes say more than a thousand words, and managers can respond to such nonverbal signals on the spot. Face-to-face communication also enables managers to receive instant feedback. Points of confusion, ambiguity, or misunderstanding can be resolved, and managers can cycle through the communication process as many times as needed to reach a common understanding.

With the growing proliferation of electronic forms of communication, such as e-mail, some managers fear that face-to-face communication is being shortchanged to the detriment of building common understandings and rapport.[35] Moreover, some messages that really should be communicated face-to-face or at least in a phone conversation, and messages that are more efficiently communicated in this manner, are nonetheless sent electronically.[36] As indicated in the following "Management Insight," managers need to carefully consider whether face-to-face communication is being shortchanged in their organizations and, if it is, take steps to rectify the situation.

Management Insight

When Face-to-Face Communication Is Best

Anyone who has participated in one of those frustrating e-mail exchanges where messages shoot back and forth and it seems to take forever to resolve a problem, reach a common understanding, or come to a resolution about an issue knows there must be a better way. In such cases, a face-to-face conversation (or if that is not possible, a phone conversation) often will lead to better outcomes all around.

According to Ron McMillan, a consultant to managers at all ranks and coauthor of best-selling books on communication, e-mail should not be relied on to communicate information that is complex, important, or sensitive.[37] In such cases, face-to-face communication (or even a phone conversation) can convey more information than e-mail can, and it is much more effective at reaching a common understanding. Research conducted by Professor Albert Mehrabian

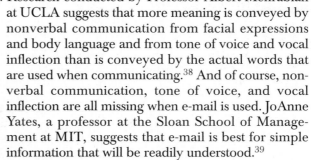

at UCLA suggests that more meaning is conveyed by nonverbal communication from facial expressions and body language and from tone of voice and vocal inflection than is conveyed by the actual words that are used when communicating.[38] And of course, nonverbal communication, tone of voice, and vocal inflection are all missing when e-mail is used. JoAnne Yates, a professor at the Sloan School of Management at MIT, suggests that e-mail is best for simple information that will be readily understood.[39]

Sara Roberts, founder and president of Roberts Golden Consulting in San Francisco, recognizes the value of face-to-face communication. Although consultants in her firm regularly communicate with each other, clients, and suppliers via e-mail and this is often efficient and effective, Roberts believes that rapport and collaboration can suffer when e-mail is used extensively. So she instituted, "No E-mail Fridays" at her firm; on Fridays, employees are not to use e-mail unless it is clearly necessary (e.g., to reply to a client who wants an urgent e-mail response).[40] As Roberts puts it, "No E-mail Friday helps us to remember we really could go over to that person sitting right over there and collaborate more."[41]

management by wandering around A face-to-face communication technique in which a manager walks around a work area and talks informally with employees about issues and concerns.

Management by wandering around is a face-to-face communication technique that is effective for many managers at all levels in an organization.[42] Rather than scheduling formal meetings with subordinates, managers walk around work areas and talk informally with employees about issues and concerns that both employees and managers may have. These informal conversations provide managers and subordinates with important information and at the same time foster the development of positive relationships. William Hewlett and David Packard, founders and former top managers of Hewlett-Packard, found management by wandering around to be a highly effective way of communicating with their employees.

Because face-to-face communication is highest in information richness, you might think that it should always be the medium of choice for managers. This is not the case, however, because of the amount of time it can take and the lack of a paper or electronic trail resulting from it. For messages that are important, personal, or likely to be misunderstood, it is often well worth managers' time to use face-to-face communication and, if need be, supplement it with some form of written communication documenting the message.

Advances in information technology are providing managers with new communication media that are close substitutes for face-to-face communication. Many organizations, such as American Greetings Corp. and Hewlett-Packard, are using *videoconferences* to capture some of the advantages of face-to-face communication (such as access to facial expressions) while saving time and money, since managers in different locations do not have to travel to meet with one another. During a videoconference, managers in two or more locations communicate with each other over large TV or video screens; they not only hear each other but also see each other throughout the meeting.

Videoconferences capture some of the advantages of face-to-face communication (such as access to facial expressions) while saving time and money because managers in different locations do not have to travel to meet with one another.

In addition to saving travel costs, videoconferences sometimes have other advantages. Managers at American Greetings have found that decisions get made more quickly when videoconferences are used, because more managers can be involved in the decision-making process and therefore fewer managers have to be consulted outside the meeting itself. Managers at Hewlett-Packard have found that videoconferences have shortened new product development time by 30% for similar reasons. Videoconferences also seem to lead to more efficient meetings. Some managers have found that their meetings are 20% to 30% shorter when videoconferences are used instead of face-to-face meetings.[43]

Taking videoconferences one step further, IBM and TelePort Corporation have joined forces to build virtual dining rooms in which top managers can actually have "power meals" with other managers in another location. Managers in one location are seated around a large, round table bisected by a huge video screen on which they are able to see (life-size) their dining partners in another location sitting around the same kind of table having the same kind of meal. Even though managers may be hundreds or thousands of miles apart, they can eat together as they discuss pressing concerns. The cameras enabling the transmission of the video images are hidden in flower arrangements so as not to unnerve the diners.[44]

Spoken Communication Electronically Transmitted

After face-to-face communication, spoken communication electronically transmitted over phone lines is second highest in information richness (see Figure 16.2). Although managers communicating over the telephone do not have access to body language and facial expressions, they do have access to the tone of voice in which a message is delivered, the parts of the message the sender emphasizes, and the general manner in which the message is spoken, in addition to the actual words themselves. Thus, telephone conversations have the capacity to convey extensive amounts of information. Managers can ensure that mutual understanding is reached because they can get quick feedback over the phone and answer questions.

Voice mail systems and answering machines also allow managers to send and receive verbal electronic messages over telephone lines. Voice mail systems are companywide systems that enable senders to record messages for members of an organization who are away from their desks and allow receivers to access their messages even when hundreds of miles away from the office. Such systems are obviously a necessity when managers are frequently out of the office, and managers on the road are well advised to periodically check their voice mail.

Personally Addressed Written Communication

Lower than electronically transmitted verbal communication in information richness is personally addressed written communication (see Figure 16.2). One of the advantages of face-to-face communication and verbal communication electronically transmitted is that they both tend to demand attention, which helps ensure that receivers pay attention. Personally addressed written communications, such as memos and letters, also have this advantage. Because they are addressed to a particular person, the chances are good that the person will actually pay attention to (and read) them. Moreover, the sender can write the message in a way that the receiver is most likely to understand. Like voice mail, written communication does not enable a receiver to have his or her questions answered immediately, but when messages are clearly written and feedback is provided, common understandings can still be reached.

Even if managers use face-to-face communication, sending a follow-up in writing is often necessary for messages that are important or complicated and need to be referred to later on. This is precisely what Karen Stracker, a hospital administrator, did when she needed to tell one of her subordinates about an important change in the way the hospital would be handling denials of insurance benefits. Stracker met with the subordinate and described the changes face-to-face. Once she was sure that the subordinate understood them, she handed her a sheet of instructions to follow, which essentially summarized the information they had discussed.

E-mail also fits into this category of communication media because senders and receivers are communicating through personally addressed written words. The words, however, are appearing on their computer screens rather than on pieces of paper. E-mail is so widespread in the business world that some managers such as Vickie Farrell in "A Manager's Challenge" are finding that they have to deliberately take time out from checking their e-mail to get their work done, think about pressing concerns, and come up with new and innovative ideas.[45] E-mail etiquette is a growing concern for managers whose in-boxes are overloaded with ever more messages. Certain etiquette norms are obvious—don't send jokes or witty passages, and don't flag messages as important just to get someone's attention or make sure they are read. Other etiquette norms may be more subtle. For example, to save time, Andrew Giangola, a manager at Simon & Schuster, a book publisher, used to type all his e-mail messages in capital letters. He was surprised when a receiver of one of his messages responded, "Why are you screaming at me?" Messages in capital letters are often perceived as being shouted or screamed, and thus Giangola's routine use of capital letters was bad e-mail etiquette. Here are some other guidelines from polite e-mailers: Always punctuate messages; do not ramble on or say more than you need to; do not act as though you do not understand something when in fact you do understand it; and pay attention to spelling and format. To avoid embarrassments like Giangola's, managers at Simon & Schuster created a task force that developed guidelines for e-mail etiquette.[46]

The growing popularity of e-mail has also enabled many workers and managers to become *telecommuters*, people who are employed by organizations and work out of offices in their own homes. There are over 45 million telecommuters in the United States.[47] Many telecommuters indicate that the flexibility of working at home enables them to be more productive and, at the same time, be closer to their families and not waste time traveling to and from the office.[48] In a recent study conducted by Georgetown University, 75% of the telecommuters surveyed said their productivity increased and 83% said their home life improved once they started telecommuting.[49]

Unfortunately, the widespread use of e-mail has been accompanied by growing abuse of e-mail. There have been cases of employees sexually harassing coworkers through e-mail, sending pornographic content via e-mail, and sending messages that disparage certain employees or groups.[50] To counter disparaging remarks making their way to employees' in-boxes (and being cc'd to coworkers), Mark Stevens, CEO of MSCO, a 40-person marketing firm in Purchase, New York, instituted a policy that forbids employees to use e-mail or Blackberrys to communicate messages that criticize someone else.[51]

Managers need to develop a clear, written policy specifying what company e-mail can and should be used for and what is out of bounds. Managers also should clearly communicate this policy to all members of the organization, as well as inform them of the procedures that will be used when e-mail abuse is suspected and the consequences that will result if the abuse is confirmed. According to a survey conducted by the ePolicy Institute, of the 79% of companies that have an e-mail policy, only about 54% are actually providing employees with training and education to ensure that they understand it.[52] Training and education are important to ensure that employees know not only what the policy is but also what it means for their own e-mail usage.

Additionally, e-mail policies should specify how much personal e-mail is appropriate and when the bounds of appropriateness have been overstepped. Just as employees make personal phone calls while on the job (and sometimes have to), so too do they send and receive personal e-mails. In fact, according to Waterford Technologies, a provider of e-mail management and archive services, based in Irvine, California, about one third of e-mail to and from companies is personal or not work-related.[53] Clearly, banning all personal e-mails is impractical and likely to have negative consequences for employees and their organizations (e.g., lower levels of job satisfaction and increased personal phone conversations). Some companies limit personal e-mails to certain times of the day or a certain amount of time per day; others have employees create lists of contacts whom they want to receive e-mails from at work (e.g., family members, children, baby-sitters); while still others want personal e-mails to be sent and received through Web-based systems like Gmail and Hotmail rather than the corporate e-mail system.[54]

According to the American Management Association, while the majority of organizations have a written policy about e-mail usage, most do not have written guidelines for instant messaging.[55] *Instant messaging* allows people who are online and linked through a buddy or contact list to send instant messages back and forth through a small window on their computer screens without having to go through the steps of sending and receiving e-mails.[56]

What about surfing the Internet on company time? According to a study conducted by Websense, approximately half of the employees surveyed indicated that they surfed the Web at work, averaging about two hours per week.[57] Most visited news and travel sites, but about 22% of the male respondents and 12% of the female respondents indicated that they visited pornographic Web sites.[58] Of all those surveyed, 56% said that they sent personal e-mails at work. The majority of those surveyed felt that sending personal e-mails and surfing the Web had no effect on their performance, and 27% thought that doing so improved their productivity.[59] Other statistics suggest that while overall there is more Internet usage at home than at work, individuals who use the Internet at work spend more time on it and visit more sites than do those who use it at home.[60] As indicated in the following "Ethics in Action," personal e-mails and Internet surfing at work present managers with some challenging ethical dilemmas.

Ethics
in Action

Monitoring E-mail and Internet Usage

A growing number of companies provide managers and organizations with tools to track the Web sites their employees visit and the e-mails they send. For example, Stellar Technologies Inc., based in Naples, Florida, sells software that managers can access anywhere to find out exactly how much time employees have spent at specific Web sites.[61] Currently, a little over half of the large corporations in the United States monitor their employees' e-mail; the percentage is higher among high-technology organizations. Only about half of the organizations that monitor e-mail let their employees know about the monitoring.[62]

Monitoring employees raises concerns about privacy. Most employees would not like to have their bosses listening to their phone conversations; similarly, some believe that monitoring e-mails and tracking Internet usage are an invasion of privacy.[63] Given the increasingly long working hours many employees are clocking in, should personal e-mails and Internet usage be closely scrutinized? Clearly, when illegal and unethical e-mail usage is suspected, such as sexually harassing coworkers or divulging confidential company information to third parties, monitoring may be called for. But should it be a normal part of organizational life, even when there are no indications of a real problem?

Essentially, this dilemma revolves around issues of trust. Procter & Gamble does not monitor individuals unless there appears to be a need to do so. P&G has close to 140,000 employees working in 80 countries, and the different countries have different laws and different internal organizational rules and norms.[64] Rather than monitoring individuals to see if they are abiding by the particular standards at the location where they work, P&G monitors electronic communication at its work sites in the aggregate to spot patterns. As Sandy Hughes, head of P&G's Global Privacy Council, puts it, "At some level, you have to trust your employees are going to be doing the right things."[65] Interestingly enough, research suggests that people are less likely to lie in e-mail than they are in phone calls or face-to-face conversations.[66]

Impersonal Written Communication

Impersonal written communication is lowest in information richness but is well suited for messages that need to reach a large number of receivers. Because such messages are not addressed to particular receivers, feedback is unlikely, so managers must make sure that messages sent by this medium are written clearly in language that all receivers will understand.

Managers often find company newsletters useful vehicles for reaching large numbers of employees. Many managers give their newsletters catchy names to spark employee interest and also to inject a bit of humor into the workplace. Managers at the pork-sausage maker Bob Evans Farms Inc. called their newsletter "The Squealer" for many years but recently changed the title to "The Homesteader" to reflect the company's broadened line of products. Managers at American Greetings Corp., at Yokohama Tire Corp., and at Eastman Kodak call their newsletters "Expressions," "TreadLines," and "Kodakery," respectively. Managers at Quaker State Corp. held a contest to rename their newsletter. Among the 1,000 names submitted were "The Big Q Review," "The Pipeline," and "Q.S. Oil Press"; the winner was "On Q."[67]

Managers can use impersonal written communication for various messages, including announcements of rules, regulations, policies, newsworthy information, changes in procedures, and the arrival of new organizational members. Impersonal written communication also can convey instructions about how to use machinery or how to process work orders or customer requests. For these kinds of messages, the paper or electronic trail left by this communication medium can be invaluable for employees.

Just as with personal written communication, impersonal written communication can be delivered and retrieved electronically, and this is increasingly the case in companies large and small. Unfortunately, the ease with which electronic messages can be spread has led to their proliferation. Many managers' and workers' electronic in-boxes are so backlogged that often they do not have time to read all the electronic work-related information available to them. The problem with such **information overload** is the potential for important information to be ignored or overlooked (even that which is personally addressed) while tangential information receives attention. Moreover, information overload can result in thousands of hours and millions of dollars in lost productivity. In "A Manager's Challenge," Vickie Farrell has gotten so overloaded with e-mail that she cannot read or respond to it all; she has told her coworkers to call her when sending an important message so that she will be sure to read and respond to it on a timely basis.[68]

information overload The potential for important information to be ignored or overlooked while tangential information receives attention.

Communication Networks

Although various communication media are utilized, communication in organizations tends to flow in certain patterns. The pathways along which information flows in groups and teams and throughout an organization are called **communication networks.** The type of communication network that exists in a group depends on the nature of the group's tasks and the extent to which group members need to communicate with one another in order to achieve group goals.

communication networks The pathways along which information flows in groups and teams and throughout the organization.

Communication Networks in Groups and Teams

As you learned in Chapter 14, groups and teams, whether they are cross-functional teams, top-management teams, command groups, self-managed work teams, or task forces, are the building blocks of organizations. Four kinds of communication networks can develop in groups and teams: the wheel, the chain, the circle, and the all-channel network (see Figure 16.3).

WHEEL NETWORK   In a wheel network, information flows to and from one central member of the group. Other group members do not need to communicate with one another to perform highly, so the group can accomplish its goals by directing all communication to and from the central member. Wheel networks are often found in command groups with pooled task interdependence. Picture a group of taxi cab drivers who report to the same dispatcher, who is also their supervisor. Each driver needs to communicate with the dispatcher, but the drivers do not need to communicate with one another. In groups such as this, the wheel network results in efficient communication, saving time without compromising performance. Although found in groups, wheel networks are not found in teams because they do not allow for the intense interactions characteristic of teamwork.

CHAIN NETWORK   In a chain network, members communicate with one another in a predetermined sequence. Chain networks are found in groups with sequential task interdependence, such as in assembly-line groups. When group work has to be performed in a predetermined order, the chain network is often found because group members need to communicate with those whose work

Figure 16.3
Communication Networks in Groups and Teams

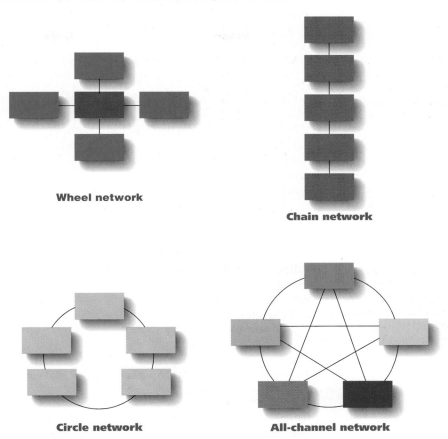

Wheel network

Chain network

Circle network

All-channel network

directly precedes and follows their own. Like wheel networks, chain networks tend not to exist in teams because of the limited amount of interaction among group members.

CIRCLE NETWORK   In a circle network, group members communicate with others who are similar to them in experiences, beliefs, areas of expertise, background, office location, or even where they sit when the group meets. Members of task forces and standing committees, for example, tend to communicate with others who have similar experiences or backgrounds. People also tend to communicate with people whose offices are next to their own. Like wheel and chain networks, circle networks are most often found in groups that are not teams.

ALL-CHANNEL NETWORK   An all-channel network is found in teams. It is characterized by high levels of communication: Every team member communicates with every other team member. Top-management teams, cross-functional teams, and self-managed work teams frequently have all-channel networks. The reciprocal task interdependence often found in such teams requires information flows in all directions. Computer software specially designed for use by work groups can help maintain effective communication in teams with all-channel networks because it provides team members with an efficient way to share information with one another.

Organizational Communication Networks

An organization chart may seem to be a good summary of an organization's communication network, but often it is not. An organization chart summarizes the *formal* reporting relationships in an organization and the formal pathways along which communication takes place. Often, however, communication is *informal* and flows around issues, goals, projects, and ideas instead of moving up and down the organizational hierarchy in an orderly fashion. Thus, an organization's communication network includes not only the formal communication pathways summarized in an organization chart but also informal communication pathways along which a great deal of communication takes place (see Figure 16.4)

Communication can and should occur across departments and groups as well as within them and up and down and sideways in the corporate hierarchy. Communication up and down the corporate hierarchy is often called *vertical* communication. Communication among employees at the same level in the hierarchy, or sideways, is called *horizontal* communication. Managers obviously cannot determine in advance what an organization's communication network will be, nor should they try to. Instead, to accomplish goals and perform at a high level, organizational members should be free to communicate with whomever they

Figure 16.4

Formal and Informal Communication Networks in an Organization

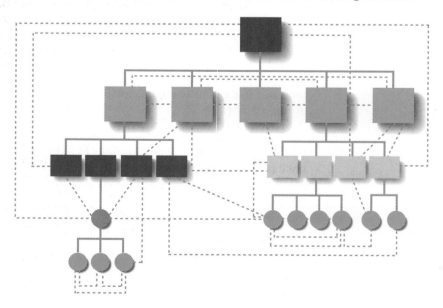

———— Formal pathways of communication summarized in an organization chart

------ Informal pathways along which a great deal of communication takes place

need to contact. Because organizational goals change over time, so too do organizational communication networks. Informal communication networks can contribute to an organization's competitive advantage because they help ensure that organizational members have the information they need when they need it to accomplish their goals.

grapevine An informal communication network along which unofficial information flows.

The **grapevine** is an informal organizational communication network along which unofficial information flows quickly, if not always accurately.[69] People in an organization who seem to know everything about everyone are prominent in the grapevine. Information spread over the grapevine can be on issues of either a business nature (an impending takeover) or a personal nature (the CEO's separation from his wife).

External Networks

In addition to participating in networks within an organization, managers, professional employees, and those with work-related ties outside their employing organization often are part of external networks whose members span a variety of companies. For example, scientists working in universities and in corporations often communicate in networks formed around common underlying interests in a particular topic or subfield. As another example, physicians working throughout the country belong to specialty professional associations that help them keep up to date on the latest advances in their fields. For some managers and professionals, participation in such interest-oriented networks is just as important, or even more important, than participation in internal company networks. Networks of contacts who are working in the same discipline or field or who have similar expertise and knowledge can be very helpful, for example, when an individual wants to change jobs or even find a job after a layoff. Unfortunately, as a result of discrimination and stereotypes, some of these networks are off-limits to certain individuals due to gender or race. For example, the term *old boys' network* alludes to the fact that networks of contacts for job leads, government contracts, or venture capital funding have sometimes been dominated by men and less welcoming of women.[70]

Information Technology and Communication

Advances in information technology have dramatically increased managers' abilities to communicate with others as well as to quickly access information to make decisions. Three advances that are having major impacts on managerial communication are the Internet, intranets, and groupware. However, as profiled in "A Manager's Challenge," managers must not lose sight of the fact that communication is essentially a human endeavor, no matter how much it may be facilitated by IT.

The Internet

Internet A global system of computer networks.

The **Internet** is a global system of computer networks that is easy to join and is used by employees of organizations around the world to communicate inside and outside their companies. Over 205 million people in the United States alone use the Internet, and the use of broadband connections (in place of dial-up service) has dramatically increased.[71] Table 16.1 lists the 20 countries with the most Internet users.[72]

On the Internet, the World Wide Web is the "business district" with multimedia capabilities. Companies' home pages on the Web are like offices that potential customers can visit. In attractive graphic displays on home pages, managers communicate information about the goods and services they offer, why customers should want to purchase them, how to purchase them, and where to purchase them. By surfing the Web and visiting competitors' home pages, managers can see what their competitors are doing.[73] Each day, hundreds of new companies add themselves to the growing number of organizations on the World Wide Web.[74] According to a recent study, the six "Web-savviest" nations (taking into account usage of broadband connections) in descending order are Denmark, Great Britain, Sweden, Norway, Finland, and the United States.[75]

By all counts, use of the Internet for communication is burgeoning. Nevertheless, some managers and organizations do not conduct business over the Internet. Ironically, the very reason why the Internet was created and why it is so popular—it allows millions of senders and receivers of messages to share vast amounts of information with one another—has hampered its use for certain business transactions because of a lack of security. Just as managers do not want to freely distribute information about their accounts to the public, some customers do not want to disclose their credit card numbers via the Internet. Experts suggest, however, that the Internet can be made reasonably secure so that accounts, credit cards, business documents, and even monetary transactions are relatively safe.[76] In addition, when considering security on the Internet, managers need to

Table 16.1

Top 20 Countries in Internet Usage

Country	Internet Users
United States	205,326,680
China	111,000,000
Japan	86,300,000
India	50,600,000
Germany	48,721,997
United Kingdom	37,800,000
Korea (South)	33,900,000
Italy	28,870,000
France	26,214,173
Brazil	25,900,000
Russia	23,700,000
Canada	21,900,000
Indonesia	18,000,000
Spain	17,142,198
Australia	14,189,557
Taiwan	13,800,000
Netherlands	10,806,328
Poland	10,600,000
Turkey	10,220,000

Source: "Top 20 Countries with the Highest Number of Internet Users," Internet World Stats and Population Statistics, www.internetworldstats.com/top20,htm, June 20, 2006. Used by permission.

compare it to the security of alternative communication media. Scott McNealy, founder and chairman of the board of Sun Microsystems, says that his e-mail is much more secure and harder for unwanted intruders to access than is his regular mail, which is just dropped into an unlocked box.[77]

Intranets

intranet A companywide system of computer networks.

Growing numbers of managers are finding that the technology on which the World Wide Web and the Internet are based has enabled them to improve communication within their own companies. These managers are using the technology that allows information sharing over the Internet to share information within their own companies through company networks called **intranets.** Intranets are being used not just in high-tech companies such as Sun Microsystems and Digital Equipment but also in companies such as Chevron, Goodyear, Levi Strauss, Pfizer, Chrysler, Motorola, and Ford.[78]

Intranets allow employees to have many kinds of information at their fingertips (or keyboards). Directories, phone books, manuals, inventory figures, product specifications, information about customers, biographies of top managers and the board of directors, global sales figures, minutes from meetings, annual reports, delivery schedules, and up-to-the minute revenue, cost, and profit figures are just a few examples of the information that can be shared through intranets. Intranets can be accessed with different kinds of computers so that all members of an organization can be linked together. Intranets are protected from unwanted intrusions, by hackers or by competitors, by means of firewall security systems that ask users to provide passwords and other pieces of identification before they are allowed to access the intranet.[79]

The advantage of intranets lies in their versatility as a communication medium. They can be used for a number of different purposes by people who may have little expertise in computer software and programming. While some managers complain that the Internet is too crowded and the World Wide Web too glitzy, informed managers are realizing that using the Internet's technology to create their own computer network may be one of the Internet's biggest contributions to organizational effectiveness.

Groupware and Collaboration Software

groupware Computer software that enables members of groups and teams to share information with one another.

Groupware is computer software that enables members of groups and teams to share information with one another to improve their communication and performance. In some organizations, such as the Bank of Montreal, managers have had success in introducing groupware into the organization; in other organizations, such as the advertising agency Young & Rubicam, managers have encountered considerable resistance to groupware.[80] Even in companies where the introduction of groupware has been successful, some employees resist using it. Some clerical and secretarial workers at the Bank of Montreal, for example, were dismayed to find that their neat and accurate files were being consolidated into computer files that would be accessible to many of their coworkers.

Managers are most likely to be able to successfully use groupware in their organizations as a communication medium when certain conditions are met:[81]

1. The work is group- or team-based, and members are rewarded, at least in part, for group performance.
2. Groupware has the full support of top management.

3. The culture of the organization stresses flexibility and knowledge sharing, and the organization does not have a rigid hierarchy of authority.

4. Groupware is being used for a specific purpose and is viewed as a tool that enables group or team members to work more effectively together, not as a personal source of power or advantage.

5. Employees receive adequate training in the use of computers and groupware.[82]

Employees are likely to resist using groupware and managers are likely to have a difficult time implementing it when people are working primarily on their own and are rewarded for their own individual performances.[83] Under these circumstances, information is often viewed as a source of power, and people are reluctant to share information with others by means of groupware.

Take the case of three salespeople who sell insurance policies in the same geographic area; each is paid based on the number of policies he or she sells and on his or her retention of customers. Their supervisor invested in groupware and encouraged them to use it to share information about their sales, sales tactics, customers, insurance providers, and claim histories. The supervisor told the salespeople that having all this information at their fingertips would allow them to be more efficient as well as sell more policies and provide better service to customers.

Even though they received extensive training in how to use the groupware, the salespeople never got around to using it. Why? They all were afraid that giving away their secrets to their coworkers might reduce their own commissions. In this situation, the salespeople were essentially competing with one another and thus had no incentive to share information. Under such circumstances, a groupware system may not be a wise choice of communication medium. Conversely, had the salespeople been working as a team and had they received bonuses based on team performance, groupware might have been an effective communication medium.

For an organization to gain a competitive advantage, managers need to keep up to date on advances in information technology such as groupware. But managers should not adopt these or other advances without first considering carefully how the advance in question might improve communication and performance in their particular groups, teams, or whole organization. Moreover, as highlighted in "A Manager's Challenge," managers need to keep in mind that all of these advances in IT are tools for people to use to facilitate effective communication; they are not replacements for face-to-face communication.

collaboration software Groupware that promotes and facilitates collaborative, highly interdependent interactions and provides an electronic meeting site for communication among team members.

Collaboration software is groupware that aims to promote collaborative, highly interdependent interactions among members of a team and provide the team with an electronic meeting site for communication.[84] Collaboration software provides members of a team with an online work site where they can post, share, and save data, reports, sketches, and other documents; keep calendars; have team-based online conferences; and send and receive messages. The software can also keep and update progress reports, survey team members about different issues, forward documents to managers, and let users know which of their team members are also online and at the site.[85] Having an integrated online work area can help to organize and centralize the work of a team, help to ensure that information is readily available as needed, and also help team members to make sure that important information is not overlooked. Collaboration software can be much more efficient than e-mail or instant messaging for managing ongoing team collaboration and interaction that is not face-to-face. Moreover, when a team does meet face-to-face, all documents the team might need in the course of the meeting are just a click away.[86]

For work that is truly team-based, entails a number of highly interdependent yet distinct components, and involves team members with distinct areas of expertise who need to closely coordinate their efforts, collaboration software can be a powerful communication tool. The New York-based public relations company Ketchum Inc. uses collaboration software for some of its projects. For example, Ketchum is managing public relations, marketing, and advertising for a new charitable program that Fireman's Fund Insurance Co. has undertaken. By using the eRoom software provided by Documentum (a part of EMC Corporation), Ketchum employees working on the project at six different locations, employee representatives from Fireman's, and a graphics company that is designing a Web site for the program can share plans, documents, graphic designs, and calendars at an online work site.[87] Members of the Ketchum-Fireman team get e-mail alerts when something has been modified or added to the site. As Ketchum's chief information officer Andy Roach puts it, "The fact that everyone has access to the same document means Ketchum isn't going to waste time on the logistics and can focus on the creative side."[88]

Another company taking advantage of collaboration software is Honeywell International Inc. Managers at Honeywell decided to use the SharePoint collaboration software provided by Microsoft, in part because it can be integrated with other Microsoft software such as Outlook.[89] So, for example, if a team using SharePoint makes a change to the team's calendar, that change will be automatically made in team members' Outlook calendars.[90] Clearly, collaboration software has the potential to enhance communication efficiency and effectiveness in teams.

Wikis, a result of the open-source software movement (see the *BusinessWeek* Case in the News accompanying Chapter 13), are a free or very low cost form of collaboration software that a growing number of organizations are using. Wikis enable the organizations not only to promote collaboration and better communication but also to cut back on the use of e-mail,[91] as indicated in the following "Information Technology Byte."

Information Technology Byte

Wikis to the Rescue

According to Postini Inc., an e-mail filtering company in Redwood, California, approximately 10% of all e-mails sent and received are legitimate. And while many organizations have invested in filtering software to keep spam from flooding employees' in-boxes, according to the Gartner Group (an Internet research firm), 60% of messages that make their way into employees' in-boxes are spam.[92] Darren Lennard, a managing director at Dresdner Kleinwort Wasserstein, an investment bank in London, was receiving approximately 250 e-mails a day, of which only 15% were relevant to his job. Every day, Lennard's first and last activities were to clear out his inbox on his BlackBerry—until frustration got the better of him, after a long and grueling workday, and he smashed his BlackBerry on the kitchen countertop in his home.[93]

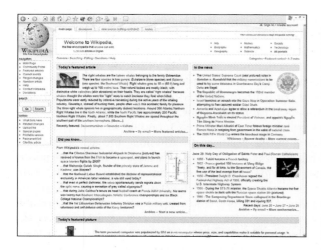

Lennard is not alone in his frustration. J. P. Rangaswani, global chief information officer at Dresdner, who particularly dislikes use of cc's and bcc's on e-mails, wants to reduce the reliance on e-mail communication at the bank. He is taking steps to implement the use of collaboration software and other electronic forms of communication such as instant messaging and RSS (really simple syndication, which enables users to subscribe for information they require). In fact, many organizations such as Yahoo, Eastman Kodak, Walt Disney, and the U.S. government are trying to reduce their reliance on e-mail by turning to other software tools that promote effective communication and collaboration.[94] While e-mail is likely to continue to be extensively used for one-on-one communication, for communication that involves collaboration within and between groups and teams, the use of other, more efficient and effective software tools is likely to dramatically increase in the coming years.[95]

In particular, wikis (in Hawaiian, the word *wiki* means "fast"), which are relatively easy to use and low cost or free, are expected to be increasingly popular as collaborative communication tools.[96] The Gartner Group predicts that by 2009, 50% of companies will be using wikis.[97] A wiki uses server software to enable users to create and revise Web pages quickly on a company intranet or through a hosted Internet site. Users who are authorized to access a wiki can log on to it and edit and update data, as well as see what other authorized users have contributed. Wikis enable collaboration in real time, and they keep a history so that users can go back and see what changes were made to, for example, a spreadsheet or a proposal.[98]

Soar Technology Inc., an artificial intelligence company in Ann Arbor, Michigan, that does work for the U.S. Office of Naval Research, has found that relying on wikis for collaboration has reduced the time it takes to complete projects by 50%.[99] According to Jacob Crossman, an engineer at Soar, wikis save time because they do away with the need for multiple e-mails with attachments and eliminate the typical confusion that surrounds multiple iterations of the same document.[100] Dresdner has found that e-mail pertaining to projects that use wikis has been reduced by about 75% and even meeting times have been significantly lowered.[101] Lennard recently created a wiki to figure out how to increase profits on a certain kind of trade. In the past, he would send e-mails with attachments to multiple colleagues, have to integrate and make sense of all the responses he received back from them, and then perhaps follow-up with subsequent e-mails. Instead, on the wiki page he created, colleagues contributed ideas, commented on each others' ideas, and revised and edited in real time. Lennard estimates that what would have taken about two weeks to accomplish through e-mail took about two days using a wiki.[102] Clearly, managers such as Lennard and Rangaswami have multiple options to ensure efficient, effective, and collaborative communication.[103]

Communication Skills for Managers

Some of the barriers to effective communication in organizations have their origins in senders. When messages are unclear, incomplete, or difficult to understand, when they are sent over an inappropriate medium, or when no provision for feedback is made, communication suffers. Other communication barriers have their origins in receivers. When receivers pay no attention to or do not listen to messages or when they make no effort to understand the meaning of a message, communication is likely to be ineffective. Sometimes advanced information technology such as automated phone systems can hamper effective communication to the extent that the human element is missing.

To overcome these barriers and effectively communicate with others, managers (as well as other organizational members) must possess or develop certain communication skills. Some of these skills are particularly important when managers *send* messages; others are critical when managers *receive* messages. These skills help ensure that managers will be able to share information, will have the information they need to make good decisions and take action, and will be able to reach a common understanding with others.

Communication Skills for Managers as Senders

Organizational effectiveness depends on the ability of managers (as well as other organizational members) to effectively send messages to people both inside and outside the organization. Table 16.2 summarizes seven communication skills that help ensure that when managers send messages, they are properly understood and the transmission phase of the communication process is effective. Let's see what each skill entails.

SEND CLEAR AND COMPLETE MESSAGES   Managers need to learn how to send a message that is clear and complete. A message is clear when it is easy for the receiver to understand and interpret, and it is complete when it contains all the information that the sender and receiver need to reach a common understanding. In striving to send messages that are both clear and complete, managers must learn to anticipate how receivers will interpret messages and must adjust messages to eliminate sources of misunderstanding or confusion.

Table 16.2
Seven Communication Skills for Managers as Senders of Messages

- Send messages that are clear and complete.
- Encode messages in symbols that the receiver understands.
- Select a medium that is appropriate for the message.
- Select a medium that the receiver monitors.
- Avoid filtering and information distortion.
- Ensure that a feedback mechanism is built into messages.
- Provide accurate information to ensure that misleading rumors are not spread.

ENCODE MESSAGES IN SYMBOLS THE RECEIVER UNDER-STANDS Managers need to appreciate that when they encode messages, they should use symbols or language that the receiver understands. When sending messages in English to receivers whose native language is not English, for example, it is important to use commonplace vocabulary and to avoid using clichés that, when translated, may make little sense and sometimes are either comical or insulting.

jargon Specialized language that members of an occupation, group, or organization develop to facilitate communication among themselves.

Jargon, specialized language that members of an occupation, group, or organization develop to facilitate communication among themselves, should never be used when communicating with people outside the occupation, group, or organization. For example, truck drivers refer to senior-citizen drivers as "double-knits," compact cars as "rollerskates," highway dividing lines as "paints," double or triple freight trailers as "pups," and orange barrels around road construction areas as "Schneider eggs." Using this jargon among themselves results in effective communication because they know precisely what is being referred to. But if a truck driver used this language to send a message to a receiver who did not drive trucks (such as "That rollerskate can't stay off the paint"), the receiver would have no idea what the message meant.[104]

SELECT A MEDIUM APPROPRIATE FOR THE MESSAGE As you have learned, when relying on verbal communication, managers can choose from a variety of communication media, including face-to-face communication in person, written letters, memos, newsletters, phone conversations, e-mail, voice mail, faxes, and videoconferences. When choosing among these media, managers need to take into account the level of information richness required, time constraints, and the need for a paper or electronic trail. A primary concern in choosing an appropriate medium is the nature of the message. Is it personal, important, nonroutine, and likely to be misunderstood and in need of further clarification? If it is, face-to-face communication is likely to be in order.

SELECT A MEDIUM THE RECEIVER MONITORS Another factor that managers need to take into account when selecting a communication medium is whether the medium is one that the receiver monitors. Managers differ in the communication media they pay attention to. Many managers simply select the medium that they themselves use the most and are most comfortable with, but doing this can often lead to ineffective communication. Managers who dislike telephone conversations and too many face-to-face interactions may prefer to use e-mail, send many e-mail messages per day, and check their own e-mail every few hours. Managers who prefer to communicate with people in person or over the phone may have e-mail addresses but rarely use e-mail and forget to check for e-mail messages. No matter how much a manager likes e-mail, sending e-mail to someone who does not check his or her e-mail is futile. Learning which managers like things in writing and which prefer face-to-face interactions and then using the appropriate medium enhances the chance that receivers will actually receive and pay attention to messages.

A related consideration is whether receivers have disabilities that hamper their ability to decode certain messages. A blind receiver, for example, cannot read a written message. Managers should ensure that employees with disabilities have resources available to communicate effectively with others. For example, deaf employees can effectively communicate over the telephone by using text-typewriters that have a screen and a keyboard on which senders can type messages. The message travels along the phone lines to special operators called *communication assistants,* who translate the typed message into words that the receiver can listen to. The receiver's spoken replies are translated into typewritten text by the communication assistants and appear on the sender's screen. The communication assistants relay messages back and forth to each sender and receiver.[105] Additionally, use of fax and e-mail instead of phone conversations can aid deaf employees.

filtering Withholding part of a message because of the mistaken belief that the receiver does not need or will not want the information.

AVOID FILTERING AND INFORMATION DISTORTION Filtering occurs when senders withhold part of a message because they (mistakenly) think that the receiver does not need the information or will not want to receive it. Filtering can occur at all levels in an organization and in both vertical and horizontal communication. Rank-and-file workers may filter messages they send to first-line managers, first-line managers may filter messages to middle managers, and middle managers may filter messages to top managers. Such filtering is most likely to take place when messages contain bad news or problems that subordinates are afraid they will be blamed for. Managers need to hear bad news and be aware of problems as soon as they occur so that they can take swift steps to rectify the problem and limit the damage it may have caused.

Some filtering takes place because of internal competition in organizations or because organizational members fear that their power and influence will be diminished if others have access to some of their specialized knowledge. By increasing levels of trust in an organization, taking steps to motivate all employees (and the groups and teams they belong to) to work together to achieve organizational goals, and ensuring that employees realize that when the organization reaches its goals and performs effectively, they too will benefit, this kind of filtering can be reduced.

information distortion Changes in the meaning of a message as the message passes through a series of senders and receivers.

Information distortion occurs when the meaning of a message changes as the message passes through a series of senders and receivers. Some information distortion is accidental—due to faulty encoding and decoding or to a lack of feedback. Other information distortion is deliberate. Senders may alter a message to make themselves or their groups look good and to receive special treatment.

Managers themselves should avoid filtering and distorting information. But how can they eliminate these barriers to effective communication throughout their organization? They need to establish trust throughout the organization. Subordinates who trust their managers believe that they will not be blamed for things beyond their control and will be treated fairly. Managers who trust their subordinates provide them with clear and complete information and do not hold things back.

INCLUDE A FEEDBACK MECHANISM IN MESSAGES Because feedback is essential for effective communication, managers should build a feedback mechanism into the messages they send. They either should include a request for feedback or indicate when and how they will follow up on the message to make sure that it was received and understood. When managers write letters and memos or send faxes, they can request that the receiver respond with comments and suggestions in a letter, memo, or fax; schedule a meeting to discuss the issue; or follow up with a phone call. By building feedback mechanisms such as these into their messages, managers ensure that they get heard and are understood.

rumors Unofficial pieces of information of interest to organizational members but with no identifiable source.

PROVIDE ACCURATE INFORMATION Rumors are unofficial pieces of information of interest to organizational members but with no identifiable source. Rumors spread quickly once they are started, and usually they concern topics that organizational members think are important, interesting, or amusing. Rumors, however, can be misleading and can cause harm to individual employees and their organizations when they are false, malicious, or unfounded. Managers can halt the spread of misleading rumors by providing organizational members with accurate information on matters that concern them.

Communication Skills for Managers as Receivers

Managers receive as many messages as they send. Thus, managers must possess or develop communication skills that allow them to be effective receivers of messages. Table 16.3 summarizes three of these important skills, which we examine here in greater detail.

PAY ATTENTION   Because of their multiple roles and tasks, managers often are overloaded and forced to think about several things at once. Pulled in many different directions, they sometimes do not pay sufficient attention to the messages they receive. To be effective, however, managers should always pay attention to messages they receive, no matter how busy they are. When discussing a project with a subordinate, an effective manager focuses on the project and not on an upcoming meeting with his or her own boss. Similarly, when managers are reading written communications, they should focus their attention on understanding what they are reading; they should not be sidetracked into thinking about other issues.

BE A GOOD LISTENER   Managers (and all other members of an organization) can do several things to be good listeners. First, managers should refrain from interrupting senders in the middle of a message so that senders do not lose their train of thought and managers do not jump to erroneous conclusions based on incomplete information. Second, managers should maintain good eye contact with senders so that senders feel their listeners are paying attention; doing this also helps managers focus on what they are hearing. Third, after receiving a message, managers should ask questions to clarify points of ambiguity or confusion. Fourth, managers should paraphrase, or restate in their own words, points senders make that are important, complex, or open to alternative interpretations; this is the feedback component so critical to successful communication.

Managers, like most people, often like to hear themselves talk rather than listen to others. Part of being a good communicator, however, is being a good listener, an essential communication skill for managers as receivers of messages transmitted face-to-face and over the telephone.

BE EMPATHETIC   Receivers are empathetic when they try to understand how the sender feels and try to interpret a message from the sender's perspective, rather than viewing the message from only their own point of view. Marcia Mazulo, the chief psychologist in a public school system in the Northwest, recently learned this lesson after interacting with Karen Sanchez, a new psychologist on her staff. Sanchez was distraught after meeting with the parent of a child she had been working with extensively. The parent was difficult to talk to and argumentative and was not supportive of her own child. Sanchez told Mazulo how upset she was, and Mazulo responded by reminding Sanchez that she was a professional and that dealing with such a situation was part of her job. This feedback upset Sanchez further and caused her to storm out of the room.

Table 16.3

Three Communication Skills for Managers as Receivers of Messages

- Pay attention.
- Be a good listener.
- Be empathetic.

In hindsight, Mazulo realized that her response had been inappropriate. She had failed to empathize with Sanchez, who had spent so much time with the child and was deeply concerned about the child's well-being. Rather than dismissing Sanchez's concerns, Mazulo realized, she should have tried to understand how Sanchez felt and given her some support and advice for dealing positively with the situation.

Understanding Linguistic Styles

Consider the following scenarios:

- A manager from New York is having a conversation with a manager from Iowa City. The Iowa City manager never seems to get a chance to talk. He keeps waiting for a pause to signal his turn to talk, but the New York manager never pauses long enough. The New York manager wonders why the Iowa City manager does not say much. He feels uncomfortable when he pauses and the Iowa City manager says nothing, so he starts talking again.

- Elizabeth compliments Bob on his presentation to upper management and asks Bob what he thought of her presentation. Bob launches into a lengthy critique of Elizabeth's presentation and describes how he would have handled it differently. This is hardly the response Elizabeth expected.

- Catherine shares with co-members of a self-managed work team a new way to cut costs. Michael, another team member, thinks her idea is a good one and encourages the rest of the team to support it. Catherine is quietly pleased by Michael's support. The group implements "Michael's" suggestion, and it is written up as such in the company newsletter.

- Robert was recently promoted and transferred from his company's Oklahoma office to its headquarters in New Jersey. Robert is perplexed because he never seems to get a chance to talk in management meetings; someone else always seems to get the floor. Robert's new boss wonders whether Robert's new responsibilities are too much for him, although Robert's supervisor in Oklahoma rated him highly and said he is a real "go-getter." Robert is timid in management meetings and rarely says a word.

What do these scenarios have in common? Essentially, they all describe situations in which a misunderstanding of linguistic styles leads to a breakdown in communication. The scenarios are based on the research of linguist Deborah Tannen, who describes **linguistic style** as a person's characteristic way of speaking. Elements of linguistic style include tone of voice, speed, volume, use of pauses, directness or indirectness, choice of words, credit taking, and use of questions, jokes, and other manners of speech.[106] When people's linguistic styles differ and these differences are not understood, ineffective communication is likely.

The first and last scenarios illustrate regional differences in linguistic style.[107] The Iowa City manager and Robert from Oklahoma expect the pauses that signal turn taking in conversations to be longer than the pauses made by their colleagues in New York and New Jersey. This difference causes communication problems. The Iowan and transplanted Oklahoman think that their eastern colleagues never let them get a word in edgewise, and the easterners cannot figure out why their colleagues from the Midwest and South do not get more actively involved in conversations.

linguistic style A person's characteristic way of speaking.

Differences in linguistic style can be a particularly insidious source of communication problems because linguistic style is often taken for granted. People rarely think about their own linguistic styles and often are unaware of how linguistic styles can differ. In the example above, Robert never realized that when dealing with his New Jersey colleagues, he could and should jump into conversations more quickly than he used to do in Oklahoma, and his boss never realized that Robert felt that he was not being given a chance to speak in meetings.

The aspect of linguistic style just described, length of pauses, differs by region in the United States. Much more dramatic differences in linguistic style occur cross-culturally.

CROSS-CULTURAL DIFFERENCES   Managers from Japan tend to be more formal in their conversations and more deferential toward upper-level managers and people with high status than are managers from the United States. Japanese managers do not mind extensive pauses in conversations when they are thinking things through or when they think that further conversation might be detrimental. In contrast, U.S. managers (even managers from regions of the United States where pauses tend to be long) find very lengthy pauses disconcerting and feel obligated to talk to fill the silence.[108]

Being aware of cross-cultural differences in communication styles will help managers when communicating with people from different cultures.

Another cross-cultural difference in linguistic style concerns the appropriate physical distance separating speakers and listeners in business-oriented conversations.[109] The distance between speakers and listeners is greater in the United States, for example, than it is in Brazil or Saudi Arabia. Citizens of different countries also vary in how direct or indirect they are in conversations and the extent to which they take individual credit for accomplishments. Japanese culture, with its collectivist or group orientation, tends to encourage linguistic styles in which group rather than individual accomplishments are emphasized. The opposite tends to be true in the United States.

These and other cross-cultural differences in linguistic style can and often do lead to misunderstandings. For example, when a team of American managers presented a proposal for a joint venture to Japanese managers, the Japanese managers were silent as they thought about the implications of what they had just heard. The American managers took this silence as a sign that the Japanese managers wanted more information, so they went into more detail about the proposal. When they finished, the Japanese were silent again, not only frustrating the Americans but also making them wonder whether the Japanese were at all interested in the project. The American managers suggested that if the Japanese already had decided that they did not want to pursue the project, there was no reason for the meeting to continue. The Japanese were truly bewildered. They were trying to carefully think out the proposal, yet the Americans thought they were not interested!

Communication misunderstandings and problems like this can be overcome if managers make themselves familiar with cross-cultural differences in linguistic styles. If the American managers and the Japanese managers had realized that periods of silence are viewed differently in Japan and in the United States, their different linguistic styles might have been less troublesome barriers to communication. Before managers communicate with people from abroad, they should try to find out as much as they can about the aspects of linguistic style that are specific to the country or culture in question. Expatriate managers who have lived in the country in question for an extended period of time can be good sources of information about linguistic styles because they are likely to have experienced firsthand some of the differences that citizens of a country are not aware of. Finding out as much as possible about cultural differences also can help managers learn about differences in linguistic styles because the two are often closely linked.

GENDER DIFFERENCES   Referring again to the four scenarios that open this section, you may be wondering why Bob launched into a lengthy critique of Elizabeth's presentation after she paid him a routine compliment on his presentation, or you may be wondering why Michael got the credit for Catherine's idea in the self-managed work team. Research conducted by Tannen and other linguists has found that the linguistic styles of men and women differ in practically every culture or language.[110] Men and women take their own linguistic styles for granted and thus do not realize when they are talking with someone of a different gender that differences in their styles may lead to ineffective communication.

In the United States, women tend to downplay differences between people, are not overly concerned about receiving credit for their own accomplishments, and want to make everyone feel more or less on an equal footing so that even poor performers or low-status individuals feel valued. Men, in contrast, tend to emphasize their own superiority and are not reluctant to acknowledge differences in status. These differences in linguistic style led Elizabeth to routinely compliment Bob on his presentation even though she thought that he had not done a particularly good job. She asked him how her presentation was so that he could reciprocate and give her a routine compliment, putting them on an equal footing. Bob took Elizabeth's compliment and question about her own presentation as an opportunity to confirm his superiority, never realizing that all she was expecting was a routine compliment. Similarly, Michael's enthusiastic support for Catherine's cost-cutting idea and her apparent surrender of ownership of the idea after she described it led team members to assume incorrectly that the idea was Michael's.[111]

Do some women try to prove that they are better than everyone else, and are some men unconcerned about taking credit for ideas and accomplishments? Of course. The gender differences in linguistic style that Tannen and other linguists have uncovered are general tendencies evident in *many* women and men, not in *all* women and men.

Where do gender differences in linguistic style come from? Tannen suggests that they begin developing in early childhood. Girls and boys tend to play with children of their own gender, and the ways in which girls and boys play are quite different. Girls play in small groups, engage in a lot of close conversation, emphasize how similar they are to one another, and view boastfulness negatively. Boys play in large groups, emphasize status differences, expect leaders to emerge who boss others around, and give one another challenges to try to meet. These differences in styles of play and interaction result in differences in linguistic styles when boys and girls grow up and communicate as adults. The ways in which men communicate emphasize status differences and play up relative strengths; the ways in which women communicate emphasize similarities and downplay individual strengths.[112]

Management in Action

Topics for Discussion and Action

Discussion

1. Which medium (or media) do you think would be appropriate for each of the following kinds of messages that a subordinate could receive from his or her boss: (a) a raise, (b) not receiving a promotion, (c) an error in a report prepared by the subordinate, (d) additional job responsibilities, and (e) the schedule for company holidays for the upcoming year? Explain your choices.

2. Discuss the pros and cons of using the Internet and World Wide Web for communication within and between organizations.

3. Why do some organizational members resist using groupware?

4. Why do some managers find it difficult to be good listeners?

5. Explain why subordinates might filter and distort information about problems and performance shortfalls when communicating with their bosses. What steps can managers take to eliminate filtering and information distortion?

6. Explain why differences in linguistic style, when not understood by senders and receivers of messages, can lead to ineffective communication.

Action

7. Interview a manager in an organization in your community to determine with whom he or she communicates on a typical day, what communication media he or she uses, and which typical communication problems the manager experiences.

Building Management Skills

Diagnosing Ineffective Communication

Think about the last time you experienced very ineffective communication with another person—someone you work with, a classmate, a friend, a member of your family. Describe the incident. Then answer the following questions:

1. Why was your communication ineffective in this incident?

2. What stages of the communication process were particularly problematic and why?

3. Describe any filtering or information distortion that occurred.

4. Do you think differences in linguistic styles adversely affected the communication

that took place? Why or why not?

5. How could you have handled this situation differently so that communication would have been effective?

Managing Ethically

Many employees use their company's Internet connections and e-mail systems to visit Web sites and send personal e-mails and instant messages.

Questions

1. Either individually or in a group, explore the ethics of using an organization's Internet connection and e-mail system for personal purposes at work and while away from the office. Should employees have some rights to use this resource? When does their behavior become unethical?

2. Some companies keep track of the way their employees use the company's Internet connection and e-mail system. Is it ethical for managers to read employees' personal e-mails or to record Web sites that employees visit? Why or why not?

Small Group Breakout Exercise

Reducing Resistance to Advances in Information Technology

Form groups of three or four people, and appoint one member as the spokesperson who will communicate your findings to the class when called on by the instructor. Then discuss the following scenario.

You are a team of managers in charge of information and communication in a large consumer products corporation. Your company has already implemented many advances in information technology. Managers and workers have access to e-mail, the Internet, your company's own intranet, groupware, and collaboration software.

Many employees use the technology, but the resistance of some is causing communication problems. A case in point is the use of groupware and collaboration software. Many teams in your organization have access to groupware and are encouraged to use it. While some teams welcome this communication tool and actually have made suggestions for improvements, others are highly resistant to sharing documents on their teams' online workspaces.

Although you do not want to force people to use the technology, you want them to at least try it and give it a chance. You are meeting today to develop strategies for reducing resistance to the new technologies.

1. One resistant group of employees is made up of top managers. Some of them seem computer-phobic and are highly resistant to sharing information online, even with sophisticated security precautions in place. What steps will you take to get these managers to have more confidence in electronic communication?

2. A second group of resistant employees consists of middle managers. Some middle managers resist using your company's intranet. Although these managers do not resist the technology per se and do use electronic communication for multiple purposes, including communication, they seem to distrust the intranet as a viable way to communicate and get things done. What steps will you take to get these managers to take advantage of the intranet?

3. A third group of resistant employees is made up of members of groups and teams who do not want to use the groupware that has been provided to them. You think that the groupware could improve their communication and performance, but they seem to think otherwise. What steps will you take to get these members of groups and teams to start using groupware?

CHAPTER 17

Managing Conflict, Politics, and Negotiation

Learning Objectives

After studying this chapter, you should be able to:

- Explain why conflict arises, and identify the types and sources of conflict in organizations.

- Describe conflict management strategies that managers can use to resolve conflict effectively.

- Understand the nature of negotiation and why integrative bargaining is more effective than distributive negotiation.

- Describe ways in which managers can promote integrative bargaining in organizations.

- Explain why managers need to be attuned to organizational politics, and describe the political strategies that managers can use to become politically skilled.

A Manager's Challenge

Bridging Cultures and Mind-Sets at Toyota

How can managers effectively bridge cultures and mind-sets to capitalize on their organizations' strengths while being responsive to customers in different markets?

Jim Press, president of Toyota Motor North America, is a master at effectively managing conflict and using power to help Toyota achieve record levels of revenues and profits from its North American operations.[1] Importantly, Press never loses sight of even bigger issues, though. Improving quality and value, protecting the natural environment and conserving resources, supporting and giving back to communities in which Toyota has operations, philanthropy, and education all figure prominently on Press's mind.[2]

While Toyota's engineering and manufacturing expertise is world-renowned, success in the U.S. market hinges on being responsive to the desires of U.S. customers. Press is highly influential within Toyota, and thus within the U.S. auto industry as a whole given Toyota's strong presence, because of his

deep understanding of this market and his ability to effectively manage conflict, bridge cultures and mind-sets, and keep Toyota in

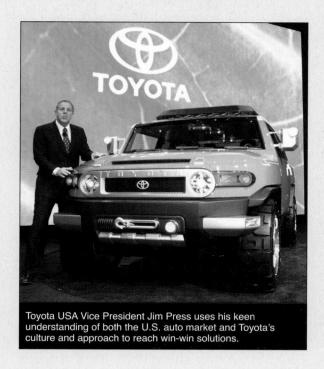

Toyota USA Vice President Jim Press uses his keen understanding of both the U.S. auto market and Toyota's culture and approach to reach win-win solutions.

tune with, and responsive to, U.S. customers while capitalizing on the company's own strengths in engineering and manufacturing.[3] Consistent with Press's power in the U.S. auto industry, he is the first top manager from an international auto company to be elected chair of the industry's main trade group, the Alliance for Automobile Manufacturers.[4]

Toyota's culture, values, and norms could result in a certain lack of responsiveness to customers in major markets outside Japan, such as the United States. Japanese engineers and managers in Toyota tend to be risk-averse and not eager to introduce new models without having a deep understanding and experience base to fall back on. Their risk aversion can lead to strong apprehensions and fears about things going wrong.[5]

Toyota's engineering and manufacturing ethos stresses efficiency, high quality, lean production, and continuous improvement. Not enamored of the bigger engines and brawny horsepower that appeal to U.S. customers, Toyota has typically concentrated on fuel-efficient, smaller engines.[6] Efficient utilization of space, avoidance of unnecessary features, and precise engineering and manufacturing have been priorities at Toyota. When it comes to engineering and manufacturing, Toyota stands out as a perfectionist among its rivals in the auto industry, and thus it has the highest profit margins.[7]

Jim Press is extremely powerful within Toyota precisely because he is so ingrained in the U.S. auto market and because he is intimately familiar with Toyota's culture and approach. Press has always loved cars: At age 13, he was tinkering with old cars as a hobby and washing cars in his uncle's car dealership; he has worked in the auto industry ever since, graduating from Kansas State University in 1967.[8]

More so than most top managers, Press seems to really understand what U.S. car buyers want and what will appeal to them. Gauging the ever-changing tastes and needs of car buyers is a never-ending pursuit for Press, so he is very close to Toyota's dealerships, as dealers are closest to customers. Press regularly visits dealerships and talks with all kinds of employees, ranging from salespeople and mechanics to receptionists, to keep on top of this dynamic market. As he puts it, "The strength of this company is its relationship with customers, and dealers are our lifeblood. . . . They see problems, issues, change. If we do something wrong, they get bruised."[9]

Press's closeness to the U.S. car buyer, an intimate familiarity with Toyota's culture and decision-making style gleaned from working at Toyota for over 35 years, and an uncanny ability to effectively manage conflict and exercise his own power within the company have proved to be a win-win situation for Press and Toyota. Press spends two weeks out of every month in Japan working with Japanese managers and engineers; he helps them appreciate the psyche of U.S. car buyers and collaboratively develop new products that are responsive to the U.S. market and embody Toyota's excellence in engineering and manufacturing. Dr. Schoichiro Toyoda, the honorary chairman of Toyota, suggests that Press, one of 44 managing officers (and one of only 5 non-Japanese managing officers) of Toyota is a "force for change."[10] For example, Press played a pivotal role in Toyota's decision to develop and manufacture the new Toyota Tundra, its first major full-size U.S. pickup truck. The new 2008 Tundra rivals the features and capabilities of mainstay U.S. trucks made by companies like Ford, Nissan, and General Motors.[11]

For an American to be a "force for change" in a Japanese company and effectively manage conflicting opinions and perspectives to reach win-win solutions is a real managerial challenge. Press's soft-spoken, patient, yet determined, demeanor, in combination with an organizational culture that emphasizes listening,[12] will likely lead Toyota USA to new heights in the U.S. auto industry.[13] As *BusinessWeek* writer David Kiley recently stated, "Jim Press is sometimes referred to as the most important auto executive you've never heard of."[14]

Overview

Successful leaders such as Jim Press in "A Manager's Challenge" are able to effectively use their power to influence others and to manage conflict to achieve win-win solutions. In Chapter 14 we described how managers, as leaders, exert influence over other people to achieve group and organizational goals and how managers' sources of power enable them to exert such influence. In this chapter we describe why managers need to develop the skills necessary to manage organizational conflict, politics, and negotiation if they are going to be effective and achieve their goals, as does Jim Press.

organizational conflict The discord that arises when the goals, interests, or values of different individuals or groups are incompatible and those individuals or groups block or thwart one another's attempts to achieve their objectives.

We describe conflict and the strategies that managers can use to resolve it effectively. We discuss one major conflict resolution technique, negotiation, in detail, outlining the steps managers can take to be good negotiators. Lastly, we discuss the nature of organizational politics, and the political strategies that managers can use to maintain and expand their power and use it effectively. By the end of this chapter, you will appreciate why managers must develop the skills necessary to manage these important organizational processes if they are to be effective and achieve organizational goals.

Organizational Conflict

Organizational conflict is the discord that arises when the goals, interests, or values of different individuals or groups are incompatible and those individuals or groups block or thwart one another's attempts to achieve their objectives.[15] Conflict is an inevitable part of organizational life because the goals of different stakeholders such as managers and workers are often incompatible. Organizational conflict also can exist between departments and divisions that compete for resources or even between managers who may be competing for promotion to the next level in the organizational hierarchy.

Tension starts to build during an office meeting. Since some degree of conflict is inevitable and desirable, conflict is a force that needs to be managed rather than eliminated.

It is important for managers to develop the skills necessary to manage conflict effectively. In addition, the level of conflict present in an organization has important implications for organizational performance. Figure 17.1 illustrates the relationship between organizational conflict and performance. At point A, there is little or no conflict and organizational performance suffers. Lack of conflict in an organization often signals that managers emphasize conformity at the expense of new ideas, are resistant to change, and strive for agreement rather than effective decision making. As the level of conflict increases from point A to point B, organizational effectiveness is likely to increase. When an organization has an optimum level of conflict (point B), managers are likely to be open to, and encourage, a variety of perspectives, look for ways to improve organizational functioning and effectiveness, and view debates and disagreements as a necessary ingredient for effective decision making. As the level of conflict increases from point B to point C, conflict escalates to the point where organizational performance suffers. When an organization has a dysfunctionally high level of conflict, managers are likely to waste organizational resources to achieve their own ends, to be more concerned about winning political battles than about doing what will lead to a

Figure 17.1
The Effect of Conflict on Organizational Performance

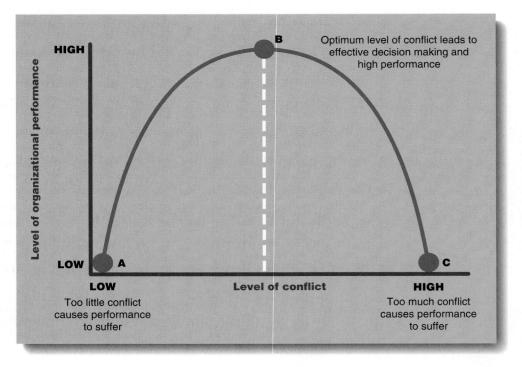

competitive advantage for their organization, and to try to get even with their opponents rather than make good decisions.

Conflict is a force that needs to be managed rather than eliminated.[16] Managers should never try to eliminate all conflict but, rather, should try to keep conflict at a moderate and functional level to promote change efforts that benefit the organization. Additionally, managers should strive to keep conflict focused on substantive, task-based issues, and minimize conflict based on personal disagreements and animosities. To manage conflict,[17] managers must understand the types and sources of conflict and be familiar with certain strategies that can be effective in dealing with it.

Types of Conflict

There are several types of conflict in organizations: interpersonal, intragroup, intergroup, and interorganizational (see Figure 17.2).[18] Understanding how these types differ can help managers to deal with conflict.

INTERPERSONAL CONFLICT   Interpersonal conflict is conflict between individual members of an organization, occurring because of differences in their goals or values. Two managers may experience interpersonal conflict when their values concerning protection of the environment differ. One manager may argue that the organization should do only what is required by law. The other manager may counter that the organization should invest in equipment to reduce emissions even though the organization's current level of emissions is below the legal limit.

Figure 17.2
Types of Conflict in Organizations

As pressures are mounting in many organizations to improve efficiency and effectiveness, sometimes conflicts and disagreements between overstretched co-workers over matters large and small can be debilitating. As indicated in the following "Management Insight," some managers are enlisting the help of outside experts to keep these interpersonal conflicts from getting out of hand.

Management Insight

Keeping Interpersonal Conflict from Getting Out of Hand

Sigmet, a small company with 10 employees headquartered in Westford, Massachusetts, makes data processors to convert radar weather information into graphic displays for meteorologists. Alan Siggia, an electrical engineer, and Richard Passarelli, a meteorologist, founded the company and serve as its head of hardware engineering and president, respectively.[19]

Siggia and Passarelli used to handle interpersonal conflicts between co-workers themselves. Some of these conflicts were over work-related matters such as whether or not a product was ready to be delivered to a customer or whose job duties and responsibilities were whose. Other times, conflicts pertained to personal idiosyncrasies and habits such as leaving dirty dishes in the office sink. And sometimes the conflicts seemed to take on a life of their own, with grudges between coworkers interfering with the smooth operation of a small business like Sigmet. As Siggia puts it, "The struggles people were having were beyond what a well-intentioned but untrained person like me could handle."[20]

Sigmet turned to Dina Beach Leach, a lawyer by training and founder of WorkWellTogether, a Boston consulting firm specializing in ombudsman services to small businesses with 500 or fewer employees.[21] Leach essentially spends a few hours a week at Sigmet, talking to employees, finding out about problems they are having and what is bothering them, and helping them come up with ways to deal with

Sometimes even seemingly small problems like dirty dishes can take on a life of their own.

interpersonal conflicts. For example, if an employee is sick and tired of a co-worker always giving unwanted advice, Leach can walk the employee through a way to get this message across to the coworker in a manner that resolves the problem without creating more hard feelings. These conversations are kept confidential (unless there is a real potential for harm to come to the company or another person), which allows employees to be much more frank that they used to be with Siggia and Passarelli.[22]

In addition to helping employees work out their differences, Lynch also advises Siggia and Passarelli about things they can do to prevent new interpersonal conflicts from arising. For example, as is sometimes the case in very small businesses, Sigmet lacked clear job descriptions, which at times caused employees to compete for responsibilities and assignments; based on Lynch's feedback and advice, Sigmet is in the process of creating job descriptions that give employees much more guidance in terms of their own responsibilities.[23] Siggia and Passarelli have found that enlisting the services of Lynch and WorkWellTogether to resolve workplace conflicts and disputes has not only led to smoother day-to-day functioning but also enabled them to have more time and energy to focus on their business.[24]

INTRAGROUP CONFLICT   Intragroup conflict is conflict that arises within a group, team, or department. When members of the marketing department in a clothing company disagree about how they should spend budgeted advertising dollars for a new line of men's designer jeans, they are experiencing intragroup conflict. Some of the members want to spend all the money on advertisements in magazines. Others want to devote half of the money to billboards and ads in city buses and subways.

INTERGROUP CONFLICT   Intergroup conflict is conflict that occurs between groups, teams, or departments. R&D departments, for example, sometimes experience intergroup conflict with production departments. Members of the R&D department may develop a new product that they think production can make inexpensively by using existing manufacturing capabilities. Members of the production department, however, may disagree and believe that the costs of making the product will be much higher. Managers of departments usually play a key role in managing intergroup conflicts such as this.

INTERORGANIZATIONAL CONFLICT   Interorganizational conflict is conflict that arises across organizations. Sometimes interorganizational conflict arises when managers in one organization feel that another organization is not behaving ethically and is threatening the well-being of certain stakeholder groups.

Sources of Conflict

Conflict in organizations springs from a variety of sources. The ones that we examine here are different goals and time horizons, overlapping authority, task interdependencies, different evaluation or reward systems, scarce resources, and status inconsistencies (see Figure 17.3).[25]

DIFFERENT GOALS AND TIME HORIZONS   Recall from Chapter 10 that an important managerial activity is organizing people and tasks into departments and divisions to accomplish an organization's goals. Almost inevitably, this

Figure 17.3

Sources of Conflict in Organizations

grouping results in the creation of departments and divisions that have different goals and time horizons, and the result can be conflict. Production and production managers, for example, usually concentrate on efficiency and cost cutting; they have a relatively short time horizon and focus on producing quality goods or services in a timely and efficient manner. In contrast, marketing and marketing managers focus on sales and responsiveness to customers. Their time horizon is longer than that of production because they are trying to be responsive not only to customers' needs today but also to their changing needs in the future to build long-term customer loyalty. These fundamental differences between marketing and production are often breeding grounds for conflict.

Suppose production is behind schedule in its plan to produce a specialized product for a key customer. The marketing manager believes that the delay will reduce sales of the product and therefore insists that the product be delivered on time even if saving the production schedule means increasing costs by paying production workers overtime. The production manager says that she will happily schedule overtime if marketing will pay for it. Both managers' positions are reasonable from the perspective of their own departments, and conflict is likely.

In "A Manager's Challenge," Jim Press's goal of being responsive to U.S. customers is sometimes different from the goals of Toyota's Japanese product designers and engineers, efficiently utilizing space and conserving fuel. These conflicting goals are illustrated by Toyota's experience in the minivan market. In the late 1980s, Toyota focused on creating an ideal minivan with precise engineering. The 1991 Previa embodied Toyota's engineering expertise and efficient use of space; the engine of the Previa was situated between the front and rear seats. While Toyota's engineers were delighted, its U.S. customers were not—they found the Previa was not spacious enough and was difficult to move around due to the bump in the floor, between the rows of seats, where the engine was.[26] Press knew that U.S. customers preferred larger, roomier minivans with many cup holders, and he convinced the Japanese product designers to give the U.S. market what it wanted. The result was the 1998 Sienna minivan, which, while roomier than the Previa, was still not big enough for U.S. tastes. With the 2004 Sienna, Press and Toyota succeeded in giving U.S. customers the space and features they want in a minivan; the model has sold remarkably well.[27] With the introduction of the new 2008 Toyota Tundra, Press and Toyota are now striving to give U.S. drivers all they want in a full-size pickup truck.[28]

OVERLAPPING AUTHORITY   When two or more managers, departments, or functions claim authority for the same activities or tasks, conflict is likely.[29] This is precisely what happened when heirs of the Forman liquor distribution company, based in Washington, D.C., inherited the company from their parents. One of the heirs, Barry Forman, wanted to control the company and was reluctant to share power with the other heirs. Several of the heirs felt that they had authority over certain tasks crucial to Forman's success (such as maintaining good relationships with the top managers of liquor companies). What emerged was a battle of wills and considerable conflict, which escalated to the point of being dysfunctional, requiring that the family hire a consulting firm to help resolve it.[30]

Have you ever been assigned a group project for one of your classes and had one group member who consistently failed to get things done on time? Whenever individuals, groups, teams, or departments are interdependent, the potential for conflict exists.

TASK INTERDEPENDENCIES   Have you ever been assigned a group project for one of your classes and had one group member who consistently failed to get things done on time? This probably created some conflict in your group because other group members were dependent on the late member's contributions to complete the project. Whenever individuals, groups, teams, or departments are interdependent, the potential for conflict exists.[31] With differing goals and time horizons, the managers of marketing and production come into conflict precisely because the departments are interdependent. Marketing is dependent on production for the goods it markets and sells, and production is dependent on marketing for creating demand for the things it makes.

DIFFERENT EVALUATION OR REWARD SYSTEMS   The way in which interdependent groups, teams, or departments are evaluated and rewarded can be another source of conflict.[32] Production managers, for example, are evaluated and rewarded for their success in staying within budget or lowering costs while maintaining quality. So they are reluctant to take any steps that will increase costs, such as paying workers high overtime rates to finish a late order for an important customer. Marketing managers, in contrast, are evaluated and rewarded for their success in generating sales and satisfying customers. So they often think that overtime pay is a small price to pay for responsiveness to customers. Thus, conflict between production and marketing is rarely unexpected.

SCARCE RESOURCES   Management is the process of acquiring, developing, protecting, and utilizing the resources that allow an organization to be efficient and effective (see Chapter 1). When resources are scarce, management is all the more difficult and conflict is likely.[33] For example, divisional managers may be in conflict over who has access to financial capital, and organizational members at all levels may be in conflict over who gets raises and promotions.

STATUS INCONSISTENCIES The fact that some individuals, groups, teams, or departments within an organization are more highly regarded than others in the organization can also create conflict. In some restaurants, for example, the chefs have relatively higher status than the people who wait on tables. Nevertheless, the chefs receive customers' orders from the wait staff, and the wait staff can return to the chefs food that their customers or they think is not acceptable. This status inconsistency—high-status chefs taking orders from low-status wait staff—can be the source of considerable conflict between chefs and the wait staff. For this reason, some restaurants require that the wait staff put orders on a spindle, thereby reducing the amount of direct order giving from the wait staff to the chefs.[34]

Conflict Management Strategies

If an organization is to achieve its goals, managers must be able to resolve conflicts in a functional manner. *Functional conflict resolution* means that the conflict is settled by compromise or by collaboration between the parties in conflict (later in the chapter we discuss other, typically less functional ways in which conflicts are sometimes resolved).[35] **Compromise** is possible when each party is concerned about not only its own goal accomplishment but also the goal accomplishment of the other party and is willing to engage in a give-and-take exchange and to make concessions until a reasonable resolution of the conflict is reached. **Collaboration** is a way of handling conflict in which the parties try to satisfy their goals without making any concessions but, instead, come up with a way to resolve their differences that leaves them both better off.[36] Jim Press and his Japanese counterparts in Toyota manage conflict through collaboration; by frequently meeting, listening to each other, and patiently working through their differences, they are able to design and manufacture cars that appeal to U.S. customers and embody the engineering and manufacturing strengths of Toyota.

In addition to compromise and collaboration, there are three other ways in which conflicts are sometimes handled: accommodation, avoidance, and competition.[37] When **accommodation** takes place, one party to the conflict simply gives in to the demands of the other party. Accommodation typically takes place when one party has more power than the other and is able to pursue its goal attainment at the expense of the weaker party. From an organizational perspective, accommodation is often ineffective, as the two parties are not cooperating with each other, they are unlikely to want to cooperate in the future, and the weaker party who gives in or accommodates the more powerful party might look for ways to get back at the stronger party in the future.

When conflicts are handled by **avoidance,** the two parties to a conflict try to ignore the problem and do nothing to resolve the disagreement. Avoidance is often ineffective since the real source of the disagreement has not been addressed, conflict is likely to continue, and communication and cooperation are hindered.

Competition occurs when each party to a conflict tries to maximize its own gain and has little interest in understanding the other party's position and arriving at a solution that will allow both parties to achieve their goals. Competition can actually escalate levels of conflict as each party tries to outmaneuver the other. As a way of handling conflict, competition is ineffective for the organization since the two sides to a conflict are more concerned about "winning" the battle than cooperating to arrive at a solution that is best for the organization

compromise A way of managing conflict in which each party is concerned about not only its own goal accomplishment but also the goal accomplishment of the other party and is willing to engage in a give-and-take exchange and make concessions.

collaboration A way of managing conflict in which both parties try to satisfy their goals by coming up with an approach that leaves them both better off and does not require concessions on issues that are important to either party.

accommodation An ineffective conflict-handling approach in which one party, typically with weaker power, gives in to the demands of the other, typically more powerful, party.

avoidance An ineffective conflict-handling approach in which the two parties try to ignore the problem and do nothing to resolve their differences.

competition An ineffective conflict-handling approach in which each party tries to maximize its own gain and has little interest in understanding the other party's position and arriving at a solution that will allow both parties to achieve their goals.

and acceptable to both sides. Handling conflicts through accommodation, avoidance, or competition is ineffective from an organizational point of view because the two parties do not cooperate with each other and work toward a mutually acceptable solution to their differences.

When the parties to a conflict are willing to cooperate with each other and, through compromise or collaboration, devise a solution that each finds acceptable, an organization is more likely to achieve its goals.[38] Conflict management strategies that managers can use to ensure that conflicts are resolved in a functional manner focus on individuals and on the organization as a whole. Below, we describe four strategies that focus on individuals: increasing awareness of the sources of conflict, increasing diversity awareness and skills, practicing job rotation or temporary assignments, and using permanent transfers or dismissals when necessary. We also describe two strategies that focus on the organization as a whole: changing an organization's structure or culture and directly altering the source of conflict.

STRATEGIES FOCUSED ON INDIVIDUALS

INCREASING AWARENESS OF THE SOURCES OF CONFLICT   Sometimes conflict arises because of communication problems and interpersonal misunderstandings. For example, differences in linguistic styles (see Chapter 16) may lead some men in work teams to talk more, and take more credit for ideas, than women in those teams. These communication differences can result in conflict when the men incorrectly assume that the women are uninterested or less capable because they participate less and the women incorrectly assume that the men are being bossy and are not interested in their ideas because they seem to do all the talking. By increasing people's awareness of this source of conflict, managers can help to resolve conflict functionally. Once men and women realize that the source of their conflict is differences in linguistic styles, they can take steps to interact with each other more effectively. The men can give the women more of a chance to provide input, and the women can be more proactive in providing this input.

Sometimes personalities clash in an organization. In these situations, too, managers can help resolve conflicts functionally by increasing organizational members' awareness of the source of their difficulties. For example, some people who are not inclined to take risks may come into conflict with those who are prone to taking risks. The non-risk takers might complain that those who welcome risk propose outlandish ideas without justification, while the risk takers might complain that their innovative ideas are always getting shot down. When both types of people are made aware that their conflicts are due to fundamental differences in their ways of approaching problems, they will likely be better able to cooperate in coming up with innovative ideas that entail only moderate levels of risk.

INCREASING DIVERSITY AWARENESS AND SKILLS   Interpersonal conflicts also can arise because of diversity. Older workers may feel uncomfortable or resentful about reporting to a younger supervisor, a Hispanic may feel singled out in a group of white workers, or a female top manager may feel that members of her predominantly male top-management team band together whenever one of them disagrees with one of her proposals. Whether these feelings are justified, they are likely to cause recurring conflicts. Many of the techniques we described in Chapter 5 for increasing diversity awareness and skills can help managers effectively manage diversity and resolve conflicts that have their origins in differences between organizational members.

PRACTICING JOB ROTATION OR TEMPORARY ASSIGNMENTS   Sometimes conflicts arise because individual organizational members simply do not have a good understanding of the work activities and demands that others in an organization face. A financial analyst, for example, may be required to submit monthly reports to a member of the accounting department. These reports have a low priority for the analyst, who typically turns them in a couple of days late. On the due date, the accountant always calls up the financial analyst, and conflict ensues as the accountant describes in detail why she must have the reports on time and the financial analyst describes everything else he needs to do. In situations such as this, job rotation or temporary assignments, which expand organizational members' knowledge base and appreciation of other departments, can be a useful way of resolving the conflict. If the financial analyst spends some time working in the accounting department, he may appreciate better the need for timely reports. Similarly, a temporary assignment in the finance department may help the accountant realize the demands a financial analyst faces and the need to streamline unnecessary aspects of reporting.

USING PERMANENT TRANSFERS OR DISMISSALS WHEN NECESSARY
Sometimes when other conflict resolution strategies do not work, managers may need to take more drastic steps, including permanent transfers or dismissals.

Suppose two first-line managers who work in the same department are always at each other's throats; frequent bitter conflicts arise between them even though they both seem to get along well with the other employees. No matter what their supervisor does to increase their understanding of each other, the conflicts keep occurring. In this case, the supervisor may want to transfer one or both managers so that they do not have to interact as frequently.

When dysfunctionally high levels of conflict occur among top managers who cannot resolve their differences and understand each other, it may be necessary for one of them to leave the company. This is how Gerald Levin managed such conflict among top managers when he was chairman of Time Warner (later Levin was CEO of AOL Time Warner). Robert Daly and Terry Semel, one of the most respected management teams in Hollywood and top managers in the Warner Brothers film company, had been in conflict with Michael Fuchs, a long-time veteran of Time Warner and head of the music division, for two years. As Semel described it, the company "was running like a dysfunctional family, and it needed one management team to run it."[39] Levin realized that Time Warner's future success rested on resolving this conflict, that it was unlikely that Fuchs would ever be able to work effectively with Daly and Semel, and that he risked losing Daly and Semel to another company if he did not resolve the conflict. Faced with that scenario, Levin asked Fuchs to resign.[40]

STRATEGIES FOCUSED ON THE WHOLE ORGANIZATION

CHANGING AN ORGANIZATION'S STRUCTURE OR CULTURE   Conflict can signal the need for changes in an organization's structure or culture. Sometimes, managers can effectively resolve conflict by changing the organizational structure they use to group people and tasks.[41] As an organization grows, for example, the *functional structure* (composed of departments such as marketing, finance, and production) that was effective when the organization was small may cease to be effective, and a shift to a *product structure* might effectively resolve conflicts (see Chapter 10).

Managers also can effectively resolve conflicts by increasing levels of integration in an organization. Recall from Chapter 15 that Hallmark Cards increased integration by using cross-functional teams to produce new cards. The use of cross-functional teams speeded new card development and helped to resolve conflicts between different departments. Now, when a writer and an artist have a conflict over the appropriateness of the artist's illustrations, they do not pass criticisms back and forth from one department to another, because they are on the same team and can directly resolve the issue on the spot.

Sometimes managers may need to take steps to change an organization's culture to resolve conflict (see Chapter 3). Norms and values in an organizational culture might inadvertently promote dysfunctionally high levels of conflict that are difficult to resolve. For instance, norms that stress respect for formal authority may create conflict that is difficult to resolve when an organization creates self-managed work teams and managers' roles and the structure of authority in the organization change. Values stressing individual competition may make it difficult to resolve conflicts when organizational members need to put others' interests ahead of their own. In circumstances such as these, taking steps to change norms and values can be an effective conflict resolution strategy.

ALTERING THE SOURCE OF CONFLICT   When the source of conflict is overlapping authority, different evaluation or reward systems, or status inconsistencies, managers can sometimes effectively resolve the conflict by directly altering its source. For example, managers can clarify the chain of command and reassign tasks and responsibilities to resolve conflicts due to overlapping authority.

negotiation A method of conflict resolution in which the two parties consider various alternative ways to allocate resources to each other in order to come up with a solution acceptable to both of them.

Negotiation

A particularly important conflict resolution technique for managers and other organizational members to use in situations where the parties to a conflict have approximately equal levels of power is negotiation. During **negotiation,** the parties to a conflict try to come up with a solution acceptable to themselves by considering various alternative ways to allocate resources to each other.[42] Sometimes the two sides involved in a conflict negotiate directly with each other. Other times, a **third-party negotiator** is relied on. Third-party negotiators are impartial individuals who are not directly involved in the conflict and have special expertise in handling conflicts and negotiations;[43] they are relied on to help the two negotiating parties reach an acceptable resolution of their conflict.[44] When a third-party negotiator acts as a **mediator,** his or her role in the negotiation process is to facilitate an effective negotiation between the two parties; mediators do not force either party to make concessions, nor can they force an agreement to resolve a conflict. **Arbitrators,** on the other hand, are third-party negotiators who can impose what they believe is a fair solution to a dispute that both parties are obligated to abide by.[45]

third-party negotiator An impartial individual with expertise in handling conflicts and negotiations who helps parties in conflict reach an acceptable solution.

mediator A third-party negotiator who facilitates negotiations but has no authority to impose a solution.

arbitrator A third-party negotiator who can impose what he or she thinks is a fair solution to a conflict that both parties are obligated to abide by.

distributive negotiation Adversarial negotiation in which the parties in conflict compete to win the most resources while conceding as little as possible.

Distributive Negotiation and Integrative Bargaining

There are two major types of negotiation—distributive negotiation and integrative bargaining.[46] In **distributive negotiation,** the two parties perceive that they have a "fixed pie" of resources that they need to divide.[47] They take a competitive, adversarial stance. Each party realizes that he or she must concede something but is out to get the lion's share of the resources.[48] The parties see no need to interact with each other in the future and do not care if their interpersonal relationship is damaged or destroyed by their competitive negotiation.[49] In distributive negotiations, conflicts are handled by competition.

In **integrative bargaining,** the parties perceive that they might be able to increase the resource pie by trying to come up with a creative solution to the conflict. They do not view the conflict competitively, as a win-or-lose situation; instead, they view it cooperatively, as a win-win situation in which both parties can gain. Trust, information sharing, and the desire of both parties to achieve a good resolution of the conflict characterize integrative bargaining.[50] In integrative bargaining, conflicts are handled through collaboration and/or compromise.

integrative bargaining Cooperative negotiation in which the parties in conflict work together to achieve a resolution that is good for them both.

Consider how Adrian Hofbeck and Joseph Steinberg, partners in a successful German restaurant in the Midwest, resolved their recent conflict. Hofbeck and Steinberg founded the restaurant 15 years ago, share management responsibilities, and share equally in the restaurant's profits. Hofbeck recently decided that he wanted to retire and sell the restaurant, but retirement was the last thing Steinberg had in mind; he wanted to continue to own and manage the restaurant. Distributive negotiation was out of the question, for Hofbeck and Steinberg were close friends and valued their friendship; neither wanted to do something that would hurt the other or their continuing relationship. So they opted for integrative bargaining, which they thought would help them resolve their conflict so that both could achieve their goals and maintain their friendship.

Strategies to Encourage Integrative Bargaining

There are five strategies that managers in all kinds of organizations can rely on to facilitate integrative bargaining and avoid distributive negotiation: emphasizing superordinate goals; focusing on the problem, not the people; focusing on interests, not demands; creating new options for joint gain; and focusing on what is fair (see Table 17.1).[51] Hofbeck and Steinberg used each of these strategies to resolve their conflict.

EMPHASIZING SUPERORDINATE GOALS   *Superordinate goals* are goals that both parties agree to regardless of the source of their conflict. Increasing organizational effectiveness, increasing responsiveness to customers, and gaining a competitive advantage are just a few of the many superordinate goals that members of an organization can emphasize during integrative bargaining. Superordinate goals help parties in conflict to keep in mind the big picture and the fact that they are working together for a larger purpose or goal despite their disagreements. Hofbeck and Steinberg emphasized three superordinate goals

Table 17.1
Negotiation Strategies for Integrative Bargaining

- Empasize superordinate goals.
- Focus on the problem, not the people.
- Focus on interests, not demands.
- Create new options for joint gain.
- Focus on what is fair.

during their bargaining: ensuring that the restaurant continued to survive and prosper, allowing Hofbeck to retire, and allowing Steinberg to remain an owner and manager as long as he wished.

FOCUSING ON THE PROBLEM, NOT THE PEOPLE   People who are in conflict may not be able to resist the temptation to focus on the other party's shortcomings and weaknesses, thereby personalizing the conflict. Instead of attacking the problem, the parties to the conflict attack each other. This approach is inconsistent with integrative bargaining and can easily lead both parties into a distributive negotiation mode. All parties to a conflict need to keep focused on the problem or on the source of the conflict and avoid the temptation to discredit one another.

Given their strong friendship, this was not much of an issue for Hofbeck and Steinberg, but they still had to be on their guard to avoid personalizing the conflict. Steinberg recalls that when they were having a hard time coming up with a solution, he started thinking that Hofbeck, a healthy 57-year-old, was lazy to want to retire so young: "If only he wasn't so lazy, we would never be in the mess we're in right now." Steinberg never mentioned these thoughts to Hofbeck (who later admitted that sometimes he was annoyed with Steinberg for being such a workaholic), because he realized that doing so would hurt their chances for reaching an integrative solution.

FOCUSING ON INTERESTS, NOT DEMANDS   Demands are *what* a person wants; interests are *why* the person wants them. When two people are in conflict, it is unlikely that the demands of both can be met. Their underlying interests, however, can be met, and meeting them is what integrative bargaining is all about.

Hofbeck's demand was that they sell the restaurant and split the proceeds. Steinberg's demand was that they keep the restaurant and maintain the status quo. Obviously, both demands could not be met, but perhaps their interests could be. Hofbeck wanted to be able to retire, invest his share of the money from the restaurant, and live off the returns on the investment. Steinberg wanted to continue managing, owning, and deriving income from the restaurant.

CREATING NEW OPTIONS FOR JOINT GAIN   Once two parties to a conflict focus on their interests, they are on the road achieving creative solutions to the conflict that will benefit them both. This win-win scenario means that rather than having a fixed set of alternatives from which to choose, the two parties can come up with new alternatives that might even expand the resource pie.

Hofbeck and Steinberg came up with three such alternatives. First, even though Steinberg did not have the capital, he could buy out Hofbeck's share of the restaurant. Hofbeck would provide the financing for the purchase, and in return Steinberg would pay him a reasonable return on his investment (the same kind of return he could have obtained had he taken his money out of the restaurant and invested it). Second, the partners could seek to sell Hofbeck's share in the restaurant to a third party under the stipulation that Steinberg would continue to manage the restaurant and receive income for his services. Third, the partners could continue to jointly own the restaurant. Steinberg would manage it and receive a proportionally greater share of its profits than Hofbeck, who would be an absentee owner not involved in day-to-day operations but would still receive a return on his investment in the restaurant.

FOCUSING ON WHAT IS FAIR Focusing on what is fair is consistent with the principle of distributive justice, which emphasizes the fair distribution of outcomes based on the meaningful contributions that people make to organizations (see Chapter 5). It is likely that two parties in conflict will disagree on certain points and prefer different alternatives that each party believes may better serve his or her own interests or maximize his or her own outcomes. Emphasizing fairness and distributive justice will help the two parties come to a mutual agreement about what the best solution is to the problem.

Steinberg and Hofbeck agreed that Hofbeck should be able to cut his ties with the restaurant if he chose to do so. They thus decided to pursue the second alternative described above and seek a suitable buyer for Hofbeck's share. They were successful in finding an investor who was willing to buy out Hofbeck's share and let Steinberg continue managing the restaurant. And they remained good friends.

When managers pursue these five strategies and encourage other organizational members to do so, they are more likely to be able to effectively resolve their conflicts through integrative bargaining. In addition, throughout the negotiation process, managers and other organizational members need to be aware of, and on their guard against, the biases that can lead to faulty decision making (see Chapter 7).[52]

As indicated in the following "Information Technology Byte," when negotiations involve complex and multiple parameters, or negotiators lack the time to engage in the negotiation process themselves, negotiation software can sometimes be beneficial.

Information Technology Byte

Computerized Negotiations

Some negotiations, especially those taking place between members of different organizations and involving multiple parameters, can be very time-consuming. For negotiations that overstretched employees simply do not have time to deal with, negotiation software can be a blessing.[53]

For example, physicians and insurance companies are often in the position of negotiating payment schedules; physicians want prompter payments for their services, while insurance companies prefer lengthier payment schedules. Using software provided by SplitTheDifference, the physicians and insurance companies can come to a mutually acceptable agreement.[54] Based on information from both parties, the software presents proposals to physicians (e.g., prompter payments for a discount on fees paid), who can accept the proposal or reject it and come back with a counteroffer. The negotiation proceeds until a deal has been struck; if after three rounds, no deal has been struck, both parties revert to the terms of the initial contract/claim between the physician and the insurance company.[55]

Other companies are developing software to deal with more complex kinds of negotiations. For example, the Project A team at Fujitsu Laboratories of America is developing software that can tabulate millions of different scenarios involving negotiations in which the two parties might initially have far more points of divergence than of agreement.[56] Computers can process information and find solutions more quickly than humans, so by using information on people's preferences, computers can come up with a vast array of potential solutions that can be cycled through. For example, the Project A team is working on software that can facilitate negotiations between a purchasing agent and a supplier by taking into account both parties' preferences and relative priorities for factors such as delivery times, quantities, reliability, quality, shipping costs and methods, size, color, and whatever else might be relevant for the negotiation at hand to come up with a solution that both parties find acceptable. Dave Marvit, who heads Project A, puts it this way, "Good negotiators know you can do better if you add more business terms to the discussions. . . . Not just price, but time and others. The computers can handle more parameters so more value can be squeezed out of the transaction. It's the opposite of a zero-sum game."[57]

Organizational Politics

Managers must develop the skills necessary to manage organizational conflict in order for an organization to be effective. Suppose, however, that top managers are in conflict over the best strategy for an organization to pursue or the best structure to adopt to utilize organizational resources efficiently. In such situations, resolving conflict is often difficult, and the parties to the conflict resort to organizational politics and political strategies to try to resolve the conflict in their favor.

Organizational politics are the activities that managers (and other members of an organization) engage in to increase their power and to use power effectively to achieve their goals and overcome resistance or opposition.[58] Managers often engage in organizational politics to resolve conflicts in their favor.

Political strategies are the specific tactics that managers (and other members of an organization) use to increase their power and to use power effectively to influence and gain the support of other people while overcoming resistance or opposition. Political strategies are especially important when managers are planning and implementing major changes in an organization: Managers need not only to gain support for their change initiatives and influence organizational members to behave in new ways but also to overcome often strong opposition from people who feel threatened by the change and prefer the status quo. By increasing their power, managers are better able to make needed changes. In addition to increasing their power, managers also must make sure that they use their power in a way that actually enables them to influence others.

organizational politics Activities that managers engage in to increase their power and to use power effectively to achieve their goals and overcome resistance or opposition.

political strategies Tactics that managers use to increase their power and to use power effectively to influence and gain the support of other people while overcoming resistance or opposition.

The Importance of Organizational Politics

The term *politics* has a negative connotation for many people. Some may think that managers who are political have risen to the top not because of their own merit and capabilities but because of whom they know. Or people may think that political managers are self-interested and wield power to benefit themselves, not their organization. There is a grain of truth to this negative connotation. Some managers do appear to misuse their power for personal benefit at the expense of their organization's effectiveness.

Nevertheless, organizational politics are often a positive force. Managers striving to make needed changes often encounter resistance from individuals and groups who feel threatened and wish to preserve the status quo. Effective managers engage in politics to gain support for and implement needed changes. Similarly, managers often face resistance from other managers who disagree with their goals for a group or for the organization and with what they are trying to accomplish. Engaging in organizational politics can help managers overcome this resistance and achieve their goals.

Indeed, managers cannot afford to ignore organizational politics. Everyone engages in politics to a degree—other managers, coworkers, and subordinates, as well as people outside an organization, such as suppliers. Those who try to ignore politics might as well bury their heads in the sand because in all likelihood they will be unable to gain support for their initiatives and goals.

Political Strategies for Gaining and Maintaining Power

Managers who use political strategies to increase and maintain their power are better able to influence others to work toward the achievement of group and organizational goals. (Recall from Chapter 14 that legitimate, reward, coercive, expert, and referent powers help managers influence others as leaders.) By controlling uncertainty, making themselves irreplaceable, being in a central position, generating resources, and building alliances, managers can increase their power (see Figure 17.4).[59] We next look at each of these strategies.

Figure 17.4
Political Strategies for Increasing Power

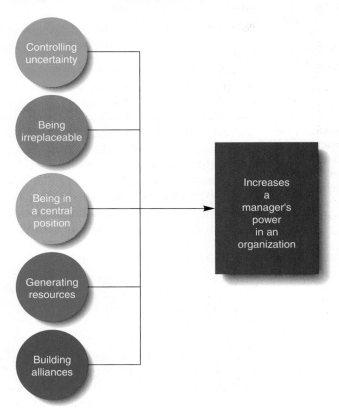

CONTROLLING UNCERTAINTY   Uncertainty is a threat for individuals, groups, and whole organizations and can interfere with effective performance and goal attainment. For example, uncertainty about job security is threatening for many workers and may cause top performers (who have the best chance of finding another job) to quit and take a more secure position with another organization. When an R&D department faces uncertainty about customer preferences, its members may waste valuable resources to develop a product, such as smokeless cigarettes, that customers do not want. When top managers face uncertainty about global demand, they may fail to export products to countries that want them and thus may lose a source of competitive advantage.

Managers who are able to control and reduce uncertainty for other managers, teams, departments, and the organization as a whole are likely to see their power increase.[60] Managers of labor unions gain power when they can eliminate uncertainty over job security for workers. Marketing and sales managers gain power when they can eliminate uncertainty for other departments such as R&D by accurately forecasting customers' changing preferences. Top managers gain power when they are knowledgeable about global demand for an organization's products. Managers who are able to control uncertainty are likely to be in demand and be sought after by other organizations.

MAKING ONESELF IRREPLACEABLE   Managers gain power when they have valuable knowledge and expertise that allow them to perform activities that no one else can handle. This is the essence of being irreplaceable.[61] The more central these activities are to organizational effectiveness, the more power managers gain from being irreplaceable. In "A Manager's Challenge," Jim Press gains power from being irreplaceable; the combination of in-depth knowledge of Toyota and its culture, an understanding of the pulse of the U.S. auto market, and his soft-spoken, patient, and determined manner of collaboratively working through conflicts for win-win solutions is hard to find in other top managers.[62]

BEING IN A CENTRAL POSITION   Managers in central positions are responsible for activities that are directly connected to an organization's goals and sources of competitive advantage and often are located in central positions in important communication networks in an organization.[63] Managers in key positions have control over crucial organizational activities and initiatives and have access to important information. Other organizational members are dependent on them for their knowledge, expertise, advice, and support, and the success of the organization as a whole is seen as riding on these managers. These consequences of being in a central position are likely to increase managers' power.

Managers who are outstanding performers, have a wide knowledge base, and have made important and visible contributions to their organizations are likely to be offered central positions that will increase their power, as is true of Jim Press in "A Manager's Challenge."

GENERATING RESOURCES   Organizations need three kinds of resources to be effective: (1) input resources such as raw materials, skilled workers, and financial capital, (2) technical resources such as machinery and computers, and (3) knowledge resources such as marketing or engineering expertise. To the extent that a manager is able to generate one or more of these kinds of resources for an organization, that manager's power is likely to increase.[64] In universities, for example, professors who win large grants to fund their research, from associations such as the National Science Foundation and the Army Research Institute, gain power because of the financial resources they are generating for their departments and the university as a whole.

Andrew C. Sigler, chairman of the board of the paper producer Champion International Corporation, gained so much power from generating resources that he remained at the top of a Fortune 500 company for 20 years despite Champion's poor returns to shareholders. A sudden rise in paper prices turned Champion's fortunes around, but insiders attribute at least part of Sigler's staying power at the top to his close relationships with major investors such as billionaires Warren Buffett and Laurence Tisch; these ties enabled him to generate capital for Champion.[65]

BUILDING ALLIANCES   When managers build alliances, they develop mutually beneficial relationships with people both inside and outside the organization. The two parties to an alliance support one another because doing so is in their best interests, and both parties benefit from the alliance. Alliances provide managers with power because they provide the managers with support for their initiatives. Partners to alliances provide support because they know that the managers will reciprocate when their partners need support. Alliances can help managers achieve their goals and implement needed changes in organizations because they increase managers' levels of power.

Many powerful top managers focus on building alliances not only inside their organizations but also with individuals, groups, and organizations in the task and general environments on which their organizations are dependent for resources. These individuals, groups, and organizations enter into alliances with managers because doing so is in their best interests and they know that they can count on the managers' support when they need it. When managers build alliances, they need to be on their guard to ensure that everything is aboveboard, ethical, and legal.

Political Strategies for Exercising Power

Politically skilled managers not only have a good understanding of, and ability to use, the five strategies to increase their power; they also have a good appreciation of strategies for exercising their power. These strategies generally focus on how managers can use their power *unobtrusively*.[66] When a manager exercise power unobtrusively, other members of an organization may not be aware that the managers are using their power to influence them. They may think that they support these managers for a variety of reasons: because they believe it is the rational or logical thing to do, because they believe that doing so is in their own best interests, or because they believe that the position or decision that the managers are advocating is legitimate or appropriate.

The unobtrusive use of power may sound devious, but managers typically use this strategy to bring about change and achieve organizational goals. Political strategies for exercising power to gain the support and concurrence of others include relying on objective information, bringing in an outside expert, controlling the agenda, and making everyone a winner (see Figure 17.5).[67]

RELYING ON OBJECTIVE INFORMATION   Managers require the support of others to achieve their goals, implement changes, and overcome opposition. One way for a manager to gain this support and overcome opposition is to rely on objective information that supports the manager's initiatives. Reliance on

MAKING EVERYONE A WINNER   Often, politically skilled managers are able to exercise their power unobtrusively because they make sure that everyone whose support they need benefits personally from providing that support. By making everyone a winner, a manager is able to influence other organizational members because these members see supporting the manager as being in their best interest.

Figure 17.5
Political Strategies for Exercising Power

Bain & Co., like bombshells. Boston Consulting proposed boosting sales by, among other things, opening outlet stores—a move that the image-obsessed Nike team feared would degrade the value of the brand. The firm wanted to cut costs by outsourcing day care, janitorial, and security services. "The intent was to raise awareness in the company to control operating expenses," Perez said. "I was trying to accelerate the pace, but most of my resistance came from Phil."

Knight and Perez also clashed over a highly charged political battle between the company and the city of Beaverton, Ore., which was trying to annex the Nike campus against the company's wishes. This summer, a friendly state legislature stopped the city from its annexation claim and gave Nike its independence for another 35 years before the issue would be reviewed again. "I thought that was fine," Perez says. "But not Phil. He wanted to sue Beaverton. I thought that was a bad idea because it would have created ill will with the public and with the lawmakers that had helped us out." But what rankled Perez even more was the larger question: Why was Knight even devoting any time to such a minor issue?

Perez, who came from a consumer-product marketing background, says he sometimes wondered if Nike's famously creative, irreverent advertising was actually conveying relevant messages about the product. The first commercial he saw was a 30-second spot aimed at last year's NCAA basketball tournament. The commercial showed ants crawling onto the basketball court. After 28 seconds, a voice would say "Nike basketball." His concern: The ad explained nothing about the product, and it had minimal brand presence. "I came from a rational world of communications," Perez said.

Nike insiders, meanwhile, were developing a parallel set of concerns about Perez. "He didn't have an intuitive sense of Nike as a brand," said one of them. "He relied more on the spreadsheet, analytical approach as opposed to having a good creative marketing sense."

In the end, Knight said that he could tolerate only so much friction. "I think the failure to really kind of get his arms around this company and this industry led to confusion on behalf of the management team," he said at the Jan. 23 press conference. In a later interview with *BusinessWeek,* Knight claimed to have learned from the misadventure. "Communication is huge, and I didn't know that would be as big of an issue with Bill," Knight said. "There is no question communication between Mark Parker and me will be better than between me and Bill." That's probably true. It's hard to see how the dialogue between Knight and Perez could have been much worse.

Questions

1. Why did Nike hire William Perez to be its new CEO in 2004?

2. What were the sources of conflict between Phil Knight and William Perez?

3. How did they manage the conflict?

4. How was the conflict ultimately resolved?

Source: S. Holmes, "Inside the Coup at Nike." Reprinted from the February 6, 2006, issue of *BusinessWeek* by special permission. Copyright © 2006 by the McGraw-Hill Companies.

CHAPTER 18

Using Advanced Information Technology to Increase Performance

Learning Objectives

After studying this chapter, you should be able to:

- Differentiate between data and information, and list the attributes of useful information.

- Describe three reasons why managers must have access to information to perform their tasks and roles effectively.

- Describe the computer hardware and software innovations that have created the IT revolution.

- Differentiate among seven different kinds of management information systems.

- Explain why managers are using IT to build strategic alliances and network structures to increase efficiency and effectiveness.

A Manager's Challenge

Bricks, Clicks, or Bricks-and-Clicks Supermarkets?

How can managers create competitive advantage through IT?

The potential uses of information technology (IT) and the Internet for improving responsiveness to customers became clear to companies in many industries in the late 1990s. One of these industries was the food delivery or supermarket industry. Entrepreneurs decided that developing an online ordering system that allowed customers to use the Internet to order their food and then creating a delivery system to package and bring the food to their homes had enormous potential. For example, virtual grocer Webvan raised more than $1 billion to develop both the IT and the physical infrastructure of warehouses and delivery trucks that it needed to deliver food to customers. Other competitors like GroceryWorks.com and Homegrocer.com made similar kinds of investments. These online stores did attract customers, and by 2000 they had more than $1 billion in sales. Bricks-and-mortar (B&M) supermarkets like Kroger Company, Albertson's, and Safeway watched with some

trepidation as the online rivals tried to perfect their operations. Should they respond with their own online stores? How else could they use IT?

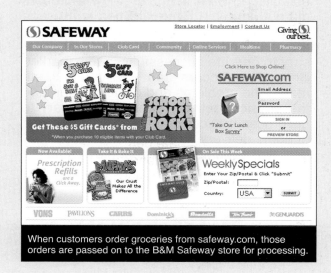

When customers order groceries from safeway.com, those orders are passed on to the B&M Safeway store for processing.

One of the first steps B&M supermarkets took was to use IT to make their customers' shopping experience more enjoyable. For example, Kroger experimented with a wide variety of self-serving technology kiosks.[1] Kiosks are physical units within the store, such as self-checkout units, check-cashing units, bill payment units, and payment terminals that perform a variety of specific services for customers. These kiosks improved operations because they helped stores eliminate lengthy checkout lines and helped the company focus more on customer service. Kroger has also installed dozens of flat-screen TV monitors in supermarket aisles and at the checkout counter to provide customers with useful information regarding its products and services. All these moves helped B&M supermarkets increase the quality of their products and improve responsiveness to customers. Some also set up pilot programs to test the idea of home delivery.

The question of whether online grocers would prove to be a threat to bricks-and-mortar stores was soon settled, however, when most of them, including Webvan, went out of business. Why? First, unlike their well-established B&M rivals, the new e-grocers did not have the IT capabilities to manage the nationwide inventory, transportation, distribution, and warehousing logistics necessary to operate successfully in this market. Second, e-grocers had totally underestimated the problems and costs of operating the physical delivery service necessary to get groceries to customers. The average cost of home delivery for Webvan and other grocers was around $30, a cost they could not pass on to the customers they were trying to attract. In B&M supermarkets, however, customers perform their own services, including, of course, selecting their own groceries and delivering them to their own homes—a major cost saving.

After the collapse of Webvan, the remaining virtual grocers took a hard look at their IT. They decided that while they could successfully use it to attract well-heeled customers who would be willing to pay a premium price for online groceries, they had to find a way to reduce operating costs. The solution adopted by a few online grocers was to focus their activities on large cities and then form alliances with B&M supermarkets to process and deliver the groceries to customers. For example, in several cities safeway.com now lets its customers order at its online store but then passes the orders onto the B&M Safeway stores for processing.[2]Safeway's trucks then deliver the orders; this avoids all the costs of sourcing and warehousing. A few Web grocers decided to focus only on one city market and then develop a delivery system to serve the needs of wealthy customers in that market. For example, vons.com serves the needs of well-heeled customers in Southern California.[3]

Overview

Webvan and other virtual grocers used IT and the Internet to create a grocery business that was highly responsive to customers, but it was also costly and inefficient compared to B&M supermarkets. The implication is clear: There are enormous opportunities for managers to find new ways to use IT to utilize organizational resources more efficiently and effectively. However, IT will help an organization achieve high performance only if it can improve the way the organization operates relative to its rivals, in other words, in a way that gives it a competitive advantage.

In this chapter we begin by looking at the relationship between information and the manager's job and then examine the ongoing IT revolution. Then we discuss six types of specific management information systems, each of which is based on a different sort of IT, which can help managers perform their jobs more efficiently and effectively. Next, we examine the impact that rapidly evolving IT is having on managers' jobs and on an organization's competitive advantage. By the end of this chapter, you will understand the profound ways in which new developments in IT are shaping managers' tasks and roles and the way organizations operate.

Information and the Manager's Job

data Raw, unsummarized, and unanalyzed facts.

information Data that are organized in a meaningful fashion.

Managers cannot plan, organize, lead, and control effectively unless they have access to information. Information is the source of the knowledge and intelligence that they need to make the right decisions. Information, however, is not the same as data.[4] **Data** are raw, unsummarized, and unanalyzed facts such as volume of sales, level of costs, or number of customers. **Information** is data that are organized in a meaningful fashion, such as in a graph showing the change in sales volume or costs over time. Data alone do not tell managers anything; information, in contrast, can communicate a great deal of useful knowledge to the person who receives it—such as a manager who sees sales falling or costs rising. The distinction between data and information is important because one of the purposes of IT is to help managers transform data into information in order to make better managerial decisions.

To further clarify the difference between data and information, consider the case of a manager in a supermarket who must decide how much shelf space to allocate to two breakfast cereal brands for children: Dentist's Delight and Sugar Supreme. Most supermarkets use checkout scanners to record individual sales and store the data on a computer. Accessing this computer, the manager might find that Dentist's Delight sells 50 boxes per day and Sugar Supreme sells 25 boxes per day. These raw data, however, are of little help in assisting the manager to decide about how to allocate shelf space. The manager also needs to know how much shelf space each cereal currently occupies and how much profit each cereal generates for the supermarket.

Suppose the manager discovers that Dentist's Delight occupies 10 feet of shelf space and Sugar Supreme occupies 4 feet and that Dentist's Delight generates 20 cents of profit a box while Sugar Supreme generates 40 cents of profit a box. By putting these three bits of data together (number of boxes sold, amount of shelf space, and profit per box), the manager gets some useful information on which to base a decision: Dentist's Delight generates $1 of profit per foot of shelf space per day [(50 boxes × $.20)/10 feet], and Sugar Supreme generates $2.50 of profit per foot of shelf space per day [(25 boxes × $.40)/4 feet]. Armed with this information, the manager might decide to allocate less shelf space to Dentist's Delight and more to Sugar Supreme.

Attributes of Useful Information

Four factors determine the usefulness of information to a manager: quality, timeliness, completeness, and relevance (see Figure 18.1).

QUALITY Accuracy and reliability determine the quality of information.[5] The greater the accuracy and reliability, the higher is the quality of information. For IT to work well, the information that it provides must be of high quality. If managers conclude that the quality of information provided by the IT they use is low, they are likely to lose confidence in it and stop using it. Alternatively, if managers base decisions on low-quality information, poor and even disastrous decision making can result. For example, the partial meltdown of the nuclear reactor at Three Mile Island in Pennsylvania during the 1970s was the result of poor information caused by an IT malfunction. While their computer screens indicated to engineers controlling the reactor that there was enough water in the

Figure 18.1
Factors Affecting the Usefulness of Information

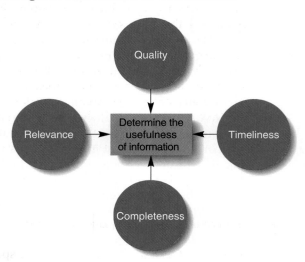

reactor core to cool the nuclear pile, this was in fact not the case. The consequences included the partial meltdown of the reactor and the release of radioactive gas into the atmosphere.

TIMELINESS   Information that is timely is available when it is needed for managerial action, not after the decision has been made. In today's rapidly changing world, the need for timely information often means that information must be available on a real-time basis.[6] **Real-time information** is information that reflects current conditions. In an industry that experiences rapid changes, real-time information may need to be updated frequently.

real-time information
Frequently updated information that reflects current conditions.

Airlines use real-time information on the number of flight bookings and competitors' prices to adjust their prices on an hour-to-hour basis to maximize their revenues. Thus, for example, the fare for flights from New York to Seattle might change from one hour to the next as fares are reduced to fill empty seats and raised when most seats have been sold. Airlines use real-time information on reservations to adjust fares at the last possible moment to fill planes and maximize revenues. U.S. airlines make more than 80,000 fare changes each day.[7] Obviously, the managers who make such pricing decisions need real-time information about the current state of demand in the marketplace.

COMPLETENESS   Information that is complete gives managers all the information they need to exercise control, achieve coordination, or make an effective decision. Recall from Chapter 7, however, that managers rarely have access to complete information. Instead, because of uncertainty, ambiguity, and bounded rationality, they have to make do with incomplete information.[8] One of the functions of information systems is to increase the completeness of the information that managers have at their disposal.

RELEVANCE   Information that is relevant is useful and suits a manager's particular needs and circumstances. Irrelevant information is useless and may actually hurt the performance of a busy manager who has to spend valuable time determining whether information is relevant. Given the massive amounts of information that managers are now exposed to and humans' limited information-processing capabilities, the people who design information systems need to make sure that managers receive only relevant information.

Today, software agents are increasingly being used by managers to scan and sort incoming e-mail and prioritize it. A *software agent* is a software program that can be used to perform simple tasks such as scanning incoming information for relevance, taking some of the burden away from managers. Moreover, by recording and analyzing a manager's own efforts to prioritize incoming information, the software agent can mimic the manager's preferences and thus perform such tasks more effectively. For example, the software agent can automatically reprogram itself to place incoming e-mail from the manager's boss at the top of the pile.[9]

What Is Information Technology?

information technology The set of methods or techniques for acquiring, organizing, storing, manipulating, and transmitting information.

Information technology is the set of methods or techniques for acquiring, organizing, storing, manipulating, and transmitting information.[10] A **management information system (MIS)** is a specific form of IT that managers select and utilize to generate the specific, detailed information they need to perform their roles effectively. Management information systems have existed for as long as there have been organizations—a long time indeed. Before the computer age, most systems were paper-based: Clerks recorded important information on documents (often in duplicate or triplicate) in the form of words and numbers; sent a copy of the document to superiors, customers, or suppliers, as the case might be; and stored other copies in files for future reference.

management information system (MIS) A specific form of IT that managers utilize to generate the specific, detailed information they need to perform their roles effectively.

Rapid advances in the power of IT—specifically, through the development of more and more sophisticated computer hardware and software—are having a fundamental impact on managers, their organizations, and their suppliers and customers, as suggested by developments in the supermarket business in "A Manager's Challenge."[11] Some new IT, such as inventory management and customer relationship management (CRM) systems, contributes so much to performance that organizations that do *not* adopt it, or that implement it ineffectively, become uncompetitive compared with organizations that do adopt it.[12] In the 2000s, much of the increasing productivity and efficiency of business in general has been attributed to advancing IT.

Managers need information for three reasons: to make effective decisions, to control the activities of the organization, and to coordinate the activities of the organization. Below we examine these uses of information in detail.

Information and Decisions

Much of management (planning, organizing, leading, and controlling) is about making decisions. For example, the marketing manager must decide what price to charge for a product, what distribution channels to use, and what promotional messages to emphasize. The manufacturing manager must decide how much of a product to make and how to make it. The purchasing manager must decide from whom to purchase inputs and what inventory of inputs to hold. The human relations manager must decide how much employees should be paid, how they should be trained, and what benefits they should be given. The engineering manager must make decisions about new product design. Top managers must decide how to allocate scarce financial resources among competing projects, how best to

To make effective decisions, managers need to acquire and process relevant information.

structure and control the organization, and what business-level strategy the organization should be pursuing. And, regardless of their functional orientation, all managers have to make decisions about matters such as what performance evaluation to give to a subordinate.

Decision making cannot be effective in an information vacuum. To make effective decisions, managers need information, both from inside the organization and from external stakeholders. When deciding how to price a product, for example, marketing managers need information about how consumers will react to different prices. They need information about unit costs because they do not want to set the price below the cost of production. And they need information about competitive strategy, since pricing strategy should be consistent with an organization's competitive strategy. Some of this information will come from outside the organization (for example, from consumer surveys) and some from inside the organization (information about unit production costs comes from manufacturing). As this example suggests, managers' ability to make effective decisions rests on their ability to acquire and process information.

Information and Control

As discussed in Chapter 11, controlling is the process whereby managers regulate how efficiently and effectively an organization and its members are performing the activities necessary to achieve organizational goals.[13] Managers achieve control over organizational activities by taking four steps (see Figure 11.2): (1) They establish measurable standards of performance or goals. (2) They measure actual performance. (3) They compare actual performance against established goals. (4) They evaluate the result and take corrective action if necessary.[14] The package delivery company DHL, for example, has a delivery goal: to deliver 95% of the packages it picks up by noon the next day.[15] Throughout the United States, DHL has thousands of ground stations (branch offices that coordinate the pickup and delivery of packages in a particular area) that are responsible for the physical pickup and delivery of packages. DHL managers monitor the delivery performance of these stations on a regular basis; if they find that the 95% goal is not being attained, they determine why and take corrective action if necessary.[16]

To achieve control over any organizational activity, managers must have information. To control ground-station activities, a DHL manager might need to know what percentage of packages each station delivers by noon. To obtain this information, the manager uses DHL's IT. All packages to be shipped to the stations have been scanned with handheld scanners by the DHL drivers who pick them up; then all this information is sent wirelessly to DHL's headquarters mainframe computer. When the packages are scanned again at delivery, this information is also transmitted to DHL's mainframe. Accessing the mainframe, the manager can quickly discover what percentage of packages were delivered by noon of the day after they were picked up and also how this information breaks down on a station-by-station basis.[17]

Management information systems are used to control all divisional and functional operations. In accounting, for example, information systems are used to monitor expenditures and compare them against budgets.[18] To track expenditures against budgets, managers need information on current expenditures, broken down by relevant organizational units; accounting IT is designed to provide managers with this information. An example of IT used to monitor and control the daily activities of employees is the online MBO information system used by T. J. Rodgers at Cypress Semiconductor, discussed in Chapter 11. Rodgers implemented IT that allows him to review the goals of all his employees in about four hours.[19] At first glance, it might seem that advances in IT would have a limited impact on the business of an office furniture maker; however, this assumption would be incorrect, as the following "Management Insight" suggests.

Management
Insight

Herman Miller's Office of the Future

Managers at Herman Miller have been finding countless ways to use IT and the Internet to give their company a competitive advantage over rival office furniture makers (OFMs) such as Steelcase and Hon.[20] Early on, Miller's managers saw the potential of the Internet for selling its furniture to business customers. Other furniture companies' Web sites were online advertisements for their products, services, and other marketing information. However, Miller's managers quickly realized the true potential of using both the company's intranet and the Internet to reach customers.

First, Miller's managers developed IT that linked all the company's dealers and salespeople to its manufacturing hub so that sales orders could be coordinated with the custom design department and with manufacturing, enabling customers to receive pricing and scheduling information promptly. Then, with this customer delivery system in place, Miller developed IT to link its manufacturing operations with its network of suppliers so that its input supply chain would be coordinated with its customer needs.

Herman Miller uses the Internet to reduce errors and time-to-market in delivering custom office furniture such as that depicted here.

When Miller's managers noticed that competitors were quickly imitating its IT, they began to search for new ways to use it to gain a competitive advantage. Soon they realized that IT could transform the office furniture business itself. When they began to define Herman Miller as a "digital" enterprise infused with e-business, they realized IT could not only improve efficiency but also change the way the customer experienced "Herman Miller" and increase value for the customer. A major Web initiative was the establishment of an e-learning tool, Uknowit.com, which became Herman Miller's online university. Via the Web thousands of Miller's employees and dealers are currently enrolled in Uknowit.com, where they choose from 85 courses covering technology, products and services, product applications, consultative/selling skills, and industry competitive knowledge. The benefits to Miller, its dealers, and its customers from this IT initiative are improved speed to market and better ability to respond to competitors' tactics. That is, salespeople and dealers now have the information and tools they need to better compete for and keep customers.

Moreover, the office furniture business offers highly customized solutions to its customers. A main source of competitive advantage is the ability to give customers exactly what they want and at the right price. Using its new IT, Miller's salespeople are giving design and manufacturing more accurate and timely information, which has reduced the incidence of sales and specification errors during the selling process. Also, with the new systems time to market has been reduced, and Miller is committed to being able to offer customers highly customized furniture in 10 business days or less.

Of course, all these IT initiatives have been costly to Herman Miller. Thousands of hours of management time have been spent developing the IT and providing content, such as information on competitors for the company's online classes. Herman Miller's managers are looking at the long term; they believe they have created a real source of competitive advantage for their company that will sustain it in the years ahead.

Information and Coordination

Coordinating department and divisional activities to achieve organizational goals is another basic task of management. As an example of the size of the coordination task that managers face, consider the coordination effort involved in building Boeing's 777 jet aircraft, which is composed of over 3 million individual parts.[21] Managers at Boeing have to coordinate the production and delivery of all of these parts so that every part arrives at Boeing's Everett, Washington, facility exactly when it is needed (for example, the wings should arrive before the engines). To achieve this high level of coordination, managers need information about which supplier is producing what part, and when it will be produced. To meet this need, managers at Boeing created IT that links Boeing to all its suppliers and can track the flow of 3 million component parts through the production process in real time—an immense task.

As we noted in previous chapters, the coordination problems that managers face in managing their global supply chains to take advantage of national differences in the costs of production are increasing. So managers have been adopting sophisticated IT that helps them coordinate the flow of materials, semifinished goods, and finished products throughout the world. Consider, for example, how Bose, which manufactures some of the world's best-known high-fidelity speakers, manages its global supply chain. Bose purchases almost all of the components for its speakers, and about 50% of its purchases are from foreign suppliers, the majority of which are in the Far East. The challenge for managers is to coordinate this globally dispersed supply chain to minimize Bose's inventory and transportation costs. Minimizing these costs requires that component parts arrive at Bose's assembly plant just in time to enter the production process and not before. Bose also has to remain responsive to customer demands, which means that the company and its suppliers have to be able to respond quickly to changes in the demand for certain kinds of speakers, increasing or decreasing production as needed.

The responsibility for coordinating the supply chain to simultaneously minimize inventory and transportation costs and respond quickly to changing customer demands belongs to Bose's logistics managers. They contracted with W. N. Procter, a Boston-based supply chain manager, to develop logistics IT that gives Bose the real-time information it needs to track parts as they move through the global supply chain. The IT is known as ProcterLink. When a shipment leaves a supplier, it is logged into ProcterLink.[22] From that point on, Bose can track the supplies as they move across the globe toward Massachusetts. This system allows Bose to fine-tune its production scheduling so that supplies enter the production process exactly when they are needed.

How well this system works was illustrated when one Japanese customer unexpectedly doubled its order for Bose speakers. Bose had to gear up its manufacturing in a hurry, but many of its components were stretched out across long distances. By using ProcterLink, Bose was able to locate the needed parts in its supply chain. It then broke them out of the normal delivery chain and moved them by air freight to get them to the assembly line in time for the accelerated schedule. As a result, Bose was able to meet the request of its customer.

The IT Revolution

Advances in IT have enabled managers to make gigantic leaps in the way they can collect more timely, complete, relevant, and high-quality information and use it in more effective ways. To better understand the ongoing revolution in IT that has transformed companies like Kroger, Herman Miller, and Bose and allowed them to improve their responsiveness to customers, minimize costs, and improve their competitive position, we need to examine several key aspects of advanced IT.

The Effects of Advancing IT

The IT revolution began with the development of the first computers—the hardware of IT—in the 1950s. The language of computers is a digital language of zeros and ones. Words, numbers, images, and sound can all be expressed in zeros and ones. Each letter in the alphabet has its own unique code of zeros and ones, as does each number, each color, and each sound. For example, the digital code for the number 20 is 10100. In the language of computers it takes a lot of zeros and ones to express even a simple sentence, to say nothing of complex color graphics or moving video images. Nevertheless, modern computers can read, process, and store millions and billions of instructions per second (an *instruction* is a line of software code) and thus vast amounts of zeros and ones. This awesome "number-crunching" power forms the foundation of the ongoing IT revolution.

The products and services that result from advancing IT are all around us. Ever more powerful microprocessors and PCs, high-bandwith wireless smart phones, sophisticated word-processing software, ever-expanding computer networks, inexpensive digital cameras and camcorders, and more and more useful online information and retailing services that did not exist a generation ago. Now these products are commonplace and being continuously improved. Many of the managers and companies that helped develop the new IT have reaped enormous gains.

However, while many companies have benefited from advancing IT, others have been threatened. Traditional telephone companies the world over have seen their market dominance threatened by new companies offering Internet, broadband, and wireless telephone technology. For example, AT&T, Verizon, and other long-distance companies have been facing increased competition because of advances in telecommunications and, like Kroger in the opening case, have been forced to use new IT to compete. So advancing IT is both an opportunity and a threat.[23]

On the one hand, IT helps create new product opportunities that managers and their organizations can take advantage of—such as online travel and vacation booking. On the other hand, IT creates new and improved products that reduce or destroy demand for older, established products—such as the services provided by bricks-and-mortar travel agents. Wal-Mart, by developing its own sophisticated proprietary IT, has been able to reduce retailing costs so much that it has put hundreds of thousands of small and medium-size stores out of business. Similarly, thousands of small, specialized bookstores have closed in the United States in the last decade as a result of advances in IT that made online bookselling possible.

IT and the Product Life Cycle

product life cycle The way demand for a product changes in a predictable pattern over time

When IT is advancing, organizational survival requires that managers quickly adopt and apply it. One reason for this is the way IT affects the length of the **product life cycle,** which is the way that the demand for a product changes in a predictable pattern over time.[24] In general, the product life-cycle consists of four stages: the embryonic, growth, maturity, and decline stages (see Figure 18.2). In the *embryonic stage* a product has yet to gain widespread acceptance; customers are unsure what a product, such as a new smart phone, has to offer, and demand for it is minimal. As a product, like Apple's iPod, becomes accepted by customers (although many products do *not*, like Dell's MP3 player), demand takes off and the product enters its growth stage. In the *growth stage* many consumers are entering the market and buying the product for the first time, and demand increases rapidly. This is the stage Apple iPods are in currently.

The growth stage ends and the *mature stage* begins when market demand peaks because most customers have already bought the product (there are relatively few first-time buyers left). At this stage demand is typically replacement demand. In the PC market, for example, people who already have a PC are trading up to a more powerful model. Products such as PCs, wireless phones, and online information services are currently in this stage. If demand for a product starts to fall, then the *decline stage* begins; this frequently happens

A young woman sports the familiar iPod earphones. In the growth stage many consumers are entering the market and buying the product for the first time and demand increases rapidly. This is the stage Apple iPods are in currently.

Figure 18.2
A Product Life Cycle

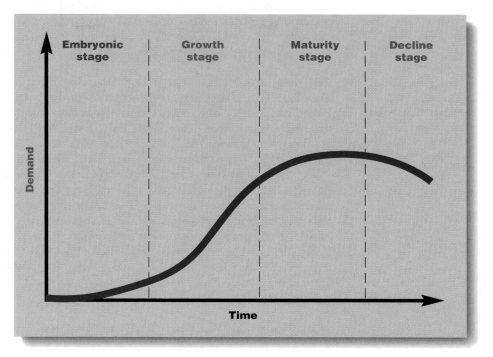

when advancing IT leads to the development of a more advanced product, making the old one obsolete. For example, demand for every generation of PC, wireless phone, or MP3 player falls off as the products are superseded by those that incorporate advances in IT, such as Apple iPods that have new video capabilities or 3G smart phones that have more powerful broadband capabilities.

Thus one reason the IT revolution has been so important for managers is that advances in IT are one of the most significant determinants of the length of a product's life cycle, and therefore of competition in an industry.[25] In some industries—such as PCs, semiconductors, and computer disk drives—technological advances are so rapid that product life cycles are very short. For example, in the disk-drive industry a new model becomes technologically obsolete about 12 months after its introduction; in the PC industry product life cycles have shrunk from three years during the 1980s to a few months today because of advancing IT.

In other industries the product life cycle is often longer. In the car industry, for example, the average product life cycle is about three to five years. But even here the life cycle has been shortening because advancing IT has led to a continual stream of incremental innovations in car design. Today, a typical car has over 300 advanced electronic microcontrollers that run most of its operating functions, such as the hybrid engine in Toyota's Prius, which is powered by gas and an electric motor but controlled by chips.

The message for managers is clear: The shorter the length of a product's life cycle because of advancing IT, the more important it is to innovate products quickly and continuously. The PC company that cannot develop a new and improved product line every three to six months will soon find itself in trouble. Increasingly, managers are trying to outdo their rivals by being the first to market with a product that incorporates some advance in IT, such as advanced stability or steering control that prevents vehicle wrecks.[26] In sum, the tumbling price of information brought about by advances in IT is at the heart of the IT revolution. So the question is, How can managers use all this computing power to their advantage?

Computer Networks

networking The exchange of information through a group or network of interlinked computers.

The tumbling price of computing power and information has facilitated computer **networking,** the exchange of information through a group or network of interlinked computers. The most common arrangement now emerging is a four-tier network consisting of personal digital assistants (PDAs), clients, servers, and a mainframe (see Figure 18.3). At the outer nodes of a typical four-tier system are the PDAs, such as wireless smart phones and electronic organizers like the Palm Pilot, which allow users to e-mail coworkers and which provide access to files on their PCs and on the company's intranet. Next in the network are the PCs that sit on the desks of individual users. These PCs, referred to as *clients,* are linked to a local server, a high-powered midrange computer that "serves" the client PCs. Servers often store power-hungry software programs that can be run more effectively on the server than on an individual's personal computer. Servers may also manage a network of printers that can be used by hundreds of clients, store data files, and handle e-mail communications between clients. The client computers linked

Figure 18.3
A Typical Four-Tier Information System

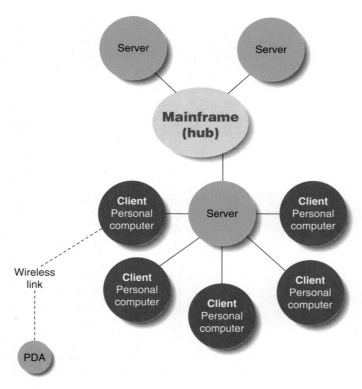

directly to a server constitute a *local area network (LAN)*. Within any organization there may be several LANs—for example, one in every division and function.

At the hub of a four-tier system are mainframe computers. *Mainframes* are large and powerful computers that can be used to store and process vast amounts of information. The mainframe can also be used to handle electronic communications between personal computers situated in different LANs. In addition, the mainframe may be connected to mainframes in other organizations and, through them, to LANs in other organizations. A manager with a PDA or PC hooked into a four-tier system can access data and software stored in the local server, in the mainframe, or through the Internet in computers based in another organization. A manager can therefore communicate electronically with other individuals hooked into the system, whether they are in the manager's LAN, in another LAN within the manager's organization, or in another organization altogether. Moreover, with wireless communication an individual with the necessary IT can hook into the system from any location—at home, on a boat, on the beach, in the air—anywhere a wireless communication link can be established. Increasingly, the Internet, a worldwide network of inter-linked computers, is used as the conduit for connecting the computer systems of different organizations, but specialist IT organizations such as IBM are also trying to provide this service, as the following "Management Insight" suggests.

Management Insight

IBM's "Business-on-Demand" IT

A company seeking to purchase new IT has to decide which components of computer hardware and software will result in the greatest gains in competitive advantage and profitability. Convincing a company to spend millions or billions of dollars to buy new kinds of software and hardware is a daunting task facing the sales force of a company that sells IT today. One company facing this challenge is IBM, which makes, sells, and services a vast array of computer hardware and software. To maintain its leading position in the highly competitive IT industry, Sam Palmisano, IBM's CEO, announced a bold new business strategy for IBM called "Business on Demand." Over the long run, he claims, companies that adopt IBM's new IT will generate millions or billions of dollars in savings in operating costs.

To promote its new strategy, IBM told its customers to think of information and computing power as being a fluid, like water, contained in the hundreds or thousands of computers that are the "reservoirs" or "lakes" of a large company's IT system. This water flows between computers in a company's computer network through the fiber-optic cables that connect them. Thus, computing power, like water, can potentially be moved between computers both inside a company and between companies, as long as all the computers are linked seamlessly together. "Seamless" means that computer hardware or software does not create information logjams, which disrupt the flow of information and computing power.

To allow the potential computing power of all a company's computers to be shared, IBM's software engineers developed new e-business software that enables computers to work seamlessly together. Among its other capabilities, this software allows computer operators to monitor hundreds of different computers at the same time and shift work from one machine to another to distribute a company's computing power to wherever it is most needed. This has several cost-saving advantages. First, companies can run their computers at a much higher level, close to capacity, thereby greatly improving IT productivity and reducing operating costs.

Second, to ensure that its customers never experience a "drought," IBM uses its own vast computer capacity as a kind of bank or reservoir that customers can tap into whenever their own systems become overloaded. For example, using IBM's e-business software, companies can shift any excess work to IBM's computers rather than investing tens of millions of dollars in extra computers—a huge cost saving. Third, when a company's computers are seamlessly networked together, they can function as a supercomputer, a computer with immense information processing power, which can easily cost upward of $50 million just to purchase and tens of millions more to maintain.

IBM decided to implement its new e-business IT in its own company to show customers the cost-saving potential of its new products. Previously, IBM had allowed its many different product divisions to choose whatever software they liked to manage their own purchasing and supply chain activities. Palmisano appointed star manager Linda Stanford to overhaul IBM's whole supply chain, which amounts to $44 billion in yearly purchases. She is responsible for developing software to link them all into a single e-business system. IBM expects this will result in a 5% productivity gain each year for the next 5 to 10 years—which translates into savings of $2 billion a year. IBM is telling its customers that they can expect to see similar savings if they purchase its software.

IBM's new e-business system also has many other performance-enhancing benefits. Its thousands of consultants are experts in particular industries, such as the car, financial services, or retail industries. They have a deep understanding of the particular problems facing companies in those industries and how to solve them. Palmisano asked IBM's consultants to work closely with its software engineers to find ways to incorporate their knowledge into advanced software that can be implanted into a customer's IT system. IBM has developed 17 industry-specific expert systems, which consist of problem-solving software managers can use to make better business decisions and control a company's operations. One expert system is being developed for the pharmaceutical industry. Using this new software, a pharmaceutical company's interlinked computers will be able to function as a supercomputer and simulate and model the potential success of new drugs under development. Currently, only 5% to 10% of new drugs make it to the market. IBM believes that its new IT could raise that rate to over 50%, which would lead to billions of dollars in cost savings.[27]

Just as computer hardware has been advancing rapidly, so has computer software. *Operating system software* tells the computer hardware how to run. *Applications software*, such as programs for word processing, spreadsheets, graphics, and database management, is software developed for a specific task or use. The increase in the power of computer hardware has allowed software developers to write increasingly powerful programs that are, at the same time, increasingly user-friendly. By harnessing the rapidly growing power of microprocessors, applications software has vastly increased the ability of managers to acquire, organize, manipulate, and transmit information. In doing so, it also has increased the ability of managers to coordinate and control the activities of their organization and to make decisions, as discussed earlier.

Types of Management Information Systems

Advancing computer hardware and software has continuously increased managers' ability to obtain the information they need to make decisions and to coordinate and control organizational resources. Next, we discuss six types of management information systems that over time have been particularly helpful to managers as they go about the task of managing: transaction-processing systems, operations information systems, decision support systems, expert systems, enterprise resource planning systems, and e-commerce systems (see Figure 18.4). These systems are arranged along a continuum according to the sophistication of the IT they are based on—IT that determines their ability to provide managers with the information they need to make nonprogrammed decisions. (Recall from Chapter 7 that nonprogrammed decision making occurs in response to unusual, unpredictable opportunities and threats.) We examine each of these systems after focusing on the management information system that preceded them all: the organizational hierarchy.

The Organizational Hierarchy: The Traditional Information System

Traditionally, managers have used the organizational hierarchy as the main system for gathering the information necessary to make decisions and coordinate and control activities (see Chapter 10 for a detailed discussion of organizational structure and hierarchy). According to business historian Alfred Chandler, the use of the hierarchy as an information network was perfected by railroad companies in the United States during the 1850s.[28] At that time, the railroads were

Figure 18.4

Six Computer-Based Management Information Systems

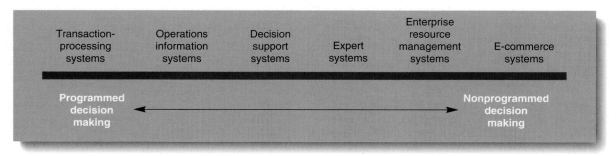

the largest industrial organizations in the United States. By virtue of their size and geographic spread, they faced unique problems of coordination and control. In the 1850s, railroad companies started to solve these problems by designing hierarchical management structures that provided senior managers with the information they needed to achieve coordination and control and to make decisions about the running of the railroads.

Daniel McCallum, superintendent of the Erie Railroad in the 1850s, realized that the lines of authority and responsibility defining the Erie's management hierarchy also represented channels of communication along which information traveled. McCallum established what was perhaps the first modern management information system. Regular daily and monthly reports were sent up the management chain so that top managers could make decisions about, for example, controlling costs and setting freight rates. Decisions were then relayed back down the hierarchy so that they could be carried out. Imitating the railroads, most other organizations used their hierarchies as systems for collecting and channeling information. This practice began to change only when computer-based IT became more reasonably priced in the 1960s.

Although hierarchy is a useful information system, it has several drawbacks. First, when an organization has many layers of managers, it takes a long time for information and requests to travel up the hierarchy and for decisions and answers to travel back down. This slow pace can reduce the timeliness and usefulness of the information and prevent an organization from responding quickly to changing market conditions.[29] Second, information can be distorted as it moves from one layer of management to another, and information distortion reduces the quality of information.[30] Third, because managers have only a limited span of control, as an organization grows larger, its hierarchy lengthens, and this tall structure can make the hierarchy a very expensive information system. The popular idea that companies with tall management hierarchies are bureaucratic and unresponsive to the needs of their customers arises from the inability of tall hierarchies to effectively process data and provide managers with timely, complete, relevant, and high-quality information. Until modern IT came along, however, the management hierarchy was the best information system available.

Transaction-Processing Systems

transaction-processing system A management information system designed to handle large volumes of routine, recurring transactions.

A **transaction-processing system** is an MIS designed to handle large volumes of routine, recurring transactions (see Figure 18.4). Transaction-processing systems began to appear in the early 1960s with the advent of commercially available mainframe computers. They were the first type of computer-based IT adopted by many organizations, and today they are commonplace. Bank managers use a transaction-processing system to record deposits into, and payments out of, bank accounts. Supermarket managers use a transaction-processing system to record the sale of items and to track inventory levels. More generally, most managers in large organizations use a transaction-processing system to handle tasks such as payroll preparation and payment, customer billing, and payment of suppliers.

Operations Information Systems

operations information system A management information system that gathers, organizes, and summarizes comprehensive data in a form that managers can use in their nonroutine coordinating, controlling, and decision-making tasks.

Many types of MIS followed hard on the heels of transaction-processing systems in the 1960s as companies like IBM advanced IT. An **operations information system** is an MIS that gathers comprehensive data, organizes them, and summarizes them in a form that is of value to managers. Whereas a transaction-processing system processes routine transactions, an operations information system provides managers with information that they can use in their nonroutine coordinating, controlling, and decision-making tasks. Most operations information systems are coupled with a transaction-processing system. An operations information system typically accesses data gathered by a transaction-processing system, processes those data into useful information, and organizes that information into a form accessible to managers. Managers often use an operations information system to get sales, inventory, accounting, and other performance-related information. For example, the information that T. J. Rodgers at Cypress Semiconductors gets on individual employee goals and performance is provided by an operations information system.

DHL uses an operations information system to track the performance of its 500 or so ground stations. Each ground station is evaluated according to four criteria: delivery (the goal is to deliver 95% of all packages by noon the day after they are picked up), productivity (measured by the number of packages shipped per employee-hour), controllable cost, and station profitability. Each ground station also has specific delivery, efficiency, cost, and profitability targets that it must attain. Every month DHL's operations information system is used to gather information on these four criteria and summarize it for top managers, who are then able to compare the performance of each station against its previously established targets. The system quickly alerts senior managers to underperforming ground stations, so they can intervene selectively to help solve any problems that may have given rise to the poor performance.[31]

Decision Support Systems

decision support system An interactive computer-based management information system that managers can use to make nonroutine decisions.

A **decision support system** provides computer-built models that help managers make better nonprogrammed decisions.[32] Recall from Chapter 7 that nonprogrammed decisions are decisions that are relatively unusual or novel, such as decisions to invest in new productive capacity, develop a new product, launch a new promotional campaign, enter a new market, or expand internationally. Although an operations information system organizes important information for managers, a decision support system gives managers a model-building capability and so provides them with the ability to manipulate information in a variety of ways. Managers might use a decision support system to help them decide whether to cut prices for a product. The decision support system might contain models of how customers and competitors would respond to a price cut. Managers could run these models and use the results as an *aid* to decision making.

The stress on the word *aid* is important, for in the final analysis a decision support system is not meant to make decisions for managers. Rather, its function is to provide managers with valuable information that they can use to improve the quality of their decisions. A good example of a sophisticated decision support system, developed by Judy Lewent, chief financial officer of the U.S. pharmaceutical company Merck, is given in the following "Manager as a Person."

Manager as a Person

How Judy Lewent Became One of the Most Powerful Women in Corporate America

With annual sales of over $40 billion, Merck is one of the world's largest developers and marketers of advanced pharmaceuticals.[33] The company spent over $3 billion a year on R&D to develop new drugs—an expensive and difficult process that is fraught with risks. Most new drug ideas fail to make it through the development process. It takes an average of $300 million and 10 years to bring a new drug to market, and 7 out of 10 new drugs fail to make a profit for the developing company.

Given the costs, risks, and uncertainties involved in the new drug development process, Judy Lewent, the former director of capital analysis at Merck, decided to develop a decision support system that could help managers make more effective R&D investment decisions. Her aim was to give Merck's top managers the information they needed to evaluate proposed R&D projects on a case-by-case basis. The system that Lewent and her staff developed is referred to in Merck as the "Research Planning Model."[34] At the heart of this decision support system is a sophisticated model. The input variables to the model include data on R&D spending, manufacturing costs, selling costs, and demand conditions. The relationships among the input variables are modeled by means of several equations that factor in the probability of a drug's making it through the development process and to market. The outputs of this modeling process are the revenues, cash flows, and profits that a project might generate.

Judy Lewent, chief financial officer of Merck, consults with managers of Sweden's Astra Pharmaceuticals, as they work out the details of their global venture.

The Merck model does not use a single value for an input variable, nor does it compute a single value for each output. Rather, a range is specified for each input variable (such as high, medium, and low R&D spending). The computer repeatedly samples at random from the range of values for each input variable and produces a probability distribution of values for each output. So, for example, instead of stating categorically that a proposed R&D project will yield a profit of $500 million, the decision support system produces a probability distribution. It might state that although $500 million is the most likely profit, there is a 25% chance that the profit will be less than $300 million and a 25% chance that it will be greater than $700 million.

Merck now uses Lewent's decision support system to evaluate all proposed R&D investment decisions. In addition, Lewent has developed other decision support system models that Merck's managers can use to help them decide, for example, whether to enter into joint ventures with other companies or how best to hedge foreign exchange risk. As for Lewent, her reward was promotion to the position of chief financial officer of Merck, and she became one of the most powerful women in corporate America.

Most decision support systems are geared toward aiding middle managers in the decision-making process. For example, a loan manager at a bank might use a decision support system to evaluate the credit risk involved in lending money to a particular client. Very rarely does a top manager use a decision support system. One reason for this may be that most electronic management information systems are not yet sophisticated enough to handle effectively the ambiguous types of problems facing top managers. To improve this situation, IT professionals have been developing a variant of the decision support system: an executive support system.

executive support system A sophisticated version of a decision support system that is designed to meet the needs of top managers.

An executive support system is a sophisticated version of a decision support system that is designed to meet the needs of top managers. Lewent's Research Planning Model is actually an executive support system. One of the defining characteristics of executive support systems is user-friendliness. Many of them include simple pull-down menus to take a manager through a decision analysis problem. Moreover, they may contain stunning graphics and other visual features to encourage top managers to use them.[35] Increasingly, executive support systems are being used to link top managers so that they can function as a team; this type of executive support system is called a group decision support system.

group decision support system An executive support system that links top managers so that they can function as a team.

Artificial Intelligence and Expert Systems

artificial intelligence Behavior performed by a machine that, if performed by a human being, would be called "intelligent."

Artificial intelligence is another interesting and potentially fruitful software development. Artificial intelligence has been defined as behavior by a machine that, if performed by a human being, would be called "intelligent."[36] Artificial intelligence has already made it possible to write programs that can solve problems and perform simple tasks. For example, software programs variously called *software agents, softbots,* or *knowbots* can be used to perform simple managerial tasks such as sorting through reams of data or incoming e-mail messages to look for the important ones. The interesting feature of these programs is that from "watching" a manager sort through such data they can "learn" what his or her preferences are. Having done this, they then can take over some of this work from the manager, freeing more time for the manager to work on other tasks. Most of these programs are still in the development stage, but they may be commonplace within a decade.[37]

expert system A management information system that employs human knowledge, embedded in a computer, to solve problems that ordinarily require human expertise.

Expert systems, the most advanced management information systems available, incorporate artificial intelligence in their design.[38] An expert system is a system that employs human knowledge, embedded in computer software, to solve problems that ordinarily require human expertise.[39] Mimicking human expertise (and

Even though Deep Blue could calculate 200 million moves a second, chess expert Garry Kasporov at first tricked the computer into foolish exchanges. But in a subsequent meeting, DB crushed him.

intelligence) requires IT that can at a minimum (1) recognize, formulate, and solve a problem; (2) explain the solution; and (3) learn from experience.

Recent developments in artificial intelligence that go by names such as "fuzzy logic" and "neural networks" have resulted in computer programs that, in a primitive way, try to mimic human thought processes. Although artificial intelligence is still at a fairly early stage of development, an increasing number of business applications are beginning to emerge in the form of expert systems. General Electric, for example, has developed an expert system to help troubleshoot problems in the diesel locomotive engines it manufactures. The expert system was originally based on knowledge collected from David Smith, GE's former top locomotive troubleshooter. A novice engineer or technician can use the system to uncover a fault by spending only a few minutes at a computer terminal. The system also can explain to the user the logic of its advice, thereby serving as a teacher as well as a problem solver. The system is based on a flexible, humanlike thought process, and it can be updated to incorporate new knowledge as it becomes available. GE has installed the system in every railroad repair shop that it serves, thus eliminating delays and boosting maintenance productivity.[40]

Enterprise Resource Planning Systems

To achieve high performance, it is not sufficient just to develop an MIS inside each of a company's functions or divisions to provide better information and knowledge. It is also vital that managers in the different functions and divisions have access to information about the activities of managers in other functions and divisions. The greater the flow of information and knowledge among functions and divisions, the more learning can take place, and this builds a company's stock of knowledge and expertise. This knowledge and expertise is the source of its competitive advantage and profitability.

In the last 25 years, another revolution has taken place in IT as software companies have worked to develop enterprise resource planning systems, which essentially incorporate most aspects of the MISs just discussed, as well as much more. **Enterprise resource planning (ERP) systems** are multimodule application software packages that allow a company to link and coordinate the entire set of functional activities and operations necessary to move products from the initial product design stage to the final customer stage. Essentially, ERP systems (1) help each individual function improve its functional-level skills and (2) improve integration among all functions so that they work together to build a competitive advantage for the company. Today, choosing and designing an ERP system to improve the way a company operates is the biggest challenge facing the IT function inside a company. To understand why almost every large global company has installed an ERP system in the last few decades, it is necessary to return to the concept of the value chain, introduced in Chapter 8.

enterprise resource planning (ERP) systems Multimodule application software packages that coordinate the functional activities necessary to move products from the product design stage to the final customer stage.

Recall that a company's value chain is composed of the sequence of functional activities that are necessary to make and sell a product. The value-chain idea focuses attention on the fact that each function, in sequence, performs its activities to add or contribute value to a product. Once one function has made its contribution, it then hands the product over to the next function, which makes its own contribution, and so on down the line.

The primary activity of marketing, for example, is to uncover new or changing customer needs or new groups of customers and then decide what kinds of products should be developed to appeal to those customers. It then shares or "hands off" its information to product development, where engineers and scientists work to develop and design the new products. In turn, manufacturing and materials management then work to find ways to produce the new products as efficiently as possible. Then, sales is responsible for finding the best way to convince customers to buy these products.

The value chain is useful in demonstrating the sequence of activities necessary to bring products to the market successfully. In an IT context, however, it suggests the enormous amount of information and communication that needs to take place to link and coordinate the activities of all the various functions. Installing an ERP system for a large company can cost tens of millions of dollars. The following "Information Technology Byte" discusses the ERP system designed and sold by the German IT company SAP.

Information Technology Byte

SAP's ERP System

SAP is the world's leading supplier of ERP software; it introduced the world's first ERP system in 1973. So great was the demand for its software that it had to train thousands of consultants from companies like IBM, HP, Accenture, and Cap Gemini to install and customize its software to meet the needs of companies in different industries throughout the world.

The popularity of SAP's ERP is that it manages all the stages of a company's value chain, both individually and as a collection. SAP's software has modules specifically devoted to each of a company's core functional activities. Each module contains a set of "best practices," or the optimum way to perform specific activities, that SAP's IT experts have found results in the biggest increases in efficiency, quality, innovation, and responsiveness to customers. SAP's ERP is therefore "the expert system of expert systems." SAP claims that when a company reconfigures its IT system to make SAP's software work, it can achieve productivity gains of 30% to 50%, which amounts to many billions of dollars of savings for large companies.[41]

For each function in the value chain, SAP has a software module that it installs on a function's LAN. Each function then inputs its data into that module in the way specified by SAP. For example, the sales function inputs all the information about customer needs required by SAP's sales module, and the materials management function inputs information about the product specifications it requires from suppliers into SAP's materials management module. These modules give functional managers real-time feedback on the status of their particular functional activities. Essentially, each SAP module functions as an expert system that can reason through the information functional managers put into it. It then provides them with recommendations as to how they can improve functional operations. However, the magic of ERP does not stop there.

SAP's ERP software also connects across functions. Managers in all functions have access to the other functions' expert systems, and SAP's software is designed to alert managers when their functional activities will be affected by changes taking place in another function. Thus, SAP's ERP allows managers across the organization to better coordinate their activities, and this can be a major source of competitive advantage. Moreover, SAP software on corporate mainframe computers takes the information from all the different functional and divisional expert systems and creates a companywide ERP system that provides top managers with an overview of the operations of the whole company. In essence, SAP's ERP creates a sophisticated top-level expert system that can reason through the huge volume of information being provided by the company's functions. It can then recognize and diagnose common problems and issues in that information and develop and recommend organizationwide solutions for those problems and issues. Top managers armed with this information can then use it to improve the fit between their strategies and the changing environment.

As an example of how an ERP system works, let's examine how SAP's software allows managers to better coordinate their activities to speed product development. Suppose marketing has discovered some new unmet customer need, suggested what kind of product needs to be developed, and forecasted that the demand for the product will be 40,000 units a year. With SAP's IT, engineers in product development use their expert system to work out how to design the new product in a way that builds in quality at the lowest possible cost. Manufacturing managers, watching product development's progress, are working simultaneously to find the best way to make the product, and thus use their expert system to find out how to keep operating costs at a minimum.

Remember, SAP's IT gives all the other functions access to this information; they can tap into what is going on between marketing and manufacturing in real time. So materials management managers watching manufacturing make its plans can simultaneously plan how to order supplies of inputs or components from global suppliers or how and when to ship the final product to customers to keep costs at a minimum. At the same time, HRM is tied into the ERP system and uses its expert system to forecast the type and cost of the labor that will be required to carry out the activities in the other functions—for example, the number of manufacturing employees who will be required to make the product or the number of salespeople who will be needed to sell the product to achieve the 40,000 sales forecast.

How does this build competitive advantage and profitability? First, it speeds up the product development process; companies can bring products to market much more quickly, thereby generating higher sales revenues. Second, SAP's IT focuses on how to drive down operating costs while keeping quality high. Third, SAP's IT is oriented toward the final customer; its CRM module watches how customers respond to the new product and then feeds back this information quickly to the other functions.

To see what this means in practice, let's jump ahead three months and suppose that the CRM component of SAP's ERP software reports that actual sales are 20% below target. Further, the software has reasoned that the problem is due to the fact that the product lacks one crucial feature that customers want. The product is a smart phone, for example, and customers must have a built-in digital camera. Sales decides this issue deserves major priority and alerts managers in all the other functions about the problem. Now managers can begin to make decisions about how to manage this unexpected situation.

Engineers in product development, for example, use their expert system to work out how much it would cost, and how long it would take, to modify the product so that it includes the missing feature, the digital camera, that customers require. Managers in other functions watch the engineers' progress through the ERP system and can make suggestions for improvement. In the meantime, manufacturing managers know about the slow sales and have already cut back on production to avoid a buildup of the unsold product in the company's warehouse. They are also planning how to phase out this product and introduce the next version, with the digital camera, to keep costs as low as possible. Similarly, materials management managers are contacting digital-camera makers to find out how much such a camera will cost and when it can be supplied. In the meantime, marketing managers are researching how they came to miss this crucial product feature and are developing new sales forecasts to estimate demand for the modified product. They announce a revised sales forecast of 75,000 units of the modified product.

It takes the engineers one month to modify the product, but because SAP's IT has been providing information on the modified product to managers in manufacturing and materials management, the product hits the market only two months later. Within weeks, the sales function reports that early sales figures for the product have greatly exceeded even marketing's revised forecast. The company knows it has a winning product, and top managers give the go-ahead for manufacturing to build a second production line to double production of the product. All the other functions are expecting this decision; in fact, they have already been experimenting with their SAP modules to find out how long it will take them to respond to such a move. Each function provides the others with its latest information so that they can all adjust their functional activities accordingly.

All this quick and responsive action has been made possible because of the ERP system. Compare this situation to that of a company which relies only on a paper-based system, in which salespeople fill in paper sales reports. In such a company, it would take many times as long to find out about slow sales; it might take six months to a year for the company to find out that its sales projections were wrong. In the meantime, manufacturing, producing according to plan, will generate a huge stock of unsold products, which is a major source of operating costs. When the sales problem is finally uncovered, managers from the different functions will have to make frantic phone calls and hold face-to-face meetings to decide what to do. It might take another six months for the modified product to come into production, so more than one year of time, and huge potential profits, will have been lost.

In the ERP example, efficiency is promoted because a company has a better control of its manufacturing and materials management activities. Quality is increased because an increased flow of information between functions allows for a better-designed product. Innovation is speeded because a company can rapidly change its products to suit the changing needs of customers. Finally, responsiveness to customers improves because using its CRM software module, sales can better manage and react to customer's changing needs and provide better service and support to back up the sales of the product. ERP's ability to promote competitive advantage is the reason why managers in so many companies, large and small, are moving to find the best ERP "solution" for their particular companies.

E-Commerce Systems

e-commerce Trade that takes place between companies, and between companies and individual customers, using IT and the Internet.

business-to-business (B2B) commerce Trade that takes place between companies using IT and the Internet to link and coordinate the value chains of different companies.

B2B marketplace An Internet-based trading platform set up to connect buyers and sellers in an industry.

business-to-customer (B2C) commerce Trade that takes place between a company and individual customers using IT and the Internet.

E-commerce is trade that takes place between companies, and between companies and individual customers, using IT and the Internet. **Business-to-business (B2B) commerce** is trade that takes place between companies using IT and the Internet to link and coordinate the value chains of different companies. (See Figure 18.5.) The goal of B2B commerce is to increase the profitability of making and selling goods and services. B2B commerce increases profitability because it allows companies to reduce their operating costs or because it may improve product quality. A principal B2B software application is **B2B marketplaces,** Internet-based trading platforms that have been set up in many industries to connect buyers and sellers. To participate in a B2B marketplace, companies adopt a common software standard that allows them to search for and share information with one another. Then companies can work together over time to find ways to reduce costs or improve quality.

Business-to-customer (B2C) commerce is trade that takes place between a company and individual customers using IT and the Internet. Using IT to connect directly to the customer means that companies can avoid having to use intermediaries, such as wholesalers and retailers, who capture a significant part of the profit being created in the value chain. The use of Web sites and online stores also allows companies to provide their customers with much more information about the value of their products. This often allows them to attract more customers and thus generate higher sales revenues. We discuss this important issue in depth in the chapters on marketing and sales.

In the last five years, computer software makers including Microsoft, Oracle, SAP, and IBM, have rushed to make their products work seamlessly with the Internet to respond to global companies' growing demand for e-commerce

Figure 18.5
Types of E-Commerce

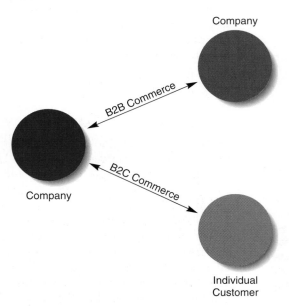

software. Previously, their software had been configured to work only on a particular company's intranet. Now, they have had to develop software that would network the computer systems of companies to their suppliers and customers.

Today, the challenge facing managers is to select the e-commerce software that allows the seamless exchange of information between companies anywhere in the world. The stakes are high; we discussed earlier how IBM's new thrust is toward on-demand software. SAP has also rushed to update its ERP modules to allow for transactions over the Internet. It calls its new B2B commerce software "mySAP," and today every one of its modules is Internet-compatible. Microsoft is promoting its .net Internet software, which is compatible with all its other Windows software, and is vigorously competing with IBM and SAP to raise its share of this growing software market.

In summary, by using computer-based MISs, managers have more control over a company's activities and operations and can work to improve its competitive advantage and profitability. Today, the IT function is becoming increasingly important because IT managers select which kind of hardware and software a company will use and also train employees to use it.

The Impact and Limitations of Information Technology

The advances in IT and management information systems described in this chapter are having important effects on managers and organizations. By improving the ability of managers to coordinate and control the activities of the organization and by helping managers make more effective decisions, modern IT has become a central component of any organization's structure. And evidence that IT can be a source of competitive advantage is growing; organizations that do not adopt leading-edge IT are likely to be at a competitive disadvantage. In this section we examine how the rapid advances in IT are affecting organizational structure and competitive advantage. We also examine problems associated with implementing management information systems effectively, as well as the limitations of MISs.

Strategic Alliances, B2B Network Structures, and IT

Recently, increasing globalization and the use of new IT has brought about two innovations that are sweeping through U.S. and European companies: electronically managed strategic alliances and B2B network structures. A **strategic alliance** is a formal agreement that commits two or more companies to exchange or share their resources in order to produce and market a product.[42] Most commonly, strategic alliances are formed because the companies share similar interests and believe they can benefit from cooperating. For example, Japanese car companies such as Toyota and Honda have formed many strategic alliances with particular suppliers of inputs such as car axles, gearboxes, and air-conditioning systems. Over time, these car companies work closely with their suppliers to improve the efficiency and effectiveness of the inputs so that the

strategic alliance An agreement in which managers pool or share their organization's resources and know-how with a foreign company and the two organizations share the rewards and risks of starting a new venture.

final product—the car produced—is of higher quality and very often can be produced at lower cost. Toyota and Honda have also established alliances with suppliers throughout the United States and Mexico because both companies now build several models of cars in these countries.

Throughout the 1990s, the growing sophistication of IT with global intranets and teleconferencing has made it much easier to manage strategic alliances and allow managers to share information and cooperate. One outcome of this has been the growth of strategic alliances into an IT-based network structure. A **B2B network structure** is a formal series of global strategic alliances that one or several organizations create with suppliers, manufacturers, and/or distributors to produce and market a product. Network structures allow an organization to manage its global value chain in order to find new ways to reduce costs and increase the quality of products—without incurring the high costs of operating a complex organizational structure (such as the costs of employing many managers). More and more U.S. and European companies are relying on global network structures to gain access to low-cost foreign sources of inputs, as discussed in Chapter 6. Shoemakers such as Nike and Adidas are two companies that have used this approach extensively.

Nike is the largest and most profitable sports shoe manufacturer in the world. The key to Nike's success is the network structure that Nike founder and CEO Philip Knight created to allow his company to produce and market shoes. As noted in Chapter 8, the most successful companies today are trying to pursue simultaneously a low-cost and a differentiation strategy. Knight decided early that to do this at Nike he needed to focus his company's efforts on the most important functional activities, such as product design and engineering, and leave the others, such as manufacturing, to other organizations.

By far the largest function at Nike's Oregon headquarters is the design and engineering function, whose members pioneered innovations in sports shoe design such as the air pump and Air Jordans that Nike introduced so successfully. Designers use computer-aided design (CAD) to design Nike shoes, and they electronically store all new product information, including manufacturing instructions. When the designers have finished their work, they electronically transmit all the blueprints for the new products to a network of Southeast Asian suppliers and manufacturers with which Nike has formed strategic alliances.[43] Instructions for the design of a new sole may be sent to a supplier in Taiwan; instructions for the leather uppers, to a supplier in Malaysia. The suppliers produce the shoe parts and send them for final assembly to a manufacturer in China with which Nike has established another strategic alliance. From China the shoes are shipped to distributors throughout the world. Ninety-nine percent of the over 100 million pairs of shoes that Nike makes each year are made in Southeast Asia.

This network structure gives Nike two important advantages. First, Nike is able to respond to changes in sports shoe fashion very quickly. Using its global IT system, Nike literally can change the instructions it gives each of its suppliers overnight, so that within a few weeks its foreign manufacturers are producing new kinds of shoes.[44] Any alliance partners that fail to perform up to Nike's standards are replaced with new partners through the regular B2B marketplace.

Second, Nike's costs are very low because wages in Southeast Asia are a fraction of what they are in the United States, and this difference gives Nike a low-cost advantage. Also, Nike's ability to outsource and use foreign manufacturers to produce all its shoes abroad allows Knight to keep the organization's U.S.

B2B network structure A series of global strategic alliances that an organization creates with suppliers, manufacturers, and/or distributors to produce and market a product.

structure flat and flexible. Nike is able to use a relatively inexpensive functional structure to organize its activities.

The use of network structures is increasing rapidly as organizations recognize the many opportunities they offer to reduce costs and increase organizational flexibility. U.S. companies spent $300 billion on global supply chain management each year in the 2000s. The push to lower costs has led to the development of B2B marketplaces in which most or all of the companies in an industry (for example, carmakers) use the same software platform to link to each other and establish industry specifications and standards. Then these companies jointly list the quantity and specifications of the inputs they require and invite bids from the thousands of potential suppliers around the world. Suppliers also use the same software platform, so electronic bidding, auctions, and transactions are possible between buyers and sellers around the world. The idea is that high-volume standardized transactions can help drive down costs at the industry level. Also, quality will increase as these relationships become stable as a B2B network structure develops.

Flatter Structures and Horizontal Information Flows

Rapid advances in IT have been associated with a "delayering" (flattening) of the organizational hierarchy, a move toward greater decentralization and horizontal information flows within organizations, and the concept of the boundary-less organization.[45]

FLATTENING ORGANIZATIONS   By electronically providing managers with high-quality, timely, relevant, and relatively complete information, modern management information systems have reduced the need for tall management hierarchies. (See Figure 18.6). Consider again the computer-based

Figure 18.6

How Computer-Based Information Systems Affect the Organizational Hierarchy

Before

Tall structure
primarily up-down
communication

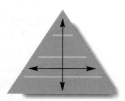

After

Flat structure
both up-down
and lateral
communication

operations information system that T. J. Rodgers uses at Cypress Semiconductor to review the performance of his 1,500 employees. Ten years ago, Rodgers might have needed 100 managers to conduct such performance reviews; now he can do them himself in four hours a week. Modern IT has reduced the need for a hierarchy to function as a means of coordinating and controlling organizational activities, Also, by reducing the need for hierarchy, modern IT can directly increase an organization's efficiency because fewer employees are required to perform organizational activities. At one time, for example, 13 layers of management separated Kodak's general manager of manufacturing and factory workers. With IT the number of layers has been cut to four. Similarly, Intel found that by increasing the sophistication of its own MIS, it could cut the number of hierarchical layers in the organization from 10 to 5.[46]

HORIZONTAL INFORMATION FLOWS   Fired by the growth of four-tier mainframe-server-client-PDA computing architecture (see Figure 18.3), expansion of organizationwide computer networks has been rapid in recent years. E-mail systems, the development of software programs for sharing documents electronically, and the development of intranets (see Chapter 16) have accelerated this trend. An important consequence has been the increase of horizontal information flows within organizations, something illustrated well by the experiences of Tel Co. and Soft Co., discussed in the following "Information Technology Byte."

Information Flows at Tel Co. and Soft Co.

Information Technology Byte

Despite being part of a high-tech company, managers at Tel Co. were slow to adopt an internal electronic mail system (e-mail) to facilitate communication throughout the company. Soft Co., by contrast, is a software company in which managers virtually "live online" and most communication between them takes place by means of e-mail. Commenting on how the two companies differ, a manager who moved from Tel Co. to Soft Co. said:

> At Tel Co. I would take two boxes of memos and company reports home with me each weekend to read. Then I had to go through all this stuff, most of which was irrelevant to my job, to find those pieces of paper that mattered to me. It was very time-consuming, very unproductive. At Soft Co. there is no paper to take home; most communication takes place via the company's email system. I use a software agent to scan all my incoming email and prioritize it [a software agent is a computer program that can perform certain tasks—such as sorting through and prioritizing incoming e-mail]. This saves a massive amount of time. The system alerts me instantly to e-mail that is relevant to my job.[47]

This manager also noted that the use of an e-mail system led to other communication differences between the two companies. At Tel Co. communication is primarily vertical; middle managers send information up the organizational hierarchy, and top managers send their responses back down. At Soft Co., however, communication between managers at different levels has become far less structured, and because of the e-mail system there is much less emphasis on formal channels of communication. E-mail allows managers at any level to communicate easily with one another, so managers at Soft Co. communicate

Figure 18.7

Communication Flows at Tel Co. and Soft Co.

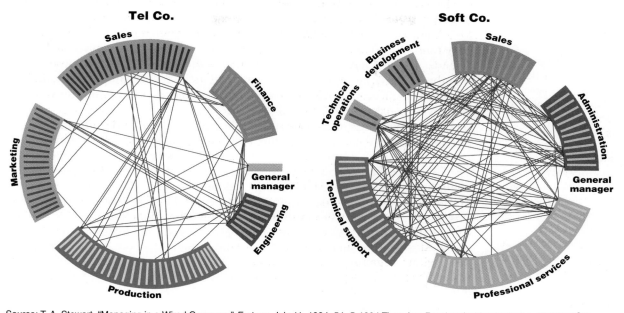

Source: T. A. Stewart, "Managing in a Wired Company," *Fortune,* July 11, 1994, 54. © 1994 Time, Inc. Reprinted with permission. NETMAP® is a registered trademark for the NETMAP Software Systems, Alta Analytics, Inc., Westerville, OH.

directly with whomever they need to contact to get the job done. Also, e-mail has resulted in much more cross-functional, horizontal communication because it is so easy for managers in different functions to communicate.

The observations of this manager about communication flows at Tel Co. and Soft Co. were confirmed in a study undertaken by Alta Analytics, a management consulting company.[48]Figure 18.7 shows maps of the communication flows between managers based in different departments at Tel Co. and Soft Co. The boxes in these two maps are employees grouped by function. To make these maps, Alta asked employees to name every manager with whom they had communication in any form—phone, meeting, memo, e-mail—in the past week. If two people agreed that they had three or more important contacts, the mapmakers drew a line between their boxes, indicating a significant link.

The differences between the two companies are immediately apparent. At Tel Co., the general manager communicated only with four senior functional managers, all of whom had a direct reporting relationship with him; there were hardly any links between the marketing and production departments; and a handful of functional managers accounted for most of the interfunctional communication. At Soft Co., there was a much richer flow of communication between managers in the different functions, as indicated by the number of lines connecting the different boxes. Clearly, boundaries between functions mean little at Soft Co., as do differences in rank. Almost everybody talks to everybody else because of Soft Co.'s e-mail system. At Soft Co. the development of organizationwide computer networks has broken down the barriers that have traditionally separated functional departments and divisions and the result has been improved performance.

THE BOUNDARYLESS ORGANIZATION The ability of IT to flatten structure and facilitate the flow of horizontal information between employees has led many researchers and consultants to popularize the idea of a **boundaryless organization.** Such an organization is composed of people linked by IT—computers, faxes, computer-aided design systems, and video teleconferencing—who may rarely, if ever, see one another face-to-face. People are utilized when their services are needed, much as in a matrix structure, but they are not formal members of an organization; they are functional experts who form an alliance with an organization, fulfill their contractual obligations, and then move on to the next project.

Large consulting companies, such as Arthur Andersen and McKinsey & Co., utilize their global consultants in this way. Consultants are connected by laptops to an organization's **knowledge management system,** its company-specific virtual information system that systematizes the knowledge of its employees and facilitates the sharing and integrating of expertise within and between functions and divisions through real-time, interconnected IT. Knowledge management systems enable employees to share their knowledge and expertise and provide them with virtual access to other employees who have the expertise to solve the problems that they encounter as they perform their jobs.

Limitations of IT

For all of their usefulness, IT in general and management information systems in particular have some limitations. A serious potential problem is that in all of the enthusiasm for management information systems, electronic communication by means of a computer network, and the like, a vital *human element* of communication might be lost. Some kinds of information cannot be aggregated and summarized on an MIS report. Henry Mintzberg noted that *thick information* is often required to coordinate and control an enterprise and to make informed decisions; Mintzberg means information rich in meaning and significance, far beyond that which can be quantified and aggregated.[49] According to Mintzberg, such information must be dug out, on-site, by people closely involved in the events they wish to influence.

The importance of thick information is a strong argument in favor of using electronic communication to support face-to-face communication, not to replace it. For example, it would be wrong to make a judgment about an individual's performance merely by "reading the numbers" provided by an MIS. Instead, the numbers should be used to alert managers to individuals who may have a performance problem. The nature of this problem should then be explored in a face-to-face meeting, during which thick information can be gathered. As a top Boeing manager noted,

> In our company, the use of e-mail and videoconferencing has not reduced the need to visit people at other sites; it has increased it. E-mail has facilitated the establishment of communications channels between people who previously would not communicate, which is good, but direct visits are still required to cement any working relationships that evolve out of these electronic meetings.[50]

At Soft Co., discussed earlier, managers were heard to complain that one drawback of their internal e-mail system is that people spend a lot of time behind closed doors looking at computer screens and communicating electronically and very little time interacting directly with other managers.[51] When this is the case in an organization, management decisions may suffer because of a lack of thick information.

Another limitation of IT in organizations is that despite its many advantages there are still technological problems to be overcome.[52] One of these is the lack of consistent technological standards, since different manufacturers of computer and communication equipment use different standards. If a company uses different kinds of hardware or software systems, made by different IT companies, throughout its divisions or functions, the inconsistency can impede communication and decision making. For example, an IBM mainframe may be manufactured according to technical standards different from those of a Sun or Compaq server or an Apple personal computer. These different standards make it difficult to integrate various machines into a seamless computer network, and machines designed according to different standards may find it difficult to "talk" to one another. One reason for the growing popularity of SAP's ERP is that it solves these problems because it provides a common IT standard throughout a company.

Managers can take several steps to make it easier and quicker to implement an MIS. First, they have to develop a list of the organization's principal goals and then decide on the major types of information they need to collect to measure how well they are achieving those goals. Second, while making this analysis, managers should audit their current MISs to determine the degree to which the information they are currently collecting is accurate, reliable, timely, and relevant. Third, managers need to investigate what other sources of information might be available to measure and improve efficiency, quality, innovation, and responsiveness to customers. For example, are organizational members using state-of-the-art IT like wireless e-mail, computer-assisted design, and four-tier designs? It is useful to benchmark competitors to determine what kinds of systems they are using.

Fourth, when this analysis is complete, managers need to build support for the introduction of an advanced MIS and convince employees that the system will help raise job and organizational performance. Fifth, managers should create formal training programs, with appropriate backup support, to help train employees to use the new information system and technology, making sure that the system is as user-friendly as possible. Sixth, managers should emphasize that the MIS is not a substitute for face-to-face communication and that employees at all levels should be involved in a continuing discussion about how best to take advantage of ongoing developments in IT to create a competitive advantage.

Summary and Review

INFORMATION AND THE MANAGER'S JOB Computer-based IT is central to the operation of most organizations. By providing managers with high-quality, timely, relevant, and relatively complete information, properly implemented IT can improve managers' ability to coordinate and control the operations of an organization and to make effective decisions. Moreover, IT can help the organization to attain a competitive advantage through its beneficial impact on productivity, quality, innovation, and responsiveness to customers. Thus, modern IT is an indispensable management tool.

THE IT REVOLUTION Over the last 30 years there have been rapid advances in the power, and rapid declines in the cost, of IT. Falling prices, wireless communication, computer networks, and software developments have all radically improved the power and efficacy of computer-based IT.

TYPES OF MANAGEMENT INFORMATION SYSTEMS   Traditionally managers used the organizational hierarchy as the main system for gathering the information they needed to coordinate and control the organization and to make effective decisions. Today, managers use six main types of computer-based information systems. Listed in ascending order of sophistication, they are transaction-processing systems, operations information systems, decision support systems, expert systems, enterprise resource planning systems, and e-commerce systems.

THE IMPACT AND LIMITATIONS OF IT   Modern IT has changed organizational structure in many ways. Using IT, managers can create a series of electronic strategic alliances and form a B2B network structure. A network structure, based on some shared form of IT, can be formed around one company, or a number of companies can join together to create an industry B2B network. Modern IT also makes organizations flatter and encourages more horizontal cross-functional communication. As this increasingly happens across the organizational boundary, the term *boundaryless organizations* has been coined to refer to virtual organizations whose members are linked electronically together.

Management in Action

Topics for Discussion and Action

Discussion

1. To be useful, information must be of high quality, be timely, be relevant, and be as complete as possible. Why does a tall management hierarchy, when used as a management information system, have negative effects on these desirable attributes?

2. What is the relationship between IT and competitive advantage?

3. Because of the growth of high-powered, low-cost wireless communications and IT such as videoconferencing, many managers soon may not need to come into the office to do their jobs. They will be able to work at home. What are the pros and cons of such an arrangement?

4. Many companies have reported that it is difficult to implement advanced management information systems such as ERP systems. Why do you think this is so? How might the roadblocks to implementation be removed?

5. How can IT help in the new product development process?

6. Why is face-to-face communication between managers still important in an organization?

Action

7. Ask a manager to describe the main kinds of IT that he or she uses on a routine basis at work.

8. Compare the pros and cons of using a network structure to perform organizational activities versus performing all activities in-house or within one organizational hierarchy.

9. What are the advantages and disadvantages of business-to-business networks?

Building Management Skills

Analyzing Management Information Systems

Pick an organization about which you have some direct knowledge. It may be an organization that you worked for in the past or are in contact with now (such as the college or school that you attend). For this organization, answer the following questions:

1. Describe the management information systems that are used to coordinate and control organizational activities and to help make decisions.

2. Do you think that the organization's existing MISs provide managers with high-quality, timely, relevant, and relatively complete information? Why or why not?

3. How might advanced IT be used to improve the competitive position of this organization? In particular, try to identify the impact that a new MIS might have on the organization's efficiency, quality, innovation, and responsiveness to customers.

Managing Ethically

The use of management information systems, such as ERPs, often gives employees access to confidential information from all functions and levels of an organization. Employees have access to important information about the company's products that is of great value to competitors. As a result, many companies monitor employees' use of the intranet and Internet to prevent an employee from acting unethically, for example, by selling this information to competitors. On the other hand, with access to this information employees might discover that their company has been engaging in unethical or even illegal practices.

Questions

1. Ethically speaking, how far should a company go to protect its proprietary information, given that it needs to also protect the privacy of its employees? What steps can it take?

2. When is it ethical for employees to give information about a company's unethical or illegal practices to a third party such as a newspaper or government agency?

Small Group Breakout Exercise
Using New Management Information Systems

Form groups of three or four people, and appoint one member as the spokesperson who will communicate your findings to the class when called on by the instructor. Then discuss the following scenario.

You are a team of managing partners of a large management consultancy company. You are responsible for auditing your firm's MISs to determine whether they are appropriate and up to date. To your surprise, you find that although your organization does have a wireless e-mail system in place and consultants are connected into a powerful local area network (LAN) at all times, most of the consultants (including partners) are not using this technology. It seems that most important decision making still takes place through the organizational hierarchy.

Given this situation, you are concerned that your organization is not exploiting the opportunities offered by new IT to obtain a competitive advantage. You have discussed this issue and are meeting to develop an action plan to get consultants to appreciate the need to learn about and use the new IT.

1. What advantages can you tell consultants they will obtain when they use the new IT?

2. What problems do you think you may encounter in convincing consultants to use the new IT?

3. What steps might you take to motivate consultants to learn to use the new technology?

Exploring the World Wide Web

Go to IBM's Web site (www.ibm.com), and under the "services" tab click "On Demand." Read about the latest developments in IBM's on-demand business, and look at the case study on Sak's Fifth Avenue. Then answer the following questions:

1. What are the main ways in which IBM's on-demand IT can help companies?

2. In what ways did IBM's IT help Sak's improve its performance? (If the Sak's case study is no longer available, pick another.)

Be the Manager

You are one of the managers of a small specialty furniture maker of custom-made tables, chairs, and cabinets. You've been charged with finding ways to use IT and the Internet to identify new business opportunities that can improve your company's competitive advantage, for example, ways to reduce costs or attract customers.

Questions

1. What are the various forces in a specialty furniture maker's task environment that have the most effect on its performance.

2. What kinds of IT or MISs can be used to help the company better manage these forces?

3. In what ways can the Internet be used to help this organization improve its competitive position?

BusinessWeek

Case in the News

The Quickening at Nissan

Ever since Carlos Ghosn became president at Nissan Motor (NSANY) in 2000, Japan's second-largest auto maker has enjoyed the kind of recovery that bosses at strugglers like GM (GM) must dream about. Just as important, though, has been the way Nissan has spiced up its product offerings. Today a river of eye-catching autos—from the stylish Murano crossover and new Infiniti M luxury sedan to the boxy Cube minivan—streams out of Nissan's factories.

Just as impressive, under a program called V3P, Nissan is halving the time needed to take new cars from design to showroom. For the Japanese market, the Note subcompact was rolled out just 10.5 months after its design was finalized, vs. the 20.75 months that the process used to take. Key to the faster delivery has been wider use of the latest in computer-aided design software and a reliance on fewer prototypes.

To find out more about how Nissan aims to give customers what they want faster, *BusinessWeek* Tokyo correspondent Ian Rowley caught up with Nissan's Carlos Tavares, the executive vice-president who supervises design, product planning, and corporate strategy, at the company's Tokyo offices. Tavares, 47, joined Renault—44% owner of Nissan—in 1981 before moving to Nissan in 2004.

How does Nissan approach new vehicle development?
Ultimately, the process is about regularly creating exciting cars without disrupting the [production] process. We don't want a situation where we are putting so much pressure on the design teams that they have to keep using the existing parts and platforms and not be able to meet customer needs. This discussion between creativity on one side and disciplined, accurate implementation on the other is one of the most exciting things within this company.

But where does the process begin? Is it with a group of engineers?
Well, we actually put a lot of energy into trying to address the automotive answer as late as possible in the process. A lot of people in our organization are engineers and we tend to think about hardware answers or hardware solutions much too soon in the process. We need to first ask who will be our focus customers.

How do you do this?
We look at different groups and demographics and decide which people we will target.

So how big are the customer segments you focus on?
It can be quite a small number of people—you might think we'd only sell 50 cars—but this [partly explains] why most of our products are very strong. It might sound a little crazy to make a tailor-made car for a small number of people, but what we look for is to make a car for a very particular type of person.

We're not talking about a million people but small groups with the same kind of emotional needs, education, mindset, and so forth. You then make a car for them. If you succeed and make the right car for these people, other people from outside the group will say they would also like to have one.

What about after you've identified the customers?

We then check that the designers and the product planners understand the concept in the same way. We listen to the designer and we listen to the product planner. We have a meeting where each one explains to us how he perceives the target customer, how he perceives the emotional values, the functional values, the mindset. If they don't see things the same way, you can be sure there will be a mess.

How do you avoid that?

We tell them to go back to work and come back when they share the same vision of the target customer. If you have to postpone [moving on to the next stage] by two, three, or four months because people are not talking about the same target customer, it's no problem.

Is there any resistance to focusing so heavily on aspects other than engineering?

It's very important that you have a very strong [production] process that gives you the possibility to combine the talent of the designers, the product planners and the market intelligence people. But I'm convinced that automotive companies that are uniquely engineering-driven are in danger.

What about speed to market?

That's the strength of our engineering and manufacturing. If you put things in the pipeline properly—and you have to do this properly and with good design, planning, and features outlining performance targets—this company has huge strengths in terms of engineering and manufacturing.

But are you getting faster?

Yes. Our engineers have worked a lot at what we call V3P, a system which involves compressing the latter stages of development and manufacturing [from the moment the designs are fixed]. We're close to ten months in some Japanese products. This is very fast—it's half of what it was before.

How do you do this?

One example is that by using sophisticated [computer software] we can decrease the number of mistakes and increase quality. That helps save time. We've also reduced the number of prototypes from three to one for the Note [a subcompact sold in Japan].

Quesions

1. How does Nissan manage the relationship between its different value-chain functions to speed product development?

2. In what ways could Nissan use IT and the management information systems discussed in the chapter to speed the product development process?

Source: Cover story, "The Quickening at Nissan ." Reprinted from the March 27, 2006 , issue of *BusinessWeek* by special permission. Copyright © 2006 by the McGraw-Hill Companies.

BusinessWeek

Case in the News

FedEx: Taking Off like "a Rocket Ship"

As soon as Motion Computing Inc. in Austin, Tex., receives an order for one of its $2,200 tablet PCs, workers at a supplier's factory in Kunshan, China, begin assembling the product. When they've finished, they individually box each order and hand them to a driver from FedEx Corp. (FDX), who trucks it 50 miles to Shanghai, where it's loaded on a jet bound for Anchorage before a series of flights and truck rides finally puts the product into the customer's hands.

Elapsed time: as little as five days. Motion's inventory costs? Nada. Zip. Zilch. "We have no inventory tied up in the process anywhere," marvels Scott Eckert, Motion's chief executive. "Frankly, our business is enabled by FedEx."

There are thousands of other Motion Computings that, without FedEx, would be crippled by warehouse and inventory costs. That value proposition has made the Memphis shipping giant an indispensable partner for companies whose products are made in China. In the past two years, the volume of goods that FedEx has shipped over its vast international network has soared 40%, with much of the growth from Asia. FedEx earnings leapt 21% last year, and its stock price has more than doubled since 2003, landing FedEx the No. 40 spot on the BusinessWeek 50. "FedEx has been a rocket ship," says Daniel Ortwerth, analyst at St. Louis brokerage Edward Jones.

That FedEx has become the preferred carrier out of China is no accident. As far back as the 1980s, FedEx founder and CEO Frederick W. Smith predicted that Asia would become an economic powerhouse. In 1989 he shelled out $895 million to buy Tiger International Inc., a struggling cargo hauler that nonetheless had assets Smith coveted: flying rights into most major Asian airports and a management team with a deep knowledge of the Pacific Rim. Wall Street roundly panned the move—many Asian economies were unstable at the time—but it was prescient, giving FedEx a 10-year jump on rivals.

These days, FedEx operates 120 flights weekly to and from Asia, including 26 out of China alone. As a result, FedEx now controls 39% of the China-to-U.S. air express market, vs. 32% for United Parcel Service Inc. (UPS) and 27% for DHL International, according to Satish Jindel, president of SJ Consulting Group Inc. in Pittsburgh.

Now Smith is doubling his bets on China. FedEx plans to close its Asian hub in the Philippines by 2008 in favor of a new $150 million superhub in Guangzhou, a city in the heart of one of China's fastest-growing manufacturing districts. Also in 2008, FedEx will take delivery of the first of up to 20 of Airbus' A380 cargo haulers, birds so massive that they hold twice the load of the Boeing (BA) MD-11. The A380 can fly nonstop from Asia to FedEx' U.S. hubs. Here again, Smith was ahead of the pack: By being the first American customer, he not only beat UPS to the punch but got to contribute to the configuration of the A380, too. "They played a pivotal role in the design," says Allan McArtor, chairman of Airbus North America Holdings Inc. and a former FedEx executive.

FedEx' ambitions in China may extend beyond exports. In January, it spent $400 million to buy out its 50-50 delivery partner in China, Datian Group. That gives FedEx full control over Datian's truck fleet and

its 89 distribution hubs. Some analysts, such as Morgan Stanley's (MWD) James Valentine, believe that the purchase is a step toward FedEx domestic service between China's largest cities, at least for large business customers. Some wonder, though, if China is ready for that, given the shabby state of its highways. "[FedEx] could run up against infrastructure problems," warns Ortwerth. Smith isn't worried. He's been right about China before.

Questions

1. How does FedEx use its IT to help other company's improve their performance?

2. Which kind of IT systems discussed in the chapter are most likely to increase FedEx's own level of performance?

Source: Dean Foust, "FedEx:Taking Off Like a Rocket Ship." Reprinted from the March 27, 2006 , issue of *BusinessWeek* by special permission. Copyright © 2006 by the McGraw-Hill Companies.

Glossary

360-DEGREE APPRAISAL A performance appraisal by peers, subordinates, superiors, and sometimes clients who are in a position to evaluate a manager's performance.

ACCOMMODATION An ineffective conflict-handling approach in which one party, typically with weaker power, gives in to the demands of the other, typically more powerful, party.

ACCOMMODATIVE APPROACH Companies and their managers behave legally and ethically and try to balance the interests of different stakeholders as the need arises.

ACHIEVEMENT ORIENTATION A worldview that values assertiveness, performance, success, and competition.

ADMINISTRATIVE MANAGEMENT The study of how to create an organizational structure and control system that leads to high efficiency and effectiveness.

ADMINISTRATIVE MODEL An approach to decision making that explains why decision making is inherently uncertain and risky and why managers usually make satisfactory rather than optimum decisions.

AGREEABLENESS The tendency to get along well with other people.

ALDERFER'S ERG THEORY The theory that three universal needs–for existence, relatedness, and growth–constitute a hierarchy of needs and motivate behavior. Alderfer proposed that needs at more than one level can be motivational at the same time.

AMBIGUOUS INFORMATION Information that can be interpreted in multiple and often conflicting ways.

ARBITRATOR A third-party negotiator who can impose what he or she thinks is a fair solution to a conflict that both parties are obligated to abide by.

ARTIFICIAL INTELLIGENCE Behavior performed by a machine that, if performed by a human being, would be called "intelligent."

ATTITUDE A collection of feelings and beliefs.

ATTRACTION-SELECTION-ATTRITION (ASA) FRAMEWORK A model that explains how personality may influence organizational culture.

AUTHORITY The power to hold people accountable for their actions and to make decisions concerning the use of organizational resources.

AVOIDANCE An ineffective conflict-handling approach in which the two parties try to ignore the problem and do nothing to resolve their differences.

B2B MARKETPLACE An Internet-based trading platform set up to connect buyers and sellers in an industry.

B2B NETWORK STRUCTURE A series of global strategic alliances that an organization creates with suppliers, manufacturers, and/or distributors to produce and market a product.

BARRIERS TO ENTRY Factors that make it difficult and costly for an organization to enter a particular task environment or industry.

BEHAVIORAL MANAGEMENT The study of how managers should behave to motivate employees and encourage them to perform at high levels and be committed to the achievement of organizational goals.

BENCHMARKING The process of comparing one company's performance on specific dimensions with the performance of other, high-performing organizations.

BIAS The systematic tendency to use information about others in ways that result in inaccurate perceptions.

BOTTOM-UP CHANGE A gradual or evolutionary approach to change in which managers at all levels work together to develop a detailed plan for change.

BOUNDARY SPANNING Interacting with individuals and groups outside the organization to obtain valuable information from the environment.

BOUNDARYLESS ORGANIZATION An organization whose members are linked by computers, faxes, computer-aided design systems, and video teleconferencing and who rarely, if ever, see one another face-to-face.

BOUNDED RATIONALITY Cognitive limitations that constrain one's ability to interpret, process, and act on information.

BRAND LOYALTY Customers' preference for the products of organizations currently existing in the task environment.

BUREAUCRACY A formal system of organization and administration designed to ensure efficiency and effectiveness.

BUREAUCRATIC CONTROL Control of behavior by means of a comprehensive system of rules and standard operating procedures.

BUSINESS-LEVEL PLAN Divisional managers' decisions pertaining to divisions' long-term goals, overall strategy, and structure.

BUSINESS-LEVEL STRATEGY A plan that indicates how a division intends to compete against its rivals in an industry.

BUSINESS-TO-BUSINESS (B2B) COMMERCE Trade that takes place between companies using IT and the Internet to link and coordinate the value chains of different companies.

BUSINESS-TO-CUSTOMER (B2C) COMMERCE Trade that takes place between a company and individual customers using IT and the Internet.

CAFETERIA BENEFIT PLAN A plan from which employees can choose the benefits that they want.

CENTRALIZATION The concentration of authority at the top of the managerial hierarchy.

CHARISMATIC LEADER An enthusiastic, self-confident leader who is able to clearly communicate his or her vision of how good things could be.

CLAN CONTROL The control exerted on individuals and groups in an organization by shared values, norms, standards of behavior, and expectations.

CLASSICAL DECISION-MAKING MODEL A prescriptive approach to decision making based on the assumption that the decision maker can identify and evaluate all possible alternatives and their consequences and rationally choose the most appropriate course of action.

CLOSED SYSTEM A system that is self-contained and thus not affected by changes occurring in its external environment.

COERCIVE POWER The ability of a manager to punish others.

COLLABORATION A way of managing conflict in which both parties try to satisfy their goals by coming up with an approach that leaves them both better off and does not require concessions on issues that are important to either party.

COLLABORATION SOFTWARE Groupware that promotes and facilitates collaborative, highly interdependent interactions and provides an electronic meeting site for communication among team members.

COLLECTIVE BARGAINING Negotiations between labor unions and managers to resolve conflicts and disputes about issues such as working hours, wages, benefits, working conditions, and job security.

COLLECTIVISM A worldview that values subordination of the individual to the goals of the group and adherence to the principle that people should be judged by their contribution to the group.

COMMUNICATION The sharing of information between two or more individuals or groups to reach a common understanding.

COMMUNICATION NETWORKS The pathways along which information flows in groups and teams and throughout the organization.

COMPETITION An ineffective conflict-handling approach in which each party tries to maximize its own gain and has little interest in understanding the other party's position and arriving at a solution that will allow both parties to achieve their goals.

COMPETITIVE ADVANTAGE The ability of one organization to outperform other organizations because it produces desired goods or services more efficiently and effectively than they do.

COMPETITORS Organizations that produce goods and services that are similar to a particular organization's goods and services.

COMPROMISE A way of managing conflict in which each party is concerned about not only its own goal accomplishment but also the goal accomplishment of the other party and is willing to engage in a give-and-take exchange and make concessions.

CONCENTRATION ON A SINGLE INDUSTRY Reinvesting a company's profits to strengthen its competitive position in its current industry

CONCEPTUAL SKILLS The ability to analyze and diagnose a situation and to distinguish between cause and effect.

CONCURRENT CONTROL Control that gives managers immediate feedback on how efficiently inputs are being transformed into outputs so that managers can correct problems as they arise.

CONSCIENTIOUSNESS The tendency to be careful, scrupulous, and persevering

CONSIDERATION Behavior indicating that a manager trusts, respects, and cares about subordinates.

CONTINGENCY THEORY The idea that the organizational structures and control systems managers choose depend on—are contingent on—characteristics of the external environment in which the organization operates.

CONTRACT BOOK A written agreement that details product development factors such as responsibilities, resource commitments, budgets, time lines, and development milestones.

CONTROL SYSTEMS Formal target-setting, monitoring, evaluation, and feedback systems that provide managers with information about how well the organization's strategy and structure are working.

CONTROLLING Evaluating how well an organization is achieving its goals and taking action to maintain or improve performance; one of the four principal tasks of management.

CORE COMPETENCY The specific set of departmental skills, knowledge, and experience that allows one organization to outperform another.

CORE MEMBERS The members of a team who bear primary responsibility for the success of a project and who stay with a project from inception to completion.

CORPORATE-LEVEL PLAN Top management's decisions pertaining to the organization's mission, overall strategy, and structure.

CORPORATE-LEVEL STRATEGY A plan that indicates in which industries and national markets an organization intends to compete.

CREATIVITY A decision maker's ability to discover original and novel ideas that lead to feasible alternative courses of action.

CROSS-FUNCTIONAL TEAM A group of managers brought together from different departments to perform organizational tasks.

CUSTOMER RELATIONSHIP MANAGEMENT (CRM) A technique that uses IT to develop an ongoing relationship with customers to maximize the value an organization can deliver to them over time.

CUSTOMERS Individuals and groups that buy the goods and services that an organization produces.

DATA Raw, unsummarized, and unanalyzed facts.

DECENTRALIZING AUTHORITY Giving lower-level managers and nonmanagerial employees the right to make important decisions about how to use organizational resources.

DECISION MAKING The process by which managers respond to opportunities and threats by analyzing options and making determinations about specific organizational goals and courses of action.

DECISION SUPPORT SYSTEM An interactive computer-based management information system that managers can use to make nonroutine decisions.

DECODING Interpreting and trying to make sense of a message.

DEFENSIVE APPROACH Companies and their managers behave ethically to the degree that they stay within the law and abide strictly with legal requirements.

DELPHI TECHNIQUE A decision-making technique in which group members do not meet face-to-face but respond in writing to questions posed by the group leader.

DEMOGRAPHIC FORCES Outcomes of changes in, or changing attitudes toward, the characteristics of a population, such as age, gender, ethnic origin, race, sexual orientation, and social class.

DEPARTMENT A group of people who work together and possess similar skills or use the same knowledge, tools, or techniques to perform their jobs.

DEVELOPMENT Building the knowledge and skills of organizational members so that they are prepared to take on new responsibilities and challenges.

DEVELOPMENTAL CONSIDERATION Behavior a leader engages in to support and encourage followers and help them develop and grow on the job.

DEVIL'S ADVOCACY Critical analysis of a preferred alternative, made in response to challenges raised by a group member who, playing the role of devil's advocate, defends unpopular or opposing alternatives for the sake of argument.

DIALECTICAL INQUIRY Critical analysis of two preferred alternatives in order to find an even better alternative for the organization to adopt.

DIFFERENTIATION STRATEGY Distinguishing an organization's products from the products of competitors on dimensions such as product design, quality, or after-sales service.

DISCIPLINE Obedience, energy, application, and other outward marks of respect for a superior's authority.

DISTRIBUTIVE JUSTICE A moral principle calling for the distribution of pay raises, promotions, and other organizational resources to be based on meaningful contributions that individuals have made and not on personal characteristics over which they have no control.

DISTRIBUTIVE NEGOTIATION Adversarial negotiation in which the parties in conflict compete to win the most resources while conceding as little as possible.

DISTRIBUTORS Organizations that help other organizations sell their goods or services to customers.

DIVERSIFICATION Expanding a company's business operations into a new industry in order to produce new kinds of valuable goods or services.

DIVERSITY Differences among people in age, gender, race, ethnicity, religion, sexual orientation, socioeconomic background, and capabilities/disabilities.

DIVISIONAL STRUCTURE An organizational structure composed of separate business units within which are the functions that work together to produce a specific product for a specific customer.

E-COMMERCE Trade that takes place between companies, and between companies and individual customers, using IT and the Internet.

ECONOMIC FORCES Interest rates, inflation, unemployment, economic growth, and other factors that affect the general health and well-being of a nation or the regional economy of an organization.

ECONOMIES OF SCALE Cost advantages associated with large operations.

EFFECTIVENESS A measure of the appropriateness of the goals an organization is pursuing and of the degree to which the organization achieves those goals.

EFFICIENCY A measure of how well or how productively resources are used to achieve a goal.

EMOTIONAL INTELLIGENCE The ability to understand and manage one's own moods and emotions and the moods and emotions of other people.

EMOTIONS Intense, relatively short-lived feelings.

EMPLOYEE STOCK OPTION A financial instrument that entitles the bearer to buy shares of an organization's stock at a certain price during a certain period of time or under certain conditions.

EMPOWERMENT The expansion of employees' knowledge, tasks, and decision-making responsibilities.

ENCODING Translating a message into understandable symbols or language.

ENTERPRISE RESOURCE PLANNING (ERP) SYSTEMS Multimodule application software packages that coordinate the functional activities necessary to move products from the product design stage to the final customer stage.

ENTREPRENEUR An individual who notices opportunities and decides how to mobilize the resources necessary to produce new and improved goods and services.

ENTREPRENEURSHIP The mobilization of resources to take advantage of an opportunity to provide customers with new or improved goods and services.

ENTROPY The tendency of a closed system to lose its ability to control itself and thus to dissolve and disintegrate.

EQUAL EMPLOYMENT OPPORTUNITY (EEO) The equal right of all citizens to the opportunity to obtain employment regardless of their gender, age, race, country of origin, religion, or disabilities.

EQUITY The justice, impartiality, and fairness to which all organizational members are entitled.

EQUITY THEORY A theory of motivation that focuses on people's perceptions of the fairness of their work outcomes relative to their work inputs.

ESCALATING COMMITMENT A source of cognitive bias resulting from the tendency to commit additional resources to a project even if evidence shows that the project is failing.

ESPRIT DE CORPS Shared feelings of comradeship, enthusiasm, or devotion to a common cause among members of a group.

ETHICAL DILEMMA The quandary people find themselves in when they have to decide if they should act in a way that might help another person or group even though doing so might go against their own self-interest.

ETHICS The inner-guiding moral principles, values, and beliefs that people use to analyze or interpret a situation and then decide what is the "right" or appropriate way to behave.

ETHICS OMBUDSMAN A manager responsible for communicating and teaching ethical standards to all employees and monitoring their conformity to those standards.

EVOLUTIONARY CHANGE Change that is gradual, incremental, and narrowly focused.

EXECUTIVE SUPPORT SYSTEM A sophisticated version of a decision support system that is designed to meet the needs of top managers.

EXPECTANCY In expectancy theory, a perception about the extent to which effort results in a certain level of performance.

EXPECTANCY THEORY The theory that motivation will be high when workers believe that high levels of effort lead to high performance and high performance leads to the attainment of desired outcomes.

EXPERT POWER Power that is based on the special knowledge, skills, and expertise that a leader possesses.

EXPERT SYSTEM A management information system that employs human knowledge, embedded in a computer, to solve problems that ordinarily require human expertise.

EXPORTING Making products at home and selling them abroad.

EXTERNAL LOCUS OF CONTROL The tendency to locate responsibility for one's fate in outside forces and to believe that one's own behavior has little impact on outcomes.

EXTINCTION Curtailing the performance of dysfunctional behaviors by eliminating whatever is reinforcing them.

EXTRAVERSION The tendency to experience positive emotions and moods and to feel good about oneself and the rest of the world.

EXTRINSICALLY MOTIVATED BEHAVIOR Behavior that is performed to acquire material or social rewards or to avoid punishment.

FACILITIES LAYOUT The strategy of designing the machine-worker interface to increase operating system efficiency.

FEEDBACK CONTROL Control that gives managers information about customers' reactions to goods and services so that corrective action can be taken if necessary.

FEEDFORWARD CONTROL Control that allows managers to anticipate problems before they arise.

FILTERING Withholding part of a message because of the mistaken belief that the receiver does not need or will not want the information.

FIRST-LINE MANAGER A manager who is responsible for the daily supervision of nonmanagerial employees.

FLEXIBLE MANUFACTURING The set of techniques that attempt to reduce the costs associated with the product assembly process or the way services are delivered to customers.

FOCUSED DIFFERENTIATION STRATEGY Serving only one segment of the overall market and trying to be the most differentiated organization serving that segment.

FOCUSED LOW-COST STRATEGY Serving only one segment of the overall market and trying to be the lowest-cost organization serving that segment.

FOLKWAYS The routine social conventions of everyday life.

FORMAL APPRAISAL An appraisal conducted at a set time during the year and based on performance dimensions and measures that were specified in advance.

FRANCHISING   Selling to a foreign organization the rights to use a brand name and operating know-how in return for a lump-sum payment and a share of the profits.

FREE-TRADE DOCTRINE   The idea that if each country specializes in the production of the goods and services that it can produce most efficiently, this will make the best use of global resources.

FUNCTIONAL STRUCTURE   An organizational structure composed of all the departments that an organization requires to produce its goods or services.

FUNCTIONAL-LEVEL PLAN   Functional managers' decisions pertaining to the goals that they propose to pursue to help the division attain its business-level goals.

FUNCTIONAL-LEVEL STRATEGY   A plan of action to improve the ability of each of an organization's functions to perform its task-specific activities in ways that add value to an organization's goods and services.

GATEKEEPING   Deciding what information to allow into the organization and what information to keep out.

GENDER SCHEMAS   Preconceived beliefs or ideas about the nature of men and women, their traits, attitudes, behaviors, and preferences.

GENERAL ENVIRONMENT   The wide-ranging global, economic, technological, sociocultural, demographic, political, and legal forces that affect an organization and its task environment.

GEOGRAPHIC STRUCTURE   An organizational structure in which each region of a country or area of the world is served by a self-contained division.

GLASS CEILING   A metaphor alluding to the invisible barriers that prevent minorities and women from being promoted to top corporate positions.

GLOBAL ENVIRONMENT   The set of global forces and conditions that operate beyond an organization's boundaries but affect a manager's ability to acquire and utilize resources.

GLOBAL ORGANIZATION   An organization that operates and competes in more than one country.

GLOBAL OUTSOURCING   The purchase of inputs from overseas suppliers or the production of inputs abroad to lower production costs and improve product quality or design.

GLOBAL STRATEGY   Selling the same standardized product and using the same basic marketing approach in each national market.

GLOBALIZATION   The set of specific and general forces that work together to integrate and connect economic, political, and social systems *across* countries, cultures, or geographical regions so that nations become increasingly interdependent and similar.

GOAL-SETTING THEORY   A theory that focuses on identifying the types of goals that are most effective in producing high levels of motivation and performance and explaining why goals have these effects.

GRAPEVINE   An informal communication network along which unofficial information flows.

GROUP DECISION SUPPORT SYSTEM An executive support system that links top managers so that they can function as a team.

GROUPTHINK   A pattern of faulty and biased decision making that occurs in groups whose members strive for agreement among themselves at the expense of accurately assessing information relevant to a decision.

GROUPWARE   Computer software that enables members of groups and teams to share information with one another.

HAWTHORNE EFFECT   The finding that a manager's behavior or leadership approach can affect workers' level of performance.

HERZBERG'S MOTIVATOR-HYGIENE THEORY   A need theory that distinguishes between motivator needs (related to the nature of the work itself) and hygiene needs (related to the physical and psychological context in which the work is performed) and proposes that motivator needs must be met for motivation and job satisfaction to be high.

HEURISTICS   Rules of thumb that simplify decision making.

HIERARCHY OF AUTHORITY   An organization's chain of command, specifying the relative authority of each manager.

HOSTILE WORK ENVIRONMENT SEXUAL HARASSMENT   Telling lewd jokes, displaying pornography, making sexually oriented remarks about someone's personal appearance, and other sex-related actions that make the work environment unpleasant.

HUMAN RELATIONS MOVEMENT   A management approach that advocates the idea that supervisors should receive behavioral training to manage subordinates in ways that elicit their cooperation and increase their productivity.

HUMAN RESOURCE MANAGEMENT (HRM)   Activities that managers engage in to attract and retain employees and to ensure that they perform at a high level and contribute to the accomplishment of organizational goals.

HUMAN RESOURCE PLANNING Activities that managers engage in to forecast their current and future needs for human resources.

HUMAN SKILLS   The ability to understand, alter, lead, and control the behavior of other individuals and groups.

HYBRID STRUCTURE   The structure of a large organization that has many divisions and simultaneously uses many different organizational structures.

HYPERCOMPETITION   Permanent, ongoing, intense competition brought about in an industry by advancing technology or changing customer tastes

ILLUSION OF CONTROL A source of cognitive bias resulting from the tendency to overestimate one's own ability to control activities and events.

IMPORTING Selling at home products that are made abroad.

INCREMENTAL PRODUCT INNOVATION The gradual improvement and refinement to existing products that occurs over time as existing technologies are perfected,

INDIVIDUAL ETHICS Personal standards and values that determine how people view their responsibilities to others and how they should act in situations when their own self-interests are at stake.

INDIVIDUALISM A worldview that values individual freedom and self-expression and adherence to the principle that people should be judged by their individual achievements rather than by their social background.

INEQUITY Lack of fairness.

INFORMAL APPRAISAL An unscheduled appraisal of ongoing progress and areas for improvement.

INFORMAL ORGANIZATION The system of behavioral rules and norms that emerge in a group.

INFORMATION Data that are organized in a meaningful fashion.

INFORMATION DISTORTION Changes in the meaning of a message as the message passes through a series of senders and receivers.

INFORMATION OVERLOAD The potential for important information to be ignored or overlooked while tangential information receives attention.

INFORMATION RICHNESS The amount of information that a communication medium can carry and the extent to which the medium enables the sender and receiver to reach a common understanding.

INFORMATION TECHNOLOGY The set of methods or techniques for acquiring, organizing, storing, manipulating, and transmitting information.

INITIATING STRUCTURE Behavior that managers engage in to ensure that work gets done, subordinates perform their jobs acceptably, and the organization is efficient and effective.

INITIATIVE The ability to act on one's own, without direction from a superior.

INNOVATION The process of creating new or improved goods and services or developing better ways to produce or provide them.

INPUT Anything a person contributes to his or her job or organization.

INSTRUMENTAL VALUE A mode of conduct that an individual seeks to follow.

INSTRUMENTALITY In expectancy theory, a perception about the extent to which performance results in the attainment of outcomes.

INTEGRATING MECHANISMS Organizing tools that managers can use to increase communication and coordination among functions and divisions.

INTEGRATIVE BARGAINING Cooperative negotiation in which the parties in conflict work together to achieve a resolution that is good for them both.

INTELLECTUAL STIMULATION Behavior a leader engages in to make followers be aware of problems and view these problems in new ways, consistent with the leader's vision.

INTERNAL LOCUS OF CONTROL The tendency to locate responsibility for one's fate within oneself.

INTERNET A global system of computer networks.

INTRANET A companywide system of computer networks.

INTRAPRENEUR A manager, scientist, or researcher who works inside an

organization and notices opportunities to develop new or improved products and better ways to make them.

INTRINSICALLY MOTIVATED BEHAVIOR Behavior that is performed for its own sake.

INTUITION Feelings, beliefs, and hunches that come readily to mind, require little effort and information gathering, and result in on-the-spot decisions.

INVENTORY The stock of raw materials, inputs, and component parts that an organization has on hand at a particular time.

JARGON Specialized language that members of an occupation, group, or organization develop to facilitate communication among themselves.

JOB ANALYSIS Identifying the tasks, duties, and responsibilities that make up a job and the knowledge, skills, and abilities needed to perform the job.

JOB DESIGN The process by which managers decide how to divide tasks into specific jobs.

JOB ENLARGEMENT Increasing the number of different tasks in a given job by changing the division of labor.

JOB ENRICHMENT Increasing the degree of responsibility a worker has over his or her job.

JOB SATISFACTION The collection of feelings and beliefs that managers have about their current jobs.

JOB SIMPLIFICATION The process of reducing the number of tasks that each worker performs.

JOB SPECIALIZATION The process by which a division of labor occurs as different workers specialize in different tasks over time.

JOINT VENTURE A strategic alliance among two or more companies that agree to jointly establish and share the ownership of a new business.

JUST-IN-TIME (JIT) INVENTORY SYSTEM A system in which parts or supplies arrive at an organization when they are needed, not before.

JUSTICE RULE An ethical decision is a decision that distributes benefits and harms among people and groups in a fair, equitable, or impartial way.

KNOWLEDGE MANAGEMENT SYSTEM A company-specific virtual information system that systematizes the knowledge of its employees and facilitates the sharing and integrating of their expertise.

LABOR RELATIONS The activities that managers engage in to ensure that they have effective working relationships with the labor unions that represent their employees' interests.

LATERAL MOVE A job change that entails no major changes in responsibility or authority levels.

LEADER An individual who is able to exert influence over other people to help achieve group or organizational goals.

LEADER–MEMBER RELATIONS The extent to which followers like, trust, and are loyal to their leader; a determinant of how favorable a situation is for leading.

LEADERSHIP The process by which an individual exerts influence over other people and inspires, motivates, and directs their activities to help achieve group or organizational goals.

LEADERSHIP SUBSTITUTE A characteristic of a subordinate or of a situation or context that acts in place of the influence of a leader and makes leadership unnecessary.

LEADING Articulating a clear vision and energizing and enabling organizational members so that they understand the part they play in achieving organizational goals; one of the four principal tasks of management.

LEARNING A relatively permanent change in knowledge or behavior that results from practice or experience.

LEARNING ORGANIZATION An organization in which managers try to maximize the ability of individuals and groups to think and behave creatively and thus maximize the potential for organizational learning to take place.

LEARNING THEORIES Theories that focus on increasing employee motivation and performance by linking the outcomes that employees receive to the performance of desired behaviors and the attainment of goals.

LEGITIMATE POWER The authority that a manager has by virtue of his or her position in an organization's hierarchy.

LICENSING Allowing a foreign organization to take charge of manufacturing and distributing a product in its country or world region in return for a negotiated fee.

LINE MANAGER Someone in the direct line or chain of command who has formal authority over people and resources at lower levels.

LINE OF AUTHORITY The chain of command extending from the top to the bottom of an organization.

LINGUISTIC STYLE A person's characteristic way of speaking.

LONG-TERM ORIENTATION A worldview that values thrift and persistence in achieving goals.

LOW-COST STRATEGY Driving the organization's costs down below the costs of its rivals.

MANAGEMENT The planning, organizing, leading, and controlling of human and other resources to achieve organizational goals efficiently and effectively.

MANAGEMENT BY OBJECTIVES (MBO) A goal-setting process in which a manager and each of his or her subordinates negotiate specific goals and objectives for the subordinate to achieve and then periodically evaluate the extent to which the subordinate is achieving those goals.

MANAGEMENT BY WANDERING AROUND A face-to-face communication technique in which a manager walks around a work area and talks informally with employees about issues and concerns.

MANAGEMENT INFORMATION SYSTEM (MIS) A specific form of IT that managers utilize to generate the specific, detailed information they need to perform their roles effectively.

MANAGEMENT SCIENCE THEORY An approach to management that uses rigorous quantitative techniques to help managers make maximum use of organizational resources.

MARKET STRUCTURE An organizational structure in which each kind of customer is served by a self-contained division; also called *customer structure.*

MASLOW'S HIERARCHY OF NEEDS An arrangement of five basic needs that, according to Maslow, motivate behavior. Maslow proposed that the lowest level of unmet needs is the prime motivator and that only one level of needs is motivational at a time.

MATRIX STRUCTURE An organizational structure that simultaneously groups people and resources by function and by product.

MECHANISTIC STRUCTURE An organizational structure in which authority is centralized, tasks and rules are clearly specified, and employees are closely supervised.

MEDIATOR A third-party negotiator who facilitates negotiations but has no authority to impose a solution.

MEDIUM The pathway through which an encoded message is transmitted to a receiver.

MENTORING A process by which an experienced member of an organization (the mentor) provides advice and guidance to a less experienced member (the protégé) and helps the less experienced member learn how to advance in the organization and in his or her career.

MERIT PAY PLAN A compensation plan that bases pay on performance.

MESSAGE   The information that a sender wants to share.

MIDDLE MANAGER   A manager who supervises first-line managers and is responsible for finding the best way to use resources to achieve organizational goals.

MISSION STATEMENT   A broad declaration of an organization's purpose that identifies the organization's products and customers and distinguishes the organization from its competitors.

MOOD   A feeling or state of mind.

MORAL RIGHTS RULE   An ethical decision is one that best maintains and protects the fundamental or inalienable rights and privileges of the people affected by it.

MORES   Norms that are considered to be central to the functioning of society and to social life.

MOTIVATION   Psychological forces that determine the direction of a person's behavior in an organization, a person's level of effort, and a person's level of persistence.

MULTIDOMESTIC STRATEGY   Customizing products and marketing strategies to specific national conditions.

NATIONAL CULTURE   The set of values that a society considers important and the norms of behavior that are approved or sanctioned in that society.

NEED   A requirement or necessity for survival and well-being.

NEED FOR ACHIEVEMENT   The extent to which an individual has a strong desire to perform challenging tasks well and to meet personal standards for excellence.

NEED FOR AFFILIATION   The extent to which an individual is concerned about establishing and maintaining good interpersonal relations, being liked, and having other people get along.

NEED FOR POWER   The extent to which an individual desires to control or influence others.

NEED THEORIES   Theories of motivation that focus on what needs people are trying to satisfy at work and what outcomes will satisfy those needs.

NEEDS ASSESSMENT   An assessment of which employees need training or development and what type of skills or knowledge they need to acquire.

NEGATIVE AFFECTIVITY   The tendency to experience negative emotions and moods, to feel distressed, and to be critical of oneself and others.

NEGATIVE REINFORCEMENT   Eliminating or removing undesired outcomes when people perform organizationally functional behaviors.

NEGOTIATION   A method of conflict resolution in which the two parties consider various alternative ways to allocate resources to each other in order to come up with a solution acceptable to them both.

NETWORKING   The exchange of information through a group or network of interlinked computers.

NOISE   Anything that hampers any stage of the communication process.

NOMINAL GROUP TECHNIQUE   A decision-making technique in which group members write down ideas and solutions, read their suggestions to the whole group, and discuss and then rank the alternatives.

NONPROGRAMMED DECISION MAKING   Nonroutine decision making that occurs in response to unusual, unpredictable opportunities and threats.

NONVERBAL COMMUNICATION   The encoding of messages by means of facial expressions, body language, and styles of dress.

NORMS   Unwritten, informal codes of conduct that prescribe how people should act in particular situations.

NORMS   Informal rules of conduct for behaviors considered important by most members of a group or organization.

NURTURING ORIENTATION   A worldview that values the quality of life, warm personal friendships, and services and care for the weak.

OBJECTIVE APPRAISAL   An appraisal that is based on facts and is likely to be numerical.

OBSTRUCTIONIST APPROACH   Companies and their managers choose *not* to behave in a socially responsible way and instead behave unethically and illegally.

OCCUPATIONAL ETHICS   Standards that govern how members of a profession, trade, or craft should conduct themselves when performing work-related activities.

ON-THE-JOB TRAINING   Training that takes place in the work setting as employees perform their job tasks.

OPEN SYSTEM   A system that takes in resources from its external environment and converts them into goods and services that are then sent back to that environment for purchase by customers.

OPENNESS TO EXPERIENCE   The tendency to be original, have broad interests, be open to a wide range of stimuli, be daring, and take risks.

OPERANT CONDITIONING THEORY   The theory that people learn to perform behaviors that lead to desired consequences and learn not to perform behaviors that lead to undesired consequences.

OPERATING BUDGET   A budget that states how managers intend to use organizational resources to achieve organizational goals.

OPERATIONS INFORMATION SYSTEM   A management information system that gathers, organizes, and summarizes comprehensive data in a form that managers can use in their nonroutine coordinating, controlling, and decision-making tasks.

OPTIMUM DECISION   The most appropriate decision in light of what managers believe to be the most desirable future consequences for the organization.

ORDER   The methodical arrangement of positions to provide the organization with the greatest benefit and to provide employees with career opportunities.

ORGANIC STRUCTURE   An organizational structure in which authority is decentralized to middle and first-line managers and tasks and roles are left ambiguous to encourage employees to cooperate and respond quickly to the unexpected.

ORGANIZATIONAL ARCHITECTURE The organizational structure, control systems, culture, and human resource management systems that together determine how efficiently and effectively organizational resources are used.

ORGANIZATIONAL BEHAVIOR   The study of the factors that have an impact on how individuals and groups respond to and act in organizations.

ORGANIZATIONAL BEHAVIOR MODIFICATION (OB MOD)   The systematic application of operant conditioning techniques to promote the performance of organizationally functional behaviors and discourage the performance of dysfunctional behaviors.

ORGANIZATIONAL CHANGE   The movement of an organization away from its present state and toward some desired future state to increase its efficiency and effectiveness.

ORGANIZATIONAL CITIZENSHIP BEHAVIORS (OCBs)   Behaviors that are not required of organizational members but that contribute to and are necessary for organizational efficiency, effectiveness, and competitive advantage.

ORGANIZATIONAL COMMITMENT   The collection of feelings and beliefs that managers have about their organization as a whole.

ORGANIZATIONAL CONFLICT   The discord that arises when the goals, interests, or values of different individuals or groups are incompatible and those individuals or groups block or thwart one another's attempts to achieve their objectives.

ORGANIZATIONAL CULTURE   The shared set of beliefs, expectations, values, norms, and work routines that

influence the ways in which individuals, groups, and teams interact with one another and cooperate to achieve organizational goals.

ORGANIZATIONAL DESIGN   The process by which managers make specific organizing choices that result in a particular kind of organizational structure.

ORGANIZATIONAL ENVIRONMENT The set of forces and conditions that operate beyond an organization's boundaries but affect a manager's ability to acquire and utilize resources.

ORGANIZATIONAL ETHICS   The guiding practices and beliefs through which a particular company and its managers view their responsibility toward their stakeholders.

ORGANIZATIONAL LEARNING   The process through which managers seek to improve employees' desire and ability to understand and manage the organization and its task environment.

ORGANIZATIONAL PERFORMANCE   A measure of how efficiently and effectively a manager uses resources to satisfy customers and achieve organizational goals.

ORGANIZATIONAL POLITICS Activities that managers engage in to increase their power and to use power effectively to achieve their goals and overcome resistance or opposition.

ORGANIZATIONAL SOCIALIZATION The process by which newcomers learn an organization's values and norms and acquire the work behaviors necessary to perform jobs effectively.

ORGANIZATIONAL STRUCTURE   A formal system of task and reporting relationships that coordinates and motivates organizational members so that they work together to achieve organizational goals.

ORGANIZING   Structuring working relationships in a way that allows organizational members to work together to achieve organizational goals; one of the four principal tasks of management.

OUTCOME   Anything a person gets from a job or organization.

OUTSOURCE   To use outside suppliers and manufacturers to produce goods and services.

OUTSOURCING   Contracting with another company, usually abroad, to have it perform an activity the organization previously performed itself.

OVERPAYMENT INEQUITY   The inequity that exists when a person perceives that his or her own outcome-input ratio is greater than the ratio of a referent.

OVERT DISCRIMINATION   Knowingly and willingly denying diverse individuals access to opportunities and outcomes in an organization.

PATH-GOAL THEORY   A contingency model of leadership proposing that leaders can motivate subordinates by identifying their desired outcomes, rewarding them for high performance and the attainment of work goals with these desired outcomes, and clarifying for them the paths leading to the attainment of work goals.

PAY LEVEL   The relative position of an organization's pay incentives in comparison with those of other organizations in the same industry employing similar kinds or workers.

PAY STRUCTURES   The arrangement of jobs into categories reflecting their relative importance to the organization and its goals, levels of skill required, and other characteristics.

PERCEPTION   The process through which people select, organize, and interpret what they see, hear, touch, smell, and taste to give meaning and order to the world around them.

PERFORMANCE APPRAISAL   The evaluation of employees' job performance and contributions to their organization.

PERFORMANCE FEEDBACK   The process through which mangers share performance appraisal information with subordinates, give subordinates an opportunity to reflect on their own performance, and develop, with subordinates, plans for the future.

PERSONALITY TRAITS Enduring tendencies to feel, think, and act in certain ways.

PLANNING Identifying and selecting appropriate goals and courses of action; one of the four principal functions of management.

POLITICAL AND LEGAL FORCES Outcomes of changes in laws and regulations, such as the deregulation of industries, the privatization of organizations, and the increased emphasis on environmental protection.

POLITICAL STRATEGIES Tactics that managers use to increase their power and to use power effectively to influence and gain the support of other people while overcoming resistance or opposition.

POSITION POWER The amount of legitimate, reward, and coercive power that a leader has by virtue of his or her position in an organization; a determinant of how favorable a situation is for leading.

POSITIVE REINFORCEMENT Giving people outcomes they desire when they perform organizationally functional behaviors.

POTENTIAL COMPETITORS Organizations that presently are not in a task environment but could enter if they so choose.

POWER DISTANCE The degree to which societies accept the idea that inequalities in the power and well-being of their citizens are due to differences in individuals' physical and intellectual capabilities and heritage.

PRACTICAL RULE An ethical decision is one that a manager has no reluctance about communicating to people outside the company because the typical person in a society would think it is acceptable.

PRIOR-HYPOTHESIS BIAS A cognitive bias resulting from the tendency to base decisions on strong prior beliefs even if evidence shows that those beliefs are wrong.

PROACTIVE APPROACH Companies and their managers actively embrace socially responsible behavior, going out of their way to learn about the needs of different stakeholder groups and utilizing organizational resources to promote the interests of all stakeholders.

PROCEDURAL JUSTICE A moral principle calling for the use of fair procedures to determine how to distribute outcomes to organizational members.

PROCESS REENGINEERING The fundamental rethinking and radical redesign of business processes to achieve dramatic improvement in critical measures of performance such as cost, quality, service, and speed.

PRODUCT CHAMPION A manager who takes "ownership" of a project and provides the leadership and vision that take a product from the idea stage to the final customer.

PRODUCT DEVELOPMENT The management of the value-chain activities involved in bringing new or improved goods and services to the market.

PRODUCT DEVELOPMENT PLAN A plan that specifies all of the relevant information that managers need in order to decide whether to proceed with a full-blown product development effort.

PRODUCT LIFE CYCLE The way demand for a product changes in a predictable pattern over time.

PRODUCT STRUCTURE An organizational structure in which each product line or business is handled by a self-contained division.

PRODUCT TEAM STRUCTURE An organizational structure in which employees are permanently assigned to a cross-functional team and report only to the product team manager or to one of his or her direct subordinates.

PRODUCTION BLOCKING A loss of productivity in brainstorming sessions due to the unstructured nature of brainstorming.

PROGRAMMED DECISION MAKING Routine, virtually automatic decision making that follows established rules or guidelines.

PUNISHMENT Administering an undesired or negative consequence when dysfunctional behavior occurs.

QUALITY CIRCLES Groups of employees who meet regularly to discuss ways to increase quality.

QUANTUM PRODUCT INNOVATION The development of new, often radically different, kinds of goods and services because of fundamental shifts in technology brought about by pioneering discoveries.

QUID PRO QUO SEXUAL HARASSMENT Asking for or forcing an employee to perform sexual favors in exchange for receiving some reward or avoiding negative consequences.

REAL-TIME INFORMATION Frequently updated information that reflects current conditions.

REALISTIC JOB PREVIEW (RJP) An honest assessment of the advantages and disadvantages of a job and organization.

REASONED JUDGMENT A decision that takes time and effort to make and results from careful information gathering, generation of alternatives, and evaluation of alternatives.

RECEIVER The person or group for which a message is intended.

RECRUITMENT Activities that managers engage in to develop a pool of qualified candidates for open positions.

REFERENT POWER Power that comes from subordinates' and coworkers' respect, admiration, and loyalty.

RELATED DIVERSIFICATION Entering a new business or industry to create a competitive advantage in one or more of an organization's existing divisions or businesses.

RELATIONSHIP-ORIENTED LEADERS Leaders whose primary concern is to develop good relationships with their subordinates and to be liked by them.

RELIABILITY The degree to which a tool or test measures the same thing each time it is used.

REPRESENTATIVENESS BIAS A cognitive bias resulting from the tendency to generalize inappropriately from a small sample or from a single vivid event or episode.

REPUTATION The esteem or high repute that individuals or organizations gain when they behave ethically.

RESTRUCTURING Downsizing an organization by eliminating the jobs of large numbers of top, middle, and first-line managers and nonmanagerial employees.

REVOLUTIONARY CHANGE Change that is rapid, dramatic, and broadly focused.

REWARD POWER The ability of a manager to give or withhold tangible and intangible rewards.

RISK The degree of probability that the possible outcomes of a particular course of action will occur.

RULES Formal written instructions that specify actions to be taken under different circumstances to achieve specific goals.

RUMORS Unofficial pieces of information of interest to organizational members but with no identifiable source.

SATISFICING Searching for and choosing an acceptable, or satisfactory, response to problems and opportunities, rather than trying to make the best decision.

SCENARIO PLANNING The generation of multiple forecasts of future conditions followed by an analysis of how to respond effectively to each of those conditions.

SCHEMA An abstract knowledge structure that is stored in memory and makes possible the interpretation and organization of information about a person, event, or situation.

SCIENTIFIC MANAGEMENT The systematic study of relationships between people and tasks for the purpose of redesigning the work process to increase efficiency.

SELECTION The process that mangers use to determine the relative qualifications of job applicants and their potential for performing well in a particular job.

SELF-EFFICACY A person's belief about his or her ability to perform a behavior successfully.

SELF-ESTEEM The degree to which individuals feel good about themselves and their capabilities.

SELF-MANAGED TEAM A group of employees who assume responsibility for organizing, controlling, and supervising their own activities and monitoring the quality of the goods and services they provide.

SELF-REINFORCER Any desired or attractive outcome or reward that a person gives to himself or herself for good performance.

SENDER The person or group wishing to share information.

SHORT-TERM ORIENTATION A worldview that values personal stability or happiness and living for the present.

SKUNKWORKS A group of intrapreneurs who are deliberately separated from the normal operation of an organization to encourage them to devote all their attention to developing new products.

SOCIAL LEARNING THEORY A theory that takes into account how learning and motivation are influenced by people's thoughts and beliefs and their observations of other people's behavior.

SOCIAL RESPONSIBILITY The way a company's managers and employees view their duty or obligation to make decisions that protect, enhance, and promote the welfare and well-being of stakeholders and society as a whole.

SOCIAL STRUCTURE The arrangement of relationships between individuals and groups in a society.

SOCIETAL ETHICS Standards that govern how members of a society should deal with one another in matters involving issues such as fairness, justice, poverty, and the rights of the individual.

SOCIOCULTURAL FORCES Pressures emanating from the social structure of a country or society or from the national culture.

SPAN OF CONTROL The number of subordinates who report directly to a manager.

STAFF MANAGER Someone responsible for managing a specialist function, such as finance or marketing.

STAGE-GATE DEVELOPMENT FUNNEL A planning model that forces managers to make choices among competing projects so that organizational resources are not spread thinly over too many projects.

STAKEHOLDERS The people and groups that supply a company with its productive resources and so have a claim on and stake in the company.

STANDARD OPERATING PROCEDURES (SOPs) Specific sets of written instructions about how to perform a certain aspect of a task.

STEREOTYPE Simplistic and often inaccurate beliefs about the typical characteristics of particular groups of people.

STRATEGIC ALLIANCE An agreement in which managers pool or share their organization's resources and know-how with a foreign company, and the two organizations share the rewards and risks of starting a new venture.

STRATEGIC HUMAN RESOURCE MANAGEMENT The process by which managers design the components of an HRM system to be consistent with each other, with other elements of organizational architecture, and with the organization's strategy and goals.

STRATEGIC LEADERSHIP The ability of the CEO and top managers to convey a compelling vision of what they want the organization to achieve to their subordinates.

STRATEGY A cluster of decisions about what goals to pursue, what actions to take, and how to use resources to achieve goals.

STRATEGY FORMULATION The development of a set of corporate-, business-, and functional strategies that allow an organization to accomplish its mission and achieve its goals.

SUBJECTIVE APPRAISAL An appraisal that is based on perceptions of traits, behaviors, or results.

SUPPLIERS Individuals and organizations that provide an organization with the input resources that it needs to produce goods and services.

SWOT ANALYSIS A planning exercise in which managers identify organizational strengths (S) and weaknesses (W) and environmental opportunities (O) and threats (T).

SYNERGY Performance gains that result when individuals and departments coordinate their actions.

SYSTEMATIC ERRORS Errors that people make over and over and that result in poor decision making.

TARIFF A tax that a government imposes on imported or, occasionally, exported goods.

TASK ENVIRONMENT The set of forces and conditions that originate with suppliers, distributors, customers, and competitors and affect an organization's ability to obtain inputs and dispose of its outputs because they influence managers on a daily basis.

TASK STRUCTURE The extent to which the work to be performed is clear-cut so that a leader's subordinates know what needs to be accomplished and how to go about doing it; a determinant of how favorable a situation is for leading.

TASK-ORIENTED LEADERS Leaders whose primary concern is to ensure that subordinates perform at a high level.

TECHNICAL SKILLS The job-specific knowledge and techniques required to perform an organizational role.

TECHNOLOGICAL FORCES Outcomes of changes in the technology that managers use to design, produce, or distribute goods and services.

TECHNOLOGY The combination of skills and equipment that managers use in the design, production, and distribution of goods and services.

TERMINAL VALUE A lifelong goal or objective that an individual seeks to achieve.

THEORY X A set of negative assumptions about workers that lead to the conclusion that a manager's task is to supervise workers closely and control their behavior.

THEORY Y A set of positive assumptions about workers that lead to the conclusion that a manager's task is to create a work setting that encourages commitment to organizational goals and provides opportunities for workers to be imaginative and to exercise initiative and self-direction.

THIRD-PARTY NEGOTIATOR An impartial individual with expertise in handling conflicts and negotiations who helps parties in conflict reach an acceptable solution.

TIME HORIZON The intended duration of a plan.

TOP MANAGER A manager who establishes organizational goals, decides how departments should interact, and monitors the performance of middle managers.

TOP-DOWN CHANGE A fast, revolutionary approach to change in which top managers identify what needs to be changed and then move quickly to implement the changes throughout the organization.

TOP-MANAGEMENT TEAM A group composed of the CEO, the COO, and the heads of the most important departments.

TOTAL QUALITY MANAGEMENT (TQM) A management technique that focuses on improving the quality of an organization's products and services.

TRAINING Teaching organizational members how to perform their current jobs and helping them acquire the knowledge and skills they need to be effective performers.

TRANSACTION-PROCESSING SYSTEM A management information system designed to handle large volumes of routine, recurring transactions.

TRANSACTIONAL LEADERSHIP Leadership that motivates subordinates by rewarding them for high performance and reprimanding them for low performance.

TRANSFORMATIONAL LEADERSHIP Leadership that makes subordinates aware of the importance of their jobs and performance to the organization and aware of their own needs for personal growth and that motivates subordinates to work for the good of the organization.

TRUST The willingness of one person or group to have faith or confidence in the goodwill of another person, even though this puts them at risk

UNCERTAINTY Unpredictability.

UNCERTAINTY AVOIDANCE The degree to which societies are willing to tolerate uncertainty and risk.

UNDERPAYMENT INEQUITY The inequity that exists when a person perceives that his or her own outcome-input ratio is less than the ratio of a referent.

UNITY OF COMMAND A reporting relationship in which an employee receives orders from, and reports to, only one superior.

UNITY OF DIRECTION The singleness of purpose that makes possible the creation of one plan of action to guide managers and workers as they use organizational resources.

UNRELATED DIVERSIFICATION Entering a new industry or buying a company in a new industry that is not related in any way to an organization's current businesses or industries.

UTILITARIAN RULE An ethical decision is a decision that produces the greatest good for the greatest number of people.

VALENCE In expectancy theory, how desirable each of the outcomes available from a job or organization is to a person.

VALIDITY The degree to which a tool or test measures what it purports to measure.

VALUE CHAIN The coordinated series or sequence of functional activities necessary to transform inputs such as new product concepts, raw materials, component parts, or professional skills into the finished goods or services customers value and want to buy.

VALUE-CHAIN MANAGEMENT The development of a set of functional-level strategies that support a company's business-level strategy and strengthen its competitive advantage.

VALUE SYSTEM The terminal and instrumental values that are guiding principles in an individual's life.

VALUES Ideas about what a society believes to be good, right, desirable, or beautiful.

VERBAL COMMUNICATION The encoding of messages into words, either written or spoken.

VERTICAL INTEGRATION Expanding a company's operations either backward into an industry that produces inputs for its products or forward into an industry that uses, distributes, or sells its products.

VICARIOUS LEARNING Learning that occurs when the learner becomes motivated to perform a behavior by watching another person perform it and be reinforced for doing so; also called *observational learning.*

WHOLLY OWNED FOREIGN SUBSIDIARY Production operations established in a foreign country independent of any local direct involvement.

Credits

Notes

Chapter 1

1. M. Moritz, *The Little Kingdom: The Private Story of Apple Computer* (New York: Morrow, 1984).

2. R. Cringely, *Accidental Empires* (New York: Harper Business, 1994); B. Dumaine, "America's Toughest Bosses," *Fortune*, October 18, 1993, 38–50.

3. www.apple.com, 2004.

4. Ibid.

5. G. Gentile, "Disney to Acquire Pixar for $7.4B in Stock," www.yahoo.com, January 24, 2006; www.pixar.com, 2006.

6. G. R. Jones, *Organizational Theory, Design, and Change* (Upper Saddle River, NJ: Pearson, 2003).

7. www.consumerreports.org, 2006.

8. J. P. Campbell, "On the Nature of Organizational Effectiveness," in P. S. Goodman, J. M. Pennings, et al., *New Perspectives on Organizational Effectiveness* (San Francisco: Jossey-Bass, 1977).

9. www.apple.com, 2006.

10. M. J. Provitera, "What Management Is: How It Works and Why It's Everyone's Business," *Academy of Management Executive* 17 (August 2003), 152–54.

11. J. McGuire and E. Matta, "CEO Stock Options: The Silent Dimension of Ownership," *Academy of Management Journal* 46 (April 2003), 255–66.

12. www.apple.com, press releases, 2000, 2001, 2003, 2006.

13. J. G. Combs and M. S. Skill, "Managerialist and Human Capital Explanations for Key Executive Pay Premium: A Contingency Perspective," *Academy of Management Journal* 46 (February 2003), 63–74.

14. H. Fayol, *General and Industrial Management* (New York: IEEE Press, 1984). Fayol actually identified five different managerial tasks, but most scholars today believe these four capture the essence of Fayol's ideas.

15. P. F. Drucker, *Management Tasks, Responsibilities, and Practices* (New York: Harper & Row, 1974).

16. D. McGraw, "The Kid Bytes Back," *U.S. News & World Report*, December 12, 1994, 70–71.

17. www..dell.com, 2006.

18. www.apple.com, press release, 2003.

19. www.xerox.com, 2006.

20. "She Put the Bounce Back into Xerox," www.businessweek.com., March 1, 2005.

21. F. Arner, "How Xerox Got Up to Speed," www.businessweek.com, March 2, 2006.

22. www.xerox.com, 2006.

23. G. McWilliams, "Lean Machine–How Dell Fine-Tunes Its PC Pricing to Gain Edge in a Slow Market," *The Wall Street Journal*, June 8, 2001, A1.

24. R. H. Guest, "Of Time and the Foreman," *Personnel* 32 (1955), 478–86.

25. L. Hill, *Becoming a Manager: Mastery of a New Identity* (Boston: Harvard Business School Press, 1992).

26. Ibid.

27. H. Mintzberg, "The Manager's Job: Folklore and Fact," *Harvard Business Review*, July–August 1975, 56–62.

28. H. Mintzberg, *The Nature of Managerial Work* (New York: Harper & Row, 1973).

29. J. Kotter, *The General Managers* (New York: Free Press, 1992).

30. C. P. Hales, "What Do Managers Do? A Critical Review of the Evidence," *Journal of Management Studies*, January 1986, 88–115; A. I. Kraul, P. R. Pedigo, D. D. McKenna, and M. D. Dunnette, "The Role of the Manager: What's Really Important in Different Management Jobs," *Academy of Management Executive*, November 1989, 286–93.

31. A. K. Gupta, "Contingency Perspectives on Strategic Leadership," in D. C. Hambrick, ed., *The Executive Effect: Concepts and Methods for Studying Top Managers* (Greenwich, CT: JAI Press, 1988), 147–78.

32. D. G. Ancona, "Top Management Teams: Preparing for the Revolution," in J. S. Carroll, ed., *Applied Social Psychology and Organizational Settings* (Hillsdale, NJ: Erlbaum, 1990); D. C. Hambrick and P. A Mason, "Upper Echelons: The Organization as a Reflection of Its Top Managers," *Academy of Management Journal* 9 (1984), 193–206.

33. T. A. Mahony, T. H. Jerdee, and S. J. Carroll, "The Jobs of Management," *Industrial Relations* 4 (1965), 97–110; L. Gomez-Mejia, J. McCann, and R. C. Page, "The Structure of Managerial Behaviors and Rewards," *Industrial Relations* 24 (1985), 147–54.

34. W. R. Nord and M. J. Waller, "The Human Organization of Time: Temporal Realities and Experiences," *Academy of Management Review* 29 (January 2004), 137–140.

35. R. L. Katz, "Skills of an Effective Administrator," *Harvard Business Review*, September–October 1974, 90–102.

36. Ibid.

37. P. Tharenou, "Going Up? Do Traits and Informal Social Processes Predict Advancing in Management," *Academy of Management Journal* 44 (October 2001), 1005–18.

38. C. J. Collins and K. D. Clark, "Strategic Human Resource Practices, Top Management Team Social Networks, and Firm Performance: The Role of Human Resource Practices in Creating Organizational Competitive Advantage," *Academy of Management Journal* 46 (December 2003), 740–52.

39. R. Stewart, "Middle Managers: Their Jobs and Behaviors," in J. W. Lorsch, ed., *Handbook of Organizational Behavior* (Englewood Cliffs, NJ: Prentice-Hall, 1987), 385–91.

40. S. C. de Janasz, S. E. Sullivan, and V. Whiting, "Mentor Networks and Career Success: Lessons for Turbulent Times," *Academy of Management Executive* 17 (November 2003), 78–92.

41. K. Labich, "Making Over Middle Managers," *Fortune*, May 8, 1989, 58–64.

42. B. Wysocki, "Some Companies Cut Costs Too Far, Suffer from Corporate Anorexia," *The Wall Street Journal*, July 5, 1995, A1.

43. www.dell.com, 2006.

44. V. U. Druskat and J. V. Wheeler, "Managing from the Boundary: The Effective Leadership of Self-Managing Work Teams," *Academy of Management Journal* 46 (August 2003), 435–58.

45. S. R. Parker, T. D. Wall, and P. R. Jackson, "That's Not My Job: Developing Flexible Work Orientations," *Academy of Management Journal* 40 (1997), 899–929.

46. B. Dumaine, "The New Non-Manager," *Fortune*, February 22, 1993, 80–84.

47. H. G. Baum, A. C. Joel, and E. A. Mannix, "Management Challenges in a New Time," *Academy of Management Journal* 45 (October 2002), 916–31.

48. A. Shama, "Management Under Fire: The Transformation of Management in the Soviet Union and Eastern Europe," *Academy of Management Executive* 10 (1993), 22–35.

49. www.apple.com, 2006; www.nike.com, 2006.

50. K. Seiders and L. L. Berry, "Service Fairness: What It Is and Why It Matters," *Academy of Management Executive* 12 (1998), 8–20.

51. T. Donaldson, "Editor's Comments: Taking Ethics Seriously–A Mission Now More Possible," *Academy of Management Review* 28 (July 2003), 363–67.

52. C. Anderson, "Values-Based Management," *Academy of Management Executive* 11 (1997), 25–46.

53. W. H. Shaw and V. Barry, *Moral Issues in Business*, 6th ed. (Belmont, CA: Wadsworth, 1995); T. Donaldson, *Corporations and Morality* (Englewood Cliffs, NJ: Prentice-Hall, 1982).

54. www.lucent.com, press release, 2004.

55. www.consumerreports.com, 2003.

56. www.fda.com, 2004.

57. www.fda.org, press releases, 2004.

58. J. Bohr, "Deadly Roses," *The Battalion*, February 13, 2006, 3.

59. S. Jackson et al., *Diversity in the Workplace: Human Resource Initiatives* (New York: Guilford Press, 1992).

60. G. Robinson and C. S. Daus, "Building a Case for Diversity," *Academy of Management Executive* 3 (1997), 21–31; S. J. Bunderson and K. M. Sutcliffe, "Comparing Alternative Conceptualizations of Functional Diversity in Management Teams: Process and Performance Effects," *Academy of Management Journal* 45 (October 2002), 875–94.

61. D. Jamieson and J. O'Mara, *Managing Workforce 2000: Gaining a Diversity Advantage* (San Francisco: Jossey-Bass, 1991).

62. www.uboc.com, 2004.

63. J. Hickman, C. Tkaczyk, E. Florian, and J. Stemple, "The 50 Best Companies for Minorities to Work For," *Fortune*, July 7, 2003, 55–58.

64. A. R. Randel and K. S. Jaussi, "Functional Background Identity, Diversity, and Individual Performance in Cross-Functional Teams," *Academy of Management Journal* 46 (December 2003), 763–75.

65. "Union Bank of California Honored by U.S. Labor Department for Employment Practices," press release, September 11, 2000.

66. Ibid.

67. T. H. Cox and S. Blake, "Managing Cultural Diversity: Implications for Organizational Competitiveness," *Academy of Management Executive*, August 1991, 49–52.

68. D. R. Tobin, *The Knowledge Enabled Organization* (New York: AMACOM, 1998).

Chapter 2

1. H. Ford, "Progressive Manufacture," *Encyclopedia Britannica*, 13th ed. (New York: Encyclopedia Co., 1926).

2. R. Edwards, *Contested Terrain: The Transformation of the Workplace in the Twentieth Century* (New York: Basic Books, 1979).

3. A. Smith, *The Wealth of Nations* (London: Penguin, 1982).

4. Ibid., 110.

5. J. G. March and H. A. Simon, *Organizations* (New York: Wiley, 1958).

6. L. W. Fry, "The Maligned F. W. Taylor: A Reply to His Many Critics," *Academy of Management Review* 1 (1976), 124–29.

7. F. W. Taylor, *Shop Management* (New York: Harper, 1903); F. W. Taylor, *The Principles of Scientific Management* (New York: Harper, 1911).

8. J. A. Litterer, *The Emergence of Systematic Management as Shown by the Literature from 1870–1900* (New York: Garland, 1986).

9. H. R. Pollard, *Developments in Management Thought* (New York: Crane, 1974).

10. D. Wren, *The Evolution of Management Thought* (New York: Wiley, 1994), 134.

11. Edwards, *Contested Terrain*.

12. J. M. Staudenmaier, Jr., "Henry Ford's Big Flaw," *Invention and Technology* 10 (1994), 34–44.

13. H. Beynon, *Working for Ford* (London: Penguin, 1975).

14. Taylor, *Scientific Management*.

15. F. B. Gilbreth, *Primer of Scientific Management* (New York: Van Nostrand Reinhold, 1912).

16. F. B. Gilbreth, Jr., and E. G. Gilbreth, *Cheaper by the Dozen* (New York: Crowell, 1948).

17. D. Roy, "Efficiency and the Fix: Informal Intergroup Relations in a Piece Work Setting," *American Journal of Sociology* 60 (1954), 255–66.

18. M. Weber, *From Max Weber: Essays in Sociology*, ed. H. H. Gerth and C. W. Mills (New York: Oxford University Press, 1946); M. Weber, *Economy and Society*, ed. G. Roth and C. Wittich (Berkeley: University of California Press, 1978).

19. C. Perrow, *Complex Organizations*, 2d ed. (Glenview, IL: Scott, Foresman, 1979).

20. Weber, *From Max Weber*, 331.

21. See Perrow, *Complex Organizations*, see chap. 1, for a detailed discussion of these issues.

22. H. Fayol, *General and Industrial Management* (New York: IEEE Press, 1984).

23. Ibid., 79.

24. T. J. Peters and R. H. Waterman, Jr., *In Search of Excellence: Lessons from America's Best-Run Companies* (New York: Harper & Row, 1982).

25. R. E. Eccles and N. Nohira, *Beyond the Hype: Rediscovering the Essence of Management* (Boston: Harvard Business School Press, 1992).

26. L. D. Parker, "Control in Organizational Life: The Contribution of Mary Parker Follett," *Academy of Management Review* 9 (1984), 736–45.

27. P. Graham, *M. P. Follett–Prophet of Management: A Celebration of Writings from the 1920s* (Boston: Harvard Business School Press, 1995).

28. M. P. Follett, *Creative Experience* (London: Longmans, 1924).

29. E. Mayo, *The Human Problems of Industrial Civilization* (New York: Macmillan, 1933); F. J. Roethlisberger and W. J. Dickson, *Management and the Worker* (Cambridge: Harvard University Press, 1947).

30. D. W. Organ, "Review of *Management and the Worker*, by F. J. Roethlisberger and W. J. Dickson," *Academy of Management Review* 13 (1986), 460–64.

31. D. Roy, "Banana Time: Job Satisfaction and Informal Interaction," *Human Organization* 18 (1960), 158–61.

32. For an analysis of the problems in determining cause from effect in the Hawthorne studies and in social settings in general, see A. Carey, "The Hawthorne Studies: A Radical Criticism," *American Sociological Review* 33 (1967), 403–16.

33. D. McGregor, *The Human Side of Enterprise* (New York: McGraw-Hill, 1960).

34. Ibid., 48.

35. Peters and Waterman, *In Search of Excellence*.

36. J. Pitta, "It Had to Be Done and We Did It," *Forbes*, April 26, 1993, 148–52.

37. www.hp.com, press release, June 2001.

38. www.hp.com, press releases, 2003–2004.

39. www.hp.com, 2006.

40. T. Dewett and G. R. Jones, "The Role of Information Technology in the Organization: A Review, Model, and Assessment," *Journal of Management* 27 (2001), 313–46.

41. W. E. Deming, *Out of the Crisis* (Cambridge: MIT Press, 1986).

42. J. D. Thompson, *Organizations in Action* (New York: McGraw-Hill, 1967).

43. D. Katz and R. L. Kahn, *The Social Psychology of Organizations* (New York: Wiley, 1966); Thompson, *Organizations in Action*.

44. T. Burns and G. M. Stalker, *The Management of Innovation* (London: Tavistock, 1961); P. R. Lawrence and

J. R. Lorsch, *Organization and Environment* (Boston: Graduate School of Business Administration, Harvard University, 1967).

45.   Burns and Stalker, *The Management of Innovation.*

46.   R. O. Crockett and S. Baker, "Suddenly, Mobile Phones Aren't Moving So Fast," *BusinessWeek Online,* November 6, 2000; S. Baker, I. Resch, and R. O. Crockett, "Commentary: Nokia's Costly Stumble," *BusinessWeek Online,* August 14, 2000.

47.   www.nokia.com, 2006.

48.   Ibid.

49.   Ibid.

50.   Ibid.

51.   C. W. L. Hill and G. R. Jones, *Strategic Management: An Integrated Approach,* 6th ed. (Boston: Houghton Mifflin, 2007).

Chapter 3

1.   "PAETEC Signs Exclusive Agreement with Los Angeles Area Hotel and Lodging Association," PAETEC News Current Press Releases, February 18, 2004; "Markets Served–PAETEC Communications, Inc.," www.paetec.com/2_1/2_1_5_2.html, May 27, 2006; "Media Center–2005 Press Releases–PAETEC Communications, Inc.," www.paetec.com/3/2005_news.html, May 27, 2006; "PAETEC SECURETEC MPLS Now Has a World–Reach," www.paetec.com, May 27, 2006.

2.   "Partnership Pays Off for OSS Player," in Ray Le Maistre, International (ed.), *Boardwatch,* January 28, 2004 (www.boardwatch.com); "PAETEC Communications, Inc.: 2005 Year in Review," www.paetec.com, May 27, 2006; "PAETEC Communications," http://en.wikipedia. org/wiki/PAETEC_Communications, May 27, 2006.

3.   "Offering the PAETEC Solutions Portfolio," www.paetec.com, March 8, 2004.

4.   D. Dorsey, "Happiness Pays," *Inc. Magazine,* February 2004, 89–94.

5.   "PAETEC Communications, Inc.: 2005 Year in Review."

6.   D. Dorsey, "Happiness Pays," *Inc. Magazine,* February 2004, 89–94.

7.   "Company Profile about PAETEC," www.paetec.com, March 8, 2004.

8.   Dorsey, "Happiness Pays."

9.   "PAETEC Receives 2005 American Business Ethics Award," www.paetec.com, May 27, 2006.

10.   R. News Staff, "Paetec Gives Bonuses," www.rnews.com, March 8, 2004.

11.   Dorsey, "Happiness Pays,"; "Media Center–Press Releases–PAETEC Communications, Inc.,"

Feb. 17, 2006 – PAETEC Employees Achieve Bonus Award"; http://www.paetec.com/3/3_1_2.html, May 27, 2006.

12.   "PAETEC Communications, Inc.: 2005 Year in Review."

13.   Dorsey, "Happiness Pays."

14.   Ibid.

15.   Ibid.

16.   Ibid.

17.   "Company Profile about PAETEC."

18.   C. Hymowitz and G. Stern, "At Procter & Gamble, Brands Face Pressure and So Do Executives," *The Wall Street Journal,* May 10, 1993, A1, A8; Z. Schiller, "Ed Artzt's Elbow Grease Has P&G Shining," *BusinessWeek,* October 10, 1994, 84–86.

19.   S. Carpenter, "Different Dispositions, Different Brains," *Monitor on Psychology,* February 2001, 66–68.

20.   J. M. Digman, "Personality Structure: Emergence of the Five-Factor Model," *Annual Review of Psychology* 41 (1990), 417–40; R. R. McCrae and P. T. Costa, "Validation of the Five-Factor Model of Personality Across Instruments and Observers," *Journal of Personality and Social Psychology* 52 (1987), 81–90; R. R. McCrae and P. T. Costa, "Discriminant Validity of NEO-PIR Facet Scales," *Educational and Psychological Measurement* 52 (1992), 229–37.

21.   Digman, "Personality Structure"; McCrae and Costa, "Validation of the Five-Factor Model"; McCrae and Costa, "Discriminat Validity"; R. P. Tett and D. D. Burnett, "A Personality Trait-Based Interactionist Model of Job Performance," *Journal of Applied Psychology* 88, no. 3 (2003), 500–17; J. M. George, "Personality, Five-Factor Model," in S. Clegg and J. R. Bailey, eds., *International Innovations Encyclopedia of Organization Studies* (Thousand Oaks, CA: Sage, forthcoming in 2007).

22.   L. A. Witt and G. R. Ferris, "Social Skills as Moderator of Conscientiousness-Performance Relationship: Convergent Results Across Four Studies," *Journal of Applied Psychology* 88, no.5, (2003), 809–20; M. J. Simmering, J. A. Colquitte, R. A. Noe, and C. O. L. H. Porter, "Conscientiousness, Autonomy Fit, and Development: A Longitudinal Study," *Journal of Applied Psychology* 88, no. 5 (2003), 954–63.

23.   M. R. Barrick and M. K. Mount, "The Big Five Personality Dimensions and Job Performance: A Meta-Analysis," *Personnel Psychology* 44 (1991), 1–26.

24.   Digman, "Personality Structure"; McCrae and Costa, "Validation of the Five-Factor Model"; McCrae and Costa, "Discriminant Validity."

25.   "Your Partner Is Finding Solutions," www.standardtextiles.com, March 20, 2006;

G. Helman, "Company Overview," *Standard Textile,* March 20, 2006, (www.standardtextile.com/company.asp).

26.   M. Fong, "Woven in China'," *The Wall Street Journal* (April 2005): B1, B4.

27.   G. Heiman, "Innovation, Not Quotas," *washingtonpost.com,* April 8, 2005, A25.

28.   M. Fong, "Woven in China," *The Wall Street Journal,* April 11, 2005, B1, B4.

29.   Ibid.

30.   Ibid.

31.   Heiman, "Innovation, Not Quotas."

32.   Fong, "Woven in China."

33.   J. B. Rotter, "Generalized Expectancies for Internal Versus External Control of Reinforcement," *Psychological Monographs* 80 (1966), 1–28; P. Spector, "Behaviors in Organizations as a Function of Employees' Locus of Control," *Psychological Bulletin* 91 (1982), 482–97.

34.   J. Brockner, *Self-Esteem at Work* (Lexington, MA: Lexington Books 1988).

35.   D. C. McClelland, *Human Motivation* (Glenview, IL: Scott, Foresman, 1985); D. C. McClelland, "How Motives, Skills, and Values Determine What People Do," *American Psychologist* 40 (1985), 812–25; D. C. McClelland, "Managing Motivation to Expand Human Freedom," *American Psychologist* 33 (1978), 201–10.

36.   D. G. Winter, *The Power Motive* (New York: Free Press 1973).

37.   M. J. Stahl, "Achievement, Power, and Managerial Motivation: Selecting Managerial Talent with the Job Choice Exercise," *Personnel Psychology* 36 (1983), 775–89; D. C. McClelland and D. H. Burnham, "Power Is the Great Motivator," *Harvard Business Review* 54 (1976), 100–10.

38.   R. J. House, W. D. Spangler, and J. Woycke, "Personality and Charisma in the U.S. Presidency: A Psychological Theory of Leader Effectiveness," *Administrative Science Quarterly* 36 (1991), 364–96.

39.   G. H. Hines, "Achievement, Motivation, Occupations and Labor Turnover in New Zealand," *Journal of Applied Psychology* 58 (1973), 313–17; P. S. Hundal, "A Study of Entrepreneurial Motivation: Comparison of Fast- and Slow-Progressing Small Scale Industrial Entrepreneurs in Punjab, India," *Journal of Applied Psychology* 55 (1971), 317–23.

40.   M. Rokeach, *The Nature of Human Values* (New York: Free Press 1973).

41.   Ibid.

42.   Ibid.

43.   "Hedge Fund Association: Who We Are," www.thehfa.org, March 19, 2004.

44.   R. D. Atlas, "Fund Inquiry Informant Discloses Her Identity," *The New York Times,* December 9, 2003.

45.   Ibid.

46. N. Harrington, "Acting with Courage," *Fast Company,* April 15, 2004 (www. fastcompany.com/fast50_04/winners/harrington.html).

47. "Council of Institutional Investors Fall 2005 Conference Speaker Biographies: Noreen Harrington–Managing Partner, Alternative Institutional Partners," www.cii.org/meetings/fall2005/speakerbios.ht m, May 27, 2006.

48. A. P. Brief, *Attitudes In and Around Organizations* (Thousand Oaks, CA: Sage, 1998).

49. M. Irvine, "In Search of the Simple Life," *Houston Chronicle,* February 1, 2004, 8A; M. Irvine, "Simple Life Holds Appeal for Young Professionals," http://the. honoluluandvertiser.com/article/2004/jan/ 26.bz/bz10a.html, January 26, 2004; "More Young People Pursuing Simpler Life," http://msnbc.msn.com/id/4062706, January 26, 2004.

50. Irvine, "In Search of the Simple Life"; Irvine, "Simple Life Holds Appeal"; "More Young People Pursuing Simpler Life"; "Diaper Rash Cream and Ointment for Babies–PINXAV," www.pinxav.com, May 28, 2006.

51. Irvine, "In Search of the Simple Life"; Irvine, "Simple Life Holds Appeal"; "More Young People Pursuing Simpler Life."

52. Ibid.

53. D. W. Organ, *Organizational Citizenship Behavior: The Good Soldier Syndrome* (Lexington, MA: Lexington Books, 1988).

54. J. M. George and A. P. Brief, "Feeling Good–Doing Good: A Conceptual Analysis of the Mood at Work–Organizational Spontaneity Relationship," *Psychological Bulletin* 112 (1992), 310–29.

55. W. H. Mobley, "Intermediate Linkages in the Relationship Between Job Satisfaction and Employee Turnover," *Journal of Applied Psychology* 62 (1977), 237–40.

56. "Managers View Workplace Changes More Positively Than Employees," *The Wall Street Journal,* December 13, 1994, A1.

57. J. E. Mathieu and D. M. Zajac, "A Review and Meta-Analysis of the Antecedents, Correlates, and Consequences of Organizational Commitment," *Psychological Bulletin* 108 (1990), 171–94.

58. E. Slate, "Tips for Negotiations in Germany and France," *HR Focus,* July 1994, 18.

59. D. Watson and A. Tellegen, "Toward a Consensual Structure of Mood," *Psychological Bulletin* 98 (1985), 219–35.

60. Ibid.

61. J. M. George, "The Role of Personality in Organizational Life: Issues and Evidence," *Journal of Management* 18 (1992), 185–213.

62. J. P. Forgas, "Affect in Social Judgments and Decisions: A Multi-Process Model," in M. Zanna, ed., *Advances in Experimental and Social Psychology,* vol. 25 (San Diego, CA: Academic Press, 1992), 227-75; J. P. Forgas and J. M. George, "Affective Influences on Judgments and Behavior in Organizations: An Information Processing Perspective," *Organizational Behavior and Human Decision Processes* 86 (2001), 3–34; J. M. George, "Emotions and Leadership: The Role of Emotional Intelligence," *Human Relations* 53 (2000), 1027–55; W. N. Morris, *Mood: The Frame of Mind* (New York: Springer-Verlag, 1989).

63. George, "Emotions and Leadership.

64. J. M. George and K. Bettenhausen, "Understanding Prosocial Behavior, Sales Performance, and Turnover: A Group Level Analysis in a Service Context," *Journal of Applied Psychology* 75 (1990), 698–709.

65. George and Brief, "Feeling Good–Doing Good"; J. M. George and J. Zhou, "Understanding When Bad Moods Foster Creativity and Good Ones Don't: The Role of Context and Clarity of Feelings," paper presented at the Academy of Management Annual Meeting, 2001; A. M. Isen and R. A. Baron, "Positive Affect as a Factor in Organizational Behavior," in B. M. Staw and L. L. Cummings, eds., *Research in Organizational Behavior,* vol. 13 (Greenwich, CT: JAI Press, 1991), 1–53.

66. J. D. Greene, R. B. Sommerville, L. E. Nystrom, J. M. Darley, and J. D. Cohen, "An FMRI Investigation of Emotional Engagement in Moral Judgment," *Science,* September 14, 2001, 2105–08; L. Neergaard, "Brain Scans Show Emotions Key to Resolving Ethical Dilemmas," *Houston Chronicle,* September 14, 2001, 13A.

67. L. Berton, "It's Audit Time! Send in the Clowns," *The Wall Street Journal,* January 18, 1995, B1, B6.

68. R. C. Sinclair, "Mood, Categorization Breadth, and Performance Appraisal: The Effects of Order of Information Acquisition and Affective State on Halo, Accuracy, Informational Retrieval, and Evaluations," *Organizational Behavior and Human Decision Processes* 42 (1988), 22–46.

69. D. Goleman, *Emotional Intelligence* (New York: Bantam Books, 1994); J. D. Mayer and P. Salovey, "The Intelligence of Emotional Intelligence," *Intelligence* 17 (1993), 433–42; J. D. Mayer and P. Salovey, "What Is Emotional Intelligence?" in P. Salovey and D. Sluyter, eds., *Emotional Development and Emotional Intelligence: Implications for Education* (New York: Basic Books, 1997); P. Salovey and J. D. Mayer, "Emotional Intelligence," *Imagination, Cognition, and Personality* 9 (1989–1990), 185–211.

70. S. Epstein, *Constructive Thinking* (Westport, CT: Praeger, 1998).

71. "Leading by Feel," *Inside the Mind of the Leader,* January 2004, 27–37.

72. P. C. Early and R. S. Peterson, "The Elusive Cultural Chameleon: Cultural Intelligence as a New Approach to Intercultural Training for the Global Manger," *Academy of Management Learning and Education* 3, no. 1 (2004), 100–15.

73. George, "Emotions and Leadership"; S. Begley, "The Boss Feels Your Pain," *Newsweek,* October 12, 1998, 74; D. Goleman, *Working with Emotional Intelligence* (New York: Bantam Books, 1998).

74. J. Bercovici, "Remembering Bernie Goldhirsh," www.medialifemagazine. com/news2003/jun03/jun30/4_thurs/ news1thursday.html, April 15, 2004.

75. B. Burlingham, "Legacy: The Creative Spirit," *INC.,* September 2003, 11–12.

76. Burlingham, "Legacy: The Creative Spirit"; "Inc. magazine," www.inc.com/magazine, May 28, 2006.

77. B. Burlingham, "Legacy: The Creative Spirit."

78. Ibid.

79. Ibid.

80. "Bernard Goldhirsh, Magazine Founder and MIT Alumnus, Dies at 63," http://web.mit.edu/newsoffice/nr/2003/goldhi rsh.html, July 1, 2003.

81. "Leading by Feel," *Inside the Mind of the Leader,* January 2004, 27–37.

82. George, "Emotions and Leadership."

83. J. Zhou and J. M. George, "Awakening Employee Creativity: The Role of Leader Emotional Intelligence," *Leadership Quarterly* 14 (2003), 545–68.

84. A. Jung, "Leading by Feel: Seek Frank Feedback," *Inside the Mind of the Leader,* January 2004, 31.

85. H. M. Trice and J. M. Beyer, *The Cultures of Work Organizations* (Englewood Cliffs, NJ: Prentice-Hall, 1993).

86. J. B. Sørensen, "The Strength of Corporate Culture and the Reliability of Firm Performance," *Administrative Science Quarterly* 47, (2002), 70–91.

87. "Personality and Organizational Culture," in B. Schneider and D. B. Smith, eds., *Personality and Organizations* (Mahway, NJ: Lawrence Erlbaum, 2004), 347–369; J. E. Slaughter, M. J. Zickar, S. Highhouse, and D. C. Mohr, "Personality Trait Inferences about Organizations: Development of a Measure and Assessment of Construct Validity," *Journal of Applied Psychology* 89, no. 1 (2004), 85–103.

88. T. Kelley, *The Art of Innovation: Lessons in Creativity from IDEO, America's Leading Design Firm* (New York: Random House, 2001).

89. "Personality and Organizational Culture."

90. B. Schneider, "The People Make the Place," *Personnel Psychology* 40 (1987), 437–53.

91. "Personality and Organizational Culture."

92.   Ibid.

93.   B. Schneider, H. B. Goldstein, and D. B. Smith, "The ASA Framework: An Update," *Personnel Psychology* 48 (1995), 747-73; J. Schaubroeck, D. C. Ganster, and J. R. Jones, "Organizational and Occupational Influences in the Attraction-Selection-Attrition Process," *Journal of Applied Psychology* 83 (1998), 869–91.

94.   Kelley, *The Art of Innovation.*

95.   Ibid.

96.   "Personality and Organizational Culture."

97.   Kelley, *The Art of Innovation.*

98.   George, "Emotions and Leadership."

99.   Kelley, *The Art of Innovation.*

100.   Ibid.

101.   D. C. Feldman, "The Development and Enforcement of Group Norms," *Academy of Management Review* 9 (1984), 47–53.

102.   G. R. Jones, *Organizational Theory, Design, and Change* (Upper Saddle River, NJ: Prentice-Hall, 2003).

103.   H. Schein, "The Role of the Founder in Creating Organizational Culture," *Organizational Dynamics* 12 (1983), 13–28.

104.   J. M. George, "Personality, Affect, and Behavior in Groups," *Journal of Applied Psychology* 75 (1990), 107–16.

105.   J. Van Maanen, "Police Socialization: A Longitudinal Examination of Job Attitudes in an Urban Police Department," *Administrative Science Quarterly* 20 (1975), 207–28.

106.   www.intercotwest.com/Disney; M. N. Martinez, "Disney Training Works Magic," *HRMagazine,* May 1992, 53–57.

107.   P. L. Berger and T. Luckman, *The Social Construction of Reality* (Garden City, NY: Anchor Books, 1967).

108.   H. M. Trice and J. M. Beyer, "Studying Organizational Culture Through Rites and Ceremonials," *Academy of Management Review* 9 (1984), 653–69.

109.   Kelley, *The Art of Innovation.*

110.   H. M. Trice and J. M. Beyer, *The Cultures of Work Organizations* (Englewood Cliffs, NJ: Prentice-Hall, 1993).

111.   B. Ortega, "Wal-Mart's Meeting Is a Reason to Party," *The Wall Street Journal,* June 3, 1994, A1.

112.   Trice and Beyer, "Studying Organizational Culture."

113.   Kelley, *The Art of Innovation.*

114.   S. McGee, "Garish Jackets Add to Clamor of Chicago Pits," *The Wall Street Journal,* July 31, 1995, C1.

115.   K. E. Weick, *The Social Psychology of Organization* (Reading, MA: Addison-Wesley, 1979).

116.   B. McLean and P. Elkind, *The Smartest Guys in the Room: The Amazing Rise and Scandalous Fall of Enron* (New York: Penguin Books, 2003); R. Smith and

J. R. Emshwiller, *24 Days: How Two Wall Street Journal Reporters Uncovered the Lies That Destroyed Faith in Corporate America* (New York: HarperCollins, 2003); M. Swartz and S. Watkins, *Power Failure: The Inside Story of the Collapse of ENRON* (New York: Doubleday, 2003).

Chapter 4

1.   "John Mackey's Blog: 20 Questions with Sunni's Salon," www.wholefoodsmarket.com, 2006.

2.   Ibid.

3.   D. McGinn, "The Green Machine," *Newsweek,* March 21, 2005, E8–E10.

4.   A. E. Tenbrunsel, "Misrepresentation and Expectations of Misrepresentation in an Ethical Dilemma: The Role of Incentives and Temptation," *Academy of Management Journal* 41 (June 1998), 330–40.

5.   D. Kravets, "Supreme Court to Hear Case on Medical Pot," www.yahoo.com, June 29, 2004; C. Lane "A Defeat for Users of Medical Marihuana," www.washingtonpost.com, June 7, 2005.

6.   www.yahoo.com, 2003; www.mci.com, 2004.

7.   J. Child, "The International Crisis of Confidence in Corporations," *Academy of Management Executive* 16 (August 2002), 145–48.

8.   T. Donaldson, "Editor's Comments: Taking Ethics Seriously–A Mission Now More Possible," *Academy of Management Review* 28 (July 2003), 463–67.

9.   R. E. Freeman, *Strategic Management: A Stakeholder Approach* (Marshfield, MA: Pitman, 1984).

10.   J. A. Pearce, "The Company Mission as a Strategic Tool," *Sloan Management Review,* Spring 1982, 15–24.

11.   C. I. Barnard, *The Functions of the Executive* (Cambridge, MA: Harvard University Press, 1948).

12.   Freeman, *Strategic Management.*

13.   http://data.bls.gov/cgi-bin/surveymost, 2006.

14.   G. Brown, "How to Embrace Change," *Newsweek,* June 12, 2006, 69.

15.   P. S. Adler, "Corporate Scandals: It's Time for Reflection in Business Schools," *Academy of Management Executive* 16 (August 2002), 148–50.

16.   T. L. Beauchamp and N. E. Bowie, eds., *Ethical Theory and Business* (Englewood Cliffs, NJ: Prentice-Hall, 1979); A. MacIntyre, *After Virtue* (South Bend, IN: University of Notre Dame Press, 1981).

17.   R. E. Goodin, "How to Determine Who Should Get What," *Ethics,* July 1975, 310–21.

18.   E. P. Kelly, "A Better Way to Think About Business" (book review), *Academy of Management Executive* 14 (May 2000), 127–129.

19.   T. M. Jones, "Ethical Decision Making by Individuals in Organizations: An Issue Contingent Model," *Academy of Management Journal* 16 (1991), 366–95; G. F. Cavanaugh, D. J. Moberg, and M. Velasquez, "The Ethics of Organizational Politics," *Academy of Management Review* 6 (1981), 363–74.

20.   L. K. Trevino, "Ethical Decision Making in Organizations: A Person-Situation Interactionist Model," *Academy of Management Review* 11 (1986), 601–17; W. H. Shaw and V. Barry, *Moral Issues in Business,* 6th ed. (Belmont, CA: Wadsworth, 1995).

21.   T. M. Jones, "Instrumental Stakeholder Theory: A Synthesis of Ethics and Economics," *Academy of Management Review* 20 (1995), 404–37.

22.   B. Victor and J. B. Cullen, "The Organizational Bases of Ethical Work Climates," *Administrative Science Quarterly* 33 (1988), 101–25.

23.   www.yahoo.com, 2006.

24.   www.napster.com, 2006.

25.   C. W. L. Hill, "Napster," in C. W. L. Hill and G. R. Jones, *Strategic Management: An Integrated Approach* (Boston: Houghton Mifflin, 2004).

26.   D. Collins, "Organizational Harm, Legal Consequences and Stakeholder Retaliation," *Journal of Business Ethics* 8 (1988), 1–13.

27.   R. C. Soloman, *Ethics and Excellence* (New York: Oxford University Press, 1992).

28.   T. E. Becker, "Integrity in Organizations: Beyond Honesty and Conscientiousness," *Academy of Management Review* 23 (January 1998), 154–62.

29.   S. W. Gellerman, "Why Good Managers Make Bad Decisions," in K. R. Andrews, ed., *Ethics in Practice: Managing the Moral Corporation* (Boston: Harvard Business School Press, 1989).

30.   J. Dobson, "Corporate Reputation: A Free Market Solution to Unethical Behavior," *Business and Society* 28 (1989), 1–5.

31.   M. S. Baucus and J. P. Near, "Can Illegal Corporate Behavior Be Predicted? An Event History Analysis," *Academy of Management Journal* 34 (1991), 9–36.

32.   Trevino, "Ethical Decision Making in Organizations."

33.   "GSK, Merck and Bristol Myers Squibb Are the World's Most Ethical Companies, Across All Sectors, Swiss Study," www.medicalnewstoday.com, January 8, 2006.

34.   A. S. Waterman, "On the Uses of Psychological Theory and Research in the Process of Ethical Inquiry," *Psychological Bulletin* 103, no. 3 (1988), 283–98.

35.   M. S. Frankel, "Professional Codes: Why, How, and with What Impact?" *Ethics* 8 (1989), 109–15.

36.   J. Van Maanen and S. R. Barley, "Occupational Communities: Culture and Control in Organizations," in B. Staw and L. Cummings, eds., *Research in Organizational Behavior,* vol. 6 (Greenwich, CT: JAI Press, 1984), 287–365.

37.   Jones, "Ethical Decision Making by Individuals in Organizations."

38.   B. Bradley, P. Jansen, and L. Silverman, "The Nonprofit Sector's $100 billion Opportunity," www.harvardbusinessonline.edu, May 1, 2003.

39.   E. Gatewood and A. B. Carroll, "The Anatomy of Corporate Social Response," *Business Horizons,* September– October 1981, 9–16.

40.   www.yahoo.com, June 7, 2006.

41.   R. Johnson, "Ralston to Buy Beechnut, Gambling It Can Overcome Apple Juice Scandal," *The Wall Street Journal,* September 18, 1989, B11.

42.   M. Friedman, "A Friedman Doctrine: The Social Responsibility of Business Is to Increase Its Profits," *New York Times Magazine,* September 13, 1970, 33.

43.   Conlin, "Where Layoffs Are a Last Resort"; Southwest Airlines Fact Sheet, www.southwest.com, 2004.

44.   G. R. Jones, *Organizational Theory: Text and Cases* (Englewood Cliffs, NJ: Prentice-Hall, 2003).

45.   P. E. Murphy, "Creating Ethical Corporate Structure," *Sloan Management Review,* Winter 1989, 81–87.

46.   C. Stavraka, "Strong Corporate Reputation at J&J Boosts Diversity Recruiting Efforts," DiversityInc.com, February 16, 2001.

47.   "Our Credo," www.jj.com, 2004.

48.   Ibid.

49.   L. L. Nash, *Good Intentions Aside* (Boston: Harvard Business School Press, 1993).

50.   Ibid.; L. L. Nash, "Johnson & Johnson's Credo," in *Corporate Ethics: A Prime Business Asset* (New York: Business Roundtable, February 1988).

51.   Nash, *Good Intentions Aside.*

52.   Stavraka, "Strong Corporate Reputation."

53.   Nash, *Good Intentions Aside.*

Chapter 5

1.   U.S. Department of Labor, Women's Bureau, "Nontraditional Occupations for Women in 2003," www.dol.gov/wb, April 28, 2004.

2.   C. Hymowitz, "In the U.S., What Will It Take to Create Diverse Boardrooms?" *The Wall Street Journal,* July 8, 2003, B1.

3.   "Calvert Online Issue Brief: Board Diversity," *Calvert Online: Investments That Make a Difference,* May 27, 2006 (www.calvert.com/sri_ib_4.html).

4.   Alliance for Board Diversity, "Women and Minorities on Fortune 100 Boards, May 17, 2005," http://216.15.17766/ABDReport.pdf, May 27, 2006.

5.   A. Joyce, "Few Women, Minorities Serve on Boards, Study Finds," *washingtonpost.com,* May 12, 2005 (www.washingtonpost.com/wp-dyn/content/article/2005/05/11/AR2005051102027).

6.   Joyce, "Few Women, Minorities Serve on Boards"; Alliance for Board Diversity, "Women and Minorities on Fortune 100 Boards."

7.   "Leonard Schaeffer Profile," *Forbes.com,* May 28, 2006, (www.forbes.com/finance/mktguideapps/personinfo/FromPersonIDPersonTearsheet.j . . .).

8.   Hymowitz, "In the U.S., What Will It Take to Create Diverse Boardrooms?"

9.   Ibid.

10.   M. Nusbaum, "Breaking into More Male Strongholds," *The New York Times,* November 15, 2003, C9.

11.   Ibid.

12.   L. M. Sixel, "Making Diversity Work a Full-Time Job for This Doctor," *Houston Chronicle,* April 16, 2004.

13.   Ibid.

14.   P. Tyre, "MS. Top Cop," *Newsweek,* April 12, 2004, 48–49.

15.   S. Janis, "Girl Power: More and More Women Entering City Police Academy," *Baltimore City Paper,* January 25, 2006 (www.citypaper.com/news).

16.   "Boston Police Department: A Message from the Police Commissioner," www.ci/boston.ma.us/police, May 28, 2006.

17.   Tyre, "MS. Top Cop"; "Biography of Thomas M. Menino, Mayor of Boston," www.cityofboston.gov/mayor/bio.asp, May 28, 2006.

18.   D. McCracken, "Winning the Talent War for Women," *Harvard Business Review,* November–December 2000, 159–67.

19.   W. B. Swann, Jr., J. T. Polzer, D. C. Seyle, and S. J. Ko, "Finding Value in Diversity: Verification of Personal and Social Self-Views in Diverse Groups," *Academy of Management Review* 29, no. 1 (2004), 9–27.

20.   "Usual Weekly Earnings Summary," *News: Bureau of Labor Statistics,* April 16, 2004 (www.bls.gov/news.release/whyeng.nr0.htm); "Facts on Affirmative Action in Employment and Contracting," *Americans for a Fair Chance,* January, 28, 2004 (fairchance.civilrights.org/research_center/details.cfm?id=18076); "Household Data Annual Averages," www.bls.gov, April 28, 2004.

21.   "Prejudice: Still on the Menu," *Business Week,* April 3, 1995, 42.

22.   "She's a Woman, Offer Her Less," *Business Week,* May 7, 2001, 34.

23.   "Glass Ceiling Is a Heavy Barrier for Minorities, Blocking Them from Top Jobs," *The Wall Street Journal,* March 14, 1995, A1.

24.   "Catalyst Report Outlines Unique Challenges Faced By African-American Women in Business," *Catalyst news release,* February 18, 2004.

25.   C. Gibson, "Nation's Median Age Highest Ever, but 65-and-Over Population's Growth Lags, Census 2000 Shows," *U.S. Census Bureau News,* May 30, 2001 (www.census.gov); "U.S. Census Press Releases: Nation's Population One-Third Minority," *U.S. Census Bureau News,* May 10, 2006 (www.census.gov/Press-Release/www/releases/archives/population/006808.html).

26.   "Table 2: United States Population Projections by Age and Sex: 2000–2050," *U.S. Census Board, International Data Base, 94,* April 28, 2004 (www.census.gov/ipc/www.idbprint.html).

27.   U.S. Equal Employment Opportunity Commission, "Federal Laws Prohibiting Job Discrimination–Questions and Answers," www.eeoc.gov, June 20, 2001.

28.   "Sex by Industry by Class of Worker for the Employed Civilian Population 16 Years and Over," *American FactFinder,* October 15, 2001 (factfinder.census.gov); "2002 Catalyst Census of Women Corporate Officers and Top Earners in the Fortune 500," www.catalystwomen.org, August 17, 2004.

29.   "Profile of Selected Economic Characteristics: 2000," *American FactFinder,* October 15, 2001 (factfinder.census.gov); "Usual Weekly Earnings Summary," www.bls.gov/news.release, August 17, 2004.

30.   "2000 Catalyst Census of Women Corporate Officers and Top Earners of the Fortune 500," www.catalystwomen.org, October 21, 2001; S. Wellington, M. Brumit Kropf, and P. R. Gerkovich, "What's Holding Women Back?" *Harvard Business Review,* June 2003, 18–19; D. Jones, "The Gender Factor," *USA Today.com,* December 30, 2003; "2002 Catalyst Census of Women Corporate Officers and Top Earners in the Fortune 500," www.catalystwomen.org, August 17, 2004.

31.   T. Gutner, "Wanted: More Diverse Directors," *BusinessWeek,* April 30, 2001, 134; "2003 Catalyst Census of Women Board Directors," www.catalystwomen.org, August 17, 2004.

32.   Ibid.

33.   R. Sharpe, "As Leaders, Women Rule," *BusinessWeek,* November 20, 2000, 75–84.

34.   Ibid.

35.   "New Catalyst Study Reveals Financial Performance Is Higher for Companies with More Women at the Top," *Catalyst news release,* January 26, 2004.

36.   B. Guzman, "The Hispanic Population," U.S. Census Bureau, May 2001; U.S. Census Bureau, "Profiles of General Demographic

Characteristics," May 2001; U.S. Census Bureau, "Revisions to the Standards for the Classification of Federal Data on Race and Ethnicity," November 2, 2000, 1–19.

37. L. Chavez, "Just Another Ethnic Group," *The Wall Street Journal*, May 14, 2001, A22.

38. Bureau of Labor Statistics, "Civilian Labor Force 16 and Older by Sex, Age, Race, and Hispanic Origin, 1978, 1988, 1998, and Projected 2008," stats.bls.gov/emp, October 16, 2001.

39. "U.S. Census Bureau, Profile of General Demographic Characteristics: 2000," *Census 2000*, www.census.gov; "U.S. Census Press Releases: Nation's Population One-Third Minority," *U.S. Census Bureau News*, May 10, 2006 (www.census.gov/Press-Release/www/releases/archives/population/006808.html).

40. *U.S. Census Bureau*, "Census Bureau Projects Tripling of Hispanic and Asian Populations in 50 Years; Non-Hispanic Whites May Drop to Half of Total Populations," www.census.gov/Press-Release/www/releases/archives/population/001720.html, March 18, 2004; "Asians Projected to Lead Next Population Growth Surge," *Houston Chronicle*, May 1, 2004, 3A.

41. "Table 1: United States Population Projections by Race and Hispanic Origin: 2000–2050," www.census.gov/Press-Release, March 18, 2004; "U.S. Census Press Releases: Nation's Population One-Third Minority."

42. "Census Bureau Projects Tripling"; "Asians Projected to Lead Next Population Growth Surge."

43. Associated Press, "Asian Population in U.S. in 2050," *Newsday.com–AP National News*, April 30, 2004, (www.newsday.com/news/nationworld/nation/wire/sns-ap-asians-glance,0,157).

44. "Table 1: United State Population Projections by Race and Hispanic Origin."

45. Ibid.

46. "Census Bureau Projects Tripling"; "Asians Projected to Lead Next Population Growth Surge."

47. "U.S. Census Press Releases: Nation's Population One-Third Minority."

48. "Reports Says Disparities Abound Between Blacks, Whites," *Houston Chronicle*, March 24, 2004, 7A.

49. Ibid.

50. J. Flint, "NBC to Hire More Minorities on TV shows," *The Wall Street Journal*, January 6, 2000, B13.

51. J. Poniewozik, "What's Wrong with This Picture?" *Time*, June 1, 2001 (www.Time.com).

52. Ibid.

53. National Association of Realtors, "Real Estate Industry Adapting to Increasing Cultural Diversity," *PR Newswire*, May 16, 2001.

54. "Toyota Apologizes to African Americans over Controversial Ad," *Kyodo News Service*, Japan, May 23, 2001.

55. J. H. Coplan, "Putting a Little Faith in Diversity," *BusinessWeek Online*, December 21, 2000.

56. Ibid.

57. Ibid.

58. J. N. Cleveland, J. Barnes-Farrell, and J. M. Ratz, "Accommodation in the Workplace," *Human Resource Management Review* 7 (1997), 77–108; A. Colella, "Coworker Distributive Fairness Judgments of the Workplace Accommodations of Employees with Disabilities," *Academy of Management Review* 26 (2001), 100–16.

59. Colella, "Coworker Distributive Fairness Judgments"; D. Stamps, "Just How Scary Is the ADA," *Training* 32 (1995), 93–101; M. S. West and R. L. Cardy, "Accommodating Claims of Disability: The Potential Impact of Abuses," *Human Resource Management Review* 7 (1997), 233–46.

60. G. Koretz, "How to Enable the Disabled," *BusinessWeek*, November 6, 2000 (BusinessWeek Archives).

61. Colella, "Coworker Distributive Fairness Judgments."

62. "Notre Dame Disability Awareness Week 2004 Events," www.nd.edu/~bbuddies/daw.html, April 30, 2004.

63. P. Hewitt, "UH Highlights Abilities, Issues of the Disabled," *Houston Chronicle*, October 22, 2001, 24A.

64. Ibid.

65. J. M. George, "AIDS/AIDS-Related Complex," in L. H. Peters, C. R. Greer, and S. A. Youngblood, eds., *The Blackwell Encyclopedic Dictionary of Human Resource Management* (Oxford, UK: Blackwell, 1997), 6–7.

66. J. M. George "AIDS Awareness Training," in L. H. Peters, C. R. Greer, and S. A. Youngblood, eds., *The Blackwell Encyclopedic Dictionary of Human Resource Management* (Oxford, UK: Blackwell, 1997), 6.

67. S. Armour, "Firms Juggle Stigma, Needs of More Workers with HIV," *USA Today*, September 7, 2000, B1.

68. Ibid.

69. Ibid; S. Vaughn, "Career Challenge; Companies' Work Not Over in HIV and AIDS Education," *Los Angeles Times*, July 8, 2001.

70. R. Brownstein, "Honoring Work Is Key to Ending Poverty," *Detroit News*, October 2, 2001, 9; G. Koretz, "How Welfare to Work Worked," *BusinessWeek*, September 24, 2001 (BusinessWeek Archives).

71. "As Ex-Welfare Recipients Lose Jobs, Offer Safety Net," *The Atlanta Constitution*, October 10, 2001, A18.

72. "Profile of Selected Economic Characteristics: 2000," *American FactFinder* (factfinder.census.gov).

73. U.S. Census Bureau, "Poverty–How the Census Bureau Measures Poverty," *Census 2000*, September 25, 2001.

74. U.S. Census Bureau, "Poverty 2000," www.census.gov, October 26, 2001.

75. I. Lelchuk, "Families Fear Hard Times Getting Worse/$30,000 in the Bay Area Won't Buy Necessities, Survey Says," *San Francisco Chronicle*, September 26, 2001, A13; S. R. Wheeler, "Activists: Welfare-to-Work Changes Needed," *Denver Post*, October 10, 2001, B6.

76. B. Carton, "Bedtime Stories: In 24-Hour Workplace, Day Care Is Moving to the Night Shift," *The Wall Street Journal*, July 6, 2001, A1, A4.

77. Ibid.

78. Ibid.

79. Ibid.

80. "Google View Question: Q: Homosexual Statistics," answers.google.com/answers/threadview?id=271269, April 30, 2004; D. M. Smith and G. Gates, "Gay and Lesbian Families in the United States," *Urban Institute*, May 28, 2006 (www.urban.org/publications/1000491.html).

81. J. Hempel, "Coming Out in Corporate America," *BusinessWeek*, December 15, 2003, 64–72.

82. Ibid.

83. J. Files, "Study Says Discharges Continue Under 'Don't Ask, Don't Tell,'" *The New York Times*, March 24, 2004, A14; J. Files, "Gay Ex-Officers Say 'Don't Ask Doesn't Work," *The New York Times*, December 10, 2003, A14.

84. Hempel, "Coming Out in Corporate America"; "DreamWorks Animation SKG Company History," www.dreamworksanimation.com/dwa/opencms/company/history/index.html, May 29, 2006; J. Chng, "Allan Gilmour: Former Vice-Chairman of Ford Speaks on Diversity," www.harbus.org/media/storage/paper343/news/2006/04/18/News/Allan.Gilmour.Former.ViceChairman.Of.Ford.Speaks.On.Diversity-1859600.shtml?norewrite200606021800&sourcedomain=www.harbus.org, April 18, 2006.

85. Hempel, "Coming Out in Corporate America."

86. Ibid.

87. Ibid.

88. "For Women, Weight May Affect Pay," *Houston Chronicle*, March 4, 2004, 12A.

89. V. Valian, *Why So Slow? The Advancement of Women* (Cambridge, MA: MIT Press, 2000).

90. S. T. Fiske and S. E. Taylor, *Social Cognition*, 2d ed. (New York: McGraw-Hill, 1991); Valian, *Why So Slow?*

91. Valian, *Why So Slow?*

92. S. Rynes and B. Rosen, "A Field Survey of Factors Affecting the Adoption and Perceived Success of Diversity Training," *Personnel Psychology* 48 (1995) 247–70; Valian, *Why So Slow?*

93. V. Brown and F. L. Geis, "Turning Lead into Gold: Leadership by Men and Women and the Alchemy of Social Consensus," *Journal of Personality and Social Psychology* 46 (1984) 811–24; Valian, *Why So Slow?*

94. Valian, *Why So Slow?*

95. J. Cole and B. Singer, "A Theory of Limited Differences: Explaining the Productivity Puzzle in Science," in H. Zuckerman, J. R. Cole, and J. T. Bruer, eds., *The Outer Circle: Women in the Scientific Community* (New York: Norton, 1991), 277–310; M. F. Fox, "Sex, Salary, and Achievement: Reward-Dualism in Academia," *Sociology of Education* 54 (1981) 71–84; J. S. Long, "The Origins of Sex Differences in Science," *Social Forces* 68 (1990) 1297–1315; R. F. Martell, D. M. Lane, and C. Emrich, "Male-Female Differences: A Computer Simulation," *American Psychologist* 51 (1996) 157–58; Valian, *Why So Slow?*

96. Cole and Singer, "A Theory of Limited Differences"; M. F. Fox, "Sex, Salary, and Achievement: Reward-Dualism in Academia," *Sociology of Education* 54 (1981) 71–84; Long, "The Origins of Sex Differences in Science"; R. F. Martell, D. M. Lane, and C. Emrich, "Male-Female Differences: A Computer Simulation," *American Psychologist* 51 (1996) 157–58; Valian, *Why So Slow?*

97. R. Folger and M. A. Konovsky, "Effects of Procedural and Distributive Justice on Reactions to Pay Raise Decisions," *Academy of Management Journal* 32 (1989) 115–30; J. Greenberg, "Organizational Justice: Yesterday, Today, and Tomorrow," *Journal of Management* 16 (1990) 399–402; "O. Janssen, "How Fairness Perceptions Make Innovative Behavior Much or Less Stressful," *Journal of Organizational Behavior* 25 (2004), 201–15.

98. Catalyst, "The Glass Ceiling in 2000: Where Are Women Now?", www.catalystwomen.org, October 21, 2001; Bureau of Labor Statistics, 1999, www.bls.gov; Catalyst, "1999 Census of Women Corporate Officers and Top Earners", www.catalystwomen.org; "1999 Census of Women Board Directors of the Fortune 1000," www.catalystwomen.org; Catalyst, "Women of Color in Corporate Management: Opportunities and Barriers, 1999," www.catalystwomen.org, October 21, 2001.

99. "Household Data Annual Averages," www.bls.gov, April 28, 2004.

100. Ibid.

101. A. M. Jaffe, "At Texaco, the Diversity Skeleton Still Stalks the Halls," *The New York Times*, December 11, 1994, sec. 3, p. 5.

102. Greenberg, "Organizational Justice"; M. G. Ehrhart, "Leadership and Procedural Justice Climate as Antecedents of Unit-Level Organizational Citizenship Behavior," *Personnel Psychology* 57 (2004) 61–94; A. Colella, R. L. Paetzold, and M. A. Belliveau, "Factors Affecting Coworkers' Procedural Justice Inferences of the Workplace Accommodations of Employees with Disabilities," *Personnel Psychology* 57 (2004) 1–23.

103. G. Robinson and K. Dechant, "Building a Case for Business Diversity," *Academy of Management Executive* (1997) 3, 32–47.

104. A. Patterson, "Target 'Micromarkets' Its Way to Success; No 2 Stores Are Alike," *The Wall Street Journal*, May 31, 1995, A1, A9.

105. "The Business Case for Diversity: Experts Tell What Counts, What Works," *DiversityInc.com*, October 23, 2001.

106. B. Hetzer, "Find a Niche—and Start Scratching," *BusinessWeek*, September 14, 1998 (BusinessWeek Archives).

107. K. Aaron, "Woman Laments Lack of Diversity on Boards of Major Companies," *The Times Union*, May 16, 2001 (www.timesunion.com).

108. "The Business Case for Diversity."

109. B. Frankel, "Measuring Diversity Is One Sure Way of Convincing CEOs of Its Value," *DiversityInc.com*, October 5, 2001.

110. A. Stevens, "Lawyers and Clients," *The Wall Street Journal*, June 19, 1995, B7.

111. B. McMenamin, "Diversity Hucksters," *Forbes*, May 22, 1995, 174–76.

112. J. Kahn, "Diversity Trumps the Downturn," *Fortune*, July 9, 2001, 114–16.

113. H. R. Schiffmann, *Sensation and Perception: An Integrated Approach* (New York: Wiley, 1990).

114. A. E. Serwer, "McDonald's Conquers the World," *Fortune*, October 17, 1994, 103–16.

115. S. T. Fiske and S. E. Taylor, *Social Cognition* (Reading, MA: Addison-Wesley, 1984).

116. J. S. Bruner, "Going Beyond the Information Given," in H. Gruber, G. Terrell, and M. Wertheimer, eds., *Contemporary Approaches to Cognition* (Cambridge, MA: Harvard University Press, 1957); Fiske and Taylor, *Social Cognition*.

117. Fiske and Taylor, *Social Cognition*.

118. Valian, *Why So Slow?*

119. D. Bakan, *The Duality of Human Existence* (Chicago: Rand McNally, 1966); J. T. Spence and R. L. Helmreich, *Masculinity and Femininity: Their Psychological Dimensions, Correlates, and Antecedents* (Austin: University of Texas Press, 1978); J. T. Spence and L. L. Sawin, "Images of Masculinity and Femininity: A Reconceptualization," in V. E. O'Leary, R. K. Unger, and B. B. Wallston, eds., *Women, Gender, and Social Psychology* (Hillsdale, NJ: Erlbaum, 1985), 35–66; Valian, *Why So Slow?*

120. Valian, *Why So Slow?*

121. Serwer, "McDonald's Conquers the World"; P. R. Sackett, C. M. Hardison, and M. J. Cullen, "On Interpreting Stereotype Threat as Accounting for African American-White Differences on Cognitive Tests," *American Psychologist* 59, no. 1, (January 2004) 7–13; C. M. Steele and J. A. Aronson, "Stereotype Threat Does Not Live by Steele and Aronson," *American Psychologist* 59, no. 1 (January 2004) 47–55; P. R. Sackett, C. M. Hardison, and M. J. Cullen, "On the Value of Correcting Mischaracterizations of Stereotype Threat Research," *American Psychologist* 59, no. 1 (January 2004), 47–49; D. M. Amodio, E. Harmon-Jones, P. G. Devine, J. J. Curtin, S. L. Hartley, and A. E. Covert, "Neural Signals for the Detection of Unintentional Race Bias," *Psychological Science* 15, no. 2 (2004), 88–93.

122. M. Loden and J. B. Rosener, *Workforce America! Managing Employee Diversity as a Vital Resource* (Burr Ridge, IL: Irwin, 1991).

123. A. Stein Wellner, "The Disability Advantage," *Inc. Magazine*, October 2005, 29–31.

124. "Habitat International: Our Products," www.habitatint.com/products.htm, April 6, 2006; "Habitat International Home Page," www.habitatint.com, April 6, 2006.

125. A. Stein Wellner, "The Disability Advantage," *Inc. Magazine*, October 2005, 29–31.

126. "Habitat International: Our People," www.habitatint.com/people/htm, April 6, 2006.

127. A. Stein Wellner, "The Disability Advantage," *Inc. Magazine*, October 2005, 29–31.

128. Ibid.

129. Ibid.

130. Ibid.

131. Ibid.

132. E. D. Pulakos and K. N. Wexley, "The Relationship Among Perceptual Similarity, Sex, and Performance Ratings in Manager Subordinate Dyads," *Academy of Management Journal* 26 (1983), 129–39.

133. Fiske and Taylor, *Social Cognition*.

134. "Hotel to Pay $8 Million in Settlement," *The Houston Chronicle*, March 22, 2000, 3A; M. France and T. Smart, "The Ugly Talk on the Texaco Tape," *Business Week*, November 18, 1996: 58; J. S. Lublin, "Texaco Case Causes a Stir in Boardrooms," *The Wall Street Journal*, November 22, 1996, B1, B6; T. Smart, "Texaco: Lessons from a Crisis-in-Progress," *BusinessWeek*, December 2, 1996, 44; "Ford Settling Bias Case, Will Hire More Women, Minorities," *The Houston Chronicle*, February 19, 2000, 8C; C. Salter, "A Reformer Who Means Business," *Fast Company*, April 2003, 102-111; A. Zimmerman, "Wal-Mart Appeals Bias-Suit Ruling," *The Wall Street Journal*, August 8, 2005, B5: C. H. Deutsch, "Chief of Unit Files Lawsuit Accusing G.E. of Racial Bias," *The New York Times*, May 18, 2005, C3.

135. N. Alster, "When Gray Heads Roll, Is Age Bias at Work?" *The New York Times*, January 30, 2005, BU3.

136. Ibid.

137. Ibid.

138. Ibid.

139. Ibid.

140. Ibid.

141. Ibid.

142. M. Freudenheim, "Help Wanted: Older Workers Please Apply," *The New York Times*, March 23, 2005, p. A1.

143. Ibid.

144. L. Corghan, "Don't Let 'Rampant' Age Bias Bring You Down in Job Hunt," *The Houston Chronicle*, August 29, 2005, p. D1.

145. A. G. Greenwald and M. Banaji, "Implicit Social Cognition: Attitudes, Self-Esteem, and Stereotypes," *Psychological Review* 102 (1995), 4–27.

146. A. Fisher, "Ask Annie: Five Ways to Promote Diversity in the Workplace," *Fortune*, April 23, 2004 (www.fortune.com/fortune/subs/print/0,15935,455997,00.html); E. Bonabeau, "Don't Trust Your Gut," *Harvard Business Review*, May 2003, 116–23.

147. A. P. Carnevale and S. C. Stone, "Diversity: Beyond the Golden Rule," *Training & Development*, October 1994, 22–39.

148. Fisher, "Ask Annie."

149. B. A. Battaglia, "Skills for Managing Multicultural Teams," *Cultural Diversity at Work* 4 (1992); Carnevale and Stone, "Diversity: Beyond the Golden Rule."

150. Swann et al., "Finding Value in Diversity."

151. Valian, *Why So Slow?*

152. A. P. Brief, R. T. Buttram, R. M. Reizenstein, S. D. Pugh, J. D. Callahan, R. L. McCline, and J. B. Vaslow, "Beyond Good Intentions: The Next Steps Toward Racial Equality in the American Workplace," *Academy of Management Executive*, November 1997, 59–72.

153. Ibid.

154. Ibid.

155. Ibid.

156. Y. Cole, "Linking Diversity to Executive Compensation," *Diversity Inc.*, August–September 2003, 58–62.

157. B. Mandell and S. Kohler-Gray, "Management Development That Values Diversity," *Personnel*, March 1990, 41–47.

158. B. Filipczak, "25 Years of Diversity at UPS," *Training*, August 1992, 42–46.

159. D. A. Thomas, "Race Matters: The Truth About Mentoring Minorities," *Harvard Business Review*, April 2001, 99–107.

160. Ibid.

161. S. N. Mehta, "Why Mentoring Works," *Fortune*, July 9, 2000.

162. Ibid.; Thomas, "Race Matters."

163. "Chevron Settles Claims of 4 Women at Unit as Part of Sex Bias Suit," *The Wall Street Journal*, January 22, 1995, B12.

164. D. K. Berman, "TWA Settles Harassment Claims at JFK Airport for $2.6 Million," *The Wall Street Journal*, June 25, 2001, B6.

165. A. Lambert, "Insurers Help Clients Take Steps to Reduce Sexual Harassment," *Houston Business Journal*, March 19, 2004 (Houston.bizjournals.com/Houston/stories/2004/03/22/focus4.html).

166. T. Segal, "Getting Serious About Sexual Harassment," *BusinessWeek*, November 9, 1992, 78–82.

167. U.S. Equal Employment Opportunity Commission, "Facts About Sexual Harassment," www.eeoc.gov/facts/fs-sex.html, May 1, 2004.

168. B. Carton, "Muscled Out? At Jenny Craig, Men Are Ones Who Claim Sex Discrimination," *The Wall Street Journal*, November 29, 1994, A1, A7.

169. R. L. Paetzold and A. M. O'Leary-Kelly, "Organizational Communication and the Legal Dimensions of Hostile Work Environment Sexual Harassment," in G. L. Kreps, ed., *Sexual Harassment: Communication Implications* (Cresskill, NJ: Hampton Press, 1993).

170. M. Galen, J. Weber, and A. Z. Cuneo, "Sexual Harassment: Out of the Shadows," *Fortune*, October 28, 1991, 30–31.

171. A. M. O'Leary-Kelly, R. L. Paetzold, and R. W. Griffin, "Sexual Harassment as Aggressive Action: A Framework for Understanding Sexual Harassment," paper presented at the annual meeting of the Academy of Management, Vancouver, August 1995.

172. B. S. Roberts and R. A. Mann, "Sexual Harassment in the Workplace: A Primer," www3.uakron.edu/lawrev/robert1.html, May 1, 2004.

173. "Former FedEx Driver Wins EEOC Lawsuit," *Houston Chronicle*, February 26, 2004, 9B.

174. Ibid.

175. J. Robertson, "California Jury Awards $61M for Harassment," http://news.Yahoo.com, June 4, 2006.

176. "2 FedEx Drivers Win Slur Lawsuit," *Houston Chronicle*, June 4, 2006, p. A9.

177. S. J. Bresler and R. Thacker, "Four-Point Plan Helps Solve Harassment Problems," *HR Magazine*, May 1993, 117–24.

178. "Du Pont's Solution," *Training*, March 1992, 29.

179. Ibid.

180. Ibid.

Chapter 6

1. L. J. Bourgeois, "Strategy and Environment: A Conceptual Integration," *Academy of Management Review* 5 (1985), 25–39.

2. M. E. Porter, *Competitive Strategy* (New York: Free Press, 1980).

3. *"Coca-Cola Versus Pepsi-Cola and the Soft Drink Industry,"* Harvard Business School Case 9-391-179.

4. www.splenda.com, 2006.

5. A. K. Gupta and V. Govindarajan, "Cultivating a Global Mind-set," *Academy of Management Executive* 16 (February 2002), 116–27.

6. "Boeing's Worldwide Supplier Network," *Seattle Post–Intelligence*, April 9, 1994, 13.

7. I. Metthee, "Playing a Large Part," *Seattle Post-Intelligence*, April 9, 1994, 13.

8. R. J. Trent and R. M. Monczke, "Pursuing Competitive Advantage Through Integrated Global Sourcing," *Academy of Management Executive* 16 (May 2002), 66–81.

9. R. B. Reich, *The Work of Nations* (New York: Knopf, 1991).

10. "Business: Link in the Global Chain," *The Economist*, June 2, 2001, 62–63.

11. M. E. Porter, *Competitive Advantage* (New York: Free Press, 1985).

12. www.walmart.com, 2004.

13. "The Tech Slump Doesn't Scare Michael Dell, *BusinessWeek*, April 16, 2001, 48.

14. T. Levitt, "The Globalization of Markets," *Harvard Business Review*, May–June 1983, 92–102.

15. "Dell CEO Would Like 40 Percent PC Market Share," www.daily news.yahoo.com, June 20, 2001.

16. For views on barriers to entry from an economics perspective, see Porter, *Competitive Strategy*. For the sociological perspective, see J. Pfeffer and G. R. Salancik, *The External Control of Organization: A Resource Dependence Perspective* (New York: Harper & Row, 1978).

17. Porter, *Competitive Strategy*; J. E. Bain, *Barriers to New Competition* (Cambridge, MA: Harvard University Press, 1956); R. J. Gilbert, "Mobility Barriers and the Value of Incumbency," in R. Schmalensee and R. D. Willig, eds., *Handbook of Industrial Organization*, vol. 1 (Amsterdam: North Holland, 1989).

18. www.amazon.com, press release, May 2001.

19. C. W. L. Hill, "The Computer Industry: The New Industry of Industries," in Hill and Jones, *Strategic Management: An Integrated Approach* (Boston: Houghton Mifflin, 2003).

20. J. Bhagwati, *Protectionism* (Cambridge, MA; MIT Press, 1988).

21. www.yahoo.com, July 18, 2004.

22. J. Schumpeter, *Capitalism, Socialism and Democracy* (London: Macmillan, 1950), 68. Also see R. R. Winter and S. G. Winter, *An Evolutionary Theory of Economic Change* (Cambridge, MA: Harvard University Press, 1982).

Decision Making (New York: Wiley, 1986). Also see Simon, *Administrative Behavior*.

July 3, 2004; I. Halvorson, "Atlantis Gets Ready to Fly: Shuttle Set for August Launch

Problems, *Strategic Management Journal* 1 (1980), 331–42.

"A Framework for Successful Adoption and Performance of Japanese Manufacturing Practices in the United States," *Academy of Management Review* 17 (1992), 677–701.

23. G. Stalk and T. M. Hout, *Competing Against Time* (New York: Free Press, 1990).

24. T. Stundza, "Massachusetts Switch Maker Switches to Kanban," *Purchasing,* November 16, 2000, 103.

25. B. Dumaine, "The Trouble with Teams," *Fortune,* September 5, 1994, 86–92.

26. See C. W. L. Hill, "Transaction Cost Economizing as a Source of National Competitive Advantage: The Case of Japan," *Organization Science,* 2 (1994); M. Aoki, *Information, Incentives, and Bargaining in the Japanese Economy* (Cambridge: Cambridge University Press, 1989).

27. J. Hoerr, "The Payoff from Teamwork," *BusinessWeek,* July 10, 1989, 56–62.

28. M. Hammer and J. Champy, *Re-engineering the Corporation* (New York: HarperBusiness, 1993), 35.

29. Ibid., 46.

30. Ibid.

31. www.dell.com, 2006.

32. Michael Dell, *Direct from Dell: Strategies That Revolutionized an Industry* (New York: HarperBusiness, 1999), 91.

33. www.google.com, 2006.

34. J. S. Adams, "The Structure and Dynamics of Behavior in Boundary Spanning Roles," in M. D. Dunnette, ed., *The Handbook of Industrial and Organizational Psychology* (Chicago: Rand McNally, 1976).

35. For a discussion of sources of organizational inertia, see M. T. Hannah and J. Freeman, "Structural Inertia and Organizational Change," *American Sociological Review* 49 (1984), 149–64.

36. L. Helm and M. Edid, "Life on the Line: Two Auto Workers Who Are Worlds Apart," *BusinessWeek,* September 30, 1994, 76–78.

37. Dumaine, "The Trouble with Teams."

Chapter 10

1. www.homedepot.com, 2006.

2. Ibid.

3. "Renovating Home Depot," www.businessweekonline.com, March 6, 2006.

4. H. R. Weber, "Profits Are Up, Sales Are Not," www.businessweekonline.com, May 16, 2006.

5. G. R. Jones, *Organizational Theory, Design and Change: Text and Cases* (Upper Saddle River: Prentice-Hall, 2003).

6. J. Child, *Organization: A Guide for Managers and Administrators* (New York: Harper & Row, 1977).

7. P. R. Lawrence and J. W. Lorsch, *Organization and Environment* (Boston: Graduate School of Business Administration, Harvard University, 1967).

8. R. Duncan, "What Is the Right Organizational Design?" *Organizational Dynamics,* Winter 1979, 59–80.

9. T. Burns and G. R. Stalker, *The Management of Innovation* (London: Tavistock, 1966).

10. D. Miller, "Strategy Making and Structure: Analysis and Implications for Performance," *Academy of Management Journal* 30 (1987), 7–32.

11. A. D. Chandler, *Strategy and Structure* (Cambridge, MA: MIT Press, 1962).

12. J. Stopford and L. Wells, *Managing the Multinational Enterprise* (London: Longman, 1972).

13. C. Perrow, *Organizational Analysis: A Sociological View* (Belmont, CA: Wadsworth, 1970).

14. F. W. Taylor, *The Principles of Scientific Management* (New York: Harper, 1911).

15. R. W. Griffin, *Task Design: An Integrative Approach* (Glenview, IL: Scott, Foresman, 1982).

16. Ibid.

17. J. R. Hackman and G. R. Oldham, *Work Redesign* (Reading, MA: Addison-Wesley, 1980).

18. J. R. Galbraith and R. K. Kazanjian, *Strategy Implementation: Structure, System, and Process,* 2d ed. (St. Paul, MN: West, 1986).

19. Lawrence and Lorsch, *Organization and Environment.*

20. Jones, *Organizational Theory.*

21. Lawrence and Lorsch, *Organization and Environment.*

22. R. H. Hall, *Organizations: Structure and Process* (Englewood Cliffs, NJ: Prentice-Hall, 1972); R. Miles, *Macro Organizational Behavior* (Santa Monica, CA: Goodyear, 1980).

23. Chandler, *Strategy and Structure.*

24. G. R. Jones and C. W. L. Hill, "Transaction Cost Analysis of Strategy-Structure Choice," *Strategic Management Journal* 9 (1988), 159–72.

25. www.gsk.com, 2006.

26. Ibid.

27. S. M. Davis and P. R. Lawrence, *Matrix* (Reading, MA: Addison-Wesley, 1977); J. R. Galbraith, "Matrix Organization Designs: How to Combine Functional and Project Forms," *Business Horizons* 14 (1971), 29–40.

28. L. R. Burns, "Matrix Management in Hospitals: Testing Theories of Matrix Structure and Development," *Administrative Science Quarterly* 34 (1989), 349–68.

29. C. W. L. Hill, *International Business* (Homewood, IL: Irwin, 2003).

30. Jones, *Organizational Theory.*

31. A. Farnham, "America's Most Admired Company," *Fortune,* February 7, 1994, 50–54.

32. P. Blau, "A Formal Theory of Differentiation in Organizations," *American Sociological Review* 35 (1970), 684–95.

33. S. Grey, "McDonald's CEO Announces Shifts of Top Executives," *The Wall Street Journal,* July 16, 2004, A11.

34. www.mcdonalds.com, 2006.

35. Child, *Organization.*

36. S. McCartney, "Airline Industry's Top-Ranked Woman Keeps Southwest's Small-Fry Spirit Alive," *The Wall Street Journal,* November 30, 1995, B1.

37. www.plexus.com, 2006.

38. W. M. Bulkeley, "Plexus Strategy: Smaller Runs of More Things," *The Wall Street Journal,* October 8, 2003, B1, B12.

39. P. M. Blau and R. A. Schoenherr, *The Structure of Organizations* (New York: Basic Books, 1971).

40. Jones, *Organizational Theory.*

41. www.microsoft.com, 2005, press release.

42. A. Linn, "Microsoft Organizes to Compete Better," www.yahoo.com, September 26, 2005.

43. www.microsoft.com, 2006.

44. Lawrence and Lorsch, *Organization and Environment,* 50–55.

45. J. R. Galbraith, *Designing Complex Organizations* (Reading, MA: Addison-Wesley, 1977), chap. 1; Galbraith and Kazanjian, *Strategy Implementation,* chap. 7.

46. Lawrence and Lorsch, *Organization and Environment,* 55.

47. S. D. N. Cook and D. Yanow, "Culture and Organizational Learning." *Journal of Management Inquiry* 2 (1993), 373–90.

48. www.walmart.com, 2006.

49. "Associates Keystone to Structure," *Chain Store Age,* December, 1999, 17.

50. www.walmart.com, 2006.

51. M. Troy, "The Culture Remains the Constant," *Discount Store News,* June 8, 1998, 95–98.

52. S. Voros, "3D Management," *Management Review,* January 2000, 45–47.

53. "Neurosis, Arkansas-Style," *Fortune,* April 17, 2000, 36.

54. B. Schneider, "The People Make the Place," *Personnel Psychology* 40 (1987), 437–53.

55. J. E. Sheriden, "Organizational Culture and Employee Retention," *Academy of Management Journal* 35 (1992), 657–92.

56. M. Hannan and J. Freeman, "Structural Inertia and Organizational Change," *American Sociological Review* 49 (1984), 149–64.

57. C. A. O'Reilly, J. Chatman, D. F. Caldwell, "People and Organizational Culture: Assessing Person-Organizational Fit," *Academy of Management Journal* 34 (1991), 487–517.

58. T. L. Beauchamp and N. E. Bowie, eds., *Ethical Theory and Business* (Englewood Cliffs, NJ: Prentice-Hall, 1979); A. MacIntyre, *After Virtue* (Notre Dame, IN: University of Notre Dame Press, 1981).

59. A. Sagie and D. Elizur, "Work Values: A Theoretical Overview and a Model of Their Affects," *Journal of Organizational Behavior* 17 (1996), 503–14.

60. G. R. Jones, "Transaction Costs, Property Rights, and Organizational Culture: An Exchange Perspective," *Administrative Science Quarterly* 28 (1983), 454–67.

61. C. Perrow, *Normal Accidents* (New York: Basic Books, 1984).

62. H. Mintzberg, *The Structuring of Organizational Structures* (Englewood Cliffs, NJ: Prentice-Hall, 1979).

63. G. Kunda, *Engineering Culture* (Philadelphia: Temple University Press, 1992).

64. www.nokia.com, 2006.

65. P. de Bendern, "Quirky Culture Paves Nokia's Road to Fortune," www.yahoo.com, 2000.

66. K. E. Weick, *The Social Psychology of Organization* (Reading, MA: Addison-Wesley, 1979).

67. J. W. Schulz, L. C. Hauck, and R. M. Hauck, "Using the Power of Corporate Culture to Achieve Results: A Case Study of Sunflower Electric Power Corporation," *Management Quarterly* 2 (2001), 2–19.

68. J. P. Kotter and J. L. Heskett, *Corporate Culture and Performance* (New York: Free Press, 1992).

69. Copyright © 2006, Gareth R. Jones.

Chapter 11

1. www.microsoft.com, 2006.

2. O. Thomas, "Microsoft Employees Feel Maligned," www.money.cnn.com, March 10 2006.

3. J. Nightingale, "Rising Frustration with Microsoft's Compensation and Review System," www.washtech.org, March 10, 2006.

4. Ibid.

5. "Microsoft's Departing Employees." www.yahoo.news.com, May 6, 2006.

6. W. G. Ouchi, "Markets, Bureaucracies, and Clans," *Administrative Science Quarterly* 25 (1980), 129–41.

7. P. Lorange, M. Morton, and S. Ghoshal, *Strategic Control* (St. Paul, MN: West, 1986).

8. H. Koontz and R. W. Bradspies, "Managing Through Feedforward Control," *Business Horizons,* June 1972, 25–36.

9. E. E. Lawler III and J. G. Rhode, *Information and Control in Organizations* (Pacific Palisades, CA: Goodyear, 1976).

10. C. W. L. Hill and G. R. Jones, *Strategic Management: An Integrated Approach,* 6th ed. (Boston: Houghton Mifflin, 2003).

11. W. M. Bulkeley and J. S. Lublin, "Xerox Appoints Insider Mulcahy to Execute Turnaround as CEO," *The Wall Street Journal,* July 27, 2001, A2.

12. E. Flamholtz, "Organizational Control Systems as a Management Tool," *California Management Review,* Winter 1979, 50–58.

13. W. G. Ouchi, "The Transmission of Control Through Organizational Hierarchy," *Academy of Management Journal* 21 (1978), 173–92.

14. W. G. Ouchi, "The Relationship Between Organizational Structure and Organizational Control," *Administrative Science Quarterly* 22 (1977), 95–113.

15. Ouchi, "Markets, Bureaucracies, and Clans."

16. W. H. Newman, *Constructive Control* (Englewood Cliffs, NJ: Prentice-Hall, 1975).

17. J. D. Thompson, *Organizations in Action* (New York: McGraw-Hill, 1967).

18. R. N. Anthony, *The Management Control Function* (Boston: Harvard Business School Press, 1988).

19. Ouchi, "Markets, Bureaucracies, and Clans."

20. Hill and Jones, *Strategic Management.*

21. R. Simons, "Strategic Orientation and Top Management Attention to Control Systems," *Strategic Management Journal* 12 (1991), 49–62.

22. G. Schreyogg and H. Steinmann, "Strategic Control: A New Perspective," *Academy of Management Review* 12 (1987), 91–103.

23. B. Woolridge and S. W. Floyd, "The Strategy Process, Middle Management Involvement, and Organizational Performance," *Strategic Management Journal* 11 (1990), 231–41.

24. J. A. Alexander, "Adaptive Changes in Corporate Control Practices," *Academy of Management Journal* 34 (1991), 162–93.

25. www.gillette.com, 2004.

26. Hill and Jones, *Strategic Management.*

27. G. H. B. Ross, "Revolution in Management Control," *Management Accounting* 72 (1992), 23–27.

28. K. Naughton, "The Blue-Collar CEO," *Newsweek,* December 5, 2005, pp. 4–6.

29. www.daimlerchrysler.com, 2005.

30. Naughton, "The Blue-Collar CEO."

31. P. F. Drucker, *The Practice of Management* (New York: Harper & Row, 1954).

32. S. J. Carroll and H. L. Tosi, *Management by Objectives: Applications and Research* (New York: Macmillan, 1973).

33. R. Rodgers and J. E. Hunter, "Impact of Management by Objectives on Organizational Productivity," *Journal of Applied Psychology* 76 (1991), 322–26.

34. M. B. Gavin, S. G. Green, and G. T. Fairhurst, "Managerial Control Strategies for Poor Performance over Time and the Impact on Subordinate Reactions," *Organizational Behavior and Human Decision Processes* 63 (1995), 207–21.

35. www.cypress.com, 2001.

36. B. Dumaine, "The Bureaucracy Busters," *Fortune,* June 17, 1991, 46.

37. D. S. Pugh, D. J. Hickson, C. R. Hinings, and C. Turner, "Dimensions of Organizational Structure," *Administrative Science Quarterly* 13 (1968), 65–91.

38. B. Elgin, "Running the Tightest Ships on the Net," *Business Week,* January 29, 2001, 125–26.

39. P. M. Blau, *The Dynamics of Bureaucracy* (Chicago: University of Chicago Press, 1955).

40. Ouchi, "Markets, Bureaucracies, and Clans."

41. Ibid.

42. www.ups.com, 2004.

43. J. Van Maanen, "Police Socialization: A Longitudinal Examination of Job Attitudes in an Urban Police Department," *Administrative Science Quarterly* 20 (1975), 207–28.

44. This section draws heavily on K. Lewin, *Field Theory in Social Science* (New York: Harper & Row, 1951).

45. L. Chung-Ming and R. W. Woodman, "Understanding Organizational Change: A Schematic Perspective," *Academy of Management Journal* 38, no. 2 (1995), 537–55.

46. D. Miller, "Evolution and Revolution: A Quantum View of Structural Change in Organizations," *Journal of Management Studies* 19 (1982), 11–151; D. Miller, "Momentum and Revolution in Organizational Adaptation," *Academy of Management Journal* 2 (1980), 591–614.

47. C. E. Lindblom, "The Science of Muddling Through," *Public Administration Review* 19 (1959), 79–88; P. C. Nystrom and W. H. Starbuck, "To Avoid Organizational Crises, Unlearn," *Organizational Dynamics* 12 (1984), 53–65.

48. L. Brown, "Research Action: Organizational Feedback, Understanding and Change," *Journal of Applied Behavioral Research* 8 (1972), 697–711; P. A. Clark, *Action Research and Organizational Change* (New York: Harper & Row, 1972); N. Margulies and A. P. Raia, eds., *Conceptual Foundations of Organizational Development* (New York: McGraw-Hill, 1978).

49. W. L. French and C. H. Bell, *Organizational Development* (Englewood Cliffs, NJ: Prentice-Hall, 1990).

50. W. L. French, "A Checklist for Organizing and Implementing an OD Effort," in W. L. French, C. H. Bell, and R. A. Zawacki, eds., *Organizational Development and Transformation* (Homewood, IL: Irwin, 1994), 484–95.

Chapter 12

1. "Who's in Charge Here? No one," *The Observer,* April 27, 2003 (http://observer.guardian.co.uk/business/story/0,6903,944138,00.html); "Ricardo Semler, CEO, Semco SA," cnn.com, June 29, 2004 (http://cnn.worldnews.printthis.clickability.com/pt/cpt&title=cnn.com); D. Kirkpatrick, "The Future of Work: An 'Apprentice'-Style

Office?" *Fortune,* April 14, 2004 (www.fortune.com/fortune/subs/print/0,15935,611068,00.html); A. Strutt and R. Van Der Beek, "Report from HR2004," www.mce.be/hr2004/reportd2.htm, July 2, 2004; R. Semler, "Seven-Day Weekend Returns Power to Employees," workopolis.com, May 26, 2004 (http://globeandmail.workopolis.com/servlet/content/qprinter/20040526/cabooks26); "SEMCO," http://semco.locaweb.com.br/ingles, May 31, 2006; "Ricardo Semler, Semco SA: What Are You Reading?" cnn.com, May 31, 2006. (www.cnn.com/2004/BUSINESS/06/29/semler.profile/index.html).

2.   R. Semler, *The Seven-Day Weekend: Changing the Way Work Works* (New York: Penguin, 2003); "SEMCO."

3.   Ibid.

4.   Ibid.

5.   R. Semler, "Managing Without Managers," *Harvard Business Review* 67, no. 5 (September-October 1989), 76–84; R. Semler, "Why My Former Employees Still Work for Me," *Harvard Business Review* 72, no. 1, (January-February 1994), 64–74; "Personal Histories: Leaders Remember the Moments and People That Shaped Them," *Harvard Business Review,* Reprint R0111B (December 2001); R. Semler, "Leading by Omission," *MITWorld,* May 31, 2006 (http://mitworld.mit.edu/video/308/); "PMI Global Congress 2005–Latin America Exceeds Expectations," www.pmi.org/prod/groups/public/documents/info/ap_news-lacongress.asp, May 31, 2006; "Leaders in London Summit 2006: Ricardo Semler," www.leadersinlondon.com/bio_Riccardo_Semler.asp, May 31, 2006.

6.   A. Strutt, "Interview with Ricardo Semler," *Management Centre Europe,* April 2004 (www.mce.be/knowledge/392/35).

7.   Semler, *The Seven-Day Weekend.*

8.   Ibid.

9.   "Extreme Flextime," *Inc.,* April 2004, 91.

10.   Semler, *The Seven-Day Weekend.*

11.   R. Semler, "How We Went *Digital* Without a *Strategy,*" *Harvard Business Review* 78, no. 5 (September–October 2000), 51–56.

12.   Ibid.

13.   Semler, *The Seven-Day Weekend.*

14.   J. E. Butler, G. R. Ferris, and N. K. Napier, *Strategy and Human Resource Management* (Cincinnati: Southwestern Publishing, 1991); P. M. Wright and G. C. McMahan, "Theoretical Perspectives for Strategic Human Resource Management," *Journal of Management* 18 (1992), 295–320.

15.   L. Clifford, "Why You Can Safely Ignore Six Sigma," *Fortune,* January 22, 2001, 140.

16.   S. J. Palmisano, "How the U.S. Can Keep Its Innovation Edge," *BusinessWeek,* November 17, 2003, 34.

17.   F. Warner, "Brains for Sale," *Fast Company,* January 2004, 88–89; www.ibm.com, June 4, 2006.

18.   Warner, "Brains for Sale"; "JPMorgan Chase," www.jpmorganchase.com/cm/cs?pagename=Templates/Page/JPMC_CacheHome&cid=8014123, May 31, 2006.

19.   Warner, "Brains for Sale."

20.   Ibid.

21.   S. Hamm, "Big Blue Shift," *BusinessWeek Online,* June 5, 2006 (www.businessweek.com/magazine/content/06_23/b3987093.htm?campaign_id=search).

22.   Ibid.

23.   Ibid.

24.   J. B. Quinn, P. Anderson, and S. Finkelstein, "Managing Professional Intellect: Making the Most of the Best," *Harvard Business Review,* March–April 1996, 71–80.

25.   Ibid.

26.   C. D. Fisher, L. F. Schoenfeldt, and J. B. Shaw, *Human Resource Management* (Boston: Houghton Mifflin, 1990).

27.   Wright and McMahan, "Theoretical Perspectives."

28.   L. Baird and I. Meshoulam, "Managing Two Fits for Strategic Human Resource Management," *Academy of Management Review* 14, 116–28; J. Milliman, M. Von Glinow, and M. Nathan, "Organizational Life Cycles and Strategic International Human Resource Management in Multinational Companies: Implications for Congruence Theory," *Academy of Management Review* 16 (1991), 318–39; R. S. Schuler and S. E. Jackson, "Linking Competitive Strategies with Human Resource Management Practices," *Academy of Management Executive* 1 (1987), 207–19; P. M. Wright and S. A. Snell, "Toward an Integrative View of Strategic Human Resource Management," *Human Resource Management Review* 1 (1991), 203–225.

29.   Equal Employment Opportunity Commission, "Uniform Guidelines on Employee Selection Procedures," *Federal Register* 43 (1978), 38290–315.

30.   R. Stogdill II, R. Mitchell, K. Thurston, and C. Del Valle, "Why AIDS Policy Must Be a Special Policy," *BusinessWeek,* February 1, 1993, 53–54.

31.   J. M. George, "AIDS/AIDS-Related Complex," in L. Peters, B. Greer, and S. Youngblood, eds., *The Blackwell Encyclopedic Dictionary of Human Resource Management* (Oxford, England: Blackwell Publishers, 1997).

32.   Ibid.

33.   J. M. George, "AIDS Awareness Training," in Peters et al., *The Blackwell Encyclopedic Dictionary;* Stogdill et al., "Why AIDS Policy Must Be a Special Policy."

34.   J. Helyar, "50 and Fired," *Fortune,* May 16, 2005, 78–90.

35.   S. Clifford, "Saying No to Retirement," *Inc. Magazine,* September 2005, 27–29; "Demographic Profile of American Baby Boomers," www.metlife.com/Applications/Corporate/WPS/CDA/PageGenerator/0,,P88 95 AP,0. . . , May 5, 2006; "Baby Boomer," www.wikipedia.org, May 2, 2006 (http://en.wikipedia.org/wiki/Baby_boomer); "The Baby Boomer Generation–Trends, Research, Discussion and Comment," *Aging Hipsters: The Baby Boomer Generation,* May 2, 2006 (www.aginghipsters.com).

36.   Helyar, "50 and Fired."

37.   Ibid.

38.   Ibid.

39.   Ibid.

40.   Ibid.

41.   Ibid.

42.   S. L. Rynes, "Recruitment, Job Choice, and Post-Hire Consequences: A Call for New Research Directions," in M. D. Dunnette and L. M. Hough, eds., *Handbook of Industrial and Organizational Psychology,* vol. 2 (Palo Alto, CA: Consulting Psychologists Press, 1991), 399–444.

43.   R. L. Sullivan, "Lawyers a la Carte," *Forbes,* September 11, 1995, 44.

44.   E. Porter, "Send Jobs to India? U.S. Companies Say It's Not Always Best," *The New York Times,* April 28, 2004, A1, A7.

45.   D. Wessel, "The Future of Jobs: New Ones Arise; Wage Gap Widens," *The Wall Street Journal,* April 2, 2004, A1, A5; "Relocating the Back Office," *The Economist,* December 13, 2003, 67–69.

46.   Porter, "Send Jobs to India?"

47.   Ibid.

48.   "Learning to Live with Offshoring," *BusinessWeek,* January 30, 2006, 122.

49.   "Offshoring: Spreading the Gospel," *BusinessWeek Online,* March 6, 2006 (www.businessweek.com/print/magazine/content/06_10/b3974074.htm?chan=gl).

50.   "Offshoring: Spreading the Gospel; "Genpact: Management Team," www.genpact.com/aboutus.asp?key=1&page=team.htm&submenu=0, April 25, 2006; "Genpact," www.genpact.com/genpact/aboutus?key=1, April 25, 2006,; "Genpact: Growth History," www.genpact.com/genpact/aboutus.asp?key=1&page=growth.htm, April 25, 2006.

51.   "Genpact: Management Team; "Genpact."

52.   "Offshoring: Spreading the Gospel."

53.   Ibid.

54.   R. J. Harvey, "Job Analysis," in Dunnette and Hough, *Handbook of Industrial and Organizational Psychology,* 71–163.

55.   E. L. Levine, *Everything You Always Wanted to Know About Job Analysis: A Job Analysis Primer* (Tampa, FL: Mariner Publishing, 1983).

56. R. L. Mathis and J. H. Jackson, *Human Resource Management*, 7th ed. (Minneapolis: West, 1994).

57. E. J. McCormick, P. R. Jeannerette, and R. C. Mecham, *Position Analysis Questionnaire* (West Lafayette, IN: Occupational Research Center, Department of Psychological Sciences, Purdue University, 1969).

58. Fisher et al., *Human Resource Management;* Mathis and Jackson, *Human Resource Management;* R. A. Noe, J. R. Hollenbeck, B. Gerhart, and P. M. *Wright, Human Resource Management: Gaining a Competitive Advantage* (Burr Ridge, IL: Irwin, 1994).

59. Fisher et al., *Human Resource Management;* E. J. McCormick, *Job Analysis: Methods and Applications* (New York: American Management Association, 1979); E. J. McCormick and P. R. Jeannerette, "The Position Analysis Questionnaire" in S. Gael ed., *The Job Analysis Handbook for Business, Industry, and Government* (New York: Wiley, 1988); Noe et al., *Human Resource Management.*

60. Rynes, "Recruitment, Job Choice, and Post-Hire Consequences."

61. R. Sharpe, "The Life of the Party? Can Jeff Taylor Keep the Good Times Rolling at Monster.com?," *BusinessWeek,* June 4, 2001 (*BusinessWeek* Archives).

62. www.monster.com, June 2001.

63. www.jobline.org, Jobline press releases, May 8, 2001, accessed June 20, 2001.

64. S. L. Premack and J. P. Wanous, "A Meta-Analysis of Realistic Job Preview Experiments," *Journal of Applied Psychology* 70, (1985) 706–19; J. P. Wanous, "Realistic Job Previews: Can a Procedure to Reduce Turnover also Influence the Relationship Between Abilities and Performance?" *Personnel Psychology* 31, (1978) 249–58; J. P. Wanous, *Organizational Entry: Recruitment, Selection, and Socialization of Newcomers* (Reading, MA: Addison-Wesley, 1980).

65. R. M. Guion, "Personnel Assessment, Selection, and Placement," in Dunnette and Hough, *Handbook of Industrial and Organizational Psychology,* 327–97.

66. T. Joyner, "Job Background Checks Surge," *Houston Chronicle,* May 2, 2005, D6.

67. "RadioShack CEO Quits in Résumé Scandal," www.cbc.ca/story/business/national/2006/02/20/shack-060220.html, February 20, 2006.

68. Joyner, "Job Background Checks Surge"; "ADP News Releases: Employer Services: ADP Hiring Index Reveals Background Checks Performed More than Tripled Since 1997," *Automatic Data Processing, Inc.,* June 3, 2006 (www.investquest.com/iq/a/aud/ne/news/adp042505background.htm).

69. "ADP News Releases."

70. J. McGregor, "Background Checks That Never End," *BusinessWeek Online,* March 20,

2006 (www.businessweek.com/magazine/content/06_12/b3976065.htm?campaign_id=search).

71. Ibid.

72. J. Gangemi, "Small Biz Screens for Work Status," *BusinessWeek Online,* June 1, 2006 (www.businessweek.com/smallbiz/content/jun2006/sb20060601_691438.htm?campaign_id=search).

73. "Form I–9, Employment Eligibility Verification," www.uscis.gov/text/formsfee/forms/i-9,htm, June 3, 2006; Gangemi, "Small Biz Screens for Work Status.

74. Gangemi, "Small Biz Screens for Work Status."

75. McGregor, "Background Checks That Never End."

76. Gangemi, "Small Biz Screens for Work Status."

77. Noe et al., *Human Resource Management;* J. A. Wheeler and J. A. Gier, "Reliability and Validity of the Situational Interview for a Sales Position," *Journal of Applied Psychology* 2 (1987), 484–87.

78. Noe et al., *Human Resource Management.*

79. J. Flint, "Can You Tell Applesauce from Pickles?" *Forbes,* October 9, 1995, 106–08.

80. Ibid.

81. "Wanted: Middle Managers, Audition Required," *The Wall Street Journal,* December 28, 1995, A1.

82. I. L. Goldstein, "Training in Work Organizations," in Dunnette and Hough, *Handbook of Industrial and Organizational Psychology,* 507–619.

83. S. Overman, "Ethan Allen's Secret Weapon," *HRMagazine,* May 1994, 61.

84. N. Banerjee, "For Mary Kay Sales Reps in Russia, Hottest Shade Is the Color of Money," *The Wall Street Journal,* August 30, 1995, A8.

85. T. D. Allen, L. T. Eby, M. L. Poteet, E. Lentz, and L. Lima, "Career Benefits Associated with Mentoring for Protégés: A Meta-Analysis," *Journal of Applied Psychology* 89, no. 1, (2004), 127–36.

86. L. A. Tyson, "Vice President, Investor Relations and Global Corporate Communications," Dell.com, June 3, 2006 (www.dell.com/content/topics/global.aspx/corp/biographies/en/lynn-tyson?c=us&l=en . . .).

87. P. Garfinkel, "Putting a Formal Stamp on Mentoring," *The New York Times,* January 18, 2004, BU10.

88. Ibid.

89. Ibid.

90. Allen et al., "Career Benefits Associated with Mentoring"; L. Levin, "Lesson Learned: Know Your Limits. Get Outside Help Sooner Rather than Later," *BusinessWeek Online,* July 5, 2004 (www.businessweek.com); "Family, Inc.," *BusinessWeek Online,* November 10, 2003 (www.businessweek.com); J. Salamon, "A Year

with a Mentor. Now Comes the Test," *The New York Times,* September 30, 2003, B1, B5.

91. Garfinkel, "Putting a Formal Stamp on Mentoring."

92. J. A. Byrne, "Virtual B-Schools," *BusinessWeek,* October 23, 1995, 64–68.

93. Fisher et al., *Human Resource Management.*

94. Ibid; G. P. Latham and K. N. Wexley, *Increasing Productivity Through Performance Appraisal* (Reading, MA: Addison-Wesley, 1982).

95. T. A. DeCotiis, "An Analysis of the External Validity and Applied Relevance of Three Rating Formats," *Organizational Behavior and Human Performance* 19 (1977), 247–66; Fisher et al., *Human Resource Management.*

96. J. Muller, K. Kerwin, D. Welch, P. L. Moore, D. Brady, "Ford: It's Worse Than You Think," *BusinessWeek,* June 25, 2001 (*BusinessWeek* Archives).

97. Ibid.

98. L. M. Sixel, "Enron Rating Setup Irks Many Workers," *Houston Chronicle,* February 26, 2001, 1C.

99. J. S. Lublin, "It's Shape-Up Time for Performance Reviews," *The Wall Street Journal,* October 3, 1994, B1, B2.

100. A. Serwer, "The Education of Michael Dell," *Fortune,* March 7, 2005, 73–82.

101. Ibid.

102. J. S. Lublin, "Turning the Tables: Underlings Evaluate Bosses," *The Wall Street Journal,* October 4, 1994, B1, B14; S. Shellenbarger, "Reviews from Peers Instruct–and Sting," *The Wall Street Journal,* October 4, 1994, B1, B4.

103. C. Borman and D. W. Bracken, "360 Degree Appraisals," in C. L. Cooper and C. Argyris, eds., *The Concise Blackwell Encyclopedia of Management* (Oxford, England: Blackwell Publishers, 1998), 17; D. W. Bracken, "Straight Talk About Multi-Rater Feedback," *Training and Development* 48 (1994), 44–51; M. R. Edwards, W. C. Borman, and J. R. Sproul, "Solving the Double-Bind in Performance Appraisal: A Saga of Solves, Sloths, and Eagles," *Business Horizons* 85 (1985), 59–68.

104. M. A. Peiperl, "Getting 360⁰ Feedback Right," *Harvard Business Review,* January 2001, 142–47.

105. A. Harrington, "Workers of the World, Rate Your Boss!" *Fortune,* September 18, 2000, 340, 342; www.ImproveNow.com, June 2001.

106. Ibid.

107. Lublin, "It's Shape-Up Time for Performance Reviews."

108. S. E. Moss and J. I. Sanchez, "Are Your Employees Avoiding You? Managerial Strategies for Closing the Feedback Gap," *Academy of Management Executive* 18, no. 1 (2004), 32–46.

109. J. Flynn and F. Nayeri, "Continental Divide over Executive Pay," *BusinessWeek,* July 3, 1995, 40–41.

110. J. A. Byrne, "How High Can CEO Pay Go?" *BusinessWeek*, April 22, 1996, 100–06.

111. "Executive Pay," *BusinessWeek*, April 19, 2004, 106–10.

112. A. Borrus, "A Battle Royal Against Regal Paychecks," *BusinessWeek*, February 24, 2003, 127; "Too Many Turkeys," *The Economist*, November 26, 2005, 75–76; G. Morgenson, "How to Slow Runaway Executive Pay," *The New York Times*, October 23, 2005, 1, 4.

113. "Executive Pay."

114. L. Lavelle, "The Gravy Train May Be Drying Up," *BusinessWeek*, April 5, 2004, 52–53.

115. C. Terhune, B. McKay, C. Mollenkamp, and J. S. Lublin, "Coke Tradition: CEOs Go Better with a Fat Send-Off," *Wall Street Journal*, June 11, 2004, B1, B3.

116. Ibid.

117. Ibid.

118. M. Liedtke, "Shareholders Sue Hewlett-Packard over Fiorina Severance Pay," *LAW.com*, June 3, 2006 (www.law.com/jsp/law/LawArticleFriendly.jsp?id=114172591292).

119. Terhune et al., "Coke Tradition."

120. "Executive Pay."

121. E. Tahmincioglu, "Paths to Better Health (On the Boss's Nickel)," *The New York Times*, May 23, 2004, BU7.

122. Ibid.

123. C. Kleiman, "Babe in Arms Benefit Pays Off in Loyalty," *Houston Chronicle*, January 26, 2004, 1D, 3D.

124. Ibid.

125. S. Shellenbarger, "Amid Gay Marriage Debate, Companies Offer More Benefits to Same-Sex Couples," *The Wall Street Journal*, March 18, 2004, D1.

126. S. Premack and J. E. Hunter, "Individual Unionization Decisions," *Psychological Bulletin* 103 (1988), 223–34.

127. M. B. Regan, "Shattering the AFL-CIO's Glass Ceiling," *BusinessWeek*, November 13, 1995, 46.

128. www.aflcio.org, June 2001.

129. G. P. Zachary, "Some Unions Step Up Organizing Campaigns and Get New Members," *The Wall Street Journal*, September 1, 1995, A1, A2.

130. Regan, "Shattering the AFL-CIO's Glass Ceiling"; www.aflcio.org, June 2001; R. S. Dunham, "Big Labor: So Out It's 'Off the Radar Screen,'" *BusinessWeek*, March 26, 2001 (*BusinessWeek* Archives).

131. "The Honorable Elaine L. Chao United States Secretary of Labor," www.dol.gov/dol/sec/public/aboutsec/chao.htm, June 25, 2001.

132. R. Blumenstein, "Ohio Strike That Is Crippling GM Plants Is Tied to Plan to Outsource Brake Work," *The Wall Street Journal*, March 12, 1996, A3–A4.

133. J. Hannah, "GM Workers Agree to End Strike," *Bryan-College Station Eagle*, March 23, 1996, A12.

Chapter 13

1. M. Duff, "Top-Shelf Employees Keep Container Store on Track," www.looksmart.com, www.findarticles.com, March 8, 2004; M. K. Ammenheuser, "The Container Store Helps People Think Inside the Box," www.icsc.org, May 2004; "The Container Store: Store Location," www.containerstore.com/find/index/jhtml, June 5, 2006.

2. "Learn About Us," www.containerstore.com, June 26, 2001.

3. Ibid.

4. J. Schlosser and J. Sung, "The 100 Best Companies to Work For," *Fortune*, January 8, 2001, 148-68. ""Fortune 100 Best Companies to Work For 2006," cnn.com, June 5, 2006, (http://money.cnn.com/magazines/fortune/bestcompanies/snapshots/359.html)."

5. "The Container Store," www.careerbuilder.com, July 13, 2004; "Tom Takes Re-imagine to PBS," *Case Studies*, www.tompeters.com, March 15, 2004; "2004 Best Companies to Work For," www.fortune.com, July 12, 2004; "Fortune 100 Best Companies to Work For 2006," cnn.com, June 5, 2006, (http://money.cnn.com/magazines/fortune/bestcompanies/snapshots/359.html).

6. D. Roth, "My Job at the Container Store," *Fortune*, January 10, 2000 (www.fortune.com, June 26, 2001).

7. "Fortune 2004: 100 Best Companies to Work For," www.containerstore.com/careers/FortunePR_2004.jhtml?message=/repository/messages/fortuneCareer.jhtml, January 12, 2004.

8. R. Levering, M. Moskowitz, and S. Adams, "The 100 Best Companies to Work For," *Fortune* 149, no. 1 (2004), 56–78.

9. T. A. Stewart, "Just Think: No Permission Needed," *Fortune*, January 8, 2001 (www.fortune.com, June 26, 2001).

10. "The Container Store Tops *Fortune*'s 100 Best List for Second Year in a Row," www.containerstore.com, December 18, 2000.

11. "The Container Store Sells Products That Are Difficult to Sell," *San Gabriel Valley Tribune*, July 12, 2004 (docs.newsbank.com); D. De Marco, "Eager Workers Train at Washington D.C.'s Soon-to-Open Container Store," *Knight Ridder Tribune Business News*, February 27, 2004 (gateway.proquest.com); "The Foundation Is Organization," *The Container Store*, June 5, 2006

(www.containerstore.com/careers/foundation.jhtml); A. Wilson, "Container Store Owner Makes Customer Service a Priority," *Rice News*, April 20, 2006, 5.

12. Roth, "My Job at the Container Store."

13. Stewart, "Just Think: No Permission Needed."

14. R. Yu, "Some Texas Firms Start Wellness Programs to Encourage Healthier Workers," *Knight Ridder Tribune Business News*, July 7, 2004 (gateway.proquest.com); Levering et al., "The 100 Best Companies to Work For."

15. Roth, "My Job at the Container Store."; "The Foundation Is Organization."

16. R. Kanfer, "Motivation Theory and Industrial and Organizational Psychology," in M. D. Dunnette and L. M. Hough, eds., *Handbook of Industrial and Organizational Psychology*, 2d ed., vol. 1 (Palo Alto, CA: Consulting Psychologists Press, 1990), 75–170.

17. Stewart, "Just Think: No Permission Needed."

18. Roth, "My Job at the Container Store."

19. G. P. Latham & M.H. Budworth, "The Study of Work Motivation in the 20th Century," in L.L. Koppes, ed., *Historical Perspectives in Industrial and Organizational Psychology* (Hillsdale, NJ: Laurence Erlbaum, 2006).

20. L. Hales, "An Environmental Problem Slipping Through the Quacks," *washingtonpost.com*, August 27, 2005 (www.washingtonpost.com/wp-dyn/content/article/2005/08/26/AR2005082601888).

21. M. Conlin and P. Raeburn, "Industrial Evolution," *Business Week*, April 8, 2002, 70–72.

22. Ibid.

23. "Masters of Design: William McDonough," *Fastcompany.com*, April 18, 2006 (www.fastcompany.com/magazine/83/mod_mcdonough.html); "William McDonough, FAIA," www.mcdonough.com, April 18, 2006.

24. "Masters of Design: William McDonough."

25. Ibid.

26. "Designing the Future," msnbc.com, April 18, 2006 (www.msnbc.com/id/7773650/site/newsweek/?artid=1130).

27. N. Nicholson, "How to Motivate Your Problem People," *Harvard Business Review*, January 2003, 57–65.

28. J. P. Campbell and R. D. Pritchard, "Motivation Theory in Industrial and Organizational Psychology," in M. D. Dunnette, ed., *Handbook of Industrial and Organizational Psychology* (Chicago: Rand McNally, 1976), 63–130; T. R. Mitchell, "Expectancy Value Models in Organizational Psychology," in N. T. Feather, ed., *Expectations*

and Actions: Expectancy Value Models in Psychology (Hillsdale, NJ: Erlbaum, 1982), 293–312; V. H. Vroom, *Work and Motivation* (New York: Wiley, 1964).

29. N. Shope Griffin, "Personalize Your Management Development," *Harvard Business Review* 8, no. 10, 2003, 113–119.

30. Stewart, "Just Think: No Permission Needed."

31. M. Copeland, "Best Buy's Selling Machine," *Business 2.0,* July 2004, 91-102; L. Heller, "Best Buy Still Turning on the Fun," *DSN Retailing Today* 43, no. 13, (July 5, 2004), 3; S. Pounds, "Big-Box Retailers Cash In on South Florida Demand for Home Computer Repair," *Knight Ridder Tribune Business News,* July 5, 2004 (gateway.proquest.com); J. Bloom, "Best Buy Reaps the Rewards of Risking Marketing Failure," *Advertising Age* 75, no. 25, (June 21, 2004), 16; L. Heller, "Discount Turns Up the Volume: PC Comeback, Ipod Popularity Add Edge," *DSN Retailing Today* 43, no. 13 (July 5, 2004), 45; www.bestbuy.com, June 8, 2006.

32. T. J. Maurer, E. M. Weiss, and F. G. Barbeite, "A Model of Involvement in Work-Related Learning and Development Activity: The Effects of Individual, Situational, Motivational, and Age Variables," *Journal of Applied Psychology* 88, no. 4 (2003), 707–24.

33. J. Kaufman, "How Cambodians Came to Control California Doughnuts," *The Wall Street Journal,* February 22, 1995, A1, A8.

34. A. H. Maslow, *Motivation and Personality* (New York: Harper & Row, 1954); Campbell and Pritchard, "Motivation Theory in Industrial and Organizational Psychology."

35. Kanfer, "Motivation Theory and Industrial and Organizational Psychology."

36. S. Ronen, "An Underlying Structure of Motivational Need Taxonomies: A Cross-Cultural Confirmation," in H. C. Triandis, M. D. Dunnette, and L. M. Hough, eds., *Handbook of Industrial and Organizational Psychology,* vol. 4 (Palo Alto, CA: Consulting Psychologists Press, 1994), 241–69.

37. N. J. Adler, *International Dimensions of Organizational Behavior,* 2d ed. (Boston: P.W.S.-Kent, 1991); G. Hofstede, "Motivation, Leadership and Organization: Do American Theories Apply Abroad?" *Organizational Dynamics,* Summer 1980, 42–63.

38. C. P. Alderfer, "An Empirical Test of a New Theory of Human Needs," *Organizational Behavior and Human Performance* 4 (1969), 142–75; C. P. Alderfer, *Existence, Relatedness, and Growth: Human Needs in Organizational Settings* (New York: Free Press, 1972); Campbell and Pritchard, "Motivation Theory in Industrial and Organizational Psychology."

39. Kanfer, "Motivation Theory and Industrial and Organizational Psychology."

40. F. Herzberg, *Work and the Nature of Man* (Cleveland: World, 1966).

41. N. King, "Clarification and Evaluation of the Two-Factor Theory of Job Satisfaction," *Psychological Bulletin* 74 (1970), 18–31; E. A. Locke, "The Nature and Causes of Job Satisfaction," in Dunnette, *Handbook of Industrial and Organizational Psychology,* 1297–1349.

42. D. C. McClelland, *Human Motivation* (Glenview, IL: Scott, Foresman, 1985); D. C. McClelland, "How Motives, Skills, and Values Determine What People Do," *American Psychologist* 40 (1985), 812–25; D. C. McClelland, "Managing Motivation to Expand Human Freedom," *American Psychologist* 33 (1978), 201–10.

43. D. G. Winter, *The Power Motive* (New York: Free Press, 1973).

44. M. J. Stahl, "Achievement, Power, and Managerial Motivation: Selecting Managerial Talent with the Job Choice Exercise," *Personnel Psychology* 36 (1983), 775–89; D. C. McClelland and D. H. Burnham, "Power Is the Great Motivator," *Harvard Business Review* 54 (1976), 100–10.

45. R. J. House, W. D. Spangler, and J. Woycke, "Personality and Charisma in the U.S. Presidency: A Psychological Theory of Leader Effectiveness," *Administrative Science Quarterly* 36 (1991), 364–96.

46. G. H. Hines, "Achievement, Motivation, Occupations, and Labor Turnover in New Zealand," *Journal of Applied Psychology* 58 (1973), 313–17; P. S. Hundal, "A Study of Entrepreneurial Motivation: Comparison of Fast- and Slow-Progressing Small Scale Industrial Entrepreneurs in Punjab, India," *Journal of Applied Psychology* 55 (1971), 317–23.

47. R. A. Clay, "Green Is Good for You," *Monitor on Psychology,* April 2001, 40–42.

48. Schlosser and Sung, "The 100 Best Companies to Work For"; Levering et al., "The 100 Best Companies to Work For,"; "Fortune 100 Best Companies to Work For 2006," CNNMoney.com, June 5, 2006 (www.money.cnn.com/magazines/fortune/best companies/snapshots/1181.html).

49. E. P. Dalesio, "Quiet Giant Ready to Raise Its Profits," *Houston Chronicle,* May 6, 2001, 4D; Levering et al., "The 100 Best Companies to Work For."; J. Goodnight, "Welcome to SAS," www.sas.com/corporate/index.html, August 26, 2003; "SAS Press Center: SAS Corporate Statistics," www.sas.com/bin/pfp.pl?=fi, April 18, 2006; "SAS Continues Annual Revenue Growth Streak," www.sas.com/news/prelease/031003/newsl.html, August 28, 2003.

50. J. Pfeffer, "SAS Institute: A Different Approach to Incentives and People Management Practices in the Software Industry," Harvard Business School Case HR-6, January 1998; "Saluting the Global Awards Recipients of Arthur Andersen's Best Practices Awards 2000," www.fortune.com, September

6, 2000; N. Stein, "Winning the War to Keep Top Talent," www.fortune.com, September 6, 2000.

51. Ibid.

52. Ibid.

53. Goodnight, "Welcome to SAS"; "By Solution," www.sas.com/success/solution.html, August 26, 2003; www.sas.com, June 8, 2006.

54. S. H. Wildstrom, "Do Your Homework, Microsoft," *BusinessWeek Online,* August 8, 2005 (www.businessweek.com/print/ magazine/content/05-b3946033-mz006.htm?chan); www.sas.com, June 8, 2006.

55. J. S. Adams, "Toward an Understanding of Inequity," *Journal of Abnormal and Social Psychology* 67 (1963), 422–36.

56. Ibid.; J. Greenberg, "Approaching Equity and Avoiding Inequity in Groups and Organizations," in J. Greenberg and R. L. Cohen, eds., *Equity and Justice in Social Behavior* (New York: Academic Press, 1982), 389–435; J. Greenberg, "Equity and Workplace Status: A Field Experiment," *Journal of Applied Psychology* 73 (1988), 606–13; R. T. Mowday, "Equity Theory Predictions of Behavior in Organizations," in R. M. Steers and L. W. Porter, eds., *Motivation and Work Behavior* (New York: McGraw-Hill, 1987), 89-110.

57. A. Goldwasser, "Inhuman Resources," *Ecompany.com,* March 2001, 154–55.

58. E. A. Locke and G. P. Latham, *A Theory of Goal Setting and Task Performance* (Englewood Cliffs, NJ: Prentice-Hall, 1990).

59. Ibid.; J. J. Donovan and D. J. Radosevich, "The Moderating Role of Goal Commitment on the Goal Difficulty-Performance Relationship: A Meta-Analytic Review and Critical Analysis," *Journal of Applied Psychology* 83 (1998), 308–15; M. E. Tubbs, "Goal Setting: A Meta Analytic Examination of the Empirical Evidence," *Journal of Applied Psychology* 71 (1986), 474–83.

60. E. A. Locke, K. N. Shaw, L. M. Saari, and G. P. Latham, "Goal Setting and Task Performance: 1969–1980," *Psychological Bulletin* 90 (1981), 125–52.

61. P. C. Earley, T. Connolly, and G. Ekegren, "Goals, Strategy Development, and Task Performance: Some Limits on the Efficacy of Goal Setting," *Journal of Applied Psychology* 74 (1989), 24–33; R. Kanfer and P. L. Ackerman, "Motivation and Cognitive Abilities: An Integrative/Aptitude-Treatment Interaction Approach to Skill Acquisition," *Journal of Applied Psychology* 74 (1989), 657–90.

62. W. C. Hamner, "Reinforcement Theory and Contingency Management in Organizational Settings," in H. Tosi and W. C. Hamner, eds., *Organizational Behavior and Management: A Contingency Approach* (Chicago: St. Clair Press, 1974).

63.   B. F. Skinner, *Contingencies of Reinforcement* (New York: Appleton-Century-Crofts, 1969).

64.   H. W. Weiss, "Learning Theory and Industrial and Organizational Psychology," in Dunnette and Hough, *Handbook of Industrial and Organizational Psychology,* 171–221.

65.   Hamner, "Reinforcement Theory and Contingency Management."

66.   F. Luthans and R. Kreitner, *Organizational Behavior Modification and Beyond* (Glenview, IL: Scott, Foresman, 1985); A. D. Stajkovic and F. Luthans, "A Meta-Analysis of the Effects of Organizational Behavior Modification on Task Performance, 1975–95," *Academy of Management Journal* 40 (1997), 1122–49.

67.   A. D. Stajkovic and F. Luthans, "Behavioral Management and Task Performance in Organizations: Conceptual Background, Meta Analysis, and Test of Alternative Models," *Personnel Psychology* 56 (2003), 155–94.

68.   Ibid.; Luthans and A. D. Stajkovic, "Reinforce for Performance: The Need to Go Beyond Pay and Even Rewards," *Academy of Management Executive* 13, no. 2 (1999), 49–56; G. Billikopf Enciina and M. V. Norton, "Pay Method Affects Vineyard Pruner Performance," www.cnr.berkeley.edu/ucce50/ag-labor/7research/7calag05.htm.

69.   A. Bandura, *Principles of Behavior Modification* (New York: Holt, Rinehart and Winston, 1969); A. Bandura, *Social Learning Theory* (Englewood Cliffs, NJ: Prentice-Hall, 1977); T. R. V. Davis and F. Luthans, "A Social Learning Approach to Organizational Behavior," *Academy of Management Review* 5 (1980), 281–90.

70.   A. P. Goldstein and M. Sorcher, *Changing Supervisor Behaviors* (New York: Pergamon Press, 1974); Luthans and Kreitner, *Organizational Behavior Modification and Beyond.*

71.   Bandura, *Social Learning Theory;* Davis and Luthans, *"A Social Learning Approach to Organizational Behavior";* Luthans and Kreitner, *Organizational Behavior Modification and Beyond.*

72.   "Fact Sheet," *The Ritz Carlton,* July 28, 2003 (www.ritzcarlton.com/corporate/about_us/fact_sheet.asp); "The Ritz Carlton: Fact Sheet," www.ritzcarlton.com/corporate/about_us/fact_sheet.asp, April 12, 2006; "Puttin' on the Glitz in Miami," *Business Week Online,* April 12, 2006 (www.businessweek.com/print/magazine/content/04_08/c3871141.htm?chan=mz).

73.   In T. Gutner, "Dividends," *Business Week Online,* July 28, 2003.

74.   "Gold Standards," *The Ritz Carlton,* July 28, 2003 (www.ritzcarlton.com/corporate/about_us/_sheet.asp).

75.   Ibid.

76.   P. Hemp, "My Week as a Room-Service Waiter at the Ritz," *Harvard Business Review,* June 2002, 50–62.

77.   Ibid.

78.   "Fact Sheet,"; "Press Release: The Ritz Carlton Company Repeats as Most Prestigious Luxury Institute," *The Ritz-Carlton Press Room,* April 12, 2006 (www.ritzcarlton.com/corporate/press_room/releases/luxury_institute_06.html).

79.   A. Bandura, "Self-Reinforcement: Theoretical and Methodological Considerations," *Behaviorism* 4 (1976), 135–55.

80.   P. Engardio, "A Hothouse of High-Tech Talent," *BusinessWeek/21st Century Capitalism* (1994), 126.

81.   R. D. Hof, "Why Tech Will Bloom Again," *BusinessWeek Online,* August 25, 2003 (www.businessweek.com); "Google Corporate Information: Quick Profile," www.google.com/corporate/facts.html, April 24, 2006; B. Elgin, "Managing Google's Idea Factory," *BusinessWeek,* October 3, 2005, 88–90; "Google Corporate Information: Company Overview," www.google.com/corporate/index.html, April 24, 2006; K. H. Hammonds, "Growth Search," *Fast Company,* April 2003, 74–81.

82.   J. Kerstetter, "Still the Center of This World," *BusinessWeek Online,* August 25, 2003 (www.businessweek.com); "Google Corporate Information: Quick Profile"; Hammonds, "Growth Search."

83.   Hammonds, "Growth Search."

84.   B. Elgin, "Managing Google's Idea Factory," *Business Week,* October 3, 2005, 88–90.

85.   "Google Corporate Information: Google Milestones," www.google.com/corporate/history.html, April 24, 2006.

86.   A. Bandura, "Self-Efficacy Mechanism in Human Agency," *American Psychologist* 37 (1982), 122–27; M. E. Gist and T. R. Mitchell, "Self-Efficacy: A Theoretical Analysis of Its Determinants and Malleability," *Academy of Management Review* 17 (1992), 183–211.

87.   E. E. Lawler III, *Pay and Organization Development* (Reading, MA: Addison-Wesley, 1981).

88.   The Risky New Bonuses," *Newsweek,* January 16, 1995, 42.

89.   Lawler, *Pay and Organization Development.*

90.   Ibid.

91.   J. F. Lincoln, *Incentive Management* (Cleveland: Lincoln Electric Company, 1951); R. Zager, "Managing Guaranteed Employment," *Harvard Business Review* 56 (1978), 103–15.

92.   Lawler, *Pay and Organization Development.*

93.   M. Gendron, "Gradient Named 'Small Business of Year," *Boston Herald,* May 11, 1994, 35.

94.   W. Zeller, R. D. Hof, R. Brandt, S. Baker, and D. Greising, "Go-Go Goliaths," *BusinessWeek,* February 13, 1995, 64–70.

95.   "Stock Option," *Encarta World English Dictionary,* June 28, 2001 (www.dictionary.msn.com); personal interview with Professor Bala Dharan, Jones Graduate School of Business, Rice University, June 28, 2001.

96.   Personal interview with Professor Bala Dharan.

97.   Ibid.

98.   A. J. Michels, "Dallas Semiconductor," *Fortune,* May 16, 1994, 81.

99.   M. Betts, "Big Things Come in Small Buttons," *Computerworld,* August 3, 1992, 30.

100.   M. Boslet, "Metal Buttons Toted by Crop Pickers Act as Mini Databases," *The Wall Street Journal,* June 1, 1994, B3.

101.   C. D. Fisher, L. F. Schoenfeldt, and J. B. Shaw, *Human Resource Management* (Boston: Houghton Mifflin, 1990); B. E. Graham-Moore and T. L. Ross, *Productivity Gainsharing* (Englewood Cliffs, NJ: Prentice-Hall, 1983); A. J. Geare, "Productivity from Scanlon Type Plans," *Academy of Management Review* 1 (1976), 99–108.

102.   J. Labate, "Deal Those Workers In," *Fortune,* April 19, 1993, 26.

103.   K. Belson, "Japan's Net Generation," *BusinessWeek,* March 19, 2001 (*BusinessWeek Archives,* June 27, 2001).

104.   K. Belson, "Taking a Hint from the Upstarts," *BusinessWeek,* March 19, 2001 (*BusinessWeek* Archives, June 27, 2001); "Going for the Gold," *BusinessWeek,* March 19, 2001 (*BusinessWeek* Archives, June 27, 2001); "What the Government Can Do to Promote a Flexible Workforce," *BusinessWeek,* March 19, 2001 (*BusinessWeek* Archives, June 27, 2001).

Chapter 14

1.   T. Lowry, "Can MTV Stay Cool?" *Business Week,* February 20, 2006, 51–60.

2.   www.viacom.com/2006/pdf/Viacom_Fact_Sheet_4_5_06.pdf, June 9, 2006; M. Gunther, "Mr. MTV Grows Up," CNNMoney.com, April 13, 2006 (http://money.cnn.com/magazines/fortune/fortune_archive/2006/04/17/8374305/index.htm); "Viacom Completes Separation into CBS Corporation and 'New' Viacom," Viacom.com, January 1, 2006 (www.viacom.com/view_release.jhtml?inID=10000040&inReleaseID=126683).

3.   Lowry, "Can MTV Stay Cool?"

4.   J. H. Higgins, "A Rockin' Role: McGrath Keeps MTV Networks Plugged In and Focused," www.broadcastingcable.com, April 10, 2006 (www.broadcastingcable.com/article/CA6323342.html?display=Search+Results&text=judy+mcgrath); "FORTUNE 50 Most Powerful Women in Business 2005," CNNMoney.com, November 14, 2005 (http://money.cnn.com/magazines/fortune/mostpowerfulwomen/snapshots/10.html); E. Levenson, "Hall of Fame: Digging a Little

Deeper into the List, We Salute the Highfliers and Share Some Facts to Inspire and Amuse," CNNMoney.com, November 14, 2005 (http://money.cnn.com/magazines/fortune/fortune_archive/2005/11/14/8360698/index.html).

5. Lowry, "Can MTV Stay Cool?"; "Welcome to Viacom–Senior Management," www.viacom.com/management.jhtml, June 9, 2006.

6. Lowry, "Can MTV Stay Cool?"

7. Ibid.

8. "The 2006 National Show Mobile Edition–Judy McGrath," www.thenationalshoe.com/Mobile/SpeakerDetail.aspx?ID=199, June 9, 2006.

9. Lowry, "Can MTV Stay Cool?"

10. Ibid.; "Viacom's MTV Networks Completes Acquisition of Xfire, Inc.," www.viacom.com/view_release.jhtml?inID=10000040&inReleaseID=227008, June 9, 2006.

11. "MTV Networks Unveils URGE Digital Music Service on Microsoft's New Windows Media Player 11 Platform," *Microsoft*, May 17, 2006 (www.microsoft.com/presspass/press/2006/may06/05-17URGEPR.mspx).

12. Lowry, "Can MTV Stay Cool?"

13. Ibid.

14. Ibid.

15. G. Yukl, *Leadership in Organizations*, 2d ed. (New York: Academic Press, 1989); R. M. Stogdill, *Handbook of Leadership: A Survey of the Literature* (New York: Free Press, 1974).

16. Lowry, "Can MTV Stay Cool?"

17. W. D. Spangler, R. J. House, and R. Palrecha, "Personality and Leadership," in B. Schneider and D. B. Smith, eds., *Personality and Organizations* (Mahwah, NJ: Lawrence Erlbaum, 2004), 251–90.

18. Ibid.; "Leaders vs. Managers: Leaders Master the Context of Their Mission, Managers Surrender to It," www.msue.msu.edu/msue/imp/modtd/visuals/tsld029.htm, July 28, 2004; *"Leadership,"* Leadership Center at Washington State University; M. Maccoby, "Understanding the Difference Between Management and Leadership," *Research Technology Mangement* 43, no. 1 (January-February 2000), 57–59 (www.maccoby.com/articles/UtDBMaL.html); P. Coutts, "Leadership vs. Management," www.telusplanet.net/public/pdcoutts/leadership/LdrVsMgnt.htm, October 1, 2000; S. Robbins, "The Difference Between Managing and Leading," www.Entrepreneur.com/article/0,4621,304743,00.html, November 18, 2002; W. Bennis, "The Leadership Advantage," *Leader to Leader* 12 (Spring 1999) (www.pfdf.org/leaderbooks/121/spring99/bennis.html).

19. Spangler et al., "Personality and Leadership"; "Leaders vs. Managers"; "Leadership"; Maccoby, "Understanding the Difference Between Management and

Leadership"; Coutts, "Leadership vs. Management"; Robbins, "The Difference Between Managing and Leading"; Bennis, "The Leadership Advantage."

20. J. Gertner, "The Virtue in $6 Heirloom Tomatoes," *The New York Times*, June 6, 2004 (www.nytimes.com); "Whole Foods Market: About Us," www.wholefoodsmarket.com/company/facts.html, June 13, 2006; "Fortune Names Whole Foods Market #15 on 100 Best Companies to Work For List," www.wholefoodsmarket.com/cgi-vin/print10pt.cgi?url=/company/pr-01-09-06.html, January 9, 2006.

21. Gertner, "The Virtue in $6 Heirloom Tomatoes"; W. Zellner, "John Mackey's Empire: Peace, Love, and the Bottom Line," *BusinessWeek Online*, December 7, 1998 (www.businessweek.com/@@cUnEBIYQB3qr3QcA/archives/1998/b3607112.arc.htm); "Whole Foods Market Expands into U.K.," www.wholefoodsmarket.com/investor/freshwild.html, January 16, 2004; "Whole Foods Market Opens Largest Supermarket in Manhattan, a Naturally Sought After Destination," www.wholefoodsmarket.com/company/pr_02-05-04.html, July 12, 2004.

22. R. Rayasam, "His Nutritious 15 Minutes," *Houston Chronicle*, July 4, 2004, D5.

23. Gertner, "The Virtue in $6 Heirloom Tomatoes."

24. Rayasam, "His Nutritious 15 Minutes."

25. "Whole Foods Market: About Us," www.wholefoodsmarket.com/company/facts.html, June 13, 2006; "Fortune Names Whole Foods Market #15."

26. Gertner, "The Virtue in $6 Heirloom Tomatoes."

27. Ibid.

28. "Declaration of Independence," www.wholefoods.com/company/declaration.html, July 28, 2004.

29. Gertner, "The Virtue in $6 Heirloom Tomatoes"; Rayasam, "His Nutritious 15 Minutes"; "Declaration of Independence."

30. "Whole Foods Market CEO, Chairman John Mackey Identified by Barron's as One of World's Top Corporate Leaders," www.wholefoodsmarket.com/cgi-bin/print10pt.cgi?url=/company/pr_04-04-06-b.html, April 4, 2006.

31. R. Calori and B. Dufour, "Management European Style," *Academy of Management Executive* 9, no. 3 (1995), 61–70.

32. Ibid.

33. H. Mintzberg, *Power in and Around Organizations* (Englewood Cliffs, NJ: Prentice-Hall, 1983); J. Pfeffer, *Power in Organizations* (Marshfield, MA: Pitman, 1981).

34. R. P. French, Jr., and B. Raven, "The Bases of Social Power," in D. Cartwright and A. F. Zander, eds., *Group Dynamics* (Evanston, IL: Row, Peterson, 1960), 607–23.

35. R. L. Rose, "After Turning Around Giddings and Lewis, Fife Is Turned Out Himself," *The Wall Street Journal*, June 22, 1993, A1.

36. E. Olson, "Adventures as a Team Sport," *The New York Times* October 23, 2005, 9; "Investor Relations–Alaska Communications System: Board of Directors," *ACS*, March 20, 2006 (www.acsalaska.com/ALSK/en-US/Board+of+Directors/Liane+Pelletier.htm).

37. Olson, "Adventures as a Team Sport."

38. Ibid.

39. "Investor Relations–Alaska Communications System."

40. "Alaska Communications," *Corporate Spotlight*, March 21, 2006 (www.redcoatpublishingcom/spotlights/s1_08_05_Alaska.asp).

41. G. G. Marcial, "Heading North To Alaska Communications," *BusinessWeek Online*, June 27, 2005 (www.businessweek.com).

42. Olson, "Adventures as a Team Sport."

43. A. Grove, "How Intel Makes Spending Pay Off," *Fortune*, February 22, 1993, 56–61; "Craig R. Barrett, Chief Executive Officer: Intel Corporation," *Intel*, July 28, 2004 (www.intel.com/pressroom/kits/bios/barrett/bio.htm).

44. M. Loeb, "Jack Welch Lets Fly on Budgets, Bonuses, and Buddy Boards," *Fortune*, May 29, 1995, 146.

45. T. M. Burton, "Visionary's Reward: Combine 'Simple Ideas' and Some Failures; Result: Sweet Revenge," *The Wall Street Journal*, February 3, 1995, A1, A5.

46. L. Nakarmi, "A Flying Leap Toward the 21st Century? Pressure from Competitors and Seoul May Transform the Chaebol," *BusinessWeek*, March 20, 1995, 78–80.

47. B. M. Bass, *Bass and Stogdill's Handbook of Leadership: Theory, Research, and Managerial Applications*, 3d ed. (New York: Free Press, 1990); R. J. House and M. L. Baetz, "Leadership: Some Empirical Generalizations and New Research Directions," in B. M. Staw and L. L. Cummings, eds., *Research in Organizational Behavior*, vol. 1 (Greenwich, CT: JAI Press, 1979), 341–423; S. A. Kirpatrick and E. A. Locke, "Leadership: Do Traits Matter?" *Academy of Management Executive* 5, no. 2 (1991), 48–60; Yukl, *Leadership in Organizations*; G. Yukl and D. D. Van Fleet, "Theory and Research on Leadership in Organizations," in M. D. Dunnette and L. M. Hough, eds., *Handbook of Industrial and Organizational Psychology*, 2d ed., vol. 3 (Palo Alto, CA: Consulting Psychologists Press, 1992), 147–97.

48. E. A. Fleishman, "Performance Assessment Based on an Empirically Derived Task Taxonomy," *Human Factors* 9 (1967), 349–66; E. A. Fleishman, "The Description of Supervisory Behavior," *Personnel Psychology* 37

(1953), 1–6; A. W. Halpin and B. J. Winer, "A Factorial Study of the Leader Behavior Descriptions," in R. M. Stogdill and A. I. Coons, eds., *Leader Behavior: Its Description and Measurement* (Columbus Bureau of Business Research, Ohio State University, 1957); D. Tscheulin, "Leader Behavior Measurement in German Industry," *Journal of Applied Psychology* 56 (1971), 28–31.

49.   S. Greenhouse, "How Costco Became the Anti-Wal-Mart," *The New York Times*, July 17, 2005, BU1, BU8.

50.   "Corporate Governance," *Costco Wholesale Investor Relations*, April 28, 2006, (http://phx.corporate-ir.net/phoenix. zhtml?c=83830&p=irol-govhighlights).

51.   Greenhouse, "How Costco Became the Anti-Wal-Mart."

52.   Ibid.

53.   Ibid.

54.   Ibid; S. C., "Because Who Knew a Big-Box Chain Could Have a Generous Soul," *INC. Magazine*, April 2005, 88.

55.   S. Holmes and W. Zellner, "Commentary: The Costco Way," *BusinessWeek Online*, April 12, 2004 (www.businessweek.com/ print/magazine/content/04_15/b3878084_ mz021.htm?chan . . .); M. Herbst, "The Costco Challenge: An Alternative to Wal-Martization?" *LRA Online*, July 5, 2005 (www. laborresearch.org/print.php?id=391).

56.   Greenhouse, "How Costco Became the Anti-Wal-Mart."

57.   Ibid.

58.   "Costco Wholesale Corporation Reports Second Quarter and Year-to-Date Operating Results Fiscal 2006 and February Sales Results," *Costco Wholesale Investor Relations: News Release*, April 28, 2006 (http://phx. corporate-ir.net/phoenix.zhtml?c=83830& p=irol-newsArticle&ID=824344&highlight=); "Costco Wholesale Corporation Reports March Sales Results and Plans for Membership Fee Increase," *Costco Wholesale Investor Relations: News Release*, April 28, 2006 (http://phx.corporate-ir.net/phoenix. zhtml?c=83830&p=irol-newsArticle& ID=839605&highlight=); "Wal-Mart Stores Post Higher January Sales," *BusinessWeek Online*, February 2, 2006 (www.businessweek. com/print/investor/conent/feb2006/ pi2006022_0732_pi004.htm).

59.   E. A. Fleishman and E. F. Harris, "Patterns of Leadership Behavior Related to Employee Grievances and Turnover," *Personnel Psychology* 15 (1962), 43–56.

60.   R. Likert, *New Patterns of Management* (New York: McGraw-Hill, 1961); N. C. Morse and E. Reimer, "The Experimental Change of a Major Organizational Variable," *Journal of Abnormal and Social Psychology* 52 (1956), 120–29.

61.   R. R. Blake and J. S. Mouton, *The New Managerial Grid* (Houston: Gulf, 1978).

62.   P. Hersey and K. Blanchard, *Management of Organizational Behavior: Utilizing Human Resources* (Englewood Cliffs, NJ: Prentice-Hall, 1982).

63.   F. E. Fiedler, *A Theory of Leadership Effectiveness* (New York: McGraw-Hill, 1967); F. E. Fiedler, "The Contingency Model and the Dynamics of the Leadership Process," in L. Berkowitz, ed., *Advances in Experimental Social Psychology* (New York: Academic Press, 1978).

64.   J. Rebello, "Radical Ways of Its CEO Are a Boon to Bank," *The Wall Street Journal*, March 20, 1995, B1, B3.

65.   J. Fierman, "Winning Ideas from Maverick Managers," *Fortune*, February 6, 1995, 66–80.

66.   Ibid.

67.   M. Schuman, "Free to Be," *Forbes*, May 8, 1995, 78–80.

68.   House and Baetz, "Leadership"; L. H. Peters, D. D. Hartke, and J. T. Pohlmann, "Fiedler's Contingency Theory of Leadership: An Application of the Meta-Analysis Procedures of Schmidt and Hunter," *Psychological Bulletin* 97 (1985), 274–85; C. A. Schriesheim, B. J. Tepper, and L. A. Tetrault, "Least Preferred Co-Worker Score, Situational Control, and Leadership Effectiveness: A Meta-Analysis of Contingency Model Performance Predictions," *Journal of Applied Psychology* 79 (1994), 561–73.

69.   M. G. Evans, "The Effects of Supervisory Behavior on the Path-Goal Relationship," *Organizational Behavior and Human Performance* 5 (1970), 277–98; R. J. House, "A Path-Goal Theory of Leader Effectiveness," *Administrative Science Quarterly* 16 (1971), 321 38; J. C. Wofford and L. Z. Liska, "Path-Goal Theories of Leadership: A Meta-Analysis," *Journal of Management* 19 (1993), 857–76.

70.   J. Rosenfeld, "Lead Softly, but Carry a Big Baton," *Fast Company* (July 2001), 46–48.

71.   Ibid.; "What Is the Music Paradigm?" www.themusicparadigm.com/what_is.asp, July 20, 2004; "Roger Nierenberg," www.goldstars. com/roger_nierenberg.htm, July 30, 2004; "Roger Nierenberg–Leading Authorities Speakers Bureau," www.leadingauthorities. com/10245/Roger_Nierenberg.htm, June 17, 2006.

72.   C. Bangle, "The Ultimate Creativity Machine: How BMW Turns *Art* into Profit," *Harvard Business Review*, January 2001, 47–55; G. Green, "The Shape of Things to Come: Controversial Auto Designer Chris Bangle Has Only Just Begun His Quest to Change the World," *Motor Trend*, January 2006 (www. motortrend.com/features/consumer/112_0601 _chris_bangle_bmw_design_chief/index.html).

73.   Bangle, "The Ultimate Creativity Machine"; www.bmw.com, September 11, 2001.

74.   S. Kerr and J. M. Jermier, "Substitutes for Leadership: Their Meaning and Measurement," *Organizational Behavior and Human Performance* 22 (1978), 375–403; P. M. Podsakoff, B. P. Niehoff, S. B. MacKenzie, and M. L. Williams, "Do Substitutes for Leadership Really Substitute for Leadership? An Empirical Examination of Kerr and Jermier's Situational Leadership Model," *Organizational Behavior and Human Decision Processes* 54 (1993), 1–44.

75.   Kerr and Jermier, "Substitutes for Leadership"; Podsakoff et al., "Do Substitutes for Leadership Really Substitute for Leadership?"

76.   K. Miller, "Siemens Shapes Up," *BusinessWeek*, May 1, 1995, 52–53.

77.   "Siemens History: Heinrich v. Pierer (*1941)," siemens.com, June 17, 2006 (http://w4siemens.de/archive/en/persoenlichk eiten/vorstaende/piere.html).

78.   B. M. Bass, *Leadership and Performance Beyond Expectations* (New York: Free Press, 1985); Bass, *Bass and Stogdill's Handbook of Leadership*; Yukl and Van Fleet, "Theory and Research on Leadership."

79.   G. E. Schares, J. B. Levine, and P. Coy, "The New Generation at Siemens," *BusinessWeek*, March 9, 1992, 46–48.

80.   Miller, "Siemens Shapes Up."

81.   Ibid.

82.   J. A. Conger and R. N. Kanungo, "Behavioral Dimensions of Charismatic Leadership," in J. A. Conger, R. N. Kanungo, and Associates, *Charismatic Leadership* (San Francisco: Jossey-Bass, 1988).

83.   Bass, *Leadership and Performance Beyond Expectations*; Bass, *Bass and Stogdill's Handbook of Leadership*; Yukl and Van Fleet, "Theory and Research on Leadership."

84.   Ibid.

85.   Miller, "Siemens Shapes Up."

86.   Bass, *Leadership and Performance Beyond Expectations*.

87.   Bass, *Bass and Stogdill's Handbook of Leadership*; B. M. Bass and B. J. Avolio, "Transformational Leadership: A Response to Critiques," in M. M. Chemers and R. Ayman, eds., *Leadership Theory and Research: Perspectives and Directions* (San Diego: Academic Press, 1993), 49–80; B. M. Bass, B. J. Avolio, and L. Goodheim, "Biography and the Assessment of Transformational Leadership at the World Class Level," *Journal of Management* 13 (1987), 7–20; J. J. Hater and B. M. Bass, "Supervisors Evaluations and Subordinates' Perceptions of Transformational and Transactional Leadership," *Journal of Applied Psychology* 73, (1988), 695–702; R. Pillai, "Crisis and Emergence of Charismatic Leadership in Groups: An Experimental Investigation," *Journal of Applied Psychology* 26 (1996), 543–562; J. Seltzer and B. M. Bass, "Transformational Leadership: Beyond Initiation and Consideration," *Journal of Management* 16 (1990), 693–703; D. A. Waldman, B. M. Bass, and W. O. Einstein, "Effort, Performance, Transformational Leadership in Industrial and

Military Service," *Journal of Occupation Psychology* 60 (1987), 1–10.

88.   R. Pillai, C. A. Schriesheim, and E. S. Williams, "Fairness Perceptions and Trust as Mediators of Transformational and Transactional Leadership: A Two-Sample Study," *Journal of Management* 25 (1999), 897–933.

89.   L. Tischler, "Where Are the Women?" *Fast Company*, February 2004, 52–60.

90.   Ibid.

91.   A. H. Eagly and B. T. Johnson, "Gender and Leadership Style: A Meta-Analysis," *Psychological Bulletin* 108 (1990), 233–56.

92.   Ibid.

93.   The Economist, "Workers Resent Scoldings from Female Bosses," *Houston Chronicle*, August 19, 2000, 1C.

94.   Ibid.

95.   Ibid.

96.   Ibid.

97.   A. H. Eagly, S. J. Karau, and M. G. Makhijani, "Gender and the Effectiveness of Leaders: A Meta-Analysis," *Psychological Bulletin* 117 (1995), 125–45.

98.   Ibid.

99.   Tischler, "Where Are the Women?"

100.   J. Porretto, "Autos Attract a Winner," *Houston Chronicle*, July 17, 2004, D2; "About Tower Automotive," www.towerautomotive.com/02.htm, June 17, 2006; "About Tower Automotive: Enterprise Leadership," www.towerautomotive.com/02_06.htm, June 17, 2006; "Tower Automotive: Investors–Corporate Governance," www.towerautomotive.com/06_12dir.htm, June 17, 2006.

101.   K. Ligocki, "From Art History Student to CEO," *Women Working 2000 and Beyond*, July 30, 2004 (www.womenworking2000.com/feature/index/php?id=29).

102.   "Biographical Sketch of Kathleen Ligocki," *Detroit Free Press*, July 3, 2004 (www.freep.com/news/statewire/sw100484_20 0407803.htm); "Biographical Sketch of Kathleen Ligocki," *The Journal Gazette*, July 3, 2004 (www.fortwayne.com/mld/journalgazette/business/9074506.htm).

103.   Porretto, "Autos Attract a Winner"; *"Biographical Sketch of Kathleen Ligocki,"* Detroit Free Press; "Biographical Sketch of Kathleen Ligocki," *The Journal Gazette*; Ligocki, "From Art History Student to CEO."

104.   Porretto, "Autos Attract a Winner."

105.   Ibid.

106.   J. M. George and K. Bettenhausen, "Understanding Prosocial Behavior, Sales Performance, and Turnover: A Group-Level Analysis in a Service Context," *Journal of Applied Psychology*, 75 (1990), 698–709.

107.   T. Sy, S. Cote, and R. Saavedra, "The Contagious Leader: Impact of the Leader's Mood on the Mood of Group Members, Group Affective Tone, and Group Processes," *Journal of Applied Psychology* 90(2), (2005), 295–305.

108.   J. M. George, "Emotions and Leadership: The Role of Emotional Intelligence," *Human Relations* 53 (2000), 1027–55.

109.   Ibid.

110.   J. Zhou and J. M. George, "Awakening Employee Creativity: The Role of Leader Emotional Intelligence," *The Leadership Quarterly* 14, no. 4 5 (August–October 2003), 545–68.

111.   Ibid.

112.   Ibid.

Chapter 15

1.   C. Matlack, R. Tiplady, D. Brady, R. Berner, and H. Tashiro, "The Vuitton Machine," *Business Week*, March 22, 2004, 98–102; "America's Most Admired Companies," *Fortune.com*, August 18, 2004 (www.fortune.com/fortune/mostadmired/snap shot/0,15020,383,00.html); "Art Samberg's Ode to Steel," *Big Money Weekly*, June 29, 2004 (http://trading.sina/com/trading/rightside/big money_weekly_040629.b5.shtml); "Nucor Reports Record Results for First Quarter of 2004," www.nucor.com/financials.asp?finpage=newsreleases, August 18, 2004; "Nucor Reports Results for First Half and Second Quarter of 2004," www.nucor.com/financials.asp?finpage=newsreleases; J. C. Cooper, "The Price of Efficiency," *BusinessWeek Online*, March 22, 2004 (www.businessweek.com/magazine/content/0 4_12/b3875603.htm); "LVHM–Fashion & Leather Goods," www.lvmh.com, June 18, 2006; C. Matlack, "Rich Times for the Luxury Sector," *BusinessWeek Online*, March 6, 2006 (www.businessweek.com/globalbiz/content/mar2006/gb20060306_296309.htm?campaign_id=search); N. Byrnes, "The Art of Motivation," *BusinessWeek*, May 1, 2006, 56–62.

2.   Matlack et al., "The Vuitton Machine"; "LVMH Key Figures," www.lvmh.com/groupe/pop_chiffres.asp?str_contenu_pop=4, June 18, 2006.

3.   C. Matlack et al., "The Vuitton Machine."

4.   Ibid.

5.   Ibid.

6.   www.nucor.com, November 21, 2001.

7.   "About Nucor," www.nucor.com/aboutus.htm, August 18, 2004; N. Byrnes, "The Art of Motivation," *BusinessWeek*, May 1, 2006, 56–62; "Nucor: About Us," www.nucor.com/aboutus.htm, June 19, 2006.

8.   M. Arndt, "Out of the Forge and into the Fire," *BusinessWeek*, June 18, 2001 (*BusinessWeek* Archives); Byrnes, "The Art of Motivation."

9.   S. Baker, "The Minimill That Acts like a Biggie," *BusinessWeek*, September 30, 1996, 101–104; S. Baker, "Nucor," *BusinessWeek* February 13, 1995, 70; S. Overman, "No-Frills at Nucor," *HRMagazine*, July 1994, 56–60.

10.   www.nucor.com, November 21, 2001; "Nucor: About Us."

11.   Baker, "The Minimill That Acts like a Biggie"; Baker, "Nucor"; Overman, "No-Frills at Nucor"; www.nucor.com; Byrnes, "The Art of Motivation"; "Nucor: About Us."

12.   Matlack et al., "The Vuitton Machine"; "About Nucor"; "America's Most Admired Companies"; "Art Samberg's Ode to Steel"; "Nucor Reports Record Results for First Quarter of 2004"; "Nucor Reports Results for First Half and Second Quarter of 2004"; Byrnes, "The Art of Motivation."

13.   W. R. Coradetti, "Teamwork Takes Time and a Lot of Energy," *HRMagazine*, June 1994, 74–77; D. Fenn, "Service Teams That Work," *Inc. Magazine*, August 1995, 99; "Team Selling Catches On, but Is Sales Really a Team Sport?" *The Wall Street Journal*, March 29, 1994, A1.

14.   T. M. Mills, *The Sociology of Small Groups* (Englewood Cliffs, NJ: Prentice-Hall, 1967); M. E. Shaw, *Group Dynamics* (New York: McGraw-Hill, 1981).

15.   R. S. Buday, "Reengineering One Firm's Product Development and Another's Service Delivery," *Planning Review*, March–April 1993, 14–19; J. M. Burcke, "Hallmark's Quest for Quality Is a Job Never Done," *Business Insurance*, April 26, 1993, 122; M. Hammer and J. Champy, *Reengineering the Corporation* (New York: HarperBusiness, 1993); T. A. Stewart, "The Search for the Organization of Tomorrow," *Fortune*, May 18, 1992, 92–98.

16.   T. Claburn, "Lockheed Finds a Way to Connect Questions with Answers," *InformationWeek*, June 14, 2004 (www.informationweek.com/showArticle.jhtml?articleID=21700462); "About Us," www.lockheedmartin.com/wms/findPage.do?dsp=fec&ci=4&sc=400&prfr=true, June 19, 2006.

17.   "Smart Organizations Choose Tacit," http://tacit.com/customers/index.html, June 19, 2006; "Tacit ActiveNet: A Powerful Way to Drive the Right Collaboration," http://tacit.com/products/index.html, June 19, 2006.

18.   "Lockheed Martin Licenses Tacit to Network Space Systems Employees," www.tacit.com/company/news/press/2004.05.24.html. May, 24, 2004.

19.   P. Kaihla, "The Matchmaker in the Machine," *Business 2.0*, February 2004, 52–55.

20.   Claburn, "Lockheed Finds a Way to Connect Questions with Answers."

21.   Kaihla, "The Matchmaker in the Machine"; "Northrop Grumman: About Us," www.northropgrumman.com/about_us/about_us.html, June 19, 2006.

22. Kaihla, "The Matchmaker in the Machine."

23. Ibid.

24. "Amazon.com Investor Relations: Officers & Directors," http://phx.corporate-ir.net/phoenix.zhtml?c=97664&p=irol-govManage, June 19, 2006.

25. A. Deutschman, "Inside the Mind of Jeff Bezos," *Fast Company,* August 2004, 50–58.

26. Ibid.

27. Ibid.; "Amazon.com Digital Media Technology," http://media-server.amazon.com/jobs/jobs.html, June 19, 2006.

28. Deutschman, "Inside the Mind of Jeff Bezos."

29. "Online Extra: Jeff Bezos on Word-of-Mouth Power," *BusinessWeek Online,* August 2, 2004 (www.businessweek.com); R. D. Hof, "Reprogramming Amazon," *BusinessWeek Online,* December 22, 2003 (www.businessweek.com); "About Amazon.com: Company Information," www.amazon.com/exec/obidos/tg/browsw/-/574562/104-0138839-3693547, June 19, 2006.

30. S. Dallas, "Rock Bottom Restaurants: Brewing Up Solid Profits," *BusinessWeek,* May 22, 1995, 74.

31. J. A. Pearce II and E. C. Ravlin, "The Design and Activation of Self-Regulating Work Groups," *Human Relations* 11 (1987), 751–82.

32. www.scjohnson.com, June 19, 2006.

33. R. Henkoff, "When to Take on the Giants," *Fortune,* May 30, 1994, 111, 114.

34. B. Dumaine, "Who Needs a Boss?" *Fortune,* May 7, 1990, 52–60; Pearce and Ravlin, "The Design and Activation of Self-Regulating Work Groups."

35. Dumaine, "Who Needs a Boss"; A. R. Montebello and V. R. Buzzotta, "Work Teams That Work," *Training and Development,* March 1993, 59–64.

36. T. D. Wall, N. J. Kemp, P. R. Jackson, and C. W. Clegg, "Outcomes of Autonomous Work Groups: A Long-Term Field Experiment," *Academy of Management Journal* 29 (1986): 280–304.

37. A. Markels, "A Power Producer Is Intent on Giving Power to Its People," *The Wall Street Journal,* July 3, 1995, A1, A12.

38. J. S. Lublin, "My Colleague, My Boss," *The Wall Street Journal,* April 12, 1995, R4, R12.

39. W. R. Pape, "Group Insurance," *Inc. Magazine* (Technology Supplement), June 17, 1997, 29–31; A. M. Townsend, S. M. DeMarie, and A. R. Hendrickson, "Are You Ready for Virtual Teams?" *HRMagazine,* September 1996, 122–126; A. M. Townsend, S. M. DeMarie, and A. M. Hendrickson, "Virtual Teams: Technology and the Workplace of the Future," *Academy of Management Executive* (1998) 12, no. 3, 17–29.

40. Townsend et al., "Virtual Teams."

41. Pape, "Group Insurance,"; Townsend et al., "Are You Ready for Virtual Teams?"

42. D. L. Duarte and N. T. Snyder, *Mastering Virtual Teams* (San Francisco: Jossey-Bass, 1999); K. A. Karl, "Book Reviews: *Mastering Virtual Teams,*" *Academy of Management Executive,* August 1999, 118–19.

43. B. Geber, "Virtual Teams," *Training* 32, no. 4 (August 1995), 36–40; T. Finholt and L. S. Sproull, "Electronic Groups at Work," *Organization Science* 1 (1990), 41–64.

44. Geber, "Virtual Teams."

45. E. J. Hill, B. C. Miller, S. P. Weiner, and J. Colihan, "Influences of the Virtual Office on Aspects of Work and Work/Life Balance," *Personnel Psychology* 31 (1998), 667–83; S. G. Strauss, "Technology, Group Process, and Group Outcomes: Testing the Connections in Computer-Mediated and Face-to-Face Groups," *Human Computer Interaction,* 12 (1997), 227–66; M. E. Warkentin, L. Sayeed, and R. Hightower, "Virtual Teams versus Face-to-Face Teams: An Exploratory Study of a Web-based Conference System," *Decision Sciences* 28, no. 4 (Fall 1997), 975–96.

46. S. A. Furst, M. Reeves, B. Rosen, and R. S. Blackburn, "Managing the Life Cycle of Virtual Teams," *Academy of Management Executive* 18, no. 2 (May 2004), 6–20.

47. Ibid.

48. A. Deutschman, "The Managing Wisdom of High-Tech Superstars," *Fortune,* October 17, 1994, 197–206.

49. J. D. Thompson, *Organizations in Action* (New York: McGraw-Hill, 1967).

50. Ibid.

51. Lublin, "My Colleague, My Boss."

52. R. G. LeFauve and A. C. Hax, "Managerial and Technological Innovations at Saturn Corporation," *MIT Management,* Spring 1992, 8–19.

53. B. W. Tuckman, "Developmental Sequences in Small Groups," *Psychological Bulletin* 63 (1965), 384–99; B. W. Tuckman and M. C. Jensen, "Stages of Small Group Development," *Group and Organizational Studies* 2 (1977), 419–27.

54. C. J. G. Gersick, "Time and Transition in Work Teams: Toward a New Model of Group Development," *Academy of Management Journal* 31 (1988), 9–41; C. J. G. Gersick, "Marking Time: Predictable Transitions in Task Groups," *Academy of Management Journal* 32 (1989), 274–309.

55. J. R. Hackman, "Group Influences on Individuals in Organizations," in M. D. Dunnette and L. M. Hough, eds., *Handbook of Industrial and Organizational Psychology,* 2d ed., vol. 3 (Palo Alto, CA: Consulting Psychologists Press, 1992), 199–267.

56. Ibid.

57. Ibid.

58. Lublin, "My Colleague, My Boss."

59. T. Kelley and J. Littman, *The Art of Innovation* (New York: Doubleday, 2001); "ideo.com: Our Work," www.ideo.com/portfolio, June 19, 2006.

60. B. Nussbaum, "The Power of Design," *BusinessWeek,* May 17, 2004, 86-94; "ideo.com: About Us: Teams," www.ideo.com/about/index.asp?x=1&y=1, June 19, 2006.

61. Ibid.

62. Nussbaum, "The Power of Design."

63. Kelley and Littman, *The Art of Innovation.*

64. Ibid; www.ideo.com; "1999 Idea Winners," *BusinessWeek,* June 7, 1999 (*BusinessWeek* Archives).

65. Nussbaum, "The Power of Design.

66. L. Festinger, "Informal Social Communication," *Psychological Review* 57 (1950), 271–82; Shaw, *Group Dynamics.*

67. Hackman, "Group Influences on Individuals in Organizations"; Shaw, *Group Dynamics.*

68. D. Cartwright, "The Nature of Group Cohesiveness," in D. Cartwright and A. Zander, eds., *Group Dynamics,* 3d ed. (New York: Harper & Row, 1968); L. Festinger, S. Schacter, and K. Black, *Social Pressures in Informal Groups* (New York: Harper & Row, 1950); Shaw, *Group Dynamics.*

69. T. F. O'Boyle, "A Manufacturer Grows Efficient by Soliciting Ideas from Employees," *The Wall Street Journal,* June 5, 1992, A1, A5.

70. Lublin, "My Colleague, My Boss."

71. Kelley and Littman, "The Art of Innovation," p. 93.

72. Kelley and Littman, "The Art of Innovation."

73. J. Guyon, "The Soul of a Moneymaking Machine," *Fortune,* October 3, 2005, 113–20.

74. Ibid.

75. Ibid.; "Valero's Bill Greehey to Focus on Role as Chairman," *Valero Energy Corporation* www.valero.com/NR/exeres/AD148F57-B714-4C01-A208-8812D4A75D9.htm, October 31, 2005.

76. Guyon, "The Soul of a Moneymaking Machine."

77. Ibid.

78. Ibid.

79. Ibid.

80. Ibid.

81. Ibid.

82. Ibid.; "Valero's Bill Greehey to Focus on Role as Chairman"; R. Barker, "Valero's Sweet Spot," *BusinessWeek Online,* October 24, 2005 (www.businessweek.com); "Valero Energy Corporation Reports Fourth Quarter and Full Year 2005 Earnings," *Valero Energy Corporation,* http://www.valero.com/NewsRoom/News+Releases/NR_20060131.htm, January 31, 2006; "Valero Receives Several Top Honors," *Valero Energy Corporation,* www.valero.com/NewsRoom/News+Releases/NR_20051230.htm, December 30, 2005.

83. "Fortune 100 Best Companies to Work For: Full List," CNNMoney.com, March 23, 2006, (http://money.cnn.com/magazines/fortune/bestcompanies/full_list); "About the 2005 Speakers," *Great Place to Work–Conference,* March 22, 2006 (www.greatplacetowork-conference.com/conference/speakers,php?id=86); "Valero Jumps to No. 3 on Fortune's List of 'America's 100 Best Companies to Work For' in America," *Valero Energy Corporation,* www.valero.com/NewsRoom/News+Releases/NR_20060109.htm, January 9, 2006; "Bill Greehey, Chairman of the Board," *Valero Energy Corporation,* www.valero.com/NewsRoom/Executive+Team, March 22, 2006.

84. "Fortune 100 Best Companies to Work For: Valero Energy," CNNMoney.com, March 23, 2006 (http://money.cnn.com/magazines/fortune/bestcompanies/snapshots/1521.html).

85. P. C. Earley, "Social Loafing and Collectivism: A Comparison of the United States and the People's Republic of China," *Administrative Science Quarterly* 34 (1989), 565–81; J. M. George, "Extrinsic and Intrinsic Origins of Perceived Social Loafing in Organizations," *Academy of Management Journal* 35 (1992), 191–202; S. G. Harkins, B. Latane, and K. Williams, "Social Loafing: Allocating Effort or Taking It Easy," *Journal of Experimental Social Psychology* 16 (1980), 457–65; B. Latane, K. D. Williams, and S. Harkins, "Many Hands Make Light the Work: The Causes and Consequences of Social Loafing," *Journal of Personality and Social Psychology* 37 (1979), 822–32; J. A. Shepperd, "Productivity Loss in Performance Groups: A Motivation Analysis," *Psychological Bulletin* 113 (1993), 67–81.

86. George, "Extrinsic and Intrinsic Origins"; G. R. Jones, "Task Visibility, Free Riding, and Shirking: Explaining the Effect of Structure and Technology on Employee Behavior," *Academy of Management Review* 9 (1984), 684–95; K. Williams, S. Harkins, and B. Latane, "Identifiability as a Deterrent to Social Loafing: Two Cheering Experiments," *Journal of Personality and Social Psychology* 40 (1981), 303–11.

87. S. Harkins and J. Jackson, "The Role of Evaluation in Eliminating Social Loafing," *Personality and Social Psychology Bulletin* 11 (1985), 457–65; N. L. Kerr and S. E. Bruun, "Ringelman Revisited: Alternative Explanations for the Social Loafing Effect," *Personality and Social Psychology Bulletin* 7 (1981), 224–31; Williams et al., "Identifiability as a Deterrent to Social Loafing"; Harkins and Jackson, "The Role of Evaluation in Eliminating Social Loafing"; Kerr and Bruun, "Ringelman Revisited."

88. M. A. Brickner, S. G. Harkins, and T. M. Ostrom, "Effects of Personal Involvement: Thought-Provoking Implications for Social Loafing," *Journal of Personality and Social Psychology* 51 (1986), 763–69; S. G. Harkins and R. E. Petty, "The Effects of Task Difficulty and Task Uniqueness on Social Loafing," *Journal of Personality and Social Psychology* 43 (1982), 1214–29.

89. B. Latane, "Responsibility and Effort in Organizations," in P. S. Goodman, ed., *Designing Effective Work Groups* (San Francisco: Jossey-Bass, 1986); Latane et al., "Many Hands Make Light the Work"; I. D. Steiner, *Group Process and Productivity* (New York: Academic Press, 1972).

Chapter 16

1. C. Hymowitz, "Missing from Work: The Chance to Think, Even to Dream a Little," *The Wall Street Journal,* March 23, 2004, B1.

2. Ibid.

3. Ibid.

4. Y. J. Yong, "CEO Message," www.samsung.com, August 22, 2004; "Yun Jong Yong: Biography," www.hwwilson.com, August 22, 2004.

5. C. Chandler, "CEO Voices: Jong-Yong Yun" *Fortune,* July 26, 2004.

6. "2004 Most Powerful People in Business: Yun Jong Yong," *Fortune,* August 22, 2004 (www.fortune.com/fortune/subs/mostpowerful/asia/snapshot/0,21105,5,00.html); "Overhauling Samsung," *BusinessWeek Online,* January 10, 2000 (www.businessweek.com:/2000/00_02/b3663060.htm?scriptFramed); J. Ewing, "The Global 1200," *BusinessWeek Online,* December 26, 2005 (www.businessweek.com/print/magazine/content/05_52/b396500.htm?chang=gl), June 20, 2006; Yun Jong Yong, "No. 9: Samsung Electronics," *BusinessWeek Online,* October 24, 2005 (www.businessweek.com/print/magazine/content/05_43/b3956415.htm?chan=gl), June 20, 2006; Telis Demos, "The World's Most Admired Companies," *CNNMoney.com,* February 28, 2006 (http://cnnmoney.printthis.clickability.com/pt/cpt?action=cpt&title=The+World%27s+Most . . . ..), June 20, 2006; Brian Bremner, "The Best Asian Performers," *BusinessWeek Online,* October 24, 2005 (www.businessweek.com/print/magazine/content/05_43/b3956401.htm?chan=gl), June 20, 2006; M. Ihlwan and L Young, "Behind Samsung's Bright Lights," *Businessweek Online,* October 24, 2005 (www.businessweek.com/print/magazine/content/05_43/b3956080.htm?chan=gl), June 20, 2006; M. Ihlwan, "Korea: Set to Duel in Digital TV," *BusinessWeek Online,* May 30, 2006 (www.businessweek.com/print/magazine/may2006/tc20060530_512280.htm), June 20, 2006; Jong-Yong Yun, "The Information Technology 100," *Businessweek Online* (www.businessweek.com/it100/2005/company/SAM.htm?campaign_id=search), June 20, 2006.

7. L. Kraar, "Asia's Businessman of the Year," *Fortune,* January 24, 2000 (www.fortune.com).

8. Chandler, "CEO Voices."

9. Kraar, "Asia's Businessman of the Year."

10. Ibid.

11. "2004 Most Powerful People in Business." Yun, "The Information Technology 100."

12. "Yun Jong Yong," *BusinessWeek Online,* January 12, 2004 (www.businessweek.com); "2004 Most Powerful People in Business"; Kraar, "Asia's Businessman of the Year"; Ewing, "The Global 1200"; Yong, "No. 9: Samsung Electronics"; Demos, "The World's Most Admired Companies"; Bremner, "The Best Asian Performers."

13. Chandler, "CEO Voices."

14. Hymowitz, "Missing from Work."

15. C. A. O'Reilly and L. R. Pondy, "Organizational Communication," in S. Kerr, ed., *Organizational Behavior* (Columbus, OH: Grid, 1979).

16. "World's First Volume Computed Tomography (VCT) System, Developed by GE Healthcare, Scanning Patients at Froedtert," www.gehealthcare.com/company/pressroom/releases/pr_release_9722.html, June 18, 2004; "GE Healthcare Fact Sheet," *GE Healthcare Worldwide,* June 20, 2006 (www.gehealthcare.com/usen/about/ge_factsheet.html); WTN News, "GE Healthcare Names New CEO," *Wisconsin Technology Network,* January 25, 2006 (http://wistechnology.com/printarticle.php?id=2639), June 20, 2006.

17. S. Kirsner, "Time [Zone] Travelers," *Fast Company,* August 2004, 60–66; "LightSpeed VCT Series," *GE Healthcare Worldwide,* June 20, 2006 (www.gehealthcare.com/usen/ct/products/vct.html).

18. "New CT Scanner by GE Healthcare Advances Imaging Technology," *Wisconsin Technology Network,* June 21, 2004 (www.wistechnology.com).

19. Kirsner, "Time [Zone] Travelers."

20. Ibid.

21. Ibid.

22. E. M. Rogers and R. Agarwala-Rogers, *Communication in Organizations* (New York: Free Press, 1976).

23. W. Nabers, "The New Corporate Uniforms," *Fortune,* November, 13, 1995, 132–56.

24. R. B. Schmitt, "Judges Try Curbing Lawyers' Body-Language Antics," *The Wall Street Journal,* September 11, 1997, B1, B7.

25. D. A. Adams, P. A. Todd, and R. R. Nelson, "A Comparative Evaluation of the Impact of Electronic and Voice Mail on Organizational Communication," *Information & Management* 24 (1993), 9–21.

26. R. Winslow, "Hospitals' Weak Systems Hurt Patients, Study Says," *The Wall Street Journal,* July 5, 1995, B1, B6.

27. B. Newman, "Global Chatter," *The Wall Street Journal,* March 22, 1995, A1, A15.

28. "Miscommunications Plague Pilots and Air-Traffic Controllers," *The Wall Street Journal,* August 22, 1995, A1.

29. P. Reinert, "Miscommunication Seen as Threat to Space Station," *Houston Chronicle,* September 24, 2003, 6A.

30. W. E. Leary, "NASA Report Says Problems Plague Space Station Program," *The New York Times,* February 28, 2004, A12.

31. R. L. Daft, R. H. Lengel, and L. K. Trevino, "Message Equivocality, Media Selection, and Manager Performance: Implications for Information Systems," *MIS Quarterly* 11 (1987), 355–66; R. L. Daft and R. H. Lengel, "Information Richness: A New Approach to Managerial Behavior and Organization Design," in B. M. Staw and L. L. Cummings, eds., *Research in Organizational Behavior* (Greenwich, CT: JAI Press, 1984).

32. R. L. Daft, *Organization Theory and Design* (St. Paul, MN: West, 1992).

33. "Lights, Camera, Meeting: Tele-conferencing Becomes a Time-Saving Tool," *The Wall Street Journal,* February 21, 1995, A1.

34. Daft, *Organization Theory and Design.*

35. A. S. Wellner, "Lost in Translation", *Inc. Magazine,* September 2005, 37–38.

36. Ibid.

37. Ibid.; R. McMillan, "Business Communication Expert and *New York Times* Bestselling Author," www.vitalsmarts.com, June 20, 2006.

38. Wellner, "Lost in Translation."

39. Ibid.

40. Ibid.; S. Roberts, "Sara Roberts, President, Roberts Golden Consulting–Biographies," www.robertsgolden.com/bios.html, June 20, 2006; "Roberts Golden Consulting," www.robertsgolden.com, June 20, 2006.

41. Wellner, "Lost in Translation."

42. T. J. Peters and R. H. Waterman, Jr., *In Search of Excellence* (New York: Harper & Row, 1982); T. Peters and N. Austin, *A Passion for Excellence: The Leadership Difference* (New York: Random House, 1985).

43. "Lights, Camera, Meeting."

44. B. Ziegler, "Virtual Power Lunches Will Make Passing the Salt an Impossibility," *The Wall Street Journal,* June 28, 1995, B1.

45. Hymowitz, "Missing from Work."

46. "E-Mail Etiquette Starts to Take Shape for Business Messaging," *The Wall Street Journal,* October 12, 1995, A1.

47. "Telecommuters Bring Home Work and Broadband," www.emarketer.com/Article.aspx?1002943, July 20, 2004; "Annual Survey Shows Americans Are Working from Many Different Locations Outside Their Employer's Office," *International Telework Association & Council,* May 10, 2006 (www.workingfromanywhere.org/news); "Itac, the Telework Advisory Group for WorldatWork," www.workingfromanywhere.org, May 10, 2006; "Virtual Business Owners Community–FAQ Center: Telecommuting/Telework," www.vsscyberoffice.com/vfaq/25.html, May 10, 2006.

48. E. Baig, "Taking Care of Business–Without Leaving the House," *BusinessWeek,* April 17, 1995, 106–07.

49. "Life Is Good for Telecommuters, but Some Problems Persist," *The Wall Street Journal,* August 3, 1995, A1.

50. "E-Mail Abuse: Workers Discover High-Tech Ways to Cause Trouble in the Office," *The Wall Street Journal,* November 22, 1994, A1; "E Mail Alert: Companies Lag in Devising Policies on How It Should Be Used," *The Wall Street Journal,* December 29, 1994, A1.

51. Wellner, "Lost in Translation."

52. "The Most Important Part of an E-mail System Isn't the Software. It's the Rules You Make About Using It," *Inc. Magazine,* October 2005, 119–22.

53. Ibid.

54. Ibid.

55. American Management Association and the ePolicy Institute's Nancy Flynn, "2004 Workplace E-Mail and Instant Messaging Survey Summary," www.amanet.org, 2004.

56. J. Tyson, "How Instant Messaging Works," computer.howstuffworks.com, August 23, 2004.

57. "Study: Workers Are Surfing on Company Time," www.medialifemagazine.com/news2004/may04/may03/3_wed/news8 wednesday.html, May 5, 2004.

58. Ibid.

59. Ibid.

60. ClikZ Stats staff, "U.S. Web Usage and Traffic, July 2004," www.clickz.com/stats/big_picture/traffic_patterns/article.php/33953 51, August 23, 2004.

61. L. Conley, "The Privacy Arms Race," *Fast Company,* July 2004, 27 28; "Migrating to Microsoft Exchange . . . or Another Mail System?" www.stellarim.com, June 20, 2006; "About Stellar Technologies, Inc.," www.stellartechnologies.com/about_us.cfm, June 20, 2006.

62. Conley, "The Privacy Arms Race."

63. Ibid.

64. "P & G Who We Are: Purpose, Values, and Principles," www.pg.com/company/who_we_are/ppv.jhtml, August 25, 2004; L. Conley, "Refusing to Gamble on Privacy," *Fast Company,* July 2004 (http://pf.fastcompany.com/magazine/84.essay_hughes.html); "Who We Are," *P&G Global Operations,* June 20, 2006 (www.pg.com/company/who_we_are/index.jhtml).

65. Conley, "The Privacy Arms Race."

66. J. O'Neil, "E-Mail Doesn't Lie (That Much)," *The New York Times,* March 2, 2004, D6.

67. "Employee-Newsletter Names Include the Good, the Bad, and the Boring," *The Wall Street Journal,* July 18, 1995, A1.

68. Hymowitz, "Missing from Work."

69. O. W. Baskin and C. E. Aronoff, *Interpersonal Communication in Organizations* (Santa Monica, CA: Goodyear, 1989).

70. T. Gutner, "Move Over, Bohemian Grove," *BusinessWeek,* February 19, 2001, 102.

71. "We've All Got Mail," *Newsweek,* May 15, 2001, 73K; "Diversity Deficit," *BusinessWeek Online,* May 14, 2001; "Dial-Up Users Converting to Broadband in Droves," www.emarketer.com/Article.aspx?1003009, August 23, 2004; "Top 20 Countries with the Highest Number of Internet Users," *Internet World Stats,* June 20, 2006 (www.internetworldstats.com/top20.htm).

72. "Top 15 Countries in Internet Usage, 2002," www.infoplease.com/ipa/A0908185.html, August 25, 2004; "Top 20 Countries with the Highest Number of Internet Users."

73. J. Sandberg, "Internet's Popularity in North America Appears to Be Soaring," *The Wall Street Journal,* October 30, 1995, B2.

74. "How to Research Companies," *Oxford Knowledge Company,* www.oxford-knowledge.co.uk, September, 16, 2004.

75. "Survey: Denmark Is Web-Savviest Nation," *MSNBC.com,* April 19, 2004 (www.msnbc.msn.com/id/4779944/1/displaymode/1 098); L. Grinsven, "U.S. Drops on Lists of Internet Savvy," *Houston Chronicle,* April 20, 2004, 6B.

76. J. W. Verity and R. Hof, "Bullet-Proofing the Net," *BusinessWeek,* November 13, 1995, 98–99.

77. Ibid.; "Corporate Governance Board of Directors," *Sun Company,* www.sun.com/company/cgov/board.html, June 20, 2006.

78. M. J. Cronin, "Ford's Intranet Success," *Fortune,* March 30, 1998, 158; M. J. Cronin, "Intranets Reach the Factory Floor," *Fortune,* June 10, 1997; A. L. Sprout, "The Internet Inside Your Company," *Fortune,* November 27, 1995, 161–68; J. B. White, "Chrysler's Intranet: Promise vs. Reality," *The Wall Street Journal,* May 13, 1997, B1, B6.

79. Ibid.

80. G. Rifkin, "A Skeptic's Guide to Groupware," *Forbes ASAP,* 1995, 76–91.

81. Ibid.

82. Ibid.

83. "Groupware Requires a Group Effort," *BusinessWeek,* June 26, 1995, 154.

84. M. Totty, "The Path to Better Teamwork," *The Wall Street Journal,* May 20, 2004, R4; "Collaborative Software," *Wikipedia,* August 25, 2004 (en.wikipedia.org/wiki/Collaborative_software); "Collaborative Groupware Software," www.svpal.org/~grantbow/groupware.html, August 25, 2004.

85. Totty, "The Path to Better Teamwork"; "Collaborative Software."

86. Ibid.; "Collaborative Groupware Software."

87. Totty, "The Path to Better Teamwork"; "Collaborative Software."

88. Ibid.

89. Microsoft Windows SharePoint Services Developer Center, "Windows SharePoint Service," http://msdn.microsoft.com/sharepoint, June 21, 2006.

90. Totty, "The Path to Better Teamwork"; "Collaborative Software."

91. M. Conlin, "E-mail Is So Five Minutes Ago," *BusinessWeek,* November 28, 2005, 111–12; D. Dahl, "The End of E-mail," *Inc. Magazine,* February 2006, 41–42; "Weaving a Secure Web Around Education: A Guide to Technology Standards and Security," http://nces.ed.gov/pubs2003/secureweb/glossary.asp, June 21, 2006; "Wikis Make Collaboration Easier," *InformationWeek,* June 20, 2006, (www.informationweek.com/shared/printable ArticleSrc.jhtml?articleID=170100392).

92. Conlin, "E-mail Is So Five Minutes Ago."

93. Ibid.

94. Ibid.

95. Ibid.

96. Dahl, "The End of E-mail"; "Wikis Make Collaboration Easier."

97. Conlin, "E-mail Is So Five Minutes Ago."

98. Dahl, "The End of E-mail."

99. Conlin, "E-mail Is So Five Minutes Ago."

100. Ibid.

101. Ibid.

102. Ibid.

103. Ibid.; Dahl, "The End of E-mail"; "Weaving a Secure Web Around Education."

104. "On the Road," *Newsweek,* June 6, 1994, 8.

105. Wakizaka, "Faxes, E-Mail, Help the Deaf Get Office Jobs," *The Wall Street Journal,* October 3, 1995, B1, B5.

106. D. Tannen, "The Power of Talk," *Harvard Business Review,* September–October 1995, 138–48; D. Tannen, *Talking from 9 to 5* (New York: Avon Books, 1995).

107. Tannen, "The Power of Talk."

108. Ibid.

109. Ibid.

110. Ibid.

111. Ibid.; Tannan, *Talking from 9 to 5.*

112. Ibid.

113. J. Cohen, "He Writes, She Writes," *Houston Chronicle,* July 7, 2001, C1–C2.

114. Ibid.

115. Ibid.

116. Tannen, "The Power of Talk," 148.

117. Kirsner, "Time [Zone] Travelers."

Chapter 17

1. A. Taylor III, "Toyota's Secret Weapon," *Fortune,* August 23, 2004, 60–66; "Toyota Sales Shake Up Big Three," *CNNMoney.com,* May 3, 2006 (http://cnnmoney.printthis.clickability.com/pt/cpt?action=cpt&title=Toyota+coule+replace . . .), June 24, 2006; A. Taylor III, "Toyota Envy," *CNNMoney.com,* May 1, 2006 (http://cnnmoney.printthis.clickability.com/pt.cpt?action=cpt&title=Plugged+in%3A+Toyo . . . . . .), June 24, 2006; A. Taylor III, "Toyota's Recipe for Success," *CNNMoney.com,* February 22, 2006 (http://cnnmoney.printthig.clickability.com/pt/cpt?action=cpt&title=Plugged+in%3A+Toyo . . .), June 23, 2006; A. Ohnsman, "Toyota Picks U.S. Sales Chief," *The Detroit News Autos Insider,* June 24, 2005 (www.detnews.com/2005/autosinsider/0506/24/F03-226647.htm), June 23, 2006; "Toyota Profits Shift into High Gear," *TheState.com,* May 11, 2006 (www.thestate.com/mld/thestate/business/14550161.htm?template=contentModules/p . . .), June 24, 2006.

2. A. Taylor III, "Toyota: The Birth of the Prius," *CNNMoney.com,* February 21, 2006 (http://cnnmoney.printthis.clickability.com/pt/cpt?action=cpt&title=FORTUNE%3A+The+ . . . .), June 23, 2006; B. Berman, "The Top Ten Hybrid Myths," *BusinessWeek Online,* February 13, 2006 (www.businessweek.com/print/autos/content/jan2006/bw20060131_870391.htm), June 23, 2006; J. Press, "Toyota's Jim Press Discusses the Future," *BusinessWeek Online,* May 17, 2006 (www.businessweek.com/print/autos/content/may2006/bw20060517_241467.htm), June 24, 2006.

3. Taylor, "Toyota's Secret Weapon."

4. Press, "Toyota's Jim Press Discusses the Future."

5. Taylor, "Toyota's Secret Weapon."

6. M. Hanley, "Toyota Shows Imposing Full-Size Truck Concept, New Highlander Hybrid," *cars.com,* January 4, 2004 (www.cars.com); D. Welch, "Commentary: Detroit Is over a ($50) Barrel," *BusinessWeek Online,* September 13, 2004 (www.businessweek.com).

7. Taylor, "Toyota's Secret Weapon."

8. Ibid.

9. Ibid.

10. Ibid.

11. J. Press, "Toyota: To the Tundra and Beyond," *BusinessWeek Online,* February 13, 2006 (www.businessweek.com/print/autos/content/feb2006/bw20060210_240045.htm), June 23, 2006; D. Kiley, "Toyota's Tundra Thunders In," *BusinessWeek Online,* February 9, 2006 (www.businessweek.com/print/autos/content/feb2006/bw20060209_359467.htm), June 23, 2006; D. Kiley, "Toyota Builds

a Truck Even Bubba May Love," *BusinessWeek Online,* February 13, 2006 (www.businesswee.com/print/magazine/content/06_07/b3971060.htm?chan=gl), June 23, 2006.

12. Taylor, "Toyota's Secret Weapon."

13. C. Dawson, "Buy a Toyota, Get a Mortgage," *BusinessWeek Online,* September 13, 2004 (www.businessweek.com).

14. Press, "Toyota: To the Tundra and Beyond."

15. J. A. Litterer, "Conflict in Organizations: A Reexamination," *Academy of Management Journal* 9 (1966), 178–86; S. M. Schmidt and T. A. Kochan, "Conflict: Towards Conceptual Clarity," *Administrative Science Quarterly* 13 (1972), 359–70; R. H. Miles, *Macro Organizational Behavior* (Santa Monica, CA: Goodyear, 1980).

16. S. P. Robbins, *Managing Organizational Conflict: A Nontraditional Approach* (Englewood Cliffs, NJ: Prentice-Hall, 1974); L. Coser, *The Functions of Social Conflict* (New York: Free Press, 1956).

17. K. A. Jehn, "A Qualitative Analysis of Conflict Types and Dimensions in Organizational Groups," Cornell University, 1997; K. A. Jehn, "A Multimethod Examination of the Benefits and Detriments of Intragroup Conflict," Cornell University, 1995.

18. L. L. Putnam and M. S. Poole, "Conflict and Negotiation," in F. M. Jablin, L. L. Putnam, K. H. Roberts, and L. W. Porter, eds., *Handbook of Organizational Communication: An Interdisciplinary Perspective* (Newbury Park, CA: Sage, 1987), 549–99.

19. J. Gill, "Squelching Office Conflict," *Inc. Magazine,* November 2005, 40-43; Vaisala Oyj, "Stock Exchange Release," December 23, 2005 (www.vaisala.com/newsanddownloads/stockexchangereleases/year2005?Id=40863& . . .), June 25, 2006.

20. Gill, "Squelching Office Conflict."

21. Ibid.; D. B. Lynch, "About the Founder," *workwelltogether.com,* June 24, 2006 (www.workwelltogether.com/public/department13.cfm). "Dispute Resolution and Ombudsman Services," *workwelltogether.com,* June 24, 2006 (www.workwelltogether.com/public/main.cfm).

22. Gill, "Squelching Office Conflict."

23. Ibid.

24. Ibid.

25. L. R. Pondy, "Organizational Conflict: Concepts and Models," *Administrative Science Quarterly* 2 (1967), 296–320; R. E. Walton and J. M. Dutton, "The Management of Interdepartmental Conflict: A Model and Review," *Administrative Science Quarterly* 14 (1969), 62–73.

26. Taylor, "Toyota's Secret Weapon."

27. Ibid.

28. Press, "Toyota: To the Tundra and Beyond"; Kiley, "Toyota's Tundra Thunders In"; Kiley, "Toyota Builds a Truck Even Bubba May Love."

29. G. R. Jones and J. E. Butler, "Managing Internal Corporate Entrepreneurship: An Agency Theory Perspective," *Journal of Management* 18 (1992), 733–49.

30. T. Petzinger, Jr., "All Happy Businesses Are Alike, but Heirs Bring Unique Conflicts," *The Wall Street Journal,* November 17, 1995, B1.

31. J. A. Wall, Jr., "Conflict and Its Management," *Journal of Management* 21 (1995), 515–58.

32. Walton and Dutton, "The Management of Interdepartmental Conflict."

33. Pondy, "Organizational Conflict."

34. W. F. White, *Human Relations in the Restaurant Industry* (New York: McGraw-Hill, 1948).

35. R. L. Pinkley and G. B. Northcraft, "Conflict Frames of Reference: Implications for Dispute Processes and Outcomes," *Academy of Management Journal* 37 (February 1994), 193–206.

36. K. W. Thomas, "Conflict and Negotiation Processes in Organizations," in M. D. Dunnette and L. M. Hough, eds., *Handbook of Industrial and Organizational Psychology,* 2d ed., vol. 3 (Palo Alto, CA: Consulting Psychologists Press, 1992), 651–717.

37. Ibid.

38. Pinkley and Northcraft, "Conflict Frames of Reference."

39. E. Shapiro, J. A. Trachtenberg, and L. Landro, "Time Warner Settles Feud by Pushing Out Music Division's Fuchs," *The Wall Street Journal,* November 17, 1995, A1, A6.

40. Ibid.

41. P. R. Lawrence, L. B. Barnes, and J. W. Lorsch, *Organizational Behavior and Administration* (Homewood, IL: Irwin, 1976).

42. R. J. Lewicki and J. R. Litterer, *Negotiation* (Homewood, IL: Irwin, 1985); G. B. Northcraft and M. A. Neale, *Organizational Behavior* (Fort Worth, TX: Dryden, 1994); J. Z. Rubin and B. R. Brown, *The Social Psychology of Bargaining and Negotiation* (New York: Academic Press, 1975).

43. C. Bendersky, "Organizational Dispute Resolution Systems: A Complementarities Model," *Academy of Management Review* 28 (October 2003), 643–57.

44. R. E. Walton, "Third Party Roles in Interdepartmental Conflicts," *Industrial Relations* 7 (1967), 29–43.

45. "Meaning of Arbitrator," *hyperdictionary,* September 4, 2004 (www.hyperdictionary. com); "Definitions of Arbitrator on the Web," www.google.com, September 4, 2004.

46. L. Thompson and R. Hastie, "Social Perception in Negotiation," *Organizational Behavior and Human Decision Processes* 47 (1990), 98–123.

47. Thomas, "Conflict and Negotiation Processes in Organizations."

48. R. J. Lewicki, S. E. Weiss, and D. Lewin, "Models of Conflict, Negotiation and Third Party Intervention: A Review and Synthesis," *Journal of Organizational Behavior* 13 (1992) 209–52.

49. Northcraft and Neale, *Organizational Behavior.*

50. Lewicki et al., "Models of Conflict, Negotiation and Third Party Intervention"; Northcraft and Neale, Organizational Behavior; D. G. Pruitt, "Integrative Agreements: Nature and Consequences," in M. H. Bazerman and R. J. Lewicki, eds., *Negotiating in Organizations* (Beverly Hills, CA: Sage, 1983).

51. R. Fischer and W. Ury, *Getting to Yes* (Boston: Houghton Mifflin, 1981); Northcraft and Neale, *Organizational Behavior.*

52. P. J. Carnevale and D. G. Pruitt, "Negotiation and Mediation," *Annual Review of Psychology* 43 (1992), 531–82.

53. K. Belson, "Digital Dealmakers Meet in the Middle," *The New York Times,* September 11, 2003, E1, E4.

54. "About Us," www.splitthedifference. com/aboutUs, September 5, 2004.

55. Belson, "Digital Dealmakers Meet in the Middle."

56. Ibid.; "Fujitsu America, Inc.," www. fujitsu.com/us/about/OtherOps/FAI, September 5, 2004; www.fujitsu.com, June 26, 2006.

57. Belson, "Digital Dealmakers Meet in the Middle."

58. A. M. Pettigrew, *The Politics of Organizational Decision Making* (London: Tavistock, 1973); Miles, *Macro Organizational Behavior.*

59. D. J. Hickson, C. R. Hinings, C. A. Lee, R. E. Schneck, and D. J. Pennings, "A Strategic Contingencies Theory of Intraorganizational Power," *Administrative Science Quarterly* 16 (1971), 216–27; C. R. Hinings, D. J. Hickson, J. M. Pennings, and R. E. Schneck, "Structural Conditions of Interorganizational Power," *Administrative Science Quarterly* 19 (1974), 22–44; J. Pfeffer, *Power in Organizations* (Boston: Pitman, 1981).

60. Pfeffer, *Power in Organizations.*

61. Ibid.

62. Taylor, "Toyota's Secret Weapon."

63. M. Crozier, "Sources of Power of Lower Level Participants in Complex Organizations," *Administrative Science Quarterly* 7 (1962), 349–64; A. M. Pettigrew, "Information Control as a Power Resource," *Sociology* 6 (1972), 187–204.

64. Pfeffer, *Power in Organizations*; G. R. Salancik and J. Pfeffer, "The Bases and Uses of Power in Organizational Decision Making," *Administrative Science Quarterly* 19 (1974), 453–73; J. Pfeffer and G. R. Salancik, *The External Control of Organizations:*

A Resource Dependence View (New York: Harper & Row, 1978).

65. J. S. Lublin, "Despite Poor Returns, Champion's Chairman Hangs On for 21 Years," *The Wall Street Journal,* October 31, 1995, A1, A5.

66. Pfeffer, *Power in Organizations.*

67. Ibid.

68. Ibid.

69. L. Kramer, "Doing Well and Good: How Social Responsibility Helped One Coffee Grower Land a Deal with Starbucks," *Inc. Magazine,* June 2006, 55–56.

70. Ibid.; "Corporate Social Responsibility," www.starbucks.com/aboutus/csr.asp, June 25, 2006.

71. "The Exceptional Cup Participating Farms Finca El Faro," www. guatemalancoffees.com/GCContent/ GCeng/auction_tec_fincas/FincaElFaro.asp, June 25, 2006.

72. Kramer, "Doing Well and Good."

73. Ibid.

74. Ibid.

75. Ibid.

76. Ibid.

77. Ibid.

78. Ibid.

Chapter 18

1. www.kroger.com, 2006.

2. www.safeway.com, 2006.

3. Ibid.

4. N. B. Macintosh, *The Social Software of Accounting Information Systems* (New York: Wiley, 1995).

5. C. A. O'Reilly, "Variations in Decision Makers' Use of Information: The Impact of Quality and Accessibility," *Academy of Management Journal* 25 (1982), 756–71.

6. G. Stalk and T. H. Hout, *Competing Against Time* (New York: Free Press, 1990).

7. L. Uchitelle, "Airlines off Course," *San Francisco Chronicle,* September 15, 1991, 7.

8. R. Cyert and J. March, *Behavioral Theory of the Firm* (Englewood Cliffs, NJ: Prentice-Hall, 1963).

9. R. Brandt, "Agents and Artificial Life," *BusinessWeek: The Information Revolution,* special issue, 1994, 64–68.

10. E. Turban, *Decision Support and Expert Systems* (New York: Macmillan, 1988).

11. R. I. Benjamin and J. Blunt, "Critical IT Issues: The Next Ten Years," *Sloan Management Review,* Summer 1992, 7–19; W. H. Davidow and M. S. Malone, The Virtual Corporation (New York: HarperBusiness, 1992).

12. Davidow and Malone, *The Virtual Corporation;* M. E. Porter, *Competitive Advantage* (New York: Free Press, 1984).

13.   S. M. Dornbusch and W. R. Scott, *Evaluation and the Exercise of Authority* (San Francisco: Jossey-Bass, 1975).

14.   J. Child, *Organization: A Guide to Problems and Practice* (London: Harper & Row, 1984).

15.   www.dhl.com, 2006.

16.   Ibid.

17.   Ibid.

18.   Macintosh, The Social Software of Accounting Information Systems.

19.   www.cypress.com, 2006.

20.   www.hermanmiller.com, 2006.

21.   www.boeing.com, 2006.

22.   P. Bradley, "Global Souring Takes Split-Second Timing," *Purchasing,* July 20, 1989, 52–58.

23.   J. A. Schumpeter, *Capitalism, Socialism and Democracy* (New York: Harper, 1942).

24.   V. P. Buell, *Marketing Management* (New York: McGraw-Hill, 1985).

25.   See M. M. J. Berry and J. H. Taggart, "Managing Technology and Innovation: A Review," *R & D Management* 24 (1994), 341–53; K. B. Clark and S. C. Wheelwright, *Managing New Product and Process Development* (New York: Free Press, 1993).

26.   See Berry and Taggart, "Managing Technology and Innovation"; M. Gort and J. Klepper, "Time Paths in the Diffusion of Product Innovations," *Economic Journal,* September 1982, 630–53. Looking at the history of 46 products, Gort and Klepper found that the length of time before other companies entered the markets created by a few inventive companies declined from an average of 14.4 years for products introduced before 1930 to 4.9 years for those introduced

after 1949–implying that product life cycles were being compressed. Also see A. Griffin, "Metrics for Measuring Product Development Cycle Time," *Journal of Production and Innovation Management* 10 (1993), 112–25.

27.   www.ibm.com, 2006.

28.   A. D. Chandler, *The Visible Hand* (Cambridge, MA: Harvard University Press, 1977).

29.   C. W. L. Hill and J. F. Pickering, "Divisionalization, Decentralization, and Performance of Large United Kingdom Companies," *Journal of Management Studies* 23 (1986), 26–50.

30.   O. E. Williamson, *Markets and Hierarchies: Analysis and Antitrust Implications* (New York: Free Press, 1975).

31.   C. W. L. Hill, "Airborne Express," in C. W. L. Hill and G. R. Jones, *Strategic Management: An Integrated Approach* (Boston: Houghton-Mifflin, 2004).

32.   Turban, *Decision Support and Expert Systems.*

33.   www.merck.com, 2006.

34.   N. A. Nichols, "Scientific Management at Merck: An Interview with CFO Judy Lewent," *Harvard Business Review,* January–February 1994, 88–91.

35.   Turban, *Decision Support and Expert Systems*.

36.   E. Rich, *Artificial Intelligence* (New York: McGraw-Hill, 1983).

37.   Brandt, "Agents and Artificial Life."

38.   Rich, *Artificial Intelligence.*

39.   Ibid., 346.

40.   P. P. Bonisson and H. E. Johnson, "Expert Systems for Diesel Electric

Locomotive Repair," *Human Systems Management* 4 (1985), 1–25.

41.   G. R. Jones, "SAP and the Enterprise Resource Planning Industry," in C. W. L. Hill and G. R. Jones, *Strategic Management: An Integrated Approach,* 6th ed. (Boston: Houghton Mifflin, 2003).

42.   B. Kogut, "Joint Ventures: Theoretical and Empirical Perspectives," *Strategic Management Journal* 9 (1988), 319–32.

43.   G. S. Capowski, "Designing a Corporate Identity," *Management Review,* June 1993, 37–38.

44.   J. Marcia, "Just Doing It," *Distribution,* January 1995, 36–40.

45.   Davidow and Malone, *The Virtual Corporation.*

46.   Ibid., 168.

47.   The companies are real, but their names are fictitious. Information was obtained from a personal interview with a senior manager who had experience with both companies' information systems.

48.   T. A. Stewart, "Managing in a Wired Company," *Fortune,* July 11, 1994, 54.

49.   H. Mintzberg, *Mintzberg on Management: Inside Our Strange World of Organizations* (New York: Free Press, 1989).

50.   From an interview conducted by C. W. L. Hill with a senior Boeing manager.

51.   Stewart, "Managing in a Wired Company," 54.

52.   See J. R. Meredith, "The Implementation of Computer Based Systems," *Journal of Operational Management,* October 1981; Turban, *Decision Support and Expert Systems;* R. J. Thierauf, *Effective Management and Evaluation of IT* (London: Quorum Books, 1994).

Photo Credits

Chapter 1
Pg.3 AP Images/Paul Sakuma
Pg.6 © Michael Newman/PhotoEdit

Pg.111 Courtesy Texas A&M University
Pg.112 © Mark Richards/PhotoEdit

Pg.228 © JUNG YEON-JE/AFP/
Getty Images
Pg.233 © Bob Daemmrich/The Image

Index

Names

Subjects

Organizations